Major Problems in American
Foreign Relations

MAJOR PROBLEMS IN AMERICAN HISTORY SERIES

GENERAL EDITOR
THOMAS G. PATERSON

Major Problems in American Foreign Relations
Volume II: Since 1914

DOCUMENTS AND ESSAYS

FIFTH EDITION

EDITED BY
DENNIS MERRILL
UNIVERSITY OF MISSOURI–KANSAS CITY

THOMAS G. PATERSON
UNIVERSITY OF CONNECTICUT

HOUGHTON MIFFLIN COMPANY
Boston   New York

Editor in Chief: Jean L. Woy
Senior Associate Editor: Frances Gay
Senior Project Editor: Julie Lane
Editorial Assistant: Jennifer O'Neill
Associate Production/Design Coordinator: Jodi O'Rourke
Senior Cover Design Coordinator: Deborah Azerrad Savona
Manufacturing Coordinator: Andrea Wagner
Senior Marketing Manager: Sandra McGuire
Marketing Assistant: Ivan Chan

Cover Designer: Rose Corbett Gordon
Cover Image: *Camp David Accords Signed at the White House,* an acrylic painting by
Franklin McMahon (CORBIS/Franklin McMahon)

Printed in the U.S.A.

Library of Congress Catalog Card Number: 99-71940

ISBN: 0-395-93885-6

3456789-FFG-05 04 03 02 01

For
Barbara Shaw Merrill
Aaron M. Paterson

Contents

CHAPTER 3
The International History of the 1920s
Page 76

CHAPTER 4
Franklin D. Roosevelt and the Origins of the Second World War in the Pacific
Page 115

CHAPTER 7
Mao's China and the Chances for Sino-American Accommodation
Page 267

CHAPTER 8
The Korean War
Page 299

C H A P T E R 1 3
The United States Encounters the Middle East
Page 530

C H A P T E R 1 4
The Cold War Ends and the Post–Cold War Era Begins
Page 591

E S S A Y S

Maps

Preface

Newspaper headlines and television reports from around the world bombard Americans every day, reminding us, sometimes to our discomfort, that the United States participates in a global community as never before. In a world made interdependent by an information revolution, instant communications, rapid transportation, economic partnerships, and a shared natural environment, we have discovered that everything from gasoline at the pump to the clothes we buy to the air we breathe carries the "international" tag. As tourists, we traverse nearly every corner of the globe engaging in economic and cultural exchange. As hosts, we annually welcome millions of overseas visitors to our own country. We express pride when our habits, styles, and values find favor among foreigners, and grumble when our best intentions go unappreciated. We know that a sizable portion of our tax dollars pays for foreign economic, military, and humanitarian aid, for overseas military and intelligence installations, and for interventions, wars, and covert operations intended to change the behavior of other peoples and governments. News of massacres, famines, and violent uprisings constantly arouse Americans' moral sensibilities. Those of us with strong ties to former homelands collect funds and lobby the U.S. government on behalf of friends and relatives abroad. Terrorist attacks bring foreign ethnic, religious, and political disputes closer to Americans. Holidays commemorate foreign events. Families worry about the hundreds of thousands of U.S. military personnel stationed abroad. Town after town in the United States pays tribute through memorial statues and plaques to uniformed men and women who have died in foreign wars and expeditions. So it is that we Americans are deeply intertwined in the affairs of the world—and thus necessarily is our government.

This book explores America's many intersections with the world from World War I to the present. It shows how Americans from various walks of life have participated in the world community. It examines why and how American leaders devised policies to protect, manage, and extend U.S. interests abroad. The documents and essays in *Major Problems in American Foreign Relations* reveal that searching debate—among Americans, among Americans and foreign peoples, and among scholars who study the past—has surrounded most issues. Indeed, Americans have spiritedly debated one another about their place in the world, their wars, their territorial expansion, their overseas commitments, and the status of their principles and power; and with comparable vigor they have debated the people of other nations about the spread of U.S. interests, culture, and ideologies. This book captures the reasoning and the passion that informed these debates by probing the factors that influence decisionmakers, the processes by which decisions are made, and the impact of those decisions on the United States and other nations.

We use the phrase *American Foreign Relations* in the title because the subject matter encompasses the myriad ways in which peoples, cultures, economies, national governments, nongovernmental organizations, regional associations, and international institutions interact. The term *foreign policy* seems inadequate to account for this wide array of activities and actors because it focuses largely on governmental decisionmaking and on policy itself. *Diplomacy* falls short because it refers primarily to negotiations or communications among states and organizations. *International history* seems so broad a term that it loses meaning, while at the same time it underplays an appropriate emphasis on an *American* foreign relations. The phrase *foreign relations* comes closest to the new emphases because it explains the totality of interactions—economic, cultural, political, military, environmental, and more—among peoples, organizations, states, and systems.

For this fifth edition we have integrated into our chapters some of the very best recent scholarship, adding selections that are based on new archival findings or which raise original, thought-provoking questions and points of debate. Following the lead of scholars in the disciplines of history and international relations, we have given greater attention to cultural relations and to the ways in which socially constructed, popular attitudes about race and gender have helped shape America's perceptions of the world and subsequently its overseas relationships. In this edition, in both essays and documents, we included more foreign voices and more statements by people of color, so as to illuminate the wide array of participants in foreign relations and to suggest the ways in which America has influenced other peoples and nations.

The ending of the Cold War and the on-going, yet still incomplete, declassification of documents in foreign archives—Russian, Cuban, and Chinese, for example—have generated new perspectives and more textured discussions of many topics, including the origins of the Cold War, Sino-American relations, the Korean War, the nuclear arms race, and the Cuban missile crisis. Recently released documents and the evolving scholarship on these questions are represented in this volume.

Like other volumes in this series, *Major Problems in American Foreign Relations* approaches its subject in two ways: first, through primary sources; and second, through the interpretations of scholars. We invite readers to contend with a diversity of viewpoints and approaches on critical issues. Documents introduce each chapter's problem, identify key questions, reveal the flavor of the times, and convey the intensity of the debate. Through encounters with documents, students can immerse themselves in the historical moment, shape their own perspectives, and test the explanations of others. The essays demonstrate that different scholars read documents differently, come to quite different conclusions, or choose to focus on different aspects of an issue. Students' interactions with the documents and essays build an appreciation for the complexity of historical problems, a fascination about historical inquiry, and a recognition that events and personalities once buried in the past carry contemporary meaning for students as both scholars and citizens. Introductions and headnotes in each chapter start this empowering and rewarding process.

Instructors and students who want to continue their study of foreign relations history are invited to join the Society for Historians of American Foreign Relations (SHAFR). This organization publishes a superb journal, *Diplomatic History,* and an informative newsletter; offers book, article, and lecture prizes and dissertation research grants; and holds an annual conference where scholars present their views and research results. Dues are very reasonable. For information, contact the SHAFR Business Office, Department of History, Wright State University, Dayton, OH 45435.

SHAFR also maintains a home page at www.ohiou.edu/~shafr/shafr.htm where you will find links to other sites related to American foreign relations. *Diplomatic History* maintains a web site at www.cohums.ohio-state.edu/history/projects/diplh. For online discussion of topics in the history of U.S. foreign relations, consult the electronic journal *H-DIPLO* web page at http://h-net2.msu.edu/~diplo.

We are very pleased to acknowledge the many generous people who have helped us with both documents and essays, advised us about content, and pointed out errors. Detailed and constructive written reviews were provided by Peter L. Hahn, Nancy Mitchell, Andrew Rotter, Thomas Schwartz, and Nancy Bernkopf Tucker. We also appreciate the assistance of J. Garry Clifford, Gregory E. Dowd, Jim Falls, Miriam Formanek-Brunell, Mary A. Giunta, Carla Klausner, Joel Rhodes, and Mary Wolfskill. The talented Houghton Mifflin staff deserves special thanks. Imaginative, thorough, and understanding, Houghton Mifflin's editors shaped this book for the better. We thank Vice President and Editor in Chief for History and Political Science Jean L. Woy; Senior Associate History Editor Frances Gay; Senior Project Editor Julie Lane; and Permissions Editor Katie Mulligan.

We are also grateful to friends, colleagues, and students who contributed in various ways to the first four editions: Lloyd E. Ambrosius, Harold Barto, Miriam Biurci, Richard Dean Burns, Richard H. Collin, Bruce Cummings, Joe Decker, Bruce dePyssler, John Dobson, Michael Ebner, Mark Gilderhus, James Goode, Gerald Gordon, Laura Grant, Kenneth J. Hagan, Peter L. Hahn, Paul W. Harris, James Hindman, Jane Hunter, Michael Hunt, Holly Izard, Donald Johnson, Lawrence Kaplan, Ellen Kerley, Warren Kimball, Karen Kupperman, Melvyn Leffler, Douglas Little, Jean Manter, Frederick Marks, James Matray, John Merrill, Jean-Donald Miller, Carl Murdoch, Brian Murphy, Charles Neu, Patrick Peebles, Stephen Pelz, Alan Perry, Carol Petillo, Eileen Rice, Kenneth E. Shewmaker, Martha Lund Smalley, Mark Stoler, Harry Stout, William Stueck, John Sylvester, Paul Varg, Marvin Zahniser, and Thomas Zoumaras.

We welcome comments, suggestions, and criticisms from students and instructors so that we can continue to improve this book.

D. M.
T. G. P.

Approaching the Study of American Foreign Relations

The study of American foreign relations encompasses several central questions. What are the key characteristics of U.S. foreign relations, and what shaped them? What is the relationship between the nation's domestic setting—ideology, core values, politics, geography, social structure, and economy—and its foreign relations? To what extent does American foreign relations owe its character not to domestic conditions and attitudes but to interaction with the wider world of the international system? Does the United States behave like other powers in international relations, or does the nation exhibit exceptional qualities? What weight should we assign to the several ways in which nations relate to one another in the international system—political, strategic, economic, military, cultural, and others? How is power distributed in the international system? And, as the twenty-first century opens, is the United States suffering the decline of its vaunted position?

Most scholars agree that the United States built on a tradition of expansionism to emerge as a prominent, even hegemonic, global power in the twentieth century. But how, and why? Was the expansionist course calculated and coherent, or accidental and haphazard? The historian William Appleman Williams's The Tragedy of American Diplomacy, *first published in 1959, profoundly influenced scholars by citing economic—or "Open Door"—expansionism as the key to understanding U.S. foreign relations. With an accompanying "Open Door" ideology that posited that their domestic welfare depended on access to markets abroad, Americans, argued Williams, exploited overseas economies and sought to remake foreign societies. Coercion of foreign peoples necessarily followed, he concluded, producing a "tragedy"—Americans' violation of their own best principles, especially the right of self-determination. Much of the scholarship of the past few decades has applied the Williams thesis, elaborated on it, amended it, or disputed it, but has never ignored it.*

Related to the many questions about U.S. expansionism and the larger world are others that highlight how policy is made and how the process of decision making itself shapes both the policy and the outcome. How have U.S. leaders gone about deciding to use the nation's power abroad, and has that exercise of power produced the results intended? In this category, scholars explore the role of domestic politics and elections, presidential-congressional relations, the Constitution, bureaucracies, interest groups and elites, and individuals whose particular personalities mold perceptions and influence decisions.

One way in which to think about the different approaches, presented very briefly in this opening chapter, is to ask how each would explain specific events or relations, such as U.S. entry into the First World War, Japanese-American disputes leading to World War II, the origins of the Cold War, the Korean War, the nuclear arms race, or U.S. participation in the search for Arab-Israeli peace in the Middle East. Does one approach or a combination of approaches carry more explanatory power than others?

The diversity of viewpoints in this introductory chapter affords an opportunity to discover and understand the complexity of major problems in American foreign relations whose legacies persist today.

 E S S A Y S

In the first essay, Thomas J. McCormick of the University of Wisconsin, Madison, emphasizes U.S. economic hegemony or dominance in a capitalist world system comprising core, periphery, and semi-periphery countries. In the twentieth century, the United States has possessed predominant economic and military power and exercised political-ideological leadership, rising to the status of the preeminent core country. McCormick notes, however, that hegemony is "impermanent"; great powers become rentier and warfare states, and decline inevitably sets in. In the second essay, Emily S. Rosenberg of Macalaster College explores a subject that is in many ways interconnected to global economics: international cultural relations. She makes the case that the export of American ideas, news headlines, music, sports, consumer products, tourists, radio broadcasts, and movies—promoted both by government agencies and through private initiative—contributed significantly to U.S. hegemony overseas. Despite regular backlashes of cultural nationalism, Rosenberg observes that American popular culture is often warmly received by others and incorporated by various classes and interest groups within recipient societies. The information revolution of the late twentieth century, she concludes, has further blurred national lines and produced a globalization of culture.

In the third essay, Andrew Rotter of Colgate University explores a specific aspect of culture: gender. Using U.S. relations with India as an example, he explains that cultural constructions of femininity and masculinity influence the ways in which diplomats perceive and relate to other peoples. For example, the gendered language of international relations undergirded a negative view of nonaligned India during the Cold War era and helped justify a vigorous policy of anti-Communist containment on the Indian subcontinent. Michael H. Hunt of the University of North Carolina, Chapel Hill, identifies three core ideas of an American foreign policy ideology, and in the fourth essay he discusses the centrality of one of them: racism.

Melvyn P. Leffler of the University of Virginia, in the fifth essay, argues that the pursuit of national security—the defense of core values and concrete interests against foreign threats—best explains U.S. behavior abroad. In highlighting the exercise of U.S. power to protect core values, Leffler points not only to the realities of material interests, territory, and ideology but also to perceptions of foreign threats. In the sixth selection, J. Garry Clifford of the University of Connecticut explains how bureaucratic politics—the give-and-take bargaining within the U.S. government—shapes the pacing, implementation, and therefore the outcome of foreign policy. Because of all the tugging and hauling in the policy process, U.S. foreign relations do not always come out as leaders intended.

The World-System, Hegemony, and Decline

THOMAS J. McCORMICK

Since modern history began in the late fifteenth century, the earth's inhabitants have lived in three distinct types of environments: the capitalist world-system (or world economy), the external world (empires), or the minisystems of subsistence communities. For the past five hundred years, the dynamic growth and expansion of the world-system has been at the expense of the other two. The Ottoman Empire of the Turks disappeared, the Russian Empire of the Romanovs and the empire of the Manchus in China collapsed in revolutionary disarray, all victims of their archaic political systems and the inability of their quasi-feudal economies to compete with or alternatively to insulate themselves from the more dynamic and efficient economies of the capitalist world-system. Likewise, the minisystems of Eastern Europe, Ireland, the Americas, Africa, and Asia were, over time and despite great resistance, wrenched away from their subsistence, village agriculture and integrated into a cash nexus and the world market. By the late twentieth century, the remnants of the external world of empires, the Soviet Union and the Peoples' Republic of China, had emerged from the containment and self-isolation of the Cold War and begun to experiment with market economies in place of command (planned) economies. Also by that time, the remaining isolated pockets of subsistence systems had virtually disappeared from the face of the earth. The revolutionary expansion of European capitalism and Mediterranean civilization, begun a half-millennium earlier, seemed about to reach its final, all-encompassing frontier. The world-system and the world itself seemed almost one—one world rather than three.

Throughout its five centuries, capitalism has been an inherently expansionistic type of economy. The key to accumulating capital, enlarging market shares, and maximizing profits has historically been long-distance trade, especially by large capitalists with political connections and economic reserves. That was true of Baltic merchant capitalists in the seventeenth century rerouting their grain ships to the Adriatic to take advantage of local famine and exorbitant prices. It was true of nineteenth-century British industrial capitalists using their superior technology and economies of scale to wipe out hand-crafted textiles in Turkey, India, and China and to enlarge the British share of the world market. It is true today of finance capitalists in New York whose overseas bank loans to newly industrializing countries give a high rate of return no longer possible at home. In short, capitalism as an economic system has always functioned most profitably and most efficiently when its universe of options has been sufficiently large and fluid for capital, goods, services, and people to move from one place to another in order to secure greater returns, even if that place be both distant and foreign. Moreover, even when capitalism has not functioned efficiently, its spatial expansion into distant empires and subsistence enclaves has fueled its rejuvenation. Periodically, crises of overproduction have resulted from the contradictory instincts of entrepreneurs to keep production high (to enlarge market shares) and wage bills low (to reduce production costs).

Historically, however, global expansion of new markets for goods and capital has helped restore demand to the level of supply, raised the rate of profit, and replaced economic depression with economic boom. The long slumps of 1680–1730, 1870–1900, and 1930–50 were all resolved in part by the creation of new economic frontiers: the mercantile empires of the eighteenth century, the new imperialism of the late nineteenth century, and the economic internationalization promoted by American foreign policy in the mid-twentieth century.

During the last decade, a number of academic observers have concluded that capitalism's tendency toward international fluidity eventually produced a configuration that could properly be described as a system, a combination of parts forming a complex, unitary whole. Fernand Braudel and Immanuel Wallerstein, in their epic studies of early European capitalism, concluded that such a system was in place by 1650. Others feel that it was not until the nineteenth century that an integrated global division of labor allowed capitalism to merit characterization as a system.

Studies advancing a world-system analysis (including this study) argue that there are three constants about that world system, even though the particular forms it takes are always changing. First, there are always implicit geographical boundaries within that system, and they are essentially defined by the spatial limits of the world market economy at any given time. In our contemporary period, the term *free world* is essentially a synonym for the capitalist world-system. Cold War rhetoric may impart a more ideological twist to the phrase, but Nelson Rockefeller's chief aide got at its root in late 1941 when he declared that America was "committed to the fight for freedom of economic life and for freedom of the seas, in a word, the fight for a free world." Second, there is always a center or pole to the system, a dominant city that acts as the coordinating point and clearing house of international capital. Its location has shifted historically from the Mediterranean to Northern Europe to North America (and perhaps yet to Northeast Asia), but there is always a central metropolis, be it London in 1845 or New York in 1945.

Finally, the system consists of three successive zones, each performing a specialized function in a complex, international division of labor. *Core* countries (the First World) own most of the high-tech, high-profit enterprises. The *periphery* (the Third World) specializes in primary production of agricultural commodities and raw materials—they are the "hewers of wood and carriers of water." Between them, the *semiperiphery* (the Second World) performs intermediate functions of transport, local capital mobilization, and less complex, less profitable forms of manufacturing. Historically, there has been some limited mobility of individual nations between zones, including America's own transformation from a semiperipheral country in 1790 to a core country by 1890. Likewise, changing technology continually redefines what constitutes high-, intermediate-, or low-value enterprises. Textiles, steel, and shipbuilding might have been high-value activities in an earlier era but have become low- or intermediate-value in the contemporary age of electrical equipment. What remains constant are the zones themselves and the specialized (and unequally rewarded) division of labor among them. Hence, in 1988 there is a world-system in which North America, Japan, and Europe constitute the core and specialize in electronics, capital goods, diversified agriculture, and finance; the less developed countries (LDCs) of Africa, Southeast Asia, and the Caribbean basin, as the periphery, specialize in non-petroleum raw materials and single-crop agriculture; and the newly industrializing countries (NICs), Mexico, Brazil, South Africa, Israel, Iran, India, China, and those of Eastern Europe and the Pacific rim, as the semiperiphery, specialize in shipping, petroleum, credit transactions, and consumer goods manufacturing.

The emergence of a capitalist world economy coincided with the emergence of the modern nation-state as the prevailing political unit of governance, and the nation-state has both fostered and inhibited the capitalist world economy. On one hand, nation-states have often provided crucial stimulation of economic growth and development: their banking, taxation, credit, and internal improvement policies have frequently aided domestic entrepreneurs in accumulating capital and minimizing risks. On the other hand, those same nation-states have often interfered with and impeded the fluidity and mobility of capital, goods, and labor across national boundaries. This nationalist bias is caused in part by nation-states being, by definition, wedded to specific territories and committed to the defense and sustenance of their citizens. In part, too, it reflects the uneven pace of capitalist development among countries, and the unequal division of labor and rewards that results from it. The frequent consequence has been an attempt by "have-not" countries to overtake "have" countries through nationalistic economic measures, often referred to as mercantilistic policies in earlier periods and, in our own time, as import-substitution policies (i.e., substitution of indigenous products for those previously imported). Whatever the cause of this nationalist bias, the resulting farm subsidies, military spending, protective tariffs, navigation laws, capital controls, and restricted currency convertibility have constituted serious obstacles to a free world of economic internationalism and interdependence in which capitalism, as a purely economic system, can realize its maximum efficiency and profitability. So, too, have the policies of territorial expansion that often accompany economic nationalism interfered, by seeking to monopolize whole regions of the earth for the benefit of a single national economy. Examples are the British mercantile empire of the eighteenth century and the Japanese Greater East Asian Co-Prosperity Sphere of the twentieth. In sum, nation-states have tended to pursue policies of economic autarky—capitalism in one country or one self-contained trading bloc—and such approaches limit the options of capital in pursuit of maximum rewards.

Hegemony historically has operated to soften the contradiction between the internationalist imperatives of capitalism and the nationalist biases of political nation-states. In the context of the world-system, hegemony means that one nation possesses such unrivaled supremacy, such predominant influence in economic power, military might, and political-ideological leadership, that no other power, or combination of powers, can prevail against it. Economic supremacy is the indispensable base of hegemony, for all other forms of power are possible with it and no others possible, for very long, without it. Any hegemonic power must, simultaneously, contain the dominant financial center, possess a clear comparative advantage in a wide range of high-tech, high-profit industries, and function commercially as both the world's major exporter and its major importer. Beyond mere economic power, it must possess clear military superiority and ideological hegemony as well. By fear or respect, it must be able to exert its political will over the rest of the system and command deference to its principles and policies.

Hegemony and the balance of power have been on opposing sides of the contradiction between economic internationalism and national autarky or self-sufficiency.

The balance of power attempts to use the alignment of forces and, if necessary, war, to prevent any one power from achieving such preponderance that it could impose economic internationalism on autarkic-minded nations. A single hegemonic power, however, has a built-in incentive to force other nations to abandon their national capitalism and economic controls and to accept a world of free trade, free capital flows, and free currency convertibility. As the world's dominant economic power, a hegemonic power has the most to gain from such a free world and the most to lose from nationalistic efforts to limit the free movement of capital, goods, and currencies. So the preponderant world power is unequivocally self-interested in using its economic power, as workshop and banker of the free world, to create institutions and ground rules that foster the internationalization of capital. It finds it inherently advantageous to use its political power as ideologue of the world-system to preach the universal virtues of freedom of the seas, free trade, open door policies, comparative advantage, and a specialized division of labor. It finds it necessary to use its military power as global policeman to protect the international system against external antagonists, internal rebellions, and internecine differences: to be judge, jury, and executioner, insuring that the ground rules of internationalism are not impeded by either friend or foe.

Only twice in the history of the capitalist world economy has hegemony triumphed over balance of power as the prevailing structure of the international system. Great Britain functioned as hegemonic center between roughly 1815 and 1870, and the United States did so between roughly 1945 and 1970. (Others argue that the Dutch republic did so as well, in the late seventeenth century, but the argument seems rather forced.) In each instance, world war was crucial to the formation of hegemony. It radically redistributed power and wealth in ironic fashion, denying hegemony to a European continental power while bestowing postwar supremacy on its balance of power adversary.

In the first instance, France attempted through its Napoleonic Wars (constituting the first truly world war) to impose its dominance on the Eurasian heartland, the very center of European capitalism. Great Britain attempted to thwart that ambition through its traditional balance of power politics, and it ultimately prevailed. But the wars and attendant revolutions were so long, so destructive, so destabilizing that they temporarily obliterated the old balance of power system and left Great Britain the tacit sovereign of the post-Napoleonic world. In the second instance (as we shall see in detail later), Germany, under both the Kaiser and Hitler, attempted to impose its dominance on the same Eurasian heartland, while Anglo-American balance of power diplomacy sought to prevent it. But the ironic consequence of World Wars I and II was, by denying hegemony to the Germans, to make it possible for the Americans to become the acknowledged leaders of the free world. In each case, hegemony made it nearly impossible for other core powers to use war as an instrument of diplomacy against each other—a Pax Britannica for the mid-nineteenth century and a Pax Americana for the mid-twentieth. In each case, hegemony blunted the forces of economic nationalism and facilitated greater global interdependence, enabling a freer and easier *exchange* of goods in the nineteenth century and the multinational *production* of goods in the twentieth.

Hegemony is always impermanent, as Great Britain discovered and the United States is discovering. Indeed, hegemony undermines the very economic supremacy upon which it necessarily must rest. Two related tendencies lead the preponderant power to neglect investment in its civilian research and production and to transform itself into a *rentier* nation and *warfare* state. There is a tendency to overinvest and lend overseas and to live off dividends and interests (renting out one's money, hence *rentier*). It happens because it is easy to do, since the hegemonic power is in a position to secure favorable treatment for its capital throughout the free world. It happens also because it is necessary, since higher wage bills make it more profitable to invest overseas than at home. The higher wage bills themselves are part of the burden of power: the necessity to demonstrate to managers and workers that there are ample economic rewards for supporting an internationalist foreign policy with their votes, tax dollars, and conscription.

The tendency to overinvest abroad is compounded by the tendency to overinvest in military production. Essential to the hegemonic power's capacity to act as global policeman, military research and production receive favored treatment from the government in the form of state-subsidized high profits. The government becomes a more predictable and more profitable customer than private individuals and corporate consumers. The end result is to divert capital from civilian to military production, to the neglect of modernization needs of the domestic industrial plant. This disinvestment, as some term it, erodes over time the economic underpinnings of hegemony and makes it more difficult to compete with other core powers who have avoided the pitfalls of similar disinvestment. Moreover, like a snowball rolling downhill, the problems compound as the hegemon grows aware of its decline. Confronted with declining profitability in the civilian sector, it is likely to stress military spending even more as the easiest way to assure its capitalists of adequate returns—often spending far in excess of any plausible military purposes. Relatedly, it is likely to exploit its continuing function as world policeman to extort special privileges from its competitors: favored treatment for its currency, its trade, and its investments in exchange for continued police protection. In short, it is likely to become even more of a rentier or warfare economy and speed up the very decline it is trying to retard.

Cultural Interactions

EMILY R. ROSENBERG

During the early conquest of the New World, a scientist in Europe prophesied that "The New World, which you have conquered, will now conquer you." The United States in the twentieth century, having become the most powerful of the states created in the New World, did indeed launch what many Europeans considered a reverse conquest. What Englishman W. T. Stead in 1901 called the "Americanization of the World," however, came less through armaments, armadas, and mass movements of population than through the exportation of cultural products. In recent years, scholars of American foreign relations, taking cues from social and cultural history, have given increased attention to this history of cultural expansion.

"Cultural Interactions," by Emily Rosenberg from Stanley Kutler, ed., *Encyclopedia of the United States in the Twentieth Century,* Volume II. (New York: Charles Scribner & Sons, 1996), pp. 695, 698–708, 710–715.

Two themes emerge from this growing body of scholarship. First, mass commercial culture, encompassing both mass-mediated entertainment and mass-consumption lifestyles, provided the most dynamic engine of U.S. expansion. In fact, over the past century, American mass culture came to provide the very definition of what was "modern": assembly-line production for a broad market, consumerism fed by advertising, and media packaging of identity, lifestyle, and taste. *America* came to signify the future, affluence, modernity, and freedom. Such power over meanings and expectations about the future should not be taken lightly; it may be a power more important than the kinds measured in throw-weights or megatons.

Second, throughout the twentieth century, the U.S. government played a significant role in promoting the expansion of cultural industries and activities. Domestic discussions about international cultural exchange have often assumed that, because the United States had a privately owned media, its cultural expansion was divorced from government policy. But the lack of public ownership over media certainly has not meant an absence of governmental involvement. Especially during times of war, the government energetically promoted U.S. cultural and informational enterprises as the advance agents of "freedom."

Analyzing American cultural expansion presents interpretive challenges. Modernization theories of the 1950s simply assumed that America's cultural influence was both "free" and benevolent. Repelled by the state-manipulated informational systems of Hitler's Germany and Stalin's USSR, intellectuals in the early Cold War era claimed that the growth of American-style, privately owned media would promote both democracy and prosperity in countries around the globe. Advocating an international open door for information and culture seemed a nearly uncontestable counterpart to the Cold War goal of advancing freedom and democracy.

During the 1960s and 1970s, more critical scholars challenged modernization theories by adapting the concept of "imperialism" to the cultural realm. Studies of America's "cultural imperialism" tended to link cultural expansion, especially by U.S.-based media, to global exploitation by American capitalism. Scholarship in this tradition raised important questions about the process of international cultural exportation and helped stimulate critical study of a subject that, too long, had been guided by unexamined faiths.

This essay departs from both the modernization and the cultural imperialism paradigms. It neither portrays America's growing cultural dominance as inexorably uplifting nor implies that cultural implantation has destroyed the world's rich cultural diversity and turned everyone into passive recipients of American capitalism. Influenced by poststructuralist theory, this essay assumes that cultural exchanges are contextually negotiated, vary considerably according to time and place, and are marked by both acceptance and resistance. It also suggests that U.S. cultural products have been important purveyors of trends that now ironically seem "international." In the late twentieth century it may be that Americanization and internationalization have actually become blended phenomena, both characterized by the simultaneous globalization and cultural fragmentation associated with postmodernity. . . .

Exportation of mass cultural products predated the Great War [World War I], but the national emergency enlarged governmental promotion of America's entertainment and informational industries. The war, and governmental assistance, formed the basis for rapid international expansion of American mass culture in the 1920s.

President Woodrow Wilson appointed George Creel, a journalist and progressive reformer, as head of the Committee on Public Information (CPI), charged with selling the war at home and abroad. Creel did not see these promotional activities as propaganda or manipulation. Rather, he insisted that he was purveying truth, information, and education. Firmly believing in what he termed the Gospel of Americanism, Creel shared Wilson's conviction that the United States had a special mission in the world to promote international harmony and peace, even if the means involved war. Creel did not try to sell the war so much as he tried to sell America as a symbol of progress and of social and industrial fairness. . . .

Creel appreciated the persuasive power of the printed word, but his true genius lay in marshaling moving images to serve the national cause. America's motion pictures were already fairly popular exports. Developed in the United States by an immigrant-influenced film industry for a largely immigrant audience, Hollywood's films of the silent era easily crossed boundaries of language and culture. . . .

. . . During the war, competition tilted decidedly in America's favor. The film industries of Britain, France, and Germany collapsed under the pressures of financially strapped governments, shortages of material such as film, and disruption of export trade. Creel, meanwhile, made sure that Hollywood producers received allotments of carefully controlled nitrate, a scarce component vital to both the film and munitions industries. Moreover, the technical and stylistic innovations of American filmmakers attracted audiences. Unlike their European counterparts, American films owed more to the streetwise influences of vaudeville and the lavish extravaganzas of nineteenth-century popular pageants (including Wild West shows) than to elite art and culture. With or without governmental assistance, Hollywood had laid the basis for a global entertainment empire. . . .

. . . American film exports boomed throughout the 1920s and came to dominate world markets: American films constituted 95 percent of those shown in Britain and Canada, 70 percent of those in France, 80 percent of those in South America. Even the advent of talkies, which many people had predicted would bring the death of film exports, had little effect. After a short period of experimentation, subtitles and dubbing began to work satisfactorily, adding little additional production cost. . . .

Like the motion picture industry, America's radio industry also received a jump-start from government during World War I and then expanded during the 1920s. Before World War I, Britain dominated international cable lines, the chief form of international communications, and could easily invade the confidentiality of both commercial and strategic cables originating in the United States. For the U.S. government, promoting a new network of point-to-point wireless communications became a priority. During the war, the government nationalized the radio industry, rapidly enlarged its capacities, and worked with business leaders to forge a global communications network. When broadcasting (as distinguished from point-to-point transmissions) of radio messages emerged as a major medium of entertainment and information after the war, American technology was in the forefront. . . .

Exports of information, film, and radio were part of a much broader outflow of products associated with American mass culture. American specialty products in the post–World War I era—electrical goods, automobiles, oil—were strong carriers of cultural values. America's giant electrical companies, for example, sold the hardware for the growth of radio broadcasting, made illumination more widespread, and pushed home consumer items such as refrigerators. The American automobile, oil, and rubber industries all reinforced each other in promoting internationally a car culture that was also developing at home. And modern advertising, given a boost by the example of Creel's wartime success in salesmanship and by new studies on the psychology of selling, introduced these lifestyle-transforming products to international markets in more compelling ways than ever before. . . .

American tourists and intellectuals of the 1920s (even those who often denounced America for its materialism) also spread consumer values. The age of mass tourism was just dawning. By the late 1920s, many middle-class Americans could afford foreign travel. Numbers of tourists to Europe—the favored destination—rose from 15,000 in 1912 to more than a quarter of a million in 1929. American intellectuals also had a growing impact, especially in Europe. The American writers and artists who migrated to Paris in the interwar period contributed to what Jean-Paul Sartre described as France's greatest literary experience. American Studies developed respectability, as the Sorbonne, inspired by the World War I alliance between France and the United States, became the first European university to establish a permanent teaching position in American Civilization (in 1917). Universities in England, Germany, Austria, the Soviet Union, and elsewhere also instituted American Studies.

Although the U.S. government promoted the expansion of American newspapers, movies, radio, and consumer products in various ways, one cultural export boomed without official encouragement: jazz. Jazz was one of the most controversial of cultural exports. Evolving from African American rhythms, jazz music and dance projected a sensuality that alarmed many middle-class, white Americans. The custodians of culture, who would have liked America represented abroad by "high" art and literature, hardly considered it an asset to America's international image. . . .

The American cultural invasion of the interwar years brought a backlash of cultural nationalism. Influential, sensational books in many countries around the world assailed the rising cultural power of the United States. . . . Critiques such as these leveled an array of charges, from German disgruntlement at a country that would enforce a constitutional ban against beer drinking to broader jabs against America's alleged crass materialism, soulless individualism, and worship of technology. A board of concerned British citizens, including the novelist Thomas Hardy, warned that the tasteless melodramatics of American films imperiled the Empire by portraying whites as fools who worshiped money and fashion and had no stable home life. . . .

The discourses of anti-Americanism that accumulated as American cultural influence grew, however, need to be treated cautiously. In the countries of Europe, and also of Asia and Latin America, the "meaning" of America came to be encoded within cultural and political debates that often had little to do with the United States itself. The European avant-garde, for example, greeted American jazz and some consumer goods as democratic impulses that could help sweep away class pretensions in a new Europe. (Many of the most fervent admirers of America, however, had never visited the country; and many others did not like it when they did.) Similarly, anti-Americanism created a foil against which presumed national virtues or characteristics could be reinforced and applauded. Anti-American critics stressed U.S. crime and violence (frequently mentioning Al Capone), materialism, and licentiousness to argue for cultural preservation at home. . . .

If economic hard times and cultural nationalism during the 1930s challenged American expansiveness, World War II brought new and unparalleled opportunities for extending U.S. influence. New wartime propaganda agencies [such as the Office of War Information], the presence of U.S. army troops around the globe, the Americanization associated with postwar occupations, postwar aid and informational programs, and the anticommunist cultural offensive launched in the early 1950s all helped the United States attain preeminent cultural, as well as military, power in the post–World War II era. . . .

The global anticommunist cultural offensive of the 1950s arose together with the economic, political, and military mobilization recommended in the important 1950 National Security Council document NSC-68. Immediately after World War II, the OWI had been disbanded and the State Department, settling into peacetime, emphasized "cultural" rather than "informational" (i.e., propaganda) initiatives. Congress provided direct funding for educational exchanges under the Smith-Mundt Act of 1948, which created the Fulbright program. As Soviet-American antagonism grew, however, those advocating more aggressive promotion of Americanism attacked expenditures for slow, elite-based cultural exchanges. In 1950 President Truman, responding to the recommendations of NSC-68 and to the Korean War, initiated a "Campaign of Truth.". . . The new initiative expanded Fulbright exchanges but also laid the foundations for more targeted propaganda by placing information offices, libraries, and mass media products in countries around the world. Nearly 300 centers were established by the late 1950s, offering English and stressing the value of American-style democracy, labor unions, and technological accomplishments. . . .

The new activism in informational diplomacy gathered even greater momentum during the Korean War. President Dwight Eisenhower, taking an aggressive stand, decided to institutionalize the Campaign of Truth in a new agency, the United States Information Agency (USIA), formed in 1953. The USIA built on the earlier informational policies of the OWI, the occupation governments, and the Campaign of Truth to design its programs. It undertook the dissemination of American books, art, music and films. It instituted and expanded programs to encourage educational exchange, American Studies curricula, educational reform, magazine publication, lectures, and exhibitions. USIA news services devised ways of getting American-slanted news into local newspapers and magazines under the by-lines of local journalists. . . .

The postwar cultural offensive, of course, also involved film. . . . The Motion Picture Export Association (MPEA), a cartel representing the American film industry, formed in 1945. In the red-baiting climate of the 1950s, major film studios extended the wartime practice of screening each film for content that might be objectionable to either the U.S. government or a friendly foreign nation. Industry leaders such as Ronald Reagan and Walt Disney regularly reported to the FBI concerning left-wing activity in Hollywood. In return for this self-regulation and demonstrated anticommunism, the American government used its economic and political muscle on behalf of "free flow" for the film trade. . . .

Historians have tended to focus on nuclear shields, alliance systems, and joint military maneuvers as the substance of "free world" alignments during the Cold War. The strength of these political/military arrangements, however, emerged within the context of another mighty force: the semiotic power that equated America with an inevitable and desirable future that was "modern." Just as anticommunism helped reinforce symbolic associations between "freedom" and American cultural products, the semiotics of America's consumer-driven, mass-mediated products also helped bind the anticommunist coalition together. Policy and business elites of the postwar era clearly understood that a "cultural offensive" powerfully served larger geopolitical and economic interests.

Creation of a permanent peacetime propaganda apparatus to spread American culture marked a significant departure for U.S. policy, but America's cultural influence abroad did not come solely from governmental design. America's mass culture seemed to have almost boundless appeal, especially to youth. Although USIA officials sometimes complained about movies that portrayed Americans as gangsters, racists, foolish millionaires, and corrupt materialists, Hollywood's America packed box offices and fed the fascination with American life. Like movies, privately sponsored radio programs, such as *Hit Parade* and *The Jack Benny Show,* attracted audiences and won friends. U.S. television networks, fearing saturation in domestic markets, aggressively invested in foreign stations and arranged syndication. . . .

As in the 1920s, U.S. consumer products continued to be successful missionaries for the American Way. American-style self-service grocery stores, chain-store retailing, and installment buying developed in Europe as well as in parts of Latin America and Asia in the 1950s. America's mass-marketed magazines, especially Henry Luce's *Life,* fed the identification between America and consumer abundance, between "freedom" and purchasing power. *Life's* 1946 feature entitled "Dreams of 1946," for example, pictured a dishwasher, radio, power lawnmower, and other household technologies. Magazines featured women with leisure time provided by electric kitchens and new prepackaged foods. Glamorous housewives with the time to dote on their husbands became another icon for "freedom" during the Cold War. . . .

Some people eagerly embraced American models. Around the world, commentators remarked about the special appeal of American culture to youth. If older generations had seen Britain or France as preeminent cultural centers, the generation born during World War II increasingly looked to the United States. The lingua franca of this global youth culture emanated from the United States in words such as "bar," "DJ," "rock 'n' roll," "sex appeal," "teenager," "be-bop," "glamour girls," "minibar." . . .

[Yet] the fear that U.S. "cultural imperialism" would facilitate its political and economic domination became even more widespread during and after the generally unpopular Vietnam War. In the 1970s, the global dominance of the American media and the formation of a "nonaligned movement" in Cold War politics prompted some international politicians to try to redefine "free flow" as having to do with the balance of information sources rather than simply with private ownership. Urho Kekkonen, the president of Finland, for example, noted in a 1973 speech that the global flow of information is "one-way, unbalanced traffic and in no way possesses the depth and range which the principles of freedom of speech require." . . .

The backlash against American "cultural imperialism" seemed to peak in the 1970s and early 1980s. Resistance to American power, however, often had a twist. Just as young protestors in the United States used rock 'n' roll songs as their protest anthems, so did youth abroad. Crowds who might one day throw stones at U.S. embassies might, the next day, gather to listen to American rock music. The worldwide student unrest of 1968 seemed interwoven in a kind of global youth culture, often with origins in the United States itself. Ironically, even when America's international policies failed to bring goodwill, its popular culture often gained converts for the future. . . .

In China, similarly, Americanization became linked to youthful protests. In the mid-1980s the Chinese government began a program to attract tourist money by developing historical sites, golf courses, theme parks, and resorts. . . . Along with displays of leisure came fashion. New designs in clothing and shoes, Chinese disco, and a burgeoning presence of advertisements by international companies showed the new influence of westernized, consumer-oriented tastes. These trends also accompanied outspokenness against Chinese officials and dissatisfaction with the structure of China's political economy.

The westernization that was cautiously encouraged by the government early in the decade took an abrupt and brutal turn with the government's massacre of student protesters in Tiananmen Square in 1989, but cultural change continued to spread. . . .

The domino-like fall of communist governments in Eastern Europe during 1989 and 1990 opened even more opportunities for U.S. cultural expansion. As Pepsi developed ads that associated their cola with images of the crumbling Berlin Wall, McDonald's gloated over the taste that Eastern Europeans were developing for American cuisine. Billboards in Prague carried the message "I am a billboard, I sell your products." *Playboy,* in a full-page ad in the *New York Times* (15 December 1989) proclaimed itself to be in the forefront of "EXPORTING THE AMERICAN DREAM.". . .

In the late twentieth century, international flows of finance, information, and entertainment—managed by computers, digitalized information networks, and satellites—are rendering national boundaries less important. Whereas major media industries in the past were clearly anchored within the nation-state system, the information revolution that will extend into the twenty-first century transcends state boundaries. . . .

The very consumer-oriented specialty commodities upon which America built both economic and cultural power in the 1920s now comprise the sectors that best exemplify the new transnational, globalized economy and culture: automobiles, electrical appliances, food processing. During the 1980s, most giant American manufacturing firms substantially cut jobs in the United States and added to their labor forces abroad. Ford now builds a "world car" from parts manufactured and assembled on four continents. Even America's signature specialty product, the Hollywood film, is now a globalized phenomenon. . . .

Throughout much of the twentieth century, Americans exported, often with significant assistance from government, a distinctive mass culture that identified America with the future and served the country's geopolitical interests. As technologies of information and entertainment have spread in the late twentieth century, however, cultural interactions are less and less amenable to an analytical frame focused on the nation state. In this postmodern era, marked by simultaneous globalization and fragmentation, Americanization and internationalization increasingly overlap, and sites of cultural interaction multiply with less and less relationship to national boundaries. One might paraphrase the older prophecy that opened this essay and direct it to the United States itself: "The world, which you have conquered, will now conquer you."

The Gendering of Peoples and Nations

ANDREW ROTTER

An analysis of gender illuminates important aspects of relations between nations; here the concern is with the United States, in relation to India and, tangentially, to Pakistan. [The scholar] Mrinalini Sinha has written, "Empires and nations are gendered ideological constructs," to which one might add that nations—reacting to the real differences between them—also construct each other. For the purposes of this article, gender, or gendering, is not a static idea, but a transnational process: it is the assignment of certain characteristics based on prevailing ideas of masculinity and femininity to a people and nation by another people and nation. Masculinity and femininity are not, in this view, biologically determined categories, but culturally and socially conditioned constructs. Nations and the people who constitute them become gendered, and this affects the policies that other nations pursue toward them.

The history of United States foreign relations is not generally held to be susceptible to gender analysis. The makers of American foreign policy, mostly men, do not talk explicitly about gender issues or intentionally use a gendered vocabulary when they discuss their policies toward other countries. They talk about strategy and geopolitics, economics and access to raw materials, and systems, ours versus theirs. Because of this, as [the historian] Joan W. Scott has written, most historians believe that gender "refers only to those areas . . . involving relations between the sexes. Because, on the face of it, war, diplomacy, and high politics have not been explicitly about those relationships, gender seems not to apply and so continues to be irrelevant to the thinking of historians concerned with issues of politics and power."

Scott herself argues that "high politics itself is a gendered concept," and at least one diplomatic historian has pursued this insight. In her two important essays, Emily S. Rosenberg has suggested that historians of United States foreign relations undertake "a quest to understand the ever-changing ideologies related to gender, and their social and political implications." . . .

Examination of the gender issue requires the use of sources not often studied by diplomatic historians, among them anthropology and psychology texts, photographs, popular literature, travelers' accounts, films . . . and plays. The study also demands an unconventional reading of conventional sources on policy making. One must look at the usual published documents, in the State Department *Foreign Relations* volumes and elsewhere, and also make the rounds of American presidential libraries and national archives in the United States, Great Britain, and India. But the researcher with gender in mind must look for odd things in the documents: stray remarks about personal style or gesture, comments about a people's alleged "emotionalism" or "effeminacy," and even references to the kinds of parties American hosts put on for their Indian or Pakistani guests. What would seem a collection of marginalia to most diplomatic historians becomes a treasure trove of information demanding thick description to someone interested in culture.

Reprinted by permission from Andrew Rotter, "Gender Relations, Foreign Relations: The United States and South Asia, 1947–1964," *Journal of American History* (81) September 1994.

Begin with the Western idea, which persists over time, that India is a female country. One of the most influential books about India written by a Westerner was Katherine Mayo's *Mother India,* published in 1927, a scathing attack on Hindu customs and practices. Mayo's choice of title was no accident; it built on a long tradition of representing India as female. The early twentieth-century American traveler Sydney Greenbie noted, apparently without irony, that on a map India "looked like the ponderous milk-bags of a cow holding the very living essence of Asia." Writers contrasted the West and India in ways that evoked gender. The West was grasping, materialistic, scientific, and calculating; India was spiritual, impulsive, and even irrational. "The masculine science of the West," wrote Greenbie, "has found out and wooed and loved or scourged this sleepy maiden of mysticism." In the discourse of India's relations with the West, concludes Richard Cronin, "one metaphor emerges as dominant. The West is a man, the East is a woman."

The Western representation of India as female conferred effeminacy on most Indian men. Caught in the enervating web of Hinduism, which Westerners regarded as less a religion than a pathology, the majority of Indian men had been deprived of their manliness and their virility. In the context of gender, it is possible to discern three features that Westerners historically assigned to most Indian men. The first of these was passivity and its more exaggerated forms; the second was emotionalism; the third was a lack of heterosexual energy. All of these features were associated with femininity, which Westerners regarded as effeminacy if exhibited by a man, and all imposed on India the Western constructions of the feminine and the masculine.

The first of these features amalgamated passivity, servility, and cowardice. Nothing, argued Westerners, could stir Hindu men out of their passive torpor. Indian men could endure anything, evidently without suffering from a sense of shame because of their inaction. They did not resist oppressors but rather regarded them with stupefying indifference. In *Mother India* Mayo wrote: "India was . . . the flaccid subject of a foreign rule. . . . Again and again conquering forces came sweeping through the mountain passes down out of Central Asia, and the ancient Hindu stock, softly absorbing each recurrent blow, quivered—and lay still." There was a "Hindu craze" in the United States during the 1920s and 1930s, and thousands of Americans became familiar with the "three levels of conduct" of Vedanta, the type of Hinduism most often brought to the country by Indian spiritual leaders, or swamis. Level one was "obedient activity"; level two "desireless activity"; the third and highest level was "pure passivity." It is not hard to imagine that such exhortations to obedience, renunciation, and quiescence could have been borrowed from prescriptive literature written for early twentieth-century American women.

The exaggerated form of passivity was servility. This, Westerners declared, Hindu men had in abundance. Many subscribed (at least implicitly) to John Stuart Mill's dictum that "in truth, the Hindu, like the eunuch, excels in the qualities of the slave." While watching a German hotel manager in Bombay discipline a servant by clouting him in the jaw and seeing the servant's taking it without protest, Mark Twain was reminded of his childhood and the "forgotten fact that this was the *usual* way of explaining one's desires to a slave." The traveler Henry M. Field was astonished and delighted with the apparent servility of Indian men. He was "surrounded and waited upon by soft-footed Hindoos, who glided about noiselessly like cats, watching every look, eager to anticipate every wish before they heard the word of command. I was never the object of such reverence before." Everyone called him "sahib," a title of respect, and the servants automatically rose in his presence. "I never knew before how great a being I was," Field wrote [in 1877]. "There is nothing like going far away from home, to the other side of the world, among Hindoos or Hottentots, to be fully appreciated." . . .

The idea that Indian men were passive, servile, and cowardly persisted into the Cold War period. British and American policy makers condemned Indian foreign policy makers for their unwillingness to take a stand in the conflict between the United States and the Soviet Union. A British official characterized Indian policy toward Indochina in 1950 as "non-interference i.e. doing nothing." Sir Archibald Nye, the perceptive British high commissioner in India during the late 1940s and early 1950s, blamed "Gandhian ethics" for what he called India's "quietist policy of non-resistance to aggression" and noted that Indian leaders were inclined to make "pronouncements which, when trouble appears on the horizon, are not acted upon." Americans agreed with this view. Officials in the Eisenhower administration reported that the Indians were "fearful" of United States arms sales to [its more openly anti-Soviet neighbor] Pakistan because "physically they are weak and fear aggression," a fear policy makers thought irrational and alarmist. . . .

A second trait that according to Americans and other Westerners revealed the effeminacy of Hindu men was emotionalism, usually associated with hypersensitivity. Rather than deal with issues logically and coolly, Hindu men flew off the handle—just as American women were allegedly apt to do. Americans constantly found verification for the cliché that the West was rational and tough, the East emotional and sensitive. In a 1948 profile, the Central Intelligence Agency (CIA) described Jawaharlal Nehru, the Indian prime minister: "Nehru is a man of broad vision and of integrity, but his character is weakened by a tendency toward emotionalism which at times destroys his sense of values. He is gracious as well as brilliant, but volatile and quick-tempered." A sense of pride came naturally with independence, but the Indians were an especially sensitive people—or so claimed ambassadors to India Loy Henderson (1948–1951) and Chester Bowles (1951–1953). In 1954, the former law partner of Secretary of State John Foster Dulles wrote that Indians had "an almost feminine hypersensitiveness with respect to the prestige of their country." President Dwight D. Eisenhower agreed. Reading of Indian objections to the administration's plan to provide arms for Pakistan, Eisenhower wrote Dulles: "This is one area of the world where, even more than most cases, emotion rather than reason seems to dictate policy."

Finally, Americans believed that Hindu men failed to show a healthy sexual interest in women. This failure was not, of course, a characteristic of American women, but of unmanly American men. Hindu men seemed inclined to homosexuality or, like the great nationalist leader Mohandas Gandhi, sexual renunciation. Visitors to India noticed Indian men hold hands, as they do still. Sculptures of beings that were bifurcated into male and female halves added to the apparent confusion of gender roles in India. . . .

Where did these American representations of India come from? Who constructed gendered India, and why? One answer, perhaps the simplest, is that the representations came from the British and were deployed to serve the purposes of empire. Americans often saw India through British eyes, and the British made a clear distinction between hard-fighting, masculine, Indian men from the north and west—usually Muslims—and weak, effeminate Hindus from the south and Bengal. These images were popularized by Rudyard Kipling, whose stories made archetypes of the loyally militant Muslim and the craven, underhanded Bengali. Kipling's verse "East is East, and West is West, and never the twain shall meet" is well known, but few remember the next two lines: "But there is neither East nor West, Border, nor Breed, nor birth / When two strong men stand face to face, though they come from the ends of earth!" Kipling was referring to the camaraderie between British soldiers and the Muslim Pathans of the northwest frontier. The British who lived in India regarded the Bengali, on the other hand, as "litigious" and "effeminate," a "troublemaker" who "doesn't appeal to many British people in the same way as the very much more manly, direct type from upper India." John Strachey's book *India* led the syllabus for British candidates training for the Indian Civil Service in the late nineteenth century. It included this passage:

> The physical organization of the Bengali is feeble even to effeminacy. He lives in a constant vapor bath. His pursuits are sedentary, his limbs delicate, his movements languid. During many ages he has been trampled on by men of bolder and more hardy breeds . . . his mind bears a singular analogy to his body. It is weak even to helplessness for purposes of manly resistance; but its suppleness and tact move the children of sterner climates to admiration not unmingled with contempt. . . . Englishmen who know Bengal, and the extraordinary effeminacy of its people, find it difficult to treat seriously many of the political declamations in which English-speaking Bengalis are often fond of indulging.

This last comment by Strachey exposed his purposes: the British characterized Bengali men as effeminate as part of the project of imperialism. Gendered British thinking about India emerged simultaneously with the rise of British imperialism. Gender inspired imperialism, allowed it to grow, and justified its frequently tortuous evolution. [The scholar] Ashis Nandy has argued that pre-modern Europe, with its agrarian economy and "peasant cosmology," valued the attributes of "femininity, childhood, and . . . 'primitivism.' " The emergence of capitalism and its concomitants "achievement and productivity" resulted in the rejection of feminine, agrarian values and caused their projection onto the so-called "low cultures of Europe" and cultures in America, Africa, and Asia. By this process, Nandy writes, west Europeans came to see "uncivilized" others paradoxically, as innocent children but also as "devious, effeminate, and passive-aggressive." In combination particularly with economic factors—it was the East India Company, not the British government, that established its rule over much of India in the late eighteenth and early nineteenth centuries—gender explained to Britons why India needed their help. The innocent children of India required the protection of the strong men of the West. Other nations, especially Russia, threatened India. Within the country, the British saw their presence as essential to protect the weakest elements of Indian society. They argued that despite their effeminate cowardliness—or perhaps because of it—Hindu men frequently brutalized the lower castes and women especially. . . . As a matter of fact, they presided over a system that promoted child marriage, abused brides who married with insufficient dowries, and encouraged *sati,* the self-immolation of widows. British imperialists argued that interposing their power between the upper castes and the helpless masses was their only humane course. . . .

Americans learned much of what they knew about empire from the British. The United States became an imperialist nation in its own right, but like the British raj, the American empire was undergirded by perceptions based on gender. Gendered imagery, linked to discourses on race, figured prominently in the white subjugation of Native Americans. The image of the noble savage, childlike and innocent and in communion with Mother Earth, largely gave way to the image of the bloodthirsty savage who threatened white womanhood and therefore had to be controlled. When American policy makers looked abroad in the late nineteenth century, they beheld nations whose populations seemed to cry out for the protection, guidance, and discipline that only white men could provide. As [the historian] Emily Rosenberg notes, "Women, nonwhite races, and tropical countries often received the same kinds of symbolic characterizations from white male policy makers: emotional, irrational, irresponsible, unbusinesslike, unstable, and childlike." Concerned, perhaps, that their own masculinity was at risk—a concern of American men at least as far back as the Revolution, when Tom Paine had charged men to awaken from "fatal and unmanly slumbers"—policy makers developed patriarchal designs on the weaker members of the family of nations. There were figurative children out there who needed help, and there were figurative women who were too soft or emotional to take care of themselves. This metaphor informed American discussions of Latin America, the countries of which were frequently depicted as women in distress, victims (as Cuba and Puerto Rico were) of Spanish villainy. Delicate Chinese mandarins required protection against the brutalities of men from Europe, Russia, and Japan. Theodore Roosevelt's emphasis on the strenuous life and the manly virtues of combat gave rhetorical substance to images of others based on gender. . . .

Like the señoritas who so often represented them in cartoons, the Latin American nations could be wooed by an appropriate suitor—Uncle Sam—and also required male protection from the lecherous Spanish. American gender perceptions of East Asian nations swung on weights and counterweights. For officials at the United States legation in Peking (Beijing) in the late nineteenth century, China was inert, weak, and therefore vulnerable to European imperialism. Chinese mandarins were soft and indolent, surrounded by eunuchs and more concerned with palace intrigue than with putting some necessary steel into the military. That vision changed with the Boxer Rebellion in 1899 and 1900; a cartoon drawn in the latter year shows Uncle Sam and President William McKinley moving against the Boxers with sword and bayonet, though too late for an American woman and child who lie dead before them. Americans viewed the Japanese with ambivalence during the first decades of the twentieth century, but American unease turned to loathing following the "Rape of Nanjing" in 1937.

In Vietnam, the United States fought for and against allegedly unmanly men. Vietnamese men were slight of build and smooth skinned. They held hands, which according to Gen. William Westmoreland, struck the American solders as "odd and effeminate." Who could feel manly fighting for men like these? Why die (in Loren Baritz's ironic phrase) "in defense of perverts"? Vietnamese women also fought the Americans, increasing the humiliation of defeat. President Lyndon B. Johnson, whose efforts to assert his manhood through his foreign policy were at least as pronounced as those of Kennedy, first castrated his chief adversary: "I have Ho Chi Minh's pecker in my pocket"; then effeminized him: "I'm going up old Ho Chi

Minh's leg an inch at a time." The inability of the United States to win in Vietnam caused great frustration, and American cultural discourse after 1973 attempted to reconstruct the shattered masculinity of American men. It may be that American manhood was restored with the United States–led coalition victory over Iraq in the 1991 Gulf War. Saddam Hussein was punished, said George Bush, for having "raped, pillaged, and plundered" Kuwait. As a result, the United States had finally "kicked the Vietnam syndrome." During the brief ground war a *New York Times* reporter saw an American soldier brandish a pair of women's underpants and exult: "*This* is what we are fighting for!" Women were thus symbolically returned to their rightful place in American society, and Kuwait joined the ranks of nations gathered under the protective arm of United States paternalism.

Racism in American Ideology

MICHAEL H. HUNT

By the early twentieth century, three core ideas relevant to foreign affairs had emerged, and they collectively began to wield a strong influence over policy. The capstone idea defined the American future in terms of an active quest for national greatness closely coupled to the promotion of liberty. It was firmly in place by the turn of the century, after having met and mastered a determined opposition on three separate occasions—in the 1790s, the 1840s, and the 1890s. A second element in the ideology defined attitudes toward other peoples in terms of a racial hierarchy. Inspired by the struggle of white Americans to secure and maintain their supremacy under conditions that differed from region to region, this outlook on race was the first of the core ideas to gain prominence. The third element defined the limits of acceptable political and social change overseas in keeping with the settled conviction that revolutions, though they might be a force for good, could as easily develop in a dangerous direction. Attitudes toward revolution, like those toward race, were fairly consistent through the formative first century, but unlike views on race, they were only sporadically evoked in that period. It was not until the 1910s, in response to an outburst of revolutionary activity abroad, that the power and the place of this element in the ideological construct was confirmed.

Now tightly interrelated and mutually reinforcing, these core ideas could provide national leaders with a clear and coherent vision of the world and the American place in it. . . .

[Theodore] Roosevelt, a New York patrician with boundless curiosity, energy, and self-confidence, offers a particularly dramatic illustration of the degree to which the "rise to world power" was an affirmation of core American policy ideas. Roosevelt believed fervently in America's mission. To doubters among his countrymen he had a characteristically forceful and direct reply: "No man is worth his salt who does not believe that the growth of his own country's influence is for the good of all those benighted people who have had the misfortune not to be born within its fold."

The road to national greatness required unremitting struggle, so Roosevelt contended. A compulsive classifier even as a youth, he took a lifelong interest in the natural order and its competitive features. By the 1880s he was avidly Darwinian in his views on international relations (as he was on domestic affairs). Conflict among nations was natural. The fit would prevail and the weak go down to defeat and extinction. . . .

Roosevelt's "strenuous" conception of national greatness dovetailed neatly with his preoccupation with race. Roosevelt read voraciously and wrote extensively on the subject; in expressing himself he could as easily employ formal pseudo-scientific language as the cruder epithets of popular discourse. He regarded the world as a competitive arena for races no less than nations. The clash between civilized races and barbarian ones was inevitable; progress came only through the civilized man "subduing his barbarian neighbor." Not surprisingly Roosevelt considered Anglo-Saxons (he later came to prefer the term "English-speaking" people) the most advanced race. In 1881, in his first foray as an author, he described them as "bold and hardy, cool and intelligent." The American branch had been further strengthened by the frontier experience where lesser races had served as its "natural prey." With the frontier gone, Americans would have to confirm their mettle by joining their English cousins in the race for overseas territory and in the "warfare of the cradle" against the more prolific lower orders, chiefly eastern Europeans, Latin Americans, and blacks.

Of the "lower orders" Roosevelt had little good to say. He found the passivity and national indiscipline and weakness of the Chinese ("Chinks") contemptible, while the Filipinos stood as no better than savages, who on their own could know only "the black chaos of savagery and barbarism." Among the Orientals, only the Japanese escaped his censure. Indeed, they earned his growing admiration for their prowess in defeating China in 1894–95 and Russia a decade later. Latinos ("dagoes") were—in the familiar clichés—hot blooded yet cowardly, politically incompetent, and shockingly miscegenated. The Indians struck Roosevelt as "squalid savages," their fate the inevitable one of a backward people engulfed by civilization. Only their manliness and their penchant for warfare saved them from his utter contempt. Roosevelt reserved the lowest rung in his hierarchy for blacks, deficient in intelligence and moral vigor and "but a few generations removed from the wildest savagery." Like an earlier generation, he took Haiti's "half-savage negroid people" as prime evidence of the political incapacity of "darkeys" in general. . . .

Older attitudes toward race also persisted little changed into the interwar era. They flourished at home in the nativism of the 1920s, itself an encore to the hyperpatriotism and attacks on hyphenates that had marred the war years. With the foreign-born and their children accounting for an alarmingly high proportion of the population (over a fifth), defenders of the old stock and ancestral virtues stirred into action. Congress passed by overwhelming margins laws to keep out undesirable immigrants—Japanese, Filipinos, and southern and eastern Europeans. In the South, Midwest, Southwest, and Far West as many as five million Americans joined the Ku Klux Klan, drawn by its doctrine of white supremacy and its attacks on Catholics, Jews, and other outsiders. The racial hatreds of the time turned most ferociously against blacks, for whom lynchings were but the most brutal of a variety of reminders of their assigned place in the hierarchy of color. . . .

These racial attitudes bore striking fruit in the feelings of condescension and contempt that policymakers occasionally revealed. Franklin D. Roosevelt, advocate of the Good Neighbor policy toward Latin America, unwittingly revealed his feelings of superiority when he offered a backhanded compliment to what he described as "these South American things." He observed, "They think they are just as good as we are," and then broadmindedly conceded that "many of them are." In Cuba in 1933 he demonstrated the strength of his paternalism when he acted on what he conceived to be "our duty" to prevent starvation or chaos among the Cuban people." China, consistent with popular notions, was viewed from Washington and even by its Asian experts as plastic, passive, and in need of American help. Japan was seen as schizoid—"the Prussia of the East," in [Henry Cabot] Lodge's phrase, as well as the best oriental student the Anglo-Saxons had. One side of this split Japanese personality was thought to reflect an indigenous warrior tradition. Treacherous and armed with modern weapons, militaristic leaders controlled their own "emotional population" and pursued a foreign policy of terror and conquest. The other side of the Japanese character was represented by forward-looking, Western-oriented civilians eager to promote international cooperation.

Japan's occupation of Manchuria in 1931 and the invasion of China proper six years later bothered the defenders of Anglo-Saxonism in the East. Stimson and later Roosevelt and his secretary of state Cordell Hull worried that the militarists were in the ascendance. But American leaders also believed that the civilians still had a chance to regain control and reverse a policy of aggression if encouraged by an admonitory and if necessary hard-line U.S. stance. Stimson, confident that his service in the Philippines had given him an insight into "the Oriental mind," was determined to defend the East Asian international order and a U.S. China policy characterized by a "real nobility." Both were threatened by the "virtually mad dogs" that had taken control in Japan. Staging public displays of disapproval, he also fussed and blustered at Japanese envoys in private. Hull, for this part, had by the late 1930s decided that the Japanese were barbarians at the gate intent on joining Hitler in driving the world back into the Dark Ages. Roosevelt bluntly told Japanese diplomats that their policy violated "the fundamental principles of peace and order." . . .

The Roosevelt administration increased the pressure on Tokyo, moved in part by the conviction that these Orientals, proverbially respectful of force, would give way. Economic sanctions, a naval buildup, aid to China, and deployment of the Pacific fleet in a more offensive position, however, produced not the desired retreat or even a slowing of the Japanese advance but the unexpected blow at Pearl Harbor. For Americans this "sneak attack" was an extraordinary outrage (though entirely consistent with assumptions about the wily oriental character). A supposedly inferior people had directly and for the moment successfully challenged a superior people carrying out their self-assigned role as arbiters of civilized behavior.

The American response to the contemporaneous crisis in Europe was also influenced by racial notions. Americans displayed increasing sympathy for their embattled British cousins. By late 1941 more than two-thirds of Americans supported any steps short of war to save Britain. During the same period antisemitism left Americans indifferent to the Holocaust then beginning to unfold. Congress, organized labor, and four-fifths of the public surveyed in 1938 opposed admitting Jewish refugees. Entry into the war did nothing to soften this opposition. Restrictive immigration regulations, interpreted by a prejudiced foreign service, held the flow of European·Jewry to a trickle. . . .

World War II led to an unprecedented, decade-long mobilization and deployment of national power. No sooner had American leaders been assured of victory over the Axis than they set to work on stabilizing and reforming the postwar political and economic order, as well as on countering what they soon concluded was a serious Soviet threat to that order. By the end of 1950 the pattern of the Cold War was set as arms costs mushroomed, aid programs and alliances multiplied, American troops fought their first limited war in Korea, and Washington made the initial commitments that would lead to the second, in Indochina. . . .

After five years of gestation a policy geared to greatness and counterrevolution had taken shape. In Europe it quickly proved a success. The Marshall Plan, the largest of the postwar assistance programs, rescued the Continent's war-ravaged economies, while American-backed Christian Democrats drove the large French and Italian Communist parties from power. The North Atlantic Treaty Organization functioned no less effectively as a shield against the Red Army. . . .

Elsewhere along the containment line stretching from the Middle East to Northeast Asia, American leaders encountered greater difficulties. Indeed, not only here but throughout the "Third World" (in other words, lands unfamiliar to Americans, even those making up the foreign-policy elite) they would find military and political problems ambiguous, complex, intractable, and in the final analysis ill suited to a straightforward policy of containment modeled on the European experience. Rural economies more sorely pinched by poverty than those in Europe, leaders still struggling to end colonial control and give form to their national aspirations, and peoples largely immune to the appeal of American political values left the lands of Asia, Latin America, and Africa in ferment. American cold warriors constantly worried about the disorder these continents were prone to. Unsettled conditions not only made for infirm allies and fickle dependents but, more troubling still, invited Communist subversion or invasion.

Realizing that the solution of these problems was the precondition for the defense of the Third World, Washington came to embrace a policy of development. Development was the younger sibling of containment. While containment focused on the immediate problems of holding the Soviets and their leftist allies at bay, development was intended to provide long-term immunity against the contagion of communism. Like containment, development policy drew inspiration from the long-established ideology. But while containment underlined the obligations of a great nation to defend liberty, development theory drew its inspiration from the old American vision of appropriate or legitimate processes of social change and an abiding sense of superiority over the dark-skinned peoples of the Third World. Social scientists and policymakers often described the goals of development in abstract, neutral catchwords. They spoke of the modernization of traditional societies, nation building, or the stimulation of self-sustaining economic growth in once stagnant economies. In practice, though, these impressive new formulations amounted to little more than a restatement of the old ethnocentric platitudes about uplift and regeneration formerly directed at the Philippines, China, and Mexico. . . .

Condescending and paternalistic, development theory . . . carried forward the long-established American views on race. Changing domestic practices and international conditions had, however, made untenable a hierarchy cast in explicitly

racial terms. From the 1940s Jim Crow laws had fallen under mounting attack, culminating in the civil-rights movement of the late 1950s and early 1960s. Over that
same period a hot war against Nazi supermen and a cold war in the name of freedom and the liberation of oppressed peoples had made racial segregation at home
and pejorative references to race in public a serious embarrassment. Moreover, scientists had by then turned their backs on grand racial theories, thereby further undermining the legitimacy of thinking in terms of race. Policymakers, whose impulse
to see the world in terms of a hierarchy was ever more at odds with the need for
political discretion, found their way out of their bind by recasting the old racial
hierarchy into cultural terms supplied by development theorists. No longer did
leaders dare broadcast their views on barbarous or backward people, race traits, or
skin color. It was instead now the attributes of modernity and tradition that fixed a
people's or nation's place on the hierarchy. . . .

The private comments of American leaders from the 1940s to the 1960s suggest
that the old stereotypes and condescension did indeed cling to the new hierarchy
of development. . . .

George Kennan, the paragon of foreign-policy expertise, revealed how deeply
his "realism" was wedded to a sense of Anglo-Saxon mission when in 1949 he
urged Americans to go "forth to see what we can do in order that stability may be
given to all of the non-communist world." He saw in the Chinese Communists in
1949 "a grievously misguided and confused people" (though he also somehow concluded that theirs was a "fluid and subtle oriental movement"). He was predictably
outraged by the Chinese intervention in the Korean War, "an affront of the greatest
magnitude to the United States." The Chinese had become "savage and arrogant."
They deserved "a lesson." Kennan's response to a tour through Latin America was
equally in keeping with past national attitudes. He was unable to imagine "a more
unhappy and hopeless background for the conduct of human life" than he found in
those "confused and unhappy societies." Latinos had retreated in "a highly personalized, anarchical make-believe," while their prospects for progress were blocked
by an intemperate climate, promiscuous interracial marriage, and the Spanish
legacy of "religious fanaticism, frustrated energy, and an addiction to the most merciless cruelty." Arabs were no better. A brief exposure to Iraq in 1944 had Kennan
recoiling in distaste from a people he regarded as not only ignorant and dirty but
also "inclined to all manner of religious bigotry and fanaticism."

The quintessential racist in the Truman administration may have been the president himself. His early correspondence is replete with racial references. Mexico was
"Greaserdom." Slavic peoples were "bohunks." Still lower in his esteem were the
"nigger" and the "Chinaman." None, the young Truman observed, belonged in the
United States. Service in World War I introduced him to "kike town" (New York),
evoked the stereotype of the avaricious Jew, widened his range of reference to in-
clude "frogeater" (the French) and "Dago," and stimulated a hatred for Germans.
"They have no hearts or no souls," he wrote home in 1918. The next world war intro-
duced "Jap" into his vocabulary and convinced him that they were, as he wrote at
Potsdam in 1945, "savages, ruthless, merciless and fanatics." Accustomed to the
Southern pattern of race relations that had prevailed in Independence, Missouri,
Truman continued to refer to blacks as "nigs" and "niggers" at least as late as 1946.
As president he also continued to express impatience with "hyphenates," those
Americans of foreign descent who refused to jump into the cultural melting pot. He

lavished on the British, whom he saw as the source of American law and as close allies, the most fulsome praise he could manage for any foreigners, noting that "fundamentally . . . our basic ideas are not far apart. . . ."

The American tendency to see the world as simple and pliable has been reinforced by geopolitics, with its conception of the globe as a chessboard, neatly demarcated and easily controlled by anyone with enough strong pieces and the proper strategy. But the world, complex and slow to change, has resisted our efforts to impose our will and enforce our rules. We have known the bewilderment of the chess master who discovers that in fact no square is like another, that pawns often disturbingly assume a life of their own, and that few contests are neatly two-sided.

The American experience in Vietnam offers examples aplenty of all these unfortunate tendencies inspired by our ideological constructs and reflected in our stereotypes. We dehumanized the Vietnamese by the everyday language applied to them. We called them "gooks" or "slopes" (just as we had earlier derided other unruly peoples as "gu-gus" and "niggers"). Reflecting our diminished sense of their humanity, we made massive and indiscriminate use of firepower and herbicides, killing noncombatants as well as combatants and poisoning the land. At the same time, we promoted a pattern of national development informed by the American experience, taught the Vietnamese how to fight and govern, and when necessary both fought and governed for them. The resulting devastation, dislocation, and subordination was the price the Vietnamese paid for our self-assigned crusade to stop communism, save a people we regarded as backward, and revitalize an outmoded culture.

The paternalism and contempt evident in the Vietnam "adventure" testifies to the continuing influence of a culture-bound, color-conscious world view that still positions nations and peoples in a hierarchy defined at the extremes by civilization and barbarism, modernity and tradition. It renders us sympathetic to forward-looking Israelis, seen largely as European, at loggerheads with swarthy, bearded, polygamous, fanatical Arabs. It supports empathy for civilized white South Africans rather than a black underclass barely removed from their "primitive" tribal origins. We wring our hands over repression of Soviet-dominated Eastern Europe, while the continuing plight of the native peoples of the Americas—of dark skin and peculiar habits—could for all the attention it gets in the United States be a problem on some yet undiscovered planet.

National Security, Core Values, and Power

MELVYN P. LEFFLER

National security policy encompasses the decisions and actions deemed imperative to protect domestic core values from external threats. The national security approach provides an overall interpretative framework for studying foreign policy, because it forces historians to analyze the foreign as well as the domestic factors shaping policy. If the inputs from both sources are faithfully studied, a great divide in the study of American diplomatic history might be overcome. Realist historians believe that diplomatic behavior responds (or should respond) mainly to the distribution of power in the international system; most revisionist and corporatist scholars assume that domestic economic forces and social structures are of overwhelming importance. A synthesis would include study of the dynamic interaction between the two sources of foreign policy behavior. By relating foreign threats to internal core values, the national security approach facilitates such assessment.

It does more. The national security approach acknowledges that power plays a key role in the behavior of nations and the functioning of the international system. Proponents of that approach believe that a nation's power depends on its political stability, social cohesion, and economic productivity as well as the number of its troops, tanks, planes, ships, missiles, and nuclear warheads. It recognizes that an overarching synthesis must integrate questions of political economy, military policy, and defense strategy. It assumes that fears of foreign threats are a consequence of both real dangers in the external environment and ideological precepts, cultural symbols, and mistaken images. . . .

In studying the systemic sources of foreign policy behavior, the national security approach demands that analysts distinguish between realities and perceptions. This task, as simple as it sounds, is fraught with difficulty because it is often harder for historians to agree on what constituted an actual danger than on what was a perceived threat. For example, the very different interpretations of American diplomacy in the 1920s and 1930s between "realists" on the one hand and "revisionists" or "corporatists" on the other hand rests in part on whether or not there were real threats to American security during the interwar years. If there were no real threats before the middle or late 1930s, then contemporary proponents of arms limitation treaties, arbitration agreements, and nonaggression pacts might be viewed as functional pragmatists seeking to create a viable liberal capitalist international order rather than as naive idealists disregarding the realities of an inherently unstable and ominous balance of power.

Perceptions of events abroad are themselves greatly influenced by the core values of the perceiver. The national security approach demands that as much attention be focused on how the American government determines its core values as on how it perceives external dangers. The term *core values* is used here rather than *vital interests* because the latter implies something more material and tangible than is appropriate for a national security imperative. The United States has rarely defined its core values in narrowly economic or territorial terms. Core values usually *fuse* material self-interest with more fundamental goals like the defense of the state's organizing ideology, such as liberal capitalism, the protection of its political institutions, and the safeguarding of its physical base or territorial integrity. [The historian] N. Gordon Levin, Jr., has beautifully described how, when faced with unrestricted German submarine warfare, Woodrow Wilson fused ideological, economic, and geopolitical considerations. Together these factors became core values and influenced his decisions for war, for intervention, and for the assumption of political obligations abroad. . . .

The protection and pursuit of core values requires the exercise of power. Power is the capacity to achieve intended results. Power may be an end in itself as well as a means toward an end. In the twentieth century, power (including military power) derives primarily from economic capabilities. Power stems from the scale, vigor, and productivity of one's internal economy and its access to or control over other countries' industrial infrastructure, skilled manpower, and raw materials. Power is relative.

The chief characteristic of twentieth-century American foreign policy has been the willingness and capacity of the United States to develop and exert its power beyond its nineteenth-century range to influence the economic, political, and military affairs of Europe and Asia. This trend has manifested itself in the evolution of the Open Door policy, in the aid to the Allies in both world wars, in the wielding of American financial leverage, in the assumption of strategic obligations, in the deployment of troops overseas, in the provision of economic and military assistance, in the undertaking of covert operations, in the huge expenditures on armaments, and in the growth of the American multinational corporation. The national security approach helps to make sense out of these developments. Alterations in the distribution of power, changes in the international system, and developments in technology influence the perception of threat and the definition of core values and impel American officials to exercise power in varying ways. . . .

Preponderance and hegemony, as Paul Kennedy [*The Rise and Fall of the Great Powers,* 1987] and Robert Gilpin [*War and Change,* 1981] have written, confer advantages and impose costs. If threats are exaggerated and commitments overextended, if one's credibility is vested in the achievement of too many goals, one's relative power will erode and one's core values may become imperiled. There is an ominous dynamic influencing the behavioral patterns of great powers. Whether or not the United States will succumb to it will depend on whether groups, bureaucracies, and individual policymakers can find a means of restoring a viable equilibrium among threats, core values, and the exercise of power.

Bureaucratic Politics and Policy Outcomes

J. GARRY CLIFFORD

In the mid-1960s, when members of the Harvard Faculty Study Group on Bureaucracy, Politics, and Policy began to write their scholarly tomes, their sometime colleague in the mathematics department, the folk singer Tom Lehrer, inadvertently gave song to what came to be called the "bureaucratic politics" approach to the study of U.S. foreign policy. In his ballad about a certain German émigré rocket scientist, Lehrer wrote: "Once the rockets are up / Who cares where they come down? / That's not my department! / Said Wernher von Braun." Lehrer's ditty, by suggesting that government is a complex, compartmentalized machine and that those running the machine do not always intend what will result, anticipated the language of bureaucratic politics. The dark humor also hinted that the perspective might sometimes excuse as much as it explains about the foreign policy of the United States.

The formal academic version of bureaucratic politics came a few years later with the publication in 1971 of Graham T. Allison's *Essence of Decision.* Building on works by Warner R. Schilling, Roger Hilsman, Richard E. Neustadt, and other political scientists who emphasized internal bargaining within the foreign policy process, and adding insights from organizational theorists like James G. March and Herbert A. Simon, Allison examined the Cuban missile crisis to refute the traditional assumption that foreign policy is produced by the purposeful acts of unified national governments. Allison argued that instead of resembling the behavior of a "rational actor," the Kennedy administration's behavior during the crisis was best explained as "outcomes" of the standard operating procedures followed by separate organizations (the navy's blockade, the Central Intelligence Agency's U-2 overflights, and the air force's scenarios for a surgical air strike) and as a result of compromise and competition among hawks and doves seeking to advance individual and organizational versions of the national interest. . . .

The Allisonian message holds that U.S. foreign policy has become increasingly political and cumbersome with the growth of bureaucracy after World War II. Diversity and conflict permeate the policy process. There is no single "maker" of foreign policy. Policy flows instead from an amalgam of large organizations and political actors who differ substantially on any particular issue and who compete to advance their own personal and organizational interests as they try to influence decisions. The president, while powerful, is not omnipotent; he is one chief among many. Even when a direct presidential decision is reached, the game does not end because decisions are often ignored or reversed. Jimmy Carter may have thought he had killed the B-1 bomber, but a decade later the weapon was still being produced and its utility still being debated. Because organizations rely on routines and plans derived from experience with familiar problems, those standard routines usually form the basis for options furnished the president. Ask an organization to do what it has not done previously, and it will usually do what the U.S. military did in Vietnam: It will follow existing doctrines and procedures, modifying them only slightly in deference to different conditions.

Final decisions are also "political resultants," the product of compromise and bargaining among the various participants. As Allison puts it, policies are "*resultants* in the sense that what happens is not chosen . . . but rather results from compromise, conflict, and confusion of officials with diverse interests and unequal influence; *political* in the sense [of] . . . bargaining along regularized channels among individual members of government." Similarly, once a decision is made, considerable slippage can occur in implementing it. What follows is hostage to standard operating procedures and the interests of the implementers. Even when a president personally monitors performance, as John F. Kennedy tried to do with the navy's blockade during the missile crisis, organizational repertoires and hierarchies are so rigid and complex that the president cannot micromanage all that happens. Kennedy's own naval background notwithstanding, he did not know that antisubmarine warfare units were routinely forcing Soviet submarines to the surface, thus precipitating the very confrontations he so painstakingly tried to avoid.

The bureaucratic politics perspective also suggests that intramural struggles over policy can consume so much time and attention that dealing effectively with external realities becomes secondary. Strobe Talbott's extraordinarily well informed accounts of arms control policy during the Carter and Reagan years [*Endgame*, 1979, and *Deadly Gambits*, 1984] confirm the truism that arriving at a consensus among the various players and agencies within the government is more complicated, if not more difficult, than negotiating with the Soviets. Ironically, officials who are finely attuned to the conflict and compartmentalism within the American government often see unitary, purposive behavior on the part of other governments. Recall the rush to judgment about the Soviet shooting down of a Korean airliner in 1983 as compared to the tortured ("rules of engagement") justifications that followed the destruction of an Iranian aircraft by the American naval cruiser *Vincennes* in 1988. . . .

Several criticisms have been leveled at the bureaucratic politics approach. Some critics contend that ideological core values shared by those whom Richard J. Barnet has called "national security managers" weigh more in determining policy than do any differences attributable to bureaucratic position. The axiom "where you stand depends on where you sit" has had less influence, they argue, than the generational mindset of such individuals as Paul Nitze, John J. McCloy, and Clark Clifford, whose participation in the foreign policy establishment spanned decades and cut across bureaucratic and partisan boundaries. Similarly, the perspective underestimates the extent to which the president can dominate the bureaucracy by selecting key players and setting the rules of the game. The Tower Commission report [1987] exposed the flaws of instant bureaucratic analysis when it simplistically blamed the Iran-contra affair on a loose cannon in the White House basement and exonerated a detached president who was allegedly cut out of the policy "loop." The historian must be careful in each case to judge how much of the buck that stops with the president has already been spent by the bureaucracy. . . .

Yet those defects in the bureaucratic politics approach may not hamper historians, who do not need models that predict perfectly. Unlike political scientists, they do not seek to build better theories or to propose more effective management techniques. Because the bureaucratic politics approach emphasizes state-level analysis, it cannot fully answer such cosmic questions as why the United States has opposed revolutions or why East-West issues have predominated over North-South issues. It is better at explaining the timing and mechanics of particular episodes, illuminating proximate as opposed to deeper causes, and showing why outcomes were not what was intended. The bureaucratic details of debacles like Pearl Harbor and the Bay of Pigs invasion are thus better understood than the long-term dynamics of war and peace. . . .

When can the perspective be most helpful? Because organizations function most predictably in a familiar environment, major transformations in the international system (wars and their aftermaths, economic crises, the Sino-Soviet split) require the analyst to study how institutional adjustments in U.S. policies resulted from the changes. Similarly propitious are transitions that bring in new players pledged to reverse the priorities of their predecessors, and particularly those administrations in which the president, deliberately or not, encourages competition and initiative from strong-willed subordinates. Fiascos like the American failure to fend off the attack on Pearl Harbor and the Iran-contra affair not only force agencies to reassess procedures and programs but, even better, often spawn official investigations that provide scholars with abundant evidence for bureaucratic analysis. Budget battles, weapons procurement, coordination of intelligence, war termination, alliance politics—in short, any foreign policy that engages the separate attentions of multiple agencies and agents should alert the historian to the bureaucratic politics perspective.

Consider, for example, the complex dynamics of American entry into World War II. Looking at the period through the lens of bureaucratic politics reveals that FDR may have had more than Congress and public opinion in mind when making his famous remark: "It's a terrible thing to look over your shoulder when you are trying to lead—and to find no one there." The institutional aversion to giving commissioned naval vessels to a foreign power delayed the destroyers-for-bases deal for several weeks in the summer of 1940, and only by getting eight British bases in direct exchange for the destroyers could Roosevelt persuade the chief of naval operations, Admiral Harold Stark, to certify, as required by statute, that these destroyers were no longer essential to national defense. According to navy scuttlebutt, the president threatened to fire Stark if he did not support what virtually every naval officer opposed and the admiral agonized before acquiescing. Similarly, the army's initial opposition to peacetime conscription, FDR's dramatic appointment of Henry L. Stimson and Frank Knox to head the War and Navy departments in June 1940, his firing of Admiral James O. Richardson for his opposition to basing the Pacific fleet at Pearl Harbor, the refusal of the army and navy to mount expeditions to the Azores and Dakar in the spring of 1941, the unvarying strategic advice not to risk war until the armed forces were better prepared—all suggest an environment in which the president had to push hard to get the bureaucracy to accept his policy of supporting the Allies by steps short of war. Even the navy's eagerness to begin Atlantic convoys in the spring of 1941 and the subsequent Army Air Corps strategy of reinforcing the Philippines with B-17s were aimed in part at deploying ships and planes that FDR might otherwise have given to the British and the Russians. . . .

In sum, this essay should be read as a modest plea for greater attention to bureaucratic politics. The perspective can enrich and complement other approaches. By focusing on internal political processes we become aware of the conflict within government before arriving at the cooperative core values posited by the corporatists or the neorealists. In its emphasis on individual values and tugging and hauling by key players, bureaucratic politics makes personality and cognitive processes crucial to understanding who wins and why. Although bureaucratic struggles may be over tactics more than over strategy, over pace rather than direction, those distinctions may matter greatly when the outcome is a divided Berlin and Korea, a second atomic bomb, an ABM [antiballistic missile] system that no one really wanted, or the failure of last-minute efforts to avert war in the Pacific. Too easily dismissed as a primer for managing crises that should be avoided, the bureaucratic politics perspective also warns national security managers that when "governments collide," the machines cannot do what they are not programmed to do. Rather than press "delete" and conceptualize policy only as a rational action, it is incumbent on historians to know how the machines work, their repertoires, the institutional rules of the game, and how the box score is kept. The processes are peculiarly American. The British ambassador Edward Lord Halifax once observed that the foreign policy establishment in Washington was "rather like a disorderly line of beaters out shooting; they do put the rabbits out of the bracken, but they don't come out where you would expect." Historians of American foreign relations need to identify the beaters and follow them into the bureaucratic forest because the game is much bigger than rabbit.

FURTHER READING

See works mentioned in the essays above.

Richard J. Barnet, *Roots of War* (1972)

William H. Becker and Samuel F. Wells, eds., *Economics and World Power* (1984)

Gail Bederman, *Manliness and Civilization* (1995)

Marshall Blonsky, *American Mythologies* (1992)

Paul H. Buhle, *William Appleman Williams, The Tragedy of Empire* (1995)

David Campbell, *Writing Security* (1992) (on postmodernism)

John M. Carroll and George C. Herring, eds., *Modern American Diplomacy* (1995)

J. Garry Clifford and Samuel R. Spencer, Jr., *The First Peacetime Draft* (1986)

Jerald A. Combs, *American Diplomatic History: Two Centuries of Changing Interpretations* (1982)

Robert Dallek, *The American Style of Foreign Policy* (1983)

Alexander DeConde, ed., *Encyclopedia of American Foreign Policy* (1978)

James Fallows, *More Like Us* (1989)

Frances FitzGerald, *America Revised* (1979)

Andre Gunder Frank and Barry Gills, *The World System* (1996)

Frank Füred, *The Silent War* (1998) (on race)

John Lewis Gaddis, "The Corporatist Synthesis: A Skeptical View," *Diplomatic History,* 10 (1986), 357–362

———, "New Conceptual Approaches to the Study of American Foreign Relations," *Diplomatic History,* 14 (1990), 403–425

Lloyd C. Gardner, ed., *Redefining the Past* (1986)

Craig Gordon, *Force and Statecraft* (1995)

Norman A. Graebner, *Ideas and Diplomacy* (1964)

Gerald K. Haines and J. Samuel Walker, eds., *American Foreign Relations* (1981)

Morton Halperin, *Bureaucratic Politics and Foreign Policy* (1974)

Michael P. Hamilton, ed., *American Character and Foreign Policy* (1986)

John Higham, *History* (1989)

Elizabeth Cobbs Hoffman, "Diplomatic History and the Meaning of Life: Toward a Global American History," *Diplomatic History,* 21 (1997), 499–518

Michael J. Hogan, ed., *America in the World* (1996)

———, ed., "Writing the History of U.S. Foreign Relations: A Symposium," *Diplomatic History,* 14 (1990), 553–605

——— and Thomas G. Paterson, eds., *Explaining the History of American Foreign Relations* (1991)

Ole Holsti, *Public Opinion and American Foreign Policy* (1996)

Michael H. Hunt, *Ideology and U.S. Foreign Policy* (1987)

———, "The Long Crisis in U.S. Diplomatic History: Coming to a Closure," *Diplomatic History,* 16 (1992), 115–140

Akira Iriye, "Culture and Power," *Diplomatic History,* 3 (1979), 115–128

———, "The Internationalization of History," *American Historical Review,* 94 (1989), 1–10

———, *Power and Culture* (1981)

Rhodri Jeffreys-Jones, *Changing Differences* (1995) (on gender)

George F. Kennan, *American Diplomacy, 1900–1950* (1951)

Charles Kindleberger, *The World Economy and National Finance in Historical Perspective* (1995)

Gabriel Kolko, *The Roots of American Foreign Policy* (1969)

———, *Century of War* (1994)

Michael L. Krenn, ed., *Race and U.S. Foreign Policy,* 5 vols. (1998)

Melvyn P. Leffler, *A Preponderance of Power* (1992)

———, "New Approaches, Old Interpretations, and Prospective Reconfigurations," *Diplomatic History,* 19 (1995), 173–196

William E. Leuchtenburg, "The Pertinence of Political History," *Journal of American History,* 73 (1986), 585–600

Thomas J. McCormick, "Drift or Mastery?" *Reviews in American History,* 10 (1982), 318–330

James McDougall, *Promised Land, Crusader State* (1995)

Charles S. Maier, "Marking Time: The Historiography of International Relations," in Michael Kamman, ed., *The Past Before Us* (1980)

Gordon Martel, ed., *American Foreign Relations Reconsidered* (1994)

Hans J. Morgenthau, *In Defense of the National Interest* (1951)

Charles E. Neu, "The Rise of the National Security Bureaucracy," in Louis Galambos, ed., *The New American State* (1987)

Richard E. Neustadt, *Presidential Power* (1990)

———— and Ernest R. May, *Thinking in Time* (1986)

Frank Ninkovich, "Interests and Discourse in Diplomatic History," *Diplomatic History,* 13 (1989), 135–161

————, "No Post-Mortems for Postmodernism, Please," *Diplomatic History,* 22 (1998), 451–466

Peter Novick, *That Noble Dream: The "Objectivity" Question and the American Historical Profession* (1988)

Thomas G. Paterson, ed., "Symposium: Explaining the History of American Foreign Relations," *Journal of American History,* 77 (1990), 93–182

Stephen E. Pelz, "A Taxonomy for American Diplomatic History," *Journal of Interdisciplinary History,* 19 (1988), 259–276

Brenda Gayle Plummer, *Rising Wind: Black Aspirations and U.S. Foreign Affairs, 1935–1960* (1997)

David Potter, *People of Plenty* (1954)

Emily S. Rosenberg, *Spreading the American Dream: American Economic and Cultural Expansion, 1898–1945* (1982)

Eugene Rostow, *Toward Managed Peace* (1993)

Arthur M. Schlesinger, Jr., *The Cycles of American History* (1986)

————, *The Imperial Presidency* (1973)

Joan W. Scott, *Gender and the Politics of History* (1988)

Robert Shaffer, "Race, Class, Gender, and Diplomatic History," *Radical History Review,* 70 (1998), 156–168

Mrinalini Sinha, "Reading *Mother India:* Empire, Nation, and the Female Voice," *Journal of Women's History,* 6 (1994), 6–44

Richard Slotkin, *Gunfighter Nation: The Myth of the Frontier in Twentieth Century America* (1992)

————, *Regeneration Through Violence* (1973)

Geoffrey S. Smith, "National Security and Personal Isolation: Sex, Gender, and Disease in Cold-War United States," *International History Review,* 14 (1992), 221–240

Tony Smith, *America's Mission* (1994)

Anders Stephanson, *Manifest Destiny* (1995)

"Symposium: African Americans and U.S. Foreign Relations," *Diplomatic History,* 20 (1996), 531–650

"Symposium: Gender and U.S. Foreign Relations," *Diplomatic History,* 18 (1994), 47–124

"Symposium: Responses to Charles S. Maier, 'Marking Time,'" *Diplomatic History,* 5 (1981), 353–371

Christopher Thorne, *Border Crossings* (1988)

Robert Tucker, *The Radical Left and American Foreign Policy* (1971)

Penny Von Eschen, *Race Against Empire: Black Americans and Anticolonialism 1937–1957* (1997)

Theodore H. von Laue, *The World Revolution of Westernization* (1987)

William O. Walker III, "Drug Control and the Issue of Culture in American Foreign Relations," *Diplomatic History,* 12 (1988), 365–382

Immanuel Wallerstein, *The Capitalist World-Economy* (1979)
Rubin F. Weston, *Racism in U.S. Imperialism* (1972)
Donald W. White, *The American Century* (1996)
William A. Williams, *The Contours of American History* (1966)
———, *Empire as a Way of Life* (1980)
———, *Tragedy of American Diplomacy* (1959)

Special Note: The journal *Diplomatic History,* published by the Society for Historians of American Foreign Relations, regularly presents essays on changing interpretations in and approaches to the field.

C H A P T E R
2

Woodrow Wilson,
the First World War,
and the League Fight

*In August 1914 Europe descended into war. Then an imperial power and a sub-
stantial trader on the high seas, the United States became ensnared in the deadly
conflict. Until April 1917, however, President Woodrow Wilson struggled to define
policies that would protect U.S. interests and principles, keep the nation out of the
war, end the bloodshed, and permit him to shape the terms of the peace settlement
and the characteristics of the postwar international system. The president protested
violations of U.S. neutral rights, lectured the belligerents to respect international
law, appealed for a "peace without victory," and offered to mediate. When his
peace advocacy faltered and Germany launched unrestricted submarine warfare,
Wilson asked a divided but ultimately obliging Congress for a declaration of war.
America's participation in the First World War elevated the nation to great-power
status and transformed U.S. foreign relations.*

*Why did the United States go to war? Historians usually point fingers at the
German U-boat, which violated neutral rights, endangered the lives of passengers
on ocean liners, and sank American merchant ships. Germany, many have argued,
forced the United States into the war. But some scholars of Wilsonian diplomacy
have asked: Would Germany have unleashed the submarine if U.S. policy had
been different? That is, was the United States truly neutral, or did it side with the
British? Did U.S. economic interests, especially the expanded wartime trade and
loans, force Wilson's hand? Did U.S. officials favor the British owing to deep-
rooted cultural affinities—shared values, language, and political institutions?*

*Studies of Woodrow Wilson have speculated about the roles of his personality,
his religious faith, his interpretation of international law, his penchant for person-
alizing issues and speaking in exaggerated terms, and his grasp of hard-nosed
world politics. Did Wilson act to protect U.S. economic and strategic interests (was
he a realist?), or did he decide on war primarily to satisfy his lofty principles about
saving humanity (was he an idealist?)? Did he take America to war in order to ensure himself a seat at the postwar peace table? Why did his calls for peace fail? Did*

Wilson have viable options other than war? Should the United States have stayed out of the European conflict?

Once the United States became a belligerent, Wilson strove not only to win the war but to shape the postwar peace. He called for a nonvindictive peace treaty and urged creation of an association of nations to deter war. The president's Fourteen Points outlined his plans for shelving balance-of-power politics in favor of disarmament, open diplomacy, Open Door trade, and self-determination. Having tipped the balance in favor of the Allies, the United States helped to force Germany to surrender on November 11, 1918. In January of the following year, Wilson went to the Versailles Palace near Paris to negotiate a peace treaty and a covenant for the League of Nations that he believed would sustain a stable world order. European leaders sneered that Wilson was a dreamer, out of touch with reality, but millions of people on the Continent cheered his arrival and his high-minded appeals for a moral and pacific future.

At home, however, many Americans began to question Wilson's handling of foreign policy, especially after they learned that he had compromised some of his principles in order to win approval for his League. Some critics listened to his lofty rhetoric and wondered if the president had deluded himself into thinking that he was a new messiah. Republican leaders, who had defeated the Democrats in the 1918 congressional elections, calculated that Wilson was politically vulnerable. Supreme nationalists feared that an international organization would undermine American sovereignty—that opting for collective security would snub George Washington's venerable advice to avoid restrictive foreign entanglements. Wilson battled back in an intense national debate, denouncing naysayers as narrow, backward-looking people who did not understand humanity's demand for a new world order. He refused to abandon the collective-security provision of Article 10 of the League covenant. He insisted that the covenant would ensure American prosperity, protect the U.S. national interest, and help the United States to take its rightful place as world leader. Unwilling to compromise with senators who demanded "reservations" (amendments), opposed by "irreconcilables" who would accept no league whatsoever, and laid low by illness, Wilson lost the fight. The Senate rejected the peace treaty and U.S. membership in the League of Nations.

Explanations for this outcome vary widely. Some scholars believe that the personal feud between Wilson and Republican senator Henry Cabot Lodge, chair of the Foreign Relations Committee, doomed Wilson's efforts; that two-party politics took its toll; or that the Wilson administration's trampling on civil liberties at home during the war and the president's abandonment of liberal allies undermined his international cause. Others have emphasized the president's personality—his arrogance, ignorance, self-righteousness, stubbornness. Wilson's deteriorating health, especially his severe stroke in October 1919, has raised the question of whether a healthy, more clear-headed Wilson might have accepted compromise. Finally, some scholars have questioned interpretations built on personality or politics. They have argued that the League fight represented a debate about the very core of American foreign policy: whether the nation would adhere to the tradition of unilateralism or instead embrace collective security.

Other questions look to the future: Did the peace treaty impose such harsh terms on Germany and create such a weak international system that another world war became inevitable? Did it matter that the United States rejected membership in the League? Is Woodrow Wilson responsible for the turmoil of international relations that followed his presidency, including the descent into the Second World War?

✪ D O C U M E N T S

When a German U-boat sank the British liner *Lusitania* on May 7, 1915, killing 1,198, including 128 Americans, President Woodrow Wilson sent a strong note to Berlin. The May 13 warning, Document 1, demands that Germany disavow submarine warfare and respect the right of Americans to sail on the high seas. On April 20, 1916, Secretary of State Robert Lansing and Count Johann-Heinrich Bernstorff, German ambassador to the United States, debated U-boat warfare. This meeting, reported in Document 2, came less than a month after the torpedoing of the French ship *Sussex* and helped to produce a German pledge not to attack merchant vessels and liners without warning. In January, 1917, Germany declared unrestricted submarine warfare, and Wilson broke diplomatic relations with Berlin. On April 2, after the sinking of several American vessels, the president asked Congress for a declaration of war. His war message, Document 3, outlines U.S. grievances against Germany. One of the few dissenters in the Senate—the war measure passed, 82 to 6—was Robert M. La Follette of Wisconsin. In his speech of April 4, Document 4, the great reform politician reveals his fear of an American "war machine."

President Wilson issued his Fourteen Points in a speech on January 8, 1918, reprinted here as Document 5. Articles 10 through 16 of the Covenant of the League of Nations hammered out at the Paris Peace Conference in 1919 are included as Document 6. Wilson explained during his busy western U.S. speaking tour in September 1919 that these provisions would prevent wars. Excerpts from his speeches are featured in Document 7. Led by Senator Henry Cabot Lodge of Massachusetts, critics worked to add "reservations" to the covenant through a Lodge resolution dated November 19, 1919, Document 8. But neither an amended peace treaty (which contained the covenant) nor an unamended treaty passed the Senate.

1. The First *Lusitania* Note, 1915

The Government of the United States has been apprised that the Imperial German Government considered themselves to be obliged by the extraordinary circumstances of the present war and the measures adopted by their adversaries in seeking to cut Germany off from all commerce, to adopt methods of retaliation which go much beyond the ordinary methods of warfare at sea, in the proclamation of a war zone from which they have warned neutral ships to keep away. This Government has already taken occasion to inform the Imperial German Government that it cannot admit the adoption of such measures or such a warning of danger to operate as in any degree an abbreviation of the rights of American shipmasters or of American citizens bound on lawful errands as passengers on merchant ships of belligerent nationality; and that it must hold the Imperial German Government to a strict accountability for any infringement of those rights, intentional or incidental. It does not understand the Imperial German Government to question those rights. It assumes, on the contrary, that the Imperial Government accept, as of course, the rule that the lives of noncombatants, whether they be of neutral citizenship or citizens of one of the nations at war, can not lawfully or rightfully be put in jeopardy by the capture or destruction of an unarmed merchantman, and recognize also, as all other nations do, the obligation to take the usual precaution of visit and search

---

This document can be found in U.S. Department of State, *Papers Relating to the Foreign Relations of the United States, 1915, Supplement* (Washington, D.C.: Government Printing Office, 1928), pp. 393–396.

to ascertain whether a suspected merchantman is in fact of belligerent nationality or is in fact carrying contraband of war under a neutral flag.

The Government of the United States, therefore, desires to call the attention of the Imperial German Government with the utmost earnestness to the fact that the objection to their present method of attack against the trade of their enemies lies in the practical impossibility of employing submarines in the destruction of commerce without disregarding those rules of fairness, reason, justice, and humanity, which all modern opinion regards as imperative. It is practically impossible for the officers of a submarine to visit a merchantman at sea and examine her papers and cargo. It is practically impossible for them to make a prize of her; and, if they can not put a prize crew on board of her, they can not sink her without leaving her crew and all on board of her to the mercy of the sea in her small boats. These facts it is understood the Imperial German Government frankly admit. We are informed that, in the instances of which we have spoken, time enough for even that poor measure of safety was not given, and in at least two of the cases cited, not so much as a warning was received. Manifestly submarines can not be used against merchantmen, as the last few weeks have shown, without an inevitable violation of many sacred principles of justice and humanity.

American citizens act within their indisputable rights in taking their ships and in traveling wherever their legitimate business calls them upon the high seas, and exercise those rights in what should be the well-justified confidence that their lives will not be endangered by acts done in clear violation of universally acknowledged international obligations, and certainly in the confidence that their own Government will sustain them in the exercise of their rights.

2. Robert Lansing and Johann-Heinrich Bernstorff Debate Submarine Warfare, 1916

L: You will recall that we said in the first *Lusitania* note that we thought it was impossible to use submarines in a really humane way and that later, in our note of July 21, we said that the way submarine warfare had been conducted for the past two months showed that it was possible and therefore we hoped that course would be pursued. Then we had the sinking of the *Arabic* right on top of that, which was another great disaster. Our position is that, if submarine warfare had been conducted in that way, that possibly there would have been no further question raised. But it has not. It has been conducted in the most indiscriminate way and we cannot help but believe that it is ruthless. In those conditions submarine warfare should stop against commercial vessels, unless visit and search is observed.

B: That, of course, is impossible. Germany cannot abandon submarine warfare. No government could come out and say—"We give up the use of submarines." They would have to resign.

This document can be found in U.S. Department of State, *Papers Relating to the Foreign Relations of the United States, The Lansing Papers 1914–1920* (Washington, D.C.: Government Printing Office, 1939), I, 555–556, 557–558.

L: What possible methods in the use of submarines, that are effective from a belligerent standpoint, can be suggested which will comply with the law?

B: I had always supposed that warning was to be given.

L: We do not consider that the people on board—the non-combatants on board the vessels—are in a place of safety when put into an open boat a hundred miles from land. It might be calm there, but in the two days it would take them to reach land there might be a severe storm. That is one of the grounds of complaint.

B: That, of course, speaking of neutral vessels—

L: The fact that we do not have Americans on these vessels does not remove the menace to American lives. The sinking of neutral vessels shows that Americans cannot travel with safety on neutral vessels even. That is the serious part of it and I do not know how your government can modify submarine warfare and make it effective and at the same time obey the law and the dictates of humanity.

B: Humanity. Of course war is never humane.

L: "Humanity" is a relative expression when used with "war" but the whole tendency in the growth of international law in regard to warfare in the past 125 years has been to relieve non-combatants of needless suffering.

B: Of course I think it would be an ideal state of affairs, but our enemies violate all the rules and you insist on their being applied to Germany.

L: One deals with life; the other with property. . . .

L: There would have to be a complete abandonment first and then if the German Government desires to discuss the matter—

B: I want to do what I can, because I am perfectly convinced they do not want to break; quite apart from the sentimental side I think they do not want a break. A break would prolong the war. It would last for years.

L: We do not any of us want to prolong the war.

B: That is exactly why I want to get out of this present difficulty. From the present state of affairs it looks as if the end is coming and if now there was a break and the United States was brought into the war it would prolong it. It would cause new complications.

L: New complications?

B: New economic difficulties.

L: I think that would be Germany's problem. The only possible course is an abandonment of submarine warfare, whether limited or not would depend on the terms. I would want to see an abandonment first and then possibly a discussion could follow as to how submarine warfare can be conducted within the rules of international law and entire safety of non-combatants, because, of course, in my viewpoint that is the chief question of international law in regard to attacks by belligerents on enemy's commerce.

B: Then I am to understand that you do not recognize the law of retaliation?

L: We do not recognize retaliation when it affects the rights of neutrals.

B: The British retaliate by stopping all commerce to Germany.

L: It is a very different thing. The right to life is an inherent right, which man has from birth; the right of property is a purely legal right.

B: Only in this case, England's methods affect the lives of non-combatants of Germany.

L: Not neutrals.

B: No, but it affects non-combatants.

3. President Woodrow Wilson's War Message, 1917

On the third of February last I officially laid before you the extraordinary announcement of the Imperial German Government that on and after the first day of February it was its purpose to put aside all restraints of law of humanity and use its submarines to sink every vessel that sought to approach either the ports of Great Britain and Ireland or the western coasts of Europe or any of the ports controlled by the enemies of Germany within the Mediterranean. That had seemed to be the object of the German submarine warfare earlier in the war, but since April of last year the Imperial Government had somewhat restrained the commanders of its undersea craft in conformity with its promise then given to us that passenger boats should not be sunk and that due warning would be given to all other vessels which its submarines might seek to destroy, when no resistance was offered or escape attempted, and care taken that their crews were given at least a fair chance to save their lives in their open boats. The precautions taken were meagre and haphazard enough, as was proved in distressing instance after instance in the progress of the cruel and unmanly business, but a certain degree of restraint was observed. The new policy has swept every restriction aside. Vessels of every kind, whatever their flag, their character, their cargo, their destination, their errand, have been ruthlessly sent to the bottom without warning and without thought of help or mercy for those on board, the vessels of friendly neutrals along with those of belligerents. Even hospital ships and ships carrying relief to the sorely bereaved and stricken people of Belgium, though the latter were provided with safe conduct through the proscribed areas by the German Government itself and were distinguished by unmistakable marks of identity, have been sunk with the same reckless lack of compassion or of principle.

I was for a little while unable to believe that such things would in fact be done by any government that had hitherto subscribed to the humane practices of civilized nations. International law had its origin in the attempt to set up some law which would be respected and observed upon the seas, where no nation had right of dominion where lay the free highways of the world. By painful stage after stage has that law been built up, with meagre enough results, indeed, after all was accomplished that could be accomplished, but always with a clear view, at least of what the heart and conscience of mankind demanded. This minimum of right the German Government has swept aside under the plea of retaliation and necessity and because it had no weapons which it could use at sea except these which it is impossible to employ as it is employing them without throwing to the winds all scruples of humanity or of respect for the understandings that were supposed to underlie the intercourse of the world. I am not now thinking of the loss of property involved, immense and serious as that is, but only of the wanton and wholesale destruction of the lives of noncombatants, men, women, and children, engaged in pursuits which have always, even in the darkest periods of modern history, been deemed innocent and legitimate. Property can be paid for; the lives of peaceful and innocent people cannot be. The present German submarine warfare against commerce is a warfare against mankind.

This document can be found in *Congressional Record*, LV (April 2, 1917), Part 1, 102–104.

It is a war against all nations. American ships have been sunk, American lives taken, in ways which it has stirred us very deeply to learn of, but the ships and people of other neutral and friendly nations have been sunk and overwhelmed in the waters in the same way. There has been no discrimination. The challenge is to all mankind. Each nation must decide for itself how it will meet it. The choice we make for ourselves must be made with a moderation of counsel and a temperateness of judgment befitting our character and our motives as a nation. We must put excited feeling away. Our motive will not be revenge or the victorious assertion of the physical might of the nation, but only the vindication of right, of human right, of which we are only a single champion. . . .

With a profound sense of the solemn and even tragical character of the step I am taking and of the grave responsibilities which it involves, but in unhesitating obedience to what I deem my constitutional duty, I advise that the Congress declare the recent course of the Imperial German Government to be in fact nothing less than war against the government and people of the United States; that it formally accept the status of belligerent which has thus been thrust upon it; and that it take immediate steps not only to put the country in a more thorough state of defense but also to exert all its power and employ all its resources to bring the Government of the German Empire to terms and end the war. . . .

Does not every American feel that assurance has been added to our hope for the future peace of the world by the wonderful and heartening things that have been happening within the last few weeks in Russia? Russia was known by those who knew it best to have been always in fact democratic at heart, in all the vital habits of her thought, in all the intimate relationships of her people that spoke their natural instinct, their habitual attitude towards life. The autocracy that crowned the summit of her political structure, long as it had stood and terrible as was the reality of its power, was not in fact Russian in origin, character, or purpose; and now it has been shaken off and the great, generous Russian people have been added in all their naive majesty and might to the forces that are fighting for freedom in the world, for justice, and for peace. Here is a fit partner for a League of Honour.

One of the things that has served to convince us that the Prussian autocracy was not and could never be our friends is that from the very outset of the present war it has filled our unsuspecting communities and even our offices of government with spies and set criminal intrigues everywhere afoot against our national unity of counsel, our peace within and without, our industries and our commerce. . . . That it means to stir up enemies against us at our very doors the intercepted note to the German Minister at Mexico City is eloquent evidence.

We are accepting this challenge of hostile purpose because we know that in such a government, following such methods, we can never have a friend; and that in the presence of its organized power, always lying in wait to accomplish we know not what purpose, there can be no assured security for the democratic governments of the world. We are now about to accept gauge of battle with its natural foe to liberty and shall, if necessary, spend the whole force of the nation to check and nullify its pretensions and its power. We are glad, now that we see the facts with no veil of false pretence about them, to fight thus for the ultimate peace of the world and for the liberation of its peoples, the German peoples included: for the rights of nations great and small and the privilege of men everywhere to choose their way of life and of obedience. The world must be made safe for democracy. . . .

It is a distressing and oppressive duty, Gentlemen of the Congress, which I have performed in thus addressing you. There are, it may be, many months of fiery trial and sacrifice ahead of us. It is a fearful thing to lead this great peaceful people into war, into the most terrible and disastrous of all wars, civilization itself seeming to be in the balance. But the right is more precious than peace, and we shall fight for the things which we have always carried nearest our hearts—for democracy, for the right of those who submit to authority to have a voice in their own governments, for the rights and liberties of small nations, for a universal dominion of right by such a concert of free peoples as shall bring peace and safety to all nations and make the world itself at last free. To such a task we can dedicate our lives and our fortunes, everything that we are and everything that we have, with the pride of those who know that the day has come when America is privileged to spend her blood and her might for the principles that gave her birth and happiness and the peace which she has treasured. God helping her, she can do no other.

4. Senator Robert M. La Follette
Voices His Dissent, 1917

The poor, sir, who are the ones called upon to rot in the trenches, have no organized power, have no press to voice their will upon this question of peace or war; but, oh, Mr. President, at some time they will be heard. I hope and I believe they will be heard in an orderly and a peaceful way. I think they may be heard from before long. I think, sir, if we take this step, when the people to-day who are staggering under the burden of supporting families at the present prices of the necessaries of the life find those prices multiplied, when they are raised a hundred percent, or 200 percent, as they will be quickly, aye, sir, when beyond that those who pay taxes come to have their taxes doubled and again doubled to pay the interest on the nontaxable bonds held by Morgan and his combinations, which have been issued to meet this war, there will come an awakening; they will have their day and they will be heard. It will be as certain and as inevitable as the return of the tides, and as resistless, too. . . .

Just a word of comment more upon one of the points in the President's address. He says that this is a war "for the things which we have always carried nearest to our hearts—for democracy, for the right of those who submit to authority to have a voice in their own government." In many places throughout the address is this exalted sentiment given expression. . . .

But the President proposes alliance with Great Britain, which, however liberty-loving its people, is a hereditary monarchy, with a hereditary ruler, with a hereditary House of Lords, with a hereditary landed system, with a limited and restricted suffrage for one class and a multiplied suffrage power for another, and with grinding industrial conditions for all the wageworkers. The President has not suggested that we make our support of Great Britain conditional to her granting home rule to Ireland, or Egypt, or India. We rejoice in the establishment of a democracy in Russia, but it will hardly be contended that if Russia was still an autocratic Government, we

---

would not be asked to enter this alliance with her just the same. Italy and the lesser powers of Europe, Japan in the Orient; in fact all of the countries with whom we are to enter into alliance, except France and newly revolutionized Russia, are still of the old order—and it will be generally conceded that no one of them has done as much for its people in the solution of municipal problems and in securing social and industrial reforms as Germany. . . .

Who has registered the knowledge or approval of the American people of the course this Congress is called upon in declaring war upon Germany? Submit the question to the people, you who support it. You who support it dare not do it, for you know that by a vote of more than ten to one the American people as a body would register their declaration against it.

In the sense that this war is being forced upon our people without their knowing why and without their approval, and that wars are usually forced upon all peoples in the same way, there is some truth in the statement; but I venture to say that the response which the German people have made to the demands of this war shows that it has a degree of popular support which the war upon which we are entering has not and never will have among our people. The espionage bills, the conscription bills, and other forcible military measures which we understand are being ground out of the war machine in this country is the complete proof that those responsible for this war fear that it has no popular support and that armies sufficient to satisfy the demand of the entente allies can not be recruited by voluntary enlistments.

5. The Fourteen Points, 1918

I. Open covenants of peace, openly arrived at, after which there shall be no private international understandings of any kind but diplomacy shall proceed always frankly and in the public view.

II. Absolute freedom of navigation upon the seas, outside territorial waters, alike in peace and in war, except as the seas may be closed in whole or in part by international action for the enforcement of international covenants.

III. The removal, so far as possible, of all economic barriers and the establishment of an equality of trade conditions among all the nations consenting to the peace and associating themselves for its maintenance.

IV. Adequate guarantees given and taken that national armaments will be reduced to the lowest point consistent with domestic safety.

V. A free, open-minded, and absolutely impartial adjustment of all colonial claims, based upon a strict observance of the principle that in determining all such questions of sovereignty the interests of the populations concerned must have equal weight with the equitable claims of the government whose title is to be determined.

VI. The evacuation of all Russian territory and such a settlement of all questions affecting Russia as will secure the best and freest cooperation of the other nations of the world in obtaining for her an unhampered and unembarrassed opportunity for the independent determination of her own political development and national policy and assure her of a sincere welcome into the society of free nations under institutions of her own choosing; and, more than a welcome, assistance also of every

This document can be found in *Congressional Record,* LVI (January 8, 1918), Part 1, 680–682.

kind that she may need and may herself desire. The treatment accorded Russia by her sister nations in the months to come will be the acid test of their good will, of their comprehension of her needs as distinguished from their own interests, and of their intelligent and unselfish sympathy.

VII. Belgium, the whole world will agree, must be evacuated and restored, without any attempt to limit the sovereignty which she enjoys in common with all other free nations. No other single act will serve as this will serve to restore confidence among the nations in the laws which they have themselves set and determined for the government of their relations with one another. Without this healing act the whole structure and validity of international law is forever impaired.

VIII. All French territory should be freed and the invaded portions restored, and the wrong done to France by Prussia in 1871 in the matter of Alsace-Lorraine, which has unsettled the peace of the world for nearly fifty years, should be righted, in order that peace may once more be made secure in the interest of all.

IX. A readjustment of the frontiers of Italy should be effected along clearly recognizable lines of nationality.

X. The peoples of Austria-Hungary, whose place among the nations we wish to see safeguarded and assured, should be accorded the freest opportunity of autonomous development.

XI. Rumania, Serbia, and Montenegro should be evacuated; occupied territories restored; Serbia accorded free and secure access to the sea; and the relations of the several Balkan states to one another determined by friendly consul along historically established lines of allegiance and nationality; and international guarantees of the political and economic independence and territorial integrity of the several Balkan states should be entered into.

XII. The Turkish portions of the present Ottoman Empire should be assured a secure sovereignty, but the other nationalities which are now under Turkish rule should be assured an undoubted security of life and an absolutely unmolested opportunity of autonomous development, and the Dardanelles should be permanently opened as a free passage to the ships and commerce of all nations under international guarantees.

XIII. An independent Polish state should be erected which should include the territories inhabited by indisputably Polish populations, which should be assured a free and secure access to the sea, and whose political and economic independence and territorial integrity should be guaranteed by international covenant.

XIV. A general association of nations must be formed under specific covenants for the purpose of affording mutual guarantees of political independence and territorial integrity to great and small states alike.

6. Articles 10 through 16 of the League Covenant, 1919

Article 10. The Members of the League undertake to respect and preserve as against external aggression the territorial integrity and existing political independence of all Members of the League. In case of any such aggression or in case of any threat or danger of such aggression the Council shall advise upon the means by which this obligation shall be fulfilled.

This document can be found in U.S. Department of State, *Papers Relating to the Foreign Relations of the United States, 1919* (Washington, D.C.: Government Printing Office, 1942–1947), XIII, 83–89.

Article 11.   Any war or threat of war, whether immediately affecting any of the Members of the League or not, is hereby declared a matter of concern to the whole League, and the League shall take any action that may be deemed wise and effectual to safeguard the peace of nations. . . .

It is also declared to be the friendly right of each Member of the League to bring to the attention of the Assembly or of the Council any circumstance whatever affecting international relations which threatens to disturb international peace or the good understanding between nations upon which peace depends.

Article 12.   The Members of the League agree that if there should arise between them any dispute likely to lead to a rupture, they will submit the matter either to arbitration or to inquiry by the Council, and they agree in no case to resort to war until three months after the award by the arbitrators or the report by the Council.

In any case under this Article the award of the arbitrators shall be made within a reasonable time, and the report of the Council shall be made within six months after the submission of the dispute.

Article 13.   The Members of the League agree that whenever any dispute shall arise between them which they recognise to be suitable for submission to arbitration and which cannot be satisfactorily settled by diplomacy, they will submit the whole subject-matter to arbitration. . . .

Article 14.   The Council shall formulate and submit to the Members of the League for adoption plans for the establishment of a Permanent Court of International Justice. The Court shall be competent to hear and determine any dispute of an international character which the parties thereto submit to it. The Court may also give an advisory opinion upon any dispute or question referred to it by the Council or by the Assembly.

Article 15.   If there should arise between Members of the League any dispute likely to lead to a rupture, which is not submitted to arbitration in accordance with Article 13, the Members of the League agree that they will submit the matter to the Council. . . .

Article 16.   Should any Member of the League resort to war in disregard of its covenants under Articles 12, 13 or 15, it shall *ipso facto* be deemed to have committed an act of war against all other Members of the League, which hereby undertake immediately to subject it to the severance of all trade or financial relations, the prohibition of all intercourse between their nationals and the nationals of the covenant-breaking State, and the prevention of all financial, commercial or personal intercourse between the nationals of the covenant-breaking State and the nationals of any other State, whether a Member of the League or not.

It shall be the duty of the Council in such case to recommend to the several Governments concerned what effective military, naval or air force the Members of the League shall severally contribute to the armed forces to be used to protect the covenants of the League.

7. Wilson Defends the Peace Treaty and League, 1919

Indianapolis, Indiana, September 4

You have heard a great deal about article 10 of the covenant of the league of nations. Article 10 speaks the conscience of the world. Article 10 is the article which goes to the heart of this whole bad business, for that article says that the members of this league, that is intended to be all the great nations of the world, engage to respect and to preserve against all external aggression the territorial integrity and political independence of the nations concerned. That promise is necessary in order to prevent this sort of war from recurring, and we are absolutely discredited if we fought this war and then neglect the essential safeguard against it. You have heard it said, my fellow citizens, that we are robbed of some degree of our sovereign independent choice by articles of that sort. Every man who makes a choice to respect the rights of his neighbors deprives himself of absolute sovereignty, but he does it by promising never to do wrong, and I can not for one see anything that robs me of any inherent right that I ought to retain when I promise that I will do right, when I promise that I will respect the thing which, being disregarded and violated, brought on a war in which millions of men lost their lives, in which the civilization of mankind was in the balance, in which there was the most outrageous exhibition ever witnessed in the history of mankind of the rapacity and disregard for right of a great armed people. We engage in the first sentence of article 10 to respect and preserve from external aggression the territorial integrity and the existing political independence not only of the other member States, but of all States, and if any member of the league of nations disregards that promise, then what happens? The council of the league advises what should be done to enforce the respect for that covenant on the part of the nation attempting to violate it, and there is no compulsion upon us to take that advice except the compulsion of our good conscience and judgment. So that it is perfectly evident that if in the judgment of the people of the United States the council adjudged wrong and that this was not a case of the use of force, there would be no necessity on the part of the Congress of the United States to vote the use of force. But there could be no advice of the council on any such subject without a unanimous vote, and the unanimous vote includes our own, and if we accepted the advice we would be accepting our own advice, for I need not tell you that the representatives of the Government of the United States would not vote without instructions from their Government at home, and that what we united in advising we could be certain that the American people would desire to do. There is in that covenant not only not a surrender of the independent judgment of the Government of the United States, but an expression of it, because that independent judgment would have to join with the judgment of the rest.

But when is that judgment going to be expressed, my fellow citizens? Only after it is evident that every other resource has failed, and I want to call your attention to the central machinery of the league of nations. If any member of that league or any nation not a member refuses to submit the question at issue either to arbitration or

This document can be found in *Congressional Record*, LVIII (September 1919): Part 5, 5001–5002, 5005; Part 6, 5593, 6244–6245, 6249, 6254; Part 7, 6417, 6422.

to discussion by the council, there ensues automatically, by the engagements of this covenant, an absolute economic boycott. There will be no trade with that nation by any member of the league. There will be no interchange of communication by post or telegraph. There will be no travel to or from that nation. Its borders will be closed. No citizen of any other State will be allowed to enter it and no one of its citizens will be allowed to leave it. It will be hermetically sealed by the united action of the most powerful nations in the world. And if this economic boycott bears with unequal weight, the members of the league agree to support one another and to relieve one another in any exceptional disadvantages that may arise out of it. . . .

. . . I want to call your attention, if you will turn it up when you go home, to article 11, following article 10 of the covenant of the league of nations. That article, let me say, is the favorite article in the treaty, so far as I am concerned. It says that every matter which is likely to affect the peace of the world is everybody's business; that it shall be the friendly right of any nation to call attention in the league to anything that is likely to affect the peace of the world or the good understanding between nations, upon which the peace of the world depends, whether that matter immediately concerns the nation drawing attention to it or not.

St. Louis, Missouri, September 5

There can hereafter be no secret treaties. There were nations represented around that board—I mean the board at which the commission on the league of nations sat, where 14 nations were represented—there were nations represented around that board who had entered into many a secret treaty and understanding, and they made not the least objection to promising that hereafter no secret treaty should have any validity whatever. The provision of the covenant is that every treaty or international understanding shall be registered, I believe the word is, with the general secretary of the league, that the general secretary shall publish it in full just so soon as it is possible for him to publish it, and that no treaty shall be valid which is not thus registered. It is like our arrangements with regard to mortgages on real estate, that until they are registered nobody else need pay any attention to them. And so with the treaties; until they are registered in this office of the league nobody, not even the parties themselves, can insist upon their execution. You have cleared the deck thereby of the most dangerous thing and the most embarrassing thing that has hitherto existed in international politics.

Sioux Falls, South Dakota, September 8

I can not understand the psychology of men who are resisting it [the treaty]. I can not understand what they are afraid of, unless it is that they know physical force and do not understand moral force. Moral force is a great deal more powerful than physical. Govern the sentiments of mankind and you govern mankind. Govern their fears, govern their hopes, determine their fortunes, get them together in concerted masses, and the whole thing sways like a team. Once get them suspecting one another, once get them antagonizing one another, and society itself goes to pieces. We are trying to make a society instead of a set of barbarians out of the governments of the world. I sometimes think, when I wake in the night, of all the wakeful nights that anxious fathers and mothers and friends have spent during those weary years of this awful war, and I seem to hear the cry, the inarticulate cry of mothers all over the world, millions of them on the other side of the sea and thousands of them on this side of the sea, "In God's name, give us the sensible and hopeful and peaceful processes of right and of justice."

America can stay out, but I want to call you to witness that the peace of the world can not be established without America. America is necessary to the peace of the world. And reverse the proposition: The peace and good will of the world are necessary to America. Disappoint the world, center its suspicion upon you, make it feel that you are hot and jealous rivals of the other nations, and do you think you are going to do as much business with them as you would otherwise do? I do not like to put the thing on that plane, my fellow countrymen, but if you want to talk business, I can talk business. If you want to put it on the low plane of how much money you can make, you can make more money out of friendly traders than out of hostile traders. You can make more money out of men who trust you than out of men who fear you.

San Francisco, California, September 17

The Monroe doctrine means that if any outside power, any power outside this hemisphere, tries to impose its will upon any portion of the Western Hemisphere the United States is at liberty to act independently and alone in repelling the aggression; that it does not have to wait for the action of the league of nations; that it does not have to wait for anything but the action of its own administration and its own Congress. This is the first time in the history of international diplomacy that any great government has acknowledged the validity of the Monroe doctrine. Now for the first time all the great fighting powers of the world except Germany, which for the time being has ceased to be a great fighting power, acknowledge the validity of the Monroe doctrine and acknowledge it as part of the international practice of the world.

They [critics] are nervous about domestic questions. They say, "It is intolerable to think that the league of nations should interfere with domestic questions," and whenever they begin to specify they speak of the question of immigration, of the question of naturalization, of the question of the tariff. My fellow citizens, no competent or authoritative student of international law would dream of maintaining that these were anything but exclusively domestic questions, and the covenant of the league expressly provides that the league can take no action whatever about matters which are in the practice of international law regarded as domestic questions.

San Francisco, California, September 18

In order that we may not forget, I brought with me the figures as to what this war [First World War] meant to the world. This is a body of business men and you will understand these figures. They are too big for the imagination of men who do not handle big things. Here is the cost of the war in money, exclusive of what we loaned one another: Great Britain and her dominions, $38,000,000,000; France, $26,000,000,000; the United States, $22,000,000,000 (this is the direct cost of our operations); Russia, $18,000,000,000; Italy $13,000,000,000; and the total, including Belgium, Japan, and other countries, $123,000,000,000. This is what it cost the Central Powers: Germany, $39,000,000,000, the biggest single item; Austria-Hungary, $21,000,000,000; Turkey and Bulgaria, $3,000,000,000; a total of $63,000,000,000, and a grand total of direct war costs of $186,000,000,000—almost the capital of the world. The expenditures of the United States were at the rate of

$1,000,000 an hour for two years, including nighttime with daytime. The battle deaths during the war were as follows: Russia lost in dead 1,700,000 men, poor Russia that got nothing but terror and despair out of it all; Germany, 1,600,000; France, 1,385,000; Great Britain, 900,000; Austria, 800,000; Italy, 364,000; the United States, 50,300 dead. The total for all the belligerents, 7,450,200 men—just about seven and a half million killed because we could not have arbitration and discussion, because the world had never had the courage to propose the conciliatory methods which some of us are now doubting whether we ought to accept or not.

San Diego, California, September 19

It is feared that our delegates will be outvoted, because I am constantly hearing it said that the British Empire has six votes and we have one. I am perfectly content to have only one when the one counts six, and that is exactly the arrangement under the league. Let us examine that matter a little more particularly. Besides the vote of Great Britain herself, the other five votes are the votes of Canada, of South Africa, of Australia, of New Zealand, and of India. We ourselves were champions and advocates of giving a vote to Panama, of giving a vote to Cuba—both of them under the direction and protectorate of the United States—and if a vote was given to Panama and to Cuba, could it reasonably be denied to the great Dominion of Canada? Could it be denied to that stout Republic in South Africa, that is now living under a nation which did, indeed, overcome it at one time, but which did not dare retain its government in its hands, but turned it over to the very men whom it had fought? Could we deny it to Australia, that independent little republic in the Pacific, which has led the world in so many liberal reforms? Could it be denied New Zealand? Could we deny it to the hundreds of millions who live in India? But, having given these six votes, what are the facts? For you have been misled with regard to them. The league can take no active steps without the unanimous vote of all the nations represented on the council, added to a vote of the majority in the assembly itself. These six votes are in the assembly, not in the council. The assembly is not a voting body, except upon a limited number of questions, and whenever those questions are questions of action, the affirmative vote of every nation represented on the council is indispensable, and the United States is represented on the council.

Salt Lake City, Utah, September 23

I am not going to stop, my fellow citizens, to discuss the Shantung provision [which shifted control of the area from Germany to Japan] in all its aspects, but what I want to call your attention to is that just so soon as this covenant is ratified every nation in the world will have the right to speak out for China. And I want to say very frankly, and I ought to add that the representatives of those great nations themselves admit, that Great Britain and France and the other powers which have insisted upon similar concessions in China will be put in a position where they will have to reconsider them. This is the only way to serve and redeem China, unless, indeed, you want to start a war for the purpose. At the beginning of the war and during the war Great Britain and France engaged by solemn treaty with Japan that if she would come into the war and continue in the war, she could have, provided she in the meantime took it by force of arms, what Germany had in China. Those are treaties already in force. They are not waiting for ratification. France and England can not withdraw from those obligations, and it will serve China not one iota if we should dissent from the Shantung arrangement; but by being parties to that arrangement we can insist upon the promise of Japan—the promise which the other Governments have not matched—that she will return to China immediately all sovereign rights within the Province of Shantung. We have got that for her now, and under the operations of article 11 and of article 10 it will be impossible for any nation to make any further inroads either upon the territorial integrity or upon the political independence of China.

Denver, Colorado, September 25

The adoption of the treaty means disarmament. Think of the economic burden and the restraint of liberty in the development of professional and mechanical life that resulted from the maintenance of great armies, not only in Germany but in France and in Italy and, to some extent, in Great Britain. If the United States should stand off from this thing we would have to have the biggest army in the world. There would be nobody else that cared for our fortunes. We would have to look out for ourselves, and when I hear gentlemen say, "Yes; that is what we want to do; we want to be independent and look out for ourselves" I say, "Well, then, consult your fellow citizens. There will have to be universal conscription. There will have to be taxes such as even yet we have not seen. There will have to be concentration of authority in the Government capable of using this terrible instrument. You can not conduct a war or command an army by a debating society. You can not determine in community centers what the command of the Commander in Chief is going to be; you will have to have a staff like the German staff, and you will have to center in the Commander in Chief of the Army and Navy the right to take instant action for the protection of the Nation." America will never consent to any such thing.

8. The Lodge Reservations, 1919

1. . . . In case of notice of withdrawal from the league of nations, as provided in said article [Article 1], the United States shall be the sole judge as to whether all its international obligations . . . have been fulfilled, and notice of withdrawal . . . may be given by a concurrent resolution of the Congress of the United States.

2. The United States assumes no obligation to preserve the territorial integrity or political independence of any other country . . . under the provisions of article 10, or to employ the military or naval forces of the United States under any article of the treaty for any purpose, unless in any particular case the Congress, which . . . has the sole power to declare war . . . shall . . . so provide.

3. No mandate shall be accepted by the United States under article 22 . . . except by action of the Congress of the United States.

4. The United States reserves to itself exclusively the right to decide what questions are within its domestic jurisdiction. . . .

5. The United States will not submit to arbitration or to inquiry by the assembly or by the council of the league of nations . . . any questions which in the judgment of

This document can be found in *Congressional Record,* LVIII (November 19, 1919), Part 9, 877–878.

the United States depend upon or relate to . . . the Monroe doctrine; said doctrine is to be interpreted by the United States alone and is . . . wholly outside the jurisdiction of said league of nations. . . .

6. The United States withholds its assent to articles 156, 157, and 158 [Shantung clauses]. . . .

7. The Congress of the United States will provide by law for the appointment of the representatives of the United States in the assembly and the council of the league of nations, and may in its discretion provide for the participation of the United States in any commission. . . . No person shall represent the United States under either said league of nations or the treaty of peace . . . except with the approval of the Senate of the United States. . . .

9. The United States shall not be obligated to contribute to any expenses of the league of nations . . . unless and until an appropriation of funds . . . shall have been made by the Congress of the United States.

10. If the United States shall at any time adopt any plan for the limitation of armaments proposed by the council of the league . . . it reserves the right to increase such armaments without the consent of the council whenever the United States is threatened with invasion or engaged in war. . . .

14. The United States assumes no obligation to be bound by any election, decision, report, or finding of the council or assembly in which any member of the league and its self-governing dominions, colonies, or parts of empire, in the aggregate have cast more than one vote.

 E S S A Y S

In the first essay, Wilson's major biographer, Arthur S. Link of Princeton University, praises the president for a "higher realism" and defends him against critics who have argued that excessive idealism blinded Wilson. Link raises questions about the meaning of realism, and he exonerates Wilson from responsibility for the tumult of international relations that followed Wilson's presidency. In the second essay, the Dutch scholar Jan Wilhelm Schulte-Nordholt disputes Link's flattering portrayal. While admiring Woodrow Wilson's commitment to peace, Schulte-Nordholt depicts a strong-willed dreamer who lost touch with reality. What drove Wilson was the belief that only he and the United States could provide an appropriate model for world peace. Unlike Link, Schulte-Nordholt concludes that Wilson failed to understand the complexities of world politics and spoke in abstract language about goals that had little chance of success because they "skipped over historical problems." At Paris, Wilson's imagination collided with reality, and the Versailles negotiators manipulated the president, who conceded much in order to save the League. The flawed peace, Schulte-Nordholt observes, helped to sow the seeds of the Second World War. The last essay, by Thomas J. Knock of Southern Methodist University, places Wilson in his intellectual-political milieu in the early twentieth century—a left-of-center progressive internationalism. Treating this body of ideas with respect, Knock probes the sources of Wilson's commitment to a league for peace. Knock argues that Wilson ultimately lost the support of both conservative and progressive internationalists (for different reasons). Wilson failed to achieve a Wilsonian league not because of poor health or an uncompromising personality but because the support of the progressive internationalists that he needed for victory eroded in the face of strong forces of reaction at home and abroad during the era of the First World War.

Wilson's Higher Realism

ARTHUR S. LINK

Europeans on the whole still view Wilson very much as many of them viewed him forty years ago at the end of the Paris Peace Conference and the great struggle in the United States over ratification of the Treaty of Versailles. This European image is, I think it is fair to say, one of a well-intentioned idealist, a man good by ordinary Christian standards, but essentially a destructive force in modern history because he was a visionary, unrealistic, provincial, and ignorant of European problems, and zealous and messianic in conceit but devoid of either practical knowledge or the humility to follow others better informed than he. I do not think that this is an essentially unfair statement of the European point of view. It was, of course, the image held by John Maynard Keynes, Georges Clemenceau, and most of the thoughtful European public at the end of the Peace Conference. It is the view still largely held by English, French, and German scholars alike, if for different reasons.

I have felt impelled to my subject not only by . . . forceful reminders of the strong survival of the old European image of President Wilson, but also . . . in our own country . . . [by a] school of historical critics, and by their work in constructing an image of President Wilson that is remarkably like the older European one. Calling themselves realists, and drawing their inspiration from the distinguished diplomat-historian, George Kennan, and the Austrian-trained authority in international relations, Hans J. Morgenthau, . . . these new American critics have found Wilson wanting because he did not think in terms of strategy, bases, and armed power, but dwelt too much in ethereal realms.

Are the old European and new American critics right, I have asked myself over and over during the past few years: is this the image that I also see, the Wilson that I know? Were the Austrians right in thinking that his irresponsible preaching of a slogan, "self-determination," was primarily responsible for the destruction of the Hapsburg Empire? Were the Germans right in holding him responsible for what they regarded as the monstrous betrayal of Versailles? Were the French right in thinking that he prevented the imposition of the only kind of peace settlement upon Germany that could endure? Were the English and new American critics near the truth when they portrayed him as a tragic figure irrelevant in the modern world?

I must confess that I have sometimes been tempted to agree. No one who has ever given any serious attention to President Wilson's life could fail to agree that he was *primarily* a Christian idealist. By this I mean a man who almost always tended to judge policies on a basis of whether they were right by Christian standards, not whether they brought immediate material or strategic advantage. I mean also a man whose foreign policies were motivated by the assumption that a nation as much as an individual should live according to the law of Christian love, and by a positive repudiation of the assumptions of the classical "realists" about international behavior.

No one who has given serious study to Wilson's career, moreover, could fail to agree that there is at least an appearance of reality about the old European and new

Reprinted by permission of the Presbyterian Historical Society from "The Higher Realism of Woodrow Wilson," by Arthur Link from *Journal of Presbyterian History*, XLI (March 1963).

American image. Wilson was not merely an idealist, but a crusading idealist. An orator of enormous eloquence and power, he was also a phrasemaker who more than once fell victim to the magic of his own words. In international relations, he did not give undue weight to material forces or base his policies upon the assumption that nations must always act selfishly. At times, he did seem to give the appearance of believing that he was a kind of messiah divinely appointed to deliver Europe from the cruel tyranny of history.

I have myself made all these criticisms and others more elaborately in my own writings. But they have never really satisfied me and do not satisfy me now. I do not think that they add up to a historical image that is accurate. Indeed, I cannot escape the conclusion that they altogether miss the main point and meaning of President Wilson's career.

The point, in my opinion, and the theme of this paper, is that among all the major statesmen and thoughtful critics of his age, President Wilson was in fact the supreme realist, and that because this is true, what he stood for and fought to accomplish has large meaning for our own generation.

This is, to be sure, a very broad, perhaps even an audacious, statement, one that does not mean very much unless we are careful to define our terms. A realist, I take it, is one who faces life and its situations without illusions, in short, one who can see realities or truth through the fog of delusion that normally shrouds the earth-bound individual. If the European and American critics of President Wilson who thought mainly in strategic and material terms, who measured national power by army divisions and naval bases, and the like, if *they* were realists, then President Wilson was a realist of a different sort. Sheerly for purposes of convenience, let us call his view of the national and international situations with which he had to cope a "higher realism," higher because more perceptive, more in accord with ultimate reality, more likely to win the long-run moral approval of societies professing allegiance to the common western, humane, Christian traditions. . . .

I am sure that in talking about Wilson's "higher realism" in meeting domestic challenges, I have simply been saying things and making judgments with which virtually every historian of the United States would readily agree. It is precisely this "higher realism" that has entitled Wilson to rank, by the agreement of American historians, among the four or five most successful Presidents in our history. In talking about Wilson's policies and contributions in the realm of foreign affairs, I am, I know, on more controversial ground. Wilson was magnificently prepared for leadership in internal affairs by long study of American history and institutions. He had little if any preparation for leadership in the world at large; indeed, at the outset of his tenure in the White House he had no serious interest in foreign affairs. At the outset and later he made mistakes that still seriously impair his record. Even so, I cannot but conclude that President Wilson on the whole showed the same kind of wisdom and long-range vision and understanding—in short, "higher realism"—in his third career as international statesman as he had already revealed in his first two careers at home.

This, I know, is a big statement, and I would like to preface it with a few generalizations about Wilson's thought and character as a diplomat in order to lay foundations for some later observations.

The first is the most obvious and the one with which most historians would agree, namely, that President Wilson was, as I have already said, above all an idealist in the conduct of foreign affairs, one who subordinated immediate goals and material interests to what he considered to be superior ethical standards and moral purposes. His idealism was perhaps best revealed in his thinking about the purposes that the United States should serve in the world. The mission of America, he said over and over and sincerely believed, was not a mission of aggrandizement of material power but one of service to mankind. It was a mission of peace, of sacrifice, of leading the nations into a new international community organized to achieve right ends.

Second, all of Wilson's thinking about international relations was conditioned, in general, by a loathing for war and, in particular, by a conviction that physical force should never be used to achieve selfish and material aims.

Third, Wilson was actually in many ways "realistic," even by conventional standards, in his thinking about and methods in the conduct of foreign relations. For example, he used armed force in the classic way to achieve certain diplomatic objectives in Mexico and the Caribbean. He understood the meaning of the term "balance of power." He was keenly aware of the relevance of material interests and had few illusions about the fundamental bases of international behavior. It is, one must say, the sheerest nonsense to talk about him as an impractical idealist and visionary.

Fourth, while admitting that there were times when a nation had no recourse but to use armed force in international disputes, and while using force himself on behalf of the American government on certain occasions, President Wilson never permitted war's neuroses and fascinations either to derange his reason or to obscure the political objectives for which force was being used. Hence he was never the victim of that greatest twentieth-century delusion, that it is necessary to win wars even at the risk of losing everything for which wars are fought.

This is a very imperfect characterization of the thought and character of Wilson the diplomatist, but it may help us to understand his policies during the greatest tragedy of the modern epoch and the event that raised the gravest challenges to his leadership—the First World War. It was for Wilson a period with three distinct stages: the period of American neutrality, from August 1914 to April 1917; the period of American belligerency, from April 1917 to November 1918; and the period of peacemaking, from November 1918 to June 1919. The challenges of each period were different, but he met them all, on the whole, with the same "higher realism" that had characterized his leadership at home.

His policies during the first period can best be briefly described by saying that from the outbreak of the war in Europe to the beginning of the German unlimited submarine campaign in early 1917, President Wilson tried as hard as any man could have done to be neutral, to make the necessary accommodations to the exercise of belligerent power, and to engage in stern defense of American rights only when they could not, because fundamental human principles were involved, be compromised.

Some of the recent American "realists" have joined the older English and French critics in charging Wilson with impractical idealism precisely because he did follow such a course—because he did not rally the American people to preparation for what they have said was an inevitable participation; because he conducted long and patient negotiations to avoid a break with Germany; because he did not undertake large and early measures of assistance to the Allies and thus help to shorten the duration of Europe's agony; because he refused throughout the period of American neutrality even to align the American people and their government morally on the Allied side.

Looking back upon the final outcome, as we are entitled to do, we well might wonder who the true realists were during this period: so-called realists, or President Wilson, who in an almost uncanny way kept himself immune from the emotional hysterias and passions that seized other men; who believed that the causes of the war were so complex and remote that it was impossible to assess the blame; who, overborne by the tragedy of the event, fought desperately to preserve American neutrality so that he could perform the healing task of reconciliation once the nations of Europe had come to some sense; who believed that an enduring peace could come only through a "peace without victory," a "peace between equals"? Who were the deluded men who had lost sight of reality? The European leaders who thought that they could win decisive victories on the battlefields and on or under the seas, and who thought that they could impose their nations' wills upon other great peoples? Or Wilson, who thought that they were momentarily mad?

The climactic confrontation, the supreme reckoning between so-called realists and the alleged impractical idealist, came, once the United States had been forced into the conflict and Germany was defeated. It did not occur earlier, because the British and French leaders had refused to permit it to occur before the Armistice was safely signed. But it could not then be long postponed, for the Allied leaders had matured their plans, and President Wilson had meanwhile formed a peace program of his own and announced it to the world in the Fourteen Points address and other speeches.

There is no need to review the turbulent events of the Paris Peace Conference here. They are familiar enough, to begin with; but a detailed account of them now would obscure my larger purpose—to look back upon the Paris settlement and, while looking back, to attempt to see who the true realists were.

The supreme task of the victors at Paris in 1919 was, obviously, to work out a peace settlement and reconstruct an international order that could endure. It had to be a peace that could survive the ebbing of passions and hatreds that consumed Europe in 1919. It had to be a peace that could survive because it could command the approval of the German people. Above all, it had to be the kind of settlement that would endure because it could retain the long-run support of the American and English peoples, even of the French people. The necessity of constructing this kind of settlement was, as we can now see clearly, the supreme reality of peacemaking in 1919. We must, therefore, judge men and measures at the Paris Conference according to whether they met this test or not.

By this criterion I do not see how any fair historian can but conclude that the so-called realists at Paris—the dedicated if cynical [Georges] Clemenceau, concerned only about the destruction of the ancient foe and the future security of France; the well-intentioned [David] Lloyd George, who had given so many hostages to war passions at home and to the Commonwealths that he was no longer a free man; and the Italians, [Sidney] Sonnino and [Vittorio] Orlando, eager only for spoils—how could they be called anything other than sublime irrationalists and dreamers? Theirs was a dream, a nightmare, of unreality. Given the task of reconstructing Europe and preventing a future war, they would have responded by attempting to perpetuate the division of Europe and by making a new war almost inevitable.

On the other side and standing usually in solitary if splendid isolation was the alleged impractical idealist fighting for the only kind of settlement that had any chance of survival—for a peace of reconciliation, for disarmament by victors as well as vanquished, against annexations and indemnities, and for a new international organization that would include former enemy states as active members from the beginning. Over and over he warned that this was the only kind of peace that would prove acceptable to the American people in the short run and to the moral opinion of the world in the long run, in short, the only kind of settlement that could endure. It should require little reference to events that followed the Paris Conference to demonstrate the "higher realism" of President Wilson's views.

If proof is needed on specific points, one could cite, for example, Wilson's point of view on the problem of reparations. Over and over he insisted, and with a steadfast consistency, that reparations should be compensation for specific willful damage only, not indemnity; that the Germans should not be saddled with a debt that was heavier than they could carry; and that there should be a time limit to the obligation that the German nation should be forced to assume. What the Allied leaders demanded and finally obtained is well known. . . . What the realistic solution of this problem was is now too obvious for comment. Or, as a second example, one might cite Wilson's attitude toward the Russian Revolution—how he saw the deeply rooted causes of that cataclysm and the futility of any western effort to suppress it by military force; and how the realism of his attitude contrasted with the egregious folly of so-called realists who thought that it lay within their power to change the course of Russian history.

The result of the clash between European so-called realism and Wilsonian so-called idealism was of course the Treaty of Versailles, that compromise that violated the terms of the agreement by which the Germans had stopped fighting and made a mockery of some of the principal planks in the American President's peace program. Why, it is fair to ask, did President Wilson permit such a peace to be made and sign the treaty embodying it? The answer, I submit, is that it was "higher realism" that drove him to this difficult decision. Having won, at least partially, many of the things for which he had been fighting, he had to give as well as to take, for he could not impose his will entirely upon his colleagues. He signed the Versailles Treaty in the conviction that the passage of time and the Treaty's new creation, the League of Nations, would almost certainly operate to rectify what he knew were the grievous mistakes of the Peace Conference. He signed the Versailles Treaty, in short, because he believed that it was the best settlement possible in the circumstances of 1919.

What President Wilson hoped would occur did of course in large part take place during the 1920s and early 1930s, even though alleged realists in the United States combined with authentic visionaries to repudiate Wilson's work and prevent their government from playing the role of mediating leadership within the League of Nations of which Wilson had dreamed. The great tragedy of the postwar period was not that the Versailles Treaty was imperfect. It was that the forces of reconciliation could not operate rapidly enough without American leadership in the League, that France and Great Britain had neither the will nor the strength to defend the Treaty alone during the 1930s and, above all, that the German people submitted to demonic forces that promised a speedy rectification of all the injustices of Versailles.

But this is precisely what President Wilson, in another flash of "higher realism," predicted would occur if the so-called realists, both in the United States and in Europe, continued to have their way.

That is the age-old question, whether the so-called realists or the higher realists shall have their way in determination of national and international policies. President Wilson survives as a more powerful force in history than when he lived because he gave us the supreme demonstration in the twentieth century of higher realism in statesmanship.

This, obviously, was no accident. Woodrow Wilson's "higher realism" was the product of insight and wisdom informed by active Christian faith. He was not, fundamentally, a moralist, as he so often seemed to be, but a man who lived in faith, trying to be guided by the Holy Spirit in meeting the complex problems of a changing nation and world. Using one of his own metaphors, we can say that the light of Heaven gleamed upon his sword. His precepts and ideals will be relevant so long as democracy endures, so long as men seek after a new international community organized for peace and the advancement of mankind.

The Peace Advocate Out of Touch with Reality

JAN WILHELM SCHULTE-NORDHOLT

We are in many respects Woodrow Wilson's heirs. That is why it is of great importance to us to make out what kind of man he was, how he came to his exalted and advanced ideas, and why in the end he failed. That is my purpose. . . . I want to examine more closely the life of a man who sought a solution to problems that are still ours, and who was therefore the first great advocate of world peace. He was, as it were, a whole peace movement all by himself.

I almost wrote "apostle of peace," but this phrase is too strong. It makes it seem that I had at least to some extent a work of hagiography in mind. Far from it! History is about people, their dreams and their failures. It would be all too easy to paint Woodrow Wilson as the great prophet who was always wiser than his fellow men. The purpose of a biography ought not to be to turn a human being into a figure of puppetry; to change the metaphor, to press him into flat uniformity. Was Wilson a prophet, an idealist, a dissembler, a practical man, a revolutionary reformer? He was to some small extent all of these. Like most great men, indeed like most people, Wilson was a bundle of contradictions. That is what makes him so fascinating. He was many things: a scholar driven by deep feelings; a poet who found his vocation in politics; a Christian consumed by his need for recognition; a lonely man who thought he understood mankind; a practical man who became fossilized in all too lofty dreams; a reasonable man full of turbulent passions. It is this paradoxical personality that I have tried to respect, . . . the irritating, moving grandeur of a self-willed man who played an immense role in history and whose importance has become extraordinarily great in our own times, even though he

From *Woodrow Wilson: A Life for Peace* (1991) by Jan W. Schulte-Nordholt, trans./ed. by Rowen, Herbert. Reprinted by permission of the University of California Press.

failed so wretchedly. That is why his life story is a dramatic tale, almost a Greek tragedy, with a catharsis at the end that still drains and raises our emotions. . . .

The outbreak of the war [in 1914] affected the president deeply. It shocked his sensitive nature. We read for example in a letter to [his assistant Edward] House in August: "I feel the burden of the thing almost intolerably from day to day." Two months later he wrote in the same vein but at greater length to Walter Page, the ambassador in London:

> The whole thing is vivid in my mind, painfully vivid, and has been almost ever since the struggle began. I think my thought and imagination contain the picture and perceive its significance from every point of view. I have to force myself not to dwell upon it to avoid the sort of numbness that comes from deep apprehension and dwelling upon elements too vast to be yet comprehended or in any way controlled by counsel.

Here we see once again in Wilson the tension between feeling and detachment.

This only emphasizes the importance of the question of how neutral he really was or wanted to be. His first personal reactions were emotionally favorable to the Allies. He was, after all, imbued with English values and ideals. The French ambassador to Washington, Jules Jusserand, wondered what "the great doctrinaire" in the White House was thinking, but the president soon gave his answer, as it were, to the English ambassador, Sir Cecil Spring-Rice. Spring-Rice informed Sir Edward Grey, the English foreign secretary, that Wilson had admitted to him that everything he held dear was now at stake. The president, he added, spoke with deep emotion. The ambassador, who knew the man he was dealing with, quoted a few lines from Wordsworth's sonnets about English freedom written during the Napoleonic wars. He knew them by heart, Wilson said with tears in his eyes. (Spring-Rice, as it happened, was also playing up to Grey, who, like Wilson, was passionately fond of Wordsworth.)

In his personal feelings Wilson was not in the slightest neutral. House heard him inveigh against everything German—government and people and what he called abstract German philosophy, which lacked spirituality! But he was quite able to separate his personal opinions and his official duties. In the first place, he understood that neutrality was necessary, that the American people were totally set against intervention. But he was also moved by the great goal that he had glimpsed since the beginning of the war, a possibility that fitted his character like a glove. It makes its appearance in his call for neutrality, for he did not merely issue a scrupulously formal official declaration, as any other president would have done. He did more, accompanying this declaration with a personal call to the people to remain truly neutral in thought and words. America, he reminded them, was composed of many peoples and too great sympathy for one or the other side could bring division among them.

Unity was even more necessary for another reason as well. This was the grand ideal that he now made public officially for the first time and which henceforth would inspire him and more and more involve him in international complications. America, he announced, was chosen to mediate, as only America could, just because it was neutral. He spoke in an exalted, religious tone, as he liked to do on so many other occasions. It was as if the war at last made possible things that all his life he had dreamed of—his country as the model and the very leader of the whole world, and himself called and chosen as the leader of his country and the maker of the future. . . .

One thing led to another. The arms shipments [to the Allies] led to loans. [William Jennings] Bryan, the pacifist-minded secretary of state, doubted that this flow of funds, which went almost entirely to the Entente, was really neutral. In good biblical fashion, he saw money as the root of all evil. Was it not written in Scripture that where one's treasure was, one's heart was too? He was able to convince Wilson that steps had to be taken against these loans, and American bankers were therefore warned on August 15, 1914, that such credits were "inconsistent with the true spirit of neutrality." But such a splendid position could not be maintained in the long run. Arms deliveries continued to grow, and the American economy could not do without them. In the spring of 1915 Bryan's idealistic approach was abandoned and one loan after another was floated in the United States. When America entered the war in 1917, the loans to the Allies had risen to more than two billion dollars, while those to the Central Powers amounted to no more than $27,000,000. . . .

War brings all international agreements into question, for war is unpredictable and full of surprises, always different from what anyone could have imagined. This was never so painfully evident as in the question of submarine warfare, since submarines were a weapon without equal, but operated effectively only by surprise. A multitude of notes discussed and debated the question of their surprise attacks. What was the status of the fine agreements about merchant ships in wartime? The answer was clear: a warship might halt, search, seize, and even sink a merchantman, but only after prior warning and giving civilian travelers the opportunity to leave safely. But a submarine that adhered to such rules would of course become defenseless and useless.

When the war broke out, German ships were swept off the seas, Germany was blockaded, and the Germans desperately turned to the submarine as a means of breaking the Allied stranglehold. The initial successes of the U-boats in the autumn of 1914 brought a sudden resurgence of hope, and the German military command slowly realized what a powerful weapon it had in its hands. On February 4, 1915, the German government published an official declaration putting a blockade around the British islands: in a zone around Great Britain, all enemy ships, including merchant vessels, would be attacked without warning. Neutral ships were advised to avoid these regions, since the Allied ships could always be disguised with neutral flags. . . .

The submarine weapon made it much more difficult for the United States, like all nonbelligerents, to remain neutral. Neutrality became a dilemma as never before. Was it neutral to waive fundamental rights of free navigation? Wasn't this itself a serious breach of international law, a grave derogation of morality in a world where morality seemed more and more on the wane?

Wilson, a man of principle, protested, but in so doing he reduced his chances for mediation. A sharp note was sent to Berlin, declaring that the policy set forth in the German note was "so unprecedented in naval warfare that this Government is reluctant to believe that the Imperial Government of Germany in this case contemplates it as possible." The American government would hold the German government fully responsible for the consequences. This seemed like plain talk, but what would happen if American rights were really challenged could not be foreseen. It was nonetheless probable that once such a stand on principle was taken, a conflict would result. . . .

Wherever the inspiration for the phrase ["peace without victory"] came from, the address that the president made to the Senate on January 22 [1917] was genuine Wilson from beginning to end. It was a plea, splendid, grandiose, and vague, for America's involvement in a future world order. That order—an organization of the peoples with its own force—had to come, he said. The question was, what kind of force? This was and remained the point of difficulty. For Wilson, the moralist who knew that without human inspiration and dedication the finest promises are empty, had in mind a "force" that was greater than the force of any country or alliance, which was "the organized major force of mankind." The nations must come to an agreement and then the old system of the "balance of power" would give way to a "community of power." And that could happen only if there was true reconciliation, upon the basis of a "peace without victory," a peace among equals.

That did not bring pleasure to everyone's ears, he realized. But he had to say it, for his intention was "only to face realities and to face them without soft concealments." Dreamers want so much to be taken for realists! . . .

. . . He spoke in the name of the United States of America, the unique and superior country, as he himself liked to call it, forward-looking and in the lead in the service of mankind. All liberal-thinking people everywhere, in Europe and in America, rejoiced at his words. But conservatives (must we call them the realists?) on both sides of the ocean shook their heads over such empty phrases. Among the first of these, as we know, were persons in Wilson's own backyard, his closest advisers. [Secretary of State Robert] Lansing had warned against the term "peace without victory." What did it really mean? And, most of all, how would these words be taken in the Allied countries? But, Lansing tells us, Wilson did not want to listen. "I did not argue the matter, especially as I knew his fondness for phrase-making and was sure that it would be useless to attempt to dissuade him." . . .

As was to be expected, Lodge surpassed all the others in his hostility to Wilson. In an angry speech to the Senate he wielded the full resources of his logic to tear apart the arguments of his enemy. What did it mean to say that America had no interest in the peace terms but only in the peace? How can men be required to wage war not to win, so that all their sacrifices were in vain, "a criminal and hideous futility"? . . . How could the "organized major force of mankind" be applied? Voluntarily, or automatically, or compulsorily? When the idea of a league was broached two years earlier, he had been greatly attracted to it, but the more he thought about it, the more problems he saw. It could not be made effective by "high-sounding phrases, which fall so agreeably upon the ear, when there is no thought behind it." Does it mean that the small nations can, by majority vote, involve the large nations in war? "Are we prepared to commit ourselves to a purely general proposition without knowing where we are going or what is to be demanded of us, except that we shall be compelled to furnish our quota of military and naval forces to the service of a league in which we shall have but one voice?" A league for peace meant readiness to wage war against any country that did not obey its decisions. What if it decided that Japan and China should have the right of migration anywhere, and Canada, Australia, and New Zealand declined to accept the decision? Or California, for that matter?

The points made by Lodge were fundamental, which is why I present them at such length. Already at this time, in January 1917, the lines of division were drawn which would define the great debate and the great tragedy of 1919. On one side stood the idealist, on the other the realist, and on both sides more than personal animosity was involved. Furthermore, a political alliance was beginning to take shape that slackened during the war years but operated with full force in 1919; it brought together the Republican isolationists from the West, who were also idealists, for the most part from the Progressive camp, and the Republican internationalist realists, [Senator William] Borah on the one side and Lodge on the other. It was an alliance that would bring disaster to Wilson, but in 1917 he could not foresee that. . . .

Wilson shrank from taking the final step [after the German decision in late January 1917 to launch unrestricted submarine warfare], not out of fear, not out of unsullied pacifism, but because his whole conception of mediating between the belligerents (and thereby saving white civilization) would be shattered. This was the principal reason for his hesitation. And so he talked during these weeks in almost pacifist terms about war and imperialism, spoke out in anger against the support for war from right-wing circles, which he described as "Junkerthum trying to creep in under the cover of the patriotic feeling of the moment." . . .

[The journalist] Walter Lippmann, who looked at him with cool rationality and was among those bitterly disappointed with him after 1919, draws for us nonetheless a portrait of Wilson in his book *Men of Destiny,* showing the orator of light learning about darkness. He gazed in March 1917, says Lippmann, "in the bottomless pit." He was "an anguished prophet," full of compassion and doubt, a man who experienced the tragedy of his time and therefore was able, with overwrought absoluteness, to see the league of nations as the only justification of his action.

With this as his justification he went into the war, not out of economic interest, not because of the violation of the neutral rights of the United States, although these played a part, but in order to bring about genuine peace. Only if America took part could it have a voice in the peace. Mediation through participation would be more effective than neutrality, he now believed. To a delegation of pacifists led by Jane Addams, he said on February 28 that "as head of a nation participating in the war, the President of the United States would have a seat at the Peace Table, but that if he remained the representative of a neutral country he could at best only 'call through a crack in the door.' " Personal ambition and general interest concurred in what we may call a mission. The man and his times seemed to fit each other like the two halves of a piece of fruit. . . .

Of all the impressive sermons that Wilson preached to his people and to the world, none became so famous as his "Fourteen Points" speech of January 8, 1918. It attained a breadth and depth, in space and in time, greater than that of all the others. Not that it is his finest address; there are others, such as the "peace without victory" speech of a year earlier and the declaration of war of April 1917, which are more splendid in rhetoric and wider in vision. But this time Wilson was more practical, adding as it were deed to words; he developed a practical program that was of importance for the whole world. . . .

All in all, the Fourteen Points seemed practical and responsible. How lightly they skipped over historical problems would only become evident in Paris. But there was also a fourteenth point, a panacea for all the shortcomings now and later, a League of Nations: "A special association of nations must be formed under specific covenants for the purpose of affording mutual guarantees of political independence and territorial integrity to great and small states alike." This short sentence carried a heavy burden, too heavy as it turned out. In these few words the future world peace was settled, totally and permanently. For Wilson everything revolved around it; he did not see the difficulties and he did not want to see them, and this would in the end bring his downfall. . . .

In general Wilson's principles more and more broke loose from reality and lived their own lives. Self-determination was one such principle. During the war it became one of the major foundations of Wilson's new world order. We shall never subject another people, he had said back in 1915, "because we believe, we passionately believe, in the right of every people to choose their own allegiance and be free of masters altogether."

Only very slowly, as the reality of Europe began to come closer, did he discover the dangerous consequences of the principle. In the discussion with Spring-Rice on January 3 . . . , he wondered whether it was in fact possible to apply it consistently. The example of the threatening dismemberment of Austria-Hungary was probably in his thoughts when he said: "Pushed to its extreme, the principle would mean the disruption of existing governments to an undefinable extent. Logic was a good and powerful thing but apart from the consideration of existing circumstances might well lead to very dangerous results." The Englishman must have heard this with satisfaction, for the British Empire was not about to grant self-determination to all its peoples.

Later, in Paris, many began to realize the difficulties and dangers in this splendid principle. Lansing hit the nail on the head in a confidential memorandum, in which he wondered what self-determination would mean for the Irish, Indians, Egyptians, and South African Boers. What would happen with the Muslims in Syria and Palestine, and how did that fit in with the idea of Zionism, to which Wilson was very sympathetic. "The phrase is simply loaded with dynamite. It will raise hopes which can never be realized." It was the dream of an idealist, he said, and it is clear whom Lansing really had in mind.

As Wilson himself came to see, he had to be very cautious in Paris when trying to put his great principles into practice. He acknowledged that when he had first spoken of self-determination he had not realized that there were so many peoples who would claim it as their right. . . .

Wilson did not underestimate the devastation in Europe, but he retained his nineteenth-century American optimism. His whole existence was tied up with it; he could not live without hope. He clung to the idea of a grand radical cure, to a mystical faith in the mankind of the future, who were purified by events and repented. He had to represent that mankind; he had to make a new peace.

That is why he had to go to Paris [after the German surrender in late 1918]. . . . He was overwhelmed by his mission. His Czech colleague Thomas Masaryk, who understood him well ("now, we were both professors") warned him about the European statesmen: "But he wouldn't listen, for he was too filled with his plan for a League of Nations to take obstacles into account." . . .

Wilson's triumphal tour of Europe took him from Paris to London and then to Rome. Everywhere he was greeted as a savior, as the "Redeemer of Humanity" (*Redentore dell' Humanità*) and "God of Peace" (*Dio di Pace*), in the words of the Italian banners. He spent weeks indulging in this pomp and circumstance, immersed in a sea of flags and songs, carried along by beautiful words that promised so much for the future. Justice! Peace! When we hear Wilson speak in these first weeks, everything is radiant. Sometimes a harsh sound breaks through, as when he replies to [Raymond] Poincaré, the president of France, who wants no reconciliation with the foe, that there exist "eternal principles of right and justice" which bring with them "the certainty of just punishment." But for the most part his outlook is peaceful. He speaks of the peoples who form "the organized moral force of men throughout the world," of the tide of good will: "There is a great tide running in the hearts of men. The hearts of men have never beaten so singularly in unison before. Men have never been so conscious of this brotherhood." . . .

. . . Alas, there was in fact no moral tide that carried all with it. There was rather a divided Europe in which the peoples were driven at least as much by muddled feelings of rage and revenge as by lofty thoughts of right and reason. Wilson himself had experienced the impact of such vindictiveness during the off-year elections in the United States, and it was at least as prevalent in Europe. [French premier Georges] Clemenceau told the Chamber of Deputies at the end of December that he disagreed with Wilson, although he had, he said, the greatest admiration for the American president's "noble candor" (which was changed in the parliamentary journal to "noble grandeur"); he thereupon won a vote of confidence by a majority of 380 to 134. [British prime minister] Lloyd George triumphed equally convincingly in elections for the House of Commons just before Christmas. His coalition of Liberals and Tories, in which the latter were dominant, ran on an electoral program of hate and revenge against Germany with slogans like "Hang the Kaiser" and "Make Germany Pay," received no less than 526 of the 707 seats. It was not Lloyd George himself but the navy minister Sir Eric Geddes who uttered the notorious words, "We shall squeeze the German lemons until the pips squeak."

Wilson's moral majority therefore existed only in his poetic imagination. He was totally out of touch with reality. The Europeans did not know what to make of his fine words. They asked themselves whether he actually meant what he said. "I am one of the few people who think him honest," said Lloyd George to his friends. But he too was exasperated when the president blew his own horn loudly and gave no sign that he understood the sacrifices England had made: "Not a word of generous appreciation issued from his lips." Wilson, the American, could not establish an accepted character and place in Europe. The Europeans thought he was American, with his smooth, streamlined face, showing no emotion behind his shining glasses. . . .

In a word, the European leaders did not like Woodrow Wilson. From the start there was tension between them. Clemenceau, an old hand in politics, was not the man to come under the influence of Wilson's lofty words. He knew the United States; he had lived there just after the Civil War, spoke English well, and had married an American woman. He had no high opinion of American idealism, as was evident in the witticisms he made at Wilson's expense. God had needed only ten commandments, but Wilson fourteen, he jibed. . . . And, in reaction to the "peace without victory" speech, he wrote: "Never before has any political assembly heard so fine a sermon on what human beings might be capable of accomplishing if only they weren't human." In brief, this was classic realism confronting classic idealism. . . .

Wilson believed in his League of Nations as a remedy for all troubles, a miraculous cure that would work precisely because it was so entwined with the peace treaty itself. The treaty might not be perfect, he said in April, but with the League of Nations as an integral part of the treaty, there was a mechanism to improve its operation.

But actually it worked the other way round, a fact that Wilson completely missed. The delegates of the Allied countries exploited his League of Nations proposal to extract concessions from him; the peace turned out very badly because he repeatedly made compromises in order to save his beloved plan, carrying it through the bustling debates to safe harbor. . . . "The fact is," wrote the deeply disappointed [diplomat Henry] White in May, "that the League of Nations, in which he had been more deeply interested than anything else from the beginning, believing it to be the best if not the only means of avoiding war in the future, has been played to the limit by France and Japan in extracting concessions from him; to a certain extent by the British too, and the Treaty as it stands is the result." . . .

The history of the Versailles peace has called forth a welter of difficult questions. Was it too harsh, a *Diktatfrieden* that automatically elicited a reaction of revanche? Or was it, on the contrary, too mild a settlement, enabling the old forces in Germany to continue? In any case, is there a direct causal link between 1919 and 1933? Does the guilt for the disastrous consequences lie with the men who, in Paris, laid down the rules for the future? These are all questions that in their nature cannot be given a conclusive or logically satisfactory answer. But they are also questions that cannot be evaded. If this peace were not accepted, Wilson said many times on his swing through the West in the fall, there would be another war in twenty years. . . .

How horribly right he proved to be! What he predicted came about just as he said. But was he himself guiltless? Hadn't he written the whole scenario for that future? The defeat [of Germany] was a humiliation, not intended as such by him in his noble naïveté, but nonetheless felt as such by the vanquished. Humiliation led to dreams of revenge; the seeds of a new war were put into the soil. Of course, they would only grow when the climate was favorable, when events, primarily the Great Depression that began in 1929, permitted. But beyond question the seeds were planted by the peace of Versailles. . . .

Historians, in their quest for consistency, have to fit Wilson into some pattern, if need be, one that takes time into account. This provides a way out: in the long run, in the future (but with what a frightful intermezzo!), Wilson would be right. This is the way Arthur Link, Wilson's outstanding biographer, approaches the question. For him, Wilson's vision might seem foolish at first sight, because it clashed with reality, but there is in fact a "higher realism." This adds a wider dimension to the problem of Wilson; his deeds then must be judged within the perspective of the future. In it his deeds accord with his words; if they were failures in the short run, all is reconciled in the perspective of a better future. It is a quite Wilsonian idea, paralleling the way Wilson himself saw the League of Nations as the panacea for all temporary compromises.

But is it possible to separate today and tomorrow from each other in this way? Is this how the relationship between realism and idealism actually works? What is the value of a prophet in politics? These are the questions we constantly encounter. There is a deep tragedy within them. Let me repeat: Wilson himself saw and warned that if there was not a just peace, there would be war again in twenty years. Does it follow from this that he personally shared in the responsibility for the horrors that would break out two decades later? Link's reply is that he did not. At Versailles there was the familiar tension between the ideal and reality, but it is inherent in all human striving. One can only ask why Wilson failed. There are more than enough reasons. After the armistice he had no means to compel France and England; he had been weakened in his own country by the elections; he had formidable opponents in Clemenceau, Lloyd George, [Italian prime minister] Orlando, and [Italian foreign minister Sidney] Sonnino; his ideal of "open covenants" was frustrated. And yet, Link maintains, he gained a reasonable peace that worked and created a new international order. He snaps at the critics:

> It is time to stop perpetuating the myth that the Paris settlement made inevitable the rise to power of Mussolini, the Japanese militarists, and Hitler, and hence the Second World War. That war was primarily the result of the Great Depression.

All the same, questions persist. If the war that came in twenty years was not the consequence of a bad peace, or if it wasn't such a bad peace after all, was Wilson's forecast just a stab in the dark? But then why reproach the others who opposed him?

Wilson's Battle for the League: Progressive Internationalists Confront the Forces of Reaction

THOMAS J. KNOCK

As the historian Frederick Jackson Turner once remarked, the age of reform in the United States was "also the age of socialistic inquiry." Indeed, by 1912, the Socialist Party of America and its quadrennial standard-bearer, Eugene Debs, had attained respectability and legitimacy. The party's membership exceeded 115,000, and some 1,200 socialists held public office in 340 municipalities and twenty-four states. As many as three million Americans read socialist newspapers on a regular basis. Julius Wayland's *Appeal to Reason,* with 760,000 weekly subscribers, ranked among the most widely read publications in the world.

The general cast of the four-way presidential campaign of 1912 also lent credence to Turner's observation. Notwithstanding the conservatism of the incumbent, William Howard Taft, the impact of progressivism on the two main parties, in tandem with the success of the Socialist party, caused a certain blurring of traditional political lines. To millions of citizens, a vote for either Woodrow Wilson, the progressive Democrat, Theodore Roosevelt, the insurgent "Bull Moose" who bolted the Republicans to form the Progressive party, or Debs, the Socialist, amounted to a protest against the status quo of industrial America. And that protest, from top to bottom, sanctioned an unfolding communion between liberals and socialists practically unique in American history.

In this new age of progressive reform and socialistic inquiry, it would be Woodrow Wilson's opportunity and challenge to reconcile and shape domestic and foreign concerns in ways that no previous chief executive had ever contemplated. . . .

. . . The League of Nations had many authors and the concept was in a constant state of metamorphosis. Wilson's essential contribution was grand synthesis and

This is an original essay written for this volume based on *To End All Wars: Woodrow Wilson and the Quest for a New World Order* (New York: Oxford University Press, 1992).

propagation. At a fairly early stage in the war, a new internationalist movement came into being in the United States. Two divergent aggregations of activists— "progressive internationalists" and "conservative internationalists"—composed this movement. Wilson's relationship with both groups was of fundamental importance.

Feminists, liberals, pacifists, socialists, and reformers of varying kinds filled the ranks of the progressive internationalists. Their leaders included many of the era's authentic heroes and heroines: Jane Addams of Hull House, the poet-journalist John Reed, Max Eastman of the *Masses,* the civil-rights crusader Oswald Garrison Villard, and Lillian Wald of New York's Henry Street Settlement, to name a few. For them the search for a peaceful world order provided a logical common ground. Peace was indispensable to change itself—to the survival of the labor movement, to their campaigns on behalf of women's rights and the abolition of child labor, and to social justice legislation in general. If the war in Europe were permitted to rage on indefinitely, progressive internationalists believed, then the United States could not help but get sucked into it; not only their great causes, but also the very moral fiber of the nation would be destroyed should its resources be diverted from reform to warfare. Thus, their first goal (and one in keeping with Wilson's policy of neutrality) was to bring about a negotiated settlement of the war.

The Woman's Peace party, founded in January 1915, in Washington, D.C., and led by Jane Addams, played a pivotal role in the progressive internationalist movement. Guided by the principle of "the sacredness of human life," the platform of the Woman's Peace party constituted the earliest manifesto on internationalism advanced by any American organization throughout the war. The party's "program for constructive peace" called for an immediate armistice, international agreements to limit armaments and nationalize their manufacture, a reduction of trade barriers, self-determination, machinery for arbitration, and a "Concert of Nations" to supersede the balance-of-power system. The platform also pressed for American mediation of the war. Its authors made sure that the president received all of their recommendations.

The ideas and activities of the Woman's Peace party cut a wide swath. Within a year, it had an active membership of 40,000, while several kindred organizations sprang up and adopted its platform. On numerous occasions, Addams and her associates met with Wilson at the White House. Although they sometimes found him evasive, his consistent example of restraint during the early submarine crises with Germany made him something of a hero in their eyes. For his part, the president was deeply impressed with the "program for constructive peace." Addams's personal record of an interview in July 1915 is particularly enlightening: "He drew out the papers I had given him, and they seem[ed] to have been much handled and read. 'You see I have studied these resolutions,' he said, 'I consider them by far the best formulation which up to the moment has been put out by any body.'" The fact of the matter was that the Woman's Peace party had furnished Wilson with a pioneering synthesis of the New Diplomacy during the critical year in which his own thinking acquired a definite shape.

The Socialist Party of America, too, devised a momentous program for a "democratic peace" and motivated a sizeable constituency to think about foreign policy in new ways. In May 1915, the party adopted and published a "Manifesto on Disarmament and World Peace." Read by millions, this analysis of the political and economic causes of the war contained statements on disarmament, self-determination, and the establishment of an international parliament to replace secret diplomacy. The Socialist party was arguably second only to the Woman's Peace party in its impact upon both radicals and reformers during the progressive internationalist movement's formative stage.

In January 1916, Wilson welcomed to the Oval Office Morris Hillquit, the primary architect of the "Manifesto"; James H. Maurer, president of the Pennsylvania State Federation of Labor; and Meyer London, a Socialist member of the House of Representatives. According to Hillquit's account, their host looked tired and preoccupied when they arrived but became animated once their conversation about the Socialist declaration got under way. Hillquit was somewhat surprised when Wilson, in confidence, "informed us that he had had a similar plan under consideration" and also "hinted at the possibility of a direct offer of mediation by . . . the United States." . . .

The question of which elements of the polity exerted the greatest influence on Wilson became especially relevant in light of the ongoing public debate over the state of the nation's military strength. Many progressive internationalists regarded the reactionary opponents of domestic reform and the advocates of militarism and imperialism as twins born of the same womb; they watched with alarm as the champions of "preparedness" mounted what they viewed as an insidious offensive to thwart social and economic progress at home, as well as disarmament and the repudiation of war as an instrument of foreign policy. In response to the preparedness movement, liberal reformers and leading socialists joined forces to establish the American Union Against Militarism (AUAM). Within months, the AUAM had branches in every major city in the country. When, in the wake of the *Lusitania* disaster, Wilson introduced legislation to increase substantially the size of the army and navy, it appeared that he had surrendered to the enemy. Then, too, a competing, conservative vision of internationalism was vying for national attention.

The program of the conservative internationalists was different in both subtle and conclusive ways. It was developed by the organizers of the League to Enforce Peace (LEP), founded in June 1915, and led by former president William Howard Taft and other Republicans prominent in the field of international law. Within two years, they had established four thousand branches in forty-seven states. The LEP's platform, "Warrant from History," called for American participation in a world parliament, which would assemble periodically to make appropriate changes to international law and employ arbitration and conciliation procedures to settle certain kinds of disputes. While more or less endorsing the general principle of collective security, most conservative internationalists also believed that the United States should build up its military complex and reserve the right to undertake independent coercive action whenever the "national interest" was threatened. Unlike progressive internationalists, the LEP did not concern itself with self-determination or advocate disarmament or even a military standoff in Europe. These internationalists were openly pro-Allied; in fact, the slogan, "The LEP does *not* seek to end the present war," appeared on their letterhead in the autumn of 1916.

Throughout that year, Wilson met and corresponded with representatives of both wings of the new internationalist movement. In May 1916, for example, he delivered an important address before a gathering of the LEP, the occasion for his first public affirmation on behalf of American membership in some kind of postwar peacekeeping organization. Yet Wilson's sympathies lay decidedly with the progressive internationalists. Two weeks earlier, for the first time, he had articulated to persons other than his absolute confidants his ideas for a "family of nations," during a lengthy White House colloquy with leaders of the AUAM.

The AUAM stood neither for "peace at any price" nor against "sane and reasonable" military preparedness, Lillian Wald explained to the president; but they were anxious about those agents of militarism who were "frankly hostile to our institutions of democracy." Wilson contended that his preparedness program conformed to his interlocutors' criteria—that it would provide adequate security "without changing the spirit of the country" and that one of his motives for it was to achieve a league of nations. "[I]f the world undertakes, as we all hope it will undertake, a joint effort to keep the peace, it will expect us to play our proportional part," he said. "Surely that is not a militaristic ideal. That is a very practical, possible ideal." . . .

Wilson could not have made a truly plausible case for a new diplomacy and a league—nor would he have been continued in office—if, at the same time, he had not been willing and able to move plainly to the left of center in American politics. Indeed, the array of social justice legislation he pushed through Congress on the eve of his reelection campaign gave legitimacy to his aspirations in foreign affairs like nothing else could have. Wilson could boast of a number of accomplishments for his first two years in office: the Underwood Tariff, the Clayton Antitrust Act, the Federal Reserve System, and the Federal Trade Commission. Then, as his polestar moved comparatively leftward with the approach of the 1916 campaign, he put two "radicals" (Louis D. Brandeis and John Hessin Clarke) on the Supreme Court. Over the protests of conservatives in and out of Congress, he secured passage of the Adamson Act, which established the eight-hour day for railroad workers, and the Keating-Owen bill, which imposed restrictions on child labor. Finally, he had defused the conservatives' appeal to jingoism with his "moderate" preparedness program, which, in conjunction with the Revenue Act of 1916, yielded the first real tax on wealth in American history. . . .

But this was only the half of it. As the complement to his advanced progressivism, Wilson also made American membership in a league of nations one of the cardinal themes of his campaign, a theme that complemented the Democratic chant, "He Kept Us Out Of War!" His utterances on the league exerted a significant impact on the outcome. [The leftist journalist] Max Eastman predicted that Wilson would win reelection because "he has attacked the problem of eliminating war, and he has not succumbed to the epidemic of militarism." Indeed, his speeches on the league constituted "the most important step that any President of the United States has taken towards civilizing the world since Lincoln." Herbert Croly, the influential editor of the *New Republic,* threw his support to Wilson not only on the grounds of the president's domestic record but also because he had "committed himself and his party to a revolutionary doctrine": American participation in a postwar league of nations. . . .

The proposed League of Nations had already begun to take on a vexatious partisan dimension, owing in part to the failure of conservative internationalists to have secured even a vague endorsement of the proposition in the Republican party platform. (Roosevelt would not hear of it, and Taft deferred to his wishes.) Moreover as the contest heated up, contempt for Wilson among Republicans and conservative internationalists grew apace. In beating the drum for Hughes, Roosevelt became the administration's most wrathful critic (and the country's most obstreperous pro-Allied extremist). Taft referred to Wilson as "a ruthless hypocrite . . . who has no convictions that he would not barter at once for votes." But what the LEP president did not realize was that his party had, in essence, handed the issue of the league, like a gift, to Wilson and the Democrats.

In any event, the election returns suggested that Wilson and the progressive internationalists had not merely checked the reactionaries; they had presided over the creation of a left-of-center coalition that seemed to hold the balance of political power in the United States. Precisely what all of this portended for future domestic struggles could hardly be predicted. As for foreign policy, the deeper meaning of their victory was unmistakable. "[T]he President we reelected has raised a flag that no other president has thought or perhaps dared to raise," [the left-liberal journalist] Amos Pinchot submitted. "It is the flag of internationalism."

American neutrality was a fragile thing. Wilson had always shared the conviction of fellow peace seekers that the best way to keep the country out of the war was to try to bring about a negotiated settlement. Twice, to that end, in 1915 and 1916, he had sent his personal emissary, Colonel Edward M. House, to Europe for direct parlays with the heads of all the belligerent governments. These appeals had proved futile. Now, fortified by reconfirmation at the polls, he decided on a bold stroke. In a climactic attempt to end the war, he went before the Senate on January 22, 1917, and called for "peace without victory." In this address, Wilson drew together the strands of progressive internationalist thought and launched a penetrating critique of European imperialism, militarism, and balance-of-power politics—the root causes of the war, he said. In their stead, he held out the promise of a "community of nations"—a new world order sustained by procedures for the arbitration of disputes between nations, a dramatic reduction of armaments, self-determination, and collective security. The chief instrumentality of this sweeping program was to be a league of nations. Thus, Wilson began his ascent to a position of central importance in the history of international relations in the twentieth century.

Responses to the address varied. The governments of both warring coalitions, still praying for decisive victory in the field, either ignored it or received it with contempt. Many pro-Allied Republicans, such as Senator Henry Cabot Lodge of Massachusetts, heaped scorn upon the very notion of "peace without victory" and wondered exactly what membership in a league might entail. Nonetheless, Wilson's manifesto met with an unprecedented outpouring of praise from progressive groups at home and abroad. . . .

One week later, Germany announced the resumption of unrestricted submarine warfare against all flags. After three American ships were sunk without warning, public opinion shifted markedly. On March 20, the cabinet unanimously recommended full-fledged belligerency. Wilson, too, had concluded that after some thirty months of neutrality, war had "thus been thrust upon" the United States. "But," the secretary of interior recorded in his diary, "he goes unwillingly."

In his address to Congress on April 2, 1917, the president explained why neutrality no longer seemed tenable and outlined the measures necessary for getting the country on a war footing. He then turned to more transcendent matters. His goals were the same as when he had addressed the Senate in January; he said, "The world must be made safe for democracy. Its peace must be planted upon the tested foundations of political liberty. We have no selfish ends to serve. We desire no conquest, no dominion. We seek no indemnities for ourselves, no material compensation for the sacrifices we shall freely make." He implied that Americans would be fighting to establish some degree of "peace without victory," or, as he put it, "for a universal dominion of right by such a concert of free nations as shall bring peace and safety to all nations and the world itself at last free"—a program now attainable apparently only through the crucible of war.

Wilson never wavered in his fundamental aim though the obstacles in his path were enormous. As the brilliant young radical, Randolph Bourne, asked of all pro-war liberals and socialists in a famous essay, "If the war is too strong for you to prevent, how is it going to be weak enough for you to control and mould to your liberal purposes?" Indeed, Wilson had to cope not only with an indeterminate measure of opposition clustered in the Senate but also with the antagonism of the Allies themselves, who all but refused to embrace his ideas for a fair and democratic peace. Then, just as the United States entered the war, Russia, staggering under the relentless blows of the German army, was seized by revolutionary upheaval. By the end of 1917, the Bolshevik leaders, V. I. Lenin and Leon Trotsky, pulled their ravaged nation out of the war. They thereupon issued proclamations on behalf of a democratic peace based on self-determination and summoned the peoples of Europe to demand that their governments—the Allies and the Central Powers alike—repudiate plans for conquest.

In the circumstances, Wilson really had no choice but to respond to the Bolshevik challenge. In his Fourteen Points Address, of January 8, 1918, the most celebrated speech of his presidency, he reiterated much of the anti-imperialist "peace without victory" formula and once again made the League of Nations the capstone. In answer to Lenin's entreaty to stop the war, he argued that German autocracy and militarism must be crushed so that humanity could set about the task of creating a new and better world. Wilson's endeavor to remove the suspicions hanging over the Allied cause and rally doubters to see the war through to the bitter end succeeded magnificently. The popular approbation that greeted the Fourteen Points in both Europe and America approached phenomenal proportions. (Even Lenin hailed the address as "a great step ahead towards the peace of the world.") But as before, the Allied governments declined to endorse or comment on Wilson's progressive war aims.

At home, Wilson's own immediate priorities inexorably shifted toward the exigencies of war mobilization. And, in part owing to stinging Republican criticism of "peace without victory" and, later, the Fourteen Points as the basis for the postwar settlement, he refused to discuss his plans for the League in any concrete detail throughout the period of American belligerency. He also neglected to lay essential political groundwork for it at home. By the autumn of 1918, important segments among both conservative and progressive internationalists had grown disenchanted with Wilson, albeit for entirely different reasons.

This development would prove to be as unfortunate as the partisan opposition led by the president's arch-nemeses, Theodore Roosevelt and Henry Cabot Lodge. For example, Wilson grievously offended Taft by frustrating the wartime efforts of the LEP and other conservative internationalists, who wanted to make formal plans for the League of Nations in cooperation with the British government. (There were, of course, serious ideological differences between his and Taft's conception of the League, but Wilson might have found a way to use the Republican-dominated LEP to defuse some of the incipient senatorial criticism.)

Perhaps just as consequential, Wilson failed to nurture the left-of-center coalition of 1916, a dynamic political force that, had it remained intact, might have made it possible for him to secure and validate American leadership in a peacekeeping organization intended to serve progressive purposes. But he began to lose his grip on his former base of support as a tidal wave of anti-German hysteria and superpatriotism swept over the country in 1917–1918. Like a giant wrecking machine, "One Hundred Percent Americanism," as it was known, had the potential to batter the progressive wing of the American internationalist movement to ruins. In every part of the United States, acts of political repression and violence (sanctioned by federal legislation) were committed against German-Americans as well as pacifists and radicals. Only at risk of life or limb did antiwar dissenters express their views in public. For example, for speaking out against American participation in the war, Eugene Debs was sentenced to ten years in prison. The postmaster general denied second-class mailing privileges to such publications as the *Milwaukee Leader,* the *Appeal to Reason,* and the *Masses,* virtually shutting them down. The majority of progressive internationalists steadfastly supported the war effort, but they could not abide these kinds of violations of basic First Amendment rights, for which, ultimately, they held Wilson responsible. And so, because he acquiesced in the suppression of civil liberties, Wilson himself contributed to a gradual unraveling of his coalition.

The circumstances in which the war ended compounded the larger problem. By September 1918, the combined might of the Allied and American armies had pushed the enemy back toward Belgium. On October 6, German Chancellor Max von Baden appealed to Wilson to take steps for the restoration of peace based on the Fourteen Points. The armistice was signed on November 11. Meanwhile, a midterm congressional election more important than most presidential elections in American history had taken place. Against the Wilsonian peace plan, the Republicans launched a fiercely partisan, ultraconservative campaign. This time around, endorsements on behalf of the administration by leading progressives outside the Democratic party hardly matched those of the 1916 contest. Even so, the centralization of the wartime economy and the core of Wilson's foreign policy placed him far enough to the left to make all Democrats vulnerable to Republican charges that they were "un-American." Most historians maintain that Wilson committed the worst blunder of his presidency in countering the attacks: He asked the public for a vote of confidence—an ostensibly partisan appeal to sustain the Democrats' control of Congress. When the Republicans won majorities of forty-five in the House and two in the Senate, they could claim that the president, who planned to attend the Paris Peace Conference personally, had been repudiated. The Republicans also thereby gained control over congressional committees, including the Senate Foreign Relations Committee, which would be chaired by Lodge.

Yet despite these political setbacks, the Fourteen Points had acquired the status of sacred text among the war-weary peoples of Europe, and "Wilson" was becoming something more than the name of a president. Italian soldiers placed his picture in their barracks. An old woman said she heard that in America "there was a great saint who is going to make peace for us." Romain Rolland, the French Nobel laureate, pronounced him the greatest "moral authority" in the world. The whole world seemed to come to a halt to honor Wilson when he arrived in Europe. Into the streets and piazzas of Paris, London, Rome, and Milan, millions of people turned out to hail "the Moses from Across the Atlantic." . . .

Whereas he could not have prevailed without the massive outpouring of public support, Wilson still had to pay a heavy price for the League. If he was adored by the "common people," the statesmen of Europe—David Lloyd George, Georges Clemenceau, and Vittorio Orlando—held grave reservations about a Wilsonian peace. They were also keen students of American politics. Fully aware of the arithmetic of the Senate, they used their acceptance of the covenant as a lever to gain concessions on other vital and contentious issues.

For instance, Wilson was compelled to swallow a less-than-satisfactory compromise on the disposition of captured enemy colonies, which the Allies (in particular, Australia and South Africa) coveted for themselves. Clemenceau, on threat of withdrawal of his certification of the League, demanded for France military occupation of the Rhineland; Orlando claimed for Italy the Yugoslav port city of Fiume; and the Japanese insisted on retaining exploitative economic privileges in China's Shantung province. On several occasions, Wilson was able to moderate the more extreme Allied demands and uphold at least the spirit of the Fourteen Points. But, then, on verge of physical collapse, he permitted the Allies to impose upon Germany a huge reparations burden and, on top of everything else, a "war-guilt" clause—saddling it with the moral responsibility for allegedly having started the war. Wilson tried to take comfort in the hope that, once the "war psychosis" had receded, the League would be in position to arbitrate and rectify the injustices contained in the peace treaty itself. After six long months of often acrimonious deliberations, however, the signing of that document in the Hall of Mirrors at Versailles, on June 28, 1919, was at best a fleeting triumph for the exhausted president.

By the time Wilson returned to the United States in the summer of 1919, thirty-two state legislatures and thirty-three governors had endorsed the covenant. According to a *Literary Digest* poll, the vast majority of nearly 1,400 newspaper editors, including a majority of Republican editors, advocated American membership in some kind of league. Had a national referendum been held at just that moment, the country almost certainly would have joined. The reasons for its failure to do so are still debated by historians. To begin, Wilson had already lost the active support of most left-wing progressives, not to mention that of the socialists. Many liberals, too, shook their heads in dismay upon reading the Versailles settlement. They believed that, regardless of his motives, he had forsaken the Fourteen Points; that he had conceded too much to the Allies in the territorial compromises; and that vindictiveness, not righteousness, had ruled at the Paris conclave. In short, they feared that the League of Nations would be bound to uphold an unjust peace.

The great debate also coincided with the opening phase of the Red Scare, an even more hysterical and pervasive manifestation of "One Hundred Percent Americanism" whose focus had shifted from the German menace to the threat of bolshevism. Deterioration of civil liberties continued to discourage many progressive internationalists from giving Wilson's crusade their full devotion, and they implored him to issue a blanket amnesty to all those who still suffered political repression and imprisonment. Such a dramatic gesture of goodwill would revitalize the coalition of 1916 and, as one of them contended, inspirit "a force great and militant enough to crush the opposition to the League." At length, however, Wilson deferred to the objections of his red-baiting attorney general, A. Mitchell Palmer. . . .

In the Senate on one hand sheer partisanship motivated much of the opposition. Until the autumn of 1918, Wilson had been the most uniformly successful (if controversial) president since Lincoln. What would become of the Republican party, a friend asked Senator Lodge, if Wilson got his League and the Democrats could boast of "the greatest constructive reform in history"? On the other hand, many of the senatorial objections were grounded in ideological principles. Most Republicans acknowledged that the United States should cooperate with the Allies and play its part in upholding the peace settlement; but they also believed that Wilson had consigned too many vital national interests to the will of an international authority. (At one point, Wilson had frankly admitted, "Some of our sovereignty would be surrendered.") The Republicans found Article X of the covenant particularly troubling. It obliged contracting nations to "preserve as against external aggression the territorial integrity and political independence of all Members of the League." Thus, at least on paper, the United States might be required to take part in some far-flung military intervention in which it had no compelling interest; at the same time, the United States apparently would be prevented from using its military power unilaterally whenever it wanted to. Although during the peace conference he had responded to early criticisms and amended the covenant—to provide for withdrawal from the League and nominally to exempt the Monroe Doctrine and domestic matters (such as immigration) from its jurisdiction—Wilson had not done enough to assuage the anxieties of the majority of Republicans.

Then, too, a small but sturdy knot of senators known as the "irreconcilables" flat-out opposed the League in any form. Not all of the fifteen or so irreconcilables were partisans or reactionaries (though most, like Albert Fall, were); several of them, including Robert La Follette and George Norris, were bona-fide progressives who based their opposition on convictions similar to those of many liberals and socialists. Irreconcilable or no, only a few of Wilson's opponents were strict isolationists. No one had cut through to the crux of the debate with more discernment than Gilbert M. Hitchcock of Nebraska, the Democratic leader in the Senate, when he observed, "Internationalism has come, and we must choose what form the internationalism is to take." The *Appeal to Reason,* though disillusioned with the president and highly dubious of his labors, was harsher: Republicans feared Wilson's League because it placed restrictions on "America's armed forces . . . [and] the commercial and territorial greed of American capitalists." The Lodge crowd hardly advocated isolationism, but rather "the internationalism of unrestrained plunder and competition."

By summer's end, the Senate Foreign Relations Committee, dominated by Republicans and irreconcilables and with Lodge at the helm, had formulated forty-six amendments as the conditions for ratification; by autumn, these had evolved into formal reservations—curiously, fourteen in number. The most controversial one pertained to Article X of the covenant: "The United States assumes no obligation to preserve the territorial integrity or political independence of any country . . . unless in any particular case the Congress . . . by act or joint resolution [shall] so provide." . . .

Meanwhile, Wilson held a series of White House meetings with groups of Republicans known as "mild reservationists" and tried to persuade them to ratify the treaty as it was written. In fact, there was very little difference between their views and those of the senators called "strong reservationists." Hence, none of these conferences changed anyone's mind. Then, against the advice of his personal physician and the pleading of the First Lady, Wilson determined that he must take his case directly to the American people and let them know what was at stake. For three weeks in September 1919, he traveled ten thousand miles by train throughout the Middle and Far West, making some forty speeches to hundreds of thousands of people.

Wilson appealed to his audiences on both the intellectual and the emotional level. Despite the importance of Article X, he told them, military sanctions probably would not have to come into play very often—in part because of the deterrent manifest within the threat of collective force, in part because of the cooling-off provisions in the arbitration features of the League, and in part because disarmament, which he heavily emphasized, would help to eliminate most potential problems from the start. He also addressed the question of sovereignty, as it related to the Senate's concern over arbitration and the hindrance to unilateral action that League membership implied: "The only way in which you can have impartial determinations in this world is by consenting to something you do not want to do." And the obvious corollary was to agree to refrain from doing something that you *want* to do, for there might be times "when we lose in court [and] we will take our medicine."

But there could be no truly effective League without America's participation. Should Americans turn their backs, he said, they would have to live forever with a gun in their hands. And they could not go in grudgingly or on a conditional basis. The "Lodge Reservations" would utterly "change the entire meaning of the Treaty." If the League were thus crippled, he would feel obliged to stand "in mortification and shame" before the boys who went across the seas to fight and say to them, " 'You are betrayed. You fought for something that you did not get.' " . . .

As the crowds grew larger and the cheers louder, Wilson looked more haggard and worn out at the end of each day. His facial muscles twitched. Headaches so excruciating that he could hardly see recurred. To keep from coughing all night, he slept propped up in a chair. At last, his doctor called a halt to the tour and rushed him back to Washington. Two days later, on October 2, he suffered a stroke that nearly killed him and permanently paralyzed the left side of his body. From that point onward, Wilson was but a fragile husk of his former self, a tragic recluse in the White House, shielded by his wife and doctor.

The Senate roll was called three times, in November 1919 and March 1920. But whether on a motion to ratify the treaty unconditionally or with the fourteen Lodge reservations attached to it, the vote always fell short of a two-thirds majority. In November 1920, Warren G. Harding, the Republican presidential candidate, won a landslide victory over the Democrat, James M. Cox. The Republicans were only too happy to interpret the returns as the "great and solemn referendum" that Wilson had earlier said he had wanted for his covenant. "So far as the United States is concerned," Lodge now declared, "that League is dead."

In surveying the ruins, many historians have cited the president's stroke as the primary factor behind the outcome. A healthy Wilson, they argue, surely would have grasped the situation and strived to find a middle ground on the question of reservations. Other historians have maintained that his refusal to compromise was consistent with his personality throughout his life, that he would never have yielded to the Republicans (especially to Lodge), regardless of the state of his health. Although there is merit in both of these interpretations—the stroke and Wilson's personality are of obvious relevance—neither provides a complete explanation. They do not take adequate account of the evolution of the League idea, the ideological gulf that had always separated progressive and conservative internationalism, or the domestic political conditions that had taken shape long before the treaty was in the Senate.

In a very real sense, Wilsonian, or progressive, internationalism had begun at home, as part of the reform impulse in the "age of socialistic inquiry." By the touchstone of Wilson's advanced reform legislation and his synthesis of the tenets of the New Diplomacy, progressive internationalists had been able to define the terms of the debate and claim title to the League until 1917–1918—that is, until "One Hundred Percent Americanism" released uncontrollable forces that overwhelmed them. Wilson contributed to this turn of events by losing sight of the relationship between politics and foreign policy—by refusing to acknowledge his administration's culpability in the wartime reaction and by declining to take any action to combat it. The results of the 1918 midterm elections were the first tangible sign of the erosion of the domestic foundation and depletion of the political environment essential to both ratification on Wilson's terms and American leadership in a progressive, as opposed to a conservative, league movement. . . .

Ray Stannard Baker, his sympathetic biographer, once commented on Wilson's fate: "He can escape no responsibility & must go to his punishment not only for his own mistakes and weaknesses of temperament but for the greed and selfishness of the world." Whatever the central cause of his historic failure, Wilson's conservative and partisan adversaries earnestly believed that his was a dangerously radical vision, a new world order alien to their own understanding of how the world worked. His severest critics among progressive internationalists believed he had not done enough to rally the people to his side and resist the forces of reaction—either in America or at the Paris Peace Conference. Wilson's response to them was a cry of anguish. "What more could I have done?" he asked historian William E. Dodd shortly before leaving the presidency. "I had to negotiate with my back to the wall. Men thought I had all power. Would to God I had had such power." His voice choking with emotion, he added, "The 'great' people at home wrote and wired every day that they were against me."

On all counts, and no doubt for all concerned, it had been, as Dodd himself concluded, "one long wilderness of despair and betrayal, even by good men."

FURTHER READING

Robert D. Accinelli, "Link's Case for Wilson the Diplomatist," *Review in American History,* 9 (1981), 285–294

Lloyd Ambrosius, *Wilsonian Statecraft* (1991)

———, *Woodrow Wilson and the American Diplomatic Tradition: The League Fight in Perspective* (1987)

———, "Woodrow Wilson and the Quest for Orderly Progress," in Norman A. Graebner, ed., *Traditions and Values: American Diplomacy, 1865–1945* (1985), pp. 73–100

Thomas A. Bailey, *Woodrow Wilson and the Great Betrayal* (1945)

————, *Woodrow Wilson and the Lost Peace* (1944)

John M. Blum, *The Progressive Presidents* (1980)

Frederick S. Calhoun, *Power and Principle: Armed Intervention in Wilsonian Foreign Policy* (1986)

John W. Chambers III, *The Tyranny of Change: America in the Progressive Era, 1890–1920* (1992)

Kendrick A. Clements, *The Presidency of Woodrow Wilson* (1992)

————, *Woodrow Wilson: World Statesman* (1987)

G. R. Conyne, *Woodrow Wilson: British Perspectives* (1992)

John W. Coogan, "Wilsonian Diplomacy in War and Peace," in Gordon Martel, ed., *American Foreign Relations Reconsidered, 1890–1993* (1994)

————, *The End of Neutrality: The United States, Britain, and Maritime Rights, 1899–1915* (1981)

John Milton Cooper, "Disability in the White House: The Case of Woodrow Wilson," in Frank Friedel and William Pencak, eds., *The White House: The First Two Hundred Years* (1994)

John M. Cooper, Jr., *The Warrior and the Priest: Woodrow Wilson and Theodore Roosevelt* (1983)

———— and Charles E. Neu, eds., *The Wilson Era* (1991)

Charles DeBenedetti, *Origins of the Modern American Peace Movement, 1915–1929* (1978)

Patrick Devlin, *Too Proud to Fight* (1975)

Richard R. Doerries, *Imperial Challenge: Ambassador Count von Bernstorff and German-American Relations, 1908–1917* (1989)

David M. Esposito, *The Legacy of Woodrow Wilson* (1996)

Robert H. Ferrell, *Woodrow Wilson and World War I* (1985)

Lloyd C. Gardner, *Safe for Democracy* (1984)

Hans W. Gatske, *Germany and the United States* (1980)

Alexander L. George and Juliette George, *Woodrow Wilson and Colonel House: A Personality Study* (1956)

————, "Woodrow Wilson and Colonel House: A Reply to Weinstein, Anderson, and Link," *Political Science Quarterly,* 96 (1981–1982), 641–665

Ross Gregory, *The Origins of American Intervention in the First World War* (1971)

George F. Kennan, *American Diplomacy, 1900–1950* (1951)

William R. Keylor, *The Legacy of the Great War* (1998)

Henry Kissinger, *Diplomacy* (1994)

Thomas J. Knock, *To End All Wars: Woodrow Wilson and the Quest for a New World Order* (1992)

Antony Lentin, *Lloyd George, Woodrow Wilson, and the Guilt of Germany* (1985)

N. Gordon Levin, *Woodrow Wilson and World Politics* (1968)

Arthur S. Link, *Wilson,* 5 vols. (1947–1965)

————, *Woodrow Wilson: Revolution, War, and Peace* (1979)

————, ed., *Woodrow Wilson and a Revolutionary World* (1982)

David W. McFadden, *Alternative Paths: Soviets and Americans, 1917–1920* (1993)

Herbert F. Margulies, *The Mild Reservationists and the League of Nations Controversy in the Senate* (1989)

John H. Mauer, *The Outbreak of the First World War* (1995)

Ernest R. May, *The World War and American Isolation, 1914–1917* (1959)

Arno Mayer, *Politics and Diplomacy of Peacemaking* (1967)

Charles E. Neu, "The Search for Woodrow Wilson," *Reviews in American History,* 10 (1982), 223–228

Robert E. Osgood, *Ideals and Self-Interest in American Foreign Relations* (1953)

Bert E. Park, *Ailing, Aging, Addicted: Studies of Compromised Leadership* (1993)

Gregory Ross, "To Do Good in the World: Woodrow Wilson," in Frank J. Merli and Theodore A. Wilson, *Makers of American Diplomacy* (1994)

Klaus Schwabe, *Woodrow Wilson, Revolutionary Germany, and Peacemaking, 1918–1919* (1985)

Tony Smith, *America's Mission* (1994)

Ralph A. Stone, *The Irreconcilables* (1970)

Roland N. Stromberg, *Collective Security and American Foreign Policy* (1963)

Marc Trachtenburg, *Reparations in World Politics* (1980)

Barbara Tuchman, *The Zimmermann Telegram* (1958)

Robert W. Tucker, "The Triumph of Wilsonianism?" *World Policy Journal,* 10 (1993–1994), 83–99

Arthur Walworth, *Wilson and His Peacemakers* (1986)

Edwin A. Weinstein, *Woodrow Wilson: A Medical and Psychological Biography* (1981)

——, James W. Anderson, and Arthur S. Link, "Woodrow Wilson's Political Personality," *Political Science Quarterly,* 93 (1978–1979), 585–598

William C. Widenor, *Henry Cabot Lodge and the Search for an American Foreign Policy* (1980)

The International History

of the 1920s

The transition from war to peace proved rough. The embittering experiences of the First World War and the Versailles peacemaking left postwar leaders with a daunting international agenda. Throughout the 1920s they worked diligently to devise plans and prescriptions that could stabilize economies and currencies, energize foreign trade and investment, facilitate payment of foreign debts and reparations, curb political extremism, reduce armaments, tame national rivalries, protect imperial interests, and prevent war. Central to the decade's contentions were the questions of how to contain yet restore Germany, whose economic health was so essential to European stability; how to reassure a skeptical France about its security as Germany revitalized itself; how to manage great-power competition in East Asia, especially how to persuade Japan to respect Western interests and China's sovereignty; and how to contain radical Soviet Russia yet integrate it into the international community.

As the 1930s opened, however, devastating events demonstrated that the quest for a peaceful world order and balance of power had failed. The Great Depression began to cripple the world economy, debts and reparations went unpaid, and trade wars broke out. Militarists in hobbled Germany and vulnerable Japan vowed destruction of the Versailles settlement and nonaggression pacts, and the League of Nations continued to struggle to define its role in world affairs. As fervent nationalism drove countries away from the once-high hopes of Wilsonian internationalism, a second world war seemed possible.

Americans reacted in many different ways to the upheaval of international relations in the 1920s. Some preferred that the country stay out of Europe and let the Old World alone contend with its self-made miseries. This so-called isolationist opinion drew on the disillusioning experience of the First World War, which fed thoughts that the United States could not provide answers to generations-long European questions. Other Americans argued that the United States simply could not retreat from worldwide responsibilities, because trade, immigration, debts, investments, colonies, and overseas allies and bases (especially in Latin America) inevitably thrust it into the maelstrom and demanded the unilateral use of power to stem threats to U.S. interests. Scholars have called such thinking "independent internationalism."

At the same time, American pacifists and internationalists intent on reviving Wilsonianism advocated multilateral agreements on disarmament and the outlawry of war and urged U.S. participation in the World Court. Business and banking expansionists, eager to maintain American supremacy in the increasingly interdependent world economy, pressed receptive Republican administrations to trumpet the "Open Door" policy and encourage private experts to craft workable debts and reparations plans. Americans who claimed that the Caribbean and Central America constituted North America's "backyard" advocated continued U.S. hegemony in Latin America, preferably through economic rather than military penetration.

As Americans participated actively in the world economy, many proudly observed that their culture gained influence abroad as other peoples became attracted to U.S. goods, productivity, movies, and technology. Although some foreigners applauded the United States as a model for the future, others rejected Americanism and Americanization as threats to national tradition and identity.

Historians continue to debate what to call U.S. foreign relations in the 1920s: isolationist, unilateralist, internationalist, expansionist, corporatist? U.S. leaders worked for peaceful change through economic reconstruction and cultural influence, but the United States, clearly the era's giant, did not succeed in establishing a stable world order. Did it fail for want of serious trying? Did it fall short because of troubles endemic to the international system—national rivalries and the legacy of Versailles, for example—that were impervious to outside solution? Was the reason for failure the U.S. government's and the American people's naive belief that appeals to principle and signatures on unenforceable agreements rather than applications of power would set things right? Did America's absence from the League of Nations matter? Did the United States let down its guard in the 1920s, refusing to maintain a strong military that might have deterred disturbers of peace? Did the United States pay too much attention to economic and financial remedies, ignoring critical political questions like the balance of power and strategic commitments?

Did Washington too often refrain from direct, effective participation in problem solving and instead let the private sector handle crises? Did failure to build a stable world order stem from selfishness on the part of private interests that too narrowly served themselves for short-term gain (making questionable loans, for example) instead of building a durable international structure? Was failure rooted in contradictory U.S. policies such as the Open Door abroad and protectionist tariffs at home? Just how wisely did American leaders address international issues? What more should *they* and could *they* have done? Put another way, did American leaders prudently understand the limits of U.S. power, avoiding overcommitment and misapplication? Or did they—and other international leaders—squander opportunities to avert the calamities that ultimately brought on the Second World War?

Many of these questions are applicable to almost any period of international history. Here they are tested in the pivotal decade of the 1920s.

DOCUMENTS

In Document 1, dated November 12, 1921, Secretary of State Charles Evans Hughes addresses the Washington Conference on naval disarmament. In making the case that arms reductions would permit public funds to be more wisely applied to economic rehabilitation and growth, Hughes boldly asks the major powers to scrap great numbers of warships. The

Five-Power Treaty of 1922 did just that. Document 2, a *Chicago Tribune* editorial of November 13, 1921, expresses what many Americans believed after the First World War: that Europe was hopelessly entrapped in rivalries and that the United States ought to stay clear until the continent set its house in order. In Document 3, a speech before the American Historical Association on December 29, 1922, Secretary Hughes identifies German reconstruction and the reparations issue as keys to European stability and recommends the mobilization of private experts to devise solutions. Hughes's proposals came to fruition in the Dawes Plan of 1924, which set a schedule for German reparations payments and provided for private American loans to alleviate Germany's economic plight.

Document 4 is a selection from the prolific Argentine anti-imperialist writer Manuel Ugarte, who identifies the United States as a "New Rome" that annexes wealth rather than territory, manipulates native politics, and creates a detrimental dependency among Latin Americans. Document 5, Edward G. Lowry's article "Trade Follows the Film" (*Saturday Evening Post,* November 7, 1925), reveals the link between economic and cultural expansion in the 1920s as American-made movies penetrated world markets. Secretary of Commerce Herbert Hoover, an ardent economic expansionist, establishes the value of foreign trade to the U.S. economy and dismisses critics of America's protective tariffs in Document 6, a speech of March 16, 1926. Document 7 is the antiwar Kellogg-Briand Pact, signed by the United States and most of the world's nations in August 1928. One of the signers was Soviet Russia, a nation that the United States refused to recognize until 1933 even though U.S. businesses invested in and traded with the communist nation.

1. Secretary of State Charles Evans Hughes on Naval Disarmament, 1921

We not only have the lessons of the past to guide us, not only do we have the reaction from the disillusioning experiences of war, but we must meet the challenge of imperative economic demands. What was convenient or highly desirable before is now a matter of vital necessity. If there is to be economic rehabilitation, if the longings for reasonable progress are not to be denied, if we are to be spared the uprisings of peoples made desperate in the desire to shake off burdens no longer endurable, competition in armament must stop. The present opportunity not only derives its advantage from a general appreciation of this fact, but the power to deal with the exigency now rests with a small group of nations, represented here, who have every reason to desire peace and to promote amity. . . . Is it not plain that the time has passed for mere resolutions that the responsible Powers should examine the question of limitation of armament? We can no longer content ourselves with investigations, with statistics, with reports, with the circumlocution of inquiry. The essential facts are sufficiently known. The time has come, and this Conference has been called, not for general resolutions or mutual advice, but for action. . . .

It is apparent that this can not be accomplished without serious sacrifices. Enormous sums have been expended upon ships under construction and building programs which are now under way can not be given up without heavy loss. Yet if

---

This document can be found in the U.S. Congress, *Senate Documents,* 67th Congress, 1st Session (Washington, D.C.: Government Printing Office, 1921), Doc. No. 77, pp. 13–17.

the present construction of capital ships goes forward other ships will inevitably be built to rival them and this will lead to still others. Thus the race will continue so long as ability to continue lasts. The effort to escape sacrifices is futile. We must face them or yield our purpose. . . .

In making the present proposal the United States is most solicitous to deal with the question upon an entirely reasonable and practicable basis, to the end that the just interests of all shall be adequately guarded and that national security and defense shall be maintained. Four general principles have been applied:

1. That all capital-ship building programs, either actual or projected, should be abandoned;
2. That further reduction should be made through the scrapping of certain of the older ships;
3. That in general regard should be had to the existing naval strength of the Powers concerned;
4. That the capital ship tonnage should be used as the measurement of strength for navies and a proportionate allowance of auxiliary combatant craft prescribed.

The principal features of the proposed agreement are as follows:

Capital Ships

United States.   The United States is now completing its program of 1916 calling for 10 new battleships and 6 battle cruisers. One battleship has been completed. The others are in various stages of construction; in some cases from 60 to over 80 per cent of the construction has been done. On these 15 capital ships now being built over $330,000,000 have been spent. Still, the United States is willing in the interest of an immediate limitation of naval armament to scrap all these ships.

The United States proposes, if this plan is accepted—

1. To scrap all capital ships now under construction. This includes 6 battle cruisers and 7 battleships on the ways and in course of building, and 2 battleships launched.

The total number of new capital ships thus to be scrapped is 15. The total tonnage of the new capital ships when completed would be 618,000 tons.

2. To scrap all of the older battleships up to, but not including, the *Delaware* and *North Dakota*. The number of these old battleships to be scrapped is 15. Their total tonnage is 227,740 tons.

Thus the number of capital ships to be scrapped by the United States, if this plan is accepted, is 30, with an aggregate tonnage (including that of ships in construction, if completed) of 845,740 tons.

Great Britain.   The plan contemplates that Great Britain and Japan shall take action which is fairly commensurate with this action on the part of the United States.

It is proposed that Great Britain—

1. Shall stop further construction of the 4 new Hoods, the new capital ships not laid down but upon which money has been spent. These 4 ships, if completed, would have tonnage displacement of 172,000 tons.
2. Shall, in addition, scrap her pre-dreadnaughts, second line battleships, and first line battleships up to, but not including, the *King George V* class.

These, with certain pre-dreadnaughts which it is understood have already been scrapped, would amount to 19 capital ships and a tonnage reduction of 411,375 tons.

The total tonnage of ships thus to be scrapped by Great Britain (including the tonnage of the 4 Hoods, if completed) would be 583,375 tons.

Japan.   It is proposed that Japan

1. Shall abandon her program of ships not yet laid down, viz., the *Kii, Owari, No. 7* and *No. 8* battleships, and *Nos. 5, 6, 7,* and *8,* battle cruisers.

It should be observed that this does not involve the stopping of construction, as the construction of none of these ships has been begun.

2. Shall scrap 3 capital ships (the *Mutsu* launched, the *Tosa,* and *Kago* in course of building) and 4 battle cruisers (the *Amagi* and *Akagi* in course of building, and the *Atoga* and *Takao* not yet laid down, but for which certain material has been assembled).

The total number of new capital ships to be scrapped under this paragraph is seven. The total tonnage of these new capital ships when completed would be 289,100 tons.

3. Shall scrap all pre-dreadnaughts and battleships of the second line. This would include the scrapping of all ships up to, but not including, the *Settsu*; that is, the scrapping of 10 older ships, with a total tonnage of 159,828 tons.

The total reduction of tonnage on vessels existing, laid down, or for which material has been assembled (taking the tonnage of the new ships when completed), would be 448,928 tons.

Thus, under this plan there would be immediately destroyed, of the navies of the three Powers, 66 capital fighting ships, built and building, with a total tonnage of 1,878,043.

It is proposed that it should be agreed by the United States, Great Britain, and Japan that their navies, with respect to capital ships, within three months after the making of the agreement shall consist of certain ships designated in the proposal and numbering for the United States 18, for Great Britain 22, for Japan 10. . . .

With the acceptance of this plan the burden of meeting the demands of competition in naval armament will be lifted. Enormous sums will be released to aid the progress of civilization. At the same time the proper demands of national defense will be adequately met and the nations will have ample opportunity during the naval holiday of 10 years to consider their future course. Preparation for offensive naval war will stop now.

2. The Isolationist *Chicago Tribune* Denounces Europe's Folly, 1921

It is natural that pacifists and excited humanitarians should stress the evil consequences of the world war at this time. It is equally natural that foreign statesmen and public agencies should join them in keeping this phase of the European situation [of famine and insurrections] before us. It gives a tremendous momentum to the pacifist propaganda, and it relieves the governments and peoples of Europe of a large part of their responsibility for the present condition of their affairs.

But the American mind should clear itself on this point. No one will deny that the war is responsible directly for a vast wastage of life and property. But what needs recognition and emphasis at this moment . . . is that had common sense and self-control governed the policies of the governments and the sentiments of the peoples of Europe their affairs would not be tottering now on the rim of chaos.

On the contrary, were there wisdom and courage in the statesmanship of Europe, were there the same selfless devotion in chancelleries and parliaments as was exhibited on the battlefield, Europe would have been today well on the way to recovery.

The expenditures of the war and the intensification of long existing animosities and jealousies undoubtedly have complicated the problems of statecraft and of government. Undoubtedly the temporary depletion of man power and the temporary exhaustion of body and spirit among the war worn peoples were a burden which recovery has had to assume. Undoubtedly the wastage of wealth and diversion of productive agencies were a handicap to expeditious restoration.

But that these are chiefly responsible for the present state of Europe we do not admit and the future judgment of history, we are confident, will deny.

It is chiefly the folly which has been persistently demonstrated by governments and people since the war that is responsible for Europe's condition today. It is because the moment hostilities ceased and the enemy was disarmed, victors and vanquished turned their backs on the healing and constructive principles they had solemnly asserted from time to time when matters were going against them at the battle front, that the European nations almost without exception have been going down hill. There never in history has been a more perfect illustration of the ancient sarcasm: "When the devil is sick, the devil a monk would be; when the devil is well, the devil a monk is he."

If we wish to know why Europe is in the present state, we cannot do better than to draw a parallel between the assertions of purpose and principle of the allies and "associated" powers in 1916, '17, and '18, and what has actually happened since Nov. 11, 1918.

The war was a gigantic folly and waste. No one will deny that. But it was not so foolish nor so wasteful as the peace which has followed it. The European governments, those who come at our invitation and those who remain away, would have us believe they are mere victims of the war. They say nothing of what the war did for them. We might remind them that they profited as well as lost by the war.

This document appeared in *Chicago Tribune*, November 13, 1921.

Many of them were freed from age long tyranny. They got rid of kaisers and saber clattering aristocracies. They were given freedom, and their present state shows how little they have known how to profit by it. They have been given new territories and new resources, and they have shown how little they deserve their good fortune. The last three years in Europe have been given not to sane efforts to heal wounds, remove hostilities, develop cooperation for the common economic restoration which is essential to the life of each. On the contrary, they have been marked by new wars and destruction, by new animosities and rivalries, by a refusal to face facts, make necessary sacrifices and compromises for financial and economic recovery, by greedy grabbing of territory and new adventures in the very imperialism which brought about the war.

It is well for Americans and their representatives to keep this in mind. The appeal to America's disinterestedness is unfairly fortified by the assumption that Europe is the innocent victim of one egotist's or one nation's ruthless ambition. We can take due account of the disastrous effects of the Prussian effort at dominance, but that should not overshadow the stubborn errors which began over again on the very threshold of peace, and which have made the peace more destructive than the war. When the European governments and peoples are ready to make a real peace, which cannot arrive until they give over the policies and attitudes that produced the world war, America will then not fail to give generous aid. But America would be foolish to contribute to the support of present methods or give any encouragement to the spirit which now prevails in the old world.

3. Debts and German Reparations: Hughes Calls on Private Experts for Help, 1922

The economic conditions in Europe give us the greatest concern. They have long received the earnest consideration of the administration. It is idle to say that we are not interested in these problems, for we are deeply interested from an economic standpoint, as our credits and markets are involved, and from a humanitarian standpoint, as the heart of the American people goes out to those who are in distress. We cannot dispose of these problems by calling them European, for they are world problems and we cannot escape the injurious consequences of a failure to settle them.

They are, however, European problems in the sense that they cannot be solved without the consent of European Governments. We cannot consent for them. The key to the settlement is in their hands, not in ours.

The crux of the European situation lies in the settlement of reparations. There will be no adjustments of other needs, however pressing, until a definite and accepted basis for the discharge of reparation claims has been fixed. It is futile to attempt to erect any economic structure in Europe until the foundation is laid.

How can the United States help in this matter? We are not seeking reparations. We are, indeed, asking for the reimbursement of the costs of our army of occupation; and with good reason, for we have maintained our army in Europe at the request

This document can be found in *Annual Report of the American Historical Association for the Year 1922* (Washington, D.C.: Government Printing Office, 1926), I, 265–268.

of the Allies and of Germany, and under an agreement that its cost with like army costs should be a first charge upon the amounts paid by Germany. Others have been paid and we have not been paid.

But we are not seeking general reparations. We are bearing our own burden and through our loans a large part of Europe's burden in addition. No demands of ours stand in the way of a proper settlement of the reparations question.

Of course we hold the obligations of European Governments and there has been much discussion abroad and here with respect to them. There has been a persistent attempt ever since the Armistice to link up the debts owing to our Government with reparations or with projects of cancellation. This attempt was resisted in a determined manner under the former administration and under the present administration. The matter is plain enough from our standpoint. The capacity of Germany to pay is not at all affected by any indebtedness of any of the Allies to us. That indebtedness does not diminish Germany's capacity, and its removal would not increase her capacity. For example, if France had been able to finance her part in the war without borrowing at all from us, that is, by taxation and internal loans, the problem of what Germany could pay would be exactly the same. Moreover, so far as the debtors to the United States are concerned, they have unsettled credit balances, and their condition and capacity to pay cannot be properly determined until the amount that can be realized on these credits for reparations has been determined. . . .

We have no desire to see Germany relieved of her responsibility for the war or of her just obligations to make reparation for the injuries due to her aggression. There is not the slightest desire that France shall lose any part of her just claim. On the other hand, we do not wish to see a prostrate Germany. There can be no economic recuperation in Europe unless Germany recuperates. There will be no permanent peace unless economic satisfactions are enjoyed. There must be hope, and industry must have promise of reward if there is to be prosperity. We should view with disfavor measures which instead of producing reparations would threaten disaster.

Some of our own people have suggested that the United States should assume the role of arbiter. There is one sufficient answer to this suggestion, and that is that we have not been asked to assume the role of arbiter. There could be no such arbitrament unless it were invited, and it would be an extraordinary and unprecedented thing for us to ask for such an invitation.

I do not think that we should endeavor to take such a burden of responsibility. We have quite enough to bear without drawing to ourselves all the ill-feeling which would result from disappointed hopes and a settlement which would be viewed as forced upon nations by this country which at the same time is demanding the payment of the debts owing to it. . . .

Why should they [statesmen] not invite men of the highest authority in finance in their respective countries—men of such prestige, experience and honor that their agreement upon the amount to be paid, and upon a financial plan for working out the payments, would be accepted throughout the world as the most authoritative expression obtainable? Governments need not bind themselves in advance to accept the recommendations, but they can at least make possible such an inquiry with their approval, and free the men who may represent their country in such a commission from any responsibility to Foreign Offices and from any duty to obey political instructions. In other words, they may invite an answer to this difficult and pressing question from men of such standing and in such circumstances of freedom as will ensure a reply prompted only by knowledge and conscience. I have no doubt that distinguished Americans would be willing to serve in such a commission.

4. Manuel Ugarte Identifies the United States as the "New Rome," 1923

The flexibility of North American imperialism in its external activities, and the diverse forms which it adopts according to circumstances, the racial composition and the social conditions of the peoples upon which its action is exercised, is one of the most significant phenomena of this century from the point of view of political science. Never in all history has such an irresistible or marvellously concerted force been developed as that which the United States are bringing to bear upon the peoples which are geographically or politically within its reach in the south of the Continent or on the shores of the sea. . . . At times imperious, at other times suave, in certain cases apparently disinterested, in others implacable in its greed, pondering like a chess-player who foresees every possible move, with a breadth of vision embracing many centuries, better-informed and more resolute than any, without fits of passion, without forgetfulness, without fine sensibilities, without fear, carrying out a world activity in which everything is foreseen—North American imperialism is the most perfect instrument of domination which has been known throughout the ages.

By adding to what we may call the scientific legacy of past imperialisms the initiative born of its own inspiration and surroundings, this great nation has subverted every principle in the sphere of politics just as it had already transformed them in the sphere of material progress. Even the European powers, when confronted with North American diplomacy, are like a rapier pitted against a revolver. In the order of ideas with which we are dealing, Washington has modified the whole perspective. The first conquerors, with their elementary type of mind, annexed the inhabitants in the guise of slaves. Those who came afterwards annexed territories without inhabitants. The United States . . . inaugurated the system of annexing wealth, apart from inhabitants or territories, disdaining outward shows in order to arrive at the essentials of domination without a dead-weight of areas to administrate and multitudes to govern. . . .

Thus there has arisen within their spheres of influence an infinite variety of forms and shades. The new imperialism, far from applying a formula or a panacea, has founded a system of special diagnosis for every case, taking into account the area of the region, its geographical situation, the density of its population, its origin, predominating racial composition, level of civilisation, customs, neighbours, whatever may favour or hinder resistance, whatever may induce assimilation or alienation by reason of affinities or differences of race, whatever has to be brought about with a view to future contingencies. The higher motives of force or healthy activity which give direction to expansionist energy, watch particularly over the racial purity of the group and reject every addition which is not identical with it. To annex peoples is to modify the composition of one's own blood, and the invader

From Manuel Ugarte, *The Destiny of a Continent,* Catherine A. Phillips (tr.), with an introduction by J. Fred Rippy (ed.) (New York: Knopf, 1925), pp. 139–148.

who does not desire to be diluted, but to perpetuate himself, avoids as far as possible any impairing or enfeebling of the superiority which he claims. . . .

That species of action which makes itself felt in the form of financial pressure, international tutelage, and political censorship admits of every advantage with no risk. In the development of these tactics imperialist policy has given evidence of that incomparable dexterity which is admired even by its victims. In the financial sphere its tendency is to control the markets to the exclusion of all competition, to take upon itself the regulation of any production to which it attaches any value, and to lead the small nations on to contract debts which afterwards provoke conflicts, give rise to claims, and prepare the way for interference favourable to the extension of its virtual sovereignty. In the sphere of external policy it appoints itself the defender of these peoples, obliging the world to accept its intervention in treating with them, and drawing them as satellites into its orbit. In the internal order it encourages the diffusion of whatever increases its prestige, forwards the ambitions of those men who favour its influence, and opposes the spread of all influences of a different nature, blocking the way peremptorily to those who, from a superior sagacity or patriotism, try to maintain their nationality unimpaired. . . .

. . . Here it foments tyrannies, there it supports attempts at revolution, always constituting itself the conciliator or the arbiter, and indefatigably pressing events in the direction of the two ends which it sets before it: first in the moral order, to increase anarchy, so as to bring discredit upon the country; and second, in the political order, to get rid of national representatives who are refractory to the dominant influence, till they meet with a weak or not very enlightened man who, out of inexperience or impatience, will make himself the accomplice of its domination. . . .

The greatest triumph of this system has consisted in the fact that it has come to be a cause of success within our own life. As the source of expedients in our civil struggles, as the dispenser of favours in official life, it has driven not only those who are impatient, but even the most incorruptible and upright to the utmost limit of what can be granted without abdication. In this manner it has proceeded to create subconsciously, in the countries it has "manipulated," a peculiar state of mind, which admits the collaboration in its civil struggles of forces not arising from their own surroundings, and allows an element of foreign life and interest to enter into every national act or project. . . .

When we consider the work of imperialism in America as a whole, it is impossible to refrain from a certain admiration for the magnitude of its effort and the clearness of its conceptions. Never in all history has such subtlety been seen, combined with such a capacity for sustained action. It is evident, I repeat, that from the Spanish-American point of view we have to do with a policy which we ought all to work together to check. A good number of us have been writing and speaking in this sense without intermission for long years. But if we are to stem the advance, our most urgent task is to arrive at a full knowledge of the truth, and to give up vain speech-making. Every strong people extends its ambitions as far as its arms can reach, and every weak people lasts just so long as its energy for defending itself endures. In sacrificing doctrines in order to favour its present and future greatness, the new Rome believes itself to be accomplishing a duty, since it is thus preparing that world dominion for which it considers itself to be set apart. By developing to its full volume and protecting itself against these risks, Latin America would preserve its personality.

5. "Trade Follows the Film," 1925

The sun, it now appears, never sets on the British Empire and the American motion picture. It is a droll companionship, and one which is beginning to evoke comment and provoke inquiry in exalted quarters in foreign parts. The world at large has become so accustomed to seeing the British Empire take this daily promenade in the sun alone that it now lifts its eyebrows and regards the scene with what the fictionists of another day used to call mixed emotions.

In the British the spectacle calls forth a touch of asperity. The French are puzzled and ask, "Is it an amour?" The Germans have begun to dig in and erect barriers. All of them are in varying degrees alarmed by the portent. They are just a teeny bit afraid of this gay, laughing, amusing hussy who parades the whole wide world with such assurance and to such applause from the diverse races and breeds of men. . . .

Our pictures are doing for us what the Prince of Wales so frankly and so capably is doing for the British. International trade is, of course, based on good will. The Prince for some years now has been going about all over the world promoting good will for his countrymen and subjects. Incidentally he has helped trade. Everybody remembers when he was last in New York he set a vogue for blue shirts with soft collars, for a style of hat that blossomed in the shop windows even before he departed, and for gray flannels. Every day what he wore was chronicled in the newspapers, and the youth who set store by styles were quick to copy him. The same thing, it is fair to suppose, happened in the colonies and in South America. The heir apparent did something to introduce and popularize English clothes, shoes, hats, pipes and what not.

Happily, or unhappily—just as you choose—we have no royal family to do that sort of thing for us. But now the word comes from abroad, from many quarters and in increasing volume, that the movie stars and their associates, and the happy and handsome environment in which they are displayed in the films are creating and stimulating a demand for American wares. We now hear that the old saying that trade follows the flag is archaic and out of joint.

"Trade follows the film" is the cry from overseas. It is the discovery of this new factor in international relationships that has caused the flutter. When the movies were simply an amusement and a relaxation and a form of entertainment for the millions, they could be laughed at by the sophisticates as examples of crude American taste, and no harm was done. But once it became clear that the films directly influenced the currents of trade—that from Spain, the Near East, Chile, the Argentine and Brazil were coming demands for American office furniture, shoes, hardware, clothing and types of California bungalows "like those we see in the movies," then the pictures became a menace and a peril to the foreign trader. His pocketbook touched, he became aroused and began to appeal to his government.

The Prince of Wales himself, as a promoter of trade and good will for his people, was among the earliest to declare and disclose the potency of our pictures as a competitor in securing foreign trade. As long ago as 1923 the Prince was saying in

Edward G. Lowry, "Trade Follows the Film," *Saturday Evening Post,* 198 (November 7, 1925), 12–13, 151, 158.

a speech before the British National Film League that the importance of the film industry deserved attention. There was the imperial aspect, he urged. Trade followed the film, he said, and films were a real aid both to the development of imperial trade and the work of individual firms. The film helped to bring together nations speaking different languages. It had no one language of its own, but could convey its ideas in all languages. And so on to the extent of nearly a column in the *London Morning Post,* in which the speech was reported. The same newspaper, commenting on the Prince's outgiving, said: "If the United States abolished its diplomatic and consular services, kept its ships in harbor and its tourists at home, and retired from the world's markets, its citizens, its problems, its towns and countryside, its roads, motor cars, counting houses and saloons would still be familiar in the uttermost corners of the world. . . . The film is to America what the flag was once to Britain. By its means Uncle Sam may hope some day, if he be not checked in time, to Americanize the world." . . .

For whatever may be said about our movies, the stubborn fact stands up that millions of all sorts of people all over the world like them and are willing to pay habitually and constantly to see them. Neither in Germany, England, France, Italy nor Scandinavia can they make pictures with such a universal appeal. I will not be put in the light of a defender or champion of the quality of the American movie; I am not a fan. But their world dominance is an incontestable fact. They are popular, they are affecting trade, they are coloring the minds and changing the desires of foreign peoples, they are the most vivid and potent projection—however distorted— of life in the United States that foreigners receive. The stay-at-homes abroad get their conception of us from our pictures. Whether that condition is or is not deplorable, it is a proved fact.

Now what is the secret of this great popularity and success? It is built on a firm economic basis. For that, the motion-picture industry can take no credit. Lady Luck dealt our producers a hand all aces. The great domestic market afforded in the United States makes it possible to have $1,000,000 superfeatures. Here we have 40 per cent of all the motion-picture theaters in the world. The average weekly attendance at these theaters in the United States is something more than 50,000,000. This great throng pays admissions of about $500,000,000 annually. That is the solid-rock basis on which the American producer has built his world-wide dominion.

With this great supporting, pleasure-loving, money-spending public at home he can afford to experiment, to develop, to lavish expenditures on his productions. If he only just breaks even on a $1,000,000 picture at home, he is still in a comfortable position, for he can count on his export for a profit. It is this domestic market, which no foreign producer has, that gives our industry its solid base. The figures prove it. In 1913, 32,000,000 linear feet of film were exported. In 1928, 200,000,000 feet were sent abroad. On the other hand, only 425 foreign pictures were sent here in 1922, and of these only six were sold and exhibited. The number of imported films has increased in the past three years, but the proportion of imports to exports remains about the same. The foreign and the domestic fan are as one in preferring the American picture to all others.

Now what quality is inherent in the American picture that causes every sort of foreigner—English, German, French, Italian, South American, Central European and Asiatic—to prefer it to his own? What is it in the American picture that has made it a trade and political factor? There is no definite answer, but the industry offers suggestions and possible explanations. One of these, made to me, is this:

> There is no laughter in the European films. They lack gayety, light-heartedness, sprightliness. They do not portray happiness. There is not in them anywhere any sense of irresponsible children at play. These lacking qualities are supplied in almost every American film. Our pictures show people having fun. They reflect freedom, prosperity, happiness, a higher standard of living in clothing, houses, interiors, motor cars—all the material appurtenances of good living.
>
> The European intelligentzia criticize the happy endings of our stories as bad art. But to peoples recovering from the shock of war, and whose financial, economic and social problems are not yet solved, these happy pictures are beacon lights of hope. They seem to show the way to peace, prosperity and happiness. They make the spectators forget their cares and worries and anxieties. They bring relaxation and give entertainment. They are an escape from the daily routine of work. They open a fresh new world of play where there are no class restrictions or the inertia that comes of despair. That is why American pictures are popular abroad. I think, too, we know more of what can be done with the camera.

It may be that that is the true reason. We are at that particular period of our history and growth that gives us happiness in youth and strength and wealth. We are an extraordinarily fortunate and blessed people. Not all of us realize it. But the rest of the world does and is constantly reminded of it by our movies. It has awakened desires in them for some of the things we possess. That is what has made the movie a factor in trade and in our international relationships. That is why trade begins to follow the film.

And it all began as a five-cent peep show. An astonishing evolution, isn't it?

6. Secretary of Commerce Herbert Hoover Extols U.S. Foreign Trade, 1926

Foreign trade has become a vital part of the whole modern economic system. The war brought into high relief the utter dependence of the life of nations upon it. The major strategy of war is to crush the enemy by depriving him of it. In peace time our exports and imports are the margins upon which our well-being depends. The export of our surplus enables us to use in full our resources and energy. The creation of a wider range of customers to each production unit gives to that unit greater stability in production and greater security to the workers.

And we may quite well view our exports from the other side of the trade balance sheet. They enable us to purchase and import those goods and raw materials which we can not produce ourselves. We could probably get along as a nation if we had to suppress the 7 to 10 per cent of our production which goes to export, but our standard of living and much of the joy of living is absolutely dependent upon certain import commodities. We could not carry on our material civilization without

This document can be found in U.S. Department of Commerce, *The Future of Our Foreign Trade* (Speech by Herbert Hoover, March 16, 1926, to the Export Manager's Club of New York), Washington, D.C.: Government Printing Office, 1926.

some of the fibers, rubber, and some metals. Without diamonds we would not be able to get satisfactorily engaged to marry. The prosperity of our people in many ways can be measured by the volume of imports. . . .

The Government can chart the channels of foreign trade and keep them open. It can assist American firms in advancing their goods. In the improvement of all the foreign services the Department of Commerce has made great progress in the past five years, and it has been developed into organizing in internal cooperation and consultation with our industries and our merchants. . . .

I believe the effect of the efforts of the department [of Commerce] in establishment of standards, elimination of waste, and the provision of wider information has been to expand the possibilities of foreign trade to many concerns not hitherto able to extend into this field. One of the interesting and encouraging facts is the rapid increase in the number of small concerns participating in export business. The surprisingly large number of inquiries now being received by the department from such firms amply proves that the virtues of high quality, specialized production, good service, precise export technique, and farsighted policy are by no means monopolized by big corporations. Literally thousands of small dealers and manufacturers, whose commodities have a strong specialty appeal and meet a definite need, are now successfully cultivating overseas markets. Foreign trade is thus becoming a national asset in the fullest sense of the word. . . .

Without entering upon any partisan discussion of the protective tariff, which I, of course, support, there is one phase of the tariff which I believe experience shows has less effect upon the volume of international movement of commodities than had at one time been assumed.

As a result of the hardships suffered by many people of both combatant and neutral nations during the war, there came to all nations a deep resolution, in so far as the resources of their countries permitted, to produce as far as possible their essential commodities. The struggle to overcome post-war unemployment has added to this impulse. The result is that 52 of the 70 nations of the world, including almost every important trading nation, increased their tariffs after the war. It might seem that these widespread protective policies would tend to localize industry and thus decrease the total volume of international trade. But it certainly appears that internal economic and social currents which make for prosperity or depression in a nation have a much larger effect upon the total volume of imports than the tariffs and thus more largely affect world trade as a whole. In our case, far from our present tariff diminishing our total imports, they have increased about 35 per cent since the higher tariff came into effect. This has also been the case with other nations which have progressed in internal economy. In any event our experience surely indicates that in considering the broad future of our trade we can dismiss the fear that our increased tariff would so diminish our total imports as to destroy the ability of other nations to buy from us.

The most commonly remarked revolution in our foreign economic relations is our shift from a debtor to a creditor nation upon a gigantic scale. It is the father of much speculative discussion as to its future effect upon our merchandise trade. Alarm has been repeatedly raised that repayment of the war debts must necessitate the increase of imports of competitive goods in order to provide for these payments— to the damage of our industry and workmen. These ideas are out of perspective. Our war debt when settled upon our own views of the capacity to pay will yield about $300,000,000 per annum, although as yet the actual payments are much less than this. The private foreign loans and investments to-day require repayments in principal and interest of about $600,000,000 annually, or nearly twice the war debt. I have heard of no suggestion that interest and repayment of these private debts will bring the disaster attributed to the war debt. The question is of importance, however, as to how this $800,000,000 or $900,000,000 of annual payments may affect our merchandise movement. There is a compensating factor in American trade relations unique to our country which has a large bearing upon this question—that is, the vast dimension of our invisible exports in the form of tourist expenditure, emigrants' remittances, and other forms of American expenditure abroad. These items in 1925 amounted to about $900,000,000, or about $100,000,000 more than our incoming payments on debts of all kinds. In other words, at this stage of calculation the balance of trade should be in our favor by about $100,000,000. But beyond this we are making, and shall long continue to make, loans abroad. For the last four years these loans have averaged nearly $700,000,000 a year, and in fact the merchandise balance in our favor has been running just about this amount.

Now the summation and purpose of all these words is the conclusion that there is no disastrous shift in our imports and exports of merchandise in prospect from debt causes. . . .

By contributing to peace and economic stability, by the loan of our surplus savings abroad for productive purposes, by the spread of inventions over the world, we can contribute to the elevation of standards of living in foreign countries and the demand for all goods.

7. The Kellogg-Briand Pact Outlaws War, 1928

Article 1.   The High Contracting Parties solemnly declare in the names of their respective peoples that they condemn recourse to war for the solution of international controversies, and renounce it as an instrument of national policy in their relations with one another.

Article 2.   The High Contracting Parties agree that the settlement or solution of all disputes or conflicts of whatever nature or of whatever origin they may be, which may arise among them, shall never be sought except by pacific means.

 E S S A Y S

In the first essay, Norman A. Graebner, long a professor at the University of Virginia, criticizes Americans and U.S. foreign policy in the 1920s for retreating from world leadership. A self-defined "realist," Graebner claims that Americans' embrace of both isolationism and internationalism left the United States incapable of using its great power to thwart aggression and sustain peace. In the second essay, John Braeman of the University of Nebraska,

This document can be found in U.S. Department of State, *Papers Relating to the Foreign Relations of the United States, 1928* (Washington, D.C.: Government Printing Office, 1942), I, 155.

Lincoln, disputes Graebner's interpretation, arguing instead that the United States sustained adequate military power, kept the nation secure, and protected its interests abroad. Braeman wonders what more the United States should have done, given the many obstacles to a more vigorous foreign policy—not only domestic reluctance to engage in foreign ventures but also the intractability of foreign crises that would likely have arisen regardless of the U.S. posture. In the last essay, Frank Costigliola of the University of Connecticut agrees with Braeman that, although the United States contributed to international problems, there was little that Washington could have done to stem the world's descent into chaos because neither Europeans nor Americans would have tolerated massive U.S. intervention. Rather than treating the 1920s as an interlude between disasters, Costigliola sees the decade as a time of relative peace and prosperity. One of his contributions to our understanding of the 1920s is the spotlighting of another dimension of foreign relations that Americans considered a success and that calls into question the label "isolationist"—cultural expansion in the form of the "Americanization" of Europe through Hollywood films and other cultural exports.

Oblivious to Reality:
The Extremes of American Isolationism and Internationalism

NORMAN A. GRAEBNER

During the critical months of debate and decision which followed the Versailles Conference, the United States deserted its wartime commitment to remake the world in its own image and retreated instead to the confines of its immediate interests. For this violent counterrevolution in the nation's outlook [Woodrow] Wilson, its primary victim, was in some measure responsible. The American involvement in the Great War had demonstrated again that the United States could not and would not escape any major European struggle that threatened the balance of power or ventured onto the Atlantic. That involvement demonstrated, furthermore, that the United States could not influence European politics with policies that avoided direct and sizeable commitments of American economic and military power to the affairs of the continent. On the other hand, Wilson's failure at Versailles to eliminate from international relations the traditional reliance on national interest and force made it clear that the world's leading nations had less interest in his idealism than in the remarkable capacity of the United States to wage total war. Thus sound American policy, in the future as in the past, would avoid the extreme goals of either attempting to escape all obligations abroad or defending the interests of oppressed humanity everywhere. Rather such policy would be directed at the definition and protection of a wide variety of specific historic and geographic interests in competition with nations which would pursue traditional interests of their own with whatever means came to hand.

Unfortunately Wilson's concepts and personality so dominated the American scene that they drove American policies toward the extremes against which the nation's experience had warned. In his wartime effort to transform world politics in

From Norman A. Graebner, "America's Twentieth-Century Search for World Order," in *The National War College Forum,* Winter 1970, pp. 36–39. Reprinted with the permission of the author.

accordance with his principles of peaceful change and self-determination, Wilson had warred with such remarkable success on the guiding traditions of national interest and balance of power that he succeeded in eliminating them almost completely from the main currents of American political thought. Only with difficulty would the nation ever again agree on the goals and assumptions which should underlie its policies abroad. At the same time Wilson's failure to restructure world politics created the foundations for a pervading postwar isolationism. The nation could measure Wilson's success by his standards alone, and by those standards he had failed. If few Americans pondered the consequences of a possible German victory, it was because the country's wartime leadership had not formulated American interventionist policy in terms of protecting the traditional balance of power. By ignoring the limited, but precise, gains that lay within the nation's capabilities, Wilson managed to transform a successful, and perhaps essential, national effort into failure. For those, in short, who accepted his assumptions of an American world role, as well as for those who rejected them totally, Wilson failed to establish the bases of a sound national response to the challenges of the future.

Unable to discover any demonstrable gain from their wartime efforts, millions of Americans emerged from the European involvement determined to prevent its repetition. Europe, the isolationists agreed, had demonstrated again the hopelessness of her politics, the bitterness of her diplomacy. Her troubles, whatever their nature, were not the concern of the United States and thus no legitimate cause for American involvement. Never again, warned the *New Republic,* should the American people become embroiled in a system of European alliances. "We ask only to live our own life in our own way," declared California's Senator, Hiram Johnson, in March, 1922, "in friendship and sympathy with all, in alliance with none." Much of the postwar cynicism toward the war focused on Britain, the nation allegedly responsible for undermining American neutrality. The powerful newspaper publisher, William Randolph Hearst, reminded his readers that Britain had often been the target of American patriotism. American isolationism, as it demolished the country's wartime pro-Allied sentiment, gained the support of those Irish and German minorities which had resented Wilson's decision to underwrite the British cause.

Isolationism took additional strength from the rebirth of nationalism with its conviction of national superiority and its faith in the country's ability to protect itself from attack. Proud of their nation's wealth and achievements, which they attributed to hard work and the relative perfection of their institutions, the spokesmen of "America first" expressed their reluctance to share again their prosperity and good fortune with peoples less deserving. What compounded this determination to preserve their favored position was the widespread notion that Europe, still engaged in petty quarrels and turmoil, was untrustworthy and corrupt. Why take responsibility for the security of the greedy and ungrateful people of Europe? For a rich and supposedly self-sufficient country what mattered was less the welfare of Europe than the quality and direction of American life. Sinclair Lewis captured the spirit of postwar America when his George Babbitt informed the Zenith Real Estate Board that the real American was "the ideal type to which the entire world must tend if there's to be a decent, well-balanced, go-ahead future for this little old planet!" A country in pursuit of nineteenth-century values could find easy intellectual and emotional rewards in contemplating the superiority of its civilization and the security afforded by both its industrial power and the existence of surrounding oceans.

Isolationism, in rejecting the importance of events abroad, could scarcely form the basis for policies that would sustain the essentials of the Versailles settlement. But internationalism, as embodied in the Wilsonian tradition, was as oblivious to political reality as was isolationism. Both were strangers to the conservative tradition of American diplomacy [the matching of ends and means and an understanding of power]. Both denied that the United States need be concerned with any specific political or military configuration in Europe or Asia. Whereas isolationism limited the nation's interests to the Western Hemisphere, internationalism assumed that American interests were universal—wherever mankind was oppressed or threatened by aggression. Isolationists preached that events outside the hemisphere were inconsequential; internationalists insisted not only that they mattered but also that the United States, in its role as a world leader, could not renounce its obligation to engage in policies of cooperation. In practice, however, the internationalists would control the world environment, not with the traditional devices of diplomacy or force, but by confronting aggressors with a combination of international law, signed agreements, and world opinion. Every program fostered by American internationalists throughout the twenties—membership in the League of Nations or the World Court, the resort to arbitration and conciliation, collective security, naval disarmament, or the outlawry of war—denied the need of any precise definition of either the ends or the means of national policy. What mattered in world politics was the limitation of change to peaceful means. Thus in the hands of the internationalists the concepts of peace and peaceful change became the bulwark of the *status quo,* for change limited to general agreement could alter the international order only on questions of little or no consequence.

Isolationism and internationalism had more in common than the conflicting rhetoric of the twenties would suggest. Americans—even the isolationists—had no desire to escape the world of commerce and investment. Businessmen, isolationists and internationalists alike, demanded that their government sustain their privileged economic position everywhere on the globe. And because a stable world environment would best serve the needs of Americans, many citizens insisted that the country accept the moral responsibility for the peace, provided that the responsibility entail no specific obligation for the defense of any foreign country or region. These limited, and generally conflicting, objectives established the bounds of popular national policy. The successive Republican administrations of the twenties, in their perennial support of American business interests abroad, satisfied the demands of nationalists who believed in "America First." The repeated involvements of the United States in the cause of peace delighted those internationalists who believed that the nation should serve, not merely the needs of its own citizens, but the needs of humanity everywhere. United States policies varied from narrow nationalism to limited internationalism, all designed to serve the specific interests of trade and investment as well as the general interest in peace.

In the roseate years of the late twenties the great democracies—the creators of Versailles—shared an illusion that the decade of peace reflected the triumph of their moral and intellectual leadership. So often had officials and editors of the English-speaking countries insisted that power had been eliminated from international relations that they began to believe it. Because war would bring disaster, they could scarcely believe that any nation would resort to war in the face of reason or an outraged world opinion. Unfortunately the peace of the twenties was no demonstration of either a general acceptance of the Versailles settlement (symbolic of the *status quo*) or even the universal rejection of force. What sustained the assumption that all wars had been fought and all issues resolved was the predominance of Western power which permitted the spokesmen of the democracies to manage the game of international politics so effortlessly that they were quite unconscious of the role which power had played in their success. Thus peace rested primarily on the weakness of those nations whose governments had already made clear their dissatisfaction with the Versailles Treaty. Any collapse of the Western monopoly of power would witness the almost immediate return of force to international life.

So precarious was the world's peace structure that an armed clash outside Mukden, Manchuria, in September 1931, could threaten it with disaster. For it quickly became apparent that Japanese officials in Manchuria were determined to exploit the crisis occasioned by the alleged destruction of tracks along the South Manchurian Railway by altering the regions political status. In part, the ensuing Japanese assault on Manchuria was defensive, for Chinese nationalism and anti-foreignism endangered Japan's special privileges in Manchuria, which included the right to station troops along the South Manchurian Railway. So successful had been Japanese investments and industrial leadership in developing the Manchurian economy that by 1931 almost thirty million people, overwhelmingly Chinese, lived in the three Eastern Japanese–occupied provinces. The large Chinese migration into Manchuria evolved into a massive effort to drive out the Japanese. For Japan, however, Manchuria had become a region of vital necessity. The Japanese islands had only limited arable land, no mineral resources, and a population increasing at the rate of a million each year. Korea and Formosa had failed to satisfy the Japanese requirements for land and resources. But Manchuria, with its abundant natural riches, promised at last to supply the food and raw materials necessary for Japan's economic existence. Rather than withdraw from the mainland under Chinese pressure, the Japanese preferred to convert Manchuria into a Japanese dependency.

What troubled official Washington in the Japanese conquest of Manchuria were not this nation's vital interests. Nelson T. Johnson, the American minister in China, observed as early as March 1931, that a possible Japanese possession of Manchuria need not embroil the United States in war. With this judgment the Hoover administration agreed. But if the United States had little interest in the disposition of Manchuria's resources, it had a profound interest in the Far Eastern peace structure embodied in the Nine Power Pact and the Kellogg-Briand Pact. In signing these documents Japan had joined other nations in agreeing to limit its ambitions to what it might achieve through peaceful means alone. In a cabinet meeting on October 9, 1931, Secretary of State Henry L. Stimson warned the President against getting into a humiliating position in case Japan refused to honor her own signatures on the paper treaties. But Stimson recorded in his diary the essential character of United States policy in the Far East:

> The question of the "scraps of paper" is a pretty crucial one. We have nothing but "scraps of paper." This fight has come on in the worst part of the world for peace treaties. The peace treaties of modern Europe made out by the Western nations of the world no more fit the three great races of Russia, Japan, and China, who are meeting in Manchuria, than, as I put it to the Cabinet, a stovepipe hat would fit an African savage. Nevertheless they are parties to these treaties and the whole world looks on to see

whether the treaties are good for anything or not, and if we lie down and treat them like scraps of paper nothing will happen, and in the future the peace movement will receive a blow that it will not recover from for a long time.

Thus Hoover and Stimson refused from the outset to accept any new arrangement in the Far East which resulted from the Japanese resort to force. At stake in Manchuria was the credibility of the whole system of collective security based on the force of world opinion as well as on the influence and prestige of the League of Nations. Johnson warned the administration in a letter of November, 1931, "The fate of Manchuria is of secondary importance compared with the fate of the League." Throughout the crisis, however, the United States attached its policy to the Kellogg Pact and the Nine Power Treaty, not to the League of Nations, and thereby limited its response to reminding the Japanese of their obligation to uphold the provisions of the two treaties. But what if such moral pressure failed to control Japan? The democracies would then face the ultimate choice of witnessing the collapse of the Versailles settlement or sustaining the world they favored with a resort to superior force.

Powerful, Secure, and Involved: What More Should the United States Have Done?

JOHN BRAEMAN

Since Pearl Harbor, American foreign policy during the Harding-Coolidge-Hoover years has received a largely negative appraisal from historians. In the aftermath of World War II, the adherents of Wilsonian internationalism dominated the writing of American diplomatic history. The crux of their indictment of the Republican administrations of the twenties was that this country's refusal to participate in collective-security arrangements for upholding the peace was responsible for the breakdown of international order in the years that followed. If the United States had joined the League of Nations, or at the minimum cooperated with the peace-loving nations, Britain, France, and, until the illusions of the wartime alliance collapsed, the Soviet Union, against would-be or actual aggressors, the Second World War could have been avoided. Although this view has continued to have its champions, the hardening of Cold War tensions—and the accompanying disillusionment with the efficacy of the United Nations—spurred a major counterattack upon what [the scholar-diplomat] George F. Kennan has termed the "legalistic-moralistic approach to international problems." With the emergence of the so-called realist school came a different—though no more positive—evaluation of the role played by the United States during the age of normalcy.

The dominant intellectual figure in the post–World War II realist movement was University of Chicago political scientist Hans J. Morgenthau. Morgenthau's starting point was a complex of assumptions about the behavior of nations and, more fundamentally, about human nature, which were in striking contrast to the

From "Power and Diplomacy: The 1920s Reappraised," *The Review of Politics,* 44 (July 1982). Reprinted with the permission of the editor of *The Review of Politics,* Notre Dame, Indiana 46556. Pp. 342–355, 358–366, 369.

nineteenth-century liberal faith in the existence of an inherent harmony of interests that underlay the Wilsonian vision of collective security.

"The primordial social fact," he postulated in *Scientific Man vs. Power Politics,* "is conflict, actual or potential. . . ." Or as he put the matter more bluntly still in his now-classic *Politics Among Nations,* "the struggle for power is universal in time and space and is an undeniable fact of experience." Within most nations, he acknowledged, there existed a community of interests and values that tended to reduce the intensity of conflict. But the international arena was different. "The history of the nations active in international politics shows them continuously preparing for, actively involved in, or recovering from organized violence in the form of war." In such an anarchical world, force remained the ultimate arbiter. Thus, whatever the long-term goals of a nation, "Power is always the immediate aim." And given this country's geopolitical situation, he defined as the American national interest "to preserve the unique position of the United States as a predominant power without rival" in the Western Hemisphere and "the maintenance of the balance of power" in Europe and Asia.

The trouble was, runs the realist indictment, few Americans in the age of normalcy grasped those truths. [The political scientist] Robert E. Osgood lamented that the post–World War I revulsion against Wilsonian utopianism had fostered a no less dangerous set of illusions: a millennialist hope for "peace by incantation," "a blind aversion to war and the instruments of war as absolute evils abstracted from the conflicts of power and national self-interest which lead to war," and, thus, a refusal to accept "the uses of force and the threat of force as indispensable instruments of national policy." . . .

Military historians deplored the lack of machinery for civilian-military consultation in formulating foreign policies, the resulting widening gap between goals and capabilities, and the flight from "reality" in the services' own strategic planning. The United States's refusal to assume a share of the burdens of economic reconstruction, its aloofness from foreign political involvements, and what [the historian] Edward W. Bennett has stigmatized as its "indifference to, or even revulsion from, the principle of the balance of power" were blamed for undercutting the Versailles settlement in Europe. Even heavier fire was directed against this country's Far Eastern policies. A minority of the postwar realists questioned the wisdom of American hostility to Japanese ambitions. . . . But the preponderant view among the post–Pearl Habor generation of historians was that the fault lay in this country's failure to maintain sufficient military strength to meet the Japanese challenge. Popular hostility to naval spending, congressional economizing, and the naval limitations agreements undercut the deterrent power of the navy. And when Japan in Manchuria launched the first major direct attack upon the world order, the United States responded with no more than words.

There is no question that the political and intellectual atmosphere in the United States during the twenties opposed large-scale military and naval expenditures. But a nation's military capability cannot be measured by any absolute standard. Even in the narrow sense of armed forces-in-being, what matters is their relative size and efficiency vis-à-vis those of potential enemies. And in the larger sense, a nation's "military potential" depends upon a number of factors: its geographical vulnerability; the kind of war to be fought; and most importantly, as World War I had demonstrated, its technological and economic capacity. Perhaps the most salient feature of the Republican era was this country's overwhelming superiority in the economic sphere. In the late 1920's, the United States produced an output of manufactures larger than that of the other six major powers—Great Britain, Germany, France, the Soviet Union, Italy, and Japan—combined. The extent to which a nation translates its available resources into mobilized strength is a political decision. That decision, as [the scholar] Klaus Knorr has pointed out, reflects a "cost-gain calculation" of the advantages and disadvantages anticipated from the maintenance of military strength at different levels. "The desirability of ready combat strength depends, first, on the importance of the prevailing goals for the achievement of which military power is a means and, secondly, on the prevailing assumptions about the amount of military resources necessary to achieve these goals." If such variables are taken into account, substantial evidence exists for a reappraisal of the conventional wisdom about American policies during the Harding-Coolidge-Hoover years.

In the first place, the extent of pacifist influence upon American policy during the 1920's should not be exaggerated. Although the organized peace groups mobilized impressive shows of public support on such issues as naval disarmament and outlawing war, the military services could, and did, rally the backing of veterans' organizations, patriotic societies, and special interest groups. Viewing the world as a competitive arena in which each nation pursued its self-interest, the increasingly influential professional careermen in the State Department had no illusions that moral force did, or could, regulate international relations. And their thinly veiled hostility toward those peace enthusiasts who hoped for a radical transformation of the international order was shared by their politically responsible superiors. Nor was there any lack of consultation with the services on matters involving national security; even Hoover, the most pacifist-minded of the chief executives of the era, took pains to do so. The crux of the services' grievance was that their advice was not always followed when purely military considerations conflicted with larger policy goals. Most important, the Republican administrations remained committed to the basic principles of military and naval policy that had been formulated during the preceding two decades: "a strong Navy and battle fleet, second to none, as a first line of defense capable of dominating the western Atlantic and the eastern Pacific"; "a small Regular Army devoted primarily to the preservation and increase of military knowledge, the training of civilian components, and the preparation of plans for future wars"; and "a strong civilian industrial economy capable of conversion to war production in an emergency."

Post–World War I army planning was based upon an "insurance" concept of preparedness resting upon a small professional force capable of emergency defense, while providing the nucleus for the mobilization and training of a mass "citizen" army. Funding limitations did keep the army's enlisted strength in the latter twenties and early thirties to 118,750 men—a far cry from the 280,000 maximum envisaged by the National Defense Act of 1920 and below the 165,000 figure estimated by the General Staff as required for carrying out the army's responsibilities. But even in the midst of the depression, appropriations were more than double the pre–World War I level. And while during the years of prosperity recruiters found difficulty in attracting and retaining high-caliber enlistees, the impact of hard times allowed the army to upgrade its standards. The officer corps remained at approximately twice the prewar level, thus providing the cadre that was able to lead the vastly expanded army of World War II. This pool of potential leaders was reinforced by the continuation of Citizens' Military Training Camps and the expansion of the Reserve Officers' Training Corps in the colleges. . . .

Nor was there any threat on the European side warranting a larger American buildup. The military establishments of all the major European powers—except for the Soviet Union—suffered during the twenties from popular suspicion, stringent budgetary limitations, and a loss of self-confidence that bordered upon defeatism. From 1919 until its abrogation in 1932, British military policy was shaped by the "Ten Year Rule" that the Empire would not become involved in a major war during the next decade. Given this assumption, the strength of pacifist sentiment, and the country's near-desperate need for financial retrenchment, the British army was cut back to a level barely capable of handling its routine peacetime responsibilities. Although France as of 1933 had 450,000 officers and men under arms—with plans to mobilize within two weeks sufficient reserves to raise the total to a million—Paris' anxiety over Germany's superior population and industry, and its potential military superiority, bred a state-of-siege mentality. The Treaty of Versailles had bound the German army by a network of restrictions down to the equipping and arming of units. Despite the growing evasion of these limitations after mid-decade, the *Reichswehr* in the years before Hitler did not envisage the possibility of mobilizing more than a maximum 300,000-man force in the event of war and doubted their ability to equip even that many. The Soviet Union was probably the most formidable military power on the continent. In the late twenties, its regular army numbered 562,000 men, and starting in 1931 a large-scale program of expansion and reequipment was launched under a leadership committed to an offensive strategy based on mobility, maneuver, and mechanization. But the USSR's technological and industrial backwardness, its continuing internal problems, and its leaders' obsession with the threat of "capitalist encirclement" made the avoidance of war the keystone of Soviet policy.

Similarly exaggerated are the charges, made then and since, that American policymakers were blind to the revolutionary potentialities of air power. The Army Reorganization Act of 4 June 1920 provided formal recognition of the Air Service as a combatant arm, while the Air Force Act of 1926 provided for a new assistant secretary of war to deal with aviation matters, added an air section to each of the General Staff divisions, and authorized a five-year program of expansion in personnel and equipment. Insufficient money prevented achievement of the authorized 1800-plane force. But appropriations did rise sharply, with the result that by 1933 the Air Corps boasted 1619 planes, of which over 1100 were regarded as first-line craft. While balking at granting the air arm full autonomy as an independent service, the General Staff in its contingency war planning from 1923 on envisaged establishment of a consolidated air strike force under a single commander directly responsible to Army General Headquarters. By the early 1930's, army officialdom was gradually moving toward acceptance of this organizational setup for peacetime. Although the most vocal champion of the supremacy of air power, Brigadier General "Billy" Mitchell, was forced out of the service, his ideas about the airplane as primarily an offensive weapon whose function was to destroy the enemy's industrial base had come to permeate Air Corps' thinking. If the air power enthusiasts failed to achieve all their goals, the reasons were not simply old-guard obstruction and congressional parsimony. The major obstacles were the limits of the existing technology, substantive differences over strategy and tactics, and the absence of any immediate threat. "Despite popular legend," World War II Air Corps chief H. H. "Hap" Arnold acknowledged, "we could not have had any real air power much sooner than we got it." . . .

Most important, aviation technology still left the oceans as safe defenses. Even the head of the Air Service acknowledged in the fall of 1925 that the United States was not in any immediate danger of air attack. Eight years later, a board headed by Major General Hugh A. Drum, the army's deputy chief of staff—pointing to the difficulties attending the flight of the highly rated Italian bombers to the Chicago World Fair—reaffirmed that this country need not fear attack by land-based planes. As late as 1935, Britain's top heavy bomber, the Hawker "Hendon," could carry 1,500 pounds of bombs for no more than a thousand miles round trip. Despite the enthusiasm of *Reichswehr* air planners from the early twenties for a long-range strategic bomber, the first steps toward implementing its development were not undertaken until late 1933, and Germany would remain without an operational heavy bomber at the beginning of World War II. Rather than lagging behind, the United States was in the forefront of long-range bomber development. The landmark breakthrough came in 1931 with the appearance of the Martin B-10, an all-metal monoplane that was the first of the modern bombers. In July 1933 the Air Corps Materiel Division began work on the plans for what would become the B-17 Flying Fortress. And what would prove decisive in the long run, the growth of civilian aviation and the aircraft industry—stimulated by the Air Mail Act of 1925, the Air Commerce Act of 1926, Charles Lindbergh's 1927 transatlantic flight, and the Air Corps's policy of encouraging private manufacturers to build up their design and engineering staffs through placing orders for experimental prototypes—gave the United States an industrial and technological infrastructure in the aeronautics field that no rival could match.

The most controversial issue involved the state of the navy. Whereas the army command acquiesced without major protest in civilian decisions about funding and manpower levels, most naval officers made no secret of their unhappiness. Their anger was first roused by the restrictions placed upon capital ships by the Five Power Treaty of the Washington Conference of 1921–1922: a ten-year ban upon new construction; maximum tonnage quotas; and a 5:5:3 ratio for the United States, Britain, and Japan. Their anxieties about the navy's deterrent capability were heightened by the agreement reached at the London Conference of 1930. That pact continued the holiday in capital ship construction until 1936 and reduced further the tonnage allowances; fixed tonnage quotas for heavy cruisers, light cruisers, destroyers, and submarines; and provided for a 10:10:7 ratio in the first three categories with parity in submarines. Domestic political realities were an important factor in the American government's championship of naval limitation. The struggle over the naval appropriations bill of 1921 demonstrated the resistance to implementing the Wilson administration's planned building program. But the key point, and what made the agreements possible, was that similar forces were at work in this country's two major sea rivals. In Britain, the mood of pacifism and the demand for financial retrenchment joined to exert tremendous pressure for major cutbacks in naval expenditures. Similarly, the balance of political forces in

Japan up until the Great Depression worked in favor of a policy of accommodation with the United States: the backlash against military interventionism spurred by the unsuccessful Siberian invasion; the growing influence of the political parties; the acceptance by the civilian decision-making elite that Japan's interests in China were primarily economic; the financial burdens of a naval arms race; Japan's dependence on this country for vital raw materials; and the sense of security given the existing favorable power balance in the western Pacific.

Qualitatively, the agreements were, as [the historian] William R. Braisted has suggested, "a service to the Navy" by requiring the service to make the most efficient use of its available resources. The reduced capital ship tonnage required by the Five Power Treaty allowed the navy to eliminate overaged and obsoletely equipped vessels. With new construction halted, the navy concentrated upon an extensive program of modernization of its remaining battleships. The installation of new engines and the conversion from coal to oil increased speed and range; new electrical power systems were developed; improvements in the elevating mechanism of turreted guns resulted in increased firing power; and the substitution of plastics and aluminum for heavier materials allowed improved armor while keeping within the tonnage limitations. Naval researchers made important advances in radio communications, in radar, and in radio-controlled torpedoes. . . . When the test came after Pearl Harbor, the American treaty-era ships proved "effective if not optimal military units, capable of performing their fundamentally defensive strategic function."

Similarly impressive were the innovations in strategy. In line with its assigned mission of capturing Japanese bases in Micronesia in support of the fleet in the western Pacific, the Marine Corps during the twenties worked out the basic principles of amphibious assault doctrine, gave increased emphasis in its training, course work, and maneuvers to landing operations, and worked out techniques of air support for such landings. The navy's most glaring weakness was in submarines. But the Naval Research Laboratory worked to improve submarine technology; submarine officers engaged in an ongoing study of design and tactics; and the London Conference's restrictions on tonnage forced a rethinking of submarine design to maximize cruising distance and torpedo power. Probably most significant for the future was the progress achieved in naval aviation. Despite its ponderousness and slowness, the airplane carrier *Langley*—a converted old fleet collier commissioned in 1922—proved invaluable for training and experimental purposes. When commissioned in 1927, the *Saratoga* and *Lexington* were the finest carriers afloat. Although the undersized *Ranger* proved a misstep, the navy in 1933 gained congressional authorization for the *Yorktown* and *Enterprise*. At the same time, a group of younger aviation-oriented officers pioneered in formulating the concept of the carrier as an independent striking force. By contrast, British carrier development lagged because of the Royal Air Force's preoccupation with long-range, land-based strategic bombers. And though more active than the British in this area, the Japanese continued to view the carrier as an auxiliary in support of the main battle fleet. This country's fleet aircraft, Rear Admiral Ernest J. King, chief of the Bureau of Aeronautics, reported in 1934, "have reached a degree of efficiency not equaled by any other power." . . .

The most important single factor shaping, and delimiting, United States foreign policymaking in the Republican era was this country's overwhelming sense of security. While favoring the expansion of overseas trade and investment, American officials were not willing to incur excessive costs and risk in their pursuit. Washington was most activist in backing American business abroad when such action coincided with its larger strategic and political goals: the World War I–inspired desire for American control over petroleum reserves, cables, and banking facilities in Latin America; defense of the traditional Open Door policy in China; and access to the oil of the Middle East and Dutch East Indies because of the feared depletion of American reserves. Where such political and strategic objectives were not at stake, State Department support for private interests was limited to routine calls for equal opportunities for American firms. Exports and overseas investments represented no more than a minor factor in the total national economy. The country remained self-sufficient in most mineral resources; by the latter 1920's even the anxieties over oil supplies had largely faded. The third world, as we now call it, remained under colonial rule; most of the underdeveloped countries that were independent, far from resisting, welcomed American investment from a wish to play this country off against more immediately threatening powers, to tap new sources of revenue, or to promote economic growth.

American strategic planning for Latin America up to the late thirties envisaged United States interests almost exclusively in terms of the Caribbean region as this country's "soft underbelly." Although plans were drawn up for intervention in each of the South American countries, these were more conceptual and intellectual exercises than operational realities. Even with regard to the Caribbean area, the absence of any meaningful danger from Europe after World War I led American policymakers to inaugurate a shift away from military intervention in favor of other methods of promoting order and stability. When temporary intervention was required to safeguard American lives and property, the forces at the disposal of the navy's Special Squadron were sufficient for the purpose. Only in Nicaragua was there significant resistance—and the *Sandinistas* were more a political embarrassment than a military threat. Nor was there—except for Mexico—any effective challenge to American primacy south of the border from the larger Latin American countries. Developments during and after World War I had strengthened the bonds of Latin American economic dependency upon this country. Notwithstanding the strain of anti-Americanism among Latin American intellectuals, most local elites welcomed the Yankee dollar. Apart from Argentina, the South American republics deferred to American leadership in political matters. The 1920's did witness major frictions with Mexico, partly because of the threat to American property rights from Mexican revolutionary nationalism, partly because of the Mexican government's anticlerical campaign. But, despite rumors to the contrary, American officials never seriously contemplated using force. And a judicious mixture of pragmatic official and unofficial diplomacy with economic pressure brought a resolution of the differences on terms satisfactory to Washington.

Despite the popular distrust of Old World entanglements, the Republican administrations of the age of normalcy were not indifferent to, nor aloof from, European problems. On the contrary, the establishment of a peaceful and prosperous Europe ranked high upon their list of priorities. American negotiators disregarded congressional guidelines to scale down substantially the Allied war debts. Convinced of the adverse political and economic effects of excessive reparations, Washington simultaneously labored to work out a "realistic" solution based upon Germany's capacity to pay. After the failure of his efforts to forestall the French occupation of the Ruhr, Secretary of State Charles Evans Hughes took the lead in arranging for the Dawes Plan settlement of the deadlock. The Federal Reserve—encouraged and supported by the Treasury—cooperated with the European central banks to achieve currency stabilization. Although the United States took no formal part in the security arrangements reached [in 1925] at Locarno [formalizing Western European borders set by the Versailles Treaty], American officials exerted behind-the-scenes pressure in favor of the accord by warning that continued American loans depended upon the return of political stability. In contrast with the later ridicule of the naiveté of outlawing war, the Kellogg-Briand treaty was hailed by contemporaries as the harbinger of a larger role by the United States in world affairs, while influential elements in this country saw in the pact an opening wedge for American cooperation with collective action against aggressors.

The question is not the fact of United States involvement in European affairs, but its extent. The promotion of European recovery did take a secondary place in the calculations of American officialdom to what was regarded as more important priorities, such as tariff protection for the home market and reducing the burden on American taxpayers. Nor did support for European political stability extend to a willingness to make binding diplomatic or military commitments. Yet, even leaving aside the domestic political constraints upon American decision-makers, what more *should* the United States have done? American political and business leaders remained confident—and here Herbert Hoover was simply the most articulate spokesman of a widely shared optimism—that the United States could prosper economically, regardless of what happened in Europe. Diplomatic and military commitments meant in the context of the time support for France against Germany. Although regarding a strong France as indispensable for a European balance of power, Washington did not accept Paris' definition of what constituted French security. American officials were convinced that the French hard line on reparations, their refusal to meet Germany's legitimate grievances, and their efforts to keep Germany down were self-defeating by undermining the possibility of a prosperous, satisfied, republican Germany. Thus, they worried that any commitments on this country's part would strengthen French intransigence. Nor were they alone in this view. Their British counterparts were no more willing to underwrite the *status quo*.

If from the vantage point of the Second World War, the failure to back up France appears misguided, was that the wisest course in the 1920's? Despite the Treaty of Versailles, Germany remained potentially the most powerful nation in Europe. Nothing short of the massing of overwhelming military force could have kept Germany in a permanently inferior status. The disastrous results of Hitler's rise to power showed the validity of the American view that future European peace depended upon the success of the Weimar Republic. More immediately relevant, American policies appeared to have been successful. The influx of American loans that followed adoption of the Dawes Plan, and the achievement of currency stabilization, led to a spurt of economic growth and a new mood of optimism in Europe. The resulting prosperity contributed to muting the social conflicts that had wracked the domestic politics of the European nations in the first half of the decade. American leaders shared the contemporary optimism about the Locarno settlement as the dawn of a new era of cooperation and peace. . . .

When this structure began to crumble under the impact of the Great Depression, the Hoover administration was not blind to the dangers. In the face of the German financial crisis in the spring of 1931, the President moved boldly to forestall the threatened collapse of the Central European banking and financial structure with his moratorium, while simultaneously working behind the scenes to promote a new debt-reparations settlement. By 1932, he had become sufficiently alarmed at the deadlock at the Geneva Disarmament Conference to take new initiatives that went far toward meeting the French demand for security guarantees. Reversing its long-standing position, Washington endorsed a system of international supervision and control as part of any new arms limitation agreement. Although Hoover continued to balk at making commitments in advance—even if no more than a formal consultative pact—American officials repeatedly assured the Western Europeans that this country would not interfere with collective action against aggressors. That Hoover's efforts to unravel the debt-reparations tangle proved a failure was due as much to the intransigence of the European powers as to domestic political impediments. The administration's decision not to go further in meeting French security anxieties reflected in part popular and congressional hostility to involvement in European power rivalries, partly the chief executive's own fear that such involvement might entangle the United States in responsibilities and dangers, such as in Eastern Europe, not commensurate with its interests.

Limited interest similarly shaped United States policy in the Far East. Although firms with a large economic stake in China, such as Standard Oil, were not without political muscle, this country's trade with and investment in China were relatively minor—and substantially below trade with and investment in Japan. Nor did American bankers, despite State Department urgings, show any enthusiasm for loans to China. American interests in China were primarily ideological, or, to put the matter more bluntly, sentimental. Captivated by the image of this country as the protector and friend of China, a vocal body of American opinion spearheaded by the missionary lobby indulged in fanciful visions of the United States as the mentor to China's evolution into a modern liberal democracy. Responsible government officials had a more realistic grasp of the rampant confusion and chaos in China, and were painfully aware of this country's limited ability to shape events in the Celestial Empire to its liking. Taking as axiomatic their duty to protect the lives, property, and rights of American citizens abroad, American diplomats kept up a drumfire of protests when those were threatened. Wishing to maintain a show of the flag, the State Department overruled the army's wish to withdraw the tiny force stationed in China. But the major thrust of American policy toward China during the twenties was toward accommodation with Chinese nationalism. The Hoover administration even accepted in principle, and entered into negotiations for, the gradual relinquishment of the keystone of the so-called unequal treaty system, the right of extraterritoriality.

Those historians who fault American policymakers for failing to take a firmer stand against Japan fail to ask what was the alternative to the attempt at a *modus vivendi* inaugurated by Secretary of State Charles Evans Hughes. China was a weak reed; Russia in the aftermath of the war was in temporary eclipse as a Far Eastern power; and Britain, painfully aware of its vulnerability in Asia, was anxious to avoid provoking the Japanese. American efforts first under Taft and then under Wilson to resist Japanese ambitions in China had antagonized the Japanese without any substantive gain for the United States. Most importantly, Hughes did not think the Open Door a sufficiently vital interest for the United States to be worth fighting for. Even if he had, the public and their representatives in Congress were not willing to make the military and naval expenditures required to deter Japan if she determined to close the door. Given this situation, Hughes achieved at the Washington Conference a diplomatic triumph that gained for the United States the abrogation of the long-suspect Anglo-Japanese Alliance, Japan's formal withdrawal of Group V of the Twenty-One Demands, and its pledge to respect the Open Door and China's independence and territorial integrity. And until 1931, Tokyo remained committed to the "Washington system" of peaceful economic expansion in China and cooperation with the Anglo-American powers. . . .

The basic flaw in the realist indictment of American foreign and military policies during the so-called age of normalcy is a case of confusing the 1920's with the 1930's. The years after 1933 did witness an extraordinary rapid shift in the world balance of power. That shift was due partly to the accelerating pace of technological innovation, but more to the differing willingness by the major powers to allocate resources to arms. If the United States was ill-prepared to meet the resulting challenges, the fault lay with the men in charge when those changes took place. In the context of 1921–1933, however, American policies were neither naive nor unwise. Perhaps at no time in its history—before or since—has the United States been more secure. Nor did his Republican successors have Wilson's messianic zeal to create a new global order. "The foreign policy of small nations is often determined for them," the British scholar A. E. Campbell has pointed out, "but in a nation complex, powerful, and unusually secure the assessment of the national interest can only rest on a general conception of the world situation. . . . Politically conscious men will have such a conception at the back of their minds, if not always at the forefront, and against that conception they will test the importance or unimportance for their nation of specific world events, and so the need for government action." Thus, what must be kept in mind about the years after World War I is that "the United States possessed a unique combination of great power and an isolated position."

U.S. Cultural Expansion in an Era of Systemic Upheaval

FRANK COSTIGLIOLA

In the quarter-century following the Great Crash, many historians wrote the 1920s off as a decade of amusing antics, precarious prosperity, and isolationist diplomacy. One example of such an approach is Frederick Lewis Allen's *Only Yesterday,* published in the midst of the Depression, which poked fun at a silly decade of flat-chested flappers, narrow-minded businessmen, and tight-fisted diplomats. All this, Allen suggested, especially when mixed with bathtub gin, had to end in a crash. Though his focus was broad, Allen denigrated the achievements of the 1920s.

However historians evaluate the years 1919–33, they must come to grips with the period's central force: political, economic, and cultural upheaval. That systemic instability has often blinded historians to the real accomplishments of the era. Much of the recent historical literature performs a valuable corrective by considering the decade on its own terms, as a period of relative peace and prosperity. These works remind us that most Americans and Europeans of the 1920s believed they could avoid the catastrophes of war and depression. To disparage the 1920s as a period of "false" prosperity and peace because those happy conditions did not endure is to distort history. Certainly the economic and political collapse in the Great Depression evidenced a terrible failure. Yet it is impossible to show how the disaster could have been avoided. By 1929 it was probably beyond the power of the United States to save the international order short of massive intervention—something neither Americans nor Europeans would have tolerated. Moreover, the dissolution of post–World War II prosperity should make us more humble and sympathetic in our criticism of those who were unable to preserve post–World War I prosperity. . . .

In the political realm, instability emerged from the Versailles, St. Germain, and Trianon treaties which made up the 1919 peace settlement. The key point was that these treaties *were* an international issue, an object of debate and struggle that ended only with the outbreak of war in 1939. The treaties imposed a settlement that the defeated nations—Germany, Austria, and Hungary—did not accept and that three of the four main victors—the United States, Great Britain, and Italy—soon saw as at least partially unwise and unsatisfactory. In opposition to the defeated nations, which wanted to overthrow the treaties, France and its eastern allies—Poland, Czechoslovakia, and Rumania—sought to preserve the 1919 settlement.

American pressures and sympathies, both official and unofficial, lay toward moderate treaty revision. Most Americans opposed a total overthrow of Versailles. They did not want to see Germany free of all fetters, nor did they appreciate any change, political, economic or social, that was drastic and destabilizing. Yet the peace treaties were too harsh, many Americans believed, and hampered integration of the defeated powers, particularly Germany, into a stable, prosperous, and peaceful Europe. Although the United States refused to form political alliances with Europeans after 1919, it consistently favored slow, moderate peace treaty revision that would ease the burdens on Germany. In the reparations conferences of 1924 and 1929, the unofficial American representatives who dominated the proceedings substantially transformed reparations from a club with which to beat Germany to a contractual debt owed by Germany. In 1924, at American and British insistence, France reluctantly relinquished its right under Versailles to march into Germany in case of reparations default. Americans encouraged Europeans to accept Germany into the Locarno Pacts and the League of Nations. In 1931, President Herbert Hoover and Secretary of State Henry L. Stimson went so far as to urge the French to pressure their Polish ally to revise the Polish corridor in Germany's favor. . . .

This American solution of peaceful change, of moderate Versailles revision, fit with the Progressive reform tradition such policymakers as Herbert Hoover and Charles E. Hughes carried with them into the postwar years. Like the Progressives of the previous decade, makers of American foreign policy in the 1920s sought stability and order through slow reform that would give repressed groups (workers in the 1910s, Germans in the 1920s) a stake in the improved, fairer system.

American leaders opposed sudden overthrow of the peace treaties just as they opposed socialist revolution at home or anywhere else. Taken in its widest context, the policy of peaceful change was part of America's effort throughout the twentieth century to combat revolutionary upheaval with moderate reform. Pacifying and rebuilding Germany was integral to containing the Bolshevik revolution. Bolshevik Russia presented both a symbolic and a substantive threat to the peaceful change alternative. Most American leaders viewed the Soviet Union as revolution incarnate, despite Moscow's caution and conservatism. If Germany's political and economic structure collapsed, its people, Americans feared, might in desperation forge a Russian alliance to overthrow both Versailles and capitalism. Their very opposition to revolution led Hoover, Hughes, and other American leaders to combat the French policy of rigidly enforcing Versailles, which would only build up pressures for change until they exploded in revolutionary upheaval. . . .

. . . Americans preferred the middle road of democratic capitalism. Yet when faced with the options of revolutionary socialism or fascist order, Americans consistently picked the latter. The United States maintained cordial relations with Benito Mussolini, funding Italy's war debt on favorable terms, allowing private bankers to make large loans, and cooperating closely in 1931 on disarmament and political issues. . . .

Confronted with disorder in the European and world economies, the United States responded with a solution parallel to the political answer of peaceful change. Orderly growth in the international capitalist economy, Americans believed, would reduce political tensions and the threat of revolution while expanding markets and investment opportunities for United States business. Although the United States carefully measured its political entanglements in Europe, its economic involvement was broad and deep. In the 1920s, moreover, economics and business enjoyed enormous popular prestige in both America and Europe. For reasons of conviction and of expedience, the United States government approached basically political questions such as reparations from an economic or business perspective. This economic emphasis was particularly suited to American policy's decentralized implementation and to its goal of a prosperous Europe. By 1923–24, government officials, central bankers, and top private businessmen forged a loose alliance. Although tactical differences often separated these leaders, they usually cooperated enough to present Europeans with a united front on war debt, loan, and other issues.

Before the crash, Americans pressed the Europeans to adopt the international gold standard, reduce government expenditures, and fund war debts and reparations. This financial program, the Yankees believed, would lay the foundation for Europe's recovery and reestablish an orderly flow of goods and capital. Responding to American and internal pressures, most European governments adopted the gold standard in the 1920s. This move boosted both international business and the power of America's huge gold reserve, but also burdened the world economy with a rigid monetary system that probably depressed prices. Similar consequences followed from American efforts to impose order upon the chaos of war debts and reparations. Under U.S. prodding, by 1929 the Allies and Germany settled these political debts on a fixed, reduced basis. This helped stabilize the world credit system, but the rigid debt settlements, like the rigid gold standard, proved brittle in the Depression. . . .

These political and economic relations can only be understood in their cultural context. The term *culture* is here comprehensively defined to include high culture such as literature, painting, and formal music; popular entertainment forms such as jazz, dancing, film, and sports; mundane matters such as household appliances, foods, and gadgets; more abstract concerns such as religion, philosophy, and language; attitudes toward work, play, money, and war; and finally technological innovations that had sociological implications, such as increased emphasis on machines, statistics, and mass assembly-line production.

Europeans interpreted virtually every manifestation of American culture, whether it was music, films, or automobiles, as the product of a society dominated by technology and the machine. America's technological superiority, moreover, made other aspects of its culture more attractive to Europeans. And it was this technological influence that persisted in Europe after the fad for Americans faded in the Great Depression. In virtually every cultural aspect, there was significant interchange between America and Europe during the 1919–33 period, with most, but not all, of the influence flowing eastward.

To war-weary Europe, struggling to cope with the problems of modern mass society, the United States, emerging from the war rich and buoyant, seemed to have the answers. Since the machine civilization was most advanced and apparently most successful in the United States, many European artists, businessmen, and politicians alike looked westward for models. To help Europe deal with the turbulence of modernization, America offered its own institutions and values, or what contemporaries termed *Americanism.*

Americanism meant a pragmatic, optimistic outlook on life; a peaceful, rational compromise of political differences; an efficient, modern way of organizing work that emphasized machines and mass assembly production; rising standards of living with declining class antagonisms; scientific use of statistics and other information; and the predominance of mass society (this meant democratic politics, widespread consumption, and popular entertainment). Many Europeans welcomed Americanism; others railed against it or were ambivalent, but nearly all believed it was in Europe's future.

In 1630, Governor John Winthrop predicted that America would become a model for the world—"a Citty Upon a Hill" with "the eies of all people" upon it. Three hundred years later Paul Claudel, ambassador from France and himself a man of letters, told Americans: "Your movies and talkies have soaked the French mind in American life, methods, and manners. American gasoline and American ideas have circulated throughout France, bringing a new vision of power and a new tempo of life. The place in French life and culture formerly held by Spain and Italy, in the nineteenth century by England, now belongs to America. More and more we are following America." Hans Joachim, a German writer, recalled the powerful influence in the 1920s of the United States as a land and as a symbol: "America was a good idea; it was the land of the future. It was at home in its age . . . we loved it. Long enough had . . . technology appeared only in the forms of tank, mine, shell-gas. . . . In America, it [technology] was at the service of human life. Our interest in elevators, radio towers, and jazz was . . . expressive of the wish to beat the sword into a plowshare. It was against cavalry but for horsepower. . . . It was an attitude that wanted to convert the flame thrower into a vacuum cleaner. . . . Our belief in

America demonstrated where we stood." Europeans in the 1920s were entranced by the image of that city upon the hill.

America's cultural influence was both a product of and a contributor to the United States' economic, political, and (in 1917–19) military power in Europe. In 1917–18 the American economy's size and technological superiority made a psychological as well as military impact on Europe. Exhausted Europeans watched as the Americans quickly raised, equipped, and transported across the Atlantic a two-million-man army. Allies and Germans alike marveled at the Yankees' modern, efficient modes of transportation and organization.

The U.S. Committee on Public Information directed propaganda campaigns at war-weary Europeans eager for new, better answers. Other agencies, such as Herbert Hoover's American Relief Administration, made promotion of America and its way of life an integral part of their operation. Hoover made sure that relief recipients understood their food was coming from a beneficent America. When labor-management strife threatened to stop coal production in central Europe, Hoover's men introduced more liberal labor practices coupled with emphasis on increased labor productivity. President Woodrow Wilson was an enormously effective propagandist, even though—like his chief rival, Vladimir Lenin—he excited European expectations which he could not fulfill.

Indeed, the propaganda war between the United States' liberal capitalism and Russia's revolutionary socialism contained not only antagonistic but complementary aspects that prepared the ground for Europe's Americanization in the 1920s. Wilson and Lenin had both told the European masses that the old imperialist regimes with their balance-of-power politics had produced the war and had to be replaced. Both proclaimed a new era of popular sovereignty, mass society, economic growth, and technological improvement. By the early 1920s, most Europeans were disillusioned with both Wilson's and Lenin's millennial visions. Yet America's enormous economic power and apparent success as a society ensured that many Europeans looking for social solutions, including some of those who had been inspired by Lenin, would turn to the United States for models. Even the Russian Bolsheviks, despite continued hostility toward capitalism, tried to adopt many of America's technological wonders. The United States government ceased propaganda efforts in 1919, but in the ensuing decade private Americans advertised their ideas, institutions, and products in Europe.

Yankee merchandise, films, aviators, artists, entertainers, and above all dollars flooded the Old World, bringing Europeans direct evidence of the United States' position as the leader of Western civilization. Economic and cultural factors intertwined in various ways. . . .

Two elements lay at the source of these cultural interactions: the United States' economic power, which captured European markets and imaginations while financing a flood of tourists and expatriate artists and giving Americans the money to buy what they wanted; and the process of Americanization. Contemporaries used *Americanization* to refer to both the United States' cultural penetration of Europe and the overlapping process of Europe's indigenous modernization. That America became a metaphor and a symbol for modernization testified to the nation's leading position in Western civilization.

In subtle yet important ways, this cultural influence and prestige enhanced the ability of the United States to conduct its political and economic policies in Europe with minimal cost and entanglement. This was especially important after 1919, when the United States government, under both Democratic and Republican administrations, shifted away from direct, official involvement in European politics. The new diplomacy was unofficial rather than official, economic rather than political, limited rather than open-ended, cautious rather than crusading. The respect that many Europeans held for American ideas and methods made such diplomacy easier to implement. At the 1924 Dawes reparations conference, for example, the unofficial American representatives conducted a successful publicity campaign in Europe that presented their plan as a pragmatic and businesslike—that is, an American—solution. Recognizing the importance of prestige (or what they termed moral power), American leaders tried to limit their intervention to instances where it would be successful, thereby enhancing their reputation for effectiveness. . . .

Just as America's prestige flowered with its impressive performance in World War I and in the 1920s, so did its cultural influence, economic power, and political leverage wilt with the Depression and the dissolution of its economy. European artists became disillusioned with their Americanist dream of permanent prosperity and progress and, with the flow of checks and tourists drying up, most American artists went home. The Depression also revealed flaws in the American reconstruction of the world economy. The United States had stabilized trade and financial relations in ways that both protected American interests and enabled Europe to recover, and Americans confidently believed that the beneficent change of economic growth would make the system work. The gold standard, the political debt settlements, the private loans, and the high U.S. tariff were burdens Europe probably could have borne had prosperity continued. But in hard times the economic structure proved too rigid and too tilted toward American interests. It collapsed. . . .

The rise of Nazi Germany and Soviet Russia during this turbulent period of a revolutionary century made mock of American attempts to implement policies of peaceful, moderate political reform and orderly, capitalist economic growth. By 1933, only the cultural leg of the triad was left standing at all, and here too both the Nazis and Soviets demonstrated that technological modernization was easily separated from the rest of the Americanization process. America could not control the chaos unloosed in 1914 after all. . . .

After 1917 American culture penetrated Europe in various ways. The American Expeditionary Force prepared the way for post-war cultural exchange by introducing Europeans to jazz and doughboys to the charm of the Old World. The doughboys' machines, their efficiency, energy, and innovativeness, impressed Europeans. Exhausted by the war, disillusioned with their own societies, many Europeans wondered whether they should not adopt the methods of these highly successful Americans. After the war, many former soldiers returned to the Old World as artists, tourists, or businessmen, each in his own way spreading U.S. culture. Along with Herbert Hoover's American Relief Administration, smaller private aid teams initiated Progressive reforms. Hollywood films stimulated demand for America's products while exposing Europeans to its speech, its manners (and mannerisms), and its values. Fads swept Europe as boxers and dance troupes pioneered this cultural and economic frontier.

Yankee popular culture excited many European artists, particularly avant-garde Germans of the *neue Sachlichkeit,* or new objective school, who sought modern cultural models to replace discredited imperial ones. Although many of these artists, like other Europeans, feared domination by the machine, they welcomed Americanism as a way to increase the Old World's economic productivity while resolving its social and ideological conflicts.

America's mass culture seemed democratic and progressive, the wave of the future. Many German leftist artists saw little contradiction in paying simultaneous allegiance to Bolshevism and Americanism. Both creeds preached popular sovereignty, mass culture, and technological development. In the heyday of U.S. influence, such German artists as Bertolt Brecht decided that Americanism, not bolshevism, offered the surer and more comfortable road to progress.

The United States was not only Europe's competitor, creditor, and occasional political mediator, but also the leader of Western civilization; and what happened in America was of intense, often personal interest to many Europeans. They watched closely, and reacted with near-hysterical joy, to [the aviator] Charles Lindbergh's solo flight across the Atlantic and, only a few months later passionately repudiated the Massachusetts trial and execution of Nicola Sacco and Bartolomeo Vanzetti.

America's influence in Europe had great impact also on its own artistic development. American painters, writers, composers, and other artists made pilgrimages to Europe, looking for freedom and esthetic inspiration. There they found many artists fascinated with the technologically dominated culture they had scorned. Moreover, significant numbers of expatriate artists ended up financing their adventures by working for compatriot businessmen and tourists. In the Old World, then, many Yankee artists found both esthetic validation and financial support for developing an indigenous American art.

Just as America's power led Europeans to heed American culture, so too did such prestige or moral power enhance the effectiveness of the United States' unofficial economic diplomacy. Washington officials realized that America's reputation for success and efficiency, coupled with its lack of interest in most European political rivalries, gave the nation a subtle but important moral authority in the Old World.

The State Department valued this asset because it yielded influence abroad with minimal cost or responsibility. Department officials tried to maximize America's moral power by making sure their foreign policy initiatives would succeed. In 1927, the department countered European resentment of U.S. power by using Charles Lindbergh as a goodwill ambassador. Like the AEF [American Expeditionary Force] a decade earlier, Lindbergh riveted Europeans' attention on Yankee boldness and technology, and thus quickened the pace of Americanization. . . .

Tourists constituted the largest and economically most important American group in Europe. The number of United States visitors jumped from roughly 15,000 in 1912 to 251,000 in 1929. In the latter year, American citizens in Europe spent close to $323 million and immigrants visiting home expended an additional $87 million. By the end of the 1920s, foreign travel became possible for middle-class Americans.

Visits to Paris nightclubs and the Louvre seemed a painless answer to America's balance-of-payments dilemma. Tourists' dollars helped Europe pay its debts and the United States maintain its tariff. Herbert Hoover's Commerce Department noted happily that worldwide American tourist expenditures of $770 million in 1927 more than matched $714 million in war and private debt receipts. In addition to the financial dividend, tourism had a beneficial "political effect," American officials told the Germans, "leading to a normal resumption of relations" between the two nations.

The flood of travelers generated resentment as well as dollars. Always the tourists' favorite, France in 1926 attracted foreigners who picked up bargains as the franc fell. Americans commonly asked waiters and shopkeepers "How much is that in real money?" A few even papered their train compartments or luggage with franc notes. Such insensitivity aggravated tensions over the war debt, and in July Paris erupted in several antiforeign, and especially anti-American demonstrations. Both French and American officials tried to calm emotions. Calvin Coolidge balanced a rebuke of "bumptious" tourists with a warning that badly treated Americans would stay home. But probably the majority of visitors had pleasant tours that never made newspaper headlines—in any case, France remained the number one American tourist attraction in Europe.

In 1929, the combined expenditure of American tourists and residents in France totaled over $137 million, creating an American economy in Paris. In the French capital one could be born in the American hospital, attend one of several American schools and churches, belong to the American Legion, the YMCA, the Cornell, Harvard, or American Women's Club; read one of three Parisian-American newspapers, in a favorite café or at the American Library; sip whiskey in the many American bars, drink milk delivered by American milkmen, eat sweet corn and ice cream produced by local Americans; go to hockey games, boxing matches, and other imported sport events; receive care from American dentists and doctors and be buried by an American undertaker. With fewer United States tourists or permanent residents, Berlin still supported an American church, student association, newspaper and, intermittently, chapters of the American Medical Association, Daughters of the American Revolution, and the Harvard Club. . . .

During the Great War, Hollywood invaded European and other world markets. YMCA representatives entertained Allied troops with American films, and the "movie habit" caught on among civilians and soldiers. In the 1920s, American films were an international box-office hit. Assured of the domestic market, which netted 60 percent of total world film revenue, Hollywood produced extravaganzas with which Europeans could not compete. By 1925, United States films made up 95 percent of the total shown in Britain, 60 percent of the total in Germany, 70 percent in France, 65 percent in Italy, and 95 percent in Australia and New Zealand. In Germany, the number of cinemas increased by 35 percent from 1920 to 1929, while the production dropped from 646 films to 175 films. Americans owned three-fourths of the most fashionable movie threatres in France. Hollywood's profits depended on foreign screenings, since domestic revenues covered only production costs, and frequently not even that.

"Trade follows the film," Americans and Europeans agreed. Greek appliance wholesalers and Brazilian furniture dealers found that their customers demanded goods like those pictured in the American movies. Although direct correlation between films and trade was hard to prove, Congress, parsimonious in most matters, established a Motion Picture Section in the Bureau of Foreign and Domestic Commerce in 1926. Bureau chief Julius Klein and his officials attested that United States films "stimulat[ed] the desire to own and use such garments, furnishing, utensils, and scientific innovations as are depicted on the screen." Will H. Hays, Hollywood czar, boasted of the power of these "silent salesmen of American goods."

American films not only sold United States goods, but, many Europeans feared, threatened independent national identity. "America has colonized us through the cinema," one Frenchman complained. Another French critic testified to the secularization of John Winthrop's city upon the hill: "Formerly US preachers . . . deluged the world with pious brochures; their more cheerful offspring, who pursue the same ends, inundate it with blonde movie stars; whether as missionaries loaded with bibles or producers well supplied with films, the Americans are equally devoted to spreading the American way of life." Charles Pomaret, a member of the Chamber of Deputies, remarked that Europeans had become "galley-slaves" to American finance and culture—appropriately, an image taken from the Hollywood hit *Ben-Hur.* British groups worried that the many Hollywood films shown throughout the empire led to "American domination in the development of national character or characteristics." After a concerned speech by the Prince of Wales, the London *Morning Post* warned: "The film is to America what the flag was once to Britain. By its means Uncle Sam may hope some day, if he be not checked in time, to Americanize the world."

After 1925, Britain, Germany, and France tried to check the trend. Governments enacted measures to limit the number of imported Hollywood films and encourage domestic production. This policy diminished but did not eliminate Hollywood's dominance in Europe. Required by law to produce domestic films if they wanted to import the popular American ones, German and other European producers responded with "quota quickies," often subgrade efforts produced only to meet the letter of the law. American filmmakers circumvented the restrictions by investing in Europe, especially Germany. They imported European directors and performers and remained preeminent in world film exports. The State and Commerce departments vigorously supported Hollywood's diplomacy. In the late twenties film exporters faced a new danger, with talkies. How could they screen English-language movies in polyglot Europe? Hollywood responded with multi-language production. In collaboration with a Berlin company, Paramount filmed *The Blue Angel* in English and German versions. In France, Paramount worked on an assembly-line basis: sixty-six features in twelve languages for the first year. Dubbed sound tracks helped, and by 1931 United States films had regained all but 10 percent of their 1927 market in England and Germany.

Hollywood films were a hit in Europe because they projected modern culture in a vivid and attractive light. Film embodied the era's emphasis on mechanical, simultaneous, and concentrated production. The message was mass entertainment. As Adolf Behne, a German avant-gardist, recognized, "Film is . . . democratic. . . . This ha[s] been recognized by the German masses, which flock to see Charlie Chaplin films." As the industry's global leaders, Hollywood producers had budgets large enough to pay for the casts of thousands and other spectacular effects calculated to please those masses. Finally, the films portrayed an image of life in fabulous America, the giant of the contemporary world and the pioneer of Europe's own future.

From Switzerland to the Soviet Union, Europeans acknowledged America's cultural leadership. "Mrs. Lenin," Anna Louise Strong reported from Moscow, "wants . . . American ideas on education through doing; manuals about . . . various things." Jean-Paul Sartre reflected, "Skyscrapers . . . were the architecture of the future, just as the cinema was the art and jazz the music of the future." André Siegfried, a French sociologist, concluded that America had replaced Europe as "the driving force of the world." . . .

What happened in America affected the whole world. The United States had become John Winthrop's city upon the hill, though not for the religious reasons that he had expected, and Europeans could not avert their gaze. Whether they welcomed the prospect or dreaded it, most Europeans believed that American civilization portrayed the future course of their own societies. The United States was the metropolis, the hub of the modern cultural system, and Europe now figured as a satellite.

 F U R T H E R   R E A D I N G

Selig Adler, *The Isolationist Impulse* (1957)

Derek H. Aldcroft, *From Versailles to Wall Street*, 1919–1929 (1977)

Harriet Hyman Alonso, *The Women's Peace Union and the Outlawry of War, 1921–1942* (1989)

Leroy Ashby, *The Spearless Leader: Senator Borah and the Progressive Movement in the 1920s* (1972)

John Braeman, "American Foreign Policy in the Age of Normalcy: Three Historiographical Traditions," *Amerikastudian/American Studies,* 26 (1981), 125–158

Thomas Buckley and Edwin B. Strong, *American Foreign and National Security Policies, 1914–1945* (1987)

Kathleen Burk, "The Lineaments of Foreign Policy: The United States and a 'New World Order,' 1919–39," *Journal of American Studies,* 26 (1992), 377–391

Bruce J. Calder, *The Impact of Intervention* (1984) (Dominican Republic)

Warren I. Cohen, *Empire Without Tears* (1987)

Frank Costigliola, "The United States and the Reconstruction of Germany in the 1920s," *Business History Review,* 50 (1976), 477–502

Charles DeBenedetti, *Origins of the Modern American Peace Movement, 1915–1929* (1978)

Roger Dingman, *Power in the Pacific: The Origins of Naval Arms Limitations, 1914–1922* (1976)

Justus D. Doenecke, *When the Wicked Rise: American Opinion-Makers and the Manchurian Crisis of 1931–1933* (1984)

L. Ethan Ellis, *Republican Foreign Policy, 1921–1933* (1968)

Richard W. Fanning, *Peace and Disarmament* (1995)

Martin L. Fausold, *The Presidency of Herbert C. Hoover* (1985)

Herbert Feis, *The Diplomacy of the Dollar* (1950)

Robert H. Ferrell, *American Diplomacy in the Great Depression* (1957)

———, *Frank B. Kellogg and Henry L. Stimson* (1963)

———, *Peace in Their Time* (1952)

Peter Filene, *Americans and the Soviet Experiment, 1917–1933* (1967)

Betty Glad, *Charles Evans Hughes and the Illusions of Innocence* (1966)

Norman A. Graebner, *Ideas and Diplomacy* (1964)

Kenneth J. Grieb, *The Latin American Policy of Warren G. Harding* (1976)

Linda B. Hall, *Oil, Banks, and Politics* (1995) (Mexico)

Ellis W. Hawley, ed., *Herbert Hoover, Secretary of Commerce, 1921–1928* (1981)

Michael J. Hogan, *Informal Entente: The Private Structure of Cooperation in Anglo-American Economic Diplomacy* (1977)

Jon Jacobson, "Is There a New International History of the 1920s?" *American Historical Review,* 88 (1983), 617–645

Robert D. Johnson, *The Peace Progressives and American Foreign Policy* (1995)

Harold Josephson, *James T. Shotwell and the Rise of Internationalism in America* (1976)

William Kamman, *A Search for Stability: United States Diplomacy Toward Nicaragua, 1925–1933* (1968)

Robert G. Kaufman, *Arms Control in the Pre-Nuclear Era: The United States and Naval Limitation Between the Two World Wars* (1990)

Bruce Kent, *The Spoils of War* (1989) (reparations)

Michael L. Krenn, *U. S. Policy Toward Economic Nationalism in Latin America, 1917–1929* (1990)

Walter LaFeber, *Inevitable Revolutions* (1993) (Central America)

Melvyn P. Leffler, *The Elusive Quest: America's Pursuit of European Stability and French Security, 1919–1933* (1979)

Brian McKercher, ed., *Anglo-American Relations in the 1920s* (1991)

———, "Reaching for the Brass Ring: The Recent Historiography of Interwar American Foreign Relations," *Diplomatic History,* 15 (1991), 565–598

Charles S. Maier, *Recasting Bourgeois Europe* (1975)

Sally Marks, *The Illusion of Peace: International Relations, 1918–1933* (1976)

Robert K. Murray, *The Harding Era* (1969)

Louis A. Pérez, Jr., *Cuba Under the Platt Amendment, 1902–1934* (1986)

Stephen J. Randall, *United States Foreign Oil Policy, 1919–1948* (1986)

Emily S. Rosenberg, *Spreading the American Dream* (1982)

——— and Norman L. Rosenberg, "The Public-Private Dynamic in United States Foreign Financial Advising, 1898–1929," *Journal of American History,* 74 (1987), 59–82

Thomas J. Saunders, *Hollywood in Berlin: American Cinema and Weimar Germany* (1994)

Stephen A. Schuker, *American "Reparations" to Germany, 1919–33* (1988)

———, *The End of French Predominance in Europe: The Financial Crisis of 1924 and the Adoption of the Dawes Plan* (1976)

Robert D. Schulzinger, *The Making of the Diplomatic Mind: The Training, Outlook, and Style of United States Foreign Service Officers, 1908–1931* (1975)

Michael S. Sherry, *The Rise of American Air Power* (1987)

Robert F. Smith, "Republican Policy and Pax Americana, 1921–1932," in William Appleman Williams, ed., *From Colony to Empire* (1972), pp. 253–292

George Soule, *Prosperity Decade* (1947)

Marc Trachtenberg, *Reparation in World Politics* (1980)

Christine A. White, *British and American Commercial Relations with Soviet Russia, 1918–1924* (1992)

William Appleman Williams, "The Legend of Isolationism in the 1920s," *Science and Society,* 18 (1954), 1–20

John Hoff Wilson, *American Business and Foreign Policy, 1920–1933* (1971)

———, *Herbert Hoover* (1975)

———, *Ideology and Economics: U.S. Relations with the Soviet Union, 1918–1933* (1974)

CHAPTER
4

Franklin D. Roosevelt
and the Origins of
the Second World War
in the Pacific

German and Japanese aggression in the 1930s presented Americans once again with questions of war and peace, neutrality or alliance. The United States protested this aggression—witness the strongly worded Stimson Doctrine after Japan invaded Manchuria in 1931—but Americans sought to avoid entanglement in the cascading crises that engulfed Europe and Asia. Congress passed neutrality acts, and President Franklin D. Roosevelt publicly endorsed the United States's neutral stance. Recalling the horrors of World War I and beset by a terrible economic depression at home, many Americans embraced "isolationism," or what historians have called "independent internationalism." After the outbreak of full-scale war in Europe in September 1939, Roosevelt and the nation gradually moved toward an interventionist posture, repealing the arms embargo and in 1941 sending Britain and the Soviet Union Lend-Lease supplies. When war came for the United States, however, it occurred six thousand miles away from Europe, in Asia.

For most of the twentieth century, the United States had opposed Japanese expansion into China. When the Japanese sought access to vital raw materials and markets to relieve their economic stress in the 1930s, taking Manchuria and renaming it Manchukuo, Americans viewed Japanese imperialism as a violation of the Open Door and a threat to world order. Later in the decade, as the Sino-Japanese war intensified, the United States gradually expanded its navy, granted loans to China, and did not invoke the neutrality acts—thereby permitting China to buy armaments from the United States. Yet Washington protested Japanese aggression in a manner designed not to provoke war with the Empire of the Sun. Certain that America's strategic priorities lay across the Atlantic in Europe, the Roosevelt administration hoped to avoid a two-front war.

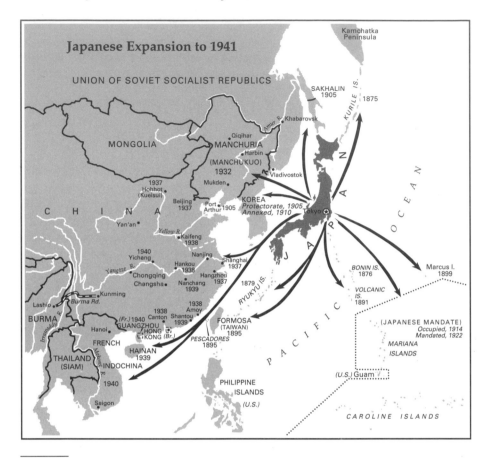

Thomas G. Paterson et al., *American Foreign Relations*, 5/e. Copyright © 2000 by Houghton Mifflin Company. Reprinted by permission of Houghton Mifflin Company.

Following conclusion of the Tripartite Pact among Japan, Germany, and Italy in September 1940 and Japan's acquisition of bases in French Indochina, the administration embargoed shipments of scrap iron and steel to the island nation. The crisis in the Pacific reached a critical juncture when Japanese troops, in July 1941, occupied French Indochina. In response, the Roosevelt administration froze Japanese assets in the United States, thereby denying Japan essential petroleum shipments. Tokyo and Washington exchanged proposals and counterproposals for the rest of the year, but to no avail. On December 7, in a surprise attack, Japanese pilots bombed the U.S. naval base at Pearl Harbor in the Hawaiian Islands. The United States declared war on Japan, and Germany declared war on the United States. Americans braced once again for world war.

Historians have grappled with weighty questions in explaining America's road to war. What at root caused the deterioration in U.S.-Japanese relations? Was the economic downturn of the 1930s the culprit? Were cultural differences a major source of conflict? Did Japan's aggressive nationalism and economic exclusiveness pose an unacceptable threat to the international system? Why did Japan's definition of a "new order" alarm other nations? Did the United States push Japan toward *war? Was Japanese-American conflict unavoidable? Did conflict have to escalate into war? Or could different policies toward Japanese expansionism have produced a different outcome? Why did the Roosevelt administration bow to "appeasement" sentiment in dealing with Germany but adopt a more confrontational stance toward Japan? What was the relationship between events in Europe and events in Asia? Was the issue of China solvable, and why was the United States so concerned about the fate of China? Could war have been delayed? How important was timing?*

Almost all historians of this subject have studied Franklin D. Roosevelt as decisionmaker, probing his ideas, leadership, and choices, and the results of his policies. Did FDR have a coherent strategy for coping with aggression in Europe and Asia, or did he deal with issues haphazardly? Was he in command of the making of foreign policy, or did he leave crucial decisions to subordinates, who complicated his diplomacy or pressed Japan harder than the president intended? What roles did the State Department and Secretary of State Cordell Hull play? What advice did military officials offer? Did bureaucratic infighting confuse matters? To what extent did public opinion influence policy?

Finally, although most historians reject any notion of a Rooseveltian conspiracy, questions of this nature persist: Did Roosevelt, eager to enter the European conflict, devise policies toward Japan that guaranteed entry into war through the Asian "back door"? Did the president deliberately set up Pearl Harbor for disaster? Or did American leaders simply err in not alerting the base to possible attack?

 ## D O C U M E N T S

Document 1, the Stimson Doctrine of January 7, 1932, was issued by Secretary of State Henry L. Stimson after the Japanese overran Manchuria. Stimson's policy of nonrecognition guided the United States for the rest of the 1930s. U.S. pressure on Tokyo escalated following a clash between Japanese and Chinese troops at the Marco Polo bridge, south of Beijing, in July 1937, and Japan's full-fledged invasion of China. In obvious reference to what Japan's leaders called the "China Incident," President Franklin D. Roosevelt told a Chicago audience on October 5, 1937, that aggressors should be "quarantined" (Document 2). Although FDR offered no concrete policies, the administration in the following months began to send modest amounts of aid to China.

Document 3, an official Japanese statement of November 3, 1938, following a string of military victories in China, proclaimed the establishment of a "new order" in East Asia. Japan's bold actions sparked debate among American policymakers over how best to halt and reverse the aggression. On November 14, 1938, Stanley K. Hornbeck, a senior adviser on Asian affairs in the State Department, urged the United States to develop a diplomatic "war plan" to punish and deter the Japanese (Document 4). An outspoken hawk, Hornbeck called for economic measures, including the abrogation of the 1911 U.S.-Japan commercial treaty. U.S. ambassador to Japan Joseph C. Grew disagreed. In a memorandum to Secretary of State Cordell Hull on December 1, 1939, Document 5, he predicted that sanctions would only alienate Japanese leaders and provoke further conquest.

On July 25, 1941, following Japan's invasion of French Indochina, the Roosevelt administration froze Japanese assets. Document 6, final negotiating points adopted by the Imperial government on November 5, 1941, sets forth two options for a settlement with the United States: Plan A, which called for a Japanese withdrawal from China only after a satisfactory Sino-Japanese truce had been reached; and Plan B, which skirted the China issue, but pledged that Japan would advance no further south than Indochina in exchange for an unfreezing of Japan's assets and resumption of normal trade with the United States. Document 7, a restatement of Washington's proposals to Japan dated November 26, 1941, rejected compromise and sought to roll back Japanese expansionism and revive the Open Door principle. The Japanese position paper (Document 8) handed to Hull on December 7, 1941, as the Japanese descended on Pearl Harbor, outlined Japan's case against the United States and for mastery of China. Document 9 is Roosevelt's war message to Congress, delivered on December 8, 1941.

1. The Stimson Doctrine, 1932

With the recent [Japanese] military operations about Chinchow, the last remaining administrative authority of the Government of the Chinese Republic in South Manchuria, as it existed prior to September 18th, 1931, has been destroyed. The American Government continues confident that the work of the neutral commission recently authorized by the Council of the League of Nations will facilitate an ultimate solution of the difficulties now existing between China and Japan. But in view of the present situation and of its own rights and obligations therein, the American Government deems it to be its duty to notify both the Imperial Japanese Government and the Government of the Chinese Republic that it cannot admit the legality of any situation *de facto* nor does it intend to recognize any treaty or agreement entered into between those Governments, or agents thereof which may impair the treaty rights of the United States or its citizens in China, including those which relate to the sovereignty, the independence, or the territorial administrative integrity of the Republic of China, or to the international policy relative to China, commonly known as the open door policy; and that it does not intend to recognize any situation, treaty or agreement which may be brought about by means contrary to the covenants and obligations of the Pact of Paris of August 27, 1928, to which Treaty both China and Japan, as well as the United States, are parties.

2. President Franklin D. Roosevelt Proposes to "Quarantine" Aggressors, 1937

Some fifteen years ago the hopes of mankind for a continuing era of international peace were raised to great heights when more than sixty nations solemnly pledged themselves not to resort to arms in furtherance of their national aims and policies. The high aspirations expressed in the Briand-Kellogg Peace Pact and the hopes for peace thus raised have of late given way to a haunting fear of calamity. The present reign of terror and international lawlessness began a few years ago.

It began through unjustified interference in the internal affairs of other nations or the invasion of alien territory in violation of treaties; and has now reached a stage where the very foundations of civilization are seriously threatened. The landmarks

---

Document 1 can be found in U.S. Department of State, *Papers Relating to the Foreign Relations of the United States, Japan: 1931–1941* (Washington, D.C.: Government Printing Office, 1943), I, 76.

Document 2 can be found in U.S. Department of State, *Papers Relating to the Foreign Relations of the United States, Japan: 1931–1941* (Washington, D.C.: Government Printing Office, 1943), I, 379–383.

and traditions which have marked the progress of civilization toward a condition of law, order and justice are being wiped away.

Without a declaration of war and without warning or justification of any kind, civilians, including vast numbers of women and children, are being ruthlessly murdered with bombs from the air. In times of so-called peace, ships are being attacked and sunk by submarines without cause or notice. Nations are fomenting and taking sides in civil warfare in nations that have never done them any harm. Nations claiming freedom for themselves deny it to others.

Innocent peoples, innocent nations, are being cruelly sacrificed to a greed for power and supremacy which is devoid of all sense of justice and humane considerations. . . .

The peace-loving nations must make a concerted effort in opposition to those violations of treaties and those ignorings of humane instincts which today are creating a state of international anarchy and instability from which there is no escape through mere isolation or neutrality.

Those who cherish their freedom and recognize and respect the equal right of their neighbors to be free and live in peace must work together for the triumph of law and moral principles in order that peace, justice and confidence may prevail in the world. There must be a return to a belief in the pledged word, in the value of a signed treaty. There must be recognition of the fact that national morality is as vital as private morality. . . .

There is a solidarity and interdependence about the modern world, both technically and morally, which makes it impossible for any nation completely to isolate itself from economic and political upheavals in the rest of the world, especially when such upheavals appear to be spreading and not declining. There can be no stability or peace either within nations or between nations except under laws and moral standards adhered to by all. International anarchy destroys every foundation for peace. It jeopardizes either the immediate or the future security of every nation, large or small. It is, therefore, a matter of vital interest and concern to the people of the United States that the sanctity of international treaties and the maintenance of international morality be restored.

The overwhelming majority of the peoples and nations of the world today want to live in peace. They seek the removal of barriers against trade. They want to exert themselves in industry, in agriculture and in business, that they may increase their wealth through the production of wealth-producing goods rather than striving to produce military planes and bombs and machine guns and cannon for the destruction of human lives and useful property.

In those nations of the world which seem to be piling armament on armament for purposes of aggression, and those other nations which fear acts of aggression against them and their security, a very high proportion of their national income is being spent directly for armaments. It runs from thirty to as high as fifty percent. We are fortunate. The proportion that we in the United States spend is far less— eleven or twelve percent.

How happy we are that the circumstances of the moment permit us to put our money into bridges and boulevards, dams and reforestation, the conservation of our soil and many other kinds of useful works rather than into huge standing armies and vast supplies of implements of war.

I am compelled and you are compelled, nevertheless, to look ahead. The peace, the freedom and the security of ninety percent of the population of the world is being jeopardized by the remaining ten percent who are threatening a breakdown of all international order and law. Surely the ninety percent who want to live in peace under law and in accordance with moral standards that have received almost universal acceptance through the centuries, can and must find some way to make their will prevail.

The situation is definitely of universal concern. The questions involved relate not merely to violations of specific provisions of particular treaties; they are questions of war and of peace, of international law and especially of principles of humanity. It is true that they involve definite violations of agreements, and especially of the Covenant of the League of Nations, the Briand-Kellogg Pact and the Nine Power Treaty. But they also involve problems of world economy, world security and world humanity.

It is true that the moral consciousness of the world must recognize the importance of removing injustices and well-founded grievances; but at the same time it must be aroused to the cardinal necessity of honoring sanctity of treaties, of respecting the rights and liberties of others and of putting an end to acts of international aggression.

It seems to be unfortunately true that the epidemic of world lawlessness is spreading.

When an epidemic of physical disease starts to spread, the community approves and joins in a quarantine of the patients in order to protect the health of the community against the spread of the disease.

It is my determination to pursue a policy of peace. It is my determination to adopt every practicable measure to avoid involvement in war. It ought to be inconceivable that in this modern era, and in the face of experience, any nation could be so foolish and ruthless as to run the risk of plunging the whole world into war by invading and violating, in contravention of solemn treaties, the territory of other nations that have done them no real harm and are too weak to protect themselves adequately. Yet the peace of the world and the welfare and security of every nation, including our own, is today being threatened by that very thing.

3. Japan Envisions a "New Order" in Asia, 1938

What Japan seeks is the establishment of a new order which will insure the permanent stability of East Asia. In this lies the ultimate purpose of our present military campaign.

This new order has for its foundation a tripartite relationship of mutual aid and co-ordination between Japan, Manchoukuo [the name Japan gave to Manchuria in February 1932], and China in political, economic, cultural and other fields. Its object is to secure international justice, to perfect the joint defence against Communism, and to create a new culture and realize a close economic cohesion throughout

---

This document can be found in U.S. Department of State, *Papers Relating to the Foreign Relations of the United States, Japan: 1931–1941* (Washington, D.C.: Government Printing Office, 1943), I, 477–478.

East Asia. This indeed is the way to contribute toward the stabilization of East Asia and the progress of the world.

What Japan desires of China is that that country will share in the task of bringing about this new order in East Asia. She confidently expects that the people of China will fully comprehend her true intentions and that they will respond to the call of Japan for their co-operation. Even the participation of the Kuomintang Government would not be rejected, if, repudiating the policy which has guided it in the past and remolding its personnel, so as to translate its re-birth into fact, it were to come forward to join in the establishment of the new order.

Japan is confident that other Powers will on their part correctly appreciate her aims and policy and adapt their attitude to the new conditions prevailing in East Asia. For the cordiality hitherto manifested by the nations which are in sympathy with us, Japan wishes to express her profound gratitude.

The establishment of a new order in East Asia is in complete conformity with the very spirit in which the Empire was founded; to achieve such a task is the exalted responsibility with which our present generation is entrusted. It is, therefore, imperative to carry out all necessary internal reforms, and with a full development of the aggregate national strength, material as well as moral, fulfill at all costs this duty incumbent upon our nation.

Such the Government declare to be the immutable policy and determination of Japan.

4. Stanley K. Hornbeck Urges Economic Sanctions Against Japan, 1938

It is an important interest of the United States that Japan not gain control of China. It therefore would be to our interest that Chinese resistance to Japan's effort to gain that control continue. The Japanese nation today is animated by concepts and is pursuing objectives which are in conflict with the concepts and the legitimate objectives of the people of the United States. The Japanese are embarked upon a program of predatory imperialism. Unless the Japanese march is halted by the Chinese or by some other nation, the time will come when Japan and the United States will be face to face and definitely opposed to each other in the international political arena. It is desirable that the development of such a situation be prevented. It therefore is desirable that the United States act toward the preventing of such a development.

The American Government should formulate and adopt a program of action (a diplomatic "war plan") toward averting an armed conflict between the United States and Japan. In the conducting of our relations with Japan and with China we should not take haphazard and unrelated steps. Such action as we may take in the realm of use of words should be related to action which we may plan to take in the realm of material pressures (positive or negative, or both). It should be our objective to have Japan's predatory march halted. Our course of action should, therefore, be a course in opposition to that march. That march will be halted only by the power

---

This document can be found in U.S. Department of State, *Foreign Relations of the United States, 1938* (Washington, D.C.: Government Printing Office, 1954), III, 572–573.

of resistance of material obstacles and material pressures. Any nation which definitely opposes that march should be prepared in last analysis to use, if it prove necessary, armed force. The Chinese have already found resort to armed force necessary. China's resistance may possibly be overcome by Japanese armed force. Resistance which may be made by other countries may in the long run have to take the form of armed force. This country, therefore, in formulating its course of action should make it its business to be prepared if necessary to use armed force.

The American Government has during recent years been opposing Japan by use of words (appeal to principles, to rules of law, to provisions of treaties, etc.). Our Department of State may be able to get the better of the Japanese Foreign Office—though even that is not certain—in the field of argumentation, but victories on our part in that field will not halt the forward march of Japan's military machine. The fact is that unless the United States expects and intends to use weapons stronger than those of argument, continuance on our part along that line is almost certain to lead to the development of a situation in which this country will have either to accept a diplomatic defeat or find itself forced to resort to arms. The more we talk and the longer we refrain from resort to some substantial measures of positive (material) pressure toward preventing the Japanese from taking or destroying our rights, titles and interests in the Far East, the more likely will it be that resort by us to such measures at some future time—if and when—will be replied to by the Japanese with resort to armed force against us, which would, in turn, compel us to respond with armed force.

The most practicable course for us to follow would be that of giving assistance to the Chinese and withholding those things which are of assistance to the Japanese, toward prolonging and strengthening China's resistance and curtailing Japan's ability to continue military operations against China. If and when, however, we commit ourselves to that line of action, we should do so wholeheartedly and with determination. We should not take some one step without expecting, intending and being able to take further steps, many further steps, in the same direction. Such steps should include a combination of diplomatic, economic and potential military pressures. If this Government wishes to embark upon such a course, it should be prepared to consider seriously the taking of such steps as denunciation of the U.S.-Japan Commercial Treaty of 1911, repeal of the Neutrality Act, retaliatory tariff measures against Japan, placing of embargoes upon trade and shipping between Japan and the United States, [and] disposal of our naval resources in such manner as to indicate to the Japanese Government and nation that we "mean business."

5. Ambassador Joseph C. Grew Warns Against Economic Sanctions, 1939

The United States is solemnly (to use that somewhat overworked Wilsonian term) committed to uphold the principles of the Nine Power Treaty, primarily to uphold the territorial and administrative integrity of China and the Open Door. Therein lies the point of principle.

This document can be found in U.S. Department of State, *Foreign Relations of the United States, 1939* (Washington, D.C.: Government Printing Office, 1955), III, 605–607, 608, 609–611.

On the other side of the picture, nothing in international affairs can be more mathematically certain (if anything in international affairs is ever certain) than that Japan is not going to respect the territorial and administrative integrity of China, now or in future, has not the slightest intention of doing so and could be brought to do so only by complete defeat. Observance in practice of the Open Door is and will continue to be a matter of degree governed by expediency, not by principle. Herein lies the point of realism.

Given the situation now existing in Europe, there does not now appear on the horizon the possibility of such a defeat being inflicted by any nation or by any set of circumstances, military, social, economic or financial. . . .

Statisticians have proved to their own satisfaction, and will continue so to prove, that Japan can be defeated by economic pressure from without. But the statisticians generally fail to include psychological factors in their estimates. Japan is a nation of hardy warriors still inculcated with the samurai do-or-die spirit which has by tradition and inheritance become ingrained in the race. The Japanese throughout their history have faced periodic cataclysms brought about by nature and by man: earthquakes, hurricanes, floods, epidemics, the blighting of crops, and almost constant wars within and without the country. By long experience they are inured to hardships and they are inured to regimentation. Every former difficulty has been overcome. Estimates based on statistics alone may well mislead.

During the months since my return from the United States I have carefully and thoroughly studied opinion in Japan, including opinion in the Government, the army, the influential elements in civil life, the business world and the masses, and on one issue that opinion can definitely be said to be unanimous: the so-called "new order in East Asia" has come to stay. That term is open to wide interpretation, but the minimum conception of the term envisages permanent Japanese control of Manchuria, Inner Mongolia, and North China. In the army and among certain elements of the Government and the public the conception is very much broader; those elements would exert Japanese control throughout all of China, or as much of China as can now or in future be grasped and held, including the treaty ports and the international settlements and concessions. . . .

To await the hoped-for discrediting in Japan of the Japanese army and the Japanese military system is to await the millenium. The Japanese army is no protuberance like the tail of a dog which might be cut off to prevent the tail from wagging the dog: it is inextricably bound up with the fabric of the entire nation; its ramifications are far too deep for any effective amputation, or any effective withering through discredit. Certainly there are plenty of Japanese who dislike the army's methods; there is plenty of restiveness at the wholesale impressment of the able-bodied young men to fight in China, of the death and crippling of many, and of the restrictions and handicaps in every-day life entailed by the expenses of the campaign. But that the army can be discredited in the eyes of the people to a degree where its power and prestige will become so effectively undermined as to deprive the army of its control or at least of its preponderant influence in shaping national policy is an hypothesis which I believe no one intimately conversant with Japan and the Japanese would for a moment entertain. . . .

So here we find ourselves squarely faced with a problem which, from all present indications, is to be permanently with us: the problem of principle versus realism. What are we going to do about it? . . .

One course envisages complete intransigence. Unless and until Japan reorientates her policy and actions, both as regards her commitments under the Nine Power Treaty (until modified by orderly processes) and her respect of American rights and interests in China, we would refuse to negotiate a new treaty of commerce and navigation and would, if public demand in the United States calls for it, impose an embargo next winter.

This course would set Japanese-American relations moving on a downward slope to a point from which it would be difficult to bring them back to normal for a long time to come; a treatyless situation, with its attending handicaps to Japanese trade, would start the movement; the imposition of an embargo would greatly accelerate it.

The other course, after endeavoring to consider the situation and outlook from all angles, I believe is in our own interests now and, so far as we can foresee the future, the wiser one to follow. We would say to Japan: "The United States concedes no right and recognizes no compromise with respect to the provisions and principles of the Nine Power Treaty. We, however, desire so far as feasible to maintain good relations with Japan. We await progressive implementation of your assurances that American rights and interests in China will be respected, not only in negative ways, such as cessation of the bombings of American property, indignities to American citizens and the more flagrant interferences with American business and trade, but also in positive ways through the presentation progressively of concrete evidence that American commercial, cultural and other rights and interests are not to be crowded out of China by Japanese measures as hitherto has appeared patently to be intentional. As soon as some definite start is made in presenting concrete evidence to the foregoing effect, we, for our part, with a view to facilitating the efforts of the Government in Tokyo to further such a program, will enter into negotiations for a new treaty of commerce and navigation and concurrently for a *modus vivendi* of limited duration to tide over a treatyless situation, it being clearly understood that the ratification of such a treaty will depend upon future developments, namely, the progressive implementation of such a program. In the meantime, also depending upon developments, we will endeavor to hold in abeyance the question of imposing an embargo against Japan. . . .

. . . A treatyless situation plus an embargo would exasperate the Japanese to a point where anything could happen, even serious incidents which could inflame the American people beyond endurance and which might call for war. The Japanese are so constituted and are just now in such a mood and temper that sanctions, far from intimidating, would almost certainly bring retaliation which, in turn, would lead to counterretaliation. Japan would not stop to weigh ultimate consequences. It would be all very well to say that Japan had brought our action on her own head, that the United States can get along without Japanese friendship and that the dignity and power of the United States cannot tolerate compromise, but such an attitude would be lacking in any constructive element. I think that our dignity and our power in themselves counsel moderation, forbearance and the use of every reasonable means of conciliation without the sacrifice of principle. . . .

It is axiomatic to say that good relations between the United States and Japan are in our own interests. No purely altruistic motives are involved. In our own interests, particularly our commercial and cultural interests, we should approach this problem from a realistic and constructive standpoint. Not only on Japan's future action but on our own future action too will depend the question whether our relations with Japan are susceptible of improvement or whether they are to go straight down hill. There is no use whatever in quibbling about this, no use in refusing to face facts. The bombings of our property, the personal indignities and interferences, and some of the more flagrant violations of our commercial rights can be stemmed, but unless we are prepared to fight for it, the Open Door, as we conceive it, is not going to be kept open. We have the choice of losing everything or of saving something from the wreckage, while opening the way to a potential building up of our relations with Japan.

6. Japanese Proposals to the United States, November 1941

Plan A

The most important pending matters in negotiations between Japan and the United States are: 1) the stationing and withdrawal of troops in China and French Indochina; 2) nondiscriminatory trade in China; 3) interpretation and observance of the Tripartite Pact; and 4) the Four Principles [see Document 7]. These matters are to be moderated to the following extent:

1) The stationing and withdrawal of troops in China.

Setting aside for the moment our reasons for stationing troops, we shall moderate our stance to the following extent, considering that the United States has (a) attached great importance to the stationing of troops for an indeterminate period of time, (b) objected to the inclusion of this item in the terms for a peace settlement, and (c) called for a clearer expression of intent regarding the withdrawal of troops:

> Japanese forces dispatched to China because of the China Incident shall occupy designated areas of north China and Mongolia and Hainan island for as long as is necessary after peace is concluded between Japan and China. The evacuation of other forces shall commence the minute peace is concluded, in accordance with separate arrangements made between Japan and China, and shall be completed within two years.
>
> Note: Should the United States ask what "for as long as is necessary" means, we shall reply to the effect that our goal is roughly 25 years.

2) The stationing and withdrawal of troops in French Indochina.

The United States entertains misgivings that Japan has territorial ambitions in French Indochina and is attempting to make it into a base for military advances

Reprinted from *Japan's Decision for War: Records of the 1941 Policy Conferences,* Edited and Translated by Nobutaka Ike with the permission of the publishers, Stanford University Press. © 1967 by the Board of Trustees of the Leland Stanford Junior University.

into adjacent territories. In recognition of this, we shall moderate our stance to the following extent:

> The Japanese government respects the territorial sovereignty of French Indochina. Japanese troops currently dispatched to French Indochina will be immediately evacuated upon the settlement of the China Incident or upon the establishment of a just peace in the Far East.

3) Nondiscriminatory treatment in trade with China.

In the event that there is no prospect of securing complete agreement to our previous proposal of September 25, we shall deal with this issue on the basis of the following proposal:

> The Japanese government acknowledges that the principle of nondiscrimination will be applied in the entire Pacific region and China as well, insofar as that principle is applied throughout the world.

4) Interpretation and observance of the Tripartite Pact.

We shall respond on this matter by making it even clearer that we have no intention of unduly broadening our interpretation of the right of self defense; that as far as interpreting and observing the Tripartite Pact is concerned, the Japanese government will act on its own discretion, as we have frequently elaborated before; and that we think that the United States already understands this fully.

5) As for what the United States calls its four principles, we shall avoid with all our might their inclusion in anything formally agreed to between Japan and the United States (whether that be the Draft Understanding or other declarations).

Plan B

1) Both Japan and the United States shall promise not to make any advances by military force into Southeast Asia and the South Pacific region, other than French Indochina.

2) The governments of Japan and the United States shall cooperate together so as to guarantee the procurement of necessary resources from the Dutch East Indies.

3) The governments of Japan and the United States shall together restore trade relations to what they were prior to the freezing of assets, and the United States will promise to supply Japan with the petroleum it needs.

4) The United States government shall not engage in such actions as may hinder efforts toward peace by Japan and China

Notes

1) If it is necessary to do so, there is no objection to promising that if the present agreement is concluded, Japanese forces now stationed in southern Indochina are prepared, with the approval of the French government, to transfer to northern French Indochina, and that these Japanese forces will withdraw from French Indochina upon settlement of the China Incident or the establishment of a just peace in the Pacific region.

2) If it is also necessary to do so, additional insertions may be made to the provisions regarding nondiscriminatory treatment in trade and those regarding interpretation and observance of the Tripartite Pact in the existing proposals (last plans).

7. American Proposals to Japan, November 1941

Section I   Draft Mutual Declaration of Policy

The Government of the United States and the Government of Japan both being solicitous for the peace of the Pacific affirm that their national policies are directed toward lasting and extensive peace throughout the Pacific area, that they have no territorial designs in that area, that they have no intention of threatening other countries or of using military force aggressively against any neighboring nation, and that, accordingly, in their national policies they will actively support and give practical application to the following fundamental principles upon which their relations with each other and with all other governments are based:

1. The principle of inviolability of territorial integrity and sovereignty of each and all nations.
2. The principle of non-interference in the internal affairs of other countries.
3. The principle of equality, including equality of commercial opportunity and treatment.
4. The principle of reliance upon international cooperation and conciliation for the prevention and pacific settlement of controversies and for improvement of international conditions by peaceful methods and processes.

The Government of Japan and the Government of the United States have agreed that toward eliminating chronic political instability, preventing recurrent economic collapse, and providing a basis for peace, they will actively support and practically apply the following principles in their economic relations with each other and with other nations and peoples:

1. The principle of non-discrimination in international commercial relations.
2. The principle of international economic cooperation and abolition of extreme nationalism as expressed in excessive trade restrictions.
3. The principle of non-discriminatory access by all nations to raw material supplies.
4. The principle of full protection of the interests of consuming countries and populations as regards the operation of international commodity agreements.
5. The principle of establishment of such institutions and arrangements of international finance as may lend aid to the essential enterprises and the continuous development of all countries and may permit payments through processes of trade consonant with the welfare of all countries.

This document can be found in U.S. Department of State, *Papers Relating to the Foreign Relations of the United States, Japan: 1931–1941* (Washington, D.C.: Government Printing Office, 1943), II, 768–769.

Section II   Steps to Be Taken by the Government of the United States and by the Government of Japan

The Government of the United States and the Government of Japan propose to take steps as follows:

1. The Government of the United States and the Government of Japan will endeavor to conclude a multilateral non-aggression pact among the British Empire, China, Japan, the Netherlands, the Soviet Union, Thailand and the United States.
2. Both Governments will endeavor to conclude among the American, British, Chinese, Japanese, the Netherland and Thai Governments an agreement whereunder each of the Governments would pledge itself to respect the territorial integrity of French Indochina and, in the event that there should develop a threat to the territorial integrity of Indochina, to enter into immediate consultation with a view to taking such measures as may be deemed necessary and advisable to meet the threat in question. Such agreement would provide also that each of the Governments party to the agreement would not seek or accept preferential treatment in its trade or economic relations with Indochina and would use its influence to obtain for each of the signatories equality of treatment in trade and commerce with French Indochina.
3. The Government of Japan will withdraw all military, naval, air and police forces from China and from Indochina.
4. The Government of the United States and the Government of Japan will not support—militarily, politically, economically—any government or regime in China other than the National Government of the Republic of China with capital temporarily at Chungking.
5. Both Governments will give up all extraterritorial rights in China, including rights and interests in and with regard to international settlements and concessions, and rights under the Boxer Protocol of 1901.

   Both Governments will endeavor to obtain the agreement of the British and other governments to give up extraterritorial rights in China, including rights in international settlements and in concessions and under the Boxer Protocol of 1901.
6. The Government of the United States and the Government of Japan will enter into negotiations for the conclusion between the United States and Japan of a trade agreement, based upon reciprocal most-favored-nation treatment and reduction of trade barriers by both countries, including an undertaking by the United States to bind raw silk on the free list.
7. The Government of the United States and the Government of Japan will, respectively, remove the freezing restrictions on Japanese funds in the United States and on American funds in Japan.
8. Both Governments will agree upon a plan for the stabilization of the dollar-yen rate, with the allocation of funds adequate for this purpose, half to be supplied by Japan and half by the United States.
9. Both Governments will agree that no agreement which either has concluded with any third power or powers shall be interpreted by it in such a way as to conflict with the fundamental purpose of this agreement, the establishment and preservation of peace throughout the Pacific area.

10. Both Governments will use their influence to cause other governments to adhere to and to give practical application to the basic political and economic
principles set forth in this agreement.

8. The Japanese Position, Presented
on December 7, 1941

Ever since the China Affair broke out owing to the failure on the part of China to
comprehend Japan's true intentions, the Japanese Government has striven for the
restoration of peace and it has consistently exerted its best efforts to prevent the extension of war-like disturbances. It was also to that end that in September last year
Japan concluded the Tripartite Pact with Germany and Italy.

However, both the United States and Great Britain have resorted to every possible measure to assist the Chungking regime so as to obstruct the establishment
of a general peace between Japan and China, interfering with Japan's constructive
endeavors toward the stabilization of East Asia. Exerting pressure on the Netherlands East Indies, or menacing French Indo-China, they have attempted to frustrate Japan's aspiration to the ideal of common prosperity in cooperation with
these regions. Furthermore, when Japan in accordance with its protocol with
France took measures of joint defence of French Indo-China, both American and
British Governments willfully misinterpreting it as a threat to their own possessions, and inducing the Netherlands Government to follow suit, they enforced the
assets freezing order, thus severing economic relations with Japan. While mani-
festing thus an obviously hostile attitude, these countries have strengthened their
military preparations perfecting an encirclement of Japan, and have brought about
a situation which endangers the very existence of the Empire. . . .

From the beginning of the present negotiation the Japanese Government has always maintained an attitude of fairness and moderation, and did its best to reach a
settlement, for which it made all possible concessions often in spite of great
difficulties. As for the China question which constituted an important subject of the
negotiation, the Japanese Government showed a most conciliatory attitude. As for
the principle of non-discrimination in international commerce, advocated by the
American Government, the Japanese Government expressed its desire to see the
said principle applied throughout the world, and declared that along with the actual
practice of this principle in the world, the Japanese Government would endeavor to
apply the same in the Pacific Area including China, and made it clear that Japan had
no intention of excluding from China economic activities of third powers pursued
on an equitable basis. Furthermore, as regards the question of withdrawing troops
from French Indo-China, the Japanese Government even volunteered, as mentioned
above, to carry out an immediate evacuation of troops from Southern French Indo-
China as a measure of easing the situation.

It is presumed that the spirit of conciliation exhibited to the utmost degree by
the Japanese Government in all these matters is fully appreciated by the American
Government.

This document can be found in *Department of State Bulletin,* V (December 13, 1941), 466–470.

On the other hand, the American Government, always holding fast to theories in disregard of realities, and refusing to yield an inch on its impractical principles, caused undue delay in the negotiation. It is difficult to understand this attitude of the American Government and the Japanese Government desires to call the attention of the American Government especially to the following points:

1. The American Government advocates in the name of world peace those principles favorable to it and urges upon the Japanese Government the acceptance thereof. The peace of the world may be brought about only by discovering a mutually acceptable formula through recognition of the reality of the situation and mutual appreciation of one another's position. An attitude such as ignores realities and imposes one's selfish views upon others will scarcely serve the purpose of facilitating the consummation of negotiations.

   Of the various principles put forward by the American Government as a basis of the Japanese-American Agreement, there are some which the Japanese Government is ready to accept in principle, but in view of the world's actual conditions, it seems only a utopian ideal on the part of the American Government to attempt to force their immediate adoption.

   Again, the proposal to conclude a multilateral non-aggression pact between Japan, United States, Great Britain, China, the Soviet Union, the Netherlands and Thailand, which is patterned after the old concept of collective security, is far removed from the realities of East Asia.

2. The American proposal contained a stipulation which states—"Both Governments will agree that no agreement, which either has concluded with any third power or powers, shall be interpreted by it in such a way as to conflict with the fundamental purpose of this agreement, the establishment and preservation of peace throughout the Pacific area." It is presumed that the above provision has been proposed with a view to restrain Japan from fulfilling its obligations under the Tripartite Pact when the United States participates in the War in Europe, and, as such, it cannot be accepted by the Japanese Government.

   The American Government, obsessed with its own views and opinions, may be said to be scheming for the extension of the war. While it seeks, on the one hand, to secure its rear by stabilizing the Pacific Area, it is engaged, on the other hand, in aiding Great Britain and preparing to attack, in the name of self-defense, Germany and Italy, two Powers that are striving to establish a new order in Europe. Such a policy is totally at variance with the many principles upon which the American Government proposes to found the stability of the Pacific Area through peaceful means.

3. Whereas the American Government, under the principles it rigidly upholds, objects to settle international issues through military pressure, it is exercising in conjunction with Great Britain and other nations pressure by economic power. Recourse to such pressure as a means of dealing with international relations should be condemned as it is at times more inhumane than military pressure.

4. It is impossible not to reach the conclusion that the American Government desires to maintain and strengthen, in coalition with Great Britain and other Powers, its dominant position it has hitherto occupied not only in China but in other areas of East Asia. It is a fact of history that the countries of East Asia for the past hundred years or more have been compelled to observe the *status quo* under the

Anglo-American policy of imperialistic exploitation and to sacrifice themselves to the prosperity of the two nations. The Japanese Government cannot tolerate the perpetuation of such a situation since it directly runs counter to Japan's fundamental policy to enable all nations to enjoy each its proper place in the world.

The stipulation proposed by the American Government relative to French Indo-China is a good exemplification of the above-mentioned American policy. Thus six countries,—Japan, the United States, Great Britain, the Netherlands, China and Thailand,—excepting France, should undertake among themselves to respect the territorial integrity and sovereignty of French Indo-China and equality of treatment in trade and commerce would be tantamount to placing the territory under the joint guarantee of the Governments of those six countries. Apart from the fact that such a proposal totally ignores the position of France, it is unacceptable to the Japanese Government in that such an arrangement cannot be considered as an extension to French Indo-China of a system similar to the Nine Power Treaty structure which is the chief factor responsible for the present predicament of East Asia.

5. All the items demanded of Japan by the American Government regarding China such as wholesale evacuation of troops or unconditional application of the principle of non-discrimination in international commerce ignored the actual conditions of China, and are calculated to destroy Japan's position as the stabilizing factor of East Asia. The attitude of the American Government in demanding Japan not to support militarily, politically or economically any regime other than the regime at Chungking, disregarding thereby the existence of the Nanking Government, shatters the very basis of the present negotiation. This demand of the American Government falling, as it does, in line with its above-mentioned refusal to cease from aiding the Chungking regime, demonstrates clearly the intention of the American Government to obstruct the restoration of normal relations between Japan and China and the return of peace to East Asia.

In brief, the American proposal contains certain acceptable items such as those concerning commerce, including the conclusion of a trade agreement, mutual removal of the freezing restrictions and stabilization of yen and dollar exchange, or the abolition of extra-territorial rights in China. On the other hand, however, the proposal in question ignores Japan's sacrifices in the four years of the China Affair, menaces the Empire's existence itself and disparages its honour and prestige. Therefore, viewed in its entirety, the Japanese Government regrets that it cannot accept the proposal as a basis of negotiations.

9. Roosevelt's War Message, 1941

Yesterday, December 7, 1941—a date which will live in infamy—the United States of America was suddenly and deliberately attacked by naval and air forces of the Empire of Japan.

The United States was at peace with that Nation and, at the solicitation of Japan, was still in conversation with its Government and its Emperor looking toward the

This document can be found in U.S. Department of State, *Papers Relating to the Foreign Relations of the United States, Japan: 1931–1941* (Washington, D.C.: Government Printing Office, 1943), II, 793–794.

maintenance of peace in the Pacific. Indeed, one hour after Japanese air squadrons had commenced bombing in Oahu, the Japanese Ambassador to the United States and his colleague delivered to the Secretary of State a formal reply to a recent American message. While this reply stated that it seemed useless to continue the existing diplomatic negotiations, it contained no threat or hint of war or armed attack.

It will be recorded that the distance of Hawaii from Japan makes it obvious that the attack was deliberately planned many days or even weeks ago. During the intervening time the Japanese Government has deliberately sought to deceive the United States by false statements and expressions of hope for continued peace.

The attack yesterday on the Hawaiian Islands has caused severe damage to American naval and military forces. Very many American lives have been lost. In addition American ships have been reported torpedoed on the high seas between San Francisco and Honolulu.

Yesterday the Japanese Government also launched an attack against Malaya.

Last night Japanese forces attacked Hong Kong.

Last night Japanese forces attacked Guam.

Last night Japanese forces attacked the Philippine Islands.

Last night the Japanese attacked Wake Island.

This morning the Japanese attacked Midway Island.

Japan has, therefore, undertaken a surprise offensive extending throughout the Pacific area. The facts of yesterday speak for themselves. The people of the United States have already formed their opinions and well understand the implications to the very life and safety of our Nation.

As Commander-in-Chief of the Army and Navy I have directed that all measures be taken for our defense.

Always will we remember the character of the onslaught against us.

No matter how long it may take us to overcome this premeditated invasion, the American people in their righteous might will win through to absolute victory.

I believe I interpret the will of the Congress and of the people when I assert that we will not only defend ourselves to the uttermost but will make very certain that this form of treachery shall never endanger us again.

Hostilities exist. There is no blinking at the fact that our people, our territory, and our interests are in grave danger.

With confidence in our armed forces—with the unbounded determination of our people—we will gain the inevitable triumph—so help us God.

I ask that the Congress declare that since the unprovoked and dastardly attack by Japan on Sunday, December seventh, a state of war has existed between the United States and the Japanese Empire.

✪ E S S A Y S

In the first essay, Akira Iriye of Harvard University places the origins of the Pacific war in the context of the global crisis of the 1930s. Economic chaos and militant nationalism put Japan on an expansionist course that challenged the structure or "system" of international relations established at the Washington Conference in 1921–1922. Iriye suggests that, although President Roosevelt sought to delay war with Japan, he ultimately had little choice but to join the international community to block aggression. Depicting Japan as relentlessly expansionistic, Iriye emphasizes the role of uncompromising military leaders who launched a poorly conceived and unwinnable war rather than submit to other powers' pressure. In the second essay, Hosoya Chihiro of the International University of Japan holds Roosevelt's hardline advisers responsible for provoking the Pacific war. Stanley K. Hornbeck and other hardliners, Hosoya argues, miscalculated badly in believing that economic sanctions would deter Japan. As Ambassador Joseph C. Grew had predicted, these restrictive measures simply emboldened the hardliners in the Tokyo government to initiate a war that could have been avoided. Hornbeck misread Japanese psychology, concluding quite wrongly that the Japanese would never dare to attack the United States. In the last essay in this chapter, Waldo Heinrichs, formerly of San Diego State University, seeks to understand why, in mid-1941, at a time when U.S. strategy emphasized defeating Germany in Europe, the Roosevelt administration took hardline steps that intensified Japanese-U.S. hostility and set both nations on a war path. Heinrichs introduces the "Russian factor." That is, eager to keep a struggling and occupied Soviet Russia in the war against Hitler's Germany, Roosevelt chose policies calculated to influence Japanese leaders, should they decide for war, to move southward rather than northward into the Soviet Union.

Clash of Systems: The International Community Confronts Japanese Aggression

AKIRA IRIYE

On 18 September 1931, a small number of Japanese and Chinese soldiers clashed outside of Fengtien (Mukden) in southern Manchuria—an event which soon developed into what was to be a long, drawn-out, intermittent war between China and Japan. Over ten years later, on 7 December 1941, Japanese air, naval, and land forces attacked American, British, and Dutch possessions throughout Asia and the Pacific. It marked the beginning of Japan's war against the combined forces of China, America, Britain, the Netherlands and, ultimately, France and the Soviet Union. . . .

Japan had not always been an international loner. On the contrary, the country's leadership and national opinion had emphasized the cardinal importance of establishing Japan as a respected member of the community of advanced powers. And in the 1920s it had enjoyed such a status. The treaties it signed during the Washington Conference (1921–22) symbolized it. In one—the naval disarmament treaty—Japan was recognized as one of the three foremost powers; together with the United States and Britain, the nation would seek to maintain an arms equilibrium in the world and contribute to stabilizing the Asian-Pacific region. Another treaty, signed by these three plus France, provided for a mechanism whereby they would consult with one another whenever the stability was threatened. Most important, the nine-power treaty (signed by Japan, the United States, Britain, France, Italy, Belgium, the Netherlands, Portugal, and China) established the principle of international co-operation in China. Eight signatories were to co-operate with respect to the ninth, China, to uphold the latter's independence and integrity, maintain the principle of equal opportunity, and to provide an environment for the development of a stable government. Japan was a full-fledged member of the new treaty regime, which historians have called the Washington Conference system. Since much of the story of the 1930s revolves around Japan's challenge to these treaties, it is well at the outset to examine what was involved in the regime.

The term "the Washington Conference system," or "the Washington system" for short, was not in current use in the 1920s, nor was it subsequently recognized as a well-defined legal concept. None the less, immediately after the conference there was much talk of "the spirit of the Washington Conference," and a country's behaviour in Asia tended to be judged in terms of whether it furthered or undermined that spirit. As such it connoted more a state of mind than an explicit mechanism; it expressed the powers' willingness to co-operate with one another in maintaining stability in the region and assisting China's gradual transformation as a modern state. It was viewed as an alternative to their unilateral policies or exclusive alliances and *ententes* aimed at particularistic objectives. Instead, the Washington system indicated a concept of multinational consultation and co-operation in the interest of regional stability. By the same token, this spirit was essentially gradualist and reformist, not radical or revolutionary. It was opposed to a rapid and wholesale transformation of Asian international relations, such as was being advocated by the Communist International and by an increasing number of Chinese nationalists. Rather, the Washington powers would stress an evolutionary process of change so as to ensure peace, order, and stability. . . .

Moreover, there was an economic system that underlay the structure. All the Washington signatories were linked to one another through their acceptance of the gold standard. More precisely called "the gold exchange standard," the mechanism called upon nations to accept gold as the medium of international economic transactions, to link their currencies to gold, and to maintain the principle of currency convertibility. Through such devices, it was believed that commercial activities across national boundaries would be carried out smoothly for the benefit of all. . . .

Till the late 1920s, the system worked by and large to bring order and stability to the Asian-Pacific region. There were few overtly unilateral acts by a Washington signatory, and the powers continued their mutual consultation as they sought to revise the old treaties with China. The latter, on its part, had come steadily to seek to realize its aspirations in co-operation with, rather than defiance of, the Washington powers. To be sure, Chinese Nationalists were initially adamantly opposed to the Washington Conference treaties, viewing them as a device for perpetuating foreign control. However, with their military and political successes, they emerged as the new leaders of the country, and with them there came a willingness to modify some of the radical rhetoric. After 1928, when they established a central government in Nanking under Chiang Kai-shek, they had to concentrate on domestic unification and economic development, tasks which necessitated foreign capital and technology, as well as a respite in international crises that would drain resources away from much-needed projects at home. . . .

The United States, Britain, Japan and others one by one recognized the Nanking regime, signed new treaties for tariff revision, and began negotiations for an ultimate abrogation of extra-territoriality, the traditional symbol of China's second-class status. Although these negotiations dragged on, by 1931 differences between China and the powers had narrowed considerably, so that a full restoration of jurisdictional authority to Chinese courts seemed to be a matter of time. It was at that juncture that the Japanese army struck, not only to oppose further concessions to Chinese nationalism, but ultimately to redefine the international system itself. . . .

The precise timing for [the Japanese] action was a matter of some deliberation. But in many ways the year 1931 appeared the right moment. For one thing, the government's commitment to the existing international order had begun to encounter widespread domestic opposition. In 1930 Japan under the cabinet of Hamaguchi Osachi had signed a new naval disarmament treaty in London. The treaty covered "auxiliary craft" such as light cruisers and submarines which had been excluded from the provisions of the Washington naval treaty, and limited the total sizes of these ships that Japan, Britain, and the United States were allowed to possess. The new treaty established the allowable tonnages in the ratio of 6.975 for Japan and 10 for the other two. This was a higher ratio for Japan than the 6 to 10 formula for capital ships adopted by the Washington treaty, but it split the Japanese navy. Those who supported the government's acceptance of the new ratio (the "treaty faction") confronted the adamant opposition of the "fleet faction," determined to wage a public campaign against the treaty. The latter made it a constitutional issue, accusing the civilian government of having violated the emperor's "right of supreme command," according to which the military presumably had direct access to the emperor as his advisers on command problems. Although no such case had been made after the Washington Conference, now the naval activists believed the public would be more receptive to this type of argument.

They judged the public mood and political climate of the country quite accurately. In 1925 Japan had instituted a universal manhood suffrage, and the political parties had become sensitive to changing moods and diverse interests of the population. Although the bulk of the newly enfranchised public may have understood or cared little for international affairs, it appears that it paid attention to and was fascinated by the kind of argument put forth by the navy's anti-government minority and its sympathizers. This receptivity reflected the economic situation, for the coming of the age of mass politics coincided with the world economic crisis that began with the Wall Street crash of October 1929. . . .

Such background explains the timing of 1931, why that year must have seemed particularly auspicious for those who had chafed under what they considered undue constraints of foreign policy and domestic politics over a legitimate assertion of national rights. A group of Kwantung Army officers, led by Ishiwara Kanji and Itagaki Seishirō, judged that the moment was ripe for bold action. Unless it were taken, they feared that the powers would continue to give in to China's demands, and Japan's position become more and more untenable. The thing to do, they reasoned, was not to seek to preserve Japanese interests within the existing system of co-operation with the Western powers, but to act unilaterally and entrench Japanese power once and for all in Manchuria. . . .

The League [of Nations] invoked the 1928 [Kellogg-Briand] pact to denounce Japan's violation of its spirit. . . . China was now clearly a victim of lawlessness, and by the same token a champion of international law and order, whereas Japan was put in the position of having to defend aggressive military action. For the first time, the United States became actively involved by sending Consul-General Prentis Gilbert to attend the Council meetings. It was symbolic that America was thus identifying itself with the League and what it stood for, thus explicitly joining China's new cause. The result was a Council resolution, with Japan alone opposing, to call on the Japanese army to return to the position it had held prior to 18 September. . . .

This did not mean, however, that there was an anti-Japanese coalition forming in the world that would support China's struggle against Japan. This remained the goal of Chinese leaders. . . .

Despite such hopes, the powers would not go beyond criticizing Japan. . . . Both Washington and London were satisfied with these steps, somehow hoping that ultimately the Japanese would see the light and mend their ways. In the meantime, neither the United States nor Britain was prepared to employ anti-Japanese sanctions to help China. . . .

The outbreak of war between China and Japan in July 1937 [also] came at a critical moment in the orientation of Japanese policy. For some months civilian officials and military leaders had been divided between those who wanted to return to some modified version of the Washington system and those who preferred to push for an alternative—albeit loosely defined—order of Asian-Pacific affairs. Chinese-Japanese skirmishes outside of Peking on 7 July added fuel to the debate, and the internal discord continued until the government decided on seeking a "new order in East Asia" by expanding the hostilities. Such action compelled other countries to take a stand, to redefine once again their respective positions not only towards the war but towards the whole issue of Asian-Pacific order. . . .

When, on 6 October [1937], the [League of Nations] Assembly denounced Japan and called for a nine-power conference, the Roosevelt administration quickly concurred, joining in the condemnation of Japan's violation of the peace and of Chinese independence. Moreover, on just the preceding day, Roosevelt had delivered an important speech in Chicago—the "quarantine address"—indicating America's interest in acting together with other countries to "quarantine" those that were "creating a state of international anarchy and instability." He did not specify which these countries were, but it was clear to his listeners at home and abroad that he had in mind Germany, Italy, and Japan. (He had privately branded them "bandit nations," in view of what Germany had done in Spain, Italy in Ethiopia, and Japan in China.) Although vague, it was not difficult to see the implications of the speech. The United States, after several years of relative passivity and lack of interest in identifying with an international structure, was once again showing signs of willingness to act together with other nations to "preserve peace.". . .

That neither London nor Washington was much interested in an Asian Munich, in the wake of the fateful conference, suggests several underlying assumptions on their part. First, the Western governments may have considered chances for an Asian appeasement much more problematical than one in Europe. Second, related to this must have been a tacit assumption that China was not quite the same thing as Austria or Czechoslovakia. Japan could not have used the German argument for a racial *Anschluss*. Japanese military action was much more of a transparent aggression. Third, at the same time, the democracies may have believed that the Asian war was less likely to develop into a world war than the European crisis brought about by Hitler's revanchism. Fourth, they may have reasoned that the Soviet Union would be more successful in checking Japanese than German expansionism, and therefore that an appeasement strategy in Asia would have to involve it as a principal actor; but the latter had not abandoned its popular front policy and would have vehemently opposed any appeasement of Fascist nations at that time. In fact, Munich impressed [Marshal Joseph] Stalin as an attempt by the West to mollify Germany, which had the effect of weakening their resolve to stand firm towards Hitler. The Soviet leader would in time respond to this turn of events by approaching Hitler himself for an understanding. But this was in the future, and for the moment the Soviet Union's adamant opposition to an international settlement in Europe made it certain that it would likewise object to an Asian Munich.

A combination of all these factors resulted in the West's lack of initiative to appease Japan in late 1938. But one should also add another significant difference between Europe and Asia. The United States was more prepared to be involved in the latter region. Opinion polls indicated that the American people were far more willing to take a stand on the Chinese-Japanese War than on any European issue at that time. With an overwhelming majority (consistently three-quarters or more of those polled) expressing their sympathy for China, the Roosevelt administration, even if it had wanted to, would have found it virtually impossible to approach Japan for some kind of agreement, unless it included the latter's withdrawal from China, an unrealistic goal. Moreover, the public was becoming alarmed over the fact, which newspapers and magazines began stressing, that American trade with Japan, especially export of arms, was growing. An inference could readily be drawn that the United States was supplying Japan with munitions which the latter used to fight against China. Japan's dependence on American scrap iron and steel was particularly noticeable, and these items could easily be pictured as being turned into tanks and aircraft for use in China. This was an appalling revelation, and a movement to stop shipments of raw materials and arms to Japan began to be organized throughout the United States. . . .

On 3 November [1937], Prime Minister [Fumimaro] Konoe issued a public statement, defining the basic national objective as the construction of "a new order for ensuring permanent stability in East Asia." This, the statement asserted, was the joint goal of Japan, Manchukuo, and China; all three must co-operate politically, economically, and culturally so as to "establish international justice, carry out a common defence against communism, create a new culture, and bring about an economic combination" in East Asia. . . .

In other words, the treaties and principles cited by the United States government were no longer valid and would not be accepted as such by the Japanese. One could date Japan's formal rejection of the Washington system from this point. The Konoe statement . . . showed that Japan, after long hesitation, finally crossed the bridge of no return. Although . . . Japanese officials would later equivocate and even try to conciliate Americans by speaking of their co-operation in Asia and the Pacific, as far as Washington was concerned an irrevocable decision had been made by the Japanese leadership, and no reconciliation could now be effected unless these statements were explicitly repudiated. . . .

It was around this time that some key officials in Washington began contemplating specific measures to sanction Japan. Rather than vaguely formulated contingency plans for naval action which Roosevelt had favoured, these officials were thinking of economic pressure. They were particularly interested in two ideas: the abrogation of the existing treaty of commerce with Japan, and the offer of loans to

China. The first began to be urged by some officials as an effective way of sanctioning Japan. The 1911 treaty of commerce and navigation had regulated trade between the two countries, and to abrogate it would mean depriving the trade of American legal protection. It would place Japanese import from and export to the United States at the mercy of the latter. This would be a drastic but necessary step, according to its advocates, now that the Japanese had explicitly repudiated the Washington treaties. The second suggestion was less dramatic: the United States might offer China loans so as to enable it to keep resisting Japan. Secretary of the Treasury Henry Morgenthau emerged as the spokesman for this alternative, pleading with Roosevelt for an initial $25 million loan to China. The "future of democracy, the future of civilization," he declared, "are at stake." Supporting Morgenthau, Stanley K. Hornbeck, adviser to Secretary of State [Cordell] Hull on Asian affairs, argued, "Unless the Japanese march is halted by the Chinese or by some other nation, the time will come when Japan and the United States will be face to face and definitely opposed to each other in the international political arena." Such a perception was shared by an increasing number of officials in Washington. But they disagreed among themselves as to specific action America should now take. Hull thought all these proposals were premature and would unnecessarily irritate Japan, but Roosevelt at least approved the loan scheme, and thus the first of what would amount to billions of dollars of credit was offered to the Chinese at the end of the year. . . .

On 26 July [1939], Washington notified Japan that it intended to abrogate the 1911 treaty of commerce and navigation between the two countries. According to the terms of the treaty, abrogation would take effect in six months after notification, namely January 1940. . . .

By August 1939, then, Japan's international position had seriously deteriorated. It was becoming more and more difficult to avoid complications with third powers while the nation tried to conclude the war with China, and the attempt to take advantage of the European situation for enhancing Japanese power in Asia was not working. In the growingly desperate situation, some in Tokyo, notably War Minister Itagaki [Seishirō], strongly argued that the best way out of the impasse was to conclude an alliance with Germany as quickly as possible, even accepting the latter's terms. Japan would then at least have one reliable ally, whereas otherwise it would be totally alone in the world. . . .

The Axis alliance, consummated among Germany, Italy, and Japan in September 1940, was to have been Japan's trump card in implementing its vision of a new Asian order directed against the Anglo-American nations. It would augment Japan's potential power by tying the nation's destiny to German military accomplishments in Europe, and to Soviet neutrality in Asia, and thereby expel Anglo-American influence from Asia. Time was soon to show, however, that this influence, if anything, grew steadily during the months following the formation of the alliance so that, by mid-1941, the Japanese would feel even more insecure than before. They would find themselves surrounded by the ABCD powers—America, Britain, China, and the Dutch East Indies. Rarely did a diplomatic initiative end in a more complete fiasco. . . .

Given [the Axis alliance], one thing that the Chinese could count on was the unswerving position of the United States and Britain *vis-à-vis* Japan. They would have been heartened if they had known that in early October Prime Minister

[Winston] Churchill confided that nothing compared "with the importance of the British Empire and the United States being co-belligerents." He believed that American entry into the war against the Axis powers would be "fully conformable with British interests." Plans were made for staff talks both in Asia and in Washington among British, American, and Dutch officials for a joint strategy against Japan. It is true that at this stage neither London nor Washington was envisaging full strategic co-ordination with Chinese forces, but the implications were clear; the coming together of Germany and Japan, and even possibly of the Soviet Union and Japan, was only confirming the solidarity of America and Britain, so that the Chinese would find themselves part of a coalition just as the Japanese were trying to establish a global alliance of their own. The Chinese-Japanese War was turning into a conflict between two groups of nations. . . .

The only issue at the end of 1940 was one of strategic priorities. Granted that America was involved in a global struggle against the Axis powers, it needed to establish a sense of where to place its emphasis in the immediate future. . . . Here all-out aid to the British home isles took precedence. Whatever London asked, Washington would provide. China came next. After the reopening of the Burma Road, shipments from America, and smaller amounts from Britain, were resumed. An agreement with Chungking for a loan of $100 million, announced on 30 November, was the most massive given China by the United States. The funds were to be used at Chiang Kai-shek's discretion. Equally important, the United States would provide him with fifty pursuit planes, and American citizens would be allowed to serve in China as aviators and aviation instructors. The planes and aviators would be assigned to a volunteer air force which Colonel Claire Chennault would create in Chungking. The air force, officially called the American Volunteer Group but popularly known as the Flying Tigers, would be in place in the autumn of 1941.

America's top military strategists, however, were unwilling to go much further at this time. They all shared Roosevelt's perception that the nation was engaged in a quasi-war, and that it must be prepared for a real war as well. But they were not yet ready to fight a two-front war, against both Germany and Japan. Although ultimately the nation would have to fight them both, the strategists at this time generally agreed with Admiral Harold R. Stark, chief of naval operations, and General George C. Marshall, army chief of staff, that the United States should first concentrate on the Atlantic theatre. Defeat of Germany would take all the nation's resources and manpower, which should not be diverted to a Pacific war with Japan. The United States should not be on the defensive in that part of the world at least until the situation definitely improved in Europe. . . .

War across the Pacific was not inevitable. At least as of June 1941, both Tokyo and Washington were intent upon avoiding such an eventuality. But whereas the Japanese thought war could be avoided if only the United States desisted from assisting Britain against Germany and intervening in Asia, American officials were fast establishing a global system of collective security to push back Germany and Japan to earlier positions. Given the success of American strategy, Japan's only hope, if it were to persist in its Asian scheme, lay in establishing an impregnable empire so as to withstand the pressures of the United States and its allies.

Developments in the summer of 1941 confirmed these two trends. On one hand, the German invasion of the Soviet Union, commenced on 22 June, had the effect of adding the latter to the global American-led coalition. On the other, Japan's decision to take advantage of the German-Russian War by invading southern Indo-China was designed to prepare the nation for an ultimate confrontation with the ABCD powers. Under these circumstances, only a break-up of that partnership or Japan's reversal of southern expansionism could have prevented a Pacific war. . . .

. . . One drastic alternative would have been for Japan to recognize frankly the failure of its pro-German policy and, as Konoe said, reorient Japanese policy to effect a *rapprochement* with the United States. He reasoned that the Axis pact had outlived its usefulness; now that it had revealed its utter bankruptcy, Japan should release itself from it and seek an accommodation with the United States. As the prime minister wrote to [Foreign Minister] Matsuoka [Yōsuke] in early July, Japan could never afford to go to war with both America and the Soviet Union; the two powers must be prevented from establishing a close relationship, and in the meantime Japan must have a continued supply of raw materials. All such aims necessitated a readjustment of Japanese relations with America. That would require that Japan make concessions in China and South-East Asia, but Konoe believed such concessions would be worth an improved relationship with the United States. In essence he was arguing for a return to an earlier pattern of Japanese foreign policy in which economic and political ties to America had been of fundamental importance. . . .

This was too drastic a scheme to be acceptable to Japan's military, or to Matsuoka. For them, to go back to the framework of co-operation with the United States would be incompatible with the Axis alliance and entail giving up the scheme for establishing an Asian co-prosperity sphere. They were right, of course, and Konoe was asking them to reorient their thinking so as to accommodate the drastic turn of events overseas. From the military's point of view, however, such reorientation was tantamount to yielding to American pressure and giving up the war in China as hopeless. They could not do so without risking loss of prestige and their privileged position in domestic affairs. . . .

Between 26 June and 2 July, [Japan's top leaders debated] the next steps Japan was to take, and the result of their deliberations was the crucial policy document ("Outlines of fundamental national policy") adopted at a meeting in the presence of the emperor, held on 2 July. According to the memorandum, Japan was to "construct the Great East Asian Co-prosperity Sphere regardless of the changes in the world situation." More specifically, Japan would concentrate on the settlement of the Chinese war, prepare for southern expansion, and try to solve the "northern problem." In other words, both southern and northern strategies were to be pursued simultaneously; which came first would depend on circumstances, particularly the course of the European war. However, greater specificity was given to [a] southern advance when the document referred to a 25 June decision by the liaison conference that had called for the stationing of Japanese troops in southern Indo-China. The 2 July memorandum stated that such action was part of the preparedness against the United States and Britain.

In other words, the policy that emerged from the deliberations of late June and early July combined a determination to extend Japanese control to southern Indo-China with, at the same time, preparing for war against the United States, Britain, and the Soviet Union. Since Japan was already fighting a war with China, what was visualized was the possibility of a war with four powers, plus probably Indo-China and the Dutch East Indies. This sort of development was the very thing the Japanese had sought to avoid, and apparently they still believed it could be prevented by acting with lightning speed to entrench Japanese power in southern Indo-China. If that could be carried out without incurring foreign intervention, then Japan would have successfully enlarged its empire and be in a better position to fight an all-front war, should it become necessary.

In retrospect, there was faulty logic behind such a decision. Since all parties in Japan were agreed on the imperative of preventing a war against the combined force of its potential enemies, in particular America, Britain, and the Soviet Union, every effort should have been made to establish clear-cut priorities and concentrate on preparedness against one enemy at a time. . . .

The last ten days of July were crucial in determining the future of Japanese-American relations. Already on 21 July, Under-Secretary of State Sumner Welles warned the Japanese that their occupation of Indo-China would be incompatible with the negotiations going on between the two countries. Through "Magic," the code-breaking device that had now become operational, American officials had known of Japan's intention to occupy southern Indo-China, an action which they believed would seriously affect the situation in South-East Asia and must be resisted. American policy after the German invasion of the Soviet Union a month earlier had been quite forceful and clear-cut. The United States welcomed the new development, Roosevelt agreeing with Churchill that, in the latter's words, "Any man or state who fights on against Nazidom will have our aid." The government in Washington immediately started planning for extending lend-lease aid to the Soviet Union, and in the meantime Roosevelt released part of the latter's assets, frozen after the latter's invasion of Finland in late 1939. "If the Russians could hold the Germans until October 1," he said, "that would be of great value in defeating Hitler." In that connection, the president wanted to discourage any Japanese attack on the Soviet Union, warning Prime Minister Konoe in a personal message on 4 July that any such action would jeopardize the negotiations in Washington and undermine the peace in the Pacific.

The United States, in short, was already seeing itself as being tied to the Soviet Union in the European war. It could help the latter by shipping aid goods and by frustrating Japanese attempts to take advantage of the German assault to attack the Soviet Union from the rear. In that connection, Japan's southern advance would be welcome inasmuch as it might divert resources from the north and make less likely an impending Japanese war with the Soviet Union. Instead of acquiescing in Japanese occupation of Indo-China, however, the Roosevelt administration decided to throw obstacles in its way, thus in effect choking off Japan from both northern and southern options. The main instrument was to be economic, in particular the freezing of Japanese assets in the United States. Just as the United States was unfreezing Soviet assets to enable the latter to fight Germany, it would make it impossible for Japan to obtain funds with which to purchase goods in America, especially much-needed oil. A total cessation of exports to Japan was not visualized, however. What Roosevelt, Hull, Welles, and others had in mind was that henceforth Japan would require an export licence whenever it wanted to buy American commodities. Moreover, some small quantities of low-octane gasoline could still be sold to Japan so as not to provide the latter with an excuse for going into the

Dutch East Indies. Nevertheless, the intent of such measures was unmistakable. The United States would take steps to deter Japan both from attacking the Soviet Union and occupying Indo-China. Such warning was explicitly communicated to Tokyo so as to leave little room for doubt about America's serious intentions. . . .

Konoe should have taken such warning seriously, but he was too weak to stop the momentum. On 14 July Japan had presented a note to the [French] Vichy regime, demanding the right to station troops in southern Indo-China, and five days later the new foreign minister, Toyoda [Teijirō], gave Vichy the deadline of 23 July. Regardless of Vichy's response, the supreme command was determined to carry out the invasion, and plans were completed for the dispatch of necessary troops on 24 July. Vichy's acceptance came on the 23rd, and thus a "peaceful" landing on the Indo-China coast was accomplished between 28 and 30 July. In retaliation, on 25 July the United States ordered the freezing of Japanese assets. The following day, Britain and the Philippines followed suit, and on 27 July New Zealand and the Netherlands did likewise. The ABCD encirclement of Japan was virtually complete. . . .

America's stiff measures had at least one effect on Japanese policy. The supreme command in Tokyo became less and less sanguine about the prospect of waging a successful campaign against the Soviet Union. Given the deteriorating condition of Japanese-American relations, the nation would have to be prepared for a grave crisis in South-East Asia which could lead to war against the ABCD powers. Under the circumstances, even the die-hard exponents of the northern strategy began showing signs of hesitancy, the more so as the German assault on the Soviet Union was not proceeding as smoothly as had at first been anticipated. . . .

Between 2 July and 9 August, then, a crucial reversal of Japanese strategy had taken place. From preparedness for an impending offensive against the Soviet Union, the supreme command reverted to a more passive stance in the north. Sixteen divisions would still be mobilized, but they would not be engaged in any action for the time being. Henceforth, Japanese strategy would focus on a possible conflict with the ABCD powers. In this sense, 9 August may be taken as the point of no return as far as Japanese-American relations were concerned.

The United States contributed to that turn of events by instituting a *de facto* embargo on oil. The freezing of Japanese assets, announced on 25 July, had been followed by a week of intensive work by State department, Treasury, and other officials to set up a machinery for implementing the order. The idea, which Roosevelt approved, was to let the Japanese apply for export licences which would then be examined on a case-by-case basis and necessary funds released from blocked Japanese monies to purchase the goods. Oil, too, would be dealt with in this fashion. But the processing of applications for licences and release of funds took time, and the matter was overseen by Dean Acheson, assistant secretary of state, who refused to release funds, intent upon punishing Japan for its southern expansionism. The result was that Japan never got any oil after 25 July, a fact that even Roosevelt did not find out till early September. But the Japanese were under no illusion about the matter. They now realized that a total oil embargo was being put into effect. Japanese strategy would now have to take that development into consideration. . . .

During the second half of August, [Roosevelt and Konoe] continued to exchange messages, and there was much talk of a possible summit conference. This was because both sides, for different reasons, clearly wanted to avoid a showdown. . . .

President Roosevelt, on his part, was interested in the idea of a summit meeting with Konoe, but not necessarily because he believed a long-lasting settlement of the crisis could be achieved. For him it would be unthinkable to give up the basic principles, but at least a meeting with Konoe would give time for the United States armed forces to be better prepared for a possible war. The president's enthusiasm, however, was not reciprocated by Hull, who believed no summit meeting would be useful until some fundamental issues had been discussed beforehand. Moreover, he was worried lest the meeting affect the solidarity of the ABCD *entente* and drive China out of desperation to the Japanese. If the Chinese should feel they were being betrayed by the Americans, such an outcome would not be unthinkable, Hull believed, and could even lead to releasing Japanese forces out of China for use southward. . . .

Given Chinese sensitivity about any sign of the weakening of the ABCD *entente,* the American government had to tread very cautiously in considering a summit meeting between Roosevelt and Konoe. Nevertheless, the United States might have gone through with the meeting if the Japanese side had been solidly behind Konoe and willing to modify significantly its policy in Asia. Such was not the case, and in the final analysis the aborting of the summit conference must be attributed to the unwillingness of Japan to change course.

For it was during the crucial weeks of late August and early September 1941 that the Japanese leadership finally decided on war. Even as Konoe and his supporters were trying desperately to avert a crisis with the United States through his meeting with President Roosevelt, the supreme command's army and navy sections began a series of intensive discussions to arrive at a consensual decision concerning the timing and scale of preparedness for war against the ABD powers. . . . [T]he navy had believed that war preparedness could be undertaken without a national decision for war, whereas the army believed a definite commitment to go to war was needed before mobilization of necessary forces could be implemented. After daily meetings, the two sides finally reached a compromise at the beginning of September. It was to the effect that Japan should complete war preparedness by late October and decide on war against the ABD powers if no diplomatic settlement had been arrived at by the first part of the month. In other words, war preparedness would be followed by a decision for war, but in the meantime diplomatic efforts would be continued to see if war could be avoided. The army's and the navy's viewpoints were neatly balanced in the compromise. The formula was written into a document, "Guidelines for implementing national policies," which was formally adopted at a leaders' conference in the presence of the emperor on 6 September.

That document may be regarded as a virtual declaration of war by Japan. It clearly implied that war would come unless a peaceful settlement could be worked out with the United States and Britain. In an appendix [annex] to the document the minimal terms acceptable to Japan were spelled out; if those terms were not met, then war would come. Japan would insist, first, that the Anglo-American powers desist from extending military and economic aid to the Chiang Kai-shek regime; second, that they refrain from establishing military facilities within Thailand, the Dutch East Indies, China, or the Far Eastern provinces of the Soviet Union and from augmenting their forces beyond their existing strength; and, third, that they provide Japan with resources needed for its existence by restoring trade relations and offering friendly co-operation with Japan as the latter undertook to collaborate economically with Thailand and the Dutch East Indies. In return for such concessions on the part of the United States and Britain, Japan would be willing to promise not to undertake further military expansion in Asia and to withdraw its troops from Indo-China "upon the establishment of a just peace in East Asia." Furthermore, it would be prepared to guarantee Philippine neutrality and refrain from hostile action against the Soviet Union so long as the latter observed the neutrality treaty. . . .

[Japan's] terms were clearly unacceptable to America. Although the language was somewhat modified, the American side was unimpressed when they were transmitted on 23 September. At a meeting with [Ambassador] Nomura [Kichisaburō] on 2 October, Hull bluntly told the ambassador that he saw little point in holding a summit conference. . . . China was the crucial question. Without further concessions on Japan's part on this point, it was extremely unlikely that any agreement could be reached with the United States—a contingency that could only mean war. If war were to be avoided, therefore, the Konoe cabinet would have somehow to persuade the army to commit itself to withdrawing from China, an impossible demand at this late hour. Thus the Japanese army seized on Hull's 2 October message as a virtual rejection of the peace efforts and pressed Konoe to give up the idea of a summit conference. . . .

On 14 October, [War Minister] Tōjō [Hideki] made an impassioned speech at a cabinet meeting against making concessions on the troop withdrawal question. If Japan should submit to American pressure, he said, the fruits of the war with China would be nullified, the existence of Manchukuo jeopardized, and colonial control over Korea itself endangered. It would signal the nation's return to "Little Japan before the Manchurian incident." That was the crux of the matter. The army refused to return to the situation existing in the 1920s, something the United States was insisting upon. . . .

Here, in stark simplicity, was the moment of decision forced upon the cabinet by the war minister. Tōjō was correct in saying that if war was not to be the decision, then the 6 September guidelines would have to be revised. Since the cabinet had been responsible for those guidelines, it was accountable for not having carried out those policies. Thus the only thing left was for the entire cabinet, including Konoe, to resign. . . . All such developments led inevitably to the cabinet's resignation on 16 October. With it the idea of a conference with President Roosevelt, on the realization of which Konoe had pinned his hopes for peace, also evaporated. . . .

What should be the absolute minimal conditions Japan could accept to maintain a peace with the United States? Much time was spent on defining those terms. Here [Foreign Minister] Tōjō [Shigenori] came up with a two-pronged approach. The first (Plan A) was to arrive at a comprehensive settlement of the major issues with the United States. Japan, according to the policy approved by the liaison conference on 1 November, would agree to withdraw its forces from most areas of China within two years of the establishment of a truce, concentrating them in certain parts of north China, Mongolia, Sinkiang, and Hainan Island. They would stay in those areas for up to twenty-five years. Once the war with China was settled, all Japanese troops would be withdrawn from Indo-China. Japan would also accept the principle of non-discrimination in trade in the Pacific and in China if the same principle were applied throughout the world. This was in response to Hull's fundamental principles; the

Japanese were in effect saying that the problem of commercial opportunity in China should not be treated in isolation from the rest of the world. It was a rather tame response and reflected a reluctance to make a firm commitment on China before the settlement of the war. As for the Axis alliance, Japan would act "in accordance with its own decisions"—an indirect way of saying that the German pact would not be applicable to the United States unless the latter attacked Germany first.

These terms still indicated a determination to retain Japan's special position in China and the rest of Asia that it had sought to establish by force. As Prime Minister Tōjō explained at the crucial 5 November meeting of the Japanese leaders in the presence of the emperor, Japan could never go back to the "constraints" of the nine-power treaty, which was what Hull's four principles signified. Since the nation had tried to free itself from these constraints by going to war in Manchuria and China, it made no sense to return to the situation existing before 1931. Because the United States appeared adamant on this point, there was little expectation in Tokyo that an agreement could be reached under Plan A. As Foreign Minister Tōjō stated frankly, there was too little time to negotiate a basic understanding on China. Since, however, every effort must be maintained to avoid war if at all possible, Japan was to present a second set of conditions (Plan B) to the United States as the absolute minimum acceptable terms. They would not try for a comprehensive agreement on China, and instead seek to prevent further deterioration of Japanese-American relations. Specifically, Japan would pledge not to advance militarily beyond French Indo-China; the two nations would co-operate in the Dutch East Indies so as to procure the resources they needed; the United States would restore its trade with Japan by lifting the freezing of Japanese assets and providing Japan with the oil it required; and the United States would not obstruct the attempts by Japan and China for peace. If an agreement could be reached on the basis of these terms, Japan would be willing to evacuate southern Indo-China and ultimately the entire peninsula. . . .

The Japanese recognized that . . . there really was little chance that the United States would give up its support of China or agree to the loosening of the ABCD *entente*. Thus virtually all who participated in the 5 November conference resigned themselves to the possibility of war against the ABCD powers. But they also realized that such a war would be an extremely difficult one to wage. Prior to meeting on 5 November, the top military leaders had conferred with the emperor on a number of occasions to apprise him of the crucial decisions that were being made. They all assumed that war would come in early December. Admiral Nagano expressed confidence that through a lightning attack on the enemy, Japan would be able to score initial victories and establish strategic bases in the south-western Pacific; however, he reiterated his earlier scepticism about Japan's chances in a prolonged war. Much would depend on the state of national mobilization as well as world conditions, he said. Japan's only hope, he went on, would lie in the possibility of British defeat through the severing of its oceanic routes by Japan and the landing of German troops on the home isles. Even so, Japan was disadvantaged in that it would never be possible to attack the United States at its source. General Sugiyama was more optimistic; he asserted that the initial southern strategy should enable the nation to establish a position of impregnability, from which to continue the war against American and British forces. At the same time, he cautioned that the United States would force the Soviet Union to offer its Asian territory for use as airfields and submarine bases, and the latter would find it impossible to resist the pressure. Thus, Sugiyama said, there was a possibility that the Soviet Union too might enter the war, especially if it became prolonged.

Given such realistic estimates, why should Japan decide on war? Prime Minister Tōjō concluded that it was now the only alternative. If the nation should simply persevere, within two years America's position would become even more strengthened as it would have extended its air power to the Pacific, whereas Japan would have exhausted its oil stock. It would then be too late to undertake a southern strategy to obtain petroleum. In China, in the meantime, American-supported movements against the Japanese forces of occupation would intensify, and even the Soviet Union might be emboldened to help China. In other words, inaction would make matters worse in two years, whereas the military were saying that at least for that duration the war would go well for the nation. Japan would have a southern empire for two years, and although the China war might still not be settled within the time span, the situation could not be worse than the certain deterioration caused by passivity. It was some such thinking that persuaded Japan's top leaders to make the fatal decision for war, on 5 November 1941.

What the discussion revealed was lack of a long-range vision. Nobody knew how the war would go after the initial successes, still less how the ABCD nations would act in two years' time. But all agreed that the continuation of the existing situation was intolerable. It would, as Tōjō declared, relegate Japan to the status of a third-rate nation, since the nation would become more and more subject to American power and will. It would be better to resist this power as much as possible and see how things developed. It was believed that Japan would suffer in a United States–dominated world order, whereas if it challenged that order, the way might be opened for an alternative arrangement of international affairs. . . .

Given such developments, the relationship between Japan and the United States was reaching an impasse. Only a comprehensive understanding would prevent their total rupture, but no comprehensive understanding could be worked out in the short span of time that Tokyo and Washington had available to make the effort. This became painfully evident in the second half of November, when negotiators in Washington made one last attempt to see if Japan's Plan B could be salvaged. That plan, in contrast to Plan A, proposed to set aside the China issue and aimed at restoring the status quo of June 1941, but for that very reason it had little chance of success. American officials, nevertheless, were willing to consider a temporary arrangement so as to postpone a showdown. Aware, through "Magic" intercepts, that the Japanese would strike unless an agreement had been reached by 1 December, and desirous of putting off a war for at least several months, they drafted a counterproposal, the so-called *modus vivendi*. A product of high-level deliberations in Washington, the proposal would call for Japanese withdrawal of troops from southern Indo-China, keeping a limited number (25,000) in northern Indo-China, in return for resumption of American shipments of oil to Japan. That was to be a three-month experiment, far from the comprehensive settlement that was needed. Even so, had the British, Chinese, and Dutch governments endorsed the plan, it would have been presented to the Japanese negotiators in Washington, now headed by Kurusu Saburō, special envoy hastily dispatched from Tokyo. Quite predictably, however, the Chinese took strong exception, and from London [Winston S.] Churchill cabled his support of the Chinese stance. After all, the maintenance of the ABCD *entente* was at stake, and the United States could not unilaterally deal with Japan. The decision not to submit the *modus vivendi* proposal, then, was added evidence that the ABCD *entente* could not be broken up to placate Japan, even for three months.

If the ABCD *entente* could not be broken up, there was little point in negotiations between Japan and the United States. . . . In the short span of time that they had available—from the middle to the end of November—it was impossible either for Japan or the United States to reorient its position. Hull's 26 November note, in which he reiterated the basic principles on which America had insisted, confirmed this state of affairs. . . .

From that point onward, what was left to the United States was not to negotiate further with Japan but to strengthen the ABCD partnership. On 1 December, President Roosevelt assured Lord Halifax, the British ambassador, that in the event of a Japanese attack on British or Dutch possessions in Asia, "we should obviously all be together." In other words, the United States would come to their assistance, so that there would be war between Japan and the ABCD powers together. Japan would get what it had been planning for. In the subsequent days, Roosevelt reiterated the commitment, explicitly stating that America's support meant "armed support," and that the ABCD powers should act together in issuing parallel warnings to Japan not to attack Thailand, Malaya, or the Indies. China, in the meantime, would continue to receive full American support. The ABCD alliance had now come into being in all but name. . . .

Postwar history was to show that the two nations [Japan and the United States] shared much in common and could co-operate for their mutual benefit. That framework of mutuality and co-operation had been the pattern through most of modern history, and reached a peak during the 1920s. Somehow, however, the framework—the Washington Conference system—had been eroded and a sense of rivalry and conflict had replaced that of friendly co-existence. In the long history of Japanese-American relations, however, the crisis and war of the late 1930s and the 1940s were but a brief interlude.

The story, however, must be put in the larger context of international relations, for Japanese-American relations were never purely bilateral ones. In the 1920s, they were the main proponents, together with Britain, of the Washington system, and during the first half of the 1930s there was little actual crisis across the Pacific as Japan managed to act forcefully in China without incurring the combined opposition of other nations. From the mid-1930s, however, there grew progressively a realignment of powers so that China no longer had to fight alone against Japanese aggression. One after another outside powers' help was obtained, and by the end of the decade there had emerged a loose coalition of the United States, Britain, the Netherlands, France, and the Soviet Union, all desirous of checking Japanese advance. In a sense this was a modified Washington system, shorn of Japan but with the addition of Russia. To counter the trend, Japan tried to detach the Soviet Union from the *entente* and enter into a solid alliance with Germany and Italy. The hope was to form an alternative alignment, consisting of Japan, Germany, Italy, and the Soviet Union to oppose the first. The attempt failed, and the result was that Japan found itself more than ever isolated, "encircled" as it was said. In the end it was an encircled Japan pitting itself against a fortified coalition. That enhanced the feeling of insecurity and crisis on the part of the Japanese. The only way out of isolation would have been to go back to the Washington Conference system, but this appeared difficult now that China and the Soviet Union were more closely involved in that system. Seeing no way out of the dilemma except through a gamble for an alternative system of Asian-Pacific affairs, Japan struck. It was, as the government declared, a struggle for a new order and for national survival. The two aims were closely linked. But the war was to demonstrate that survival within the old framework would have been just as plausible.

Miscalculation and Economic Sanctions: U.S. Hardliners Ensure War with Japan

HOSOYA CHIHIRO

Hard-liners in the U.S. government such as Stanley Hornbeck, Cordell Hull, Henry Stimson, and Henry Morgenthau, who favored economic sanctions against Japan in the years immediately preceding the Japanese attack on Pearl Harbor, seriously miscalculated the impact of such a policy on Japan. Instead of deterring the Japanese from pursuing an expansionist policy, these economic sanctions exacerbated U.S.-Japanese relations, encouraged Japan's southward expansion, and provoked Japanese hard-liners to risk war with the United States. The advocates of the hard-line policy toward Japan misunderstood the psychology of the Japanese, particularly the middle levels of the military, the Japanese decision-making process, and Japanese economic realities. They also rode roughshod over the prudent proposals of the soft-liners in the U.S. State Department such as the director of the Far Eastern Division, Maxwell Hamilton, and Ambassador Joseph Grew in Japan.

The demand of the hard-liners for economic sanctions against Japan played into the hands of the ultranationalists in the Japanese government. The latter argued that the imposition of economic sanctions by the United States necessitated risk and expansion by Japan. In such a climate Japanese moderates found it impossible to counsel caution and accommodation. Their counterparts in the U.S. government similarly learned that they were no match for those who foolishly believed that Japan would not dare attack the United States and that economic reprisals would so cripple Japan that she would acquiesce to American pressures.

After the Marco Polo Bridge Incident of July 7, 1937, Japan adopted an increasingly aggressive course in China. After the *Panay* incident on December 12 [in which Japanese planes attacked a U.S. gunboat, the *Panay*, on China's Yangtze River], the Japanese occupation forces there increasingly interfered with U.S. economic interests. These actions stiffened the American attitude and led to diplomatic protests. When these actions had limited effect on the Japanese military, hard-liners in the U.S. government favored an imposition of economic sanctions against Japan. They believed that Japan's economic dependence on the United

From "Miscalculation in Deterrent Policy: U.S.-Japanese Relations, 1938–1941," by Hosoya Chihiro, in Hilary Conroy and Harry Wray, eds., *Pearl Harbor Reexamined: Prologue to the Pacific War,* © 1990. Reprinted by permission of the University of Hawai'i Press.

States gave them a decided advantage in restraining Japanese expansion. Hence they counseled strong, punitive economic actions against Japan such as prohibiting the importing and exporting of selected goods, suspending credit, restricting monetary exchange, and even imposing a total economic boycott. The legal obstacle confronting them was the 1911 U.S.-Japanese Treaty of Commerce and Navigation.

The first official to advocate the abrogation of this treaty was Hornbeck in a memorandum of July 19, 1938. Initially, he had few supporters. The mood in Washington, D.C., changed, however, when the Japanese government announced on November 3, 1938, a "New Order in East Asia" and Foreign Minister Arita Hachirō stated on November 18 that the large-scale involvement of Japan in China could not help violating U.S. economic interests and that pre-war standards and principles would need to be altered to fit the present and future conditions in Asia. These Japanese actions were taken to be a violation of the Nine-Power Treaty. They created a majority opinion within the State Department that was favorable to an abrogation of the U.S.-Japanese Treaty of Commerce and Navigation. In a curiously argued report issued on December 5, Francis Sayre, assistant secretary of state, maintained correctly that full-scale economic reprisals against Japan posed the serious danger of a military conflict and would create widespread domestic economic disturbances. Paradoxically, however, he went on to maintain that the commercial treaty should be abolished and that steps should be taken to end the granting of credits and loans.

In rapid succession the U.S. government announced on January 14, 1939, a "moral embargo" on airplanes and parts and on February 7, 1939, a cessation of credit to Japan. However, soft-liners in the State Department, represented by Grew and Hamilton, argued that a moderate policy would lead to a revival of the moderate faction (Shidehara diplomacy) in Japan and would also blunt the efforts of the hard-liners who were advocating a strengthened coalition with Nazi Germany. These moderate arguments temporarily bore fruit. Further study by the State Department led to a decision to hand Japan an *aide memoire* proposing a new commercial treaty that would exclude articles five and fourteen [which guaranteed most-favored-nation treatment with respect to tariffs and prohibited export/import restrictions] in the existing treaty. Such a move would be a less severe shock to Japan but would still make it possible to impose embargoes and discriminatory duties.

Unfortunately, on April 27, before the *aide memoire* could be submitted to Japan, the chairman of the Foreign Relations Committee, Key Pitman, submitted a resolution to the Senate that scuttled the State Department's plans. This resolution gave the president the "power to effect an embargo and limit credits against a country which infringes the Nine-Power Treaty and injures American lives and interests." Hamilton feared that the planned revision of the commercial treaty would appear to be connected to the Senate bill and would produce too strong an impression concerning U.S. policy toward Japan. As a result the State Department decided in May to postpone the *aide memoire*.

The hard-line faction in the State Department, led by Hornbeck, could not prevail in 1938 and 1939 because the moderates were supported at that time by the [U.S.] military. The military leaders did not feel the country was sufficiently ready for a conflict with Japan. A Hornbeck memorandum to Sayre on December 29, 1938, argued a position that would be repeated incessantly until the Pearl Harbor attack, namely that a strong U.S. stand of "comprehensive and thoroughgoing program of measures of material pressure" could prevent military conflict and lead to a revision in Japanese policy. Hornbeck's view was echoed in the Senate and by the general populace. A Gallup poll survey showed 66 percent in favor of a boycott on Japanese goods and 78 percent in favor of an embargo on weapons and munitions to Japan. When Japan blockaded the Tientsin settlement in June over Britain's refusal to return four accused Chinese to the Japanese and news circulated of Japan's intention to remove English interests from China, an aroused American public opinion strengthened the hard-line faction's stand on Japanese policy. On July 26, 1939, President Roosevelt announced that the treaty of commerce would be void after January 26, 1940. Hull and Sayre believed that the U.S. ability to impose economic sanctions thereafter would have a "sobering effect" on Japan because of her economic dependence on America.

In Japan Foreign Minister Arita [Hachirō] was more optimistic about the American announcement than were those from the anxious economic circles engaged in trade with the United States or the pro-Anglo-American groups. Arita assessed the American move as largely political, "first in order to settle the question of its rights and interests in China, and second as a gesture in connection with the coming elections this fall." Although he thought a solution could be found, a document developed by the foreign office, which reflected the more hard-line approach of its middle-level officials, opposed a passive "wait and see policy." Instead, the document demanded that Japan should "denounce the unfriendly attitude of the U.S. Government" and appeal to the American public and isolationist faction there.

The hard-liners in Japan suffered a temporary setback when the Nazis signed a non-aggression pact with the Soviet Union. The Hiranuma cabinet fell in late August, and the new Prime Minister, Abe Nobuyuki, by his own volition as well as orders from the emperor, sought to improve U.S.-Japanese relations. Documents developed on October 4 and October 20 by, respectively, the foreign office (based on an army plan) and the Japanese navy argued for bettering U.S.-Japanese relations through the favorable treatment of U.S. interests in China and U.S. citizens residing there. The navy document also advocated holding a U.S.-Japanese conference in Tokyo to conclude a new commercial treaty or at least to obtain a "generalized, temporary agreement even if it fails to affirm specifically the principle of non-discriminatory treatment." It called for avoiding discussion of the Nine-Power Treaty, opening the Yangtze and Canton rivers, compensating U.S. interests in China, and moderating restrictions on U.S. cultural work. Here was an opportunity for the U.S. government to improve U.S.-Japanese relations, but the Japanese conciliatory attitude did not bear fruit because of miscalculations by the hard-liners in the U.S. government.

On the surface, it appeared that these conciliatory Japanese decisions confirmed the thesis of the U.S. hard-liners that a tough approach against Japan would be effective. But two points mitigate against acceptance of this view. First, the German-Soviet non-aggression pact had frightened many Japanese. Second, the same navy document mentioned above also incorporated a hard-line policy. It warned that non-diplomatic measures might have to be adopted against the United States to counter U.S. pressure. The argument was that if Japan were to advance southward or to make more rapid war preparations, Japan would have to enter into arrangements with other countries to obtain necessary raw materials. Furthermore, the document claimed that the alleged tendency of U.S. foreign policy to change rapidly forced Japan to accelerate her war preparations to meet all contingencies.

As a result of the Abe government's effort to improve relations with the United States, Japanese concessions were made at the Tokyo conference in meetings of November 4 and December 18, 1939. The Japanese promised that talks about concessions to U.S. citizens for losses sustained in China through Japanese bombings, settlement problems, and taxes and currency problems would prove satisfactory to the United States and that the Yangtze and Canton rivers would be opened in two months. In return the Japanese wanted mutual concessions and negotiations for the concluding of a new commercial treaty of *modus vivendi*. On December 22 the Japanese ambassador to the United States, Horinouchi Kensuke, presented the details of the *modus vivendi* to Hull. It called for: (1) the principle of the most-favored-nation treatment for commerce, navigation, and tariffs; (2) freedom of entry, travel, and residence where the purpose was that of trade; (3) the handling of taxes, duties, and commissions, direct or indirect, on the basis of non-discrimination or the most-favored-nation principle.

Diametrically opposite reactions to Abe's efforts to improve U.S.-Japanese relations occurred within the U.S. government. Ambassador Grew consistently called for a conciliatory policy. In support of the *modus vivendi* proposed by Japan he said the following in a strongly worded telegram to Washington on December 18, 1939:

> The simple fact is that we are here dealing not with a unified Japan but with a Japanese Government which is endeavoring courageously, even with only gradual success, to fight against a recalcitrant Japanese Army, a battle which happens to be our own battle. . . . If we now rebuff the Government we shall not be serving to discredit the Japanese Army but rather to furnish the Army with powerful arguments to be used in its own support. I am convinced that we are in a position either to direct American-Japanese relations into a progressively healthy channel or to accelerate their movement straight down hill.

The strong reaction of the hard-liners to the *modus vivendi* was demonstrated repeatedly over the next two years. In a memorandum issued the next day Hornbeck argued:

> In my opinion adoption as a major premise of the thought that the "civilian" element in the Japanese nation, may gain an ascendancy over the "military" element and, having done so, would alter the objectives of Japanese policy can lead to nothing but confusion and error in reasoning. . . . Practically the whole of the Japanese population believes in and is enthusiastic over the policy of expansion and aggrandisement of the Japanese empire.

He urged policymakers to believe that the Japanese were insincere; within them "there is a change neither of attitude nor of heart." He and Grew were far apart in their assessments. Grew, however, had been on the Japanese scene for almost a decade; Hornbeck did not know Japan and was strongly pro-Chinese.

Secretary Hull became increasingly sympathetic to Hornbeck's view. Although he did not support the hard-line faction's argument (stated in a December 11, 1939, memorandum to Roosevelt) to impose duties on Japanese commerce upon the termination of the commerce treaty, he refused to heed Grew's advice to implement a new treaty or a *modus vivendi* (December 20). The consequent failure of the Tokyo conference was the final straw that brought about the collapse of the Abe cabinet. The new cabinet headed by Admiral Yonai Mitsumasa and Foreign

Minister Arita submitted the same proposal with no new approaches. That effort failed, and the Treaty of Commerce and Navigation lapsed on January 26, 1940.

Despite the Japanese awareness that a lapse of the treaty did not mean an automatic levy of discriminatory tariffs or restrictions on Japanese products, the psychological impact was profound. Immediately, the foreign office concluded that they "must end as quickly as possible the present high level of economic dependence on the U.S. and press on for a policy to establish an economic system which would not be endangered by the U.S. attitude." When the Nazi Blitzkrieg defeated Norway, the Netherlands, Belgium, Luxemburg, and France between April and June, 1940, many Japanese feared that Japan "might miss the bus." They saw an opportunity by a quick southward movement to obtain oil and other materials from the Dutch East Indies and to prevent the transport of war supplies to Chiang Kai-shek from French Indochina.

All factions in the U.S. government were opposed to a Japanese southern advance and an alliance with Germany, but they differed on how to prevent these possibilities. Grew wanted the United States to break the deadlock with Japan by discussing a new commercial treaty and by extending credit to Japan for non-military supplies. At a meeting of Hull, Hamilton, and Hornbeck on May 24, the latter feared that American concessions would be perceived as a sign of weakness and would encourage new Japanese aggression. He opposed any new moves. In May and June, however, Hull seemed to have adopted a more conciliatory attitude. He even allowed the opening of conferences by Grew with Foreign Minister Arita to discuss the promotion of trade and the strengthening of relations between the two countries. These talks failed because Grew had to assert that the *sine qua non* for improved U.S.-Japanese relations was non-interference in U.S. interests and the halting of the use of force in effecting national policy. Foreign Minister Arita was just as adamant that the obstacle to that goal was the lack of a commercial treaty. Grew, at least, sought to initiate talks in support of a *modus vivendi* from Washington, but by July Hull was no longer interested. He may have been interested in these talks in May and June only because of the altered condition in Europe and Hornbeck's advice that such talks might stall the feared Japanese advance southward.

The failure of the Grew-Arita talks contributed to the fall of the Yonai cabinet and to the creation of a more aggressive cabinet led by Konoe Fumimaro with Matsuoka Yōsuke as foreign minister. It was recognized that such a cabinet would be more favorable to both a southern advance and a coalition with Italy and Germany. When Japan closed the Burma Road, Hornbeck advocated either immediate export restrictions on aviation gasoline or the implementation of a full-scale embargo on exports. The rationale was that these actions would "retard or prevent new adventuring."

In the meantime the U.S. government took a number of steps beyond diplomatic action. It ordered the continued stationing of the fleet in Hawaii on May 4 to deter a Japanese attack on the Dutch Indies and also passed the National Defense Act, which gave the president power to license the export of arms, munitions, raw materials, airplane parts, optical instruments, and other items. Scrap iron and petroleum were omitted because, as Hamilton put it, "such restrictions or prohibition would tend to impel Japan towards moving into the Dutch East Indies. . . ."

The appointment of Henry Stimson as secretary of war also hardened the U.S. position. Stimson had been advocating a strong policy of economic sanctions against

Japan since the Manchurian Incident of 1931. He was very close to the Secretary of the Treasury Morgenthau and to Hornbeck and other hard-liners. From hindsight we can see that he and Hornbeck suffered from the same two misconceptions: (1) that Japan would never dare wage war against the United States despite American actions against her, and (2) that Japan's southern advance would prove unlikely because of her deeper involvement in the Chinese quicksand. Stimson argued to prohibit the export of munitions and war materials to Japan as well as imports from Japan. At a dinner party at the British embassy on July 18 he said, "The only way to treat Japan is not to give in to her on anything."

The soft-liners fought an ever-losing battle. A conference requested by President Roosevelt to discuss Morgenthau's proposed moratorium on petroleum was held in late July. It included Morgenthau, the secretaries of the army and navy, and Acting Secretary of State Sumner Welles. Although Welles argued vigorously for Hull against Morgenthau regarding a proposed export licensing system for products including petroleum and scrap iron, he was able to achieve only a small compromise on July 26. The compromise on petroleum limited export restrictions to aviation motor fuel and lubricants; scrap iron restrictions were limited to Number 1 heavy melting iron and steel scrap. Stimson was elated and wrote in his diary: "We have won . . . a long battle, which we have been waging against Japan for about four years." In fact, however, given developments in Japan, they had not won at all.

The severe economic sanctions deeply shocked citizens in every quarter of Japan. The army's general staff argued strongly on August 2 for strengthening the southern expansion policy. The first section of the navy's general staff on August 1 drew up "A Study Relating to Policy Towards French Indo-China" that echoed the army's response to the economic sanctions imposed by the United States. The conviction of the Japanese military that a "U.S. imposition of complete embargo" would make the "use of military forces toward the south . . . a matter of life and death" was confirmed by the navy's general staff toward the end of August. Such a policy also received unanimous support at a round-table conference of the middle-echelon officers of the army and navy. Although the minister for naval affairs, Yoshida Zengo, opposed the use of force in the event of a complete embargo, the middle-echelon officers of the Japanese army and navy did not. . . .

The enforcement of U.S. economic sanctions had stiffened the attitude of the middle-echelon officers and provoked them to execute the plan for a southern advance. Their action, however, escalated things further. Far from learning anything from the results of their hard-line action, the American proponents of this approach now demanded more economic sanctions to halt Japanese aggression. . . .

On September 6, when the Japanese troops caused an incident on the Indochina border, the U.S. cabinet witnessed a sharp exchange of words between Morgenthau and Stimson on the one hand and Hull on the other concerning the question of an embargo on petroleum. Hornbeck on September 11 stressed to Stimson the need for a more active policy of restraining Japanese actions and promoting friendly relations with the Soviet Union. On September 19, after hearing about the latest Japanese ultimatum regarding Indochina, the American cabinet met again to examine the question of a complete embargo on aviation gasoline. Although Hull feared that an oil embargo would incite Japan to attack the Dutch East Indies, Stimson and Morgenthau demanded a complete embargo on oil. State Department opposition limited economic sanctions to a prohibition on the export of all grades of scrap iron.

On October 5, Foreign Minister Matsuoka expressed his displeasure to Ambassador Grew at this U.S. action. He stated that "such embargoes would intensely anger the Japanese people." On October 8, Ambassador Horinouchi, in a hand-delivered note to Hull, heatedly protested restrictions that he claimed constituted a "virtual embargo" and an "unfriendly act" that "may cause future relations between the United States and Japan to become 'unpredictable.' "

In Japan the hard-liners now made their own miscalculations. On September 27 [1940] the Tripartite Pact between Japan, Germany, and Italy was signed. Matsuoka expected that the strengthening of the Axis would enhance Japan's position. He believed the pact would frustrate the U.S. intention to intervene in a Japanese southern advance and would lessen the possibility of the outbreak of war with the United States.

The U.S. reaction was completely contrary to what Matsuoka had divined. According to a U.S. public opinion survey of late September, the attitude toward Japan had worsened. The number of Americans favoring strong action against Japan had greatly increased. A cabinet meeting on October 4 led to the consensus that the United States would not yield one inch to Japanese intimidation. A navy squadron was proposed for sailing to the Dutch East Indies or Singapore. Furthermore, Roosevelt stated on October 12 that the United States would not be intimidated. The Tripartite Pact had failed dismally to produce the impact the Japanese hard-liners had predicted. Instead, it had exacerbated relations with the United States. Middle-echelon army officers intensified their cry for an acceleration of southern expansion. Even before the enactment of the Tripartite Pact, Japan had demanded permission to move troops into southern Indochina and did so on July 28 [1941].

The Japanese pressures on Indochina led the U.S. government on July 25 to freeze Japanese assets in the United States and to impose an embargo against Japan. The lines were drawn. Hull wrote: "Nothing will stop them except force. . . . The point is how long we can maneuver the situation until the military matter in Europe is brought to a conclusion." From hindsight it is curious why Hull stated such an objective but pursued policies that played into the hands of Japanese hard-liners and contributed to their escalated aggression.

Middle-echelon officers in the Japanese navy were resolved to go to war because of the oil embargo. They were anxious about the existing supply of oil turning the Japanese navy into a "scarecrow navy." A secret war diary of the army general staff noted on August 1 that the "atmosphere of the inevitability of war with England and the U.S. had gradually deepened" and on August 2 "the Military Affairs Section of the Ministry of War proposed an Imperial Conference to determine to go to war with England and the United States." Simultaneously, Ambassador Grew was in a state of despair as a result of the oil embargo. He wrote, "The vicious circle of reprisals and counter reprisals is on. The obvious conclusion is eventual war."

Thus, the American hard-liners' policy of first proposing and then imposing economic sanctions to deter a Japanese southern advance and war failed badly. To understand how it produced the opposite effect it is necessary to consider two miscalculations about the Japanese made by the hard-line faction of the U.S. government. One was that Japan would seek to avoid war with the United States at all costs. The other assumption followed from the first, namely that Japan would inevitably submit to unbending American resolution. However, economic pressure did not restrain Japan from a southern advance. Instead it accelerated a Japanese southern policy even at the risk of possible war with the United States.

Why had the hard-liners miscalculated? First, their predictions of Japan's reactions were based on an analysis of Japan's upper-level policymakers. They lacked an understanding of the important role played by the middle-echelon military officers in the making of Japanese foreign policy. This middle-echelon group was more adventurous, more contemptuous of compromise, and more militaristic.

Second, the hard-liners were prone to making false analogies from the past. For example, Hornbeck argued that the exaggerated gestures of men such as Matsuoka in the past actually reflected a lack of Japanese resolve to wage war. . . .

Third, the hard-line faction concluded that, in light of the disparity in strength between Japan and the United States, Japanese decision makers could not rationally decide on war. In this regard they made the mistake of applying to the Japanese in unaltered form the western model of decision making based upon rational behavior. Lack of knowledge about the psychology of the Japanese people and especially of the middle-echelon military officers in the period immediately preceding the war led the hard-line faction to miscalculate Japanese psychology. That psychology was marked by a predisposition to making crucial decisions in the face of extremely great, even illogical, risks—as was expressed in Tōjō Hideki's often quoted statement that "sometimes a man has to jump with his eyes closed, from the temple of Kiyomizu into the ravine below." This predisposition was also characterized by an absolute abhorrence of submission. They would choose "death rather than humiliation." Grew understood that mentality. He wrote, "Japan is a nation of hard warriors, still inculcated with the samurai do-or-die spirit which has by tradition and inheritance become ingrained in the race." He was correct in warning the decision makers at home not to miscalculate the peculiarities in the Japanese mode of action. Had his advice been followed the Pacific War might very well have been avoided. Grew was prudent. The same thing could not be said for the hard-liners.

Roosevelt's Global Perspective: The Russian Factor in Japanese-American Relations

WALDO HEINRICHS

Despite all we know about the road to Pearl Harbor, it is still hard to fathom why the United States brought matters to a head with Japan in July–August 1941 when it was supposedly pursuing a strategy of concentration against Germany and strict defense in the Pacific. In particular, it is difficult to understand why the United States imposed a total embargo on the shipment of petroleum products to Japan when officials from the president on down recognized that such an act might propel Japan into a grab for Dutch East Indies oil, the very southern advance the United States hoped to prevent. The various explanations at hand—sentimentalism over China,

From Waldo Heinrichs, "The Russian Factor in Japanese-American Relations, 1941," in Hilary Conroy and Harry Wray, eds., *Pearl Harbor Reexamined: Prologue to the Pacific War,* © 1990. Reprinted by permission of The University of Hawai'i Press.

naive hopes about the deterrent capacity of air power in the Philippines, a coup by hawkish bureaucrats while the president was at the Atlantic Conference, chaotic decision making in the Roosevelt administration—simply do not alone or together provide satisfying answers.

Perhaps we are looking in the wrong direction. It is true that East Asia–Pacific policy had its own parameters, as did Atlantic-European policy, and that American policies East and West tended to be the reciprocals of one another. Yet this was not the only framework of policy. The great question for world leaders in the first half of 1941 was whether Hitler would attack the Soviet Union, and the great question in the latter half was whether he would succeed. This was the central dynamic of world politics from which hung in large measure the strategic decisions of Japan, Great Britain, and the United States, not to mention the USSR, which had its own East-West reciprocals, standing as it did between Germany and Japan.

A chain of reciprocals encircled the globe, and every link was relevant to Roosevelt and his advisers; their framework of policy was truly worldwide by 1941. So we may hypothesize that the German-Soviet conflict had a direct bearing on Japanese-American relations. Within this wider canvas we may find better answers to nagging questions.

A decisive change—one needing greater emphasis—occurred in American foreign and strategic policy in mid-1941. It occurred at the time of, and partly as a result of, the Atlantic Conference between Churchill and Roosevelt but was not bounded by the time frame or agenda of that conference.

From January until well into July of 1941 Roosevelt's policy had been extremely cautious and hesitant. Fear of encouraging isolationist sentiment during the Lend-Lease debate was undoubtedly one factor. So was a scarcity of military resources. The U.S. Atlantic Fleet simply did not have the ships and readiness to make an important contribution to the Battle of the Atlantic before mid-summer. Japan's threat of southward advance, reinforced by the Soviet-Japanese neutrality treaty, delayed the transfer of reinforcements from the Pacific Fleet to the Atlantic.

What most worried Roosevelt, however, was uncertainty about Hitler's intentions. The United States did not, as we thought was the case, receive an unambiguous warning early in 1941 of the forthcoming German attack on the Soviet Union. In these months an invasion of England remained the most likely possibility. From April on German troop movements to the East made a decisive outcome of Soviet-German tensions seem inevitable, but the overwhelming belief was that the German concentration was for the purpose of intimidation, that Hitler would finally present an ultimatum demanding concessions, and that Stalin would bow. The German blitz in the Balkans in April and the seizure of Crete in May pointed the way to Suez and the Middle East, and at all times intelligence flowed into Washington, which was especially sensitive on the score, of a possible German southwestern drive through Spain and Gibraltar to northwestern Africa and Dakar.

Roosevelt and his advisers were truly uncertain about which set of reports to believe until early June. No possible vector of German advance seemed sure enough to build policy on, and so the tendency was to guard against the worst case and protect the Atlantic. After a year of devastating events, a German attack on Russia looked too good to be true. Even if an attack occurred, the war was not expected to last longer than four to eight weeks, allowing time for further campaigning that year. The aura of German power before the Russian campaign was little short of overwhelming.

Beginning with the Japanese acquisition of bases in southern Indochina at the end of July, American policy changed dramatically. It is hard to imagine how Roosevelt could have avoided some demonstration of firmness in the face of this latest Japanese move, obviously penultimate to an attack on Malaya and the Dutch East Indies and taken despite American warnings and mounting trade curbs stopping just short of oil. What is difficult to account for solely in an East Asian or any other regional context is the sweeping nature and boldness of his moves. He ordered a suspension of petroleum exports to Japan before leaving for the Atlantic Conference and converted it into an embargo upon his return. At the conference he established that no significant secret agreements yet existed between Britain and the USSR and worked out with [Winston S.] Churchill a set of war aims that were congruent with American Wilsonian values and that formed a basis for risking or waging war. He agreed to undertake an escort of convoys in the western Atlantic. He ordered maximum assistance to the Soviet Union before winter set in and pushed for a conference in Moscow to arrange for further deliveries in amounts acceptable to the Soviets. He agreed to Churchill's plea for a warning to Japan that any further move would lead to war, and he gave it, although in diluted form. Finally, he began reinforcement of the Philippines, especially with air power.

The assertion that Roosevelt temporarily suspended oil exports contradicts the conclusion of well-accepted, independent studies of the question and requires an explanation. [The historians] Jonathan Utley and Irvine Anderson have been most helpful in showing the extent to which shipments of petroleum products had already been virtually halted by various means such as the withdrawal of tankers and a ban on shipment of oil in drums. They contend that despite Roosevelt's declared intent of permitting the shipment of some kinds and amounts of petroleum products, Dean Acheson and other second-level officials managed to discover bureaucratic devices to shut the tap completely while the president was away at the Atlantic Conference.

On the point of presidential knowledge and intent, I disagree. Declarations to the contrary notwithstanding, Roosevelt left for the Atlantic Conference determined to withhold further shipments of oil until he had discussed this and related questions with Churchill. Sumner Welles, acting secretary of state and long-time confidant of Roosevelt, told Assistant Secretary [Dean] Acheson on July 29 that the "happiest solution" would be to withhold action on Japanese applications for dollars to buy oil for the "next week or so." Evidence suggests that the time frame he meant was in fact two weeks, or not far short of the time during which Welles and the president would be at the Atlantic Conference.

It is difficult to imagine Welles not speaking for Roosevelt or Acheson acting without authorization on so sensitive an issue. Acting on orders fits with Acheson's account in his memoirs and with his discontent at his own performance eight years earlier when, as undersecretary of the treasury, he had refused to sign an order legalizing the devaluation of the dollar and had been fired for it. The lesson he drew and undoubtedly applied on this his second chance was that an assistant to the president must be "very alert and watchful" of the president's position and interests, indeed "twice as much as your own." Acheson was under orders to stall and found ways to comply.

The president was temporizing but moving in a direction he knew entailed great risk. Why would he do so just when he was about to enter into the Battle of the Atlantic? Surely the logic of Plan Dog and Rainbow 5, of concentration against Germany and defense in the Pacific, would argue against so severe an oil policy.

We begin to understand Roosevelt's intent if we consider an event that coincided with the Japanese move into southern Indochina and war at least as significant: a pause in the German advance on Moscow beginning July 19 and lasting into mid-August, occasioned by the need for resupply and a disagreement among Hitler and his generals about a strategy for the next stage. While Roosevelt was considering what to do about Japan he was seeing the first evidence that the Soviet Union might, after all, survive the German onslaught until winter and so into 1942. The press reported "Nazi drives halted," "blitzkrieg braked." On July 29 the *Washington Post* described the German invasion timetable as "completely upset." The same day Hanson Baldwin, under a headline, "Winter Looms as Red Ally," wrote: "The future history of the world is being written in the struggling melee of tanks and planes and men on the 2,000 mile front." Diplomatic reports reinforced the emerging optimism. The American embassy in Berlin learned that German plans were awry due to the discovery of a second Soviet defense line of more than 100 fresh divisions east of the so-called Stalin Line. The general feeling in Germany now was that the war would go into another winter. At his conference with Churchill, Roosevelt heard [presidential assistant] Harry Hopkins' encouraging report of his meeting with Stalin.

From the depths of despair, morale bounded higher than circumstances at the moment justified, but even the possibility of Russian survival made all the difference. The reversal of fortunes from as late as March 1941 when an alignment of the Axis with the Soviet Union seemed quite possible was near miraculous. A coalition of the United States, Great Britain, and the Soviet Union had the power to defeat Germany. This was the time to get Hitler, said Treasury Secretary Henry Morgenthau. "We will never have a better chance. . . . [W]e can't count on the good Lord and just plain dumb luck forever." Roosevelt began pressing his aides to allocate and speed shipments of arms to the Soviet Union in the strongest possible way, as a matter of vital national safety.

Support for the Soviet Union and the grand coalition to defeat Hitler had serious implications for American East Asian policy. The question before the Japanese government in the wake of the German attack was whether to join Germany, as requested, in attacking the Soviet Union or to pursue its southward advance. The decision of the Imperial Conference of July 2 was to move into southern Indochina but to prepare in the north and to attack if circumstances favored it, that is, if the Germans were clearly winning and the Soviets transferred enough of their Far Eastern forces to the western front. Preparing in the north meant mobilizing 850,000 men, causing an inflow of troops carefully monitored by American consuls in Manchuria. It was difficult to decide whether Japan would go north or south, or when and under what conditions, but an attack on Russia became a distinct possibility.

Opposite were thirty tough, experienced Soviet divisions, three cavalry brigades, sixteen tank brigades, and 2,000 tanks and aircraft. A great deal depended on whether a crisis in the west would compel Stalin to withdraw these forces. American leaders undoubtedly asked themselves what conditions would provide Stalin with sufficient assurance about Siberia to withdraw enough of these forces to survive in the west. Foreign Minister V. M. Molotov sought an American warning that the United States would come to Russia's assistance if it were attacked by Japan. Roosevelt was not prepared to offer such a commitment, to join the war and send an army to the Russian front, as invited, to provide more than token aid in 1941. What could he do to help?

To do nothing regarding Japan would not only leave the resources of southeast Asia and Britain's connections to Australia and New Zealand at Japan's mercy but would offer no discouragement to a Japanese attack on the Soviet rear. To pursue diplomacy might prevent or delay a southward advance, but any agreement at China's expense was likely to weaken China's will to resist and permit further redeployment of Japanese forces north or south or both. Furthermore, any evidence of American appeasement was likely to undermine American credibility and reliability in the eyes of the anti-Hitler coalition. Any security Japan might gain in the south by an agreement with the United States could well encourage Japan to strike northward. Any assurance of American petroleum supplies, a probable requirement of agreement, would provide the wherewithal. Even reducing allocations to Japan's peacetime levels would allow the import of more than five million barrels of crude oil and nearly half a million barrels of gasoline in the remainder of 1941.

Roosevelt could also apply maximum pressure: not a drop of oil. Let Japan's oil supplies dry up and its capacity for military operations anywhere shrink. Seek closer collaboration with the British, Dutch, and Australians and provide further assistance to the Chinese. Reinforce the Philippines, especially with long-range bombers capable of raiding Japanese cities. Create such uncertainty and concern among Japanese decision makers regarding the south and relations with America that they did not dare go north. This was a line of argument advanced by an officer in the Far Eastern division of the State Department a few days after the German attack on the Soviet Union.

Containment was Roosevelt's preferred way of dealing with Japanese aggression. Victory in any struggle between the two nations, he wrote in 1923, was bound to lie with the United States, which had vast economic superiority. In 1937 he had commented approvingly on a suggestion by the U.S. Asiatic Fleet commander, Admiral Harry Yarnell, that the way to fight Japan was to form a common front with Britain, France, the Netherlands, and the Soviet Union to cut off all trade with Japan, simply attacking Japanese commerce from distant encircling bases, while China tied down Japanese troops. The result would be the "strangulation" of Japan without the cost of huge armies or Jutland-style naval battles.

Containment on this order, of course, remained only an idea as the threat of Hitler supervened and conceivable Asian partners fell by the wayside, weakened or turned in other directions. Now, however, the British-American alignment with the Soviet Union, even if only implicit as far as Japan was concerned, the growing possibility of establishing a British Eastern Fleet, and the availability of B-17 bombers and their success in flying the longest hop to Hawaii in a possible ferry route to the Philippines revived the idea of containment.

July was a wonderful clarifying month for Roosevelt and his advisers. Hitler's attack on the Soviet Union together with the first evidence of the Russians' ability to sustain resistance made it conceivable, realistic, and calculable to marshal forces sufficient to defeat Nazi Germany. On July 9 the president ordered the services to estimate how much total production would be required to defeat the nation's potential enemies.

The incalculable component of this global scheme was Japan. The Soviet-German war had intensified Japanese expansionism, opportunism, and unpredictability. Whether Japan went north or south—and who could tell which?—it threatened to upset the improving balance of forces. This careening expansionism must be stopped. Japan must be boxed in, contained, immobilized. Embargo, coalition diplomacy, military aid, demonstrations of firmness, and air and naval deployments would, it was hoped, keep Japan within bounds. The risks of war would increase, but the risks of inaction, in the global calculus, seemed greater. Roosevelt could see the whole picture now. He was forceful, impatient of delay, pressing upon events, so different from the reserved, withdrawn president of the spring.

Let no one mistake the severity of American policy toward Japan. Acheson reported to Welles upon the latter's return from the Atlantic Conference that none of Japan's applications for funds had been approved. No countervailing directive came down; Roosevelt had promised Churchill to maintain his economic measures in full force, and he did. Utley and Anderson have shown that Acheson and his colleagues, by insisting that the Japanese pay from sequestered funds before dollars could be unblocked and by other devices, managed to bring trade to a halt without any formal order. They could point out, Acheson explained with relish to a British diplomat, that the Japanese had "imposed [an] embargo upon themselves by their lack of loyalty" to the American order to freeze their dollars.

Roosevelt's dilution of the war warning was not a weakening but a means of delay. The Japanese suggestion of a leaders' meeting provided too good an opportunity of stringing out talks while reinforcement of the Philippines proceeded and the de facto embargo took hold. Careful examination of the American documents and negotiating position reveals not a whit of evidence that Roosevelt or Hull intended compromise or summit. Somewhat like Acheson and his trade officials, the Far Eastern officers of the State Department questioned, compared, and criticized Japanese terms, asking always for further clarification and explanation without registering progress or impasse. The object was, as Roosevelt had told Churchill, to gain a delay of thirty to sixty days. Upon the fall of the Konoe cabinet in October he wrote Churchill that he had gained "two months of respite in the Far East."

Before meeting Churchill at the Atlantic Conference, Roosevelt met with his military advisers and authorized sending thirty-six B-17's to the Philippines. "That was a distinct change of policy," General H. H. Arnold later reminisced. "It was the start of a thought to give General MacArthur weapons for offensive operations." As General George Marshall, chief of staff, explained, these planes would act as a "serious deterrent" to Japan, especially in the winter months that were suitable for high altitude bombing.

After the Atlantic Conference, from the middle of August through September, news from the Russian front was dismal; the Germans besieged Leningrad and encircled Kiev, capturing two-thirds of a million Soviet troops. The Ukraine and Odessa were lost, the Crimea cut off, the crossings of the Dnieper seized. Beyond lay the riches of the Donetz Basin and the Caucasus. Every major city of European Russia except, for the moment, Moscow, was imperiled. Stalin admitted in a letter to Churchill that the Soviet Union was in "mortal menace" and would be defeated or rendered useless as an ally unless the British mounted a second front in the Balkans or France and provided large quantities of aluminum, aircraft, and tanks. The Soviet ambassador, in conveying the message, Churchill informed Roosevelt, used language implying a separate peace if Soviet demands could not be met.

A second front was out of the question, but Roosevelt and Churchill were determined to do what they could by way of supply. They hastened a conference in Moscow and cobbled together a commitment of 500 tanks per month, which meant stretching out the equipping of the U.S. Third, Fourth, and Fifth Armored Divisions and fifteen independent tank battalions, and postponing the activation of the Sixth Armored Division. They also promised 1,800 planes. Roosevelt supplied the three largest U.S. troop transports to take a British division to Basra, Iraq, from where it might reinforce the Russians in the Caucasus or, in case they collapsed, defend against a German thrust from that direction.

On September 5, the day Roosevelt received Stalin's message, besides approving arrangements for the first escort of convoys and the Basra transports, the president saw Hull, who converted Acheson's undercover stalling tactics into a de facto embargo. On that same day nine B-17's departed from Hawaii for the Philippines, and twenty-seven more received orders to depart in October. As Churchill had informed Stalin on August 28, Roosevelt "seemed disposed . . . to take a strong line against further Japanese aggression whether in the South or in the Northwest Pacific." General [George C.] Marshall urged the president to authorize a buildup of air power in the Philippines to restrain Japan "from advance into Malaysia or Eastern Siberia." On September 12, when the first nine B-17's arrived safely, the army ordered thirty-five more across in December, totaling seventy, together with dive bombers, more fighters, and command, air warning, reconnaisance, ordnance, and engineering units for the air force as well as tanks, antiaircraft, and artillery. About this time, according to the British ambassador Lord Halifax, Roosevelt sent a verbal message to [Josef] Stalin (possibly through Averell Harriman) advising that in case of an acute crisis in the west he should withdraw his troops from Siberia and not worry about what the Japanese did, because any incursion could be corrected later. Support for the Soviet Union correlated with a stiffening policy toward Japan.

In October a powerful, concentrated German assault on Moscow made the Russian situation even more precarious. The question returned of how to get Japan "off Russia's back," as one diplomat put it. An army intelligence estimate of October 2 warned against any agreement with Japan that would permit Japan to withdraw the bulk of its army from China. Any liberation of Japanese forces "for action against Russia's rear in Siberia would be foolhardy." The Army War Plans Division advised a continuation of existing pressures "with a view to rendering Japan incapable of offensive operations against Russia or against possessions of the associated powers in the Far East."

The fall of the Konoe cabinet on October 16 and the appointment of General Tōjō as premier increased fears of Japanese aggression. Some signs pointed south, but the balance of opinion in October, including the president's, was that Japan would strike to the north. With the embargo now complete, with persistent warnings already given to Japan against an attack to the north as well as to the south, the only further means of pressure was to strengthen American military power in the region. With the president's approval the army had increased the number of B-17's planned for the Philippines to 170. The dispatch of these aircraft, however, was scheduled over many months, and the force would not be complete until October 1942. On October 16, 1941, in the wake of the fall of the Konoe cabinet and after an emergency meeting of the president and his military advisers, the dispatch of the bombers was accelerated so that 165 would arrive by March 1942. Now also for the first time the army committed an additional ground combat unit, an infantry regiment, and another tank battalion, an antiaircraft regiment, and a field artillery brigade. The navy dispatched Submarine Squadron Two, twelve newly commissioned boats, pushing the Asiatic Fleet's submarine force to twenty-nine, the largest in the navy.

As the establishment of American air power in East Asia progressed, the American military leadership warmed to the idea. The Army War Plans Division argued that "strong offensive air forces" in the Philippines, prepared to operate from British and Dutch bases, would provide a crucial deterrent to Japanese expansion southward. Deterring a Japanese attack on Siberia would be American, British, and Dutch forces in Japan's rear, as well as the possibility of American entry into the war and the use of Russian bases for bombardment of Japan's cities.

Secretary of War Henry Stimson was enthusiastic about the capability of the B-17's to deter an attack on Singapore. He was skeptical about northward deterrence but nevertheless advised the president that Vladivostock was crucial for the supply of Russian troops because the Archangel route was in jeopardy from the German advance and the Persian corridor was undeveloped. He presented an exciting picture of these long-range bombers sweeping from the Philippines across Japan to Soviet bases on the Kamchatka Peninsula and onward to Alaska and back, after the fashion of the German Condors shuttling between bases in western France and Norway.

General Marshall showed unaccustomed enthusiasm in describing the new possibilities. In a phone conversation he pointed out that the B-17's could operate from Australia, New Britain, Singapore, and the Dutch East Indies, "possibly even Vladivostock." They could cover the whole area of possible Japanese operations and "exercise a more determining influence on the course of events right now than anything else." This force, he said, "practically backs the Japanese off and would certainly stop them on the Malaysian thing. It probably would make them feel they didn't dare take the Siberian thing and I think it has a better than 50 percent chance of forcing them to practically drop the Axis." By acting quickly the United States might give Japan "a complete pause."

Similar thinking was occurring in London. The fall of the Konoe cabinet and what Foreign Minister Anthony Eden described as the "Russian defeats," and the Admiralty as "the deterioration of the Russian situation," precipitated a decision pressed by Churchill and Eden to send H.M.S. *Prince of Wales* with the new carrier *Indomitable* to join the battlecruiser *Repulse* in the Indian Ocean. "The firmer your attitude and ours," Churchill wrote Roosevelt, "the less chance of their taking the plunge."

In early November it appeared that the threat to the survival of Russia had passed, and a change occurred. The German offensive against Moscow bogged down in bad weather at the end of October. Winter seemed to have finally arrived. Optimism about Russia's ability to survive reemerged. Now the Soviet problem could be disengaged from Japanese-American relations. This was fortunate, too, because evidence was now accumulating about a Japanese attack to the south. Plan Dog thinking revived, and the president and Hull seriously attempted to reach a temporary accommodation with the Japanese that would permit the completion of the reinforcement of the Philippines. This foundered on Chinese and British objections, and the road then led directly to Pearl Harbor. Confidence that the Russian campaign was over for the winter lasted only briefly. The German offensive resumed on November 15, and by November 25, the day the *modus vivendi* project was cancelled, Moscow was imperiled. The Red Army was said to be fighting "one of the most critical battles of its history." The Russian situation looked "awful" to Roosevelt; Moscow, he said, was "falling." The time called for solidarity and steadfastness. Critical in the final defense of Moscow and the Russian counteroffensive launched December 4 were the Siberian troops withdrawn from the Far East.

It was not a case of Roosevelt's saving Moscow. Stalin withdrew half his Far Eastern forces on information gathered in October by his spy Richard Sorge in the German embassy in Tokyo that the Japanese were headed south not north. The Japanese decided on August 9, at the time of the Atlantic Conference and before Roosevelt had settled on a full-scale embargo, not to attack Siberia unless the Soviets collapsed. The embargo did not contain; it precipitated a decision to attack southward. Only a small portion of the air-power deterrent arrived in time and was soon wiped out. Submarine Squadron Two's torpedoes did not work. The *Indomitable* went on reef in Jamaica, the *Prince of Wales* and *Repulse* to the bottom of the South China Sea. Fallacies about air power, confusion between deterrence (the B-17's) and coercion (the embargo), gross underestimation of Japanese military capability and desperate determination, and racist notions of firmness in dealing with Asians: all these errors occurred.

Yet what other reasonable courses lay open to Roosevelt and his advisers? Was serious negotiation possible with a Japanese government that was so opportunistic, unpredictable, and given to force? What would be the consequences of negotiation in light of information available to the American government, which by no means ruled out an attack northward? Circumstances can outpace men's ability to avoid war.

However one judges the wisdom of the containment of Japan, the Russian factor goes a long way toward answering the questions raised here. Roosevelt engaged in an oil embargo to immobilize Japan and prevent any attack north or south. This entailed a risk—more than he knew—of an attack southward but less of a risk than a Japanese attack northward because the survival of the Soviet Union was crucial to a victory over Germany. Roosevelt rejected negotiation with Japan except to gain time because any measure of stability Japan might secure in the south might encourage an attack northward. It pays to think beyond Plan Dog and the Atlantic-Pacific options and to see the problem the way FDR saw it, in a global perspective.

 F U R T H E R   R E A D I N G

Selig Adler, *The Isolationist Impulse* (1957)

Irvine H. Anderson, *The Standard-Vacuum Oil Company and United States East Asia Policy* (1975)

Michael Barnhart, *Japan Prepares for Total War* (1987)

————, *Japan and the World Since 1868* (1995)

————, "The Origins of the Second World War in Asia and the Pacific: Synthesis Impossible?" *Diplomatic History,* 20 (1996), 241–260

Charles A. Beard, *President Roosevelt and the Coming of the War, 1941* (1948)

Michael Beschloss, *Kennedy and Roosevelt* (1980)

Günter Bischof and Robert L. Dupont, eds., *The Pacific War Revisited* (1997)

Dorothy Borg, *The United States and the Far Eastern Crisis of 1933–1938* (1964)

————and Shumpei Okamoto, eds., *Pearl Harbor as History* (1973)

Russell D. Buhite, *Nelson T. Johnson and American Policy Toward China* (1968)

James M. Burns, *The Lion and the Fox* (1956)

Richard D. Burns and Edward M. Bennett, eds., *Diplomats in Crisis* (1974)

Robert J. C. Butow, *The John Doe Associates* (1974)

————, "Marching Off to War on the Wrong Foot: The Final Note Tokyo Did Not Send to Washington," *Pacific Historical Review,* 63 (1994), 67–79

————, *Tojo and the Coming of the War* (1961)

Mark Chadwin, *The Hawks of World War II* (1968)

J. Garry Clifford and Samuel R. Spencer, Jr., *The First Peacetime Draft* (1986)

————, "Both Ends of the Telescope: New Perspectives on FDR and American Entry into World War II," *Diplomatic History,* 13 (1989), 213–230

Warren I. Cohen, *America's Response to China* (1990)

Wayne S. Cole, *America First: The Battle Against Intervention, 1940–1941* (1953)

————, *Roosevelt and the Isolationists, 1932–1945* (1983)

James Crowley, *Japan's Quest for Autonomy* (1966)

David H. Culbert, *News for Everyman* (1976) (radio and foreign affairs)

Robert Dallek, *Franklin D. Roosevelt and American Foreign Policy* (1979)

Kenneth R. Davis, *FDR* (1993)

Roger Dingman, *Power in the Pacific* (1976)

Robert A. Divine, *The Reluctant Belligerent* (1979)

Justus D. Doenecke and John E. Wilz, *From Isolation to War* (1991)

John Dower, *Japan in War and Peace* (1993)

Herbert Feis, *The Road to Pearl Harbor* (1950)

Frank Freidel, *Franklin D. Roosevelt: A Rendezvous with Destiny* (1990)

Lloyd Gardner, *Economic Aspects of New Deal Diplomacy* (1964)

Martin Gilbert, *Winston S. Churchill: Finest Hour, 1939–1941* (1983)

John M. Haight, Jr., *American Aid to France, 1938–1940* (1970)

Patrick Hearden, *Roosevelt Confronts Hitler* (1987)

Waldo H. Heinrichs, Jr., *American Ambassador* (1966) (Joseph Grew)

Saburō Ienaga, *The Pacific War* (1978)

Akira Iriye, *Across the Pacific* (1967)

————, *After Imperialism* (1969)

———— and Warren Cohen, eds., *American, Chinese, and Japanese Perspectives on Wartime Asia, 1931–1949* (1990)

Manfred Jonas, *Isolationism in America* (1966)

Kenneth P. Jones, *U.S. Diplomats in Europe, 1919–1941* (1981)

Warren F. Kimball, *The Most Unsordid Act: Lend-Lease, 1939–1941* (1969)

Charles P. Kindleberger, *The World in Depression, 1929–1939* (1973)

William E. Kinsella, Jr., *Leadership in Isolation* (1978)

Walter LaFeber, *The Clash* (1997) (on Japan)

William L. Langer and S. E. Gleason, *The Challenge to Isolation, 1937–1940* (1952)

————, *The Undeclared War, 1940–1941* (1953)

William E. Leuchtenburg, *Franklin D. Roosevelt and the New Deal* (1963)

Robert D. Lowe, ed., *Pearl Harbor Revisited* (1994)

Mark A. Lowenthal, *Leadership and Indecision* (1988) (war planning)

Thomas R. Maddux, *Years of Estrangement* (1980) (Soviet Union)

Frederick W. Marks III, *Wind over Sand* (1988) (FDR)

Jonathan Marshall, *To Have and Have Not* (1995) (raw materials and war)

Gorden Martel, ed., *The Origins of the Second World War Reconsidered* (1986)

Martin V. Melosi, *The Shadow of Pearl Harbor* (1977)

James W. Morley, ed., *Deterrent Diplomacy* (1976)

————, ed., *The Fateful Choice* (1979) (Japan and Southeast Asia)

————, ed., *Japan's Road to the Pacific War: The Final Confrontation* (1994)

Charles Neu, *The Troubled Encounter* (1975)

William L. Neumann, *America Encounters Japan* (1963)

Arnold Offner, *American Appeasement* (1969)

————, *The Origins of the Second World War* (1975)

Stephen Pelz, *Race to Pearl Harbor* (1974)

Gordon W. Prange, *At Dawn We Slept: The Untold Story of Pearl Harbor* (1981)

————, *Pearl Harbor* (1986)

Julius Pratt, *Cordell Hull* (1964)

David Reynolds, *The Creation of the Anglo-American Alliance, 1937–41* (1982)

Bruce Russett, *No Clear and Present Danger* (1972)

Michael Schaller, *The U.S. Crusade in China, 1938–1945* (1978)

Arthur M. Schlesinger, Jr., "The Man of the Century," *American Heritage,* May/June 1994, 82–93 (on FDR)

David F. Schmitz, *The United States and Fascist Italy, 1922–1940* (1988)

Paul W. Schroeder, *Axis Alliance and Japanese-American Relations, 1941* (1958)

Raymond Sontag, *A Broken World, 1919–1939* (1971)

Richard Steele, *Propaganda in an Open Society* (1985) (FDR and media)

Youli Sun, *China and the Origins of the Pacific War* (1993)

Charles C. Tansill, *Back Door to War* (1952)

James C. Thomson, Jr., et al., *Sentimental Imperialists* (1981)

John Toland, *Infamy: Pearl Harbor and Its Aftermath* (1982)

Jonathan G. Utley, *Going to War with Japan, 1937–1941* (1985)

Cornelis A. Van Minnen and John F. Sears, eds., *FDR and His Contemporaries* (1992) (foreign views)

Paul A. Varg, *The Closing of the Door* (1973)

D. C. Watt, *How War Came* (1989)

Lawrence Wittner, *Rebels Against War* (1984)

Roberta Wohlstetter, *Pearl Harbor: Warning and Decision* (1962)

Defeating the Axis, Planning the Peace: The Second World War

After American entry into the Second World War, Great Britain, the United States, and the Soviet Union formed the fifty-nation Grand Alliance, which in time would force the Axis to surrender. Through extensive correspondence and summit meetings, the Allied leaders Winston S. Churchill, Franklin D. Roosevelt, and Joseph Stalin not only plotted military strategy to defeat Germany, Italy, and Japan but also shaped plans for the postwar era. Big Three decisions about war and peace, and the upending results of the war, transformed the international system: power shifted from some states to others, wartime destruction battered economies, decolonization eroded traditional empires, social divisions widened, political stability in both defeated and victorious nations fractured, new world organizations emerged, and the atomic bomb terrified all. Soon after defeating the Axis, the Grand Alliance broke apart, already having generated the sources of a new conflict—the Cold War.

Although the Allies cooperated sufficiently to win the war, they bickered a great deal over both war strategy and the postwar structure of international relations. Legacies of distrust from hostile prewar relations and opposing ideologies impeded harmony. Allied goals also differed: Britain sought to resurrect its empire, to blunt Soviet expansion, and to direct European affairs; the Soviet Union coveted the Baltic states and friendly communist governments in Eastern Europe; the United States eyed new influence, especially in Asia and the Pacific, worked for the Open Door in trade, and looked to great-power postwar control through what Roosevelt called the "Four Policemen," with the United States, of course, ranking first among these international sheriffs.

The Allies exchanged sharp views during the war on the opening of a second, or western, military front. They squabbled over the location of new military campaigns and the timely availability of U.S. supplies under the U.S. Lend-Lease program. They suspected each other of flirting with separate peaces. They jockeyed for political position in the countries liberated from Nazi and Japanese control, such as

Poland and China. The Allies, moreover, debated the colonial question—should France return to imperial rule in Indochina, for example? They also created the United Nations Organization, the World Bank, the International Monetary Fund, and the United Nations Relief and Rehabilitation Administration. Then they competed for influence in the new bodies, in the process shattering unity. All the while, three bold individuals of exceptional power—Churchill, Roosevelt, and Stalin— alternately clashed and cooperated, nipped and purred, in extraordinary episodes of personal diplomacy.

The foreign policy of President Franklin D. Roosevelt stands at the center of any discussion of the Grand Alliance. Some scholars treat his record favorably, emphasizing his grasp of power realities, his understanding of both the limits and the opportunities of power, his deft handling of Churchill and Stalin to keep the alliance together, his highminded desire to free colonies, and his skill in negotiating the unique complexities of conducting a global war. After all, the Allies did achieve the impressive feat of smashing powerful enemies, and they did sketch promising plans for the future. In the eventual faltering of those plans, the responsibility perhaps lies with Roosevelt's successors. Some historians argue, furthermore, that the United States used the opportunity of war to weaken the British Empire, to expand American interests, including overseas bases and new markets and economic holdings, and to thwart a rising political left. Under Roosevelt's leadership, then, the United States deliberately developed and protected a larger American sphere of influence while offering to honor the spheres of other great powers. Without recognized spheres, some defenders of Roosevelt suggest, the world would have descended into even deeper chaos than that it in fact did.

Roosevelt's management of wartime and postwar issues has also drawn considerable criticism. Some writers believe that the president made military decisions without adequately considering their long-term political impact. Some critics hold Roosevelt responsible for the postwar Soviet domination of Eastern Europe, faulting him for not using American power to blunt Stalin's aggressive push into neighboring nations. The president's negotiations at summit conferences have particularly sparked debate, in large part because many of the agreements did not hold and because, in the case of the Yalta Conference, Roosevelt's deteriorating health raises questions about his performance. Critics, too, challenge his spheres-of-influence approach to world politics, noting that it trampled on weak or small nations. Some conclude that Roosevelt said much about decolonization but did little. Others charge that the president, fearing a rebirth of isolationism, did not prepare the American people for the global role they would have to play and the compromises they would be called on to accept after the war. Even more, some claim, Roosevelt deceived people and ignored his advisers, holding his cards close to the vest, arrogantly thinking that he would fix everything in the long run. But for him, there was no long run; he died in April 1945, before the war ended. Thus is prompted a perennial question in history: What if he had lived?

  ## D O C U M E N T S

The timing of the opening of a second front in Europe troubled Allied relations until June 6, 1944, when British, American, and Canadian troops crossed the English Channel to attack German forces in France. Until that time, bearing the brunt of the European war, the Soviets pressed for action. In Document 1, a U.S. report on the Washington, D.C., meeting

of May 30, 1942, between President Franklin D. Roosevelt and Soviet foreign minister
V. M. Molotov, FDR promised a second front before year's end. But delays set in. Marshal
Joseph Stalin's letter of June 24, 1943, to Churchill reveals the embittered Soviet leader's
impatience. A Soviet record, it is reprinted here as Document 2. At the Allied conference
held at Teheran, Iran, Roosevelt and Stalin discussed the president's concept of "Four
Policemen." The American record of the Roosevelt-Stalin meeting on November 29, 1943,
is reprinted as Document 3. Allied interest in spheres of influence is illustrated by Document 4—the Churchill-Stalin percentages agreement, which delineated British and Soviet
roles in liberated nations. This account of the Moscow meeting of October 1944 is drawn
from Churchill's memoirs.

Document 5 and Document 6—agreements struck at the Yalta Conference of February
4–11, 1945—demonstrate a high degree of Allied compromise and unity on many issues as
the Big Three neared victory over Germany. In Document 7, a letter dated April 4, 1945,
Roosevelt chided Stalin for charging that U.S. officials were negotiating with German
authorities in Switzerland behind Soviet backs. Just before Roosevelt's death, in response
to Churchill's warnings about Soviet manipulation of Polish politics, the president wrote
the prime minister a reassuring letter of April 11, 1945, reprinted here as Document 8.

1. Roosevelt Promises a Second Front, 1942

Mr. [V. M.] Molotov . . . remarked that, though the problem of the second front was
both military and political, it was predominantly political. There was an essential
difference between the situation in 1942 and what it might be in 1943. In 1942
Hitler was the master of all Europe save a few minor countries. He was the chief
enemy of everyone. To be sure, as was devoutly to be hoped, the Russians might
hold and fight on all through 1942. But it was only right to look at the darker side
of the picture. On the basis of his continental dominance, Hitler might throw in
such reinforcements in manpower and material that the Red Army might *not* be
able to hold out against the Nazis. Such a development would produce a serious situation which we must face. The Soviet front would become secondary, the Red
Army would be weakened, and Hitler's strength would be correspondingly greater,
since he would have at his disposal not only more troops, but also the foodstuffs
and raw materials of the Ukraine and the oil-wells of the Caucasus. In such circumstances the outlook would be much less favorable for all hands, and he would not
pretend that such developments were all outside the range of possibility. . . .

Mr. Molotov therefore put this question frankly: could we undertake such offensive action as would draw off 40 German divisions which would be, to tell the
truth, distinctly second-rate outfits? If the answer should be in the affirmative, the
war would be decided in 1942. If negative, the Soviets would fight on alone, doing
their best, and no man would expect more from them than that. He had not, Mr.
Molotov added, received any positive answer in London. Mr. [Winston] Churchill
had proposed that he should return through London on his homeward journey from
Washington, and had promised Mr. Molotov a more concrete answer on his second
visit. Mr. Molotov admitted he realized that the British would have to bear the

This document can be found in U.S. Department of State, *Foreign Relations of the United States: Diplomatic Papers, 1942* (Washington D.C.: Government Printing Office, 1961), III, 576–577.

brunt of the action if a second front were created, but he also was cognizant of the role the United States plays and what influence this country exerts in questions of major strategy. . . .

The difficulties, Mr. Molotov urged, would not be any less in 1943. The chances of success were actually better at present while the Russians still have a solid front. "If you postpone your decision," he said, "you will have eventually to bear the brunt of the war, and if Hitler becomes the undisputed master of the continent, next year will unquestionably be tougher than this one."

The President then put to General [George C.] Marshall the query whether developments were clear enough so that we could say to Mr. Stalin that we are preparing a second front. "Yes," replied the General. The President then authorized Mr. Molotov to inform Mr. Stalin that we expect the formation of a second front this year.

2. Joseph Stalin Conveys Impatience over a Second Front, 1943

From your [Winston Churchill's] messages of last year and this I gained the conviction that you and the President [FDR] were fully aware of the difficulties of organising such an operation and were preparing the invasion accordingly, with due regard to the difficulties and the necessary exertion of forces and means. Even last year you told me that a large-scale invasion of Europe by Anglo-American troops would be effected in 1943. In the Aide-Memoire handed to V. M. Molotov on June 10, 1942, you wrote:

> Finally, and most important of all, we are concentrating our maximum effort on the organization and preparation of a large-scale invasion of the Continent of Europe by British and American forces in 1943. We are setting no limit to the scope and objectives of this campaign, which will be carried out in the first instance by over a million men, British and American, with air forces of appropriate strength.

Early this year you twice informed me, on your own behalf and on behalf of the President, of decisions concerning an Anglo-American invasion of Western Europe intended to "divert strong German land and air forces from the Russian front." You had set yourself the task of bringing Germany to her knees as early as 1943, and named September as the latest date for the invasion.

In your message of January 26 you wrote:

> We have been in conference with our military advisers and have decided on the operations which are to be undertaken by the American and British forces in the first nine months of 1943. We wish to inform you of our intentions at once. We believe that these operations together with your powerful offensive, may well bring Germany to her knees in 1943.

This document can be found in Ministry of Foreign Affairs of the U.S.S.R., *Correspondence Between the Chairman of the Council of Ministers of the U.S.S.R. and the President of the U.S.A. and the Prime Minister of Great Britain During the Great Patriotic War of 1941–1945* (Moscow: Foreign Languages Publishing House, 1957), pp. 74–76.

In your next message, which I received on February 12, you wrote, specifying the date of the invasion of Western Europe, decided on by you and the President:

> We are also pushing preparations to the limit of our resources for a cross-Channel operation in August, in which British and United States units would participate. Here again, shipping and assault-landing craft will be the limiting factors. If the operation is delayed by the weather or other reasons, it will be prepared with stronger forces for September.

Last February, when you wrote to me about those plans and the date for invading Western Europe, the difficulties of that operation were greater than they are now. Since then the Germans have suffered more than one defeat: they were pushed back by our troops in the South, where they suffered appreciable loss; they were beaten in North Africa and expelled by the Anglo-American troops; in submarine warfare, too, the Germans found themselves in a bigger predicament than ever, while Anglo-American superiority increased substantially; it is also known that the Americans and British have won air superiority in Europe and that their navies and mercantile marines have grown in power.

It follows that the conditions for opening a second front in Western Europe during 1943, far from deteriorating, have, indeed, greatly improved.

That being so, the Soviet Government could not have imagined that the British and U.S. Governments would revise the decision to invade Western Europe, which they had adopted early this year. In fact, the Soviet Government was fully entitled to expect the Anglo-American decision would be carried out, that appropriate preparations were under way and that the second front in Western Europe would at last be opened in 1943. . . .

So when you now declare: "I cannot see how a great British defeat and slaughter would aid the Soviet armies," is it not clear that a statement of this kind in relation to the Soviet Union is utterly groundless and directly contradicts your previous and responsible decisions, listed above, about extensive and vigorous measures by the British and Americans to organise the invasion this year, measures on which the complete success of the operation should hinge.

I shall not enlarge on the fact that this [ir?]responsible decision, revoking your previous decisions on the invasion of Western Europe, was reached by you and the President without Soviet participation and without inviting its representatives to the Washington conference, although you cannot but be aware that the Soviet Union's role in the war against Germany and its interest in the problems of the second front are great enough.

There is no need to say that the Soviet Government cannot become reconciled to this disregard of vital Soviet interests in the war against the common enemy.

You say that you "quite understand" my disappointment. I must tell you that the point here is not just the disappointment of the Soviet Government, but the preservation of its confidence in its Allies, a confidence which is being subjected to severe stress. One should not forget that it is a question of saving millions of lives in the occupied areas of Western Europe and Russia and of reducing the enormous sacrifices of the Soviet armies, compared with which the sacrifices of the Anglo-American armies are insignificant.

3. Roosevelt and Stalin Discuss the "Four Policemen," at the Teheran Conference, 1943

The President then said the question of a post-war organization to preserve peace had not been fully explained and dealt with and he would like to discuss with the Marshal the prospect of some organization based on the United Nations.

The President then outlined the following general plan:

1. There would be a large organization composed of some 35 members of the United Nations which would meet periodically at different places, discuss and make recommendations to a smaller body.

Marshal Stalin inquired whether this organization was to be world-wide or European, to which the President replied, world-wide.

The President continued that there would be set up an executive committee composed of the Soviet Union, the United States, United Kingdom and China, together with two additional European states, one South American, one Near East, one Far Eastern country, and one British Dominion. He mentioned that Mr. Churchill did not like this proposal for the reason that the British Empire only had two votes. This Executive Committee would deal with all non-military questions such as agriculture, food, health, and economic questions, as well as the setting up of an International Committee. This Committee would likewise meet in various places.

Marshal Stalin inquired whether this body would have the right to make decisions binding on the nations of the world.

The President replied, yes and no. It could make recommendations for settling disputes with the hope that the nations concerned would be guided thereby, but that, for example, he did not believe the Congress of the United States would accept as binding a decision of such a body. The President then turned to the third organization which he termed "The Four Policemen," namely, the Soviet Union, United States, Great Britain, and China. This organization would have the power to deal immediately with any threat to the peace and any sudden emergency which requires this action. He went on to say that in 1935, when Italy attacked Ethiopia, the only machinery in existence was the League of Nations. He personally had begged France to close the Suez Canal, but they instead referred it to the League which disputed the question and in the end did nothing. The result was that the Italian Armies went through the Suez Canal and destroyed Ethiopia. The President pointed out that had the machinery of the Four Policemen, which he had in mind, been in existence, it would have been possible to close the Suez Canal. The President then summarized briefly the idea that he had in mind.

Marshal Stalin said that he did not think that the small nations of Europe would like the organization composed of the Four Policemen. He said, for example, that a European state would probably resent China having the right to apply certain machinery to it. And in any event, he did not think China would be very powerful at the

---

This document can be found in U.S. Department of State, *Foreign Relations of the United States: Diplomatic Papers, The Conferences at Cairo and Teheran, 1943* (Washington, D.C.: Government Printing Office, 1961), pp. 530–532.

end of the war. He suggested as a possible alternative, the creation of a European or a Far Eastern Committee and a European or a Worldwide organization. He said that in the European Commission there would be the United States, Great Britain, the Soviet Union and possibly one other European state.

The President said that the idea just expressed by Marshal Stalin was somewhat similar to Mr. Churchill's idea of a Regional Committee, one for Europe, one for the Far East, and one for the Americas. Mr. Churchill had also suggested that the United States be a member of the European Commission, but he doubted if the United States Congress would agree to the United States' participation in an exclusively European Committee which might be able to force the dispatch of American troops to Europe.

The President added that it would take a terrible crisis such as at present before Congress would ever agree to that step.

Marshal Stalin pointed out that the world organization suggested by the President, and in particular the Four Policemen, might also require the sending of American troops to Europe.

The President pointed out that he had only envisaged the sending of American planes and ships to Europe, and that England and the Soviet Union would have to handle the land armies in the event of any future threat to the peace. He went on to say that if the Japanese had not attacked the United States, he doubted very much if it would have been possible to send any American forces to Europe.

4. Winston S. Churchill and Stalin Cut Their Percentages Deal, 1944

The moment was apt for business, so I [Churchill] said, "Let us settle about our affairs in the Balkans. Your armies are in Rumania and Bulgaria. We have interests, missions, and agents there. Don't let us get at cross-purposes in small ways. So far as Britain and Russia are concerned, how would it do for you to have ninety per cent predominance in Rumania, for us to have ninety per cent of the say in Greece, and go fifty-fifty about Yugoslavia?" While this was being translated I wrote out on a half-sheet of paper:

Rumania	
Russia	90%
The others	10%
Greece	
Great Britain (in accord with U.S.A.)	90%
Russia	10%
Yugoslavia	50–50%
Hungary	50–50%
Bulgaria	
Russia	75%
The others	25%

I pushed this across to Stalin, who had by then heard the translation. There was a slight pause. Then he took his blue pencil and made a large tick upon it, and passed it back to us. It was all settled in no more time than it takes to set down.

Of course, we had long and anxiously considered our point, and were only dealing with immediate war-time arrangements. All larger questions were reserved on both sides for what we then hoped would be a peace table when the war was won.

After this there was a long silence. The pencilled paper lay in the centre of the table. At length I said, "Might it not be thought rather cynical if it seemed we had disposed of these issues, so fateful to millions of people, in such an offhand manner? Let us burn the paper." "No, you keep it," said Stalin.

5. The Yalta Protocol of Proceedings, 1945

I. World Organization

It was decided:

1. that a United Nations Conference on the proposed world organization should be summoned for Wednesday, 25th April, 1945, and should be held in the United States of America.
2. the Nations to be invited to this Conference should be:
   a. the United Nations as they existed on the 8th February, 1945; and
   b. such of the Associated Nations as have declared war on the common enemy by 1st March, 1945. (For this purpose by the term "Associated Nations" was meant the eight Associated Nations and Turkey). When the Conference on World Organization is held, the delegates of the United Kingdom and United States of America will support a proposal to admit to original membership two Soviet Socialist Republics, i.e. the Ukraine and White Russia.
3. that the United States Government on behalf of the Three Powers should consult the Government of China and the French Provisional Government in regard to decisions taken at the present Conference concerning the proposed World Organization.
4. that the text of the invitation to be issued to all the nations which would take part in the United Nations Conference should be as follows:

Invitation

The Government of the United States of America, on behalf of itself and of the Governments of the United Kingdom, the Union of Soviet Socialist Republics, and the Republic of China and the Provisional Government of the French Republic, invite the Government of —————— to send representatives to a Conference of the United Nations to be held on 25th April, 1945, or soon thereafter, at San Francisco in the United States of America to prepare a Charter for a General International Organization for the maintenance of international peace and security.

The above named governments suggest that the Conference consider as affording a basis for such a Charter the Proposals for the Establishment of a General International Organization, which were made public last October as

This document can be found in U.S. Department of State, *Foreign Relations of the United States: The Conferences at Malta and Yalta, 1945* (Washington, D.C.: Government Printing Office, 1955), pp. 975–982.

a result of the Dumbarton Oaks Conference, and which have now been supplemented by the following provisions for Section C of Chapter VI:

C. Voting

1. Each member of the Security Council should have one vote.
2. Decisions of the Security Council on procedural matters should be made by an affirmative vote of seven members.
3. Decisions of the Security Council on all other matters should be made by an affirmative vote of seven members including the concurring votes of the permanent members; provided that, in decisions under Chapter VIII, Section A, and under the second sentence of paragraph 1 of Chapter VIII, Section C, a party to a dispute should abstain from voting.

Further information as to arrangements will be transmitted subsequently. In the event that the Government of ———— desires in advance of the Conference to present views or comments concerning the proposals, the Government of the United States of America will be pleased to transmit such views and comments to the other participating Governments.

Territorial Trusteeship.   It was agreed that the five Nations which will have permanent seats on the Security Council should consult each other prior to the United Nations Conference on the question of territorial trusteeship.

The acceptance of this recommendation is subject to its being made clear that territorial trusteeship will only apply to (a) existing mandates of the League of Nations; (b) territories detached from the enemy as a result of the present war; (c) any other territory which might voluntarily be placed under trusteeship; and (d) no discussion of actual territories is contemplated at the forthcoming United Nations Conference or in the preliminary consultations, and it will be a matter for subsequent agreement which territories within the above categories will be placed under trusteeship.

II. Declaration on Liberated Europe

The following declaration has been approved:

> The Premier of the Union of Soviet Socialist Republics, the Prime Minister of the United Kingdom and the President of the United States of America have consulted with each other in the common interests of the peoples of their countries and those of liberated Europe. They jointly declare their mutual agreement to concert during the temporary period of instability in liberated Europe the policies of their three governments in assisting the peoples of the former Axis satellite states of Europe to solve by democratic means their pressing political and economic problems.
>
> The establishment of order in Europe and the rebuilding of national economic life must be achieved by processes which will enable the liberated peoples to destroy the last vestiges of Nazism and Fascism and to create democratic institutions of their own choice. This is a principle of the Atlantic Charter—the right of all peoples to choose the form of government under which they will live—the restoration of sovereign rights and self-government to those peoples who have been forcibly deprived of them by the aggressor nations.
>
> To foster the conditions in which the liberated peoples may exercise these rights, the three governments will jointly assist the people in any European liberated state or former Axis satellite state in Europe where in their judgment conditions require (a) to

establish conditions of internal peace; (b) to carry out emergency measures for the relief of distressed peoples; (c) to form interim governmental authorities broadly representative of all democratic elements in the population and pledged to the earliest possible establishment through free elections of governments responsible to the will of the people; and (d) to facilitate where necessary the holding of such elections.

The three governments will consult the other United Nations and provisional authorities or other governments in Europe when matters of direct interest to them are under consideration.

When, in the opinion of the three governments, conditions in any European liberated state or any former Axis satellite state in Europe make such action necessary, they will immediately consult together on the measures necessary to discharge the joint responsibilities set forth in this declaration.

By this declaration we reaffirm our faith in the principles of the Atlantic Charter, our pledges in the Declaration by the United Nations, and our determination to build in cooperation with other peace-loving nations world order under law, dedicated to peace, security, freedom and general well-being of all mankind.

In issuing this declaration, the Three Powers express the hope that the Provisional Government of the French Republic may be associated with them in the procedure suggested.

III. Dismemberment of Germany

It was agreed that Article 12 (a) of the Surrender Terms for Germany should be amended as follows:

> The United Kingdom, the United States of America and the Union of Soviet Socialist Republics shall possess supreme authority with respect to Germany. In the exercise of such authority they will take such steps, including the complete disarmament demilitarization and dismemberment of Germany as they deem requisite for future peace and security. . . .

IV. Zone of Occupation for the French and Control Council for Germany

It was agreed that a zone in Germany, to be occupied by the French Forces, should be allocated to France. This zone would be formed out of the British and American zones and its extent would be settled by the British and Americans in consultation with the French Provisional Government.

It was also agreed that the French Provisional Government should be invited to become a member of the Allied Control Council of Germany.

V. Reparation

The heads of the three governments agreed as follows:

1. Germany must pay in kind for the losses caused by her to the Allied nations in the course of the war. Reparations are to be received in the first instance by those countries which have borne the main burden of the war, have suffered the heaviest losses and have organized victory over the enemy.
2. Reparation in kind to be exacted from Germany in three following forms:
   a. Removals within 2 years from the surrender of Germany or the cessation of organized resistance from the national wealth of Germany located on the

territory of Germany herself as well as outside her territory (equipment, machine-tools, ships, rolling stock, German investments abroad, shares of industrial, transport and other enterprises in Germany etc.), these removals to be carried out chiefly for purpose of destroying the war potential of Germany.

  b. Annual deliveries of goods from current production for a period to be fixed.

  c. Use of German labor.

3. For the working out on the above principles of a detailed plan for exaction of reparation from Germany, an Allied Reparation Commission will be set up in Moscow. It will consist of three representatives—one from the Union of Soviet Socialist Republics, one from the United Kingdom and one from the United States of America.

4. With regard to the fixing of the total sum of the reparation as well as the distribution of it among the countries which suffered from the German aggression the Soviet and American delegations agreed as follows:

> The Moscow Reparation Commission should take in its initial studies as a basis for discussion the suggestion of the Soviet Government that the total sum of the reparation in accordance with the points (a) and (b) of the paragraph 2 should be 20 billion dollars and that 50% of it should go to the Union of Soviet Socialist Republics.

The British delegation was of the opinion that pending consideration of the reparation question by the Moscow Reparation Commission no figures of reparation should be mentioned.

The above Soviet-American proposal has been passed to the Moscow Reparation Commission as one of the proposals to be considered by the Commission.

VI. Major War Criminals

The Conference agreed that the question of the major war criminals should be the subject of enquiry by the three Foreign Secretaries for report in due course after the close of the Conference.

VII. Poland

The following Declaration on Poland was agreed by the Conference:

> A new situation has been created in Poland as a result of her complete liberation by the Red Army. This calls for the establishment of a Polish Provisional Government which can be more broadly based than was possible before the recent liberation of [the] Western part of Poland. The Provisional Government which is now functioning in Poland should therefore be reorganized on a broader democratic basis with the inclusion of democratic leaders from Poland itself and from Poles abroad. This new Government should then be called the Polish Provisional Government of National Unity.
>
> M. Molotov, Mr. Harriman and Sir A. Clark Kerr are authorized as a commission to consult in the first instance in Moscow with members of the present Provisional Government and with other Polish democratic leaders from within Poland and from abroad, with a view to the reorganization of the present Government along the above lines. This Polish Provisional Government of National Unity shall be pledged to the holding of free and unfettered elections as soon as possible on the basis of universal suffrage and secret ballot. In these elections all democratic and anti-Nazi parties shall have the right to take part and to put forward candidates.

When a Polish Provisional Government of National Unity has been properly formed in conformity with the above, the Government of the U.S.S.R., which now maintains diplomatic relations with the present Provisional Government of Poland, and the Government of the United Kingdom and the Government of the United States of America will establish diplomatic relations with the new Polish Provisional Government of National Unity, and will exchange Ambassadors by whose reports the respective Governments will be kept informed about the situation in Poland.

The three Heads of Government consider that the Eastern frontier of Poland should follow the Curzon Line with digressions from it in some regions of five to eight kilometers in favor of Poland. They recognize that Poland must receive substantial accession of territory in the North and West. They feel that the opinion of the new Polish Provisional Government of National Unity should be sought in due course on the extent of these accessions and that the final delimitation of the Western frontier of Poland should therefore await the Peace Conference.

[Following this declaration, but omitted here for reasons of space, are brief statements on Yugoslavia, the Italo-Yugoslav frontier and Italo-Austrian frontier, Yugoslav-Bulgarian relations, Southeastern Europe, Iran, meetings of the three foreign secretaries, and the Montreux Convention and the Straits.]

6. The Yalta Agreement on Soviet Entry into the War Against Japan, 1945

The leaders of the three Great Powers—the Soviet Union, the United States of America and Great Britain—have agreed that in two or three months after Germany has surrendered and the war in Europe has terminated the Soviet Union shall enter into the war against Japan on the side of the Allies on condition that:

1. The *status quo* in Outer-Mongolia (The Mongolian People's Republic) shall be preserved;
2. The former rights of Russia violated by the treacherous attack of Japan in 1904 shall be restored, viz:
   a. the southern part of Sakhalin as well as all the islands adjacent to it shall be returned to the Soviet Union,
   b. the commercial port of Dairen shall be internationalized, the preeminent interests of the Soviet Union in this port being safeguarded and the lease of Port Arthur as a naval base of the USSR restored,
   c. the Chinese-Eastern Railroad and the South-Manchurian Railroad which provides an outlet to Dairen shall be jointly operated by the establishment of a joint Soviet-Chinese Company; it being understood that the preeminent interests of the Soviet Union shall be safeguarded and that China shall retain full sovereignty in Manchuria;
3. The Kurile islands shall be handed over to the Soviet Union.

It is understood, that the agreement concerning Outer-Mongolia and the ports and railroads referred to above will require concurrence of Generalissimo Chiang

---

This document can be found in U.S. Department of State, *Foreign Relations of the United States:The Conferences at Malta and Yalta* (Washington, D.C.: Government Printing Office, 1955), p. 984.

Kai-shek. The President will take measures in order to obtain this concurrence on advice from Marshal Stalin.

The Heads of the three Great Powers have agreed that these claims of the Soviet Union shall be unquestionably fulfilled after Japan has been defeated.

For its part the Soviet Union expresses its readiness to conclude with the National Government of China a Pact of friendship and alliance between the USSR and China in order to render assistance to China with its armed forces for the purpose of liberating China from the Japanese yoke.

7. Roosevelt's Anger with Stalin, 1945

I have received with astonishment your message of April 3 containing an allegation that arrangements which were made between Field Marshals [Harold] Alexander and [Albert] Kesselring at Berne [Switzerland] "permitted the Anglo-American troops to advance to the East and the Anglo-Americans promised in return to ease for the Germans the peace terms."

In my previous messages to you in regard to the attempts made in Berne to arrange a conference to discuss a surrender of the German army in Italy I have told you that: (1) No negotiations were held in Berne, (2) The meeting had no political implications whatever, (3) In any surrender of the enemy army in Italy there would be no violation of our agreed principle of unconditional surrender, (4) Soviet officers would be welcomed at any meeting that might be arranged to discuss surrender.

For the advantage of our common war effort against Germany, which today gives excellent promise of an early success in a disintegration of the German armies, I must continue to assume that you have the same high confidence in my truthfulness and reliability that I have always had in yours.

I have also a full appreciation of the effect your gallant army has had in making possible a crossing of the Rhine by the forces under General [Dwight D.] Eisenhower and the effect that your forces will have hereafter on the eventual collapse of the German resistance to our combined attacks.

I have complete confidence in General Eisenhower and know that he certainly would inform me before entering into any agreement with the Germans. He is instructed to demand and will demand unconditional surrender of enemy troops that may be defeated on his front. Our advances on the Western Front are due to military action. Their speed has been attributable mainly to the terrific impact of our air power resulting in destruction of German communications, and to the fact that Eisenhower was able to cripple the bulk of the German forces on the Western Front while they were still west of the Rhine.

I am certain that there were no negotiations in Berne at any time and I feel that your information to that effect must have come from German sources which have made persistent efforts to create dissension between us in order to escape in some measure responsibility for their war crimes. If that was [General Karl] Wolff's purpose in Berne, your message proves that he has had some success.

This document can be found in U.S. Department of State, *Foreign Relations of the United States, 1945* (Washington, D.C.: Government Printing Office, 1968), III, 745–746.

With a confidence in your belief in my personal reliability and in my determination to bring about, together with you, an unconditional surrender of the Nazis, it is astonishing that a belief seems to have reached the Soviet Government that I have entered into an agreement with the enemy without first obtaining your full agreement.

Finally I would say this, it would be one of the great tragedies of history if at the very moment of the victory, now within our grasp, such distrust, such lack of faith should prejudice the entire undertaking after the colossal losses of life, material and treasure involved.

Frankly I cannot avoid a feeling of bitter resentment toward your informers, whoever they are, for such vile misrepresentations of my actions or those of my trusted subordinates.

8. Roosevelt's Last Letter to Churchill, 1945

I would minimize the general Soviet problem as much as possible because these problems, in one form or another, seem to arise every day and most of them straighten out as in the case of the Berne meeting.

We must be firm, however, and our course thus far is correct.

 E S S A Y S

In the first essay, a positive appraisal of President Franklin D. Roosevelt's wartime diplomacy, the historian Warren F. Kimball of Rutgers University at Newark argues that Roosevelt possessed a coherent vision of America's role in the world and practiced considerable diplomatic skill in pursuing his goals. During the war, according to Kimball, the president won allied backing to launch a second military front in France that eased pressures on the Soviet Union, contained British imperialism, and ensured an Anglo-American presence in postwar Europe. Although Roosevelt recognized that the Second World War presented an opportunity to restructure international politics, he did not advocate a Wilsonian League of Nations, but instead worked to negotiate a balance of power between the victorious states. At the same time, the president hoped that open rather than closed spheres of influence, gradual decolonization, and a United Nations that entrusted veto power to the alliance leaders would promote a liberal world order conducive to U.S. security and economic needs. Although the Yalta accords, signed in February 1945, were later criticized for sanctioning Soviet domination of Eastern Europe, Kimball concludes that the agreements struck by both Roosevelt and British Prime Minster Winston Churchill with Soviet Marshal Joseph Stalin were the best that could be had given the U.S.S.R.'s military presence in Poland and other states at the time.

The second essay, in contrast, attempts to deflate Roosevelt's reputation as an adept manager of Allied relations. Joseph L. Harper of The Johns Hopkins University School of Advanced International Studies portrays FDR as a narrow-minded American nationalist, whose Jeffersonian outlook made him contemptuous of Europe and eager to disengage the United States from the continent's postwar affairs. Harper maintains that Roosevelt planned to erect two regional pillars, Britain and the Soviet Union, in lieu of a continued

---

This document can be found in U.S. Department of State, *Foreign Relations of the United States, 1945* (Washington, D.C.: Government Printing Office, 1967), V, 210.

U.S. presence on the continent. As evidence grew that Stalin would clamp down on Poland and other East European states Roosevelt refused to alter his plans for U.S. withdrawal and ignored Churchill's advice to toughen his stance against Soviet expansionism. As the war drew to a close, discrepancies between Roosevelt's Wilsonian rhetoric and his cynical practice of power politics had diminished prospects for Allied cooperation and aroused a suspicious American public opinion. Harper concludes that Roosevelt's policies sowed the seeds of postwar instability.

Franklin D. Roosevelt's Successful Wartime Diplomacy

WARREN F. KIMBALL

[President Franklin D.] Roosevelt had come into the war with vague but what proved to be consistent views on how to restructure international relations. The United States had to work with other nations to preserve peace, but it also had to avoid commitments that would drag it into every little argument and local squabble. Woodrow Wilson's League of Nations concept had fallen into that trap, and the American public and Congress had rejected the scheme, insisting that the United States retain its freedom of action. That experience, and FDR's assessment of the causes of the two world wars, left him convinced that only the Great Powers could maintain the peace. As he had told one of [French leader Charles] De Gaulle's emissaries a few months earlier, "I am not a Wilsonian idealist, I have problems to resolve."

Like hereditary aristocrats throughout history, Roosevelt assumed that power and responsibility justified each other, a geopolitical version of noblesse oblige. During the Atlantic Conference in August 1941 he had suggested to [British prime minister] Churchill that the two Great Powers, the United States and Great Britain, would have to act as policemen after the war, although some sort of international organization might be possible later on. That same month he casually repeated the idea to dinner guests, saying that the two nations would "have to police the entire world—not on a sanction basis but in trust." Only the Great Powers would have arms, and there would be "complete economic and commercial and boundary liberty, but America and England would have to maintain the peace." Disarmament would be key—"the smaller powers might have rifles but nothing more dangerous," he once commented—though he had to make a virtue of vice by entrusting enforcement to the Great Powers, which would never accept disarmament. Small nations would have to trust in the Great Powers; "another League of Nations with 100 different signatories" would mean "simply too many nations to satisfy." He had spoken similarly to [Soviet foreign minister V. M.] Molotov in May–June 1942, and the concept received Stalin's strong endorsement. . . . [On another occasion,] Roosevelt wondered why smaller nations needed arms. "Will it be necessary for these states to defend themselves after this war?" he asked. . . .

FDR's four policemen would also act as trustees for colonial societies not ready for full independence. The Pacific islands held by the Japanese (usually old League of Nations mandates), Korea (despite its being independent for centuries before the United States existed), and Indochina were his favorite examples, but the idea tended to be Roosevelt's catchall answer for any difficult territorial problem, as in the case of the Croatians and Serbs. When he spoke to [Anthony] Eden of trusteeships for Japan's Pacific island empire, French Indochina, and Portuguese Timor, Eden knew the president meant all European empires. . . .

The Atlantic Charter and FDR's subsequent scheme for bringing the Soviets into his group of world policemen have routinely been dismissed as unrealistic "Wilsonian nonsense." And "Wilsonianism," that catchall term for anything less than untrammeled power politics, was supposedly dangerous daydreaming.

But the Americans saw it differently. The Atlantic Charter was more than mere moral posturing. It was a call for reform, for the new world order, a consistent theme in American foreign policy before and since. Economic liberalism may have promised tangible benefits for the United States, but Americans had pursued economic liberalism since their Revolution; was that merely two centuries of cynicism? The decolonization of European empires could, and sometimes did, enhance American power and interests. Shall we then conclude that Franklin Roosevelt and all his predecessors plotted to "succeed John Bull"? The United Nations organization became, for more than a decade after the Second World War, an instrument of American foreign policy. Does that mean internationalism in the United States was just a ploy? . . .

Roosevelt had assumed a great peace conference would come after the fighting, just as after the First World War, but it would be a meeting of the Great Powers, not all the United Nations. Like Wilson, Roosevelt was determined that "something 'big' will come out of this war: a new heaven and a new earth." The president was convinced that only the New World—the United States—offered any innovative thinking in international relations. . . .

The discussions [held between the three alliance leaders] at Teheran [in November and December 1943] had an air of cordiality. . . .

But a tension existed that is apparent even in the dry, printed records of the talks. FDR was expansive and optimistic, but he failed in his efforts to get Stalin to preserve at least the appearances of self-determination in Eastern Europe. Nor did the president trust his Soviet counterpart enough to mention the atomic bomb, despite knowing that the Soviet leader already knew about the Manhattan Project. Stalin pushed the Anglo-Americans politely but relentlessly on Overlord [the Anglo-American cross-channel invasion of northern France], dismissing [British-led] operations in the Aegean as a diversion, then baiting Churchill and the British during two supposedly festive dinners. Yet he was obviously aware of and uncomfortable with the Soviet Union's dependence on the Anglo-Americans. Churchill, fearful that Britain was being relegated to lesser status, later described "the poor little English donkey," caught between "the great Russian bear" on one side and the "Great American buffalo" on the other. . . .

The talks went quickly to the key issues. Overlord was the initial focus and produced the easiest decision of the conference. FDR gave Stalin an opportunity to endorse the British strategy [of concentrating Anglo-American forces in the Aegean area]. "One of the questions to be considered here," said the president, was how to use Allied forces in the Mediterranean "to bring the maximum aid to the Soviet armies on the Eastern front." Stalin, assuming that the Americans tied the second front to a commitment to enter the Pacific war, promised to create a "common front" against Japan once Germany surrendered. Next he exploited the advantage of having a victorious army by summarizing the situation on the Russian front. Only then did he casually dismiss the campaign in Italy, where it seemed to him that Hitler had succeeded in tying up a large number of Allied divisions. He was equally dismissive of a Balkans campaign. That would require Turkey's entry into the war, which Stalin repeatedly insisted would not happen. Moreover, "the Balkans were far from the heart of Germany." . . .

Churchill had done his best to look to Britain's postwar interests. Throughout the war he expressed little concern for, and even dislike of, formal postwar planning, but that did not mean he had no postwar goals. He paid little heed to structure but gave much attention to using the war to develop and maintain his nation's interests. Italy might not ever be Great Britain's satellite, but British-led campaigns in the Mediterranean offered one last opportunity to enhance the U.K.'s prestige and protect its influence in the region. It was one last chance to appear like a Great Power.

Because the Americans generally assumed Britain's Great Power status, particularly the opulence of its empire, they interpreted the motives for the Mediterranean option more narrowly. As FDR pointed out to his military chiefs, "the British look upon the Mediterranean as an area under British domination." One American naval attaché expressed the common sentiment: "Now 168 years later [after the American Revolution] we are again being taxed hundreds of thousands of lives and billions of dollars to save the British Empire. . . ."

But it was more than just formal empire. Perhaps the prime minister truly hoped that victory in Italy, military action in the Aegean and Adriatic, and Turkish entry into the war would stimulate uprisings in the Balkans against the Germans, uprisings that could also liberate those countries before Stalin could apply his axiom ["that everyone imposes his own system" on occupied territories] to their political reconstruction, though Churchill never said so by the time of the Teheran meeting. The Americans viewed Churchill's policy as power politics, not ideological conflict. . . .

The details of the postwar settlements were not agreed on at Teheran. The three leaders preferred to paper over the cracks rather than endanger the Grand Alliance, which all believed still necessary in order to defeat Germany and Japan. But the Teheran talks prefigured the decisions that would come, particularly at Yalta, although the devil was in the details, particularly for FDR, whose bureaucracy, already embarked on postwar planning, had little understanding of his thinking.

One of the papered-over cracks was the matter of France, which stood as a symbol for weakness in both Europe and in the colonial world. On the first day of the talks Stalin roundly condemned "the entire French ruling class" for being "rotten to the core" and for having "delivered over France to the Germans." FDR agreed, saying anyone over forty should be kept out of the postwar French government. When Stalin suggested that the Allies should not "shed blood to restore Indochina" to France, FDR agreed and then implied that China, which had forsworn any "designs" on Indochina, should act as a trustee while Indochina prepared for independence, which would take "20 to 30 years." No sense in talking to Churchill about India, Roosevelt commented privately to Stalin, but perhaps reform from the bottom up, "somewhat on the Soviet line," was the best solution. That would mean "revolution," was the candid reply. The president made no reply but then seized on Stalin's comment that the French should not control any strategic points to insist that Dakar, on the bulge of West Africa, had to be "under the trusteeship of the United Nations." . . .

The partitioning of Germany remained something that both Roosevelt and Stalin supported, though the Soviet leader's primary concern was with making Germany "impotent ever again to plunge the world into war." Churchill agreed that Prussia should be "detached" from the rest of Germany but backed away from much more than that. They could agree that the European Advisory Commission (EAC) had to deal with the details, but that led ineluctably to the question of postwar frontiers, and that brought the Polish question to the table.

Stalin's proposal, offered on the first day and never modified, was that Poland should have a western boundary on the Oder River [formerly within Germany's boundaries] and generally along the old Curzon Line in the east [which assured Soviet control over eastern Poland and the Balkan states]. Pounds of paper and gallons of ink have since been expended in arguments over just which Oder River line should apply and what adjustments were needed to the Curzon Line, which Churchill accurately but cantankerously insisted on calling the "Ribbentrop-Molotov Line." But the basic agreement was crystal clear. For the British prime minister's part, "he would like to see Poland moved westward in the same manner as soldiers at drill execute the drill 'left close' and illustrated his point with three matches representing the Soviet Union, Poland and Germany." His instinctive solution to the dangers of postwar confrontation was to establish clearly defined boundaries and spheres of influence. Churchill, whose sense of history underpinned his policies, reckoned that such arrangements had worked in the nineteenth century, why not again? . . .

Roosevelt was not assuming that the Red Army would liberate and occupy Eastern Europe all the way to Germany; that eventuality was, in December 1943, only a possibility. The reality for FDR was that the Soviet Union would be the major player in the politics of that region. The choice seemed clear: Try to work with that dominant power or adopt Churchill's approach of setting up clear, and exclusive, spheres of influence. But when FDR suggested that some sort of plebiscite in the Baltic states would be "helpful to him personally" and then expressed confidence that the people would vote to be part of the Soviet Union, Stalin seemed less confident and rejected any "international" role in the Baltic region. The president's attempt to separate security from ownership was either too subtle or too unthinkable for the Soviet leader.

FDR's concern for appearances unpinned his supposed concern for "'the Polish vote'—six to seven million Polish-Americans," he told Stalin. But that number was "evidently plucked from the air." There were less than half that number of Polish-Americans, many of whom were not voters. FDR's hyperbole was perhaps a bit more calculated and less casual than it appeared, for it allowed him to escape public responsibility for the political fact that he, Churchill, and Stalin's Red Army together ensured that in the short run Poland's independence would depend on Moscow's self-restraint, not on Anglo-American guarantees.

There were ways to push the Russians to exercise that self-restraint. The Anglo-Americans had long assumed that the Soviet Union would be dependent on postwar aid for economic reconstruction. In January 1942 Churchill had written of "the United States and the British Empire" being "the most powerfully armed and economic *bloc* the world has ever seen, and that the Soviet Union will need our aid," although by late 1943 Britain had begun to take its own place in line for such postwar assistance. FDR presumed that the Soviet Union's need for postwar economic aid would give the United States continued leverage, although perhaps thinking of the remarkable Soviet industrial performance, he seems not to have placed as much faith in that mechanism as some others. . . .

The next afternoon, during a tête-à-tête with Stalin, the president sketched out his concept of the four policemen. When the Soviet leader questioned having China play a role in European affairs, FDR warned that the United States could not participate in an exclusively European committee that might try to force the dispatch of American troops to Europe, a comment that suggests [British foreign secretary Anthony] Eden was correct when he surmised that the president was using the American public's "feeling for China" to "lead his people to accept international responsibilities." When Stalin pressed him about an American response to a request from the other policemen, FDR resorted to his prewar notion of sending only planes and ships from the United States to keep the peace in Europe. Then he slipped back another couple of years to 1937, suggesting that the "quarantine method" might be best. . . .

Stalin got the message and the next day agreed that any international organization should be worldwide, not regional, although FDR remained uncertain of Stalin's conversion. But trying to work out the details could derail the concept, and the four policemen then nearly disappeared from the American record of the conference. . . .

"We leave here friends in fact, in spirit, and in purpose," said Roosevelt at the closing dinner. Churchill used more relative terms when he cabled Attlee that "relations between Britain, United States and USSR have never been so cordial and intimate. All war plans are agreed and concerted." . . .

The Normandy invasion [the following June, 1944] was the largest amphibious attack in history, a logistical tour de force. Men and equipment were landed on the beaches, at adjacent small ports, and later using the Mulberries (floating harbors) constructed once the beachheads were secure. . . . Within three weeks the Allies managed to land more than 850,000 men, nearly 150,000 vehicles, and some 570,000 tons of supplies. . . .

What the cross-Channel invasion did ensure was an Anglo-American presence on the Continent at war's end, a presence that would provide stability, order, and the opportunity to exercise Stalin's axiom and determine the course of political (and hence economic and social) reconstruction in Western Europe. At the same time the invasion of Western Europe also preserved the Grand Alliance, at least for the rest of the war. The implication that Overlord aimed at getting into Western and Central Europe before the Russians writes Cold War thinking into World War II, since the decision to invade at Normandy came well before the Red Army began to roll inexorably across Central Europe. But fear of the Soviet Union was there. Roosevelt and Churchill hedged their bets by drawing up the Rankin plans [for an earlier invasion of France in the event of a sudden German collapse] and by keeping the atomic bomb secret from everyone else. Yet even while the president admitted that "he didn't know what to do about Russia," he pursued goals that went against a get-tough approach toward the Soviet Union. . . .

By mid-autumn 1944, as the Germans were crushing the Warsaw uprising, Churchill . . . found a spheres of influence arrangement more practical than confrontation, despite his intense dislike of bolshevism. In 1939 he had sought to limit German expansion by exploiting Nazi-Soviet rivalry. Now, in 1944, he sought to protect British interests in the Mediterranean and Central Europe; that necessitated limiting Soviet expansion. In each case he proposed diplomacy and compromise to accomplish what Britain could not achieve by arms.

Churchill had tried to arrange an immediate Big Three conference, but Roosevelt insisted that he could not attend until after the American presidential election in early November. The prime minister contemptuously dismissed further delay with the comment that the Red Army would not wait for the election results. He cabled Stalin and suggested a meeting in Moscow, with a tripartite conference, possibly in The Hague, to follow the presidential election. Stalin agreed to the Moscow meeting, though he firmly rebuffed any proposal for a Big Three meeting that would take him out of the Soviet Union. . . .

With Roosevelt not in Moscow to preach his own hybrid form of "open" spheres of influence, Churchill and Stalin got down to serious horse trading. The talks, code-named Tolstoy, were long (October 9–17, 1944), but the key discussions came early. Taking advantage of [U.S. ambassador Averell] Harriman's absence from the first meeting (Roosevelt had agreed that Churchill should conduct some private discussions), the prime minister offered his notorious "percentages" proposal—what he later called a "naughty document." The note, which he slid across the table to Stalin, seemed a callous return to an era when princes swapped chunks of territory like pieces on a chessboard. Ninety percent influence for the Soviets in Romania; the same for Britain in Greece. Seventy-five percent in Bulgaria went to Moscow, while Yugoslavia and Hungary were split fifty-fifty. Churchill warned that they should "express these things in diplomatic terms and not to use the phrase 'dividing into spheres,' because the Americans might be shocked" and suggested destroying the paper; Stalin "ticked" the proposal and told the prime minister to keep it. When Stalin agreed that "Britain must be the leading Mediterranean power," Churchill endorsed a request that the Soviet Union gain unrestricted access to the Mediterranean from the Black Sea, despite a long-standing British-sponsored international agreement that allowed Turkey to close the Dardanelles to warships. Both the British and the Soviets took the percentages formula seriously, with Eden and Molotov subsequently haggling over 5 percent here and 10 percent there.

Like Roosevelt, Churchill could see no way to prevent the Russians from dominating Eastern Europe. Why not make the best of a bad situation and protect British prestige and interests in the Mediterranean and, at the same time, get the Soviet Union to agree to limit its expansion?

Churchill also tried to play Soviet power against that of the United States (just as Roosevelt's advisers had feared). Obviously having little faith in the United Nations Organization, the prime minister ignored FDR's request not to discuss the results of the Dumbarton Oaks talks [on establishing the United Nations in August 1943] and came out in favor of Great Power unanimity (the veto) in any postwar international organization. Without it, he feared, if "China asked Britain to give up Hong Kong, China and Britain would have to leave the room while Russia and the U.S.A. settled the question."

Churchill found the combination of nationalism and Roosevelt's calls for Britain to grant independence to its empire as great a threat to British interests as was Soviet expansion into Eastern Europe. Britain's place in East Asia, specifically, China, deeply concerned the prime minister. Seeking Stalin's support, or at least neutrality, in a region of intensifying nationalism, he outlined concessions he thought should go to the Soviet Union in the Far East. The deal between Stalin and Churchill was implied, not the sort of explicit arrangement they had made over Greece and Romania, but the approach was the same. The Soviet Union should have "effective rights at Port Arthur," said Churchill. Why worry about Soviet naval power in the Far East? he told his chiefs of staff; the Soviet fleet was "vastly inferior" and would be "hostages to the stronger Naval Powers." More important, "any claim by Russia for indemnity at the expense of China, would be favourable to our resolve about Hong Kong." The Hong Kong issue led Churchill quickly to instruct that no agreements be reached with the United States to oppose a "restoration of Russia's position in the Far East."

Four months later, at Yalta, Roosevelt worked out a Far Eastern settlement with Stalin that paralleled the quid pro quo Churchill had floated at Moscow, but FDR's reasons were a bit different. First and foremost, the Soviet Union's entry into what all expected to be a long and bloody war against Japan had always been framed to include something for Russia. Roosevelt had no doubt Stalin would live up to his promise so long as the United States and Great Britain lived up to theirs. Beyond that, FDR was, like Churchill, concerned about China, although it was the impending conflict between Mao [Zedong] and Chiang [Kai-shek (Jiang Jieshi)], not the decolonization of Hong Kong, that worried him. Persuading Stalin not to throw in with the Chinese Communists and thus give the Kuomintang a chance to consolidate its rule was Roosevelt's goal. . . .

Eight years after the Yalta Conference, at the height of Cold War tensions, Churchill distanced himself from the Far Eastern settlement at Yalta. Since the State Department had released the Far Eastern protocol to the public in February 1946, Churchill could only pretend that Britain had played no role in the arrangement, claiming the matter was, for Britain, "remote and secondary." We signed the agreement, but "neither I nor Eden took any part in making it," Churchill wrote. "In the United States there have been many reproaches about the concessions made to Soviet Russia. The responsibility rests with their own representatives. To us the problem was remote and secondary." This was technically correct. Churchill had not helped draft the language adopted at Yalta. Why bother? He had cut his deal five months earlier. . . .

Although Churchill and Stalin saved their most sensitive conversations for the times Harriman was excluded, the American "observer," a confidant of the prime minister and a close friend of many of the Churchills (he and Randolph Churchill's wife, Pamela, had an affair while Harriman was in London), soon found out what was going on. When the ambassador accurately reported the spheres of influence arrangement that was developing for the Balkans, Roosevelt blandly replied that his concern was to take practical steps "to insure against the Balkans getting us into a future international war." Spheres of influence were neither endorsed nor rejected. Since Stalin's insistence on a "friendly" government in Poland meant that Poles in the West would be unhappy, FDR asked Churchill for a two-week delay in

any announcement of an agreement, should one be reached. Roosevelt had no expectations of a change of heart on Stalin's part, but two weeks would take him past
the presidential election. "I am delighted," he cabled Stalin, "to learn from your
message and from reports by Ambassador Harriman of the success attained by you
and Mr. Churchill. . . ." FDR reserved the right to disagree when the Big Three next
met but gave no hint of concern about the results of the Churchill-Stalin talks. . . .

At the beginning of 1945 had the Anglo-Americans sought to redirect the
thrust of the postwar settlement that had already emerged, they had very little military leverage. The Trinity test of the atomic bomb was five months away, a lifetime
in the midst of frantic postwar peacemaking. As the [Yalta] conference opened, the
Red Army stood on the Oder River, a mere 40 miles from Berlin, having rolled
some 250 miles westward in only three weeks. Soviet forces had liberated almost
all of Poland, and the Anglo-Americans assumed the final assault on Berlin was
only a few days or weeks away. Meanwhile, Eisenhower's armies were still recovering from the disruption caused by the German offensive in the Ardennes (the
Battle of the Bulge). Nervous American diplomats, unaware that the Red Army
needed time to consolidate its positions and let its supply system catch up, advised
Roosevelt to endorse the occupation zone boundaries for Germany worked out by
the European Advisory Commission before Stalin could claim that no agreement
existed and moved his forces into the western part of Germany. . . .

Roosevelt and Churchill tried during and after the Crimea talks [at the Black
Sea resort of Yalta] to get Stalin to make concessions in Eastern Europe that
would improve appearances rather than substance, an approach they had taken
since autumn 1944. The Soviet leader, either hostile toward or unbelieving about
their domestic political concerns, conceded a few words and phrases but not an
inch of control. A vague promise to allow "all democratic and anti-Nazi parties" to
participate in "free and unfettered elections" guaranteed nothing for the London
Poles since those elections would be supervised by Soviet officials. A tripartite
commission for Poland turned out to be just like the one in Italy, only this time the
Anglo-Americans here excluded. Stalin was nothing if not a fast learner. Little
wonder, then, that Roosevelt and Churchill admitted that implementation of the
Yalta accords depended on Stalin's goodwill, for it did. . . .

Although most of the discussions at Yalta about Germany's future took place
among the three foreign ministers—Molotov, Eden, and [Edward] Stettinius—the
attitudes of the Big Three set the context. Unconditional surrender, agreed upon
from the outset, remained tripartite policy. They all agreed that nazism had to be ex-
tirpated and that Germany must never again threaten the peace of Europe. But each
had a different take on how best to accomplish that. Stalin's solution was a weak
Germany, unable to threaten the Soviet Union. Roosevelt's was a reformed Germany, uninterested in threatening peace. Churchill seemed to see nazism as a veneer
imposed by a powerful few. Fearful of the changing power relationships in Europe,
he argued against any permanent partitioning of Germany and toyed with the idea of
Germany's again acting as Prussia had in the eighteenth and nineteenth centuries: as
a British-financed barrier to any powerful rival, this time against Soviet expansion.

Stalin remained quietly adamant that Germany must never be able to threaten
Russia, but faced with the enormous task of rebuilding a devastated nation, he
talked most about reparations, proposing a ten-year reparations-in-kind program

and extensive removals of German industrial plants. Churchill considered the plan unreasonable and impractical. Roosevelt, uncertain about what policy to pursue, avoided specifics. Remembering the American experience following World War I, he rejected any notion that the United States should or would provide aid to assist the Germans in meeting reparations demands or to prevent the collapse of the German economy. He never brought up the issue of postwar reconstruction aid to the Soviet Union—despite, or perhaps because of, Harriman's arguments that the promise of loans could be used to pry concessions out of Stalin. Then, in typically contradictory Roosevelt fashion, he endorsed large short-term reparations from Germany, with half of an estimated twenty billion dollars' worth going to the Soviet Union. But even that agreement was vaguely labeled a "basis for discussion" by a "reparation commission." The tough decisions on German dismemberment and its economy were postponed. . . .

[The] Yalta agreement on the Far East, vilified later for "giving away" so much of China to Stalin, did little more than spell out what had been agreed to earlier. Territory and privilege Russia claimed it had lost in 1905 after the Russo-Japanese War were returned: the southern part of Sakhalin Island, the Kurile Islands, and control of railroads in Manchuria. The Big Three confirmed the status of Outer Mongolia, which had been a Soviet-sponsored "people's republic" since the 1920s. Stalin was guaranteed use of two ports, Dairen (Dalian) and Port Arthur (now Lushun), on the Liaotung Peninsula, just west of Korea. (Roosevelt understood the desire for naval bases, although he wanted both ports internationalized, which Stalin rejected in the case of Port Arthur.) All this was to be done with Chiang Kai-shek's approval, but getting that approval was Roosevelt's job. . . .

The only "new" agreement at Yalta was the Declaration on Liberated Europe, and it proved the most disillusioning agreement of all. Signed by the Big Three, it called for free elections. Yet it was not new, only a restatement of the Atlantic Charter principle: "the right of all people to choose the form of government under which they will live." But the persistent Soviet demand for a "friendly" government in Warsaw demonstrated that none of the anti-Soviet Poles in London would be acceptable in a new Polish government, elected or not, while British actions in Greece and American policy in Italy demonstrated that Stalin's axiom still governed. The declaration was put together with a minimum of time and bargaining, suggesting that all three leaders understood full well what it meant—or did not mean. "It was the best I could do," Roosevelt told one adviser. . . .

Stalin's performance following Yalta fell far short of the "responsible" behavior expected of one of the world's policemen, and Churchill had no more prepared his public for the gap between ideals and reality than did Roosevelt his. The Soviets took control in Romania, Hungary, and Bulgaria with speed and brutality—an impression strengthened by the growing controversy over Stalin's demands for forcible repatriation of German-held Soviet prisoners of war. Many of those POWs, often from the Baltic states and the Ukraine, refused to return to a homeland now dominated by a "foreign" power, the Soviet Union.

But Poland remained the litmus test. Molotov, who handled the "diplomacy" of the situation, had refused to allow the London Poles [non-Communist Poles who had established a government-in-exile in London] any role in the new government, leaving no alternative but the Lublin committee [Communist Poles]. Since Soviet control over all those areas had long been agreed to by the British, as well as the Americans, style rather than substance was the only cause for concern. Yet a mere two weeks after Yalta Churchill shifted from support of those agreements to arguing that he had been deceived by Stalin. With an election coming up the prime minister found an immediate reason to back away from agreements he could not change but did not like. He could now take the position that Eden and a number of Foreign Office officials (as well as Labour leaders) had begun to advocate: that compromise with Stalin only increased the Russian's appetite, an obvious variation on the critique of appeasing Hitler in the 1930s. The time had come to confront the Soviet Union. . . .

For the next two months [February–April, 1945] Churchill repeatedly pushed the president to challenge Stalin, but FDR's responses were consistent: Let us not be hasty; give the Yalta accords a chance to work. "I cannot agree that we are confronted with a breakdown of the Yalta agreements until we have made the effort to overcome the obstacles," said Roosevelt in a message drafted in the State Department. He, and those drafting his messages, repeated that practical advice over and over, for the only other choice seemed confrontation and the collapse of any hope for postwar cooperation.

Nor could Churchill persuade FDR to enter the "race" for Berlin, even if the president had himself raised that possibility more than a year earlier. Roosevelt's refusal to order a dash for the German capital followed the recommendations of his military advisers who disliked the very idea of a president's interfering with the field commander. Moreover, American generals argued that there was little military advantage in attacking Berlin since the Red Army was in position to launch an offensive. Eisenhower, with Marshall's strong support, insisted on pursuing the military objective, the German Army. Rumors of a last-ditch stand by fanatical Nazis holed up in an strong redoubt somewhere in southern Germany made Ike even more cautious. . . .

Churchill later pretended to blame the [U.S.] decision[s] on Roosevelt's deteriorating health. "We can now see the deadly hiatus which existed between the fading of President Roosevelt's strength and the growth of President Truman's grip of the vast world problem. In this melancholy void one President could not act and the other could not know." . . .

But FDR's health was not why American policy remained constant. He did not have to make significant changes to the draft messages provided him by aides in the White House. The advisers who had been with Roosevelt at Yalta—[Harry] Hopkins, [James] Byrnes, Admiral [William D.] Leahy—had returned home believing the president's approach had been successful. Even Harriman in Moscow had not lost faith in Roosevelt's dream of Soviet cooperation, although he was cautious, telling FDR that if the United States was "definite and firm" the Soviets will "make substantial concessions." Avoiding tension and confrontation with the Soviets was the tactic. Within the context of the dispute over the makeup of the "new" Polish government and with the Soviets preparing for an assault on the German capital, a "race" for Berlin in spring 1945 would have had the wrong effect. Perhaps if the Arnhem operation [allied air attacks on the strategic Dutch town of Arnhem in October 1944] had worked, or if the German counterattack in the Ardennes [forest of Belgium in December 1944] had not delayed the Anglo-Americans, things would have been different. But in April 1945 it was too late—if it had ever mattered. . . .

[The scholar and former Secretary of State] Henry Kissinger, writing as a self-confessed realist, has used the Far Eastern settlement after World War II to disparage the apparent contradictions in FDR's actions: "Roosevelt had granted Stalin a sphere of influence in northern China to encourage him to participate in a world order that would make spheres of influence irrelevant." Kissinger, apparently unaware that Churchill had outlined the Far Eastern settlement before the president agreed to Stalin's requests, understood that Roosevelt hoped to persuade the Soviets to take part in a new world order, but concluded that the president knew full well it would have spheres of influence. Why else his four policemen?

But the nature of Roosevelt's spheres of influence was different from what Stalin established in Eastern Europe (though not in Manchuria and North Korea, where direct Soviet military intervention was not a factor during the postwar era). Nor were Roosevelt's ideas what Churchill had in mind for Britain's colonial and neocolonial empires.

Roosevelt's awkward, imprecise, poorly articulated distinction between "closed" or "exclusive" spheres of influence and what might be called "open" spheres was the bridge he tried to construct between the structure proposed by Churchill and Stalin and the one suggested twenty-five years earlier by Woodrow Wilson. FDR tried to make Wilsonian idealism practical. "Open spheres" would permit the flow of culture, trade, and the establishment of what he called "free ports of information." He seems casually to have assumed that such openness would, in the fullness of time, expand American-style political and economic liberalism since those concepts worked. He had seen Wilson's experiment collapse under the weight of nationalism and political insecurity. Why bother to re-create that system if it would only fail? . . .

[T]he structure that Churchill and Roosevelt helped create, even if it was not what either had in mind, what historians have come to call the Yalta system, lasted for nearly fifty years—until the early 1990s, when the Soviet Empire crumbled. During that time the old colonial empires collapsed only to be replaced by less formal ones, nationalism changed the maps time and again, and the Great Powers—the Anglo-Americans and the Soviets—confronted each other. But they never went to war directly, and Europe, the cockpit of war for the first half of the twentieth century, avoided that horror. In one sense Yalta firmed up a settlement that, like the Congress of Vienna, created an era of peace—or, more precisely, an era without war. . . .

. . . Caught up in the celebratory atmosphere of the 1990s, Britons and Americans have focused on all that went wrong with the results of the Second World War, forgetting that few, if any, of those "mistakes" could have been made if Hitler's Germany and militaristic Japan had won or even survived the war intact. Winning the Second World War was the prerequisite to all the failures, and all the successes, that followed. Had Churchill and Roosevelt chosen to fight the war solely for postwar advantage against Russia, communism, and the left, they could not have won the struggle. But almost always, when faced with crucial choices about victory versus postwar political advantage, Roosevelt, Churchill, or both made the decision to keep the Grand Alliance together and to defeat the Axis. They could not solve all the political, social, and economic problems of the world, but they could lead their nations to victory and prevent a far worse set of problems.

And they did.

The Failure of Roosevelt's Wartime Diplomacy

JOSEPH L. HARPER

Roosevelt's solution—his mature vision of Europe—was Jeffersonian in its Europhobic spirit. . . . Like the Jefferson Memorial, which rose during the war at FDR's behest within view of the White House, the vision took definite shape over several years. Like Jefferson's, FDR's vision was inspired by a fundamental cynicism, compounded by the vexation of his failure to insulate America from Europe or to influence it from a distance. FDR sketched in the details, calling up concepts and sentiments that had accumulated over a lifetime and now became the brick and mortar of a culminating structure. To pursue the metaphor, FDR's eventual design for Europe consisted of three mutually reinforcing levels or components: a new political and territorial groundwork, two regional pillars bearing direct responsibility for peace, and an overarching structure in which the United States would occupy the position of keystone or *primus inter pares*. The purpose of these arrangements was to bring about a radical reduction in the weight of Europe, in effect to preside over its indefinite retirement from the international scene. As such, it was conceived as a set of arrangements drastic and definitive enough to allow the United States to return to its natural Western Hemisphere and Pacific habitat and preoccupations— but with one eye cocked toward Europe and able to exercise long-range striking power. The trick, which had been beyond America's power in Jefferson's time, was to be able to arbitrate from afar. . . .

Like Jefferson, FDR was less interested in saving Europe from itself than in rescuing the rest of the world from Europe. "Fractionization" was the path to a weak and harmless Europe, and one subject to outside manipulation. Decentralization and renewal from below meant removal of the old forces that had pursued destructive foreign policies. The new political forces would be in no position to resist the restructuring of Europe's world position through disarmament and decolonization. FDR's ideal was an Indian Raj writ in European terms: a fragmented continent over which the two remaining powers, Britain and the Soviet Union, could conduct a game of *divide et impera* [divide and rule] without depending on the United States.

The logic of decentralization and territorial rearrangement pervades FDR's discussion of postwar problems. To [Britain's foreign secretary Anthony] Eden in March 1943 he expressed his "opinion that the Croats and Serbs had nothing in common" and that it was "ridiculous to try to force them to live together." Belgium was another "artificial bilingual state" that might share the fate of Yugoslavia. The same argument applied to the chief troublemakers, Germany and France. He considered detaching Alsace and Lorraine from both, perhaps incorporating the contested areas into a new entity including Belgium and Luxembourg. He also asked, "After Germany is disarmed, what is the reason for France having a big military establishment?" . . .

From Joseph L. Harper, *American Visions of Europe: Franklin D. Roosevelt, George F. Kennan, and Dean G. Acheson*. © 1994 Cambridge University Press. Reprinted with the permission of Cambridge University Press.

FDR's solution to the German problem was dismemberment of a kind that went well beyond the detachment of East Prussia and the restoration of Austria. He was encouraged by [Under Secretary of State Sumner] Welles, [Treasury Secretary Henry] Morgenthau, [presidential adviser Harry] Hopkins, and former ambassadors James Gerard and Hugh Wilson, but the notion was very much his own. In March 1943, he told Eden, "We should encourage the differences and ambitions that will spring up within Germany." Even if "that spontaneous desire [should] not spring up . . . Germany must be divided into several states." At [the wartime summit in] Tehran [in November and December 1943], FDR suggested a five-state Germany, with the Kiel Canal–Hamburg area, the Ruhr, and the Saar under international control. He privately accepted the cession to Poland of German territory up to the Oder River to compensate for Polish territory lost to the Soviet Union. FDR agreed with Stalin that most of the differences among the Germans had been eliminated by the experience of unity, but thought religious, dynastic, linguistic, and cultural divisions could be revived. According to [Secretary of the Interior Harold] Ickes, he toyed with the idea of a Roman Catholic southern German state under Archduke Otto of Austria. He believed the German people themselves were redeemable within a looser, pre-1870 political framework and did not lose sleep over the possibility that they would go communist "in the Russian manner." The important thing was "not to leave in the German mind the concept of the Reich." The word itself "should be stricken from the language." . . .

In 1943 [former U.S. ambassador to the Soviet Union] William Bullitt wrote Roosevelt several letters on the subject of Russia. They are of considerable interest because they are links in a chain connecting the turn-of-the-century protocontainment outlook with the post–World War II strategy of the United States. According to Bullitt, Stalin aimed to dominate all of Europe, but he put "out pseudopodia like an amoeba rather than leaping like a tiger. If the pseudopodia meet no obstacle, the Soviet Union flows in." What he tactfully referred to as British policy—it was actually FDR's—Bullitt called the "Balance of Impotence." "Europe cannot be made a military vacuum for the Soviet Union to flow into." FDR should try personal diplomacy with Stalin, but the best way to deal with him was the "prior arrival of American and British Armies in the Eastern Frontiers of Europe . . . by way of Salonika and Constantinople." In August, he repeated that "the first step toward preventing Soviet domination of Europe is the creation of a British–American line in Eastern Europe."

FDR's subsequent actions suggest that he was not converted by Bullitt's thesis but was alarmed by its appearance. In May, he tried to arrange a tête-à-tête with Stalin in Alaska (Stalin declined) and pledged his support—this time definite—to the plan for a cross-channel invasion in the spring of 1944. In August, he won a commitment to plan "Overlord" [the cross-channel invasion of France] from the British. Roosevelt said, "We could if necessary carry out the operation ourselves." He was "anxious to have American preponderance . . . starting from the first day of the assault." A second plan ("Rankin") was developed in case of sudden German collapse, reflecting Roosevelt's desire "to be ready to get to Berlin as soon as did the Russians" (and the British). These decisions indicate a sense of urgency about forging a direct relationship with Stalin while harnessing the British to his will. . . .

In May, [British prime minister Churchill] proposed a "Supreme World Council" including the United States, Russia, Britain (and, if the United States insisted,

China) and regional councils for Europe, the Western Hemisphere, and Pacific. Members of the Supreme Council would "sit on the Regional Councils in which they were directly interested." Thus "in addition to being represented on the American Regional Council the United States would be represented on the European Regional Council." Churchill also wanted a strong France and thought Coudenhove-Kalergi's ideas "had much to recommend them." . . .

Such proposals created a basic dilemma for Roosevelt. On one hand, Theodore Roosevelt's notion of great-power regional hegemony was central to his vision. FDR said: "Russia would be charged with keeping peace in Europe. The United States would be charged with keeping peace in the Western Hemisphere." Pan-American and European councils might facilitate the regional policemen's work. In the first public airing of the four-policeman concept, [the journalist] Forrest Davis's April 1943 article in the *Saturday Evening Post,* FDR let it be known that his basic approach to foreign policy was closer to Theodore Roosevelt's than to Wilson's. He floated the idea of "a security commission" of Britain, the United States, and Russia "to police the peace of Europe . . . until the political reorganization of the Continent is completed." At the same time, Roosevelt feared Churchill's council as a device for tying the United States down in Europe. FDR did not foresee "the U.S. forever embroiled in foreign quarrels and required to keep large military forces abroad." He was "very emphatic" that the United States could not join "any independent regional body such as a European Council." America's military assets were to be committed elsewhere; FDR had commissioned elaborate studies for an expanded chain of postwar U.S. bases in the Atlantic and Pacific. But a European council to which the United States did not belong presented a different set of problems: it might resist U.S. influence or evolve into an anti-Soviet combination. On balance, regional bodies were not a good idea.

FDR's shift away from regionalism, embodied in the Moscow Conference Four Power Declaration of October 1943, was also a victory for [Secretary of State Cordell] Hull and his advisers. They had argued, with regrettable accuracy from FDR's standpoint, that domestic and world opinion would support only a "general international organization based on the principle of sovereign equality"—as opposed to a cabal of the big powers. . . . FDR was obliged to juggle once again. If in his frank secret dealings with Churchill and Stalin he continued to think in terms of great-power regional hegemony, he henceforth had to cater to public and congressional support for an egalitarian United Nations. Such an organization, hatched by Hull's inner circle, would prove to be the secretary's fitting, if unintended, revenge for years of humiliation by the White House. . . .

Roosevelt's purpose at Tehran, and throughout 1944, was to put himself in an intermediary position between Great Britain and the Soviet Union. At Tehran, FDR played the card of the second front to the embarrassment of the British, who wanted to delay it once more in favor of Mediterranean operations. "The trip was *almost* a complete success," he wrote, "specially the Russians." He referred to the personal relationship established with Stalin, as well as the latter's pledge to enter the war against Japan.

Roosevelt was always on guard against what he saw as British efforts to entangle the United States in Europe. He flatly rejected the U.S. occupation zone—southern Germany, France, and Austria—contained in a plan that gave the British northwest

Germany, Belgium, Holland, and Denmark. Since, according to the invasion plans, U.S. forces would occupy the right (south) side of the line and the British the left (north), FDR insisted that there would have to be a "cross-over" of U.S. and British armies after they entered Germany to allow the United States to occupy the northwest zone and channel ports. He cabled Churchill, "I am absolutely unwilling to police France and possibly Italy and the Balkans as well." He dismissed Churchill's answer that "the question of policing" France did not arise:

> "Do please don't" ask me to keep any American forces in France. I just cannot do it! . . . As I suggested before, I denounce and protest the paternity of Belgium, France and Italy. You really ought to bring up and discipline your own children. In view of the face that they may be your bulwark in future days, you should at least pay for their schooling now.

Roosevelt accepted an Anglo-Soviet proposal to settle the boundary between the Soviet occupation zone and the western zones in Germany, but he was adamant that the United States would take the northern zone.

There is little need to emphasize that 1944 was a presidential election year: "political considerations in the United States" made his decision final. But Roosevelt's aversion to entrapment in Europe went beyond electoral politics, as did his intention to force the British to accept the consequences of a rapid U.S. pullout. They would have no choice, as Churchill himself put it, except "to make friends with Stalin," and this was one of the purposes of forcing Churchill to face the nakedness of the British position at Tehran. FDR's reservations about Britain's 1944 approach to the Russians on Eastern Europe had to do with the possible domestic fallout and with his abiding suspicion of the British. Though the two were supposedly "95 percent together," FDR knew perfectly well that Eden opposed his plans for the weakening and fragmentation of Europe. Eden, in any case, was far too stereotypical a Tory creature to be trusted by FDR.

Roosevelt's relationship with Churchill himself has been "much romanticized." When Churchill took power in 1940, FDR reportedly considered him a "playboy and a drunkard." Churchill the nationalist, imperialist, Russophobe, and purveyor of Anglo-American brotherhood deeply irritated Roosevelt, even if the prime minister was too much of a "museum piece, a rare relic," to be taken altogether seriously. It is also true that Churchill's "un-English" exuberance—he was after all half-American—allowed for a kind of informality and companionship that FDR found impossible with most Britons. The only precedent was the young Nigel Law, whose rapt courtship of FDR during the First World War had won him a similar condescending warmth. Roosevelt remarked, "I have a feeling when I am with Winston that I am twenty years older than he is." Churchill recalled, "I always looked up to him as an older man, though he was eight years my junior." If there was a basic element of trust in the relationship, it was based on a tacit acceptance of Roosevelt's dominant position: in effect, FDR trusted Churchill as long as he thought he could control him.

In April 1944, Churchill began to explore an arrangement whereby the Russians would "take the lead" in Romania and the British in Greece. He asked FDR's "blessing" on May 31. Ostensibly temporary, the arrangement was supposed to formalize what FDR himself favored: the predominance of the British on the

Mediterranean littoral and of the Russians in Eastern Europe. When Hull objected, FDR allowed the State Department to draft a disapproving cable, but the next day he unilaterally approved Churchill's suggestion that the arrangement be tried for three months. FDR complained that the Foreign Office had decided to tell the United States about its Balkan negotiations only after the Russians had broached the subject with the State Department, but he did not oppose the idea. FDR accepted Hopkin's suggestion that Stalin and Churchill be told that any decisions made during Churchill's visit to Moscow in October 1944 were subject to his approval, but his intuition told him that the mission was worthwhile. He soon knew the gist of the sphere-of-influence arrangements and there is little evidence that he objected. . . .

. . . At Dumbarton Oaks [a private estate in Washington, D.C., where the first conference on the United Nations convened in August 1943], meanwhile, he tried to erect an overarching structure that would permit America to remain aloof from Europe while retaining a decisive voice in the determination of its fate. FDR's reluctant acceptance of a universal world organization had to do with the development of wide support for such a body in 1943. In deference to the claims of smaller countries, FDR also agreed that the organization's executive council would have three or more revolving as well as four permanent members. Still, FDR stuck to his conviction that only the "four policemen" would be armed and would enforce peace on the basis of regional assignments. The real problem was how to ensure collaboration among the great powers themselves. FDR had said, "The United States will have to *lead*" and use its "good offices always to conciliate, to help solve the differences which will arise between the others." . . .

The crucial problem at Dumbarton Oaks was whether the four policemen could veto decisions in cases where they were directly involved. If the big powers possessed an absolute veto, the kind of United States-led coalitions suggested by FDR's poker allusion could not materialize within the council. The organization would become a mere debating society, and "a poor one at that." There were obvious counterarguments: no country would accept restrictions when its vital interests were involved. The United States and Britain decided to support the principle that the big four should not vote on questions involving the peaceful settlement of a dispute to which they were a party, while retaining the right to veto enforcement measures. . . .

How should one interpret Roosevelt's decision in the same context to initial the secret aide-mémoire [in 1944 with British prime minister Winston Churchill] on atomic energy at Hyde Park? The agreement [which called for full atomic collaboration between Britain and the U.S.] is the chief exhibit in the case that far from being naive or too optimistic, FDR was now preparing to contain the Russians. According to [the historian] Martin Sherwin, FDR saw an atomic-armed Britain as "America's outpost on the European frontier." Sherwin and [the historian] Barton Bernstein emphasize the importance that the weapon had acquired: FDR was "reserving the option of using it in the future as a bargaining lever, threat, military counter-weight, or even as a weapon again the Soviets." . . .

In all likelihood, FDR's real preference was an American monopoly. As someone concerned to allay Soviet suspicion of Britain and of Anglo-American collusion, he probably saw exclusive American control as more palatable to Moscow that independent British possession of the bomb. In a more visceral way, he no doubt coveted the bomb as the symbol and instrument of American supremacy and independence. At this level, the bomb was the rod of yore that someday "we may shake . . . over the heads of all [the Europeans]," the means by which America could remain remote and secure from Europe, as well as the arbiter of its fate. The air-delivered atomic bomb was the ultimate Jeffersonian weapon. . . .

. . . The Quebec agreement [reached by FDR and Churchill in August 1943, which called for a full exchange of atomic information], to which the Hyde Park aide-mémoire was essentially a codicil, came about after Churchill threatened to pursue the bomb on his own and in a way that might have negative consequences for the United States. FDR's choice was now a possibly serious delay in the Manhattan Project and crisis with Britain versus an agreement restoring a flow of information that would allow the British to build a bomb at some point in the future. Anglo-American atomic diplomacy is another instance in which FDR made a valiant effort to eat his cake and have it. . . .

The final meeting of Roosevelt and Churchill [at the Yalta Conference in February 1945], though it gave rise to a brief euphoria, did not reestablish trust. At the center of the negotiations were the questions of the future Polish regime and the United Nations voting formula. The Americans agreed to the mere broadening of the [Communist] Lublin cabinet, through the inclusion of additional democratic elements, rather than a genuinely new government. FDR's earlier resistance on this point melted away once Stalin had accepted the U.S. voting formula for the United Nations and dropped a demand for membership for all fifteen Soviet republics. The British, who held out for more concrete guarantees on Poland, had no choice but to go along. FDR approached the question, in his words, as the inhabitant "of another hemisphere" and once again reminded those present that U.S. troops would leave Europe within two years after the war. Stalin and FDR reiterated the Tehran decision to proceed with the dismemberment of Germany; the British were reluctant. On the question of German reparations, the U.S. and Soviet sides agreed to the figure of $20 billion as a basis of discussion, with the Russians to receive half. Churchill was appalled. FDR and Stalin conducted secret talks resulting in territorial gains by the Soviet Union in the Far East. . . .

Churchill later said of the president at Yalta, "He was a tragic figure." He was referring to FDR's shrunken, world-weary appearance, but the remark conveys the regret that he felt over the fading of a relationship based, at least for Churchill, on affection as well as self-interest. When it came in April, FDR's was "an enviable death." He "had brought his country through the worst of its perils and the heaviest of its toils." But it was enviable also because it prevented further estrangement and more violent disagreement. Churchill, with his sense of the drama of history, was suggesting that Roosevelt's decline had been tragic in the deeper, classical meaning of the term—a great figure brought down by a fatal flaw of character. Roosevelt's vision of America's relationship to the Old World was animated by a combination of animosity and hubris. Both impulses, along with a dose of sadism, were present in his personal relationships with Churchill and de Gaulle. At bay in 1944, the two exponents of old-fashioned European power politics turned and defied the New World. Their resistance opened cracks in Roosevelt's "monumental conception," even as the Soviet pillar seemed to be rising in its place. . . .

The unexpected controversy occurred during the two months between Yalta and Roosevelt's death. Stalin's mid-April remark ("Everyone imposes his own system. . . . It cannot be otherwise") was not a declaration of strategy but a reflection on what, willy-nilly, was actually taking place. It rings like an epitaph for Roosevelt and the Rooseveltian vision of Europe. What Stalin meant was, "From now on, it cannot be otherwise." Without Roosevelt, Rooseveltian policies were certainly doomed.

What went wrong? Who was responsible? [The historian] Robert Messer makes a convincing case that initial post-Yalta troubles had to do with the manner in which the agreements were presented to the public in the United States. James Byrnes, FDR's "Yalta salesman," returned from the conference, where, thanks to FDR, he had received a selective impression of what had happened and proceeded to portray the Declaration on Liberated Europe and the Polish settlement as the triumph of self-determination. FDR was pleased by the performance, at least by the positive public reaction to Yalta that resulted. In private remarks immediately after Yalta, Roosevelt denounced the U.S. Senate as incompetent and obstructionist, affirming that the only way to accomplish anything was to circumvent it. But the Russians were bound to take a dim view of the Wilsonian love feast being staged by FDR. Vice Foreign Minister [Andrei] Vishinsky's brutal ultimatum to the Romanian government on February 27 was a reminder that the Declaration on Liberated Europe was something less than an instrument to foster bourgeois democracy in Eastern Europe. Other historians argue that FDR was naive to assume that the Russians would behave in a way that would not create undue embarrassment for him at home, while his own vagueness at Yalta had only encouraged Stalin to make new demands. But if Soviet behavior after Yalta was partly a reaction to distorted public claims arising from FDR's domestic requirements, Roosevelt's responsibility appears in a somewhat different light. It is hard to avoid the conclusion that Roosevelt had been sincere with Stalin (with whom he had tended to deal as if he himself were a kind of absolute monarch) and was trying to deceive his Wilsonian public. The Russians appear not to have understood this and believed somebody was trying to deceive them.

FDR's, arguably, was another case of "useful deceit" and in any event unavoidable given his ambiguous, instrumental relationship to Wilson and the Wilsonians all along. By 1945, [the historian] William McNeill notes, "Roosevelt embodied a myth." Partly through his own doing, the myth was essentially Wilsonian. To be sure, FDR had occasionally tried to explain to the public . . . that his was a hardheaded and "partial internationalism," closer to Theodore Roosevelt than to Wilson. Privately he had said, "You can't invoke high moral principles when high moral principles don't exist." But since the twenties—and never more so than in 1944— he had prospered as a politician by wrapping himself in Wilson's mantle. While he shared Wilson's dream of abolishing the centrality of Europe, his postwar plans had little to do with the self-determination of nations. As the gap between right hand and left, between public expectations and the Eastern European reality, plainly widened after Yalta, the helpless juggler was hoist aloft on his Wilsonian petard.

Controversy erupted after the February 23 meeting of the "Moscow Commission" set up to consult the various Polish groups with a view to reorganizing the

Polish government. While disturbed, Roosevelt recognized the predominance of the Communist Poles and was determined not to allow a secondary issue to destroy his foreign policy. For his part, however, Churchill asked Parliament on February 27:

> Are they [the Poles] to be free, as we in Britain and the United States or France are free? Are their sovereignty and independence to be untrammeled, or are they to become a mere projection of the Soviet State, forced against their will by an armed minority to adopt a command or totalitarian system. I am putting the case in all its bluntness.

Privately he said, "I have not the slightest intention of being cheated over Poland, not even if we go to the verge of war with Russia." Churchill was now in revolt against FDR's foreign policy. . . .

. . . The laws of physics decreed that FDR's structure would not stand: his two telemones [supporting columns], Russia and Britain, emerged from the war profoundly inimical and disproportionate in stature. Britain and Russia did not believe that, even acting together, they had the strength to keep Europe in the reduced and fragmented condition that Roosevelt envisioned. "Give them [the Germans] twelve to fifteen years and they'll be on their feet again," Stalin told [the Yugoslav Communist Milovan] Djilas in April 1945. "We shall recover in fifteen or twenty years, and then we'll have another go at it." The prospect of the American withdrawal, brutally reiterated by Roosevelt at Yalta, the absence of an American pillar in Europe, weighed heavily in the calculations of both Churchill and Stalin in 1945. Every instinct drove Churchill to try to force the Americans to confront the dominant Continental power and re-create the Anglo-American intimacy of 1940–41. . . .

The progressive hardening of the British and Soviet positions in Europe weighed heavily on Roosevelt in the last days of his life. There could have been no more eloquent signal of the collapse of his design. Stalin's behavior was a bitter cup to swallow. . . . It is impossible to say whether with approaching death came self-knowledge, whether, in other words, Roosevelt recognized the Jeffersonian hubris and fatal ambivalence about entanglement in Europe that lay at the heart of his monumental failure. He had tried to concoct the transformation and retirement of Europe—a solution to the European Question—without American responsibility and entanglement. Only someone of Roosevelt's profoundly solipsistic nationalism and sense of American superiority—incorporating a turn-of-the-century certainty of the Old World's moral bankruptcy—could have seriously entertained the idea.

🌐 *F U R T H E R   R E A D I N G*

Stephen E. Ambrose, *Eisenhower and Berlin, 1945* (1967)
——— and Douglas Brinkley, *Rise to Globalism* (1993)
Edward M. Bennett, *Franklin D. Roosevelt and the Search for Victory* (1990)
Robert Blake and Wm. Roger Louis, eds., *Churchill* (1993)
Richard Breitman and Alan M. Kraut, *American Refugee Policy and European Jewry, 1933–1945* (1987)
Susan Brewer, *To Win the Peace* (1997)
Douglas Brinkley and David Facey-Crowther, eds., *The Atlantic Charter* (1994)
Charles Brower, ed., *World War II in Europe* (1998)
Russell Buhite, *Decisions at Yalta* (1986)

James M. Burns, *Roosevelt: The Soldier of Freedom* (1970)
Thomas M. Campbell, *Masquerade Peace: America's UN Policy, 1944–1945* (1973)
Diane Shaver Clemens, *Yalta* (1970)
Wayne S. Cole, *Roosevelt and the Isolationists, 1932–1945* (1983)
Mark J. Conversino, *Fighting with the Soviets* (1997)
Kenneth R. Crispell and Carlos F. Gomez, *Hidden Illness in the White House* (1988)
R. D. Cuff and J. L. Granatstein, *Canadian-American Relations in Wartime* (1975)
Robert Dallek, *Franklin D. Roosevelt and American Foreign Policy, 1933–1945* (1979)
Kenneth R. Davis, *FDR* (1993)
Robert A. Divine, *Roosevelt and World War II* (1969)
———, *Second Chance* (1967)
John W. Dower, *War Without Mercy* (1986)
Robin Edmonds, *The Big Three* (1991)
Carol Eisenberg, *Drawing the Line: The American Decision to Divide Germany,
     1944–1949* (1996)
Herbert Feis, *Between War and Peace* (1960)
———, *Churchill, Roosevelt, Stalin* (1957)
Robert H. Ferrell, *Ill-Advised* (1992)
Frank Freidel, *Franklin D. Roosevelt* (1990)
Lloyd C. Gardner, *Spheres of Influence* (1993)
Martin Gilbert, *Winston S. Churchill* (1986)
Mary N. Hampton, *The Wilsonian Impulse* (1996) (Germany)
Gary R. Hess, *America Encounters India, 1941–1947* (1971)
———, *The United States at War, 1941–1945* (1986)
———, *The United States' Emergence as a Southeast Asian Power, 1940–1950* (1987)
Robert C. Hilderbrand, *Dumbarton Oaks* (1990)
Townsend Hoopes and Douglas Brinkley, *FDR and the Creation of the UN* (1997)
Julian C. Hurstfield, *America and the French Nation, 1939–1945* (1986)
Akira Iriye, *Power and Culture* (1981)
Warren Kimball, *The Juggler* (1991)
Richard H. Kohn, ed., "The Scholarship on World War II," *Journal of Military History,* 55
     (1991), 365–393
Gabriel Kolko, *The Politics of War* (1968)
Eric Larrabee, *Commander in Chief* (1987)
Clayton D. Laurie, *The Propaganda Warriors* (1996)
Lloyd E. Lee, *World War II: Crucible of the Contemporary World* (1991)
Michael Leigh, *Mobilizing Consent* (1976) (public opinion)
Ralph B. Levering, *American Opinion and the Russian Alliance* (1976)
Wm. R. Louis, *Imperialism at Bay* (1978) (decolonization)
Richard Lukas, *The Strange Alliance* (1978) (Poland)
Frederick W. Marks III, *Over Sand: The Diplomacy of Franklin Roosevelt* (1988)
Vojtech Mastny, *Russia's Road to the Cold War* (1979)
Steven M. Miner, *Between Churchill and Stalin* (1988)
Samuel Eliot Morison, *Strategy and Compromise* (1958)
William L. Neumann, *After Victory* (1967)
Robert Nisbet, *Roosevelt and Stalin* (1988)
Raymond G. O'Connor, *Diplomacy for Victory* (1971) (unconditional surrender)
William O'Neill, *A Democracy at War* (1993)
Forrest C. Pogue, *George C. Marshall* (1963–1987)
William A. Renzi and Mark D. Roehrs, *Never Look Back* (1991)
David Reynolds et al., eds., *Allies at War* (1994)
———, *Churchill and Roosevelt at War* (1994)
———, *Rich Relations: The American Occupation of Britain* (1995)
——— and David Dimbleby, *An Ocean Apart* (1989) (Anglo-American relations)
Keith Sainsbury, *Churchill and Roosevelt at War* (1994)
———, *The Turning Point* (1985)

John Sbrega, *Anglo-American Relations and Colonialism in East Asia* (1983)
Michael Schaller, *The U.S. Crusade in China, 1938–1945* (1978)
Georg Schild, *Bretton Woods and Dumbarton Oaks* (1995)
Michael S. Sherry, *Preparing for the Next War* (1977)
———, *The Rise of American Air Power* (1987)
Bradley F. Smith, *Sharing Secrets with Stalin* (1996)
Gaddis Smith, *American Diplomacy During the Second World War, 1941–1945* (1985)
Ronald H. Spector, *Eagle Against the Sun* (1984)
Mark A. Stoler, "A Half Century of Conflict: Interpretations of U.S. World War II Diplo-
    macy," *Diplomatic History, 18 (1994), 375–403*
———, *George Marshall* (1989)
———, *The Politics of the Second Front* (1977)
Kenneth W. Thompson, *Winston Churchill's World View* (1983)
Christopher Thorne, *Allies of a Kind* (1978)
———, *The Issue of War* (1985)
Adam Ulam, *Expansion and Coexistence* (1974) (Soviet foreign policy)
Cornelius Van Minnen and John F. Sears, eds., *FDR and His Contemporaries* (1992)
Gerhard L. Weinberg, *A World at Arms* (1993)
Randall Woods, *A Changing of the Guard* (1990)
Llewellyn Woodward, *British Foreign Policy in the Second World War* (1970–1971)
David S. Wyman, *The Abandonment of the Jews* (1984)

CHAPTER
6

The Origins of the
Cold War

The Grand Alliance collapsed soon after the Second World War. Strife had developed
during the war itself, and the scramble for postwar position accentuated differences
of power, interests, and ideology, especially between the United States and the Soviet
Union. As they defined their postwar goals, each side in the unfolding contest drew
different lessons from the 1930s and pushed aside the plans devised at the Yalta and
Potsdam conferences near the end of the war.

While Soviet leaders came to see the United States as an expansionist power
seeking world supremacy, threatening USSR security, and manipulating weaker
states, U.S. leaders increasingly read the Soviet Union as a bullying aggressor bent
on grabbing territory, subjugating neighbors, and disturbing the postwar peace
through subversion. The Kremlin charged the United States with trying to encircle
the Soviet Union; Washington claimed that it was only trying to contain the Soviet
Union. Each side saw offense when the other saw defense. Fearful about the future,
the adversaries competed to build and enlarge spheres of influence, to attract allies,
to enhance military capabilities, and to gain economic advantage. Shortly after the
Second World War, a new, long global war began that would endure for more than
four decades—the Cold War.

Poland, Germany, Iran, Czechoslovakia, Greece, China, Korea, and many
other nations became the diplomatic and military battlegrounds for the Cold War
by midcentury. The Soviet Union and the United States never sent their troops into
battle directly against one another. Instead, they started an expensive arms race,
cultivated and at times intimidated client states, constructed overseas bases and
intelligence posts, intervened in civil wars, launched covert operations, constructed
rival alliance systems, sponsored exclusionist economic partnerships and foreign
aid programs, and initiated propaganda campaigns in which they charged one
another with conspiracy. Soon such designations as "West" and "East" and "Third
World" (nonaligned nations in the developing world) reflected global divisions.

The end of the Cold War in the late 1980s and early 1990s, and the question of
who won or lost it, are treated in the last chapter of this book. Here, we strive to
understand why and how the Cold War began. The scholarship on this subject is in
transition because post–Cold War Russian, Eastern European, Chinese, and other

archives have only recently opened for the first time, providing illuminating but still limited new documentation. The Cold War International History Project Bulletin, *published by the Woodrow Wilson International Center for Scholars in Washington, D.C., has since 1992 reprinted many declassified Soviet and Communist documents. The new evidence, at times clarifying and at other times ambiguous (because Soviet leaders rarely stated their motives, even to one another, in unguarded terms), has by no means brought closure in debates about the Cold War. The documents of "the other side" nonetheless enable scholars to consider the interactive nature of Soviet-American relations, to understand better the impact of the superpower rivalry on client states, and to present new or revised perspectives on the origins of the Cold War. The traditional view that the Cold War was all the Soviet Union's fault, the revisionist view that both the United States and the Soviet Union caused it and that U.S. expansionism stands as a major catalyst, and the postrevisionist view that the USSR was primarily responsible for disrupting international relations and prompting the United States to build a global empire—all these views will necessarily be tested anew.*

Three sets of questions have guided and will continue to guide scholars as they explore the sources of the Cold War. First is the international context: Was postwar conflict inevitable because of the wrenching changes wrought in the international system by the Second World War? How was power redistributed in that system, and which nation held most? What restraints and opportunities did the state of the world present to the United States and the Soviet Union? Which of the two was more responsible for the Cold War—or must they share responsibility? And why did a conflict that began largely in Europe spread to the rest of the world?

The second set of questions studies the national context of the Soviet Union and the United States. What drove them to become international activists? Power? Security interests? Economic needs? Ideology? Culture and distorted perceptions of the other's value system and behavior? Lessons from the past? To what extent did domestic politics or governmental organization shape their policies? Especially in the case of the United States, to what extent did public opinion contribute to the deepening antagonisms? Why did Americans ultimately see the Soviets as an unparalleled menace to standards of civilization? Because of Moscow's influence in Eastern Europe, because of communist ideology, because of Stalinist authoritarianism, because of social and economic instability in Europe that communists might exploit? Because the Soviet Union stood out as the one major obstacle to a U.S.-ordered and U.S.-centered postwar world? Or, because the USSR had the potential, in a disorderly world, to shut off the United States from overseas bases, from raw materials such as oil, and from lucrative markets? For their part, why did Soviet leaders think the worst of the United States? Which historical legacies and postwar issues influenced Soviet interpretations and behavior? Why did Moscow come to believe that the United State practiced a reprehensible atomic diplomacy and economic imperialism? Finally, did the Cold War evolve because the two sides simply misunderstood one another, or because they understood each other very well, including their quite different national interests?

The third set of questions addresses the role of individuals, whose personalities, political ambitions, and styles of diplomacy influenced their nation's foreign relations. The personal imprints of President Harry S. Truman and Marshal Joseph Stalin stand out. Individual leaders usually define their nation's needs and goals, shape ideologies, decide whether to negotiate, and play politics with foreign policy. Some leaders are wise and patient, others shallow and impatient; some understand nuance and gray areas, others see extreme blacks and whites; some decisionmakers are driven blindly by ideology, entrenched interests, or ignorance, while others are more knowledgeable, practical, and flexible. In an accounting of the origins of the Cold War, how much weight should scholars give to Truman and Stalin as compared to systemic and national sources of conflict? More precisely, to ask a counterfactual question in the case of the United States, would Franklin D. Roosevelt have handled Soviet-American relations differently?

To end with an overarching question: Was the Cold War inevitable, or were there viable alternatives to the long war?

 # D O C U M E N T S

As the Second World War neared its end, President Harry S. Truman sent a special representative to Moscow to explain U.S. policies to Joseph Stalin and reduce growing tensions. Harry Hopkins, who had served for years as an adviser to President Franklin D. Roosevelt, already knew the Soviet leader, and Stalin apparently trusted him. On May 27, 1945, as Document 1 reveals, they talked frankly about two rancorous issues: the abrupt American termination of Lend-Lease aid to the Soviet Union, and the USSR's manipulation of Polish politics.

On June 11, 1945, a group of scientists in Chicago who had been secretly developing an atomic bomb petitioned Secretary of War Henry L. Stimson to recognize the importance of future international (especially Soviet) agreement to prevent nuclear warfare. Headed by James Franck, the scientists' committee recommended against a surprise atomic attack on Japan and instead advocated a noncombatant use of the bomb on an island or in a desert, with international observers. But President Truman and his advisers rejected the Franck Committee's advice, presented as Document 2. On September 11, 1945, Stimson sent Truman a memorandum in which the secretary of war argued that "the problem" of the atomic bomb "dominated" Soviet-American relations. Stimson now urged that the United States approach the Soviet Union to discuss controls in order to reduce distrust, as Document 3 indicates.

Document 4, written by George F. Kennan, is his "long telegram" sent to Washington on February 22, 1946, from his post as attaché in the U.S. embassy in Moscow. Kennan pessimistically speculated on the motivations for Soviet behavior. His critique proved persuasive among Truman officials, and Kennan went on to serve as head of the State Department's Policy Planning Staff, where he helped to establish "containment" as U.S. Cold War doctrine. Document 5 is former British Prime Minister Winston S. Churchill's "iron curtain" speech of March 5, 1946, delivered in Fulton, Missouri, with an approving President Truman present. Secretary of Commerce Henry A. Wallace disapproved of the trend toward an American "get tough" policy and appealed to Truman to seek accommodation, not confrontation, with the Soviets. Wallace's memorandum of July 1946 is printed as Document 6. When Wallace went public with his criticisms in September, Truman fired him from the cabinet. On September 27, 1946, Nikolai Novikov, Soviet ambassador to the United States, sent his own long telegram to his superiors in Moscow. Included as Document 7, Novikov's report described the United States as an expansionist power bent on world supremacy.

On March 12, 1947, the president addressed Congress to announce the "Truman Doctrine," or containment doctrine, in conjunction with a request for aid to Greece and Turkey. Much of the significant speech is reprinted here as Document 8. The Marshall Plan for European reconstruction soon followed. Suggested by Secretary of State George C. Marshall in June 1947, the aid program took form in the Economic Cooperation Act of 1948, which the president signed on April 3; the introduction to this legislation is included as Document 9. An excerpt from National Security Council Paper No. 68 (NSC-68), dated April 7, 1950, is reprinted as Document 10. Requested by the president, this alarmist report represented high-level American thinking about the Cold War and argued the need for a large military buildup.

Changes in Europe After World War II

Territorial Changes After World War II

Notes: -The United States, British, and French Zones of Germany merged in 1949 as the Federal Republic of Germany.

-The Russian Zone of Germany became the German Democratic Republic in 1949.

-The four zones of Austria merged in 1955 to become the Federal Republic of Austria.

1. Harry Hopkins and Joseph Stalin
Discuss Lend-Lease and Poland, 1945

Marshal Stalin said he would not attempt to use Soviet public opinion as a screen but would speak of the feeling that had been created in Soviet government circles as a result of recent moves on the part of the United States Government. He said these circles felt a certain alarm in regard to the attitude of the United States Government. It was their impression that the American attitude towards the Soviet Union had perceptibly cooled once it became obvious that Germany was defeated, and that it was as though the Americans were saying that the Russians were no longer needed. He said he would give the following examples: . . .

[1] 3. The attitude of the United States Government towards the Polish question. He said that at Yalta it had been agreed that the existing government was to be reconstructed and that anyone with common sense could see that this meant that the present government was to form the basis of the new. He said no other understanding of the Yalta Agreement was possible. . . .

[2] 4. The manner in which Lend Lease had been curtailed. He said that if the United States was unable to supply the Soviet Union further under Lend Lease that was one thing but that the manner in which it had been done had been unfortunate and even brutal. For example, certain ships had been unloaded and while it was true that this order had been cancelled the whole manner in which it had been done had caused concern to the Soviet Government. If the refusal to continue Lend Lease was designed as pressure on the Russians in order to soften them up then it was a fundamental mistake. He said he must tell Mr. [Harry] Hopkins frankly that [if] the Russians were approached frankly on a friendly basis much could be done but that reprisals in any form would bring about the exact opposite effect. . . .

Mr. Hopkins replied that what disturbed him most about Marshal's statement was the revelation that he believed that the United States would use Lend Lease as a means of showing our displeasure with the Soviet Union. He wished to assure the Marshal that however unfortunate an impression this question had caused in the mind of the Soviet Government he must believe that there was no attempt or desire on the part of the United States to use it as a pressure weapon. He said the United States is a strong power and does not go in for those methods. Furthermore, we have no conflict of immediate interests with the Soviet Union and would have no reason to adopt such practices. . . .

Mr. Hopkins concluded the discussion of Lend Lease by stating that he thought it would be a great tragedy if the greatest achievement in cooperation which the Soviet Union and the United States had on the whole worked out together on the basis of Lend Lease were to end on an unsatisfactory note. He said he wished to add that we had never believed that our Lend Lease help had been the chief factor in the Soviet defeat of Hitler on the eastern front. That this had been done by the heroism and blood of the Russian army. . . .

This document can be found in U.S. Department of State, *Foreign Relations of the United States: Diplomatic Papers, The Conference of Berlin* (Washington, D.C.: Government Printing Office, 1960), I, 31–41.

Mr. Hopkins then said with the Marshal's permission he would like to review the position of the United States in regard to Poland. He said first of all he wished to assure the Marshal that he had no thought or indeed any right to attempt to settle the Polish problem during his visit here in Moscow, nor was he intending to hide behind American public opinion in presenting the position of the United States.

Marshal Stalin said he was afraid that his remark concerning Soviet public opinion has cut Mr. Hopkins to the quick and that he has not meant to imply that Mr. Hopkins was hiding behind the screen of American public opinion. In fact he knew Mr. Hopkins to be an honest and frank man.

Mr. Hopkins said that he wished to state this position as clearly and as forcibly as he knew how. He said the question of Poland per se was not so important as the fact that it had become a symbol of our ability to work out problems with the Soviet Union. He said that we had no special interests in Poland and no special desire to see any particular kind of government. That we would accept any government in Poland which was desired by the Polish people and was at the same time friendly to the Soviet Government. He said that the people and Government of the United States felt that this was a problem which should be worked out jointly between the United States, the Soviet Union and Great Britain and that we felt that the Polish people should be given the right to free elections to choose their own government and their own system and that Poland should genuinely be independent. The Government and people of the United States were disturbed because the preliminary steps towards the reestablishment of Poland appeared to have been taken unilaterally by the Soviet Union together with the present Warsaw Government and that in fact the United States was completely excluded. . . .

Marshal Stalin replied that he wished Mr. Hopkins would take into consideration the following factors: He said it may seem strange although it appeared to be recognized in United States circles and Churchill in his speeches also recognized it, that the Soviet Government should wish for a friendly Poland. In the course of twenty-five years the Germans had twice invaded Russia via Poland. Neither the British nor American people had experienced such German invasions which were a horrible thing to endure and the results of which were not easily forgotten. He said these German invasions were not warfare but were like the incursions of the Huns. He said that Germany had been able to do this because Poland had been regarded as a part of the cordon sanitaire around the Soviet Union and that previous European policy had been that Polish Governments must be hostile to Russia. In these circumstances either Poland had been too weak to oppose Germany or had let the Germans come through. . . . He said there was no intention on the part of the Soviet Union to interfere in Poland's internal affairs, that Poland would live under the parliamentary system which is like Czechoslovakia, Belgium and Holland and that any talk of an intention to Sovietize Poland was stupid. . . . Mr. Hopkins had spoken of Russian unilateral action in Poland and United States opinion concerning it. It was true that Russia had taken such unilateral action but they had been compelled to. He said the Soviet Government had recognized the Warsaw Government and concluded a treaty with it at a time when their Allies did not recognize this government. These were admittedly unilateral acts which would have been much better left undone but the fact was they had not met with any understanding on the part of their Allies. The need for these actions has arisen out of the presence of Soviet troops in Poland and it would have been impossible to have waited until such time as the Allies had come to an agreement on Poland. The logic of the war against Germany demanded that the Soviet rear be assured and the Lublin Committee had been of great assistance to the Red Army at all times and it was for this reason that these actions had been taken by the Soviet Government. . . . He said he wished to emphasize that these steps had not been taken with any desire to eliminate or exclude Russia's Allies. He must point out however that Soviet action in Poland had been more successful than British action in Greece and at no time had they been compelled to undertake the measures which they had done in Greece. Stalin then turned to his suggestion for the solution of the Polish problem.

Marshal Stalin said that he felt that we should examine the composition of the future Government of National Unity. He said there were eighteen or twenty ministries in the present Polish Government and that four or five of these portfolios could be given representatives of other Polish groups taken from the list submitted by Great Britain and the United States (Molotov whispered to Stalin who then said he meant four and not five posts in the government). He said he thought the Warsaw Poles would not accept more than four ministers from other democratic groups. He added that if this appears a suitable basis we could then proceed to consider what persons should be selected for these posts. He said of course that they would have to be friendly to the U.S.S.R. and to the Allies. . . .

Marshal Stalin then said it might be wise to ask some of the Warsaw leaders to come to Moscow now and to hear what they had to say and to learn more of what had been decided. He added that if we are able to settle the composition of the new government he felt that no differences remained since we were all agreed on the free and unfettered elections and that no one intended to interfere with the Polish people.

2. The Franck Committee Predicts a Nuclear-Arms Race If the Atomic Bomb Is Dropped on Japan, 1945

The way in which the nuclear weapons, now secretly developed in this country, will first be revealed to the world appears of great, perhaps fateful importance.

One possible way—which may particularly appeal to those who consider the nuclear bombs primarily as a secret weapon developed to help win the present war—is to use it without warning on an appropriately selected object in Japan. It is doubtful whether the first available bombs, of comparatively low efficiency and small in size, will be sufficient to break the will or ability of Japan to resist, especially given the fact that the major cities like Tokyo, Nagoya, Osaka and Kobe already will largely be reduced to ashes by the slower process of ordinary aerial bombing. Certain and perhaps important tactical results undoubtedly can be achieved, but we nevertheless think that the question of the use of the very first available atomic bombs in the Japanese war should be weighed very carefully, not only by military authority, but by the highest political leadership of this country. If we consider international agreement on total prevention of nuclear warfare as the

This document can be found in "Political and Social Problems," June 11, 1945, Manhattan Engineering District Papers, National Archives, Washington, D.C. It can also be found in The Committee of Social and Political Implications, A Report to the Secretary of War, June 1945, *Bulletin of the Atomic Scientists,* I (May 1, 1946), 2–4, 16.

paramount objective, and believe that it can be achieved, this kind of introduction of atomic weapons to the world may easily destroy all our chances of success. Russia, and even allied countries which bear less mistrust of our ways and intentions, as well as neutral countries, will be deeply shocked. It will be very difficult to persuade the world that a nation which was capable of secretly preparing and suddenly releasing a weapon, as indiscriminate as the rocket bomb and a thousand times more destructive, is to be trusted in its proclaimed desire of having such weapons abolished by international agreement. . . .

Thus, from the "optimistic" point of view—looking forward to an international agreement on prevention of nuclear warfare—the military advantages and the saving of American lives, achieved by the sudden use of atomic bombs against Japan, may be outweighed by the ensuing loss of confidence and wave of horror and repulsion, sweeping over the rest of the world, and perhaps dividing even the public opinion at home.

From this point of view a demonstration of the new weapon may best be made before the eyes of representatives of all United Nations, on the desert or a barren island. The best possible atmosphere for the achievement of an international agreement could be achieved if America would be able to say to the world, "You see what weapon we had but did not use. We are ready to renounce its use in the future and to join other nations in working out adequate supervision of the use of this nuclear weapon."

This may sound fantastic, but then in nuclear weapons we have something entirely new in the order of magnitude of destructive power, and if we want to capitalize fully on the advantage which its possession gives us, we must use new and imaginative methods. After such a demonstration the weapon could be used against Japan if a sanction of the United Nations (and of the public opinion at home) could be obtained, perhaps after a preliminary ultimatum to Japan to surrender or at least to evacuate a certain region as an alternative to the total destruction of this target.

It must be stressed that if one takes a pessimistic point of view and discounts the possibilities of an effective international control of nuclear weapons, then the advisability of an early use of nuclear bombs against Japan becomes even more doubtful—quite independently of any humanitarian considerations. If no international agreement is concluded immediately after the first demonstration, this will mean a flying start of an unlimited armaments race.

3. Henry L. Stimson Appeals for Atomic Talks with the Soviets, 1945

In many quarters it [atomic bomb] has been interpreted as a substantial offset to the growth of Russian influence on the continent. We can be certain that the Soviet Government has sensed this tendency and the temptation will be strong for the Soviet political and military leaders to acquire this weapon in the shortest possible

This document can be found in Henry L. Stimson, Memorandum for the President, 11 September 1945, "Proposed Actions for Control of Atomic Bombs," Harry S. Truman Papers, PSF: General File, Folder: Atomic Bomb, Box 112, Harry S. Truman Presidential Library, Independence, MO. It can also be found in Henry L. Stimson and McGeorge Bundy, *On Active Service in Peace and War* (New York: Harper & Brothers, 1948), pp. 642–646.

time. Britain in effect already has the status of a partner with us in the development of this weapon. Accordingly, unless the Soviets are voluntarily invited into the partnership upon a basis of cooperation and trust, we are going to maintain the Anglo-Saxon bloc over against the Soviet in the possession of this weapon. Such a condition will almost certainly stimulate feverish activity on the part of the Soviet toward the development of this bomb in what will in effect be a secret armament race of a rather desperate character. There is evidence to indicate that such activity may have already commenced. . . .

To put the matter concisely, I consider the problem of our satisfactory relations with Russia as not merely connected with but as virtually dominated by the problem of the atomic bomb. Except for the problem of the control of that bomb, those relations, while vitally important, might not be immediately pressing. The establishment of relations of mutual confidence between her and us could afford to await the slow progress of time. But with the discovery of the bomb, they became immediately emergent. Those relations may be perhaps irretrievably embittered by the way in which we approach the solution of the bomb with Russia. For if we fail to approach them now and merely continue to negotiate with them, having this weapon rather ostentatiously on our hip, their suspicions and their distrust of our purposes and motives will increase. . . .

If the atomic bomb were merely another though more devastating military weapon to be assimilated into our pattern of international relations, it would be one thing. We could then follow the old custom of secrecy and nationalistic military superiority relying on international caution to prescribe the future use of the weapon as we did with gas. But I think the bomb instead constitutes merely a first step in a new control by man over the forces of nature too revolutionary and dangerous to fit into the old concepts. I think it really caps the climax of the race between man's growing technical power for destructiveness and his psychological power of self-control and group control—his moral power. If so, our method of approach to the Russians is a question of the most vital importance in the evolution of human progress. . . .

My idea of an approach to the Soviets would be a direct proposal after discussion with the British that we would be prepared in effect to enter an arrangement with the Russians, the general purpose of which would be to control and limit the use of the atomic bomb as an instrument of war and so far as possible to direct and encourage the development of atomic power for peaceful and humanitarian purposes. Such an approach might more specifically lead to the proposal that we would stop work on the further improvement in, or manufacture of, the bomb as a military weapon, provided the Russians and the British would agree to do likewise. It might also provide that we would be willing to impound what bombs we now have in the United States provided the Russians and the British would agree with us that in no event will they or we use a bomb as an instrument of war unless all three Governments agree to that use. We might also consider including in the arrangement a covenant with the U.K. and the Soviets providing for the exchange of benefits of future developments whereby atomic energy may be applied on a mutually satisfactory basis for commercial or humanitarian purposes. . . .

I emphasize perhaps beyond all other considerations the importance of taking this action with Russia as a proposal of the United States—backed by Great Britain but peculiarly the proposal of the United States. Action of any international group of nations, including many small nations who have not demonstrated their potential power or responsibility in this war would not, in my opinion, be taken seriously by the Soviets. . . .

. . . The use of this bomb has been accepted by the world as the result of the initiative and productive capacity of the United States, and I think this factor is a most potent lever toward having our proposals accepted by the Soviets, whereas I am most skeptical of obtaining any tangible results by way of any international debate. I urge this method as the most realistic means of accomplishing this vitally important step in the history of the world.

4. George F. Kennan's "Long Telegram," 1946

At bottom of Kremlin's neurotic view of world affairs is traditional and instinctive Russian sense of insecurity. Originally, this was insecurity of a peaceful agricultural people trying to live on vast exposed plain in neighborhood of fierce nomadic peoples. To this was added, as Russia came into contact with economically advanced West, fear of more competent, more powerful, more highly organized societies in that area. But this latter type of insecurity was one which afflicted rather Russian rulers than Russian people; for Russian rulers have invariably sensed that their rule was relatively archaic in form, fragile and artificial in its psychological foundation, unable to stand comparison or contact with political systems of Western countries. For this reason they have always feared foreign penetration, feared direct contact between Western world and their own, feared what would happen if Russians learned truth about world without or if foreigners learned truth about world within. And they had learned to seek security only in patient but deadly struggle for total destruction of rival power, never in compacts and compromises with it.

It was no coincidence that Marxism, which had smouldered ineffectively for half a century in Western Europe, caught hold and blazed for first time in Russia. Only in this land which had never known a friendly neighbor or indeed any tolerant equilibrium of separate powers, either internal or international, could a doctrine thrive which viewed economic conflicts of society as insoluble by peaceful means. After establishment of Bolshevist regime, Marxist dogma, rendered even more truculent and intolerant by Lenin's interpretation, became a perfect vehicle for sense of insecurity with which Bolsheviks, even more than previous Russian rulers, were afflicted. In this dogma, with its basic altruism of purpose, they found justification for their instinctive fear of outside world, for the dictatorship without which they did not know how to rule, for cruelties they did not dare not to inflict, for sacrifices they felt bound to demand. In the name of Marxism they sacrificed every single ethical value in their methods and tactics. Today they cannot dispense with it. It is fig leaf of their moral and intellectual respectability. Without it they would stand before history, at best, as only the last of that long succession of cruel and wasteful Russian rulers who have relentlessly forced country on to ever new heights of military power in order to guarantee external security of their internally weak regimes. This is why

This document can be found in U.S. Department of State, *Foreign Relations of the United States, 1946, Eatern Europe: The Soviet Union* (Washington, D.C.: Government Printing Office, 1969), VI, 699–701, 706–707.

Soviet purposes must always be solemnly clothed in trappings of Marxism, and why no one should underrate importance of dogma in Soviet affairs. Thus Soviet leaders are driven [by?] necessities of their own past and present position to put forward a dogma which [apparent omission] outside world as evil, hostile and menacing, but as bearing within itself germs of creeping disease and destined to be wracked with growing internal convulsions until it is given final *coup de grace* by rising power of socialism and yields to new and better world. This thesis provides justification for the increase of military and police power of Russian state, for that isolation of Russian population from outside world, and for that fluid and constant pressure to extend limits of Russian police power which are together the natural and instinctive urges of Russian rulers. Basically this is only the steady advance of uneasy Russian nationalism, a centuries old movement in which conceptions of offense and defense are inextricably confused. But in new guise of international Marxism, with its honeyed promises to a desperate and war torn outside world, it is more dangerous and insidious than ever before.

It should not be thought from above that Soviet party line is necessarily disingenuous and insincere on part of all those who put it forward. Many of them are too ignorant of outside world and mentally too dependent to question [apparent omission] self-hypnotism, and who have no difficulty making themselves believe what they find it comforting and convenient to believe. Finally we have the unsolved mystery as to who, if anyone, in this great land actually receives accurate and unbiased information about outside world. In atmosphere of oriental secretiveness and conspiracy which pervades this Government, possibilities for distorting or poisoning sources and currents of information are infinite. The very disrespect of Russians for objective truth—indeed, their disbelief in its existence—leads them to view all stated facts as instruments for furtherance of one ulterior purpose or another. There is good reason to suspect that this Government is actually a conspiracy within a conspiracy; and I for one am reluctant to believe that Stalin himself receives anything like an objective picture of outside world. Here there is ample scope for the type of subtle intrigue at which Russians are past masters. Inability of foreign governments to place their case squarely before Russian policy makers—extent to which they are delivered up in their relations with Russia to good graces of obscure and unknown advisers who they never see and cannot influence—this to my mind is most disquieting feature of diplomacy in Moscow, and one which Western statesmen would do well to keep in mind if they would understand nature of difficulties encountered here. . . .

In summary, we have here a political force committed fanatically to the belief that with US there can be no permanent *modus vivendi,* that it is desirable and necessary that the internal harmony of our society be disrupted, our traditional way of life be destroyed, the international authority of our state be broken, if Soviet power is to be secure. This political force has complete power of disposition over energies of one of world's greatest peoples and resources of world's richest national territory, and is borne along by deep and powerful currents of Russian nationalism. In addition, it has an elaborate and far flung apparatus for exertion of its influence in other countries, an apparatus of amazing flexibility and versatility, managed by people whose experience and skill in underground methods are presumably without parallel in history. Finally, it is seemingly inaccessible to considerations of reality in its basic reactions. For it, the vast fund of objective fact about human society is not, as with us, the measure against which outlook is constantly being tested and reformed, but a grab bag from which individual items are selected arbitrarily and tendenciously to bolster an outlook already preconceived. This is admittedly not a pleasant picture. Problem of how to cope with this force [is] undoubtedly greatest task our diplomacy has ever faced and probably greatest it will ever have to face. It should be point of departure from which our political general staff work at present juncture should proceed. It should be approached with same thoroughness and care as solution of major strategic problem in war, and if necessary, with no smaller outlay in planning effort. I cannot attempt to suggest all answers here. But I would like to record my conviction that problem is within our power to solve—and that without recourse to any general military conflict. And in support of this conviction there are certain observations of a more encouraging nature I should like to make:

1. Soviet power, unlike that of Hitlerite Germany, is neither schematic nor adventuristic. It does not work by fixed plans. It does not take unnecessary risks. Impervious to logic of reason, and it is highly sensitive to logic of force. For this reason it can easily withdraw—and usually does—when strong resistance is encountered at any point. Thus, if the adversary has sufficient force and makes clear his readiness to use it, he rarely has to do so. If situations are properly handled there need be no prestige-engaging showdowns.
2. Gauged against Western World as a whole, Soviets are still by far the weaker force. Thus, their success will really depend on degree of cohesion, firmness and vigor which Western World can muster. And this is factor which it is within our power to influence.
3. Success of Soviet system, as form of internal power, is not yet finally proven. It has yet to be demonstrated that it can survive supreme test of successive transfer of power from one individual or group to another. Lenin's death was first such transfer, and its effects wracked Soviet state for 15 years. After Stalin's death or retirement will be second. But even this will not be final test. Soviet internal system will now be subjected, by virtue of recent territorial expansions, to series of additional strains which once proved severe tax on Tsardom. We here are convinced that never since termination of civil war have mass of Russian people been emotionally farther removed from doctrines of Communist Party than they are today. In Russia, party has now become a great and—for the moment—highly successful apparatus of dictatorial administration, but it has ceased to be a source of emotional inspiration. Thus, internal soundness and permanence of movement need not yet be regarded as assured.
4. All Soviet propaganda beyond Soviet security sphere is basically negative and destructive. It should therefore be relatively easy to combat it by any intelligent and really constructive program.

5. Winston S. Churchill's "Iron Curtain" Speech, 1946

A shadow has fallen upon the scenes so lately lighted by the Allied victory. Nobody knows what Soviet Russia and its Communist international organization intends to do in the immediate future, or what are the limits, if any, to their expansive and proselytizing tendencies. I have a strong admiration and regard for the valiant Russian

---

This document can be found in *Congressional Record,* XCII (1946, Appendix), A1145–A1147.

people and for my wartime comrade, Marshal Stalin. There is sympathy and good will in Britain—and I doubt not here also—toward the peoples of all the Russias and a resolve to persevere through many differences and rebuffs in establishing lasting friendships.

We understand the Russian need to be secure on her western frontiers from all renewal of German aggression. We welcome her to her rightful place among the leading nations of the world. Above all, we welcome constant, frequent, and growing contacts between Russian people and our own people on both sides of the Atlantic. It is my duty, however, to place before you certain facts about the present position in Europe.

From Stettin in the Baltic to Trieste in the Adriatic, an iron curtain has descended across the continent. Behind that line lie all the capitals of the ancient states of Central and Eastern Europe. Warsaw, Berlin, Prague, Vienna, Budapest, Belgrade, Bucharest, and Sofia, all these famous cities and the populations around them lie in the Soviet sphere and all are subject, in one form or another, not only to Soviet influence but to a very high and increasing measure of control from Moscow. Athens alone, with its immortal glories, is free to decide its future at an election under British, American, and French observation.

The Russian-dominated Polish government has been encouraged to make enormous and wrongful inroads upon Germany, and mass expulsions of millions of Germans on a scale grievous and undreamed of are now taking place. The Communist parties, which were very small in all these eastern states of Europe, have been raised to preeminence and power far beyond their numbers and are seeking everywhere to obtain totalitarian control. Police governments are prevailing in nearly every case, and so far, except in Czechoslovakia, there is no true democracy.

Turkey and Persia are both profoundly alarmed and disturbed at the claims which are made upon them and at the pressure being exerted by the Moscow government. An attempt is being made by the Russians in Berlin to build up a quasi-Communist party in their zone of occupied Germany by showing special favors to groups of left-wing German leaders. At the end of the fighting last June, the American and British Armies withdrew westward, in accordance with an earlier agreement, to a depth at some points of 150 miles on a front of nearly 400 miles, to allow the Russians to occupy this vast expanse of territory which the Western democracies had conquered.

If now the Soviet government tries, by separate action, to build up a pro-Communist Germany in their areas, this will cause new serious difficulties in the British and American zones, and will give the defeated Germans the power of putting themselves up to auction between the Soviets and the Western democracies. Whatever conclusions may be drawn from these facts—and facts they are—this is certainly not the liberated Europe we fought to build up. Nor is it one which contains the essentials of permanent peace.

In front of the iron curtain which lies across Europe are other causes for anxiety. In Italy the Communist party is seriously hampered by having to support the Communist-trained Marshall Tito's claims to former Italian territory at the head of the Adriatic. Nevertheless, the future of Italy hangs in the balance. Again, one cannot imagine a regenerated Europe without a strong France. . . .

However, in a great number of countries, far from the Russian frontiers and throughout the world, Communist fifth columns are established and work in complete unity and absolute obedience to the directions they receive from the Communist center. Except in the British Commonwealth, and in the United States, where communism is in its infancy, the Communist parties or fifth columns constitute a growing challenge and peril to Christian civilization. These are somber facts for anyone to have to recite on the morrow of a victory gained by so much splendid comradeship in arms and in the cause of freedom and democracy, and we should be most unwise not to face them squarely while time remains.

The outlook is also anxious in the Far East and especially in Manchuria. The agreement which was made at Yalta, to which I was a party, was extremely favorable to Soviet Russia, but it was made at a time when no one could say that the German war might not extend all through the summer and autumn of 1945 and when the Japanese war was expected to last for a further eighteen months from the end of the German war. In this country you are all so well informed about the Far East and such devoted friends of China that I do not need to expatiate on the situation there. . . .

Our difficulties and dangers will not be removed by closing our eyes to them; they will not be removed by mere waiting to see what happens; nor will they be relieved by a policy of appeasement. What is needed is a settlement, and the longer this is delayed, the more difficult it will be and the greater our dangers will become. From what I have seen of our Russian friends and allies during the war, I am convinced that there is nothing they admire so much as strength, and there is nothing for which they have less respect than for military weakness. For that reason the old doctrine of a balance of power is unsound. We cannot afford, if we can help it, to work on narrow margins, offering temptations to a trial of strength. If the Western democracies stand together in strict adherence to the principles of the United Nations Charter, their influence for furthering these principles will be immense and no one is likely to molest them. If, however, they become divided or falter in their duty, and if these all-important years are allowed to slip away, then indeed catastrophe may overwhelm us all.

6. Henry A. Wallace Questions the "Get Tough" Policy, 1946

How do American actions since V-J Day appear to other nations? I mean by actions the concrete things like $13 billion for the War and Navy Departments, the Bikini tests of the atomic bomb and continued production of bombs, the plan to arm Latin America with our weapons, production of B-29s and planned production of B-36s, and the effort to secure air bases spread over half the globe from which the other half of the globe can be bombed. I cannot but feel that these actions must make it look to the rest of the world as if we were only paying lip service to peace at the conference table. These facts rather make it appear either (1) that we are preparing ourselves to win the war which we regard as inevitable or (2) that we are trying to build up a predominance of force to intimidate the rest of mankind. How

Henry A. Wallace, "The Path to Peace with Russia," *New Republic,* 115 (1946), 401–406.

would it look to us if Russia had the atomic bomb and we did not, if Russia had ten thousand-mile bombers and air bases within a thousand miles of our coast lines and we did not?

Some of the military men and self-styled "realists" are saying: "What's wrong with trying to build up a predominance of force? The only way to preserve peace is for this country to be so well armed that no one will dare attack us. We know that America will never start a war."

The flaw in this policy is simply that it will not work. In a world of atomic bombs and other revolutionary new weapons, such as radioactive poison gases and biological warfare, a peace maintained by a predominance of force is no longer possible. . . .

Insistence on our part that the game must be played our way will only lead to a deadlock. The Russians will redouble their efforts to manufacture bombs, and they may also decide to expand their "security zone" in a serious way. Up to now, despite all our outcries against it, their efforts to develop a security zone in Eastern Europe and in the Middle East are small change from the point of view of military power as compared with our air bases in Greenland, Okinawa and many other places thousands of miles from our shores. We may feel very self-righteous if we refuse to budge on our plan and the Russians refuse to accept it, but that means only one thing—the atomic armament race is on in deadly earnest. . . .

I should list the factors which make for Russian distrust of the United States and of the Western world as follows: The first is Russian history, which we must take into account because it is the setting in which Russians see all actions and policies of the rest of the world. Russian history for over a thousand years has been a succession of attempts, often unsuccessful, to resist invasion and conquest—by the Mongols, the Turks, the Swedes, the Germans and the Poles. The scant thirty years of the existence of the Soviet government has in Russian eyes been a continuation of their historical struggle for national existence. The first four years of the new regime, from 1917 through 1921, were spent in resisting attempts at destruction by the Japanese, British and French, with some American assistance, and by the several White Russian armies encouraged and financed by the Western powers. Then, in 1941, the Soviet state was almost conquered by the Germans after a period during which the Western European powers had apparently acquiesced in the rearming of Germany in the belief that the Nazis would seek to expand eastward rather than westward. The Russians, therefore, obviously see themselves as fighting for their existence in a hostile world.

Second, it follows that to the Russians all of the defense and security measures of the Western powers seem to have an aggressive intent. Our actions to expand our military security system—such steps as extending the Monroe Doctrine to include the arming of the Western Hemisphere nations, our present monopoly of the atomic bomb, our interest in outlying bases and our general support of the British Empire—appear to them as going far beyond the requirements of defense. I think we might feel the same if the United States were the only capitalistic country in the world and the principal socialistic countries were creating a level of armed strength far exceeding anything in their previous history. From the Russian point of view, also, the granting of a loan to Britain and the lack of tangible results on their request to borrow for rehabilitation purposes may be regarded as another evidence of strengthening of an anti-Soviet bloc.

Finally, our resistance to her attempts to obtain warm water ports and her own security system in the form of "friendly" neighboring states seems, from the Russian point of view, to clinch the case. After twenty-five years of isolation and after having achieved the status of a major power, Russia believes that she is entitled to recognition of her new status. Our interest in establishing democracy in Eastern Europe, where democracy by and large has never existed, seems to her an attempt to reestablish the encirclement of unfriendly neighbors which was created after the last war and which might serve as a springboard of still another effort to destroy her.

If this analysis is correct, and there is ample evidence to support it, the action to improve the situation is clearly indicated. The fundamental objective of such action should be to allay any reasonable Russian grounds for fear, suspicions and distrust. We must recognize that the world has changed and that today there can be no "one world" unless the United States and Russia can find some way of living together. For example, most of us are firmly convinced of the soundness of our position when we suggest the internationalization and defortification of the Danube or of the Dardanelles, but we would be horrified and angered by any Russian counterproposal that would involve also the internationalizing and disarming of Suez or Panama. We must recognize that to the Russians these seem to be identical situations. . . .

It is of the greatest importance that we should discuss with the Russians in a friendly way their long-range economic problems and the future of our cooperation in matters of trade. The reconstruction program of the USSR and the plans for the full development of the Soviet Union offers tremendous opportunities for American goods and American technicians. . . .

Many of the problems relating to the countries bordering on Russia could more readily be solved once an atmosphere of mutual trust and confidence is established and some form of economic arrangements is worked out with Russia. These problems also might be helped by discussions of an economic nature. Russian economic penetration of the Danube area, for example, might be countered by concrete proposals for economic collaboration in the development of the resources of this area, rather than by insisting that the Russians should cease their unilateral penetration and offering no solution to the present economic chaos there.

This proposal admittedly calls for a shift in some of our thinking about international matters. It is imperative that we make this shift. We have little time to lose. Our postwar actions have not yet been adjusted to the lessons to be gained from experience of Allied cooperation during the war and the facts of the atomic age.

7. Soviet Ambassador Nikolai Novikov Identifies a U.S. Drive for World Supremacy, 1946

The foreign policy of the United States, which reflects the imperialist tendencies of American monopolistic capital, is characterized in the postwar period by a striving for world supremacy. This is the real meaning of the many statements by President Truman and other representatives of American ruling circles: that the United States

From *Origins of the Cold War: The Novikov, Kennan, and Roberts "Long Telegram" of 1946,* Kenneth M. Jensen, editor, Washington: United States Institute of Peace, 1991. Translated by Kenneth M. Jensen and John Glad.

has the right to lead the world. All the forces of American diplomacy—the army, the air force, the navy, industry and science—are enlisted in the service of this foreign policy. . . .

Europe has come out of the war with a completely dislocated economy, and the economic devastation that occurred in the course of the war cannot be overcome in a short time. All of the countries of Europe and Asia are experiencing a colossal need for consumer goods, industrial and transportation equipment, etc. Such a situation provides American monopolistic capital with prospects for enormous shipments of goods and the importation of capital into these countries—a circumstance that would permit it to infiltrate their national economies. . . .

At the same time the USSR's international position is currently stronger than it was in the prewar period. Thanks to the historical victories of Soviet weapons, the Soviet armed forces are located on the territory of Germany and other formerly hostile countries, thus guaranteeing that these countries will not be used again for an attack on the USSR. In formerly hostile countries, such as Bulgaria, Finland, Hungary, and Romania, democratic reconstruction has established regimes that have undertaken to strengthen and maintain friendly relations with the Soviet Union. In the Slavic countries that were liberated by the Red Army or with its assistance—Poland, Czechoslovakia, and Yugoslavia—democratic regimes have also been established that maintain relations with the Soviet Union on the basis of agreements on friendship and mutual assistance. . . .

Such a situation in Eastern and Southeastern Europe cannot help but be regarded by the American imperialists as an obstacle in the path of the expansionist policy of the United States.

The foreign policy of the United States is not determined at present by the circles in the Democratic party that (as was the case during Roosevelt's lifetime) strive to strengthen the cooperation of the three great powers that constituted the basis of the anti-Hitler coalition during the war. The ascendance to power of President Truman, a politically unstable person but with certain conservative tendencies, and the subsequent appointment of [James F.] Byrnes as Secretary of State meant a strengthening of the influence on U.S. foreign policy of the most reactionary circles of the Democratic party. The constantly increasing reactionary nature of the foreign policy course of the United States, which consequently approached the policy advocated by the Republican party, laid the groundwork for close cooperation in this field between the far right wing of the Democratic party and the Republican party. . . .

At the same time, there has been a decline in the influence on foreign policy of those who follow Roosevelt's course for cooperation among peace-loving countries. Such persons in the government, in Congress, and in the leadership of the Democratic party are being pushed farther and farther into the background. The contradictions in the field of foreign policy existing between the followers of [Henry] Wallace and [Claude] Pepper, on the one hand, and the adherents of the reactionary "bi-partisan" policy, on the other, were manifested with great clarity recently in the speech by Wallace that led to his resignation from the post of Secretary of Commerce. . . .

In the summer of 1946, for the first time in the history of the country, Congress passed a law on the establishment of a peacetime army, not on a volunteer basis but on the basis of universal military service. The size of the army, which is supposed to amount to about one million persons as of July 1, 1947, was also increased significantly. The size of the navy at the conclusion of the war decreased quite insignificantly in comparison with wartime. At the present time, the American navy occupies first place in the world, leaving England's navy far behind, to say nothing of those of other countries.

Expenditures on the army and navy have risen colossally, amounting to 13 billion dollars according to the budget for 1946–47 (about 40 percent of the total budget of 36 billion dollars). This is more than ten times greater than corresponding expenditures in the budget for 1938, which did not amount to even one billion dollars.

Along with maintaining a large army, navy, and air force, the budget provides that these enormous amounts also will be spent on establishing a very extensive system of naval and air bases in the Atlantic and Pacific oceans. According to existing official plans, in the course of the next few years 228 bases, points of support, and radio stations are to be constructed in the Atlantic Ocean and 258 in the Pacific. . . .

One of the stages in the achievement of dominance over the world by the United States is its understanding with England concerning the partial division of the world on the basis of mutual concessions. The basic lines of the secret agreement between the United States and England regarding the division of the world consist, as shown by facts, in their agreement on the inclusion of Japan and China in the sphere of influence of the United States in the Far East, while the United States, for its part, has agreed not to hinder England either in resolving the Indian problem or in strengthening its influence in Siam and Indonesia.

In connection with this division, the United States at the present time is in control of China and Japan without any interference from England. . . .

In recent years American capital has penetrated very intensively into the economy of the Near Eastern countries, in particular into the oil industry. At present there are American oil concessions in all of the Near Eastern countries that have oil deposits (Iraq, Bahrain, Kuwait, Egypt, and Saudi Arabia). American capital, which made its first appearance in the oil industry of the Near East only in 1927, now controls about 42 percent of all proven reserves in the Near East, excluding Iran. Of the total proven reserves of 26.8 billion barrels, over 11 billion barrels are owned by U.S. concessions. . . .

In expanding in the Near East, American capital has English capital as its greatest and most stubborn competitor. The fierce competition between them is the chief factor preventing England and the United States from reaching an understanding on the division of spheres of influence in the Near East, a division that can occur only at the expense of direct British interests in this region. . . .

It must be kept in mind, however, that incidents such as the visit by the American battleship *Missouri* to the Black Sea straits, the visit of the American fleet to Greece, and the great interest that U.S. diplomacy displays in the problem of the straits have a double meaning. On the one hand, they indicate that the United States has decided to consolidate its position in the Mediterranean basin to support its interests in the countries of the Near East and that it has selected the navy as the tool for this policy. On the other hand, these incidents constitute a political and military demonstration against the Soviet Union. The strengthening of U.S. positions in the Near East and the establishment of conditions for basing the American navy at one or more points on the Mediterranean Sea (Trieste, Palestine, Greece, Turkey) will therefore signify the emergence of a new threat to the security of the southern regions of the Soviet Union. . . .

The current relations between England and the United States, despite the temporary attainment of agreements on very important questions, are plagued with great internal contradictions and cannot be lasting.

The economic assistance from the United States conceals within itself a danger for England in many respects. First of all, in accepting the [U.S.] loan, England finds herself in a certain financial dependence on the United States from which it will not be easy to free herself. Second, it should be kept in mind that the conditions created by the loan for the penetration by American capital of the British Empire can entail serious political consequences. The countries included in the British Empire or dependent on it may—under economic pressure from powerful American capital—reorient themselves toward the United States, following in this respect the example of Canada, which more and more is moving away from the influence of England and orienting itself toward the United States. The strengthening of American positions in the Far East could stimulate a similar process in Australia and New Zealand. In the Arabic countries of the Near East, which are striving to emancipate themselves from the British Empire, there are groups within the ruling circles that would not be averse to working out a deal with the United States. It is quite possible that the Near East will become a center of Anglo-American contradictions that will explode the agreements now reached between the United States and England.

The "hard-line" policy with regard to the USSR announced by [Secretary of State James F.] Byrnes after the rapprochement of the reactionary Democrats with the Republicans is at present the main obstacle on the road to cooperation of the Great Powers. It consists mainly of the fact that in the postwar period the United States no longer follows a policy of strengthening cooperation among the Big Three (or Four) but rather has striven to undermine the unity of these countries. The objective has been to impose the will of other countries on the Soviet Union. This is precisely the tenor of the policy of certain countries, which is being carried out with the blessing of the United States, to undermine or completely abolish the principle of the veto in the Security Council of the United Nations. This would give the United States opportunities to form among the Great Powers narrow groupings and blocs directed primarily against the Soviet Union, and thus to split the United Nations. Rejection of the veto by the Great Powers would transform the United Nations into an Anglo-Saxon domain in which the United States would play the leading role.

The present policy of the American government with regard to the USSR is also directed at limiting or dislodging the influence of the Soviet Union from neighboring countries. In implementing this policy in former enemy or Allied countries adjacent to the USSR, the United States attempts, at various international conferences or directly in these countries themselves, to support reactionary forces with the purpose of creating obstacles to the process of democratization of these countries. In so doing, it also attempts to secure positions for the penetration of American capital into their economies. . . .

One of the most important elements in the general policy of the United States, which is directed toward limiting the international role of the USSR in the postwar world, is the policy with regard to Germany. In Germany, the United States is taking measures to strengthen reactionary forces for the purpose of opposing democratic reconstruction. Furthermore, it displays special insistence on accompanying this policy with completely inadequate measures for the demilitarization of Germany.

The American occupation policy does not have the objective of eliminating the remnants of German Fascism and rebuilding German political life on a democratic basis, so that Germany might cease to exist as an aggressive force. The United States is not taking measures to eliminate the monopolistic associations of German industrialists on which German Fascism depended in preparing aggression and waging war. Neither is any agrarian reform being conducted to eliminate large landholders, who were also a reliable support for the Hitlerites. Instead, the United States is considering the possibility of terminating the Allied occupation of German territory before the main tasks of the occupation—the demilitarization and democratization of Germany—have been implemented. This would create the prerequisites for the revival of an imperialist Germany, which the United States plans to use in a future war on its side. One cannot help seeing that such a policy has clearly outlined anti-Soviet edge and constitutes a serious danger to the cause of peace.

The numerous and extremely hostile statements by American government, political, and military figures with regard to the Soviet Union and its foreign policy are very characteristic of the current relationship between the ruling circles of the United States and the USSR. These statements are echoed in an even more unrestrained tone by the overwhelming majority of the American press organs. Talk about a "third war," meaning a war against the Soviet Union, and even a direct call for this war—with the threat of using the atomic bomb—such is the content of the statements on relations with the Soviet Union by reactionaries at public meetings and in the press. . . .

Careful note should be taken of the fact that the preparation by the United States for a future war is being conducted with the prospect of war against the Soviet Union, which in the eyes of American imperialists is the main obstacle in the path of the United States to world domination. This is indicated by facts such as the tactical training of the American army for war with the Soviet Union as the future opponent, the siting of American strategic bases in regions from which it is possible to launch strikes on Soviet territory, intensified training and strengthening of Arctic regions as close approaches to the USSR, and attempts to prepare Germany and Japan to use those countries in a war against the USSR.

8. The Truman Doctrine, 1947

The gravity of the situation which confronts the world today necessitates my appearance before a joint session of the Congress.

The foreign policy and the national security of this country are involved.

One aspect of the present situation, which I present to you at this time for your consideration and decision, concerns Greece and Turkey.

The United States has received from the Greek Government an urgent appeal for financial and economic assistance. Preliminary reports from the American Economic Mission now in Greece and reports from the American Ambassador in

---

This document can be found in *Public Papers of the Presidents of the United States, Harry S. Truman, 1947* (Washington, D.C.: U.S. Government Printing Office, 1963), pp. 176–180.

Greece corroborate the statement of the Greek Government that assistance is imperative if Greece is to survive as a free nation. . . .

The British Government has informed us that, owing to its own difficulties, it can no longer extend financial or economic aid to Turkey.

As in the case of Greece, if Turkey is to have the assistance it needs, the United States must supply it. We are the only country able to provide that help.

I am fully aware of the broad implications involved if the United States extends assistance to Greece and Turkey, and I shall discuss these implications with you at this time.

One of the primary objectives of the foreign policy of the United States is the creation of conditions in which we and other nations will be able to work out a way of life free from coercion. This was a fundamental issue in the war with Germany and Japan. Our victory was won over countries which sought to impose their will, and their way of life, upon other nations.

To ensure the peaceful development of nations, free from coercion, the United States has taken a leading part in establishing the United Nations. The United Nations is designed to make possible lasting freedom and independence for all its members. We shall not realize our objectives, however, unless we are willing to help free peoples to maintain their free institutions and their national integrity against aggressive movements that seek to impose upon them totalitarian regimes. This is no more than a frank recognition that totalitarian regimes imposed upon free peoples, by direct or indirect aggression, undermine the foundations of international peace and hence the security of the United States.

The peoples of a number of countries of the world have recently had totalitarian regimes forced upon them against their will. The Government of the United States has made frequent protests against coercion and intimidation, in violation of the Yalta agreement, in Poland, Rumania, and Bulgaria. I must also state that in a number of other countries there have been similar developments.

At the present moment in world history nearly every nation must choose between alternative ways of life. The choice is too often not a free one.

One way of life is based upon the will of the majority, and is distinguished by free institutions, representative government, free elections, guarantees of individual liberty, freedom of speech and religion, and freedom from political oppression.

The second way of life is based upon the will of a minority forcibly imposed upon the majority. It relies upon terror and oppression, a controlled press and radio, fixed elections, and the suppression of personal freedoms.

I believe that it must be the policy of the United States to support free peoples who are resisting attempted subjugation by armed minorities or by outside pressures.

I believe that we must assist free peoples to work out their own destinies in their own way.

I believe that our help should be primarily through economic and financial aid which is essential to economic stability and orderly political processes.

The world is not static, and the *status quo* is not sacred. But we cannot allow changes in the *status quo* in violation of the Charter of the United Nations by such methods as coercion, or by such subterfuges as political infiltration. In helping free and independent nations to maintain their freedom, the United States will be giving effect to the principles of the Charter of the United Nations.

It is necessary only to glance at a map to realize that the survival and integrity of the Greek nation are of grave importance in a much wider situation. If Greece should fall under the control of an armed minority, the effect upon its neighbor, Turkey, would be immediate and serious. Confusion and disorder might well spread throughout the entire Middle East.

Moreover, the disappearance of Greece as an independent state would have a profound effect upon those countries in Europe whose peoples are struggling against great difficulties to maintain their freedoms and their independence while they repair the damages of war.

It would be an unspeakable tragedy if these countries, which have struggled so long against overwhelming odds, should lose that victory for which they sacrificed so much. Collapse of free institutions and loss of independence would be disastrous not only for them but for the world. Discouragement and possibly failure would quickly be the lot of neighboring peoples striving to maintain their freedom and independence.

Should we fail to aid Greece and Turkey in this fateful hour, the effect will be far reaching to the West as well as to the East.

We must take immediate and resolute action.

I therefore ask the Congress to provide authority for assistance to Greece and Turkey in the amount of $400,000,000 for the period ending June 30, 1948. In requesting these funds, I have taken into consideration the maximum amount of relief assistance which would be furnished to Greece out of the $350,000,000 which I recently requested that the Congress authorize for the prevention of starvation and suffering in countries devastated by the war.

In addition to funds, I ask the Congress to authorize the detail of American civilian and military personnel to Greece and Turkey, at the request of those countries, to assist in the tasks of reconstruction, and for the purpose of supervising the use of such financial and material assistance as may be furnished. I recommend that authority also be provided for the instruction and training of selected Greek and Turkish personnel. . . .

This is a serious course upon which we embark.

I would not recommend it except that the alternative is much more serious. The United States contributed $341,000,000,000 toward winning World War II. This is an investment in world freedom and world peace.

The assistance that I am recommending for Greece and Turkey amounts to little more than 1/10 of 1 percent of this investment. It is only common sense that we should safeguard this investment and make sure that it was not in vain.

The seeds of totalitarian regimes are nurtured by misery and want. They spread and grow in the evil soil of poverty and strife. They reach their full growth when the hope of a people for a better life has died.

We must keep that hope alive.

The free peoples of the world look to us for support in maintaining their freedoms.

If we falter in our leadership, we may endanger the peace of the world—and we shall surely endanger the welfare of this Nation.

Great responsibilities have been placed upon us by the swift movement of events.

I am confident that the Congress will face these responsibilities squarely.

9. The Marshall Plan (Economic Cooperation Act of 1948)

Recognizing the intimate economic and other relationships between the United States and the nations of Europe, and recognizing that disruption following in the wake of war is not contained by national frontiers, the Congress finds that the existing situation in Europe endangers the establishment of a lasting peace, the general welfare and national interest of the United States, and the attainment of the objectives of the United Nations. The restoration or maintenance in European countries of principles of individual liberty, free institutions, and genuine independence rests largely upon the establishment of sound economic conditions, stable international economic relationships, and the achievement by the countries of Europe of a healthy economy independent of extraordinary outside assistance. The accomplishment of these objectives calls for a plan of European recovery, open to all such nations which cooperate in such plan, based upon a strong production effort, the expansion of foreign trade, the creation and maintenance of internal financial stability, and the development of economic cooperation, including all possible steps to establish and maintain equitable rates of exchange and to bring about the progressive elimination of trade barriers. Mindful of the advantages which the United States has enjoyed through the existence of a large domestic market with no internal trade barriers, and believing that similar advantages can accrue to the countries of Europe, it is declared to be the policy of the people of the United States to encourage these countries through a joint organization to exert sustained common efforts as set forth in the report of the Committee of European Economic Cooperation signed at Paris on September 22, 1947, which will speedily achieve that economic cooperation in Europe which is essential for lasting peace and prosperity. It is further declared to be the policy of the people of the United States to sustain and strengthen principles of individual liberty, free institutions, and genuine independence in Europe through assistance to those countries of Europe which participate in a joint recovery program based upon self-help and mutual cooperation: *Provided,* That no assistance to the participating countries herein contemplated shall seriously impair the economic stability of the United States. It is further declared to be the policy of the United States that continuity of assistance provided by the United States should, at all times, be dependent upon continuity of cooperation among countries participating in the program.

10. National Security Council Paper No. 68 (NSC-68), 1950

Within the past thirty-five years the world has experienced two global wars of tremendous violence. It has witnessed two revolutions—the Russian and the Chinese—of extreme scope and intensity. It has also seen the collapse of five empires—the Ottoman, the Austro-Hungarian, German, Italian, and Japanese—and the drastic

Document 9 can be found in *United States Statutes at Large, 1948* (Washington, D.C.: Government Printing Office, 1949), Vol. 62, p. 137.

Document 10 can be found in U.S. Department of State, *Foreign Relations of the United States, 1950, National Security Affairs; Foreign Economic Policy* (Washington, D.C.: Government Printing Office, 1977), I, 237, 252–253, 262–263, 264, 282, 290.

decline of two major imperial systems, the British and the French. During the span of one generation, the international distribution of power has been fundamentally altered. For several centuries it had proved impossible for any one nation to gain such preponderant strength that a coalition of other nations could not in time face it with greater strength. The international scene was marked by recurring periods of violence and war, but a system of sovereign and independent states was maintained, over which no state was able to achieve hegemony.

Two complex sets of factors have now basically altered this historical distribution of power. First, the defeat of Germany and Japan and the decline of the British and French Empires have interacted with the development of the United States and the Soviet Union in such a way that power has increasingly gravitated to these two centers. Second, the Soviet Union, unlike previous aspirants to hegemony, is animated by a new fanatic faith, antithetical to our own, and seeks to impose its absolute authority over the rest of the world. Conflict has, therefore, become endemic and is waged, on the part of the Soviet Union, by violent or nonviolent methods in accordance with the dictates of expediency. With the development of increasingly terrifying weapons of mass destruction, every individual faces the ever-present possibility of annihilation should the conflict enter the phase of total war. . . .

Our overall policy at the present time may be described as one designed to foster a world environment in which the American system can survive and flourish. It therefore rejects the concept of isolation and affirms the necessity of our positive participation in the world community.

This broad intention embraces two subsidiary policies. One is a policy which we would probably pursue even if there were no Soviet threat. It is a policy of attempting to develop a healthy international community. The other is the policy of "containing" the Soviet system. These two policies are closely interrelated and interact on one another. Nevertheless, the distinction between them is basically valid and contributes to a clearer understanding of what we are trying to do. . . .

As for the policy of "containment," it is one which seeks by all means short of war to (1) block further expansion of Soviet power, (2) expose the falsities of Soviet pretentions, (3) induce a retraction of the Kremlin's control and influence and (4) in general, so foster the seeds of destruction within the Soviet system that the Kremlin is brought at least to the point of modifying its behavior to conform to generally accepted international standards.

It was and continues to be cardinal in this policy that we possess superior overall power in ourselves or in dependable combination with other like-minded nations. One of the most important ingredients of power is military strength. In the concept of "containment," the maintenance of a strong military posture is deemed to be essential for two reasons: (1) as an ultimate guarantee of our national security and (2) as an indispensable backdrop to the conduct of the policy of "containment." Without superior aggregate military strength, in being and readily mobilizable, a policy of "containment"—which is in effect a policy of calculated and gradual coercion—is no more than a policy of bluff.

At the same time, it is essential to the successful conduct of a policy of "containment" that we always leave open the possibility of negotiation with the U.S.S.R. A diplomatic freeze—and we are in one now—tends to defeat the very purposes of "containment" because it raises tensions at the same time that it makes Soviet retractions and adjustments in the direction of moderated behavior more difficult. It also tends to inhibit our initiative and deprives us of opportunities for maintaining a moral ascendancy in our struggle with the Soviet system.

In "containment" it is desirable to exert pressure in a fashion which will avoid so far as possible directly challenging Soviet prestige, to keep open the possibility for the U.S.S.R. to retreat before pressure with a minimum loss of face and to secure political advantage from the failure of the Kremlin to yield or take advantage of the openings we leave it.

We have failed to implement adequately these two fundamental aspects of "containment." In the face of obviously mounting Soviet military strength ours has declined relatively. Partly as a byproduct of this, but also for other reasons, we now find ourselves at a diplomatic impasse with the Soviet Union, with the Kremlin growing bolder, with both of us holding on grimly to what we have and with ourselves facing difficult decisions. . . .

It is apparent from the preceding sections that the integrity and vitality of our system is in greater jeopardy than ever before in our history. Even if there were no Soviet Union we would face the great problem of the free society, accentuated many fold in this industrial age, of reconciling order, security, the need for participation, with the requirements of freedom. . . .

It is quite clear from Soviet theory and practice that the Kremlin seeks to bring the free world under its dominion by the methods of the cold war. The preferred technique is to subvert by infiltration and intimidation. Every institution of our society is an instrument which it is sought to stultify and turn against our purposes. Those that touch most closely our material and moral strength are obviously the prime targets, labor unions, civic enterprises, schools, churches, and all media for influencing opinion. . . .

At the same time the Soviet Union is seeking to create overwhelming military force, in order to back up infiltration with intimidation. In the only terms in which it understands strength, it is seeking to demonstrate to the free world that force and the will to use it are on the side of the Kremlin, that those who lack it are decadent and doomed. In local incidents it threatens and encroaches both for the sake of local gains and to increase anxiety and defeatism in all the free world.

The possession of atomic weapons at each of the opposite poles of power, and the inability (for different reasons) of either side to place any trust in the other, puts a premium on a surprise attack against us. It equally puts a premium on a more violent and ruthless prosecution of its design by cold war, especially if the Kremlin is sufficiently objective to realize the improbability of our prosecuting a preventive war. It also puts a premium on piecemeal aggression against others, counting on our unwillingness to engage in atomic war unless we are directly attacked. . . .

A more rapid build-up of political, economic, and military strength and thereby of confidence in the free world than is now contemplated is the only course which is consistent with progress toward achieving our fundamental purpose. The frustration of the Kremlin design requires the free world to develop a successfully functioning political and economic system and a vigorous political offensive against the Soviet Union. These, in turn, require an adequate military shield under which they can develop. It is necessary to have the military power to deter, if possible, Soviet expansion, and to defeat, if necessary, aggressive Soviet or Soviet-directed actions of a limited or total character. The potential strength of the free world is great; its ability to develop these military capabilities and its will to resist Soviet expansion will be determined by the wisdom and will with which it undertakes to meet its political and economic problems. . . .

Our position as the center of power in the free world places a heavy responsibility upon the United States for leadership. We must organize and enlist the energies and resources of the free world in a positive program for peace which will frustrate the Kremlin design for world domination by creating a situation in the free world to which the Kremlin will be compelled to adjust. Without such a cooperative effort, led by the United States, we will have to make gradual withdrawals under pressure until we discover one day that we have sacrificed positions of vital interest.

It is imperative that this trend be reversed by a much more rapid and concerted build-up of the actual strength of both the United States and the other nations of the free world. The analysis shows that this will be costly and will involve significant domestic financial and economic adjustments.

 E S S A Y S

In the opening essay, Barton J. Bernstein, a professor of history at Stanford University, analyzes the Roosevelt and Truman administrations' thinking about the atomic bomb's place both as a weapon to defeat Japan and as a lever to pry diplomatic concessions from the Soviet Union. Bernstein agrees with most historians that Truman ordered the use of the atomic bomb against Japanese civilians primarily to end the war quickly and to save American lives. But Bernstein also explores the bomb as a diplomatic "bonus" that American leaders believed would enhance U.S. bargaining power in the Cold War, and he explains the detrimental effect of the bomb and atomic diplomacy on Soviet-American relations.

In the second essay, based in part on newly released materials from Russian archives, John Lewis Gaddis of Yale University observes that the Second World War produced two distinctively different Cold War empires. Gaddis highlights the Soviet Union's thirst for security through territorial expansion, motivated both by traditional Russian nationalism and by Joseph Stalin's authoritarian Marxism-Leninism. The U.S. empire, by contrast, reflected America's democratic traditions and allowed more give and take between the imperial power and its clients. Whereas Stalin used military force to impose the Soviet Union's will on occupied Eastern Europe, Washington negotiated with its West European allies, compromised differences, and extended its influence primarily at its partners' invitation. Therefore, according to Gaddis, the Soviet empire was the more dangerous and destabilizing of the two and more directly responsible for the onset of the Cold War.

In the last essay Frank Costigliola of the University of Connecticut uses gender studies and psychology to analyze the Cold War thinking of George F. Kennan, the State Department official instrumental in formulating the U.S. strategy of anti-Communist containment in 1946 and 1947. Costigliola finds in Kennan's choice of words and tone of language a tendency to describe the Soviet Union in gendered and highly eroticized terms. Traditional Russia with its rural simplicity and charm seemed to Kennan, and other U.S. officials, to possess qualities of feminine beauty and sensuality, making it more acceptable to the United States. By contrast, Kennan equated the brutal, expansionistic policies of Stalin's Soviet Union with the actions of a pathologically violent male rapist. These powerful, emotionally charged images and discourses, Costigliola concludes, contributed to Washington's exaggeration of Soviet behavior and legitimized the Truman administration's decision to abandon negotiations with Moscow and engage in Cold War.

Secrets and Threats: Atomic Diplomacy and Soviet-American Antagonism

BARTON J. BERNSTEIN

Ever since the publication in 1965 of Gar Alperovitz's *Atomic Diplomacy,* scholars and laymen have developed a new interest in the relationship of the atomic bomb to wartime and postwar diplomacy and to the origins of the Cold War. This bold book revived and sometimes recast old themes and thereby sparked renewed interest in questions that once seemed settled: Why was the atomic bomb dropped on Japan? Why weren't other alternatives vigorously pursued? How did the bomb influence American policy before and after Hiroshima? Did the dropping of the bomb and postwar American atomic policies contribute to the cold war?

Unfortunately many studies of these questions have focused exclusively on the Truman period and thereby neglected the Roosevelt administration, which bequeathed to Truman a legacy of assumptions, options, and fears. Acting on the assumption that the bomb was a legitimate weapon, Roosevelt initially defined the relationship of American diplomacy and the atomic bomb. He decided to build the bomb, to establish a partnership on atomic energy with Britain, to bar the Soviet Union from knowledge of the project, and to block any effort at international control of atomic energy. These policies constituted Truman's inheritance—one he neither wished to abandon nor could easily escape. He was restricted politically, psychologically, and institutionally from critically reassessing this legacy.

Like Roosevelt, Truman assumed that the bomb was a legitimate weapon and also understood that it could serve as a bargaining lever, a military counterweight, a threat, or a combat weapon in dealing with the Soviet Union in the postwar world. In addition to speeding the end of the war, the combat use of the bomb, the Truman administration understood, offered the United States great advantages in the postwar world. Policy makers assumed that use of the bomb would help shape the world in a desirable mold: The bomb would impress the Soviets and make them more tractable. Contrary to some contentions, this consideration about the postwar world was not the controlling reason why the United States used the bomb. Rather, it was an additional reason reinforcing an earlier analysis. Ending the war speedily was the primary purpose; impressing the Soviet Union was secondary. This secondary aim did constitute a subtle deterrent to reconsidering combat use of the bomb and to searching for alternative means of ending the war. Had the use of the bomb threatened to impair, rather than advance, American aims for the postwar peace, policy makers would have been likely to reassess their assumptions and perhaps to choose other alternatives. . . .

From "Roosevelt, Truman, and the Atomic Bomb, 1941–1945: A Reinterpretation," by Barton J. Bernstein from *Political Science Quarterly* 90 (Spring 1975), pp. 23–24, 30–32, 34–43, 44–54, 57–69. Reprinted by permission.

When Harry S. Truman became president on April 12, 1945, he was only dimly aware of the existence of the Manhattan Project and unaware that it was an atomic-bomb project. Left uninformed of foreign affairs and generally ignored by Roosevelt in the three months since the inaugural, the new president inherited a set of policies and a group of advisers from his predecessor. While Truman was legally free to reverse Roosevelt's foreign policies and to choose new advisers on foreign policy, in fact he was quite restricted for personal and political reasons. Because Truman was following a very prestigious president whom he, like a great many Americans, loved and admired, the new president was not free psychologically or politically to strike out on a clearly new course. Only a bolder man, with more self-confidence, might have tried critically to assess the legacy and to act independently. But Truman lacked the confidence and the incentive. When, in fact, he did modify policy—for example, on Eastern Europe—he still believed sincerely, as some advisers told him, that he was adhering to his predecessor's agreements and wishes. When seeking counsel on foreign affairs, he usually did not choose new advisers but simply drew more heavily upon those members of Roosevelt's staff who were more anti-Soviet and relied less upon those who were more friendly to the Soviet Union. Even in this strategy, he believed that he was adhering to the policies of his predecessor, who, in his last weeks, Truman stressed, had become more suspicious of Stalin, more distressed by Soviet action in Eastern Europe, and more committed to resisting Soviet encroachments.

In the case of the international-diplomatic policy on the bomb, Truman was even more restricted by Roosevelt's decisions, for the new president inherited a set of reasonably clear wartime policies. Because Roosevelt had already decided to exclude the Soviets from a partnership on the bomb, his successor could not *comfortably* reverse this policy during the war—unless the late president's advisers pleaded for such a reversal or claimed that he had been about to change his policy. They did neither. Consider, then, the massive personal and political deterrents that blocked Truman from even reassessing this legacy. What price might he have paid at home if Americans learned later that he had reversed Roosevelt's policy and had launched a bold new departure of sharing with the Soviets a great weapon that cost the United States $2 billion? Truman, in fact, was careful to follow Roosevelt's strategy of concealing from Congress even the dimensions of the secret partnership on atomic energy with Britain.

Truman, depending as he did upon Roosevelt's advisers, could not easily reassess the prevailing assumption that the bomb was a legitimate weapon to be used in combat against Japan. Truman lacked the will and the incentive to reexamine this assumption, and his dependence upon Roosevelt's advisers and the momentum of the project confirmed this tendency. Only one close adviser, Admiral William Leahy, may have later challenged the use of the bomb, but he was an old "war horse," an expert on explosives of another era, who had often proclaimed that the bomb would not work, that the scientists were duping the administration, and that they were squandering $2 billion. His counsel could not outweigh the continuing legacy of assumptions and commitments, of advisers and advice, that Truman had inherited from Roosevelt. It was a subtle legacy, one that infiltrated decisions and shaped actions, so that Truman accepted it as part of his unquestioned inheritance. For Truman, the question would never be how openly to challenge this legacy, only how to fulfill it, how to remain true to it.

During his first weeks in office, Truman learned about the project from Stimson and from James F. Byrnes, Roosevelt's former director of the Office of War Mobilization and Reconversion who was to become Truman's secretary of state. Byrnes, despite his recent suspicions that the project might be a scientific boondoggle, told Truman, in the president's words, that "the bomb might well put us in a position to dictate our own terms at the end of the war." On April 25, Stimson discussed issues about the bomb more fully with Truman, especially the "political aspects of the S-1 [atomic bomb's] performance." The bomb, the secretary of war explained in a substantial memorandum, would probably be ready in four months and "would be the most terrible weapon ever known in human history [for it] . . . could destroy a whole city." In the future, he warned, other nations would be able to make atomic bombs, thereby endangering the peace and threatening the world. The bomb could be either a threat to or a guarantor of peace. "[I]n the light of our present position with reference to this weapon, the question of sharing it with other nations and, if so shared, upon what terms, becomes a primary question of our foreign relations," Stimson lectured the president. If "the problem of the proper use of this weapon can be solved, we would have the opportunity to bring the world into a pattern in which the peace of the world and our civilization can be saved."

The entire discussion, judging from Stimson's daily record and Groves's memorandum, assumed that the bomb was a legitimate weapon and that it would be used against Japan. The questions they discussed were not *whether* to use the bomb, but its relationship to the Soviet Union and the need to establish postwar atomic policies. Neither Stimson nor Truman sought then to resolve these outstanding issues, and Truman agreed to his secretary's proposal for the establishment of a high-level committee to recommend "action to the executive and legislative branches of our government when secrecy is no longer in full effect." At no time did they conclude that the committee would also consider the issue of whether to use the bomb as a combat weapon. For policy makers, that was not a question; it was an operating assumption.

Nor did Stimson, in his own charge to the Interim Committee, ever *raise* this issue. Throughout the committee's meetings, as various members later noted, all operated on the assumption that the bomb would be used against Japan. They talked, for example, about drafting public statements that would be issued after the bomb's use. They did not discuss *whether* but how to use it. Only one member ultimately endorsed an explicit advance warning to Japan, and none was prepared to suggest that the administration should take any serious risks to avoid using the bomb. At lunch between the two formal meetings on May 31, some members, perhaps only at one table, briefly discussed the possibility of a noncombat demonstration as a warning to Japan but rejected the tactic on the grounds that the bomb might not explode and the failure might stiffen Japanese resistance, or that Japan might move prisoners of war to the target area.

What impact would the bomb have on Japan? At the May 31 meeting, the Interim Committee, joined by its four-member scientific advisory panel discussed this question. Some felt, according to the minutes, that "an atomic bomb on an arsenal would not be much different in effect" from present bombing attacks. J. Robert Oppenheimer, the eminent physicist and member of the scientific panel, expecting that the bomb would have an explosive force of between 2,000 and 20,000 tons of TNT, stressed its visual effects ("a brilliant luminescence which would run to a height of 10,000 to 20,000 feet") and its deadly power ("dangerous to life for a radius of at least two-thirds of a mile"). Oppenheimer's predictions did not answer the question. There were too many unknowns—about the bomb and Japan. According to the official minutes, Stimson concluded, with unanimous support: "that we could not concentrate on a civilian area; but we should seek to make a profound psychological impression on as many of the inhabitants as possible." At [the scientist James B.] Conant's suggestion, "the Secretary agreed that the most desirable target would be a vital war plant employing a large number of workers and closely surrounded by workers' houses." . . .

Two weeks later, after the Franck Committee recommended a noncombat demonstration, Stimson's assistant submitted this proposal to the four-member scientific advisory panel for advice. The panel promptly rejected the Franck Committee proposal: "we can propose no technical demonstration likely to bring an end to the war; we see no acceptable alternative to direct military use." Had the four scientists known that an invasion was not scheduled until November, or had they even offered their judgment after the unexpectedly impressive Alamogordo test on July 16, perhaps they would have given different counsel. But in June, they were not sure that the bomb explosion would be so dramatic, and, like many others in government, they were wary of pushing for a change in tactics if they might be held responsible for the failure of those tactics—especially if that failure could mean the loss of American lives.

A few days after the panel's report, the issue of giving Japan an advance warning about the bomb was raised at a White House meeting with the president, the military chiefs, and the civilian secretaries. On June 18, after they agreed upon a two-stage invasion of Japan, beginning on about November 1, Assistant Secretary of War John J. McCloy became clearly troubled by the omission of the bomb from the discussion and planning. When Truman invited him to speak, the assistant secretary argued that the bomb would make the invasion unnecessary. Why not warn the emperor that the United States had the bomb and would use it unless Japan surrendered? "McCloy's suggestion had appeal," the official history of the AEC [Atomic Energy Commission] later recorded, "but a strong objection developed" to warning Japan in advance, "which no one could refute—there was no assurance the bomb would work." Presumably, like the Interim Committee, they too feared that a warning, followed by a "dud," might stiffen Japan's morale. There was no reason, policy makers concluded, to take this risk.

Though the Interim Committee and high administration officials found no reason not to use the bomb against Japan, many were concerned about the bomb's impact, and its later value, in Soviet-American relations. "[I]t was already apparent," Stimson later wrote, "that the critical questions in American policy toward atomic energy would be directly connected with Soviet Russia." At a few meetings of the Interim Committee, for example, members discussed informing the Soviets of the bomb before its use against Japan. When the issue first arose, [the scientist Vannevar] Bush and Conant estimated that the Soviet Union could develop the bomb in about four years and argued for informing the Soviets before combat use as a preliminary to moving toward international control and thereby avoiding a postwar nuclear arms race. Conant and Bush had been promoting this strategy since the preceding September. Even though Roosevelt had cast them to the side in 1943, when he cemented the Anglo-American alliance, the two scientist-administrators had not abandoned hope for their notions. They even circulated to the Interim Committee one of their memoranda on the subject. But at the meetings of May 18 and 31 they again met defeat. General Groves, assuming that America was far more advanced technologically and scientifically and also that the Soviet Union lacked uranium, argued that the Soviets could not build a bomb for about twenty years. He contributed to the appealing "myth" of the atomic secret—that there was a secret and it would long remain America's monopoly. James Byrnes, with special authority as secretary of state–designate and Truman's representative on the committee, accepted Groves's analysis and argued for maintaining the policy of secrecy— which the committee endorsed. Byrnes was apparently very pleased, and Stimson agreed, as he told Truman on June 6, "There should be no revelation to Russia or anyone else of our work on S-1 [the atomic bomb] until the first bomb has been laid successfully on Japan."

At a later meeting on June 21, the Interim Committee, including Byrnes, reversed itself. Yielding to the pleas of Bush and Conant, who were strengthened by the scientific panel's recommendations, the Interim Committee advised Truman to inform the Soviets about the bomb before using it in combat. Like the Franck Committee, the Interim Committee concluded (as the minutes record):

> In the hope of securing effective future control and in view of the fact that general information concerning the project would be made public shortly after the [Potsdam] conference, the Committee *agreed* that there would be considerable advantage, if suitable opportunity arose, in having the President advise the Russians that we were working on this weapon with every prospect of success and that we expected to use it against Japan.
>
> The president might say further that he hoped this matter might be discussed some time in the future in terms of insuring that the weapon would become an aid to peace.

Because of this recommendation, and perhaps also because of the continuing prodding of Bush and Conant, Stimson reversed his own position. He concluded that if the United States dropped the bomb on Japan without first informing the Soviet Union, that act might gravely strain Soviet-American relations. Explaining the committee's position to Truman, Stimson proposed that if the President "thought that Stalin was on good terms with him" at the forthcoming Potsdam conference, he would inform Stalin that the United States had developed the bomb, planned to use it against Japan, knew the Soviets were working on the bomb, and looked forward to discussing international control later. This approach left open the option of "atomic diplomacy."

The issues of the bomb and the Soviet Union had already intruded in other ways upon policy and planning. Awaiting the bomb, Truman had postponed the Potsdam conference, delayed negotiations with Russia, and hoped that atomic energy would pry some concessions from Russia. Truman explained in late May to Joseph Davies, an advocate of Soviet-American friendship, and in early June to Stimson that he was delaying the forthcoming Potsdam conference until the Alamogordo test, when he would know whether the United States had a workable atomic bomb—what Stimson repeatedly called the "mastercard." . . .

For the administration, the atomic bomb, if it worked, had great potential value. It could reduce the importance of early Soviet entry into the war and make American concessions unnecessary. It could also be a lever for extracting concessions from the Soviet Union. On June 6, for example, Stimson discussed with Truman "quid pro quos which should be established for our taking them [Russia] into [a nuclear] partnership. He [Truman] said that he had been thinking of the same things that I was thinking of, namely the settlement of the Polish, Rumanian, Yugoslavian, and Manchurian problems." There is no evidence that they were planning explicitly to threaten the Soviets to gain these concessions, but, obviously, they realized that the Soviets would regard an American nuclear monopoly as threatening and would yield on some issues in order to terminate that monopoly and thereby reduce, or eliminate, the threat. . . .

For policy makers, the atomic weapons scheduled for combat use against Japan were intimately connected with the problem of Russia. In recent years some historians have focused on this relationship and raised troubling questions: Did the bomb, for policy makers, constitute an alternative to Soviet intervention in the Pacific war? Did they delay or even try to prevent Soviet entry because the bomb made it unnecessary? If so, did they do this in order to use the bomb? Was the bomb dropped on Japan primarily to influence Russia? Did the bomb influence American policy at Potsdam?

At Yalta, Roosevelt had granted the Soviet Union concessions in China in order to secure Soviet entry into the Pacific war, which Stalin promised, within two to three months after V-E Day (May 8). Stalin made it clear that Soviet entry would await a Sino-Soviet pact ratifying these concessions. At the time of Yalta, American military planners were counting on a Soviet attack in Manchuria to pin down the Kwantung army there and hence stop Japan from shifting these forces to her homeland to meet an American invasion.

But by April, war conditions changed and military planners revised their analysis: Japan no longer controlled the seas and therefore could not shift her army, so Soviet entry was not essential. In May, the State Department asked Stimson whether Soviet participation "at the earliest possible moment" was so necessary that the United States should abide by the Far East section of the Yalta agreement. Stimson concluded that the Soviets would enter the war for their own reasons, at their schedule, and with little regard to any American action, that the Yalta concessions would be largely within the grasp of Soviet military power, and that Soviet assistance would be useful, but not essential, if an American invasion was necessary. If there is an invasion, "Russian entry," he wrote, "will have a profound military effect in that almost certainly it will materially shorten the war and thus save American lives." But if the bomb worked, he implied in other discussions, then an invasion would probably not be necessary and Soviet help would be less important. As a result, he urged a delay in settling matters with Russia on the Far East until after the Alamogordo test, and the President apparently followed this counsel. . . .

Truman claimed that he went to Potsdam to secure Soviet entry and that he never changed his position. The first part of that claim is correct, but the second part is dubious, for Truman did nothing substantive at Potsdam to encourage Soviet intervention and much to delay or prevent it. The successful test at Alamogordo emphasized to policy makers that prompt Soviet entry was no longer necessary and that the United States might even be able to end the war without Soviet entry. After the unexpectedly glowing report of the test, Truman wanted to know whether Marshall considered Soviet entry necessary. "Marshall felt," Stimson recorded, "that now with our new weapon we would not need the assistance of the Russians to conquer Japan." "The bomb as a merely probable weapon had seemed a weak reed on which to rely, but the bomb as a colossal reality was very different," Stimson later explained. From Potsdam on July 23, Churchill cabled London: "It is quite clear that the United States do not at the present time desire Russian participation in the war against Japan." The bomb had eliminated the importance of Russia's prompt entry, since the planned American invasion no longer seemed necessary. Invasion and the bomb were the likely alternatives. As a result, Truman had no reason to offer concessions to secure early Soviet entry.

Could the United States keep the Soviet Union out of the war? Did policy makers try to do this? In mid-July Soviet troops were stationed on the Manchurian border and would soon be ready to intervene. Marshall concluded that even if Japan surrendered on American terms before Soviet entry, Russia could still march into Manchuria and take virtually whatever she wanted there in the surrender terms. Truman, if he believed Marshall's analysis, had nothing to gain politically from deterring Soviet entry, unless he feared, as did Stimson, that the Soviets might try to reach the Japanese homeland and put in a "claim to occupy and help rule it." Perhaps Truman followed the counsel of Stimson and Byrnes, who, for slightly different reasons, were eager to restrain the Soviets.

Byrnes, unlike Stimson, was sometimes naively optimistic. Part of the time he hoped to keep the Soviet Union out of the war, and not simply delay her entry, in order to protect China. On July 28, he explained to Secretary of the Navy James Forrestal (in Forrestal's words): "Byrnes said he was most anxious to get the Japanese affair over with before the Russians got in, with particular reference to Dairen and Port Arthur." These were the areas that both Stimson and Marshall acknowledged the Soviets could seize. Walter Brown, the friend who accompanied the secretary to Potsdam, recorded in his diary notes for July 20 Byrnes's strategy: "JFB determined to outmaneuver Stalin on China. Hopes Soong [the Chinese foreign minister] will stand firm and then Russians will not go in war. Then he feels Japan will surrender before Russia goes to war and this will save China." On July 24, four days later, Brown noted that Byrnes was linking the bomb and Japan's surrender but was less optimistic about excluding Russia: "JFB still hoping for time, believing after atomic bombing Japan will surrender and Russia will not get in so much on the kill, thereby [not] being in a position to press for claims against China."

Byrnes purposely impeded Sino-Soviet negotiations in order to *prevent* the Soviets from entering the war. Did Truman support Byrnes for the *same* reasons?— as Byrnes claimed later and as Truman obliquely denied. Perhaps. But, more likely, Truman supported his secretary's strategy for a different reason: the early entry of the Soviets was no longer important and, therefore, Truman did not want Chiang to make the required concessions, which would later weaken Chiang's government. In addition, Truman *may* have concluded that Russia's delayed entry would weaken her possible claims for a role in the postwar occupation government in Japan.

Why didn't Truman invite Stalin to sign the Potsdam Proclamation of July 26 calling for Japan's surrender? Some analysts argued later that this omission was part of a devious strategy: that Truman wanted to use the bomb and feared that Stalin's signature, tantamount to a declaration of war, might catapult Japan to surrender, thereby making a nuclear attack impossible. The major difficulty with this interpretation is that it exaggerates occasional, sometimes ambiguous, statements about the *possible* impact of Soviet entry and ignores the fact that this possible shock was not a persistent or important theme in American planning. Truman did not exclude the Soviets from the Proclamation in order to use the bomb. The skimpy, often oblique evidence *suggests* a more plausible explanation and a less devious pattern: he wanted to avoid requesting favors from the Soviets. As a result, he did not try this one possible, but not very likely, way of ending the war without using atomic weapons.

At Potsdam, on July 24, Truman told Stalin casually that the United States had developed "a new weapon of unusual destructive force" for use against Japan but did not specify an atomic weapon. Why didn't Truman explicitly inform Stalin about the atomic bomb? Was Truman, as some have suggested, afraid that the news would prompt Stalin to hasten Soviet intervention and therefore end the war and make combat use of the bomb impossible? Did Truman simply want to delay Soviet entry and did he, like Byrnes, fear that his news would have the opposite effect? Did Truman think that the destruction wrought by the bomb would not impress the Soviets as forcefully if they were informed in advance? Why did Truman reject the counsel of the Interim Committee, of Stimson, and even of Churchill, who, after the glowing news of the Alamogordo test, "was not worried about giving the Russians information on the matter but was rather inclined to use it as an argument in our favor in the negotiations"?

Many of these questions cannot be definitively answered on the basis of the presently available evidence, but there is enough evidence to refute one popular interpretation: that Truman's tactic was part of an elaborate strategy to prevent or retard Soviet entry *in order* to delay Japan's surrender and *thereby* make combat use of the bomb possible. That interpretation claims too much. Only the first part can be supported by some, albeit indirect, evidence: that he was probably seeking to delay or prevent Soviet entry. Byrnes later said that he feared that Stalin would order an immediate Soviet declaration of war if he realized the importance of this "new weapon"—advice Truman dubiously claimed he never received. Truman was not trying to postpone Japan's surrender *in order* to use the bomb. In addition to the reasonable theory that he was seeking to prevent or retard Soviet entry, there are two other plausible, complementary interpretations of Truman's behavior. First, he believed, as had some of his advisers earlier, that a combat demonstration would be more impressive to Russia without an advance warning and therefore he concealed the news. Second, he was also ill-prepared to discuss atomic energy with Stalin, for the president had not made a decision about postwar atomic policy and how to exploit the bomb, and probably did not want to be pressed by Stalin about sharing nuclear secrets. Perhaps all three theories collectively explained Truman's evasive tactics.

Even without explicit disclosure, the bomb strengthened American policy at Potsdam. The Alamogordo test stiffened Truman's resolve, as Churchill told Stimson after the meeting of the Big Three on July 22: "Truman was evidently much fortified . . . and . . . he stood up to the Russians in a most emphatic and decisive manner, telling them as to certain demands that they absolutely could not have." Probably, also, the bomb explains why Truman pushed more forcefully at Potsdam for the Soviets to open up Eastern Europe. It is less clear whether the bomb changed the substance of American policy at Potsdam. Probably Byrnes endorsed a reparations policy allowing the division of Germany because the bomb replaced Germany as a potential counterweight to possible Soviet expansion. . . .

Scholars and laymen have criticized the combat use of the atomic bomb. They have contended, among other points, that the bombs were not necessary to end the war, that the administration knew or should have known this, that the administration knew that Japan was on the verge of defeat and *therefore* close to surrender, and that the administration was either short-sighted or had other controlling international-political motives (besides ending the war) for using the bomb. These varying contentions usually focus on the alleged failure of the United States to pursue five alternatives, individually or in combination, in order to achieve Japanese surrender before using the bomb: (1) awaiting Soviet entry, a declaration of war, or a public statement of intent (already discussed); (2) providing a warning and/or a noncombat demonstration (already discussed); (3) redefining unconditional surrender to guarantee the Imperial institution; (4) pursuing Japan's "peace feelers"; or (5) relying upon conventional warfare for a longer period. These contentions assume that policy makers were trying, or should have tried, to avoid using atomic bombs—precisely what they were not trying to do. . . .

There were powerful reasons why the fifth alternative—the use of conventional weapons for a longer period *before* using atomic bombs—seemed undesirable to policy makers. The loss of American lives, while perhaps not great, would have been unconscionable and politically risky. How could policy makers have justified to themselves or to other Americans delaying the use of this great weapon and squandering American lives? Consider the potential political cost at home. In contrast, few Americans were then troubled by the mass killing of enemy citizens, especially if they were yellow. The firebombings of Tokyo, of other Japanese cities, and even of Dresden had produced few cries of outrage in the United States. There was no evidence that most citizens would care that the atomic bomb was as lethal as the raids on Dresden or Tokyo. It was unlikely that there would be popular support for relying upon conventional warfare and not using the atomic bomb. For citizens and policy makers, there were few, if any, moral restraints on what weapons were acceptable in war.

Nor were there any powerful advocates within the high councils of the administration who wanted to delay or not use the bomb and rely instead upon conventional warfare—a naval blockade, continued aerial bombings, or both. The advocates of conventional warfare were not powerful, and they did not directly oppose the use of the bomb. Admiral Ernest L. King, chief of Naval Operations, did believe that the invasion and the atomic bomb were not the only alternative tactics likely to achieve unconditional surrender. A naval blockade, he insisted, would be successful. The army, however, he complained, had little faith in sea power and, hence, Truman did not accept his proposal. Leahy had serious doubts about using the bomb, but as an old explosives expert who had long claimed that the bomb would never work, he carried little weight on this matter. Surprisingly, perhaps, he did not forcefully press his doubts on the president. . . .

For policy makers, the danger was not simply the loss of a few hundred American lives *prior* to the slightly delayed use of the bombs if the United States relied upon conventional warfare for a few more weeks. Rather the risk was that, if the nuclear attacks were even slightly delayed, the scheduled invasion of Kyushu, with perhaps 30,000 casualties in the first month, would be necessary. After the war, it became fashionable to assume that policy makers clearly foresaw and comfortably expected that an atomic bomb or two would shock Japan into a speedy surrender. But the evidence does not support this view. "The abrupt surrender of Japan came more or less as a surprise," Henry H. Arnold, commanding general of the air force, later explained. Policy makers were planning, if necessary, to drop at least three atomic bombs in August, with the last on about August 24, and more in September. . . .

There have been criticisms of the administration for failing to pursue two other alleged opportunities: (1) redefining the unconditional surrender demands before Hiroshima to guarantee the Imperial institution; (2) responding to Japan's "peace feelers," which stressed the need for this guarantee. Byrnes and apparently Truman, however, were fearful at times that concessions might strengthen, not weaken, the Japanese military and thereby prolong, not shorten, the war. Some critics imply that Byrnes and Truman were not sincere in presenting this analysis and that they rejected concessions consciously in order to use the bomb. That is incorrect. Other critics believe that these policy makers were sincere but disagree with their assessment—especially since some intelligence studies implied the need for concessions on peace terms to shorten the war. Probably the administration was wrong, and these latter critics right, but either policy involved risks and some were very unattractive to Truman.

Truman, as a new president, was not comfortable in openly challenging Roosevelt's policy of unconditional surrender and modifying the terms. That was risky. It could fail and politically injure him at home. Demanding unconditional surrender meant fewer risks at home and, according to his most trusted advisers at times, fewer risks in ending the war speedily. Had his most powerful and trusted advisers pushed for a change in policy, perhaps he might have found reason and will to modify Roosevelt's policy well before Hiroshima. But most of Truman's closest advisers first counseled delay and then some moved into opposition. As a result, he too shifted from delay to opposition. At Potsdam, when Stimson pushed unsuccessfully for providing the guarantee in the proclamation, Truman refused but told Stimson that he would carefully watch Japan's reactions on this issue and implied that he would yield if it seemed to be the only impediment to surrender. After August 10, when Japan made the guarantee the only additional condition, Truman yielded on the issue. He deemed it a tactical problem, not a substantive one. But even then, Byrnes was wary of offering this concession, despite evidence that it would probably end the war promptly—precisely what he wanted in order to forestall Soviet gains in the Far East. . . .

Let us look at the remaining, but connected, alternative—pursuing Japan's "peace feelers." Japan's so-called peace feelers were primarily a series of messages from the foreign minister to his nation's ambassador in Moscow, who was asked to investigate the possibility of having the Soviets serve as intermediaries in negotiating a peace. American intelligence intercepted and decoded all the messages. Most, if not all, were sent on to Potsdam, where Truman and Byrnes had access to them. Both men showed little interest in them, and may not even have read all of them, apparently because the proposed concessions were insufficient to meet American demands and because Truman and Byrnes had already decided that the peace party in Japan could not succeed until American attacks—including atomic bombs—crushed the military's hopes. The intercepted and decoded messages fell short of American expectations. Not only did Japan's foreign minister want to retain the Imperial institution, which was acceptable to some policy makers, but he also wanted a peace that would maintain his nation's "honor and existence," a phrase that remained vague. As late as July 27, the day after the Potsdam Proclamation, when Japan's foreign minister was planning a special peace mission to Russia, he was still unwilling or unable to present a "concrete proposal" for negotiations. What emerges from his decoded correspondence is a willingness by some elements in Japan's government to move toward peace, their fear of opposition from the military, and their inability to be specific about terms. Strangely, perhaps, though they feared that Stalin might be on the verge of entering the war, they never approached the United States directly to negotiate a peace settlement. For Truman and Byrnes, Japan was near defeat but not near surrender when the three powers issued the Potsdam Proclamation on July 26. When Japan's premier seemed to reject it, the president and secretary of state could find confirmation for their belief that the peace party could not triumph in Japan without more American "aid"—including nuclear attacks.

Given the later difficulties of Japan's peace party, even after the atomic bombings, after Soviet entry, and after more large-scale conventional bombings, top American policy makers could find evidence in the ambiguous record for their assessment that Japan's leaders were not ready to surrender before Hiroshima. More troubling were American policy makers' wartime convictions that any concessions or pursuit of unsure "peace feelers" might stiffen resistance. Most American leaders were fearful of softening demands. War had bred an attitude that any efforts at compromise might indicate to the enemy America's flaccidity of spirit and weakness of will. Toughness, for most policy makers, seemed to promise success.

Looking back upon these years, Americans may well lament the unwillingness of their leaders to make some concessions at this time and to rely upon negotiations before using the bombs. That lament, however, is logically separable from the unfounded charges that policy makers consciously avoided the "peace feelers" *because* they wanted to drop the bombs in order to intimidate the Soviets. It is true that American leaders did not cast policy in order to avoid using the atomic bombs. Given their analysis, they had no reason to avoid using these weapons. As a result, their analysis provokes ethical revulsion among many critics, who believe that policy makers should have been reluctant to use atomic weapons and should have sought, perhaps even at some cost in American lives, to avoid using them. . . .

Had policy makers concluded that the use of the bomb would impair Soviet-American relations and make the Soviets intransigent, they might have reconsidered their assumption. But their analysis indicated that the use of the bomb would aid, not injure, their efforts to secure concessions from the Soviets. The bomb offered a bonus. The promise of these likely advantages probably constituted a subtle deterrent to any reconsideration of the use of the atomic bomb. Policy makers rejected the competing analysis advanced by the Franck Committee:

> Russia, and even allied countries which bear less mistrust of our ways and intentions, as well as neutral countries, will be deeply shocked. It will be very difficult to persuade the world that a nation which was capable of secretly preparing and suddenly releasing . . . [the bomb] is to be trusted in its proclaimed desire of having such weapons abolished by international agreement.

Instead, policy makers had come to assume that a combat demonstration would advance, not impair, the interests of peace—a position shared by Conant, Oppenheimer, Arthur H. Compton, Nobel laureate and director of the Chicago Metallurgical Laboratory, and Edward Teller, the physicist and future father of the hydrogen bomb. In explaining the thinking of the scientific advisory panel in recommending combat use of the bomb, Oppenheimer later said that one of the two "overriding considerations . . . [was] the effect of our actions on the stability . . . of the postwar world." Stimson's assistant, Harvey H. Bundy, wrote in 1946, that some thought "that unless the bomb were used it would be impossible to persuade the world that the saving of civilization in the future would depend on a proper international control of atomic energy." The bomb, in short, would impress the Soviets.

In addition, there was another possible advantage to using the bomb: retribution against Japan. A few days after Nagasaki, Truman hinted at this theme in a private letter justifying the combat use of the bombs:

> Nobody is more disturbed over the use of Atomic bombs than I am but I was greatly disturbed over the unwarranted attack by the Japanese on Pearl Harbor. The only language they seem to understand is the one that we have been using to bombard them. When you have to deal with a beast you have to treat him as a beast. It is most regrettable but nevertheless true.

In this letter, one can detect strains of the quest for retribution (the reference to Pearl Harbor), and some might even find subtle strains of racism (Japan was "a beast"). The enemy was a beast and deserved to be destroyed. War, as some critics would stress, dehumanized victors and vanquished, and justified inhumanity in the name of nationalism, of justice, and even humanity.

In assessing the administration's failure to challenge the assumption that the bomb was a legitimate weapon to be used against Japan, we may conclude that Truman found no reason to reconsider, that it would have been difficult for him to challenge the assumption, and that there were also various likely benefits deterring a reassessment. For the administration, in short, there was no reason to avoid using the bomb and many reasons making it feasible and even attractive. The bomb was used primarily to end the war *promptly* and thereby to save American lives. There were other ways to end the war, but none of them seemed as effective. They would not produce victory as promptly and seemed to have greater risks. Even if Russia had not existed, the bombs would have been used in the same way. How could Truman, in the absence of overriding contrary reasons, justify not using the bombs, or even delaying their use, and thereby prolonging the war sacrificing American lives? . . .

On August 9, the day that Nagasaki was bombed, the president delivered a national address on the Potsdam meeting. The United States, he declared, "would maintain military bases necessary for the complete protection of our interests and of world peace." The secret of the bomb, he promised, would be retained until the world ceased being "lawless." "We must constitute ourselves trustees of this new force—to prevent its misuse, and to turn it into the channels of service to mankind." He also emphasized that the Balkan nations "are not to be the spheres of influence of any one power"—a direct warning to the Soviet Union. Here was the first, albeit muted, statement of atomic diplomacy: the implicit threat that the bomb could roll back Soviet influence from Eastern Europe.

"In many quarters," Stimson lamented in late August and early September, the bomb is "interpreted as a substantial offset to the growth of Russian influence on the continent." He complained that Byrnes was wearing the bomb ostentatiously on his hip and hoping to use the weapon to secure his program at the September Conference of Foreign Ministers in London. "His mind is full of his problems," Stimson wrote in his diary. Byrnes "looks to having the presence of the bomb in his pocket, so to speak, as a great weapon to get through the thing. . . . " Assistant Secretary of War John J. McCloy concluded, after a long discussion with Byrnes, that he "wished to have the implied threat of the bomb in his pocket during the conference . . . [in London]." This evidence is unambiguous as to Byrnes's intent, and it cannot be ignored or interpreted as misleading. Byrnes had no reason to seek to deceive Stimson and McCloy about his hopes and tactics. Byrnes had no incentive to posture with them or to appear militant, since they opposed his vigorous tactics and instead counseled moderation and international control of atomic energy. . . .

At the London Conference, an uneasy Vyacheslav Molotov, the Soviet foreign minister, twitted Byrnes about America's nuclear monopoly and tried uneasily to minimize its importance. Molotov's humor betrayed Soviet fears. On September 13, three days into the conference, "Molotov asks JFB if he has an atomic bomb in his side pocket. 'You don't know Southerners,' Byrnes replied. 'We carry our artillery in our hip pocket. If you don't cut out all this stalling and let us get down to work I am going to pull an atomic bomb out of my hip pocket and let you have it.' " In response to this veiled threat, according to the informal notes, "Molotov laughed as did the interpreter." Byrnes's barb emphasized American power. A few nights later, after a stormy session during the day, Molotov commented once more, with strained jocularity, that Byrnes had two advantages that the Soviet minister could not match—eloquence and the atomic bomb.

In this period, the Soviets never officially admitted great concern or anxiety about America's nuclear monopoly. They never claimed that it actually constituted a threat to their welfare, and they publicly minimized its strategic value. Presumably they adopted these tactics because they did not want to reveal their fears and encourage the United States to continue atomic diplomacy. They even devised stratagems to suggest that they had also developed the bomb. At the London Conference, for example, Molotov contrived a scene where he "accidentally" let slip the statement, "You know we have the atomic bomb," and then was quickly hustled out of the room by an associate. In November, this time in a national address, he implied that the Soviet Union had nuclear weapons. During this period, as later sources made clear, Soviet scientists were rushing to build the bomb.

Though Soviet officials at this time never publicly charged the United States with conducting atomic diplomacy, the Soviet media carried oblique charges. A Soviet columnist contended, for example, "The atomic bomb served as a signal to the incorrigible reactionaries all over the world to launch a lynching campaign against the Soviet Union." After Truman's militant Navy Day address in late October, Moscow radio charged that the United States was keeping the bomb as part of the American program "to pursue power." . . .

Some British and American observers stressed that the bomb frightened the Soviets and injured Soviet-American relations. The bomb "overshadowed" the unsuccessful London Conference, Prime Minister Clement Attlee told Truman in October. Clark Kerr, the British ambassador to the Soviet Union, explained the growing bitterness of the Soviet Union toward the United States in terms of the bomb. "When the bomb seemed to them to become an instrument of . . . [American policy, the reaction was] spleen." Writing from Moscow, the American ambassador, W. Averell Harriman, outlined a similar diagnosis:

> Suddenly the atomic bomb appeared and they recognized that it was an offset to the power of the Red Army. This must have revived their old feeling of insecurity. . . .

The combat use of the bomb against Japan added weight to American demands for freer elections in Eastern Europe and may have helped bring about some Soviet concessions—especially delay of the scheduled election in Bulgaria in August and a broadening of the multiparty ticket there to enlarge the representation of noncommunist groups. When the American public and Congress compelled partial demobilization after the war, the bomb constituted a valued counterweight to the large armies that policy makers mistakenly thought the Soviet Union possessed. The military use of the bomb, policy makers presumably assumed, provided some credibility that the United States might use it again, in still undefined situations against the Soviet Union.

Though the bomb strengthened American policy and partly compensated for reductions in conventional forces, Truman had private doubts about whether he could use atomic weapons against the Soviet Union. On October 5, in talking with Harold Smith, his budget director, the president worried about the international situation and that the United States might be demobilizing too fast. "There are some people in the world who do not seem to understand anything except the number of divisions you have," he complained. Smith replied, "You have the atomic bomb up your sleeve." "Yes," Truman acknowledged, "but I am not sure it can ever be used." He did not explain his thinking, but presumably he meant that, short of a Soviet attack on Western Europe or on the United States, the American people, given the prevailing sentiments of late 1945, would not tolerate dropping atomic bombs on the Soviet Union. Certainly, they would not then countenance the military use of the bomb to roll back the Soviets from Eastern Europe. Few Americans then cared enough about Eastern Europe or were willing to endorse war against the Soviet Union. The bomb, rather than conferring omnipotence on the United States, had a more restricted role: it was a limited threat. Perhaps partly because of popular attitudes, policy makers felt restrained from employing explicit threats. Implicit threats, however, may have seemed equally useful and have allowed more flexibility: Policy makers were not committed publicly to using the bomb as a weapon in future situations.

Did the bomb make a critical difference in shaping the early Cold War? Roosevelt's repeated decisions to bar the Soviets from the nuclear project and Truman's decision to use the bomb in combat without explicitly informing the Soviet Union and inviting her to join in postwar control of atomic energy undoubtedly contributed to the Cold War and helped shape the form that it took. Yet, in view of the great strains in the fragile wartime Soviet-American alliance, historians should not regard America's *wartime* policy on the bomb as *the* cause, but only as one of the causes, of the Cold War. The wartime policy on atomic energy represented one of a number of missed opportunities at achieving limited agreements and at testing the prospects for Soviet-American cooperation on a vital matter.

The atomic bomb, first as prospect and then as reality, did influence American policy. The bomb reduced the incentives for compromise and even stiffened demands by the time of the Potsdam meeting in July 1945 because the weapon gave the United States enhanced power. Without the bomb, policy makers probably would have been more conciliatory after V-J Day in dealing with the Soviet Union, especially about Eastern Europe. The president certainly would have been unable to try to use atomic diplomacy (implied threats) to push the Soviets out of Eastern Europe. Rather, he might have speedily, though reluctantly, agreed to the dominance of Soviet power and to the closed door in that sector of the world. The bomb, as potential or actual weapon, did *not* alter the administration's conception of an ideal world, but possession of the weapon did strengthen the belief of policy makers in their capacity to move toward establishing their goal: an "open door" world with the Soviets acceding to American demands. This ideal world included free elections, an open economic door, and the reduction of Soviet influence in Eastern Europe. Without the bomb, the Truman administration would not have surrendered these ultimate aims, but policy makers would have had to rely primarily on economic power as a bargaining card to secure concessions from the Soviet Union. And economic power, taken alone, would probably have seemed insufficient—as the record of lend-lease and the Russian loan suggests. . . .

Without the bomb, in summary, American policy after V-J Day would have been more cautious, less demanding, less optimistic. Such restraint would not have prevented the breakdown of the Soviet-American alliance, but probably the cold war would not have taken the form that it did, and an uneasy truce, with less fear and antagonism, might have been possible.

Two Cold War Empires: Imposition vs. Invitation

JOHN LEWIS GADDIS

Leaders of both the United States and the Soviet Union would have bristled at having the appellation "imperial" affixed to what they were doing after 1945. But one need not send out ships, seize territories, and hoist flags to construct an empire: "informal" empires are much older than, and continued to exist alongside, the more "formal" ones Europeans imposed on so much of the rest of the world from the fifteenth through the nineteenth centuries. During the Cold War years Washington and Moscow took on much of the character, if never quite the charm, of old imperial capitals like London, Paris, and Vienna. And surely American and Soviet influence, throughout most of the second half of the twentieth century, was at least as ubiquitous as that of any earlier empire the world had ever seen. . . .

Let us begin with the structure of the Soviet empire, for the simple reason that it was, much more than the American, deliberately designed. It has long been clear that, in addition to having had an authoritarian vision, [Joseph] Stalin also had an imperial one, which he proceeded to implement in at least as single-minded a way. No comparably influential builder of empire came close to wielding power for so long, or with such striking results, on the Western side.

It was, of course, a matter of some awkwardness that Stalin came out of a revolutionary movement that had vowed to smash, not just tsarist imperialism, but all forms of imperialism throughout the world. The Soviet leader constructed his own logic, though, and throughout his career he devoted a surprising amount of attention to showing how a revolution and an empire might coexist. Bolsheviks could never be imperialists, Stalin acknowledged in one of his earliest public pronouncements on this subject, made in April 1917. But surely in a *revolutionary* Russia nine-tenths of the non-Russian nationalities would not *want* their independence. Few among those minorities found Stalin's reasoning persuasive after the Bolsheviks did seize power later that year, however, and one of the first problems [Vladimir] Lenin's new government faced was a disintegration of the old Russian empire not unlike what happened to the Soviet Union after communist authority finally collapsed in 1991.

Whether because of Lenin's own opposition to imperialism or, just as plausibly, because of Soviet Russia's weakness at the time, Finns, Estonians, Latvians, Lithuanians, Poles, and Moldavians were allowed to depart. Others who tried to do so— Ukrainians, Belorussians, Caucasians, Central Asians—were not so fortunate, and in 1922 Stalin proposed incorporating these remaining (and reacquired) nationalities into the Russian republic, only to have Lenin as one of his last acts override this recommendation and establish the multi-ethnic Union of Soviet Socialist Republics. After Lenin died and Stalin took his place it quickly became clear, though, that whatever its founding principles the USSR was to be no federation of equals. Rather, it would function as an updated form of empire even more tightly centralized than that of the Russian tsars. . . .

Stalin's fusion of Marxist internationalism with tsarist imperialism could only reinforce his tendency, in place well before World War II, to equate the advance of world revolution with the expanding influence of the Soviet state. He applied that linkage quite impartially: a major benefit of the 1939 pact with Hitler had been that it regained territories lost as a result of the Bolshevik Revolution and the World War I settlement. But Stalin's conflation of imperialism with ideology also explains the importance he attached, following the German attack in 1941, to having his new Anglo-American allies confirm these arrangements. He had similar goals in East Asia when he insisted on bringing the Soviet Union back to the position Russia had occupied in Manchuria prior to the Russo-Japanese War: this he finally achieved at the 1945 Yalta Conference in return for promising to enter the war against Japan. . . .

Stalin had been very precise about where he wanted Soviet boundaries changed; he was much less so on how far Moscow's sphere of influence was to extend. He insisted on having "friendly" countries around the periphery of the USSR, but he failed to specify how many would have to meet this standard. He called during the war for dismembering Germany, but by the end of it was denying that he had ever done so: that country would be temporarily divided, he told leading German communists in June 1945, and they themselves would eventually bring about its reunification. He never gave up on the idea of an eventual world revolution, but he expected this to result—as his comments to the Germans suggested—from an expansion of influence emanating from the Soviet Union itself. "[F]or the Kremlin," a well-placed spymaster recalled, "the mission of communism was primarily to consolidate the might of the Soviet state. Only military strength and domination of the countries on our borders could ensure us a superpower role."

But Stalin provided no indication—surely because he himself did not know—of how rapidly, or under what circumstances, this process would take place. He was certainly prepared to stop in the face of resistance from the West: at no point was he willing to challenge the Americans or even the British where they made their interests clear. Churchill acknowledged his scrupulous adherence to the famous 1944 "percentages" agreement confirming British authority in Greece, and Yugoslav sources have revealed Stalin's warnings that the United States and Great Britain would never allow their lines of communication in the Mediterranean to be broken. He quickly backed down when confronted with Anglo-American objections to his ambitions in Iran in the spring of 1946, as he did later that year after demanding Soviet bases in the Turkish Straits. . . .

What all of this suggests, though, is not that Stalin had limited ambitions, only that he had no timetable for achieving them. [Foreign minister Vyacheslav] Molotov retrospectively confirmed this: "Our ideology stands for offensive operations when possible, and if not, we wait." Given this combination of appetite with aversion to risk, one cannot help but wonder what would have happened had the West tried containment earlier. To the extent that it bears partial responsibility for the coming of the Cold War, the historian Vojtech Mastny has argued, that responsibility lies in its failure to do just that. . . .

. . . The fact that Stalin was able to *expand* his empire when others were contracting and while the Soviet Union was as weak as it was required explanation. Why did opposition to this process, within and outside Europe, take so long to develop?

One reason was that the colossal sacrifices the Soviet Union had made during the war against the Axis had, in effect, "purified" its reputation: the USSR and its leader had "earned" the right to throw their weight around, or so it seemed. Western governments found it difficult to switch quickly from viewing the Soviet Union as a glorious wartime ally to portraying it as a new and dangerous adversary. President Harry S. Truman and his future Secretary of State Dean Acheson—neither of them sympathetic in the slightest to communism—nonetheless tended to give the Soviet Union the benefit of the doubt well into the early postwar era. . . .

Resistance to Stalin's imperialism also developed slowly because Marxism-Leninism at the time had such widespread appeal. It is difficult now to recapture the admiration revolutionaries outside the Soviet Union felt for that country before they came to know it well. "[Communism] was the most rational and most intoxicating, all-embracing ideology for me and for those in my disunited and desperate land who so desired to skip over centuries of slavery and backwardness and to bypass reality itself," [Milovan] Djilas recalled, in a comment that could have been echoed throughout much of what came to be called the "third world." Because the Bolsheviks themselves had overcome one empire and had made a career of condemning others, it would take decades for people who were struggling to overthrow British, French, Dutch, or Portuguese colonialism to see that there could also be such a thing as Soviet imperialism. European communists—notably the Yugoslavs—saw this much earlier, but even to most of them it had not been apparent at the end of the war.

Still another explanation for the initial lack of resistance to Soviet expansionism was the fact that its repressive character did not become immediately apparent to all who were subjected to it. With regimes on the left taking power in Eastern and Central Europe, groups long denied advancement could now expect it. For many who remembered the 1930s, autarchy within a Soviet bloc could seem preferable to exposure once again to international capitalism, with its periodic cycles of boom and bust. Nor did Moscow impose harsh controls everywhere at the same time. Simple administrative incompetence may partially account for this: one Russian historian has pointed out that "[d]isorganization, mismanagement and rivalry among many branches of the gigantic Stalinist state in Eastern Europe were enormous." But it is also possible, at least in some areas, that Stalin did not expect to *need* tight controls; that he anticipated no serious challenge and perhaps even spontaneous support. Why did he promise free elections after the war? Maybe he thought the communists would win them.

One has the impression that Stalin and the Eastern Europeans got to know one another only gradually. The Kremlin leader was slow to recognize that Soviet authority would not be welcomed everywhere beyond Soviet borders; but as he did come to see this he became all the more determined to impose it everywhere. The Eastern Europeans were slow to recognize how confining incorporation within a Soviet sphere was going to be; but as they did come to see this they became all the more determined to resist it, even if only by withholding, in a passive but sullen manner, the consent any regime needs to establish itself by means other than coercion. Stalin's efforts to consolidate his empire therefore made it at once more repressive and less secure. Meanwhile, an alternative vision of postwar Europe was emerging from the other great empire that established itself in the wake of World War II, that of the United States, and this too gave Stalin grounds for concern.

The first point worth noting, when comparing the American empire to its Soviet counterpart, is a striking reversal in the sequence of events. Stalin's determination to create his empire preceded by some years the conditions that made it possible: he had first to consolidate power at home and then defeat Nazi Germany, while at the same time seeing to it that his allies in that enterprise did not thwart his long-term objectives. With the United States, it was the other way around: the conditions for establishing an empire were in place long before there was any clear intention on the part of its leaders to do so. Even then, they required the support of a skeptical electorate, something that could never quite be taken for granted.

The United States had been poised for global hegemony at the end of World War I. Its military forces played a decisive role in bringing that conflict to an end.

Its economic predominance was such that it could control both the manner and the rate of European recovery. Its ideology commanded enormous respect, as Woodrow Wilson found when he arrived on the Continent late in 1918 to a series of rapturous public receptions. The Versailles Treaty fell well short of Wilson's principles, to be sure, but the League of Nations followed closely his own design, providing an explicit legal basis for an international order that was to have drawn, as much as anything else, upon the example of the American constitution itself. If there was ever a point at which the world seemed receptive to an expansion of United States influence, this was it.

Americans themselves, however, were not receptive. The Senate's rejection of membership in the League reflected the public's distinct lack of enthusiasm for international peace-keeping responsibilities. Despite the interests certain business, labor, and agricultural groups had in seeking overseas markets and investment opportunities, most Americans saw few benefits to be derived from integrating their economy with that of the rest of the world. . . .

This isolationist consensus broke down only as Americans began to realize that a potentially hostile power was once again threatening Europe: even their own hemisphere, it appeared, might not escape the consequences this time around. After September 1939, the Roosevelt administration moved as quickly as public and Congressional opinion would allow to aid Great Britain and France by means short of war; it also chose to challenge the Japanese over their occupation of China and later French Indochina, thereby setting in motion a sequence of events that would lead to the attack on Pearl Harbor. . . .

. . . Americans had begun to suspect, late in the nineteenth century, that the internal behavior of states determined their external behavior; certainly it is easy to see how the actions of Germany, Italy, and Japan during the 1930s could have caused this view to surface once again, much as it had in relations with tsarist Russia and imperial Germany during World War I. Once that happened, the Americans, not given to making subtle distinctions, began to oppose authoritarianism everywhere, and that could account for their sudden willingness to take on several authoritarians at once in 1941. . . .

It did not automatically follow, though, that the Soviet Union would inherit the title of "first enemy" once Germany and Japan had been defeated. A sense of vulnerability preceded the identification of a source of threat in the thinking of American strategists: innovations in military technology—long-range bombers, the prospect of even longer-range missiles—created visions of future Pearl Harbors before it had become clear from where such an attack might come. Neither in the military nor the political-economic planning that went on in Washington during the war was there consistent concern with the USSR as a potential future adversary. The threat, rather, appeared to arise from war itself, whoever might cause it, and the most likely candidates were thought to be resurgent enemies from World War II.

The preferred solution was to maintain preponderant power for the United States, which meant a substantial peacetime military establishment and a string of bases around the world from which to resist aggression if it should ever occur. But equally important, a revived international community would seek to remove the fundamental causes of war through the United Nations, a less ambitious version of Wilson's League, and through new economic institutions like the International

Monetary Fund and the World Bank, whose task it would be to prevent another global depression and thereby ensure prosperity. The Americans and the British assumed that the Soviet Union would want to participate in these multilateral efforts to achieve military and economic security. The Cold War developed when it became clear that Stalin either could not or would not accept this framework.

Did the Americans attempt to impose their vision of the postwar world upon the USSR? No doubt it looked that way from Moscow: both the Roosevelt and Truman administrations stressed political self-determination and economic integration with sufficient persistence to arouse Stalin's suspicions—easily aroused, in any event—as to their ultimate intentions. But what the Soviet leader saw as a challenge to his hegemony the Americans meant as an effort to salvage multilateralism. At no point prior to 1947 did the United States and its Western European allies abandon the hope that the Russians might eventually come around; and indeed negotiations aimed at bringing them around would continue at the foreign ministers' level, without much hope of success, through the end of that year. The American attitude was less that of expecting to impose a system than one of puzzlement as to why its merits were not universally self-evident. It differed significantly, therefore, from Stalin's point of view, which allowed for the possibility that socialists in other countries might come to see the advantages of Marxism-Leninism as practiced in the Soviet Union, but never capitalists. They were there, in the end, to be overthrown, not convinced.

The emergence of an opposing great power bloc posed serious difficulties for the principle of multilateralism, based as it had been on the expectation of cooperation with Moscow. But with a good deal of ingenuity the Americans managed to *merge* their original vision of a single international order built around common security with a second and more hastily improvised concept that sought to counter the expanding power and influence of the Soviet Union. That concept was, of course, containment, and its chief instrument was the Marshall Plan. . . .

. . . The danger here came not from the prospect that the Red Army would invade and occupy the rest of the continent, as Hitler had tried to do: rather, its demoralized and exhausted inhabitants might simply vote in communist parties who would then do Moscow's bidding. The initial steps in the strategy of containment—stopgap military and economic aid to Greece and Turkey [requested by President Truman before Congress on March 12, 1947], the more carefully designed and ambitious Marshall Plan—took place within this context: the idea was to produce instant intangible reassurance as well as eventual tangible reinforcement. Two things had to happen in order for intimidation to occur, [diplomat George F.] Kennan liked to argue: the intimidator had to make the effort, but, equally important, the target of those efforts had to agree to be intimidated. The initiatives of 1947 sought to generate sufficient self-confidence to prevent such acquiescence in intimidation from taking place.

Some historians have asserted that these fears of collapse were exaggerated: that economic recovery on the continent was already underway, and that the Europeans themselves were never as psychologically demoralized as the Americans made them out to be. Others have added that the real crisis at the time was within an American economy that could hardly expect to function hegemonically if Europeans lacked the dollars to purchase its products. Still others have suggested that the

Marshall Plan was the means by which American officials sought to project overseas the mutually-beneficial relationship between business, labor, and government they had worked out at home: the point was not to make Wilsonian values a model for the rest of the world, but rather the politics of productivity that had grown out of American corporate capitalism. All of these arguments have merit: at a minimum they have forced historians to place the Marshall Plan in a wider economic, social, and historical context; more broadly they suggest that the American empire had its own distinctive internal roots, and was not solely and simply a response to the Soviet external challenge.

At the same time, though, it is difficult to see how a strategy of containment could have developed—with the Marshall Plan as its centerpiece—had there been nothing to contain. . . . The American empire arose *primarily,* therefore, not from internal causes, as had the Soviet empire, but from a perceived external danger powerful enough to overcome American isolationism.

Washington's wartime vision of a postwar international order had been premised on the concepts of political self-determination and economic integration. It was intended to work by assuming a set of *common* interests that would cause other countries to *want* to be affiliated with it rather than to resist it. The Marshall Plan, to a considerable extent, met those criteria. . . .

The American empire, therefore, reflected little imperial consciousness or design. An anti-imperial tradition dating back to the American Revolution partially accounted for this: departures from that tradition, as in the Spanish–American War of 1898 and the Philippine insurrection that followed, had only reinforced its relevance—outside the Western hemisphere. So too did a constitutional structure that forced even imperially minded leaders like Wilson and the two Roosevelts to accommodate domestic attitudes that discouraged imperial behavior long after national capabilities had made it possible. And even as those internal constraints diminished dramatically in World War II—they never entirely dropped away—Americans still found it difficult to think of themselves as an imperial power. The idea of remaking the international system in such a way as to transcend empires altogether still lingered, but so too did doubts as to whether the United States was up to the task. In the end it was again external circumstances—the manner in which Stalin managed his own empire and the way in which this pushed Europeans into preferring its American alternative—that brought the self-confidence necessary to administer imperial responsibilities into line with Washington's awareness of their existence.

The test of any empire comes in administering it, for even the most repressive tyranny requires a certain amount of acquiescence among its subjects. Coercion and terror cannot everywhere and indefinitely prop up authority: sooner or later the social, economic, and psychological costs of such measures begin to outweigh the benefits. . . .

It is apparent now, even if it was not always at the time, that the Soviet Union did not manage its empire particularly well. Because of his personality and the structure of government he built around it, Stalin was—shall we say—less than receptive to the wishes of those nations that fell within the Soviet sphere. He viewed departures from his instructions with deep suspicion, but he also objected to manifestations of independent behavior where instructions had not yet been given. As a result, he put his European followers in an impossible position: they could satisfy

him only by seeking his approval for whatever he had decided they should do—
even, at times, before he had decided that they should do it.

An example occurred late in 1944 when the Yugoslavs—then the most powerful but also the most loyal of Stalin's East European allies—complained politely to
Soviet commanders that their troops had been raping local women in the northern
corner of the country through which they were passing. Stalin himself took note of
this matter, accusing the Yugoslavs—at one point tearfully—of showing insufficient respect for Soviet military sacrifices and for failing to sympathize when "a
soldier who has crossed thousands of kilometers through blood and fire and death
has fun with a woman or takes some trifle." The issue was not an insignificant one:
the Red Army's behavior was a problem throughout the territories it occupied, and
did much to alienate those who lived there. . . .

Similar questions arose regarding Yugoslav plans for a postwar Balkan federation. Stalin had initially supported this idea, perhaps as an excuse for removing
American and British military representatives from former enemy states like
Romania, but he soon developed reservations. The Yugoslavs themselves might
become too powerful; and their propensity for hot-headedness—evident in their
claims to Trieste and their shooting down of two American Air Force plans in
1946—might provoke the West. Orders went out that the Yugoslavs were to proceed slowly in their plans to take over Albania, and were to stop assisting the Greek
guerrillas altogether. . . .

Stalin did little better managing Western European communists, despite the
fact that they still regarded themselves as his loyal supporters. In May 1947, the
French Communist Party voted no confidence in the government of Premier Paul
Ramadier, only to have him expel their representatives from his cabinet. The Italians, with strong American encouragement, threw out their own communists later
that month. Andrei Zhdanov, who managed the Soviet Communist Party's relations
with its foreign counterparts, sharply reprimanded the French comrades for acting
without Moscow's authorization and therefore arousing concerns in the minds of
"Soviet workers." He then passed on this communication to all other European
communist parties. . . .

The Americans' unexpected offer of Marshall Plan aid to the Soviet Union and
Eastern Europe in June 1947, caused even greater difficulties for Stalin's management of empire—which is precisely what Kennan hoped for when he recommended making it. In one of the stranger illusions arising from their ideology,
Soviet leaders had always anticipated United States economic assistance in some
form. Lenin himself expected American capitalists, ever in search of foreign markets, to invest eagerly in the newly formed USSR, despite its official antipathy
toward them. Stalin hoped for a massive American reconstruction loan after World
War II, and even authorized Molotov early in 1945 to offer acceptance of such
assistance in order to help the United States stave off the economic crisis that
Marxists analysis showed must be approaching. When the Marshall Plan was
announced Stalin's first reaction was that the capitalists must be desperate. He concluded, therefore, that the Soviet Union and its East European allies should indeed
participate in the plan, and quickly dispatched Molotov and a large delegation of
economic experts to Paris to take part in the conference that was to determine the
nature and extent of European needs.

But then Stalin began to reconsider. His ambassador in Washington, Nikolai Novikov, warned that the American offer to the Soviet Union could not be sincere: "A careful analysis of the Marshall Plan shows that ultimately it comes down to forming a West European bloc as a tool of US policy. All the good wishes accompanying the plan are demagogic official propaganda serving as a smokescreen." Soviet intelligence picked up reports—accurate enough—that American Under-Secretary of State William Clayton had been conspiring with British officials on using the Marshall Plan to reintegrate Germany into the West European economy and to deny further reparations shipments to the Soviet Union. This information, together with indications at Paris that the Americans would require a coordinated European response, caused Stalin to change his mind and order his own representatives to walk out. "The Soviet delegation saw those claims as a bid to interfere in the internal affairs of European countries," Molotov explained lamely, "thus making the economies of these countries dependent on US interests." . . .

The United States, in contrast, proved surprisingly adept at managing an empire. Having attained their authority through democratic processes, its leaders were experienced—as their counterparts in Moscow were not—in the arts of persuasion, negotiation and compromise. Applying domestic political insights to foreign policy could produce embarrassing results, as when President Truman likened Stalin to his old Kansas City political mentor, Tom Pendergast, or when Secretary of State James F. Byrnes compared the Russians to the US Senate: "You build a post office in their state, and they'll build a post office in our state." But the habits of democracy had served the nation well during World War II: its strategists had assumed that their ideas would have to reflect the interests and capabilities of allies; it was also possible for allies to advance proposals of their own and have them taken seriously. That same pattern of mutual accommodation persisted after the war, despite the fact that all sides acknowledged—as they had during most of the war itself—the disproportionate power the United States could ultimately bring to bear.

Americans so often deferred to the wishes of allies during the early Cold War that some historians have seen the Europeans—especially the British—as having managed *them*. The new Labour government in London did encourage the Truman administration to toughen its policy toward the Soviet Union; Churchill—by then out of office—was only reinforcing these efforts with his March 1946 "Iron Curtain" speech. The British were ahead of the Americans in pressing for a consolidation of Western occupation zones in Germany, even if this jeopardized prospects for an overall settlement with the Russians. Foreign Secretary Ernest Bevin determined the timing of the February 1947 crisis over Greece and Turkey when he ended British military and economic assistance to those countries, leaving the United States little choice but to involve itself in the eastern Mediterranean and providing the occasion for the Truman Doctrine. And it was the desperate economic plight of the West Europeans generally that persuaded newly appointed Secretary of State George C. Marshall, in June 1947, to announce the comprehensive program of American assistance that came to bear his name.

But one can easily make too much of this argument. Truman and his advisers were not babes in the woods. They knew what they were doing at each stage, and did it only because they were convinced their actions would advance American interests. They never left initiatives entirely up to the Europeans: they insisted on an integrated plan for economic recovery and quite forcefully reined in prospective recipients when it appeared that their requests would exceed what Congress would approve. "[I]n the end we would not *ask* them," Kennan noted, "we would just *tell* them, what they would get." The Americans were flexible enough, though, to accept and build upon ideas that came from allies; they also frequently let allies determine the timing of actions taken. . . .

The habits of democracy were no less significant when it came to defeated adversaries. The Roosevelt administration had planned to treat Germany harshly after the war; and even after the President himself backed away from the punitive Morgenthau Plan in late 1944, its spirit lingered in the occupation directive for American forces, JCS 1067, which prohibited doing anything to advance economic rehabilitiation beyond the minimum necessary to avoid disease or disorder. The American design for a postwar world based on economic integration and political self-determination seemed not to apply, or so at first it appeared, to occupied Germany.

Uneasiness about this inconsistency soon developed, though; and in any event Americans far from Washington customarily maintained a certain irreverence toward orders emanating from it. General Clay concluded almost at once that his instructions were unworkable and that he would either get them changed, sabotage them, or ignore them. Here he followed the lead of his own troops who, having found prohibitions against fraternizing with the Germans to be ridiculous, quickly devised ways of circumventing them. Confronted with inappropriate directives in a difficult situation, the American occupiers—with a breezy audacity that seems remarkable in retrospect—fell back upon domestic instincts and set about transplanting democracy into the part of Germany they controlled. . . .

The Americans simply did not find it necessary, in building a sphere of influence, to impose unrepresentative governments or brutal treatment upon the peoples that fell within it. Where repressive regimes already existed, as in Greece, Turkey, and Spain, serious doubts arose in Washington as to whether the United States should be supporting them at all, however useful they might be in containing Soviet expansionism. Nor, having constructed their empire, did Americans follow the ancient imperial practice of "divide and rule." Rather, they used economic leverage to overcome nationalist tendencies, thereby encouraging the Europeans' emergence as a "third force" whose obedience could not always be assumed. It was as if the Americans were projecting abroad a tradition they had long taken for granted at home: that civility made sense; that spontaneity, within a framework of minimal constraint, was the path to political and economic robustness; that to intimidate or to overmanage was to stifle. The contrast to Stalin's methods of imperial administration could hardly have been sharper.

Stalin saw the need, after learning of the Marshall Plan, to improve his methods of imperial management. He therefore called a meeting of the Soviet and East European communist parties, as well as the French and the Italian communists, to be held in Poland in September 1947, ostensibly for the purpose of exchanging ideas on fraternal cooperation. Only after the delegations had assembled did he reveal his real objective, which was to organize a new coordinating agency for the international communist movement. Stalin had abolished the old Comintern as a wartime gesture of reassurance to the Soviet Union's allies in 1943, and the International Department of the Soviet Communist Party, headed by the veteran Comintern leader, the Bulgarian Georgii Dimitrov, had taken over its functions. What had happened during the spring and summer of 1947 made it clear, though, that these arrangements provided insufficient coordination from Stalin's point of view.

Delegations arriving at Szklarska Poreba were greeted by a militant speech from Zhdanov, picturing the world as irrevocably divided into two hostile camps: "The frank expansionist program of the United States," he charged, was "highly reminiscent of the reckless program, which failed so ignominiously, of the fascist aggressors, who, as we know, also made a bid for world supremacy." The attendees were then invited to consider—and after some reservations on the part of the Poles unanimously approved—a Soviet proposal for the creation of a "Cominform," its headquarters to be located in Belgrade, a pointed gesture in the light of Stalin's earlier concerns about independent tendencies among the Yugoslavs. The French communist leader Jacques Duclos summed up the new procedures succinctly: "Paris and Rome will be able to submit their proposals, but they shall have to be content with the decisions to be adopted in Belgrade."

Even with the Cominform in place, the momentary independence Czechoslovakia demonstrated must have continued to weigh on Stalin's mind. That country, more than any other in Eastern Europe, had sought to accommodate itself to Soviet hegemony. Embittered by how easily the British and French had betrayed Czech interests at the Munich conference in 1938, President Eduard Beneš welcomed the expansion of Soviet influence while reassuring Marxist-Leninists that they had nothing to fear from the democratic system the Czechs hoped to rebuild after the war. "If you play it well," he told Czech Communist Party leaders in 1943, "you'll win."

But Beneš meant "win" by democratic means. Although the Communists had indeed done well in the May 1946 parliamentary elections, their popularity began to drop sharply after Stalin forbade Czech participation in the Marshall Plan the following year. Convinced by intelligence reports that the West would not intervene, they therefore took advantage of a February 1948 government crisis to stage a *coup d'état*—presumably with Stalin's approval—that left them in complete control, with no further need to resort to the unpredictabilities of the ballot box. . . .

Because of its dramatic impact, the Czech coup had consequences Stalin could hardly have anticipated. It set off a momentary—and partially manufactured—war scare in Washington. It removed the last Congressional objections to the Marshall Plan, resulting in the final approval of that initiative in April 1948. It accelerated plans by the Americans, the British, and the French to consolidate their occupation zones in Germany and to proceed toward the formation of an independent West German state. And it caused American officials to begin to consider, much more seriously than they had until this point, two ideas Bevin had begun to advance several months earlier: that economic assistance alone would not restore European self-confidence, and that the United States would have to take on direct military responsibilities for defending that portion of the Continent that remained outside Soviet control.

Stalin then chose the late spring of 1948 to attempt a yet further consolidation of the Soviet empire, with even more disastrous results. Reacting to the proposed establishment of a separate West German state, as well as to growing evidence that the East German regime had failed to attract popular support, and to the introduction of a new currency in the American, British, and French sectors of Berlin over which the Russians would have no control, he ordered a progressively tightening blockade around that city, which lay within the Soviet zone. "Let's make a joint effort," he told the East German leaders in March. "Perhaps we can kick them out." Initial indications were that the scheme was working. "Our control and restrictive measures have dealt a strong blow at the prestige of the Americans and British in Germany," Soviet occupation authorities reported the following month. The Germans believed that "the Anglo-Americans have retreated before the Russians," and that this testified to the latter's strength. Suspend the new currency and the plans for a West German state, a self-confident Stalin told Western diplomats early in August, "and you shall no longer have any difficulties. That may be done even tomorrow. Think it over."

But the Soviet leader's plans, by this time, had already begun to backfire. There was now a quite genuine war scare in the West, one that intensified pressures for an American–West European military alliance, accelerated planning for an independent West Germany, further diminished what little support the communists still had outside the Soviet zone, and significantly boosted President Truman's reelection prospects in a contest few at the time thought he could win. Nor did the blockade turn out to be effective. "Clay's attempts to create 'an airlift' connecting Berlin with the western zones have proved futile," Soviet officials in that city prematurely reported to Moscow in April. "The Americans have admitted that the idea would be too expensive." In fact, though, the United States and its allies astonished themselves as well as the Russians by improvising so successful a supply of Berlin by air that there was no need to make concessions. Stalin was left with the choice he had hoped to avoid—capitulation or war—and in May 1949, in one of the most humiliating of all setbacks for Soviet foreign policy, he selected the first alternative by lifting the blockade. . . .

There remained, though, the task of consolidating Soviet control over those territories where communists already ruled, and here too 1948 proved to be a turning point, because for the first time this process provoked open resistance. Despite appearances of solidarity, Soviet–Yugoslav relations had become increasingly strained following earlier disagreements over the Red Army's abuse of Yugoslav civilians, plans for a Balkan federation, and support for the Greek communists. The fiercely independent Yugoslavs were finding it difficult to defer to the Soviet Union, whose interests seemed increasingly at odds with those of international communism. Stalin himself alternated between cajoling and bullying their leaders, sometimes including them in lengthy late-night eating and drinking sessions at his dacha, at other times upbraiding them rudely for excessive ideological militance and insufficient attention to Moscow's wishes. Tensions came to a head early in 1948 when the Yugoslavs and the Albanians began considering the possibility of unification. Stalin let it be known that he would not object to Yugoslavia "swallowing" Albania, but this only aroused suspicions among the Yugoslavs, who remembered how the Soviet Union had "swallowed" the Baltic States in 1940 and feared that the precedent might someday apply to them. Their concerns grew when Stalin then reversed course and condemned Belgrade bitterly for sending troops into Albania without consulting Moscow. By June of 1948, these disagreements had become public, and the communist world would never be the same again. . . .

. . . But the Yugoslavs alone had the capacity to resist: this communist government had not been installed by the Red Army and did not depend upon Soviet support to remain in power. Their experiences with Stalin had gradually transformed [Josip] Tito and the other top Yugoslav communists from worshipful acolytes into schismatic heretics: the Soviet leader's personality proved no more "winning" for those who were in a position to make independent judgments than was the system he had created. The Soviet empire, it now appeared, would be able to maintain itself only by imposition; Tito's defection showed that whatever invitations might have been extended were likely to be withdrawn upon more intimate acquaintance. . . .

West Europeans were meanwhile convincing themselves that they had little to lose from living within an American sphere of influence. The idea of a European "third force" soon disappeared, not because Washington officials lost interest in it, but because the Europeans themselves rejected it. The North Atlantic Treaty Organization, which came into existence in April 1949, had been a European initiative from the beginning: it was as explicit an invitation as has ever been extended from smaller powers to a great power to construct an empire and include them within it. When Kennan, worried that NATO would divide Europe permanently, put forward a plan later that spring looking toward an eventual reunification and neutralization of Germany as a way of ending both the Soviet and American presence on the continent, British and French opposition quickly shot it down. The self-confidence he and other American officials had set out to restore in Western Europe could now manifest itself, or so it appeared, only from within a framework of reassurance that only the United States could provide.

Since incorporation with the Soviet empire reassured no one, it is worth asking: why the difference? Why were allies of the United States willing to give up so much autonomy in order to enhance their own safety? How did the ideas of sovereignty and security, which historically have been difficult to separate, come to be so widely seen as divisible in this situation?

The answer would appear to be that despite a postwar polarization of authority quite at odds, in its stark bilateralism, from what wartime planners had expected, Americans managed to retain the multilateral conception of security they had developed during World War II. They were able to do this because Truman's foreign policy—like Roosevelt's military strategy—reflected the habits of domestic democratic politics. Negotiation, compromise, and consensus building abroad came naturally to statesmen steeped in the uses of such practices at home: in this sense, the American political tradition served the country better than its realist critics—Kennan definitely among them—believed it did. . . .

It would become fashionable to argue, in the wake of American military intervention in Vietnam, the Soviet invasions of Czechoslovakia and Afghanistan, and growing fears of nuclear confrontation that developed during the early 1980s, that there were no significant differences in the spheres of influence Washington and Moscow had constructed in Europe after World War II: these had been, it was claimed, "morally equivalent," denying autonomy quite impartially to all who lived under them. Students of history must make their own judgments about morality, but even a cursory examination of the historical record will show that these imperial structures could hardly have been more different in their origins, their composition, their tolerance of diversity, and as it turned out their durability. It is important to specify just what these differences were. . . .

One empire arose . . . by invitation, the other by imposition. *Europeans* made this distinction, very much as they had done during the war when they welcomed armies liberating them from the west but feared those that came from the east. They did so because they saw clearly at the time—even if a subsequent generation would not always see—how different American and Soviet empires were likely to be. It is true that the *extent* of the American empire quickly exceeded that of its Soviet counterpart, but this was because *resistance* to expanding American influence was never as great. The American empire may well have become larger, paradoxically, because the American *appetite* for empire was less that of the USSR. The United States had shown, throughout most of its history, that it could survive and even prosper without extending its domination as far as the eye could see. The logic of Lenin's ideological internationalism, as modified by Stalin's Great Russian nationalism and personal paranoia, was that the Soviet Union could not.

The early Cold War in Europe, therefore, cannot be understood by looking at the policies of either the United States or the Soviet Union in isolation. What evolved on the continent was an interactive system in which the actions of each side affected not only the other but also the Europeans; their responses, in turn, shaped further decisions in Washington and Moscow. It quickly became clear—largely because of differences in the domestic institutions of each superpower—that an American empire would accommodate far greater diversity than would one run by the Soviet Union: as a consequence most Europeans accepted and even invited American hegemony, fearing deeply what that of the Russians might entail.

Two paths diverged at the end of World War II. And that, to paraphrase an American poet, really did make all the difference.

George F. Kennan and the Gendering of Soviet Russia

FRANK COSTIGLIOLA

In the *New York Times Book Review* of April 7, 1996, Fareed Zakaria, managing editor of *Foreign Affairs,* reviewed the latest book by George F. Kennan, the ninety-two-year-old former diplomat and author of the containment doctrine. Zakaria began his review by praising the "clarity" and the "gripping, declarative prose" of Kennan's "famous long telegram from Moscow in 1946." In that 5,540-word telegram, Kennan laid out the argument for deemphasizing negotiations with Moscow on issues arising from World War II and for instead emphasizing the containment of the Soviet Union. Ever since Kennan's cable reached the State Department a half-century ago, officials and scholars have been pointing to Kennan's prose—without, however, examining why his language appeared so clear and so gripping or how his emotions and rhetorical strategies infused his writings, particularly the long telegram (LT), with such persuasive force. A close reading of Kennan's

From Frank Costigliola, "Unceasing Pressure for Penetration: Gender, Pathology, and Emotion in George Kennan's Formation of the Cold War," *Journal of American History* 83(4) (March 1997), pp. 1309–1318, 1323, 1327–1338. Reprinted with permission.

writings demonstrates that the language is neither transparent nor value-free, and that Kennan's figures of speech—which scholars have quoted as "colorful language" but have not fully analyzed—emotionalize and condition the interpretation of his ostensibly realistic prose.

Kennan wrote the LT on February 22, 1946, after two decades of deep, conflicted feelings about the Soviet people and their government. For much of that period, he longed to immerse himself in Russian society even as he felt alienated from United States society. Perhaps his deepest aspiration was to use what he saw as the primitive vitality of Russian culture to revitalize the United States. The exuberance and sensuality that Kennan and other United States diplomats such as [Ambassador] William C. Bullitt and [embassy official] Charles E. Bohlen had enjoyed in Moscow in 1933–1934 sharpened the bitterness with which they approached United States–Soviet relations at the onset of the Cold War. Kennan expressed his intense feelings in his writing, often in metaphors of gender and pathology. Because these emotion-laden tropes remained camouflaged by Kennan's expertise on Soviet affairs and his claim to realism, they offered a particularly effective rhetorical strategy for demonizing the leadership of the Soviet Union in a supposedly dispassionate analysis.

In the LT, Kennan portrayed the Soviet government as a rapist exerting "insistent, unceasing pressure for penetration and command" over Western societies. A few months later he compared the Soviet people to "a woman who had been romantically in love with her husband and who had suddenly seen his true colors revealed. . . . There was no question of a divorce. They decided to stay together for the sake of the children. But the honeymoon was definitely over." The analogy fit a favorite narrative of Kennan in which the Russian people figured as feminine (and often an object of desire), the Soviet government appeared as a cruel masculine authority, and he stood forth as the unrequited but true lover of the Russian people.

Kennan also represented the Soviet leadership as mentally ill, suffering "a psychosis which permeates and determines [the] behavior of [the] entire Soviet ruling caste." The discourse of psychological pathology privileged Kennan and his listeners—they had the authoritative gaze of physicians—while it positioned the Soviet Union as a mental patient without a legitimate subjectivity. If the Soviet government could not reason normally, why try to cooperate with it? . . .

When Kennan wrote the LT, in February 1946, Americans were searching for a clear-cut, simple explanation of Soviet foreign policy. Joseph Stalin's government, however, displayed a confusing mixture of caution and self-aggrandizement. The Soviets angered the United States by their continued occupation of northern Iran and Manchuria, by their pressure on Turkey for base rights in the Dardanelles, and by their defense of Soviet spies caught in Canada. Yet they evacuated northern Norway and the Danish island of Bornholm in the Baltic Sea, discouraged revolution in Western Europe, offered no leadership to Communist revolutionaries in Southeast Asia, and played to both sides in the Chinese civil war; further, they went on to allow free elections in Hungary, Czechoslovakia, and Finland. What was the pattern in these events? Americans wondered. Was it possible and desirable to extend wartime cooperation into the postwar era? There was "great confusion" in Washington, observed Dwight D. Eisenhower. The British ambassador reported that American leaders suffered "uneasy bewilderment," "fear of the unknown," and "baffled dismay."

American officials also debated whether to make the concessions necessary for a possible deal with Moscow. In December 1945, Secretary of State James F. Byrnes made a preliminary agreement with Stalin on control of the atomic bomb, only to have the accord killed by President Harry S. Truman and Republican senator Arthur Vandenberg. Soviet ambivalence continued. On January 25, 1946, Stalin met with Igor Kurchatov, head of the Soviet atomic bomb project, and told him to spare no expense in quickly building a bomb. Four days later, Byrnes reported to the cabinet that although the Soviets still wanted "to discuss stability and peace with the United States alone" without Britain, and although "they were always eager to do so. . . . he had discontinued the practice of having private meetings with the Russians."

Kennan's long telegram helped the Truman administration arrive at a reductive but clear picture of Soviet policy. The emotive force of this document helped delegitimate what Kennan called "intimate collaboration" with Moscow, making containment, a policy that already had strong support in the Truman administration, seem the only realistic, healthy, and manly alternative. At a time when the United States priority was already shifting away from dealing with Moscow and toward building a viable "free world," the LT convinced many that the Soviet government was a monstrous force, fanatically committed to destroying the United States and the American way of life.

Although Kennan disliked the Soviet government, he loved to melt into a Russian crowd or savor the old Russia at an untouched monastery. He felt happiest, he said, when "I could have the sense of Russia all about me, and could give myself, momentarily, the illusion that I was part of it." Kennan's involvement with Russia had the insistence of a physical need. He wrote of his "consuming curiosity to know it in the flesh," of his returning to Russia "like a thirsting man on a stream of clear water." In a "flashback," he remembered: "I drink it all in, love it intensely, and feel myself for a time an inhabitant of that older Russia."

Intensity characterized Kennan's relationships in Russia and with Russia. In December 1933 he and Ambassador Bullitt, who had negotiated with Lenin and who had been married to [the American Communist activist and author] John Reed's widow, received a warm welcome as Washington's first official envoys to the Soviet Union. It seemed a time of promise. The Soviet famine was ending, and rightist figures such as Nikolai Bukharin were reappearing. Stalin reassured a party congress that "there is nothing more to prove and, it seems, no one to fight." For embassy officials such as Kennan, Bullitt, Bohlen, and Charles Thayer, Moscow was "immensely exciting." Kennan remembered 1933–1934 as the "high point of [his] life . . . in comradeship, in gaiety, in intensity of experience." He threw himself into investigations of the Soviet economy, research for a biography of Anton Chekhov, and all-night parties of "endless talk, in the Russian manner." Kennan escaped from what he called the "social discipline of the Western world" into a "true Boheme" of journalists and others. "I loved it. I felt at home with these people," said Kennan, who rarely felt at home in United States society. In turn, Soviet officials were "delighted by young Kennan," Bullitt reported. Soviet president Mikhail Kalinin, whom Kennan remembered as "old Daddy Kalinin," "kindly" told him that the book about Siberia written by his elder cousin, another George Kennan, had been "the bible of the early Bolsheviks." . . .

Although Kennan's published memoirs emphasize distaste for the Soviet government, his unpublished writings suggest more ambiguity. In 1938, he described the commissars he had met in 1933 as "unforgettable" and macho masculine: "strong-nerved, lean, ruthlessly competent"—not "paunchy and flabby like their bourgeois counterparts abroad." Although Kennan never subscribed to Marxism, he affirmed that he and his colleagues had "read a good deal of our Marx and Lenin. We had thrilled to the exploits of John Reed, to the tales of the Revolution." In 1933–1934, Kennan found it hard to hold himself back from involvement in Russian society, to only "witness with detachment the spectacle of a generation of young Russians engaged with the realities of life." During these early years Bohlen enthused about "young Russians . . . with a lack of self consciousness that is amazing. They really are in a great many ways a new type of human being." Although Kennan was a conservative, he did not champion the marketplace. Instead he sympathized with the project of building a rational society with a group ethic. Kennan's villains were the "political bosses" such as Stalin, who had betrayed revolutionary idealism, and the fanatical Bolsheviks, who carried revolution to excess.

By December 1934, Kennan was becoming "too fascinated by Russia." Losing the balance between his duties and his engagement with Russian society, he felt that "Moscow had me somewhat on the run." Kennan confessed to Thayer that he chafed under the "restrictions of a diplomatic status," particularly "the compulsion to political inactivity, self-restraint and objectivity." In revealing language, Kennan worried that he would "end up at an early age mentally, physically and emotionally sterile." Kennan's correlations between holding himself back from Russian life and "sterility" and, by extension, between engagement with Russia and virility, perhaps referred to some sexual component in his passion for Russia. He appeared happy in his marriage to Annelise Sorensen, a Norwegian woman whom he had wed in 1931. More significant than the issue of Kennan's sexual behavior, however, is his use of sexualized or eroticized discourse for matters that intensely concerned him, particularly those relating to the Soviet Union. Moreover, his linkage of virility with involvement with Russia conformed to the narrative in which he cast himself as the male lover and Russia or the Russian people as the feminine beloved. . . .

In 1933–1934, Kennan was not the only American diplomat whose mission to Moscow was eroticized during what those diplomats labeled the "honeymoon" period of Soviet-American relations. The early Soviet women's liberation movement still flourished, and many of Kennan's colleagues had affairs with Russian women. Among the men in the embassy, talking about and sharing these heterosexual relationships tightened the friendships that arose from their work together in the pioneering Moscow mission.

The concept of homosociality hypothesizes that there is a continuum—not an equivalence but a continuous spectrum—between male friendship and male homosexual desire. Homosociality can occur in various circumstances. Bonding may come from collective effort in play or work. In an erotic or competitive triangle, the feeling linking the two rivals, or collaborators, for the attention of the third member may be stronger than the bond between either of them and the person they both desire. There can be a complex interplay of heterosexual and homosocial relations if, for example, two men have the same female partner or if they both share vicariously in the sexual activity of the same third parties. Homosocial emotion may have heightened both the exuberance of United States embassy officials during the honeymoon period in United States–Soviet relations and their letdown and resentment at the Soviet government, whose subsequent obstinacy and repression soured both diplomatic relations and their lives in Moscow.

Bullitt set the fraternity-like atmosphere when he handpicked forty men for his staff on the assumption that "there is absolutely nothing for a woman to do here." "There were usually two or three ballerinas running around the Embassy," Bohlen remembered, "the ballerinas were given free run of the diplomatic corps, and many temporary liaisons were formed." Bohlen's formulation "given free run," which suggested domestic animals being allowed to roam in a larger than usual enclosure, underplayed the agency of men such as himself who sought sexual relationships. Bohlen's use of the passive voice also camouflaged the homosociality between the Soviet authorities, who encouraged such liaisons for information, and the United States authority, in the person of Bullitt, who "constantly urged us to mix with the Russians." Bohlen left no doubt as to the kind of "mixing" when he added that, "as a bachelor, I eagerly carried out his instructions." . . .

The more enjoyment "the new boys in town," as Bohlen called his colleagues and himself, had in 1933–1934, the more they would feel assaulted—personally, professionally, and politically—when Stalin shut down contact with foreigners and denied the Americans the privileges they had enjoyed. They felt Stalin's efforts to isolate the Soviet people as a kind of aggression against them, and this sentiment contributed to what became their visceral anticommunism. For Kennan, who would wistfully remember the embassy drawing rooms filled with a "numerous, curious and friendly company of Russian guests"—including such members of the Bolshevik elite destroyed in Stalin's purges as Bukharin and Karl Radek—Stalin's repression left those rooms, and a vital aspect of his life, "emptier and emptier."

Kennan also witnessed the brief exuberance and long resentment of Ambassador Bullitt. In December 1933 at his first meeting with Bullitt, Stalin stressed the near certainty of a Japanese attack on the Soviet Union in the spring of 1934. Bullitt assured him that the United States would put its moral support behind preserving peace in the Far East. Stalin may have read more into this assurance than Bullitt intended, and Bullitt, influenced by the gala circumstances of their meeting, may have promised more than he reported to President Franklin D. Roosevelt.

That meeting, a dinner on December 20, had elements of seduction and initiation as well as of diplomacy. The difference between Bullitt's report on the dinner immediately after it occurred and his account thirteen years later suggests how exuberant homosociality, once transmuted by disappointment, could intensify resentment and hostility toward the Soviets. Bullitt reported to Roosevelt that at the nearly all-male gathering, "everyone . . . got into the mood of a college fraternity banquet, and discretion was conspicuous by its absence." Commissar for Foreign Affairs Maxim Litvinov whispered to the delighted American, "Do you realize that everyone at this table has completely forgotten that anyone is here except the members of the inner gang?" Bullitt carefully noted not just Stalin's message, but also his fingers, hand, mustache, mouth, lips, nostrils, and especially, his eyes, which, he reported to Roosevelt, appeared "a dark brown filmed with a dark blue. . . . intensely shrewd and continuously smiling." Unlike many other observers, he did not mention Stalin's bad teeth or pockmarked face. Bullitt recorded that as he was leaving, Stalin "took my head in his two hands and gave me a large kiss! I swallowed my astonishment, and, when he turned up his face for a return kiss, I delivered it." Kennan recalled that the ambassador was so "thrilled" by his "evening with Stalin and the inner circle" that he woke Kennan up and sat on the latter's bed dictating an account of the events—and thereby shared them in another intimate setting.

Thirteen years afterward, by which time Bullitt had become fiercely anticommuist, the remembered intensity powered a different discourse. Speaking as if he had been seduced and betrayed, Bullitt warned [Secretary of Commerce] Henry Wallace in February 1946 that "these Bolsheviks are charming people." He could not resist describing Stalin's eyes and mentioning that "Stalin at one time was very affectionate toward me." Bullitt related that "he kissed me full on the mouth," but he did not mention the return kiss. Instead, he exclaimed, "What a horrible experience that was!" Bullitt then shifted the discussion to Stalin's bloody purges and explained that "the Russians were like an amoeba, sending out pseudopods, surrounding" others. This conversation, which took place when Kennan was writing the LT, demonstrated how a nascent Cold War discourse could slide from a conflicted personal experience, to reference to Stalin's domestic brutality, to construction of an inhuman international threat. . . .

From 1937 until his return to Moscow in 1944, Kennan developed critiques of . . . the Soviet Union. . . . Although grounded in rational expertise, Kennan's ideas were shaped by emotion: his sensualized attachment to the Russian people, his antipathy to the Soviet government, and his alienation from American society. In 1942, lecturing to American officials interned with him in Nazi Germany, he applied to the Soviet Union the psychoanalytic "theory of the parellel [*sic*] between the childhood psychology of people[s] and of individuals . . . which has been extensively developed by Freud." Kennan, who sought out Anna Freud in London in 1944, found that the discourse of psychology buttressed his claim to special insights, offering knowledge that was "objective" even if not discernible by others. Kennan examined "the childhood of the Russian people," the development of "adolescent Russia," and Russia's fall after 1917 "right back into the psychology of the XVII century. . . . with all the strength and freshness of their youth." He coupled his psychoanalysis with a theory of racial development: under communism, the Russians had regressed into a "semi-Asiatic people." In the LT, Kennan's psychoanalytic jargon would have two implications: the Soviet government suffered from a mental pathology that made major negotiations unfeasible and unnecessary, and Russia was an enigma that could be interpreted only by specialists such as Kennan and Bohlen. . . .

As Soviet-American relations deteriorated in 1944–1946, Kennan's emotive rhetoric helped delegitimate the wartime policy of striving to cooperate with the Soviets. Bitter at Soviet restrictions on his access to the Russian people and to officials, Kennan disparaged and discouraged the ties that others might develop with Soviet leaders. He depicted those Americans seeking postwar cooperation with the Soviets as prone to "gushing assumptions of chumminess." The phrase called up an image of gullible United States officials, almost inevitably men, emasculating themselves and their nation with uncontrolled flows of homosocial feeling. . . .

Kennan did his best to distance the United States from the Soviet Union. On a variety of issues he advised the State Department against informing, consulting with, inquiring from, or otherwise engaging with the Soviets. Shortly before the February 1945 Yalta conference, he wrote Bohlen that the United States should adopt a spheres-of-influence policy, writing off Eastern Europe and abandoning efforts at cooperation. Characteristically, Kennan loaded and polarized the issue of cooperation by employing gendered/sexualized language. He contrasted the "political manliness" of those who would isolate the Soviets with the emotionalism and implied femininity and/or homosexuality of those who "yearn" for "intimate collaboration" with the Soviets. Kennan urged aloofness from what he regarded as an immoral Soviet domination of Poland. Presidential adviser Harry Hopkins concluded from a talk with Kennan: "Then you think it's just sin, and we should be agin it." "That's just about right," Kennan replied. At the December 1945 Allied foreign ministers conference, when Secretary of State Byrnes stood on a public balcony and shook hands with a Soviet leader, sparking cheers from the Moscow crowd below, Kennan became "furious," an embassy official observed, "because such gestures masked the true nature of Soviet-American relations." By the time Kennan wrote the LT, his concept of isolating the Soviets had expanded into containing the Soviets.

Although bitterness did not alone lead Kennan to advocate isolating and containing the Soviet Union, such emotion made it difficult for him to see cooperation or close contact with Stalin's government as anything but debased "collaboration." In the LT, Kennan channeled his complex feelings about the Soviet government, the Russian people, American society, and his own career into an emotional sermon that helped shape the meaning of the Cold War. As he recalled, "I am a person who rouses himself to intellectual activity only when he is stung. The more outraged I become at the preposterousness of the things other people say, the better I do." Although Kennan reported in his memoir that he had written the LT in a state of outrage, this memory misses part of the documentary record. With United States sentiment already concerned about Stalin's [harsh anti-capitalist] election speech of February 9, 1946, State Department colleagues Harrison Freeman "Doc" Matthews and Elbridge Durbrow advised Kennan that the department would welcome a major "interpretive analysis" from him. . . .

The "whole truth" of the LT actually invoked a fantastic reality in which leaders of the Soviet Union appeared as an inhuman force, without morality, beyond the appeal of reason, unable to appreciate objective fact or truth, and compelled to destroy almost every decent aspect of life in the West. Echoing his painful experience with Stalin's crackdown in the late 1930s, Kennan asserted that the "most disquieting feature of diplomacy in Moscow" was the isolation from Soviet policy makers, whom one cannot "see and cannot influence."

At the end of the LT, Kennan assured his readers that the Soviet Union did not want war, was weaker than the United States, and could be contained without war if the United States and the West took the necessary steps. Yet it was his emotionalized picture of the Soviet threat and his militarized language that grabbed the attention of readers. Kennan described the Soviet Union as "impervious to [the] logic of reason and . . . highly sensitive to [the] logic of force." The United States should determine how to apply such logic of force with "political general staff work. . . . approached with [the] same thoroughness and care as [the] solution of [a] major strategic problem in war." To Kennan's later consternation, many people concluded that containment required a massive military buildup.

Kennan's reliance on the discourse of pathological psychology to describe Soviet leaders dramatized his argument that the United States could not expect, and should not try, to have mutually understanding relations with Moscow. Kennan described Soviet leaders as "afflicted" with acute insecurity and "mentally too dependent to question [their] self-hypnotism." He urged Americans to observe the Soviet Union with the attitude "with which [a] doctor studies [an] unruly and unreasonable individual." In a sentence that was itself tortured, he portrayed Soviet leaders as mentally confined by the Marxist dogma that justified "the dictatorship without which they did not know how to rule," the "cruelties they did not dare not to inflict." Morally as well as mentally crippled, the Soviet leadership had "in the name of Marxism . . . sacrificed every single ethical value." Extending the imagery of pathology and dehumanization, he likened "world communism" to a "malignant parasite." . . .

Other rhetorical strategies, including the near absence in the text of recognizable people and the intensive use of the passive voice, helped construct this drama of polarization. The 5,540 words of the LT included the names of only two persons: Lenin, who was mentioned once in passing, and Stalin, who was quoted once and mentioned twice. The principal agents in the LT were not people, but abstract noun phrases, such as the "steady advance of uneasy Russian nationalism," the "instinctive urges of Russian rulers," and the "official propaganda machine." The monster of the LT was so scary and such an unlikely negotiating partner because it was not a person who, however cruel and ambitious, was nevertheless human and able to compromise, but a soulless "machine" or "force."

In one of the most widely quoted sentences of the LT, Kennan wrote: "In summary, we have here a political force committed fanatically to the belief that with [the] US there can be no permanent *modus vivendi,* that it is desirable and necessary that the internal harmony of our society be disrupted, our traditional way of life be destroyed, the international authority of our state be broken, if Soviet power is to be secure." Because the agent here was an abstract "political force" and because much of the sentence was in the passive voice and the archaic subjunctive, it was difficult to challenge its underlying premises by asking whether the leaders of the Soviet Union had such designs, how capable they were of achieving them, and how Kennan came to know of them. The prospects for American resistance appeared particularly grim because the reader could glean little idea of how the United States would "be disrupted" and "be destroyed." The LT had many sentences with similar construction: "Poor will be set against rich, black against white, young against old. . . ." "No effort will be spared to discredit and combat. . . ." The repetition of passive sentences—all with an archaic tone and all conveying the message of unlimited action by an evil force—suggested a religious text or a fairy tale. Such "realism" one had to accept largely on faith.

The tropes of gender in the LT were more nuanced that the representations of pathology. Throughout the document, the Soviet leadership, whether portrayed as a machine, a force, or as persons, engaged in the driving, aggressive behavior conventionally associated with masculinity. Kennan underscored this association in the LT by repeating the word "penetration" five times in reference to the Soviets' insistent, unwanted intrusion. The Soviet leadership appeared as monstrously masculine. Kennan represented the Communist objective as splitting open Western societies that were already too divided. "Efforts will be made . . . to disrupt national self confidence . . . to stimulate all forms of disunity."

Juxtaposed to this image of the Soviet government as a masculine rapist was Kennan's representation of the West as dangerously accessible through "a wide variety of national associations or bodies which can be dominated or influenced by such [Communist] penetration." Kennan listed such potentially subversive elements: "labor unions, youth leagues, women's organizations, racial societies, religious societies. . . . liberal magazines."

Kennan proposed that the West respond to the monstrous hypermasculinity of the Soviet Union by itself acting more masculine. He urged that the United States "tighten" up, achieve greater "cohesion, firmness and vigor," and approach the Soviet Union with the conventionally masculine virtues of "courage, detachment, objectivity, and . . . determination not to be emotionally provoked or unseated." The United States should play the "doctor" and calm the "hysterical anti-Sovietism" of those who expected or who wanted a war with Moscow. In the LT, implicitly gendered language helped construct an attention-grabbing morality tale.

Despite the organization of the LT in five sections, the most significant turn of argument appears midway through the last part, where Kennan moved from demonizing the Soviet Union to prescribing how the United Sates and the West should respond to this threat. Although scholars have long noted Kennan's reassurance that Soviet power could be held back without a war, they have not noted the significance of the very next sentence, in which Kennan shifted focus from the Soviet threat to the West's internal divisions, while linking these two problems. Characteristically, he signaled this move, and the leap of logic that it required, with the word "really." He wrote that the Soviets' "success will really depend on [the] degree of cohesion, firmness and vigor which [the] Western World can muster."

The most decisive arena lay, not in foreign lands, but in the United States: "Every courageous and incisive measure to solve [the] internal problems of our own society . . . is a diplomatic victory over Moscow worth a thousand diplomatic notes and joint communiqués." . . .

The LT's message about domestic problems reflected a long-held ambition. In 1933–1934, Kennan had hoped to use the "freshness" of Russian society somehow to revitalize American society. In 1938, he had advocated restricted suffrage and authoritarian government to counter what he saw as the nation's self-indulgence, political corruption, and crass commercialism. In the conclusion of the 1947 "X" article, Kennan depicted the deterioration in United States–Soviet relations as a fair trial of America's "national quality. . . . The issue of Soviet-American relations is in essence a test of the over-all worth of the United States." He expressed "gratitude" that the "implacable challenge" of the Kremlin forced Americans to "pull themselves together." Although he would soon deplore the excesses of the Cold War, Kennan at first welcomed that cataclysm. . . .

The LT was seized upon by United States officials, some of whom were already warning of the "Soviet threat" but with less effective rhetoric. A State Department colleague observed that Matthews, who had encouraged Kennan to write the LT, "engineered" distribution of the text to United States officials in Washington and around the world. Understanding that Kennan's language was intrinsic to his message, the usually parsimonious department reproduced the entire document, explaining that it was "not subject to condensation." The copies went out on March 5, 1946, coincidentally the day of Winston Churchill's Iron Curtain speech. An observer found United States diplomats in Europe "very excited" by the LT's "new line." With masculine-inflected language, Henry Norweb, the United States ambassador to Cuba, lauded Kennan's "masterpiece of 'thinking things out,'" his "realism devoid of hysteria," and his "courageous approach to a problem."

Another promoter of the LT was Navy Secretary James Forrestal, who had been trying to persuade others of the Soviet threat. Forrestal's biographers noted that he found in Kennan's analysis the "authoritative explanation he had been seeking." Forrestal sent copies to Truman, the cabinet, newspapers, and people in Congress and in business, and he made the LT required reading for navy officers. With this sudden acclaim, Kennan became a "transformed person," according to a colleague. Brought back from Moscow in April 1946, he gave some thirty department-sponored lectures across the United States, seeking to "instill into our public appreciation for basic realities"—"realities" that echoed the LT. With Forrestal's backing, Kennan became deputy commander and a teacher at the National War College in August 1946 and the first director of the State Department's Policy Planning Staff in 1947.

Although the LT alone did not cause the shift in United States policy toward the Soviets, the cable helped restrict debate. With its simplified, emotional, and yet authoritative explanation of Soviet behavior, the LT encouraged United States officials to bypass the vexing problems of understanding and accommodating the Soviets. Citing the LT, Bohlen, then special assistant to the secretary of state and a chief adviser on relations with the Soviet Union, recommended that rather than agonizing over the possibility of cooperating with the Soviets, the United States government should "take as accepted" the imperative of containing them. . . .

The pervasiveness of emotion, sensuality, and personal aspiration in shaping Kennan's attitudes and policies toward the Soviet Union suggests that historians need to deepen the debate about the origins of the Cold War and to widen diplomatic history by exploring the connections between the personal and public lives of foreign policy makers. While Kennan's "florid showmanship in prose" makes a close reading of his language particularly rewarding, we should also examine the language of other historical subjects. We can gain a fuller understanding of both text and context if we understand that the text, such as the LT, often creates its own context by the use of allusive language that conditions—although it does not determine—how we interpret the text. This is especially the case with tropes of gender and pathology, which mobilize powerful emotions because they touch on the body, on personal fears and fantasies, and on unquestioned beliefs that take as "natural" relationships that are socially constructed.

The language of the LT fostered feelings that delegitimated cooperation with the Soviets. Emotions reframed the question from whether the United States and the Soviet Union could reach compromises that would safeguard the vital interests of both nations, to whether it was realistic and manly to deal with a regime fanatically committed to destroying the United States and everything else decent. Kennan's rhetorical strategies in the LT worked so effectively because the Truman administration was looking for a clarifying statement and because Kennan—with the authority of his expertise and his ostensible realism—was able to appeal to emotions in the name of reason.

FURTHER READING

Gar Alperovitz, *Atomic Diplomacy* (1965 and 1985)
———, *The Decision to Use the Atomic Bomb* (1995)
———, "Why the U.S. Dropped the Atomic Bomb," *Technology Review,* 93 (1990), 22–34
Stephen Ambrose and Douglas Brinkley, *Rise to Globalism* (1997)
Terry H. Anderson, *The United States, Great Britain, and the Cold War* (1981)
Barton J. Bernstein, ed., *The Atomic Bomb* (1975)
———, "The Atomic Bombings Reconsidered," *Foreign Affairs,* 74 (1995), 135–142
———, ed., *Politics and Policies of the Truman Administration* (1970)
Paul Boyer, *By the Bomb's Early Light* (1986)
H. W. Brands, *The Devil We Knew* (1993)
Douglas Brinkley, ed., *Dean Acheson and the Making of U.S. Foreign Policy* (1993)
Bulletin of the Atomic Scientists, 41 (1985), entire issue for August
McGeorge Bundy, *Danger and Survival* (1990) (nuclear-arms race)
David Callahan, *Dangerous Capabilities* (1990) (on Paul Nitze)
James Chace, *Acheson* (1998)
Warren I. Cohen, *America in the Age of Soviet Power* (1995)
Committee for the Compilation of Materials on Damage Caused by the Atomic Bombs in
    Hiroshima and Nagasaki, *Hiroshima and Nagasaki* (1981)
Richard Crockatt, *The Fifty Years War* (1995)
James E. Cronin, *The World the Cold War Made* (1996)
Jeffrey M. Diefendorf et al., eds., *American Policy and the Reconstruction of West
    Germany* (1993)
Robert J. Donovan, *Conflict and Crisis* (1977)
———, *Tumultuous Years* (1982)
Christopher Duggan and Christopher Wagstaff, eds., *Italy in the Cold War* (1996)
Carol Eisenberg, *Drawing the Line* (1996) (Germany)
David Ellwood, *Rebuilding Europe* (1992)
Herbert Feis, *The Atomic Bomb and the End of World War II* (1966)
———, *From Trust to Terror* (1970)
Robert H. Ferrell, *Harry S. Truman* (1994)
John Lewis Gaddis, *The Long Peace* (1987)
———, *Russia, the Soviet Union, and the United States* (1990)
———, *Strategies of Containment* (1982)
———, *The United States and the Origins of the Cold War* (1972)
Lloyd C. Gardner, *Architects of Illusion* (1970)
Richard Gardner, *Sterling-Dollar Diplomacy* (1969)
John Gimbel, *The American Occupation of Germany* (1968)
———, *The Origins of the Marshall Plan* (1976)
———, *Science, Technology, and Reparations* (1990)
James L. Gormly, *The Collapse of the Grand Alliance, 1945–1948* (1987)
Alonzo Hamby, *Man of the People* (1995) (Truman biography)
Fraser J. Harbutt, *The Iron Curtain* (1986)
John L. Harper, *American Visions of Europe* (1994)
———, *America and the Reconstruction of Italy* (1986)
Robert M. Hathaway, *Ambiguous Partnership: Britain and America, 1944–1947* (1981)
Gregg Herken, *The Winning Weapon* (1981)

George Herring, *Aid to Russia, 1941–1946* (1973)

James Hershberg, *James B. Conant and the Birth of the Nuclear Age* (1994)

Walter Hixson, *George F. Kennan* (1990)

———, *Parting the Curtain: Propaganda, Culture, and the Cold War* (1997)

Michael J. Hogan, *A Cross of Iron: Harry S. Truman and the Origins of the National Security State* (1998)

———, ed., *Hiroshima in History and Memory* (1996)

———, *The Marshall Plan* (1987)

David Holloway, *The Soviet Union and the Arms Race* (1984)

———, *Stalin and the Bomb* (1994)

John O. Iatrides, *Revolt in Athens* (1972)

———, ed., *Greece in the 1940s* (1981)

——— and Linda Wrigley, eds., *Greece at the Crossroads* (1995)

Walter Isaacson and Evan Thomas, *The Wise Men* (1986)

Howard Jones, *"A New Kind of War"* (1989)

Lawrence S. Kaplan, *The United States and NATO* (1984)

Frank Kofsky, *Harry S. Truman and the War Scare of 1948* (1993)

Gabriel Kolko and Joyce Kolko, *The Limits of Power* (1972)

Bruce Kuniholm, *The Origins of the Cold War in the Near East* (1980)

Walter LaFeber, *America, Russia, and the Cold War* (1997)

Deborah Larson, *Anatomy of Distrust* (1997)

Melvyn Leffler, *A Preponderance of Power* (1992)

———, *The Specter of Communism* (1994)

———, "Inside Enemy Archives: The Cold War Reopened," *Foreign Affairs,* 75 (1996), 120–135

——— and David S. Painter, eds., *Origins of the Cold War* (1994)

Ralph Levering, *The Cold War* (1994)

Geir Lundestad, *The American "Empire"* (1990)

———, *The American Non-Policy Towards Eastern Europe, 1943–1947* (1975)

Thomas J. McCormick, *America's Half Century* (1995)

David McLellan, *Dean Acheson* (1976)

Robert J. McMahon, *The Cold War on the Periphery* (1994) (India and Pakistan)

——— and Thomas G. Paterson, eds., *The Origins of the Cold War* (1999)

Robert H. McNeal, *Stalin* (1988)

Robert J. Maddox, *Weapons for Victory* (1995) (atomic bombings)

Michael Mandlebaum, *The Fate of Nations* (1988)

Vojtech Mastny, *The Cold War and Soviet Insecurity* (1996)

David Mayers, *The Ambassadors and America's Soviet Policy* (1995)

Richard L. Merritt, *Democracy Imposed* (1995) (Germany)

Robert L. Messer, *The End of an Alliance* (1982)

James E. Miller, *The United States and Italy, 1940–1950* (1986)

Alan Milward, *The Reconstruction of Western Europe, 1945–51* (1984)

Wilson D. Miscamble, *George F. Kennan and the Making of American Foreign Policy* (1992)

Robert P. Newman, "Ending the War with Japan: Paul Nitze's Early Surrender Counter-factual," *Pacific Historical Review,* 64 (1995), 167–194

Frank Ninkovich, *Modernity and Power* (1994)

David S. Painter, *The Cold War* (1999)

Thomas G. Paterson, ed., *Cold War Critics* (1971)

———, *Meeting the Communist Threat* (1988)

———, *On Every Front: The Making and Unmaking of the Cold War* (1992)

———, *Soviet-American Confrontation* (1973)

James T. Patterson, *Great Expectations: The United States, 1945–1974* (1996)

William E. Pemberton, *Harry S. Truman* (1989)

Edward Pessen, *Losing Our Souls: The American Experience in the Cold War* (1993)

Edvard Radzinsky, *Stalin* (1996)

David Reynolds, ed., *The Origins of the Cold War in Europe* (1994)
T. Michael Ruddy, *The Cautious Diplomat* (1986) (on Bohlen)
Thomas A. Schwartz, *America's Germany* (1991)
Michael S. Sherry, *In the Shadow of War* (1995)
Martin Sherwin, *A World Destroyed* (1975)
E. Timothy Smith, *The United States, Italy, and NATO* (1991)
Gaddis Smith, *Dean Acheson* (1972)
Joseph Smith, ed., *The Origins of NATO* (1990)
John Spanier, *American Foreign Policy Since World War II* (1997)
Ronald Steel, *Walter Lippmann and the American Century* (1980)
Mark A. Stoler, *George C. Marshall* (1989)
"Symposium: Soviet Archives: Recent Revelations and Cold War Historiography,"
    Diplomatic History, 21 (1997), 215–305
Ronald Takaki, *Hiroshima* (1995)
William Taubman, *Stalin's American Policy* (1982)
Athan G. Theoharis, *The Yalta Myths* (1970)
Hugh Thomas, *Armed Truce* (1987)
Kenneth W. Thompson, *Cold War Theories* (1981)
Adam Ulam, *The Rivals* (1971)
Dimitri Volkogonov, *Stalin* (1991)
Reinhold Wagnleitner, *Coca-Colonization of the Cold War* (1994) (U.S.-Austria)
J. Samuel Walker, "The Decision to Use the Bomb: A Historiographical Update,"
    Diplomatic History, 14 (1993), 97–114
———, *Henry A. Wallace and American Foreign Policy* (1976)
———, *Prompt and Utter Destruction* (1997) (atomic bombings)
Irwin M. Wall, *The United States and the Making of Postwar France* (1991)
Piotr S. Wandycz, *The United States and Poland* (1980)
Imanuel Wexler, *The Marshall Plan Revisited* (1983)
Graham White and John Maze, *Henry A. Wallace* (1995)
Stephen J. Whitfield, *The Culture of the Cold War* (1996)
Allan M. Winkler, *Life Under a Cloud* (1993)
Lawrence S. Wittner, *American Intervention in Greece, 1943–1949* (1982)
———, *One World or None* (1993) (disarmament movement)
Daniel Yergin, *Shattered Peace* (1977)
Vladislav Zubok and Constantine Pleshakov, *Inside the Kremlin's Cold War* (1996)

Mao's China and the Chances for Sino-American Accommodation

The landmark Chinese Communist revolution reshaped one of the world's oldest, most populous civilizations, reconfigured Asian foreign relations, and initiated a new phase of the Cold War. The United States intervened substantially in the conflict during the 1940s. At the height of the Second World War, massive U.S. assistance flowed to the regime of Jiang Jieshi (Chiang Kai-shek), leader of the Guomindang (GMD) or Nationalists to assist China's resistance to Japanese expansionism. In July 1944, the first official American representatives, known as the Dixie Mission, established a presence in the territory controlled by Mao Zedong's Communist Party and began providing military aid and advice to that faction as well. Once the war ended, however, prospects for Chinese unity dimmed, as the two rival groups quickly turned their guns on each other.

Hopeful that a non-Communist China could play a pivotal, stabilizing role in postwar Asia, Washington continued to bolster Jiang's GMD with large-scale economic and military aid, approximately $3 billion from 1945 to 1949. But the corrupt Jiang squandered much of the aid and stubbornly resisted recommendations for reform. He also obstructed American mediation between the warring parties, most notably during the Marshall Mission (December 1945 to December 1946) when presidential envoy General George C. Marshall negotiated a temporary cease-fire but failed to bring about a sharing of political power. Washington nonetheless continued to back the Nationalist cause, even after a string of Communist military victories. After two decades of civil war, Mao's communists claimed victory in October 1949 and established the People's Republic of China (PRC).

In this politically electric atmosphere, the Truman administration groped for an appropriate response to revolutionary change. What was the new Chinese government's relationship with the Soviet Union? Would Mao's China emulate Josip Tito's Yugoslavia and reject alignment with Moscow? Or would it become a dangerous member of the Soviet camp in the Cold War? Would the new PRC leaders make good on China's treaty obligations? Would they restart trade and respect foreign investment with the West? Or would Communist party officials seek a radical restructuring of foreign relations that greatly diminished U.S. interests? Could China's Marxism coexist peacefully with the capitalist world? Could the PRC's suspicions of Western imperialism and its ardent nationalism be moderated so as to allow peaceful relations? How should Washington treat the defeated Guomindang, exiled to the island of Formosa (Taiwan)? What implications did China's revolution have for the rest of East Asia—especially such volatile areas as the Korean peninsula, occupied Japan, and colonial French Indochina? Would China's revolution inspire similar unrest all across the non-Western world?

The most pressing issue was U.S. recognition of the People's Republic of China. As with the origins of the Soviet-American Cold War, recently released documents and newly published memoirs from the Communist side, Chinese and Soviet alike, have brought more texture to the subject. Yet the new sources have by no means resolved all points of debate. Whether President Harry S. Truman and Secretary of State Dean Acheson withheld recognition from Mao because of their fear of the domestic political repercussions remains a point of disagreement among historians. Some scholars suggest instead that the Truman administration had been so inveterately anticommunist that it interpreted Mao's victory as a Soviet advance in Asia and hence passed up Chinese overtures for negotiations. Others have argued that strong Chinese anti-Americanism and attractions to Soviet Communism made chances of Sino-American accommodation minimal. Historians agree, however, that the Korean War killed all chances for an accommodation. The origins of American nonrecognition policy, which lasted until 1979, is the subject of this chapter.

 D O C U M E N T S

In May and June 1949, the U.S. ambassador in China, John Leighton Stuart, met with Huang Hua, a communist foreign-affairs official. Stuart's two telegrams to Washington, which constitute Document 1, reported the conversations and the tender of an "invitation" from Mao Zedong and Zhou Enlai to talk with them. In late May, Zhou Enlai, Mao's chief foreign-policy adviser, indirectly approached the U.S. consulate in Beijing. Consul General O. Edmund Clubb reported this *démarche* to Washington in a June 1 telegram, reprinted as Document 2. The State Department's initial answer to the Zhou *démarche,* dated June 14, is Document 3, followed by Document 4, President Truman's cool response toward the *démarche,* on June 16.

On July 30, 1949, the Department of State issued a "White Paper"—a huge volume of documents and analysis that defended pre-1949 American policies toward China against charges that the United States had "lost" China. Secretary of State Dean Acheson's public letter transmitting the book to the president is included as Document 5. Document 6 is a speech of August 18 by Mao Zedong. Several weeks earlier, he had announced that China was "leaning to one side"—the Soviet side—in the Cold War. In his August speech, he vented his strong anti-American views, accusing the United States of aggression. In Document 7, from the memoir of Bo Yibo (first published in China in 1991), the PRC's first finance minister explains the ideological and strategic assumptions behind Mao's decision to "lean to one side" and describes Mao's late 1949 trip to Moscow to sign the Sino-Soviet Treaty of Friendship and Alliance. Although the People's Republic jealously guarded its independence and held out the possibility of relations with all nations, the defense of the revolution, Bo insisted, required friendship with the Soviet Union. In Document 8, a speech of January 5, 1950, Senator William Knowland of California, a McCarthyite anticommunist and member of the "China lobby," argues against U.S. recognition of the People's Republic.

1. U.S. Ambassador John Leighton Stuart
Reports Mao's Overture, 1949

Telegram of May 14, 1949

Huang [Hua] called my residence last evening remaining almost 2 hours. Our conversation was friendly and informal. I refrained from political remarks until he opened way which he did after few personal exchanges. I then spoke earnestly of great desire that peoples of all countries had for peace, including, emphatically, my own, of dangerous situation developing despite this universal popular will; of indescribable horrors of next war; of my conviction that much, but not all, present tension due to misunderstandings, fears, suspicions which could be cleared away by mutual frankness; of fears Americans and other non-Communists had of Marxist-Leninist doctrine, subscribed to by CCP [Chinese Communist party], that world revolution and overthrow of capitalistic governments necessary, thus proclaiming subversive interference or armed invasion as fixed policy. Huang spoke of Chinese people's resentment at American aid to Kmt [Kuomintang, or Nationalist party] and other "mistakes" of US Policy to which I briefly replied.

Huang asked about my plans and I told him of my instructions, adding that I was glad to stay long enough for symbolic purpose of demonstrating American people's interest in welfare of Chinese people as whole; that I wished to maintain friendly relations of past; that being near end of my active life I hoped to be able somewhat to help restore these relations as I knew my Government and people desired; that my aim was unity, peace, truly democratic government and international good will for which Huang knew I had worked all my life in China.

Huang expressed much interest in recognition of Communist China by USA on terms of equality and mutual benefit. I replied that such terms together with accepted international practice with respect to treaties would be only proper basis. He was greatly surprised at my explanation of status of armed forces in China particularly Marines in Shanghai. Our side of story, that is desire to protect American lives during civil disturbances and chaotic conditions brought on by war, appeared never to have occurred to him. He was obviously impressed. I explained question of national government was internal; that Communists themselves at present had none; that it was customary to recognize whatever government clearly had support of people of country and was able and willing to perform its international obligations; that therefore USA and other countries could do nothing but await developments in China. I hinted that most other nations would tend to follow our lead. I explained functions of foreign consulates in maintaining informal relations with *de facto* regional authorities.

Huang expounded upon needs of China for commercial and other relations with foreign countries. He said instructions had been issued to all military units to protect safety and interests of foreigners. Intrusion into my bedroom [by Communist soldiers] was discussed and he promised to do his best in constantly shifting military situation to trace offenders. He explained that first Communist troops in city had not been prepared or properly instructed on treatment of foreigners.

This document can be found in U.S. Department of State, *Foreign Relations of the United States, 1949* (Washington, D.C.: Government Printing Office, 1978), VIII, 745–746.

Telegram of June 30, 1949

Huang Hua called on me by appointment June 28. He reported that he had received message from Mao Tse-tung and Chou En-lai assuring me that they would welcome me to Peiping if I wished to visit Yenching University. Background of this suggestion is as follows:

In early June Philip Fugh, in one of his conversations with Huang, asked casually, and not under instructions from me, if it would be possible for me to travel to Peiping to visit my old University as had been my habit in previous years on my birthday and Commencement. At that time Huang made no comment. However, 2 weeks later, June 18 to be precise, in discussing my return to Washington for consultation, Huang himself raised question with Fugh of whether time permitted my making trip to Peiping. Fugh made no commitment, commenting only that he himself had made this suggestion 2 weeks earlier. Neither Fugh nor I followed up this suggestion but apparently Huang did. Present message (almost an invitation) is reply.

Regardless whether initiation of this suggestion is considered [by] Peiping to have come from me or from Communists, I can only regard Huang's message as veiled invitation from Mao and Chou to talk with them while ostensibly visiting Yenching. To accept would undoubtedly be gratifying to them, would give me chance to describe American policy; its anxieties regarding Communism and world revolution; its desires for China's future; and would enable me to carry to Washington most authoritative information regarding CCP intentions. Such trip would be step toward better mutual understanding and should strengthen more liberal anti-Soviet element in CCP. It would provide unique opportunity for American official to talk to top Chinese Communists in informal manner which may not again present itself. It would be imaginative, adventurous indication of US open-minded attitude towards changing political trends in China and would probably have beneficial effect on future Sino-American relations.

On negative side, trip to Peiping before my return to US on consultation would undoubtedly start rumors and speculations in China and might conceivably embarrass Department because of American criticism. It would probably be misunderstood by my colleagues in Diplomatic Corps who might feel that US representative was first to break united front policy which we have sponsored toward Communist regime and might prove beginning of trek of chiefs of mission to Peiping on one pretext or another. Trip to Peiping at this time invariably suggests idea of making similar one to Canton [temporary Nationalist capital] before my return to US.

While visiting both capitals might effectively dramatize American interest in Chinese people as a whole, it might also appear as peace-making gesture, unwarranted interference in China's internal affairs, and would probably be misunderstood by Chinese Communists, thus undoing any beneficial effects of visit north. Finally, trip of US Ambassador to Peiping at this time would enhance greatly prestige, national and international, of Chinese Communists and Mao himself and in a sense would be second step on our part (first having been my remaining Nanking) toward recognition of Communist regime.

This document can be found in U.S. Department of State, *Foreign Relations of the United States, 1949* (Washington, D.C.: Government Printing Office, 1978), VIII, 766–767.

I received clear impression that Mao, Chou and Huang are very much hoping that I make this trip, whatever their motives. I, of course, gave Huang no answer to Mao's message. . . .

I have made this rather full statement of case for Department's consideration and decision. I am, of course, ready to make journey by either means should Department consider it desirable, and should be grateful for instructions earliest and nature of reply to Huang.

2. Zhou Enlai's (Chou En-lai's) *Démarche,* 1949

Following message given Assistant Military Attaché [David D.] Barrett May 31 by reliable intermediary, origin being Chou En-lai. Chou desired message be transmitted highest American authorities on top secret level without his name being mentioned, said in fact that if it were attributed him he would positively disavow it. Essential there be no leak his name to outside channels. Chou approved transmittal via Barrett who gave message me to transmit, but wanted name unmentioned even to Barrett. Chou desired what he said be conveyed to British, expressed preference transmittal be through Department.

There were few disagreements in CCP Party [*sic*] during agrarian stage revolution but with arrival at urban stage there have now developed disagreements of serious nature primarily re industrial-commercial policies and questions international relations. There is still no actual split within party but definite separation into liberal and radical wings, with Chou being of liberal, and Liu Shao-chi of radical wing. Chou however said it would be as big [a] mistake to base any policy toward China on idea there would develop major split in party as it was to attempt stop Communism in China by aiding Kmt [Kuomintang or Nationalist party] para-liberal group; feels that country is in such bad shape that most pressing need is reconstruction without regard political theories and that Mao Tse-tung concepts regarding private capital should be effected. Group feels there should have been coalition with Kmt because of party lack necessary knowledge regarding reconstruction, did not favor coalition with elements Ho Ying-chin-Chen Li-fu type but felt that without coalition reconstruction might be so delayed that party would lose support people. Realistic coalition advocated by group failed after big dispute involving most of higher figures in party with exception Mao (Chou was most careful in references to Mao). Coalition having failed, party must make most of bad job and obtain aid from outside. USSR cannot give aid which, therefore, must come from USA or possibly Britain. Chou favors getting help from USA and does not accord Soviet attitude regarding USA. Chou professedly sincere Communist but feels there has developed in USA economy something which is outside Marxist theories and that present American economic situation is, therefore, not susceptible Marxian interpretation. Therefore, Soviet attitude this respect wrong, feels American economy will continue without internal collapse or revolution and that there is no real bar to relations between USA and other governments, different political type. Unequivocally opposed

---

This document can be found in U.S. Department of State, *Foreign Relations of the United States, 1949* (Washington, D.C.: Government Printing Office, 1978), VIII, 357–360.

to American aid to Kmt but feels this was given from mistaken motives altruism rather than American viciousness. Feels USA has genuine interest in Chinese people which could become basis friendly relations between two countries.

Chou, speaking for liberal group, felt China should speedily establish *de facto* working relations with foreign governments.

This question will be prime issue in struggle between two wings. Radicals wish alliance with USSR, sort now existing between US and Britain, while liberals regard Soviet international policy as "crazy." Chou feels USSR is risking war which it is unable fight successfully and that good working relations between China and USA would have definite softening effect on party attitude toward Western countries. Chou desires these relations because he feels China desperately needs that outside aid which USSR unable give. Feels China on brink complete economic and physical collapse, by "physical" meaning breakdown physical well-being of people.

Chou feels USA should aid Chinese because: (1) China still not Communist and if Mao's policies are correctly implemented may not be so for long time; (2) democratic China would serve in international sphere as mediator between Western Powers and USSR; (3) China in chaos under any regime would be menace to peace Asia and world. Chou emphasized he spoke solely for certain people personally and not as member party, that he was not in position make formal or informal commitments or proposals. He hoped American authorities would recall wartime contacts with Communists and character and opinions of many whom they knew at that time. He hoped American authorities remembering this would believe there were genuine liberals in party who are concerned with everything connected with welfare Chinese people and "peace in our time" rather than doctrinaire theories. As spokesman for liberal wing he could say that when time came for Communist participation in international affairs his group would work within party for sensible solution impasse between USSR and west and would do its best make USSR discard policies leading to war. . . .

Chou emphasized that despite deficiencies, errors, disagreements, Communists had won military victory and in spite of same drawbacks would win future victory in reconstruction. Chou said Mao Tse-tung stands aside from party disputes using Chou, Liu Shao-chi and other liberals and radicals for specific purposes as he sees fit. Mao is genius in listening arguments various sides, then translating ideas into practical working policies.

Chou per source appeared very nervous and worried.

3. The State Department Responds to the *Démarche,* 1949

US has traditionally maintained close and friendly relations with China and has thruout past 100 years Sino-US relations, particularly since end last century, taken lead in efforts obtain internatl respect for Chi territorial and administrative integrity to end that China might develop as stable, united and independent nation. Unique record US relations with China gives clear evidence US had no territorial

This document can be found in U.S. Department of State, *Foreign Relations of the United States, 1949* (Washington, D.C.: Government Printing Office, 1978), VIII, 357–360.

designs on China and has sought no special privileges or rights which were not granted other fon [foreign] nations; US has sought maintain relations on basis mutual benefit and respect. Basic US objectives and principles remain unchanged.

In present situation US hopes maintain friendly relations with China and continue social, economic and polit relations with that country insofar as these relations based upon principle mutual respect and understanding and principle equality and are to mutual benefit two nations. In absence these basic principles, it can hardly be expected that full benefit Sino-US relations can be attained.

In this connection, US Govt and people are naturally disturbed and seriously concerned over certain recent occurrences which represent significant departure from these principles and some of which, in fact, widely at variance with accepted internatl custom and practice: Repeated bitter propaganda misrepresenting US actions and motives in China and elsewhere in world; arbitrary restrictions on movement and denial communications ConGen [U.S. consul general] Mukden and Commie failure reply to ConGen Peiping repeated representations this matter, including request withdraw ConGen and staff Mukden; and Commie failure take action release two US Marine flyers or reply ConGen Peiping representations this matter.

While we welcome expressions friendly sentiments, he must realize that they cannot be expected bear fruit until they have been translated into deeds capable of convincing American people that Sino-US relations can be placed upon solid basis mutual respect and understanding to benefit both nations.

4. President Harry S. Truman Downplays the *Démarche*, 1949

I brought the President up to date with respect to the Chou En-lai *Démarche* and read to him the pertinent sections of our reply. He approved this course of action and directs us to be most careful not to indicate any softening toward the Communists but to insist on judging their intentions by their actions.

5. Secretary of State Dean Acheson Presents the "White Paper," 1949

When peace came the United States was confronted with three possible alternatives in China: (1) it could have pulled out lock, stock and barrel; (2) it could have intervened militarily on a major scale to assist the Nationalists to destroy the Communists; (3) it could, while assisting the Nationalists to assert their authority over as much of China as possible, endeavor to avoid a civil war by working for a compromise between the two sides.

The first alternative would, and I believe American public opinion at the time so felt, have represented an abandonment of our international responsibilities and

---

Document 4 can be found in U.S. Department of State, *Foreign Relations of the United States, 1949* (Washington, D.C.: Government Printing Office, 1978), VIII, 388.

Document 5 can be found in U.S. Department of State, *United States Relations with China* (Washington, D.C.: Department of State Publication 3573, Far Eastern Series 30, 1949), pp. x, xiv–xvii.

of our traditional policy of friendship for China before we had made a determined effort to be of assistance. The second alternative policy, while it may look attractive theoretically and in retrospect, was wholly impracticable. The Nationalists had been unable to destroy the Communists during the 10 years before the war. Now after the war the Nationalists were . . . weakened, demoralized, and unpopular. They had quickly dissipated their popular support and prestige in the areas liberated from the Japanese by the conduct of their civil and military officials. The Communists on the other hand were much stronger than they had ever been and were in control of most of North China. Because of the ineffectiveness of the Nationalist forces which was later to be tragically demonstrated, the Communists probably could have been dislodged only by American arms. It is obvious that the American people would not have sanctioned such a colossal commitment of our armies in 1945 or later. We therefore came to the third alternative policy whereunder we faced the facts of the situation and attempted to assist in working out a *modus vivendi* which would avert civil war but nevertheless preserve and even increase the influence of the National Government. . . .

The reasons for the failures of the Chinese National Government appear in some detail in the attached record. They do not stem from any inadequacy of American aid. Our military observers on the spot have reported that the Nationalist armies did not lose a single battle during the crucial year of 1948 through lack of arms or ammunition. The fact was that the decay which our observers had detected in Chungking early in the war had fatally sapped the powers of resistance of the Kuomintang. Its leaders had proved incapable of meeting the crisis confronting them, its troops had lost the will to fight, and its Government had lost popular support. The Communists, on the other hand, through a ruthless discipline and fanatical zeal, attempted to sell themselves as guardians and liberators of the people. The Nationalist armies did not have to be defeated; they disintegrated. History has proved again and again that a regime without faith in itself and an army without morale cannot survive the test of battle. . . .

Fully recognizing that the heads of the Chinese Communist Party were ideologically affiliated with Moscow, our Government nevertheless took the view, in the light of the existing balance of forces in China, that peace could be established only if certain conditions were met. The Kuomintang would have to set its own house in order and both sides would have to make concessions so that the Government of China might become, in fact as well as in name, the Government of all China and so that all parties might function within the constitutional system of the Government. Both internal peace and constitutional development required that the progress should be rapid from one party government with a large opposition party in armed rebellion, to the participation of all parties, including the moderate noncommunist elements, in a truly national system of government.

None of these conditions has been realized. The distrust of the leaders of both the Nationalist and Communist Parties for each other proved too deep-seated to permit final agreement, notwithstanding temporary truces and apparently promising negotiations. The Nationalists, furthermore, embarked in 1946 on an over-ambitious military campaign in the face of warnings by General [George C.] Marshall that it not only would fail but would plunge China into economic chaos and eventually destroy the National Government. General Marshall pointed out that though Nationalist armies could, for a period, capture Communist-held cities, they could not destroy the Communist armies. Thus every Nationalist advance would expose their communications to attack by Communist guerrillas and compel them to retreat or to surrender their armies together with the munitions which the United States has furnished them. No estimate of a military situation has ever been more completely confirmed by the resulting facts.

The historic policy of the United States of friendship and aid toward the people of China was, however, maintained in both peace and war. Since V-J Day, the United States Government has authorized aid to Nationalist China in the form of grants and credits totaling approximately 2 billion dollars, an amount equivalent in value to more than 50 percent of the monetary expenditures of the Chinese Government and of proportionately greater magnitude in relation to the budget of that Government than the United States has provided to any nation of Western Europe since the end of the war. In addition to these grants and credits, the United States Government has sold the Chinese Government large quantities of military and civilian war surplus property with a total procurement cost of over 1 billion dollars, for which the agreed realization to the United States was 232 million dollars. A large proportion of the military supplies furnished the Chinese armies by the United States since V-J Day has, however, fallen into the hands of the Chinese Communists through the military ineptitude of the Nationalist leaders, the defections and surrenders, and the absence among their forces of the will to fight.

It has been urged that relatively small amounts of additional aid—military and economic—to the National Government would have enabled it to destroy communism in China. The most trustworthy military, economic, and political information available to our Government does not bear out this view.

A realistic appraisal of conditions in China, past and present, leads to the conclusion that the only alternative open to the United States was full-scale intervention in behalf of a Government which had lost the confidence of its own troops and its own people. Such intervention would have required the expenditure of even greater sums than have been fruitlessly spent thus far, the command of Nationalist armies by American officers, and the probable participation of American armed forces—land, sea, and air—in the resulting war. Intervention of such a scope and magnitude would have been resented by the mass of the Chinese people, would have diametrically reversed our historic policy, and would have been condemned by the American people.

It must be admitted frankly that the American policy of assisting the Chinese people in resisting domination by any foreign power or powers is now confronted with the gravest difficulties. The heart of China is in Communist hands. The Communist leaders have foresworn their Chinese heritage and have publicly announced their subservience to a foreign power, Russia, which during the last 50 years, under czars and Communists alike, has been most assiduous in its efforts to extend its control in the Far East. In the recent past, attempts at foreign domination have appeared quite clearly to the Chinese people as external aggression and as such have been bitterly and in the long run successfully resisted. Our aid and encouragement have helped them to resist. In this case, however, the foreign domination has been masked behind the facade of a vast crusading movement which apparently has seemed to many Chinese to be wholly indigenous and national. Under these circumstances, our aid has been unavailing.

The unfortunate but inescapable fact is that the ominous result of the civil war in China was beyond the control of the government of the United States. Nothing that this country did or could have done within the reasonable limits of its capabilities could have changed that result; nothing that was left undone by this country has contributed to it. It was the product of internal Chinese forces, forces which this country tried to influence but could not. A decision was arrived at within China, if only a decision by default. . . .

In the immediate future, however, the implementation of our historic policy of friendship for China must be profoundly affected by current developments. It will necessarily be influenced by the degree to which the Chinese people come to recognize that the Communist regime serves not their interests but those of Soviet Russia and the manner in which, having become aware of the facts, they react to this foreign domination. One point, however, is clear. Should the Communist regime lend itself to the aims of Soviet Russian imperialism and attempt to engage in aggression against China's neighbors, we and the other members of the United Nations would be confronted by a situation violative of the principles of the United Nations Charter and threatening international peace and security.

Meanwhile our policy will continue to be based upon our own respect for the Charter, our friendship for China, and our traditional support for the Open Door and for China's independence and administrative and territorial integrity.

6. Mao Zedong (Mao Tse-tung) Denounces U.S. "Imperialism," 1949

The war to turn China into a U.S. colony, a war in which the United States of America supplies the money and guns and Chiang Kai-shek the men to fight for the United States and slaughter the Chinese people, has been an important component of the U.S. imperialist policy of world-wide aggression since World War II. The U.S. policy of aggression has several targets. The three main targets are Europe, Asia and the Americas. China, the centre of gravity in Asia, is a large country with a population of 475 million; by seizing China, the United States would possess all of Asia. With its Asian front consolidated, U.S. imperialism could concentrate its forces on attacking Europe. U.S. imperialism considers its front in the Americas relatively secure. These are the smug over-all calculations of the U.S. aggressors. . . .

U.S. naval, ground and air forces did participate in the war in China. There were U.S. naval bases in Tsingtao, Shanghai and Taiwan. U.S. troops were stationed in Peiping, Tientsin, Tangshan, Chinwangtao, Tsingtao, Shanghai and Nanking. The U.S. air force controlled all of China's air space and took aerial photographs of all China's strategic areas for military maps. At the town of Anping near Peiping, at Chiutai near Changchun, at Tangshan and in the Eastern Shantung Peninsula, U.S.

This document can be found in *Selected Works of Mao Tse-Tung* (Peking: Foreign Language Press, 1961), IV, 433–436, 438–439.

troops and other military personnel clashed with the People's Liberation Army and on several occasions were captured. [Colonel Claire] Chennault's air fleet took an extensive part in the civil war. Besides transporting troops for Chiang Kai-shek, the U.S. air force bombed and sank the cruiser *Chungking*, which had mutinied against the Kuomintang. All these were acts of direct participation in the war, although they fell short of an open declaration of war and were not large in scale, and although the principal method of U.S. aggression was the large-scale supply of money, munitions and advisers to help Chiang Kai-shek fight the civil war.

The use of this method by the United States was determined by the objective situation in China and the rest of the world, and not by any lack of desire on the part of the Truman-Marshall group, the ruling clique of U.S. imperialism, to launch direct aggression against China. Moreover, at the outset of its help to Chiang Kai-shek in fighting the civil war, a crude farce was staged in which the United States appeared as mediator in the conflict between the Kuomintang and the Communist Party; this was an attempt to soften up the Communist Party of China, deceive the Chinese people and thus gain control of all China without fighting. The peace negotiations failed, the deception fell through and the curtain rose on the war.

Liberals or "democratic individualists" who cherish illusions about the United States and have short memories! Please look at Acheson's own words:

> When peace came the United States was confronted with three possible alternatives in China: (1) it could have pulled out lock, stock and barrel; (2) it could have intervened militarily on a major scale to assist the Nationalists to destroy the Communists; (3) it could, while assisting the Nationalists to assert their authority over as much of China as possible, endeavor to avoid a civil war by working for a compromise between the two sides.

Why didn't the United States adopt the first of these policies? Acheson says:

> The first alternative would, and I believe American public opinion at the time felt, have represented an abandonment of our international responsibilities and of our traditional policy of friendship for China before we had made a determined effort to be of assistance.

So that's how things stand: the "international responsibilities" of the United States and its "traditional policy of friendship for China" are nothing but intervention against China. Intervention is called assuming international responsibilities and showing friendship for China; as to non-intervention, it simply won't do. Here Acheson defiles U.S. public opinion; his is the "public opinion" of Wall Street, not the public opinion of the American people.

Why didn't the United States adopt the second of these policies? Acheson says:

> The second alternative policy, while it may look attractive theoretically and in retrospect, was wholly impracticable. The Nationalists had been unable to destroy the Communists during the 10 years before the war. Now after the war the Nationalists were, as indicated above, weakened, demoralized and unpopular. They had quickly dissipated their popular support and prestige in the areas liberated from the Japanese by the conduct of their civil and military officials. The Communists on the other hand were much stronger than they had ever been and were in control of most of North China. Because of the ineffectiveness of the Nationalist forces which was later to be tragically demonstrated, the Communists probably could have been dislodged only by

American arms. It is obvious that the American people would not have sanctioned such a colossal commitment of our armies in 1945 or later. We therefore came to the third alternative policy. . . .

What a splendid idea! The United States supplies the money and guns and Chiang Kai-shek the men to fight for the United States and slaughter the Chinese people, to "destroy the Communists" and turn China into a U.S. colony, so that the United States may fulfill its "international responsibilities" and carry out its "traditional policy of friendship for China.". . .

When the People's Liberation Army crossed the Yangtse River, the U.S. colonial government at Nanking fled helter-skelter. Yet His Excellency Ambassador Stuart sat tight, watching wide-eyed, hoping to set up shop under a new signboard and to reap some profit. But what did he see? Apart from the People's Liberation Army marching past, column after column, and the workers, peasants, and students rising in hosts, he saw something else—the Chinese liberals or democratic individualists turning out in force, shouting slogans and talking revolution together with the workers, peasants, soldiers and students. In short, he was left out in the cold, "standing all alone, body and shadow comforting each other." There was nothing more for him to do, and he had to take to the road, his briefcase under his arm. . . .

Leighton Stuart has departed and the White Paper has arrived. Very good. Very good. Both events are worth celebrating.

7. Bo Yibo Remembers the Origins of China's "Lean to One Side" Policy (1949–1950), 1991

Both to clarify the ambiguous thoughts of some non-party people and to lay the foundation for the new China's foreign policy, Chairman Mao, on June 30, 1949 proclaimed in his article "On People's Democratic Dictatorship":

> Leaning to one side stems from the lessons we have learned from the forty years of Sun Yat-sen and the twenty-eight years of the Communist Party. We are keenly aware that we must lean to one side in order to achieve and consolidate victory. According to the experience of (Sun Yat-sen's) forty years and (our party's) twenty-eight years, the Chinese have either leaned toward imperialism or toward socialism. There has been no exception. To sit on the fence is to go nowhere. There is no third path. We oppose the Jiang Jieshi reactionaries who leaned toward imperialism. We also oppose the illusion of taking a third path. . . . Internationally, we belong to the anti-imperialist front headed by the Soviet Union. We can only seek true friendship from this front, not from the imperialist front.

Why did we propose this diplomatic strategic principle at the time? What was its background and at whom was it directed? What was its long-term significance? In his letter to the comrades in the Party's East China Bureau on July 19, Comrade

"Bo Yibo Remembers the Origins of China's 'Lean to One Side' Policy (1949–1950)" from *Chinese Historians* 5 (Spring 1992), pp. 59–62, translated by Zhai Qiang. Reprinted with the permission of Chinese Historians of the United States, Inc.

Deng Xiaoping, who was directing military operations in East China, wrote a brilliant exposition, which can still help us today, especially young comrades, to deepen our understanding of the "leaning to one side" decision. For that purpose, I am quoting his exposition here:

> The purpose of the various plots of imperialism including blockade is to force us to submit to imperialism. Likewise, the aim of our struggle is to force imperialism to give in to us. Judging by the lessons of the past month, however, we can see that it will not be an easy matter for imperialism to give in to us. In fact, during that period both sides had been testing the water until Britain and the United States decided to institute a blockade. Though for the moment the blockade has exasperated the many difficulties we face, it was nevertheless advantageous for us as well. However, if the blockade lasts too long, it will be very disadvantageous. In order to break the blockade, Chairman Mao stresses that we should quickly occupy Guangdong, Guangxi, Yunnan, Guizhou, Sichuan, Xikang, Qinghai and Ningxia and strive to take the offshore islands and Taiwan as soon as possible. At the same time, we propose a foreign policy of "leaning to one side." The earlier we put this into practice, the better our position will be (Chairman Mao says that this leaning is on our initiative, and is better than being forced to lean to one side in the future). . . .

The newly-established People's Republic of China faced the serious problem of breaking the imperialist blockade. Therefore, it became all the more important to consolidate and develop the friendship and cooperation between the two great countries of China and the Soviet Union. On November 12, Chairman Mao cabled Stalin: "Thank you for inviting me to visit Moscow." On December 16, Chairman Mao reached Moscow, and was given a grand welcoming reception by the Soviet party and government. When Chairman Mao delivered a speech at the party celebrating Stalin's seventieth birthday on December 21, the entire audience rose three times. On December 22, Chairman Mao wrote to the Party Central Committee: "In preparation for the trade agreement with the Soviet Union, we should take the over-all situation into consideration. Of course, the Soviet Union has the priority, but we should also be ready to do business with such countries as Poland, Czechoslovakia, Germany, Britain, Japan and the United States." Chairman Mao also told the Central Committee that he had "already made an appointment with Stalin to have a talk either on the 23rd or on the 24th." Right at this moment (December 24, 1949), Soviet General Advisor to China I. V. Kovalev, who was accompanying Chairman Mao during his trip to the Soviet Union, presented Stalin with a written report, "On Certain Policy and Practical Matters Concerning the CCP Central Committee." This report claimed that within the Chinese Communist Party and among members of the Central Committee there were some people who had been pro-American and anti-Soviet in the past, and now received support from the leadership of the Central committee. . . .

For a period of time after Chairman Mao's arrival in the Soviet Union, the Soviet side did not take the initiative and Chairman Mao stayed in his quarters. This situation might have been the result of Kovalev's report. Chairman Mao lost his temper in front of the Soviet officials in charge of organizing his visit, and he said: "I came to the Soviet Union not just to celebrate Stalin's birthday, but to discuss important matters concerning bilateral relations between the two countries." After learning this, Stalin quickly started negotiations with Chairman Mao and gave him

General Advisor Kovalev's report, thus improving mutual understanding, although unresolved suspicions remained.

On January 2, 1950, Chairman Mao sent a telegram to the Party Central Committee: "In the past two days there has been an important development here. Comrade Stalin has agreed to let Comrade Zhou Enlai come to Moscow to sign the new Sino-Soviet Friendship and Alliance Treaty and other agreements regarding loans, trade, and civil aviation.". . .

Subsequently on April 11, Chairman Mao chaired the Sixth Meeting of the Central People's Government Committee. Premier Zhou delivered "The Report on the Sino-Soviet Treaty." The treaty [signed February 14, 1950] was approved at the meeting. In his speech Chairman Mao pointed out: "Under what circumstances did we conclude this treaty? We have defeated one enemy, that is, the reactionary forces at home. We have driven the international reactionary forces out of China. But there are still reactionaries in the world, that is, imperialists outside China. Internally, we still face difficulties. . . . Under these conditions, we need friends. . . . We should solidify our relations and our friendship with the Soviet Union in a legal manner, that is, through a treaty. To solidify the friendship between the Soviet Union and China and to establish an alliance relationship. . . . If imperialists prepare to attack us, we already have help."

Speaking of the great significance of the treaty and agreements, Chairman Mao asserted: "The recently-concluded Sino-Soviet Treaty and agreements have solidified in a legal way the friendship between the two great countries, China and the Soviet Union, and have enabled us to secure a reliable ally. Therefore, we can carry out domestic reconstruction freely, deal with possible imperialist aggression together, and win world peace." In sum, "this action will place the People's Republic in a more advantageous position, enable us to force capitalist countries to submit, and to force foreign countries to recognize China without conditions, . . . making capitalist countries hesitate to take aggressive action."

8. Senator William Knowland Argues Against Recognition, 1950

Mr. President and Members of the Senate, within the last 90 days two catastrophic events have taken place. These are the Soviet success in atomic development, as announced by the President of the United States on September 23, 1949, and the establishment of a Soviet-recognized Communist regime in China. Only in retrospect will we be able to finally determine which event will have the most far-reaching influence. Both have set off chain reactions that have not yet run their full course.

Fifty years of friendly interest on the part of our people and our Government in a free and independent China and the overwhelming contribution made by our Army, Navy, and Air Force in the Pacific during World War II gave us the power, the prestige, and the opportunity for constructive action no western nation had

This document can be found in *Congressional Record*, XCVI (January 5, 1950), 79–82.

ever before possessed. We could have pioneered in exporting the ideals that inspired men who loved freedom everywhere following our own breakaway from colonial status.

All this opportunity has been frittered away by a small group of willful men in the Far Eastern Division of the State Department who had the backing of their superiors. . . .

Communism is destructive of human liberty everywhere in the world. It is no less destructive in China or Korea than it is in Poland, Czechoslovakia, Latvia, Estonia, Lithuania, Hungary, Rumania, or Bulgaria. The pattern may differ slightly. In Poland the opposition leader, Mikolajczyk, was forced to flee; in Bulgaria Petkov was hanged; in Rumania the King was given a 2-hour ultimatum to change the government regardless of the constitution; in Czechoslovakia Masaryk's life was forfeited when it became apparent that coalition with communism would not work.

A Chinese official put it clearly by saying to me recently that there can be no real coalition with a tiger unless you are inside the tiger.

The President's State of the Union message of January 4 was notable for its silence on the question of China. In what we hope will be a free world of freemen does the administration have less concern with human liberty in Asia than it does in Europe? On what basis does the administration write off freemen in China? . . .

In Europe we have had a foreign policy in which the Republicans and the Democrats have contributed to the initiation and formulation of doctrines that are understandable. In the Far East there has been no bipartisan foreign policy. The Republicans in Congress have not been consulted in the moves leading up to the bankrupt policy which now stands revealed in all its sorry detail. . . .

Our long-standing far eastern policy was first compromised at Yalta. We gave to the Soviet Union vital rights in Manchuria which were not ours to give. It was done without the consent or approval of the American Congress or the American people. It was done in violation of the open-door policy of John Hay and of Woodrow Wilson's concept of "open covenants, openly arrived at." The Yalta agreement made Soviet domination of Manchuria and other border provinces inevitable. It made possible Chinese Communist domination of the balance of continental China and has opened the door to bringing the entire continent of Asia, with more than a billion people and vast resources, into the orbit of international communism. Sitting with our American delegation at Yalta was Alger Hiss [a State Department official who in 1948 was accused of conducting espionage for the Soviet Union].

Following VJ-day the representatives of our Department of State persistently tried to get the Government of the Republic of China to form a coalition with the Communists. When they refused we placed an embargo against the shipments of any arms or ammunition to the legal government of the country while during those same months the Soviet army of occupation in Manchuria, as the result of the Yalta agreement, was turning over to the Communist forces large amounts of captured Japanese war stocks.

Like a person with a bad conscience, the State Department on August 6 released the China white paper. All the blame was placed on the National Government, then with its back to the wall. It was apparently issued with the hope that our own sorry part and share of responsibility might be overlooked. . . .

The basic objective the United States should have kept constantly in mind was to preserve a free, independent, united non-Communist China. In the postwar illness of that nation we prescribed that the strychnine of communism be taken. The State Department having contributed greatly to the Chinese disaster, still proclaims that we must follow a hands off policy, or that we must wait for the dust to settle, or we must investigate some more. Are they preparing for a post mortem rather than a consultation? . . .

Like Mr. Chamberlain at Munich, there are some in this country and in Great Britain who believe that by appeasing the Communists they may change their way of life. This is naive, and such a viewpoint is dangerous to the peace of the world and the security of this country. . . .

The question is asked "Can anything be done at this late date?" I believe that it can. While desperate, the situation is not more desperate than it was at the time of Dunkerque or Valley Forge.

First, of course, we need a foreign policy in the Far East. We have none there today. As a basis for such a foreign policy, I suggest the following:

First. That we make clear that we have no intention of recognizing the Communist regime in China at this time nor in the immediate future and that we make known to the powers associated with us that we do not look with favor upon such recognition by others.

It is of course not sufficient merely to delay our own recognition if, with a wink of the eye or tongue in cheek the State Department leaves doubt in the minds of others as to the course of action we may pursue.

Second. That we have a major shakeup in the Far Eastern Division of the State Department. We cannot expect to get inspired leadership for a new policy in the Far East from those who have been receivers of the bankrupt policy we have been following.

Third. Our policy itself, of course, will have to be set by our constitutional officers, the President, his advisers, and the Congress. Once we have a foreign policy there is great need for it to be coordinated in both its economic and defense phases. As coordinator, either Gen. Douglas MacArthur or some other comparable figure should be selected so that in that area of the world the right hand will know what the left is doing.

Fourth. We should give supervised aid to the legal Government of China in the same way we gave it to the legal Governments of Greece and Korea when they were threatened by communism.

✪ E S S A Y S

In the first essay, Jian Chen of Southern Illinois University uses newly released Chinese and Soviet sources to probe Chinese perspectives on Sino-American relations. Chen dismisses speculation that Washington missed a chance in 1949 to establish diplomatic relations with the People's Republic. According to Chen, Mao's insistence that the United States immediately sever ties to the Guomindang, the Chinese Communist Party's strong ideological and political links to the Soviet Union, China's historic quest for great-power status, and its resentment of Western imperialism precluded fruitful negotiations with Washington.

In the second essay, Thomas J. Christensen of Cornell University concedes that U.S. support for Jiang Jieshi, and the CCP's ideological zeal, generated deep hostility in Beijing and undermined any chance for amiable relations. He emphasizes, however, that Mao Zedong and the CCP held out the possibility of normal diplomatic ties and initiated high-level contacts with U.S. officials during the final stages of China's revolution. Christensen argues that the Truman administration's refusal to sever relations with Jiang, a byproduct of the escalating Soviet-American Cold War, constituted the primary obstacle to accommodation with the newly formed People's Republic of China. He concludes that by not responding positively to Mao's overtures, Washington lost a chance to unsettle the Sino-Soviet alliance, establish reliable lines of communication with Beijing, and prevent war from breaking out between the United States and China on the Korean peninsula in November 1950.

No Lost Chance: The Chinese Communists Rejected Accommodation

JIAN CHEN

Did there exist a chance in 1949–50 for the Chinese Communist Party (CCP) and the United States to reach an accommodation or, at least, to avoid a confrontation? Scholars who believe that Washington "lost a chance" to pursue a non-confrontational relationship with the CCP generally base their argument on two assumptions—that the Chinese Communists earnestly sought U.S. recognition to expedite their country's postwar economic reconstruction and that the relationship between the CCP and the Soviet Union was vulnerable because of Moscow's failure to offer sufficient support to the Chinese Revolution. These scholars thus claim that it was Washington's anti-Communist and pro-Guomindang (the Nationalist party or GMD) policy that forced the CCP to treat the United States as an enemy. This claim, though seemingly critical of Washington's management of relations with China, is ironically American centered, implying that the CCP's policies toward the United States were simpy passive reactions to what Washington was doing toward China. This essay, with insights gained from new Chinese and, in some places, Russian materials, argues that, in the final analysis, the CCP's confrontation with the United States originated in the Party's need to enhance the inner dynamics of the Chinese Revolution after its nationwide victory, and that from a Chinese perspective, no chance existed for Communist China and the United States to reach an accommodation in 1949–50.

Contrary to the assumption of the advocates of the "lost chance" thesis, Chinese materials now available demonstrate that in 1949–50, Mao Zedong and the CCP leadership were unwilling to pursue Western recognition, let alone to establish diplomatic relations with Western countries. In November 1948, shortly after Communist troops occupied Shenyang (Mukden), the largest city in China's northeast (Manchuria), the CCP leadership initiated a policy of "squeezing out" (*jizhou*)

From Jian Chen, "The Myth of American 'Lost Chance' in China: A Chinese Perspective in Light of New Evidence," *Diplomatic History,* 21 (Winter 1997), 77–86. Reprinted with permission.

American and other Western diplomats in the "liberated zone." A Central Committee telegram (drafted by Zhou Enlai) to the party's Northeast Bureau on 10 November maintained that because the British, American, and French governments had not recognized Chinese Communist authorities, the CCP would not grant official status to their diplomats, treating them as common foreigners without diplomatic immunity. The telegram further instructed the Northeast Bureau to take "certain measures" to confine the "freedom of action" of the Western diplomats, so that "they will have to withdraw from Shenyang." On 17 November, Mao Zedong instructed Gao Gang, the CCP leader in the northeast, to act resolutely to force the British, American, and French diplomats out of Shenyang. The next day, Mao authorized the Communists in Shenyang to seize the radio transmitters in the Western consulates. When the Americans refused to hand over their radio equipment to Communist authorities, the Communists, following Soviet advice, placed Angus Ward, the American consul, and his staff under house detention on 20 November and would not allow them to leave China until December 1949.

The CCP's challenge to Western presence in Shenyang resulted in part from immediate concerns that Western diplomats might use their radio transmitters to convey military intelligence to the GMD in the ongoing Chinese civil war. But, in a deeper sense, the challenge reflected the Party leadership's determination to "make a fresh start" in China's external relations, which required the Party to "clean the house before entertaining guests," as well as to "lean to one side" (the side of the Soviet Union).

The above three principles became the guidelines of Communist China's early diplomacy. In a telegram to the Northeast Bureau on 23 November 1948, the CCP Central Committee expounded its view that the Party would refuse to recognize diplomatic relations between the GMD government and the West. In the Central Committee's "Directive on Diplomatic Affairs" of 19 January 1949, Mao Zedong declared that "with no exception will we recognize any of those embassies, legations, and consulates of capitalist countries, as the diplomatic establishments and personnel attached to them accredited to the GMD." The directive also made clear that the CCP would treat American and Soviet diplomats differently "as the foreign policy of the Soviet Union and the other new democratic countries has differed totally from that of the capitalist countries." At the Central Committee's Second Plenary Session in March 1949, the CCP leadership reached the consensus that the new Chinese Communist regime should neither hastily seek recognition from, nor pursue diplomatic relations with the United States and other Western countries. "As for the question of the recognition of our country by the imperialist countries," asserted Mao, "we should not be in a hurry to solve it now and need not be in a hurry to solve it even for a fairly long period after country-wide victory." During 1949–50, CCP leaders repeatedly emphasized that establishing diplomatic relations with the United States or other Western countries was not a priority.

As is well known, after the Chinese Communists occupied Nanjing, the capital of Nationalist China, in late April 1949, John Leighton Stuart, the American ambassador to China, remained. In May and June, Stuart held a series of meetings with Huang Hua, director of the Foreign Affairs Office under the Communist Nanjing Municipal Military Control Commission. They discussed, among other things, conditions on which relations between the CCP and the United States might be established. In the meantime, CCP leaders asserted on several occasions that if Western capitalist countries cut off their connections with the GMD and treated China and the Chinese people as "equals" the CCP would be willing to consider establishing relations with them. Advocates of the "lost chance" thesis use these exchanges and statements to support their position.

It is true that for a short period in the spring of 1949, Mao and the CCP leadership showed some interest in having contacts with the United States, which, we now know, was probably triggered by a secret message Stuart sent to the CCP through his personal friend Chen Mingshu, a pro-Communist "democratic figure." A previously unknown memorandum kept at the Chinese Central Archives indicates that on 25 and 26 March, Stuart had two secret meetings with Chen in Shanghai. The American ambassador, according to the memorandum, expressed two major concerns on the part of the United States: "(1) that the CCP might attach itself to the side of the Soviet union in a confrontation with the United States . . . , and (2) that the CCP, after unifying China by force, would stop its cooperation with the democratic figures and give up a democratic coalition government." Stuart promised that "if a genuine coalition government committed to peace, independence, democracy and freedom was to be established in China and if the CCP would change its attitude toward the United States by, among other things, stopping the anti-American campaign" the United States would be willing to "maintain friendly relations with the CCP and would provide the new government with assistance in new China's economic recovery and reconstruction."

After receiving Chen Mingshu's report, Mao and the CCP leadership speculated that because "the old U.S. policy of supporting the GMD and opposing the CCP has failed," Washington "is turning toward adopting a policy of establishing diplomatic relations with us." As long-time players of the "united front" strategy, Mao and his comrades were determined to stick to their principles, but they could not at the same time ignore an opportunity to weaken the threat from enemies and potential enemies. Mao therefore authorized Huang Hua's May–June contacts with Stuart, instructing him "to listen more and talk less." The CCP chairman also made clear that unless the Americans were willing to sever relations with the GMD and to treat China equally, the CCP would not consider having relations with the United States.

In retrospect, these two conditions were impossible for the Americans to meet. Fulfilling the first condition, cutting off connections with the GMD, would require the complete turnover of America's China policy since the end of World War II, and realizing the second, treating the Chinese as "equals," presented the Americans with a profound challenge in a historical-cultural sense. Indeed, Mao viewed "equality" as a historical problem, pointing out that Sino-American relations had been dominated by a series of unequal treaties since China's defeat in the Opium War of 1839–1842. He believed that in a moral sense the United States and other Western powers owed the Chinese a heavy debt. As the first step toward establishing an equal relationship, he argued, the United States had to end, as well as apologize for, its "unequal" treatment of China. Only when the historical phenomenon of unequal exchanges between China and the West ended would it be possible for the new Chinese Communist regime to establish relations with Western countries. So, Mao's definition of "equality" meant a total negation of America's roles in

China's modern history and also posed a crucial challenge to the existing principles of international relations followed by the United States and other Western
countries. In Mao's opinion, America's willingness to change its attitude toward
China represented a pass-or-fail test for policymakers in Washington, and he
simply did not believe that they would pass the test.

Thus, it is not surprising that the Huang-Stuart meetings failed to bring the
CCP and the United States any closer. Stuart emphasized the legitimacy of American interests in China and tried to convince the Chinese Communists that they had
to accept widely recognized international regulations and principles. Huang, on the
other hand, stressed that the CCP's two conditions were the prerequisites for any
further discussion of establishing relations. In late June, with the Stuart-Huang
contacts still under way, the CCP publicly charged Ward and his staff in Shenyang
with espionage activities and then initiated a new wave of anti-American propaganda. When Stuart returned to the United States and the U.S. State Department
published the *China White Paper* in August 1949, Mao personally directed an anti-
American propaganda campaign in the CCP media, a central theme of which was
that it did not matter if the Americans were unwilling to treat China and its people
as equals because the Chinese people would gain their equality in the international
community through their revolution.

As the CCP's relations with the United States reached an impasse, its relations
with the Soviet Union grew closer. Indeed, new Chinese and Russian evidence reveals that the relationship between the CCP and Moscow in 1949 was much more
intimate and substantial than many Western scholars realized. While it is true that
problems and disagreements (sometimes even serious ones) existed between the
Chinese and Soviet Communists, as well as between Mao Zedong and Stalin (as in
any partnership), the new evidence clearly points out that cooperation, or the willingness to cooperate, was the dominant aspect of CCP-Soviet relations in 1949.

During China's civil war in 1946–1949, the CCP's relations with Moscow
were close but not harmonious. When it became clear that the Chinese Communists were going to win the civil war, both the CCP and the Soviet Union felt the
need to further strengthen their relationship. From late 1947, Mao actively prepared to visit the Soviet Union to "discuss important domestic and international
issues" with Stalin. The extensive telegraphic exchanges between Mao and Stalin
resulted in two important secret missions in 1949. From 31 January to 7 February,
Stalin sent Anastas Mikoyan, a Soviet Politburo member to visit Xibaipo, CCP
headquarters at that time. Mao and other CCP leaders had extensive discussions
with him, introducing to him the CCP's strategies and policies. Mao particularly
explained to Mikoyan the CCP's foreign policy of "making a fresh start" and
"cleaning the house before entertaining guests." From late June to mid-August,
Liu Shaoqi, the CCP's second most important person, visited Moscow. During the
Visit, Stalin apologized for failing to give sufficient assistance to the CCP during
the civil war and promised that the Soviet Union would give the Chinese Communists political support and substantial assistance in military and other fields. Moreover, the Soviets and the Chinese discussed a "division of labor" to promote the
world revolution and reached a general consensus: While the Soviet Union would
remain the center of the international proletarian revolution, promoting revolution
in the East would become primarily China's duty. Liu left Moscow in mid-August,

accompanied by ninety-six Russian experts who were to assist China's military buildup and economic reconstruction. Mikoyan's mission to China and Liu's visit to Moscow greatly promoted Sino-Soviet cooperation.

During this period, the CCP frequently exchanged opinions with Moscow on how to evaluate the "American threat" and how to deal with relations with the United States. In November 1948, the CCP Northeast Bureau accepted Soviet advice to seize the radio transmitters of the American consulate in Shenyang. Early in January 1949, when Jiang Jieshi (Chiang Kai-shek) and the GMD started a "peace initiative" to end the civil war, Mao originally intended to rebuff it completely. But, Stalin advised the CCP leaders that the Americans were behind Jiang and that it would better serve the Party's interests if, instead of simply rebuffing Jiang's proposals, it proposed its own conditions for ending the war through non-military means. (Stalin emphasized that the CCP should make these conditions unacceptable to Jiang.) After a few exchanges, Mao Zedong "completely agreed with" Stalin's opinions and acted accordingly. In the spring of 1949, Stalin warned the CCP about possible American landing operations in the People's Liberation Army's rear, convincing the CCP leadership to maintain a strategic reserve force in northern coastal China when the PLA's [Peoples Liberation Army's] main force was engaged in the campaign of crossing the Yangzi (Yangtze) River. During Liu Shaoqi's visit to the Soviet Union in June–August 1949, the CCP presented to Stalin a detailed memorandum, summarizing the Party's domestic and, particularly, international policies (including policy toward the United States).

Particularly revealing are Mao's communications with Stalin on how the CCP should handle Huang Hua's contacts with Stuart. After receiving Chen Minshu's report about his secret meetings with Stuart in Shanghai, the CCP immediately informed Moscow of the contact. In a meeting with I.V. Kovalev, Stalin's representative to China, on 9 April 1949, Mao Zedong asked him to report to Stalin that the CCP was preparing to make minor adjustments in its foreign policy by conducting some "limited contacts" with Western capitalist countries, including the United States. But Mao also promised that the CCP would not formalize these contacts; nor would it legalize the relationship emerging from them. On 19 April, Stalin instructed Kovalev to advise Mao: "(1) We believe that China's democratic government should not refuse to establish formal relations with capitalist countries, including the United States, given that these countries formally abandon military, economic, and political support to Jiang and the GMD government. . . . (2) We believe that, under some conditions, [the CCP] should not refuse to accept foreign loans or to do business with capitalist countries." During the Huang-Stuart meetings, Mao informed Stalin about the substance of the meetings, emphasizing that "it is unfavorable that the embassies of the United States and other [capitalist] countries remain in Nanjing, and we will be happy to see that the embassies of all capitalist countries get out of China." Stalin, while expressing his gratitude to Mao for informing him about the meetings, advised him that for tactical considerations, "we do not think this is the proper time for the Soviet Union and Democratic China to demonstrate extensively the friendship between them."

One may argue that when Mao informed Stalin of the contacts between the CCP and the United States, he might have been trying to pressure Stalin so that the Soviet Union would strengthen its support to the CCP. Yet, this interpretation cannot explain the extensive and substantive exchanges between the two Communist leaders concerning CCP-U.S. contacts. Judging from the contents of the Mao-Stalin exchanges, it is more logical to regard these exchanges as a means to strengthen the foundation of the relationship between the CCP and the Soviet Union. From a Chinese perspective, the CCP's "lean-to-one-side" policy was more than lip service.

There is no doubt that Washington's continuous support of the GMD during China's civil war played an important role in the CCP's anti-American policy. But America's pro-Jiang policy alone does not offer a comprehensive explanation for the origins of the CCP-American confrontation. In order to comprehend the CCP's policy toward the United States, we must explore the historical-cultural environment in which it emerged, thus understanding the dynamics and logic underlying it.

The Chinese Communist Revolution emerged in a land that was historically known as the "Central Kingdom." The Chinese during traditional times viewed China as civilization in toto. In modern times, this Chinese view of the world had been severely challenged when China had to face the cruel reality that its door was opened by the superior forces of Western powers, and that the very survival of the Chinese nation was at stake. The generation of Mao and his comrades became indignant when they saw Western powers, including the United States, treat the old, declining China with arrogance and a strong sense of superiority. They also despised the Chinese governments from the Manchu dynasty [the last of a long series of feudalistic dynasties that collapsed in 1911] to the regimes of the warlords, which had failed to protect China's national integrity and sovereignty. An emotional commitment to national liberation provided a crucial momentum in Mao and his comrades' choice of a Marxist-Leninist style revolution. For Mao and his comrades, the final goal of their revolution was not only the total transformation of the old Chinese state and society they saw as corrupt and unjust; they would also pursue changing China's weak power status, proving to the world the strength and influence of Chinese culture, and redefining the values and rules underlying the international system. In short, they wanted to restore China's *central* position in the international community.

Therefore, Mao and his comrades never regarded the Communist seizure of power in China in 1949 as the revolution's conclusion. Rather, Mao was very much concerned about how to maintain and enhance the revolution's momentum after its nationwide victory. Indeed, this concern dominated Mao's thinking during the formation of the People's Republic and would occupy his primary attention during the latter half of his life. Consequently, Mao's approach toward China's external relations in general and his policy toward the United States in particular became heavily influenced by this primary concern. Throughout 1949–50, the Maoist discourse challenged the values and codes of behavior attached to "U.S. imperialism," pointing out that they belonged to the "old world" that the CCP was determined to destroy. While defining the "American threat," Mao and his fellow CCP leaders never confined their vision to the possibility of direct American military intervention in China; they emphasized long-range American hostility toward the victorious Chinese Revolution, especially the U.S. imperialist attempt to sabotage the revolution from within. Indeed, when Mao justified the CCP's decision not to pursue relations with the United States, his most consistent and powerful argument was that doing so would deprive the Americans of a means of sabotaging the Chinese Revolution.

It is also important to point out that while Washington's hostility toward the Chinese Revolution offended Mao and his comrades, the perceived American disdain for China as weak and the Chinese as inferior made them angry. In the anti-American propaganda campaign following the publication of the *China White Paper,* Mao sought to expose the "reactionary" and "vulnerable" nature of U.S. imperialism and encourage the ordinary Chinese people's national self-respect. In other words, Mao changed the anti-American discourses into means of mobilizing the masses for his "continuous revolution," a practice that would reach its first peak during the "Great War of Resisting America and Assisting Korea" (the Chinese name of China's participation in the Korean War) in 1950–1953.

It is apparent that the CCP's adoption of an anti-American policy in 1949–50 had deep roots in China's history and modern experiences. Sharp divergences in political ideology (communism versus capitalism) and perceived national interests did contribute to the shaping of the Sino-American confrontation; and suspicion and hostility were further crystallized as the result of Washington's continuous support to the GMD and the CCP's handling of such events as the Ward case. But, from a Chinese perspective, the most profound cause underlying the CCP's anti-American policy lay in its connection to Mao's grand plans of transforming China's state, society and international outlook, and the policy was made an integral component of these plans from the very beginning. Even though it might have been possible for Washington to change the concrete course of its China policy (which was highly unlikely given the policy's own complicated background), it would have been impossible for the United States to alter the processes and goals of the Chinese Revolution, let alone the historical-cultural environment that gave birth to it. America's "lost chance" in China must therefore be regarded as a myth.

The Lost Chance for Peace: Washington Rejected Chinese Communist Overtures

THOMAS J. CHRISTENSEN

In light of the documentary evidence from China and the United States, we can detect a causal link between two key American China policies of 1949–50—nonrecognition of Beijing and the blocking of the Taiwan Straits—and the disastrous escalation of the Korean War that occurred when China crossed the Yalu in the fall of 1950. To demonstrate this link, below I offer a new version of the "lost chance" in China thesis, arguing that while friendship between China and the

Thomas J. Christensen, *Useful Adversaries: Grand Strategy, Domestic Mobilization, and Sino-American Conflict, 1947–1958.* Copyright © 1996 by Princeton University Press. Reprinted by permission of Princeton University Press.

United States was precluded by their ideological differences, peace between the two nations was not. A plausible argument can be made that Sino-American combat in Korea could have been avoided if the United States had recognized Beijing and had honored Truman's January pledge to stay out of the Chinese Civil War. . . .

The question of whether the Truman administration wasted a chance for friendly relations with the Chinese Communists has spawned as much scholarship and debate as any issue in the history of China's foreign relations. Those who support the lost-chance thesis point to Mao's pragmatism, the ideological differences between Mao and Stalin, and the highly nationalistic nature of Chinese communism. In its original and simplest form, the lost-chance thesis posits that Mao could have befriended either camp in the Cold War. American belligerence, not ideological hardwiring, determined Mao's hostility toward Washington and alliance with Moscow. Those who reject the lost-chance thesis point to Mao's ideological hatred and distrust of the United States and the CCP's desire to secure spiritual as well as practical leadership from Stalin.

Scholarship on documentary evidence from China suggests that the critics of the lost-chance thesis are basically right. Given Mao's fundamental mistrust of the United States and early affinity for Moscow, it would have been impossible for Washington to woo the Chinese Communists away from the Soviets and toward the Western camp. In fact, Mao's "lean to one side" policy seemed set in stone as early as the 1930s. While some have argued that modified American behavior in 1948–49 might have changed Mao's fundamental perceptions of America, Chinese archival materials demonstrate that Mao would have been extremely suspicious of the Americans, even if the United States had adopted maximally conciliatory policies: cutting aid to the KMT [Guomindang] and recognizing the Communists in 1949.

A major limitation of the original lost-chance debate is its focus on the possibility for amicable relations or alignment between the United States and China. A large number of other potential outcomes fall between Sino-American alignment, as witnessed after 1972, and direct military conflict, as occurred in Korea in 1950. Just because there was no chance for friendship does not mean that there was no chance for peace. The same holds true for Sino-Soviet relations. There is a spectrum of possibilities between the high level of Sino-Soviet cooperation in Korea and the out-and-out enmity of the late 1960s. In 1950 the Chinese Communists were going to ally with the Soviets regardless of American behavior; but the tightness of the Sino-Soviet alliance still may have depended in large part on American actions.

The original lost-chance debate too often focused on Washington's ability to replace the Soviets as a friend and benefactor. In the early 1980s scholars began to address the lost-chance question more subtly, asking whether Sino-American relations could not have been somewhat better, even if they could not have been friendly. But despite these contributions, there has not been enough exploration of just how American policies, if different, might have reduced conflict between the two sides. This is not coincidental. The lack of documentary evidence on the Chinese side rendered speculation highly problematic. Using such evidence—including Mao's military and diplomatic manuscripts—below I analyze Mao's attitudes toward the United States in order to determine whether there was a lost chance for peace between the United States and China in 1949–50. I conclude that, while Mao viewed the United States as unquestionably hostile to the CCP in this period, he believed that American hostility might manifest itself in more or less threatening ways. American recognition of Beijing and abandonment of Chiang Kai-shek would not have provided a panacea for the many ills facing Sino-American relations. Still, those policies might have prevented the escalation of the Korean War in fall 1950.

In January 1949 Mao advised the Central Committee of its responsibilities in bringing the civil war to a successful conclusion. Mao's assessment of the American threat was a central element in his presentation. His view of America's future policies toward China was complex. On the level of intentionality, Mao saw the United States as unalterably hostile to his revolution. He saw no chance for friendship with Washington. On the other hand, he viewed the United States as a somewhat rational actor that eventually would recognize the futility of armed intervention in China. He went so far as to speculate that the United States might end direct military assistance to the KMT and then recognize the CCP regime. Still, Mao believed that even if the United States withdrew entirely from the civil war and recognized the Communists, Washington would still support covertly all available domestic opponents to his regime.

Despite intermittent notes of caution, Mao's talk was generally quite optimistic. He believed that American leaders, relative newcomers to "imperialism," were becoming wiser, recognizing the futility of significant assistance to Chiang Kai-shek. Therefore, in the future, Mao believed the United States would likely limit its activities to subversion. Mao said:

> In our strategic planning, we have always calculated in the possibility that the United States would directly send troops, occupying several coastal cities and engaging in warfare with us. We still must not dismiss this type of possibility. . . . *But, as the Chinese people's revolutionary strength increases and becomes more resolute, the possibility that the United States will carry out a direct military intervention also decreases, and moreover, in the same vein, the American involvement in financial and military assistance to the KMT may also decrease.* In the past year, especially in the past three months, the multiple changes in and unsteadiness of the American government's attitudes prove this point. *Among the Chinese people and in the Party there still exists a mistaken viewpoint which overestimates the power of American imperialism. It is essential [that we] continue to uncover and overcome [this tendency].*

Although he was hardly calling for laxity among his military forces, Mao's major purpose in this section of the speech was to allay fears within the party that the United States was about to invade Communist-held areas.

The optimism about the United States in Mao's speech should not be overstated. Mao believed that the United States would modify its behavior, but he believed this reflected a moderation in strategy, not a change in American intentions. He continued:

> The China policy of the American imperialists has changed from pure support of the KMT's military opposition to the Communist Party to a two-sided policy. This [policy] consists of, on the one hand, supporting the remnant KMT military forces and regional warlords [so as] to continue to oppose the People's Liberation Army; [and] on the other hand, dispatching their running dogs to infiltrate the revolutionary camp, [so as] to

organize a so-called opposition party and to break up the revolution from the inside. When the People's Liberation Army is about to achieve victory throughout the country, they may not even hesitate to use the method of recognizing the People's Republic, adopting a legitimate position [in China], and thereby implementing this policy of "internal break up." We need to increase our vigilance toward this imperialist conspiratorial plot, and resolutely smash it.

Counter to the earlier versions of the lost-chance thesis, conciliatory American moves would not have changed Mao's beliefs about America's opposition to his revolution. Consistent with his overall ideology, Mao attributed Washington's hostility to an imperialist national character. He associated any potential American conciliation in the future with environmental constraints—increased CCP power—rather than a change of heart in Washington. But for our purposes, the chairman's statements also demonstrate that, in his mind, there was a scale of hostility ranging in declining order from direct military involvement on the side of domestic adversaries, to military aid to domestic adversaries, to recognition of a Communist China followed by subversive activities. In early 1949 Mao believed that, faced with growing CCP strength and KMT collapse, the United States was rationally moving down the scale to the strategy of subversion.

The acquiescence of the U.S. Pacific Command to Chinese victories in Shanghai and Tianjin in spring 1949 demonstrated that Mao's first and most important prediction about the United States was basically correct: the United States was not going to involve itself directly in defending the remaining KMT forces on the mainland. The historical importance of Mao's predictions should not be underestimated. In April 1949 Mao decided to cross the Yangzi despite the warnings of Stalin's emissary, Anastas Mikoyan, that such an action should not be taken hastily lest the United States enter the Chinese Civil War. It was the crossing of the Yangzi that drove Chiang's government to Taiwan and ended the KMT's reign on the mainland.

After seizing Nanjing, Mao was impressed that the American embassy did not flee to Canton along with the KMT government. Mao stated on April 28:

> We should educate our troops to protect British and American residents . . . as well as foreign ambassadors, ministers, consuls, and other diplomats, especially those from the United States and Britain. Now the American side is asking a third party to contact us for the purpose of establishing diplomatic relations. We think that, if the United States and Britain can cut off their relations with the KMT, we can consider the question of establishing diplomatic relations with them. . . . The old U.S. policy of assisting the KMT and opposing the CCP is bankrupt. It seems that its policy is turning to one of establishing diplomatic relations with us.

Mao was actively considering the establishment of relations with the United States and, on April 30, he stated that the CCP would establish diplomatic relations with any country that broke with the KMT, removed its forces from China, and treated China "fairly."

Various Communist Party actions were in accord with these statements. . . . [I]n April, [a leading Chinese Communist official] Yao Yilin sought trade ties through [U.S. General Consul O. Edmund] Clubb's offices in Shanghai. In May and June,

[Zhou Enlai's assistant] Huang Hua responded positively to the overture from Ambassador [John Leighton] Stuart's office. These policies were not a sign of CCP factionalism, as was previously believed by many foreign analysts. It is clear that Mao directly controlled Huang's mission to the American embassy in Nanjing. In fact, a May 10 telegram from Mao to the Nanjing Municipal Bureau gives specific instructions to Huang Hua about what issues were to be raised with Stuart regarding the establishing of diplomatic relations with a CCP government. Huang was ordered to be firm and to emphasize that American support for the KMT, not the lack of American aid to CCP-held areas, was the main stumbling block to improved relations. Huang's apology for the Stuart incident, complaints about American relations with the KMT, and offers of detente all represented the CCP line, not simply the view of a minority faction under Zhou Enlai.

The events of April through July convinced the CCP leadership that, while Mao may have been right that the United States would not enter the Chinese Civil war directly, in the near term American distancing from the KMT was likely to be extremely limited. Despite the Huang mission and the CCP's July dispatch of Chen Mingshu, the United States rejected rapprochement with the CCP. Stuart did more than refuse to meet with Mao in Beiping, he also failed to respond satisfactorily to Huang Hua's main criticism of American behavior: that the United States was still actively involved in the civil war on the side of the KMT. Despite Stuart's assurances that American aid to Chiang was small and decreasing, Chinese Communist leaders believed that American involvement with Chiang Kai-shek was even greater than it actually was. For example, a leading Chinese Communist, Bo Yibo, reports that in July 1949 Chinese leaders believed (falsely) that the American and British navies were participating directly in the KMT naval blockade of China's southern and eastern ports. In a July 1949 report, [CCP official] Deng Xiaoping argued that China's experience "in the last month or so" had shown that forcing the "imperialists" to submit to CCP control of China would not be simple. Although the United States had not intervened to prevent PLA [People's Liberation Army] control of coastal cities, in the CCP's mind it had not come far down Mao's ladder of hostility. The CCP still believed that the United States would only recognize the KMT, would continue to grant the KMT economic and military aid, and would remain actively involved in military harassment of Communist-controlled coastal areas.

Some authors argue that Mao did not seek recognition from the United States in 1949 and that he did not plan to do so for years to come. This is correct if, by this, we mean that Mao was not going to revise the goals of his revolution in order to persuade the Americans to recognize the PRC. But the CCP was willing to accept, and in fact formally requested, recognition from the Western powers. The CCP's actions, party documents, and leaders' memoirs all suggest that Mao would have accepted recognition from all countries, including the United States, albeit with suspicion and on China's terms.

Mao's metaphor for China's policy toward foreign powers in 1949–50 was to "sweep China clean before inviting guests." The CCP was to eliminate all imperialist power in China before allowing real foreign influence to return to the mainland. But despite the image of foreigners flying out of China like swept dust and a virulent anti-American propaganda campaign, Mao's strategy did not preclude direct relations with Western powers. . . . [W]hile Mao was preparing to announce the founding of the People's Republic, the CCP sent an emissary to the American consul general, O. Edmund Clubb, in order to explain again the CCP's attitude toward establishing relations with outside countries. On October 1, 1949, Clubb was given the same request for the establishment of relations as other foreign representatives in China.

The Chinese conditions for accepting recognition and beginning a dialogue that would lead to diplomatic relations were not extremely arduous. In a December 1949 telegram regarding the establishment of relations with Burma, Mao laid out the two conditions for establishing relations with nonsocialist countries. The recognizing country must be willing to break diplomatic relations with the KMT and to enter a negotiation process to hammer out the terms of diplomatic exchanges. In his memoirs, Bo Yibo states that in late 1949 Mao had consistent criteria for the establishment of relations with any country: the recognition of the sole legitimacy of the PRC and respect for Chinese sovereignty. Bo emphasizes that "it is self-evident that Western countries were included under this principle." Huang Hua made similar statements about CCP preconditions in midyear. In Mao's hierarchy of nations there were distinctions between typical nonsocialist countries, such as Burma, and "imperialist" countries, such as Britain and the United States. In fact, on December 16 Mao is reported to have said to Stalin that China should not rush to be recognized by Britain and other imperialist powers. But it is significant to note that Britain recognized China and established official contacts in January 1950 despite Britain's long history of imperialism in China.

For practical purposes, a nation could establish high-level contacts merely by recognizing the CCP as the sole legitimate government, halting assistance to Chiang, and sending a team of representatives to negotiate the formalizing of relations. The British did this successfully in January. Although Britain fell far short of meeting Mao's terms for the exchange of ambassadors, the British still were able to dispatch a team of representatives to Beijing and to undertake long-term negotiations over the details of "unequal treaties" and other matters. These types of contacts, while not ideal, still provide direct channels of communication, which are critical in times of crisis.

But even if such contacts had been possible between Washington and Beijing, there is no reason to believe that friendship and significant economic relations would have flowed from them. Given what we now know about his deep-seated caution about the United States, Mao would have been extremely suspicious of the motives behind American recognition. But these concerns apparently would not have led him to denounce American attempts to establish more normal relations. While in Moscow, rather than worrying about the possible negative effects of recognition by nonsocialist countries, Mao seemingly welcomed the possibility, decreeing that, when nonsocialist countries agree to recognize China, the Chinese media should announce the news promptly. Three days later, Mao discussed plans for increased trade with the West, including the United States, although in no sense did he believe that the West would or should supplant the Soviet Union as China's main economic partner. Even after Mao made his decision to enter the Korean War and troops had begun crossing the Yalu, Mao still held some outside hope that a major blow to UN forces (the killing of tens of thousands of troops) might compel the Americans to open diplomatic talks with the PRC. In 1949–50, Mao saw no contradiction between diplomatic contacts and severe forms of mutual hostility.

There is a good deal of evidence that the Soviets expected the development of American relations with the CCP. In May 1950, after returning from Moscow, UN Secretary General Trygve Lie informed [Secretary of State Dean] Acheson that the Soviets had walked out of the UN in January 1950 only because they fully expected the United States to recognize the PRC in the short term. Stalin thought that if the Soviets made a principled stand at the UN, they could "take a bow for helping get the Chinese Communists into the Security Council." The Soviets may secretly have wanted to prevent Chinese entrance, but they also would have liked to take credit for that outcome if it were viewed as inevitable. There is documentary evidence from China demonstrating that, in January, China and the Soviet Union were carefully coordinating their efforts regarding the UN. While in Moscow Mao seemed hopeful that, at a minimum, the PRC would soon enter the Security Council, actually directing Liu Shaoqi to ready a PRC delegation to the UN.

While the Chinese and the Soviets may have anticipated improved relations with the United States in early January, for their part the Soviets felt that any improvement in Sino-American relations was detrimental to Soviet interests. If Lie's account is correct, by protesting at the UN the Soviets were only trying to take credit for what they falsely saw as an inevitable outcome. We now know from Russian archival discoveries and interview research that [Soviet marshal Joseph] Stalin actually feared improved relations between Beijing and Washington. From all accounts Stalin's cognitive biases about Mao's Titoism were even stronger than the Americans' oft-cited bias that Mao was a tool of Moscow. Stalin believed that Mao was a Titoist nationalist or, even worse, a rival leader of international communism. Mao's own later reflections about relations with Moscow in this period fully conform with the evidence from Russia. Mao's 1959 internal review of Sino-Soviet relations states that, until 1951, when the Chinese were fully engaged in Korea, the Soviets "doubted that ours was a real revolution."

Even though American recognition of China in the period December 1949–January 1950 would not have made Mao view the United States as a friendly power, it may have indirectly damaged Sino-Soviet relations. Stalin almost certainly would have objected vigorously to Chinese contacts with Washington. Fearing Chinese Titoism, the Soviets put a great deal of pressure on Mao to shun any overtures from the United States. They pointed to American support for the KMT as a reason to reject any such overtures. Interestingly, Acheson was well aware of this problem. On January 23, American intelligence officers informed Acheson of the potentially divisive effects of American recognition on Sino-Soviet relations, concluding that the "Soviets could not brook American recognition."

Stalin's protestations and pressure would have appeared to Mao as increased Soviet interference in China's sovereign affairs, particularly if the United States had already broken relations with the KMT. Mao, however, clearly did want to prove to Stalin that he was no Tito. Although the Chinese evidence suggests otherwise, it is possible that Mao would have denounced American attempts at recognition in order to curry favor with Stalin. But even in the event that Mao decided to buckle to Soviet pressure and react belligerently to such an American overture, this episode would have exacerbated existing tensions between the two sides, tensions that an internal CCP history chalks up to Stalin's "great power chauvinism." . . .

The only chance of avoiding significant Sino-American conflict in Korea [moreover] was missed in late September and early October [1950], before American troops crossed the 38th parallel [into North Korea]. This failure was at least partially due to the poor communication channels available to leaders in Beijing and Washington. There is evidence that suggests some possibility for successful deterrence if Chinese threats had been better communicated. Before Inchon [where General Douglas MacArthur staged in September 1950 a successful amphibious landing of U.S. and United Nations troops], civilian and military leaders wanted to avoid actions in Korea that might cause a Chinese or Soviet entry and sap America's strategic reserves in an area of little geostrategic value. On September 8 the NSC viewed favorably the crossing of the 38th parallel, "provided MacArthur's plans could be carried out without risk of a major war with the Chinese Communists or the Soviet Union." Even after Inchon, on September 27 Truman authorized MacArthur to proceed north only if he was certain that there would be no significant Soviet or Chinese intervention in Korea. The qualifications in Truman's September 27 orders demonstrate that his willingness to go north was not unconditional. Moreover, in his memoirs Truman himself recalled that the lack of direct and reliable communication channels caused him to discount [indirect warnings issued by Beijing]. . . . Documentary evidence from 1950 supports his recollections. This implies that Truman might have placed more weight on a more clearly communicated threat. . . .

It is, however, impossible to determine with certainty whether better communications would have prevented the disaster in North Korea. Given the American incentives to end the Korean problem once and for all, Truman might very well have ignored even the most direct Chinese warnings. By deciding to discount the weak and indirect October . . . warnings from Beijing, Washington squandered the last chance for peace. Once Americans crossed the 38th parallel on October 7, no coercive or reassuring acts by Truman or MacArthur could have prevented a wider war.

The history of Mao's Korean War decision making demonstrates the vital importance of the two American policy problems, . . . Truman's inability to abandon Chiang Kai-shek and his related failure to establish working relations with Beijing. For both political and strategic reasons, Truman's June [1950] decision to protect Chiang [by positioning the U.S. Seventh fleet in the Taiwan Strait] intensified Mao's sense that any long-term American presence in North Korea would threaten his new nation's security. The possibility of a future two-front war against the United States not only led Mao to fight but also counseled him to adopt an extremely offensive strategy designed to drive the Americans completely off the Korean peninsula. Finally, the lack of direct government-to-government channels complicated China's last genuine attempt to deter an expansion of the Korean conflict. . . . Truman's assistance to Chiang and his lack of contacts in Beijing were rooted in the American domestic politics of Cold War mobilization. These two policies played a more important role in Korean War escalation than the details of American military operations or the nuances of Truman's coercive threats and assurances in fall and winter 1950.

🌐 *F U R T H E R   R E A D I N G*

Robert Accinelli, *Crisis and Commitment* (1996) (U.S.–Taiwan)

Robert M. Blum, *Drawing the Line* (1982)

Robert Boardman, *Britain and the People's Republic of China* (1976)

Dorothy Borg and Waldo Heinrichs, eds., *Uncertain Years: Chinese-American Relations, 1947–1950* (1980)

Russell Buhite, *Patrick J. Hurley and American Foreign Policy* (1973)

———, *Soviet-American Relations in Asia, 1945–1954* (1982)

Carolle Carter, *Mission to Yenan* (1997)

James Chace, *Acheson* (1998)

Gordon H. Chang, *Friends and Enemies* (1990)

Jian Chen, *China's Road to the Korean War* (1994)

Warren I. Cohen, *America's Response to China* (1990)

———, "The United States and China Since 1945," in Warren I. Cohen, ed., *New Frontiers in American East Asian Relations* (1983)

John P. Davies, *Dragon by the Tail* (1972)

John K. Fairbank, *The United States and China* (1979)

Herbert Feis, *The China Tangle* (1953)

Rosemary Foot, *The Practice of Power* (1995) (Britain)

Marc S. Gallicchio, *The Cold War Begins in Asia* (1988)

Harry Harding and Yuan Ming, eds., *Sino-American Relations* (1989)

Michael H. Hunt, *The Genesis of Chinese Communist Foreign Policy* (1996)

Akira Iriye, *The Cold War in Asia* (1974)

——— and Warren Cohen, eds., *American, Chinese, and Japanese Perspectives on Wartime Asia, 1931–1949* (1990)

Christopher T. Jesperson, *American Images of China* (1996)

Arnold Xiangze Jiang, *The United States and China* (1988)

E. J. Kahn, *The China Hands* (1972)

Robert C. Keith, *The Diplomacy of Zhou Enlai* (1989)

Ross Koen, *The China Lobby in American Politics* (1974)

Paul G. Lauren, ed., *The China Hands Legacy* (1987)

Ronald L. McGlothlen, *Controlling the Waves: Dean Acheson and U.S. Foreign Policy in Asia* (1993)

Edwin Martin, *Divided Counsel: The Anglo-American Response to Communist Victory in China* (1986)

Ernest R. May, ed., *The Truman Administration and China, 1945–1949* (1975)

Gary May, *China Scapegoat: The Diplomatic Ordeal of John Carter Vincent* (1979)

David Mayers, *Cracking the Monolith: U.S. Policy Against the Sino-Soviet Alliance* (1986)

Brian Murray, "Stalin, the Cold War, and the Division of China," Working Paper #12 (June 1995), Cold War International History Project, Woodrow Wilson International Center for Scholars

Robert P. Newman, *Owen Lattimore and the "Loss" of China* (1992)

Thomas G. Paterson, *Meeting the Communist Threat* (1988)

James Reardon-Anderson, *Yenan and the Great Powers* (1980)

Michael Schaller, *The U.S. Crusade in China, 1938–1945* (1978)

———, *The United States and China in the Twentieth Century* (1990)

Yu-Ming Shaw, *John Leighton Stuart and Twentieth Century China-America Relations* (1992)

Michael Sheng, *Battling Western Imperialism: Mao, Stalin, and the United States* (1998)

William W. Stueck, Jr., *The Road to Confrontation* (1981)

"Symposium: Rethinking the Lost Chance in China," *Diplomatic History*, 21 (1997), 71–115

James C. Thomson et al., *Sentimental Imperialists* (1981)

Tang Tsou, *America's Failure in China, 1941–1950* (1963)

Barbara Tuchman, "If Mao Had Come to Washington," *Foreign Affairs,* 51 (1972), 44–64
———, *Stilwell and the American Experience in China, 1911–1945* (1971)
Nancy B. Tucker, "Continuing Controversies in the Literature of US-Chinese Relations Since 1945," in Warren I. Cohen, ed., *Pacific Passages* (1996)
———, *Patterns in the Dust: Chinese-American Relations and the Recognition Controversy, 1949–1950* (1983)
———, *Taiwan, Hong Kong, and the United States* (1994)
Paul Varg, *The Closing of the Door: Sino-American Relations, 1936–1947* (1973)
Arthur N. Waldron, *The Chinese Civil Wars, 1911–1949* (1995)
Odd Arne Westad, *Cold War and Revolution* (1993)
Donald Zagoria, "Choices in the Postwar World: Containment and China," in Charles Gati, ed., *Caging the Bear* (1974)
Shu Guang Zang, *Deterrence and Strategic Culture* (1992)
———, *Mao's Military Romanticism* (1995)

CHAPTER
8

The Korean War

Before the outbreak of the Korean War in June 1950, the United States had launched a number of Cold War strategies and programs—the Truman Doctrine, the Marshall Plan, and NATO—and had participated in crises in Iran, Turkey, Greece, Berlin, and elsewhere. Crisis also rocked China, where Mao Zedong's (Mao Tse-tung's) communists unseated Jiang Jieshi's (Chiang Kai-shek's) Nationalists in late 1949 and created the People's Republic of China.

A powerful shock wave hit the United States in August 1949 when the Soviet Union successfully exploded an atomic device, thereby ending America's atomic monopoly. Many Americans jumped to the conclusion that the United States was losing the Cold War. The phenomenon of McCarthyism, driven by an exaggerated fear of communism on the home front, surfaced in early 1950. Then in June of that year, the Korean War erupted. The Truman administration quickly decided to intervene in the conflict—to apply the containment doctrine.

U.S. intervention in Korea had actually begun in 1945, during the closing days of the Second World War, when Washington and Moscow drew a line at the thirty-eighth parallel and occupied the former Japanese colony. The two superpowers had agreed to a temporary division, but Korea soon became contested Cold War territory, an arena where the Soviets and the Americans competed to establish client states. In South Korea the United States threw its support behind the conservative government of Syngman Rhee, and in North Korea the Soviets backed Kim Il Sung's communist regime. Both Korean leaders considered themselves devout nationalists, and each envisioned himself as the head of a unified, independent Korea. As American and Soviet forces pulled back from the peninsula in 1949 and 1950, the two Koreas clashed in frequent border skirmishes and headed for a showdown. War came on June 25, 1950, when 75,000 Soviet-equipped North Korean troops punched through the thirty-eighth parallel and invaded South Korea.

The Korean War significantly altered the Cold War's course. In addition to dispatching U.S. forces to Korea, the Truman administration redoubled its efforts to contain communism around the globe and increasingly relied on military power to do the job. At home the administration raised annual defense expenditures from some $17 billion in 1950 to more than $50 billion in 1953, implementing the military buildup envisioned by the authors of NSC-68. In Europe military aid assumed priority over economic aid as Washington sought to give NATO more muscle. *U.S. officials also laid plans for regional defense arrangements in the Middle East and East Asia. In Southeast Asia the Truman administration increased military assistance to noncommunist forces in French Indochina, thus deepening U.S. intervention in Vietnam's struggle for independence. After battling Chinese troops in Korea, moreover, the United States recoiled from diplomatic recognition of the People's Republic of China. The Korean War of 1950–1953 thus transformed international relations.*

Since then, a number of complex questions have challenged historians, and the opening of Soviet, Chinese, and Korean documents has enabled new perspectives. One set of questions centers on the origins of the war. Did the Korean War spring from global, Soviet-engineered communist aggression? Or did its sources lie in a Korean civil war? Which social and political conditions on the Korean peninsula during the months leading up to the North Korean invasion of South Korea contributed to the war's outbreak? Did Soviet leaders plan and order the North Korean attack? Did they give the "green light"? Or did their North Korean allies initiate the conflict? What, exactly, was China's role, and why did it decide to intervene in the fall of 1950? Why did the United Nations take action? Was the military operation to stop North Korean aggression truly an international undertaking—or primarily a U.S. effort?

A second set of questions focuses on decisionmaking in Washington. Why did the Truman administration intervene? Should the United States have intervened? Who made the key decisions in the Truman administration during the height of the crisis? Did President Truman maintain control of policymaking? Or did subordinates, among them General Douglas MacArthur, pursue independent initiatives? What role did Congress and domestic politics play? Did administration officials carefully study the ramifications of U.S. intervention? Or did they rush to simplistic conclusions and make hurried, ill-considered decisions? How thoroughly did administration officials understand Korea's political and cultural context? Did they grasp Chinese intentions? Why did Truman change U.S. war goals—that is, why did he order American troops to cross the thirty-eighth parallel? Did the United States seriously contemplate the use of atomic weapons in Korea, or were American strategists simply dangling the nuclear threat to force diplomatic concessions? Why was General MacArthur fired? Should the United States have conducted a "limited" war, or should the war have been enlarged, as MacArthur advised?

The fighting dragged on until July 1953, when lengthy negotiations finally produced a cease-fire and peace terms that reestablished the status quo that had existed before June 25, 1950. Korea remained a divided nation, each side heavily armed and destined to live in a constant state of readiness and alert. Although Korea had been a limited war, the final casualty rate proved staggering. An estimated 3 million Koreans, nine hundred thousand Chinese, and thirty-five thousand Americans had perished.

⊕ D O C U M E N T S

On January 12, 1950, Secretary of State Dean Acheson delivered a major speech, Document 1, defining the American defense perimeter in Asia, from which he excluded Korea. Critics later charged that his omission gave the Soviet Union the incentive to use its North Korean allies to attack South Korea. Recently available Soviet sources, however, suggest that the Kremlin remained cautious. In Document 2, a telegram of January 19, 1950, the Soviet ambassador in Pyongyang, Terenti Shtykov, relays to Moscow the intent of the North Korean leader Kim Il Sung to use force to "liberate" South Korea and unify the two Koreas. Shtykov at the time warned Kim that an attack would not be advisable, but that the matter could be taken up again with Marshal Joseph Stalin. Kim visited Moscow in April, where Stalin finally endorsed his plan, pending the cooperation of the People's Republic of China.

Immediately following the North Korean attack of June 25, 1950, President Harry S. Truman met with key advisers at Blair House, a building near the White House. Document 3 is a record of the June 26, 1950, meeting in which Acheson recommended several important policies, not only for Korea but also for the Philippines, Formosa, and French Indochina. In August 1950, the Truman administration approved military plans to send U.N. troops across the thirty-eighth parallel into North Korea. On September 15, American marines landed at Inchon and soon marched north.

Meanwhile, in Beijing, Chinese authorities watched the United States's advance northward with deep concern. They decided to launch a counteroffensive. On October 2, 1950, Mao Zedong sent a cable, Document 4, to Stalin in Moscow. Describing the danger posed by the American "invaders," Mao informed the Soviet leader of China's decision for war and asked for the U.S.S.R.'s support for the mission. Yet around this same time, at a meeting with Truman on Wake Island on October 15, 1950, head of the United Nations Command General Douglas MacArthur, supremely confident of U.S. power, assured the president that the Chinese would not enter the war. This official U.S. account of this conversation is printed below as Document 5. Six weeks later, U.N. and U.S. troops frantically retreated down the Korean peninsula following China's entry into the war.

On November 30, 1950, President Truman told a press conference (an excerpt of which appears here as Document 6) that the United States had not ruled out the use of atomic weapons in the Korean theater. Washington nonetheless opted to avoid further escalation and to limit its goals to the reestablishment of a non-Communist Korea, south of the thirty-eighth parallel. Truman summarized American policy in a speech on April 11, 1951 (Document 7), shortly after he relieved MacArthur of his command. Document 8 is MacArthur's rebuttal of April 19, delivered as a speech to Congress.

1. Secretary of State Dean Acheson Defines the Defense Perimeter in Asia, 1950

What is the situation in regard to the military security of the Pacific area, and what is our policy in regard to it?

In the first place, the defeat and the disarmament of Japan has placed upon the United States the necessity of assuming the military defense of Japan so long as that is required, both in the interest of our security and in the interests of the security of the entire Pacific area and, in all honor, in the interest of Japanese security. We have American—and there are Australian—troops in Japan. I am not in a position to speak for the Australians, but I can assure you that there is no intention of any sort of abandoning or weakening the defenses of Japan and that whatever arrangements are to be made either through permanent settlement or otherwise, that defense must and shall be maintained.

This document can be found in *Department of State Bulletin*, XXII (January 23, 1950), 115–116.

The Korean War, 1950–1953

➤ United States (United Nations) forces
⇨ North Korean forces

This defensive perimeter runs along the Aleutians to Japan and then goes to the Ryukyus. We hold important defense positions in the Ryukyu Islands, and those we will continue to hold. In the interest of the population of the Ryukyu Islands, we will at an appropriate time offer to hold these islands under trusteeship of the United Nations. But they are essential parts of the defensive perimeter of the Pacific, and they must and will be held.

The defensive perimeter runs from the Ryukyus to the Philippine Islands. Our relations, our defensive relations with the Philippines are contained in agreements between us. Those agreements are being loyally carried out and will be loyally carried out. Both peoples have learned by bitter experience the vital connections between our mutual defense requirements. We are in no doubt about that, and it is hardly necessary for me to say an attack on the Philippines could not and would not be tolerated by the United States. But I hasten to add that no one perceives the imminence of any such attack.

So far as the military security of other areas in the Pacific is concerned, it must be clear that no person can guarantee these areas against military attack. But it must also be clear that such a guarantee is hardly sensible or necessary within the realm of practical relationship.

Should such an attack occur—one hesitates to say where such an armed attack could come from—the initial reliance must be on the people attacked to resist it and then upon the commitments of the entire civilized world under the Charter of the United Nations which so far has not proved a weak reed to lean on by any people who are determined to protect their independence against outside aggression. But it is a mistake, I think, in considering Pacific and Far Eastern problems to become obsessed with military considerations. Important as they are, there are other problems that press, and these other problems are not capable of solution through military means. These other problems arise out of the susceptibility of many areas, and many countries in the Pacific area, to subversion and penetration. That cannot be stopped by military means. . . .

That leads me to the other thing that I wanted to point out, and that is the limitation of effective American assistance. American assistance can be effective when it is the missing component in a situation which might otherwise be solved. The United States cannot furnish all these components to solve the question. It can not furnish determination, it can not furnish will, and it can not furnish the loyalty of a people to its government. But if the will and if the determination exists and if the people are behind their government, then, and not always then, is there a very good chance. In that situation, American help can be effective and it can lead to an accomplishment which could not otherwise be achieved. . . .

In Korea, we have taken great steps which have ended our military occupation, and in cooperation with the United Nations, have established an independent and sovereign country recognized by nearly all the rest of the world. We have given that nation great help in getting itself established. We are asking the Congress to continue that help until it is firmly established, and that legislation is now pending before the Congress. The idea that we should scrap all of that, that we should stop half way through the achievement of the establishment of this country, seems to me to be the most utter defeatism and utter madness of our interests in Asia. . . .

So after this survey, what we conclude, I believe, is that there is a new day which has dawned in Asia. It is a day in which the Asian peoples are on their own, and know it, and intend to continue on their own. It is a day in which the old relationships between east and west are gone, relationships which at their worst were exploitation, and which at their best were paternalism. That relationship is over, and the relationship of east and west must now be in the Far East one of mutual respect and mutual helpfulness. We are their friends. Others are their friends. We and those others are willing to help, but we can help only where we are wanted and only where the conditions of help are really sensible and possible. So what we can see is that this new day in Asia, this new day which is dawning, may go on to a glorious noon or it may darken and it may drizzle out. But that decision lies within the countries of Asia and within the power of the Asian people. It is not a decision which a friend or even an enemy from the outside can decide for them.

2. Kim Il Sung Pleads for Soviet Support, January 1950

[On January 17, 1950,] Kim, addressing the advisers Ignatiev and Pelishenko in an excited manner, began to speak about how now, when China is completing its liberation, the liberation of the Korean people in the south of the country is next in line. In connection with this he said:

"The people of the southern portion of Korea trust me and rely on our armed might. Partisans will not decide the question. The people of the south know that we have a good army. Lately I do not sleep at night, thinking about how to resolve the question of the unification of the whole country. If the matter of the liberation of the people of the southern portion of Korea and the unification of the country is drawn out, then I can lose the trust of the people of Korea." Further Kim stated that when he was in Moscow, Comrade Stalin said to him that it was not necessary to attack the south, in case of an attack on the north of the country by the army of Rhee Syngman [South Korean leader Syngman Rhee], then it is possible to go on the counteroffensive to the south of Korea. But since Rhee Syngman is still not instigating an attack, it means that the liberation of the people of the southern part of the country and the unification of the country are being drawn out, that he (Kim Il Sung) thinks that he needs again to visit Comrade Stalin and receive an order and permission for offensive action by the Peoples' Army for the purpose of the liberation of the people of Southern Korea. Further Kim said that he himself cannot begin an attack, because he is a communist, a disciplined person and for him the order of Comrade Stalin is law. Then he stated that if it is [not] possible to meet with Comrade Stalin, then he will try to meet with Mao Zedong, after his return from Moscow. Kim underscored that Mao Zedong promised to render him assistance after the conclusion of the war in China. (Apparently Kim Il Sung has in mind the conversation of his representative Kim Il with Mao Zedong in June 1949, about which I reported by ciphered telegram.) Kim said that he also has other questions for Mao Zedong, in particular the question of the possibility of the creation of an eastern bureau of the Cominform. He further stated that on all these questions he will try to meet with Comrade Shtykov and to secure through him a meeting with Comrade Stalin.

The advisers of the embassy Ignatiev and Pelishenko, avoiding discussing these questions, tried to switch the discussion to a general theme, then Kim Il Sung came toward me, took me aside and began the following conversation: can he meet with Comrade Stalin and discuss the question of the position in the south and the

This document can be found in *Cold War International History Project Bulletin*, Woodrow Wilson International Center for Scholars, Washington, D.C., No. 5 (Spring 1995), 8.

question of aggressive actions against the army of Rhee Syngman, that their people's army now is significantly stronger than the army of Rhee Syngman. Here he stated that if it is impossible to meet with Comrade Stalin, then he wants to meet with Mao Zedong, since Mao after his visit to Moscow will have orders on all questions.

Then Kim Il Sung placed before me the question, why don't I allow him to attack the Ongjin peninsula, which the People's Army could take in three days, and with a general attack the People's Army could be in Seoul in several days.

I answered Kim that he has not raised the question of a meeting with Comrade Stalin and if he raises such a question, then it is possible that Comrade Stalin will receive him. On the question of an attack on the Ongjin peninsula I answered him that it is impossible to do this. Then I tried to conclude the conversation on these questions and, alluding to a later time, proposed to go home. With that the conversation was concluded. . . .

In the process of this conversation Kim Il Sung repeatedly underscored his wish to get the advice of Comrade Stalin on the question of the situation in the south of Korea, since [Kim Il Sung] is constantly nurturing his idea about an attack.

3. President Harry S. Truman and His Advisers Confer at the "Blair House Meeting," June 26, 1950

GENERAL [HOYT S.] VANDENBERG reported that the First Yak [North Korean] plane had been shot down.

THE PRESIDENT remarked that he hoped that it was not the last.

GENERAL VANDENBERG read the text of the orders which had been issued to our Air Forces calling on them to take "aggressive action" against any planes interfering with their mission or operating in a manner unfriendly to the South Korean forces. He indicated, however, that they had been avoiding combat where the direct carrying-out of their mission was not involved.

MR. [DEAN] ACHESON suggested that an all-out order be issued to the Navy and Air Force to waive all restrictions on their operations in Korea and to offer the fullest possible support to the South Korean forces, attacking tanks, guns, columns, etc., of the North Korean forces in order to give a chance to the South Koreans to reform.

THE PRESIDENT said he approved this.

MR. [FRANK] PACE inquired whether this meant action only south of the thirty-eighth parallel.

MR. ACHESON said this was correct. He was making no suggestion for any action across the line.

GENERAL VANDENBERG asked whether this meant also that they should not fly over the line.

MR. ACHESON said they should not.

This document can be found in U.S. Department of State, *Foreign Relations of the United States, 1950, Korea* (Washington, D.C.: Government Printing Office, 1976), VII, 179–183.

THE PRESIDENT said this was correct; that no action should be taken north of the thirty-eighth parallel. He added "not yet.". . .

MR. ACHESON said that the second point he wished to bring up was that orders should be issued to the Seventh Fleet to prevent an attack on Formosa.

THE PRESIDENT said he agreed.

MR. ACHESON continued that at the same time the National Government of China should be told to desist from operations against the mainland and that the Seventh Fleet should be ordered to see that those operations would cease.

MR. ACHESON said his third point was an increase in the United States military forces in the Philippines and an acceleration of aid to the Philippines in order that we might have a firm base there.

THE PRESIDENT said he agreed.

MR. ACHESON said his fourth point was that aid to Indochina should be stepped up and that a strong military mission should be sent. . . .

THE PRESIDENT said that he had a letter from the Generalissimo [Jiang Jieshi] about one month (?) ago to the effect that the Generalissimo might step out of the situation if that would help. He said this was a private letter and he had kept it secret. He said that we might want to proceed along those lines in order to get Chinese forces helping us. He thought that the Generalissimo might step out if MacArthur were put in.

MR. ACHESON said that the Generalissimo was unpredictable and that it was possible that he might resist and "throw the ball game." He said that it might be well to do this later.

THE PRESIDENT said that was alright. He himself thought that it was the next step. . . .

MR. ACHESON added in regard to the Formosan situation that he thought it undesirable that we should get mixed up in the question of the Chinese administration of the Island.

THE PRESIDENT said that we were not going to give the Chinese "a nickel" for any purpose whatever. He said that all the money we had given them is now invested in United States real estate. . . .

MR. [JOHN D.] HICKERSON read the draft of the Security Council resolution recommending that UN members render such assistance as was needed to Korea to repel the attack.

THE PRESIDENT said that was right. He said we wanted everyone in on this, including Hong Kong.

GENERAL [OMAR] BRADLEY reported that British Air Marshall Tedder had come to see him, was generally in accord with our taking the firm position, and gave General Bradley a full report of the forces which the British have in that area.

MR. [DEAN] RUSK pointed out that it was possible the Russians would come to the Security Council meeting and cast a veto. In that case we would still take the position that we could act in support of the Charter.

THE PRESIDENT said that was right. He rather wished they would veto. He said we needed to lay a base for our action in Formosa. He said that he would work on the draft of his statement tonight and would talk to the Defense and State Departments in the morning regarding the final text.

Mr. Rusk pointed out that it was Mr. [George F.] Kennan's estimate that Formosa would be the next likely spot for a Communist move.

Secretary [Louis A.] Johnson reported that SCAP's [Supreme Commander to the Allied Powers] guess was that the next move would be on Iran. He thought there should be a check on this.

General [J. Lawton] Collins said that SCAP did not have as much global information as they have in Washington. He and Mr. Pace stated that they have asked for full reports all over the world in regard to any developments, particularly of Soviet preparations.

Secretary Johnson suggested to Mr. Acheson that it would be advisable to have some talks with the UK regarding possible action in Iran.

Mr. Acheson said he would talk with both the British and French. . . .

Mr. Acheson suggested that the President might wish to get in Senator [Tom] Connally and other members of the Senate and House and tell them what had been decided.

The President said that he had a meeting scheduled for 10:00 tomorrow morning with the Big Four [congressional leaders] and that he would get in any others that the Secretary thought should be added. He suggested that Secretaries Acheson and Johnson should also be there. . . .

General Collins stated that the military situation in Korea was bad. It was impossible to say how much our air can do. The Korean Chief of Staff has no fight left in him.

Mr. Acheson stated that it was important for us to do something even if the effort were not successful.

Mr. Johnson said that even if we lose Korea this action would save the situation. He said this action "suits me." He then asked whether any of the military representatives had any objection to the course of action which had been outlined. There was no objection.

General Vandenberg, in response to a question that Mr. [Thomas] Finletter, said that he bet a tank would be knocked out before dark.

The President said he had done everything he could for five years to prevent this kind of situation. Now the situation is here and we must do what we can to meet it. He had been wondering about the mobilization of the National Guard and asked General Bradley if that was necessary now. If it was he must go to Congress and ask for funds. He was merely putting the subject on the table for discussion. He repeated we must do everything we can for the Korean situation—"for the United Nations."

General Bradley said that if we commit our ground forces in Korea we cannot at the same time carry out our other commitments without mobilization. He wondered if it was better to wait now on the question of mobilization of the National Guard. He thought it would be preferable to wait a few days.

The President said he wished the Joint Chiefs to think about this and to let him know in a few days time. He said "I don't want to go to war."

General Collins stated that if we were going to commit ground forces in Korea we must mobilize.

Mr. Acheson suggested that we should hold mobilization in reserve. . . .

GENERAL COLLINS remarked that if we had had standing orders we could have stopped this. We must consider this problem for the future.

THE PRESIDENT said he agreed.

4. Mao Zedong Informs Joseph Stalin of China's Decision to Enter the Korean War, 1950

(1) We have decided to send a portion of our troops, under the name of [the Chinese] Volunteers, to Korea, assisting the Korean comrades in fighting the troops of the United States and its running dog Syngman Rhee. We regarded the mission as necessary. If Korea were completely occupied by the Americans and the Korean revolutionary forces were substantially destroyed, the American invaders would be more rampant, and such a situation would be very unfavorable to the whole East.

(2) We realize that since we have decided to send Chinese troops to Korea to fight the Americans, we must first be able to solve the problem, that is, that we are prepared to annihilate the invaders from the United States and from other countries, and to drive them out [of Korea]; second, since Chinese troops will fight American troops in Korea (although we will use the name the Chinese Volunteers), we must be prepared for an American declaration of war on China. We must be prepared for the possible bombardments by American air forces of many Chinese cities and industrial bases, and for attacks by American naval forces on China's coastal areas.

(3) Of the two issues, the first one is whether the Chinese troops would be able to defeat American troops in Korea, thus effectively resolving the Korean problem. If our troops could annihilate American troops in Korea, especially the Eighth Army (a competent veteran U.S. army), the whole situation would become favorable to the revolutionary front and China, even though the second question ([the possibility] that the United States would declare war on China) would still remain as a serious issue. In other words, the Korean problem will end in fact with the defeat of American troops (although the war might not end in name, because the United States would not recognize the victory of Korea for a long period). If this occurs, even though the United States had declared war on China, the ongoing confrontation would not be on a large-scale, nor would it last very long. We consider that the most unfavorable situation would be that the Chinese forces fail to destroy American troops in large numbers in Korea, thus resulting in a stalemate, and that, at the same time, the United States openly declares war on China, which would be detrimental to China's economic reconstruction already under way, and would cause dissatisfaction among the national bourgeoisie and some other sectors of the people (who are absolutely afraid of war).

(4) Under the current situation, we have decided, starting on October 15, to move the twelve divisions, which have been earlier transferred to southern Manchuria, into suitable areas in North Korea (not necessarily close to the thirty-eighth parallel); these troops will only fight the enemy that venture to attack areas

From *Chinese Historians* 5 (Spring 1992), 67–68, translated by Li Xiaobing, Wang Xi, and Jian Chen. Reprinted with the permission of Chinese Historians of the United States, Inc.

north of the thirty-eighth parallel; our troops will employ defensive tactics, while engaging small groups of enemies and learning about the situation in every respect. Meanwhile, our troops will be awaiting the arrival of Soviet weapons and being equipped with those weapons. Only then will our troops, in cooperation with the Korean comrades, launch a counter-offensive to destroy the invading American forces.

(5) According to our information, every U.S. army (two infantry divisions and one mechanized division) is armed with 1500 pieces of artillery of various calibers ranging from 70mm to 240mm, including tank guns and anti-aircraft guns, while each of our armies (three divisions) is equipped with only 36 pieces of artillery. The enemy would control the air while our air force, which has just started its training, will not be able to enter the war with some 300 planes until February 1951. Therefore, at present, we are not assured that our troops will be able to annihilate an entire U.S. army once and for all. But since we have decided to go into the war against the Americans, we should be prepared that, when the U.S. high command musters up one complete army to fight us in a campaign, we should be able to concentrate our forces four times greater than those of the enemy (that is, to use four of our armies to fight against one enemy army) and to marshal firing power one and a half to two times stronger than that of the enemy (that is, to use 2200 to 3000 pieces of artillery of 70mm calibre and upward to deal with the enemy's 1500 pieces of artilleries of the same calibers), so that we can guarantee a complete and thorough destruction of one enemy army.

(6) In addition to the above-mentioned twelve divisions, we are transferring another twenty-four divisions, as the second and third echelons to assist Korea, from south of the Yangzi River and the Shaanxi-Ganshu areas to the Long-hai, Tianjin-Pukuo, and Beijing–Southern Manchuria railways; we expect to gradually employ these divisions next spring and summer in accordance with the situation at the time.

5. General Douglas MacArthur Dismisses the Likelihood of Chinese Intervention, 1950

The President: What are the chances for Chinese or Soviet interference?

General MacArthur: Very little. Had they interfered in the first or second months it would have been decisive. We are no longer fearful of their intervention. We no longer stand hat in hand. The Chinese have 300,000 men in Manchuria. Of these probably not more than 100/125,000 are distributed along the Yalu River. Only 50/60,000 could be gotten across the Yalu River. They have no Air Force. Now that we have bases for our Air Force in Korea, if the Chinese tried to get down to Pyongyang there would be the greatest slaughter.

With the Russians it is a little different. They have an Air Force in Siberia and a fairly good one, with excellent pilots equipped with some jets and B-25 and B-29

This document can be found in U.S. Department of State, *Foreign Relations of the United States, 1950, Korea* (Washington, D.C.: U.S. Government Printing Office, 1976), VII, 179–183.

planes. They can put 1,000 planes in the air with some 2/300 more from the Fifth and Seventh Soviet Fleets. They are probably no match for our Air Force. The Russians have no ground troops available for North Korea. They would have difficulty in putting troops into the field. It would take six weeks to get a division across and six weeks brings the winter. The only other combination would be Russian air support of Chinese ground troops. Russian air is deployed in a semicircle through Mukden and Harbin, but the coordination between the Russian air and the Chinese ground would be so flimsy that I believe Russian air would bomb the Chinese as often as they would bomb us. Ground support is a very difficult thing to do. Our Marines do it perfectly. They have been trained for it. Our own Air and Ground Forces are not as good as the Marines but they are effective. Between untrained Air and Ground Forces an air umbrella is impossible without a lot of joint training. I believe it just wouldn't work with Chinese Communist ground and Russian air. We are the best.

6. Truman Discusses the Possible Use of Atomic Weapons in Korea, 1950

Q. Mr. President, will attacks in Manchuria depend on action in the United Nations?

The President. Yes, entirely.

Q. In other words, if the United Nations resolution should authorize General MacArthur to go further than he has, he will—

The President. We will take whatever steps are necessary to meet the military situation, just as we always have.

Q. Will that include the atomic bomb?

The President. That includes every weapon that we have.

Q. Mr. President, you said "every weapon that we have." Does that mean that there is active consideration of the use of the atomic bomb?

The President. There has always been active consideration of its use. I don't want to see it used. It is a terrible weapon, and it should not be used on innocent men, women, and children who have nothing whatever to do with this military aggression. That happens when it is used. . . .

Q. Mr. President, I wonder if we could retrace that reference to the atom bomb? Did we understand you clearly that the use of the atomic bomb is under active consideration?

The President. Always has been. It is one of our weapons.

Q. Does that mean, Mr. President, use against military objectives, or civilian—

The President. It's a matter that the military people will have to decide. I'm not a military authority that passes on those things.

Q. Mr. President, perhaps it would be better if we are allowed to quote your remarks on that directly?

The President. I don't think—I don't think that is necessary.

This document can be found in *Public Papers of the Presidents of the United States, Harry S. Truman, 1950* (Washington, D.C.: U.S. Government Printing Office, 1965), pp. 726–727.

Q. Mr. President, you said this depends on United Nations action. Does that mean that we wouldn't use the atomic bomb except on a United Nations authorization?

The President. No, it doesn't mean that at all. The action against Communist China depends on the action of the United Nations. The military commander in the field will have charge of the use of the weapons, as he always has.

7. Truman Defends U.S. Policy, 1951

In the simplest terms, what we are doing in Korea is this: We are trying to prevent a third world war.

I think most people in this country recognized that fact last June. And they warmly supported the decision of the Government to help the Republic of Korea against the Communist aggressors. Now, many persons, even some who applauded our decision to defend Korea, have forgotten the basic reason for our action.

It is right for us to be in Korea. It was right last June. It is right today.

I want to remind you why this is true.

The Communists in the Kremlin are engaged in a monstrous conspiracy to stamp out freedom all over the world. If they were to succeed, the United States would be numbered among their principal victims. It must be clear to everyone that the United States cannot—and will not—sit idly by and await foreign conquest. The only question is: When is the best time to meet the threat and how?

The best time to meet the threat is in the beginning. It is easier to put out a fire in the beginning when it is small than after it has become a roaring blaze.

And the best way to meet the threat of aggression is for the peace-loving nations to act together. If they don't act together, they are likely to be picked off, one by one.

If they had followed the right policies in the 1930's—if the free countries had acted together, to crush the aggression of the dictators, and if they had acted in the beginning, when the aggression was small—there probably would have been no World War II.

If history has taught us anything, it is that aggression anywhere in the world is a threat to peace everywhere in the world. When that aggression is supported by the cruel and selfish rulers of a powerful nation who are bent on conquest, it becomes a clear and present danger to the security and independence of every free nation.

This is a lesson that most people in this country have learned thoroughly. This is the basic reason why we joined in creating the United Nations. And since the end of World War II we have been putting that lesson into practice—we have been working with other free nations to check the aggressive designs of the Soviet Union before they can result in a third world war.

That is what we did in Greece [in 1947], when that nation was threatened by the aggression of international communism.

The attack against Greece could have led to general war. But this country came to the aid of Greece. The United Nations supported Greek resistance. With our help, the determination and efforts of the Greek people defeated the attack on the spot.

This document can be found in *Public Papers of the Presidents of the United States, Harry S. Truman, 1951* (Washington, D.C.: U.S. Government Printing Office, 1965), pp. 223–227.

Another big Communist threat to peace was the Berlin blockade. That too could have led to war. But again it was settled because free men would not back down in an emergency.

The aggression against Korea is the boldest and most dangerous move the Communists have yet made.

The attack on Korea was part of a greater plan for conquering all of Asia. . . .

The whole Communist imperialism is back of the attack on peace in the Far East. It was the Soviet Union that trained and equipped the North Koreans for aggression. The Chinese Communists massed 44 well-trained and well-equipped divisions on the Korean frontier. These were the troops they threw into battle when the North Korean Communists were beaten. . . .

So far, by fighting a limited war in Korea, we have prevented aggression from succeeding and bringing on a general war. And the ability of the whole free world to resist Communist aggression has been greatly improved. . . .

Our resolute stand in Korea is helping the forces of freedom now fighting in Indochina and other countries in that part of the world. It has already slowed down the timetable of conquest. . . .

But you may ask: Why can't we take other steps to punish the aggressor? Why don't we bomb Manchuria and China itself? Why don't we assist Chinese Nationalist troops to land on the mainland of China?

If we were to do these things, we would be running a very grave risk of starting a general war. If that were to happen, we would have brought about the exact situation we are trying to prevent.

If we were to do these things, we would become entangled in a vast conflict on the continent of Asia and our task would become immeasurably more difficult all over the world.

What would suit the ambitions of the Kremlin better than for our military forces to be committed to a full-scale war with Red China? . . .

First of all, it is clear that our efforts in Korea can blunt the will of the Chinese Communists to continue the struggle. The United Nations forces have put up a tremendous fight in Korea and have inflicted very heavy casualties on the enemy. Our forces are stronger now than they have been before. These are plain facts which may discourage the Chinese Communists from continuing their attack.

Second, the free world as a whole is growing in military strength every day. In the United States, in Western Europe, and throughout the world, free men are alert to the Soviet threat and are building their defenses. This may discourage the Communist rulers from continuing the war in Korea—and from undertaking new acts of aggression elsewhere. . . .

I believe that we must try to limit the war to Korea for these vital reasons: to make sure that the precious lives of our fighting men are not wasted; to see that the security of our country and the free world is not needlessly jeopardized; and to prevent a third world war.

A number of events have made it evident that General MacArthur did not agree with that policy. I have therefore considered it essential to relieve General MacArthur so that there would be no doubt or confusion as to the real purpose and aim of our policy.

The Korean War 313

It was with the deepest personal regret that I found myself compelled to take this action. General MacArthur is one of our greatest military commanders. But the cause of world peace is more important than any individual.

8. MacArthur's "No Substitute for Victory" Speech, 1951

While I was not consulted prior to the President's decision to intervene in the support of the Republic of Korea, that decision from a military standpoint proved a sound one. As I say, a brief and sound one as we hurled back the invaders and decimated his forces. Our victory was complete and our objectives within reach when Red China intervened with numerically superior ground forces. This created a new war and an entirely new situation, a situation not contemplated when our forces were committed against the North Korean invaders, a situation which called for new decisions in the diplomatic sphere to permit the realistic adjustment of military strategy. Such decisions have not been forthcoming.

While no man in his right mind would advocate sending our ground forces into continental China—and such was never given a thought—the new situation did urgently demand a drastic revision of strategic planning if our political aim was to defeat this new enemy as we had defeated the old.

Apart from the military need as I saw it to neutralize sanctuary, protection given to the enemy north of the Yalu, I felt that military necessity in the conduct of the war made necessary:

First, the intensification of our economic blockade against China.

Second, the imposition of a naval blockade against the China coast.

Third, removal of restrictions on air reconnaissance of China's coastal areas and of Manchuria.

Fourth, removal of restrictions on the forces of the Republic of China on Formosa with logistical support to contribute to their effective operation against the Chinese mainland.

For entertaining these views all professionally designed to support our forces committed to Korea and bring hostilities to an end with the least possible delay and at a saving of countless American and Allied lives, I have been severely criticized in lay circles, principally abroad, despite my understanding that from a military standpoint the above views have been fully shared in the past by practically every military leader concerned with the Korean campaign, including our own Joint Chiefs of Staff.

I called for reinforcements, but was informed that reinforcements were not available. I made clear that if not permitted to utilize the friendly Chinese force of some 600,000 men on Formosa; if not permitted to blockade the China coast to prevent the Chinese Reds from getting succor from without; and if there were to be

This document can be found in *Congressional Record,* XCVII (April 19, 1951), 4124–4125.

no hope of major reinforcements, the position of the command from the military standpoint forbade victory. We could hold in Korea by constant maneuver and at an approximate area where our supply advantages were in balance with the supply line disadvantages of the enemy, but we could hope at best for only an indecisive campaign, with its terrible and constant attrition upon our forces if the enemy utilized his full military potential. I have constantly called for the new political decisions essential to a solution. Efforts have been made to distort my position. It has been said in effect that I was a warmonger. Nothing could be further from the truth. I know war as few other men now living know it, and nothing to me is more revolting. . . .

But once war is forced upon us, there is no other alternative than to apply every available means to bring it to a swift end. War's very object is victory—not prolonged indecision. In war, indeed, there can be no substitute for victory.

There are some who for varying reasons would appease Red China. They are blind to history's clear lesson. For history teaches with unmistakable emphasis that appeasement but begets new and bloodier war. . . .

The tragedy of Korea is further heightened by the fact that as military action is confined to its territorial limits, it condemns that nation, which it is our purpose to save, to suffer the devastating impact of full naval and air bombardment, while the enemy's sanctuaries are fully protected from such attack and devastation. Of the nations of the world, Korea alone, up to now, is the sole one which has risked its all against communism. . . .

I am closing my 52 years of military service. When I joined the Army even before the turn of the century, it was the fulfillment of all my boyish hopes and dreams. The world has turned over many times since I took the oath on the plain at West Point, and the hopes and dreams have long since vanished. But I since remember the refrain of one of the most popular barrack ballads of that day which proclaimed most proudly that—

"Old soldiers never die; they just fade away." And like the old soldier of that ballad, I now close my military career and just fade away—an old soldier who tried to do his duty as God gave him the light to see that duty.

 E S S A Y S

In the first essay, Professor Bruce Cumings of the University of Chicago analyzes the origins of the Korean War and the roots of U.S. intervention. He challenges Cold War interpretations that blame the Soviet Union exclusively for igniting the war, and he concludes that the conflict began as a civil war between rival Korean governments, north and south, both of which sought to unify their country following its arbitrary division in 1945. Cumings faults the Truman administration for supporting an oppressive political and social hierarchy in South Korea and then leading the United Nations to contain a monolithic Communist threat that did not exist.

In the second essay, two Russian scholars, Vladislav Zubok, a senior fellow at the National Security Archive in Washington, D.C., and Constantine Pleshakov, a writer who lives in Moscow, use recently released Communist sources to probe Russian, Chinese, and North Korean policies. They place the responsibility for the war on Soviet leader Joseph Stalin. Zubok and Pleshakov argue that Stalin in early 1950 gave his backing to Kim Il

Sung's war plans hoping to demonstrate Moscow's leadership among Communist states. Stalin, they observe, was surprised by Washington's strong response and, in order to avoid direct confrontation with the United States, pressed his Chinese Communist ally Mao Zedong to intervene on Kim's behalf. In the end, Zubok and Pelshakov suggest, the Truman administration's astute countermeasures and global military buildup foiled Stalin's expansionist gamble.

Korea's Civil War and the Roots of U.S. Intervention

BRUCE CUMINGS

A Cold War narrative is all too imbedded in American histories of the liberation period (Koreans call August 15, 1945, *haebang,* meaning liberation from Japan). The accounts begin with Japan's surrender, move quickly to the December 1945 agreements on Korea with the Soviets and the two U.S.-Soviet "joint commissions" of 1946 and 1947 that followed them; they then detail the United Nations's role in sponsoring elections that established the Republic of Korea in 1948, and conclude with the war in 1950. The literature lays most of the problems in these five years at the door of Soviet obstructionism or Korean political immaturity. In fact, Koreans were the prime historical actors in this period, shaping American and Soviet power to their ends and generally ignoring all the "externals" I have just mentioned, unless they appeared to serve Korean purposes. The national division, however, was not their doing: it is Americans who bear the lion's share of the responsibility for the thirty-eighth parallel.

In the days just before Koreans heard the voice of Emperor Hirohito for the first time, broadcasting Japan's surrender and Korea's liberation on August 15, 1945, John J. McCloy of the State-War-Navy Coordinating Committee (SWNCC) directed two young colonels, Dean Rusk and Charles H. Bonesteel, to withdraw to an adjoining room and find a place to divide Korea. It was around midnight on August 10–11, the atomic bombs had been dropped, the Soviet Red Army had entered the Pacific War, and American planners were rushing to arrange the Japanese surrender throughout the region. Given thirty minutes to do so, Rusk and Bonesteel looked at a map and chose the thirty-eighth parallel because it "would place the capital city in the American zone"; although the line was "further north than could be realistically reached . . . in the event of Soviet disagreement," the Soviets made no objections—which "somewhat surprised" Rusk. General Douglas MacArthur, the hero of the Pacific campaigns, issued General Order Number One for the Japanese surrender on August 15, including in it (and thus making public) the thirty-eighth parallel decision. The Russians accepted in silence this division into spheres, while demanding a Russian occupation of the northern part of Hokkaido in Japan (which MacArthur refused).

American officials consulted no Koreans in coming to this decision, nor did they ask the opinions of the British or the Chinese, both of whom were to take part in a planned "trusteeship" for Korea. Instead, the decision was unilateral and hasty. Still, it grew out of previous American planning. The United States had taken the initiative in great-power deliberations on Korea during the war, suggesting a multilateral trusteeship for postwar Korea to the British in March 1943, and to the Soviets at the end of the same year. President Franklin D. Roosevelt worried about the disposition of enemy-held colonial territories and aware of colonial demands for independence, sought a gradualist, tutelary policy of preparing colonials (like the Koreans) for self-government and independence. He knew that since Korea touched the Soviet border, the Russians would want to be involved in the fate of postwar Korea; he hoped to get a Soviet commitment to a multilateral administration, to forestall unilateral solutions and provide an entry for American interests in Korea. Korean independence would come only at an appropriate time, or "in due course"—a phrase famous to Koreans, having been used in the 1943 declaration of the Cairo conference (where Roosevelt had met with Winston Churchill and Chiang Kai-shek) and by Prime Minister Hara Kei to justify Japan's "cultural policy" after the March First movement in 1919. The British and the French resisted Roosevelt's trusteeship idea because it threatened their empires; so did the Korean people, who were humiliated by the prospect of yet more great-power "tutelage." Stalin made no commitments to the policy, but seemed to enjoy watching Roosevelt and Churchill wrangle over the future of empire in the postwar world. Stalin was mostly silent in wartime discussions with Roosevelt about Korea, tending either to humor FDR and his pet trusteeship projects (which Stalin no doubt considered naive) or to say that the Koreans would want independence. . . .

. . . The United States gained Soviet adherence to a modified version of the trusteeship idea at the foreign ministers' conference in December 1945, an important agreement that eliminated irrelevant British and Chinese influence, while suggesting that the two powers might ultimately come to terms on how to reunify Korea. Roosevelt, basing himself on the experience of American colonialism in the Philippines, had argued that a Korean trusteeship might last as long as forty or fifty years, but the December 1945 agreement shortened the period of great-power involvement in Korean affairs to no more than five years and called for a unified provisional government of Korea. But even by that early date the agreement was still too late, because the de facto policies of the two occupations had identified the Soviets with Kim Il Sung and the people's committees [leftist governing units organized at the local level in both North Korea and South Korea], while the Americans backed Syngman Rhee and opposed the committees and widespread Korean demands for a thorough renovation of colonial legacies. Washington's internationalist policy was undermined not so much by the Soviets as by the determination of Americans on the scene in Korea to begin an early version of the Cold War "containment" doctrine.

The American military command, along with such high-ranking emissaries dispatched from Washington as John J. McCloy, tended to interpret resistance to U.S. desires in the South as radical and pro-Soviet. In particular the United States saw the [indigenously organized] "People's Republic" as part of a Soviet master plan to dominate all of Korea. Radical activity, such as the ousting of landlords and attacks on Koreans in the colonial police, was usually a matter of settling scores left over from the colonial period, or of demands by Koreans to run their own affairs. But it immediately became wrapped up with Soviet-American rivalry, such that the Cold War arrived in Korea in the last months of 1945. . . .

The problem was that Korean society had no base for either a liberal or a democratic party as Americans understood it; it had a population the vast majority of which consisted of poor peasants, and a tiny minority of which held most of the wealth: landowners, who formed the real base of the KDP [South Korea's noncommunist political power structure]. The elite of Korean society during the colonial period, nearly all of them were widely perceived to have fattened under colonial rule while everybody else suffered. The historical documentation could not be clearer: the United States intervened on behalf of the smallest group in Korea. . . .

The main problem for the [U.S. backed] conservatives was their lack of nationalist credentials. Therefore they wanted to bring back some of the exiled nationalists who had resisted the Japanese, while keeping the far more numerous exiled communists at bay. They succeeded in convincing [U.S. commanding General John Reed] Hodge that Syngman Rhee in the United States and Kim Ku in China (still in the wartime capital of Chungking with Chiang Kai-shek) should be brought back to head the southern conservatives. With Rhee there was no problem, since he had befriended wartime intelligence people in Washington and they were already trying to bring him back to Seoul. The most important of these was M. Preston Goodfellow, who had been deputy director of the Office of Strategic Services (forerunner of the CIA) under William "Wild Bill" Donovan and had a background in army intelligence; like Donovan, he was known for his interest and expertise in clandestine warfare. Goodfellow thought Rhee had more of "the American point of view" than other Korean leaders, and arranged to deposit him back in Korea in October, with MacArthur's support (but over the objections of the State Department, which had long disliked Rhee). Goodfellow then arrived in Korea himself, seeking to set up a separate, anticommunist southern government. Rhee flew into Korea on MacArthur's personal plane on October 16, 1945, and four days later General Hodge introduced him to the Korean public. . . .

With fifty years of hindsight—or even five, in 1950—we can imagine a cauterizing fire that would have settled Korea's multitude of social and political problems caused by the pressure cooker of colonial rule and instant "liberation," a purifying upheaval that might have been pretty awful, but nothing like the millions of lives lost in 1950–53. . . .

Had the Americans and the Russians quit Korea, a leftist regime would have taken over quickly, and it would have been a revolutionary nationalist government that, over time, would have moderated and rejoined the world community—as did China, as Vietnam is doing today. But we have to imagine this, because Americans do not understand the point of social revolutions, never having had one themselves; to allow this to happen would have meant that Hodge and many other Americans would have occupied Korea only to "turn it over to the communists." . . . The Americans would not turn Korea over to the Koreans, and so they got on with the "positive action" necessary to create an anticommunist South Korea. Korea thus became a harbinger of policies later followed throughout the world—in Greece, Indochina, Iran, Guatemala, Cuba, Nicaragua—where Americans came to defend any group calling itself anticommunist, because the alternative was thought to be worse. And fifty years later the Korean problem remains unsolved.

The establishment of official organizations for the South alone went on apace. The ROK was not proclaimed until August 15, 1948, but the southern political system was built in the first few months of the occupation, and did not substantially change until the 1960s. In November and December 1945 Hodge and his advisers chose to take four steps: first, to build up an army to defend the thirty-eighth parallel; second, to buttress the Korean National Police (KNP) as the primary political weapon for pacifying the South; third, to strengthen the alliance with rightist parties; and fourth, to suppress Koreans who didn't like such policies. An army that occupied Korea to disarm the Japanese was now intensively shaping a containment bulwark in South Korea. . . .

The effective opposition to the developing southern system was almost wholly on the left, mainly because Japanese policies had left Korea with such a tiny middle class. A mass popular resistance from 1945 to 1950 mingled raw peasant protest with organized labor union activity and, finally, armed guerrilla resistance. I have written much about this elsewhere, but we can see the general picture in some of the first CIA reports on Korea. In one 1948 document, CIA analysts wrote that South Korean political life was "dominated by a rivalry between Rightists and the remnants of the Left Wing People's Committees," which the CIA termed a "grass-roots independence movement which found expression in the establishment of the People's Committees throughout Korea in August 1945," led by "Communists" who based their right to rule on the resistance to the Japanese. . . .

Although membership in communist and left-wing organizations was ostensibly legal under the American occupation, "the police generally regarded the Communists as rebels and traitors who should be seized, imprisoned, and sometimes shot on the slightest provocation." . . .

American policy, of course, never set out to create one of the worst police states in Asia. The Korean problem was what we would now call a Third World problem or a North-South problem, a conflict over how best to overcome the debilities of colonial rule and comparative backwardness. In the Cold War milieu of the time, however, it was always seen by Americans as an East-West problem. The Soviets, we might say, pushed the North-South angle as a way of besting the United States in the East-West conflict on the peninsula. That is, they stayed in the background and let Koreans run the government, they put anti-Japanese resistance leaders out front, and they supported radical reforms of the land system, labor conditions, and women's rights—all of which were pushed through by the end of 1946. Although very active behind the scenes, the Russians made it seem that Kim Il Sung was in charge—especially after they withdrew their troops from Korea in late 1948.

The Americans could not withdraw their troops so easily, because they were worried about the viability of the southern regime, its dictatorial tendencies, and its oft-stated bluster about marching north. But much more important was Korea's growing importance to American global policy, as part of a new, dual strategy of containing communism and reviving the Japanese industrial economy as a motor of the world economy, but one now shorn of its previous political and military clout. In early 1947 officials in Washington decided to revive Japanese heavy industries and end the purges of wartime leaders, a policy long known as the reverse course. They all thought the solution to the sluggish European and Japanese recovery lay in lifting restrictions on heavy industry and finding ways to combine Germany and Japan with their old providers of raw materials and markets. [The historian] William Borden wrote that Germany and Japan thus formed "the key to the balance of power," and shrewdly observed that whereas Germany was merely "the pivot" of the larger Marshall Plan program, "the Japanese recovery program formed the sole large-scale American effort in Asia."

Secretary of State George Marshall scribbled a note to Dean Acheson in late January 1947 that said, "Please have plan drafted of policy to organize a definite government of So. Korea and *connect up [sic]* its economy with that of Japan," a stunning mouthful. A few months later Secretary of the Army William Draper said that Japanese influence may again develop in Korea, "since Korea and Japan form a natural area for trade and commerce." Acting Secretary of State Dean Acheson remarked in secret congressional testimony in early 1947 that the United States had drawn the line in Korea, and sought funding for a major program to turn back communism there on the model of "Truman Doctrine" aid to Greece and Turkey. Acheson understood containment to be primarily a political and economic problem, of positioning self-supporting, viable regimes around the Soviet periphery; he thought the truncated Korean economy could still serve Japan's recovery, as part of what he called a "great crescent" linking Japan with Korea, Taiwan, Southeast Asia, and ultimately the oil of the Persian Gulf. Congress and the Pentagon balked at a major commitment to Korea, however, and so Acheson and his advisers took the problem to the United Nations, in order to reposition and contain Korea through collective security mechanisms. It was at this time, in early 1947, that Washington finally got control of Korea policy from the occupation; the effect was essentially to ratify the de facto containment policies that the occupation had been following since September 1945. . . .

The United Nations, dominated by the United States at the time, agreed to form a committee (the United Nations Temporary Commission on Korea, or UNTCOK) to observe democratic elections in Korea. Its members included representatives of the Philippines and Nationalist China, who could be counted on to follow American directions, and representatives from Australia and Canada, who, although more recalcitrant once they got a taste of South Korean politics, came from allied governments subject to American influence and pressure. The North Koreans and Soviets opposed UNTCOK and refused to participate in such elections. . . .

The UNTCOK-observed elections in May 1948 presaged the final emergence of a separate southern government and thus raised the issue of Korea's permanent division. For that reason, and because of the right-wing cast of the Rhee government, virtually all the major politicians and political parties to the right of Rhee refused to participate—including Kim Kyu-sik, a rare Korean centrist, and Kim Ku, a man probably to the right of Rhee. The election went forward even though the outcome, according to several members of UNTCOK, was a foregone conclusion. The National Police and associated right-wing auxiliaries organized the voting, requiring that peasants have their food ration cards stamped at the polls (if they did not vote, they would lose their rations). On May 10, 1948, the ROK's first National Assembly was elected, composed mostly of supporters of Rhee or Kim Sŏng-su.

The ROK was inaugurated on August 15, 1948, with General MacArthur on the podium—it was only the second time he had left Japan since September 1945. Soon the Truman administration replaced the military government with the 500-man Korean Military Advisory Group (KMAG), established an aid mission (known a the Economic Cooperation Administration, or ECA), pushed big aid bills through Congress to get the Korean economy moving and to equip an army capable of defending South Korea, and arranged for KMAG to retain operational control of the Korean police and military as long as American combat troops remained. The State Department successfully delayed the final withdrawal of American troops until June 30, 1949, mainly because of worries about South Korean security. . . .

Americans knew they had a volatile charge in the new president, Syngman Rhee, and his relations with the embassy were often tempestuous. In small doses, Rhee came off as a handsome, warm, charming gentleman; he was a past master of flattery and disarming, endearing use of the democratic symbolism that stirs American hearts. It took a measure of experience with Rhee to disabuse Americans of their first impressions of him. Hodge knew him best, and by 1948 Hodge thought of Rhee about what "Vinegar Joe" Stilwell thought of Chiang Kai-shek. Hodge's politics in the abstract were similar to Rhee's; he had a typical American visceral disgust for anything that looked like communism. But he was an honest, unpretentious career military officer who, though he occupied the palatial governor-general's residence (thereafter known as the Blue House, because of its blue tile roof), moved several of his staff in with him and was well known for hard work and plain living. Within a year of his arrival in Korea, if not earlier, he developed a profound disgust with and distrust for Rhee; it is the measure of his bonehard pragmatic anticommunism that he backed him anyway, having no alternative. . . .

The critical background to the establishment of separate governments in Korea was . . . in the social and political conflict between left and right throughout the peninsula. This conflict went on at the national level in 1945 and at the provincial and county levels in 1946, as local people's committees controlled county seats and fought with their antagonists. The suppression of the massive autumn harvest uprisings in 1946 consolidated state control in the county seats, making the seizure of power by county people's committees unlikely thereafter. Villages continued to be isolated from central power, however, and leftists therefore migrated downward through the bureaucratic reaches of the system in search of space for organization.

By 1947 most leftists were members of the South Korean Labor Party (SKLP). This party was always indigenous to the South, drawing its members especially from the southwest and southeast, but it was more independent of northern or Soviet influence in 1947 than after the formation of the Rhee government. Only vague and unreliable evidence existed on northern or Soviet provision of funding for the party, and American intelligence sources did not believe that the North directed the activity of the SKLP—instead that the two worked toward common goals.

It appears, however, that by mid-1948, if not earlier, the party was under northern guidance. Intercepted instructions from the North urged members to infiltrate into "all important bureaus" of the Rhee government, to secrete food and other supplies for guerrillas in the mountains, and to "infiltrate into the South Korean Constabulary and begin political attacks aimed at causing dissension and disorder." Up until the Korean War, however, it cannot be said that southern communists were mere creatures of Kim Il Sung, and there was much conflict between the two parties and their leaders (Pak Hŏn-yŏng was the southern communist head).

Rhee and his allies formed counterorganizations at the village level to fight the left. Roy Roberts of the Associated Press wrote in August 1947 that U.S. intelligence got an average of five police reports a day, "telling of fights in villages, fights between villages, beatings of rightists, beatings of leftists, burning of granaries, attacks on village officials, attacks on police, stoning of political meetings." . . .

These village battles occurred in regions of previous people's committee strength; an American intelligence survey in September 1947 found "an underground People's Committee government" still existing "in certain parts of South Korea." . . .

When the Korean War broke out, few people knew anything about North Korea, but generally assumed it to be a typical Soviet satellite, a "people's democracy" like those in Eastern Europe. The Red Army occupied the territory, rode herd on the emergence of a socialist state with a planned economy, and installed Kim Il Sung as its handpicked puppet: what else could it be? Recent studies based on a treasure trove of documents seized when United Nations forces occupied North Korea, however, support different interpretations, which we can summarize as follows. First, North Korea evolved an indigenous political system in the late 1940s, and its basic structure has never changed substantially, so that in the fundamentals what you see in 1949 or 1950 is what you get in the 1990s. Second, the closest comparisons to North Korea were Romania and Yugoslavia—not the states under complete Soviet hegemony, such as East Germany. Third, Soviet influence competed with Chinese influence, and both conflicted with indigenous political forms and practices. The Democratic People's Republic of Korea (DPRK) was and is a divergent case among postwar Marxist-Leninist systems, representing a profound reassertion of native Korean political practice—from the superordinate role of the leader to his self-reliant ideology, to the Hermit Kingdom foreign policy. . . .

The number of Soviet advisers was never very high in the North, even in the military. British sources estimated that Soviet advisers to the central government dropped from 200 in 1946 to a mere 30 in April 1947, the greatest number of those, predictably, being in the Ministry of the Interior. The South Korean defense minister put the number of Soviet military advisers at only 120 before the war, which accords with intelligence estimates after the war began, saying the Soviets used "approximately fifteen advisory officers per NK division," there being fewer than ten divisions before June 1950. There were only fifteen Soviet advisers to the Korean Air Force. . . .

North Korea was never simply a Soviet satellite in the 1940s, but evolved from a coalition regime based on widespread people's committees in 1945–46 to one under relative Soviet dominance in 1947–48, thence in 1949 to one with important links to China, which in turn enabled the DPRK to maneuver between the two communist giants. Kim Il Sung was not a handpicked Soviet puppet, but maneuvered politically first to establish his leadership, then to isolate and defeat the communists who had remained in Korea during the colonial period, then to ally with Soviet-aligned Koreans for a time, then to create a powerful army under his own leadership (in February 1948) that melded Koreans who had fought together in Manchuria and China proper with those who remained at home. . . .

. . . [T]he North Koreans soon eliminated all nonleftist political opposition with a draconian thoroughness. A couple of united-front noncommunist parties were still allowed to exist, but they had no power. The intent was the same as that of the right wing in the South, to squash alternative centers of power. But the northerners did it much more thoroughly, because of their superior organization and the general weakness of the opposition. . . .

The Korean War did not begin on June 25, 1950, much special pleading and argument to the contrary. If it did not begin then, Kim Il Sung could not have "started" it then, either, but only at some earlier point. As we search backward for that point, we slowly grope toward the truth that civil wars do not start: they come. They originate in multiple causes, with blame enough to go around for everyone. . . .

Organized guerrilla warfare on the Korean mainland dates from November 1948. . . . This movement began the armed conflict on the peninsula, carrying the urban political turmoil and rural peasant protest of 1945–47 to the level of unconventional warfare. In early 1949 the CIA estimated that the total number of guerrillas in the South was somewhere between 3,500 and 6,000, not counting several thousand more on Cheju Island [off Korea's southeast coast]. Some were armed with rifles, mostly Japanese and American, but many just carried clubs and bamboo spears. Food and other supplies came from foraging, contributions in villages, or theft of rice stocks. KMAG advisers thought overall strategy was in North Korean hands, passed through the South Korean Labor Party headquarters in Haeju, just across the thirty-eighth parallel. One team of 60 guerrillas was known to have been dispatched from the North, and defectors estimated that another 1,000 or so were undergoing training for missions in the South. . . .

Walter Sullivan of the *New York Times* was almost alone among foreign journalists in seeking out the facts of this guerrilla war. Large parts of southern Korea, he wrote in early 1950, "are darkened today by a cloud of terror that is probably unparalleled in the world." In the "hundreds of villages across the guerrilla areas," local village guards "crouch in pyramided straw shelters," and nights "are a long, cold vigil of listening." Guerrillas make brutal assaults on police, and the police take the guerrillas to their home villages and torture them for information. Then the police shoot them and tie them to trees as an object lesson. The persistence of the guerrillas, Sullivan wrote, "puzzles many Americans here," as does "the extreme brutality" of the conflict. But Sullivan went on to argue that "there is great divergence of wealth" in the country, with both middle and poor peasants living "a marginal existence." He interviewed ten peasant families; none owned all their own land, and most were tenants. The landlord took 30 percent of the tenant produce, but additional exactions—government taxes and various "contributions"—ranged from 48 to 70 percent of the annual crop. . . .

There was little evidence of Soviet or North Korean support for the southern guerrillas. . . . No Soviet weapons had ever been authenticated in South Korea, except near the parallel; most guerrillas had Japanese and American arms. Another report found that the guerrillas "apparently receive little more than moral support from North Korea."

The principal source of external involvement in the guerrilla war was, in fact, American. Americans usually perceive an important gap between the withdrawal of U.S. combat forces in July 1949 and the war that came a year later, such that the question becomes, Why did the Americans suddenly return to defend the ROK? In reality they never left. American advisers were all over the war zones in the South, constantly shadowing their Korean counterparts and urging them on to greater effort. . . .

At the end of September 1949 the KMAG chief, General W. L. Roberts, said that it was of the "utmost importance" that the guerrillas "be cleared up as soon as possible," and asked Washington to dispatch more infantry officers to work with the ROK Army. Every division in the army, he told General MacArthur, was being diverted in part or in full from the parallel to the interior and "ordered to exterminate guerrilla bands in their zones." Roberts later said that 6,000 guerrillas had been killed in the November 1949–March 1950 period, in what he called an "all-out mop-up campaign [that] broke the backbone of the guerrilla movement." Internal reports as of mid-April put the total guerrilla dead since October 1 at 4,996, so Roberts's figure seems plausible. The ROK claimed to have engaged a total of 12,000 KPA soldiers and guerrillas in January 1950, killing 813 and losing but 51. . . .

The war that came in June 1950 followed on the guerrilla fighting and nine months of battles along the thirty-eighth parallel in 1949. Border conflict lasted from early May until late December, taking hundreds of lives and embroiling thousands of troops. . . .

. . . [T]he important border battles began at Kaesŏng on May 4, 1949, in an engagement that the South started. It lasted about four days and took an official toll of 400 North Korean and 22 South Korean soldiers, as well as upwards of 100 civilian deaths in Kaesŏng, according to American and South Korean figures. The South committed six infantry companies and several battalions, and two of the companies defected to the North. . . .

On the last Sunday in June 1949, heavy fighting opened up in the dawn hours on the Ongjin peninsula; three days later the South sent about 150 "Horim" (forest tiger) guerrillas on a long foray across the parallel . . . but [they] were wiped out by July 5. The Sunday, June 26, battle bears some scrutiny because the UN Commission on Korea (UNCOK) sent a delegation to Ongjin after hearing reports of "heavy fighting." It arrived courtesy of an ROK naval vessel and was guided around by ROKA personnel. UNCOK members remained on the peninsula for a day or so and then returned on Monday evening to Seoul, from which they then filed a report to the UN blaming "northern invaders" for the trouble. It is probable that the North was to blame, but what is remarkable is UNCOK's failure to investigate and report upon provocations by the South as well. After all, just before this incident Kim Sŏk-wŏn gave UNCOK a briefing in his status as commander of ROKA forces at the thirty-eighth parallel: North and South "may engage in major battles at any moment," he said; Korea has entered into "a state of warfare." "We should have a program to recover our lost land, North Korea, by breaking through the 38th border which has existed since 1945"; the moment of major battles, Kim told UNCOK, is rapidly approaching.

The worst fighting of 1949 occurred in early August, when North Korean forces attacked ROKA units occupying a small mountain north of the thirty-eighth parallel. It went on for days, right through an important summit conference between Syngman Rhee and Chiang Kai-shek. . . .

When we now look at both sides of the parallel with the help of some new (if scattered and selective) Soviet materials, we learn that Kim Il Sung's basic conception of a Korean War was quite similar to Rhee's and was influenced deeply by the August 1949 fighting: namely, attack the cul de sac of Ongjin, move eastward and grab Kaesŏng, and then see what happens. At a minimum, this would establish a much more secure defense of P'yŏngyang, which was quite vulnerable from Ongjin and Kaesŏng. At a maximum, it might open Seoul to his forces. That is, if the southern army collapses, move on to Seoul and occupy it in a few days. . . .

The critical issue in the Soviet documents is a military operation to seize the Ongjin peninsula. According to these documents, Kim Il Sung first broached the idea of an operation against Ongjin to the Soviet ambassador to P'yŏngyang, Terenti Shtykov, on August 12, 1949, right on the heels of the August 4 battle. Like southern leaders, Kim Il Sung wanted to bite off a chunk of exposed territory or grab a small city—all of Kaesŏng, for example, or Haeju just above the parallel on Ongjin, which southern commanders wanted to occupy in 1949–50. We also see how similar the Russians were in seeking to restrain hotheaded Korean leaders, including the chief of state. When Kim spoke about an invasion of Ongjin, two key Russian embassy officials "tried to switch the discussion to a general theme." The Soviet documents also demonstrate the hard-won, *learned* logic of this civil war by late 1949, namely, that both sides understood that their big-power guarantors would not help them if they launched an unprovoked general attack. . . . A telegram from Shtykov to Moscow in January 1950 has Kim Il Sung impatient that *the South* "is still not instigating an attack" (thus to justify his own), and the Russians in P'yŏngyang tell him once again that he cannot attack Ongjin without risking general civil war.

Thus the 1950 logic for both sides was to see who would be stupid enough to move first, with Kim itching to invade and hoping for a clear southern provocation, and hotheads in the South hoping to provoke an "unprovoked" assault, in order to get American help—for that was the only way the South could hope to win. Kim already had begun playing Moscow off against Beijing, too; for example, he let Shtykov overhear him say, at an apparently drunken luncheon on January 19, 1950, that if the Russians would not help him unify the country, "Mao Zedong is his friend and will always help Korea." In general these materials underline that the victory of the Chinese revolution had a great influence on North Korea and that the latter's China connection was a trump card Kim could play to create some breathing room for his regime between the two communist giants. . . .

The point is not that North Korea was an innocent party to this fighting but that both sides were at fault—and according to several statements by General Roberts, the KMAG commander, the South started more of the battles than did the North. . . . Also important is the opening of the fighting in the Ongjin and Kaesŏng areas, for this is where the war began a year later. . . .

In late February 1949, Kim Il Sung left P'yŏngyang for his only official, publicized visit to the Soviet Union before the Korean War. When he returned in March, Kim brought with him an economic and cultural agreement and, intelligence rumor had it, a secret military agreement. In 1948 the Soviets left quite a bit of surplus military equipment behind for the North Koreans (as did the Americans when their troops pulled out), but in 1949 the Soviets made the Koreans pay for everything, including a 220 million-ruble loan at 2 percent interest, which was about what mortgages returned to American banks in 1949—that is, there was profit in it. A January 1950 document shows Stalin appearing to be more interested than at any previous point in Kim Il Sung's invasion plans for South Korea, without a hint of what Stalin's own strategic thinking might be. Meanwhile, the North engaged in public bond drives to buy more and more equipment from Moscow. . . .

American influence in the South had reached new heights by 1950. The British minister Vyvyan Holt eloquently captured this a few weeks before the war broke out: "Radiating from the huge ten-storied Banto Hotel," American influence "penetrates into every branch of administration and is fortified by an immense outpouring of money." Americans kept the government, the army, the economy, the railroads, the airports, the mines, and the factories going, supplying money, electricity, expertise, and psychological succor. American gasoline fueled every motor vehicle in the country. American cultural influence was "exceedingly strong," ranging from scholarships to study in the United States, to several strong missionary denominations, to "a score of traveling cinemas" and theaters that played mostly American films, to the Voice of America, to big-league baseball: "America is the dream-land" to thousands if not millions of Koreans.

At this time South Korea was getting more than $100 million a year from the United States, most of it in the form of outright grants. (The entire southern national budget for 1951 was $120 million.) The ECA aid mission and the KMAG contingent were the biggest of their type in the world. The U.S. Information Service had, by its own testimony, "one of the most extensive country programs that we are operating anywhere," with nine centers in Korea, parlaying libraries, mobile units, a variety of publications, films, and Americanism before the Korean people. American officials ran Kimp'o International Airport, controlling the entry and exit of American citizens. Besides the official presence, private Americans often advised or directed private industry. . . .

The UN Commission on Korea had not liked its role in the summer of 1949, sandwiched between an indifferent United Nations and a bubbling civil war, and it wanted out. But it did not get out. It is of signal importance that the decision to install the military observers, who later reported on the outbreak of the war, grew out of worries about aggression emanating from the South more than from the North. . . .

UNCOK military observers did not arrive in Korea until May 1950. The two observers completed a survey of the parallel on the afternoon of June 23, 1950. They reported this to UNCOK on Friday and set about "the shaping up of the report" on Saturday, not out of a sense of urgency "but because it was something nice and tangible" to do on a lazy weekend. The observers slept mainly in Seoul and went up to the parallel on nine of the days between June 9 and 23. They returned to Seoul from the parallel on June 17, and stayed in Seoul until the twenty-first. But they were on the Ongjin peninsula from the twenty-first to Friday morning, the twenty-third, and that is where the war began on Sunday.

A few weeks before the South had held its second National Assembly elections. The result was a disastrous loss for the Rhee regime, bringing into the assembly a strong collection of middle-of-the-roaders and moderate leftists, several of them associated with Yŏ Un-hyŏng's political lineage, and most of them hoping for unification with the North. The Korean ambassador to the United States, John Chang, informed American officials of a resulting crisis in his regime in early June, prompting John Foster Dulles (then an adviser to Truman) to decide to visit Korea on his way to see MacArthur in Tokyo.

During Dulles's visit to Seoul (which began on June 18), Rhee not only pushed for a direct American defense but advocated an attack on the North. Dulles invited along with him a favorite reporter, William Mathews, editor of the *Arizona Daily Star;* Mathews wrote just after the meeting between Rhee and Dulles, "He is militantly for the unification of Korea. Openly says it must be brought about soon . . . Rhee pleads justice of going into North country. Thinks it could succeed in a few days. . . . [I]f he can do it with our help, he will do it." And Mathews noted that Rhee said he would "do it," even if "it brought on a general war." All this is yet more proof of Rhee's provocative behavior, but it is not different from his threats to march North made many times before. Rhee hoped that a military alliance with the United States would come out of his meetings will Dulles, but got only some pro forma reassurances of U.S. support. In P'yŏngyang, Dulles's long-standing pro-Japan positions raised the gravest suspicions. But the Dulles visit merely brought out the vintage Rhee: there is no evidence that Dulles was in collusion with him, as the North Koreans have always claimed—while featuring a famous photo of Dulles peering into the North, across the thirty-eighth parallel.

It may be, however, that Chinese Nationalists on Taiwan were willing to collude with Rhee. Taiwan was a hotbed of intrigue in June 1950. From New Year's Day onward, American and British intelligence agencies predicted that the "last battle" of the Chinese civil war would come in June 1950. In January, British Foreign Office sources predicted an invasion of Taiwan "by the end of June." Interestingly enough, Guy Burgess, infamous spy for Moscow and director of the Far Eastern Office of Britain's Foreign Office in 1950, watched this situation closely. In April, Burgess said the invasion would come in May–June or September–October. Some Americans wanted to defend Chiang's regime, while others were hoping to say good riddance—President Truman among them, or so the newspapers said. MacArthur hoped that Dulles's visit would bring a change in U.S. policy in the Far East, especially in regard to Taiwan (which he thought should be defended). Chiang Kai-shek hoped that the high-level talks in Tokyo would herald an American commitment to his regime. In Moscow, the Kremlin would monitor the journey to the East of the very personification of the "Wall Street master."

William Pawley, Charles Cooke, and other Americans with intelligence backgrounds had organized an "informal" military advisory group in the autumn of 1949 to help with the defense of Taiwan. Pawley later became a key CIA operative, influential in the overthrow of the Arbenz regime in Guatemala in 1954, and the Bay of Pigs adventure in 1961. Pawley and Cooke operated outside the established channels of American foreign policy, seeking to retrieve Chiang and his regime from their impending demise. Chiang Kai-shek also faced maturing plans by American clandestine officers for a coup d'état against him, something that has long been shrouded in secrecy. Like the Rhee regime, the Chiang regime was gravely at risk in June 1950. In May the Nationalists seemed to have played out their string; even American partisans of Chiang's regime appeared to draw back after the Nationalists failed to defend Hainan Island. Intelligence estimates continued to predict an invasion in June; the American consul, Robert Strong, reported from Taipei on May 17, "Fate of Taiwan sealed, Communist attack can occur between June 15 and end July."

In an interview the late Dean Rusk said that some elements of the Nationalist military were preparing to move against Chiang on the last weekend in June 1950, but then the Korean War intervened. In fact, Rusk was a key mover in this coup attempt and met with several important Chinese figures at the Plaza Hotel in New York on June 23, seeking to get them to form a government to replace the Kuomintang. Just after the war broke out, Kennan told a top-secret NSC meeting that "Chiang might be overthrown at any time." Guy Burgess read everything coming in from Taiwan in May and June 1950, it would appear, including unclassified press reports. The British chancery in Moscow had earlier noted that Soviet newspapers took an inordinate interest in any scraps of information on the Taiwan question. Burgess's judgment on June 24, 1950, was that "the Soviets seem to have made up their minds that the U.S.A. have a finally decided policy [not to defend Taiwan]. This *we [sic]* have never quite come to believe."

For over a decade I have been trying to get documents on this episode and various others through the Freedom of Information Act. . . . We still lack critical documents on the coup against Chiang, on American intelligence-gathering overflights of North Korean and Chinese territory that began before June 1950, and the signals intelligence that the United States collected on North Korea, China, and the USSR. We still do not know why the Pentagon approved and distributed in the week of June 19, 1950, a war plan known as SL-17, which assumed a KPA invasion, a quick retreat to and defense of a perimeter at Pusan, and then an amphibious landing at Inch'ŏn.

With all this bubbling activity, the last weekend in June 1950 nonetheless dawned on a torpid, somnolent, and very empty Washington. Harry Truman was back home in Independence. Acheson was at his Sandy Spring country farm, Rusk was in New York, Kennan had disappeared to a remote summer cottage without so much as a telephone, Paul Nitze was salmon fishing, the Joint Chiefs of Staff were occupied elsewhere, and even the United Nations representative, Warren Austin, was not at his post.

Most accounts of the outbreak of fighting in June 1950 leave the impression that a North Korean attack began all along the parallel at dawn, against an enemy taken completely unawares. But the war began in the same, remote locus of much of the 1949 fighting, the Ongjin peninsula, and some hours later spread along the parallel eastward, to Kaesŏng, Ch'unch'ŏn, and the east coast. As an official American history put it,

> On the Ongjin Peninsula, cut off from the rest of South Korea, soldiers of the 17th Regiment stood watch on the quiet summer night of 24–25 June 1950. For more than a week, there had been no serious incident along the 38th parallel. . . . Then at 0400, with devastating suddenness . . . [artillery and mortar fire] crashed into the ROK lines.

The North's official radio had it differently. It said (on June 26) that South Korean forces began shelling the Ŭnp'a Mountain area (scene of several 1949 battles, especially the big one on August 4) on June 23 at 10 P.M. and continued until June 24 at 4 A.M., using howitzers and mortars. A unit commanded by Kang To-gŏn was defending Turak Mountain on Ongjin in the early hours of June 25, when it was attacked by the Maengho, or "fierce tiger," unit of the ROK's Seventeenth Regiment, which it proceeded to destroy. By 2:30 P.M. on June 25, the unit had advanced as far as Sudong, on the Ongjin peninsula; meanwhile, guerrillas sprang forward to disrupt South Korean police stations and units in Ongjin.

South Korean sources asserted, on the contrary, that elements of the Seventeenth Regiment had counterattacked and were in possession of Haeju city, the only important point north of the thirty-eighth parallel claimed to have been taken by the South's army. Chae Pyŏng-dŏk announced this at 11:00 A.M. on June 26, a timing that would account for numerous newspaper articles saying that elements of the ROKA had occupied Haeju, articles that have since been used to suggest that the South might have attacked first. . . .

. . . MacArthur's command reported through the UN at the end of July that at the eastern and western portions of the parallel the North attacked with reinforced border constabulary brigades, at Kaesŏng and Ch'unch'ŏn with a division each (but, as we have seen, not at the start), and ran through the Ŭijŏngbu corridor with

8,000 to 10,000 troops and fifty tanks—in other words a total force of about 38,000. Thus the initial attacking force was not terribly large; the KPA had mobilized less than half its forces on June 25. Arrayed against them were five ROKA divisions located near Seoul or north of it, some 50,000 troops.

The official American position has always been that the Soviets and the North Koreans stealthily prepared an attack that was completely unprovoked, one that constituted an all-out invasion. On June 26, Kim Il Sung, on the contrary, accused the South of making "a general attack" across the parallel. Rhee had long sought to touch off a fratricidal civil war, he said, having "incessantly provoked clashes" at the front line; in preparing a "northern expedition," he had "even gone so far as to collude with our sworn enemy, Japanese militarism." Some of these charges were true, but the charge of making a general attack across the parallel is false: the North attacked, and all along the parallel, by 6 A.M. at the latest. The book still cannot be closed on the possibility that the south opened the fighting on Ongjin, with an eye to seizing Haeju, but there is no evidence that it intended a general invasion of the North on June 25.

The evidence that scholars now have (there is much more to come from unopened archives) is compatible both with an unprovoked North Korean invasion (one prefigured in North Korean and Soviet planning as we have seen) and with an interpretation linking the summer of 1949 to June 1950: that the North, like the South, wanted to seize the Ongjin peninsula and Kaesŏng and then see what happened next, but waited until it had the majority of its crack soldiers back from China, and the support or acquiescence of Stalin and Mao. It positioned its troops to take advantage of the first southern provocation in June 1950 or merely to attack and claim a direct provocation. (As we saw, new Soviet documents show Kim anxious for the South to make a move.) Kim Il Sung bears the grave responsibility for raising the civil conflict in Korea to the level of general war, with intended and unintended consequences that no one could have predicted. To say that this was the culmination of previous struggles and that Rhee wanted to do the same thing is true, but does not gainsay Kim's responsibility for the horrible consequences.

Scattered Soviet materials have shown that Soviet involvement in preparing and planning an invasion after Stalin gave his reluctant endorsement in January 1950 was higher than previous writers had thought, but we still know too little to determine the respective North Korean, Soviet, and Chinese roles in initiating the June fighting. Even when we have every document the Soviets ever produced, we will still need the South Korean archives, the North Korean archives, the Chinese archives on both sides of the Taiwan Strait, and the American intelligence, signals, and cryptography archives before we will be able to argue on truly solid ground the question we ought all try to forget, namely, "Who started the Korean civil war?"

Whatever happened on or before June 25, it was immediately clear that this war was a matter of "Koreans invading Korea"; it was not aggression across generally accepted international lines. Nor was this the point at which the civil conflict began. The question pregnant with ideological dynamite "Who started the Korean War?" is the wrong question. It is not a civil war question; it only holds the viscera in its grasp for the generations immediately afflicted by fratricidal conflict. Americans do not care any more that the South fired first on Fort Sumter; they do still care about slavery and secession. No one wants to know who started the Vietnam War. Someday Koreans in North and South will reconcile as Americans eventually did, with the wisdom that civil wars have no single authors. It took Americans about a century to do so; it is therefore not surprising that Korean reconciliation is still pending after fifty years.

Word of fighting in Korea arrived in Washington on Saturday night, June 24. In succeeding days Dean Acheson dominated the decision making that soon committed American air and ground forces to the fight. Acheson, along with Dean Rusk, made the decision to take the Korean question to the UN, before he had notified President Truman of the fighting (Acheson told Truman there was no need to have him back in Washington until the next day); at the famous Blair Hosue meetings on the evening of June 25, Acheson argued for increased military aid to the ROK, American air cover for the evacuation, and the interposition of the Seventh Fleet between Taiwan and the mainland; and on the afternoon of June 26 Acheson labored alone on the fundamental decisions committing American air and naval power to the Korean War, approved that evening at Blair House. Thus the decision to intervene was Acheson's decision, supported by the president but taken before United Nations, Pentagon, or congressional approval.

The military representatives at Blair House offered the only serious opposition to American intervention. General Omar Bradley supported Acheson's containment policy at the first Blair House meeting, remarking, "We must draw the line somewhere." But he questioned "the advisability" of introducing American ground troops in large numbers, as did Secretary of the Army Frank Pace and Defense Secretary Louis Johnson. At the second meeting on June 26, Generals Bradley and Lawton Collins again expressed the view that committing ground troops would strain American combat troop limits, unless a general mobilization was undertaken.

The United Nations merely ratified American decisions. In 1950 the General Assembly was a legislature more amenable to Truman's policies than the U.S. Congress was, so he got his war resolution out of the former. As an official Joint Chiefs of Staff study later put it, "Having resolved upon armed intervention for itself, the U.S. Government the next day sought the approval and the assistance of the United Nations." Truman called his intervention in Korea a "police action" so that he would not have to get a declaration of war; this inaugurated the pattern for the subsequent conflicts in Vietnam and the Persian Gulf, of war by executive decision rather than through proper constitutional procedure.

Korea: Stalin's Catastrophe

VLADISLOV ZUBOK AND CONSTANTINE PLESHAKOV

During their fateful meeting in Moscow in April 1950, [Soviet marshal Joseph] Stalin agreed with Kim [Il Sung] that, though he had opposed a "reunification" of Korea before, now it could be accomplished "in light of the changed international situation." Earlier, Stalin had feared that the Americans would intervene. What, then, caused him to reassess the situation?

Reprinted by permission of the publisher from *Inside the Cold War: From Stalin to Khrushchev* by Vladislov Zubok and Constantine Pleshakov, Cambridge, Mass.: Harvard University Press. Copyright © 1996 by the President and Fellows of Harvard College.

The new alliance with Communist China must have been the biggest cause for reassessment. From Stalin's viewpoint, this treaty was a watershed: the Yalta-Potsdam agreement on the spheres of influence had been broken. The world was now open for a redivision of spheres of influence on the basis of new, ideologically drawn alliances. As a Leninist, Stalin knew that this redivision meant global war. He said to Mao [Zedong]: "If we make a decision to revise treaties, we must go all the way." This phrase, in a nutshell, contained the origins of the Korean War. As the world headed for its third global confrontation, the Korean peninsula acquired new strategic meaning. Stalin worried that should the United States rearm Japan in the future, South Korea could become a dangerous beachhead for enemy forces. Therefore, it had to be captured before Japan could get back on its feet.

Several factors made the Soviet leader believe that the United States might not defend South Korea. On August 29, 1949, the Soviet Union broke the American monopoly on atomic weapons. At about the same time, the last American troops withdrew from South Korea—a development that was closely watched from Moscow. Early in 1950 some key figures in U.S. governmental circles, particularly Secretary of State Dean Acheson, made statements that excluded South Korea from the American "defense perimeter" in the Pacific arena and even hinted that the regime of Syngman Rhee was expendable. On January 28 intelligence sources reported to Stalin that the South Korean government had "little hope of American assistance" and expected that "President Truman would leave Formosa as he had left China." The report quoted Syngman Rhee as saying that "America has shown from the very beginning that it does not intend to fight for the interests of South Korea." Stalin must have felt that the Truman leadership was in disarray, incapable of mobilizing domestically. In this view, the United States failed to make use of its atomic diplomacy, could not prevent the collapse of the Guomindang, its primary ally in Asia, and now it was withdrawing from the Asian mainland altogether, returning to its traditional role of defending the islands.

Another consideration had never been spoken. Had Stalin said no to North Korea, it would have looked as if again, as during the civil war in China, he were putting the brakes on the revolutionary process in the Far East. And Mao Zedong was autonomous and unpredictable. The Chinese could start supporting Kim without the sanction of Moscow, in the same way [Josip] Tito's Yugoslavia had supported the Albanians and the Greek guerrillas, ignoring Moscow's objections. Taking issue with the PRC just months after the much-trumpeted conclusion of the Sino-Soviet treaty in Moscow would be unacceptable and ruinous. Equally so would be the recognition of Mao's revolutionary supremacy in Asia. That could lead the Chinese comrades to think too much about their international role, and to revive their nationalist ambitions. Stalin knew that Korea, before it was occupied by Japan in the late nineteenth century, had been a traditional sphere of Chinese imperial influence.

When, in early April 1950, Stalin supported Kim's invasion plan, he believed that he was preventing both of these developments, while maintaining the appearance of parity with Mao. He told Kim that North Korea could "get down to action" only after their plans were cleared "with Comrade Mao Zedong personally." The North Korean offensive could be postponed if the Chinese leadership objected. Kim then returned to Pyongyang and made another trip, this time to Beijing. On May 13

Mao sent [Foreign Minister] Zhou Enlai to the Soviet ambassador N. V. Roshchin, asking urgently for the "personal clarifications of Comrade Filippov [a pseudonym of Stalin in correspondence among Communist leaders] on this question." Stalin's answer, a masterpiece of political astuteness, was that "the question should ultimately be decided by the Chinese and Korean comrades together, and in the event the Chinese comrades should disagree, the decision on the question should be postponed until a new discussion can take place." Never secure about communications, Stalin refused to be specific about his talks with Kim in Moscow. "The Korean comrades," he wrote, "can relay to you the details of the conversation."

Stalin protected his credentials as the pontiff of world Communist revolution, responsive to the aspirations of the Korean people. At the same time he shared with Mao the burden of responsibility for the risky enterprise. Mao complained later that when he was in Moscow signing the Sino-Soviet treaty, Stalin "did not say a word about the conquest of South Korea." When Stalin invited Kim to Moscow, "nobody took pains to ask [Mao's] advice in advance."

Stalin's logic provides an explanation as to why he recalled the Soviet representative from the United Nations in the spring of 1950. Stalin boycotted the United Nations because it refused to recognize the PRC as a legitimate successor to the Chinese seat on the Security Council. In Stalin's view, the risk of the Soviets' absence was less than the strategic advantages of stressing the Sino-Soviet alliance and unmasking the United Nations as a "voting machine" obedient to America. It bears repeating that Stalin's reading of the United States' withdrawal from South Korea led him to believe that the Americans would not intervene in the Korean civil war.

Stalin and Mao were completely surprised when the Truman administration took advantage of the Soviet absence in the United Nations to obtain international approval for U.S. intervention in Korea. It was, ironically, the desire in the Kremlin to make a quick and victorious war, which the Western allies "so feared would happen in Europe," that "prompted the United States to respond with precisely the intervention in Korea that Moscow wanted above all to avoid." After the successful U.N. counterattack at Inchon in September 1950 and the resulting collapse of the North Korean army, American troops advanced to the Sino-Korean border.

Very soon the Kremlin leader concluded that the Inchon operation was a "strategic breakthrough by the U.N. forces fraught with fatal consequences." But he and his Soviet advisors had no control over the distant war. Kim's army got stuck south of the Korean peninsula, was cut off by enemy troops, and eventually disintegrated. Despite the gathering thunder in the Far East, Stalin took a train to his dacha at Sochi, on the Black Sea. As in June 1941, when developments went against his expectations, he took a time-out. What's more, the Generalissimo's physical condition necessitated a long rest. At Sochi, on October 1, after midnight, Stalin received an urgent cable from Pyongyang with a panicky letter from Kim Il Sung and the second-ranked man in the North Korean leadership, Pak Hong-yong. The letter informed him that the U.S.-led forces had taken Seoul and would probably capture North Korea, and that the North Korean army ceased to exist and thus would not be able to offer serious resistance. "The moment enemy troops cross the 38th parallel," Kim and Pak wrote, "we will desperately need immediate military assistance from the Soviet Union. If, for some reason, this help is not possible, then [would you] assist us in organizing international volunteer units in China and other people's democracies to provide military assistance in our struggle?"

This must have been a hard moment for Stalin: Kim turned out to be a bad military leader, but he was a loyal puppet who vowed to continue a protracted war to prevent, in the name of the strategic interests of the USSR and the whole Communist camp, the emergence of an American military springboard on the Korean peninsula. In the event of defeat, Stalin faced the ultimate responsibility for the deterioration of Sino-Soviet strategic positions and, as the Communist pontiff, the blame for losing the Korean "revolutionary" regime. His whole crafty strategy in the Far East had backfired. Nevertheless, Stalin must have been expecting this moment, for he had made his tactical decision in advance. It took him only a few minutes to dictate a telegram to Mao Zedong and Zhou Enlai, advising the Chinese to "move immediately at least five or six divisions to the 38th parallel" to shield Kim's regime from the advancing U.N. troops and enable him to mobilize a new army. Stalin mentioned almost elegiacally that he was "far from Moscow and somewhat cut off from the events in Korea." He wrote that the Chinese troops "could pose as volunteers [but], of course, with the Chinese command at the helm." He left it to the discretion of the leadership in Beijing to tell "the Korean comrades" about their decision on this question. In a matter of minutes, Stalin passed the buck to the Chinese, making them responsible for Kim's regime and the war.

Stalin's real "master plan" at that time was not a counterattack in Europe, as many in the West had thought, but postponement of a head-on collision with the West. He had taken precautions: his cables to Kim and Mao were all in military intelligence codes (considered to be "safe"), and he signed them with the Chinese alias Pheng Xi. He also had forbidden Soviet advisors to travel south of the 38th parallel, and Soviet pilots, flying over Korea, to speak Russian! He now refused to send Soviet troops back to North Korea, because that would lead to direct war with the Americans. Let the brave Chinese fight, with Soviet arms and Soviet air cover.

Some Chinese politicians, particularly the Communist boss of Manchuria, Gao Gang, had spoken in favor of Chinese intervention, to prevent the return of the United States (and, potentially, a remilitarized Japan) to the Asian mainland. There were, however, serious reservations in Beijing about starting another war barely a year after the end of the civil war. Mao's position was ambiguous, to say the least. He argued for intervention before his colleagues at home. At the same time, on October 2, he wrote back to Stalin that the PRC could not enter the war because several Chinese divisions would not be enough to stop the Americans. Always careful to appear Stalin's loyal ally, Mao also expressed his fear that the United States might declare war on China, which would mean a Soviet-American war as well. Feeling the urgency of the moment, Stalin stopped mincing words and, on October 5, dispatched to Mao the most remarkable cable in their whole correspondence, displaying the full force of his realpolitik logic.

The United States, Stalin wrote, "was not prepared at the present time for a big war," and Japan was still incapable of rendering any military assistance to the Americans. Therefore, if the United States faced the threat of such a war, they would "have to give in to China, backed by its Soviet ally, in [the settlement] of the Korean question." They would also be forced to leave Taiwan and renounce "a separate peace with Japanese reactionaries." Stalin warned that "without serious struggle and a new impressive display of its strength, China would not obtain all these concessions" from the Americans.

Stalin finished his seduction of the Chinese comrades with a stunning passage: "Of course I had to reckon with the fact that, despite its unpreparedness, the United States still may pull itself into a big war, [acting] out of prestige; consequently, China would be dragged into the war, and the USSR, which is bound to China by the pact of mutual assistance, would be dragged into the war as well. Should we fear this? In my opinion, we should not, since together we will be stronger than the United States and Great Britain. Other European capitalist states do not possess any serious military power, save Germany, which cannot provide assistance to the United States now. If war is inevitable, let it happen now, and not in a few years, when Japanese militarism will be restored as a U.S. ally, and when the United States and Japan will have a beach-head on the continent ready, in the form of Syngman Rhee's Korea."

Arguably, deep down Stalin hoped for just the opposite: that the Sino-Soviet treaty would be a sufficient deterrent and that the United States would hesitate to declare war on the PRC, knowing it would automatically bring in the Soviet Union. But he made a point of demonstrating to Mao that the Kremlin "father" of the Communist world had a sober vision of World War III and was not afraid of it. In this way, also, Stalin denied Mao his strongest argument against China's intervention.

Mao seemed to have surrendered to Stalin's logic: he agreed to send nine divisions to fight in Korea. Zhou Enlai flew by Soviet military plane to Sochi, allegedly to discuss with Stalin the terms under which the Soviets would supply armaments, ammunition, and particularly air cover for the Chinese "volunteers" in North Korea. The Stalin-Zhou meeting took place on October 9–10, and here again, as in the case of the Sino-Soviet treaty, the existing Chinese versions differ significantly from the newly available Soviet documents. According to Chinese sources, including Mao himself, at some point Stalin changed his mind: he would *not* supply military equipment and provide air cover. The Chinese leadership in Beijing was stunned by this act of perfidy but, *despite* it, decided to enter the war. According to Soviet records, however, Zhou told Stalin that the Politburo of the Chinese Communist party's Central Committee had decided not to send troops to Korea, restating the same old arguments. It is not clear what happened in Beijing: was Mao really facing strong opposition, or was Zhou deliberately playing the role of "bad messenger" assigned to him by Mao? One analyst of the Chinese evidence concludes that Mao and Zhou deliberately played "games" with Stalin. They were determined to send volunteers to Korea, but at the same time they were seeking the best possible deal from him. Yet another dramatic scenario is likely: the majority of Chinese leaders at that time strongly opposed the war and still hoped that Stalin was bluffing and would come to Kim's rescue once U.S. troops moved to the Soviet borders. Stalin, at least, interpreted the Chinese "game" in this light.

Stalin decided to call the Chinese bluff. The Soviet Union, he told Zhou, was not ready to fight a large-scale war in the Far East so soon after the Second World War. Besides, the Soviet–North Korean border was too narrow to allow massive troop transfers. If the U.S. actions were to jeopardize the fate of world socialism, however, the Soviet Union would be ready to take up the American challenge. Stalin began to lose his temper. The Chinese comrades should know, he said, that should they refuse to intervene, "socialism in Korea would collapse within a very short period of time." What Stalin in fact did was directly challenge the PRC's self-legitimacy from the high ground of the Soviet revolutionary-imperial paradigm. The USSR, he implied, should save itself for an ultimate battle with the forces of imperialism, whereas it is the duty of the PRC, as the major Soviet ally in Asia and the hegemon of the Asian revolutionary process, to fend off a regional imperialist offensive. In the light of the PRC's failure to perform its historic role, all Stalin could suggest was that the Soviet Union and China should work out specific plans to help the Korean comrades and their forces withdraw from North Korea and move to shelters in Manchuria and the Soviet Far East. When the stunned Zhou asked Stalin if China could count on Soviet air cover should it decide to fight in Korea, Stalin answered yes, and assured him that the Soviet Union would take care of all supplies of arms and equipment as soon as the PRC defined its actual needs. Despite all this, the Sino-Soviet talks ended without the establishment of any joint policy.

This episode showed Stalin displaying, under duress, the best of his realpolitik side. He was willing to swallow a serious regional defeat and even the loss of a "Socialist" regime on the Soviet borders rather than risk a military clash with U.N. forces. He saw to it that this policy would be shared by all his lieutenants by passing several Politiburo decisions. In [Nikita] Khrushchev's [future premier of the Soviet Union] presence he once said, "So what? If Kim Il Sung fails, we are not going to intervene with our troops. Let the Americans be our neighbors in the Far East." On October 12, Stalin surprised Kim, who expected Soviet military assistance, with a letter advising evacuation of the rest of Kim's forces to the Soviet and Chinese sanctuaries. Interestingly, Stalin referred to the "recommendations" of the "conference of the Chinese [and] Soviet leading comrades" (that is, to his talks with Zhou in Sochi). He didn't forget to blame Mao for what was solely his decision! At that moment, argues one Russian historian, the Korean War could have ended in a victory for the West.

The Chinese opposition to war crumbled under the weight of Stalin's stand, however. Within hours, on October 13, Mao informed the Kremlin leader that the CCP Politburo had decided to fight. Stalin, barely concealing his delight, sent another message to Kim, ordering him "to postpone temporarily" the evacuation, in expectation of "detailed reports from Mao Zedong about this matter." The next day Stalin announced to Kim that "after hesitation and a series of provisional decisions, the Chinese comrades at last made a final decision to render assistance to Korea with troops." He had quite a nerve to wish the Korean leader "luck." Less than a week later, on October 19, 1950, Chinese troops crossed the Yalu River. One week later they fought their first battle with U.S. troops. This seemed to many Western observers to be the prelude to a third world war.

Soviet documents dispel the myth that Stalin had allegedly been moved to the point of tears by how "good the Chinese comrades were." They reveal not a trace of revolutionary romanticism in the Soviet leader and show that, as in 1941–1945, he was even ready to act as a hard-nosed realist. The Chinese intervention, however, bore out Stalin's revolutionarism in a different way. Cynical as the Stalin-Mao bargaining may look today, its outcome was a great victory from the viewpoint of the revolutionary-imperial paradigm embraced by Stalin. The war helped wash away the ambiguity in Stalin-Mao relations: the Soviet leader accepted Mao without reservations, as long as the latter fought American power and depended on Soviet aid.

But the price of that new friendship and the continuation of the Korean War was high and tragic; it resulted in a huge setback for the USSR. The U.S. leadership adopted the view that the Sino-Soviet bloc was bent on global conquest. In turn, it was determined to destroy the aggressor and, if necessary, to embark on a large-scale campaign of mobilization and armament. The military budget of the United States quadrupled, and the arms race on the Western side did not slow down until the late 1980s.

The Korean War allowed the United States to exclude the Soviet Union from a peace settlement with Japan. Incensed by the conditions insisted upon by the Americans and careful to foil Western attempts to ruin the Sino-Soviet alliance, Stalin boycotted a final peace treaty with Japan. Immediately, the United States signed a treaty of defense and alliance with Japan—Stalin's prophecy fulfilled. With Stalin's refusal to sign the Japanese peace treaty in San Francisco, Soviet territorial acquisitions did not acquire international recognition de jure. Therefore, the ground remained for controversy over four tiny islands in the Kuriles— Shikotan, Kunashiri, Iturup, and Habomai, which to this day poison relations between Moscow and Tokyo.

Another of Stalin's worst nightmares came true. The hostilities in the Far East gave a decisive impulse to the rearmament of West Germany, with the help of some of Hitler's former generals—an idea unthinkable not long before. With the Bundeswehr, a new West German army, NATO was on the way to becoming a full-fledged military force in Europe. And the U.S. government, through the CIA and other means, intensified covert operations to assist the anti-Communist underground in Eastern Europe, the Baltic states, and Ukraine. In a word, the Americans began to wage the Cold War in earnest, with all available means short of outright attack on the USSR.

Did Stalin acknowledge these setbacks? He never gave any indication that he did. Several times after June 1951, when the frontline in Korea stabilized along the 38th parallel, the North Koreans, suffering mounting casualties from U.S. air strikes, begged Stalin for peace. Kim Il Sung told Stalin that the protracted war allowed "the enemy, who suffers almost no casualties, to cause continuous and terrible damage" to North Korea. Yet each time Stalin advised Kim to hold on, because the enemy, according to him, would capitulate first and soon. In fact, Stalin must have believed that the war of attrition would best serve the USSR's interests: it would tie down the United States in the Far East, and it would make both North Korea and the PRC even more dependent on Soviet economic and military power, which would guarantee the Kremlin a monolithic bloc and undisputed hegemony in the Communist universe. . . .

The Korean War proved to be the same for Stalin as the Crimean War had been for Czar Nicholas I a century earlier. The reign of Nicholas had started when Russia was an unquestionable great power, respected and envied in all European capitals. It ended in a shameful defeat for the czar's empire on its own territory, the Crimea, from the technologically superior coalition of Great Britain, France, and Turkey. Nicholas, however, refused to recognize defeat: only after the sudden death of the czar (suicide was suspected) did his successor end the war. Stalin had a similar decline from the Great Victory of 1945 to the deadlock on the Korean peninsula, virtually at the Soviets' doorstep.

🌐 FURTHER READING

Frank Baldwin, ed., *Without Parallel* (1975)

Barton J. Bernstein, "The Truman Administration and the Korean War," in Michael Lacey, ed., *The Truman Presidency* (1989), pp. 410–444

Clay Blair, *The Forgotten War* (1988)

William B. Breuer, *Shadow Warriors: The Covert War in Korea* (1996)

Ronald J. Caridi, *The Korean War and American Politics* (1969)

Jian Chen, "China's Changing Aims During the Korean War, 1950–1951," *Journal of East Asian-American Relations,* 1 (1992), 8–41

——, *China's Road to the Korean War* (1994)

Thomas J. Christensen, "Threats, Assurances, and the Last Chance for Peace: The Lessons of Mao's Korean War Telegrams," *International Security,* 17 (1992), 122–154

Bruce Cumings, ed., *Child of Conflict* (1983)

——, *The Origins of the Korean War,* 2 vols. (1981–1990)

—— and Jon Halliday, *Korea: The Unknown War* (1988)

Roger Dingman, "Atomic Diplomacy During the Korean War," *International Security,* 13 (1988–1989), 50–91

Charles Dobbs, *The Unwanted Symbol* (1981)

Rosemary J. Foot, "Making Known the Unknown War: Policy Analysis of the Korean Conflict in the Last Decade," *Diplomatic History,* 15 (1991), 411–431

——, *A Substitute for Victory* (1990)

——, *The Wrong War* (1985)

Alexander L. George and Richard Smoke, *Deterrence in American Foreign Policy* (1974)

Sergei N. Goncharov et al., *Uncertain Partners: Stalin, Mao, and the Korean War* (1993)

Joseph Goulden, *Korea* (1982)

Karunaker Gupta, "How Did the Korean War Begin?" *China Quarterly,* 52 (1972), 699–716. Critics' comments in 54 (1973), 354–368

Francis H. Heller, ed., *The Korean War* (1977)

Hoa Yufan and Zhai Zhihai, "China's Decision to Enter the Korean War: History Revisited," *China Quarterly,* 121 (1990), 94–114

Michael H. Hunt, "Beijing and the Korean Crisis, June, 1950–June, 1951," *Political Science Quarterly,* 107 (1992), 457–474

D. Clayton James, *Refighting the Last War* (1992)

——, *The Years of MacArthur* (1985)

Burton I. Kaufman, *The Korean War* (1986)

Edward C. Keefer, "President Dwight D. Eisenhower and the End of the Korean War," *Diplomatic History,* 10 (1986), 267–289

Nam G. Kim, *From Enemies to Allies* (1997) (Japan)

Yuen Foong Khong, *Analogies at War* (1992)

Gabriel Kolko and Joyce Kolko, *The Limits of Power* (1972)

Peter Lowe, *The Origins of the Korean War* (1986)

Callum A. MacDonald, *Korea* (1987)

David McLellan, *Dean Acheson* (1976)

James I. Matray, ed., *Historical Dictionary of the Korean War* (1991)

——, *The Reluctant Crusade* (1985)

——, "Truman's Plan for Victory: National Self-Determination and the Thirty-Eighth Parallel Decision in Korea," *Journal of American History,* 66 (1979), 314–33

Ernest R. May, *"Lessons" of the Past* (1973)

John Merrill, *Korea: The Peninsular Origins of the War* (1989)

Yonosuke Nagai and Akira Iriye, eds., *The Origins of the Cold War in Asia* (1977)

Glenn D. Paige, *The Korean Decision* (1968)

———, ed., *1950: Truman's Decision* (1970)

David Rees, *Korea, The Limited War* (1964)

Mark A. Ryan, *Chinese Attitudes Toward Nuclear Weapons: China and the United States During the Korean War* (1989)

Michael Schaller, *Douglas MacArthur: The Far Eastern General* (1989)

Gaddis Smith, *Dean Acheson* (1972)

John W. Spanier, *The Truman-MacArthur Controversy* (1959)

Russell Spurr, *Enter the Dragon: China's Involvement in the Korean War* (1988)

I. F. Stone, *The Hidden History of the Korean War* (1952)

William Stueck, "The Korean War as International History," *Diplomatic History,* 10 (1986), 291–309

———, *The Korean War* (1995)

———, *The Road to Confrontation* (1981)

John Tolland, *In Mortal Combat* (1991)

Rudy Tomedi, *No Bugle, No Drums* (1993)

Kathryn Weathersby, "To Attack, or Not to Attack? Stalin, Kim Il Sung, and the Prelude to War," *Cold War International History Bulletin,* 5 (1995), 1–9

———, "The Soviet Role in the Early Phase of the Korean War: New Documentary Evidence," *The Journal of American-East Asian Relations,* 2 (1993), 425–458

Philip West, "Confronting the West," *Journal of American-East Asian Relations,* 2 (1993), 5–28

———, "Interpreting the Korean War," *American Historical Review,* 94 (1989), 80–96

Richard Whelan, *Drawing the Line* (1990)

Allen Whiting, *China Crosses the Yalu* (1960)

John E. Wiltz, "Truman and MacArthur, The Wake Island Meeting," *Military Affairs,* 42 (1978), 169–176

Zhang Shu Guang, *Mao's Military Romanticism* (1996)

Dwight D. Eisenhower
and Nuclear Arms

In 1952 Americans elected Dwight D. Eisenhower as president. The popular World War II hero, known to many simply as Ike, named John Foster Dulles as his secretary of state and promised to oppose communism vigorously and to assert American leadership around the globe. Yet in line with his conservative, Republican principles, the president also pledged to keep taxes low and to contain spiraling military costs.

Eisenhower found a way to realize his twin goals in the doctrine of "massive retaliation." Buttressed by America's overwhelming superiority in nuclear arms at the time, Eisenhower and Dulles proclaimed that the United States reserved the right to counter communist aggression wherever it occurred with a swift, decisive nuclear response. Massive retaliation, they hoped, would allow the United States to block aggressive nations, defend its interests, and at the same time cut back on expensive conventional weapons and troops. The "New Look" for the American armed forces, sloganeers concluded, would provide the United States with "more bang for the buck," or, as the Soviets put it, "more rubble for the ruble."

As the Eisenhower administration's policies took shape, the world witnessed an ever accelerating nuclear-arms race. The United States had enjoyed an atomic monopoly until September 1949, when Moscow had detonated its first atomic bomb. The Truman administration had responded by immediately speeding up development of the hydrogen bomb, a nuclear weapon that packed nearly eight hundred times the destructive force of the original atom bomb dropped on Hiroshima, Japan. But the successful test of that awesome weapon on November 1, 1952, was duplicated by the Soviet Union in less than a year's time.

Technological innovations during the 1950s further fueled the arms race. U.S. scientists and military officials engineered more powerful warheads and produced and deployed sophisticated intercontinental jet bombers such as the B-52 to serve as "delivery vehicles." Also in the early 1950s, the U.S. Army began to develop and deploy nuclear weapons for battlefield use. Then, in 1957, the Soviet Union stunned the world when it used a ballistic missile to lift an artificial satellite, Sputnik, into outer space. The achievement revealed that Moscow had developed the ability to place a nuclear warhead atop a long-range missile and strike targets as far away as the United States. Meanwhile, atmospheric nuclear tests conducted by both sides showered poisonous, radioactive fallout on the earth. When U.S. tests at Bikini atoll in the western Pacific in March 1954 infected unsuspecting Japanese fishermen with radiation poisoning, pressure mounted for a nuclear test ban. Cities and towns rushed to construct shelters for civil defense, but arms-race critics believed that few people would survive a nuclear war. By the time Eisenhower left office in 1961, the two superpowers together possessed more than twenty thousand nuclear weapons with enough firepower to inflict millions of casualties and incalculable damage.

Cold War politics during the Eisenhower era heightened tensions. In the Soviet Union, Joseph Stalin died, and eventually Premier Nikita Khrushchev took command. Although the new regime in Moscow hinted that it wanted improved relations with the West, the two superpowers continued to quarrel over familiar problems: Korea, Indochina, Berlin, China, and Eastern Europe. At the same time, problems arose in the Third World, where emerging nations were asserting their independence. The Middle East, Asia, Africa, and Latin America became more unsettled, and hence more dangerous, to international stability. The people of the world shuddered during Cold War crises—Korea (1953), the Taiwan Strait (1954 and 1958), and Berlin (1959)—when leaders went to the nuclear brink.

Eisenhower and Khrushchev, however, did participate in summit conferences at Geneva (1955) and Camp David (1959), and they evidently shared a profound unease with reliance on nuclear weapons and with the terrible consequences of nuclear competition. In 1955 the Soviets advanced a proposal for step-by-step nuclear disarmament. Eisenhower countered with a program called Open Skies to allow air surveillance and inspection of nuclear facilities as a first step toward arms control. The concrete results of summit diplomacy, however, proved meager, and the arms race continued to gather frightening momentum. In the United States, a group of antinuclear and peace activists formed the Committee for a Sane Nuclear Policy (SANE) in 1957 to press the United Nations to oversee a cessation in nuclear testing and to initiate disarmament negotiations. Although the critics raised public awareness of nuclear issues, they carried little weight with U.S. and Soviet policymakers. And despite some analysts' conclusion that nuclear arms stabilized international politics, client-state wars, civil wars, and interventions proliferated. To cite but two examples, Khrushchev dispatched troops to Hungary in 1956, and Eisenhower sent troops to Lebanon in 1958.

Several questions inform scholarly study of Eisenhower's doctrine of massive retaliation and the nuclear-arms race. One set of questions centers on the impact of nuclear arms on superpower relations. Would the administration actually have used nuclear weapons against the Soviet Union or China? Or did it assume that the mere threat of nuclear war provided adequate deterrence? Did the Eisenhower-Dulles policy of nuclear retaliation intimidate Moscow and reduce the danger of a superpower confrontation? Or did it lead the Soviets to expand their arsenal, to speed up the arms race, and to increase the likelihood of a showdown? How did Moscow view the arms race? Did Khrushchev seek serious disarmament negotiations? Or did the Soviet political and economic system preclude compromise and peaceful coexistence? Did the growing Soviet strength in nuclear arms, especially the development of the Sputnik missile, heighten the danger of a surprise, preemptive strike against the United States? Or did American alarmists exaggerate the threat? Did growing Soviet power undermine the massive retaliation strategy because it gave Moscow the capability to retaliate? Could the superpowers fight a limited nuclear war? Or would such a conflict inevitably escalate into a full-fledged Armageddon? Would a winner emerge from a

Soviet-American nuclear war? Or would the devastation be so great that neither side could claim victory?

The impact of the arms race went beyond Soviet-American relations. How did Eisenhower's nuclear saber-rattling affect U.S. relations with its allies, many of whom grew alarmed at the arms buildup and feared that they might become the battleground in a nuclear exchange? Would the United States use nuclear weapons in limited wars in the Third World even though such conflicts usually sprang from local conditions rather than Soviet aggression? Would the United States deploy nuclear weapons or make a nuclear threat over relatively insignificant places—the offshore islands of the Taiwan Strait, for example? Did the Eisenhower administration's reliance on nuclear deterrence leave it ill prepared for smaller, localized conflicts?

A third set of questions focuses on nuclear policymaking. How did nuclear strategy evolve? Did President Eisenhower play the dominant role in planning and deploying nuclear weapons? Did the hawkish views of Secretary of State Dulles prevail? What advice did the nation's military brass give the president? Did defense contractors and military leaders, the "military-industrial complex" as President Eisenhower termed it, collude to feed the arms race by lobbying Congress for unnecessarily large defense budgets? Did Democrats exploit the issue of the "missile gap" in the late 1950s for domestic political gain and in doing so contribute to the arms-race momentum? Why did antinuclear groups such as SANE have little impact on public opinion and policy deliberation?

A major question hung over the era: Why could not American and Soviet leaders find a way to halt, slow, or at least control the arms race? Had Cold War politics and the march of technology made them prisoners of a headlong race they could not stop?

 D O C U M E N T S

The Eisenhower administration struggled to balance the nation's need for military defense with budgetary constraints. Document 1, tagged NSC 162/2, approved by the president and adopted on October 30, 1953, concluded that the United States should rely on cost-effective nuclear weapons to safeguard its interests. In Document 2, from a speech of January 12, 1954, Secretary of State John Foster Dulles announced the policy of "massive retaliation."

The Eisenhower administration publicly threatened to use nuclear weapons during the Taiwan Strait crisis of late 1954 and early 1955. Document 3 consists of two parts: an official account of Secretary of State John Foster Dulles's press conference on March 15, 1955, in which the secretary discussed the possible use of tactical nuclear weapons to resolve the Taiwan Strait crisis; and an excerpt from a press conference the next day in which President Eisenhower reiterated the nuclear threat. Some of the tensions of the times temporarily dissipated in 1955 when U.S. and Soviet leaders agreed to hold their first summit meeting since World War II.

Despite a thaw in the Cold War tensions following the Geneva Conference, the super-powers' stockpiling and testing of nuclear weapons went on apace. On October 4, 1957, the Soviet Union placed its *Sputnik* satellite into outer space, a feat that intensified Cold War fears and generated charges that Eisenhower's conservative spending policies had caused the country to lag behind in missile and satellite development. The National Security Council met on October 10, 1957, to discuss the political, scientific, and military ramifications of the Soviet achievement. Document 4 is an excerpt from that discussion. Document 5 is a public proclamation, published by the National Committee for a Sane Nuclear Policy (SANE) in the *New York Times* on November 15, 1957, that questioned the rationality and morality of the nuclear arms race and called for an immediate halt to nuclear testing and United Nations efforts to promote arms control and disarmament.

In Document 6, an excerpt from Nikita Khrushchev's memoirs, the former Soviet premier explains how he came to depend on nuclear-tipped ballistic missiles to implement a Soviet version of massive retaliation. Khrushchev also recalls his conversations with Eisenhower and their mutual lament over how both the Soviet and American military establishments continually lobbied for more weapons. Domestic politics also increased the pressure for a buildup. In a speech delivered on February 29, 1960, Document 7, Democratic senator and presidential hopeful John F. Kennedy charged that the Eisenhower administration's tight-fisted budgets had made the nation vulnerable to Soviet attack. Kennedy's criticisms echoed those of others who decried the existence of a missile gap in the Soviets' favor at the end of the Eisenhower era. (The "gap" actually favored the United States.) Document 8 is Eisenhower's farewell address of January 17, 1961, whose warning against a "military-industrial complex" aroused wide interest.

1. National Security Council Paper No. 162/2 (NSC-162/2) Promotes Atomic Power, 1953

The capability of the USSR to attack the United States with atomic weapons has been continuously growing and will be materially enhanced by hydrogen weapons. The USSR has sufficient bombs and aircraft, using one-way missions, to inflict serious damage on the United States, especially by surprise attack. The USSR soon may have the capability of dealing a crippling blow to our industrial base and our continued ability to prosecute a war. Effective defense could reduce the likelihood and intensity of a hostile attack but not eliminate the chance of a crippling blow. . . .

The USSR does not seem likely deliberately to launch a general war against the United States during the period covered by current estimates (through mid-1955). The uncertain prospects for Soviet victory in a general war, the change in leadership, satellite unrest, and the U.S. capability to retaliate massively, make such a course improbable. Similarly, an attack on NATO [North Atlantic Treaty Organization] countries or other areas which would be almost certain to bring on general war in view of U.S. commitments or intentions would be unlikely. The Soviets will not, however, be deterred by fear of general war from taking the measures they consider necessary to counter Western actions which they view as a serious threat to their security. . . .

Although Soviet fear of atomic reaction should still inhibit local aggression, increasing Soviet atomic capability may tend to diminish the deterrent effect of U.S. atomic power against peripheral Soviet aggression. It may also sharpen the reaction of the USSR to what it considers provocative acts of the United States. If either side should miscalculate the strength of the other's reaction, such local conflicts could grow into general war, even though neither seeks nor desires it. To avoid this, it will in general be desirable for the United States to make clear to the USSR the kind of actions which will be almost certain to lead to this result, recognizing, however, that as general war becomes more devastating for both sides the threat to resort to it becomes less available as a sanction against local aggression. . . .

This document can be found in U.S. Department of State, *Foreign Relations of the United States, 1952–1954* (Washington, D.C: Government Printing Office, 1984), II, 579, 580–581, 583, 588, 589, 593.

Within the free world, only the United States can provide and maintain, for a period of years to come, the atomic capability to counterbalance Soviet atomic power. Thus, sufficient atomic weapons and effective means of delivery are indispensable for U.S. security. Moreover, in the face of Soviet atomic power, defense of the continental United States becomes vital to effective security: to protect our striking force, our mobilization base, and our people. Such atomic capability is also a major contribution to the security of our allies, as well as of this country.

The United States cannot, however, meet its defense needs, even at exorbitant cost, without the support of allies. . . .

The United States must maintain a sound economy based on free private enterprise as a basis both for high defense productivity and for the maintenance of its living standards and free institutions. Not only the world position of the United States, but the security of the whole free world, is dependent on the avoidance of recession and on the long-term expansion of the U.S. economy. Threats to its stability or growth, therefore, constitute a danger to the security of the United States and of the coalition which it leads. Expenditures for national security, in fact all federal, state and local governmental expenditures, must be carefully scrutinized with a view to measuring their impact on the national economy. . . .

The requirements for funds to maintain our national security must thus be considered in the light of these dangers to our economic system, including the danger to industrial productivity necessary to support military programs, arising from excessive levels of total Government spending, taxing and borrowing. . . .

In specific situations where a warning appears desirable and feasible as an added deterrent, the United States should make clear to the USSR and Communist China, in general terms or with reference to specific areas as the situation requires, its intention to react with military force against any aggression by Soviet bloc armed forces.

In the event of hostilities, the United States will consider nuclear weapons to be as available for use as other munitions. Where the consent of an ally is required for the use of these weapons from U.S. bases on the territory of such ally, the United States should promptly obtain the advance consent of such ally for such use. The United States should also seek, as and when feasible, the understanding and approval of this policy by free nations.

This policy should not be made public without further consideration by the National Security Council.

2. Secretary of State John Foster Dulles Explains Massive Retaliation, 1954

The Soviet Communists are planning for what they call "an entire historical era," and we should do the same. They seek, through many types of maneuvers, gradually to divide and weaken the free nations by overextending them in efforts which, as Lenin put it, are "beyond their strength, so that they come to practical bankruptcy." Then, said Lenin, "our victory is assured." Then, said Stalin, will be "the moment for the decisive blow."

This document can be found in *Department of State Bulletin*, XXX (January 25, 1954), 107–108.

In the face of this strategy, measures cannot be judged adequate merely because they ward off an immediate danger. It is essential to do this, but it is also essential to do so without exhausting ourselves.

When the Eisenhower administration applied this test, we felt that some transformations were needed.

It is not sound military strategy permanently to commit U.S. land forces to Asia to a degree that leaves us no strategic reserves.

It is not sound economics, or good foreign policy, to support permanently other countries; for in the long run, that creates as much ill will as good will.

Also, it is not sound to become permanently committed to military expenditures so vast that they lead to "practical bankruptcy." . . .

We need allies and collective security. Our purpose is to make these relations more effective, less costly. This can be done by placing more reliance on deterrent power and less dependence on local defensive power.

This is accepted practice so far as local communities are concerned. We keep locks on our doors, but we do not have an armed guard in every home. We rely principally on a community security system so well equipped to punish any who break in and steal that, in fact, would-be aggressors are generally deterred. That is the modern way of getting maximum protection at a bearable cost.

What the Eisenhower administration seeks is a similar international security system. We want, for ourselves and the other free nations, a maximum deterrent at a bearable cost.

Local defense will always be important. But there is no local defense which alone will contain the mighty landpower of the Communist world. Local defenses must be reinforced by the further deterrent of massive retaliatory power. A potential aggressor must know that he cannot always prescribe battle conditions that suit him. Otherwise, for example, a potential aggressor, who is glutted with manpower, might be tempted to attack in confidence that resistance would be confined to manpower. He might be tempted to attack in places where his superiority was decisive.

The way to deter aggression is for the free community to be willing and able to respond vigorously at places and with means of its own choosing.

So long as our basic policy concepts were unclear, our military leaders could not be selective in building our military power. If an enemy could pick his time and place and method of warfare—and if our policy was to remain the traditional one of meeting aggression by direct and local opposition—then we needed to be ready to fight in the Arctic and in the Tropics; in Asia, the Near East, and in Europe; by sea, by land, and by air; with old weapons and with new weapons. . . .

But before military planning could be changed, the President and his advisers, as represented by the National Security Council, had to take some basic policy decisions. This has been done. The basic decision was to depend primarily upon a great capacity to retaliate, instantly, by means and at places of our choosing. Now the Department of Defense and the Joint Chiefs of Staff can shape our military establishment to fit what is *our* policy, instead of having to try to be ready to meet the enemy's many choices. That permits of a selection of military means instead of a multiplication of means. As a result, it is now possible to get, and share, more basic security at less cost.

3. Dulles and President Dwight D. Eisenhower Threaten to Use Nuclear Weapons: The Taiwan Strait Crisis, 1955

Dulles Statement, March 15, 1955

A correspondent said that in his speech, the secretary had referred to the existence in the hands of our forces in the Far East of new and powerful weapons which he had indicated would be used if necessary under other conditions or conditions of war out there. Asked if he could tell them anything about the nature of those weapons or the circumstances under which they might be used, the secretary replied that he thought it was generally known that certain types of atomic missiles were becoming conventional in the United States armed services. He stated that those were weapons of relatively small dimensions with considerably more explosive power than was contained in the conventional weapons. He added that, however, they were weapons of precision.

Mr. Dulles continued that he imagined that if the United States became engaged in a major military activity anywhere in the world that those weapons would come into use because, as he had said, they were more and more becoming conventional and replacing what used to be called conventional weapons. He commented that they might recall that at the meeting of the NATO Council, which had been held in Paris last December, there had been pretty much agreement at that time that atomic missiles would be treated as a conventional and normal means for the defense of Europe. He explained that what he was speaking of was merely another application of that basic policy.

Asked if he would regard United States defense of Quemoy and Matsu a major military effort in that context, Mr. Dulles answered that he could not tell that in advance because it depended upon what the effort was which we had to meet. He added that if that was a major effort on the part of the Chinese Communists, it might take a major effort on our part to counter it.

A correspondent inquired if in the case of these atomic weapons which the secretary had described as having become or in the state of becoming conventional, he was referring to what we ordinarily called tactical atomic weapons. The secretary responded that that was right.

Eisenhower Statement, March 16, 1955

Q. Mr. President, yesterday at his news conference, Secretary of State Dulles indicated that in the event of general war in the Far East, we would probably make use of some tactical small atomic weapons. Would you care to comment on this and, possibly, explain it further?

The Dulles Statement can be found as Secretary of State John F. Dulles Press Conference, 15 March, 1955: Charles McCardle papers, Box 7, Folder "1955 Secretary's Press Conferences," Dwight D. Eisenhower Presidential Library, Abilene, Kansas.

The Eisenhower Statement can be found in *Public Papers of the Presidents, Dwight D. Eisenhower, 1955* (Washington, D.C.: U.S. Government Printing Office, 1950), 332.

The President. I wouldn't comment in the sense that I would pretend to foresee the conditions of any particular conflict in which you might engage; but we have been, as you know, active in producing various types of weapons that feature nuclear fission ever since World War II.

Now, in any combat where these things can be used on strictly military targets and for strictly military purposes, I see no reason why they shouldn't be used just exactly as you would use a bullet or anything else.

I believe the great question about these things comes when you begin to get into those areas where you cannot make sure that you are operating merely against military targets. But with that one qualification, I would say, yes, of course they would be used.

4. The National Security Council Discusses the Ramifications of *Sputnik,* 1957

Mr. Allen Dulles [director of the Central Intelligence Agency] stated that . . . on October 4 the Soviets had fired their earth satellite from the Tyura Tam range. Its initial path followed the range, crossing approximately over the range's other end at Klyuchi. . . . [A]fter the successful orbiting of the earth satellite and after the second circuit of the earth by the satellite, the Soviets announced their achievement. This delay in the announcement was in line with the previous statements of the Soviet Union that they would not announce an attempt to orbit their satellite until they had been assured that the orbiting had been successful. . . .

Mr. Dulles then turned to the world reaction to the Soviet achievement. He first pointed out that Khrushchev had moved all his propaganda guns into place. The launching of an earth satellite was one of a trilogy of propaganda moves, the other two being the announcement of the successful testing of an ICBM [intercontinental ballistic missile] and the recent test of a large-scale hydrogen bomb at Novaya Zemlya. . . .

Larded in with Khrushchev's propaganda statements had been a number of interesting remarks, such as the one in which Khrushchev consigned military aircraft to museums in the future. With respect to this remark, Mr. Dulles pointed out that U.S. intelligence had not observed as many Soviet heavy bombers on airfields as had been expected. This raised the question as to whether the Soviets are in the process of de-emphasizing the role of the heavy bomber. There had been no clear verdict yet by the intelligence community on this question.

Mr. Dulles thought that there was no doubt that in gearing up all this propaganda of recent days and weeks, the Soviets had had an eye to the situation in the Middle East, and wished to exert the maximum influence they could summon on that situation. Much of the Soviet propaganda comment is following closely the original Soviet boast relating their scientific accomplishments to the effectiveness of the

This document can be found in U.S. Department of State, *Foreign Relations of the United States, 1955–1957* (Washington, D.C.: U.S. Government Printing Office, 1958), XI, 757–758, 759, 761–762.

Communist social system. The target for this particular thrust, thought Mr. Dulles, was evidently the underdeveloped nations in the world. . . .

At the conclusion of Mr. Allen Dulles' briefing, [National Security Affairs Advisor] Mr. [Robert] Cutler asked [Deputy Defense] Secretary [Donald] Quarles to speak. Secretary Quarles began by stating that much of what he was going to say would be familiar to the President and other members of the Council. The President quipped that this was indeed the case, and he was beginning to feel somewhat numb on the subject of the earth satellite. Thereafter, Secretary Quarles outlined briefly the development of satellite programs beginning with the period of World War II. . . .

As to the implications of the Soviet achievement, Secretary Quarles said he would not comment on the [C]old [W]ar aspects, since they had been dealt with by the Director of Central Intelligence. Beyond this, it was clear that the Soviets possess a competence in long-range rocketry and in auxiliary fields which is even more advanced than the competence with which we had credited them; although, of course, we had always given them the capability of orbiting an earth satellite. Finally, said Secretary Quarles, the outer space implications of the launching of this satellite were of very great significance, especially in relation to the development of reconnaissance satellites. . . .

Mr. Cutler then called on Dr. [Detlev W.] Bronk [president of the U.S. National Academy of Sciences], who stated initially that there was one thing about which he was very greatly concerned—that is, that we avoid getting our whole scientific community into a race to accomplish everything before the Russians do. He therefore thought we should adhere strictly to our stated earth satellite program and not be deflected from our course merely by the fact that the Russians had been the first to launch an earth satellite.

The President pointed out that all those around the table and others could anticipate before very long being obliged to testify before Congressional committees, to talk to the press, and the like. In the circumstances, he could imagine nothing more important than that anybody so involved should stand firmly by the existing earth satellite program which was, after all, adopted by the Council after due deliberation as a reasonable program. In short, we should answer inquiries by stating that we have a plan—a good plan—and that we are going to stick to it.

Mr. Cutler then called on Secretary [of State Christian] Herter for an appraisal of the foreign policy implications for U.S. security of the successful launching of the Soviet satellite. Secretary Herter initially stated that it was extremely difficult to make such an assessment because there was such a mass of information pouring into the Department of State. While there had been insufficient time to analyze this intake, there were already some indications of the serious effects of the Soviet success which we hope to be able to counteract.

Thereafter, Secretary Herter read selected quotations to illustrate his point, with particular reference to Turkey, Morocco, and the Philippines. He also pointed out the probable repercussions of the Soviet success in the United Nations. The United States may now encounter much greater difficulty in defending its disarmament position.

By and large, continued Secretary Herter, the reaction of our allies had been pretty firm and good, though even the best of them require assurance that we have not been surpassed scientifically and militarily by the USSR. The neutralist countries are chiefly engaged in patting themselves on the back and insisting that the

Soviet feat proves the value and the wisdom of the neutralism which these countries have adopted.

Summing up, Secretary Herter described the first foreign policy reactions as "pretty somber." The United States will have to do a great deal to counteract them and, particularly, to confirm the existence of our own real military and scientific strength. . . .

Mr. Cutler then called on Mr. [Arthur] Larson [director of the U.S. Information Agency], who said that he was hesitant to say what he was going to say because he was not sure that he really believed it. He then went on to say that while we could not permit ourselves to be panicked by the Soviet achievement, he did wonder whether our U.S. plans were now adequate with regard to the next great break-through. If we lose repeatedly to the Russians as we have lost with the earth satellite, the accumulated damage would be tremendous. We should accordingly plan, ourselves, to accomplish some of the next great break-throughs first—for example, the achievement of a manned satellite, or getting to the moon. Do we have any such plans, asked Mr. Larson. If not, our people should begin to think about them.

The President replied to Mr. Larson by stating that while he could hardly quarrel with Mr. Larson's conclusions if the Soviets were to win every time, the fact remained that the United States couldn't possibly set up a whole vast scientific program of basic research in areas about which we don't know anything, and then attempt to outdo the Russians in each aspect of such a program. We must, above all, still seek a military posture that the Russians will respect.

5. SANE Protests the Nuclear-Arms Race, 1957

A deep uneasiness exists inside Americans as we look out on the world. . . .

We are facing a danger unlike any danger that has ever existed. In our possession and in the possession of the Russians are more than enough nuclear explosives to put an end to the life of man on earth.

Our uneasiness is the result of the fact that our approach to the danger is unequal to the danger. Our response to the challenge of today's world seems out of joint. The slogans and arguments that belong to the world of competitive national sovereignties—a world of plot and counter-plot—no longer fit the world of today or tomorrow.

Just in front of us opens a grand human adventure into outer space. But within us and all around us is the need to make this world whole before we set out for other ones. We can earn the right to explore other planets only as we make this one safe and fit for human habitation.

The sovereignty of the human community comes before all others—before the sovereignty of groups, tribes, or nations. In that community, man has natural rights. He has the right to live and to grow, to breathe unpoisoned air, to work on uncontaminated soil. He has the right to his sacred nature.

If what nations are dong has the effect of destroying these natural rights, whether by upsetting the delicate balances on which life depends, or fouling the air, or devitalizing the land, or tampering with the genetic integrity of man himself; then it becomes necessary for people to restrain and tame the nations.

Indeed, the test of a nation's right to survive today is measured not by the size of its bombs or the range of its missiles, but by the size and range of its concern for the human community as a whole.

There can be no true security for America unless we can exert leadership in these terms, unless we become advocates of a grand design that is directed to the large cause of human destiny.

There can be no true security for America unless we can establish and keep vital connections with the world's people, unless there is some moral grandeur to our purposes, unless what we do is direct to the cause of human life and the free man.

There is much that America has said to the world. But the world is still waiting for us to say and do the things that will in deed and in truth represent our greatest strength.

What are these things?

That we pledge ourselves to the cause of peace with justice on earth, and that there is no sacrifice that we are not prepared to make, nothing we will not do to create such a just peace for all peoples;

That we are prepared to support the concept of a United Nations with adequate authority under law to prevent aggression, adequate authority to compel and enforce disarmament, adequate authority to settle disputes among nations according to principles of justice;

That the earth is too small for intercontinental ballistic missiles and nuclear bombs, and that the first order of business for the world is to bring both under control;

That the development of satellites or rocket stations and the exploration of outer space must be carried on in the interests of the entire human community through a pooling of world science;

That because of the grave unanswered questions with respect to nuclear test explosions—especially as it concerns the contamination of air and water and food, and the injury to man himself—we are calling upon all nations to suspend such explosions at once;

That while the abolition of testing will not by itself solve the problem of peace or the problem of armaments, it enables the world to eliminate immediately at least one real and specific danger. Also, that the abolition of testing gives us a place to begin on the larger question of armaments control, for the problems in monitoring such tests are relatively uncomplicated;

That none of the differences separating the governments of the world are as important as the membership of all peoples in the human family;

That the big challenge of the age is to develop the concept of a higher loyalty— loyalty by man to the human community;

That the greatest era of human history on earth is within reach of all mankind, that there is no area that cannot be made fertile or habitable, no disease that cannot be fought, no scarcity that cannot be conquered;

That all that is required for this is to re-direct our energies, re-discover our moral strength, re-define our purposes.

6. Soviet Premier Nikita Khrushchev Reflects on the Nuclear-Arms Race, 1970

Even honest people who want to avoid the use of atomic and hydrogen weapons can't ignore the question of how many such arms are available to us in case a global war should break out. That's why we must decide realistically on priorities for the allocation of funds.

When I was the leader of the Party and the Government, I decided that we had to economize drastically in the building of homes, the construction of communal services, and even in the development of agriculture in order to build up our defenses. I even suspended the construction of subways in Kiev, Baku, and Tblisi so that we could redirect those funds into strengthening our defense and attack forces. We also built fewer athletic stadiums, swimming pools, and cultural facilities. I think I was right to concentrate on military spending, even at the expense of all but the most essential investments in other areas. If I hadn't put such a high priority on our military needs, we couldn't have survived. I devoted all my strength to the rearmament of the Soviet Union. It was a challenging and important stage of our lives. . . .

Our potential enemy—our principal, our most powerful, our most dangerous enemy—was so far away from us that we couldn't have reached him with our air force. Only by building up a nuclear missile force could we keep the enemy from unleashing war against us. As life has already confirmed, if we had given the West a chance, war would have been declared while Dulles was alive. But we were the first to launch rockets into space; we exploded the most powerful nuclear devices; we accomplished those feats first, ahead of the United States, England, and France. Our accomplishments and our obvious might had a sobering effect on the aggressive forces in the United States, England, France, and, of course, inside the Bonn [West German] government. They knew that they had lost their chance to strike at us with impunity.

Now that it's the size of our nuclear missile arsenal and not the size of our army that counts, I think the army should be reduced to an absolute minimum. There's no question in my mind that we have indeed reached the stage where that's possible. When I led the Government and had final authority over our military allocations, our theoreticians calculated that we had the nuclear capacity to grind our enemies into dust, and since that time our nuclear capacity has been greatly intensified. During my leadership we accumulated enough weapons to destroy the principal cities of the United States, not to mention our potential enemies in Europe. . . .

I have always been against war, but at the same time I've always realized full well that the fear of nuclear war in a country's leader can paralyze that country's defenses. And if a country's defenses are paralyzed, then war really is inevitable: the enemy is sure to sense your fright and try to take advantage of it. . . .

However, we must also keep in mind the true character of all imperialists, capitalists, monopolists, and militarists who are interested in making money out of the political tension between nations. We must make sure that we don't allow ourselves to get involved in a lot of senseless competition with the West over military spending. If we try to compete with America in any but the most essential areas of military preparedness, we will be doing two harmful things. First, we will be further enriching wealthy aggressive capitalist circles in the United States who use our own military buildups as a pretext for overloading their own country's arms budget. Second, we will be exhausting our material resources without raising the living standard of our people. We must remember that the fewer people we have in the army, the more people we will have available for other, more productive kinds of work. This realization would be a good common point of departure for the progressive forces of the world in their struggle for peaceful coexistence. If one side were to curtail its accumulation of military means, it would be easier for the other side to do the same. We must be prepared to strike back against our enemy, but we must also ask, "Where is the end to this spiraling competition?"

I know from experience that the leaders of the armed forces can be very persistent in claiming their share when it comes time to allocate funds. Every commander has all sorts of very convincing arguments why he should get more than anyone else. Unfortunately there's a tendency for people who run the armed forces to be greedy and self-seeking. They're always ready to throw in your face the slogan "If you try to economize on the country's defenses today, you'll pay in blood when war breaks out tomorrow." I'm not denying that these men have a huge responsibility, and I'm not impugning their moral qualities. But the fact remains that the living standard of the country suffers when the budget is overloaded with allocations to unproductive branches of consumption. And today as yesterday, the most unproductive expenditures are all of those made on the armed forces. That's why I think that military leaders can't be reminded too often that it is the government which must allocate funds, and it is the government which must decide how much the armed forces can spend.

Apparently the control of military spending is a universal problem. I remember a conversation I once had with President Eisenhower when I was a guest at his dacha at Camp David [in September 1959]. We went for walks together and had some useful informal talks. During one of these talks, he asked, "Tell me, Mr. Khrushchev, how did you decide the question of funds for military expenses?" Then, before I had a chance to say anything, he said, "Perhaps first I should tell you how it is with us."

"Well, how is it with you?"

He smiled, and I smiled back at him. I had a feeling what he was going to say. "It's like this. My military leaders come to me and say, 'Mr. President, we need such and such a sum for such and such a program.' I say, 'Sorry, we don't have the funds.' They say, 'We have reliable information that the Soviet Union has already allocated funds for their own such program. Therefore if we don't get the funds we need, we'll fall behind the Soviet Union.' So I give in. That's how they wring money out of me. They keep grabbing for more and I keep giving it to them. Now tell me, how is it with you?"

"It's just the same. Some people from our military department come and say, 'Comrade Khrushchev, look at this! The Americans are developing such and such a system. We could develop the same system, but it would cost such and such.' I tell them there's no money; it's all been allotted already. So they say, 'If we don't get the money we need and if there's a war, then the enemy will have superiority over us.' So we discuss it some more, and I end up by giving them the money they ask for."

"Yes," he said, "that's what I thought. You know, we really should come to some sort of an agreement in order to stop this fruitless, really wasteful rivalry."

"I'd like to do that. Part of my reason for coming here was to see if some sort of an agreement would come out of these meetings and conversations."

But we couldn't agree then, and we can't agree now. I don't know. Maybe it's impossible for us to agree.

7. Senator John F. Kennedy Presses for More Military Spending to Close the Missile Gap, 1960

Winston Churchill said: "We arm—to parley." We prepare for war—in order to deter war. We depend on the strength of armaments, to enable us to bargain for disarmament. It is my intention, later this week, to make a second address on what positive preparations for disarmament we can make now. We compare our military strength with the Soviets, not to determine whether we should use it, but to determine whether we can persuade them that to use theirs would be futile and disastrous, and to determine whether we can back up our own pledges in Berlin, Formosa, and around the world.

In short, peace, not politics, is at the heart of the current debate—peace, not war, is the objective of our military policy. But peace would have no meaning if the time ever came when the deterrent ratio shifted so heavily in favor of the Soviet Union that they could destroy most of our retaliatory capacity in a single blow. It would then be irrelevant as to whether the Soviets achieved our demise through massive attack, through the threat of such attack, or through nibbling away gradually at our security.

Will such a time come?

The current debate has too often centered on how our retaliatory capacity compares today with that of the Soviets. Our striking force, the President said one week ago Sunday night, is "ample for today—far superior to any other" and large enough to deter any aggressor. But the real issue is not how we stand today but tomorrow—not in 1960 but in 1961, 1962 and particularly 1963 and thereafter. Nineteen hundred and sixty is critical because this is the year that the money must be appropriated—by this session of this Congress—if we are to obtain initial results in subsequent years. . . .

Whether the missile gap—that everyone agrees now exists—will become critical in 1961, 1962, or 1963—whether during the critical years of the gap the Russian lead will be 2 to 1, 3 to 1, or 5 to 1—whether the gap can be brought to a close—by the availability in quantity of Polaris and Minuteman missiles—in 1964 or in 1965 or ever—on all these questions experts may sincerely differ. I do not challenge the accuracy of our intelligence reports—I do not charge anyone with intentionally

This document can be found in *Congressional Record*, CVI (February 29, 1960), 3801–3803.

misleading the public for purposes of deception. For whichever figures are accurate, the point is that we are facing a gap on which we are gambling with our survival—and this year's defense budget is our last real chance to do something about it. . . .

Unless immediate steps are taken, failure to maintain our relative power of retaliation may in the near future expose the United States to a nuclear missile attack. Until our own mobile solid-fuel missiles are available in sufficient quantities to make it unwise for an enemy to consider an attack we must scrape through with what we can most quickly make available. At the present time there are no Polaris submarines on station ready for an emergency. There are no hardened missile bases. There is no adequate air defense. There is no capacity for an airborne alert in anything like the numbers admittedly needed. . . .

Time is short. This situation should never have been permitted to arise. But if we move now, if we are willing to gamble with our money instead of our survival, we have, I am sure, the wit and resource to maintain the minimum conditions for our survival, for our alliances, and for the active pursuit of peace.

8. Eisenhower Warns Against the "Military-Industrial Complex," 1961

A vital element in keeping the peace is our military establishment. Our arms must be mighty, ready for instant action, so that no potential aggressor may be tempted to risk his own destruction.

Our military organization today bears little relation to that known by any of my predecessors in peacetime, or indeed by the fighting men of World War II or Korea.

Until the latest of our world conflicts, the United States had no armaments industry. American makers of plowshares could, with time and as required, make swords as well. But now we can no longer risk emergency improvisation of national defense; we have been compelled to create a permanent armaments industry of vast proportions. Added to this, three and a half million men and women are directly engaged in the defense establishment. We annually spend on military security more than the net income of all United States corporations.

This conjunction of an immense military establishment and a large arms industry is new in the American experience. The total influence—economic, political, even spiritual—is felt in every city, every State house, every office of the Federal government. We recognize the imperative need for this development. Yet we must not fail to comprehend its grave implications. Our toil, resources and livelihood are all involved; so is the very structure of our society.

In the councils of government, we must guard against the acquisition of unwarranted influence, whether sought or unsought, by the military-industrial complex. The potential for the disastrous rise of misplaced power exists and will persist.

We must never let the weight of this combination endanger our liberties or democratic processes. We should take nothing for granted. Only an alert and knowledgeable citizenry can compel the proper meshing of the huge industrial and

This document can be found in *Public Papers of the Presidents, Dwight D. Eisenhower, 1960–1961* (Washington, D.C.: U.S. Government Printing Office, 1961), pp. 1037–1040.

military machinery of defense with our peaceful methods and goals, so that security and liberty may prosper together.

Akin to, and largely responsible for the sweeping changes in our industrial-military posture, has been the technological revolution during recent decades.

In this revolution, research has become central; it also becomes more formalized, complex, and costly. A steadily increasing share is conducted for, by, or at the direction of, the Federal government.

Today, the solitary inventor, tinkering in his shop, has been overshadowed by task forces of scientists in laboratories and testing fields. In the same fashion, the free university, historically the fountainhead of free ideas and scientific discovery, has experienced a revolution in the conduct of research. Partly because of the huge costs involved, a government contract becomes virtually a substitute for intellectual curiosity. For every old blackboard there are now hundreds of new electronic computers.

The prospect of domination of the nation's scholars by Federal employment, project allocations, and the power of money is ever present—and is gravely to be regarded.

Yet, in holding scientific research and discovery in respect, as we should, we must also be alert to the equal and opposite danger that public policy could itself become the captive of a scientific-technological elite.

It is the task of statesmanship to mold, to balance, and to integrate these and other forces, new and old, within the principles of our democratic system—ever aiming toward the supreme goals of our free society. . . .

Down the long lane of the history yet to be written America knows that this world of ours, ever growing smaller, must avoid becoming a community of dreadful fear and hate, and be, instead, a proud confederation of mutual trust and respect.

Such a confederation must be one of equals. The weakest must come to the conference table with the same confidence as do we, protected as we are by our moral, economic, and military strength. That table, though scarred by many past frustrations, cannot be abandoned for the certain agony of the battlefield.

 # E S S A Y S

In the first essay, Michael S. Sherry, a professor of history at Northwestern University, renders a sympathetic portrayal of President Dwight D. Eisenhower's struggle to avoid war and contain Cold War militarization. Sherry argues that Eisenhower's "New Look" strategy, which relied on nuclear weapons and the threat of "massive retaliation" to prevent Communist aggression, balanced the nation's long-term security needs with its budgetary constraints. More compelling, according to Sherry, the "New Look" grew from Eisenhower's conviction that a more expansive military buildup would ultimately create a garrison state that undermined democracy at home and threatened the world with nuclear annihilation. Sherry maintains that even at the time of the Taiwan Strait crises in 1954–1955 and 1958, during which the administration exaggerated the Communist threat and threatened massive retaliation against the People's Republic of China, Eisenhower ultimately backed away from a dangerous gamble. Yet in the end, Eisenhower slowed but could not reverse the trend toward militarism. Sherry concludes that America's political culture and domestic insecurities, the march of technology, and Eisenhower's own failure to articulate an alternative to Cold

War containment and nuclear security fed the Soviet-American arms race and accounted for the president's failure to rein in the swelling military industrial complex.

In the second essay, Gordon H. Chang of Stanford University and He Di of the Institute of American Studies, Chinese Academy of Social Sciences in Beijing, use both American and Chinese sources to explore in depth the Taiwan Strait crisis of 1954–1955 and advance a more critical analysis of Eisenhower's policies. They assert that the administration's strategy of threatening massive retaliation without clarifying what the United States would and would not defend ("deterrence through uncertainty") led the People's Republic of China to conclude that its controlled military campaign against Jinmen (Quemoy), Mazu (Matsu), and other offshore islands would not draw a U.S. military response. When Mao Zedong subsequently launched an invasion of the island of Yijiangshan in the Tachens, Eisenhower and Secretary of State John Foster Dulles misinterpreted the action as likely to lead to an offensive against Taiwan itself. Rather than defusing the Taiwan Strait crisis, Eisenhower's threat to use nuclear weapons and his plans for a naval blockade of China's coast carried the United States to the nuclear brink over relatively insignificant territories and spurred China's nuclear program.

Eisenhower's Heroic but Failed Crusade Against Militarization

MICHAEL S. SHERRY

Eisenhower faced sharply different options for national security [from those faced by Harry S. Truman]. Truman's ambitious policy, laid out in NSC-68 and implemented during the Korean War, presumed protracted struggle with communism, posited abundant American resources to wage it, and prized American ability to respond symmetrically to any aggression. Nuclear intimidation or attack, conventional war and covert action, economic and political pressure—each would be met by similar forms of American power. An alternative, advanced mostly by conservative Republicans who recoiled at the costs and compromises of protracted struggle, prized asymmetry: the United States should not meet the enemy gun for gun but instead rely on those forms of power, above all atomic and aerial, at which it excelled and which might provide quick victory.

As in many areas of policy, Ike chose a "middle way" between conflicting options, grafting his limited view of resources to the Truman administration's assumptions about global struggle. For him, too, the Cold War was a protracted conflict promising no quick victory (campaign rhetoric aside), but precisely for that reason the United States had to hoard its resources, limit its efforts, and spread its burdens, or else exhaust itself over the long haul. "To amass military power without regard to our economic capacity would be to defend ourselves against one kind of disaster by inviting another," his 1953 State of the Union message declared. "We can't afford to let the negative actions of the Communists force us into world-wide deployment," he argued in 1954. "We need to be free to decide where we can strike most effectively."

The result was the much-touted "New Look," an effort to limit defense spending by relying on enhanced nuclear forces, as well as alliances and covert action, rather than on costly conventional forces to counter enemy initiatives. Confrontation with the enemy was to be selective, focused on conflicts in which American power was superior and available at limited cost. At times Eisenhower still echoed the previous administration's expansive view: "As there is no weapon too small, no arena too remote, to be ignored, there is no free nation too humble to be forgotten." But the emphasis was on American freedom "to respond vigorously at places and with means of its own choosing," in Dulles's famous phrasing, or in the National Security Council's words, it was "on the capability of inflicting massive retaliatory damage by offensive striking power." Truman's programs to mass-produce nuclear weapons and bombers created the means for this strategy—so abundantly "that the margin of American superiority seemed if anything greater than it had been in the days of the American atomic monopoly."

Why did Eisenhower take this approach? Critics once singled out his fear of deficit spending and bloated government, but many considerations were at play, their weight varying among members of the administration. For Ike, those considerations all reflected his anxiety about militarization, which defined his outlook as much as the Cold War itself. He was perilously alone in that anxiety. Dulles talked of Cold War and diplomacy; Treasury Secretary George Humphrey of budgets and fiscal prudence; Defense Secretary Charles Wilson of preparedness and efficiency. Eisenhower too spoke in those terms, but also transcended them. No unbending aversion to war guided him—he had waged war and never ruled out doing so again—but a complex aversion to militarization did sustain him.

It indeed derived partly from his economic conservatism. He worried that the taxes, capital, and expertise needed for an expensive defense program, and the inflation and government debt that might flow from it, would stifle economic entrepreneurship and growth, in turn weakening the economic base needed to sustain national security. Rejecting dire Joint Chiefs of Staff warnings of national peril if cuts in the defense budget were maintained, Ike angrily proposed that the National Security Council "should have a report as to whether national bankruptcy or national destruction would get us first." The same outlook informed his denunciations of "paternalistic government" and Truman's Fair Deal, and his neo-Hooverian view of government's role as coordinator and catalyst of national energies, not regulator or financier. Because Ike's worry about militarization was shaped in part by orthodox Republican conservatism and linked to its view on domestic policies, liberals derided it as narrow-minded penny-pinching oblivious to the expansive possibilities outlined in Keynesian economics.

But not only would many Americans later find Eisenhower's economic reasoning more persuasive, his worries went far beyond economic effects. Truman's proposed defense budget, he argued, would lead to "a permanent state of mobilization" destroying "our whole democratic way of life." "If we let defense spending run wild," he told a confidant, "you get inflation . . . then controls . . . then a garrison state . . . and *then* we've lost the very values we were trying to defend." "Should we have to resort to anything resembling a garrison state," he declared on another occasion, "then all that we are striving to defend would be weakened." His repeated warnings of a "garrison state" indicated concerns far broader than rock-ribbed Republican fears for free enterprise.

Those concerns also derived from his cautious grand strategy, which he feared that bellicose national impulses could disrupt. Like other leaders, Eisenhower worried about the impatience and immaturity of ordinary Americans, but he feared more the lunge for the quick fix and the propensity to panic he saw among hawkish Republicans, money-hungry generals, and other well-placed people. . . .

Eisenhower feared strategic disaster less through communist victory, about which his warnings were few, than through nuclear war. No President worried more about the dangers of initiating or stumbling into nuclear conflict. His concern drew in part on his doubts as an army man about air power. Already "damn tired of Air Force sales programs" in his first months in office, he lectured congressmen: "We pulverized Germany . . . but their actual rate of production was as big at the end as at the beginning." Even if—especially if—bombers could destroy the Soviet Union, he could see no real victory, as he told senior officers: "Gain such a victory, and what do you do with it? Here would be a great area from the Elbe to Vladivostok and down through Southeast Asia torn up and destroyed without government, without its communications, just an area of starvation and disaster. I ask you what would the civilized world do about it? I repeat there is no victory in any war except through our imaginations, through our dedication and through our work to avoid it." . . .

Ike's resistance to militarization probably drew most on his fear of its consequences even if war were avoided. He was reasonably confident that war would be avoided, at least on his watch—his view of himself in such matters was not modest. He was less confident of resisting a broader political process that nurtured anxiety, swollen budgets, economic stagnation, and constraints on freedom—the evils of the "garrison state." His resounding statement of those dangers came in an April 16, 1953, address. Though blaming communists for the Cold War, he warned that even if atomic war were averted, the arms race offered "a life of perpetual fear and tension; a burden of arms draining the wealth and labor of all peoples. . . . Every gun that is made, every warship launched, every rocket fired, signifies, in the final sense, a theft from those who hunger and are not fed, those who are cold and not clothed. This world in arms is not spending money alone. It is spending the sweat of its laborers, the genius of its scientists, the hopes of its children." As he eloquently concluded: "This is not a way of life at all, in any true sense. Under the cloud of threatening war, it is humanity hanging from a cross of iron." Proposing what a post–Cold War generation would call a "peace dividend," he promised to devote "a substantial percentage of the savings achieved by disarmament to a fund for world aid and reconstruction." The savings would be used for "a new kind of war . . . a declared total war, not upon any human enemy but upon the brute forces of poverty and need."

Critics often applauded these broad sentiments but attacked the strategy that flowed from them, above all its reliance on threats of massive retaliation. They decried the creation of a technologically muscle-bound America so dependent on nuclear weapons that it had no choice between capitulation and catastrophe in the face of communist aggression—a strategy at once helpless and horrifying. As the 1950s wore on, the New Look seemed a feeble bulwark against the limited wars and subversive efforts waged by communist and leftist forces in the Third World.

Ike himself acknowledged the force of this criticism even before becoming President. "What should we do if Soviet *political* aggression, as in Czechoslovakia, successively chips away exposed positions in the free world?" he wrote Dulles in 1952. "To my mind this is the case where the theory of 'retaliation' falls down." He never devised a satisfactory solution to the problem.

Still, critics of the New Look also tended to caricature it—it hardly denied the administration a non-nuclear capability. Between 1954 and 1958, the army fell from 1,404,598 to 898,925 personnel, but remained 50 percent larger than at its low point in the late 1940s. Other "conventional" forces, the navy and marines, shrank only by 10 percent, as did the air force. The 2.6 million personnel of 1958 marked a 30 percent decline from the Korean War peak, but the military reserves had grown and the nation was no longer at war. This force was far more capable of limited war than any previous peacetime force. It was backed up by the CIA's enhanced capacity for paramilitary and covert action, and by military resources given allies and clients (Ike insisted on foreign military and economic aid in the face of conservatives furious about fiscal imprudence and liberals suspicious of aiding despots).

If Eisenhower never plunged conventional forces into major combat after Korea, that was by choice more than because he denied himself the means. There was virtue in self-denial—he could plead incapacity to wage another Korean War—but the self-denial was more apparent than real. Most important, critics assumed that there *was* some way to challenge communist aggression militarily at little cost—a successful strategy avoiding both the agony of Korea and the insanity of nuclear war. Hanging over the arcane debates of the 1950s was a possibility few acknowledged—that military power in any form might be of little use to America, or any great power. Eisenhower came as close as any national figure to acknowledging that dilemma, although he never fully addressed the strategic and political consequences that flowed from it.

In addition to force levels, budgets measured Eisenhower's approach to national security. Defense spending fell 20 percent between fiscal 1953 and 1955 and, though rising later in the 1950s, continued to move within a narrow range. It also declined as a fraction of the national budget (from two-thirds to one-half by 1960) and as percentage of GNP (from 13.8 to 9.1 percent). Taft wanted sharper cuts, but Eisenhower did not listen, "partly because the clamor from the other side—demanding more spending on the military—was so much louder." Indeed, Ike sustained his defense budgets in the face of heated protests from the armed forces and, after 1957, widespread pressure to spend more. . . .

As other situations showed, no refusal to use power guided Eisenhower, only a shrewd determination to act when the odds were favorable and the costs low—unless misjudged. In the nail-biting crises of 1955 and 1958 over Quemoy and Matsu—small islands near China's coast held by Taiwan's Nationalist government—the administration threatened a nuclear response if Mao's government attacked, while Dulles equated Mao's "aggressive fanaticism" with that of Hitler. Ike gained apparent victory for brinkmanship, but also "thoroughly discredited it in the eyes of the American public and allies overseas by revealing how little it would take to push the administration into a war with China," by showing the administration's "bland self-confidence that it could use nuclear weapons without setting off an all-out nuclear war," and by doing so in a crisis over real estate of purely symbolic value (although Dulles later boasted that "his most brilliant" achievement had been "to save Quemoy and Matsu").

Moreover, the outcome seemed to rest on one man whose judgment, however assessed, would have to falter on occasion. The Formosa crises showed the administration's penchant for recklessness in small matters as against restraint in larger ones. Only when the 1955 crisis threatened to explode did Ike show caution. After the Soviet foreign minister said that nuclear war would not threaten "world civilization" but only "that rotten social system with its imperialist basis soaked in blood," Eisenhower publicly reminisced about his 1945 friendship with Marshal (now Defense Minister) Zhukov, who had given him an "enormous bear hug" on his birthday. "It is necessary," comments [the historian] Paul Carter, "to think and feel one's way back into the mood of the fifties to realize how remarkable a statement this was." . . .

. . . A complex crisis in the Mideast developed when the administration misjudged Egyptian nationalism and Anglo-French foolishness: Egypt's Nasser seized the Suez Canal from Britain, Egyptian-Israeli tensions swelled, and Britain, France, and Israel moved to invade Egypt, without informing Eisenhower. Just as that crisis worsened in October, Hungarians rebelled against Soviet rule, and just as they seemed about to prevail, the Red Army crushed the revolt. Given GOP talk of liberating enslaved peoples and American propaganda urging "captive nations" to throw off their shackles, Ike's refusal to aid the rebels in Hungary was embarrassing. In the Middle East, his outrage forced France, Britain, and Israel to cease their invasion of Egypt and earned the gratitude of many smaller nations, but NATO and American Mideast interests seemed imperiled.

Relief at the avoidance of war helped Eisenhower gain an election landslide in November, but avoidance seemed to hinge perilously on one man, a perception already underscored by Ike's heart attack in 1955. In the Suez crisis Eisenhower showed "a kind of good sense we can now wish had been shown by more recent presidents who were considered more worldly-wise than Ike"—or had been shown at the time by Adlai Stevenson, who favored Israel and the imperial powers in Egypt rather than the UN resolution ordering a cease-fire. Still, militarization was contained and war avoided by a balance of forces—between the "free world" and its enemies, between Eisenhower and his critics, between the administration's own conflict tendencies—that was indeed uneasy. . . .

Eisenhower also maintained, as public reactions confirmed, that the United States now valued diplomacy with the enemy, though diplomacy rarely yielded concrete results. A 1955 treaty made Austria a permanent neutral and required withdrawal of occupying Soviet and Western forces, a significant precedent not followed for solving the weightier problem of divided Germany. The United States did not even sign the 1954 Geneva Accords on Indochina. Eisenhower offered a much-touted "Atoms for Peace" program and later an imaginative "Open Skies" proposal—foreshadowing the spirit of later mutual surveillance—whereby the superpowers would give each other "a complete blueprint of our military establishments" and allow each to photograph the other from the air. Every such proposal led to a nasty round of public posturing, Soviet and American leaders blaming each other for the arms race. Even more ballyhoo, but no agreements, accompanied the

1955 Geneva "Big Four" meeting of Ike and the Soviet, French, and British leaders. Eisenhower, and sometimes his counterparts elsewhere, were duly criticized for performing empty rituals that masked growing perils.

There was something to be said for ritual, however. Reminiscent of FDR's summit diplomacy, Eisenhower's version, undertaken in the face of shrill prophecies of "appeasement," established expectations and processes for superpower consultation that no later President could ignore. The lavish media attention given the Geneva summit reflected the substantive shallowness of the event, but also the hopes it aroused. As Eisenhower aide Emmet John Hughes said, Geneva "was widely understood to signalize, without articulating, the acceptance by the major powers of the common necessity to shun recourse to nuclear war." A similar signal arose from lofty and now-forgotten aspirations, earnestly supported by Eisenhower among others, that the United Nations become an effective instrument of world peace and prosperity.

Nonetheless, beneath the surface of international crisis and consultation ran currents that undermined Eisenhower's hopes to contain militarization. In the sprawling national security apparatus, pressure kept mounting to develop new weapons and to subvert arms control. Through the budget process, Ike exercised general control over defense policy but not over its qualitative shift toward new, expensive weapons. By bringing scientists into the White House, he gained access to experts skeptical about new programs, but also subjected himself to more direct pressure from scientists championing an aggressive course. The administration, complained Treasury Secretary Humphrey in 1957, had been "led astray by scientists and by vested interests." By denunciations of nuclear overkill or sheer explosions of temper, Eisenhower could interrupt the momentum. He could not or would not stop it. Nuclear warheads swelled in numbers and power, their megatonnage (destructive power) soaring from 150 in 1953 to 19,000 in 1960, the historic peak. By mid-decade the United States was plunging into the next stage of the arms race, intercontinental rockets for delivering nuclear weapons. A nuclear arms race whose logic had "no connection to experience or reality" was taking over. Eisenhower and the American people insisted on "clear American superiority. How they would use that lead—except to insure deterrence, which could be assured with one hundred bombs anyway—they did not know."

Historians [such as H. W. Brands] have faulted "the inadequacy of [Eisenhower's] leadership, combined with the intractable problems he faced" and his administration's "overblown rhetoric," for creating "an atmosphere in which consideration of defense issues became nearly impossible." Beyond that was a dilemma that Eisenhower barely grasped. The New Look involved a resort to technology to contain militarization—new weapons were to cut costs by minimizing force levels and averting limited wars. Drawing on an American tradition of seeking technological solutions to problems created in part by technology, it aggravated the very militarization that Ike hoped to arrest. Militarization was a qualitative phenomenon, not just a quantitative one measurable by the size of budgets or armies. The New Look accelerated it at its most technically exquisite, and exquisitely dangerous, nuclear core. Any other President might have done worse in that regard, but the higher standard of success Eisenhower set for himself makes the judgment on him more severe—as he soon felt.

Since his successors rarely did better in these matters, however, he alone was obviously not the problem. Beyond him lay a political culture hardly his to control. Humphrey's private complaint about "scientists" and "vested interests" suggested one facet of the problem. Ike could claim greater wisdom than generals and admirals, but for him to complain publicly about the pressures of scientists and other experts was virtually impossible—it would have smacked of the anti-intellectualism and cramped vision already imputed to Eisenhower and his associates too often for their political comfort. To challenge Gen. Maxwell Taylor was one thing; to dispute Edward Teller was another at a time when so much wisdom and objectivity were attributed to scientists.

One controversy over nuclear weapons did give Ike a chance to challenge the scientists' authority. A test in the Pacific of an American hydrogen bomb in 1954 stirred alarm about its sheer explosive power, but even more about the fallout that contaminated Americans, area natives, and nearby Japanese fishermen (their fate ominously resonant with August 1945). Eisenhower publicly doubted scientists' infallibility, announcing that "this time something must have happened that we have never experienced before, and must have surprised and astonished the scientists." Privately, he said that after the current American tests he would be "willing to have a moratorium on all further experimentation" with nuclear weapons.

Instead he vacillated, then drifted with the tide of experts seeking more tests, more bombs, and more vehicles to carry them. His New Look strategy was one reason, but also his desire for elite control, which public debate now threatened to erode. Dissident scientists and grass-roots activists formed new organizations. Books— Nevil Shute's *On the Beach* (1957), Walter Miller's *A Canticle for Leibowitz* (1959), Mordecai Roshwald's *Level 7* (1959)—widened debate. The Soviets grandstanded with new proposals to end the arms race. Neutrals like India, hardly wishing to bathe in the fallout of Soviet and American tests, enlivened a global debate. Charged cultural symbols were at play—Strontium-90 was entering the food chain, poisoning the milk mothers fed babies.

Eisenhower was not immune to the anxieties expressed in this widening debate. Had a strong challenge to nuclear policy emerged within his policy apparatus, he might have acted forcefully: in that arena, similar to the one he knew as a commander, he could be confident and courageous. But insiders critical of the arms race were few—Eisenhower as much as anyone, and he discouraged the criticism he also sought by his choice of scientific advisors and by his willingness to see [the Manhattan Project physicist and H-bomb opponent J. Robert] Oppenheimer forced out. A lifetime's habits made him distrust the unpredictable anxieties of outsiders. Repeatedly he considered blunt efforts to inform Americans of the nuclear danger. Repeatedly he backed away, sensing that public alarm was as likely to undermine efforts at disarmament as to strengthen them. Already in 1953, when the scientist Vannevar Bush had taken up "the case for scaring the people into a big tax program to build bomb defenses," Ike had seen "the dangers in telling too much of the truth." His distrust of public candor was not unfounded, but his chosen course served him no better. . . .

Earth's first artificial satellite went into orbit on October 4, 1957, on a Soviet rocket. Weighing less than two hundred pounds, it had no practical utility, although larger Soviet satellites and canine cosmonauts soon followed, but its symbolic import seemed incalculable, as Soviet premier Nikita Khrushchev appreciated, so eager was he to change the perception of Soviet backwardness.

If Sputnik was bait in a propaganda war, leading Americans swallowed it whole, naively or for calculated purposes. A cascade of dire warnings, expressions of humiliation, and calls for action flowed. Sen. Henry Jackson called for a "national week of shame and danger." Congressman Daniel Flood, rejecting fiscal limits on national action, cried, "I would rather have red ink in the books than red blood on the streets of America." Senate Majority Leader Lyndon Johnson proclaimed that "control of space means control of the world," with its possessor able to impose "tyranny" or "freedom." Foreseeing the miraculous developments Americans often have expected of technological change, Johnson argued that the winners in space would be "masters of infinity" able to "control the earth's water, to cause drought and flood, to change the tides and raise the levels of the sea, to divert the gulf stream and change the climates to frigid." . . .

Hard issues of power and survival were ostensibly at stake. If Soviet rockets were powerful enough to launch satellites, it was reasoned, they could strike the United States: massive retaliation seemed hollow, Khrushchev's boasts about his rockets irrefutable, Eisenhower's defense policy bankrupt. Given that dire situation, some members of the Eisenhower-appointed Gaither committee saw as the only recourse an attack on the Soviet Union before its lead in rocketry became insurmountable. Less trigger-happy Cold Warriors rejected that option, only to see a different danger. The Soviets, John Kennedy warned, now had a "shield" of bombs and rockets "behind which they will slowly, but surely, advance—through Sputnik diplomacy, limited brush-fire wars, indirect nonovert aggression, intimidation and subversion, internal revolution, increased prestige or influence, and the vicious blackmail of our allies. The periphery of the Free World will slowly be nibbled away. The balance of power will gradually shift against us." The United Sates, argued politicians like Kennedy, could only return to the principles of NSC-68, building up both strategic forces and conventional ones capable of "flexible response."

Few doubted that the stakes in space involved prestige as well as raw power. Just as wavering Third World peoples presumably watched America's sorry record in race relations, they scanned the skies for signs of America's triumph or failure, for evidence that it could live up to is promise to be more creative and productive than its totalitarian competitor. That promise was also in doubt among Americans. "Gaps" between Americans and Soviets in education and science, in discipline and imagination, seemed more alarming than the missile gap itself because they threatened the possibility that the Soviets' military lead could not be overcome, and even that Americans did not deserve to overcome it.

That fear seemed borne out in December 1957, when the American answer to Sputnik was to take to the skies from Cape Canaveral in Florida. As television sets across the land tuned in and millions of children crowded school auditoriums to watch, a navy rocket with a tiny satellite lifted a few feet from its pad, then sank back and exploded, prompting jokes about "Stayputnik," "Flopnik," and "Kaputnik" that vented national humiliation. Meanwhile, Eisenhower was briefly reduced by a stroke to uttering literal gibberish.

In a few weeks, the balance between contending forces—Soviets and Americans, Republicans and Democrats, Eisenhower and the groaning engines of militarization—seemed destroyed. In truth, it long had been precarious, so dependent on Ike's personal authority, or else one Soviet ball in space could not have upended it, exposing the fragility of Eisenhower's compromises and of Americans' sense of superiority. He rightly pleaded that American military and scientific superiority remained intact. His pleas fell on deaf ears—because he would not reveal his evidence for them, but even more because most Americans did not want to believe. . . .

Old worries that the United States was becoming an empty, hedonistic nation also surfaced again, yielding calls to recapture the frontier spirit and jeremiads against complacency and materialism that Puritan divines might have admired. Once emblems of its superiority, the nation's cars and television sets now seemed tokens of its rot. "If America ever crashes, it will be in a two-tone convertible," the venerable financier-politician Bernard Baruch predicted; the United States had to worry less about the "height of the tail fin in the new car and be more prepared to shed blood, sweat, and tears if this country and the free world are to survive," argued one senator. Although the space program was later sold as a fountainhead of technological abundance, unease about that abundance deepened the Sputnik panic.

Like most panics, this one was not a reaction to a single event but a state of mind built over time. That was evident in an array of proposed crash programs for fallout shelters, new weapons, and new strategies. Scientists aggravated and exploited the panic, as when one group approached Eisenhower with a plan to reach the moon by using "elegant little [nuclear] bombs to drive an elegant little spaceship around the solar system," as one scientist later put it. Reworking fears of a closed society and world-system that had haunted Americans for decades, scientists promoting new ventures in space thought it "essential to the growth of any new and high civilization that small groups of people can escape from their neighbors and from their governments, to go and live as they please in the wilderness." Panic also sanctioned lavish military schemes, as [the journalist] I. F. Stone discovered in the congressional testimony of an air force general who proposed that warheads "could be catapulted from shafts sunk deep into the moon's surface" and argued that if a lunar balance of terror then developed between the superpowers, stations could be built "on planets far more distant, from which control over the moon might then be exercised." Such schemes hardly enjoyed unanimous military support, but Stone could be excused for concluding: "Thus, as the Pentagon maps it, peace by mutual terror would spread outward toward the far stars." The Sputnik panic seemed to have no boundaries.

Eisenhower tried mightily to reestablish them. The psychology of the panic should not have shocked him, insofar as his strategy of massive retaliation already had rested on the psychological mysteries of deterrence and the symbolic import of new technology. Nonetheless, he was baffled by the Sputnik scare, partly because of his attachment to elite control and his reluctance to admit its erosion. His inability to articulate a visionary alternative to Cold War and militarization compounded his problems. For all its banality and hysteria, reactions to Sputnik did reveal a broad yearning for something more daring than he could provide. For good reasons, he would not embrace a race to the moon, agreeing with his first National Aeronautics and Space Administration director that if the nation's prestige rested on "'When do we get a man on the moon?'" then "all sense of perspective has gone out the window." But Ike offered no substitute. . . . Four years later, Ike was still uncomprehending, contemptuous of JFK's decision to stake national prestige on a race to the moon.

Uncomprehending he may have been, uncertain he was not. His effort to dampen hysteria and restrain militarization dominated the rest of his presidency. His primary asset was the enormous authority in military matters he still commanded. A general abandoned by most of his lieutenants (though not by Dulles and the CIA), he still gained a tactical victory in a losing campaign against the forces of militarization. "It was one of his finest hours," writes [the Eisenhower biographer] Stephen Ambrose. "The demands for shelters, for more bombers, for more bombs, for more research and development of missiles and satellites, [were] nearly irresistible," but Eisenhower rejected them. "He thereby saved his country untold billions of dollars and no one knows how many war scares."

A cold calculation of strategic realities guided him. Khrushchev might threaten the United States with extinction, but Ike knew it was a bluff. Secret flights by American U-2 aircraft—the evidence Ike would not make public, lest it infuriate the Soviets or terminate the reconnaissance—revealed that the Soviets were deploying few long-range rockets and could not match America's formidable heavy bombers. Knowing that, Eisenhower decided to leapfrog large-scale production of costly and combustible first-generation rockets in favor of advanced solid-fuel rockets (land-based Minuteman and sub-based Polaris missiles). Tied to that decision was a broader acceptance shared by Dulles of rough strategic parity with the Soviets, a heresy that helped prompt the strident charges of appeasement. Hardly neglecting America's military might, he was keen to maintain its qualitative lead, but numbers alone, nuclear "overkill" as it was now called, counted for little with him as he questioned, "How many times do we have to destroy Russia?" The armed forces were getting "into an incredible position—of having enough to destroy every conceivable target all over the world, plus a three-fold reserve," he complained. Even if the United States escaped direct attack and won a nuclear war, "there just might be nothing left of the Northern Hemisphere" because of fallout (atmospheric tests alone, he worried, might produce that result). . . .

His public utterances had the same substance. He upheld distinctions fast disappearing amid the panic: "There is much more to science than its function in strengthening our defense, and much more to our defense than the part played by science." Science's "peaceful contributions" and the nation's "spiritual powers" were "the most important stones in any defense structure." "We face," Ike wrote one concerned group, "not a temporary emergency . . . but a long-term responsibility," and he deplored hasty actions done "under the impetus of sudden fear." Elitist condescension could also flare up in public. At the start of the Sputnik panic, Ike spoke sneeringly to a hostile press of the Soviets' "one small ball in the air." During the 1958 election campaign, in "the most harsh and graceless partisan speeches of his political life," as [Ike's former speechwriter] Emmet John Hughes termed them, Eisenhower insisted that there would be "no appeasing Communist aggression," that "the so-called missile gap is being rapidly filled" (unwittingly suggesting it was real), and that "political radicals" and "self-styled liberals" had an "irresistible impulse . . . to squander money—your money." . . .

Sometimes grudgingly, Eisenhower did agree to changes: a new National Aeronautics and Space Administration (NASA); a presidential science advisor (James Killian and then George Kistiakowsky, who helped offset science hawks like Teller); modest increases in weapons and space programs; reorganization of the Department of Defense. But, as he commented on one supplemental budget he accepted, two-thirds of it went "more to stabilize public opinion than to meet any real need." As before Sputnik, he supported space programs meeting scientific curiosity and military needs—the reconnaissance capacities of satellites were especially alluring—but scorned the prestige-driven race in space.

Despite his effort to restrain militarization—and because of the exceptions he allowed in order to placate public opinion and meet his own test of vigilant defense—his success was only rearguard and temporary. By one standard it was considerable: defense budgets rose only modestly in Ike's last years. Pressure kept building for more money, programs, and forceful action, however, its power emerging more sharply under his successors.

Defense-related spending on science and technology measured those forces. Such spending remained hard to calculate because much of it was buried in non-defense budgets, went to technologies with both civilian and military uses, or had little military payoff. Moreover, the share of federal research and development spending devoted to defense was declining (the National Institutes of Health budget increased tenfold over the decade). But since total R&D budgets increased dramatically (to 15.6 percent of the budget by 1965), defense-related spending still swelled: the Defense Department's R&D budget nearly doubled between 1958 and 1961, while NASA's multiplied tenfold.

The character of this spending was as important as its size. Although championed by many scientists, basic research gained a tiny portion of the federal budget. The money flowed instead to vast engineering programs like NASA's effort to get Americans into space and then to the moon. These were public works projects on an imperial scale. . . .

As his policy on nuclear weapons showed, Ike had difficulty grappling with these forces. One of his first reactions to Sputnik had been to renew his interest in suspension of nuclear tests and in disarmament generally. His motives were a familiar mix: to lock in America's advantage in nuclear weapons, cut defense costs, counter the panicky mood, and score propaganda points to offset the Soviets' success in space. Familiar forces stalled his effort. Scientists like Teller nominally subscribed to disarmament but offered a host of objections to any moratorium on testing: the Soviets would cheat, steal "our secrets," and "surpass us"; progress would stop on "clean" (radiation-free) nuclear weapons that would benefit humankind; atomic scientists themselves "would lose tone, impetus, and personnel" during a moratorium. Then, just when new technology made seismic monitoring of a moratorium easier, science hawks countered with new nightmares: the Russians would resort to "decoupling"—conducting nuclear tests within mammoth underground caves in order to reduce their seismic shock—or even to testing bombs on the back side of the moon.

Some progress in Soviet-American negotiations was made, but it was bedeviled by many obstacles. Britain and France, eager to develop their own nuclear weapons (and, in the French case, to aid Israel's development as well), threw up roadblocks. Leaders vacillated: Eisenhower worried that a unilateral suspension of American tests would prompt Democrats to say, "This is our Munich"; Khrushchev worried that on-site inspections would expose Soviet weakness and bluster. . . .

. . . Strategic doctrine mirrored and exacerbated the pressures involved, as theorists, officers, and policymakers scrambled to impart rationality and equilibrium to a system spinning out of control. From one vantage point, stability seemed foreseeable. Prevailing American doctrine assumed a balance of terror in which each superpower deterred the other's initiation of nuclear war with its threat of a devastating response. Refined as "mutual assured destruction" (MAD), this doctrine implied that once superpowers gained rough parity, they would have powerful incentives to stabilize the competition—money would be saved, worried constituencies reassured, and the dangers of surprise minimized. Superiority might even be dangerous if it led the weaker power, fearful it could never survive a first strike, to launch such a strike itself.

Despite that finely spun argument, stability was unattainable: external pressures disrupted it, logical inconsistencies arose within it, and logic never fully governed strategy anyway. Given the Soviet rocket capability supposedly revealed by Sputnik, American strategists argued for a "second-strike" force able to survive an enemy first strike and still respond devastatingly. Building such a force, however, required missiles on submarines and in hardened silos, cost billions, drove the Soviets to reply in kind, and further ratcheted up the arms race. Costs went still higher as strategy shifted from "city-busting" to destroying enemy military forces. It seemed more humane and effective to target those forces, but since they were far more numerous, scattered, and protected than cities, "counterforce" strategy required far more missiles with far more sophisticated guidance systems. . . .

Still, the balance of terror held, and perhaps underwrote what [the historian] John Gaddis has called the "long peace" of the Cold War. The symbolic value of nuclear weapons certainly implied a kind of functional restraint: they were there for show, not for use, it often seemed. Did peace endure because of the balance of terror or despite it? The answer may be both: the terror that stayed the nuclear powers from plunging into the abyss also drove them to its edge. It also encouraged them to tolerate, promote, or enter non-nuclear wars that scared many other nations; this was a "long peace" only by the essential but singular standard of avoiding nuclear war. And what restrained the superpowers was less some *balance* of terror than mutual terror at the prospect of nuclear war, regardless of whether one side had an edge in it. They were, that is, deterred as much by their own weapons as by the enemy's, not because Americans were restrained while Soviets were reckless, or because American superiority forced a truculent enemy to back away from war. A psychological more than a military construct, the balance of terror rested less on forces than on attitudes, ones shared by superpower elites who proclaimed hatred of each other.

And it barely did hold, never more precarious than in the late 1950s and early 1960s. No episode demonstrated its fragility more than the Berlin crisis of the winter of 1958–1959. Berlin itself still stood oddly close to 1945: even in West Berlin the rubble of wartime bombing remained evident; no border guards stopped traffic between the east and west sectors; and both sectors still seemed "the pets of the occupation powers." But the dazzle of the West's Kurfurstendamm [West Berlin's commercial shopping area] mocked the drabness of Communist East Berlin, however prosperous it was by East European standards. Khrushchev, for various possible reasons—frustration and embarrassment over the drain of population and talent out of East Berlin into the West, or fear that West Germany might soon gain control of NATO nuclear weapons—precipitated the crisis, issuing a stream of menacing metaphors: "West Berlin has become a sort of malignant tumor" and "we have decided to do some surgery"; Berlin was "a bone in my throat" and "the testicles of the West. Every time I give them a yank, they holler." Many did holler when he demanded an agreement to end the Allied occupation of Berlin, make West Berlin a demilitarized free city, and establish East Berlin as East Germany's capital—and when he hinted at another Berlin blockade if he did not get his way.

Eisenhower's response was measured in the face of formidable pressures. Most NATO allies supported his cautious response, but not so many Americans. A dying Dulles spoke bitterly of spending billions on defense only to have "appeasement and partial surrender" threaten "to be our attitude." The armed forces pressed Ike to plan a military effort to break any blockade. Congressional leaders renewed their calls to increase the defense budget. Journalists asked about using NATO forces or nuclear weapons in the event of blockade. In all cases, Eisenhower rejected the pressures outright or sharply scaled back the plans urged on him. Keen to ease "pressures at home for precipitous action," he responded to questions about liberating Berlin with nuclear weapons in his typically flat style: "Well, I don't know how you could free anything with nuclear weapons." If Congress forced fifty thousand more troops on him, "Where will I put them?" he snidely asked reporters. "Well, just some place where it's nice to keep them out of the way, because I don't know what else to do with them." Moreover, he "spared no effort to assure Khrushchev a retreat with honor." Publicly he held fast to Allied rights and privately he weighed the nuclear option, but Khrushchev's ultimatum passed without incident in May. Essentially, Eisenhower talked his way out of the crisis—indeed, refused to treat it as crisis—but not before many Americans thought a nuclear war might begin. Stability, and peace itself, again seemed to pivot on him.

Berlin was only one tilt in the see-saw of events that sent hopes for detente alternately soaring and sinking. Nixon's visit to Moscow in July 1959 yielded the Kitchen Debate and a stream of vulgarities: Khrushchev likened one recent congressional action to "fresh horse shit, and nothing smells worse than that!"; Nixon retorted that "the Chairman is mistaken. There is something that smells worse than horse shit—and that is pig shit." A visit by Khrushchev to the United States produced the celebrated "spirit of Camp David," plus fury on the American right (William F. Buckley, Jr., condemned having a visitor who "profanes the nation"). Eisenhower embarked on globe-trotting diplomacy to round up allies for detente, but just as hopes for a breakthrough peaked in the spring of 1960, the Soviets shot down an American U-2 spy plane. When Khrushchev and Eisenhower bungled into a loud exchange of lies, accusations, and threats about the incident, the fragile process of summit diplomacy shattered. . . .

With his inauguration [in January 1961], John Kennedy said, the torch "passed to a new generation of Americans," those "tempered by war" and "disciplined by a hard and bitter peace." But the generational change JFK proclaimed was unclear.

His youth was striking, but he also drew for advice on elders like [former High Commissioner to West Germany] John McCloy and [former Secretary of State] Dean Acheson. Both generations had experienced World War II, but older men like Eisenhower had held high rank in it and were familiar with prewar suspicions of militarism, while men like Kennedy knew little of those suspicions, waged war from lesser positions, and had their outlook more decisively shaped by the war. Proud of their ability to break from their elders, they were nonetheless more the prisoners of World War II than Eisenhower's generation.

Moreover, the very notion of a torch passed also presumed continuity: the newcomers stood in Eisenhower's shadow and sought his blessing. When Eisenhower and Kennedy discussed Southeast Asia on January 19, complex political and generational relationships were at play. Kennedy insiders later recalled that Eisenhower's insistence on Laos as "the most important problem facing the United States" had done "a disservice to the incoming Administration," in Clark Clifford's summary. "You might have to go in there and fight it out," perhaps " 'unilaterally,' " Ike warned, according to Ted Sorensen and Arthur Schlesinger, Jr. But other accounts show that Eisenhower used such phrases to more ambiguous effect. Unilateral intervention, while not ruled out, "would be very bad for our relations" in Asia, he said, at best "a last desperate effort" in a region where communists had many advantages. . . .

Whatever the thrust of Eisenhower's advice on the 19th, his televised farewell address to the nation two days earlier had a different focus. Ike told Americans they were in a global conflict that "absorbs our very beings" and—again urging the long view—"promises to be of indefinite duration." As a result, the United States had been "compelled to create a permanent armaments industry of vast proportions," along with huge, costly armed forces. "The total influence" of this new system— "economic, political, even spiritual—is felt in every city, every State house, every office of the Federal government." He enjoined Americans to "guard against the acquisition of unwarranted influence, whether sought or unsought, by the military-industrial complex. The potential for the disastrous rise of misplaced power exists and will persist." Alarming also was "the prospect of domination of the nation's scholars by Federal employment, project allocations, and the power of money" and "the equal and opposite danger that public policy could itself become the captive of a scientific-technological elite." And as he had before, he linked these dangers to ecological perils, warning against "the impulse to live only for today, plundering, for our own ease and convenience, the precious resources of tomorrow."

What did he mean? In one way, his comments were shrewdly exculpatory. Militarization had been forced on America by dangerous enemies and technologies—it was not *his* nation's fault. What happened on his watch was "compelled," while avoidable dangers (the "*potential* for the disastrous *rise* of misplaced power") lay ahead. *He* had held the line; lesser men might not.

Yet his farewell address also held a darker view of militarization and his own role in it. By describing its influence as "economic, political, even spiritual," he suggested that whatever its origins, militarization was taking on a life of its own apart from the world scene, becoming woven into the fabric of American life. Moreover, "the conjunction of an immense military establishment and a large arms industry" had already occurred, while *he* was President, whatever abuses lay in the future. And regarding disarmament, acknowledged Eisenhower, "I confess that I lay down my official responsibilities in this field with a definite sense of disappointment." Just as striking were the omissions in the address—no summons to greater vigilance against the enemy, no recitation of trouble spots in the world, and little talk of the enemy's evil. The address was remarkably inward-looking, calling for Americans to be vigilant not against enemies but themselves. Just as the Cold War was reaching a new intensity, he directed attention away from it.

Eisenhower had left behind a memorable characterization of militarization. He added to it the next day at his final press conference, when asked how to counter "the danger that public policy could become the captive of a scientific technological elite." His first response seemed lame—he named no specific steps, only urging "an alert and informed citizenry"—yet it was appropriate given his large view of the problem, for "this misuse of influence and power could come about unwittingly . . . just by the nature of the thing," against which any single step would be puny. "When you see almost every one of your magazines, no matter what they are advertising, has a picture of the Titan missile or the Atlas [missile] or solid fuel or other things, there is becoming a great influence, almost an insidious penetration of our own minds that the only thing this country is engaged in is weaponry and missiles." . . .

Yet unwittingly Eisenhower had also aggravated that problem. By skillfully balancing conflicting needs and by keeping cold war from erupting into hot war, he had made the pursuit of national security congruent with dominant aspirations for peace and prosperity. His successors could turn his success against him: if power abroad and prosperity at home were compatible, how much more could be—had to be—achieved regarding both if greater efforts were made? The Kennedy administration was just as keen to balance "the defense effort against the other demands of the economy," wrote Schlesinger in 1965, but like many liberals who saw national resources as expansive, "it believed—correctly—that the balance could be achieved at a much higher level." Ike's message about limited resources and balancing goals ("balance" appeared seven times in one sentence of his farewell) was undercut by his own success in juggling peace, prosperity, and power.

Eisenhower's Reckless Nuclear Gamble over the Taiwan Strait

GORDON H. CHANG AND HE DI

Eisenhower and most American historians have given September 3, 1954, when Chinese Communist shore batteries opened fire on the Nationalist-held offshore island of Quemoy, as the beginning of a crisis that lasted for almost nine months. Most Western accounts have assumed that the Communist leadership ordered the shelling as part of a centrally directed military campaign that was at least a probe of the strength of the U.S. security commitment to Quemoy, if not the beginning of an

Reprinted by permission of the authors from Gordon H. Chang and He Di, "The Absence of War in the U.S.-China Confrontation Over Quemoy and Matsu in 1954–1955; Contingency, Luck, Deterrence?" *American Historical Review* 98 (December 1993), 1502, 1504–1505, 1507–1523.

actual effort to seize the island. Washington reacted to the shelling by dramatically increasing the U.S. military presence in the Taiwan Strait, strengthening Nationalist defenses, and issuing increasingly stern warnings to Beijing over the following months. To bolster its commitment to the Nationalists, the Eisenhower administration completed negotiation of a mutual defense treaty and received a blank check from Congress in early 1955, the so-called Formosa Resolution, for the use of American forces to defend Taiwan island and the nearby Pescadores.

The Chinese documentary record of high-level decision making at that time, however, does not indicate that Beijing considered September 3 shelling a precipitant event or even an unintentional initiation of a confrontation with the United States. Furthermore, the Chinese documentary record does not show that China's leaders considered the period from September 1954 to late April 1955 to be especially tense. In contrast to former U.S. officials who vividly recollected the main events, high-level Communist officials and advisers active during the 1950s and interviewed for this essay did not recall the September 3 bombardment or consider the time one of sharp conflict with America. . . .

Because Nationalist and Communist military forces had frequently clashed in the southeastern China coastal area during and after the Korean War in 1953 and 1954, Beijing did not consider the September 3 shelling, though dramatic, to be a radical departure from the pattern or level of hostilities in the area. Other observers at the time, including forces friendly to the United States, also evaluated the September 3 shelling of Quemoy, and the subsequent events in the offshore island area, in a different light than did Washington. The British government saw the activity as part of the latest round of feuding between the Nationalists and the Communists that had broken out during the summer of 1954, and it was not convinced that the Communists intended to attack Quemoy or were even principally interested in the island. The Nationalist military high command also expressed in private its belief that the Communists were only probing U.S. intentions with the shelling and were not about to launch an all-out assault on Quemoy. On September 10, the Chinese Nationalist Party organ, *Central Daily News,* dismissed the mainland's "Liberate Taiwan" campaign, which began in late July 1954, as simple propaganda and the Quemoy shelling as part of a political, rather than military, campaign.

Why, then, did the Eisenhower administration mistakenly assess the situation and consider the shelling the start of a deliberate military confrontation? In September 1954, U.S. antipathy toward the Chinese Communists and fear of their international ambitions ran high in the aftermath of the Korean War and the Vietnamese Communist defeat of the French in Indochina during the spring of 1954. The United States had steadily increased its attention to the South China Sea and China mainland offshore area for some time before September 3. U.S. ambassador to the Nationalists, Karl Rankin, and military intelligence had both warned of the possibility of trouble, including the danger of a Communist attack on Quemoy months earlier. And two U.S. men in uniform, members of the Military Assistance Advisory Group, had been killed in the Communist bombardment, which was more serious than previous sporadic shelling.

In addition, and perhaps more important, the Eisenhower administration became alarmed because the September 3 attack apparently demonstrated the failure of previous U.S. efforts at deterrence. In the spring and summer of 1954, the United States had twice sent ships of the Seventh Fleet to the Dachens (offshore islands along the Zhejiang coast) in a show of force to impress the Communists. As late as August 20, less than two weeks before the Quemoy shelling, Secretary of State John Foster Dulles sent a strong message of reassurance to the U.S. ambassador to Japan, who had communicated to Washington his own and the Japanese government's worries about possible Communist military activity in the offshore area. Dulles pointed out that because of his recent article in *Foreign Affairs,* which advanced the doctrine that later became known as "massive retaliation," he was certain that Beijing and Moscow fully appreciated the U.S. resolve to oppose Communist aggression. . . .

Thus the September 3 shelling most likely came as a rude shock for Washington, considering Dulles's expressed confidence in the power of U.S. deterrent force. Assistant Secretary of State for Far Eastern Affairs Walter Robertson explicitly interpreted events as a failure of deterrence in a September 4 memo to Dulles, arguing that the shelling had proved earlier U.S. efforts could "no longer be relied upon to deter Communist attacks" and that "more positive action by the United Sates [was] necessary if these [offshore] islands are not to be swallowed up by the Communists." Specifically, Robertson pressed for direct U.S. involvement in the event of a Communist assault on a major offshore island.

What was the actual purpose of the shelling that so disturbed U.S. officials? The memoir of General Ye Fei, the Communist commander of the Fujian forces responsible for the bombardment of Quemoy, reveals that orders Beijing sent on August 25 instructed Ye Fei to shell Quemoy, not as a preliminary to an assault on the island but as a specific and limited response to what was perceived as an increase in U.S. and Nationalist military provocations in the area and the rumored negotiation of a mutual defense treaty between Washington and Taibei [Taipei, capital city of the Republic of China (ROC)]. It was Ye Fei personally, not the central authorities, who recommended September 3 for the shelling for the simple reason, General Ye believed, that the Nationalists planned to supply the island by ship on that day. Communist shelling of Quemoy after September 3 in 1954 and 1955 was, in fact, infrequent and light. . . .

The order to Ye Fei reflected the thinking of Mao Zedong, China's commander-in-chief, about the Taiwan Strait. Convinced that the United States fully endorsed the Nationalist harassment of the mainland, Mao held Washington responsible for the mounting tensions in the area before September 1954 and firmly believed that Beijing was the defender, not the aggressor, in the Strait. Isolated in the international community, with relatively limited information, and with Leninist assumptions about the relationship of imperialism and semi-colonies, Mao could not know that there were serious strains in the U.S.-Nationalist relationship or that Washington, uneasy about the Nationalist activities, wanted to limit Chiang Kai-shek's attacks on mainland forces. He mistakenly assumed that Chiang was little more than a puppet of the United States. In addition, Mao questioned the sincerity of Washington's professed desire to reduce tensions with the Communist world after the 1954 Geneva Conference. As a result, he concluded that China had to respond to the perceived U.S.-Nationalist provocations that occurred in late 1953 and early 1954.

Mao was especially worried that a U.S.-Nationalist mutual defense treaty, reports of which began to circulate in China in mid-1954, would play a role similar to that of the cease-fire in Korea and the Geneva agreement on Vietnam, which had formalized the division of those two close neighbors of China. He had no idea that substantial differences existed between the Eisenhower administration and Chiang over the proposed treaty. Thus, on July 23, Mao sent a telegram to Zhou Enlai, who was en route from Geneva to Beijing, which admonished,

> in order to break up the collaboration between the United States and Chiang and to keep them from joining military and political forces, we must announce to our country and the world the slogan of the Liberation of Taiwan. It was improper of us not to raise the slogan in a timely manner after the cease-fire in Korea. If we were to continue dragging our heels now, we would be making a serious political mistake.

After Zhou's return to China, Mao convened a political bureau meeting at the leadership retreat at Beidaihe, where he presented, in his typically grand style, general guidelines for a propaganda campaign for the Liberation of Taiwan, the first such campaign against Taiwan in the history of the People's Republic.

In Mao's view, the conflict with the Nationalists in the Strait occurred on political, diplomatic, and propaganda fronts. Politically, acquisition of Taiwan was central to the unification of Chinese territory, and China could not accept any treaty arrangement between the United States and the Nationalists that formally separated Taiwan from the mainland or established an independent status for Taiwan. Diplomatically, the conflict was part of the struggle with the United States and a test of whether Washington's announced intention to relax tensions with the socialist camp was real. Militarily, the People's Liberation Army could respond to Taiwan's military harassment, gain control over the Dachen offshore islands, and use the opportunity to train its forces. In terms of domestic propaganda, the campaign for Taiwan would help rekindle the enthusiasm of the Chinese people for New China after the conclusion of the Korean and Vietnam conflicts. The country would have the slogan "We Must Liberate Taiwan" to rally around, providing both a goal for which to strive and a new external enemy to oppose. . . .

. . . Over the years, [Mao] had accumulated much experience in using controlled military action for discrete political purposes. He often used his armed forces to raise tensions and to dramatize his political position, such as in the offensives of the People's Liberation Army in northeast China during George C. Marshall's mission to China in 1945–1946 and during the armistice negotiations in Korea. The bombardment of Quemoy was exactly such a political-military demonstration, as the Chinese Nationalist observers on Taiwan had correctly surmised in the *Central Daily News*. Large-scale "armed propaganda" might be another description of the effort. The shelling was part of Mao's attempt to focus world attention on the Taiwan issue and what he believed was U.S. interference in Chinese internal affairs.

In contrast to the shelling of Quemoy for political purposes, Mao saw the campaign to take the Dachen Islands as essentially a military operation. To be clear, Mao saw the two theaters, Quemoy and the Dachens (which were under two separate military commands), in very different ways. He considered the shelling of Quemoy to be essentially political and low risk, since he believed he could easily control the action and avoid widescale conflict in the region, as there would be no direct military contact between Communist and U.S. personnel. The assault on the Dachens was another matter. Mao estimated that it carried a higher risk, since the possibility of direct clashes with U.S. armed forces was much greater. Thus Mao and the Chinese central command, unlike the Eisenhower administration, paid almost no attention to Quemoy but closely followed the Dachens campaign. The Central Committee's confidential instruction on the Liberate Taiwan campaign, circulated on July 24, stated, "At present, the direct target of our military struggle is Chiang Kai-shek [Jiang Jieshi] and his cohorts in Taiwan. The United States should not be treated as our direct target; we should confine the conflicts with the United States to the diplomatic arena only."

As for the relationship of the activities directed against the offshore islands to the military liberation of Taiwan, China's leaders were under no illusion that they could soon successfully assault Chiang's main island fortress. In a leadership directive on September 25, the CCP Central Committee observed that the capture of Taiwan was a "long-term and complex struggle" and was a strategic rather than immediate task. "We are not able to liberate Taiwan without a powerful navy and air force and need time to build them up." . . .

Eisenhower, assuming that the Communists did present a military challenge, described his own policy in the offshore area after the September 3 shelling as one of "keeping the enemy guessing" whether the United States would actually involve itself in a battle over Quemoy and Matsu. Dulles later aptly described this policy in private as deterrence through uncertainty. This strategy was adopted for several reasons, which included Washington's own questions about overall Communist objectives, Eisenhower's insistence on avoiding rigid commitments and maintaining flexibility of action, and administration concern about the lack of domestic and international support for further U.S. involvement in the offshore island area. At the heart of the matter, though, was the U.S. dilemma that the president, while supporting Chiang on Taiwan, did not want to be pinned down to a commitment of indefinite length to any of the offshore islands, over a hundred miles away from Taiwan and insignificant militarily in his eyes. . . .

If Washington, instead of avoiding explicit commitments to the defense of the offshore islands, had consistently demonstrated its determination to defend the islands, Mao would not have been likely to approve the assault on the Dachens. For example, in the middle of July 1954, the Central Military Commission ordered the Yijiangshan campaign to begin in September or October, and on August 10, the East Military Headquarters approved preparations for the actual attack on Yijiangshan. On August 20, the Headquarters asked the Central Military Commission to approve the assault for sometime between September 1 and 5. But, on August 21, when Mao learned of the high level of American attention to the area, he ordered that the campaign start only when there were no U.S. ships and aircraft present. In this instance, U.S. military deterrence was successful; its naval presence raised the strong possibility of direct American involvement and made the Communists pause. The attack was delayed for several months.

But U.S. deterrent efforts were not consistent. In early December, release of the terms of the Mutual Defense Treaty revealed that its provisions expressly covered only Taiwan and the Pescadores, not the Dachens and other offshore islands. Before the treaty's provisions were known and because of the vagueness of the Eisenhower administration's position, Mao had wondered whether Washington would directly involve itself in combat over the offshore islands; after the disclosure of the treaty terms, he and his military commanders concluded that the United States would not join in active defense, since the treaty omitted specific mention of the offshore islands. He therefore allowed the commanders to go ahead with their military campaign. Mao drew conclusions directly opposite to those Eisenhower and Dulles had hoped to encourage with the treaty.

Mao nevertheless proceeded cautiously. On November 30, just before the release of the terms of the Mutual Defense Treaty, Su Yu, the chief of staff of the People's Liberation Army, ordered the Yijiangshan attack to start around December 20. But, on December 11, because of a new U.S. naval maneuver in the Dachens, Mao countermanded Su Yu's order and again postponed the campaign for a month. Even on the eve of the assault on Yijiangshan, the central leaders in Beijing considered further delaying the operation, as they worried about U.S. intervention if the campaign did not end quickly. Beijing asked General Zhang Aiping if he could guarantee success in the operation, and if he could not, he was to wait longer. Zhang, however, argued that "the arrow was in the bow" and had to be shot. He maintained that the United States, according to his intelligence sources, would not become involved; that technical and morale considerations required action; that it would not be possible to keep the plan to take Yijiangshan secret much longer; and that he had the "right" to select the specific timing for a local campaign. His insistence moved Mao to compromise and, thus, he deferred to Peng Dehuai, head of the army, to make the final decision. Peng approved Zhang's request, and the assault took place the next day. On January 18, 10,000 PLA troops in the People's Republic's first large-scale coordinated air, sea, and land operation overwhelmed 1,086 Kuomingtang soldiers on Yijiangshan, inflicting heavy losses.

On February 8, Chiang, under mounting pressure from the United States, announced he would withdraw from the vulnerable Dachens, which he did with U.S. help on February 12. In a major operation, U.S. ships evacuated 14,000 civilians and 10,000 Nationalist troops with their equipment from the islands; and People's Liberation Army troops, without firing a single shot, then occupied them and the Nanji, the last of the Zhejiang offshore islands. While the quick and smooth military victories achieved by the People's Liberation Army greatly encouraged and emboldened some local commanders (they wanted to continue and expand the campaign to include bombing Taiwan itself), Mao stopped such thinking and criticized their proposals as adventurist. What is more, he came to conclude that while the Zhejiang coastal operations had been military successes, they had been political failures, since they attracted more U.S. attention than expected and raised the danger of direct military conflict with the United States. Mao decided it was time to try to reduce tensions in the region; he did not want military operations to press any further.

Mao was right about the adverse consequences of the Dachens campaign. The capture of the Zhejiang islands by the People's Liberation Army led Washington to conclude that the Communists, rather than ending their "Liberate Taiwan" campaign, were intent on escalating the crisis and perhaps even assaulting Taiwan itself. The subsequent dramatic U.S. response, in turn, increased tensions. Ironically, Mao believed that he had taken a cautious and restrained path, while U.S. leaders concluded that China's leaders were aggressive and bent on war. As Eisenhower wrote in his diary on March 26, "the Red Chinese appear to be completely reckless, arrogant, possibly overconfident, and completely indifferent as to human losses."

Rather than deterring Communist action, Eisenhower's policy of keeping the enemy guessing had sent mixed signals to Beijing, which contributed to the Communist decision to assault Yijiangshan. For his part, Mao had underestimated the effect Beijing's actions and propaganda would have on Washington. Although attentive to the U.S. reaction, he had little sense of the extreme measures Eisenhower officials were then discussing (such as widespread bombing of Chinese industrial and military facilities and the use of nuclear weapons) as a response to what Washington believed was China's preparation for large-scale hostilities in the Strait. By misinterpreting each other's intentions and signals, both sides, in taking what each considered to be prudent and justifiable actions, contributed to an increasingly dangerous situation.

In addition to displaying military support for the Nationalists and making other deterrent efforts, the United States also energetically explored diplomatic means of negotiating an end to the crisis. . . .

But factors on the Chinese Communist side, of which Eisenhower was apparently not aware or to which he was not entirely sensitive, also made efforts at a negotiated approach problematic, if not virtually impossible. Washington had taken what it considered were serious measures to meet what it perceived as China's military challenge in the Strait, such as making shows of force there, strengthening the Nationalist defenses on the offshore islands, and issuing repeated warnings to the Communists. Nevertheless, by February 1955, Mao concluded that Washington would not go to war over the offshore islands, and therefore the enhanced U.S. military posture was primarily for psychological purposes. . . .

Beijing also concluded that the non-coercive efforts pursued by Washington indicated it was not ready to engage again in direct, widespread military conflict with China. These efforts included having third parties such as Britain, Sweden, and India urge China and Taiwan to take their dispute to the UN; having Nationalists withdraw from the Dachens with U.S. help; and urging China through the UN and various other channels to accept a cease-fire proposal. Not only Mao interpreted Washington's behavior as contradictory and as sending mixed signals; U.S. ambassador Karl Rankin also made this point in a personal note to assistant secretary Walter Robertson after the Nationalists withdrew from the Dachens. "It is almost impossible," he wrote, "to overestimate the danger of confirming the Reds in a belief that, despite recent strong statements by the Secretary and others, we are for peace at any price. Withdrawal from the Dachens undoubtedly strengthened them in this belief." To correct this misimpression, Rankin advocated a military engagement with the Communists to convince "the enemy that we mean business." Rankin had accurately anticipated Mao's reaction—U.S. diplomatic efforts were undercutting the credibility of its coercive efforts.

Since the United States did not pose a genuine threat to China in Mao's eyes, Beijing could continue to keep pressure on to split the allied camp and weaken the main enemy, the United States, without risking widespread conflict. As a Central Committee comment on British-Chinese relations put it, maintaining the campaign against Taiwan would "enlarge the contradiction between England and the United States."

The effort to divide the enemy camp was part of Mao's version of "brinksmanship," what Dulles described as his own policy of averting war by going to the edge of war to intimidate one's adversary. Mao had a similar view of war and war avoidance, reflected in the CCP's instruction titled "U.S. Interference in the Question of Our Liberation of Taiwan," issued on February 21, while Dulles was on tour in Asia. "Regarding Washington's call for a 'cease-fire' and its threat to start a war," the instruction pointed out, "if we show any fear, the enemy will consider us weak and easy to bully. In other words, if we give them an inch, they will take a mile and intensify their military expansion. Only by adopting an unyielding, resolute, and calm stance can we force the enemy to retreat." In its interpretation of the lessons of history, the Chinese Communist Party observed that the September 18th Incident, when Japan invaded Manchuria in 1931, and the 1938 Munich compromise showed that peace cannot be obtained through appeasement: "Therefore, we must adopt an intransigent stance against the United States." As part of that stance, Beijing rejected Washington's diplomatic efforts, advanced formal diplomatic proposals that it knew were unacceptable to the United States (although, at the same time, Zhou Enlai quietly suggested direct bilateral talks between the United States and China; his initiative will be discussed below), and persisted with a strident anti-U.S. campaign and a "Liberate Taiwan" campaign at home, which was one of Mao's main interests in the first place.

Thus Mao's own brinksmanship and China's inflexible declared position had little to do with "maintaining face," as Eisenhower once argued in an effort to explain Chiang's and "Oriental" behavior during the crisis. Instead, the perceived absence of a fully credible U.S. threat, Beijing's own tactical considerations, and concern for Chinese domestic politics all contributed to frustrating the diplomatic efforts of the United States. Eisenhower's dismissal of the diplomatic stalemate as being a result of Chinese preoccupation with "face" and of fanaticism was obviously too simple and avoided confronting the political complexity of the dispute between the Nationalists and Communists and the sophistication of the tactics each Chinese side employed.

After the People's Liberation Army ended its large-scale military operations off the Zhejiang coast with the taking of the Dachens, the situation in the Taiwan Strait should have stabilized. Dulles himself observed on March 9 that there was a "lull" in activity in the Strait, and some U.S. intelligence reports noted that the amount of belligerent Communist propaganda in late February and early March had fallen to its lowest point since the summer of 1954. The Eisenhower administration, however, again misjudged the situation and concluded that the Communists were continuing their preparation for aggression. Dulles saw the lull not as Beijing's effort to lessen tensions but as just the opposite. He concluded that the Communists were engaged in "a large-scale build up." It was this misassessment that led the United States to escalate tensions in mid-March, and the crisis lurched toward open hostilities. . . .

Dulles's alarm, however, appears to have been unfounded and was based on inaccurate intelligence reports that grossly overestimated the ability of the People's

Liberation Army to attack Quemoy, let alone Taiwan. According to Chinese documentary sources, the army had no air and sea force in the region except in Zhejiang, and it employed only two regiments of artillery troops in the shelling of Quemoy in September. These regiments even had to change their positions after the bombardment to create confusion and avoid a punishing Nationalist counterattack. Zhang Aiping and Ye Fei also point out that China's local military capability was so limited that commanders could only plan for one small field campaign at a time. . . .

. . . The administration began to think increasingly about preemptive military options to end the threat, including the use of nuclear weapons against Communist capabilities in the offshore area. The administration's alarm was reflected in dramatic White House discussions on March 10 and 11 during which the use of military force, including nuclear weapons, was extensively discussed and in the administration's repeated public warnings that it was prepared to use nuclear weapons against China. On March 16, Eisenhower himself frightened an American public by stating at a press conference that he saw no reason why nuclear weapons could not be used "as you use a bullet or anything else," in the event of war in the Taiwan Strait. . . .

The administration's belief that the situation required decisive steps led to the formulation of a secret Eisenhower-Dulles plan that included Chiang's withdrawal from Quemoy and Matsu, a U.S. blockage of five hundred miles of China's coastal waters opposite Taiwan, and the stationing of nuclear weapons on Taiwan so long as Beijing called for the "liberation" of the island. At the climax of the crisis, Eisenhower sent [Chairman of the Joint Chiefs of Staff Admiral Arthur] Radford and Robertson to present the proposal to Chiang in mid-April, but Chiang, not wanting to surrender any further territory and not fully trusting Washington, rejected it.

Neither Beijing nor Washington had wanted direct conflict, and Chiang's acceptance of the evacuation and blockade plan would have brought the situation precipitously close to inadvertent war. As a provocative "fait accompli," the blockade would have invited Communist retaliation, including clashes between U.S. and Chinese forces. Even Radford himself anticipated such a turn of events. The proposal "meant war," the U.S. ambassador to Taiwan remarked when he heard the details of the plan, just before it was presented to Chiang.

American specialists suggest that Chinese Premier Zhou Enlai delivered his famous statement at the Bandung Conference [of nonaligned nations in Indonesia] in late April 1955 about China's peaceful intentions as a direct response to Washington's coercive efforts and that it constitutes evidence of the effectiveness of Dulles's threat of "massive retaliation." It hardly seemed coincidental that Zhou spoke at virtually the same moment that Radford and Robertson, known to be hardliners against China, were in Taiwan talking with Chiang. Soon after Zhou offered his remarks, however, Dulles confidentially told associates that "diplomacy and not merely force" had played a large part in producing Zhou's statement. Dulles claimed that U.S. political work with Asian allies had led China to "follow a pacific rather than belligerent course." It appears that Dulles's surmise was right, at least partly. Zhou's speech was an impromptu response to discussion he had had with Asian delegates at Bandung, but it was neither specifically planned by the Beijing leadership before Bandung nor presented as a response to U.S. nuclear threats.

In early April 1955, before Zhou Enlai's departure for Bandung, Indonesia, the political bureau of the Chinese Communist Party met to discuss general policy toward the conference. Party leaders at this meeting decided that China's delegation was to seek common ground between China and other Asian countries and keep differences to a minimum. Zhou was to try to establish new relationships with China's neighbors [such as nonaligned India and Indonesia] based on the recently formulated five principles of peaceful coexistence. In order to achieve this goal, the Chinese delegation decided that they would not raise controversial issues, including the Taiwan question, at the conference. Zhou was given full power to handle the situation during the meeting, which was held from April 18 to 24.

Despite Zhou's desire to avoid discussing Taiwan, and although he barely mentioned the issue publicly at the conference, many Asian leaders privately asked Zhou about the situation in the Strait. Finally, the day before the meeting's conclusion, toward the end of a luncheon with a number of Asian delegation leaders at the residence of the Indonesian prime minister, Zhou was again asked about the tensions in the offshore area. Zhou responded that China distinguished the conflict between the mainland and Taiwan from that between China and the United States. Taiwan was an internal question and linked to the Chinese civil war, he stressed, but the tension between China and the United States was an international matter, which China was willing to discuss with Washington. Zhou's off-the-cuff conciliatory comments surprised many of those present, who were urged not to speak publicly about them to avoid creating misunderstandings. Zhou was also asked, however, if he would make a general public statement, and later in the afternoon of the same day, China's delegation issued a brief press release containing his views. The haphazard manner by which Zhou's comments were delivered indicate that the presentation of his proposal was unplanned. Zhou himself believed his statement reflected general policy that had already been expressed, that adhered to Mao's point of view, and that was not a departure from China's previous position.

Upon learning of Zhou's remarks, the Eisenhower administration responded positively to what it considered to be a significant step on China's part, and tensions quickly subsided in the offshore island area. Although the build-up of military capabilities by both the Nationalists and Communists continued, direct talks between Washington and Beijing soon began. . . .

. . . Zhou's conciliatory statement appeared to the Eisenhower administration by late April to be the last possible way off the "horns of the dilemma," as Dulles had put it. The Radford-Robertson mission to Chiang had failed, military tensions were high, European and Asian allies of the United States were deeply fearful of war, and Zhou's comments had won widespread support among Asian nations. The Eisenhower administration, under tremendous domestic and international pressure, finally had to respond positively.

With the material now available from the Chinese side, it is possible to advance a number of revised or new historical evaluations of the crisis. Beijing was partially successful in conducting a controlled military campaign to achieve political ends (bringing world attention to the Taiwan issue) and limited territorial objectives (the capture of Yijiangshan, the Dachens, and other Zhejiang offshore islands). The campaign also resulted in direct discussions between China and the United States, something in which Beijing had been interested for some time.

However, it could also be said, as Mao himself acknowledged, that the campaign set back China's interests in certain respects. Mao had been mistaken about

U.S.-Nationalist relations and did not anticipate that his campaign would help push ahead the conclusion of the Mutual Defense Treaty or the Formosa Resolution that gave the president unrestricted authority to deploy U.S. forces in the defense of Taiwan. The treaty became a major political link between Washington and Taibei and later was one of the last obstacles to the eventual rapprochement between China and the United States in the 1970s. (The Formosa Resolution also formed a historical precedent for the 1964 Gulf of Tonkin Resolution that handed over war-making powers to President Lyndon Johnson in Vietnam.) Moreover, the Strait campaign contradicted Mao's wish to reduce tensions in the Southeast Asia region and damaged China's prestige with some of its Asian neighbors.

Beijing also did not understand the serious effect its activity and statements would have in the United States; it did not realize how close Washington came to escalating the crisis to widespread military action. Local Chinese military commanders, and some top officials in Beijing, believed that, since the offshore islands and Taiwan were China's own internal matter, the political reaction of the United States should be ignored.

As for the Eisenhower administration, it, too, made mistakes during the crisis. It fundamentally misunderstood the political nature of China's "Liberate Taiwan" campaign and thus played into it. It was the U.S. escalation of the crisis that helped bring world attention to the Strait, as well as dangerously exacerbated tensions there, especially in April 1955. But, most important, the Eisenhower administration erred in its belief that its effort at deterring China from assaulting Quemoy and Matsu was effective. The Quemoy-Matsu crisis of 1954–1955 is not an example of successful deterrence, since there was not an immediate, specific threat to these two island groups. (While it could be said that the United States succeeded in a general effort at deterrence of Chinese military activity in the Strait, since the U.S. presence did make Beijing cautious in its plans toward Taiwan island, this is another matter.) In addition, the Eisenhower administration made important concessions to both the Nationalists (namely, the Mutual Defense Treaty) and the Communists (bilateral talks). Its nuclear threats against the mainland not only stiffened Communist resolve, they also helped convince Beijing to launch its own nuclear weapons program. And through it all, the status of Quemoy and Matsu remained contested, ready to draw the United States into other highly charged confrontations with the mainland, as eventually happened in 1958 and in 1962.

🌐 F U R T H E R   R E A D I N G

Robert Accinelli, *Crisis and Commitment* (1996) (Taiwan)
Charles C. Alexander, *Holding the Line* (1975)
Stephen E. Ambrose, *Eisenhower: The President* (1984)
Manuela Aquilar, *Cultural Diplomacy and Foreign Policy* (1996) (Germany)
Robert Axelrod, *The Evolution of Cooperation* (1984)
Howard Ball, *Justice Downwind: America's Atomic Testing Program in the 1950s* (1986)
Michael R. Beschloss, *Mayday: Eisenhower, Khrushchev, and the U-2 Affair* (1986)
Timothy J. Botti, *Ace in the Hole* (1996)
Robert Bowie and Richard H. Immerman, *Waging Peace* (1998)

H. W. Brands, "The Age of Vulnerability: Eisenhower and the National Insecurity State," *American Historical Review,* 94 (1989), 963–989

———, *Cold Warriors* (1988)

McGeorge Bundy, *Danger and Survival* (1988)

Craig Campbell, *Destroying the Village: Eisenhower and Thermonuclear War* (1998)

Gordon H. Chang, *Friends and Enemies* (1992) (China)

Thomas J. Christensen, *Useful Adversaries* (1996) (China)

Ian Clark, *Nuclear Diplomacy and the Special Relationship* (1994)

Blanche Weisen Cook, *The Declassified Eisenhower* (1981)

Frank Costigliola, "The Nuclear Family: Tropes of Gender and Pathology in the Western Alliance," *Diplomatic History,* 21 (1997), 163–184

Robert A. Divine, *Blowing on the Wind: The Nuclear Test Ban Debate* (1978)

———, *Eisenhower and the Cold War* (1981)

———, "John Foster Dulles: What You See Is What You Get," *Diplomatic History,* 15 (1991), 277–285

———, *The Sputnik Challenge* (1993)

Saki Dockrill, *Eisenhower's New Look National Security Policy* (1996)

Michael Evangelista, "Cooperation Theory and Disarmament Negotiations in the 1950s," *World Politics,* 42 (1990), 502–528

———, *Innovation and the Arms Race* (1988)

Lawrence Freedman, *The Evolution of Nuclear Strategy* (1981)

John Lewis Gaddis, *The Long Peace* (1987)

———, *Strategies of Containment* (1982)

Alexander L. George and Richard Smoke, *Deterrence in American Foreign Policy* (1974)

Alexander L. George et al., eds., *U.S.-Soviet Security Cooperation* (1988)

Fred I. Greenstein, *The Hidden-Hand Presidency* (1982)

Morton H. Halperin, *Nuclear Fallacy* (1987)

Margot Henriksen, *Dr. Strangelove's America: Society and Culture in the Atomic Age* (1997)

Greg Herken, *Counsels of War* (1985)

Richard G. Hewlett and Jack M. Holl, *Atoms for Peace and War* (1989)

David Holloway, *The Soviet Union and the Arms Race* (1983)

Townsend Hoopes, *The Devil and John Foster Dulles* (1973)

Samuel P. Huntington, *The Common Defense* (1961)

Richard H. Immerman, "Confessions of an Eisenhower Revisionist," *Diplomatic History,* 14 (1990), 319–342

———, *John Foster Dulles* (1998)

———, ed., *John Foster Dulles and the Diplomacy of the Cold War* (1990)

Robert Jervis, *The Meaning of the Nuclear Revolution* (1989)

Robert H. Johnson, *Improbable Dangers* (1994)

Fred Kaplan, *The Wizards of Armageddon* (1983)

Milton S. Katz, *Ban the Bomb: A History of SANE* (1986)

Douglas Kinnard, *President Eisenhower and Strategy Management* (1977)

Henry Kissinger, *Nuclear Weapons and Foreign Policy* (1957)

Stewart W. Leslie, *The Cold War and American Science* (1992)

Peter Lyon, *Eisenhower* (1974)

Walter A. McDougall, *The Heavens and the Earth* (1985)

Michael Mandlebaum, *The Nuclear Revolution* (1981)

Frederick W. Marks III, *Power and Peace* (1993)

George T. Mazuzan, "American Nuclear Policy," in John M. Carroll and George C. Herring, eds., *Modern American Diplomacy* (1986), pp. 147–163

Richard A. Melanson and David Mayer, eds., *Reevaluating Eisenhower* (1987)

Charles R. Morris, *Iron Destinies, Lost Opportunities* (1988)

John Newhouse, *War and Peace in the Nuclear Age* (1988)

Frank A. Ninkovich, *Modernity and Power* (1994)

Chester J. Pach, Jr., and Elmo Richardson, *The Presidency of Dwight D. Eisenhower* (1991)

Herbert S. Parmet, *Eisenhower and the Great Crusades* (1972)

Richard Pfau, *No Sacrifice Too Great: The Life of Lewis L. Strauss* (1984)

William B. Pickett, *Dwight David Eisenhower and American Power* (1995)

Joseph E. Pilate et al., *Atoms for Peace* (1986)

Ronald E. Powaski, *March to Armageddon* (1987)

Ronald W. Pruessen, *John Foster Dulles* (1982)

Stephen G. Rabe, "Eisenhower Revisionism: A Decade of Scholarship," *Diplomatic History,*
17 (1993), 97–115

Peter J. Roman, *Eisenhower and the Missile Gap* (1995)

David Alan Rosenberg, "The Origins of Overkill," *International Security,* 7 (1983), 3–71

———, "Reality and Responsibility: Power and Process in the Making of United States
Nuclear Strategy, 1945–68," *Journal of Strategic Studies,* 9 (1986), 35–52

Walt W. Rostow, *Open Skies* (1982)

Gerard Smith, *Disarming Diplomat* (1996)

Thomas F. Soapes, "A Cold Warrior Seeks Peace: Eisenhower's Strategy for Nuclear
Disarmament," *Diplomatic History,* 4 (1980), 55–71

"Symposium: The Soviet Threat to Western Europe: A Roundtable," *Diplomatic History,* 22
(1998), 399–449

Strobe Talbott, *The Master of the Game: Paul Nitze and the Nuclear Peace* (1988)

Marc Trachtenberg, *History and Strategy* (1991)

———, "A 'Wasting Asset': American Strategy and Shifting Nuclear Balance, 1949–1954,"
International Security (1988–1989), 5–49

Sheldon Ungar, *The Rise and Fall of Nuclearism* (1992)

Samuel F. Wells, "The Origins of Massive Retaliation," *Political Science Quarterly,* 96
(1981), 31–52

Andreas Wenger, *Living with Peril: Eisenhower, Kennedy, and Nuclear Weapons* (1997)

Samuel Williamson and Steven L. Rearden, eds., *The Origins of U.S. Nuclear Strategy* (1993)

Pascaline Winand, *Eisenhower, Kennedy and the United States of Europe* (1993)

Lawrence Wittner, *The Struggle Against the Bomb* (1998)

CHAPTER

10

Cuba and the Missile Crisis

In October 1962, American U-2 reconnaissance planes photographed missile sites installed by the Soviets on the Caribbean island of Cuba. The missiles could carry nuclear weapons, and they could reach the United States. After meeting with his advisers and deciding to announce U.S. policy in a television address, President John F. Kennedy demanded withdrawal of the missiles and imposed a blockade around Cuba. A chilling war scare gripped Moscow, Havana, and Washington—and terrified the world. This was the closest the United States and the Soviet Union had ever come to nuclear war. Exchanges of diplomatic letters, rallying of allies, exhausting meetings, military preparations, and operational accidents soon followed.

In the end, deeply frightened by the prospect of nuclear disaster, Premier Nikita Khrushchev and President Kennedy settled the crisis without consulting Cuban premier Fidel Castro. The United States promised not to invade Cuba (as it had done using Cuban exiles in April 1961, at the Bay of Pigs) and assented to the removal of its Jupiter missiles from Turkey. In return, the Soviet Union agreed to withdraw its missiles from Cuba. The U.S. no-invasion pledge in fact never took effect because Castro refused to permit U.S.-stipulated United Nations follow-up inspections. But the Soviets dismantled their missiles and sent them home, and the Jupiters in Turkey also came down.

Beneath the Cuban missile crisis—or the "Caribbean crisis," as Soviet leaders called it—lay years of Cuban-American antagonism. On taking power in 1959, Fidel Castro launched a revolution that challenged major U.S. interests on the island, including mob-run casinos, U.S. military missions, and investments worth a billion dollars. Castro decried U.S. hegemony and Cuban dependency, and he vowed a restructuring of economic and political life to reduce U.S. influence that had grown especially since the interventionist Platt Amendment at the start of the century. Washington became alarmed, too, because the Cuban Revolution gained popularity throughout the Western Hemisphere and because Castro declared as one of his missions the spread of revolution across Latin America. In 1960 economic relations deteriorated severely when the United States instituted trade sanctions. The Cubans increasingly turned for help to the Soviet Union, which became the island's economic and military partner. In January 1961 the United States broke diplomatic relations with Havana. In 1961–1962 came the Bay of Pigs expedition, covert operations designed to cripple the Cuban economy through sabotage, Central Intelligence Agency (CIA) assassination plots against Castro, diplomatic efforts to isolate Cuba, and military maneuvers and plans that seemed to portend a U.S.

invasion. Because these regional events occurred during a particularly tense time in the Cold War, the U.S.-Cuba contest held international consequences.

In recent years a greater portion of the documentary record on the missile crisis in the archives of the United States, Russia, and Cuba has opened for research, and, using newly released documents, crisis participants have gathered in meetings to reexamine the 1962 confrontation. Several sets of questions remain central to understanding this dangerous episode in world history, beginning with questions about the origins of the crisis. Why did this nuclear showdown occur in Cuba and not somewhere else? Which nation was most responsible for generating the missile crisis? To what extent are the sources of the missile crisis found in the U.S.-Cuba contest? Why did Cuba welcome the Soviet missiles? Was Castro reasonable or off base in his fear that the United States would invade his country? What did the Soviets hope to gain from their installation of nuclear-tipped missiles in Cuba? Did the missiles in Cuba change the strategic balance of power, giving the U.S.S.R. a stronger position?

The second set of questions studies the management of the crisis. How well did the decisionmaking processes in Washington, Moscow, and Havana work? How well did the three belligerents communicate with one another? Why did Kennedy initially shun private negotiations in favor of public confrontation? Why did he choose a naval blockade over an air strike and military invasion? Does Kennedy's handling of the emergency rank as an excellent example of rational crisis management? To what extent should scholars study the personalities of the participants to understand the outcome of the crisis? What role did miscalculations, human error, and operational accidents play in the crisis? Just how dangerous was the episode— how close to nuclear war did the world come?

The third set of issues centers on the settlement of the crisis. Why did Kennedy and Khrushchev compromise in the end? Why did they exclude Castro from their agreement? What reasons did Castro have for rejecting the settlement? Why did all three leaders fail to write a formal agreement? Why did Kennedy promise to dismantle the U.S. Jupiter missiles in Turkey yet insist that this agreement not become public? What if Khrushchev had refused to pull his missiles out of Cuba? What next? Finally: Did anybody win?

The last questions speak to the aftermath: Why did the crisis continue into late November as the three nations squabbled over Soviet bombers and inspections? What lessons did leaders draw from their experience in the Cuban missile crisis? To what extent did the outcome change the Cold War, the nuclear-arms race, or the U.S.-Cuba relationship? Why did the United States enter new crises with the Soviet Union over Cuba in 1970 and 1979?

🌐 D O C U M E N T S

Document 1 is drawn from a November 1975 report by the U.S. Senate Select Committee to Study Governmental Operations with Respect to Intelligence Activities. Chaired by Senator Frank Church of Idaho, this committee detailed CIA assassination plots against Fidel Castro. Document 2, dated March 14, 1962, constitutes the initial guidelines for Operation Mongoose, the CIA's conspiracy to overthrow the Castro government through "indigenous sources" and possibly U.S. military intervention. President Kennedy apparently approved this secret document, and his brother, Attorney General Robert F. Kennedy, became the primary overseer of the spoiling operation.

Document 3 is a speech by Cuban president Osvaldo Dorticos. In these remarks, delivered to the United Nations on October 18, 1962, just a few days before the crisis publicly erupted, Dorticos defended Cuba's military buildup as necessary to counter U.S. aggression.

Document 4 includes significant parts of the transcribed record of Kennedy's first two meetings with his high-level advisers on October 16, 1962, the day intelligence officials presented him with photographs showing Soviet missile sites under construction in Cuba. In Document 5, a record of another senior advisers' meeting on October 17 (from the notes of CIA head John A. McCone), Charles E. Bohlen, former ambassador to the Soviet Union and then ambassador to France, unsuccessfully argues the case for private diplomacy to defuse the crisis. Document 6 is Kennedy's October 22 television address to the nation and the world. The president insisted on removal of the missiles and announced the U.S. "quarantine" of Cuba. On October 26 Premier Khrushchev replied to a Kennedy letter of the preceding day that had reiterated the U.S. case against the missile bases. The Khrushchev letter, reprinted here as Document 7, denounces the blockade and claims that the Soviet weapons had been sent to defend Cuba against a U.S. invasion. The Soviet leader also offered a deal: He would remove the "armaments" from Cuba if the United States pledged not to invade Cuba.

On October 27 Khrushchev sent another letter to Kennedy, included here as Document 8. Adding to his earlier request for a no-invasion promise, Khrushchev asked for the removal of American Jupiter missiles from Turkey. President Kennedy again convened his advisers—now called the Executive Committee (ExComm)—to discuss this new request. A record of part of their meeting of October 27 is found in Document 9. Kennedy decided to pull the Jupiters out of Turkey; Robert Kennedy soon privately conveyed this concession to the Soviets, and the crisis dissipated. Document 10, from Russian archives, reports conversations between the high-ranking Soviet official Anastas I. Mikoyan and Fidel Castro in Havana on November 4 and 5. Standing out in these intense exchanges are Soviet claims of victory and Cuban protests against both superpowers for their ending the crisis without consulting the Cuban government.

1. CIA Assassination Plots Against Fidel Castro (1960–1965), 1975

Efforts against Castro did not begin with assassination attempts.

From March through August 1960, during the last year of the Eisenhower Administration, the CIA considered plans to undermine Castro's charismatic appeal by sabotaging his speeches. According to the 1967 Report of the CIA's Inspector General, an official in the Technical Services Division (TSD) recalled discussing a scheme to spray Castro's broadcasting studio with a chemical which produced effects similar to LSD, but the scheme was rejected because the chemical was unreliable. During this period, TSD impregnated a box of cigars with a chemical which produced temporary disorientation, hoping to induce Castro to smoke one of the cigars before delivering a speech. The Inspector General also reported a plan to destroy Castro's image as "The Beard" by dusting his shoes with thallium salts, a strong depilatory that would cause his beard to fall out. The depilatory was to be

This document can be found in U.S. Senate, Select Committee to Study Governmental Operations with Respect to Intelligence Activities, *Alleged Assassination Plots Involving Foreign Leaders: An Interim Report* (Washington, D.C.: Government Printing Office, November 1975), pp. 71–77, 79–80, 83–85, 148.

administered during a trip outside Cuba, when it was anticipated Castro would leave his shoes outside the door of his hotel room to be shined. TSD procured the chemical and tested it on animals, but apparently abandoned the scheme because Castro cancelled his trip. . . .

A notation in the records of the Operations Division, CIA's Office of Medical Services, indicates that on August 16, 1960, an official was given a box of Castro's favorite cigars with instructions to treat them with lethal poison. The cigars were contaminated with a botulinum toxin so potent that a person would die after putting one in his mouth. The official reported that the cigars were ready on October 7, 1960; TSD notes indicate that they were delivered to an unidentified person on February 13, 1961. The record does not disclose whether an attempt was made to pass the cigars to Castro.

In August 1960, the CIA took steps to enlist members of the criminal under-world with gambling syndicate contacts to aid in assassinating Castro. . . .

The earliest concrete evidence of the operation is a conversation between DDP [Deputy Director for Plans Richard] Bissell and Colonel Sheffield Edwards, Director of the Office of Security. Edwards recalled that Bissell asked him to locate someone who could assassinate Castro. Bissell confirmed that he requested Edwards to find someone to assassinate Castro and believed that Edwards raised the idea of contacting members of a gambling syndicate operating in Cuba.

Edwards assigned the mission to the Chief of the Operational Support Division of the Office of Security. The Support Chief recalled that Edwards had said that he and Bissell were looking for someone to "eliminate" or "assassinate" Castro.

Edwards and the Support Chief decided to rely on Robert A. Maheu to recruit someone "tough enough" to handle the job. Maheu was an ex-FBI agent who had entered into a career as a private investigator in 1954. A former FBI associate of Maheu's was employed in the CIA's Office of Security and had arranged for the CIA to use Maheu in several sensitive covert operations in which "he didn't want to have an Agency person or a government person get caught.". . .

Sometime in late August or early September 1960, the Support Chief approached Maheu about the proposed operation. As Maheu recalls the conversation, the Support Chief asked him to contact John Rosselli, an underworld figure with possible gambling contacts in Las Vegas, to determine if he would participate in a plan to "dispose" of Castro. The Support Chief testified, on the other hand, that it was Maheu who raised the idea of using Rosselli. . . .

According to Rosselli, he and Maheu met at the Brown Derby Restaurant in Beverly Hills in early September 1960. Rosselli testified that Maheu told him that "high government officials" needed his cooperation in getting rid of Castro, and that he asked him to help recruit Cubans to do the job. Maheu's recollection of that meeting was that "I informed him that I had been asked by my Government to solicit his cooperation in this particular venture." . . .

A meeting was arranged for Maheu and Rosselli with the Support Chief at the Plaza Hotel in New York. The Inspector General's Report placed the meeting on September 14, 1960. Rosselli testified that he could not recall the precise date of the meeting, but that it had occurred during Castro's visit to the United Nations, which the New York Times Index places from September 18 through September 28, 1960. . . .

It was arranged that Rosselli would go to Florida and recruit Cubans for the operation. Edwards informed Bissell that contact had been made with the gambling syndicate.

During the week of September 24, 1960 the Support Chief, Maheu, and Rosselli met in Miami to work out the details of the operation. Rosselli used the cover name "John Rawlston" and represented himself to the Cuban contacts as an agent of ". . . some business interests of Wall Street that had . . . nickel interests and properties around in Cuba, and I was getting financial assistance from them."

Maheu handled the details of setting up the operation and keeping the Support Chief informed of developments. After Rosselli and Maheu had been in Miami for a short time, and certainly prior to October 18, Rosselli introduced Maheu to two individuals on whom Rosselli intended to rely: "Sam Gold," who would serve as a "back-up man," or "key" man and "Joe," whom "Gold" said would serve as a courier to Cuba and make arrangements there. The Support Chief, who was using the name "Jim Olds," said he had met "Sam" and "Joe" once, and then only briefly.

The Support Chief testified that he learned the true identities of his associates one morning when Maheu called and asked him to examine the "Parade" supplement to the *Miami Times*. An article on the Attorney General's ten-most-wanted criminals list revealed that "Sam Gold" was Momo Salvatore Giancana, a Chicago-based gangster, and "Joe" was Santos Trafficante, the Cosa Nostra chieftain in Cuba. The Support Chief reported his discovery to Edwards, but did not know whether Edwards reported this fact to his superiors. The Support Chief testified that this incident occurred after "we were up to our ears in it," a month or so after Giancana had been brought into the operation, but prior to giving the poison pills to Rosselli.

Maheu recalled that it was Giancana's job to locate someone in Castro's entourage who could accomplish the assassination, and that he met almost daily with Giancana over a substantial period of time. Although Maheu described Giancana as playing a "key role," Rosselli claimed that none of the Cubans eventually used in the operation were acquired through Giancana's contacts. . . .

The Inspector General's Report described conversations among Bissell, Edwards, and the Chief of the Technical Services Division (TSD), concerning the most effective method of poisoning Castro. There is some evidence that Giancana or Rosselli originated the idea of depositing a poison pill in Castro's drink to give the "asset" a chance to escape. The Support Chief recalled Rosselli's request for something "nice and clean, without getting into any kind of out and out ambushing," preferably a poison that would disappear without a trace. The Inspector General's Report cited the Support Chief as stating that the Agency had first considered a "gangland-style killing" in which Castro would be gunned down. Giancana reportedly opposed the idea because it would be difficult to recruit someone for such a dangerous operation, and suggested instead the use of poison.

Edwards rejected the first batch of pills prepared by TSD because they would not dissolve in water. A second batch, containing botulinum toxin, "did the job expected of them" when tested on monkeys. The Support Chief received the pills from TSD, probably in February 1961, with assurances that they were lethal, and then gave them to Rosselli.

The record clearly establishes that the pills were given to a Cuban for delivery to the island some time prior to the Bay of Pigs invasion in mid-April 1961. There are discrepancies in the record, however, concerning whether one or two attempts were made during that period, and the precise date on which the passage[s] occurred. The Inspector General's Report states that in late February or March 1961, Rosselli reported to the Support Chief that the pills had been delivered to an official close to Castro who may have received kickbacks from the gambling interests. The Report states that the official returned the pills after a few weeks, perhaps because he had lost his position in the Cuban Government, and thus access to Castro, before he received the pills. The Report concludes that yet another attempt was made in April 1961, with the aid of a leading figure in the Cuban exile movement. . . .

In early April 1962, Harvey, who testified that he was acting on "explicit orders" from [Director of Operations Richard] Helms, requested Edwards to put him in touch with Rosselli. The Support Chief first introduced [Operation Mongoose task force chief William K.] Harvey to Rosselli in Miami, where Harvey told Rosselli to maintain his Cuban contacts, but not to deal with Maheu or Giancana, whom he had decided were "untrustworthy" and "surplus." The Support Chief recalled that initially Rosselli did not trust Harvey although they subsequently developed a close friendship.

Harvey, the Support Chief and Rosselli met for a second time in New York on April 8–9, 1962. A notation made during this time in the files of the Technical Services Division indicates that four poison pills were given to the Support Chief on April 18, 1962. The pills were passed to Harvey, who arrived in Miami on April 21, and found Rosselli already in touch with the same Cuban who had been involved in the pre–Bay of Pigs pill passage. He gave the pills to Rosselli, explaining that "these would work anywhere and at any time with anything." Rosselli testified that he told Harvey that the Cubans intended to use the pills to assassinate Che Guevara as well as Fidel and Raul Castro. According to Rosselli's testimony, Harvey approved of the targets, stating "everything is all right, what they want to do."

The Cuban requested arms and equipment as a *quid pro quo* for carrying out the assassination operation. With the help of the CIA's Miami station which ran covert operations against Cuba (JM/WAVE), Harvey procured explosives, detonators, rifles, handguns, radios, and boat radar costing about $5,000. . . .

Rosselli kept Harvey informed of the operation's progress. Sometime in May 1962, he reported that the pills and guns had arrived in Cuba. On June 21, he told Harvey that the Cuban had dispatched a three-man team to Cuba. The Inspector General's report described the team's mission as "vague" and conjectured that the team would kill Castro or recruit others to do the job, using the poison pills if the opportunity arose.

Harvey met Rosselli in Miami on September 7 and 11, 1962. The Cuban was reported to be preparing to send in another three-man team to penetrate Castro's bodyguard. Harvey was told that the pills, referred to as "the medicine," were still "safe" in Cuba.

Harvey testified that by this time he had grave doubts about whether the operation would ever take place, and told Rosselli that "there's not much likelihood that this is going anyplace, or that it should be continued." The second team never left for

Cuba, claiming that "conditions" in Cuba were not right. During early January 1963, Harvey paid Rosselli $2,700 to defray the Cuban's expenses. Harvey terminated the operation in mid-February 1963. At a meeting with Rosselli in Los Angeles, it was agreed that Rosselli would taper off his communications with the Cubans. Rosselli testified that he simply broke off contact with the Cubans. However, he never informed them that the offer of $150,000 for Castro's assassination had been withdrawn. . . .

As [for the question of authorization], both Helms and the high Kennedy Administration officials who testified agreed that no direct order was ever given for Castro's assassination and that no senior Administration officials, including McCone, were informed about the assassination activity. Helms testified, however, that he believed the assassination activity was permissible and that it was within the scope of authority given to the Agency. McCone and other Kennedy Administration officials disagreed, testifying that assassination was impermissible without a direct order and that Castro's assassination was not within the bounds of the MONGOOSE operation [the covert U.S. operation designed to undermine the Castro government].

As DDP, Helms was in charge of covert operations when the poison pills were given to Rosselli in Miami in April 1962. Helms had succeeded to this post following Bissell's retirement in February 1962. He testified that after the Bay of Pigs:

> Those of us who were still [in the agency] were enormously anxious to try and be successful at what we were being asked to do by what was then a relatively new Administration. We wanted to earn our spurs with the President and with other officers of the Kennedy Administration.

2. Guidelines for Operation Mongoose, 1962

1. Operation Mongoose will be developed on the following assumptions:
   a. In undertaking to cause the overthrow of the target government, the U.S. will make maximum use of indigenous resources, internal and external, but recognizes that final success will require decisive U.S. military intervention.
   b. Such indigenous resources as are developed will be used to prepare for and justify this intervention, and thereafter to facilitate and support it.
2. The immediate priority objective of U.S. efforts during the coming months will be the acquisition of hard intelligence on the target area. Concurrently, all other political, economic and covert actions will be undertaken short of those reasonably calculated to inspire a revolt within the target area, or other development which would require armed U.S. intervention. These actions, insofar as possible, will be consistent with overt policies of isolating the [two words

This document can be found in "The Cuban Missile Crisis: The Making of U.S. Policy," National Security Archive Microfiche Collection, National Security Archives, Washington, D.C. It can also be found in Lawrence Chang and Peter Kornbluh, eds., *The Cuban Missile Crisis: A National Security Archive Documents Reader* (New York: The New Press, 1992), pp. 38–39.

illegible on the document but probably are "Cuban leader"] and of neutralizing his influence in the Western Hemisphere.

3. Cuba Protests U.S. Aggression, October 8, 1962

It was enough for us to promulgate laws which affected the United States monopolistic interests in our country, it was enough to promulgate the land reform act at a period when our revolutionary development was not yet shaped by socialist principles, for aggressive action against our homeland to be undertaken by the United States Government.

That was the start of the insolent diplomatic notes and piratical flights over our territory. Then the Cuban sugar quota was eliminated from the United States market, supplies of petroleum to our country were stopped, and diplomatic measures were taken aimed at isolating Cuba from the continent. Finally there was a whole series of eminently aggressive activities which generated this tension, long before—I repeat—long before we proclaimed that our revolution was a socialist one.

And what has happened since?

It would be unduly tedious, I think, to recapitulate all the acts of aggression committed by the United States against Cuba. Suffice it to mention all the efforts designed to subvert our country from within, the acts of sabotage, the attacks on persons and the espionage activities on our soil. In brief, suffice it to recall the armed invasion of our country by mercenary forces financed, trained in warfare, militarily protected and commanded by the Government of the United States: the invasion of Playa Girón [Bay of Pigs]. And what happened after Playa Girón, that ridiculous fiasco? Did they perchance learn a great lesson of history from it? Did they perchance have sufficient perception and knowledge to realize what immense forces can be marshalled by a nation firmly resolved to preserve its freedom and independence? That is not what happened. We immediately became the victims of further acts of aggression with the infiltration of agents landed on our coasts and trained by the Central Intelligence Agency, new attempts at sabotage, the military training of groups to carry out the hitherto unsuccessful internal subversion of our country and the increase of economic pressure on our homeland—tenaciously and doggedly applied in the hope that it would undermine our revolution and that, as a result, their sole objective would be attained: the downfall of the Revolutionary Government of Cuba. . . .

These aggressive acts continue, like the United States warships that lie near the coast off our harbours. Every day those of us who live in Havana must see with our own eyes these warships lurking around our island, making a show of war or of preparation for war.

This is the situation today but we can also say that it is qualitatively different from the situation which existed before the invasion of our country at Playa Girón, for the following reasons. Before Playa Girón, the Government of the United States

This document can be found in "Address by Mr. Dorticos, President of the Republic of Cuba," 8 October 1962, *United Nations General Assembly, 17th Session, 1145th Plenary Meeting* (A/PV. 1145), Official Record. New York: United Nations, 1962.

had on more than one occasion stated that it had no aggressive intentions towards our country. It is obvious that after Playa Girón even the President of the United States publicly and officially acknowledged his responsibility and his sympathy and support for that invasion.

Today the situation is different, for while it is true that once again it is being asserted—as the Head of the United States delegation has stated here [in the United Nations]—that there are no aggressive designs on our country, on the other hand there are records, and there have been statements and official resolutions which authorize armed aggression against Cuba and seek to justify it in advance. The fact is that the object—as acknowledged recently in a statement by the State Department of the United States—of the foreign policy of the United States Government in regard to Cuba is clearly and obviously the overthrow of the revolutionary Government and the destruction of our glorious revolution. . . .

By way of [further] proof it is sufficient to take a brief look at the operative part of the joint resolution [September 1962] of the United States Congress.

"Resolved by the Senate and House of Representatives of the United States of America in Congress assembled,

"That the United States is determined

"*(a)* To prevent by whatever means may be necessary, including the use of arms"—I repeat, including the use of arms—"the Marxist-Leninist regime in Cuba from extending, by force or the threat of force, its aggressive or subversive activities to any part of this hemisphere.". . .

Of course we should have preferred to devote all those human and material resources, all the energies we have had to employ in strengthening our military defences, to the development of our economy and culture. We have armed ourselves against our wishes and contrary to our aspirations, because we were driven to strengthen our military defences lest we should jeopardize the sovereignty of our nation and the independence of our homeland. We have armed ourselves because the people of Cuba have a legitimate right, sanctioned by history, to defend their sovereign decisions and to steer their country on the historic course which, in the exercise of their sovereignty, they have chosen. . . .

Cuba does not, as has been stated here, represent a problem between the East and the West. Cuba poses a problem of sovereignty and independence. The Cuban problem is a problem involving the sovereign decision of a people and the right of that people to self-determination. Cuba has not wanted to be drawn into the cold war. Cuba merely wants to pursue its economic and cultural development and to shape its own future in peace, and it is ready to demonstrate these intentions at any time. And if it is not true that there is an intention to attack our country—although we consider that such an intention certainly exists—we urge the head of the United States delegation specifically to guarantee before this Assembly that his Government does not intend to attack Cuba. We urge him, however, to back up these guarantees not merely by words, but more especially by deeds. Verbal guarantees were given before Playa Girón, and when the invasion took place, many Members of the Assembly heard the representative of the United States Government state that there was no such invasion and that his Government had not planned one; yet only a few days later, the President of the United States himself publicly and officially assumed the responsibility for that invasion.

4. Missiles Photographed in Cuba: President John F. Kennedy Meets with His Advisers, October 16, 1962

Meeting of 11:50 A.M.–12:57 P.M.

Lundahl*: This is a result of the photography taken Sunday, sir.

JFK: Yeah.

Lundahl: There's a medium-range ballistic missile launch site and two new military encampments on the southern edge of Sierra del Rosario in west central Cuba.

JFK: Where would that be?

Lundahl: Uh, west central, sir. That. . . .

JFK: Yeah. . . .

Lundahl: Well, one site on one of the encampments contains a total of at least fourteen canvas-covered missile trailers measuring 67 feet in length, 9 feet in width. The overall length of the trailers plus the tow-bars is approximately 80 feet. The other encampment contains vehicles and tents but with no missile trailers. . . .

JFK: How far advanced is this? . . . How do you know this is a medium-range ballistic missile?

Lundahl: The length, sir.

JFK: The what? The length?

Lundahl: The length of it. Yes.

JFK: The length of the missile? Which part? I mean which . . .

Lundahl: . . . the missile [word unintelligible] indicates which one is [words unintelligible]. . . .

JFK: Is this ready to be fired?

Graybeal**: No, sir.

JFK: How long have we got. . . . We can't tell, I take it . . .

Graybeal: No, sir.

JFK: . . . how long before it can be fired?

Graybeal: That depends on how ready the . . .

JFK: But, what does it have to be fired from?

Graybeal: It would have to be fired from a stable hard surface. This could be packed dirt; it could be concrete or, or asphalt. The surface has to be hard, then you put a flame deflect-, a deflector plate on there to direct the missile.

McNamara***: Would you care to comment on the position of nuclear warheads—this is in relation to the question from the president—explain when these can be fired?

This document can be found in Presidential Records, Transcripts, President's Office Files, John F. Kennedy Presidential Papers, John F. Kennedy Library, Boston, MA. It can also be found in U.S. Department of State, *Foreign Relations of the United States, 1961–1963, Cuban Missile Crisis and Aftermath* (Washington, D.C.: Government Printing Office, 1996), XI, 31–45, 49–93.

*Art Lundahl, National Photograhic Interpretation Center.

**Sidney Graybeal.

***Robert McNamara, secretary of defense.

Graybeal: Sir, we've looked very hard. We can find nothing that would spell nuclear warhead in terms of any isolated area or unique security in this particular area. The mating of the nuclear warhead to the missile from some of the other short range missiles there would take about, uh, a couple of hours to do this.

McNamara: This is not defensed, I believe, at the moment?

Lundahl: Not yet, sir. . . .

Rusk*: Don't you have to assume these are nuclear? . . .

McNamara: There's no question about that. The question is one of readiness of the, to fire and—and this is highly critical in forming our plans—that the time between today and the time when the readiness to fire capability develops is a very important thing. To estimate that we need to know where these warheads are, and we have not yet found any probable storage of warheads and hence it seems extremely unlikely that they are now ready to fire or may be ready to fire within a matter of hours or even a day or two. . . .

JFK: Secretary Rusk?

Rusk: Yes. [Well?], Mr. President, this is a, of course, a [widely?] serious development. It's one that we, all of us, had not really believed the Soviets could, uh, carry this far. . . . Now, uhm, I do think we have to set in motion a chain of events that will eliminate this base. I don't think we [can?] sit still. The questioning becomes whether we do it by sudden, unannounced strike of some sort, or we, uh, build up the crisis to the point where the other side has to consider very seriously about giving in, or, or even the Cubans themselves, uh, take some, take some action on this. The thing that I'm, of course, very conscious of is that there is no such thing, I think, as unilateral action by the United States. It's so [eminently or heavily?] involved with 2 allies and confrontation in many places, that any action that we take, uh, will greatly increase the risks of direct action involving, uh, our other alliances and our other forces in other parts of the world. Uhm, so I think we, we have to think very hard about two major, uh, courses of action as alternatives. One is the quick strike. The point where we [make or think?], that is the, uh, overwhelming, overriding necessity to take all the risks that are involved doing that. I don't think this in itself would require an invasion of Cuba. I think that with or without such an invasion, in other words if we make it clear that, uh, what we're doing is eliminating this particular base or any other such base that is established. We ourselves are not moved to general war, we're simply doing what we said we would do if they took certain action. Uh, or we're going to decide that this is the time to eliminate the Cuban problem by actually eliminating the island.

The other would be, if we have a few days—from the military point of view, if we have the whole time—uh, then I would think that, uh, there would be another course of action, a combination of things that, uh, we might wish to consider. Uhm, first, uh, that we, uh, stimulate the OAS [Organization of American States] procedure immediately for prompt action to make it quite clear that the entire hemisphere considers that the Rio Pact has been violated [and actually?] what acts should [we take or be taken?] in, under the terms of the Rio Pact. . . .

---

*Dean Rusk, secretary of state.

I think also that we ought to consider getting some word to Castro, perhaps through the Canadian ambassador in Havana or through, uh, his representative at the U.N. Uh, I think perhaps the Canadian ambassador would be best, the better channel to get to Castro [apart?] privately and tell him that, uh, this is no longer support for Cuba, that Cuba is being victimized here, and that, uh, the Soviets are preparing Cuba for destruction or betrayal. . . .

And I think there are certain military, uhm, uh, actions that we could, we might well want to take straight away. First, to, uh, to call up, uh, highly selective units [no more than?] 150,000. Unless we feel that it's better, more desirable to go to a general national emergency so that we have complete freedom of action. If we announce, at the time that we announce this development—and I think we do have to announce this development some time this week—uh, we announce that, uh, we are conducting a surveillance of Cuba, over Cuba, and we will enforce our right to do so. We reject the mission of secrecy in this hemisphere in any matters of this sort. We, we reinforce our forces in Guantánamo. We reinforce our forces in the southeastern part of the United States—whatever is necessary from the military point of view to be able to give, to deliver an overwhelming strike at any of these installations, including the SAM [surface-to-air missile] sites. And, uh, also, to take care of any, uh, MiGs or bombers that might make a pass at Miami or at the United States. Build up heavy forces, uh, if those are not already in position. . . .

I think also that we need a few days, uhm, to alert our other allies, for consultation with NATO [North Atlantic Treaty Organization]. I'll assume that we can move on this line at the same time to interrupt all air traffic from free world countries going into Cuba, insist to the Mexicans, the Dutch, that they stop their planes from coming in. Tell the British, who, and anyone else who's involved at this point, that, uh, if they're interested in peace, that they've got to stop their ships from Cuban trade at this point. Uh, in other words, isolate Cuba completely without at this particular moment a, uh, a forceful blockade. . . .

But I think that, by and large, there are, there are these two broad alternatives: one, the quick strike; the other, to alert our allies and Mr. Khrushchev that there is utterly serious crisis in the making here, and that, uh. . . . Mr. Khrushchev may not himself really understand that or believe that at this point. I think we'll be facing a situation that could well lead to general war. . . .

McNamara: Mr. President, there are a number of unknowns in this situation I want to comment upon, and, in relation to them, I would like to outline very briefly some possible military alternatives and ask General Taylor to expand upon them.

But before commenting on either the unknowns or outlining some military alternatives, there are two propositions I would suggest that we ought to accept as, uh, foundations for our further thinking. My first is that if we are to conduct an air strike against these installations, or against any part of Cuba, we must agree now that we will schedule that prior to the time these missile sites become operational. I'm not prepared to say when that will be, but I think it is extremely important that our talk and our discussion be founded on this premise: that any air strike will be planned to take place prior to the time they become operational. Because, if they become operational before the air strike, I do not believe we can state we can knock them out before they can be launched; and if they're launched there is almost certain to be, uh, chaos in part of the east coast or the area, uh, in a radius of six hundred to a thousand miles from Cuba.

Uh, secondly, I, I would submit the proposition that any air strike must be directed not solely against the missile sites, but against the missile sites plus the airfields plus the aircraft which may not be on the airfields but hidden by that time plus all potential nuclear storage sites. Now, this is a fairly extensive air strike. It is not just a strike against the missile sites; and there would be associated with it potential casualties of Cubans. . . .

Taylor*: Uh, we're impressed, Mr. President, with the great importance of getting a, a strike with all the benefits of surprise, uh, which would mean *ideally* that we would have all the missiles that are in Cuba above ground where we can take them out. Uh, that, that desire runs counter to the strong point the secretary made if the other optimum would be to get every missile before it could, becomes operational. Uh, practically, I think the, our knowledge of the timing of the readiness is going to be so, so, uh, difficult that we'll never have the, the exact permanent, uh, the perfect timing. . . . It's a little hard to say in terms of time how much I'm discussing. But we must do a good job the first time we go in there, uh, pushing a 100 percent just as far, as closely as we can with our, with our strike. . . .

I would also mention among the, the military actions we should take that once we have destroyed as many of these offensive weapons as possible, we should, should prevent any more coming in, which means a naval blockade. . . .

JFK: What is the, uh, advant-. . . . Must be some major reason for the Russians to, uh, set this up as a. . . . Must be that they're not satisfied with their ICBMs [Intercontinental Ballistic Missiles]. What'd be the reason that they would, uh. . . .

Taylor: What it'd give 'em is primary, it makes the launching base, uh, for short range missiles against the United States to supplement their rather [deceptive?] ICBM system, for example. . . .

Rusk: Still, about why the Soviets are doing this, uhm, Mr. McCone** suggested some weeks ago that one thing Mr. Khrushchev may have in mind is that, uh, uh, he knows that we have a substantial nuclear superiority, but he also knows that we don't really live under fear of his nuclear weapons to the extent that, uh, he has to live under fear of ours. Also we have nuclear weapons nearby, in Turkey and places like that.

JFK: How many weapons do we have in Turkey?

Taylor?: We have Jupiter missiles. . . .

McNamara?: About fifteen, I believe it is. . . .

Rusk: Uhm, and that Mr. McCone expresses the view that Khrushchev may feel that it's important for us to learn about living under medium-range missiles, and he's doing that to sort of balance that, uh, that political, psychological [plank?]. I think also that, uh, Berlin is, uh, very much involved in this. Uhm, for the first time, I'm beginning really to wonder whether maybe Mr. Khrushchev is entirely rational about Berlin. We've [hardly?] talked about his obsession with it. And I think we have to, uh, keep our eye on that element. But, uh, they may be thinking that they can either

---

*General Maxwell Taylor, chairman of the Joint Chiefs of Staff.
**John A. McCone, director of the Central Intelligence Agency.

bargain Berlin and Cuba against each other, or that they could provoke us into a kind of action in Cuba which would give an umbrella for them to take action with respect to Berlin. In other words like the Suez-Hungary combination. If they could provoke us into taking the first overt action, then the world would be confused and they would have, uh, what they would consider to be justification for making a move somewhere else. But, uh, I must say I don't really see the rationality of, uh, the Soviets' pushing it this far unless they grossly misunderstand the importance of Cuba to this country. . . .

JFK: Uh, eh, well, this, which . . . What you're really talking about are two or three different, uh, [tense?] operations. One is the strike just on this, these three bases. One, the second is the broader one that Secretary McNamara was talking about, which is on the airfields and on the SAM sites and on anything else connected with, uh, missiles. Third is doing both of those things and also at the same time launching a blockade, which requires really the, uh, the, uh, third and which is a larger step. And then, as I take it, the fourth question is the, uh, degree of consultation.

RFK*: Mr. President.

JFK: Yes.

RFK: We have the fifth one, really, which is the invasion. I would say that, uh, you're dropping bombs all over Cuba if you do the second, uh, air, the airports, knocking out their planes, dropping it on all their missiles. You're covering most of Cuba. You're going to kill an awful lot of people, and, uh, we're going to take an awful lot of heat on it . . .

JFK: I don't believe it takes us, at least, uh. . . . How long did it take to get in a position where we can invade Cuba? Almost a month? Two months?

McNamara: No, sir. . . .

JFK: I think we ought to, what we ought to do is, is, uh, after this meeting this afternoon, we ought to meet tonight again at six, consider these various, uh, proposals. In the meanwhile, we'll go ahead with this maximum, whatever is needed from the flights, and, in addition, we will. . . . I don't think we got much time on these missiles. They may be. . . . So it may be that we just have to, we can't wait two weeks while we're getting ready to, to roll. Maybe just have to just take *them out,* and continue our other preparations if we decide to do that. That may be where we end up. I think we ought to, beginning right now, be preparing to. . . . Because that's what we're going to do *anyway.* We're certainly going to do number one; we're going to take out these, uh, missiles. Uh, the questions will be whether, which, what I would describe as number two, which would be a general air strike. That we're not ready to say, but we should be in preparation for it. The third is the, is the, uh, the general invasion. At least we're going to do number one, so it seems to me that we don't have to wait very long. We, we ought to be making *those* preparations.

Bundy**: You want to be clear, Mr. President, whether we have *definitely* decided *against* a political [i.e., diplomatic] track. I, myself, think we ought . . .

Taylor?: Well, we'll have . . .

Bundy: . . . to work out a contingency on that.

Taylor?: We, we'll develop both tracks.

---

*Robert F. Kennedy.
**McGeorge Bundy, assistant for national security affairs.

Meeting of 6:30–7:55 P.M.

McNamara: Mr. President, could I outline three courses of action we have considered and speak very briefly on each one? The first is what I would call the political course of action, in which we, uh, follow some of the possibilities that Secretary Rusk mentioned this morning by approaching Castro, by approaching Khrushchev, by discussing with our allies. An overt and open approach politically to the problem [attempting, or in order?] to solve it. This seemed to me likely to lead to no satisfactory result, and it almost stops subsequent military action. . . .

A second course of action we haven't discussed but lies in between the military course we began discussing a moment ago and the political course of action is a course of action that would involve declaration of open surveillance; a statement that we would immediately impose an, uh, a blockade against *offensive* weapons entering Cuba in the future; and an indication that with our open-surveillance reconnaissance which we would plan to maintain indefinitely for the future. . . .

But the third course of action is any one of these variants of military action directed against Cuba, starting with an air attack against the missiles. The Chiefs are strongly opposed to so limited an air attack. But even so limited an air attack is a very extensive air attack. It's not twenty sorties or fifty sorties or a hundred sorties, but probably several hundred sorties. Uh, we haven't worked out the details. It's very difficult to do so when we lack certain intelligence that we hope to have tomorrow or the next day. But it's a substantial air attack. . . . I don't believe we have considered the consequences of any of these actions satisfactorily, and because we haven't considered the consequences, I'm not sure we're taking all the action we ought to take now to minimize those. I, I don't know quite what kind of a world we live in after we've struck Cuba, and we, we've started it. . . .

Taylor: And you'll miss some [missiles].

McNamara: And you'll miss some. That's right. Now after we've launched sorties, what kind of a world do we live in? How, how do we stop at that point? I don't know the answer to this. I think tonight State and we ought to work on the consequences of any one of these courses of actions, consequences which I don't believe are entirely clear. . . .

JFK: If the, uh, it doesn't increase very much their strategic, uh, strength, why is it, uh, can any Russian expert tell us why they. . . . After all Khrushchev demonstrated a sense of caution [thousands?] . . .

Speaker?: Well, there are several, several possible . . .

JFK: . . . Berlin, he's been cautious, I mean, he hasn't been, uh . . .

Ball*: Several possibilities, Mr. President. One of them is that he has given us word now that he's coming over in November to, to the UN. If, he may be proceeding on the assumption, and this lack of a sense of *apparent* urgency would seem to, to support this, that this *isn't* going to be discovered at the moment and that, uh, when he comes over this is something he can do, a ploy. That here is Cuba armed against the United States, or possibly use it to try to trade something in Berlin, saying he'll

---

*George W. Ball, under secretary of state.

disarm Cuba, if, uh, if we'll yield some of our interests in Berlin and some arrangement for it. I mean, that this is a, it's a trading ploy.

Bundy: I would think one thing that I would still cling to is that he's not likely to give Fidel Castro nuclear warheads. I don't believe that has happened or is likely to happen.

JFK: Why does he put these in there though?

Bundy: Soviet-controlled nuclear warheads [of the kind?] . . .

JFK: That's right, but what is the advantage of that? It's just as if we suddenly began to put a major number of MRBMs [Medium-Range Ballistic Missiles] in Turkey. Now that'd be goddam dangerous, I would think.

Bundy: Well, we *did,* Mr. President. . . .

JFK: Yeah, but that was five years ago. . . .

Ball: Yes, I think, I think you, you look at this possibility that this is an attempt to, to add to his strategic capabilities. A second consideration is that it is simply a trading ploy, that he, he wants this in so that he could, he could [words unintelligible]. . . .

JFK: Well, it's a goddam mystery to me. I don't know enough about the Soviet Union, but if anybody can tell me any other time since the Berlin blockade where the Russians have given us so clear provocation, I don't know when it's been, because they've been awfully cautious really. The Russians, I never. . . . Now, maybe our mistake was in not saying some time *before* this summer that if they do this we're [word unintelligible] to act.

5. Ambassador Charles E. Bohlen's Call for Diplomacy Is Rejected, October 17, 1962

Ambassador [Charles E.] Bohlen warned against any action against Cuba, particularly an air strike without warning, stating such would be divisive with all Allies and subject us to criticism throughout the world. He advocated writing both Khrushchev and Castro; if their response was negative or unsatisfactory then we should plan action; advise our principal allies, seek a two-thirds vote from the OAS and then act. The Attorney General [Robert F. Kennedy] and Bohlen exchanged views as to just what type of an answer we could expect from Khrushchev and what he might do if we threatened an attack. During this discussion Secretary Rusk seemed to favor asking Congress for a declaration of a state of war against Cuba and then proceed with OAS, NATO, etc., but always preserve flexibility as to the type of action. Bohlen consistently warned that world opinion would be against us if we carried out a military strike. [Under] Secretary Ball emphasized the importance of time, stating that if action was over quickly, the repercussions would not be too serious.

This document can be found in John A. McCone, Memorandum for the File, October 19, 1962, in Mary S. McAuliffe, ed., *CIA Documents on the Cuban Missile Crisis 1962* (Washington, D.C.: History Staff, Central Intelligence Agency, 1992), pp. 169–172.

The Attorney General raised the question of the attitude of Turkey, Italy, Western European countries, all of which have been "under the gun" for years, and would take the position that now that the U.S. has a few missiles in their backyard, they become hysterical. This point was discussed back and forth by various people throughout both days of discussion.

Secretary McNamara made the point that missiles in Cuba had no great military consequence because of the stalemate mentioned in my October 18th memorandum. General Taylor supported this view in the early parts of the discussion, but in the later meetings expressed increasing concern over the importance of the missile threat from Cuba. [Under Secretary of Defense Roswell] Gilpatric supported McNamara's position. [CIA director John A.] McCone doubted it, stating that McNamara's facts were not new as they had appeared in estimates months ago (which McNamara questioned). Nevertheless, he and McCone felt that a complex of MRBMs and IRBMs in Cuba would have very important military significance. McNamara took issue claiming that the military equation would not be changed by the appearance of these missiles.

Bohlen and [former ambassador to the Soviet Union Llewellyn] Thompson questioned the real purpose of the Soviets' actions in Cuba and seemed to feel that their acts may be in preparation for a confrontation with President Kennedy at which time they would seek to settle the entire subject of overseas bases as well as the Berlin question. McCone indicated this might be one of several objectives and undoubtedly would be the subject of discussion at the time of confrontation; however, McCone doubted that this was the prime purpose of such an elaborate and expensive installation as the Soviets were going forward with in Cuba. Bohlen seemed to favor precipitating talks, and was supported by Thompson.

SecDef [McNamara] and Taylor both objected to political talks because it would give time for threatening missiles to become operational and also give the Soviets an opportunity to camouflage the missiles. McCone presented most recent photographs and indicated CIA opinion that the first missiles will be operational within one or two weeks.

Bohlen again raised the question of opening up discussions. McNamara agreed that this would be desirable but emphasized the importance of developing [a] sequence of events which would lead to military action. . . .

Dean Acheson then expressed his views as follows:

We should proceed at once with the necessary military actions and should do no talking. The Soviets will react some place. We must expect this; take the consequences and manage the situations as they evolve. We should have no consultations with Khrushchev, Castro, or our allies, but should fully alert our allies in the most persuasive manner by high level people. This would include all NATO partners, and the OAS. The President should forget about the elections and should cancel all future campaign speeches.

As an alternate to military action, a plan was discussed involving a declaration of war and the creation of an all-out blockade. Thompson spoke strongly in favor of a blockade. General Taylor at this point indicated that he favored a blockade although in subsequent meetings he seemed inclined towards a military strike. McCone gave an intelligence estimate on the effects of a blockade, indicating its seriousness would depend upon how "hard" a blockade it turned out to be, and finally stated that the main objective of taking Cuba away from Castro had been lost and we have been overly consumed with the missile problem. McCone stated that we must all bear in mind that we have two objectives, one, disposing of the missile sites, and the other, getting rid of Castro's communism in the Western Hemisphere.

The meeting adjourned for dinner and in the evening Secretary Rusk came forward with the following plan.

The United States cannot accept operational MRBMs in Cuba. There is not much profit in preliminary exchanges with Khrushchev and Castro because the President has said that the establishment of Soviet bases and offensive weapons in the Western Hemisphere would raise serious problems and therefore on September 5th and 13th the President has in effect warned both Khrushchev and Castro.

Rusk continued that more talks with Khrushchev would result in extended parlays and therefore he recommended against such an approach. Rusk then proposed that we hold until the middle of next week and then follow the OD course No. 1 (52 sorties against MRBMs). Prior, we inform key allies probably on Tuesday. . . . On Wednesday, we strike with missiles and simultaneously send a message to Khrushchev, NATO, OAS, etc. We should be alert for an attack on Turkey and be prepared for the consequences in Berlin, Quemoy, Matsu, Korea, etc. Rusk made the estimate that world opinion would go along, 42 allies would go along and some neutrals would be favorable. Latin Americans must be told that we are acting in the interests of the Western Hemisphere. Rusk advocated that the first step—we take out the missiles and thus remove the immediate problem of the establishment of an offensive capability, but that we be prepared for subsequent steps. He emphasized the United States cannot accept missiles in our security interests and in view of statements made by the President and others and our various policy declarations. Bohlen continued to persist for diplomatic approach but Rusk and several others were not at this point persuaded. McNamara raised innumerable questions concerning military operations; the manner in which the strike could be properly covered with protective air and how it might be restricted.

6. Kennedy Addresses the Nation, October 22, 1962

This urgent transformation of Cuba into an important strategic base—by the presence of these large, long-range, and clearly offensive weapons of sudden mass destruction—constitutes an explicit threat to the peace and security of all the Americas, in flagrant and deliberate defiance of the Rio Pact of 1947, the traditions of this nation and hemisphere, the Joint Resolution of the 87th Congress, the Charter of the United Nations, and my own public warnings to the Soviets on September 4 and 13.

This action also contradicts the repeated assurances of Soviet spokesmen, both publicly and privately delivered, that the arms buildup in Cuba would retain its

This document can be found in *Department of State Bulletin*, XLVII (November 12, 1962), 715–720.

original defensive character and that the Soviet Union had no need or desire to station strategic missiles on the territory of any other nation.

The size of this undertaking makes clear that it has been planned for some months. Yet only last month, after I had made clear the distinction between any introduction of ground-to-ground missiles and the existence of defensive antiaircraft missiles, the Soviet Government publicly stated on September 11 that, and I quote, "The armaments and military equipment sent to Cuba are designed exclusively for defensive purposes," and, and I quote the Soviet Government, "There is no need for the Soviet Government to shift its weapons for a retaliatory blow to any other country, for instance Cuba," and that, and I quote the Government, "The Soviet Union has no powerful rockets to carry these nuclear warheads that there is no need to search for sites for them beyond the boundaries of the Soviet Union." That statement was false.

Only last Thursday, as evidence of this rapid offensive buildup was already in my hand, Soviet Foreign Minister Gromyko told me in my office that he was instructed to make it clear once again, as he said his Government had already done, that Soviet assistance to Cuba, and I quote, "pursued solely the purpose of contributing to the defense capabilities of Cuba," that, and I quote him, "training by Soviet specialists of Cuban nationals in handling defensive armaments was by no means offensive," and that "if it were otherwise," Mr. Gromyko went on, "the Soviet Government would never become involved in rendering such assistance." That statement also was false.

Neither the United States of America nor the world community of nations can tolerate deliberate deception and offensive threats on the part of any nation, large or small. We no longer live in a world where only the actual firing of weapons represents a sufficient challenge to a nation's security to constitute maximum peril. Nuclear weapons are so destructive and ballistic missiles are so swift that any substantially increased possibility of their use or any sudden change in their deployment may well be regarded as a definite threat to peace.

For many years both the Soviet Union and the United States, recognizing this fact, have deployed strategic nuclear weapons with great care, never upsetting the precarious *status quo* which insured that these weapons would not be used in the absence of some vital challenge. Our own strategic missiles have never been transferred to the territory of any other nation under a cloak of secrecy and deception; and our history, unlike that of the Soviets since the end of World War II, demonstrates that we have no desire to dominate or conquer any other nation or impose our system upon its people. Nevertheless, American citizens have become adjusted to living daily on the bull's eye of Soviet missiles located inside the U.S.S.R. or in submarines.

In that sense missiles in Cuba add to an already clear and present danger—although it should be noted the nations of Latin America have never previously been subjected to a potential nuclear threat.

But this secret, swift, and extraordinary buildup of Communist missiles—in an area well known to have a special and historical relationship to the United States and the nations of the Western Hemisphere, in violation of Soviet assurances, and in defiance of American and hemispheric policy—this sudden, clandestine decision to station strategic weapons for the first time outside of Soviet soil—is a deliberately provocative and unjustified change in the *status quo* which cannot be accepted by this country if our courage and our commitments are ever to be trusted again by either friend or foe.

The 1930's taught us a clear lesson: Aggressive conduct, if allowed to grow unchecked and unchallenged, ultimately leads to war. This nation is opposed to war. We are also true to our word. Our unswerving objective, therefore, must be to prevent the use of these missiles against this or any other country and to secure their withdrawal or elimination from the Western Hemisphere.

Our policy has been one of patience and restraint, as befits a peaceful and powerful nation, which leads a worldwide alliance. We have been determined not to be diverted from our central concerns by mere irritants and fanatics. But now further action is required—and it is underway; and these actions may only be the beginning. We will not prematurely or unnecessarily risk the costs of the world-wide nuclear war in which even the fruits of victory would be ashes in our mouth—but neither will we shrink from that risk at any time it must be faced.

Acting, therefore, in the defense of our own security and of the entire Western Hemisphere, and under the authority entrusted to me by the Constitution as endorsed by the resolution of the Congress, I have directed that the following *initial* steps be taken immediately:

First: To halt this offensive buildup, a strict quarantine on all offensive military equipment under shipment to Cuba is being initiated. All ships of any kind bound for Cuba from whatever nation or port will, if found to contain cargoes of offensive weapons, be turned back. This quarantine will be extended, if needed, to other types of cargo and carriers. We are not at this time, however, denying the necessities of life as the Soviets attempted to do in their Berlin blockade of 1948.

Second: I have directed the continued and increased close surveillance of Cuba and its military buildup. The Foreign Ministers of the OAS in their communiqué of October 3 rejected secrecy on such matters in this hemisphere. Should these offensive military preparations continue, thus increasing the threat to the hemisphere, further action will be justified. I have directed the Armed Forces to prepare for any eventualities; and I trust that, in the interest of both the Cuban people and the Soviet technicians at the sites, the hazards to all concerned of continuing this threat will be recognized.

Third: It shall be the policy of this nation to regard any nuclear missile launched from Cuba against any nation in the Western Hemisphere as an attack by the Soviet Union on the United States, requiring a full retaliatory response upon the Soviet Union.

Fourth: As a necessary military precaution I have reinforced our base at Guantánamo, evacuated today the dependents of our personnel there, and ordered additional military units to be on a standby alert basis.

Fifth: We are calling tonight for an immediate meeting of the Organ of Consultation, under the Organization of American States, to consider this threat to hemispheric security and to invoke articles 6 and 8 of the Rio Treaty in support of all necessary action. The United Nations Charter allows for regional security arrangements—and the nations of this hemisphere decided long ago against the military presence of outside powers. Our other allies around the world have also been alerted.

Sixth: Under the Charter of the United Nations, we are asking tonight that an emergency meeting of the Security Council be convoked without delay to take action against this latest Soviet threat to world peace. Our resolution will call for the prompt dismantling and withdrawal of all offensive weapons in Cuba, under the supervision of U.N. observers, before the quarantine can be lifted.

Seventh and finally: I call upon Chairman Khrushchev to halt and eliminate this clandestine, reckless, and provocative threat to world peace and to stable relations between our two nations. I call upon him further to abandon this course of world domination and to join in an historic effort to end the perilous arms race and transform the history of man. He has an opportunity now to move the world back from the abyss of destruction—by returning to his Government's own words that it had no need to station missiles outside its own territory, and withdrawing these weapons from Cuba—by refraining from any action which will widen or deepen the present crisis—and then by participating in a search for peaceful and permanent solutions.

This nation is prepared to present its case against the Soviet threat to peace, and our own proposals for a peaceful world, at any time and in any forum—in the OAS, in the United Nations, or in any other meeting that could be useful—without limiting our freedom of action. . . .

But it is difficult to settle or even discuss these problems in an atmosphere of intimidation. That is why this latest Soviet threat—or any other threat which is made either independently or in response to our actions this week—must and will be met with determination. Any hostile move anywhere in the world against the safety and freedom of peoples to whom we are committed—including in particular the brave people of West Berlin—will be met by whatever action is needed.

Finally, I want to say a few words to the captive people of Cuba, to whom this speech is being directly carried by special radio facilities. I speak to you as a friend, as one who knows of your deep attachment to your fatherland, as one who shares your aspirations for liberty and justice for all. And I have watched and the American people have watched with deep sorrow how your nationalist revolution was betrayed and how your fatherland fell under foreign domination. Now your leaders are no longer Cuban leaders inspired by Cuban ideals. They are puppets and agents of an international conspiracy which has turned Cuba against your friends and neighbors in the Americas—and turned it into the first Latin American country to become a target for nuclear war, the first Latin American country to have these weapons on its soil.

These new weapons are not in your interest. They contribute nothing to your peace and well-being. They can only undermine it. But this country has no wish to cause you to suffer or to impose any system upon you. We know that your lives and land are being used as pawns by those who deny you freedom.

Many times in the past the Cuban people have risen to throw out tyrants who destroyed their liberty. And I have no doubt that most Cubans today look forward to the time when they will be truly free—free from foreign domination, free to choose their own leaders, free to select their own system, free to own their own land, free to speak and write and worship without fear or degradation. And then shall Cuba be welcomed back to the society of free nations and to the associations of this hemisphere.

My fellow citizens, let no one doubt that this is a difficult and dangerous effort on which we have set out. No one can foresee precisely what course it will take or what costs or casualties will be incurred. Many months of sacrifice and self-discipline lie ahead—months in which both our patience and our will will be tested, months in which many threats and denunciations will keep us aware of our dangers. But the greatest danger of all would be to do nothing.

7. Premier Nikita Khrushchev Asks for a U.S. No-Invasion Pledge, October 26, 1962

I see, Mr. President, that you too are not devoid of a sense of anxiety for the fate of the world, [not without an] understanding . . . of what war entails. What would a war give you? You are threatening us with war. But you well know that the very least which you would receive in reply would be that you would experience the same consequences as those which you sent us. And that must be clear to us, people invested with authority, trust, and responsibility. We must not succumb to intoxication and petty passions, regardless of whether elections are impending in this or that country, or not impending. These are all transient things, but if indeed war should break out, then it would not be in our power to stop it, for such is the logic of war. I have participated in two wars and know that war ends when it has rolled through cities and villages, everywhere sowing death and destruction.

In the name of the Soviet Government and the Soviet people, I assure you that your conclusions regarding offensive weapons on Cuba are groundless. It is apparent from what you have written me that our conceptions are different on this score, or rather, we have different estimates of these or those military means. Indeed, in reality, the same forms of weapons can have different interpretations.

You are a military man and, I hope, will understand me. Let us take for example a simple cannon. What sort of means is this: offensive or defensive? A cannon is a defensive means if it is set up to defend boundaries or a fortified area. But if one concentrates artillery, and adds to it the necessary number of troops, then the same cannons do become an offensive means, because they prepare and clear the way for infantry to attack. The same happens with missile-nuclear weapons as well, with any type of this weapon. . . .

This document can be found in *Problems of Communism,* Special Issue: "Back from the Brink," XLI (Spring 1992), 37–45. It can also be found in U.S. Department of State, *Foreign Relations of the United States, 1961–1963, Cuban Missile Crisis and Aftermath* (Washington, D.C.: Government Printing Office, 1996), XL 235–240.

You have now proclaimed piratical measures, which were employed in the Middle Ages, when ships proceeding in international waters were attacked, and you have called this "a quarantine" around Cuba. Our vessels, apparently, will soon enter the zone which your Navy is patrolling. I assure you that these vessels, now bound for Cuba, are carrying the most innocent peaceful cargoes. Do you really think that we only occupy ourselves with the carriage of so-called offensive weapons, atomic and hydrogen bombs? Although perhaps your military people imagine that these [cargoes] are some sort of special type of weapon, I assure you that they are the most ordinary peaceful products.

Consequently, Mr. President, let us show good sense. I assure you that on those ships, which are bound for Cuba, there are no weapons at all. The weapons which were necessary for the defense of Cuba are already there. I do not want to say that there were not any shipments of weapons at all. No, there were such shipments. But now Cuba has already received the necessary means of defense. . . .

Let us normalize relations. We have received an appeal from the Acting Secretary General of the UN, U Thant, with his proposals. I have already answered him. His proposals come to this, that our side should not transport armaments of any kind to Cuba during a certain period of time, while negotiations are being conducted— and we are ready to enter such negotiations—and the other side should not undertake any sort of piratical actions against vessels engaged in navigation on the high seas. I consider these proposals reasonable. This would be a way out of the situation which has been created, which would give the peoples the possibility of breathing calmly.

You have asked what happened, what evoked the delivery of weapons to Cuba? You have spoken about this to our Minister of Foreign Affairs. I will tell you frankly, Mr. President, what evoked it.

We were very grieved by the fact—I spoke about it in Vienna [at the 1961 summit meeting]—that a landing took place [Bay of Pigs], that an attack on Cuba was committed, as a result of which many Cubans perished. You yourself told me then that this had been a mistake. . . .

Why have we proceeded to assist Cuba with military and economic aid? The answer is: we have proceeded to do so only for reasons of humanitarianism. At one time, our people itself had a revolution, when Russia was still a backward country. We were attacked then. We were the target of attack by many countries. The USA participated in that adventure. . . .

You once said that the United States was not preparing an invasion. But you also declared that you sympathized with the Cuban counterrevolutionary emigrants, that you support them and would help them to realize their plans against the present government of Cuba. It is also not a secret to anyone that the threat of armed attack, aggression, has constantly hung, and continues to hang over Cuba. It was only this which impelled us to respond to the request of the Cuban government to furnish it aid for the strengthening of the defensive capacity of this country.

If assurance were given by the President and the government of the United States that the USA itself would not participate in an attack on Cuba and would restrain others from actions of this sort, if you would recall your fleet, this would immediately change everything. I am not speaking for Fidel Castro, but I think that he and the government of Cuba, evidently, would declare demobilization and would appeal to the people to get down to peaceful labor. Then, too, the question of armaments would disappear, since, if there is no threat, then armaments are a burden for every people. Then, too, the question of the destruction, not only of the armaments which you call offensive, but of all other armaments as well, would look different. . . .

Let us therefore show statesmanlike wisdom. I propose: we, for our part, will declare that our ships, bound for Cuba, will not carry any kind of armaments. You would declare that the United States will not invade Cuba with its forces and will not support any sort of forces which might intend to carry out an invasion of Cuba. Then the necessity for the presence of our military specialists in Cuba would disappear.

Mr. President, I appeal to you to weigh well what the aggressive, piratical actions, which you have declared the USA intends to carry out in international waters, would lead to. You yourself know that any sensible man simply cannot agree with this, cannot recognize your right to such actions.

If you did this as the first step towards the unleashing of war, well then, it is evident that nothing else is left to us but to accept this challenge of yours. If, however, you have not lost your self-control and sensibly conceive what this might lead to, then, Mr. President, we and you ought not now to pull on the ends of the rope in which you have tied the knot of war, because the more the two of us pull, the tighter that knot will be tied. And a moment may come when that knot will be tied so tight that even he who tied it will not have the strength to untie it, and then it will be necessary to cut that knot. And what that would mean is not for me to explain to you, because you yourself understand perfectly of what terrible forces our countries dispose.

Consequently, if there is no intention to tighten that knot and thereby to doom the world to the catastrophe of thermonuclear war, then let us not only relax the forces pulling on the ends of the rope, let us take measures to untie that knot. We are ready for this.

8. Khrushchev Requests U.S. Removal
of Jupiter Missiles from Turkey, October 27, 1962

You are worried over Cuba. You say that it worries you because it lies at a distance of 90 miles across the sea from the shores of the United States. However, Turkey lies next to us. Our sentinels are pacing up and down and watching each other. Do you believe that you have the right to demand security for your country and the removal of such weapons that you qualify as offensive, while not recognizing this right for us?

You have stationed devastating rocket weapons, which you call offensive, in Turkey literally right next to us. How then does recognition of our equal military

---

This document can be found in *Problems of Communism,* Special Issue: "Back from the Brink," XLI (Spring 1992), 45–50. It can also be found in U.S. Department of State, *Foreign Relations of the United States, 1961–1963, Cuban Missile Crisis and Aftermath* (Washington, D.C.: Government Printing Office, 1996), XI, 257–260.

possibilities tally with such unequal relations between our great states? This does not tally at all. . . .

This is why I make this proposal: We agree to remove those weapons from Cuba which you regard as offensive weapons. We agree to do this and to state this commitment in the United Nations. Your representatives will make a statement to the effect that the United States, on its part, bearing in mind the anxiety and concern of the Soviet state, will evacuate its analogous weapons from Turkey. . . .

The U.S. Government will . . . declare that the United States will respect the integrity of the frontiers of Cuba, its sovereignty, undertakes not to intervene in its domestic affairs, not to invade and not to make its territory available as place d'armes for the invasion of Cuba, and also will restrain those who would think of launching an aggression against Cuba either from U.S. territory or from the territory of other states bordering on Cuba.

9. Kennedy and ExComm Consider Trading the Jupiter Missiles in Turkey, October 27, 1962

JFK (reading): "Premier Khrushchev told President Kennedy yesterday he would withdraw offensive missiles from Cuba if the United States withdrew its rockets from Turkey."

Speaker?: He didn't really say that, did he? . . .

JFK: That wasn't in the letter [of October 26] we received, was it?

Speaker?: No. . . .

JFK: We're going to be in an insupportable position on this matter if this becomes his proposal. In the first place, we last year tried to get the [Jupiter] missiles out of there [Turkey] because they're not militarily useful, number one. Number two, it's going to—to any man at the United Nations or any other rational man it will look like a very fair trade. . . .

I think you're going to find it very difficult to explain why we are going to take hostile military action in Cuba, against these [missile] sites—what we've been thinking about—the thing that he's saying is, if you'll get yours out of Turkey, we'll get ours out of Cuba. I think we've got a very tough one here. . . .

He's put this out in a way that's caused maximum tension and embarrassment. It's not as if it was a private proposal, which would give us an opportunity to negotiate with the Turks. He's put it out in a way that the Turks are bound to say they don't agree to this. . . .

They've got a very good card. This one is going to be very tough, I think, for us. It's going to be tough in England, I'm sure—as well as other places on the continent—we're going to be forced to take action, that might seem, in my opinion, not a blank check but a pretty good check to take action in Berlin on the grounds that we were wholly unreasonable. Most think—people think that if you're allowed

This document can be found in Presidential Recordings, Transcripts, President's Office Files, John F. Kennedy Presidential Papers, John F. Kennedy Library, Boston, MA. It can also be found in David A. Welch and James G. Blight, "October 27, 1962: Transcript of the Meetings of the ExComm," *International Security,* XII (Winter 1987–1988), 30–92.

an even trade you ought to take *advantage* of it. Therefore it makes it much more difficult for us to move with world support. These are all the things that—uh—why this is a pretty good play of his. . . .

I'm just thinking about what—what we're going to have to do in a day or so, which is [deleted] sorties and [deleted] days, and possibly an invasion, all because we wouldn't take missiles out of Turkey, and we all know how quickly everybody's courage goes when the blood starts to flow, and that's what's going to happen in NATO, when they—we start these things, and they grab Berlin, and everybody's going to say, "Well that was a pretty good proposition." Let's not kid ourselves that we've got—that's the difficulty. Today it sounds great to reject it, but it's not going to, after we do something. . . .

Thompson*: The important thing for Khrushchev, it seems to me, is to be able to say, I saved Cuba, I stopped an invasion—and he can get away with this, if he wants to, and he's had a go at this Turkey thing, and that we'll discuss later. . . .

LBJ**: Bob [McNamara], if you're willing to give up your missiles in Turkey, you think you ought to [words unclear] why don't you say that to him and say we're cutting a trade—make the trade there? [mixed voices] save all the invasion, lives and—

Speaker?: The State Department, they invite them—we talked about this, and they said they'd be *delighted* to trade those missiles in Turkey for the things in Cuba.

McNamara: I said I thought it was the realistic solution to the problem.

LBJ: Sure. What we were afraid of was he'd never offer this, but what he'd want to do was trade [mixed voices] *Berlin.* . . .

JFK: We can't very well invade Cuba with all its toil, and long as it's going to be, when we could have gotten them out by making a deal on the same missiles in Turkey. If that's part of the record I don't see how we'll have a very good war. . . .

Well, let's see—uh—let's give him [Khrushchev] an explanation of what we're trying to do. We're trying to get it back on the original proposition of last night, and—because we don't want to get into this trade. If we're unsuccessful, then we—it's *possible* that we may have to get back on the Jupiter thing.

10. Anastas I. Mikoyan and Fidel Castro Debate and Review the Crisis, November 4–5, 1962

Mikoyan-Castro Meeting in Havana, November 4, 1962

[Mikoyan:] I remember that after visiting Bulgaria [in May 1962], Nikita Khrushchev told you that all through his stay in that country he had been thinking of Cuba, fearing that the Americans might mount armed intervention with the aid of reactionary Latin American governments or commit outright aggression. They

This document can be found in, "Documents: Dialogue in Havana. The Caribbean Crisis," *International Affairs* (Moscow). No. 10 (1992), pp. 109–111, 114, 115, 116, 117, 122, 123.

*Llewellyn E. Thompson, U.S. ambassador to the Soviet Union, July 16, 1957–July 27, 1962; U.S. ambassador-at-large, October 3, 1962–1966.

**Lyndon B. Johnson, vice president.

refuse to allow Cuba to grow stronger, Nikita Khrushchev told us, and if Cuba were defeated, the whole world revolutionary movement would suffer a heavy blow. We must thwart the American imperialists' plans, he said. . . .

The only purpose of shipping Soviet troops and strategic arms to Cuba was to strengthen your defences. Ours was a containment plan, a plan intended to discourage the imperialists from playing with fire in regard to Cuba. Had we developed strategic arms in secrecy, with America knowing nothing about those arms' presence in Cuba, they would have served as a strong deterrent. That was the assumption we started from. Our military told us that Cuba's palm forests made it possible to dependably camouflage strategic missiles against detection from the air. . . .

In such a situation [U.S. invasion], we would have been unable to refrain from responding to aggression from the United States. That attack would have amounted to an attack on both you and us because we had Soviet troops and strategic missiles stationed in Cuba. A collision would inevitably have triggered a nuclear war. To be sure, we would have destroyed America and suffered severely for our part, but then our country is larger than America. Cuba would have been destroyed first. The imperialists would have done their utmost to destroy it.

We had 10 to 12 hours to go before the United States attacked Cuba. It was indispensable to use the art of diplomacy. Failure would have led to war. We had to use diplomatic means. . . .

As Kennedy agreed to Soviet troops being left in Cuba and as the Cubans kept powerful weapons and anti-aircraft missiles, we may consider that he made a concession for his part.

Kennedy's statement about nonaggression against Cuba by the United States and Latin American countries is another concession. If we take these reciprocal concessions and all other factors into account, we will see that we've won a big victory. Never before have the Americans made such statements. This is why we came to the conclusion that we were achieving the main goal, which is to preserve Cuba. There will be no attack on Cuba. Nor will there be any war. We are winning more favourable positions.

Of course, we should have sent our draft decision to Cuba, should have consulted you and secured your consent before publishing it. We would actually have done so in a normal situation. Fidel Castro wrote us in his letter [of October 26] that aggression within the next 24 hours was imminent. When we received the letter and discussed the situation, the start of aggression was only 10 to 12 hours away.

Let us compare the situation today with what it was before the crisis. At that time the Americans were planning armed intervention against Cuba. But now they have committed themselves not to attack Cuba. This is a great achievement. . . .

Frankly speaking, we had not at all been thinking about the bases in Turkey. But when discussing the dangerous situation that had developed, we received information from the United States saying that, from what [Walter] Lippmann wrote in his column, the Russians might raise the question of abolishing the US bases in Turkey. The possibility of our putting forward such a demand was discussed among Americans. The idea was debated in the United States. That was how that demand came to be advanced. Subsequently, however, we stopped insisting on it because the US bases in that country are no problem for us. The Turkish bases are of little significance as we see it. They will be destroyed in case of war. Of course, they have some political significance but we don't pay them any particular attention although we plan to press for their elimination.

Mikoyan-Castro Meeting in Havana, November 5, 1962

[*Castro:*] We have no doubt that had the siting of the strategic weapon been completed in secret, we would have obtained in that way a powerful deterrent against American plans for attack on our country. That would have meant achieving goals pursued by both the Soviet government and the government of the Republic of Cuba. We consider, however, that the deployment of Soviet missiles in Cuba was important in that it served the interests of the whole socialist camp. Even assuming that their deployment provided no military advantage, it was important politically and psychologically for the effort to contain imperialism and prevent it from implementing its plans for aggression. It follows that the strategic weapon was deployed in Cuba in the interest of defending not only Cuba but the socialist camp as a whole. It was a move made with our full consent.

We were well aware of the significance of that move and consider that it was the right thing to do.

We fully agree that war is inadmissible. We are not against the fact that the measures adopted had a twofold purpose, namely, preventing an attack on Cuba and staving off a world war. We fully subscribe to these aims pursued by the Soviet Union.

What gave rise to misunderstanding was the form in which the matter was discussed. We realise, however, that there were circumstances demanding prompt action and that the situation was not normal. . . .

The United States could have been told that the Soviet Union was ready to dismantle the facility but wanted to discuss the matter with the Cuban government. We believe you should have decided the question that way rather than issuing instructions at once on the removal of the strategic weapon. Such an approach would have eased international tension and made it possible to discuss the problem with the Americans in a more favourable context. It would have enabled us not only to bring about a lessening of international tension and discuss the matter in more favourable conditions but to secure the signing of a declaration.

 E S S A Y S

In the first essay, Ernest R. May of Harvard University and Philip D. Zelikow of the University of Virginia use the recently released tape-recorded minutes of President Kennedy's Executive Committee of the National Security Council, as well as selective Soviet records, to explain the Cuban Missile Crisis in the context of Soviet-American relations and the nuclear arms race. Downplaying the impact of Cuba's desire for defense against the United States, they argue that Premier Nikita Khrushchev initiated the crisis when he decided to remedy the Soviet Union's disadvantage in nuclear weapons and gain leverage in bargaining over Berlin by placing medium and intermediate range missiles in Cuba. Examining the administration's decisionmaking, May and Zelikow highlight the president's willingness to listen to an eclectic array of advisers, his ability to control U.S. military actions, and his coolheadedness under pressure in resolving the crisis. They particularly praise the Kennedy administration's application of historical lessons, which led to a firm U.S. stand against Soviet provocation.

Thomas G. Paterson of the University of Connecticut disagrees. In the second essay, Paterson studies the origins of the missile crisis in the context of tense Cuban-American relations and the Cold War. Conspicuous, repeated, and threatening U.S. actions incited Cuban fears of an invasion. Cuba's quest for defense joined Soviet objectives to prompt the mid-1962 Cuban-Soviet agreement to deploy missiles on the island. Paterson next explores the management of the crisis. Noting near misses and accidents, the severe stress experienced by administration officials, and the Executive Committee's inflated record, Paterson questions the thesis that Kennedy's leadership represents a superb example of calculated crisis management. Rather, fear of events spinning out of control—of a nuclear doomsday—mattered as much as anything else in bringing the crisis to a close, Paterson concludes. Finally, he studies the aftermath of the crisis to demonstrate that the U.S. "fixation" with Fidel Castro's Cuba persisted.

Kennedy's Controlled Response to Khrushchev's Cuban Gamble

ERNEST R. MAY AND PHILIP D. ZELIKOW

On the morning when he first saw photographs of Soviet missiles in Cuba, John Fitzgerald Kennedy was 4 months and 18 days past his forty-fifth birthday. During the 13 days of crisis that followed, he would ask advice from some men older than he and from a few who were younger. (From no women, so far as we know.) All had been molded by World War II and the Cold War. "Munich," "Pearl Harbor," "the iron curtain," "containment," "the Berlin blockade," "Korea," "McCarthyism," "Suez-Hungary," "Sputnik," and other such shorthand references to recent history called up shared memories and shared beliefs. . . .

"Munich" captured a world of meaning, especially for Kennedy. His father had played a role in the drama. He himself had published a book analyzing it. "Munich," of course, referred not to a single event but to a series of events and to their supposed lesson or lessons. The Munich conference of 1938 capped efforts by Britain to appease Nazi Germany, arguably making up for too-harsh peace treaties imposed after World War I. Czechoslovakia had been created by those treaties. At Munich, Britain compelled Czechoslovakia to cede to Germany borderlands populated by German speakers. When the Nazi dictator, Adolf Hitler, subsequently seized non-German Czechoslovakia and invaded Poland, Britain changed policy. World War II commenced. "Munich" and "appeasement" became synonyms for failure to stand firm in the face of aggression.

Kennedy's father, Joseph Patrick Kennedy, a famous stock speculator and one of the few millionaires openly to back Franklin Roosevelt, was Roosevelt's ambassador to Britain at the time of the Munich conference. Both in cables to the State

Reprinted by permission of the publisher from *The Kennedy Tapes: Inside the White House During the Cuban Missle Crisis* by Ernest R. May and Phillip D. Zelikow, Cambridge, Mass.: The Belknap Press of Harvard University Press, Copyright © 1997 by the President and Fellows of Harvard College.

Department and in public speeches and interviews, Joe Kennedy backed Britain's appeasement of Germany. He continued to do so. Well into World War II, he argued that Britain had been right to conciliate Hitler and that the best interests of the world would be served by a compromise peace. . . .

John Kennedy was twenty-one and a third-year undergraduate at Harvard at the time of the Munich conference. During the actual period of the conference, he seemed to agree with his father. The coming of war gave him second thoughts. Previously a desultory student, preoccupied with games and girls, he turned in his final college year to writing a long honors thesis, with the laborious title "Appeasement at Munich (the Inevitable Result of the Slowness of Conversion of the British Democracy to Change from a Disarmament Policy to a Rearmament Policy)." Family friends helped him polish the manuscript and publish it under the improved title *Why England Slept.* Appearing in 1940, only weeks after the fall of France, it became a surprise best-seller. It did not entirely contradict his father's line. Indeed, Joe Kennedy read and approved the final draft. But the book struck a different stance. Declaring "appeasement" a weak policy forced upon British governments by British public opinion, it called on America to arm so as not to have to follow a similar policy if challenged by totalitarianism.

All his life, Kennedy would carry the burden of being Joe Kennedy's son. Robert Lovett, Truman's Secretary of Defense and one of the elder statesmen whom Kennedy would consult during the missile crisis, voted against Kennedy in 1960 because Joe Kennedy was his father. George Ball, who would be Under Secretary of State and a regular member of Kennedy's missile crisis circle, writes in his memoirs that he joined the Kennedy administration only after assuaging doubts similar to Lovett's. . . .

"Pearl Harbor" was another historical reference point for Kennedy and his advisers. Practically all Americans had been shocked to learn on December 7, 1941, that Japanese planes had bombed the American naval base at Pearl Harbor and sunk or severely damaged the warships anchored there. Most could recall ever afterward exactly where they had been when they heard this news. Kennedy and a friend with whom he shared an apartment in the District of Columbia had just finished a pickup game of touch football on the grounds near the Washington Monument. They heard the first bulletins on their car radio while driving home. . . .

. . . Recollections of Pearl Harbor had helped to make worst-case worry about surprise attack a guiding theme for postwar U.S. military planning and procurement. Absent Pearl Harbor, the whole debate about the Soviet missiles in Cuba might have been different, for supposed lessons from the Pearl Harbor attack shaped the intelligence collection apparatus that informed Kennedy of the missiles and kept him and his advisers abreast of day-to-day developments. Most important of all, Pearl Harbor served as a conclusive example of the proposition that a secretive government might pursue its ambitions, or relieve its frustrations, by adopting courses of action that objectively seemed irrational or even suicidal. This proposition haunts discussion of Soviet motives and possible Soviet reactions during the missile crisis. . . .

During the final year of World War II and the early postwar years, Kennedy and the men who would surround him during the missile crisis moved into the era of the Cold War. . . .

Kennedy ran successfully for Congress in 1946. There he supported President Truman's efforts to put containment into practice by giving aid to European countries threatened either by the Soviet Union or by domestic Communist parties. While his father spoke out publicly against wasting money or running risks on behalf of foreigners unable to solve their own problems, Kennedy made a well-publicized speech in the House, declaring that the United States had a duty not only "to prevent Europe and Asia from becoming dominated by one great military power" but to prevent "the suffering people of Europe and Asia from succumbing to the soporific ideology of Red totalitarianism." . . .

In 1948 the Truman administration set an example. Berlin, the former German capital, lay well inside eastern Germany, occupied by the Soviets under wartime agreements. Berlin itself, however, had American, British, and French sectors too, creating a populous Western island within the Soviet zone. In June the Soviets suddenly imposed a blockade, stopping all rail and road traffic from the West into Berlin. After reflecting on alternatives, President Truman ordered a round-the-clock airlift to deliver food and supplies to the city. If the Soviets had interfered, the result could well have been war. The Soviets let the planes go through. After some months, they suspended the blockade. From then on Berlin stood as a symbol of U.S. determination to put American lives on the line against forceful Soviet takeover of any part of Europe. . . .

Time and again during the missile crisis debates, one person or another would make reference to the blockade and airlift. For some reason, everyone tended to misdate it, placing it in 1947–48 instead of 1948–49. . . .

After the Berlin blockade crisis, the Cold War intensified. In 1949 the Soviets surprised the West by testing an atomic bomb. It became clear that Soviet dictator Joseph Stalin, instead of giving priority to repairing war damage, was pouring resources into military modernization. In late June 1950 came the Korean War. . . .

Apart from its particular lessons for individuals, the Korean War had lasting effects on American policymaking. Until World War II, the military establishment had had almost no voice in foreign policy decisions. After the war, Congress made provision for a National Security Council, intending it to ensure that Presidents would not totally ignore military considerations when making decisions about international relations. Besides the President, the principal members were the Secretary of State and the civilian Secretary of Defense. . . .

The period of the Korean War had also been the high phase of "McCarthyism." The label came from Joseph R. McCarthy, a loutish Senator from Wisconsin, who had taken to its outer limit the tactic of detecting domestic U.S. Communists and Communist sympathizers as the chief sources of trouble both in the United States and in the world. But McCarthy's success in capturing headlines and terrorizing individuals and agencies reflected widespread public anxiety fed by, among other things, proof that prominent officials of the Roosevelt administration had been secret Soviet agents. Alger Hiss, Rusk's immediate predecessor in managing UN affairs in the State Department, had gone to the penitentiary. . . .

By October 1962 McCarthyism itself would seem far in the past. Memories of its virulence, however, persisted. So did public anxiety. A hit film of 1962, John Frankenheimer's *The Manchurian Candidate,* starring Kennedy's friend Frank Sinatra, was based on the premise that Communists could manipulate American political processes through their own mind-controlled puppets. When Kennedy and his advisers talked at the White House about possible public reactions to one option or another, many of them had in the backs of their minds hysteria such as that which had risen during the first decade of the Cold War. . . .

In the course of seeking the presidency, Kennedy confronted three clusters of issues that would become central concerns for him after being elected and that would bear critically on his management of the missile crisis. Their catchwords were "the strategic balance," "European security," and "the Third World."

"Strategic balance" referred to the relationship between the U.S. and Soviet nuclear arsenals. The years between Hiroshima and Kennedy's swearing-in as President saw dizzying advances in nuclear weapons and related military technologies. Having cracked the secret of making bombs based on the power of nuclear fission, scientists and engineers in both the West and the Soviet Union turned successfully to exploiting the vastly greater potential energy of nuclear fusion. The blast of an atomic bomb, a fission weapon, had been calculated in kilotons, each kiloton equivalent to 1,000 tons of TNT. The blast of a hydrogen bomb, a fusion weapon, was calculated in megatons, each equivalent to 1,000 kilotons, or a million tons of TNT. . . .

The rationale for continuing to accumulate new and improved nuclear weapons resided in another watchword of the Cold War: "second strike." During the 1950s some of the best minds in the world tried to untangle the logic of using nuclear weapons to defend territory despite the likelihood that their actual use would obliterate the territory and be suicidal for the defender. One early insight was that a nuclear arsenal might not achieve any deterrent effect—indeed, might encourage both aggression and nuclear war—if it could be destroyed in a disarming first strike, for a state might be tempted to rid itself at once of resistance to its aggression and any danger of its own annihilation. It followed that a nuclear arsenal served as an effective deterrent if so configured that significant forces would survive any attempt at a disarming first strike. This "second strike" capability would guarantee the attacker's devastation, no matter what. . . .

On the missile crisis tapes, the language of nuclear strategic debates rarely appears. Kennedy and many of those around him had, however, steeped themselves in those debates. The inherent dilemmas that many had studied but that no one had resolved can be heard in insistent undertone in what they said to each other during the Cuban crisis. "Do they really believe that they can cow us into not using our nuclear weapons?" they are often asking implicitly about the Soviets. "Are we willing to take actions that could set in train a nuclear war?" they are continually asking of themselves. And one cannot fully comprehend their discussions without awareness of these unspoken questions and of their perception that hundreds of millions of lives hung on the answers. . . .

The second key issue complex—European security—linked inseparably with the strategic balance. The United States had become engaged in the Cold War primarily from concern lest the Soviet Union expand into Western Europe. Increased concern, fueled by evidence of the Soviet arms buildup and especially by the Korean War, caused the United States in the 1950s to station American military forces in Europe and to press successfully for West German membership in NATO and for West Germany to provide troops and other forces for NATO.

Always anxious as to whether the Americans would actually live up to their promises of military support, given the history of the two world wars, Europeans became newly nervous as they observed the accelerating nuclear arms race. On the one hand, they feared that the Americans would decide to save themselves and let Europe go—would refuse, as the phrase went, to trade Chicago for Bonn. On the other hand, Europeans feared that the United States might either take some rash action that would precipitate a Soviet attack on Europe or, trying to protect the American homeland while at the same time sticking by the commitment to Europe, would make a war for the rescue of Europe a nonnuclear war, the result of which could be a replay of World War II. . . .

For Europeans, the Suez crisis of 1956 provided the strongest evidence that the United States might put its own national and global interests ahead of the interest of its NATO allies. This crisis, which would be cited repeatedly in missile crisis debates, originated with Egypt's nationalization of the Suez Canal. Ignoring advice to the contrary from Eisenhower, the British and French conspired with the Israelis and commenced military operations that surprised Washington no less than Cairo. Through ruthless use of diplomatic economic pressure, Eisenhower forced the British and French to desist. Meanwhile, the Soviets sent tanks into Hungary to suppress a rebellion that had briefly offered promise of that country's liberation from tight Soviet control. . . .

From that time onward, the U.S. government had increasing difficulty coping with the question of how credibly to assure Europeans that it would actually defend them and would do so without bringing on their ruin. As the Soviets acquired more and more capacity for attacking the continental United States, Americans searched for strategies that would continue to reassure Europeans but also reduce the risk of nuclear cataclysm. . . .

The U.S. positioning of IRBMs [Intermediate Range Ballistic Missiles] in Britain, Italy, and Turkey was part of this effort to allay European fears of being left in the lurch. But so fast was the evolution both of missile technology and of thinking about nuclear weapons that the Thors and Jupiters were to seem obsolete before they became operational. . . .

From the late 1950s into the early 1960s, the key pressure point testing the firmness of American guarantees to Europe was, as early in the Cold War, Berlin. Stalin's successor, Nikita Khrushchev, threatened in 1958 to sign a separate peace treaty with East Germany, turn over to the East Germans control of Berlin, and declare that, so far as he was concerned, Westerners no longer had any legal rights within the city. Meeting unbending opposition from Eisenhower, Khrushchev postponed action. He revived the threat during 1960, then let it be known that he would hold off action until the United States had a new President. Kennedy would therefore take office under warning that difficulties over Berlin, possibly a crisis, loomed ahead. . . .

[Another] development, of signal importance for understanding the debates recorded here, was the revolution in Cuba. It originated with a relatively small band of guerrillas operating from mountain bases in eastern Cuba. The existing Cuban government, headed by Fulgencio Batista, had become more and more corrupt, partly as a result of alliances with American gangsters who operated casinos in Havana. Whatever popular support Batista had once possessed he lost. Though his regime had been generally incompetent, his police had been relatively success-ful in rooting out all organized opposition other than that of the guerrillas and of underground factions such as the Cuban Communist Party. The result was that the Cuban populace had no one to whom to turn as an alternative to Batista other than the flamboyant guerrilla leader, Fidel Castro.

When Batista's regime collapsed at the very end of 1958, Castro easily took control of Havana. . . .

By mid-1959, if not earlier, U.S. feeling toward Castro had cooled. He was not only expropriating American property without compensation; he was also taking property from and jailing Cubans who criticized him. He had developed a working alliance with the now largely aboveground Communist Party, and the very long speeches to which he was prone became increasingly critical of the United States. During the following year he began openly to align himself with the Soviet Union and to accept Soviet aid. The Eisenhower administration retaliated with economic sanctions. American ports, particularly in Florida, received streams of refugees, mostly members of the middle class and intellectuals whom Castro had either dis-possessed or silenced. Castro's Cuba came increasingly to be characterized in the United States as a base for Communist subversion in the hemisphere. . . .

The first crisis of the Kennedy administration concerned Cuba. It was the Bay of Pigs affair. When Kennedy had charged that the Eisenhower administration was doing far too little for Cuban exile "freedom fighters," he had done so in ignorance that the Central Intelligence Agency, with active encouragement from Vice President Nixon, was arming and training Cuban exiles for an effort to unseat Castro. . . .

[After becoming president,] Kennedy approved the expanded CIA plan, but with misgivings. The Alliance for Progress [a $10 billion foreign aid program for Latin America] announced in his inaugural address aimed at helping non-Marxists gain the initiative in Latin American reform movements. He feared that evident U.S. intervention in Cuba would revive denunciation of Yankee imperialism and frustrate the Alliance. He also feared that U.S. military engagement in Cuba might encourage Khrushchev to make a move somewhere else, perhaps against Laos or Berlin. The Director of Central Intelligence, Allen Dulles, had, however, an im-pressive reputation as an engineer of covert action. The actual man in charge was Richard Bissell, whom Kennedy knew as creator and manager of the program for U-2 reconnaissance, and with whom Bundy had studied economics as an under-graduate at Yale. After repeatedly saying to Dulles and Bissell that he wanted the noise level kept down and that he would in no circumstances commit U.S. military forces, Kennedy gave a final go-ahead.

On April 17, 1961, 1,400 Cubans arrived off the south coast of Cuba and em-barked in small boats for the nearby beach around the Bay of Pigs. Everything that could go wrong had already started to go wrong. B-26 aircraft that had bombed Cuban airfields landed in Miami, with the pilots claiming to be defectors from the Cuban air force. Their story came apart almost at the moment reporters began to quiz them. They and their planes were identified as belonging to the CIA. In Cuba, they had missed most of their targets. Much of Castro's air strength survived. Its planes strafed the landing parties and sank 2 of the exiles' 4 freighters, including the one with most of their communications equipment. Meanwhile Castro's land forces arrived in the area in overwhelming force. And the rest of Cuba remained free of any uprisings. The 1,000 survivors soon surrendered.

Even though U.S. sponsorship of the landing had been effectively proved by the unmasking of the pilots, Kennedy stuck to the position he had taken earlier. He rejected pleas from Bissell and others that he order U.S. Navy and Air Force units into action to support the exiles. When asked at a press conference, he declined to criticize the CIA. "There's an old saying that victory has a hundred fathers and defeat is an orphan," he replied. "I am the responsible officer of this government." Later he told Dulles and Bissell that, after a decent interval, they would have to leave. "In a parliamentary system I would resign," he said. "In our system the President can't and doesn't. So you . . . must go."

The Bay of Pigs affair had many consequences important for the subsequent missile crisis. . . . Hard-line Cuban exiles never came close to forgiving [President Kennedy]. Nor did Americans who were as much old-fashioned nationalists as anti-Communists. For them, Cuba was as American as apple pie. Its being Communist was intolerable. In their eyes, Kennedy was a gutless appeaser. In varying degrees, this was also a common verdict among senior military officers, particularly in the Navy and Air Force, and in the CIA's Clandestine Service. Awareness of anger and contempt carrying over from the Bay of Pigs affair would affect Kennedy and others during the crisis of October 1962.

A second, closely related consequence of the affair was the development within Kennedy's inner circle of personal animus against Castro. Kennedy, and his brother even more, longed for some redeeming opportunity. They organized a new set of covert operations, code-named Mongoose, to stir up trouble in Cuba and, if opportunity offered, to bring down Castro. Some looked to assassination of Castro. . . .

Anxious to be ready in case anything came of Mongoose, the President and the Attorney General saw to it that the military services prepared for possible intervention. As a result, the JCS put on a "first priority basis" the drafting of contingency plans. The U.S. Air Force's Tactical Air Command, which had responsibility for providing air support for ground operations, drew up specifications for an air campaign designed to precede amphibious landings. [General Curtis] LeMay, as Chief of Staff of the Air Force, approved it. On October 6, 1962, his government agitated by shipments of Soviet arms to Cuba, the Commander-in-Chief of U.S. Forces in the Atlantic (CINCLANT), Admiral Robert L. Dennison, ordered urgent preparations to carry out the landings themselves. Thus, when Kennedy and his advisers considered invasion of Cuba, it was an option that the military services were much better prepared to carry out than might have been the case, absent the earlier Bay of Pigs affair. . . .

Kennedy also made changes in his relationship with the military establishment. The behavior of the JCS regarding the Bay of Pigs affair enraged him. "Those sons-of-bitches with all the fruit salad just sat there nodding, saying it would work," he complained. Kennedy was particularly angry at the JCS Chairman, Army General Lyman Lemnitzer. He added [General] Maxwell Taylor to his White House staff as someone to interpret for him communications from the Chiefs. As soon as Lemnitzer's term ran out, Kennedy made Taylor JCS Chairman. During the missile crisis, Kennedy could know that what he heard about the views of military leaders came form a man whom he had chosen and whom he had calibrated.

The Bay of Pigs affair also had effects on Kennedy's style of decision-making. Afterward, he recognized that he had not only listened to too few advisers but that he had given the issues too little time. . . .

When the missile crisis arrived, Kennedy applied the lessons taught him by the Bay of Pigs affair. From the outset, he assembled a comparatively large circle of advisers, not all of whom were obvious choices. He included Treasury Secretary [Douglas] Dillon. He brought in State Department experts on both the Soviet Union and Latin America. To be sure that knowledge and wisdom from the past were not ignored, he also brought in Dean Acheson, Robert A. Lovett, and John J. McCloy, key figures from the Truman administration. And, as the records . . . testify, he squeezed from these advisers everything they could say about the options open to him. If there were flaws in Kennedy's decision-making during the missile crisis, they are the exact opposite of those in the Bay of Pigs affair. . . .

By early 1962, Kennedy's own feelings about Castro and Cuba seemed to have cooled. At the very beginning of the year, his brother was pushing Mongoose with undiminished energy. The overthrow of Castro had "top priority," Robert Kennedy reportedly told the Mongoose team; "No time, money, effort—or manpower is to be spared." But the operating head of the team, General Edward Lansdale, complained not long afterward that there had actually been no high-level decision for follow-on military intervention. By the beginning of March, Lansdale understood that he was to cut back to a program of limited action not inconsistent with stated U.S. policy, which denied any intention of going beyond isolating Cuba and limiting Cuban influence. At the end of April Kennedy held a meeting—the last of 1962, so far as we know—with Cuban exile leaders who were supposed to have formed a government, had the Bay of Pigs landing succeeded. They went away frustrated, because Kennedy refused either to set up training camps for a new landing attempt or to indicate that he would eventually approve an armed invasion.

The probable reason for Kennedy's lessened interest in Cuba was rising concern about Berlin [where in August 1961 the East German government began erecting the Berlin Wall]. . . .

In March 1962 Khrushchev returned to the attack, telling Kennedy in a private communication that, in his view, Berlin had to become a demilitarized free city. State Department experts told the President that they thought Khrushchev had given up hope of negotiating satisfactory terms for Berlin. In July Kennedy received another private letter from Khrushchev, in which the Soviet leader rambled on about possibly replacing Western military forces in Berlin with UN police units. The U.S. ambassador in Moscow and experts in the State Department voiced worry, as did European leaders. . . .

In August Kennedy's attention was pulled back to Cuba. On New Year's Day 1962, when Castro paraded his military forces, U.S. informants in Havana had reported his display of Soviet-built MiG fighters, mostly of comparatively out-of-date design. They saw no other weaponry worth special comment. In July, however, Cuba's Defense Minister, Castro's brother, Raul, spent two weeks in Moscow. Not long afterward the CIA reported Soviet freighters steaming for Cuba with what appeared to be military cargo on board, and CIA informants in Cuba relayed numerous reports of military equipment arriving at Cuban ports and moving to interior areas under Soviet guard.

Noting that the reports from informants were scattered and contradictory, CIA analysts offered a cautious judgment that the Soviet shipments were probably surface-to-air air defense missiles (SAMs) and that some of the other equipment consisted of radar and electronic gear associated with such missiles. [John A.] McCone, the Director of Central Intelligence (DCI), nevertheless began to send Kennedy, Rusk, and others a stream of communications stating his personal opinion that the Soviets might be planning to base medium-range ballistic missiles (MRBMs) in Cuba. He made the point that the longest range Soviet SAMs, the SA-2s, were indistinguishable from MRBMs with a 350-mile range. . . .

Even if Kennedy felt as much concern about Cuba as McCone . . . that concern was probably short-lived. . . . Kennedy learned that U-2 flights over Cuba had discerned nothing except work on SAM sites and emplacements of short-range cruise missiles (or pilotless aircraft) designed for shore defense. Intelligence data thus reinforced the earlier assurances from Khrushchev. And these assurances were repeated by the amiable Soviet ambassador, Anatoly Dobrynin, who spoke with Robert Kennedy and soon afterward with U.S. Ambassador to the UN Adlai Stevenson, saying flatly to each that the Soviet government had no intention whatever of using Cuba as an offensive military base. What Dobrynin said privately was then said publicly out of Moscow by the authoritative official TASS news service.

Kennedy now had reason for wanting to believe what the Russians were saying, for Republicans had begun to charge the administration with looking the other way while the Soviets converted Cuba into a missile base. Probably on the basis of human intelligence reports leaked to or summarized for him by a disgruntled Navy intelligence officer, Republican Senator Kenneth Keating of New York charged on the floor of the Senate that there were "Soviet rocket installations in Cuba." This charge by Keating provoked Kennedy's public declaration that Soviet weaponry in Cuba was all defensive but that, were it to be otherwise, "the gravest issues would arise." Given what he had been told by the CIA and by the Russians themselves, he probably felt confident then that Keating was wrong and that his statement was safe. . . .

By mid-October Kennedy and members of his circle had reason to expect a crisis. To them, Khrushchev remained a mystifying figure. In early 1962, they knew, Khrushchev had suffered domestic setbacks. He had had to admit to shortfalls in his announced goals for increased food production and, indeed, to raise state-controlled food prices. He had also backed away from previously announced plans to reduce spending on traditional branches of the armed forces in order to strengthen the new Strategic Rocket Forces. This evidence suggested that Khrushchev might need an offsetting foreign policy success. Other evidence suggested that he might not have taken at full value U.S. efforts to demonstrate determination not to yield on Berlin. . . .

. . . That the focus of crisis turned out to be Cuba must have come as a shock to all of them, except possibly McCone. . . .

Throughout the crisis, the Americans asked themselves repeatedly why the Soviets had decided to put missiles in Cuba despite Kennedy's explicit and repeated warnings. They differed in their guesses as to how the Soviets would react to U.S. statements and actions and why the Soviets did what they actually did. Why, for example, did most ships subject to Moscow's orders stop sailing for Cuba while some, particularly the *Gronzy,* kept going? Why did Soviet-manned SAM crews do nothing about U-2 flights from October 14 through October 26, then shoot one down on October 27? Why did Khrushchev change his terms for withdrawing the missiles? In the long private message received late on October 26, he seemed to say his only condition was a U.S. promise not to invade Cuba. In the message publicly broadcast on the morning of October 27 (U.S. time), he called in addition for removal of U.S. "offensive means" from Turkey. Why? And why, having publicly adopted this position, did Khrushchev back down on October 28?

Owing to the passage of time, the publication of memoirs by Khrushchev and others, and, most recently, a study by [the scholars] Aleksandr Fursenko and Timothy Naftali, based not only on newly opened archives but on Presidium and KGB files not yet accessible to other scholars, we have information on these questions well beyond that available to Kennedy and his circle. The two main findings are these. First, Kennedy and his advisers did not make any serious misjudgments about the Soviets; most of what we know now confirms what was surmised by Kennedy's "demonologists," especially [U.S. ambassador to Moscow Llewellyn E.] Thompson. Second, our best retrospective judgments about the Soviet side still entail guesswork; in all probability, no one will ever be able to answer with complete confidence *any* of the questions about the Soviets that bothered Kennedy and his advisers. . . .

To explain the original Soviet decision, Kennedy and his advisers considered several hypotheses. Their favorite was that Khrushchev intended the missiles in Cuba as levers to loosen U.S. concessions regarding Berlin. A second hypothesis focused on the strategic balance. The Joint Chiefs of Staff, for example, presumed that Khrushchev had gambled as he did in order to get wider target coverage against the United States and offset the American lead in ICBMs [Intercontinental Ballistic Missiles]. A third hypothesis was that Khrushchev had acted in order to protect Cuba from invasion. The only person in the Executive Committee who came close to asserting this view was Thompson, who argued, in the afternoon meeting of October 27, that the Jupiters in Turkey were of secondary interest to the Soviets. "The important thing for Khrushchev," he said, "is to be able to say: I saved Cuba. I stopped an invasion." (But Thompson was speaking then of how Khrushchev could save face; he was not necessarily saying that defense of Cuba had been uppermost among Khrushchev's original motives.) A fourth hypothesis presumed factional interplay in the Kremlin. Thus, whatever the motive or motives, they might not be Khrushchev's own. To account for the difference in content between Khrushchev's private letter and broadcast message, [National Security Affairs Adviser McGeorge] Bundy hazarded that the former was Khrushchev's, the latter that of "hard-nosed people overruling him."

Since 1962 no other hypotheses have been advanced to supplement the four voiced by Kennedy and his advisers. But they have had different fates. Berlin, oddly, dropped from sight. Hardly anyone writing retrospectively about the crisis, except the participants, stressed Berlin as a possible primary factor in Soviet decisions. The strategic-balance hypothesis proved more hardy. Two RAND analysts wrote a book not long after the crisis, developing at length the strategic-balance rationale for Khrushchev's actions. This argument has remained an important strain in writings about the crisis by historians and political scientists specializing in international relations or security studies. But the defense-of-Cuba hypothesis has proved the most robust and longest-lived, especially among historians. This view has derived its strength and longevity not only from the United States' demonstrated "arrogance of power" (in Senator Fulbright's phrase) before, during, and since the Vietnam War but also from documentary revelations concerning Operation Mongoose and precrisis invasion planning, as well as testimony from Khrushchev and other Russians.

What we now know indicates that Kennedy and his advisers understood the reasoning in the Kremlin better than have most scholars writing about the crisis in retrospect. While Khrushchev and his colleagues did indeed care a great deal about Cuba, the thought of deterring a U.S. invasion figured only incidentally in their discussions about the missile deployments. Calculations about the strategic nuclear balance were much more in evidence. Berlin was an omnipresent and dominating concern.

To summarize what we now know about Soviet deliberations in 1962 is not, however, to state a final verdict on the motives guiding Soviet behavior before and during the crisis. The more we learn about Soviet decision-making in the Khrushchev era, the less confidence we can feel in any analyses that explain decisions in terms of a hierarchy of interest calculations. Eight points emerge from the accumulating evidence:

1. To interpret Soviet decisions is to interpret Khrushchev. He alone decided on policy. Other members of the Soviet elite who favored other policies could have their way only when Khrushchev was not around or not paying attention. No one could overrule him—yet.

2. Khrushchev made decisions largely on his own. Now and then, he would talk over a question with a fellow member of the Politburo or someone from the bureaucracy, but he did not systematically seek even advice, let alone policy analysis. He looked upon other members of the Politburo as potential enemies. He may have had some respect for military leaders; he treasured memories of working with generals on the Ukrainian front in World War II. But he probably heeded military men only with regard to narrowly military issues . . .

3. Khrushchev acted more from instinct than from calculation. Whether Berlin or the strategic balance or concern about Cuba was uppermost in is mind at the time he ordered the missiles sent to Cuba, he himself could probably not have said. Having made a decision, however, he tended not to entertain second thoughts unless and until he had no choice. In both foreign and domestic affairs, he behaved like a roulette player who chooses a number and puts chips on the number until it produces a big payoff or the stack of chips has disappeared. . . .

4. Khrushchev's instincts in foreign affairs were disciplined by relatively little experience or knowledge. Sixty-eight in 1962, he had been a coal miner as a youth and then a party functionary for most of his life. He was a party boss in Moscow at the time of Stalin's death, when, by outmaneuvering better-educated and less plebeian rivals, he became number one in the hierarchy. For practical purposes, he did not think at all about the world outside the Soviet Union until the mid-1950s, when

it fell to him to test whether Stalin had been right in prophesying that the capitalist-imperialists would wring the necks of his successors. His first encounter with capitalist-imperialist leaders came when he met Eisenhower at the Geneva summit conference in 1955.

5. The framework into which Khrushchev fitted what he learned about the outside world was built around a rather simplistic version of Marxism-Leninism. Although he was intelligent, quick, shrewd, and capable of subtlety, his observations of the outside world were influenced by tenets he had absorbed and taught in his decades of party work. . . .

6. Because of his narrow experience of the outside world, Khrushchev probably misread Kennedy. At Geneva in 1955, he had been a bit awed by Eisenhower. He changed his estimate a bit when he visited the United States in 1959 and saw an Eisenhower weakened by medical problems and on his way out of power. When he saw Kennedy in 1961 at [a summit meeting in] Vienna, Khrushchev was more impressed than he had expected to be by the "young millionaire and . . . son of a millionaire," but whereas he had come away from Geneva crediting Eisenhower with toughness, he came away from Vienna crediting Kennedy with "flexibility." He would later praise Kennedy for being "realistic enough to see that now the might of the socialist world equaled that of the capitalist world."

7. Khrushchev's thinking about foreign affairs had been molded by the Suez-Hungary crisis of 1956. Before that crisis, the United States had treated the Soviet Union as on a par with Britain and France. During the crisis, the United States temporarily broke with the British and French, deploring their surprise attack on Egypt and demanding that they desist. Khrushchev joined in this demand. Blustering, he threatened the British that, if they did not pull out of Egypt, the Soviet Union might use its "modern destructive weapons." The British and French did withdraw, largely because of diplomatic and economic pressure from Washington, but Khrushchev credited his threats with having had decisive effect. . . .

8. Khrushchev's decisions were influenced by Kremlin politics, but not in the way suggested by Bundy's reference to his "hard-nosed people." Although Khrushchev was in absolute control in Moscow, he knew that he might on almost any day find himself absolutely not in control. After Stalin's death, police head Lavrenti Beria and Premier Georgi Malenkov had formed, along with Khrushchev, a ruling triumvirate. Beria had been removed from power by gunfire, arranged for him by Khrushchev and Malenkov. As indication that Soviet politics were becoming more humane, Malenkov's removal involved mere demotion. Similar things happened to other Khrushchev opponents. Murder went out of fashion. But Khrushchev could never for a single day forget that he, too, might receive the Soviet equivalent of the black spot. . . .

A few years later, as he dictated his memoirs, Khrushchev remembered that during an official visit to Bulgaria, from May 14 to 20, 1962, "one thought kept hammering at my brain: what will happen if we lose Cuba?" We now know that Soviet-Cuban relations were deeper and much more complex than Americans realized. The Soviets had begun providing covert assistance to the Castro government in the spring of 1959, and secretly arranged the first sales of arms that autumn, well before the U.S. government had decided whether Castro would be a friend or foe.

Some Americans and many Cubans suspected that the Castro regime harbored a secret radical agenda, that the security ministries were being brought under the control of pro-Soviet Communists in order to pursue this revolutionary agenda at home and abroad, and that this faction included Fidel Castro's brother, Raul, and [the legendary Marxist] Che Guevara, if not Fidel himself. Evidence from Soviet files shows that these suspicions were well founded. . . .

[However,] on May 12, in the midst of the key decisions about sending missiles to Cuba, Khrushchev spent about 14 hours with Kennedy's press aide, Pierre Salinger, then visiting Moscow. He barely mentioned Cuba. The central issue, Khrushchev said, was Berlin. Dobrynin, who took up his post at about this time, remembered that "Germany and Berlin overshadowed everything." Describing what he expected to be his position when negotiations on Berlin resumed, Khrushchev had written to Kennedy in 1961: "You have to understand, I have no ground to retreat further, there is a precipice behind."

The expression "precipice behind" vividly conveys the value Khrushchev now attached to success on Berlin. In another letter to Kennedy, Khrushchev protested that Washington's willingness to threaten a nuclear war to protect Berlin "can rest, excuse my harsh judgments, only on the megalomania, on an intention to act from the position of strength." In March 1962 he had promised Kennedy that "one way or another" he would force the Western troops out. In late April the negotiations in Geneva between [foreign minister Andrei] Gromyko and [Secretary of State Dean] Rusk had reached a stalemate over Berlin. Angering his West German allies, Kennedy had been willing to offer a *modus vivendi* that might allow the status quo to continue. But this had not been good enough for the Soviet government, which denounced the failure of the talks at the end of April.

Thus, in late April and early May 1962, when Khrushchev was in the final stages of his decision to send missiles to Cuba, Berlin clearly had a large place in his thinking. Having issued ultimatums in 1958 and again in 1961, demanding Western departure from Berlin by specified deadlines, and having let those deadlines pass with the promise of successful negotiations to the same end, he was being forced to acknowledge failure publicly. East Germans were demanding a tougher Soviet policy. The Americans, relying on their nuclear superiority, were pursuing a "policy of strength." In March 1962 Khrushchev told Dobrynin, just before the new ambassador left for Washington, that Berlin was the principal issue in U.S.-Soviet relations, said the U.S. was acting "particularly arrogant" about its nuclear deterrent, and concluded, "It's high time their long arms were cut shorter." He liked Kennedy and considered him a man of character, yet he also clearly believed "that putting pressure on Kennedy might bring us some success."

In Moscow, Ambassador Thompson, ignorant of Khrushchev's plans to send missiles to Cuba, was puzzled. No American knew Khrushchev better or had followed his positions more closely. Thompson could not understand why Khrushchev was increasing pressure on Berlin. "He must surely know our position is firm," and "it does not seem reasonable that he would wish further to commit his personal prestige which [is] already deeply engaged." And the pressure just kept increasing. The Soviets began telling Americans that, though they would wait until after the U.S. congressional elections, the Berlin issue would be forced to a conclusion in November.

By the beginning of September 1962 Khrushchev had arranged to unveil the existence of the missiles in Cuba and publicly sign a treaty with Castro in late November, after the congressional elections. He also planned, probably in a speech to the United Nations on the same trip, to renew his ultimatum for final resolution of the Berlin crisis, demanding the withdrawal of Western troops from their sectors. Khrushchev knew the United States would threaten war if he carried out his ultimatum. But by that time Khrushchev would have the missiles, poised in Cuba, to help him call America's bluff and finally carry his 4-year-old Berlin policy to a successful conclusion. . . .

. . . We believe, with Thompson and the experts in London, that key to Khrushchev's strategy for Berlin in 1962 was missiles in Cuba. The Cuban gamble can thus be seen as a climax in the Cold War. Khrushchev had embarked on a risky Soviet effort to change the way the world perceived the balance of power and then ride that achievement to victory on the great diplomatic issue of the time. Instead Khrushchev failed both in the immediate gamble and in his plans for Berlin. It is not farfetched to characterize the missile crisis as the Pearl Harbor *and* Midway of the Cold War. Never again, even in the crisis years of 1979–1983, would the Soviet challenge or the Western response be so direct and so intense.

Certainly Berlin was never far from President Kennedy's thoughts. He refers to it constantly, calculating every move in light of its probable impact there. Only after the peak of the crisis does he voice his frustration with the ways Berlin has constrained his freedom of action at every turn. The creative solution Kennedy sought to this problem never really emerged. . . .

Another revelation is the extent of President Kennedy's own role in the management of the crisis. Naturally this role is enhanced by the fact of recordings made at the White House, with the President selectively choosing what to record for posterity. Kennedy is also reticent during the first day of the crisis, mostly letting others reason through the problems. Yet by the meeting of October 18 he is shaping the discussion and thinking ahead, and the results of this are apparent in his October 19 meeting with the Joint Chiefs of Staff, in which, alone, he takes on the combined weight of their arguments and has apparently gone far toward making up his mind, even before the oft-recounted discussions later that day at the State Department. From October 22 onward Kennedy is dominating the meetings. . . .

. . . We come to know Kennedy better in these recordings, and his advisers too. Robert Kennedy, whether alone with his brother or in a group, is quick and insightful. Sorensen usually stays in the background. Bundy is unsettled during the first week about what to do, offering many questions but fewer answers, but seems to become stronger and more focused as the crisis develops.

Rusk, too, seems to offer clearer advice later in the crisis. He is often the voice of caution. Though at the outset of the crisis [Secretary of Defense Robert S.] McNamara slows the rush toward military action with his pointed questions and forceful presentations, he becomes increasingly consumed, as the crisis wears on, by the task of managing the spiraling military preparations, and he becomes more expectant of the need to use them. Referring to the missiles, he comments on October 25, "I'd never have thought we'd get them out of Cuba without the application of substantial force."

Taylor and McCone have a consistent stand that President Kennedy understands, and for which he always has some sympathy. Kennedy respects their professional opinion. He apparently has little faith in the judgment of Taylor's colleagues, who, unlike Taylor, appear to make little effort to understand the President's problems. This quality of empathy was one that President Kennedy valued highly and often practiced in his clinical, ironic way.

Once the blockade is securely in place, after October 24, the crisis moves toward the climactic issue of whether or not Khrushchev will agree to stop construction and pull out the "offensive weapons" he has already deployed in Cuba. The Americans are plainly feeling time pressure to resolve the matter, with the military planning for a strike before the end of the month. The pressure seems to be related to the missile buildup. . . .

The turning point of the crisis may have been October 25, the day that Khrushchev decided that he would withdraw the missiles on terms that would abandon his most important original goals for the deployment. At that moment Khrushchev had made the fundamental decision that he could not so readily change the strategic balance of missile power; nor would he be able to use this new position to break the stalemate over Berlin. The Americans talked with relief about being able to discuss trading useless Jupiters [in Turkey] rather than trading Berlin. What would have happened, had Khrushchev not made this bitter choice, is awful to contemplate. . . .

Perhaps, above all, we observe in this record—more clearly than in any other documents we have ever seen—the contrary pulls of detail on the one hand and belief (or conviction or ideology) on the other. Almost from minute to minute, new information or recognition of some previously unperceived implication in information already at hand or a new argument will change in subtle or sometimes not subtle ways the form or even the character of the issue being addressed. When Kennedy and his advisers learn that the Soviets are putting up IRBMS as well as MRBMs, their understanding of what is at stake clearly changes, though they might have been hard put to explain how or why. Similarly, though they have talked about the possibility of a U-2 being attacked, they have to take stock anew when they face the reality that Major [Rudolph] Anderson's plane actually has been shot down [over Cuba]. . . .

. . . [R]ecall the care taken on the afternoon of October 27 to draft a particular kind of letter to Khrushchev. It is not quite the draft letter suggested by [the U.S. ambassador to the U.N. Adlai] Stevenson or the one suggested by McCone, and the manner of its delivery—through Robert Kennedy—is a deliberate choice. At the same time McNamara is sent out to announce a callup of Air Force reservists. This complex combination of judgments resulted in a particular set of signals sent to Khrushchev, inadequately captured by the conventional assertion: "Kennedy chose to accept Khrushchev's initial offer of October 26." We know that the particular set of signals sent from the White House helped drive Khrushchev to a particular action. He had decided to give in *before* the report came in of Robert Kennedy's talk with Dobrynin. The actual terms of the subsequent settlement were driven, too, by the particular way the American position had been crafted in Kennedy's letter of October 27. . . .

Auxiliary interests, political, bureaucratic, or personal, probably had less to do with how the decisionmakers acted than did filters in their minds formed by their own past experiences. Intellect and conscience alike tell Kennedy and Rusk and others that they cannot be—or seem to be—"appeasers." Kennedy, however, is not unsettled, as someone else might have been, when LeMay says to him on the morning of October 19 regarding the quarantine option, "This is almost as bad as the appeasement at Munich." The author of *Why England Slept* knows that the quarantine is not "Munich." The son of Joe Kennedy also probably feels some empathy when he reads Adlai Stevenson's agonized plea that *everything* be considered negotiable. And Stevenson probably felt steeled to give such advice because he, after all, had been an arch anti-appeaser back when Munich had been news, not shibboleth. . . .

We come away from this study convinced that major policymaking episodes repay the closet possible examination. Only such examination can reconstruct key judgments within the little worlds in which they are made. Only by penetrating these worlds can we truly understand and evaluate that extraordinary human faculty that we label "judgment." And only by doing that can we learn to do better. Reconstruction that oversimplifies or ignores the incessant tension between realities and beliefs makes us no wiser. By coming fully to grips with the particulars of past moments of choice, we may become better able to handle our own.

Spinning Out of Control: Kennedy's War Against Cuba and the Missile Crisis

THOMAS G. PATERSON

"My God," muttered Richard Helms of the Central Intelligence Agency, "these Kennedys keep the pressure on about [Fidel] Castro." Another CIA officer heard it straight from John F. and Robert F. Kennedy: "Get off your ass about Cuba." Defense Secretary Robert McNamara remembered that "we were hysterical about Castro at the time of the Bay of Pigs and thereafter." When White House assistant Arthur Schlesinger, Jr., returned from an early 1962 overseas trip, he told the president that people abroad thought that the administration was "obsessed with Cuba." President Kennedy himself acknowledged during the missile crisis that "most allies regard [Cuba] as a fixation of the United States."

This essay seeks, first, to explain the U.S. "fixation" with Cuba in the early 1960s, identifying the sources and negative consequences of the Kennedy administration's multitrack war against Cuba. Second, to demonstrate the considerable American responsibility for the onset of the dangerous missile crisis of fall 1962. Third, to explore Kennedy's handling of the crisis, questioning the thesis of deft, cautious management. And, last, to illustrate the persistence of the "fixation" by studying the

Revised for this fifth edition, this essay is based on Thomas G. Paterson, "Fixation with Cuba: The Bay of Pigs, Missile Crisis, and Covert War Against Castro," in Thomas G. Paterson, ed., *Kennedy's Quest for Victory: American Foreign Policy, 1961–1963* (New York: Oxford University Press, 1989), 123–155, 343–352; Thomas G. Paterson, "The Defense-of-Cuba Theme and the Missile Crisis," *Diplomatic History,* XIV (Spring 1990), 249–256; Thomas G. Paterson, *Contesting Castro: The United States and the Triumph of the Cuban Revolution* (New York: Oxford Univeristy Press, 1994); and documents declassified and studies published since the publication of these works.

aftermath of the missile crisis, when the revitalization of the U.S. war against Castro's government set Cuban-American relations on a collision course for decades.

A knowledgeable and engaged President Kennedy spent as much or more time on Cuba as on any other foreign-policy problem. Cuba stood at the center of his administration's greatest failure, the Bay of Pigs, and its alleged greatest success, the missile crisis. Why did President Kennedy and his chief advisers indulge such an obsession with Cuba and direct so many U.S. resources to an unrelenting campaign to monitor, harass, isolate, and ultimately destroy Havana's radical regime? One answer springs from a candid remark by the president's brother, Robert F. Kennedy, who later wondered "if we did not pay a very great price for being more energetic than wise about a lot of things, especially Cuba." The Kennedys' famed eagerness for action became exaggerated in the case of Cuba. They always wanted to get moving on Cuba, and Castro dared them to try. The popular, intelligent, but erratic Cuban leader, who in January 1959 overthrew the U.S. ally Fulgencio Batista, hurled harsh words at Washington and defiantly challenged the Kennedy model of evolutionary, capitalist development so evident in the Alliance for Progress. As charismatic figures charting new frontiers, Kennedy and Castro often personalized the Cuban-American contest. To Kennedy's great annoyance, Castro could not be wheedled or beaten.

Kennedy's ardent war against *fidelismo* may also have stemmed from his feeling that Castro had double-crossed him. As a senator, Kennedy had initially joined many Americans in welcoming the Cuban Revolution as an advancement over the "oppressive" Batista dictatorship. Kennedy had urged a "patient attitude" toward the new government, which he did not see as Communist. Denying repeatedly that he was a Communist, Castro had in fact proclaimed his allegiance to democracy and private property. But in the process of legitimizing his revolution and resisting U.S. pressure, Castro turned more and more radical. Americans grew impatient with the regime's highly-charged anti-Yankeeism, postponement of elections, jailing of critics, and nationalization of property. The president rejected the idea that intense U.S. hostility toward the Cuban Revolution may have contributed to Castro's tightening political grip and flirtation with the Soviet Union. Nor did Kennedy and other Americans wish to acknowledge the measurable benefits of the revolution—improvements in education, medical care, and housing, and the elimination of the island's infamous corruption that once had been the American mafia's domain. Instead, Kennedy officials concluded that Cuba's was a "betrayed revolution."

Richard N. Goodwin, the young White House and State Department official, provided another explanation for the Kennedy "fixation" with Cuba. He remarked that "the entire history of the Cold War, its positions and assumptions, converged upon the 'problem of Cuba.'" The Cold War dominated international politics, and as Cuban-American relations steadily deteriorated, Cuban-Soviet relations gradually improved. Not only did Americans come to believe that a once-loyal ally had jilted them for the tawdry embrace of the Soviets; they also grew alarmed that Castro sneered at the Monroe Doctrine by inviting the Soviet military to the island. When Castro, in late 1961, declared himself a Marxist-Leninist, Americans who had long denounced him as a Communist then felt vindicated. . . .

American politics also influenced the administration's Cuba policy. In the 1960 presidential campaign, Kennedy had seized the Cuban issue to counter

Richard Nixon's charge that the inexperienced Democratic candidate would abandon Zinmen (Quemoy) and Mazu (Matsu) to Communism and prove no match for the hard-nosed Khrushchev. "In 1952 the Republicans ran on a program of rolling back the Iron Curtain in Eastern Europe," Kennedy jabbed. "Today the Iron Curtain is 90 miles off the coast of the United States." He asked in private, "How would *we* have saved Cuba if we had [had] the power," but he nonetheless valued the political payback from his attack. "What the hell," he informed his aides, "they never told us how they would have saved China." Apparently unaware that President Dwight D. Eisenhower had initiated a clandestine CIA program to train Cuban exiles for an invasion of the island, candidate Kennedy bluntly called for just such a project. After exploiting the Cuban issue, Kennedy, upon becoming president, could not easily have retreated.

Overarching all explanations for Kennedy's obsession with Cuba is a major phenomenon of the second half of the twentieth century: the steady erosion of the authority of imperial powers, which had built systems of dependent, client, and colonial governments. The strong currents of decolonization, anti-imperialism, revolutionary nationalism, and social revolution, sometimes in combination, undermined the instruments the imperial nations had used to maintain control and order. The Cuban Revolution exemplified this process of breaking up and breaking away. American leaders reacted so hostilely to this revolution not simply because Castro and his 26th of July Movement taunted them or because domestic politics and the Cold War swayed them, but also because Cuba, as symbol and reality, challenged U.S. hegemony in Latin America. The specter of "another Cuba" haunted President Kennedy, not just because it would hurt him politically, but because "the game would be up through a good deal of Latin America," as Under Secretary of State George Ball put it. The Monroe Doctrine and the U.S. claim to political, economic, and military leadership in the hemisphere seemed at stake. As Castro once remarked, "the United States *had* to fight his revolution."

The Eisenhower Administration bequeathed to its successor an unproductive tit-for-tat process of confrontation with Cuba and a legacy of failure. In November 1959, President Eisenhower decided to encourage anti-Castro groups within Cuba to "replace" the revolutionary regime and thus end an anti-Americanism that was "having serious adverse effects on the United States position in Latin America and corresponding advantages for international Communism." In March 1960 Eisenhower ordered the CIA to train Cuban exiles for an invasion of their homeland—this shortly after Cuba signed a trade treaty with the Soviet Union. The CIA, as well, hatched assassination plots against Castro and staged hit-and-run attacks along the Cuban coast. As Cuba undertook land reform that struck at American interests and nationalized American-owned industries, the United States suspended Cuba's sugar quota and forbade American exports to the island, drastically cutting a once-flourishing commerce. On January 3, 1961, fearing an invasion and certain that the U.S. embassy was a "nest of spies" aligned with counterrevolutionaries who were burning cane fields and sabotaging buildings, Castro demanded that the embassy staff be greatly reduced. Washington promptly broke diplomatic relations with Havana.

Eisenhower failed to topple Castro, but U.S. pressure accelerated the radicalization of the revolution and helped open the door to the Soviets. Moscow bought sugar, supplied technicians, armed the militia, and offered generous trade terms. Although the revolution's radicalization was probably inevitable given Cuban conditions, it was not inexorable that Cuba would end up in the Soviet camp. Hostile U.S. policies helped ensure that outcome.

To be sure, Kennedy inherited the Cuban problem from Eisenhower. But he did not simply continue his predecessor's anti-Castro policies. Kennedy greatly exaggerated the Cuban threat, attributing to Castro a capability to export revolution that the Cuban leader never had. Castro was "an affront to our pride" and a "mischief maker," the journalist Walter Lippmann wisely wrote, but he was not a "mortal threat" to the United States. Kennedy significantly increased the pressures against the upstart island. He inherited the Cuban problem—and he made it worse.

The questions of whether and under what conditions to approve an exile expedition dominated the president's discussion of Cuba in his first few months in office. Although Kennedy always reserved the authority to cancel the operation right up to the moment of departure, his choices pointed in one direction: Go. National security affairs adviser McGeorge Bundy later said that the president "really was looking for ways to make it work . . . and allowed himself to be persuaded it would work and the risks were acceptable."

The plan to invade Cuba at the Bay of Pigs began to unravel from the start. As the brigade's old, slow freighters plowed their way to the island, B-26 airplanes took to the skies from Nicaragua. On April 15, D-Day-minus-2, the brigade pilots destroyed several parked planes of Castro's meager air force. That same day, as part of a pre-invasion ploy, a lone, artificially damaged B-26 flew directly to Miami, where its pilot claimed that he had defected from the Cuban military and had just bombed his country's airfields. But the cover story soon cracked. Snooping journalists noticed that the nose cone of the B-26 was metal; Cuban planes had plastic noses. They observed too that the aircraft's guns had not been fired. The American hand was being exposed. The president, still insistent upon hiding U.S. complicity, decided to cancel a second D-Day strike against the remnants of the Cuban air force.

Shortly after midnight on April 17, more than 1,400 commandoes motored in small boats to the beaches at Bahía de Cochinos. The invaders immediately tangled with Castro's militia. Some commandoes never made it, because their boats broke apart on razor-sharp coral reefs. In the air, Castro's marauding airplanes shot down two brigade B-26s and sank ships carrying essential communications equipment and ammunition. Fighting ferociously, the brigade nonetheless failed to establish a beachhead. Would Washington try to salvage the mission? Kennedy turned down desperate CIA appeals to dispatch planes from the nearby U.S.S. *Essex,* but he did permit some jets to provide air cover for a new B-26 attack from Nicaragua. Manned this time by American CIA pilots, the B-26s arrived an hour after the jets had come and gone. Cuban aircraft downed the B-26s, killing four Americans. With Castro's boasting that the *mercenarios* had been foiled, the final toll proved grim: 114 of the exile brigade dead and 1,189 captured. One hundred-and-fifty Cuban defenders died.

Failures in intelligence, operations, decisionmaking, and judgment doomed the Bay of Pigs undertaking. Arrogant CIA architects knew too little about the landing site and assumed too much about Cuba. The agency's inspector general, for example, wrote in a post-invasion critique that the CIA "had no intelligence evidence that Cubans in significant numbers could or would join the invaders. . . ." The CIA also failed to assassinate Fidel Castro. As a CIA official admitted, the agency had intended "that Castro would be dead before the landing."

The most controversial operational question remains the cancelled second D-day air strike. Post-crisis critics have complained that the president lost his nerve and made a decision that condemned the expedition to disaster. Cuban air supremacy did prove important to Cuba's triumph. But was it decisive? A preemptive strike on D-Day against the Cuban air force would not have delivered victory to the invaders. After the first air attack, Castro had dispersed his planes; the brigade's B-26s would have encountered considerable difficulty in locating and destroying them. And, even if a D-Day assault had disabled all of Castro's planes, then what? The brigade's 1,400 warriors would have had to face Castro's army of 25,000 and the nation's 200,000 militia. The commandoes most likely would not have survived the overwhelming power of the Cuban military. . . .

Defeat did not chasten the Kennedys. On April 20, the president spoke out. "Let the record show," he boomed, "that our restraint is not inexhaustible." Indeed, the United States intended to defend the Monroe Doctrine and carry on a "relentless" struggle with Communism in "every corner of the globe." In familiar words, Kennedy declared that "the complacent, the self-indulgent, the soft societies are about to be swept away with the debris of history. Only the strong . . . can possibly survive." Attorney General Robert Kennedy remarked that the Bay of Pigs "insult needed to be redressed rather quickly."

Critical to understanding the frightening missile crisis of fall 1962 is the relationship between post–Bay of Pigs U.S. activities and the Soviet/Cuban decisions to place on the island nuclear-tipped missiles that could strike the United States, endangering the lives of 92 million people. In late April, after hearing from Cuban leaders that they expected a direct U.S. invasion and sought Soviet help to resist an attack, and after protesting the deployment of U.S. intermediate-range Jupiter missiles in Turkey, Nikita Khrushchev began to think about a missile deployment in Cuba; in late May, after dismissing the skepticism of some key advisers who judged his plan provocative to the United States and therefore highly explosive, he made the offer of missiles to Fidel Castro, who quickly accepted them; in early July, Raúl Castro initialed a draft agreement in Moscow; and in late August and early September, during a trip by Che Guevara to Moscow, the two nations put the treaty into final form. The plan called for the Soviets' installation on the island of forty-eight medium-range ballistic missiles (SS-4s with a range of 1,020 miles), thirty-two intermediate-range ballistic missiles (SS-5s with a range of 2,200 miles), 144 surface-to-air missiles (SAMs), theater-nuclear weapons (Lunas), forty-eight IL-28 light bombers (with a range of 600 miles), and 42,000 Soviet combat troops.

After the Bay of Pigs, the Kennedy administration launched a multitrack program of covert, economic, diplomatic, and propagandistic elements calculated to overthrow the Castro government. This multidimensional project prompted the Cuban/Soviet decisions of mid-1962. Secretary of Defense Robert McNamara said later: "If I had been in Moscow or Havana at that time [1961–1962], I would have believed the Americans were preparing for an invasion." Indeed, Havana had to fear a successful Bay of Pigs operation conducted by U.S. forces.

Encouraged by the White House, the CIA created a huge station in Miami called JMWAVE to recruit and organize Cuban exiles. In Washington, Robert Kennedy became a ramrod for action. At a November 4, 1961, White House meeting, the Attorney General insisted: "stir things up on the island with espionage, sabotage, general disorder. . . ." The president himself asked Colonel Edward Lansdale to direct Operation Mongoose—"to use our available assets . . . to help Cuba overthrow the Communist regime." Operation Mongoose and JMWAVE, although failing to unseat Castro, punished Cubans. CIA-handled saboteurs burned cane fields and blew up factories and oil storage tanks. In a December 1961 raid, for example, a seven-man team blasted a railroad bridge, derailed an approaching train, and torched a sugar warehouse. One group, Agrupacíon Montecristi, attacked a Cuban patrol boat off the northern coast of the island in May 1962. Directorio Revolucionario Estudiantil, another exile organization, used two boats to attack Cuba in August, hoping to hit a hotel where Castro was dining.

The CIA, meanwhile, devised new plots to kill Castro with poisonous cigars, pills, and needles. To no avail. Did the Kennedys know about these death schemes? In May 1961, Federal Bureau of Investigation Director J. Edgar Hoover informed Robert Kennedy that the CIA had hired mafia boss Sam Giancana to do some "dirty business" in Cuba. Kennedy noted on the margin of the Hoover memorandum that this information should be "followed up vigorously." A year later, the CIA briefed the attorney general about its use of mafia gangsters to assassinate Castro. If his brother Robert knew about these CIA assassination plots, the president surely did, for Robert was John's closest confidant. They kept little if anything from one another. President Kennedy apparently never directly ordered the assassination of Castro—at least no trail of documents leads to the White House. But, of course, nobody uttered the word "assassination" in the presence of the president or committed the word to paper, thereby honoring the principle of plausible deniability. Advisers instead simply mentioned the need to remove Castro. "And if killing him was one of the things that was to be done in this connection," assassination was attempted because "we felt we were acting within the guidelines," said the CIA's Richard Helms.

Intensified economic coercion joined these covert activities. The Kennedy administration, in February 1962, banned most imports of Cuban products. Washington also pressed its North Atlantic Treaty Organization allies to support the "economic isolation" of Cuba. The embargo hurt. Cuba had to pay higher freight costs, enlarge its foreign debt, and suffer innumerable factory shut-downs due to the lack of spare parts once bought in the United States. Cuba's economic woes also stemmed from the flight of technicians and managers, a decline in tourism, high workers' absenteeism rates, the drying up of foreign capital investment, hastily conceived policies to diversify the economy, and suffocating government controls.

The Kennedy administration also engineered the ouster of Cuba from the Organization of American States in early 1962. The expulsion registered loudly in Havana, which interpreted it as "political preparation for an invasion." By spring 1962, moreover, fifteen Latin American states had answered Washington's call to break relations with Cuba.

At about the same time, American military planning and activities, some public, some secret, demonstrated a determination to cripple the Castro government.

Operation Mongoose director Lansdale noted in a top-secret memorandum to the president that he designed his schemes to "help the people of Cuba overthrow the Communist regime from within Cuba and institute a new government." But, he asked: "If conditions and assets permitting a revolt [timed for October 1962] are achieved in Cuba, and if U.S. help is required to sustain this condition, will the U.S. respond promptly with military force to aid the Cuban revolt?" Lansdale gave the answer he preferred: "The basic plan requires complete and efficient support of the military." A U.S. Army memorandum dated March 1 proposed several ways to upend Castro, including Operation Bingo (staging a fake attack on the U.S. naval base at Guantánamo, at the eastern end of Cuba, and then using it as a pretext to assault Havana), Operation Dirty Trick (should the Mercury manned space flight fail, blaming the disaster on Cuban sabotage), and Operation Good Times (distributing phony photographs of "an obese Castro" with attractive women and plates full of food, with the caption "my ration is different").

Another contemporary document, this one from the chairman of the Joint Chiefs of Staff, General Maxwell Taylor, noted in spring 1962 that the Mongoose plan to overthrow the Cuban government would be undertaken largely by "indigenous resources," but "recognizes that final success will require decisive U.S. military intervention." Because the plan also required close cooperation with Cuban exiles, it is very likely that Castro's spies picked up from the Cuban community in Miami leaks that the U.S. military contemplated military action against Cuba. As CIA agents liked to joke, there were three ways to transmit information rapidly: telegraph, telephone, and tell-a-Cuban. Cuban officials have claimed, in fact, that their intelligence agency had infiltrated anti-Castro exile groups and had learned about some of the activities associated with Lansdale's scheme. Although they surely did not know the details of President Kennedy's National Security Action Memorandum No. 181 (NSAM-181), dated August 23, a directive to engineer an internal revolt that would be followed by U.S. military intervention, the Cubans no doubt began to observe accelerated U.S. actions to achieve that goal.

American military maneuvers heightened Cuban fears. One well publicized U.S. exercise, "Quick-Kick," staged during April and May, included 40,000 troops, seventy-nine ships, and 300 aircraft along the U.S. southeastern coast. An earlier exercise in April included an amphibious Marine landing on a small island near Puerto Rico. Havana protested these exercises as provocations, tests of U.S. war plans against Cuba. Some noisy American politicians, throughout 1962, called for the real thing: an invasion of Cuba. In summer 1962, moreover, the U.S. Army began a program to create Spanish-speaking units; the Cuban exiles who signed up had as their "primary" goal a "return to Cuba to battle against the Fidel Castro regime."

By the late spring and early summer of 1962, then, when Havana and Moscow discussed defensive measures that included missiles with nuclear warheads, Cuba felt besieged from several quarters. The Soviet Union had become its trading partner, and the Soviets, after the Bay of Pigs, had begun military shipments of small arms, howitzers, machine guns, armored personnel carriers, patrol boats, tanks, and MiG jet fighters. Yet all of this weaponry had not deterred the United States. And, given the failure of Kennedy's multitrack program to unseat Castro, "were we right or wrong to fear direct invasion" next, asked Fidel Castro. As he said in mid-1962, shortly after striking the missile-deployment agreement with the Soviets: "We must prepare ourselves for that direct invasion."

Had there been no exile expedition at the Bay of Pigs, no destructive covert activities, no assassination plots, no military maneuvers and plans, and no economic and diplomatic steps to harass, isolate, and destroy the Castro government in Havana, there would not have been a Cuban missile crisis. The origins of the October 1962 crisis derived largely from the concerted U.S. campaign to quash the Cuban Revolution. To stress only the global dimension (Soviet-American competition in the nuclear arms race) is to slight the local origins of the conflict. To slight these sources by suggesting from very incomplete declassified Soviet records that the "thought of deterring a U.S. invasion figured only incidentally" in Moscow's calculations, as argued by Ernest R. May and Philip D. Zelikow, editors of the tape recordings that Kennedy made during the crisis, is to overlook the substantial evidence of Soviet (and Cuban) preoccupation with the defense of Cuba and is to miss the central point that Premier Nikita Khrushchev would never have had the opportunity to install dangerous missiles in the Caribbean if the United States had not been attempting to overthrow the Cuban government. This interpretation does not dismiss the view that the emplacement of nuclear missiles in Cuba also served the Soviet strategic goal of catching up in the nuclear arms race. Rather, the interpretation in this essay emphasizes that both Cuba and the Soviet Union calculated that their interests would be served by putting nuclear-capable rockets on the island. Havana hoped to gain deterrent power to thwart an expected American invasion, and Moscow hoped to save a new socialist ally while enhancing the USSR's deterrent power in the Cold War.

Why did the Cubans and Soviets decide on nuclear-tipped ballistic missiles instead of a military pact, conventional (non-nuclear) forces, or just the battlefield Lunas—in short, weapons that Washington could not label "offensive" because they could not reach the United States? The Cubans sought effective deterrence, or what the historian Mark White has called "the *ultimate* deterrent." One thinks here of similar American thinking, near the end of the Second World War, that the Japanese were so fanatical that only the threat of annihilation from atomic bombs would persuade them to surrender. The Cubans, in fact, looking for an immediate deterrent effect, had wanted to make the 1962 missile agreement public, but the Soviets, guessing that the deployment could be camouflaged until the missiles became operational, preferred secrecy.

On October 14, an American U-2 plane photographed missile sites in Cuba, thus providing the first "hard" evidence, as distinct from the "soft" reports of exiles, that the island was becoming a nuclear base. "He can't do that to me!" snapped Kennedy when he saw the pictures on the 16th. He had warned the Soviets that the United States would not suffer "offensive" weapons in Cuba, although the warnings had come after the Cuban-Soviet agreement of early summer. Shortly before noon on October 16, the president convened his top advisers (a group eventually called the Executive Committee, or ExComm). His first questions focused on the firing readiness of the missiles and the probability that they carried nuclear warheads. The advisers gave tentative answers. All agreed that the missiles could become operational in a brief time. Discussion of military options (invasion? air strike?) dominated this first meeting. Kennedy's immediate preference became clear: "We're certainly going . . . to take out these . . . missiles." Kennedy showed little interest in negotiations. Perhaps his initial tilt toward military action derived from his knowledge of the significant U.S. military plans, maneuvers, and movement of forces and equipment undertaken after he signed NSAM-181, thus making it possible for the United States to respond with military effectiveness.

At a second meeting on the 16th, Secretary of State Dean Rusk argued against the surprise air strike that General Taylor had bluntly advocated. Rusk recommended instead "a direct message to Castro." At the close of Rusk's remarks, Kennedy immediately asked: "Can we get a little idea about what the military thing *is*?" Bundy then asked: "How gravely does this change the strategic balance?" McNamara, for one, thought "not at all," but Taylor disputed him. Kennedy himself seemed uncertain, but he did complain that the missile emplacement in Cuba "makes them look like they're co-equal with us." And, added Treasury Secretary C. Douglas Dillon, who obviously knew the president's competitive personality, the presence of the missiles made it appear that "we're scared of the Cubans."

Then the rambling discussion turned to Khrushchev's motivation. The Soviet leader had been cautious on Berlin, Kennedy said. "It's just as if we suddenly began to put a major number of MRBMs in Turkey," the President went on. "Now that'd be goddam dangerous. . . ." Bundy jumped in: "Well, we *did,* Mr. President." Not liking the sound of a double standard, Kennedy lamely answered, "Yeah, but that was five years ago." Actually, the American Jupiter missiles in Turkey were IRBMs (intermediate-range ballistic missiles) which, under a 1959 agreement with Ankara, had gone into launch position in mid-1961—during the Kennedy administration—and were turned over to Turkish forces on October 22, 1962, the very day Kennedy informed Moscow that it must withdraw its missiles from Cuba.

For the next several days, ExComm met frequently in tight secrecy and discussed four policy options: "talk them out," "squeeze them out," "shoot them out," or "buy them out." In exhausting sessions marked by frank disagreement and changing minds, the president's advisers weighed the advantages and disadvantages of invasion, bombing, quarantine, and diplomacy. The president gradually moved with a majority of ExComm toward a quarantine or blockade of Cuba: incoming ships would be stopped and inspected for military cargo. When queried if an air strike would knock out all of the known missiles General Taylor said that "the best we can offer you is to destroy 90%. . . ." In other words, some missiles in Cuba would remain in place for firing against the United States. Robert Kennedy also worried that the Soviets might react unpredictably with military force, "which could be so serious as to lead to general nuclear war." In any case, the attorney general insisted, there would be no "Pearl Harbor type of attack" on his brother's record.

By October 22 the president had made two decisions. First, to quarantine Cuba to prevent further military shipments and to impress the Soviets with U.S. resolve to force the missiles out. If the Soviets balked, other, more drastic, measures would be undertaken. Second, Kennedy decided to inform the Soviets of U.S. policy through a television address rather than through diplomatic channels. Several advisers dubiously argued that a surprise public speech was necessary to rally world opinion behind U.S. policy and to prevent Khrushchev from issuing an ultimatum, but some ExComm participants recommended that negotiations be tried first. Former ambassador to the Soviet Union Charles Bohlen advised that Moscow would have to retaliate against the United States if its technicians died from American bombs. A stern letter to Khrushchev should be "tested" as a method to gain withdrawal of the missiles. "I don't see the urgency of military action," Bohlen told the president. And ambassador to the United Nations Adlai Stevenson appealed to an unreceptive Kennedy: "the existence of nuclear missile bases anywhere is negotiable before we start anything." Stevenson favored a trade: withdrawing the U.S. Jupiter missiles from Turkey and evacuating the Guantánamo naval base, turning it over to Cuba, in exchange for withdrawal of the Soviet missiles from Cuba. The president, according to the minutes of an October 20 ExComm meeting, "sharply rejected" Stevenson's proposal, especially on the issue of Guantánamo. Two days later, Kennedy once again scolded the ambassador, claiming that withdrawal from the naval base would indicate to Khrushchev "that we were in a state of panic." Going into the crisis, Kennedy refused to negotiate with either Khrushchev or Castro.

In his evening television speech of October 22, Kennedy demanded that the Soviets dismantle the missiles in Cuba, and he announced the Caribbean quarantine as an "initial" step. Later that evening, in a telephone conversation, he told British prime minister Harold Macmillan that U.S. credibility was on the line; if he had not acted, America's resolve to defend Berlin might be questioned and Soviet success in deploying the missiles "would have unhinged us in all of Latin America." The missile crisis soon became an international war of nerves. More than sixty American ships began patrols to enforce the blockade. The Strategic Air Command went on nuclear alert, moving upward to Defense Condition (DEF-CON) 2 for the first time ever (the next level is deployment for combat). B-52 bombers, loaded with nuclear weapons, stood ready, while men and equipment moved to the southeastern United States to prepare for an invasion. The Soviets did not mobilize or redeploy their huge military, nor did they take measures to make their strategic forces less vulnerable. The Soviets also refrained from testing the quarantine: Their ships turned around and went home. But what next? On the 26th, Kennedy and some ExComm members, thinking that the Soviets were stalling, soured on the quarantine. Sentiment for military action strengthened.

On the afternoon of the 26th, an intelligence officer attached to the Soviet embassy, Aleksandr Feklisov (alias Fomin), met with ABC television correspondent John Scali and suggested a solution to the crisis: The Soviet Union would withdraw the missiles if the United States would promise not to invade Cuba. Scali scurried to Secretary of State Dean Rusk, who sent him back to Feklisov with the reply that American leaders were interested in discussing the proposal. As it turns out, and unbeknownst to American leaders, Feklisov was acting on his own and a report of his conversations with Scali did not reach the Soviet foreign secretary in Moscow until the late afternoon of October 27. Feklisov's independent intervention, in other words, did not influence the writing of the two critical letters that Khrushchev sent to Washington on the 26th and 27th, but ExComm thought the Feklisov initiative and Khrushchev's letters were linked, thus clearly signaling an earnest Soviet desire to settle.

Khrushchev's first letter, a rambling emotional private message that ruminated on the horrors of war, offered to withdraw the missiles if the United States pledged not to invade Cuba. The Soviet premier defended the initial installation of the missiles with the argument that the United States had been threatening the island. In the morning of October 27, another Khrushchev letter reached the president. Khrushchev now upped the stakes: He would trade the missiles in Cuba for the American missiles in Turkey. Kennedy felt boxed, because "we are now in the position of risking war in Cuba and in Berlin over missiles in Turkey which are of little military value." At first, Kennedy hesitated to accept a swap—because he did not want to appear to be giving up anything in the face of Soviet provocation; because he knew that the proud Turks would recoil from the appearance of being "traded off in order to appease an enemy"; and because acceptance of a missile trade would lend credence to charges that the United States all along had been applying a doubling standard. Kennedy told ExComm that Khrushchev's offer caused "embarrassment," for most people would think it "a very fair trade." Indeed, Moscow had played "a very good card."

In the afternoon of the 27th, more bad news rocked the White House. An American U-2 plane overflew the eastern part of the Soviet Union, probably because its equipment malfunctioned. "There is always some son of a bitch who doesn't get the word," the president remarked. Soviet fighters scrambled to intercept the U-2, and American fighter jets from Alaska, carrying Falcon missiles with nuclear warheads, took flight to protect the errant aircraft. Although the spy plane flew home without having sparked a dog fight, the incident carried the potential of sending the crisis to a more dangerous level.

Also on the 27th, a U-2 was shot down over Cuba and its pilot killed by a surface-to-air missile (SAM). The shoot-down constituted a serious escalation. A distressed McNamara, not knowing that the order to shoot was made independently by the Soviet air defense commander in Cuba without orders from Moscow, now thought "invasion had become almost inevitable." He urged that U.S. aircraft "go in and take out that SAM site." But Kennedy hesitated to retaliate, surely scared about taking a step in toward a nuclear nightmare. The president decided to ignore Khrushchev's second letter and answer the first. The evening of the 27th, he also dispatched his brother Robert to deliver an ultimatum to Soviet Ambassador Anatoly Dobrynin: Start pulling out the missiles within forty-eight hours or "we would remove them." After Dobrynin asked about the Jupiters in Turkey, Robert Kennedy presented an important American concession: They would be dismantled if the problem in Cuba were resolved. As the president had said in an ExComm meeting, "we can't very well invade Cuba with all its toil . . . when we could have gotten them out by making a deal on the same missiles in Turkey." But, should the Soviets leak word of a "deal," Robert Kennedy told the Soviet ambassador, the United States would disavow the offer. Dobrynin, who judged President Kennedy a "hot-tempered gambler," cabled an account of the meeting to Moscow, pointing out that the "very upset" president's brother insisted that "time is of the essence" and that if another U.S. plane were shot at, the United States would return fire and set off "a chain reaction" toward "a real war."

On October 28, faced with an ultimatum and a concession, and fearful that the Cubans might precipitate a greater Soviet-American conflagration, Khrushchev retreated and accepted the American offer: the Soviet Union would dismantle its missiles under United Nations supervision and the United States would pledge not to invade Cuba. The crisis had ended—just when the nuclear giants seemed about to stumble over the brink. . . .

Many analysts give John F. Kennedy high marks for his handling of the Cuban missile crisis, applauding a stunning success, noble statesmanship, and model of crisis management. Secretary Rusk lauded Kennedy for having "ice water in his veins." The journalist Hugh Sidey has gushed over "the serene leader who guides the nation away from nuclear conflict." Arthur Schlesinger, Jr., has effusively written that Kennedy's crisis leadership constituted a "combination of toughness and restraint, of will, nerve, and wisdom, so brilliantly controlled, so matchlessly calibrated." May and Zelikow celebrate Kennedy's "finest hours," sketching a "lucid" and "calm" president, who, in the end, steps back from the brink.

Kennedy's stewardship of policymaking during the crisis actually stands less as a supreme display of careful crisis management and more as a case of near misses, close calls, narrow squeaks, physical exhaustion, accidents, and guesses that together scared officials on both sides into a settlement, because, in the words of McGeorge Bundy, the crisis was "so near to spinning out of control." When McNamara recalled those weeks, he questioned the entire notion of crisis management because of "misinformation, miscalculation, misjudgment, and human fallibility." "We were in luck," Ambassador John Kenneth Galbraith ruminated, "but success in a lottery is no argument for lotteries."

During the hair-trigger days of the crisis, much went wrong, the level of danger constantly rose, and weary and irritable decisonmakers sensed that they were losing their grip. "A high risk of uncontrollable escalation" dogged the crisis, McNamara recalled. So much came apart; so much could not be reined in. The two U-2 incidents—the shootdown over Cuba and the straying over Soviet territory—rank high on the list. Vice President Lyndon Johnson remarked at an ExComm meeting on October 27: "Imagine some crazy Russian captain" shooting down another American spy plane. Seeing American flares during a night reconnaissance flight, "he might just pull a trigger. Looks like we're playing Fourth of July over there or something. I'm scared of that." There was also the serious possibility that an exile group would attempt to assassinate Castro or raid the island. Operation Mongoose sabotage teams actually maneuvered inside Cuba during the crisis and could not be reached by their CIA handlers. What if this "half-assed operation," Robert Kennedy worried, ignited trouble? One of these teams actually did blow up a Cuban factory on November 8.

Danger lurked too in the way the commander of the Strategic Air Command issued DEFCON 2 alert instructions. He did so in the clear, instead of in code, because he wanted to impress the Soviets. Alerts serve to prepare American forces for war, but they may also provoke an adversary to think that the United States might launch a first strike. Under such circumstances, the adversary might be tempted to strike first. The Navy's antisubmarine warfare activities also carried the potential of escalating the crisis. Soviet submarines prowled near the quarantine line, and, following standing orders, Navy ships forced several of them to surface. In one case, a Navy commander exercised the high-risk option of dropping a depth charge on a Soviet submarine. As in so many of these examples, decisionmakers in Washington actually lost some control of the crisis to personnel at the operational level.

ExComm members represented considerable intellectual talent and experience, but a mythology of grandeur, illusion of control, and embellishment of performance have obscured the history of the committee. ExComm debated alternatives under "intense strain," often in a "state of anxiety and emotional exhaustion," recalled Under Secretary Ball. McGeorge Bundy told Ball on October 24 that he (Bundy) was getting "groggy." Two advisers may have suffered such stress that they became less able to perform their responsibilities. An assistant to Adlai Stevenson recalled that he had had to become an ExComm "back-up" for the ambassador because, "while he could speak clearly, his memory wasn't very clear. . . ." Asked if failing health produced this condition, Vice Admiral Charles Wellborn answered that the "emotional state and nervous tension that was involved in it [missile crisis] had this effect." Stevenson was feeling "pretty frightened." So apparently was Dean Rusk. The president scratched on a notepad during an October 22 meeting: "Rusk rather quiet & somewhat fatigued." Robert Kennedy remembered that the secretary of state "had a virtually complete breakdown mentally and physically." Once, when Rusk's eyes swelled with tears, Dean Acheson barked at him: "Pull yourself together, . . . you're the only secretary of state we have." We cannot determine how stress affected the advice ExComm gave Kennedy, but at least we know that its members struggled against time, sleep, exhaustion, and themselves, and they did not always think clearheadedly at a time when the stakes were very high.

What about the president himself, gravely ill from Addison's disease and often in severe pain because of his ailing back? Dr. Max Jacobson, known as "Dr. Feelgood" by the Hollywood crowd that paid for his services, and a frequent visitor to the White House, administered amphetamines and steroids to President Kennedy during the first days of the missile crisis. Medical doctors have reported that the effect of these unorthodox injections might have been supreme confidence and belligerence. One might speculate that JFK's inclination toward a bold military response at the start of the crisis was influenced by the doses of potent drugs he was taking. As the historian Michael Hunt has noted about ExComm meetings, moreover, the president at times "struggled to put a clear, complete sentence together." Indeed, "the proceedings degenerated at times into a babble that makes ExComm seem more like a kindergarten than a crisis-management team."

As for the Soviets, they too worried about their decisionmaking process and the crisis spinning out of control. Khrushchev, of course, had miscalculated from the outset. He somehow thought that the Americans would not discover the missiles until after all of them had become operational. He had no fallback plan once they were photographed. Because he had never informed his own embassy in Washington that missiles were being placed in Cuba, he had cut himself off from critical advice—counsel that would have alerted him to the certain vigorous U.S. response to the emplacement. "He was so confused," Dobrynin remarked after the crisis. Khrushchev's letter of October 26 to Kennedy betrayed desperation, if not disarray in the Kremlin: "You and I should not now pull on the ends of the rope in which you have tied a knot of war, because . . . [we might unleash the] dread forces our two countries possess." As the shootdown of the U-2 over Cuba demonstrated, Khrushchev also had to wonder if *his* field officers got the word to be cautious.

Add to these worries the Soviet premier's troubles with Fidel Castro, who demanded a bold Soviet response to U.S. actions and who might provoke an incident with the United States that could escalate the crisis. Castro pressed the Soviets to use nuclear weapons to save Cuba should the United States attack. Soviet leaders urged Castro not to "initiate provocations" and to practice "self-restraint." Such "adventurists," remarked a Soviet decisionmaker about the Cubans. Khrushchev sternly told his advisers: "You see how far things can go. We've got to get those missiles out of there before a real fire starts."

President Kennedy helped precipitate the missile crisis by harassing Cuba through his multitrack program. Then he reacted to the crisis by suspending diplomacy in favor of public confrontation. In the end, with the management of the crisis disintegrating, he frightened himself. In order to postpone doomsday, or at least to prevent a high-casualty invasion of Cuba, he moderated the American response and compromised. Khrushchev withdrew his mistake, while gaining what ExComm member Ambassador Llewellyn Thompson thought was the "important thing" all along for the Soviet leader: being able to say, "I saved Cuba. I stopped an invasion."

Although during the crisis such utterances as "Castro has to go," "cause something to crack" in Cuba, "I'd take Cuba away from Castro," and "dump" Castro punctuated ExComm meetings, the president said that restarting the task of removing Castro would have to wait until after achieving the immediate objective of dismantling the missile sites. After the missile imbroglio, the pre-crisis "fixation" reasserted itself. For example, the State Department's Policy Planning Council on November 7 urged a "maximal U.S. strategy" to eliminate the Castro regime. The messy ending to the crisis—no formal accord was reached, no formal document signed—also left the Kennedy administration room to hedge on the no-invasion promise. Using the argument that the United States had agreed not to invade the island only if the missiles were withdrawn under United Nations inspection and that Castro had blocked such inspection, Kennedy refused to give an unqualified no-invasion pledge. On November 20, the president told a press conference that "if all offensive weapons system are removed from Cuba and kept out of the hemisphere in the future, under adequate verification and safeguards, and if Cuba is not used for the export of aggressive Communist purposes, there will be peace in the Caribbean. . . . We will not, of course, abandon the political, economic, and other efforts of this hemisphere to halt subversion from Cuba nor our purpose and hope that the Cuban people shall some day be truly free. But these policies are very different from any intent to launch a military invasion of the island." Kennedy seemed to be adding a new condition—that Cuba must not stir up revolution in Latin America—and promising to continue efforts, short of military assault, to overthrow the Castro government.

Kennedy's retreat to an ambiguous no-invasion promise reflected his administration's unrelenting determination to oust Castro. In early January 1963, the CIA director noted that "Cuba and the Communist China nuclear threat" were the two most prominent issues on Kennedy's foreign-policy agenda. Later that month, the president himself told the National Security Council that Cuba must become a U.S. hostage. "We must always be in a position to threaten Cuba as a possible riposte to Russian pressure against us in Berlin. We must always be ready to move immediately against Cuba" should the Soviets move against Berlin. "We can use Cuba to limit

Soviet actions," he concluded. The administration set about once again to threaten Cuba, to "tighten the noose" around Cuba, although Kennedy grew impatient with exile attacks, because they did not deliver "any real blow at Castro."

In June 1963, the National Security Council approved a new sabotage program. The CIA quickly cranked up destructive plots and revitalized its assassination option by making contact with a traitorous Cuban official, Rolando Cubela. Code-named AM/LASH, he plotted with CIA operatives to kill Fidel Castro. In the fall of 1963, after Cuba probed for an accommodation with the United States, President Kennedy let preliminary steps be taken to open a Cuban-American dialogue through contacts at the United Nations. Yet, on the very day that Kennedy was assassinated, AM/LASH rendezvoused with CIA agents in Paris, where he received a ball-point pen rigged with a poisonous hypodermic needle. Like other assassination plots against Castro, this one failed.

After President Kennedy's death, the new Johnson administration decided to put the "marginal" and "tenuous" Cuban-American contacts "on ice." President Johnson also instructed his advisers to avoid "high risk actions" toward Cuba. Throughout the 1960s, as the United States became hostage to the war in Vietnam, Cuba receded as a top priority. Fidel Castro may have been correct when he remarked a decade after the missile crisis that Cuba "was saved by Vietnam. Who can say whether the immense American drive that went into Vietnam . . . would not have been turned against Cuba?" Except for a thaw in the mid to late-1970s, U.S.-Cuba relations remained frozen in hostility. Kennedy's "fixation" with Cuba fixed itself on U.S. Cuba policy for decades.

FURTHER READING

Graham Allison, *Essence of Decision* (1971)
———— and Philip Zelikow, *Essence of Decision* (1999; 2nd ed.)
Jules Benjamin, *The United States and the Origins of the Cuban Revolution* (1990)
Barton J. Bernstein, "The Cuban Missile Crisis: Trading the Jupiters in Turkey?" *Political Science Quarterly,* 95 (1980), 97–125
Michael Beschloss, *The Crisis Years* (1991)
James A. Bill, *George Ball* (1977)
Cole Blasier, *The Hovering Giant* (1976)
James G. Blight, *The Shattered Crystal Ball* (1990)
———— and Peter Kornbluh, eds., *Politics of Illusion: The Bay of Pigs Invasion Reexamined* (1977)
———— and David A. Welch, *On the Brink* (1989)
———— et al., *Cuba on the Brink* (1993)
Philip Brenner, "Cuba and the Missile Crisis," *Journal of Latin American Studies,* 22 (1990), 115–142
Dino Brugioni, *Eyeball to Eyeball* (1991)
McGeorge Bundy, *Danger and Survival* (1988)
Laurence Chang and Peter Kornbluh, eds., *The Cuban Missile Crisis, 1962* (1992)
Abram Chayes, *The Cuban Missile Crisis: International Crisis and the Role of Law* (1974)
David Detzer, *The Brink* (1979)
Herbert Dinerstein, *The Making of a Missile Crisis: October 1962* (1976)
Jorge I. Domínguez, *Cuba: Order and Revolution* (1978)
————, *To Make a World Safe for Revolution* (1989)

Theodore Draper, *Castroism* (1965)

Aleksandr Fursenko and Timothy Naftali, *"One Hell of a Gamble" : Khrushchev, Castro, and Kennedy, 1958–1964* (1997)

Raymond L. Garthoff, "Berlin 1961: The Record Corrected," *Foreign Policy,* 84 (1991), 142–156

Raymond L. Garthoff, *Reflections on the Cuban Missile Crisis* (1989)

Alexander George, *Avoiding War: Problems of Crisis Management* (1991)

James N. Giglio, *The Presidency of John F. Kennedy* (1991)

Piero Gleijeses, "Ships in the Night: The C.I.A., The White House, and the Bay of Pigs," *Journal of Latin American Studies,* 27 (1995), 1–42

A. A. Gromyko, "The Caribbean Crisis," *Soviet Law and Government,* 11 (1972), 3–53

Maurice Halperin, *The Rise and Decline of Fidel Castro* (1972)

———, *The Taming of Fidel Castro* (1981)

Mary N. Hampton, *The Wilsonian Impulse* (1996) (U.S.-Germany)

Hope Harrison, "Ulbricht and the Concrete 'Rose': New Archival Evidence on the Dynamics of Soviet-East German Relations and the Berlin Crisis, 1958–1961," Working Paper #5 (May 1993), *Cold War International History Project Bulletin,* Woodrow Wilson International Center for Scholars

Seymour Hersh, *The Dark Side of Camelot* (1997)

James G. Hershberg, "Before 'The Missiles of October': Did Kennedy Plan a Military Strike Against Cuba?" *Diplomatic History,* 14 (1990), 163–198

Trumbull Higgins, *The Perfect Failure* (1987) (Bay of Pigs invasion)

Irving L. Janis, *Groupthink* (1982)

Haynes B. Johnson et al., *The Bay of Pigs* (1964)

Donna Rich Kaplowitz, *Anatomy of a Failed Embargo: U.S. Sanctions Against Cuba* (1998)

Montague Kern, Patricia W. Levering, and Ralph B. Levering, *The Kennedy Crises: The Press, the Presidency, and Foreign Policy* (1983)

Richard Ned Lebow, *Between Peace and War* (1981)

——— and Janice Gross Stein, *We All Lost the Cold War* (1993)

Lee Lockwood, *Castro's Cuba, Cuba's Fidel* (1967)

Frank Mankiewicz and Kirby Jones, *With Fidel* (1975)

Frank A. Mayer, *Adenauer and Kennedy: A Study in German-American Relations, 1961–1963* (1996)

Morris Morley, *Imperial State and Revolution: The United States and Cuba, 1952–1987* (1987)

Philip Nash, *The Other Missiles of October* (1997) (Jupiters)

James A. Nathan, ed., *The Cuban Missile Crisis Revisited* (1992)

———, "The Missile Crisis," *World Politics,* 27 (1975), 256–281

Kendrick Oliver, *Kennedy, Macmillan, and the Nuclear Test Ban Treaty* (1998)

Herbert S. Parmet, *JFK* (1983)

Thomas G. Paterson, *Contesting Castro* (1994)

———, ed., *Kennedy's Quest for Victory* (1989)

——— and William T. Brophy, "October Missiles and November Elections: The Cuban Missile Crisis and American Politics, 1962," *Journal of American History,* 73 (1986), 87–119

Louis A. Pérez, Jr., *Cuba and the United States* (1990)

Steven G. Rabe, *The Most Dangerous Area in the World* (1999)

Scott D. Sagan, *The Limits of Safety* (1993)

Arthur M. Schlesinger, Jr., *Robert Kennedy and His Times* (1978)

———, *A Thousand Days* (1965)

Thomas J. Schoenbaum, *Waging Peace and War* (1988) (on Rusk)

Len Scott and Steve Smith, "Lessons of October: Historians, Political Scientists, Policymakers, and the Cuban Missile Crisis," *International Affairs,* 70 (1994), 659–684

Glenn T. Seaborg and Benjamin J. Loeb, *Kennedy, Khrushchev, and the Test Ban* (1981)

Ronald Steel, "Endgame," *New York Review of Books,* March 13, 1969, pp. 15–22
Tad Szulc, *Fidel* (1986)
———— and K. E. Meyer, *The Cuban Invasion* (1962)
Marc Trachtenberg, *History and Strategy* (1991)
Lucien S. Vandenbroucke, "Anatomy of a Failure: The Decision to Land at the Bay of
     Pigs," *Political Science Quarterly,* 99 (1984), 471–491
————, *Perilous Options* (1993)
Richard E. Welch, Jr., *Response to Revolution* (1985)
Mark J. White, *The Cuban Missile Crisis* (1996)
————, *Missiles in Cuba* (1997)
Peter Wyden, *Bay of Pigs* (1979)

The Vietnam War

After World War II, the United States's engagement in the Indochinese country of Vietnam deepened over a thirty-year period. In 1945 the Truman administration tolerated the reimposition of French colonialism, and in 1950 Washington began giving massive aid to the French to quell the patriot Ho Chi Minh's nationalist, communist-led insurgency. After the French defeat in 1954, the United States supported the division of Vietnam at the seventeenth parallel, and the Eisenhower administration helped to organize, and to prop up, a noncommunist regime in the South. In 1961 President John F. Kennedy sent U.S. military personnel to fight in Vietnamese jungles; then in 1964, under Kennedy's successor, Lyndon B. Johnson, American bombers launched an air war against North Vietnam. The Johnson administration significantly increased the level of ground forces in South Vietnam in 1965. Following the North Vietnamese–Vietcong Tet offensive in 1968, peace talks began, and in 1973 Washington and Hanoi reached a peace settlement that permitted the United States to continue to support the South Vietnamese regime. But in 1975 communist forces drove Americans pell-mell from Vietnam and seized Saigon, the southern capital, which they renamed Ho Chi Minh City.

With each passing year, the war's costs had mounted. By the end, more than 58,000 American servicemen and women had died in Vietnam, and the United States had spent more than $175 billion in Southeast Asia. Millions of Asians perished, hundreds of thousands of others became refugees, and the countries of Indochina—Vietnam, Cambodia, and Laos—lay in ruins. The war also polarized Americans at home. Peace demonstrations swept the United States during the 1960s and early 1970s. U.S. leaders ultimately responded by withdrawing American forces, but the passionate Vietnam debate nonetheless unhinged a twenty-five-year-old Cold War consensus on foreign policy.

Considering the war's length and historical significance, it is not surprising that scholars vigorously debate all aspects of the conflict. One set of questions probes the causes or motivations for U.S. intervention. Put simply, why did the United States become so deeply entangled in Vietnam and stay so long? Did U.S. security interests, especially the goal of anticommunist containment, lead to intervention? Did Vietnam become a test of the United States's credibility overseas, a place for America to demonstrate its willingness and ability to stand by its allies? To what extent did a misunderstanding of Vietnamese society and politics account for American behavior? Did U.S. officials mistakenly view Vietnamese communism, and Vietnamese nationalism, as Soviet directed? If so, what accounts for their blurred vision: A misguided desire to help Vietnam? Cultural arrogance? A lack of information? Did bureaucratic decisionmaking, which places a premium on consensus, inhibit critical thought on Vietnam? Did the imperial presidency undermine congressional oversight? Or did intervention in Vietnam arise from a determined drive for global hegemony, an urge to secure access to markets and raw materials, military bases, and political influence?

A second set of questions centers on the military conduct of the war and the question of winning. Why did the United States lose the Vietnam War? Did the antiwar movement and an investigative press undermine American resolve? Did civilian authorities err in choosing to fight a "limited war"? To what extent was the military restrained from unleashing all of its firepower, especially airstrikes? Should U.S. troops have invaded North Vietnam? Did the U.S. military wrongly rely on conventional battlefield engagement instead of counterinsurgency and a pacification program better geared to a guerrilla war? Did the U.S. strategy of attrition and massive "search and destroy" campaigns, which measured success through "body counts" of dead Vietnamese, encourage atrocities against civilians and make U.S. officials overconfident of military progress? Would a change in military tactics have brought victory? Or did corruption and instability in, and the lack of popular support for, the South Vietnamese government make victory impossible, especially when combined with the skill and motivation of the Vietnamese communists? Did the United States make a fundamental error by deciding to intervene in an anticolonial struggle in the first place, fighting against people determined to defend their homeland?

🌐 D O C U M E N T S

Resistance to foreigners is an enduring theme in Vietnamese history. During World War II, the Vietnamese battled the Japanese. On September 2, 1945, Ho Chi Minh and other nationalists wrote a Declaration of Independence for the Democratic Republic of Vietnam. The document, reprinted here as Document 1, resembled the 1776 American declaration. But the French denied independence and reclaimed their colony, and from 1945 to 1954 an anticolonial rebellion convulsed Vietnam. In Document 2, the transcript of a press conference of April 7, 1954, President Dwight D. Eisenhower explains his "domino theory," which posited that a communist takeover of Indochina would lead inexorably to communist domination throughout Asia. The beleaguered French ultimately decided to withdraw from Vietnam, and at the Geneva Conference of May 8–July 21, 1954, the warring parties and their allies, including the United States, prepared peace terms and long-range plans for Indochina. The Geneva Accords that were set down in the final declaration are reprinted here as Document 3. Thereafter, Ho's communists governed North Vietnam, and the United States, which refused to accept the Geneva agreements, backed a regime in the south.

Despite U.S. aid, the government of South Vietnam was plagued by rampant corruption, inefficiency, and inadequate popular support. By 1960 a communist-led insurgency, the National Liberation Front (NLF), had gained a widespread following in the South and secured North Vietnamese assistance. In Document 4, dating from 1961, North Vietnamese general Vo Nguyen Giap explains the strategy of "people's war," whereby a smaller, weaker force could achieve military victory over a stronger, imperialist power. The Tonkin Gulf Resolution, Document 5, which the U.S. Senate passed on August 10, 1964, with only two dissenting votes, authorized the president to use the force he deemed necessary in Vietnam.

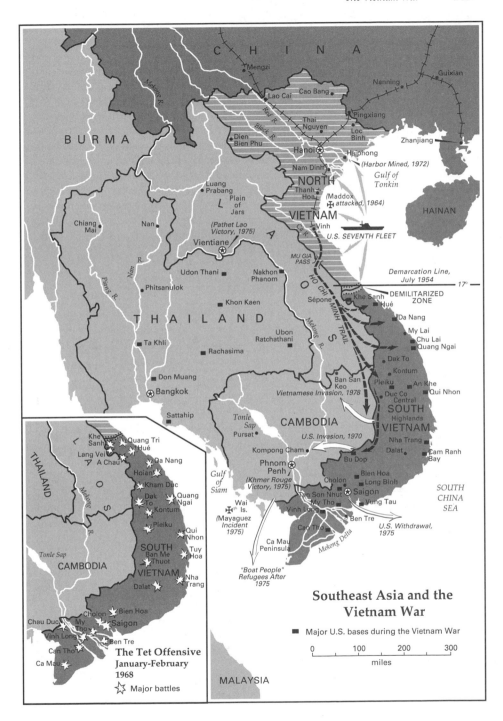

Southeast Asia and the Vietnam War

■ Major U.S. bases during the Vietnam War

0   100   200   300
miles

The Tet Offensive
January–February 1968

☆ Major battles

CHINA

BURMA

Mengzi

Nanning

Guixian

Lao Cai · Cao Bang · Pingxiang · Loc Binh

Zhanjiang

Thai Nguyen

Dien Bien Phu

Hanoi · Haiphong

(Harbor Mined, 1972)

Nam Dinh

Gulf of Tonkin

NORTH VIETNAM

Thanh Hoa

(Maddox attacked, 1964)

HAINAN

Luang Prabang

Plain of Jars

Chiang Mai · Nan

Vinh

U.S. SEVENTH FLEET

(Pathet Lao Victory, 1975)

Vientiane

L A O S

MU GIA PASS

Udon Thani · Nakhon Phanom

Demarcation Line, July 1954

17°

Phitsanulok

Khe Sanh

DEMILITARIZED ZONE

Sépone · Hué

T H A I L A N D

Khon Kaen

Da Nang

My Lai

Chu Lai

Ta Khli

Ubon Ratchathani

Quang Ngai

Dak To

Rachasima

Kontum

Don Muang

Ban San Keo

Pleiku · An Khe

⊛ Bangkok

Vietnamese Invasion, 1978

Duc Co

Qui Nhon

Central Highlands

SOUTH VIETNAM

Sattahip

Tonle Sap · Pursat

CAMBODIA

Nha Trang

Dalat

Cam Ranh Bay

U.S. Invasion, 1970

Bu Dop

Kompong Cham

Bien Hoa · Long Binh

Phnom Penh

(Khmer Rouge Victory, 1975)

Gulf of Siam

Cholon

Tan Son Nhut · Saigon

SOUTH CHINA SEA

Wai Is.

(Mayaguez Incident 1975)

My Tho

Vung Tau

Vinh Long

Ben Tre

U.S. Withdrawal, 1975

Cao Tho

Ca Mau Peninsula

Mekong Delta

"Boat People" Refugees After 1975

MALAYSIA

Tet Offensive inset map

THAILAND

Khe Sanh · Quang Tri · Hué

Lang Vei · A Chau

Da Nang

Hoian

LAOS

Kham Duc

Dak To · Quang Ngai

Kontum

Pleiku

Qui Nhon

Tonle Sap

CAMBODIA

SOUTH VIETNAM

Ban Me Thuot

Tuy Hoa

Nha Trang

Dalat

Cholon · Bien Hoa

Chau Duc

My Tho · Saigon

Vinh Long

Can Tho · Ben Tre

Ca Mau

American war managers interpreted this important document as equivalent to a declaration of war. Document 6, President Lyndon B. Johnson's passionate speech at The Johns Hopkins University on April 7, 1965, gives the reasons why the United States was fighting in Vietnam. During June and July, 1965, the Johnson administration discussed America's options in Vietnam and chose to adopt a policy of military escalation. Document 7 presents notes of an exchange between President Johnson and Under Secretary of State George Ball on July 21, during a meeting of high-level advisers, when Ball dissented from a policy of military build-up.

J. William Fulbright, chair of the Senate Foreign Relations Committee, became a vocal critic of the Vietnam War. In Document 8, a speech of May 5, 1966, he protests an American "arrogance of power." Document 9 is an excerpt from a 1969 article by former Defense Secretary Clark M. Clifford, recalling his disconcerting conferences with military leaders in the bewildering aftermath of the Tet offensive in early 1968. In Document 10, an excerpt from Robert S. McNamara's controversial 1995 memoir, *In Retrospect*, the former secretary concludes that he and the Johnson administration erred badly in July 1965 when they escalated U.S. military intervention in Vietnam.

1. The Vietnamese Declaration of Independence, 1945

All men are created equal. They are endowed by their Creator with certain inalienable rights, among these are Life, Liberty and the pursuit of Happiness.

This immortal statement was made in the Declaration of Independence of the United States of America in 1776. In a broader sense, this means: All the peoples on the earth are equal from birth, all the peoples have a right to live, to be happy and free.

The Declaration of the French Revolution made in 1791 on the Rights of Man and the Citizen also states: "All men are born free and with equal rights, and must always remain free and have equal rights."

Those are undeniable truths.

Nevertheless, for more than eighty years, the French imperialists, abusing the standard of Liberty, Equality and Fraternity, have violated our Fatherland and oppressed our fellow-citizens. They have acted contrary to the ideals of humanity and justice.

In the field of politics, they have deprived our people of every democratic liberty.

They have enforced inhuman laws; they have set up three distinct political regimes in the North, the Centre and the South of Viet Nam in order to wreck our national unity and prevent our people from being united.

They have built more prisons than schools. They have mercilessly slain our patriots; they have drowned our uprisings in rivers of blood.

They have fettered public opinion; they have practised obscurantism against our people.

To weaken our race they have forced us to use opium and alcohol.

This document can be found in Information Service, Viet-Nam Delegation in France, *The Democratic Republic of Viet-Nam* (Paris: Imprimerie Centrale Commerciale, 1948), pp. 3–5.

In the field of economics, they have fleeced us to the backbone, impoverished our people and devastated our land.

They have robbed us of our ricefields, our mines, our forests and our raw materials. They have monopolized the issuing of banknotes and the export trade.

They have invented numerous unjustifiable taxes and reduced our people, especially our peasantry, to a state of extreme poverty.

They have hampered the prospering of our national bourgeoisie; they have mercilessly exploited our workers. . . .

For these reasons, we, members of the Provisional Government, representing the whole Vietnamese people, declare that from now on we break off all relations of a colonial character with France; we repeal all the international obligation[s] that France has so far subscribed to on behalf of Viet Nam and we abolish all the special rights the French have unlawfully acquired in our Fatherland.

The whole Vietnamese people, animated by a common purpose, are determined to fight to the bitter end against any attempt by the French colonialists to reconquer their country.

We are convinced that the Allied nations which at Teheran and San Francisco have acknowledged the principles of self-determination and equality of nations, will not refuse to acknowledge the independence of Viet Nam.

A people who have courageously opposed French domination for more than eighty years, a people who have fought side by side with the Allies against the fascists during these last years, such a people must be free and independent.

For these reasons, we, members of the Provisional Government of the Democratic Republic of Vietnam, solemnly declare to the world that Viet Nam has the right to be a free and independent country—and in fact it is so already. The entire Vietnamese people are determined to mobilize all their physical and mental strength, to sacrifice their lives and property in order to safeguard their independence and liberty.

2. President Dwight D. Eisenhower Advances the Domino Theory, 1954

Q. Robert Richards, Copley Press: Mr. President, would you mind commenting on the strategic importance of Indochina to the free world? I think there has been, across the country, some lack of understanding on just what it means to us.

The President: You have, of course, both the specific and the general when you talk about such things.

First of all, you have the specific value of a locality in its production of materials that the world needs.

Then you have the possibility that many human beings pass under a dictatorship that is inimical to the free world.

This document can be found in *Public Papers of the Presidents, Dwight D. Eisenhower, 1954* (Washington, D.C.: U.S. Government Printing Office, 1960), pp. 382–383.

Finally, you have broader considerations that might follow what you would call the "falling domino" principle. You have a row of dominoes set up, you knock over the first one, and what will happen to the last one is the certainty that it will go over very quickly. So you could have a beginning of a disintegration that would have the most profound influences.

Now, with respect to the first one, two of the items from this particular area that the world uses are tin and tungsten. They are very important. There are others, of course, the rubber plantations and so on.

Then with respect to more people passing under this domination, Asia, after all, has already lost some 450 million of its peoples to the Communist dictatorship, and we simply can't afford greater losses.

But when we come to the possible sequence of events, the loss of Indochina, of Burma, of Thailand, of the Peninsula, and Indonesia following, now you begin to talk about areas that not only multiply the disadvantages that you would suffer through loss of materials, sources of materials, but now you are talking about millions and millions and millions of people.

Finally, the geographical position achieved thereby does many things. It turns the so-called island defensive chain of Japan, Formosa, of the Philippines and to the southward; it moves in to threaten Australia and New Zealand.

It takes away, in its economic aspects, that region that Japan must have as a trading area or Japan, in turn, will have only one place in the world to go—that is, toward the Communist areas in order to live.

So, the possible consequences of the loss are just incalculable to the free world.

3. Final Declaration of the Geneva Conference on Indochina, 1954

1. The Conference takes note of the agreements ending hostilities in Cambodia, Laos and Viet Nam and organising international control and the supervision of the execution of the provisions of these agreements. . . .

4. The Conference takes note of the clauses in the agreement on the cessation of hostilities in Viet Nam prohibiting the introduction into Viet Nam of foreign troops and military personnel as well as of all kinds of arms and munitions. . . .

5. The Conference takes note of the clauses in the agreement on the cessation of hostilities in Viet Nam to the effect that no military base under the control of a foreign State may be established in the regrouping zones of the two parties [above and below the seventeenth parallel], the latter having the obligation to see that the zones allotted to them shall not constitute part of any military alliance and shall not be utilised for the resumption of hostilities or in the service of an aggressive policy. . . .

6. The Conference recognises that the essential purpose of the agreement relating to Viet Nam is to settle military questions with a view to ending hostilities and that the military demarcation line [at the seventeenth parallel] is provisional

---

This document can be found in *Department of State Bulletin*, XXXI (August 2, 1954), p. 164.

and should not in any way be interpreted as constituting a political or territorial boundary. The Conference expresses its conviction that the execution of the provisions set out in the present declaration and in the agreement on the cessation of hostilities creates the necessary basis for the achievement in the near future of a political settlement in Viet Nam.

7. The Conference declares that, so far as Viet Nam is concerned, the settlement of political problems, effected on the basis of respect for the principles of independence, unity and territorial integrity, shall permit the Vietnamese people to enjoy the fundamental freedoms, guaranteed by democratic institutions established as a result of free general elections by secret ballot. In order to ensure that sufficient progress in the restoration of peace has been made, and that all of the necessary conditions obtain for free expression of the national will, general elections shall be held in July 1956, under the supervision of an international commission composed of representatives of the Member States of the International Supervisory Commission, referred to in the agreement on the cessation of hostilities. Consultations will be held on this subject between the competent representative authorities of the two zones from July 20, 1955, onwards. . . .

12. In their relations with Cambodia, Laos and Viet Nam, each member of the Geneva Conference undertakes to respect the sovereignty, the independence, the unity and the territorial integrity of the above-mentioned States, and to refrain from any interference in their internal affairs.

4. General Vo Nguyen Giap Outlines His People's War Strategy, 1961

The Vietnamese people's war of liberation [against France] was a just war, aiming to win back the independence and unity of the country, to bring land to our peasants and guarantee them the right to it, and to defend the achievements of the August [1945] Revolution. That is why it was first and foremost a people's war. To educate, mobilise, organise and arm the whole people in order that they might take part in the Resistance was a crucial question.

The enemy of the Vietnamese nation was aggressive imperialism, which had to be overthrown. . . .

A backward colonial country which had only just risen up to proclaim its independence and install people's power, Viet Nam only recently possessed armed forces, equipped with still very mediocre arms and having no combat experience. Her enemy, on the other hand, was an imperialist power which has retained a fairly considerable economic and military potentiality despite the recent German occupation [during World War II] and benefited, furthermore, from the active support of the United States. The balance of forces decidedly showed up our weaknesses against the enemy's power. The Vietnamese people's war of liberation had, therefore, to be a hard and long-lasting war in order to succeed in creating conditions for victory. All

---

This document can be found in Vo Nguyen Giap, *People's War, People's Army* (Hanoi: Foreign Languages Publishing House, 1961), pp. 27–30.

the conceptions born of impatience and aimed at obtaining speedy victory could only be gross errors. It was necessary to firmly grasp the strategy of a long-term resistance, and to exalt the will to be self-supporting in order to maintain and gradually augment our forces, while nibbling at and progressively destroying those of the enemy; it was necessary to accumulate thousands of small victories to turn them into a great success, thus gradually altering the balance of forces in transforming our weakness into power and carrying off final victory. . . .

From the point of view of directing operations, our *strategy and tactics had to be those of a people's war and of a·long-term resistance.*

Our strategy was, as we have stressed, to wage a long-lasting battle. A war of this nature in general entails several phases; in principle, starting from a stage of contention, it goes through a period of equilibrium before arriving at a general counter-offensive. In effect, the way in which it is carried on can be more subtle and more complex, depending on the particular conditions obtaining on both sides during the course of operations. Only a long-term war could enable us to utilise to the maximum our political trump cards, to overcome our material handicap and to transform our weakness into strength. To maintain and increase our forces, was the principle to which we adhered, contenting ourselves with attacking when success was certain, refusing to give battle likely to incur losses to us or to engage in hazardous actions. We had to apply the slogan: to build up our strength during the actual course of fighting.

The forms of fighting had to be completely adapted that is, to raise the fighting spirit to the maximum and rely on heroism of our troops to overcome the enemy's material superiority. In the main, especially at the outset of the war, we had recourse to guerilla fighting. In the Vietnamese theatre of operations, this method carried off great victories: it could be used in the mountains as well as in the delta, it could be waged with good or mediocre material and even without arms, and was to enable us eventually to equip ourselves at the cost of the enemy. Wherever the Expeditionary Corps came, the entire population took part in the fighting; every commune had its fortified village, every district had its regional troops fighting under the command of the local branches of the Party and the people's administration, in liaison with the regular forces in order to wear down and annihilate the enemy forces.

Thereafter, with the development of our forces, guerilla warfare changed into a mobile warfare—a form of mobile warfare still strongly marked by guerilla warfare—which would afterwards become the essential form of operations on the main front, the northern front. In this process of development of guerilla warfare and of accentuation of the mobile warfare, our people's army constantly grew and passed from the stage of combats involving a section or company, to fairly large-scale campaigns bringing into action several divisions. Gradually, its equipment improved, mainly by the seizure of arms from the enemy—the materiel of the French and American imperialists.

From the military point of view, *the Vietnamese people's war of liberation proved that an insufficiently equipped people's army, but an army fighting for a just cause, can, with appropriate strategy and tactics, combine the conditions needed to conquer a modern army of aggressive imperialism.*

5. The Tonkin Gulf Resolution, 1964

To promote the maintenance of international peace and security in southeast Asia.

Whereas naval units of the Communist regime in Vietnam, in violation of the principles of the Charter of the United Nations and of international law, have deliberately and repeatedly attacked United States naval vessels lawfully present in international waters, and have thereby created a serious threat to international peace; and

Whereas these attacks are part of a deliberate and systematic campaign of aggression that the Communist regime in North Vietnam has been waging against its neighbors and the nations joined with them in the collective defense of their freedom; and

Whereas the United States is assisting the peoples of southeast Asia to protect their freedom and has no territorial, military or political ambitions in that area, but desires only that these peoples should be left in peace to work out their own destinies in their own way: Now, therefore, be it *Resolved by the Senate and House of Representatives of the United States of America in Congress assembled,* That the Congress approves and supports the determination of the President, as Commander in Chief, to take all necessary measures to repel any armed attack against the forces of the United States and to prevent further aggression.

Sec. 2. The United States regards as vital to its national interest and to world peace the maintenance of international peace and security in southeast Asia. Consonant with the Constitution of the United States and the Charter of the United Nations and in accordance with its obligations under the Southeast Asia Collective Defense Treaty, the United States is, therefore, prepared, as the President determines, to take all necessary steps, including the use of armed force, to assist any member or protocol state of the Southeast Asia Collective Defense Treaty requesting assistance in defense of its freedom.

Sec. 3. This resolution shall expire when the President shall determine that the peace and security of the area is reasonably assured by international conditions created by action of the United Nations or otherwise, except that it may be terminated earlier by concurrent resolution of the Congress.

6. President Lyndon B. Johnson Explains Why Americans Fight in Vietnam, 1965

Why must this nation hazard its ease, its interest, and its power for the sake of a people so far away?

We fight because we must fight if we are to live in a world where every country can shape its own destiny, and only in such a world will our own freedom be finally secure.

Document 5 can be found in *Department of State Bulletin*, LI (August 24, 1964), 268.

Document 6 can be found in *Public Papers of the Presidents, Lyndon B. Johnson, 1965* (Washington, D.C.: U.S. Government Printing Office, 1966), pp. 394–398.

This kind of world will never be built by bombs or bullets. Yet the infirmities of man are such that force must often precede reason and the waste of war, the works of peace.

We wish that this were not so. But we must deal with the world as it is, if it is ever to be as we wish.

The world as it is in Asia is not a serene or peaceful place.

The first reality is that North Viet-Nam has attacked the independent nation of South Viet-Nam. Its object is total conquest.

Of course, some of the people of South Viet-Nam are participating in attack on their own government. But trained men and supplies, orders and arms, flow in a constant stream from North to South.

This support is the heartbeat of the war.

And it is a war of unparalleled brutality. Simple farmers are the targets of assassination and kidnaping. Women and children are strangled in the night because their men are loyal to their government. And helpless villages are ravaged by sneak attacks. Large-scale raids are conducted on towns, and terror strikes in the heart of cities.

The confused nature of this conflict cannot mask the fact that it is the new face of an old enemy.

Over this war—and all Asia—is another reality: the deepening shadow of Communist China. The rulers in Hanoi are urged on by Peking. This is a regime which has destroyed freedom in Tibet, which has attacked India and has been condemned by the United Nations for aggression in Korea. It is a nation which is helping the forces of violence in almost every continent. The contest in Viet-Nam is part of a wider pattern of aggressive purposes.

Why are these realities our concern? Why are we in South Viet-Nam?

We are there because we have a promise to keep. Since 1954 every American President has offered support to the people of South Viet-Nam. We have helped to build, and we have helped to defend. Thus, over many years, we have made a national pledge to help South Viet-Nam defend its independence.

And I intend to keep that promise.

To dishonor that pledge, to abandon this small and brave nation to its enemies, and to the terror that must follow, would be an unforgivable wrong.

We are also there to strengthen world order. Around the globe from Berlin to Thailand are people whose well being rests in part on the belief that they can count on us if they are attacked. To leave Viet-Nam to its fate would shake the confidence of all these people in the value of an American commitment and in the value of America's word. The result would be increased unrest and instability, and even wider war.

We are also there because there are great stakes in the balance. Let no one think for a moment that retreat from Viet-Nam would bring an end to conflict. The battle would be renewed in one country and then another. The central lesson of our time is that the appetite of aggression is never satisfied. To withdraw from one battlefield means only to prepare for the next. We must say in Southeast Asia—as we did in Europe—in the words of the Bible: "Hitherto shalt thou come, but no further.". . .

In recent months attacks on South Viet-Nam were stepped up. Thus, it became necessary for us to increase our response and to make attacks by air. This is not a change of purpose. It is a change in what we believe that purpose requires.

We do this in order to slow down aggression.

We do this to increase the confidence of the brave people of South Viet-Nam who have bravely borne this brutal battle for so many years with so many casualties.

And we do this to convince the leaders of North Viet-Nam—and all who seek to share their conquest—of a simple fact:

We will not be defeated.

We will not grow tired.

We will not withdraw, either openly or under the cloak of a meaningless agreement. . . .

Stability and peace do not come easily in such a land. Neither independence nor human dignity will ever be won though by arms alone. It also requires the works of peace. The American people have helped generously in times past in these works, and now there must be a much more massive effort to improve the life of man in that conflict-torn corner of our world.

The first step is for the countries of Southeast Asia to associate themselves in a greatly expanded co-operative effort for development. We would hope that North Viet-Nam would take its place in the common effort just as soon as peaceful co-operation is possible.

The United Nations is already actively engaged in development in this area, and as far back as 1961 I conferred with our authorities in Viet-Nam in connection with their work there. And I would hope tonight that the Secretary General of the United Nations could use the prestige of his great office and his deep knowledge of Asia to initiate, as soon as possible, with the countries of that area, a plan for co-operation in increased development.

For our part I will ask the Congress to join in a billion dollar American investment in this effort as soon as it is underway.

And I would hope that all other industrialized countries, including the Soviet Union, will join in this effort to replace despair with hope and terror with progress.

The task is nothing less than to enrich the hopes and existence of more than a hundred million people. And there is much to be done.

The vast Mekong River can provide food and water and power on a scale to dwarf even our own T.V.A. [Tennessee Valley Authority].

The wonders of modern medicine can be spread through villages where thousands die every year from lack of care.

Schools can be established to train people in the skills needed to manage the process of development.

And these objectives, and more, are within the reach of a cooperative and determined effort.

I also intend to expand and speed up a program to make available our farm surpluses to assist in feeding and clothing the needy in Asia. We should not allow people to go hungry and wear rags while our own warehouses overflow with an abundance of wheat and corn and rice and cotton.

So I will very shortly name a special team of outstanding, patriotic, and distinguished Americans to inaugurate our participation in these programs. This team will be headed by Mr. Eugene Black, the very able former president of the World Bank.

This will be a disorderly planet for a long time. In Asia, and elsewhere, the forces of the modern world are shaking old ways and uprooting ancient civilizations. There will be turbulence and struggle and even violence. Great social change—as we see in our own country—does not always come without conflict.

We must also expect that nations will on occasion be in dispute with us. It may be because we are rich, or powerful, or because we have made some mistakes, or because they honestly fear our intentions. However, no nation need ever fear that we desire their land, or to impose our will, or to dictate their institutions.

But we will always oppose the effort of one nation to conquer another nation. We will do this because our own security is at stake.

But there is more to it than that. For our generation has a dream. It is a very old dream. But we have the power, and now we have the opportunity to make that dream come true.

For centuries nations have struggled among each other. But we dream of a world where disputes are settled by law and reason. And we will try to make it so.

For most of history men have hated and killed one another in battle. But we dream of an end to war. And we will try to make it so.

For all existence most men have lived in poverty, threatened by hunger. But we dream of a world where all are fed and charged with hope. And we will help to make it so.

7. Johnson Questions Dissenting Under Secretary of State George Ball, 1965

Morning Meeting of July 21

The President: Is there anyone here of the opinion we should not do what the [Joint Chiefs of Staff] memorandum says [increase U.S. troops in Vietnam by 100,000]? If so, I want to hear from him now, in detail.

Ball: Mr. President, I can foresee a perilous voyage, very dangerous. I have great and grave apprehensions that we can win under these conditions. But let me be clear. If the decision is to go ahead, I am committed.

The President: But, George, is there another course in the national interest, some course that is better than the one [Defense Secretary] McNamara proposes? We know it is dangerous and perilous, but the big question is, can it be avoided?

Ball: There is no course that will allow us to cut our losses. If we get bogged down, our cost might be substantially greater. The pressures to create a larger war would be inevitable. The qualifications I have are not due to the fact that I think we are in a bad moral position.

This document can be found in "Cabinet Room, Wednesday, July 21, 1965," Johnson Papers, Meeting Notes File, Box 2, Lyndon B. Johnson Presidential Library, Austin, Texas.

The President: Tell me then, what other road can I go?

Ball: Take what precautions we can, Mr. President. Take our losses, let their government fall apart, negotiate, discuss, knowing full well there will be a probable take-over by the Communists. This is disagreeable, I know.

The President: I can take disagreeable decisions. But I want to know can we make a case for your thoughts? Can you discuss it fully?

Ball: We have discussed it. I have had my day in court.

The President: I don't think we can have made any full commitment, George. You have pointed out the danger, but you haven't really proposed an alternative course. We haven't always been right. We have no mortgage on victory. Right now, I am concerned that we have very little alternatives to what we are doing. I want another meeting, more meetings, before we take any definitive action. We must look at all other courses of possibility carefully. Right now I feel it would be more dangerous to lose this now, than endanger a great number of troops. But I want this fully discussed.

Afternoon Meeting of July 21

Ball: We cannot win, Mr. President. The war will be long and protracted. The most we can hope for is a messy conclusion. There remains a great danger of intrusion by the Chinese. But the biggest problem is the problem of the long war. The Korean experience was a galling one. The correlation between Korean casualties and public opinion showed support stabilized at 50 percent. As casualties increase, the pressure to strike at the very jugular of North Vietnam will become very great. I am concerned about world opinion. If we could win in a year's time, and win decisively, world opinion would be alright. However, if the war is long and protracted, as I believe it will be, then we will suffer because the world's greatest power cannot defeat guerrillas. Then there is the problem of national politics. Every great captain in history was not afraid to make a tactical withdrawal if conditions were unfavorable to him. The enemy cannot even be seen in Vietnam. He is indigenous to the country. I truly have serious doubts that an army of Westerners can successfully fight Orientals in an Asian jungle.

The President: This is important. Can Westerners, in the absence of accurate intelligence, successfully fight Asians in jungle rice paddies? I want McNamara and General [Earle] Wheeler [chairman of the Joint Chiefs of Staff] to seriously ponder this question.

Ball: I think we all have underestimated the seriousness of this situation. It is like giving cobalt treatment to a terminal cancer case. I think a long, protracted war will disclose our weakness, not our strength. The least harmful way to cut losses in SVN [South Vietnam] is to let the government decide it doesn't want us to stay there. Therefore, we should put proposals to the GVN [government of Vietnam (South)] that they can't accept. Then, it would move to a neutralist position. I have no illusions that after we were asked to leave South Vietnam, that country would soon come under Hanoi control. . . .

The President: But George, wouldn't all these countries say that Uncle Sam was a paper tiger, wouldn't we lose credibility breaking the word of three presidents, if we did as you have proposed? It would seem to be an irresponsible blow. But I gather you don't think so?

Ball: No sir. The worse blow would be that the mightiest power on earth is unable to defeat a handful of guerrillas.

8. Senator J. William Fulbright Decries the "Arrogance of Power," 1966

The attitude above all others which I feel sure is no longer valid is the arrogance of power, the tendency of great nations to equate power with virtue and major responsibilities with a universal mission. The dilemmas involved are preeminently American dilemmas, not because America has weaknesses that others do not have but because America is powerful as no nation has ever been before and the discrepancy between its power and the power of others appears to be increasing. . . .

We are now engaged in a war to "defend freedom" in South Vietnam. Unlike the Republic of Korea, South Vietnam has an army which [is] without notable success and a weak, dictatorial government which does not command the loyalty of the South Vietnamese people. The official war aims of the United States Government, as I understand them, are to defeat what is regarded as North Vietnamese aggression, to demonstrate the futility of what the communists call "wars of national liberation," and to create conditions under which the South Vietnamese people will be able freely to determine their own future. I have not the slightest doubt of the sincerity of the President and the Vice President and the Secretaries of State and Defense in propounding these aims. What I do doubt—and doubt very much—is the ability of the United States to achieve these aims by the means being used. I do not question the power of our weapons and the efficiency of our logistics; I cannot say these things delight me as they seem to delight some of our officials, but they are certainly impressive. What I do question is the ability of the United States, or France or any other Western nation, to go into a small, alien, undeveloped Asian nation and create stability where there is chaos, the will to fight where there is defeatism, democracy where there is no tradition of it and honest government where corruption is almost a way of life. Our handicap is well expressed in the pungent Chinese proverb: "In shallow waters dragons become the sport of shrimps."

Early last month demonstrators in Saigon burned American jeeps, tried to assault American soldiers, and marched through the streets shouting "Down with the American imperialists," while one of the Buddhist leaders made a speech equating the United States with the communists as a threat to South Vietnamese independence. Most Americans are understandably shocked and angered to encounter such hostility from people who by now would be under the rule of the Viet Cong but for the sacrifice of American lives and money. Why, we may ask, are they so shockingly ungrateful? Surely they must know that their very right to parade and protest and demonstrate depends on the Americans who are defending them.

The answer, I think, is that "fatal impact" of the rich and strong on the poor and weak. Dependent on it though the Vietnamese are, our very strength is a reproach to their weakness, our wealth a mockery of their poverty, our success a reminder of their failures. What they resent is the disruptive effect of our strong culture upon

---

This document can be found in the *Congressional Record,* CXII (May 17, 1966), 10805–10810.

their fragile one, an effect which we can no more avoid than a man can help being bigger than a child. What they fear, I think rightly, is that traditional Vietnamese society cannot survive the American economic and cultural impact. . . .

The cause of our difficulties in southeast Asia is not a deficiency of power but an excess of the wrong kind of power which results in a feeling of impotence when it fails to achieve its desired ends. We are still acting like boy scouts dragging reluctant old ladies across the streets they do not want to cross. We are trying to remake Vietnamese society, a task which certainly cannot be accomplished by force and which probably cannot be accomplished by any means available to outsiders. The objective may be desirable, but it is not feasible. . . .

If America has a service to perform in the world—and I believe it has—it is in large part the service of its own example. In our excessive involvement in the affairs of other countries, we are not only living off our assets and denying our own people the proper enjoyment of their resources; we are also denying the world the example of a free society enjoying its freedom to the fullest. This is regrettable indeed for a nation that aspires to teach democracy to other nations, because, as [Edmund] Burke said, "Example is the school of mankind, and they will learn at no other.". . .

There are many respects in which America, if it can bring itself to act with the magnanimity and the empathy appropriate to its size and power, can be an intelligent example to the world. We have the opportunity to set an example of generous understanding in our relations with China, of practical cooperation for peace in our relations with Russia, of reliable and respectful partnership in our relations with Western Europe, of material helpfulness without moral presumption in our relations with the developing nations, of abstention from the temptations of hegemony in our relations with Latin America, and of the all-around advantages of minding one's own business in our relations with everybody. Most of all, we have the opportunity to serve as an example of democracy to the world by the way in which we run our own society; America, in the words of John Quincy Adams, should be "the well-wisher to the freedom and independence of all" but "the champion and vindicator only of her own.". . .

If we can bring ourselves so to act, we will have overcome the dangers of the arrogance of power. It will involve, no doubt, the loss of certain glories, but that seems a price worth paying for the probable rewards, which are the happiness of America and the peace of the world.

9. Former Secretary of Defense Clark M. Clifford Recalls His Post-Tet Questions (1968), 1969

I took office on March 1, 1968. The enemy's Tet offensive of late January and early February had been beaten back at great cost. The confidence of the American people had been badly shaken. The ability of the South Vietnamese government to restore order and morale in the populace, and discipline and esprit in the armed forces, was being questioned. At the President's direction, General Earle G. Wheeler, Chairman of the Joint Chiefs of Staff, had flown to Viet Nam in late February for an on-the-spot conference with General [William] Westmoreland. He had just returned and presented the military's request that over 200,000 troops be prepared for deployment to Viet Nam. These troops would be in addition to the 525,000 previously authorized. I was directed, as my first assignment, to chair a task force named by the President to determine how this new requirement could be met. We were not instructed to assess the need for substantial increases in men and materiel; we were to devise the means by which they could be provided.

My work was cut out. The task force included Secretary [of State Dean] Rusk, Secretary [of the Treasury] Henry Fowler, Under Secretary of State Nicholas Katzenbach, Deputy Secretary of Defense Paul Nitze, General Wheeler, CIA Director Richard Helms, the President's Special Assistant, Walt Rostow, General Maxwell Taylor and other skilled and highly capable officials. All of them had had long and direct experience with Vietnamese problems. I had not. I had attended various meetings in the past several years and I had been to Viet Nam three times, but it was quickly apparent to me how little one knows if he has been on the periphery of a problem and not truly in it. Until the day-long sessions of early March, I had never had the opportunity of intensive analysis and fact-finding. Now I was thrust into a vigorous, ruthlessly frank assessment of our situation by the men who knew the most about it. Try though we would to stay with the assignment of devising means to meet the military's requests, fundamental questions began to recur over and over.

It is, of course, not possible to recall all the questions that were asked nor all of the answers that were given. Had a transcript of our discussions been made—one was not—it would have run to hundreds of closely printed pages. The documents brought to the table by participants would have totalled, if collected in one place—which they were not—many hundreds more. All that is pertinent to this essay are the impressions I formed, and the conclusions I ultimately reached in those days of exhausting scrutiny. In the colloquial style of those meetings, here are some of the principal issues raised and some of the answers as I understood them:

"Will 200,000 more men do the job?" I found no assurance that they would.

"If not, how many more might be needed—and when?" There was no way of knowing.

"What would be involved in committing 200,000 more men to Viet Nam?" A reserve call-up of approximately 280,000, an increased draft call and an extension of tours of duty of most men then in service.

"Can the enemy respond with a build-up of his own?" He could and he probably would.

"What are the estimated costs of the latest requests?" First calculations were on the order of $2 billion for the remaining four months of that fiscal year, and an increase of $10 to $12 billion for the year beginning July 1, 1968.

"What will be the impact on the economy?" So great that we would face the possibility of credit restrictions, a tax increase and even wage and price controls. The balance of payments would be worsened by at least half a billion dollars a year.

"Can bombing stop the war?" Never by itself. It was inflicting heavy personnel and materiel losses, but bombing by itself would not stop the war.

"Will stepping up the bombing decrease American casualties?" Very little, if at all. Our casualties were due to the intensity of the ground fighting in the South. We had already dropped a heavier tonnage of bombs than in all the theaters of World War II. During 1967, an estimated 90,000 North Vietnamese had infiltrated into South Viet Nam. In the opening weeks of 1968, infiltrators were coming in at three to four times the rate of a year earlier, despite the ferocity and intensity of our campaign of aerial interdiction.

"How long must we keep on sending our men and carrying the main burden of combat?" The South Vietnamese were doing better, but they were not ready yet to replace our troops and we did not know when they would be.

When I asked for a presentation of the military plan for attaining victory in Viet Nam, I was told that there was no plan for victory in the historic American sense. Why not? Because our forces were operating under three major political restrictions: The President had forbidden the invasion of North Viet Nam because this could trigger the mutual assistance pact between North Viet Nam and China; the President had forbidden the mining of the harbor at Haiphong, the principal port through which the North received military supplies, because a Soviet vessel might be sunk; the President had forbidden our forces to pursue the enemy into Laos and Cambodia, for to do so would spread the war, politically and geographically, with no discernible advantage. These and other restrictions which precluded an all-out, no-holds-barred military effort were wisely designed to prevent our being drawn into a larger war. We had no inclination to recommend to the President their cancellation.

"Given these circumstances, how can we win?" We would, I was told, continue to evidence our superiority over the enemy; we would continue to attack in the belief that he would reach the stage where he would find it inadvisable to go on with the war. He could not afford the attrition we were inflicting on him. And we were improving our posture all the time.

I then asked, "What is the best estimate as to how long this course of action will take? Six months? One year? Two years?" There was no agreement on an answer. Not only was there no agreement, I could find no one willing to express any confidence in his guesses. Certainly, none of us was willing to assert that he could see "light at the end of the tunnel" or that American troops would be coming home by the end of the year.

After days of this type of analysis, my concern had greatly deepened. I could not find out when the war was going to end; I could not find out the manner in which it was going to end; I could not find out whether the new requests for men and equipment were going to be enough, or whether it would take more and, if more, when and how much; I could not find out how soon the South Vietnamese forces would be ready to take over. All I had was the statement, given with too little self-assurance to be comforting, that if we persisted for an indeterminate length of time, the enemy would choose not to go on.

And so I asked, "Does anyone see any diminution in the will of the enemy after four years of our having been there, after enormous casualties and after massive destruction from our bombing?"

The answer was that there appeared to be no diminution in the will of the enemy. . . .

And so, after these exhausting days, I was convinced that the military course we were pursuing was not only endless, but hopeless. A further substantial increase in American forces could only increase the devastation and the Americanization of the war, and thus leave us even further from our goal of a peace that would permit the people of South Viet Nam to fashion their own political and economic institutions. Henceforth, I was also convinced, our primary goal should be to level off our involvement, and to work toward gradual disengagement.

10. Former Secretary of Defense Robert S. McNamara Concludes That He Erred, 1995

We of the Kennedy and Johnson administrations who participated in the decisions on Vietnam acted according to what we thought were the principles and traditions of this nation. We made our decisions in light of those values.

Yet we were wrong, terribly wrong. . . .

. . . Looking back, I clearly erred by not forcing—then or later, in either Saigon or Washington—a knock-down, drag-out debate over the loose assumptions, un-asked questions, and thin analyses underlying our military strategy in Vietnam. I had spent twenty years as a manager identifying problems and forcing organizations—often against their will—to think deeply and realistically about alternative courses of action and their consequences. I doubt I will ever fully understand why I did not do so here.

On July 21 [1965], I returned to Washington and presented the report I had prepared along the way to the president. It began with a frank but disturbing assessment:

> The situation in South Vietnam is worse than a year ago (when it was worse than a year before that). After a few months of stalemate, the tempo of the war has quickened. A hard VC push is now on to dismember the nation and to maul the army. . . . Without further outside help, the ARVN* is faced with successive tactical reverses, loss of key communication and population centers particularly in the highlands, piecemeal destruction of ARVN units . . . and loss of civilian confidence.

I continued:

> There are no signs that we have throttled the inflow of supplies for the VC or can throttle the flow while their material needs are as low as they are. . . . Nor have our air attacks in North Vietnam produced tangible evidence of the willingness on the part of Hanoi to come to the conference table in a reasonable mood. The DRV/VC [Democratic Republic of North Vietnam/Vietcong] seem to believe that South Vietnam is on the run and near collapse; they show no signs of settling for less than a complete take-over.

I then reviewed the three alternatives we had examined so many times before: (1) withdraw under the best conditions obtainable—almost certainly meaning something close to unconditional surrender; (2) continue at the present level—almost certainly forcing us into Option 1 later; or (3) expand our forces to meet Westy's request** while launching a vigorous effort to open negotiations—almost certainly staving off near-term defeat but also increasing the difficulty and cost of withdrawal later.

---

*The Army of the Republic of South Vietnam
**General William Westmoreland requested 175,000 troops by year's end and another 100,000 in 1966.

I was driven to Option 3, which I considered "prerequisite to the achievement of any acceptable settlement." I ended by expressing my judgment that "the course of action recommended in this memorandum—if the military and political moves are properly integrated and executed with continuing vigor and visible determination—stands a good chance of achieving an acceptable outcome within a reasonable time." Subsequent events proved my judgment wrong.

 E S S A Y S

In the first essay, George C. Herring of the University of Kentucky studies the reasons for U.S. military escalation in Vietnam, and analyzes why America's military mission ultimately failed. He traces the roots of the disaster to Washington's misapplication of anticommunist containment to Vietnam's struggle against colonialism. According to Herring, U.S. officials, from the 1940s forward, underestimated the power of Vietnamese nationalism, exaggerated communist leader Ho Chi Minh's ideological ties to Moscow and Beijing, and assigned a symbolic importance to Vietnam that exceeded concrete U.S. interests. When U.S. aid to France, and later to the newly established state of South Vietnam, failed to defeat the communists, the Johnson administration adopted a strategy of gradual military escalation. The air war and land war proved costly in U.S. lives and dollars, and counterproductive against Vietcong guerrillas and North Vietnam. Yet an unrestricted use of military power, Herring argues, would have only increased the war's cost and might have provoked Soviet and Chinese intervention. In the absence of a viable regime in South Vietnam, and the unacceptable prospect of annihilating North Vietnam, Herring concludes that the war may have been unwinnable.

Herring's autopsy of the subject differs from the radical perspective of Gabriel Kolko of York University in Canada. In the second essay, Kolko acknowledges the importance of Cold War politics and strategic thinking, but argues that U.S. intervention grew primarily from a deliberate quest, from 1945 on, to fashion an integrated world capitalist order. In the 1960s, as Vietnam's revolution seemed to weaken America's credibility as a world power, the Johnson administration moved decisively and confidently to intervene militarily and to turn back the challenge. According to Kolko, the Vietnam War became so expensive that it ultimately sapped the nation's economic strength and reduced U.S. power around the world.

Why the United States Failed in Vietnam

GEORGE C. HERRING

Understanding Vietnam requires addressing two fundamental questions. First, why did the United States commit billions of dollars and a large part of its military power to an area so remote and seemingly so insignificant? And second, why, despite this huge commitment, did the world's richest and most powerful nation fail to achieve its objective—the preservation of an independent, non-Communist South Vietnam? . . .

In the broadest sense, U.S. involvement in Vietnam stemmed from the inter-action of two major phenomena of the post-World War II era: decolonization—the breakup of the old colonial empires—and the Cold War. The rise of nationalism and the weakness of the European colonial powers combined at the end of World War II to destroy a system that had been an established feature of world politics for centuries. Changes of this magnitude do not occur smoothly, and in this case the result was turmoil and, in some areas, war. In Asia, the British and Dutch grudg-ingly recognized the inevitable and granted independence to their colonies within several years after World War II. The French, on the other hand, refused to concede the inevitability of decolonization. They attempted to regain control of their Indo-chinese colonies and to put down the Vietnamese revolution by force, sparking in 1946 a war that in its various phases would not end until the fall of Saigon in the spring of 1975.

What was unique—and from the American standpoint most significant—about the conflict in Vietnam was that the nationalist movement, the Vietminh, was led by Communists. The father of the revolution, the charismatic Ho Chi Minh, was a longtime Communist operative who had devoted his life to gaining indepen-dence and national unit for his country. Well organized and tightly disciplined, the Communists took advantage of the fragmentation among the other nationalist groups to establish their own preeminence. During World War II they exploited popular opposition to the French and to Japanese occupation forces to build support for the revolution, and they moved adeptly to fill the vacuum when the Japanese surrendered in August 1945. During the ensuing war with France, the Vietminh solidified its claim to the mantle of Vietnamese nationalism. In all the former Euro-pean colonies in Asia, only in Vietnam did Communists direct the nationalist movement, and this would have enormous long-range implications, transforming what began as a struggle against French colonialism into an international conflict of vast proportions.

At the very time that the Communist-led Vietminh was engaged in a bloody struggle with France, the Cold War was assuming global dimensions, and from an early stage Washington perceived the war in Vietnam largely in terms of its conflict with the Soviet Union. As early as 1946, Americans viewed Ho and the Vietminh as instruments of the Soviet drive for world domination, directed and controlled by the Kremlin. This view was not seriously questioned in or out of government until the United States was involved in full-scale war in Vietnam. . . .

In this context of a world divided into two hostile power blocs in a fragile bal-ance, a zero-sum game in which any gain for communism was automatically a loss for the United States, areas such as Vietnam, which had been of no more than mar-ginal importance suddenly took on great significance. The onset of the Korean War in June 1950 seemed to confirm the assumptions of NSC-68 and also suggested that the Communists were now prepared to use military invasion to upset the balance of power. Faced with this challenge, the Truman administration in 1950 extended to East Asia a containment policy that had been restricted to Europe. The first American commitment to Vietnam, a commitment to assist the French in suppressing the Viet-minh revolution, was part of this broader attempt to contain Communist expansion in Asia.

There were other, more specific reasons why U.S. policymakers attached growing significance to Vietnam after 1950. The first, usually called the "domino theory," was the idea that the fall of Vietnam could cause the fall of Indochina and then the rest of Southeast Asia, with repercussions extending west to India and east to Japan and the Philippines. This fear of a chain reaction in Southeast Asia was initially set forth by the Joint Chiefs of Staff in 1950, and events in the late 1940s and early 1950s seemed to give it credence. Mao Zedong's Communists had just taken over in China. The departure of the colonial powers left a vacuum in southeast Asia; Indochina, Burma, and Malaya were swept by revolution; and the newly independent government of Indonesia seemed highly vulnerable. Because of its location on China's southern border and because it appeared in the most imminent danger, Vietnam was considered the most important—"the keystone in the arch," as Senator John F. Kennedy put it, "the finger in the dike." If it fell, all of Southeast Asia might be lost, costing the United States access to vital raw materials and strategic bases. Primarily for this reason the United States went to the aid of France in 1950, despite its compunctions about supporting colonialism, and it stepped into the breach when France was defeated in 1954.

The domino theory was reinforced and in time supplanted by the notion that the United States must stand firm in Vietnam to demonstrate its determination to defend vital interests across the world. Acceptance of this principle of credibility reflected the intensity of the Cold War, the influence of certain perceived lessons of history, and the desire on the part of American policymakers to find a means of averting nuclear catastrophe. During the most intense period of Cold War confrontation, these policymakers felt certain that what they did in one area of the world might have a decisive impact in others. If they showed firmness, it might deter Soviet or Chinese aggression; if they showed weakness, the adversary would be tempted to take steps that might ultimately leave no option but nuclear war. The so-called Manchurian or Munich analogy—the idea that the failure of the Western democracies to stand firm against Japanese or German aggression in the 1930s had encouraged further aggression—reinforced the idea of credibility. The obvious lesson was that to avoid war a firm stand must be taken at the outset. . . .

In searching for the roots of commitment in Vietnam, a second factor deserves attention: the assumption shared by administrations from Truman to Johnson that the fall of Vietnam to communism would have disastrous consequences at home. This assumption also stemmed from perceived lessons of history, in this case the rancorous and divisive debate following the fall of China in 1949 and Republican exploitation of it at the polls in 1952. Again, the conclusion was that no administration could survive the loss of Vietnam. Although a Democrat, President Kennedy had attacked Harry S. Truman for losing China. He had been a participant in the debate and vividly remembered it. He seems to have been sufficiently frustrated by Vietnam in late 1963 that he at least considered the possibility of withdrawal, but he was convinced that he could not do so until after he had been reelected. "If I tried to pull out now," Kennedy said, "we would have another Joe McCarthy Red Scare on our hands." Lyndon B. Johnson shared similar fears on numerous occasions, exclaiming that he was not going to be the president who saw "Southeast Asia go the way China went." . . .

The containment policy now seems misguided, both generally and in its application to Vietnam. Soviet goals were more the product of traditional Russian nationalism than ideology. The so-called Communist bloc was never a monolith; it was torn by division from the start, and the fragmentation became more pronounced. There was never a zero-sum game. What appeared to be a major victory for the Soviet Union in China in 1949, for example, turned out to be something quite different. In most parts of the world neither the Soviet Union nor the United States prevailed, and pluralism was the norm.

In applying containment to Vietnam, the United States drastically misjudged the internal dynamics of the conflict. It attributed to an expansionist communism a war that began as a revolution against French colonialism. It exaggerated as well the consequences of doing nothing. There is reason to doubt whether the domino theory would have operated if Vietnam had fallen earlier. Nationalism has proven the most potent and enduring force in recent history, and the nations of Southeast Asia, long suspicious of China and Vietnam, would have resisted mightily. Moreover, by making the war a test case of American credibility, U.S. policymakers may have made its consequences greater than they would have otherwise. In short, by rigidly adhering to a narrow, one-dimensional worldview, without taking into account the nature and importance of local forces, the United States placed itself in an untenable position in Vietnam from the start.

Another perplexing question is: Why, despite its vast power, did the United States fail to achieve its objective? It became fashionable in the aftermath of the war to argue that it failed because it did not use its military power wisely and decisively. Johnson and Defense Secretary Robert S. McNamara placed restrictions on the military that prevented it from winning the war. Such an argument is shortsighted in terms of the long history of U.S. involvement in Vietnam. It ignores the fact that the military solution sought after 1965 followed fifteen years of policy failure. It is therefore necessary to look to the period from 1950 to 1965 to understand fully America's ultimate failure in Vietnam.

During those years, U.S. policy went through three distinct phases. Between 1950 and 1954 the United States supported French efforts to suppress the Vietminh revolution, to the extent by 1954 of paying close to 80 percent of the war's cost. From 1954 to 1959, America helped ease the defeated French out of Vietnam, served as midwife for the birth of South Vietnam, and, violating the letter and spirit of the Geneva Accords, tried to sustain an independent government below the 17th parallel. From 1959 to 1965, through increased economic and military aid and eventually thousands of military "advisers," the United States tried to help the South Vietnamese government put down the insurgency, which began in the South and by 1965 enjoyed large-scale support from North Vietnam. With each step along the way, its policy failed to produce the desired results, leading to escalation of the U.S. commitment. In July 1965, Johnson was left the unpleasant choice of calling in American combat forces or accepting a South Vietnamese defeat.

In the case of the French, the so-called First Indochina War, the explanation for failure seems reasonably clear. France's goal, the retention of some level of imperial control in Vietnam, ran against one of the main currents of post-World War II history. Throughout Asia and Africa, nationalist revolutions eventually prevailed, and even when imperial nations were able to win wars against insurgencies, as the

French later did in Algeria, they were forced to concede independence. American policymakers understood the problem all too well, but they could find no way to resolve it. They pressed the French to fight on to victory in Vietnam while at the same time urging them to leave as soon as the war ended. This contradiction made little sense from the French point of view, and, when faced with the choice of fighting for Vietnamese independence or withdrawing, the French chose the latter. After their disastrous defeat at the battle of Dienbienphu in May 1954, they agreed at Geneva to a negotiated settlement that provided for their ultimate withdrawal from Vietnam.

While Paris was negotiating, Washington was planning ways to create a bulwark against further Communist expansion in Southeast Asia by making permanent the temporary partition of Vietnam. For a variety of reasons this effort to create an independent, non-Communist South Vietnam also eventually failed. First, and probably most important, was the magnitude of the challenge itself. Had the United States looked all over the world it might not have found a less promising place for an experiment in nation building. The economy of South Vietnam was shattered from ten years of war, the departure of the French had left a gaping political vacuum, and France had destroyed the traditional structure of Vietnamese politics but had left nothing to replace it. As a result, there was no firmly established political tradition, no institutions of government, and no native elite capable of exercising effective leadership. In addition, South Vietnam was fragmented by a multitude of conflicting political, religious, and ethnic groups, and the emigration of nearly one million Catholics from North Vietnam after 1954 added to the already complex and conflict-ridden picture. Under these circumstances, there may have been built-in limits to what the United States or any nation could have accomplished in South Vietnam.

Second, America's nation-building policies were often misguided or misapplied. In the early years, U.S. advisers concentrated on building a South Vietnamese army to meet the threat of invasion from the North, a logical step in terms of the situation in Vietnam and earlier experience in Korea but one that left the South Vietnamese poorly equipped to cope with the developing insurgency in the late 1950s. By contrast, too little attention was devoted during these years to mobilizing the peasantry and promoting pacification in the countryside. When the United States attempted to deal with these problems in the early 1960s, it applied methods that had worked elsewhere but adapted poorly to Vietnam. The strategic hamlet program, promoted by the Kennedy administration with great enthusiasm, is a case in point. The idea of bringing peasants from isolated villages into settlements where they could be protected from insurgents had worked earlier in Malaya. However, in Malaya the insurgents were Chinese, and it was relatively easy to guard against infiltration; in Vietnam the insurgents were Vietnamese who had lived and worked with the villagers for years, and the hamlets were infiltrated with ease. In Malaya, moreover, the peasants were resettled without major disruption, but in Vietnam they had to be removed from lands on which their families had lived for centuries and that were regarded as sacred. Sometimes they had to be forcibly removed and their old homes burned behind them. They were left rootless and resentful, easy prey for recruiters from the insurgency.

A third important reason was South Vietnam's leadership, a problem all too clearly revealed in the frustrating and ultimately tragic American partnership with its first president, Ngo Dinh Diem. In terms of his anticommunism and his nationalism, Diem appeared to fit Washington's needs perfectly, and in his first years in power he seemed to be a miracle worker, stabilizing a chaotic South Vietnam in a way no one had thought possible. In time, however, his deficiencies became all too apparent. It was not simply that his government was corrupt and undemocratic. Such governments have survived for years, and Diem may have had logic and history on his side when he insisted that democracy would not work in Vietnam. The problems were more basic. He was a poor administrator who tolerated far too much from his family, particularly his notorious brother, Ngo Dinh Nhu. Most important, Diem lacked any real blueprint for Vietnam. He seemed content simply to preside over the government, but he proved incapable of leading his country, mobilizing the peasantry, or coping with the insurgency.

Diem was also fiercely independent, and this attribute posed a dilemma that the United States never resolved. Americans came in time to see his weaknesses, but they could not persuade him to change or impose their will on him. They saw no alternative to Diem, however, and feared that if he were removed it would only lead to greater chaos. Thus, the United States, with some reluctance, stood by him for nine years as the political and military situation in South Vietnam deteriorated. "Sink or swim with Ngo Dinh Diem," a critical journalist summed up American policy. It was only when Diem's actions produced a full-scale political upheaval among Buddhists in South Vietnam's major cities in 1963, and when it was learned that he and his brother were secretly negotiating with North Vietnam, that the United States finally concluded that he must go.

As many observers had predicted, the overthrow of Diem in November 1963 offered no real solutions, only more problems. The army generals who replaced Diem were, for the most part, Western educated. They lacked close touch with their own people and even less than Diem had the capacity to unify a fragmented society. Divided among themselves, they spent their energy on intrigue, and one coup followed another in such rapid fashion that it was almost impossible to keep up with the daily changes in government. Thus, by mid-1965 the United States found itself in a position that it never really had wanted and whose dangers it recognized—that of an imperial power seeking to fill a political and military vacuum.

Focusing on American and South Vietnamese failures provides only a partial picture. It is also necessary to analyze why the South Vietnamese insurgents and their northern supporters had reached the verge of victory by 1965. It is now evident from captured documents that, by 1957, Diem had nearly exterminated the remnants of the Vietminh in South Vietnam. Alarmed by their plight and the growing certainty that the elections called for at Geneva would not be held, they began to mobilize to salvage the revolution of 1945. The insurgents effectively exploited the unrest caused by Diem's heavy-handed methods. In many areas they implemented land reform programs and lowered taxes, policies that contrasted favorably with those instituted by the government. They also skillfully employed selective violence by assassinating unpopular government officials and also mobilized the peasantry. Organizing themselves into the National Liberation Front (NLF) in 1960, the insurgents not only controlled large segments of the land and the population but developed a formidable army as well.

North Vietnam's role remains a matter of controversy. It seems clear that Hanoi did not instigate the revolution in the South, as the U.S. government claimed at the time, nor did it remain an innocent and even indifferent bystander, as American critics of the war insisted. The revolution did begin spontaneously in the South, perhaps even against Hanoi's instructions. Once it started, however, Hanoi did not stand by and watch. Fearful that the southern revolution might fail—or succeed—without its help, it began to send cadres into the South to assume leadership of the insurgency. In 1959 the Democratic Republic of Vietnam approved the initiation of "armed struggle" against the Diem regime. In the aftermath of the overthrow of Diem, North Vietnam decided to undertake a major escalation of the conflict, even to the point of sending its own military units into South Vietnam to fight intact. It apparently took this step in the expectation that the United States, when faced with certain defeat, would withdraw as it had in China in 1949 rather than risk its own men and resources.

The North Vietnamese gravely miscalculated. Confronting the collapse of South Vietnam in 1965, Johnson never seriously considered withdrawing. Determined to uphold a commitment of more than a decade's standing and certain that tiny North Vietnam could not defy the will of the world's greatest power, the president in February 1965 initiated a regular systematic bombing of the North and then in July made what amounted to an open-ended commitment to use whatever ground combat forces were needed to determine the outcome of the war. In making this latter commitment, Johnson also miscalculated. He rejected the proposal of Joint Chiefs of Staff to mobilize the reserves. To avoid any risk of confrontation with China and the Soviet Union and, more important, to prevent what he called that "bitch of a war" from interfering with "the woman I really love"—the Great Society reform program at home—he escalated the war quietly while imposing the lightest possible burden on the American people. He did so in the expectation that the gradual increase of military pressure on North Vietnam would persuade it to abandon the struggle in the South. "I'm going up old Ho Chi Minh's leg an inch at a time," he explained.

Johnson's strategy of gradual escalation did not work. The United States expanded the tonnage of bombs dropped on North Vietnam from 63,000 in 1965 to 226,000 in 1967, inflicting an estimated $600 million in damages on a primitive economy. The gradualist approach gave the North Vietnamese time to disperse their vital resources, repair the damage, develop an effective air defense system, and adapt in other ways. It encouraged—and probably permitted—them to persevere, and China and the Soviet Union helped make up the losses that they sustained. As a result, the bombing did not decisively affect North Vietnam's will to resist, and its very intensity and the fact that it was carried out by a rich, advanced nation against a poor, small one gave the North Vietnamese a propaganda card that they played with consummate skill. In the United States, and indeed throughout the world, the bombing became a major target of criticism and a symbol of the alleged immorality of American intervention in Vietnam.

The strategy of attrition implemented by General William C. Westmoreland on the ground in South Vietnam also failed. The availability of sanctuaries in Laos, Cambodia, and across the demilitarized zone permitted North Vietnam to control its losses, dictate the pace and intensity of the war, and hold the strategic initiative. If at any point losses became excessive, the enemy could withdraw and take time to recover. If, on the other hand, it wished to step up the war, it could do so at times and places of its own choosing. It even had the ability to control the level of American casualties, and in time this became of considerable importance. The attrition strategy thus represented an open-ended commitment that required increasing manpower and produced growing casualties without any signs of victory. By the end of 1967 the United States had more than 500,000 troops in Vietnam and nothing to show for it except a bloody stalemate. . . .

As the war dragged on, opposition in the United States assumed major proportions. "Hawks" protested President Johnson's policy of gradual escalation, urging the use of any means necessary to achieve victory. On the other side, a heterogeneous group of "doves" increasingly questioned the wisdom and morality of the war and began to conduct protest marches and encourage draft resistance and other forms of antiwar activity. The mounting cost of the conflict was more important than the antiwar movement in causing opposition among the general public. Increased casualties, indications that more troops would be required, and Johnson's belated request for new taxes combined by late 1967 to produce a sharp decline in public support for the war and the president's handling of it.

The Tet offensive of 1968 brought Johnson's gradual escalation of the war to an inglorious end. In a strictly military sense, the United States and South Vietnam prevailed, repelling a series of massive NLF assaults against the urban areas of the South and inflicting huge casualties. At the same time, Tet had a tremendous psychological impact in the United States, raising serious questions about whether anything could be achieved that would be worth the cost. In March 1968, responding to growing signs of public frustration and impatience, Johnson rejected General Westmoreland's request for an additional two hundred thousand troops and for expansion of the war, cut back the bombing of North Vietnam, launched a diplomatic initiative eventually leading to peace negotiations in Paris, and withdrew from the presidential race.

It would be seven more years before the war finally ended. Recognizing that public frustration required him at least to scale down U.S. involvement, Johnson's successor, Richard M. Nixon, pursued an approach that he called Vietnamization, initiating a series of phased withdrawals of American troops while expanding aid to the South Vietnamese army to prepare it to take over the brunt of the fighting. Nixon also escalated the war by authorizing "incursions" into the North Vietnamese sanctuaries in Cambodia and Laos to bolster Vietnamization. When the North Vietnamese in the spring of 1972 launched a major offensive against South Vietnam, he resumed the bombing of North Vietnam and mined Haiphong harbor. Nixon was able to save South Vietnam, but opposition at home continued to grow. In 1973, without resolving the fundamental issue of the war—the political future of South Vietnam—he was forced to agree to a settlement permitting extrication of U.S. forces. That issue was settled two years later when North Vietnam launched a massive conventional invasion of the South. By that time, Nixon had resigned as a result of the Watergate scandal, and the United States stood by helplessly while an ally of twenty years went down to defeat.

Although American strategies in Vietnam were clearly flawed, the argument that an unrestricted use of military power could have produced victory at an acceptable cost is not persuasive. The capacity of air power to cripple a preindustrial nation was probably quite limited, and there is considerable evidence to suggest that, even though its cities and industries were destroyed, North Vietnam was prepared to fight on, underground if necessary. Invasion of the sanctuaries and ground operations in the North might have made the strategy of attrition more workable, but they also would have enormously increased the costs of the war at a time when American resources were already stretched thin. Neither of these approaches would have solved what was always the central problem: the political viability of South Vietnam. Each ran serious risks of Soviet and Chinese intervention. Also, even if the United States had been able to subdue North Vietnam militarily without provoking outside intervention, it still would have faced the dangerous and costly task of occupying a hostile nation along China's southern border while simultaneously containing an insurgency in South Vietnam.

In the final analysis, the causes of American failure must be found as much in Vietnam as in Washington. In South Vietnam the United States attempted a truly formidable undertaking on the basis of a very weak foundation. For nearly twenty years, Americans struggled to establish a viable nation in the face of internal insurgency and external invasion, but the rapid collapse of South Vietnam after their withdrawal suggests how little was really accomplished. The United States could never find leaders capable of mobilizing the disparate population of South Vietnam. It launched a vast array of ambitious and expensive programs to promote sound government, win the hearts and minds of the people, and wage war against the insurgents. When its client state was on the verge of collapse in 1965, it filled the vacuum by putting in its own military forces. The more it did, however, the more it induced a state of dependency among those whom it was trying to help. Tragically, right up to the fall of Saigon in 1975, South Vietnamese leaders expected the Americans to return and save them from defeat.

The United States also drastically underestimated the determination of its adversary. The North Vietnamese made huge blunders of their own and paid an enormous price for their success. At the same time, they were tightly mobilized and regimented, and they were fanatically committed to their goals. They were fighting on familiar soil and used methods perfected in the war against France. They skillfully employed the strategy of protracted war, perceiving that the Americans, like the French, could become impatient and that, if they bled long enough, they might grow weary of the war. "You will kill ten of our men, but we will kill one of yours," Ho once remarked, "and in the end it is you who will tire." The comment was made to a French official on the eve of the First Indochina War, but it just as easily could have been said of the American phase.

The circumstances of the war thus posed a dilemma that Washington never really understood, much less resolved. The attainment of American goals would probably have required the physical annihilation of North Vietnam, a distasteful and extremely costly course of action that held out a serious threat of Soviet and Chinese intervention. The only other way was to establish a viable South Vietnam, but, given the weak foundation it worked from, not to mention the strength of the internal revolution, this course was probably beyond its capability. The United States very well may have placed itself in a no-win situation.

America's Quest for a Capitalist World Order

GABRIEL KOLKO

The Vietnam War was the United States' longest and most divisive war of the post-1945 epoch, and in many regards its most important conflict in the twentieth century. Obviously, the Vietnamese Communist Party's resiliency made Vietnam distinctive after 1946, but that the United States should have become embroiled with such formidable adversaries was a natural outcome of the logic and objectives of its role in the modern era. . . .

The hallmark of American foreign policy after 1945 was the universality of its intense commitment to create an integrated, essentially capitalist world framework out of the chaos of World War Two and the remnants of the colonial systems. The United States was the major inheritor of the mantle of imperialism in modern history, acting not out of a desire to defend the nation against some tangible threat to its physical welfare but because it sought to create a controllable, responsive order elsewhere, one that would permit the political destinies of distant places to evolve in a manner beneficial to American goals and interests far surpassing the immediate needs of its domestic society. The regulation of the world was at once the luxury and the necessity it believed its power afforded, and even if its might both produced and promised far greater prosperity if successful, its inevitable costs were justified, as all earlier imperialist powers had also done, as a fulfillment of an international responsibility and mission.

This task in fact far transcended that of dealing with the USSR, which had not produced the world upheaval but was itself an outcome of the first stage of the protracted crisis of the European and colonial system that had begun in 1914, even though the United States always held Moscow culpable to a critical extent for the many obstacles it was to confront. The history of the postwar era is essentially one of the monumental American attempts—and failures—to weave together such a global order and of the essentially vast autonomous social forces and destabilizing dynamics emerging throughout the world to confound its ambitions.

Such ambitions immediately brought the United States face to face with what to this day remains its primary problem: the conflict between its inordinate desires and its finite resources, and the definition of realistic priorities. Although it took years for the limits on American power to become clear to its leaders, most of whom only partly perceived it, it has been this problem of coherent priorities, and of the means to implement them, rather than the ultimate abstract goals themselves that have divided America's leaders and set the context for debates over policy. What was most important for much of the post-1945 era was the overweening belief on the part of American leaders that regulating all the world's political and economic problems was not only desirable but also possible, given skill and power. They would not and could not concede that the economic, political, and social dynamics of a great part of the world exceeded the capacities of any one or even a group of nations to control. At stake

From Gabriel Kolko, *Anatomy of a War: Vietnam, the United States, and the Modern Historical Experience,* Pantheon, 1985, pp. 72–77, 79, 113, 123–125, 149, 166–168, 283–284, 286, 547–548. Reprinted by permission of Gabriel Kolko.

were the large and growing strategic and economic interests in those unstable nations experiencing the greatest changes. . . .

By the late 1940s the United States had begun to confront the basic dilemmas it was to encounter for the remainder of the century. The formulation of priorities was an integral part of its reasoning, and so was resistance to communism in whatever form it might appear anywhere in the world. Its own interests had been fully articulated, and these found expression in statements of objectives as well as in the creation of international political, military, and economic organizations and alliances the United States effectively dominated, with American-led "internationalism" becoming one of the hallmarks of its postwar efforts. . . .

The domino theory was to be evoked initially more than any other justification in the Southeast Asian context, and the concept embodied both strategic and economic components which American leaders never separated. "The fall of Indochina would undoubtedly lead to the fall of the other mainland states of Southeast Asia," the Joint Chiefs of Staff argued in April 1950, and with it Russia would control "Asia's war potential. . . . affecting the balance of power." Not only "major sources of certain strategic materials" would be lost, but also communications routes. The State Department maintained a similar line at this time, writing off Thailand and Burma should Indochina fall. Well before the Korean conflict this became the United States' official doctrine, and the war there strengthened this commitment.

The loss of Indochina, Washington formally articulated in June 1952, "would have critical psychological, political and economic consequences. . . . the loss of any single country would probably lead to relatively swift submission to or an alignment with communism by the remaining countries of this group. Furthermore, an alignment with communism of the rest of Southeast Asia and India, and in the longer term, of the Middle East (with the probable exceptions of at least Pakistan and Turkey) would in all probability progressively follow. Such widespread alignment would endanger the stability and security of Europe." It would "render the U.S. position in the Pacific offshore island chain precarious and would seriously jeopardize fundamental U.S. security interests in the Far East." The "principal world source of natural rubber and tin, and a producer of petroleum and other strategically important commodities" would be lost in Malaya and Indonesia. The rice exports of Burma and Thailand would be taken from Malaya, Ceylon, Japan, and India. Eventually, there would be "such economic and political pressures in Japan as to make it extremely difficult to prevent Japan's eventual accommodation to communism." This was the perfect integration of all the elements of the domino theory, involving raw materials, military bases, and the commitment of the United States to protect its many spheres of influence. In principle, even while helping the French to fight for the larger cause which America saw as its own, Washington's leaders prepared for greater intervention when it became necessary to prop up the leading domino—Indochina.

There were neither private nor public illusions regarding the stakes and goals for American power. Early in 1953 the National Security Council reiterated, "The Western countries and Japan need increased supplies of raw materials and foodstuffs and growing markets for their industrial production. Their balance of payments difficulties are in considerable part the result of the failure of production of raw materials and foodstuffs in non-dollar areas to increase as rapidly as industrial production." "Why is the United States spending hundreds of millions of dollars supporting the forces of the French Union in the fight against communism?" Vice-President Richard Nixon explained publicly in December 1953. "If Indo-china falls, Thailand is put in an almost impossible position. The same is true of Malaya with its rubber and tin. The same is true of Indonesia. If this whole part of South-east Asia goes under Communist domination or Communist influence, Japan, who trades and must trade with this area in order to exist, must inevitably be oriented towards the Communist regime." Both naturally and logically, references to tin, rubber, rice, copra, iron ore, tungsten, and oil were integral to American policy considerations from the inception. As long as he was President, Eisenhower never forgot his country's dependence on the importation of raw materials and the need to control their sources. When he first made public the "falling domino" analogy, in April 1954, he also discussed the dangers of losing the region's tin, tungsten, and rubber and the risk of Japan's being forced into dependence on communist nations for its industrial life—with all that implied. Always implicit in the doctrine was the assumption that the economic riches of the neighbors of the first domino, whether Greece or Indochina, were essential, and when the United States first intervened in those hapless and relatively poor nations, it kept the surrounding region foremost in its calculations. This willingness to accept the immense overhead charges of regional domination was constantly in the minds of the men who made the decisions to intervene.

The problem with the domino theory was, of course, its intrinsic conflict with the desire to impose priorities on U.S. commitments, resources, and actions. If a chain is no stronger than its weakest link, then that link has to be protected even though its very fragility might make the undertaking that much more difficult. But so long as the United States had no realistic sense of the constraints on its power, it was ready to take greater risks. . . .

It was in this larger context of a search for a decisive global strategy and doctrine throughout the 1950s that the emerging Vietnam issue was linked to so many other international questions. Washington always saw the challenge of Indochina as just one part of a much greater problem it confronted throughout the world: the efficacy of limited war, the danger of dominoes, the credibility of American power, the role of France in Europe, and much else. Vietnam became the conjunction of the postwar crisis of U.S. imperialism at a crucial stage of America's much greater effort to resolve its own doubts about its capacity to protect the larger international socioeconomic environment in which its interests could survive and prosper. By 1960 every preceding event required that the credibility of U.S. power be tested soon, lest all of the failures and dilemmas since 1946 undermine the very foundations of the system it was seeking to construct throughout the world. It was mainly chance that designated Vietnam as the primary arena of trial, but it was virtually preordained that America would try somewhere to attain successes—not simply one but many—to reverse the deepening pattern of postwar history. . . .

This perception of Vietnam from 1961 onward gave it a symbolic global significance that far outweighed the specific U.S. interests there, but behind this notion there nonetheless existed more tangible goals, which varied somewhat in importance but always remained a part of a justification of the effort. Raw materials, though less publicly cited than earlier, were still prominent in the decision makers' vision. This included the preservation of existing markets. The retention of South Vietnam was invariably linked to U.S. relations with other nations in the region, particularly with Indonesia, where Washington considered [President] Sukarno the most important threat to its interests.

Credibility rose in importance with the successive failures of each escalation of advisers and resources in Vietnam, reaching 11,000 by the end of 1962 and 23,000 two years later. The domino and the global contexts were incorporated into all justifications of the war. The concepts finally merged late in 1964, when General Maxwell Taylor, a leading limited-war theorist and the ambassador to Saigon, argued typically, "If we leave Vietnam with our tail between our legs, the consequences of this defeat in the rest of Asia, Africa, and Latin America would be disastrous.". . .

The desire in Washington for important new escalations culminated in the National Security Council's March [1964] commitment to make Vietnam a test case of U.S. credibility. In March, too, William Bundy, assistant secretary of state and McGeorge's brother, argued that serious punitive measures against the DRV [Democratic Republic of Vietnam (North)] for the NLF's [National Liberation Front's] action in the south would require congressional approval, and a resolution was drawn up modeled after the Offshore Islands Resolution of January 1955, sanctioning the defense of Formosa. Comparable Cuban and Middle Eastern resolutions also existed for "continuing crises."

The President's advisers debated the exact pressures that would cause the DRV to cease its support of the NLF, fully conscious that they might not work. As William Bundy conceded, "the Viet Cong *do* have a lot of appeal in South Vietnam and *do* rely heavily on captured US weapons," though he nonetheless considered the DRV's role crucial. In any case, McNamara and others could argue, action against the DRV would be good for the otherwise sagging morale and fortunes of the fast-sinking . . . [South Vietnamese] regime. At a conference in Honolulu during the first days of June, the key advisers approved a variety of contingency plans for air strikes against the DRV, including preparation to continue them on a sustained basis, and various options for an increased buildup of U.S. troops and equipment for the beginning of what was clearly going to be a larger, longer war. . . .

It was throughout this June–July period that the United States resumed its OPLAN 34A [Top Secret Operation Plan 34A] operations in the coastal DRV areas, utilizing, as the Pentagon Papers later described it, "South Vietnamese or hired personnel and supported by U.S. training and logistical efforts." OPLAN 34A was in fact always an American project and was active in the DRV coastal region around the nineteenth parallel when the USS *Maddox* on July 31 was sent on a DESOTO patrol, with a special electronic-intelligence crew aboard, planning to electronically simulate an air attack and gather information not closer than four miles off the DRV coast. There is no question it was ordered to draw DRV boats away from 34A operations. It was this combination which caused the forewarned DRV authorities correctly to conclude that the OPLAN 34A and DESOTO boats were collaborating and to attack the *Maddox,* leading to the so-called Tonkin Gulf incident on August 2. George Ball later accurately described the DESOTO missions as serving "primarily for provocation." The U.S. air attack on the patrol boat sites and oil storage facilities was the beginning of the air war against the north, and the passage of the long-prepared Tonkin Gulf Resolution on August 7, with virtually no dissent, authorized the President "to take all necessary steps, including the use of armed force," to aid any Southeast Asian state. . . .

The events leading to the Tonkin Gulf affair had left the United States with no doubt that its alternative to defeat was a much heavier use of military power, and the Tonkin Gulf Resolution had cleared the way for a sustained escalation of the war. . . .

Once the decision to bomb the DRV had been made, the whole paralytic, dangerous logic of credibility extended to it as well. Once initiated, the escalatory process cannot be terminated until it delivers success, lest it, too, appear an implausible and ineffective instrument—thereby depriving military power of its ultimate menace and role as a deterrent. The Tonkin Resolution was in fact the critical threshold regarding the use of U.S. military resources. . . .

While several senior advisers, like Maxwell Taylor, expressed skepticism about phases of this air-ground program, all save George Ball thought persistence essential to the maintaining of credibility. All who counted, their differences notwithstanding, favored some degree of escalation. It is important to stress that there was a continuity in the many steps after summer 1964, some of them quite obscure, leading to the maximum U.S. war effort. No one decision or discussion was a critical turning point, just as the events of 1964 have their antecedents in more fundamental strategic and political commitments. On March 1, 1965, for example, McNamara discussed aid to the RVN [Republic of Vietnam (South)]—whether it should be in the form of goods or of U.S. forces—and informed his service secretaries, "I want it clearly understood that there is an unlimited appropriation available for the financing of aid to Vietnam," a "blank check," as the Army's chief financial manager later described it, "which military leaders normally expected to receive when preparing for a war." In early April and again in mid-June, troop authorizations increased, and between the end of March and the end of June the actual number of American military personnel in Vietnam doubled to 60,000, with over 10,000 more authorized to go.

By April 1965 both McNamara and the JCS were committed to major escalations of both ground and air war. [Assistant national security affairs adviser] W. W. Rostow at the end of May argued that total victory was now possible—indeed, that it was nearer than anyone could imagine. McNamara thought 200,000 or so men would be the maximum needed to reverse the tide of the war before reducing U.S. forces. By June, Taylor's earlier reticence melted before the desire of the JCS and McNamara to assign 175,000 men to the war immediately, a commitment later climbing to forty-four American battalions. It could keep the NLF from winning, they claimed, and shift the balance of power by the end of the year. McNamara and Westmoreland argued that with yet more troops in 1966 and 1967 the United States could take the initiative—the higher the number of troops, the sooner success. The President prudently decided to pause at thirty-four battalions and 175,000 men for the time being, shrewdly refusing the Pentagon's request to take the politically unpopular step of calling up the Reserves. Nonetheless, convinced that the NLF was winning, the President became increasingly eager to send a massive U.S. force to turn the tide of the war, allowing him to return to his domestic program without being accused of having caused the nation's failure overseas and of having undermined its credibility. By the end of the year, there were 184,000 American military personnel in South Vietnam, and the logic of the vast escalation of American involvement in the war between the summer of 1964 and one year later had yet to reach its climax.

To comprehend the freedom and constraints on Washington's policy choices, one must also compare the events and decisions of the 1964–67 period with those after 1968. Until 1968 the war consisted for America of responding to a series of challenges, above all to the imminent victory of the NLF, and the administration had few institutional or ideological inhibitions on it. After Tet 1968 the very economic and political health of the United States was involved, starkly revealing the ultimate institutional parameters of the system as it approached its economic and social limits. During the three years of escalation, the weaknesses of American foreign policy emerged, proving that however unifying the broad consensus among decision makers on goals and general methods, specific realities eventually could—with growing failure—produce important differences on concrete tactics and unavoidable choices of priorities which acknowledged the limits of power. In this confrontation with a materially far weaker Revolutionary movement, directed by men with a relatively high degree of unity and analytic realism to guide their actions, the importance of the leadership equation on both adversaries in the war began to mount. The degree of combined cohesion and clarity on each side of the war was a possibly decisive factor, if only because the structural limit of the American system was also translated eventually into a prolonged crisis of leadership in which a materially great but increasingly confused and disunited United States found itself outmaneuvered by the physically much poorer Communists.

Precisely because conventional wisdom on the war has stressed the importance of differences among decision makers, it is worth focusing on the nature of leadership in foreign policy, the consensual values shaping it, and the context in which to place normal differences within American foreign policy circles. Whatever the convoluted way command decisions were made after 1946, or the personal chemistry of each set of men of power, in the end the consistency of responses far outweighed any rare deviations from it, and Vietnam was no exception. . . .

President Johnson's often bizarre personal conduct is not unimportant, but the case that his boorish manners were crucial to policy has yet to be made. A shrewd politician who could see the weaknesses of his sycophantic advisers very clearly, a consummate, instinctive fixer, he self-confidently played off people and problems to attain his elusive goals. His commitment to his domestic program was no more his obsession than it had been for other Presidents; the tension between foreign and domestic priorities has repeatedly broken up reform efforts. Whatever the technical differences among key presidential advisers, as a group during 1965–66 they minimized the extent to which earlier dilemmas of the limits of American power and weapons were reappearing. When they acknowledged them, it was only to reinforce the need to redeem prior failures in a new context, with new resources. Few attempted to predict the losses that might arise from the intervention in Vietnam, and they responded to such economic and political costs quite differently until 1968, when external forces and raw facts constrained their choices immeasurably. In this relatively narrow interregnum of 1965–67, the foreign policy consensus did not eliminate real tactical differences. But far more important than the essentially minor eddy of colorful anecdotes and rumor of the sort that makes good journalistic copy, let alone the personal frustrations of those like McNamara who were to lose confidence in themselves or be outmaneuvered by rivals, was the central reality of another massive failure of an essentially consensual system. The drama of this failure, ultimately, was institutional rather than individual, infringing on the very rationality of American imperialism, its postwar foreign policy, its perceptions of the world, itself, and the disparity between its desires and interests on the one hand and the limits of its power on the other. . . .

Imperialism in modern world history has never been an exclusively economic phenomenon, and that reality has been the main source of its demise. Although the economic rationale was crucial at its inception, the justification for imperialism transcended strictly materialist factors to take on geopolitical, cultural, and military dimensions and to form a character and motive too complex and convoluted for simplification. The importance of each element varied among key decision makers. Militarily and politically, Vietnam and, above all, Southeast Asia formed a crucial test for the United States as an imperialist power seeking militarily to impose its geopolitical as well as economic hegemony over major political, economic, and social developments throughout the Third World. By 1965, however, the economic basis for American imperialism in Southeast Asia had created its own fatal contradictions, and these proved to be crucial in inflicting defeat even when, militarily, the United States still appeared capable of success.

Economic factors of imperialism cannot be divorced from the political context in which they operate, and immediate economic consequences may quickly subvert the long-range economic rationality of an action. Economic costs of war always interact with other contemporaneous problems and may undermine a coherent ultimate objective, such as U.S. integration of Third World economies into the world capitalist system. . . .

The massive 1965 intervention in Vietnam began well into the longest sustained period of expansion in the postwar American economy. Starting in 1961, long before outlays for Southeast Asia further stimulated it, it lasted until 1969. The growth of the military budget in this context could only increase inflation. Rather than creating prosperity, it jeopardized it. Internationally, the United States was highly vulnerable. It attempted to play the role of stabilizer of the world economic structure, which was geared to the strength of the dollar, while it simultaneously exported investment funds and goods on the one hand and made costly political and military commitments which undermined its economic role in the world on the other. . . .

The United States' failure to recognize the limits of its economic power and its relation to its military and diplomatic policy was surely not unique in the mid-1960s and remains today a fundamental issue troubling American imperialism. Recognition of one's weaknesses is more difficult for a nation than for an individual, since states have conflicting interests and ample means of procrastinating. In 1965 the United States chose to do so, falling into an economic imbroglio through both naiveté and ignorance, becoming entangled in self-deception and cynical political maneuvering, and eventually reaching a predictable economic impasse, one which only a quick victory could keep from evolving into a prolonged military and political struggle whose economic costs would greatly accelerate America's defeat.

However Washington administered its war effort, its military strategy in limited war by the mid-1960s was certain to be expensive. Nearly half the war's cost arose from its reliance on air activities, not to mention the immense cost of high firepower. Still, the United States took the most expensive way out when McNamara gave a virtual blank check to the generals in March 1965. . . .

The Vietnam War was for the United States the culmination of its frustrating postwar effort to merge its arms and politics to halt and reverse the emergence of states and social systems opposed to the international order Washington sought to establish. It was not the first serious trial of either its military power or its political strategy, only the most disastrous. Despite America's many real successes in imposing its hegemony elsewhere, Vietnam exposed the ultimate constraints on its power in the modern era: its internal tensions, the contradictions between overinvolvement in one nation and its interests and ambitions elsewhere, and its material limits. Precisely because of the unmistakable nature of the defeat after so long and divisive an effort and because of the war's impact on the United States' political structure and aspirations, this conflict takes on a significance greater than that of either of the two world wars. Both of them had only encouraged Washington's ambition to guide and integrate the world's political and economic system—a goal which was surely the most important cause of its intervention in the Vietnam conflict after 1950.

While the strategic implications of the war for the future of American military power in local conflicts was the most obvious dimension of its defeat, it had confronted these issues often since 1946. What was truly distinctive was the collapse of a national consensus on the broad contours of America's role in the world. The trauma was intense; the war ended without glory and with profound remorse for tens of millions of Americans. Successive administrations fought the war so energetically because of these earlier frustrations, of which they were especially conscious in the early 1960s, scarcely suspecting that rather than resolving them, they would only leave the nation with a far larger set of military, political, and economic dilemmas to face for the remainder of this century. But by 1975 the United States was weaker than it had been at the inception of the war in the early 1960s, a lesson hardly any advocate of new interventions could afford to ignore.

The limits of arms and armies in Vietnam were clear by Tet 1968. Although the United States possessed nominally good weapons and tactics, it lacked a military strategy capable of overcoming its enemy's abilities and appropriate to its economic resources, its global priorities, and its political constraints in Vietnam, at home, and in the rest of the world. Although its aims in South Vietnam were never to alter, it was always incapable of coping with the countless political complexities that irrevocably emerge from protracted armed conflict. America's political, military, and ideological leaders remained either oblivious or contemptuous of these until the war was essentially lost. Even today they scarcely dare confront the war's meaning as Washington continues to assert aggressively its classic postwar objectives and interests in Latin America and elsewhere. America's failure was material, of course, but it was also analytic, the result of a myopia whose importance greatly transcended bureaucratic politics or the idiosyncrasies of Presidents and their satraps. The dominating conventional wisdom of American power after 1946 had no effective means of inhibiting a system whose ambitions and needs increasingly transcended its resources for achieving them. They remained unable and unwilling to acknowledge that these objectives were intrinsically unobtainable and irrelevant to the socioeconomic forms much of the Third World is adopting to resolve its economic and human problems, and that the United States' effort to alter this pervasive reality was certain to produce conflict.

FURTHER READING

David L. Anderson, ed., *Shadow on the White House* (1993)

———, *Trapped by Success: The Eisenhower Administration and Vietnam, 1953–1961* (1991)

Christian Appy, *Working-Class War* (1993)

Loren Baritz, *Backfire* (1985)

Richard J. Barnet, *Intervention and Revolution* (1972)

David M. Barrett, *Uncertain Warriors* (1993)

Lawrence Bassett and Stephen Pelz, "The Failed Search for Victory," in Thomas G. Paterson, ed., *Kennedy's Quest for Victory* (1989), pp. 223–252, 367–374

Eric M. Bergerud, *The Dynamics of Defeat* (1991)

———, *Red Thunder, Tropic Lightning* (1993)

Larry Berman, *Planning a Tragedy* (1982)

———, *Lyndon Johnson's War* (1989)

William C. Berman, *William Fulbright and the Vietnam War* (1988)

Irving Bernstein, *Guns or Butter: The Presidency of Lyndon Johnson* (1996)

Michael R. Beschloss, *Taking Charge* (1997) (LBJ White House)

Melanie Billings-Yun, *Decision Against War: Eisenhower and Dien Bien Phu, 1954* (1988)

Anne Blair, *Lodge in Vietnam* (1995)

Peter Braestrup, *Big Story* (1977)

———, ed., *Vietnam as History* (1984)

Robert Brigham, *The NLF's Foreign Relations and the Vietnam War* (1999)

Robert Buzzanco, *Masters of War* (1996)

———, "U.S. Military Opposition to Vietnam, 1950–1954," *Diplomatic History,* 17 (1993), 201–222

Larry Cable, *Unholy Grail* (1991)

Timothy Castle, *At War in the Shadow of Vietnam* (1993) (Laos)

Noam Chomsky, *Rethinking Camelot* (1993) (JFK and Vietnam)

James W. Clinton, *The Loyal Opposition* (1995)

Warren I. Cohen, *Dean Rusk* (1980)

Warren I. Cohen and Nancy Bernkopf Tucker, eds., *Lyndon Johnson Confronts the World* (1995)

Chester Cooper, *The Lost Crusade* (1970)

Robert Dallek, *Flawed Giant* (1998) (LBJ)

Charles DeBenedetti with Charles Chatfield, *An American Ordeal: The Antiwar Movement of the Vietnam Era* (1990)

Robert A. Divine, "Vietnam Reconsidered," *Diplomatic History,* 12 (1988), 79–93

William J. Duiker, *Sacred War* (1995)

Bernard Fall, *The Two Vietnams* (1967)

———, *Vietnam Witness, 1953–1966* (1966)

Frances FitzGerald, *Fire in the Lake* (1972)

Ilya V. Gaiduk, *The Soviet Union and the Vietnam War* (1996)

Robert L. Gallucci, *Neither Peace nor Honor* (1975)

Lloyd C. Gardner, *Pay Any Price* (1995) (LBJ)

———, *Approaching Vietnam* (1988)

Leslie H. Gelb and Richard K. Betts, *The Irony of Vietnam* (1979)

William C. Gibbons, *The U.S. Government and the Vietnam War* (1986–1987)

James William Gibson, *The Perfect War* (1986)

Daniel P. O'C. Greene, "John Foster Dulles and the End of Franco-American Entente in Indochina," *Diplomatic History,* 16 (1992), 551–572

Fred I. Greenstein and Richard H. Immerman, "What Did Eisenhower Tell Kennedy About Indochina? The Politics of Misperception," *Journal of American History,* 79 (1992), 568–587

David Halberstam, *The Best and the Brightest* (1972)

Daniel C. Hallin, *The "Uncensored War"* (1986)

Ellen J. Hammer, *A Death in November: America in Vietnam, 1963* (1988)

David Harris, *Our War* (1996)

James P. Harrison, ed., *The Endless War* (1989)

Patrick L. Hatcher, *The Suicide of an Elite* (1990)

Kenneth Heineman, *Campus Wars* (1993)

John Hellman, *American Myth and the Legacy of Vietnam* (1986)

Herbert Hendin and Ann P. Haas, *Wounds of War: The Psychological Aftermath of Combat in Vietnam* (1985)

George C. Herring, *America's Longest War* (1996)

———, *LBJ and Vietnam* (1994)

———, "The 'Vietnam Syndrome' and American Foreign Policy," *Virginia Quarterly Review,* 57 (1981), 594–612

———, "The Wrong Kind of Loyalty: McNamara's Apology for Vietnam," *Foreign Affairs,* 74 (1995), 154–158

Gary R. Hess, *The United States' Emergence as a Southeast Asian Power* (1987)

———, *Vietnam and the United States* (1990)

———, "The Military Perspective on Strategy in Vietnam," *Diplomatic History,* 10 (1986), 91–106

Michael H. Hunt, *Lyndon Johnson's War* (1996)

Richard H. Immerman, "The United States and the Geneva Conference of 1954: A New Look," *Diplomatic History,* 14 (1990), 43–66

——— and George Herring, "Eisenhower, Dulles, and Dienbienphu: The Day We Didn't Go to War," *Journal of American History,* 71 (1984), 343–363

Maurice Isserman, *Witness to War* (1995)

Susan Jeffords, *The Remasculinization of America: Gender and the Vietnam War* (1989)

George McT. Kahin, *Intervention* (1986)

——— and John W. Lewis, *The United States in Vietnam* (1969)

Lawrence S. Kaplan, Denise Artaud, and Mark R. Rubin, eds., *Dienbienphu and the Crisis in Franco-American Relations, 1954–1955* (1990)

Stanley Karnow, *Vietnam* (1983)

Ben Kiernan, "The Vietnam War: Alternative Endings," *American Historical Review,* 97 (1992), 1118–1137

Douglas Kinnard, *The Certain Trumpet: Maxwell Taylor and the American Experience in Vietnam* (1991)

Andrew F. Krepinevich, Jr., *The Army and Vietnam* (1986)

Diane B. Kunz, ed., *The Diplomacy of the Crucial Decade* (1994)

Alan J. Levine, *The U.S. and the Struggle for Southeast Asia* (1995)

David W. Levy, *The Debate over Vietnam* (1991)

Guenter Lewy, *America in Vietnam* (1978)

Fredrik Logevall, *Choosing War* (1999)

Robert J. McMahon, "U.S.-Vietnamese Relations: A Historiographical Survey," in Warren I. Cohen, ed., *Pacific Passages* (1996)

H. R. McMaster, *Dereliction of Duty* (1997)

James W. Mooney and Thomas R. West, *Vietnam* (1994)

Richard R. Moser, *The New Winter Soldiers* (1996)

Terry Nardin and Jerome Slater, "Vietnam Revised," *World Politics,* 33 (1981), 436–448

Gregory A. Olson, *Mansfield and Vietnam* (1995)

James S. Olson and Randy Roberts, *Where the Domino Fell* (1996)

Robert E. Osgood, *Limited War Revisited* (1979)

Bruce Palmer, Jr., *The 25-Year War* (1984)

Thomas G. Paterson, "Historical Memory and Elusive Victories: Vietnam and Central America," *Diplomatic History,* 12 (1988), 1–18

Achimedes L. A. Patti, *Why Viet Nam?* (1980)

Douglas Pike, *History of Vietnamese Communism* (1978)

———, *PAVN: People's Army of Vietnam* (1986)

———, *Viet Cong* (1972)

———, *Vietnam and the Soviet Union* (1987)

Norman Podhoretz, *Why We Were in Vietnam* (1982)

John Prados, *The Hidden History of the Vietnam War* (1993)

William Prochnau, *Once Upon a Distant Star* (1995)

Andrew J. Rotter, *The Path to Vietnam* (1987)

William J. Rust, *Kennedy in Vietnam* (1985)

Thomas J. Schoenbaum, *Waging Peace and War* (1988) (on Rusk)

Robert D. Schulzinger, *A Time for War* (1997)

Robert Shaplen, *Time Out of Hand* (1970)

———, *A Turning Wheel* (1979)

William Shawcross, *Sideshow: Kissinger, Nixon, and the Destruction of Cambodia* (1979)

Neil Sheehan, *A Bright Shining Lie* (1988)

Anthony Short, *The Origins of the Vietnam War* (1989)

Melvin Small, *Johnson, Nixon, and the Doves* (1988)

——— and William D. Hoover, eds., *Give Peace a Chance* (1992)

Ronald H. Spector, *After Tet* (1992)

———, *The United States Army in Vietnam* (1983)

Shelby L. Stanton, *The Rise and Fall of an American Army* (1985)

Harry G. Summers, *On Strategy* (1981)

James C. Thomson, "How Could Vietnam Happen? An Autopsy," *Atlantic Monthly,* 221 (1968), 47–53

———, *Rolling Thunder* (1980)

William S. Turley, *The Second Indochina War* (1986)

Kathleen J. Turner, *Lyndon Johnson's Dual War* (1985) (on the press)

Brian VanDeMark, *Into the Quagmire* (1991)

Francis X. Winters, *The Year of the Hare* (1997)

Randall Woods, *Fulbright* (1995)

Marilyn B. Young, *The Vietnam Wars* (1991)

Nancy Zaroulis and Gerald Sullivan, *Who Spoke Up?* (1984)

CHAPTER

12

Richard M. Nixon,
Henry A. Kissinger,
the Grand Strategy, and Détente

By the late 1960s the United States no longer dominated global affairs as it had during the two decades immediately following World War II. Defeat in Vietnam, the Soviet Union's achievement of parity in nuclear weapons, and the rise of a multipolar world order—characterized by America's relative decline and a diffusion of global economic and political power—spurred the Nixon administration to reconfigure the nation's foreign policy. President Richard M. Nixon and Henry A. Kissinger designed a grand strategy for achieving stability in the international environment. As self-described realists, they sought to make U.S. diplomacy less ideological and more adaptive to balance-of-power diplomacy. As an influential assistant for national security affairs (1969–1973) and secretary of state (1973–1977), Kissinger worked closely with Nixon to pursue détente with both the People's Republic of China and the Soviet Union. Their management of the Strategic Arms Limitation Talks (SALT) produced major agreements. Secret negotiations helped to extricate the United States from Vietnam. And Kissinger's "shuttle diplomacy" temporarily cooled the Arab-Israeli crisis in the Middle East. Admirers and critics alike applauded the Nixon administration's apparent diplomatic achievements in the 1970s.

But the Nixon-Kissinger team compiled a mixed record, as scholars have shown. Interventions and crises in Indochina, Chile, Cyprus, Bangladesh, Angola, and elsewhere sidetracked détente and undermined global stability. The White House's soft selling of human rights and emphasis on power politics raised doubts about the administration's morality and judgment. The Nixon Doctrine, which tried to reduce U.S. obligations abroad by relying on allies to promote stability, often hinged on U.S. ties to unsavory clients such as the Shah of Iran, Mohammad Reza Pahlavi, and the Philippine dictator Ferdinand Marcos. The international economy meanwhile continued to deteriorate, and, despite SALT, the nuclear-arms race accelerated. Nixon and Kissinger claimed too much for détente, and the public felt disappointed every time the Cold War heated up. Congress, resentful of being shut off from policymaking, increasingly contested Nixon's "imperial presidency." Nixon eventually resigned and the administration fell because of the array of corruptions revealed in the Watergate crisis.

Although scholarship on the Nixon-Kissinger diplomacy remains at an early stage, it has already generated spirited debate. One set of questions centers on the grand design and the policy of détente. Did détente represent a significant departure from traditional Cold War diplomacy? Or did it amount to little more than a change in tactics within the framework of anticommunist containment—a "new Cold War," as some have put it? In other words, how much did Soviet-American relations change during the Nixon era? Did SALT reduce the likelihood of nuclear war? Or did the continued military buildup that SALT allowed actually undermine arms control? Why did the Nixon administration continue to view local and regional conflicts in the Third World through a Cold War prism even as it sought accommodations with the Soviet Union and China? Was the administration's ending of the Vietnam War in 1973 a diplomatic triumph? Or could the war have been concluded earlier, saving tens of thousands of American and Asian lives? Did Nixon and Kissinger understand the limits of American power and successfully adjust to the new international setting of the late 1960s and early 1970s? Or did they continue to make commitments abroad that overstretched the nation's financial and military resources and exacerbated U.S. decline?

A second set of questions focuses on diplomatic style, especially Nixon's and Kissinger's practice of cutting Congress and the State Department out of the policymaking process. Did conservative opposition to détente and popular division over the Vietnam War force Nixon and Kissinger to conceal their controversial tactics and objectives? Or did their penchant for secrecy reflect a paranoia or insecurity deepseated in each man's personality? Are the achievements of the Nixon-Kissinger years, such as SALT and rapprochement with China, so impressive that we should restrain criticism of the abuses of presidential power evident in Indochina, Chile, and elsewhere? Might a more open relationship with Congress and the public have produced stronger support for détente and made the policy more enduring? In short, could the United States have adjusted more successfully to global change by adhering more consistently to its democratic values and honoring constitutional procedures? And, to which standard, if any, should the administration be held accountable?

As this chapter's selections suggest, Nixon and Kissinger share an ambiguous legacy that invites searching debate.

🌐 D O C U M E N T S

Richard M. Nixon, elected president in November 1968, assumed office with a reputation as a hardline Cold Warrior. But Document 1, from his memoirs, shows that he recognized new diplomatic opportunities to contain the Soviet Union and to end the war in Vietnam. One method of gaining these objectives was the exploitation of the Sino-Soviet split, sometimes called the "China card." Document 2, a Nixon statement on Asian self-help given during an interview on July 25, 1969, became known as the Nixon Doctrine. Nixon also acknowledged changes in the international economy during his presidency. Document 3 is an excerpt from a speech he gave in Kansas City, Missouri, on July 6, 1971, in which he discussed the five economic superpowers and America's role in the new global economy. In 1972 the Soviet Union and the United States signed the Strategic Arms Limitation Talks agreement, or SALT-I. In a September 19, 1974, appearance before the Senate Foreign

Relations Committee, Henry A. Kissinger defined détente and its accomplishments. His statement is reprinted here as Document 4.

Chile became a trouble spot from the Nixon-Kissinger perspective in 1970 when a Marxist, Salvador Allende, was elected president of that South American nation. The United States had attempted to block his election through covert operations but had failed. The Nixon administration then plotted to destabilize Allende's government. Document 5 is a 1975 report from the U.S. Senate Select Committee on Intelligence Activities—the Church Committee, named for its chair, Idaho Democrat Frank Church—on covert activities in Chile, 1963–1973. Document 6 is a January 13, 1977, editorial by Anthony Lewis of the *New York Times,* a writer who sharply indicted Kissinger's diplomatic record.

1. President Richard M. Nixon Recalls His Initial Goals (1968), 1978

For twenty-five years, I had watched the changing face of communism. I had seen prewar communism, luring workers and intellectuals with its siren call of equality and justice, reveal itself as an aggressive imperialistic ideology during the postwar period of the Marshall Plan. Despite the most nobly ringing rhetoric, the pattern was tragically the same: as soon as the Communists came to power, they destroyed all opposition. I had watched the Soviets' phenomenal recovery from the devastation of war and their costly but successful struggle to achieve for communism the selling point of potential prosperity. At home I had seen the face of underground subversive communism when it surfaced in the [Alger] Hiss case, reminding people not only that it existed, but that its purpose was deadly serious.

In the late 1940s and during the 1950s I had seen communism spread to China and other parts of Asia, and to Africa and South America, under the camouflage of parties of socialist revolution, or under the guise of wars of national liberation. And, finally, during the 1960s I had watched as Peking and Moscow became rivals for the role of leadership in the Communist world.

Never once in my career have I doubted the Communists mean it when they say that their goal is to bring the world under Communist control. Nor have I ever forgotten [Alger Hiss's accuser] Whittaker Chamber's chilling comment that when he left communism, he had the feeling he was leaving the winning side. But unlike some anticommunists who think we should refuse to recognize or deal with the Communists lest in doing so we imply or extend an ideological respectability to their philosophy and their system, I have always believed that we can and must communicate and, when possible, negotiate with Communist nations. They are too powerful to ignore. We must always remember that they will never act out of altruism, but only out of self-interest. Once this is understood, it is more sensible—and also safer—to communicate with the Communists than it is to live in icy cold-war isolation or confrontation. In fact, in January 1969 I felt that the relationship between the United States and the Soviet Union would probably be the single most important factor in determining whether the world would live at peace during and after my administration.

I felt that we had allowed ourselves to get in a disadvantageous position vis-à-vis the Soviets. They had a major presence in the Arab states of the Middle East, while we had none; they had Castro in Cuba; since the mid-1960s they had supplanted the Chinese as the principal military suppliers of North Vietnam; and except for Tito's Yugoslavia they still totally controlled Eastern Europe and threatened the stability and security of Western Europe.

There were, however, a few things in our favor. The most important and interesting was the Soviet split with China. There was also some evidence of growing, albeit limited, independence in some of the satellite nations. There were indications that the Soviet leaders were becoming interested in reaching an agreement on strategic arms limitation. They also appeared to be ready to hold serious talks on the anomalous situation in Berlin, which, almost a quarter century after the war had ended, was still a divided city and a constant source of tension, not just between the Soviets and the United States, but also between the Soviets and Western Europe. We sensed that they were looking for a face-saving formula that would lessen the risk of confrontation in the Mideast. And we had some solid evidence that they were anxious for an expansion of trade.

It was often said that the key to a Vietnam settlement lay in Moscow and Peking rather than in Hanoi. Without continuous and massive aid from either or both of the Communist giants, the leaders of North Vietnam would not have been able to carry on the war for more than a few months. Thanks to the Sino-Soviet split, however, the North Vietnamese had been extremely successful in playing off the Soviets and the Chinese against each other by turning support for their war effort into a touchstone of Communist orthodoxy and a requisite for keeping North Vietnam from settling into the opposing camp in the struggle for domination within the Communist world. This situation became a strain, particularly for the Soviets. Aside from wanting to keep Hanoi from going over to Peking, Moscow had little stake in the outcome of the North Vietnamese cause, especially as it increasingly worked against Moscow's own major interests vis-à-vis the United States. While I understood that the Soviets were not entirely free agents where their support for North Vietnam was concerned, I nonetheless planned to bring maximum pressure to bear on them in this area. . . .

During the transition period Kissinger and I developed a new policy for dealing with the Soviets. Since U.S.-Soviet interests as the world's two competing nuclear superpowers were so widespread and overlapping, it was unrealistic to separate or compartmentalize areas of concern. Therefore we decided to link progress in such areas of Soviet concern as strategic arms limitation and increased trade with progress in areas that were important to us—Vietnam, the Mideast and Berlin. This concept became known as linkage.

Lest there be any doubt of my seriousness in pursuing this policy, I purposely announced it at my first press conference when asked a question about starting SALT talks. I said, "What I want to do is to see to it that we have strategic arms talks in a way and at a time that will promote, if possible, progress on outstanding political problems at the same time—for example, on the problem of the Mideast and on other outstanding problems in which the United States and the Soviet Union acting together can serve the cause of peace."

Linkage was something uncomfortably new and different for the Soviets, and I was not surprised when they bridled at the restraints it imposed on our relationship.

It would take almost two years of patient and hard-nosed determination on our part before they would accept that linkage with what we wanted from them was the price they would have to pay for getting any of the things they wanted from us. . . .

The most pressing foreign problem I would have to deal with as soon as I became President was the war in Vietnam. During the transition Kissinger began a review of all possible policies toward Vietnam, distilling them into specific options that ran the gamut from massive military escalation to immediate unilateral withdrawal. A strong case could be made for each option.

For example, it could be argued that military victory was still possible if I would remove the restrictions [President Lyndon B.] Johnson had placed on our commanders in the field and allow them to use our massive power to defeat the enemy. The most serious of these constraints was the bombing halt; because of it the Communists had been able to regroup their forces and amass supplies for a new offensive. Those who favored the escalation option argued that just the threat of an invasion of North Vietnam would tie down North Vietnamese troops along the DMZ [Demilitarized Zone]; that mining Haiphong Harbor would cripple the enemy's supply lines; and that free pursuit of the Communist forces into Laos and Cambodia would blunt their ability to continue making hit-and-run attacks against our forces in South Vietnam. Renewed bombing would reinforce these other moves. That, in essence, was the escalation option. It was an option we ruled out very early.

The opinion polls showed a significant percentage of the public favored a military victory in Vietnam. But most people thought of a "military victory" in terms of gearing up to administer a knockout blow that would both end the war and win it. The problem was that there were only two such knockout blows available to me. One would have been to bomb the elaborate systems of irrigation dikes in North Vietnam. The resulting floods would have killed hundreds of thousands of civilians. The other possible knockout blow would have involved the use of tactical nuclear weapons. Short of one of these methods, escalation would probably have required up to six months of highly intensified fighting and significantly increased casualties before the Communists would finally be forced to give up and accept a peace settlement. The domestic and international uproar that would have accompanied the use of either of these knockout blows would have got my administration off to the worse possible start. And as far as escalating the conventional fighting was concerned, there was no way that I could hold the country together for that period of time in view of the numbers of casualties we would be sustaining. Resorting to the escalation option would also delay or even destroy any chance we might have to develop a new relationship with the Soviet Union and Communist China.

At the other end of the spectrum from escalation was the case for ending the war simply by announcing a quick and orderly withdrawal of all American forces. If that were done, the argument went, the Communists would probably respond by returning our POWs [Prisoners of War] after the last American had departed. . . .

I began my presidency with three fundamental premises regarding Vietnam. First, I would have to prepare public opinion for the fact that total military victory was no longer possible. Second, I would have to act on what my conscience, my experience, and my analysis told me was true about the need to keep our commitment. To abandon South Vietnam to the Communists now would cost us inestimably in our search for a stable, structured, and lasting peace. Third, I would have to end the war as quickly as was honorably possible. . . .

The Vietnam war was complicated by factors that had never occurred before in America's conduct of a war. Many of the most prominent liberals of both parties in Congress, having supported our involvement in Vietnam under Kennedy and Johnson, were now trying to back off from their commitment. Senators and congressmen, Cabinet members and columnists who had formerly supported the war were now swelling the ranks of the antiwar forces. In 1969 I still had a congressional majority on war-related votes and questions, but it was a bare one at best, and I could not be sure how long it would hold. Another unusual aspect of this war was that the American news media had come to dominate domestic opinion about its purpose and conduct and also about the nature of the enemy. The North Vietnamese were a particularly ruthless and cruel enemy, but the American media concentrated primarily on the failings and frailties of the South Vietnamese or of our own forces. In each night's TV news and in each morning's paper the war was reported battle by battle, but little or no sense of the underlying purpose of the fighting was conveyed. Eventually this contributed to the impression that we were fighting in military and moral quicksand, rather than toward an important and worthwhile objective.

More than ever before, television showed the terrible human suffering and sacrifice of war. Whatever the intention behind such relentless and literal reporting of the war, the result was a serious demoralization of the home front, raising the question whether America would ever again be able to fight an enemy abroad with unity and strength of purpose at home. As *Newsweek* columnist Kenneth Crawford wrote, this was the first war in our history when the media was more friendly to our enemies than to our allies. I felt that by the time I had become President the way the Vietnam war had been conducted and reported had worn down America's spirit and sense of confidence.

As I prepared to enter the presidency, I regarded the antiwar protesters and demonstrators with alternating feelings of appreciation for their concerns, anger at their excesses, and, primarily, frustration at their apparent unwillingness to credit me even with a genuine desire for peace. But whatever my estimation of the demonstrators' motives—and whatever their estimate of mine—I considered that the practical effect of their activity was to give encouragement to the enemy and thus prolong the war. They wanted to end the war in Vietnam. So did I. But they wanted to end it immediately, and in order to do so they were prepared to abandon South Vietnam. That was something I would not permit.

2. The Nixon Doctrine, 1969

I believe that the time has come when the United States, in our relations with all of our Asian friends, [must] be quite emphatic on two points: One, that we will keep our treaty commitments, our treaty commitments, for example, with Thailand under SEATO [Southeast Asia Treaty Organization]; but, two, that as far as

This document can be found in *Public Papers of the Presidents: Richard Nixon, 1969* (Washington, D.C.: U.S. Government Printing Office, 1971), p. 549.

the problems of internal security are concerned, as far as the problems of military defense, except for the threat of a major power involving nuclear weapons, that the United States is going to encourage and has a right to expect that this problem will be increasingly handled by, and the responsibility for it taken by, the Asian nations themselves.

I believe, incidentally, from my preliminary conversations with several Asian leaders over the past few months that they are going to be willing to undertake this responsibility. It will not be easy, but if the United States just continues down the road of responding to requests for assistance, of assuming the primary responsibility for defending these countries when they have internal problems or external problems, they are never going to take care of themselves.

3. Nixon Explains the Five Power Centers of the New Global Economy, 1971

Many of you, a few of you, are old enough to remember what America was 24 years ago.

We were number one in the world militarily, with no one who even challenged us because we had a monopoly on atomic weapons. We also at that point, of course, were number one economically by all odds. In fact, the United States of America was producing more than 50 percent of all the world's goods.

That was just 25 years ago. Now, 25 years having passed, let's look at the situation today and what it may be 5 years from now or 10 years from now. I will not try to limit myself to 5 or 10 years except to say that in the next decade we are going to see changes that may be even greater than what have occurred in the last 25 years, and very great ones have occurred in that respect.

First, instead of just America being number one in the world from an economic standpoint, the preeminent world power, and instead of there being just two super powers, when we think in economic terms and economic potentialities, there are five great power centers in the world today. Let's look at them very briefly.

There is, of course, the United States of America. There is, second, Western Europe—Western Europe with Britain in the Common Market. That means 300 million of the most advanced people in the world, with all the productivity and all the capacity that those people will have and, of course, with the clout that they have when they will act together, as they certainly will. That is a new factor in the world scene that will come, and come very soon, as we all know.

Then in the Pacific, looking also at free world countries, we have a resurgent Japan. I met with steel leaders this morning—leaders of industry and leaders of unions. I pointed out what had happened to Japan in terms of their business: Just 20 years ago Japan produced 5 million tons of steel a year; this year they produced 100 million tons of steel; 2 years from now Japan will produce more steel than the United States of America.

This document can be found in *Public Papers of the Presidents: Richard Nixon, 1971* (Washington, D.C.: U.S. Government Printing Office, 1972), pp. 804–807.

That is what has happened. It has happened in the case of Japan, in the case of Germany, our two major enemies in World War II, partly as a result of our help in getting them on their feet. But it has happened since that time as a result of their own energy and their own ability. . . .

Now we turn to the other two super powers, economic super powers I will say for the moment. The Soviet Union, of course, first comes to mind. Looking at the Soviet Union, we are entering a period which only time will tell may be successful in terms of creating a very new relationship or a very different relationship than we have had previously.

I referred to the need for an era of negotiation rather than confrontation when I made my inaugural speech. . . . I am not suggesting that these negotiations are going to lead to instant peace and instant relationships with the Soviet Union such as we presently have with our friends in Western Europe and with our friends in Asia who may be allied with us, or who may have systems of government that are more closely aligned to ours. What we have to recognize is that even as we limit arms, if we do reach an agreement in that field, and even if we find ways to avoid confrontation in other areas, and perhaps work out negotiated settlements for mutual force reductions in Europe, the problem of Berlin, all the others that come to mind, we must recognize that the Soviet Union will continue to be a very potent, powerful, and aggressive competitor of the United States of America. And, ironically—and this is also true of Mainland China, as I will point out in a moment—as we have more and more success on the negotiation front, as for example the Soviet Union, like the United States, may be able if we have a limitation in nuclear arms, if we are able to turn our eyes more toward our economic development and our economic problems, it simply means that the competition changes and becomes much more challenging in the economic area than it has been previously. . . .

Mainland China is, of course, a very different situation. First in terms of its economic capacity at the present time, a pretty good indication of where it is is that Japan, with 100 million people, produces more than Mainland China, with 800 million people. But that should not mislead us, and it gives us, and should give none of the potential competitors in world markets of Mainland China, any sense of satisfaction that it will always be that way. Because when we see the Chinese as people—and I have seen them all over the world, and some of you have, too, whether in Hong Kong, or whether in Taiwan, or whether they are in Singapore or Bangkok, any of the great cities, Manila, where Chinese are there—they are creative, they are productive, they are one of the most capable people in the world. And 800 million Chinese are going to be, inevitably, an enormous economic power, with all that that means in terms of what they could be in other areas if they move in that direction.

That is the reason why I felt that it was essential that this Administration take the first steps toward ending the isolation of Mainland China from the world community. We had to take those steps because the Soviet Union could not, because of differences that they have that at the present time seem to be irreconcilable. We were the only other power that could take those steps. . . .

Now, I do not suggest, in mentioning these five, that Latin America is not important, that Africa is not important, that South Asia is not important. All nations are important, and all peoples in underdeveloped or less developed countries will play their role. But these are the five that will determine the economic future and, because economic power will be the key to other kinds of power, the future of the world in other ways in the last third of this century.

Now let's see what this means to the United States. It means that the United States, as compared with that position we found ourselves in immediately after World War II, has a challenge such as we did not even dream of. Then we were talking about the dollar gap; then we were talking about the necessity of—putting it in terms of a poker game—that the United States had all the chips and we had to spread a few of the chips around so that others could play.

We did it. One hundred billion dollars worth to Western Europe, for example, to rebuild them, and billions of others to other countries, and it was the correct policy as it turned out. But now when we see the world in which we are about to move, the United States no longer is in the position of complete preeminence or predominance. That is not a bad thing. As a matter of fact, it can be a constructive thing. The United States, let us understand, is still the strongest nation in the world; it is still the richest nation in the world. But now we face a situation where four other potential economic powers have the capacity, have the kind of people— if not the kind of government, but at least the kind of people—who can challenge us on every front.

4. Secretary of State Henry A. Kissinger Defines Détente, 1974

There can be no peaceful international order without a constructive relationship between the United States and the Soviet Union. There will be no international stability unless both the Soviet Union and the United States conduct themselves with restraint and unless they use their enormous power for the benefit of mankind.

Thus, we must be clear at the outset on what the term "détente" entails. It is the search for a more constructive relationship with the Soviet Union. It is a continuing process, not a final condition. And it has been pursued by successive American leaders though the means have varied as have world conditions.

Some fundamental principles guide this policy:

The United States does not base its policy solely on Moscow's good intentions. We seek, regardless of Soviet intentions, to serve peace through a systematic resistance to pressure and conciliatory responses to moderate behavior.

We must oppose aggressive actions, but we must not seek confrontations lightly.

We must maintain a strong national defense while recognizing that in the nuclear age the relationship between military strength and politically usable power is the most complex in all history.

Where the age-old antagonism between freedom and tyranny is concerned, we are not neutral. But other imperatives impose limits on our ability to produce internal changes in foreign countries. Consciousness of our limits is a recognition of

This document can be found in U.S. Senate, Committee on Foreign Relations, *Détente* (Washington, D.C.: U.S. Government Printing Office, 1975), pp. 247–248, 251–254, 256.

the necessity of peace—not moral callousness. The preservation of human life and human society are moral values, too.

We must be mature enough to recognize that to be stable a relationship must provide advantages to both sides and that the most constructive international relationships are those in which both parties perceive an element of gain. . . .

To set forth principles of behavior in formal documents is hardly to guarantee their observance. But they are reference points against which to judge actions and set goals.

The first of the series of documents is the Statement of Principles signed in Moscow in 1972. It affirms: (1) the necessity of avoiding confrontation; (2) the imperative of mutual restraint; (3) the rejection of attempts to exploit tensions to gain unilateral advantages; (4) the renunciation of claims of special influence in the world; and (5) the willingness, on this new basis, to coexist peacefully and build a firm long-term relationship.

An Agreement on the Prevention of Nuclear War based on these Principles was signed in 1973. But it emphasizes that this objective presupposes the renunciation of any war or threat of war not only by the two nuclear superpowers against each other, but also against allies or third countries. In other words, the principle of restraint is not confined to relations between the United States and the U.S.S.R. It is explicitly extended to include all countries.

These statements of principles are not an American concession; indeed, we have been affirming them unilaterally for two decades. Nor are they a legal contract; rather, they are an aspiration and a yardstick by which we assess Soviet behavior. We have never intended to rely on Soviet compliance with every principle; we do seek to elaborate standards of conduct which the Soviet Union would violate only to its cost. And if over the long term the more durable relationship takes hold, the basic principles will give it definition, structure, and hope.

One of the features of the current phase of United States–Soviet relations is the unprecedented consultation between leaders either face to face or through diplomatic channels. . . .

It was difficult in the past to speak of a United States–Soviet bilateral relationship in any normal sense of the phrase. Trade was negligible. Contacts between various institutions and between the peoples of the two countries were at best sporadic. Today, by joining our efforts even in such seemingly apolitical fields as medical research or environmental protection, we and the Soviets can benefit not only our two peoples, but all mankind.

Since 1972 we have concluded agreements on a common effort against cancer, on research to protect the environment, on studying the use of the ocean's resources, on the use of atomic energy for peaceful purposes, on studying methods for conserving energy, on examining construction techniques for regions subject to earthquakes, and on devising new transportation methods. . . .

We have approached the question of economic relations with deliberation and circumspection and as an act of policy not primarily of commercial opportunity. As political relations have improved on a broad basis, economic issues have been dealt with on a comparably broad front. A series of interlocking economic agreements with the U.S.S.R. has been negotiated, side by side with the political

progress already noted. The 25-year-old lend-lease debt was settled; the reciprocal extension of the most-favored-nation treatment was negotiated, together with
safeguards against the possible disruption of our markets and a series of practical
arrangements to facilitate the conduct of business; our Government credit facilities
were made available for trade with the U.S.S.R.; and a maritime agreement regulating the carriage of goods has been signed. . . .

Over time, trade and investment may leaven the autarkic tendencies of the Soviet system, invite gradual association of the Soviet economy with the world economy, and foster a degree of interdependence that adds an element of stability to the
political relationship.

We cannot expect to relax international tensions or achieve a more stable international system should the two strongest nuclear powers conduct an unrestrained
strategic arms race. Thus, perhaps the single most important component of our
policy toward the Soviet Union is the effort to limit strategic weapons competition.

The competition in which we now find ourselves is historically unique:

Each side has the capacity to destroy civilization as we know it.

Failure to maintain equivalence could jeopardize not only our freedom but our
very survival. . . .

The prospect of a decisive military advantage, even if theoretically possible, is
politically intolerable; neither side will passively permit a massive shift in the nuclear balance. Therefore, the probable outcome of each succeeding round of competition is the restoration of a strategic equilibrium, but at increasingly higher and
more complex levels of forces.

The arms race is driven by political as well as military factors. While a decisive
advantage is hard to calculate, the appearance of inferiority—whatever its actual
significance—can have serious political consequences. Thus, each side has a high
incentive to achieve not only the reality but the appearance of equality. In a very real
sense each side shapes the military establishment of the other.

If we are driven to it, the United States will sustain an arms race. But the political or military benefit which would flow from such a situation would remain
elusive. Indeed, after such an evolution it might well be that both sides would be
worse off than before the race began.

The Soviet Union must realize that the overall relationship with the United
States will be less stable if strategic balance is sought through unrestrained competitive programs. Sustaining the buildup requires exhortations by both sides that
in time may prove incompatible with restrained international conduct. The very
fact of a strategic arms race has a high potential for feeding attitudes of hostility
and suspicion on both sides, transforming the fears of those who demand more
weapons into self-fulfilling prophecies. . . .

Détente is admittedly far from a modern equivalent to the kind of stable peace
that characterized most of the 19th century. But it is a long step away from the bitter
and aggressive spirit that has characterized so much of the post-war period. When
linked to such broad and unprecedented projects as SALT, détente takes on added
meaning and opens prospects of a more stable peace. SALT agreements should be
seen as steps in a process leading to progressively greater stability. It is in that light
that SALT and related projects will be judged by history.

5. U.S. Covert Action in Chile
(1963–1973), 1975

The pattern of United States covert action in Chile is striking but not unique. It arose in the context not only of American foreign policy, but also of covert U.S. involvement in other countries within and outside Latin America. The scale of CIA involvement in Chile was unusual but by no means unprecedented. . . .

The most extensive covert action activity in Chile was propaganda. It was relatively cheap. In Chile, it continued at a low level during "normal" times, then was cranked up to meet particular threats or to counter particular dangers.

The most common form of a propaganda project is simply the development of "assets" in media organizations who can place articles or be asked to write them. The Agency provided to its field Stations several kinds of guidance about what sorts of propaganda were desired. For example, one CIA project in Chile supported from one to five media assets during the seven years it operated (1965–1971). Most of those assets worked for a major Santiago daily which was the key to CIA propaganda efforts. . . .

The covert propaganda efforts in Chile also included "black" propaganda—material falsely purporting to be the product of a particular individual or group. In the 1970 election, for instance, the CIA used "black" propaganda to sow discord between the Communists and the Socialists and between the national labor confederation and the Chilean Communist Party.

In some cases, the form of propaganda was still more direct. The Station financed Chilean groups who erected wall posters, passed out political leaflets (at times prepared by the Station) and engaged in other street activities. . . .

Of thirty-odd covert action projects undertaken [in] Chile by the CIA between 1961 and 1974, approximately a half dozen had propaganda as their principal activity. Propaganda was an important subsidiary element of many others, particularly election projects. (See Table 1.) Press placements were attractive because each placement might produce a multiplier effect, being picked up and replayed by media outlets other than the one in which it originally came out.

Table 1   Techniques of Covert Action: Expenditures in Chile, 1963–73*

TECHNIQUES	AMOUNT
Propaganda for elections and other support for political parties	$8,000,000
Producing and disseminating propaganda and supporting mass media	4,300,000
Influencing Chilean institutions (labor, students, peasants, women) and supporting private sector organizations	900,000
Promoting military coup d'etat	<200,000

*Figures rounded to nearest $100,000.

This document can be found in U.S. Senate, Select Committee to Study Governmental Operations with Respect to Intelligence Activities, Staff Report, *Covert Action in Chile (1963–1973)* (Washington, D.C.: U.S. Government Printing Office, 1975).

In addition to buying propaganda piecemeal, the Station often purchased it wholesale by subsidizing Chilean media organizations friendly to the United States. Doing so was propaganda writ large. Instead of placing individual items, the CIA supported—or even founded—friendly media outlets which might not have existed in the absence of Agency support. . . .

By far, the largest—and probably the most significant—instance of support for a media organization was the money provided to *El Mercurio,* the major Santiago daily, under pressure during the Allende regime. . . . A CIA project renewal memorandum concluded that *El Mercurio* and other media outlets supported by the Agency had played an important role in setting the stage for the September 11, 1973, military coup which overthrew Allende.

Through its covert activities in Chile, the U.S. government sought to influence the actions of a wide variety of institutions and groups in Chilean society. The specific intent of those activities ran the gamut from attempting to influence directly the making of government policy to trying to counter communist or leftist influence among organized groups in the society. That most of these projects included a propaganda component is obvious. . . .

Projects were directed, for example, toward:

• Wresting control of Chilean university student organizations from the communists;
• Supporting a women's group active in Chilean political and intellectual life;
• Combating the communist-dominated *Central Unica de Trabajadores Chilenos* (CUTCh) and supporting democratic labor groups; and
• Exploiting a civic action front group to combat communist influence within cultural and intellectual circles.

Covert American activity was a factor in almost every major election in Chile in the decade between 1963 and 1973. In several instances the United States intervention was massive.

The 1964 presidential election was the most prominent example of a large-scale election project. The Central Intelligence Agency spent more than $2.6 million in support of the election of the Christian Democratic candidate, in part to prevent the accession to the presidency of Marxist Salvador Allende. More than half of the Christian Democratic candidate's campaign was financed by the United States, although he was not informed of this assistance. . . .

In Washington, an inter-agency election committee was established, composed of State Department, White House and CIA officials. That committee was paralleled by a group in the embassy in Santiago. No special task force was established within the CIA, but the Station in Santiago was reinforced. The Station assisted the Christian Democrats in running an American-style campaign, which included polling, voter registration and get-out-the-vote drives, in addition to covert propaganda.

The United States was also involved in the 1970 presidential campaign. That effort, however, was smaller and did not include support for any specific candidate. It was directed more at preventing Allende's election than at insuring another candidate's victory. . . .

Most covert American support to Chilean political parties was furnished as part of specific efforts to influence election outcomes. However, in several instances the CIA provided subsidies to parties for more general purposes, when elections were not imminent. Most such support was furnished during the Allende years, 1970–1973, when the U.S. government judged that without its support parties of the center and right might not survive either as opposition elements or as contestants in elections several years away.

In a sequence of decisions in 1971 through 1973, the 40 Committee [a sub-cabinet body of the executive branch which reviewed covert plans] authorized nearly $4 million for opposition political parties in Chile. Most of this money went to the Christian Democratic Party (PDC), but a substantial portion was earmarked for the National Party (PN), a conservative grouping more stridently opposed to the Allende government than was the PDC. An effort was also made to split the ruling Popular Unity coalition by inducing elements to break away. . . .

As part of its program of support for opposition elements during the Allende government, the CIA provided money to several trade organizations of the Chilean private sector. In September 1972, for instance, the 40 Committee authorized $24,000 in emergency support for an anti-Allende businessmen's organization. At that time, supporting other private sector organizations was considered but rejected because of the fear that those organizations might be involved in anti-government strikes. . . .

United States covert efforts to affect the course of Chilean politics reached a peak in 1970: the CIA was directed to undertake an effort to promote a military coup in Chile to prevent the accession to power of Salvador Allende [a project known as Track II]. . . . A brief summary here will demonstrate the extreme in American covert intervention in Chilean politics.

On September 15, 1970—after Allende finished first in the election but before the Chilean Congress had chosen between him and the runner-up, [Jorge] Alessandri—President Nixon met with Richard Helms, the Director of Central Intelligence, Assistant to the President for National Security Affairs Henry Kissinger and Attorney General John Mitchell. Helms was directed to prevent Allende from taking power. This effort was to be conducted without the knowledge of the Department of State and Defense or the Ambassador. Track II was never discussed at a 40 Committee meeting.

It quickly became apparent to both White House and CIA officials that a military coup was the only way to prevent Allende's accession to power. To achieve that end, the CIA established contact with several groups of military plotters and eventually passed three weapons and tear gas to one group. The weapons were subsequently returned, apparently unused. The CIA knew that the plans of all groups of plotters began with the abduction of the constitutionalist Chief of Staff of the Chilean Army, General René Schneider. The Committee has received conflicting testimony about the extent of CIA/White House communication and of White House officials' awareness of specific coup plans, but there is no doubt that the U.S. government sought a military coup in Chile.

On October 22, one group of plotters attempted to kidnap Schneider. Schneider resisted, was shot, and subsequently died. The CIA had been in touch with that group of plotters but a week earlier had withdrawn its support for the group's specific plans.

The coup plotting collapsed and Allende was inaugurated President. After his election, the CIA and U.S. military attachés maintained contacts with the Chilean military for the purpose of collecting intelligence. Whether those contacts strayed into encouraging the Chilean military to move against Allende; or whether the Chilean military—having been goaded toward a coup during Track II—took encouragement to act against the President from those contacts even though U.S. officials did not intend to provide it: these are major questions which are inherent in U.S. covert activities in the period of the Allende government. . . .

In addition to providing information and cover to the CIA, multinational corporations also participated in covert attempts to influence Chilean politics. . . .

A number of multinational corporations were apprehensive about the possibility that Allende would be elected President of Chile. Allende's public announcements indicated his intention, if elected, to nationalize basic industries and to bring under Chilean ownership service industries such as the national telephone company, which was at that time a subsidiary of ITT [International Telephone and Telegraph].

In 1964 Allende had been defeated, and it was widely known both in Chile and among American multinational corporations with significant interests in Chile that his opponents had been supported by the United States government. John McCone, a former CIA Director and a member of ITT's Board of Directors in 1970, knew of the significant American government involvement in 1964 and of the offer of assistance made at that time by American companies. Agency documents indicate that McCone informed Harold Geneen, ITT's Board Chairman, of these facts.

In 1970 leaders of American multinational corporations with substantial interests in Chile, together with other American citizens concerned about what might happen to Chile in the event of an Allende victory, contacted U.S. government officials in order to make their views known.

In July 1970, a CIA representative in Santiago met with representatives of ITT and, in a discussion of the upcoming election, indicated that Alessandri could use financial assistance. The Station suggested the name of an individual who could be used as a secure channel for getting these funds to the Alessandri campaign.

Shortly thereafter John McCone telephoned CIA Director Richard Helms. As a result of this call, a meeting was arranged between the Chairman of the Board of ITT and Chief of the Western Hemisphere Division of the CIA. Geneen offered to make available to the CIA a substantial amount of money to be used in support of the Alessandri campaign. In subsequent meetings ITT offered to make $1 million available to the CIA. The CIA rejected the offer. The memorandum indicated further that CIA's advice was sought with respect to an individual who might serve as a conduit of ITT funds to the Alessandri campaign.

The CIA confirmed that the individual in question was a reliable channel which could be used for getting funds to Alessandri. A second channel of funds from ITT to a political party opposing Allende, the National Party, was developed following CIA advice as to a secure funding mechanism utilizing two CIA assets in Chile. These assets were also receiving Agency funds in connection with the "spoiling" operation.

During the period prior to the September election, ITT representatives met frequently with CIA representatives both in Chile and in the United States and CIA advised ITT as to ways in which it might safely channel funds both to the Alessandri campaign and to the National Party. CIA was kept informed of the extent and the mechanism of the funding. Eventually at least $350,000 was passed by ITT to this campaign. A roughly equal amount was passed by other U.S. companies; the CIA learned of this funding but did not assist in it.

6. The Journalist Anthony Lewis Blasts Kissinger's Record, 1977

Henry Kissinger is leaving office in a blaze of adulation. The National Press Club produces a belly dancer for him and gives standing applause to his views on world peace. The Harlem Globetrotters make him an honorary member. Senators pay tribute to his wisdom.

Historians of the next generation will find it all very puzzling. Because they will not have seen Mr. Kissinger perform, they will have to rely on the record. And the record of his eight years in Washington is likely to seem thin in diplomatic achievement and shameful in human terms.

The one outstanding accomplishment is Mr. Kissinger's Middle East diplomacy. He restored United States relations with the Arab world, and he set in motion the beginnings of an Arab-Israeli dialogue. Of course, the work is incomplete. But to start something after so many years of total failure was a great breakthrough and it was essentially the work of one man: Henry Kissinger.

The other undoubtedly positive entry on the record is the opening to China, but that was in good part Richard Nixon's doing. Also, the beginnings of a relationship with the People's Republic were not followed up as they might have been, and the failure may prove damaging.

With the Soviet Union, Mr. Kissinger took the familiar idea of easing tensions and glamorized it as détente. The glamor was dangerous. It fostered the illusion that détente could prevent conflict all over the world, and many Americans turned sour on the whole idea when it did not. At times Mr. Kissinger himself seemed to believe the illusion—and became apoplectic when it failed as in Angola. Détente's real achievements are scant; not much more than a halting step toward nuclear arms control.

Ignorance and ineptitude marked his policy in much of the rest of the world. In Cyprus, his blundering led to human tragedy and left America's reputation damaged in both Greece and Turkey. His insensitivity to Japanese feelings had traumatic effects on a most important ally.

In dealing with Portugal and its African territories Mr. Kissinger decided in succession that (1) the Portuguese were in Africa to stay, (2) the U.S. should help Portugal's dictatorship, (3) after the dictatorship's fall the Communists were bound to prevail in Portugal and (4) the U.S. could decide the outcome in Angola by covert aid. That parade of folly was matched in his African policy generally: years of malign neglect, then last-minute intervention for majority rule in Rhodesia.

He often talked about freedom, but his acts show a pre-eminent interest in order. Millions lost their freedom during the Kissinger years, many to dictatorships that had crucial support from his policies, as in Chile and the Philippines. He expressed little open concern for the victims of Soviet tyranny, and he did little to enforce the human rights clauses of the Helsinki Agreement.

The American constitutional system of checks and balances he treated as an irritating obstacle to power. In his valedictory to the Press Club his only reference to Watergate was an expression of regret at "the disintegration of Executive authority that resulted."

Secrecy and deceit were levers of his power; he had no patience for the democratic virtues of openness and consultation. By keeping all the facts to himself and a few intimates, he centralized control. He practiced deceit with a kind of gusto, from petty personal matters to "peace is at hand."

His conduct in the wiretapping of his own staff gave ugly insight into his character. He provided names for investigation—and then, when the story came out, wriggled and deceived in order to minimize his role. He never expressed regret, even to those who had been closest to him, for the fact that their family conversations had been overheard for months. But when someone ransacked his garbage, he said his wife had suffered "grave anguish."

History will remember him most of all for his policy in Indochina. In the teeth of evidence well known by 1969, this supposed realist pressed obsessively for indefinite maintenance of the status quo. To that end, in his time, 20,492 more Americans died in Vietnam and hundreds of thousands of Vietnamese. The war was expanded into Cambodia, destroying that peaceable land. And all for nothing.

With such a record, how is it that people vie to place laurels on the head of the departing Secretary of State? The answer became clear the other night during an extraordinarily thoughtful Public Broadcasting television program on Mr. Kissinger's career: He has discovered that in our age publicity is power, and he has played the press as Dr. Miracle played his violin. He is intelligent and hard-working and ruthless, but those qualities are common enough. His secret is showmanship.

Henry Kissinger is our P. T. Barnum—a Barnum who plays in a vastly larger tent and whose jokes have about them the air of the grave. That we honor a person who has done such things in our name is a comment on us.

 E S S A Y S

In the first essay, Joan Hoff, a professor of history at Ohio University and a Nixon biographer, presents a positive appraisal of Nixon's Grand Design. Although Hoff faults the administration for conducting foreign policy under a veil of secrecy, particularly when combating suspected communism in the Third World, she places much of the blame for the administration's shortcomings on the president's adviser, Henry A. Kissinger. She praises Nixon, on the other hand, for his bold and imaginative policy of détente toward the People's Republic of China and the Soviet Union, his pursuit of arms control, and his ability to adjust U.S. policy to the realities of a more competitive world economy. Nixon, according to Hoff, deserves credit for initiating a foreign policy that transcended constraints imposed by Cold War ideology, deftly balanced détente with U.S. security goals in Western Europe, and effectively managed a Democratic Congress. Détente broke down, according to Hoff, largely because Moscow did not seek at the time to end the Cold War, and détente's opponents exploited popular distaste for Soviet human-rights violations.

In the second essay, Raymond L. Garthoff, a former foreign service officer and ambassador who is currently a senior fellow at the Brookings Institution in Washington, D.C., advances a more negative interpretation, finding détente a failure. He criticizes the Nixon-Kissinger team for not defining the meaning of détente more clearly and for not developing with Moscow a viable code of conduct and collaborative measures for managing the superpower rivalry. Each side expected too much from détente and misperceived the other's continued military buildup and interventions as threatening and destabilizing. The United States, Garthoff argues, maintained a particularly idealized concept of détente that condemned aggressive Soviet behavior but failed to acknowledge that the vigorous foreign policy of the United States itself at times violated the spirit of détente.

The last selection is drawn from Walter Isaacson's lengthy biography of Henry A. Kissinger. In the excerpt, Isaacson, an editor at *Time* magazine, examines Kissinger's foreign policy "realism." In contrast to Hoff, Isaacson respects Kissinger's intellectual brilliance and political savvy. Isaacson, however, emphasizes that Kissinger's concern for U.S. credibility led to imprudent interventions in the Third World. Most important, according to Isaacson, Kissinger's European style of diplomacy clashed with America's democratic traditions and moral values and thus weakened public backing for détente.

Nixon's Innovative Grand Design and the Wisdom of Détente

JOAN HOFF

Any revisionist approach to Nixon's management of foreign policy must begin by attempting to place in perspective the complex interaction developed between Nixon and Kissinger, whose "advanced megalomania remains legendary." In retrospect, I believe that one of the most unfortunate decisions the president-elect made during the interregnum was to appoint Kissinger, about whom he knew only that, as a Nelson Rockefeller supporter, Kissinger had been openly disdainful of Nixon and his bid for the Republican nomination in 1968. If Nixon thought Kissinger's views on U.S. policy were important, he could have employed him as consultant to the NSC, as the Kennedy administration had briefly done. This opinion, however, is not shared by Nixon or most of his former advisers, one of whom defended Kissinger's appointment by saying that "the care and feeding of Henry" was worth all the paranoia, backbiting, leaking, rumor-mongering, and pseudo-intellectual posturing that he brought to the White House.

Many of the wiretaps and much of the obsession with covert actions that Nixon exhibited in his first year in office can be attributed to Kissinger's ingratiating presence and self-aggrandizing influence. The combination of these two men, while occasionally resulting in dazzling achievements, had a dark, devious underside, from which to date only one of them has walked away unscathed. During the early Nixon years, for example, it was Henry Kissinger, not the president, who entertained at cocktail parties, to the delight of liberals and conservatives alike, with popular one-liners such as: "The illegal, we do right away; the unconstitutional takes a little longer." . . .

On the surface Nixon and Kissinger—an American Quaker and a German-American Jew—appear to have been the odd couple of U.S. foreign policy. Given his long personal and professional association with the Rockefeller family and his blunt criticisms of Nixon, Kissinger apparently did not think he would last even six months in the new Nixon administration. Yet when these two men came together in 1968, they actually shared many viewpoints and had developed similar operational styles. Both relished covert activity and liked making unilateral decisions; both distrusted bureaucracies; both resented any attempt by Congress to interfere with initiatives; and both agreed that the United States could impose order and stability on the world only if the White House controlled policy by appearing conciliatory but acting tough. While neither had headed any complex organization, both thought "personalized executive control" and formal application of procedures would lead to success. Even more coincidental, perhaps, each had a history of failure and rejection, which made them susceptible to devising ways of protecting themselves and their positions of power. Often the concern for protection appeared as obsession with eavesdropping, whether wiretaps or reconnaissance flights. They even eavesdropped on themselves: Nixon by installing an automatic taping system in the Oval Office, Kissinger by having some of his meetings and all of his phone conversations taped or transcribed from notes. In a word, instead of compensating for each other's weaknesses and enhancing strengths, Nixon and Kissinger shared their worst characteristics. . . .

Kissinger did not share Nixon's optimistic approach to diplomacy and proclivity for taking risky, far-reaching foreign policy actions. As vice president under Eisenhower, Nixon had said: "I am not necessarily a respecter of the *status quo* in foreign affairs. I am a *chance taker* in foreign affairs. I would take chances for peace." Along these same lines, Nixon told Kissinger in August 1969: "just because [I] supported [something] as a private individual does not mean [I] will as president." In contrast, practically every analyst of Kissinger's ideas points out their essentially conservative (and profoundly pessimistic), nineteenth-century European roots. When he joined the Nixon administration, Kissinger seems not to have changed his ideas (and dense writing style) much from the time he wrote his Ph.D. dissertation, in which he recommended the Metternichian [in reference to the nineteenth century Austrian count Klemens von Metternich] system of alliances among conservative regimes to check the forces of revolution in the modern, Western world. Kissinger's early writings presaged what his memoirs confirmed: the mind of "a middle-level manager who has learned to conceal vacuity with pretentious verbiage." His pre-1968 political science writings convey very conventional cold warrior ideas about Vietnam, anti-Communist views that opposed ideologically driven grand designs in foreign policy and at best paid only occasional lip service to the necessity for some risk taking. And as an "inveterate conceptualizer," he was seldom on top of specific contemporary issues in his search for global solutions. . . .

It remained for the president to lead the way toward genuinely innovative, grand designs for redirecting of U.S. diplomacy. . . . Henry Kissinger was a geopolitical follower rather than a leader, although his talent for dramatic, back-channel diplomacy may have made the execution of some of Nixon's policies exemplary rather than simply ordinary. The scholar Richard Falk, among a variety of contemporary commentators, noted specifically that "Nixon deserves the main credit, and bore the main responsibility, for shifts in political direction implicit in the moves toward accommodation with China and détente with the Soviet Union. In both instances there had been receptivity on the Sino-Soviet side . . . [but] it was Nixon who decided to respond affirmatively." In addition, Washington aficionados as politically and socially diverse as [Nixon cabinet member] Elliot Richardson and Ralph de Toledano (biographer of the rich and famous) agreed that Nixon's diplomacy was, indeed, "his own." "When I was involved [in the government]," Richardson has recalled, in at least two separate interviews, "I was directly exposed to the development of the Nixon foreign policy. I constantly saw Kissinger. But it was the *Nixon* foreign policy." The president "drew on Henry Kissinger as a knowledgeable, sophisticated source of historic learning . . . [but] Nixon was, from the outset, the principal architect of a foreign policy resting on a series of quite clearly formulated strategic aims." Other White House aides and cabinet-level officers agreed with the assessment that Kissinger "was taking orders, not creating policy." One went so far as to say that Kissinger was the "student" and Nixon, the "foreign policy professor."

Ralph de Toledano realized that Kissinger "was strictly Nixon's messenger boy . . . it was Nixon who made the policy." Contrary to Kissinger's claims, he was "not a great conceptualizer but . . . a brilliant tactician, the negotiator nonpareil, the supreme practitioner of the art of bureaucratic politics." Nonetheless, many newspaper people accepted (then and now) Kissinger's "lone cowboy" projection of himself as the sole force behind Nixonian foreign policy, when his entire career before 1969 was constructed upon the safe premise of never acting alone or being too far out of step with the eastern establishment. In truth, "the cowboy doesn't have to be courageous," Kissinger said in a notorious 1972 interview with Oriana Fallaci that caused him to be banished from Nixon's inner circle for the next month; "all he needs is to be alone to show others that he rides into town alone and does everything himself. . . . This amazing romantic character suits me precisely because to be alone is part of my style, if you like, my technique."

Contrary to Kissinger's public relations coup in this interview, he remained the Tonto, not the Lone Ranger, of U.S. foreign policy. Without Nixon's broad initiatives, international credibility, and, most important, ability to provide at least minimum domestic political consensus for his foreign policy until the fall of 1973, Kissinger, when finally on his own as both national security adviser and secretary of state, "was caught intellectually naked"—a messenger boy without a message. But members of the American press corps never realized that his macho, playboy image impressed them more than it did foreign heads of state, who were looking for more consistent and less idiosyncratic foreign policies and actions. As Leslie Gelb correctly observed in 1977: "Kissinger understood better than most men who come to Washington that politics is theater . . . he had to be seen and heard." And heard he was—ultimately to the dismay of Nixon and his closest aides. . . .

In Kansas City on July 6, 1971, Nixon announced his five-power, or "northern tier" strategy, which he hoped would replace the bipolar, confrontational aspects of the cold war. Instead of continuing to deal only bilaterally with the Soviet Union, Nixon wanted to bring the five great economic regions of the world—the United States, the USSR, mainland China, Japan, and Western Europe—into constructive negotiation and mutually profitable economic competition. Admitting that the United States could not long maintain its post–World War II position of "complete preeminence or predominance," Nixon outlined a "pentagonal strategy" for promoting peace and economic progress by linking the interests of the major regional powers. Kissinger never officially endorsed this plan, preferring the more exclusive Rockefeller "trilateral" approach that included only the U.S., Japan, and the Common Market nations of Western Europe (including the United Kingdom).

Before joining the administration, Kissinger also had not accepted the manner in which Nixon wanted to link global interests, especially the linking of Moscow to any successful settlement of the war in Vietnam. Ultimately, however, it was Kissinger who coined the word *linkage* for this strategy and who broadened it to include other issues such as trade, food policy, arms control, and Third World competition with the Soviet Union. Linkage became associated more with Kissinger than Nixon during the years they formulated policy together, and the concept certainly fit Kissinger's penchant for grandiose schemes described in impenetrable language. As a political plan, it posed more problems than it resolved. First and foremost, it never worked with respect to the Soviet Union in negotiations with Vietnam or the SALT I talks, and it made Nixinger policy look indifferent to Third World concerns except insofar as they could be linked to relationships between major powers.

This meant, of course, that from the beginning of the Nixon administration, entire areas of the Third World—southern Asia, the Middle East, Africa, Latin America—occupied a secondary place in the president's (and his national security adviser's) political approach to foreign policy. In particular, Nixon and Kissinger largely ignored economic foreign policy considerations in dealing with the Third World, preferring instead to link events in such countries to power relations among the major nations. "Linkage," therefore, accounts for many of the seemingly erratic aspects of U.S. foreign policy in Third World areas that fell outside the parameters of pentagonal strategy. Nixon was more interested in maintaining American spheres of influence in the Third World than in the economic needs of these developing nations. Thus, the United States promoted the overthrow of [Salvador] Allende in Chile; restrained Egyptian and Syrian aggression in the Middle East, while ignoring the potential instability of the shah's [(Mohammed Reza Pahlavi)] regime in Iran and indirectly encouraging the rise in OPEC oil prices; continued to oppose [Fidel] Castro in Cuba; and supported Pakistan against India [in their 1971 war]. The "grand design" may have been grand by superpower standards, but it remained ineffectual with respect to the Third World.

Nixon's and Kissinger's respective geopolitical divisions of the world became compatible, regardless of how poorly linkage served them. Both assumed it was the responsibility of major regional powers to keep order in their respective spheres of influence and not to intrude in areas dominated by others. Thus Nixon thought that détente based on linkage would prevent small Third World nations from setting the great powers against one another, by making the possibility of outside aid more remote if they did. He and Kissinger also thought that détente would help the United States deal simultaneously with the USSR and the People's Republic of China by taking advantage of their differences to create a triangular relationship in which American leverage could be exerted. Circumstances in all five (or three) areas of the world simultaneously fostered détente between 1969 and 1972. Consequently, the United States and the Soviet Union capitalized upon the favorable international atmosphere that developed during the first Nixon administration to improve Soviet-American relations. . . .

Long before Nixon and Kissinger formally adopted the word *détente* to describe their diplomatic strategies and goals, the president's use of the term in early foreign policy statements and in private notes for speeches clearly indicates that he thought the relationship between NATO and détente with the USSR problematic. This uncertainty was considerably exacerbated when the bilateral, back-channel methods used to achieve rapprochement with China and détente with the Soviet Union bypassed the North Atlantic Treaty countries. In particular, both the ABM [Anti Ballistic Missile] and SALT I [Strategic Arms Limitation Treaty] agreements were negotiated with a minimum of consultation with NATO nations. The same was true of the New Economic Policy announced by Nixon in August 1971. Among other things, the NEP unilaterally "floated" the U.S. dollar on international financial markets, setting the stage for its subsequent devaluation and ending the post–World War II Bretton Woods international monetary system.

In preparation for his first presidential trip to Europe from late February to March (scarcely a month after assuming office), Nixon's private handwritten notes convey the distinct impression that while he recognized the complex relationship among adequate NATO defenses, disarmament, and détente, he thought that U.S. relations with Europe stood "at a great watershed. Now is the time to move. We must seize the moment. I shall do it." Moreover, in his predeparture notes Nixon repeatedly reminded himself to stress that the United States was initiating "a new era of consultation" with its European allies and that "no demonstrations shall deter me at home or abroad. . . .[T]he demonstrators cannot hurt me—only themselves and the cause of peace . . . [which is] too important to be derailed by irresponsible [demonstrators]."

It would also appear, however, that by the spring of 1969 Nixon thought that the 1968 intervention into Czechoslovakia by the USSR made continued European and Soviet proclamations favoring détente somewhat hollow, even though he believed that up to then moves toward "détente [had] produced less fear." Upon his return from Europe, Nixon told legislative leaders that he recognized how "dangerous" détente would be if it were not based on something "real," and that there could be no reduction of U.S. support to NATO or arms negotiations between America and the Soviet Union until there had been "progress on political issues . . . because most wars start as [the] result of political issues." In the interim, however, he maintained that talks "should go forward on all fronts." According to these private notes, Nixon also returned from his first trip abroad as president ostensibly convinced that NATO member countries should be consulted "in advance of East-West negotiations," but at the same time he became more selective about dealing with individual NATO nations. In a March 2, 1970, "eyes-only" memorandum, for example, Nixon outlined his priorities in foreign policy, indicating that with respect to Western Europe he would direct his attention only to those problems "where NATO . . . and where major countries (Britain, Germany and France) are affected. The only minor countries in Europe which I want to pay attention to in the foreseeable future will be Spain, Italy, and Greece. *I do not want to see any papers of the other countries unless their problems are directly related to NATO."* . . .

. . . Nixon almost immediately resorted to sporadic back-channel dealings with, or neglect of, NATO nations. For example, he told Kissinger on February 4, 1969, that he wanted "to go forward with a heads of government meeting" during the NATO twentieth-anniversary gathering in April, but that this plan should be "very closely held until we complete our European trip. I will discuss this matter of other NATO heads of government and then make the announcement on my return from the trip." Not until he and Kissinger proclaimed 1973 to be the Year of Europe did the president concentrate on concrete ways to improve relations with NATO. By that time they thought they had secured relations with both China and the Soviet Union and successfully ended the war in Vietnam.

The United States was on the verge of developing a defensive antiballistic missile system just as LBJ and Soviet Premier Alexei Kosygin had agreed in the summer of 1967 to discussions about reducing their countries' respective nuclear arsenals. It was obvious to both Nixon and Kissinger that the ABM might prove counterproductive if it resulted in an increased number of missiles (as did indeed occur later with the multiple independently targeted reentry vehicles, or MIRVs), but the president, in particular, was convinced that he had to have the ABM as a "bargaining chip" because intelligence reports indicated a buildup in Soviet offensive nuclear weapons. Unable to reveal these reports, the administration had to rationalize the ABM system to critics on Capitol Hill on other grounds. Consequently, Nixon publicly said that opposition from Congress to the ABM system threatened the possibility of détente and continued U.S. conventional arms support for the North Atlantic Treaty nations. Liberal, Democratic senators who opposed ABM tended to be the same senators who wanted to reduce U.S. troop contributions to NATO through what was known at the time as the Mansfield amendment. So he ordered the Departments of Defense and State to close ranks behind the ABM, instead of encouraging more dissent among senators with "informed sources leaks."

The administration also did not place as much emphasis as its opponents within Congress and the arms-control community on the danger of the ABM system jeopardizing the ongoing negotiations between Gerard C. Smith, head of the U.S. Arms Control and Disarmament Agency (ACDA), and his Soviet counterpart, Vladimir Semenov, who were meeting in Vienna. As head of the U.S. SALT delegation as well, Smith wanted the development and deployment of MIRVs and ABM systems to be limited. This placed him immediately in opposition with Nixingerism [the Nixon-Kissinger policy] on two counts because the administration was in the process of striking a private bargain with the Joint Chiefs of Staff in which they would receive MIRVs in exchange for their agreement to limit ABM sites. (Smith was to add a third point of opposition in 1972, when he disagreed with specific provisions of SALT I.) But in 1970 the administration tried its best to downplay disagreement with Smith because he could sway so many congressional votes.

Facing Smith's criticisms, difficulty with the JCS, and intelligence reports saying that the USSR was deploying more intercontinental ballistic missiles (ICBMs) and building its own ABM system around Moscow, Nixon decided that he had to initiate back-channel talks directly through Kissinger with Soviet Ambassador Anatoly Dobrynin. This approach would outflank both the State Department bureaucracy (of which he considered Smith but the tip of the iceberg) and

Congress in the formulation of foreign policy. Arms control, like all other diplomatic endeavors, was to be the preserve of the White House, even if it meant avoiding needed expert advice on this technically complicated topic. Nixon's only public concession on the issue was to downgrade the "extensive ABM coverage" known as Sentinel under the Johnson administration to a "reduced version" he called Safeguard. As with so many of Nixon's other foreign policy initiatives, Kissinger, who had never been an advocate of arms control because he thought that nuclear weapons had both a strategic and a tactical usefulness, became the secret conduit between Dobrynin and the president and, paradoxically, between the president and the arms-control community, with whom Kissinger had been at odds since the 1950s.

During the spring and summer of 1969, Nixon dealt publicly and privately with NATO nations and his gradually emerging détente policy while battling senators over the ABM. The president's handwritten comments and memoranda testify to his personal involvement in the domestic political fight over the ABM issue. From telling his staff to "raise hell with CBS" for its anti-ABM television coverage when polls showed 64 percent of the American public in favor, to criticizing members of his own cabinet, like Secretary of Defense Laird, for not "doing enough," he alternately cajoled his supporters and berated his opponents. After informing Congress on March 14 of his decision to go forward with a "substantial modification in the ABM system submitted by the previous administration," Nixon privately called [Democratic] Senator Edmund Muskie's proposal to use the $6.6 billion proposed for the ABM on hunger and poverty at home and abroad "unbelievable nonsense from a national leader!" When he read that [another Democrat,] Senator John Glenn, the former astronaut, had called the ABM a "false hope" because "no one knows if it works," the president sarcastically asked: "did he know the first space shot would absolutely work?" These private outbursts notwithstanding, Nixon, always the hardball politician, told Haldeman, "this is war," and issued heavy-handed orders to his staff to "concentrate on those [senators] who are on the fence and *only* on those where we have a chance to win." Nonetheless, on August 6 he only narrowly won the battle on this antiballistic missile system in three separate amendment votes, with Vice President [Spiro T.] Agnew breaking a tie on the crucial amendment providing "spending for Safeguard deployment." The struggle left bitterness on both sides that did not bode well for future White House–Capitol Hill cooperation on other foreign or domestic issues, and the press treated it "as an anticlimactic victory for the administration."

While carefully monitoring and refusing to compromise his basic ABM proposal, Nixon authorized back-channel meetings between Kissinger and Anatoly Dobrynin, garnered support for the ABM from NATO nations, and decided to go ahead with MIRV testing despite the opposition of nonmilitary experts—all before leaving for his June 8 meeting with South Vietnamese President Nguyen Van Thieu on Midway Island in the Pacific. Then a month later, on July 25, at the beginning of a trip around the world, the president informally presented to reporters what became known as the Nixon Doctrine, noting that the United States would no longer commit U.S. troops to East Asia, although it continued to support regional security and national self-sufficiency in the area. Hence, the Nixon Doctrine was more necessary from an American perspective as a foundation block upon which to build the détente agreements with the Soviet Union (and China) than was the ABM legislation, despite the greater domestic attention that the latter received in the United States during the spring and summer of 1969. . . .

As a defense system, the ABM was more important to Soviet foreign policy than it was to the American grand design. The relative unimportance of the ABM issue for Nixingerism became more evident after Kissinger and Dobrynin agreed to divide the issues of the defensive weapons (the ABM) and offensive weapons (ultimately SALT I) in May 1971. By that time, the president and his national security adviser had decided that it would be easier to come to an agreement over future deployment of their respective ABM systems, which primarily existed only on paper, than it would be to conclude a treaty limiting the deployment of existing nuclear weapons. After campaigning against congressmen who opposed the ABM in the 1970 midterm elections, Nixon continued his "war" against Capitol Hill in the spring of 1971 by deciding it was time to "break the back of the establishment and Democratic leadership . . . [and] then build a strong defense in [our] second term" When the president wrote this to Kissinger, he faced stiff opposition in Congress over three military issues: U.S. NATO troop commitments, suspicion about a Soviet ABM system, and, of course, the ongoing Strategic Arms Limitation Talks. Even under this domestic political duress, the president did not forget the dual nature of détente; from his perspective, despite its public call for arms limitations and economic exchanges with the USSR, it privately meant continued military buildup—except in Vietnam. . . .

While European and Soviet conditions favored détente during Nixon's first term, an unfavorable congressional climate toward continued U.S. troop support of NATO complicated things for Nixon. Beginning in 1966 Senator Mike Mansfield (Dem.-Mont.) had periodically introduced "a sense of the Senate resolution" to reduce substantially the number of American soldiers stationed in Europe. Support for Mansfield's NATO Troop Reduction Amendment to the Military Selective Service Act grew during the last half of the 1960s in direct proportion to the rise of the anti-Vietnam/peace movement. Thus, two years into his presidency Nixon faced the distinct possibility that the Mansfield amendment, calling for an outright reduction of U.S. troops by one-half, or 150,000, by the end of the year, would pass.

The president's staff closely monitored the various troop reduction amendments that arose during the spring and summer of 1971. The president himself personally made telephone calls to individual senators to ensure a negative vote, and even wrote to former occupants of the White House asking them to reassert their support for NATO, while Kissinger desperately drew upon the support of such notables of American foreign policy as [former Secretary of State] Dean Rusk and listened to advice (and criticism) from individual senators such as Charles Mathias, Jr. (Rep.-Md.).

Part of the administration's problem with Congress stemmed from its refusal to rely on the 1967 Harmel Report in formulating NATO or détente policies. This NATO report, entitled "The Future Tasks of the Alliance," not only called for a "détente in East-West relations" but also specifically argued that "military security and a policy of détente are not contradictory but complementary." This report produced the first NATO studies on troop reductions, which by the early 1970s had turned into a formal NATO call for negotiations on mutual and balanced force reductions (MBFR) with the nations of the Warsaw Pact. Individual congressmen seemed to pay more attention to this NATO material than the White House did.

During the same time, the Warsaw Pact nations began advocating a conference on European security. Both sides were aware (and wary) of the other's proposals, and reciprocal acceptance was considerably delayed by the intervention into Czechoslovakia by the USSR and some of the Warsaw Pact nations. Then, in the course of 1970–71, Willy Brandt, West Germany's chancellor, initiated a policy of *Ostpolitik* by entering into a treaty with the Soviet Union that officially recognized the existence of two Germanys. This gave new life to these mutual force reduction proposals and made Nixon and Kissinger worry that West Germany would achieve détente with the Soviet Union before the United States. So when Mansfield used Brandt's *Ostpolitik* (in addition to the U.S. balance-of-payments problem) to justify his 1971 Nato troop-reduction amendment, they tried to thwart both. Because Nixon and Kissinger understood that NATO support of MBFR was cynically designed to guarantee the existence of a large number of American troops in Europe, they made sure that at a November 19, 1970, meeting of the National Security Council a decision was reached not to reduce U.S. forces in Europe, "except in the context of mutual reductions negotiated with the East."

The administration was also prepared to prevent passage of the Mansfield amendment (which required unilateral withdrawal of American troops from NATO) with a Republican counteramendment introduced by Senator Mathias that requested the president to negotiate a MBFR agreement "consistent with balance of payments situation and to report to Congress the results every six months commencing September 15, 1971." Mansfield had already accepted a friendly amendment to his resolution, saying that his called-for U.S. troop reductions would "become inoperative if prior to December 30, 1971, representatives of the Warsaw Pact countries . . . entered into negotiations, or . . . entered into formal discussions, regarding a mutual reduction by such organizations of their military forces stationed in Europe."

Before the final vote on the Mansfield amendment in May 1971, the administration received some unexpected help toward its defeat from Soviet Premier Leonid Brezhnev—for which Kissinger later tried to give the administration credit. In March and again in May 1971, Brezhnev indicated that the Soviet Union was willing to begin discussing mutual arms reductions in central Europe. While the administration took advantage of his May statement to undercut support for the Mansfield amendment by arguing that a unilateral withdrawal of U.S. troops would preclude taking Brezhnev up on his MBFR offer, there is no documentary proof for Kissinger's assertion that "carefully calibrated measures of the Administration toward the Soviet Union . . . [and] our willingness to discuss détente had lured Brezhnev into an initiative about mutual force reductions that saved our whole European defense structure from Congressional savaging." This was simply one of many of Kissinger's attempts after the fact to imply that "linkage" was working when it wasn't. . . .

. . . Kissinger's claims notwithstanding, what is significant about the defeat of the Mansfield amendment and similar ones until 1973 was Nixon's ability to outmaneuver a Democratically-controlled Congress between 1969 and 1971—not his (or Kissinger's) ability to outmaneuver the Soviet Union, which, after all, had been pursuing détente longer than the United States. . . .

From 1949 until 1979 the United States refused to recognize the Communist government of the People's Republic of China. Not until the early 1970s, during

Nixon's first administration, did the U.S. government begin to reverse this standard cold war policy of nonrecognition with a number of unilateral gestures of reconciliation, which ultimately brought about rapprochement (the establishment of friendly relations) under Nixon and recognition under Jimmy Carter in 1979. Setting in motion a process that ended in recognition of China remains one of Nixon's longest-lasting diplomatic accomplishments. Normalization of U.S. relations with China was part of Nixon's grand design to bring this giant Communist nation into the ranks of the superpowers. Long before Nixon sent Kissinger on a secret mission to Peking in July 1971 to arrange the details of his own visit there the following year, the president had used the State Department and other government agencies to make various unilateral gestures of reconciliation, indicating that he wanted fundamental improvements in relations between the United States and the People's Republic of China. It remains one of the best examples of a "Presidentially imposed, Presidentially-initiated policy."

Opening relations with China also appears to have been on Nixon's mind from the beginning of his presidency. By the mid-1960s China specialists had openly begun to complain about continuing to isolate the People's Republic and, even though anti-Chinese sentiments loomed large in the public mind because of China's support for the North Vietnamese, China had been gaining international credibility for over twenty years and was recognized by over fifty countries when Nixon assumed office. As leader of the nonaligned nations, China challenged the superpowers' right to dictate to Third World nations. Its ties with the Soviet Union had been severely strained, if not actually broken, by 1969. And the cultural revolution inside China had subsided.

Thus, conditions were propitious for rethinking Chinese-American relations—a fact not lost on Nixon. It was time to bring China into the international fold of civilized nations, along with the Soviet Union through rapprochement. There was even the slight possibility that, despite Soviet and U.S. military advantages over China, that country might launch an irrational attack against one of them. In rationalizing his new approach to the Chinese, Nixon argued to his top foreign policy adviser in April 1969 that "the tragic fact of history [is] that most of the great wars were not started by responsible men and that we have to base our assumptions on what potentially irresponsible or irrational men may do, rather than simply on what we, as responsible leaders, might do." Rapprochement might help make "irrational" Communist Chinese leaders more rational, or so the president ethnocentrically implied. . . .

By the time Nixon became president he had decided to establish a new policy toward the People's Republic of China in several stages. First, American anti-Chinese rhetoric had to be toned down in order to bring about a more rational discourse than had prevailed in fifteen years of discussion largely conducted through the mediation of Poland. Second, trade and visa restrictions needed to be reduced. Third, the number of U.S. troops at bases surrounding China and in Vietnam would be reduced. Finally, Nixon wanted the Communist leaders to know that he would personally consider revising the rigid cold war position of the United States on Taiwan and its heretofore unstinting support of Chiang. These attitude changes and low-level diplomatic actions initially took place without fanfare. Nixon underscored this approach in a memorandum to Kissinger on February 1, 1969, wanting "to give every encouragement to the attitude that this Administration is 'exploring the possibilities of rapprochement with the Chinese.' This should be done privately and under no circumstances get into public prints from this direction." Around the same time, Nixon privately told Senate majority leader Mike Mansfield that he wanted to involve China in "global responsibility." Then, on February 18, 1969, he instructed Secretary of State William Rogers to make a public announcement that the United States now favored a program of cultural and scientific exchanges with the People's Republic.

The Chinese ignored all these private and public signals until 1970. By that time Nixon had repeatedly commented publicly on "what a dangerous world . . . and . . . unhappy world it would be if those seven hundred million [Chinese] people [continued to] live in angry isolation from all the rest of the world." In a rambling monologue, he even told uncomprehending students demonstrating at the Lincoln Memorial over the Kent State student killings that he hoped one day China would be opened up so they could visit "one of the most remarkable people on earth."

Peking's slow response was fortunate in that it allowed Kissinger to come up to speed on Nixon's rapprochement policy. In August 1969, Kissinger finally invited Allen S. Whiting, a former State Department specialist on China, to brief him personally about Sino-Soviet border clashes that had occurred in March. Up to this point Kissinger had only generally endorsed Nixon's idea of rapprochement, but did not contribute specifically to it. Whiting convinced Kissinger that the administration had reacted to these military skirmishes much too casually, and that it was inaccurate to think that China would attack Russia. In fact, China so feared a Soviet attack that this was a historic opportunity to change traditional U.S. cold war policy, which had been more "favorably" disposed toward the USSR than toward China. "Belatedly, Kissinger became a convert—a latter-day Marco Polo discovering the new China," according to Marvin and Bernard Kalb, "and he plunged into his subject with all of the eagerness and occasional naiveté of the newcomer to Asia." . . .

The Chinese agreed to resume the discontinued Warsaw talks [with the United States], but after the first meeting in January 1970, they canceled the next two—one when a Chinese diplomat defected and another over the extension of the Vietnam War into Cambodia. By May, however, Peking had begun tentatively to respond positively to Nixon's first Foreign Policy Report to Congress which had been issued in February 1970. Nixon, in turn, had been trying to reassure the Chinese through two unlikely (and, as it turned out, unsavory) contacts: the Romanian leader, Nicolae Ceauşéscu, and the president of Pakistan, Yahya Khan. By October indirect contact had been established. The next month the president issued the following memorandum to Kissinger:

> On a very confidential basis, I would like you to have prepared in your staff—without any notice to people who might leak—a study of where we are with regard to the admission of Red China to the UN. It seems to me that the time is approaching sooner than we might think when we will not have the votes to block admission.
>
> The question we really need an answer to is how we can develop a position in which we keep our commitments to Taiwan and yet will not be rolled on by those who favor admission of Red China.
>
> There is no hurry on this study but within two or three months I would like to see what you come up with.

The stage was set for a breakthrough in Sino-American relations. An encouraging message from China through Romania at the beginning of 1971 prompted the United States in March and April to terminate all restrictions on American travel to the Chinese mainland and the twenty-year-old embargo on trade. Following the highly publicized Ping-Pong games between Chinese and American teams in April, the Pakistan ambassador to the United States also delivered a message from Chinese Premier Chou En-lai [Zhou Enlai] to Nixon (replying to one from the president on January 5), asking him to send a representative to China for direct discussions. The message noted that "the Chinese government reaffirms its willingness to receive publicly in Peking a special envoy of the President of the United States . . . for direct meetings and discussions."

It has never been made absolutely clear by either Nixon or Kissinger why the contacts after this note had to be conducted in secret. The obvious reasons are that the mission might have failed and that it might have provoked both the Russians and the Japanese—neither of whom knew about the previously secret contacts with the Chinese. Thus secrecy bred secrecy. Additionally, Nixon paid lip service in his memoirs to the realization that there would be conservative opposition to open, direct contacts; Kissinger gives no reason for keeping his mission secret. He does, however, manage to exaggerate both his initial role in the policy and its potential danger: "I felt immense relief [at being chosen as envoy] after so long a preoccupation with its design I would be able to bring the enterprise to fruition. . . . Assisted only by his security adviser, without the alibi provided by normal processes of bureaucratic clearance, [Nixon] authorized a mission that, had it failed, would surely have produced a political catastrophe for him and an international catastrophe for his country." More likely, covert foreign policy operations had simply become so common that Kissinger was the obvious choice as secret envoy, even though others mentioned for the mission were more qualified. Secrecy certainly made Nixon's July 15, 1971, announcement of Kissinger's undercover trip and of his own decision to visit China early in 1972 more dramatic. . . .

. . . Just before Kissinger made a second, this time public, trip to Peking in October 1971, [presidential aide H. R.] Haldeman's lengthy handwritten notes indicate that the president and his staff worried about Kissinger grabbing the spotlight by giving too many backgrounders to the press. At one point Nixon said bluntly, we "need to get Kissinger under control. . . . [I] don't want to escalate Kissinger's trip." Nixon already knew that the "press will try to give Kissinger the credit and say the President had nothing to do with it." (Ironically, Kissinger's lack of knowledge about China was painfully revealed on this second trip when he met in Peking with the former U.S. diplomat John Service. He dismissed Service with some perfunctory remarks, apparently not knowing that he "had campaigned for Chinese Communist–American détente twenty-five years before Nixon and Kissinger.") The president had no more success in containing Kissinger at the end of 1971 over China, however, than he would over Vietnam at the end of 1972.

Despite the obvious importance and success of rapprochement with the People's Republic of China, Nixon believed that the media never gave it as much credit as it deserved. As late as 1988 he was still trying to claim as much personal credit for rapprochement as possible: "We changed the world. If it had not been for the China initiative, which only I could do at that point, we would be in a terrible situation today with China aligned with the Soviet Union and with the Soviet Union's power."

Although various government officials denied that Nixon courted China in order to bring pressure to bear on the Soviet Union, the president's triumphant visit to the People's Republic of China in February 1972 (with its attendant joint "Shanghai Communiqué") was clearly part of the Nixinger "triangularization" policy. Moreover, in July 1971 when Nixon announced the visit, there is some indication that possible Sino-American rapprochement made the Soviets more amenable to moving ahead with détente in the fall of 1971. It is often forgotten, however, that the original purpose behind improved relations with both China and the USSR was to bring leverage to bear on both nations to improve the situation for the United States in Vietnam. Like so many other attempts at linkage, this one did not prove successful.

There is no direct evidence that because of Soviet concern over the results of Nixon's trip to China, rapprochement became indirectly linked to the success of negotiations leading to the ten formal summit agreements signed in Moscow between the United States and the USSR in May 1972. . . . They provided for prevention of military incidents at sea and in the air; scholarly cooperation and exchange in the fields of science and technology; cooperation in health research; cooperation in environmental matters; cooperation in the exploration of outer space; facilitation of commercial and economic relations; and, most important, the Anti-Ballistic Missile Treaty, the Interim Agreement on the Limitations on Strategic Arms (SALT I), and the Basic Principles of U.S.-Soviet Relations.

In the area of arms control, Nixinger détente policy contained the potential not only to substitute for containment—the standard way the United States had fought the cold war against the Soviet Union since the late 1940s—but also to transcend the procrustean ideological constraints at the very heart of the post–World War II conflict between these two nations. This potential was never fully realized, in large measure because Nixon and Kissinger chose to give priority to SALT talks over MIRV talks. To a smaller extent it was never realized because, until the collapse of communism in central and eastern Europe and the Soviet Union almost thirty years later, their immediate successors proved unable (or unwilling) to build upon the delicate distinction between containment and détente that they left behind. Also, there was no changed leadership or structural base in the USSR (or the former Soviet bloc countries) to reinforce the concept of détente inside or outside its borders during the last half of the 1970s, as there began to appear at the end of the 1980s. It must be remembered that the Nixon-Brezhnev détente remained essentially tactical because the cold war had not yet significantly begun to recede. Hence, there was no basic change in conflicting cold war strategies under Nixingerism—only a temporary blurring of hostilities that Reagan revived to a fever pitch in the 1980s.

SALT I, conducted in Helsinki in 1969 and Vienna in 1970, led to two arms-control documents at the 1972 Moscow summit—both in keeping with the tactical aspects of Nixon's détente. These included a treaty limiting the deployment of antiballistic missile systems (ABMs) to two for each country, and an agreement freezing the number of offensive intercontinental ballistic missiles (ICBMs) at the level of those then under production or deployed. Unlike SALT I, the ABM Treaty was of "unlimited duration . . . and not open to material unilateral revision," despite attempts by the Reagan administration to do just this beginning in 1985. Until the Strategic Defense Initiative (SDI) efforts in the last half of the 1980s, however, the

ABM Treaty essentially succeeded in relegating deployment of conventional ballistic missile defense systems to minor strategic significance.

SALT I, on the other hand, was an agreement of limited, five-year duration that attempted to establish a rough balance or parity between the offensive nuclear arsenals of the two superpowers, despite the "missile gaps" that continued to exist between them in specific weapons. For example, when Nixon signed SALT I, the United States had a total of 1,710 missiles: 1,054 land-based ICBMs and 656 on submarines (sub-launched ballistic missiles, or SLBMs). The USSR had a total of 2,358 missiles: 1,618 landbased ICBMs and 740 SLBMs. SALT I not only recognized the strategic parity of the USSR but gave it a numerical edge in missiles and a slight throw-weight [a measurement of rocket thrust] advantage. The United States retained a numerical advantage in warheads and a superiority in strategic bombers—460 in 1972 to 120 for the Soviets. SALT I by no means stopped the nuclear arms race, but it recognized that unregulated weapons competition between the two superpowers could no longer be rationally condoned. By freezing further missile buildup, SALT I meant that by the time SALT II was signed in 1979, total American-Soviet missile strength remained essentially unchanged: 2,283 to 2,504, respectively. From 1972 until the mid-1980s, therefore, SALT talks were regarded as a barometer of relations between the two countries, contrary to the claims of critics, even though the "MIRVing" engaged in by both sides has tended to obscure their generally parallel buildup since 1972.

While it is relatively easy to generalize about the meaning of SALT I so many years after its announcement, there was much controversy and confusion at the time over specific terms. The controversy was largely partisan, but the confusion was legitimate because, in terms of sheer complexity and scope, this summit meeting between Nixon and Brezhnev was an unprecedented contrast from the previous five summits following World War II. Complicating matters, we now know from those who participated in the multilevel negotiations and in the drafting of the various technical provisions that Nixon and Kissinger did not completely understand all the terms, let alone the implications, of arms control, especially the sections concerning submarine-based missiles. This was because Kissinger had erred during his initial back-channel negotiations by not insisting that these missiles be included in SALT I. By the time they were added, the Soviets had benefited from the agreed-upon formula. Additionally, as just mentioned, MIRVing, which allowed the Soviets (and the U.S.) to modernize their missile fleets, was not limited in any way by SALT I, and the original protocol had to be rewritten and signed again by Nixon and Brezhnev after the formal ceremony.

Nixon and Kissinger returned from the May 1972 Moscow summit meeting triumphant, but more vulnerable than ever on three fronts: military, economic, and moral and ideological. All three boded ill for the SALT II talks that would begin six months later. Critics immediately asserted that the United States had been "hoodwinked" by the Soviet Union into a disadvantageous military deal with respect to SLBMs. With Helsinki CSCE agreements still three years away and no mutual and balanced force reductions in sight, as negotiations over SALT II dragged on into the 1970s, an additional military criticism became that the Soviets were violating the terms of both the ABM and SALT I agreements. . . . Moral criticism of Nixingerism based on ideological hostility to the USSR became more credible in the wake of Watergate, but had always been strong in the minds of particular Republican and

Democratic conservatives in Congress and across the country. It was this criticism that Nixon and Kissinger found the hardest to answer, because their approach to détente had not, in fact, been based on moral or ideological considerations, but on very pragmatic ones.

The situation did not improve with Nixon's resignation. In the summer of 1975, with Gerald Ford as president, Kissinger went on a national speaking tour to convince people that détente was more important than "blind assertions of moral absolutes." But the time had passed for such Nixinger arguments to carry the day. Between 1972 and 1974, there was a decline in popular support for détente despite all the hard-sell tactics used to promote it, including a controversial grain deal with the Soviets in 1972, which caused domestic prices of grain to rise. . . .

Beginning in 1972 certain members of Congress insisted that in return for most-favored-nation treatment (MFN), the Soviet Union should liberalize emigration policies affecting Jews. As late as March 1974, Kissinger referred to "domestic obstacles, some of a highly irresponsible nature," after Brezhnev brought up [Democratic] Senator "Scoop" Jackson's opposition to granting MFN status to the USSR. When Brezhnev said that Jackson was linking "something [the question of Jewish migration] that bears no relation to this entire matter [MFN]," Kissinger agreed, saying: "We don't consider this a proper subject of inquiry by the United States Government." The general secretary's fears, which he had expressed the previous year to [Treasury Secretary] George Shultz, proved more realistic than the secretary of state's optimism on this question.

Once again, as on NATO troop reductions and arms control, Senator Jackson orchestrated a Senate amendment to counter the Soviet-American trade agreement. After two and a half years of haggling over various versions of the Jackson-Vanik amendment, which was extended in 1974 to include a ceiling on loans to the Soviet Union from the Export-Import Bank, Ford signed the Trade Reform Bill with the amendment on January 3, 1975, and the Soviet government officially refused to comply with it on January 10. Later that month the president withdrew his support for the MFN treatment of the USSR because of Soviet intervention into the Angolan civil war. Thus ended the move toward liberalizing trade with the Communist world (at least as represented by the Soviet Union) in the name of détente that had begun so optimistically under the Nixon administration with the passage of the Export Administration Act of 1969, liberalizing export controls.

In the interim, the October 1973 war in the Middle East not only misleadingly contributed to the popular impression in the United States that détente was not working with the Soviet Union; it also exacerbated all the underlyng differences between the European and American conceptions of détente—placing even more strain on the Atlantic Alliance. . . .

In July 1975, with American-Soviet trade relations temporarily on hold and NATO allies restive over having been bypassed at the Moscow summit and uncertain over how the United States would respond to talk of increasing Soviet military strength, the long-awaited Conference on Security and Cooperation in Europe began. The declaration of ten principles signed by thirty-five nations at Helsinki on August 1 was important to the United States and the Soviet Union for different reasons. Consequently, they differed over how best to implement the Final Act of the CSCE because they each emphasized different sections of it. This had not been the case in 1974 when Kissinger and [Soviet foreign minister Andrei] Gromyko frankly agreed to thwart the "impossible proposals" for "military détente" being put forward by the Western allies of the United States at CSCE and MBFR meetings. The Soviet Union, for example, opposed supplying such information about troop maneuvers. "I have told you we will not support this proposal," Kissinger assured Gromyko with Brezhnev listening, adding, "we can weaken these proposals substantially." Kissinger even assured the Soviet foreign minister and secretary general in this 1974 meeting that the United States would "use its influence [at CSCE meetings in Helsinki] not to embarrass the Soviet Union or raise provocative issues" with respect to Basket III, which called for humanitarian and cultural cooperation, including the freer movement of people, which the Soviets opposed.

By the time President Ford traveled to Helsinki to sign the CSCE agreements before the election of 1976, Basket III had been not only included in them but "linked" to further East-West economic cooperation at the insistence of Western Europe. Significantly, Ford's political opponents within the Republican party, such as Ronald Reagan and members of his own staff, implied in press statements that the Helsinki Accords represented "another Kissinger deal that was forced down the President's throat." They simply didn't understand how much these agreements differed from the promises Kissinger had made to Gromyko in 1974. Gone were the halcyon days of détente under the Nixon administration. . . .

The U.S. government, especially under President Carter, stressed the human rights provision of the CSCE and used it as a standard by which to measure the treatment of citizens in foreign countries, including the USSR and its satellite nations. This principle became a bone of contention between the United States and the Soviet Union in ways not anticipated by the Nixon administration. Moscow, on the other hand, logically preferred to focus on those segments of the Final Act that granted implied recognition of Soviet hegemony in eastern Europe. A major legacy of Nixinger foreign policy from 1975 until the disintegration of the Soviet Union has been manifested by agreement to disagree over the importance of the Helsinki Accords. Little wonder that Nixon's successors (including Ford) quickly retreated from a defense of Nixon's brand of détente to the point of dropping the use of the word. Yet, in light of the fall of communism, it deserved more credit than it received before Nixon's death. Détente was more than "deals with Moscow in return for no demonstrable Soviet restraint," as some commentators in the early 1990s asserted.

Why Détente Failed

RAYMOND L. GARTHOFF

The mix of cooperation and competition in American-Soviet relations makes it difficult to define the period of détente precisely. Despite President Nixon's early call for an era of negotiation, a series of confrontations in the ensuing three-and-a-half years made progress toward that goal slow. Then, in mid-1972, the first Nixon-Brezhnev summit meeting took place, and détente suddenly blossomed. During the next few

From *Détente and Confrontation: American-Soviet Relations from Nixon to Reagan* by Raymond L. Garthoff. Copyright © 1994. Reprinted by permission of The Brookings Institution.

years, a flood of cooperative ventures was inaugurated, culminating symbolically in 1975 in a joint space rendezvous, and accompanied by a great deal of rhetoric about peaceful coexistence and partnership in building a structure of peace.

Although cooperation developed in a number of areas, particularly from 1972 to 1975, it never supplanted ongoing competition nor offered sufficient guarantee against renewed confrontation. From the American perspective, one important cause of the decline of détente was the active Soviet role in Africa and South Asia after 1975. Growing concern over the strategic balance from 1976 on was an equally important source of disenchantment. From the Soviet perspective, successive U.S. administrations were seen as conducting a vigorous policy of containing and curtailing Soviet influence, especially in the Middle East, from the very beginning of détente. Moreover, the U.S. Congress had dashed expectations for economic benefits promised and even granted by the Nixon administration by making them conditional on unacceptable and humiliating concessions concerning internal Soviet affairs, specifically, escalating demands for Jewish emigration. Finally, in the period from 1977 on, the Soviet leaders perceived a growing American attempt to regain strategic superiority.

Was détente a potential solution to the risks and costs of confrontation, a solution undercut by actions of the Soviet Union, or of the United States, or both? Or did détente exacerbate the problem by providing only a disarming illusion of an alternative? Was détente a Soviet snare to lull American sensitivity to a buildup of Soviet military power and political-military expansion? Did the United States and the Soviet Union ever have a common understanding of détente—or did they hold differing conceptions that were incompatible from the start? Did détente fail? Was it ever really tested? . . .

Détente, while the shorthand description for the policies subscribed to by both powers in the 1970s, was not a clearly defined concept held in common. It became increasingly evident, beginning even in the early 1970s when détente was at a high point, that Washington and Moscow had very different conceptions of what a détente policy entailed, and had had from the outset. The expectations of both sides in turn differed greatly. And as their respective expectations were not met, disillusionment with the performance of the other side followed. Moreover, in the United States (although not in the Soviet Union) disillusionment with the very idea of détente itself also followed. . . .

Détente is a French word that actually means a "relaxation of tension" in a literal way—as with the release of a bowstring. Long ago it came to be used in diplomatic parlance to represent an easing of strained or tense relations between states. It is distinguished from another French word, *entente*, which represents a positive development of close and cooperative relations. Much of the confusion in American understanding seems to have stemmed from a tendency to interpret détente as though it meant entente. The Soviets have used a term of their own, *razryadka napryazhennosti,* or simply *razryadka,* also meaning a lessening or relaxation of tension.

The term détente had been used in the 1960s to describe steps aimed at lessening tension in East-West relations. In particular, it had been used by President Charles de Gaulle [of France] in the mid-1960s, and in the North Atlantic Treaty Organization (NATO) in the latter 1960s as one element in an alliance policy calling for balancing defense and détente. The first use of the term to describe the specific efforts launched by President Richard M. Nixon in 1969 (and, in a sense, by the Soviet Union at about the same time) to improve American-Soviet relations is elusive.

Indeed, the Nixon administration went to some lengths to avoid using the word détente. Instead, Nixon and his assistant for national security affairs, Henry A. Kissinger, spoke of "a new era," of substituting negotiations for confrontation, and of pursuing a "structure of peace" through mutual accommodation. By 1973–74, however, détente came to be used in the United States officially as well as popularly as a shorthand term describing the new policy. . . .

Foremost among the causes of the ultimate failure of détente in the 1970s was a fatal difference in the conception of its basic role by the two sides. The American leaders saw it (in Kissinger's words) as a way of "managing the emergence of Soviet power" into world politics in an age of nuclear parity. The Soviet leaders envisaged it as a way of managing the transition of the United States from its former superiority to a more modest role in world politics in an age of nuclear parity. Thus each saw itself as the manager of a transition of the other. Moreover, while the advent of parity ineluctably meant some decrease in the ability of the United States to manage world affairs, this fact was not sufficiently appreciated in Washington. And while it meant a relatively more important role for the Soviet Union, it did not mean acquisition of the kind of power the United States wielded. Finally, both had diverging images of the world order, and although that fact was well enough understood, its implications were not. Thus, underlying the attempts by each of the two powers to manage the adjustment of the other to a changing correlation of forces in the world there were even more basic parallel attempts by both to modify the fundamental world order—in different directions.

The Soviet leaders, conditioned by their Marxist-Leninist ideology, believed that a certain historical movement would ultimately lead to the replacement of capitalism (imperialism) in the world by socialism (communism). But they realized this transition would have to occur in a world made incalculably more dangerous by massive arsenals of nuclear weapons. Peaceful coexistence and détente were seen as offering a path to neutralize this danger by ruling out war between states, permitting historical change to occur, as the Soviets believed it must, through fundamental indigenous social-economic-political processes within states. While Marxist-Leninists did not shun the use of any other instrument of power if it was expedient, they did not see military power as the fundamental moving force of history. On the contrary, they saw it as a possible ultimate recourse of the doomed capitalist class ruling the imperialist citadels of the West. There was, therefore, no ideological barrier to or reservation about pursuing a policy of détente aimed at preventing nuclear war. Quite the contrary—détente represented a policy aimed at providing stability to a world order that allowed progressive historical change.

The American leadership and the American people, not holding a deterministic ideology, while self-confident, were much less sure of the trend of history. Insofar as they held an ideology for a global order, it was one of pluralism. That ideology did not assume the whole world would choose an American-style democratic and free enterprise system. The world order has been seen as one that should provide stability and at least protect the democratic option for peoples. Occasionally during the Cold War there were crusades to extirpate communism in the world. . . . But the dominant

American aim was to contain and deter Soviet or Soviet-controlled communist expansion at the expense of a pluralistic and, in that sense, "free" world order. What varied and periodically was at issue was the relative weight to be placed, on the one hand, on containment achieved by building positions of counterposing power, and on the other, on cooperation, pursued by seeking common ground for mutual efforts to reduce tension and accommodate the differing interests of the two sides. There were varied judgments in both countries about whether objective circumstances permit the latter approach or require the former, and therefore about whether détente was feasible or confrontation was necessary.

When Nixon and Kissinger developed a strategy of détente to replace a strategy of confrontation, the underlying expectation was that as the Soviet Union became more and more extensively engaged in an organic network of relations with the existing world order, it would gradually become reconciled to that order. Ideological expectations of global revolutionary change would become attenuated and merely philosophical rather than actively political. Avoidance of the risks of nuclear war was essential; hence there was acceptance of peaceful coexistence and of efforts at strategic arms limitations and other negotiations to reduce the risks.

The common American and Soviet recognition of the need to avert war was . . . of fundamental significance. But there remained radically different visions of the course world history would follow and, therefore, of the pattern of world politics. This divergence in their worldviews naturally affected the policies of the two powers. The difference was well-known in a general way; its implications for the two superpowers' respective actions, and therefore for their mutual relations and for détente, were not, however, sufficiently understood. And this gap led to unrealistic expectations that were not met and that undermined confidence in détente. . . .

The United States did not analyze critically the underlying postulates of either American or Soviet conceptions—nor, indeed, could that be done before they were more clearly articulated. For example, consider the proposition held by the Soviet leaders until 1986 that "the class struggle" and "national liberation struggle" were not and could not be affected by détente. With the exception of a minuscule minority that accepted the Soviet line uncritically, almost all Americans saw that proposition as communist mumbo jumbo being used as a transparently self-serving argument to excuse pursuit of Soviet interests. In fact, Soviet leaders considered that proposition to be a self-evident truth: détente was a policy, while the class struggle was an objective phenomenon in the historical process that could not be abolished by policy decision, even if the Soviet leaders wanted to do so. While there *was* a self-serving dimension to the Soviet proposition, it was not cynical artifice. To the contrary, it was sincerely believed. On a logical plane, to whatever extent the Soviet premise was true, it was crystal clear that any inevitable historical process could not be stopped by any state's policy or agreement between the two states.

It was not necessary to assume a prior meeting of the minds of the leaders of the two powers on ideological conceptions as a prerequisite to agreements based on calculated mutual advantage. While ideological conditioning and belief did influence policy, they did not determine it. Questions about the historical process can and should be left to history. The critical question was not whether there was a global class struggle or national liberation struggle, as defined by Marxism-Leninism, but what the Soviet leadership was going to do about it. While the Soviet leadership accepted a moral commitment to aid the world revolutionary process, it was also ideologically obliged to do so only in ways that did not weaken or risk the attainments of socialism in the USSR. Moreover, the ideology also held that world revolutionary processes were indigenous. Revolution could not be exported. Neither could counterrevolution. But both could be aided by external forces. . . .

In approaching the question of what was a proper and consistent code of conduct with respect to Soviet—and American—behavior in the third world, each side needed to understand the perspective of the other. Each, naturally, retained its own view of the historical process, as well as its own national interests. Differences of concrete interests remained to be reconciled, but failure to understand each other's viewpoint seriously compounded the problem.

A second cause of the collapse of détente was the failure to turn to greater use of collaborative measures to meet the requirements of security. National military power was bound to remain a foundation of national security in the foreseeable future. But it did not need to be the first, or usual, or sole, recourse. The American-Soviet détente involved efforts to prevent and to manage crises, and to regulate the military balance through arms control and arms limitation. In the final analysis, however, those efforts—while useful and potentially significant—were almost entirely dependent on the political relationship, and in large measure withered with it.

The effort to achieve strategic arms limitations marked the first, and the most daring, attempt to follow a collaborative approach in meeting military security requirements. It involved an unprecedented joint consideration of ways to control the most vital (or fatal) element of national power—the arsenals of strategic nuclear weaponry. Early successes held great promise—but also showed the limits of readiness of both superpowers to take this path. SALT [Strategic Arms Limitation Talks] generated problems of its own and provided a focal point for objection by those who did not wish to see either regulated military parity or political détente. The final lesson of the failure to ratify SALT II was that arms control could not stand alone nor sustain a political détente that did not support itself. Indeed, even the early successes of SALT I, which contributed to an upsurge of détente and were worthwhile on their own merits, became a bone of contention as détente came under fire.

The widely held American view that SALT tried to do too much was a misjudgment: the *real* flaw was the failure of SALT to do enough. There were remarkable initial successes in the agreement on parity as an objective and on stability of the strategic arms relationship as a necessary condition, and the control imposed on strategic defensive competition in ABM [Anti-Ballistic Missile] systems. But there was insufficient political will (and perhaps political authority) to bite the bullet and ban or sharply limit MIRVs [Multiple Independently-targetable Reentry Vehicles]— the key to controlling the strategic offensive arms race. Both sides share the blame for this failure, but especially the United States because it led a new round of the arms competition when it could safely have held back (in view of the ABM Treaty) long enough to make a real effort to ban MIRVs. The failure to control MIRVs was ultimately the key to the essential failure in the 1970s to stabilize the military dimension of parity, and it contributed indirectly to the overall fall of détente.

Too little attention has been paid to the efforts in the 1970s to devise a regime of crisis management and crisis avoidance. Paradoxically, the relatively more successful steps in this direction are rarely remembered because they do not seize attention as do political frictions. The agreements of 1971 on averting war by accident or miscalculation and on upgrading the hot line, the agreement of 1972 on avoiding incidents at sea between the U.S. and Soviet navies, and the agreement of 1973 on prevention of nuclear war played a positive role. (In addition, so did multilateral confidence-building measures in the European security framework.) The one instance sometimes charged to have been a failure of collaboration was in fact, if anything, a success: the defusing of the pseudocrisis between the two superpowers in October 1973 at the climax of the fourth Arab-Israeli war.

A third cause of the failure of American-Soviet détente in the 1970s was the inability of the superpowers to transform the recognition of strategic parity into a common political standard to govern their competitive actions in the world. The divergent conceptions of détente and of the world order underlay this failure, but these were compounded by other factors. One was the unreadiness of the United States, in conceding nominal strategic parity, also to concede political parity. Another was a reciprocated hubris in which each superpower applied a one-sided double standard in perceiving, and judging, the behavior of the other. The basic principles of mutual relations and a code of conduct were never thrashed out with the necessary frank discussion of differing views, a failure that gave rise to a facade of agreement that not only affected public, but to some extent even leadership, expectations. Expectations based on wishful thinking about the effects of the historical process, or based on overconfidence about a country's managerial abilities to discipline the behavior of the other side, were doomed to failure. Paradoxically, these inflated expectations coexisted—on both sides—with underlying excessive and projected fears and imputations of aggressive hostility, which resurfaced when the expectations were not met. That this process influenced wider political constituencies (a much wider body politic in the United States) only compounded a situation that affected the leadership as well. . . .

The consistent failure of each side to sense and recognize the different perspectives and perceptions of the other was strongly detrimental to the development of their relations, compounding their real differences. The dangers of the failure of each side to recognize the effects of its own misperceptions were also too little appreciated, as were the dangers of its failure to perceive the implications of differing perceptions and misperceptions. . . . Rather than recognize a differing perception, judging it to be a valid alternative perception, or misperception, both sides typically ascribed a different and usually malevolent purpose to each other. This tendency, for example, characterized the assessments each made of the military programs of the other, as well as of many of its political moves. Even when attempts were made to take account of different ways of thinking, on each side the usual approach was to apply respective stereotypes of "communist" or "imperialist" modes of calculation to the other side, but in a superficial way that stressed the expansionist or aggressive image of the adversary. The result was usually no more than to provide a self-satisfying illusion that the perceptual factor had been taken into account.

In the United States, many in the 1970s saw a cumulative series of Soviet interventions, involving military means, often with proxies—Angola, Ethiopia, Kampuchea, Afghanistan—that they believed formed a pattern of Soviet expansion and aggrandizement inconsistent with the Basic Principles [a May 1972 Soviet-American agreement to practice restraint in their relations] and détente. Moreover, many believed that these expansionist moves were encouraged by détente, or were at least induced by a weakness of U.S. will and military power. Hence the need to rebuild that power and reassert that will; hence the heightened suspicion of détente.

In fact, the history of diplomatic, political, and interventionist activity during the last decade [1970s] is much more extensive and complex—and much less one-sided. Certainly from the Soviet perspective, not only was the Soviet role more limited and more justified than the United States would concede, but the American role was more active and less benign. . . .

In the Middle East, the United States arranged the defection of Sadat's Egypt—and of the Sudan, Somalia, and to some degree Iraq. It effectively squeezed the Soviet Union out of a role in the Middle East peace process, despite repeated assurances that it would not do so. . . . In Africa, U.S. allies and proxies repeatedly and blatantly intervened with military force—Portugal before 1974; France in numerous cases; France, Belgium, Morocco, and Egypt in Zaire; Zaire, South Africa and others in Angola in 1975–76, albeit unsuccessfully; and so forth. Using covert operations, the United States assisted in the overthrow of an elected Marxist, [Salvador] Allende, in Chile and, with European assistance, of the Marxist-supported [Arelino] Gonçalves in Portugal. . . .

The deterioration of relations during the latter half of the 1970s not only reflected some of these developments but also contributed to them. For the most part the actions of the two powers stemmed not from Soviet or American initiatives, but as responses to local events.

There were, however, also conscious policies of assertive competition by both powers throughout the period of nominal détente. Recall, for example, the U.S. policy initiatives in the immediate aftermath of the first summit meeting in Moscow in 1972, the summit that launched détente. President Nixon flew directly from the Soviet Union to Iran. One purpose of his visit was to establish the shah [of Iran] as, in effect, American proconsul in the region, in keeping with the Nixon Doctrine. The shah was promised virtually any American arms he wanted. A contributory reason for the shah's deputation that was not apparent was to follow through on some conversations with the Chinese and to signal to them U.S. intention to build regional positions of strength around the Soviet Union, détente notwithstanding. In addition, while in Tehran the president accepted the shah's proposal covertly to arm the Iraqi Kurds. (Iraq had just signed a Treaty of Friendship with the Soviet Union.) Thus the Kurds became proxies of the United States and Iran (and of Israel, which joined in providing support in order to tie the Iraqi army down). And there was a later chapter to this American initiative: the shah persuaded and induced President Mohammad Daoud of Afghanistan in 1975–78 to move away from his previous close alignment with the Soviet Union, to improve relations with Pakistan, and to crack down on Afghan leftists. . . . That led the [pro-Soviet] Khalq military faction to mount a coup and depose him, turning the government over to the People's Democratic Party and setting in train the developments within Afghanistan that culminated in the Soviet intervention.

From Iran President Nixon flew to Poland, where he was greeted by stirring public acclaim, demonstratively showing not only that the United States would support more or less nonaligned communist regimes (Nixon had visited Romania in 1969 and Yugoslavia in 1970, as well as China in 1972), but also that no part of the Soviet alliance was out of bounds to American interest under détente.

As a direct result of the U.S. handling of the Middle East question at the détente summit meeting, [Anwar el-]Sadat [president of Egypt]—who was already secretly in touch with the United States—six weeks later expelled the 20,000 Soviet military advisers (and Soviet reconnaissance aircraft) from Egypt.

Only a few months later, in September 1972, China and Japan—with American encouragement—renewed diplomatic relations. And in December new armed clashes occurred on the Sino-Soviet border.

Further, upon President Nixon's return to Washington from the summit he urged not only ratification of the SALT I agreements, but also an increase in strategic arms. Secretary of Defense [Melvin R.] Laird even conditioned his support for SALT on congressional approval of new military programs, which he justified as necessary so as to be able to negotiate "from a position of strength," wittingly or not invoking a key symbol of the Cold War.

It is not the purpose of this brief recapitulation of some examples of vigorous American competitive activity to argue either that the *Soviet* perception of American responsibility for the decline and fall of détente is justified, or that the United States was wrong to compete with the Soviet Union (individual actions were wise or unwise on their merits, and good or bad in their consequences—as is true of various Soviet actions). But Americans need to recognize that not only the Soviet Union but also the United States was "waging détente" in the 1970s—and that it was not justified in concluding that the Soviet Union was violating some agreed, clear, and impartial standard to which the United States in practice adhered. This same point about the application of a double standard equally needed to be recognized in the Soviet Union, and equally was not.

Both sides in fact sought advantages. Surely Nixon and Kissinger, and Brezhnev and [Soviet foreign minister Andrei] Gromyko, never believed that the other side, or that *either* side, would fail to seek advantages at the expense of the other just because they had agreed, in a document on Basic Principles on Mutual Relations, that "efforts to obtain unilateral advantage at the expense of the other, directly or indirectly, are inconsistent with these objectives" (those objectives being "reciprocity, mutual accommodation and mutual benefit"). . . .

Both the United States and the Soviet Union acted in ways contrary to the spirit and letter of a code of conduct for détente as set forth in the Basic Principles to which both had committed themselves in 1972. Each saw its own actions as compatible with pursuit of a *realistic* policy of détente. Each, however, sought to hold the other side to its own *idealized* view of détente. As a result, each was disappointed in and critical of the actions of the other. The Soviet leaders, however, adjusted their expectations more realistically, seeing no better alternative than to continue an imperfect détente. This was the Soviet judgment even though the United States was seen as taking advantage of détente in the continuing competition, and even though détente proved less of a restraint on the United States than the Soviets had hoped and expected. . . .

The essence of détente, as a practical proposition, was an agreement on mutual accommodation to a political competition in which each side would limit its actions in important (but unfortunately not well-defined) ways in recognition of the common shared interest in avoiding the risks of uncontrolled confrontation. Détente called for political adjustments, both negotiated and unilateral. It did not involve a classical division of the world into spheres of hegemonic geopolitical interests. Rather, it was a compact calling for self-restraint on each side in recognition of the interests of the other to the extent necessary to prevent sharp confrontation. While this general concept and approach were accepted by both sides, regrettably each side had differing conceptions of the proper restraint it—and the other side—should assume. This discrepancy led later to reciprocal feelings of having been let down by the other side. From the outset there was insufficient recognition of the need for more frank exchanges of views and collaboration in dealing with differences of interest. With time, these efforts collapsed. Both sides showed that they were not ready to accommodate the interests of the other. An additional complicating factor was the inability of the U.S. leadership to manage and control its own policy. But more important, on both sides there was a serious gap, even inability, to perceive the viewpoint and interests of the other. This gap grew, rather than lessened, with time and experience. As a consequence, trust—which was never very great—declined. . . .

Many developments during the period under review bear witness to the importance of evaluating correctly the intentions, and not merely the capabilities or ambitions, of the other power. . . . If one side is in fact motivated by an expansionist impulse, then a forceful advance stand in opposition or retaliatory response *is* called for and can sometimes be effective. If, however, the action—no matter how reprehensible and forcible—is motivated by fear of a threat or loss, a vigorous show of strength and threats of counteraction may in fact *contribute* to the perceived threat and hence to the very moves that the other side wants to deter. By contrast, measures to allay the unfounded fears might have been a more effective course. It thus becomes highly important to assess, and assess correctly, the intentions and motivations of the other side.

The importance of assessment is that it not only applies to a specific situation, but also affects the lessons drawn from that experience. The easy conclusion often reached about Soviet moves adverse to American interests (especially by critics but sometimes also by incumbent administrations) was to question whether the United States possessed sufficient strength and had demonstrated clearly enough its readiness to use it. Sometimes that may have been the relevant question. But the record strongly suggests that more often it was not American strength and resolve that Soviet leaders have doubted, but American restraint and recognition of Soviet interests.

If international tension is seen as the product of perceived threats, détente can be characterized as the reduction of threat perceptions. . . .

Both powers also were reluctant to acknowledge, even to recognize, failures of their own political systems. Instead, they were only too ready to project responsibility onto the other side. Thus, for example, Soviet claims of American responsibility for internal opposition in Afghanistan and Poland served (among other purposes) as an alibi for failures of Soviet-style socialism. American charges of Cuban and Soviet responsibility for revolution in Central America were similarly more convenient than acknowledging failures of reactionary regimes to provide for needed peaceful change. In addition to reflecting genuine fears based on perceived vulnerabilities, it was simply easier to project hostile intervention than to admit failures to facilitate or permit peaceful change within respective areas of predominant influence.

Thus, apart from differing conceptions of détente, there were very important differences in perceptions not only of the motivations of the other side, but of the very reality of world politics. Détente should have been recognized as one complex *basis* for a competitive relationship, not as an alternative to competition. That was the reality, and the fact should have been recognized.

During much of the 1970s American perceptions of what was occurring in the world failed to reflect reality. One example was the failure of the United States to see that it was waging a vigorous competition along with the Soviet Union. And the U.S. leadership to varying degrees was more aware of the realities than the public. . . . But even the practitioners of hardheaded détente often failed to recognize the whole reality. Political critics also either did not see, or did not wish to acknowledge, reality. The desire to sustain public support for policy by using a myth of détente (and of conformity with idealistic goals) also inhibited public awareness that the United States was competing as much as the Soviet Union. The result was a shift of public opinion as détente *seemed* not to be safeguarding and serving American interests. Ronald Reagan's challenge to President Ford in 1976 marked the first significant political manifestation of this shift. Although the challenge did not succeed, it did lead Ford to shelve SALT and to jettison the very word détente. By 1980 this shift contributed (along with domestic economic and other concerns, and President Carter's ineptness and plain bad luck) to Reagan's victory and open American renunciation of détente.

Naiveté was charged to the advocates of détente. But while some may have had unrealistic aims and expectations, the American leaders and practitioners of détente . . . were not as naive as were the critics and challengers who preferred to remain blind both to the strength and vigor of U.S. global competition and to the limits on Soviet power and policy. The critics of détente saw both American and Soviet power and its exercise from opposite ends of a telescope—a greatly exaggerated image of relentless Soviet buildup and use of power in a single-minded offensive expansionist policy, and a grossly distorted image of U.S. passivity and impotence in the world.

This U.S. perspective contributed to American-European differences and frictions. The European powers (and most other countries in the world as well) had a much more balanced perception. Although they still exaggerated the Soviet threat, at least they recognized more accurately the active American role in competition—often they were concerned over what they saw as excessive competition. For the Europeans had (and have) a very different view of the cooperative element in détente, valuing more highly than most Americans the potential for economic, political, social, and arms control gains and the realities of cooperation under détente. . . . Even as such key European countries as Britain and West Germany turned to conservative governments in the early 1980s, support for East-West détente (and criticism of American confrontational policies, for example in the Caribbean basin) continued, to the perplexity, dismay and sometimes anger of leaders in Washington.

An additional reason for European satisfaction with détente, and a diverging American view, was that one important but little remarked consequence of détente in Europe from 1969 through 1979 was that the focus of U.S.-Soviet and general East-West competition shifted from Europe to the third world. The Europeans welcomed this shift, which they correctly (if not usually articulately) perceived as a fruit of détente. The United States, with little European support in the third world competition, was less grateful to détente. . . .

A fourth cause of the decline in confidence in détente in the 1970s was the view widely held on both sides that the other side was acquiring military capabilities in excess of what it needed for deterrence and defense, and therefore was not adhering to détente. This is a complex question. For example, the limits under SALT reduced some previously important areas of concern and uncertainties in projecting the military balance—notably with respect to ABMs. But another effect was that the rather complex *real* strategic balance was artificially simplified in the general understanding (and not just of the general public) to certain highlighted indexes, thereby increasing sensitivity to a symbolic arithmetical "balance." And national means of intelligence, which were given high credibility when it came to identifying a threat, were regarded with a more jaundiced eye when called upon to monitor and verify compliance with an arms limitation agreement.

In any event, during the latter half of the 1970s concern mounted in the United States over why the Soviet Union was engaged in what has been termed a relentless continuing arms buildup. At the same time U.S. military programs were justified as meeting that buildup. In turn the Soviet Union saw the American buildup as designed to restore the United States to a position of superiority.

Throughout the preceding two decades of Cold War and cold peace, the United States had maintained a clear strategic nuclear superiority. As the Soviet Union continued to build its strategic forces, despite earlier agreed strategic arms limitations, new fears and suspicions arose in the United States. Unfortunately, the actual consolidation of parity in the latter 1970s was not in synchronization with the political acceptance and public impression of parity in the early 1970s. What the Soviets saw as finally closing the gap through programs of weapons deployment, which they saw as fully consonant both with the terms of the SALT agreement and with achievement of parity, many in the United States saw as a Soviet pursuit of advantages that violated at least the spirit, if not the letter, of SALT and that threatened to go beyond parity to superiority. The real inconsistency was between the continuing Soviet deployments and the American public's *expectation* derived from SALT. The interim freeze of 1972 had set a level with respect to the deployment of forces, including some construction under way that had not yet been completed by the Soviet Union. In addition, it had limited only the level of strategic missile launchers, not of warheads, and the Soviets, who were behind in terms of arming their strategic missile force with MIRVs, sought to catch up in the years following. If the Soviet strategic deployments had occurred more nearly at the time of American deployment, and both countries had agreed to accept parity and stop at the same time (and not merely at the same level), the public perception would have been quite different.

While a desire to influence public opinion played a part in inflating presentations of the military threat posed by the other side, there were real buildups on both sides. In part, then, perceptions on both sides of a hostile arms buildup were genuine. But both sides were unduly alarmist in exaggerating the military capabilities—and imputed intentions—of the other. . . .

In addition to major gaps in mutual understanding of such key elements of détente as behavior in international politics and in managing the arms race, a fifth cause of the decline of détente was a failure to understand its crucial relationship to the internal politics of the two countries. In part this failure was reflected in errors, in particular by the Soviet Union, in comprehending the domestic political processes and dynamics of the other country. There was also some failure by political leaders, especially in the United States, to gauge the degree of their own authority. The Soviet leaders also put too much trust in the ability of an American president to carry out policy. This situation was true in the whole matter of normalization of trade and repeatedly with SALT II from 1975 to 1980. While Nixon, Kissinger, and Ford were careful to relate linkages to foreign policy issues, Congress attempted to make its own linkages with Soviet internal affairs. It failed in the effort, creating in the process new issues in U.S.-Soviet relations and reducing support for détente in the United States. The Soviet leaders also had difficulty understanding the sudden changes and discontinuities between (and occasionally within) administrations. On the other hand, American leaders, especially Presidents Carter and Reagan, . . . had little understanding of the Soviet political leadership or of Soviet political processes. President Carter was especially insensitive to the necessary limits on détente as a medium for influencing the internal political affairs of the Soviet Union.

Leaders on both sides, especially the Soviet leaders, frequently and seriously underestimated the impact of their own actions on the perceptions and policy of the other side, and the extent to which the actions of one side have been responses to real or perceived challenges. And again, Soviet secrecy, and self-serving justifications on both sides, compounded this problem.

Finally, the failure in the United States to sustain a political consensus in support of détente also ranked as a major cause of its collapse. This conclusion is particularly clear when the role of domestic political factors in the United States in torpedoing the attempt at détente is considered. Most blatant, but far from unique, was the attempt to tie trade, and thus the whole economic dimension of détente, to what amounted to interference in the internal affairs of the Soviet Union. The approach was all the more tragic but no less lethal because of the high moral motivations of many of the supporters of the effort. In this respect, the Soviet leaders were more successful in the less difficult, though not easy, task of maintaining a consensus in their quite different political process.

One reason for the disintegration of the consensus in favor of détente in the United States was the failure of the leadership to explain its limits as well as its promises to the public. To the extent that the leaders themselves failed to gauge the differences in conceptions about détente and were prisoners of their own view of the world order, they could not make this limitation clear to others. But Nixon and Kissinger did understand very well at least that there was a continuing active competition—not only in the Soviet conception, but in their own policy— a competition that was, however, masked by too much talk about a new structure of peace. When the expectations of the public, aroused by the hyperbole about the benefits of peace and détente, were not met, disillusion set in—and so did a natural temptation to blame the other side. This reaction against détente, based on disillusionment (in the pure meaning of the term), was thus in part engendered by both Nixon's and Kissinger's overestimation of their ability to manipulate and manage both international and national affairs. It should also be noted that the public (including the broader congressional and active political constituencies) has been little aware of or prepared to understand the subtleties of international politics, or even the basic idea of a political relationship of mixed cooperation and competition with the Soviet Union. In addition, the political process in the United States not only does not provide a tradition of continuity or cushion against sudden changes in foreign policy, but invites domestic political exploitation of apparent and actual adversities in the course of international relations.

The decade of détente in American-Soviet relations was in fact one of mixed confrontation and détente, of competition and cooperation, with a remarkable if ill-starred attempt to build—too rapidly—a structure for peaceful coexistence between powerful adversaries.

Kissinger's Realism Without Morality

WALTER ISAACSON

"Americans," he [Henry A. Kissinger] once wrote, "are comfortable with an idealistic tradition that espouses great causes, such as making the world safe for democracy, or human rights." But it was not in the country's nature, he often lamented, to sit still for the unedifying work of tending to imperfect alliances or the never-ending meddling necessary to maintain a balance of power. The U.S. has historically been, in [the political scientist] Stanley Hoffmann's words "traditionally hostile to balance of power diplomacy with its closets of partitions, compensations, secret treaties and gunboats."

To Kissinger, this excessive aversion to secret treaties and gunboats, and to all the other trappings of realpolitik and balance-of-power diplomacy, stemmed from the simple, often simplistic, naiveté and decency of most Americans. With a jarring use of the first-person plural that belies the fact that the descriptions scarcely apply to him, Kissinger once wrote that "our native inclination for straightforwardness, our instinct for open, noisy politics, our distrust of European manners and continental elites, all brought about an increasing impatience with the stylized methods of European diplomacy and with its tendency toward ambiguous compromise."

This idealistic streak in the American character, this desire to seek moral perfection rather than messy accommodations, was what caused the nation to lurch over the years between isolationism and interventionism, to embark on crusades (World War I, Vietnam), and then to recoil into self-righteous withdrawal. "Emotional slogans, unleavened by a concept of the national interest, had caused us to oscillate between excesses of isolation and overextension," Kissinger wrote. The way to moderate these pendulum swings, he said, was "by making judgments according to some more permanent conception of national interest."

One key component of Kissinger's brand of realism was his special emphasis on the role of military might. "Throughout history," he once wrote, "the influence of nations has been roughly correlative to their military power." This view led him to favor great displays and pretenses of power: bombings, incursions, aircraft carriers steaming toward trouble spots, nuclear alerts.

Even from a realist perspective, this emphasis on military power was subject to criticism. Other sophisticated realists, such as George Kennan and Hans Morgenthau, emphasized that economic vitality and political stability are equally important elements of national power. Kissinger's best diplomacy came in China, the Middle East, and later Africa, where the direct threat of American force played little role; his greatest failures came in Vietnam, Cambodia, and Pakistan, where displays of force abounded. There was also a political constraint: the brutal and cold application of force was incompatible with America's self-conception and what its citizenry in the 1970s was willing to countenance.

Another component of Kissinger's realism was the stress he put on the role that "credibility" played in determining a nation's influence and power. An emphasis on credibility is why realism in foreign policy is not always the same thing as pragmatism. In dealing with Vietnam, for example, a pragmatist would have come more quickly to the conclusion that the war was simply not worth the effort, that the costs were greater than any potential benefits. Realists such as Kissinger, however, emphasized that America could not abandon its commitments or else it would undermine its influence elsewhere in the world.

From his *Foreign Affairs* piece [on Vietnam negotiations] in 1968, to his analysis of Vietnam options in 1969, to his arguments in early 1975 as Saigon was falling, Kissinger put enormous weight on the credibility argument. The problem with an emphasis on credibility is that it can—and in the case of Vietnam did—result in an inability to discriminate between vital interests and ones that are merely peripheral.

A third aspect of Kissinger's realism was his lack of concern about supporting democratic forces and human rights movements in authoritarian countries. He was more comfortable dealing with strong rulers—Brezhnev, Zhou Enlai, the shah of Iran, [Syrian leader Hafez] Assad, and [Egyptian president Anwar el-]Sadat—than with the messy democracies in Europe and Israel.

In office and after, he opposed the crusades of moral activists who wanted the U.S. to push for domestic reforms in the Soviet Union, China, Pakistan, and the shah's Iran. "Why is it our business how they govern themselves?" an annoyed Kissinger asked at a meeting in 1971 when State Department bureaucrats were recommending pressure on Pakistan. This attitude was later reflected when Kissinger refused to join in the criticism of China after the 1989 crackdown in Tiananmen Square.

Though complex, even ingenious, in its design, Kissinger's realism began with a simple premise: any event should be judged foremost by whether it represented a gain for the Soviets or for the West in the overall global balance. That was the basis of his credibility argument in Vietnam: the war would show the rest of the world whether Washington had the will to stand up to Soviet expansion elsewhere. He embarked on the Middle East peace process partly as a way to undermine Soviet influence there. In the India-Pakistan war, the U.S. became involved on the losing side partly because Kissinger insisted on viewing the regional war as a proxy struggle between a Soviet and an American client.

This tendency to see global disputes through an East-West prism provided his foreign policy with a coherent framework, but it could also be distorting, as he later admitted. "We must outgrow the notion that every setback is a Soviet gain or every problem is caused by Soviet action," he said in May 1975, after setbacks in Vietnam, Cambodia, Portugal, and the Middle East put him on the defensive about his policy of détente with the Soviets. Yet the "we" in his speech fit snugly, for he had spent six years pushing that notion. . . .

At an emotional press conference in Salzburg in 1974, when he brooded about resigning because of stories about the wiretaps [of aides], Kissinger became unusually maudlin. He had been identified, he said, as someone who cared more about stabilizing the balance of power than about moral issues. "I would rather like to think," he added, "that when the record is written, one may remember that perhaps some lives were saved and perhaps some mothers can rest more at ease. But I leave that to history."

This historical judgment is unlikely ever to be a simple one. The structure of peace that Kissinger designed places him with Henry Stimson, George Marshall, and Dean Acheson atop the pantheon of modern American statesmen. In addition, he was the foremost American negotiator of this century and, along with George Kennan, the most influential foreign policy intellectual.

But Kissinger never had an instinctive feel for American values and mores, such as the emphasis that a Stimson would place on honor over intrigue or on idealism over national interests. Nor did he have an appreciation of the strengths to be derived from the healthy raucousness of American politics or from open decision-making in a democratic society. "Henry is a balance-of-power thinker," said Lawrence Eagleburger, one of his closest colleagues. "He deeply believes in stability. These kind[s] of objectives are antithetical to the American experience. Americans tend to want to pursue a set of moral principles. Henry does not have an intrinsic feel for the American political system, and he does not start with the same basic values and assumptions."

Kissinger came to power at a perilous moment for the foreign policy of his adoptive nation. America's isolationist reflexes were twitching as a result of its ill-conceived involvement in Vietnam. Congress and the public were in no mood to pay for new weapons or to engage the Soviets in marginal confrontations in the third world.

By ushering in an era of détente, Kissinger helped to assure that the competition with the Soviets would be more manageable and the showdowns less dangerous. And by devising a web of linkages, he provided the U.S. with some diplomatic leverage to compensate for its loss of military resolve. Looking back twenty years later, he could claim with some justification that "we perhaps deserve some credit for holding together the sinews of America at a time of fundamental collapse."

Some of the initiatives that he pursued along the way were enlightened and imaginative, others impulsively brutal and blunt. Some were clever, others too clever by half. As the only European-style realist ever to guide U.S. foreign policy, a power practitioner unencumbered by the sentimental idealism that suffuses American history, he seemed painfully amoral at times. But he was able to take a clear-eyed approach to the creation of a new global balance, one that helped to preserve American influence in the post-Vietnam era and eventually contributed to the end of the cold war.

Although he was too likely to see a Moscow-inspired threat in every regional crisis, Kissinger was correct in resisting the dovish and isolationist forces of the period that sought to abandon the competition with the Soviets. And he was equally correct in resisting the hawkish and neoconservative pressure to abandon cooperation with the Soviets. As Kennan had pointed out in the late 1940s—and Kissinger had reiterated in the early 1970s—the rulers in the Kremlin could prop up their system only by expanding their empire or by invoking foreign threats. If denied these opportunities, the Soviet system would eventually disintegrate, as it did.

In addition, Kissinger and Nixon turned the world's bipolar tug-of-war into a three-dimensional chess game that provided the U.S. with more opportunities for creative diplomacy. The new relationship with China, which previous presidents had barely contemplated, gave both of the world's communist giants an incentive to maintain better relations with the U.S. than they had with one another.

It added up to a fundamental change in America's postwar foreign policy: for the first time since the Potsdam Conference of 1945, cooperation as well as competition with both Moscow and Beijing could be part of a great-power strategy of balance. That alone was a triumph of hard-edged realism worthy of a Metternich [the nineteenth-century Austrian prince Klemens von Metternich].

This new framework incorporated a recognition of America's limits with a belief that the nation still had a major role to play in resisting the spread of Soviet influence. Less ardently anti-Soviet than his conservative critics desired, and more interventionist than most liberals could abide, Kissinger was able to create an American role that kept the pendulum from careening too rapidly in one direction or the other after Vietnam.

The main lines of this policy were followed for the next two decades: a blend of containment and cooperation with Moscow that allowed the internal contradictions of the Soviet system to play out; a step-by-step process in the Middle East that kept the U.S. the dominant player in the region; and a realistic attitude toward China that created a global balance that was more stable and gave Washington more leverage. When the cold war ended, this dose of realism would help the U.S. operate in a new global environment based on multiple power centers and balances.

But Kissinger's power-oriented realism and focus on national interests faltered because it was too dismissive of the role of morality. The secret bombing and then invasion of Cambodia, the Christmas bombing of Hanoi, the destabilization of Chile—these and other brutal actions betrayed a callous attitude toward what Americans like to believe is the historic foundation of their foreign policy: a respect for human rights, international law, democracy, and other idealistic values. The setbacks Kissinger encountered as a statesman, and the antagonism he engendered as a person, stemmed from the perceived amorality of his geopolitical calculations.

Kissinger's approach led to a backlash against détente; the national mood swung toward both the moralism of Jimmy Carter and the ideological fervor of Ronald Reagan. As a result, not unlike Metternich, Kissinger's legacy turned out to be one of brilliance more than solidity, of masterful structures built of bricks that were made without straw.

To Kissinger, an emphasis on realism and national interests—even though it might seem callous in its execution—was not a rejection of moral values. Rather, he saw it as the best way to pursue the stable world order that he believed was the ultimate moral imperative, especially in a nuclear age.

He tried to explain this relationship between realism and morality at a Paris gathering of Nobel Prize laureates in 1988. After being attacked in a closed-door session for his power-oriented and amoral approach—Argentine Adolfo Perez Esquivel, a former Peace Prize winner, accused him of "genocide and collective massacre"—Kissinger began to talk about his childhood. The room hushed.

More than a dozen of his relatives had been killed in the holocaust, he said, so he knew something of the nature of genocide. It was easy for human rights crusaders and peace activists to insist on perfection in this world. But the policymaker who has to deal with reality learns to seek the best that can be achieved rather than the best that can be imagined. It would be wonderful to banish the role of military power from world affairs, but the world is not perfect, as he had learned as a child. Those with true responsibility for peace, unlike those on the sidelines, cannot afford pure idealism. They must have the courage to deal with ambiguities and accommodations, to realize that great goals can be achieved only in imperfect steps. No side has a monopoly on morality.

But Kissinger's realpolitik was ill-suited to an open and democratic society, where it is difficult to invoke distant ends to justify unpalatable means. A belief that America's actions are moral and noble is necessary to rally a naturally isolationist people. Whether marching off to war or rousing itself to counter the spread of communism, America draws its motivation from a desire to defend its values—rather than from a cold calculation of its geopolitical interests. Even when an American involvement is partly based on economic self-interest, such as the Persian Gulf War of 1991, the more high-minded goals are the ones that tend to be publicly emphasized.

Kissinger considered this idealistic aspect of the American spirit a weakness in terms of sustaining policies in a messy world. To some extent he was right—but it was also a source of strength. The greatest triumph of political influence in the modern age was that of democratic capitalism over communism in the early 1990s. This occurred partly because Kissinger and others helped to create a new global balance during the 1970s, one that preserved American influence in the post-Vietnam era. But the main reason that the United States triumphed in the cold war was not because it won a competition for military power and influence. It was because the values offered by its system—among them a foreign policy that could draw its strength from the ideals of its people—eventually proved more attractive.

🌐 *F U R T H E R   R E A D I N G*

Robert J. Alexander, *The Tragedy of Chile* (1978)
Dana H. Allin, *Cold War Illusions* (1995)
Stephen E. Ambrose, *Nixon* (1987–1991)
Richard J. Barnet, *The Giants* (1977)
———, *The Lean Years* (1980)
Robert L. Beisner, "History and Henry Kissinger," *Diplomatic History,* 14 (1990), 511–527
Coral Bell, *The Diplomacy of Détente* (1977)

Henry Brandon, *The Retreat of American Power* (1973)

George W. Breslauer, "Why Détente Failed: An Interpretation," in Alexander L. George, ed., *Managing Soviet-American Relations* (1983)

Seyom Brown, *The Faces of Power* (1983)

William Bundy, *A Tangled Web* (1998)

Anne H. Cahn, *Killing Détente: The Right Attacks the C.I.A.* (1998)

Dan Caldwell, ed., *Henry Kissinger* (1983)

David Calleo, *The Imperious Economy* (1982)

Gregory D. Cleva, *Henry Kissinger and the American Approach to Foreign Policy* (1989)

Thomas M. Franck and Edward Weisband, *Foreign Policy by Congress* (1979)

Edward Friedland et al., *The Great Détente Disaster* (1975)

Leon Friedman and William F. Levantrosser, eds., *Cold War Patriot and Statesman: Richard M. Nixon* (1993)

Michael B. Froman, *The Development of the Idea of Détente* (1992)

John L. Gaddis, *Russia, the Soviet Union, and the United States* (1990)

———, *Strategies of Containment* (1982)

Lloyd C. Gardner, ed., *The Great Nixon Turnaround* (1973)

Raymond L. Garthoff, *The Great Transition* (1994)

Charles Gati and Toby Trister Gati, *The Debate over Détente* (1977)

Michael Genovese, *The Nixon Presidency* (1990)

Matti Golan, *The Secret Conversations of Henry Kissinger* (1976)

Stephen Graubard, *Kissinger: Portrait of a Mind* (1973)

John Robert Greene, *The Limits of Power* (1992)

Seymour M. Hersh, *The Price of Power: Kissinger in the White House* (1983)

Stanley Hoffmann, "The Case of Dr. Kissinger," *New York Review of Books,* November 2, 1972

———, *Primacy or World Order* (1978)

———, "The Return of Henry Kissinger," *New York Review of Books,* April 29, 1982

Joan Hoff-Wilson, " 'Nixingerism,' NATO, and Détente," *Diplomatic History,* 13 (1989), 501–526.

William G. Hyland, *Mortal Rivals* (1987)

Robert C. Johansen, *The National Interest and the Human Interest* (1980)

Loch K. Johnson, *A Season of Inquiry: The Senate Intelligence Investigation* (1985)

Bernard Kalb and Marvin Kalb, *Kissinger* (1974)

Jeffrey Kimball, *Nixon's Vietnam War* (1999)

David Landau, *Kissinger: Uses of Power* (1972)

Thomas B. Larson, *Soviet-American Rivalry* (1978)

Robert S. Litwak, *Détente and the Nixon Doctrine* (1984)

Michael Mandelbaum, *The Nuclear Question* (1979)

Roger Morris, *Richard Milhous Nixon* (1989)

———, *Uncertain Greatness: Henry Kissinger and American Foreign Policy* (1977)

Fred Warner Neal, ed., *Détente or Debacle* (1979)

Keith L. Nelson, *The Making of Détente* (1995)

John Newhouse, *Cold Dawn: The Story of SALT* (1973)

———, *War and Peace in the Nuclear Age* (1988)

Herbert S. Parmet, *Richard Nixon and His America* (1990)

James Petras and Morris Morley, *The United States and Chile* (1975)

Richard Pipes, *U.S.-Soviet Relations in the Era of Détente* (1981)

Walter F. Sater, *Chile and the United States* (1990)

Robert D. Schulzinger, *Henry Kissinger* (1989)

———, "The Naive and Sentimental Diplomat: Henry Kissinger's Memoirs," *Diplomatic History,* 4 (1980), 303–315

Franz Schurmann, *The Foreign Politics of Richard Nixon* (1987)

David Shambaugh, *Beautiful Imperialist* (1991) (Sino-U.S. relations)

Edward R. F. Sheehan, *The Arabs, Israelis, and Kissinger* (1976)

Paul E. Sigmund, *The Overthrow of Allende and the Politics of Chile, 1964–1976* (1977)

———, *The United States and Democracy in Chile* (1993)

Lewis Sorley, *Arms Transfers Under Nixon* (1983)

Harvey Starr, *Henry Kissinger* (1984)

Richard Stevenson, *The Rise and Fall of Détente* (1985)

John G. Stoessinger, *Henry Kissinger: The Anguish of Power* (1976)

Gerald S. Strober and Deborah Hart Strober, *Nixon: An Oral History of His Presidency* (1996)

Tad Szulc, "How Kissinger Did It: Behind the Vietnam Cease-Fire Agreement," *Foreign Policy,* No. 15 (1974), 21–61

———, *The Illusion of Peace* (1978)

Terry Terriff, *The Nixon Administration and the Making of U.S. Nuclear Policy* (1995)

Adam B. Ulam, *Dangerous Relations: The Soviet Union in World Politics, 1970–1982* (1983)

Garry Wills, *Nixon Agonistes* (1970)

CHAPTER
13

The United States
Encounters the Middle East

The United States is only the most recent external power to exercise influence in the Middle East. From the sixteenth century until World War I, the Ottoman Turks ruled most of the Arab lands of the region. World War I sounded the death knell of Ottoman rule, which was superseded by European domination. Between the world wars, Great Britain and France forged a new political order in the Middle East by creating new states, redrawing boundaries, and striking alliances with local rulers. The Europeans sought access to oil, worked to safeguard the strategic Suez Canal (completed in the 1880s), and used their conspicuous presence in the Middle East to enhance their status as world powers. They left a legacy of ill-defined borders, simmering ethnic and religious disputes, and nationalist resentments against Western imperialism.

Before World War II the United States had only minimal interests in the Middle East, limited for the most part to a few private oil concessions and a modest degree of Protestant missionary activity. World War II severely weakened the European colonial powers and ushered in U.S. power to the region. In 1946, after blunting Soviet influence in Iran, Washington initiated a strategic marriage with the dynasty of the Shah Mohammed Reza Pahlavi. American oil companies soon broke down British monopolies in Iran and Iraq and expanded their dealings with the oil sheiks of Saudi Arabia and Kuwait. In 1947, an exhausted Great Britain surrendered its mandate over Palestine and handed over to the United Nations an increasingly violent dispute between Jewish settlers (including a growing number of displaced Holocaust survivors) and the area's Arab Palestinian inhabitants. The United Nations called for the division of Palestine into two states, one Jewish and one Palestinian. Before partition could be implemented, however, Israel declared its sovereignty in May 1948 and gained diplomatic recognition from the United States and the Soviet Union. Not long after, Egyptian, Jordanian, and Syrian armies entered Palestine and engaged Israeli forces in the first Arab-Israeli War (1948–1949). Although Washington rebuffed Israel's requests for military aid, the United States gradually established a commitment to the new state, based on humanitarian sympathy for the victims of Nazi genocide, effective political lobbying by Jewish Americans, and strategic Cold War considerations.

   The growing instability and violence that accompanied decolonization steadily drew the United States into the region's affairs. When in 1953 the Iranian nationalist Mohammed Mossadegh seized the country's British-led oil industry and forced the Shah from power, a U.S. Central Intelligence Agency covert plot overthrew Mossadegh and reinstalled the Shah. American oil companies subsequently enjoyed liberalized access to Iranian oil fields; and Iran joined Britain, Turkey, Iraq, and Pakistan in an anti-Soviet military alliance known as the Baghdad pact. During the 1950s and 1960s, under Gamel Abdul Nasser's Pan-Arabist leadership, Egypt denounced American-sponsored military alliances, spurned negotiations with Israel (which likewise rejected negotiations), and accepted Soviet arms. In 1955, President Dwight D. Eisenhower and Secretary of State John Foster Dulles wooed Egypt by promising foreign assistance for the construction of the High Aswan Dam on the Nile River, but when Cairo went ahead and purchased Soviet-bloc arms, Washington abruptly withdrew the offer. Nasser's nationalization of the British- and French-run Suez Canal in 1956, from which he hoped to acquire revenue to finance Aswan, and stout defense against a British-French-Israeli invasion, encouraged Arab nationalists. In July 1958, a coup overthrew the pro-Western monarchy in Iraq, and that same year Egypt and Syria merged to form the United Arab Republic (UAR). Although the Eisenhower administration had exerted economic and diplomatic pressure to help turn back the British-French-Israeli invasion of Suez, it viewed Nasser's pan-Arabism with increasing alarm. In 1957 Congress approved the Eisenhower Doctrine, authorizing the president to dispatch U.S. troops to any Middle Eastern nation that requested them to resist international Communism. The following year, U.S. Marines landed on Lebanon's shores to bolster a pro-Western regime.

   Nasser's dream of a Pan-Arab alliance faded when disagreements over domestic policy led to Syria's secession from the UAR in 1961. A Baathist Socialist regime ultimately took power in Syria and rivaled Nasser's Egypt for leadership in the Arab world. At the same time, pro-Western monarchies, such as Saudi Arabia, Kuwait, and Iran, distrusted Nasser's radicalism and opposed his bid for regional leadership. The Egyptian leader suffered a devastating setback in the Six Day War of June 1967, in which Israel won a stunning victory and seized Jordan's West Bank—including the Holy City of Jerusalem, Syria's Golan Heights, and Egypt's Sinai Peninsula and Gaza Strip (see maps on page 545.). Impressed by Israel's military success, Washington after 1967 increasingly viewed Israel as a staunch Cold War ally and increased U.S. military assistance to Tel Aviv (Israel's capital city). The U.S.-Israeli relationship, however, often became a stormy one. Israel remained cool to U.S.-sponsored peace talks, based on U.N. Resolution 242 (passed November 22, 1967, with Washington's backing), which called for Israeli withdrawal from the occupied territories, Arab recognition of Israel's right to exist, and the establishment of secure borders for all belligerents. Instead, Tel Aviv undertook an ambitious settlement program in the territories and deployed military force to quell Palestinian resistance. Evidence also mounted that Israel, much to Washington's disapproval, had transferred fissionable materials from its Dimona nuclear facility to a secret weapons-development program.

   Palestinians living under Israeli rule in the West Bank and Gaza, meanwhile, looked to Yasir Arafat and the Palestinian Liberation Organization (PLO) for leadership. The PLO, formed in 1964, vowed to destroy the Jewish state and retake the captured territories. During 1969–1970, Egypt and Israel fought a limited "war of attrition" across the boundary lines of the occupied Sinai near Suez, but the Israeli occupation stood. In another clash, the Yom Kippur War of October 1973, also known as the October War, Egypt, Syria, and their Arab and Soviet backers failed again to dislodge the Israelis. The Arab world nonetheless demonstrated the power of petroleum when it organized through the Organization of Petroleum Exporting Countries (OPEC) a reduction in production and an embargo on oil exports to the United States and other supporters of Israel. The resulting four-fold increase in oil prices rocked the world economy. The Nixon administration's decision to place U.S. forces on Defense Condition 3 (just two steps short of launching a war), to prevent possible Soviet entry into the war on the Arab side, also illustrated the global ramifications of the region's conflicts. Thus, when Egyptian president Anwar el-Sadat maneuvered his country into the U.S. camp and sought normalized relations with Israel, President Richard M. Nixon (1969–1974) and Secretary of State Henry A. Kissinger responded by providing Egypt with aid and arranging a cease-fire with Israel.

As tensions mounted in the region, the PLO and other Palestinian groups increasingly resorted to terrorism. Conducted mainly from sanctuaries in Lebanon and Syria, Palestinian terrorist attacks often victimized civilians. The United States condemned the violence and refused to recognize the PLO. Secretary Kissinger nonetheless mediated bilateral disputes between Israel, Egypt, and Syria following the October War. President Jimmy Carter's administration (1977–1981) brokered the Camp David Accords between Sadat and Israel's prime minister Menachem Begin in 1978. In exchange for Israel's withdrawal from the Sinai (completed in 1982), Egypt became the first Arab nation to recognize the Jewish state. Carter closed the deal by promising generous economic and military aid to both Egypt and Israel. But Camp David left the future of the occupied territories and the issue of a Palestinian homeland undetermined.

Meanwhile, Ayatollah Ruhollah Khomeini's Islamic fundamentalist revolution in 1979 unleashed a torrent of anti-American fury traceable to Washington's unbending support for the secular, authoritarian Shah Pahlavi. When the Shah fled his country and gained admission to the U.S. for medical treatment for cancer, Iranian students occupied the U.S. embassy in Tehran, took many Americans hostage, and with government support extended the siege until January 1981. In December 1979, the Soviet Union invaded its southern neighbor Afghanistan. Concerned that Moscow might exploit the region's instability, the president enunciated in January 1980 the Carter Doctrine, which declared that the United States would deploy military force to oppose outside aggression in the Persian Gulf region.

Tumult in the Middle East has shown little sign of abating since 1980, in spite of America's increasing role in the area's affairs. War between Iran and Iraq (1980–1988), the Israeli invasion of Lebanon (1982), and a persistent cycle of terrorism have all undermined efforts to achieve regional stability. Iraq's invasion of Kuwait in the summer of 1990 momentarily transformed the Middle East's political landscape, bringing states as disparate as Israel, Egypt, Saudi Arabia, and Syria into a U.S.-led coalition that turned back Saddam Hussein's war machine. The administrations of Presidents George Bush (1989–1993) and Bill Clinton (1993–) took advantage of the diplomatic momentum generated by the Gulf War and America's enhanced leverage following the end of the Cold War to broker a settlement of the long-standing Arab-Israeli conflict. In 1994, an accord signed by the PLO and Israel brought Israel's withdrawal from the Gaza Strip and the West Bank town of Jericho. Further concessions have been only sparingly advanced, and efforts to achieve a lasting peace have been undermined by terrorism, including the

*November 1995 assassination of Israeli prime minister Yitzhak Rabin by a fellow
Israeli who opposed the peace process. On October 23, 1998, Israeli Prime Minister
Benjamin Netanyahu and Palestinian leader Yasir Arafat met at an estate outside
Washington, D.C., at the invitation of President Clinton, and signed an accord that
handed over additional portions of the West Bank to Palestinian rule, but the
measure faced staunch opposition from factions on both sides and again left the
question of Palestinian statehood unresolved. Nor did the Persian Gulf triumph
bring any liberalization of dynastic rule in Kuwait or Saudi Arabia, or a normalization of U.S. relations with Iran.*

*U.S. policy toward the Middle East provides a revealing study of American
attempts to manage difficult, historically rooted regional disputes during the
Cold War. Given the complexities of this subject, and the passion it stirs, it is not
surprising that scholars have disagreed in their evaluation of U.S. policy. Why
did U.S. leaders think it necessary for the United States to participate actively in
Mideast affairs? What was at stake? Was U.S. policy driven mainly by economic
interests—or by issues of Cold War security? What impact did pro-Israeli Jewish
Americans make on policy? What effect did the pro-Arab oil lobby have? How
have cultural differences, and popular perceptions of Jews and Arabs, influenced
U.S. thinking and decisionmaking? To what extent did Soviet support for radical
Arab states threaten U.S. interests? Did American policymakers exaggerate the
Soviet threat?*

*Scholars also debate the strengths and weaknesses of U.S. diplomatic strategies
once Washington became fully engaged in Middle East affairs. Has U.S. support
for Israel been based primarily on concrete security interests, or has it been influenced by sentiment, emotion, and domestic politics? Did American support for
Israel in the 1960s and 1970s help or hinder the Arab-Israeli peace process? How
successfully did Washington accommodate Arab nationalism? Did U.S. policymakers adequately address the issue of Palestinian rights? Why did Washington
stand behind the faltering leadership of the Shah in Iran? And what were the
strengths and weaknesses of lining up squarely with Saudi Arabia and Kuwait?
How might the United States have promoted democratization and economic development in the area? The answers to these questions vary widely, as this chapter's
readings indicate.*

 D O C U M E N T S

U.S. support for the creation of Israel after World War II was not a foregone conclusion.
The Truman administration backed a United Nations Resolution passed on November 29,
1947, to partition Palestine into separate Jewish and Arab states. But many State Department and Pentagon officials feared that partition would drive angry Arabs into the Soviet
camp and jeopardize western oil supplies. Thus, in March 1948 the United States shifted its
position and voted in the United Nations to delay partition and establish a trusteeship over
Palestine. President Harry S. Truman ultimately overruled his foreign policy advisers, and
extended diplomatic recognition to Israel within hours of its proclamation of independence
on May 14, 1948. Many observers at the time suspected that domestic politics explained
Truman's action; that is, the president hoped to win the American Jewish vote in certain
key states in his battle for re-election in 1948. Truman maintained he had acted in the best
interest of Middle East peace and out of concern for the oppressed Jewish people. In

Document 1, a letter of November 5, 1948, Israel's president Chaim Weizmann congratulates Truman on his re-election, presses for support against Israel's Arab enemies, and characterizes the new nation—perhaps to impress the president—as a society of "yeomen pioneers" determined to civilize the Negev desert.

The mid-1950s represented another turning point in U.S. policy toward the Middle East. When the Egyptian president Gamel Abdul Nasser accepted arms from the Soviet camp, President Dwight D. Eisenhower and Secretary of State John Foster Dulles abruptly canceled promised loans to help Egypt build the High Aswan Dam on the Nile River. Nasser in turn nationalized the British-French owned Suez Canal. Document 2 is drawn from a July 28, 1956, speech in which Nasser blasts European imperialism and justifies Egypt's takeover of the canal. Nasser's initiative was followed in November 1956 by an Anglo-French-Israeli invasion of the Sinai Peninsula. When the Eisenhower administration condemned the action and applied financial pressure against the aggressors, Nasser emerged an even more powerful spokesperson for Arab nationalism. Concerned over the potency of Third World nationalism and the prospect of Soviet support for radicalism in the region, President Eisenhower introduced to Congress on January 5, 1957, the Eisenhower Doctrine. The Congress quickly approved the resolution, Document 3, which allowed the president to use military force to defend Middle Eastern nations that requested aid against communist aggression.

Middle East tension nonetheless continued to escalate. Israel was not the only nation in the region to register its concern over Nasserism. In Document 4, a memorandum of conversation held on October 5, 1962, between Saudi Crown Prince Faisal and President John Kennedy, the conservative Arab leader denounces Nasser's meddling in Yemen and castigates his ties with communist states. In June 1967, after months of mutual recrimination that culminated in Nasser's closure of the strategic Gulf of Aqaba, Israel launched a preemptive attack against Egypt and its allies Syria and Jordan. In six days, the Israelis routed their opponents and occupied Jordan's West Bank, the Golan Heights along the Israeli-Syrian border, and Egypt's Sinai Peninsula and Gaza Strip. Viewing Nasser and the Soviet Union as largely responsible for the outbreak of the conflict, the administration of Lyndon Johnson strongly backed Israel. Johnson explained his policy in his memoirs, excerpted as Document 5. Although the Johnson administration remained a stalwart friend of Israel, it did back U.N. Resolution 242, adopted on November 22, 1967 (reprinted here as Document 6), which called upon Israel to relinquish control of the occupied territories in exchange for official recognition and peace. The Palestinian Liberation Organization (PLO) took up the cause of Arabs displaced by Israel's policies, and issued its National Covenant, Document 7, in July 1968. Although the covenant does not mention Israel by name, it denounces a "Zionist invasion" as a tool of Western imperialism and calls for military and political action to regain Palestine for its Arab inhabitants.

During the 1970s, Americans directly felt the wrath of Middle East nationalism when Islamic fundamentalism swept Iran, a long-time ally of the United States. In November 1979, America's troubles with Iran reached the boiling point when Iranian students invaded the U.S. embassy in Tehran and took U.S. citizens hostage. The excruciating hostage crisis lasted fourteen months until January 1981. Meanwhile, in December 1979, Moscow sent 75,000 Soviet troops into neighboring Afghanistan to bolster a client Marxist government. Document 8 is an excerpt from President Jimmy Carter's State of the Union address delivered on January 23, 1980. In that speech, the president lamented the ongoing Iranian hostage crisis, denounced Soviet military actions, and enunciated the "Carter Doctrine": the United States would use military force to counter aggression by any outside force in the oil-rich and strategically significant Persian Gulf. He also called attention to the need for action to reduce America's dependence on imported oil.

1. President Chaim Weizmann Requests U.S. Help for Israel's "Pioneers," 1948

Permit me to extend to you most hearty congratulations and good wishes on your re-election. We in this country have been watching the progress of the Presidential contest with bated breath and I am sure that I am speaking the mind of the bulk of my people when I say that we feel deeply thankful that the people of the United States have given you the opportunity of shaping the policies of your country and the affairs of humanity at large during the next critical four years. . . .

We have special cause to be gratified at your re-election because we are mindful of the enlightened help which you gave to our cause in these years of our struggle. We particularly remember your unflinching advocacy of the admission of Jewish refugees to Palestine [after World War II], your determined stand against the attempts to deflect you from your course, your staunch support of our admission to statehood at Lake Success [temporary meeting place of the United Nations at the time, located just outside New York City on Long Island], and your recognition of the fact of its establishment within an hour of our proclamation of independence. We pray that your assistance and guidance may be extended to us also in the coming years. We have succeeded in the past twelve months in defending our independence against enemies from every quarter—north, south and east, as in Biblical times—and in setting up the framework of our State. . . .

I pray with all my heart that you, Mr. President, may use your high authority to put an end to these hostile manoeuvres. We have successfully withstood the onslaught of the Arab States, who were sent against us by the British, almost like a pack of hired assassins. I am saying this with deep pain because I have throughout my life been deeply attached to Great Britain and have suffered for that attachment. But the evidence unfortunately all points in this direction, and even as I write we are receiving constant reports of Great Britain rearming the Arabs to enable them to re-start hostilities against us. Having failed in her efforts to wipe out our young commonwealth, she now appears bent on detaching the Negev from our State. I feel emboldened to ask for your intervention in this matter, remembering the deep sympathy and understanding which you displayed when I had the privilege of stating to you our case on the Negev and displaying to you maps showing its potentialities for settlement. It was with a deep feeling of elation that I left you on that day and it is this which now encourages me to plead for your intervention to prevent this part of the country, which was allotted to us last November, from being detached from our State. Sheer necessity compels us to cling to the Negev. Our pioneers have done yeoman work in opening up this semi-arid country; they have built pipe lines through the desert, set up agricultural settlements, planted gardens and orchards in what was for many centuries a barren land. They will not give up this land unless they are bodily removed from it.

This document can be found in "Chaim Weizmann to Harry S. Truman, 5 November 1948," Papers of Harry S. Truman, White House Central Files, Confidential Files, Box 43, Harry S. Truman Presidential Library, Independence, MO.

I venture to hope that clear and firm instructions be issued on this vital matter to the American Delegation in Paris which has of late, apparently, not received directives corresponding to the views which, I know, you hold on the subject. I would further plead that you may find it possible to direct the competent authorities to enable us to secure that long-term financial assistance which is urgently needed for the execution of the great scheme of reconstruction which I had the privilege of submitting to you in the Summer.

2. Egypt's Gamel Abdul Nasser Justifies Nationalizing the Suez Canal, 1956

The uproar which we anticipated has been taking place in London and Paris. This tremendous uproar is not supported by reason or logic. It is backed only by imperialist methods, by the habits of blood-sucking and of usurping rights, and by interference in the affairs of other countries. An unjustified uproar arose in London, and yesterday Britain submitted a protest to Egypt. I wonder what was the basis of this protest by Britain to Egypt? The Suez Canal Company is an Egyptian company, subject to Egyptian sovereignty. When we nationalized the Suez Canal Company, we only nationalized an Egyptian limited company, and by doing so we exercised a right which stems from the very core of Egyptian sovereignty. What right has Britain to interfere in our internal affairs? What right has Britain to interfere in our affairs and our questions? When we nationalized the Suez Canal Company, we only performed an act stemming from the very heart of our sovereignty. The Suez Canal Company is a limited company, awarded a concession by the Egyptian Government in 1865 to carry out its tasks. Today we withdraw the concession in order to do the job ourselves.

Although we have withdrawn this concession, we shall compensate shareholders of the company, despite the fact that they usurped our rights. Britain usurped 44 per cent of the shares free of charge. Today we shall pay her for her 44 per cent of the shares. We do not treat her as she treated us. We are not usurping the 44 per cent as she did. We do not tell Britain that we shall usurp her right as she usurped ours, but we tell her that we shall compensate her and forget the past.

The Suez Canal would have been restored to us in 12 years. What would have happened in 12 years' time? Would an uproar have been raised? What has happened now has disclosed hidden intentions and has unmasked Britain. If the canal was to fall to us in 12 years, why should it not be restored to us now? Why should it cause an uproar? We understand by this that they had no intention of fulfilling this pledge 12 years from now. What difference is it if the canal is restored to us now or in 12 years' time? Why should Britain say this will affect shipping in the canal? Would it have affected shipping 12 years hence?

Shipping in the Suez Canal has been normal for the past 48 hours from the time of nationalization until now. Shipping continued and is normal. We nationalized the

This document can be found in the *Summary of World Broadcasts,* Part IV, Daily Series, 6, 30 July 1956, British Broadcasting Corporation, London, UK. It can also be found in T. G. Faser, *The Middle East, 1914–1979* (New York: St. Martin's Press, 1980), pp. 88–89.

company. We have not interfered with shipping, and we are facilitating shipping matters. However, I emphatically warn the imperialist countries that their tricks, provocations and interference will be the reason for any hindrance to shipping. I place full responsibility on Britain and France for any curtailment of shipping in the Suez Canal when I state that Egypt will maintain freedom of shipping in the Suez Canal, and that since Egypt nationalized the Suez Canal Company shipping has been normal. Even before that we maintained freedom of shipping in the canal. Who has protected the canal? The canal has been under Egyptian protection because it is part of Egypt and we are the ones who should ensure freedom of shipping. We protect it today, we protected it a month ago, and we protected it for years because it is our territory and a part of our territory. Today we shall continue to protect the canal. But, because of the tricks they are playing, I hold Britain and France responsible for any consequences which may affect shipping.

Compatriots, we shall maintain our independence and sovereignty. The Suez Canal Company has become our property, and the Egyptian flag flies over it. We shall hold it with our blood and strength, and we shall meet aggression with aggression and evil with evil. We shall proceed towards achieving dignity and prestige for Egypt and building a sound national economy and true freedom. Peace be with you.

3. The Eisenhower Doctrine, 1957

Resolved by the Senate and House of Representatives of the United States of American in Congress assembled.

Sec. 1. That the President be and hereby is authorized to cooperate with and assist any nation or group of nations in the general area of the Middle East desiring such assistance in the development of economic strength dedicated to the maintenance of national independence.

Sec. 2. The President is authorized to undertake, in the general area of the Middle East, military assistance programs with any nation or group of nations of that area desiring such assistance. Furthermore, the United States regards as vital to the national interest and world peace the preservation of the independence and integrity of the nations of the Middle East. To this end, if the President determines the necessity thereof, the United States is prepared to use armed force to assist any such nation or group of nations requesting assistance against armed aggression from any country controlled by international communism:

Provided, that such employment shall be constant with the treaty obligations of the United States and the Constitution of the United States.

Sec. 3. The President is hereby authorized to use during the balance of this fiscal year 1957 for economic and military assistance under this joint resolution not to exceed $200,000,000 from any appropriation now available for carrying out the provisions of the Mutual Security Act of 1954. . . .

Sec. 4. The President should continue to furnish facilities and military assistance, within the provisions of the applicable law and established policies, to the

---

This document can be found in the *Department of State Bulletin,* XXVI (March 25, 1957), p. 481.

United Nations Emergency Force in the Middle East, with a view to maintaining the truce in that region.

Sec. 5. The President shall within the months of January and July of each year report to the Congress his actions hereunder.

Sec. 6. This joint resolution shall expire when the President shall determine that the peace and security of the nations in the general area of the Middle East are reasonably assured by international conditions created by action of the United Nations or otherwise except that it may be terminated earlier by a concurrent resolution of the two Houses of Congress.

4. Conservative Saudi Prince Faisal Voices Opposition to Nasser, 1962

After welcoming his guest, the President asked [Saudi Crown Prince] Faysal about his views on what was going on in Yemen. Faysal replied that because of the dearth of up-to-date information, the situation was still vague. Asked what the outcome might be, Faysal replied that, if the insurgents were not given any outside help, they would not be able to retain authority. President Kennedy asked if by outside help the Prince meant help from the UAR [United Arab Republic]. Faysal replied "Not only from the UAR but also from the Soviet Union." Elaborating, Faysal mentioned that the elements which carried out the coup in Yemen are a mixture of military and civilian zealots, who enjoyed the support and help of the UAR and the Communists. They were not really representative of the majority of the people or their desires. Faysal admitted conditions in Yemen during the late Imam Ahmad's life needed improving and improvement was slow in forthcoming. However, the moment Imam Muhammad al-Badr ascended the throne, he announced quite a deep and comprehensive program of social reform for the country.

"Badr's announced reforms gave the lie to proclamations of the rebels that they carried out the coup in order to bring about improvement and reform," said Faysal. Saudi Arabia's concern is that, unless the situation in Yemen is reversed, fertile ground for the entrenchment and spread of Communism and its attendant subversive activities will be provided in the area. Asked how much help Saudi Arabia is giving Prince Hassan in his efforts to reverse the present situation, Faysal replied he is not fully conversant with what the Saudi Government is actually doing. However, he felt sure Saudi Arabia would not hesitate to give Hassan any assistance which was within the modest capabilities of his country. Prince Faysal asserted that Prince Hassan enjoys the loyalty and support of most of the tribes in Yemen. The tribes, however, are armed only with light weapons such as rifles, revolvers and machine guns. In reply to a question from Mr. Johnson, Prince Faysal added that the Yemen army numbered between three and five thousand. Numerically speaking, therefore, Hassan has greater support from the tribes than the revolutionaries have from the Army. The President remarked that the UAR's and USSR's interest in Yemeni developments was evident in their prompt recognition of the revolutionary government.

This document can be found in U.S. Department of State, *Foreign Relations of the United States, 1962–1963, Middle East* (Washington, D.C.: Government Printing Office, 1995), XVIII, 162–164.

Prince Faysal reiterated his pleasure at having had the chance to meet the President, climaxing deliberations Faysal had had with other officials of the United States Government. This was Faysal's sole purpose in coming over to the United States. He wanted to learn clearly the policy of the United States vis-à-vis the Middle East generally, and Saudi Arabia in particular. The President expressed his realization of the concern Saudi Arabia felt over the situation in Yemen and over President Nasser's reported activities, which were deemed inimical to the interests of neighboring countries. The President explained that United States help to the UAR consisted mainly of food grains which went to the people of the UAR. Prince Faysal interjected that no Arab person or country could legitimately object to America's policy of helping other Arab countries, or, indeed, any other country whose people needed such help. What is a source of anxiety to Saudi Arabia, however, is that United States help to the UAR is being used indirectly by Nasser and his agents for injurious and subversive activities. Money which otherwise would have been spent on food is set free for Nasser's subversive efforts in other Middle Eastern countries.

Faysal went on to enumerate the different facets of Nasser's interference in the internal affairs of other Arab countries, in particular, Saudi Arabia. The facets include covert intelligence gathering by impermissible means, sabotage, incitement, and the organization of assassination attempts. In Faysal's view, it is obvious Nasser had one sole aim, namely, to crush the authority of the Saudi Arabian Government. This was the strongest cause of apprehension and nervous tension in Saudi Arabia. His country would wish for nothing more than to be allowed a long stretch of time marked by stability, tranquility and peace of mind so that it can move ahead with the job of carrying out needed reforms, raising standards of living, and achieving progress and prosperity.

Saudi Arabia, however, is prevented from achieving its goals by the extreme condition of terror that surrounds it. This condition of unease and fear in the area is beginning increasingly to manifest itself within his country. Prince Faysal emphatically made the point that the concern and fear he expressed does not stem from the fact that he belongs to the ruling family of Saudi Arabia. The Saudi Royal Family is just one Arabian family, which history accorded a role of leadership for the past number of years. Animatedly Faysal declared that if he had for one moment thought that the Saudi Royal Family or its existence in Saudi Arabia were damaging to the interests of his country or its people he, although a member of that Family, would not cooperate with it and would, in fact, turn against it.

5. Lyndon Johnson Blames Moscow and the Arab States for the June 1967 War, 1971

In an effort to gain influence in the radical Arab states, the Soviet Union shifted in the mid-1950s from its original support of Israel to an attempt to push moderate Arab states toward a more radical course and to provide a Middle East base for expanding its role in the Mediterranean, in Africa, and in the areas bordering on the Indian

Ocean. The Soviets used Arab hostility toward Israel to inflame Arab politics to the boiling point. Country after country had shifted to the Russian view. The expanding Soviet presence in this strategic region threatened our position in Europe. Soviet leaders called publicly for the withdrawal of our Sixth Fleet from the Mediterranean, as well as for the liquidation of NATO. If they gained control of the seas, the oil, and the air space of the vast arc between Morocco and Iran, all that had been done since President Truman's time to achieve stability and balance in world politics would have been endangered. . . .

The danger implicit in every border incident in the Middle East was not merely war between Israelis and Arabs but an ultimate confrontation between the Soviet Union and the United States and its NATO allies. This was the danger that concerned me, as well as the tragedy of war itself, in those hours before dawn on June 5, 1967.

The backdrop to the war that began that day was crowded with the diplomatic maneuvering, pent-up tensions, and explosions of the past twenty years. The most important events, stripped to bare essentials, were these: War had erupted between Israel and the Arabs twice before, in 1948 and 1956. Both times Israeli military forces showed remarkable strength and ability. Both times hostilities ended because of pressures brought to bear in the United Nations, but there was no permanent settlement. In the 1956 war Israeli troops overran the Sinai peninsula. They agreed to withdraw from the area for two reasons: first, a UN decision to put in a peacekeeping force to patrol the borders between Israel and Egypt and, second, President Eisenhower's assurance that the Gulf of Aqaba, Israel's only outlet to the Indian Ocean would remain open as an international waterway. To symbolize this assurance, the United Nations sent forces to Sharm el Sheikh. These understandings were contained in public statements at the time as well as in diplomatic exchanges. They were handled this way to satisfy [Egyptian president Gamel Abdul] Nasser's sensitivity to the appearance of making peace, or even negotiating, with Israel. . . .

Egypt had been trying to dominate the Arab world since Nasser came to leadership in 1954. For a time, in the early 1960s, we hoped that he was beginning to concentrate instead on improving the lot of his own people. On this assumption, we gave substantial aid to Egypt, mainly wheat to feed the people in its teeming cities. In the end, Nasser persisted in his imperial dream. While his strained economy slowed down, he sent troops into Yemen to support revolutionaries trying to take over that country. To support his ambitions, he became increasingly dependent on Soviet arms. Nasser's attitude toward the United States grew more and more hostile and his speeches more inflammatory. It became impossible to maintain congressional support for even token assistance to Egypt.

Through it all Nasser's prestige in the Arab world declined. So even though initial reports indicated that he preferred not to fight, he was susceptible to taunts that he was failing to protect Syria [a base for Arab terrorist raids against Israel] in the face of an alleged Israeli threat to Egypt's ally. And once he moved, events had a tragic inevitability of their own. It was not clear in mid-May of 1967 that any government actually wanted war, but after May 14 the Arab states began to act in ways inconsistent with preserving peace.

On that date, May 14, 1967, Nasser mobilized his armed forces. Two days later Egypt asked the United Nations to withdraw its peacekeeping force in the Sinai. In an action that shocked me then, and that still puzzles me, Secretary General U Thant announced that UN forces could not remain in the Sinai without Egyptian approval. Even the Egyptians were surprised. Nasser's Ambassador in Washington, Dr. Mostafa Kamel, told us that his government thought and hoped that U Thant would play for time. But he did not, and tension increased.

We threw the full weight of U.S. diplomacy into an effort to forestall war. The first necessity was to persuade the Israelis not to act hastily. I knew they would feel anxious about the withdrawal of UN forces, but I also knew that if open conflict was to be avoided, the Israelis would have to remain cool. On May 17, 1967, I cabled Prime Minister [Levi] Eshkol, spelling out our deep concern over the situation and urging restraint. "I am sure you will understand," I wrote, "that I cannot accept any responsibilities on behalf of the United States for situations which arise as the result of actions on which we are not consulted."

On May 18 UN forces withdrew. Egyptian troops entered the Sinai peninsula and took up positions on Israel's borders. Despite his ill-conceived first maneuver, U Thant then announced that he was going to Cairo to try to preserve peace. We fully supported his effort. As far as possible, I wanted the main thrust of our diplomacy to be through the United Nations. At the same time, I was prepared to use American influence in any way that might be effective and helpful. On May 22, I sent a message to Soviet Chairman [Aleksei] Kosygin suggesting a joint effort to calm the situation. . . .

On the 22nd, I also sent a letter to Nasser assuring him of America's basic friendship for Egypt and my own understanding of "the pride and aspirations of your people." I urged him to avoid war as his first duty and expressed the hope that "if we come through these days without hostilities," I could send Vice President Humphrey to talk to him and other Middle East leaders in a new attempt to find a solution to the old problems there.

That same day, after I sent my letter to Nasser but before it was actually delivered and while U Thant was flying to Cairo, the Egyptian government made its fateful announcement: Egypt was closing the Gulf of Aqaba to Israeli shipping. Although we cannot be sure, it seems likely that Nasser took this mortally dangerous action independently of the Soviet Union. . . .

On the evening of May 26 I met with Israel's Foreign Minister Abba Eban, who had just flown to Washington. Our conversation was direct and frank. Eban said that according to Israeli intelligence, the United Arab Republic (UAR) was preparing an all-out attack. I asked Secretary [of Defense Robert] McNamara, who was present, to give Mr. Eban a summary of our findings. Three separate intelligence groups had looked carefully into the matter, McNamara said, and it was our best judgment that a UAR attack was not imminent. "All of our intelligence people are unanimous," I added, "that if the UAR attacks, you will whip hell out of them."

Eban asked what the United States was willing to do to keep the Gulf of Aqaba open. I reminded him that I had defined our position on May 23. We were hard at work on what to do to assure free access, and when to do it. "You can assure the Israeli Cabinet," I said, "we will pursue vigorously any and all possible measures to keep the strait open." . . .

I told him that I saw some hope in the plan for an international naval force in the strait area, but that before such a proposal could be effective I had to be sure Congress was on board. . . .

Early in June we sensed that the Israelis might be moving toward a decision to reopen Aqaba on their own, but we still believed that we had time to reach a settlement through diplomacy. . . .

I have always had a deep feeling of sympathy for Israel and its people, gallantly building and defending a modern nation against great odds and against the tragic background of Jewish experience. I can understand that men might decide to act on their own when hostile forces gather on their frontiers and cut off a major port, and when antagonistic political leaders fill the air with threats to destroy their nation. Nonetheless, I have never concealed my regret that Israel decided to move when it did. I always made it equally clear, however, to the Russians and to every other nation, that I did not accept the oversimplified charge of Israeli aggression. Arab actions in the weeks before the war started—forcing UN troops out, closing the port of Aqaba, and assembling forces on the Israeli border—made that charge ridiculous.

When I was first called early on the morning of June 5 with news that war had broken out, the available information was sketchy. The only clear fact was that Israeli and Egyptian forces were fighting. Each side had accused the other of aggression. Whatever the truth proved to be, I knew that tragic consequences could follow.

6. United Nations Security Council Resolution 242, 1967

Expressing its continuing concern with the grave situation in the Middle East,

Emphasizing the inadmissibility of the acquisition of territory by war and the need to work for a just and lasting peace in which every State in the area can live in security.

Emphasizing further that all Member States in their acceptance of the Charter of the United Nations have undertaken a commitment to act in accordance with Article 2 of the Charter,

1. *Affirms* that the fulfillment of Charter principles requires the establishment of a just and lasting peace in the Middle East which should include the application of both the following principles:

(i) Withdrawal of Israel armed forces from territories occupied in the recent conflict;

(ii) Termination of all claims or states of belligerency and respect for and acknowledgement of the sovereignty, territorial integrity and political independence of every State in the area and their right to live in peace within secure and recognized boundaries free from threats or acts of force;

2. *Affirms further* the necessity

(a) For guaranteeing freedom of navigation through international waterways in the area;

(b) For achieving a just settlement of the refugee problem;

This document can be found in United Nations Security Council, 22nd Year, "Resolution 242 [The Situation in the Middle East]," 22 November 1967, *Resolutions and Decisions of the Security Council 1967* (S/INF/22/REV.2), Official Record. New York: United Nations, 1968, p. 8.

(c) For guaranteeing the territorial inviolability and political independence of every State in the area, through measures including the establishment of demilitarized zones;

3. *Requests* the Secretary-General to designate a Special Representative to proceed to the Middle East to establish and maintain contacts with the States concerned in order to promote agreement and assist efforts to achieve a peaceful and accepted settlement in accordance with the provisions and principles in this resolution;

4. *Requests* the Secretary-General to report to the Security Council on the progress of the efforts of the Special Representative as soon as possible.

7. The Palestinian National Covenant, 1968

Palestine is the homeland of the Palestinian Arab people and an integral part of the great Arab homeland, and the people of Palestine is a part of the Arab nation.

Palestine with its boundaries that existed at the time of the British mandate is an integral regional unit.

The Palestinian Arab people possesses the legal right to its homeland, and when the liberation of its homeland is completed it will exercise self-determination solely according to its own will and choice.

The Palestinian personality is an innate, persistent characteristic that does not disappear, and it is transferred from fathers to sons. The Zionist occupation, and the dispersal of the Palestinian Arab people as a result of the disasters which came over it, do not deprive it of its Palestinian personality and affiliation and do not nullify them.

The Palestinians are the Arab citizens who were living permanently in Palestine until 1947, whether they were expelled from there or remained. Whoever is born to a Palestinian Arab father after this date, within Palestine or outside it, is a Palestinian.

Jews who were living permanently in Palestine until the beginning of the Zionist invasion will be considered Palestinians.

The Palestinian affiliation and the material, spiritual and historical tie with Palestine are permanent realities. The upbringing of the Palestinian individual in an Arab and revolutionary fashion, the undertaking of all means of forging consciousness and training the Palestinian, in order to acquaint him profoundly with his homeland, spiritually and materially, and preparing him for the conflict and the armed struggle, as well as for the sacrifice of his property and his life to restore his homeland, until the liberation of all this is a national duty.

The phase in which the people of Palestine is living is that of national struggle for the liberation of Palestine. Therefore, the contradictions among the Palestinian national forces are of secondary order which must be suspended in the interest of the fundamental contradiction between Zionism and colonialism on the one side and the Palestinian Arab people on the other. On this basis, the Palestinian masses, whether in the homeland or in places of exile, organizations and individuals,

---

This document can be found in Walter Laqueur and Barry Rubin, eds., *The Israel-Arab Reader: A Documentary History of the Middle East Conflict* (New York: Penguin Books, 1995), pp. 218–222.

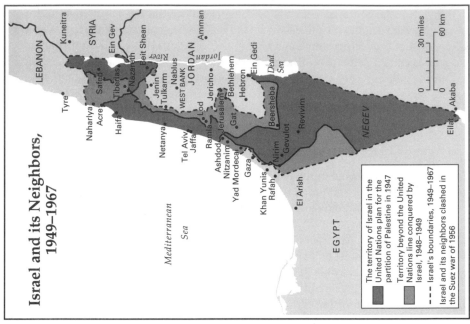

Israel and its Neighbors, 1949–1967

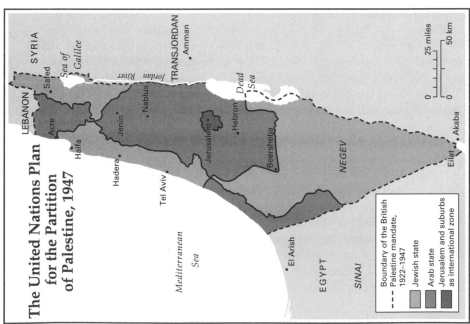

The United Nations Plan for the Partition of Palestine, 1947

Thomas G. Paterson et al., *American Foreign Relations,* Fifth Edition. Copyright © 2000 by Houghton Mifflin Company. Reprinted with permission.

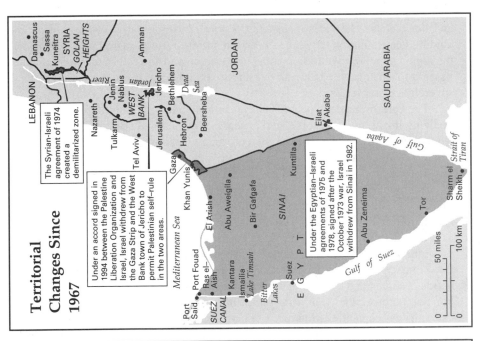

Territorial Changes Since 1967

The Syrian-Israeli agreement of 1974 created a demilitarized zone.

Under an accord signed in 1994 between the Palestine Liberation Organization and Israel, Israel withdrew from the Gaza Strip and the West Bank town of Jericho to permit Palestinian self-rule in the two areas.

Under the Egyptian-Israeli agreements of 1975 and 1978, signed after the October 1973 war, Israel withdrew from Sinai in 1982.

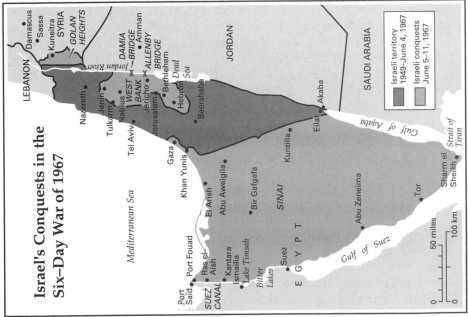

Israel's Conquests in the Six–Day War of 1967

Israeli territory 1949–June 4, 1967

Israeli conquests June 5–11, 1967

Thomas G. Paterson et al., *American Foreign Relations*, Fifth Edition. Copyright © 2000 by Houghton Mifflin Company. Reprinted with permission.

comprise one national front which acts to restore Palestine and liberate it through armed struggle.

Armed struggle is the only way to liberate Palestine and is therefore a strategy and not tactics. The Palestinian Arab people affirms its absolute resolution and abiding determination to pursue the armed struggle and to march forward towards the armed popular revolution, to liberate its homeland and return to it [to maintain] its right to a natural life in it, and to exercise its right of self-determination in it and sovereignty over it. . . .

The Palestinian Arab people believes in Arab unity. In order to fulfill its role in realizing this, it must preserve, in this phase of its national struggle, its Palestinian personality and the constituents thereof, increase consciousness of its existence and resist any plan that tends to disintegrate or weaken it. . . .

The destiny of the Arab nation, indeed the very Arab existence, depends upon the destiny of the Palestine issue. The endeavour and effort of the Arab nation to liberate Palestine follows from this connection. The people of Palestine assumes its vanguard role in realizing this sacred national aim.

The liberation of Palestine, from an Arab viewpoint, is a national duty to repulse the Zionist, Imperialist invasion from the great Arab homeland and to purge the Zionist presence from Palestine. Its full responsibility falls upon the Arab nation, peoples and governments, with the Palestinian Arab people at their head. For this purpose, the Arab nation must mobilize all its military, human, material and spiritual capacities to participate actively with the people of Palestine in the liberation of Palestine. They must especially in the present stage of armed Palestinian revolution, grant and offer the people of Palestine all possible help and every material and human support, and afford it every sure means and opportunity enabling it to continue to assume its vanguard role in pursuing its armed revolution until the liberation of its homeland.

The liberation of Palestine, from a spiritual viewpoint, will prepare an atmosphere of tranquillity and peace for the Holy Land in the shade of which all the Holy Places will be safeguarded, and freedom of worship and visitation to all will be guaranteed, without distinction or discrimination of race, colour, language or religion. For this reason, the people of Palestine looks to the support of all the spiritual forces in the world.

The liberation of Palestine, from a human viewpoint, will restore to the Palestinian man his dignity, glory and freedom. For this, the Palestinian Arab people looks to the support of those in the world who believe in the dignity and freedom of man.

The liberation of Palestine, from an international viewpoint is a defensive act necessitated by the requirements of self-defence. For this reason the Arab people of Palestine, desiring to befriend all peoples, looks to the support of the states which love freedom, justice and peace in restoring the legal situation to Palestine, establishing security and peace in its territory, and enabling its people to exercise national sovereignty and national freedom. . . .

To realize the aims of this covenant and its principles the Palestine Liberation Organization will undertake its full role in liberating Palestine.

The Palestine Liberation Organization, which represents the forces of the Palestinian revolution, is responsible for the movement of the Palestinian Arab people in its struggle to restore its homeland, liberate it, return to it and exercise the right of self-determination in it. This responsibility extends to all military, political and financial matters, and all else that the Palestine issue requires in the Arab and international spheres.

The Palestine Liberation Organization will cooperate with all Arab States, each according to its capacities, and will maintain neutrality in their mutual relations in the light of and on the basis of, the requirements of the battle of liberation and will not interfere in the internal affairs of any Arab State.

8. The Carter Doctrine, 1980

This last few months has not been an easy time for any of us. As we meet tonight, it has never been more clear that the state of our Union depends on the state of the world. And tonight, as throughout our own generation, freedom and peace in the world depend on the state of our Union. . . .

At this time in Iran, 50 Americans are still held captive, innocent victims of terrorism and anarchy. Also at this moment, massive Soviet troops are attempting to subjugate the fiercely independent and deeply religious people of Afghanistan. These two acts—one of international terrorism and one of military aggression—present a serious challenge to the United States of America and indeed to all the nations of the world. Together, we will meet these threats to peace. . . .

Three basic developments have helped to shape our challenges: the steady growth and increased projection of Soviet military power beyond its own borders; the overwhelming dependence of the Western democracies on oil supplies from the Middle East; and the press of social and religious and economic and political change in the many nations of the developing world, exemplified by the revolution in Iran. . . .

In response to the abhorrent act in Iran, our nation has never been aroused and unified so greatly in peacetime. Our position is clear. The United States will not yield to blackmail.

We continue to pursue these specific goals: first, to protect the present and long-range interests of the United States; secondly, to preserve the lives of the American hostages and to secure, as quickly as possible, their safe release, if possible, to avoid bloodshed which might further endanger the lives of our fellow citizens; to enlist the help of other nations in condemning this act of violence, which is shocking and violates the moral and the legal standards of a civilized world; and also to convince and to persuade the Iranian leaders that the real danger to their nation lies in the north, in the Soviet Union and from the Soviet troops now in Afghanistan, and that the unwarranted Iranian quarrel with the United States hampers their response to this far greater danger to them.

If the American hostages are harmed, a severe price will be paid. We will never rest until every one of the American hostages are released.

This document can be found in "President Jimmy Carter's State of the Union Address Before Congress, 23 January 1980," *Public Papers of the Presidents, 1980–1981* (Washington, D.C.: Government Printing Office, 1981), pp. 194–199.

But now we face a broader and more fundamental challenge in this region because of the recent military action of the Soviet Union. . . .

. . .The Soviet Union has taken a radical and an aggressive new step. It's using its great military power against a relatively defenseless nation. The implications of the Soviet invasion of Afghanistan could pose the most serious threat to the peace since the Second World War. . . .

While this invasion continues, we and the other nations of the world cannot conduct business as usual with the Soviet Union. That's why the United States has imposed stiff economic penalties on the Soviet Union. . . .

The region which is now threatened by Soviet troops in Afghanistan is of great strategic importance: It contains more than two-thirds of the world's exportable oil. The Soviet effort to dominate Afghanistan has brought Soviet military forces to within 300 miles of the Indian Ocean and close to the Straits of Hormuz, a waterway [connecting the Persian Gulf to the Indian Ocean] through which most of the world's oil must flow. The Soviet Union is now attempting to consolidate a strategic position, therefore, that poses a grave threat to the free movement of Middle East oil.

This situation demands careful thought, steady nerves, and resolute action, not only for this year but for many years to come. It demands collective efforts to meet this new threat to security in the Persian Gulf and in Southwest Asia. It demands the participation of all those who rely on oil from the Middle East and who are concerned with global peace and stability. And it demands consultation and close cooperation with countries in the area which might be threatened.

Meeting this challenge will take national will, diplomatic and political wisdom, economic sacrifice, and, of course, military capability. We must call on the best that is in us to preserve the security of this crucial region.

Let our position be absolutely clear: An attempt by any outside force to gain control of the Persian Gulf region will be regarded as an assault on the vital interests of the United States of America, and such an assault will be repelled by any means necessary, including military force.

. . .We are working with our allies to prevent conflict in the Middle East. The peace treaty between Egypt and Israel [framed at Camp David and finalized in March 1979] is a notable achievement which represents a strategic asset for America and which also enhances prospects for regional and world peace. We are now engaged in further negotiations to provide full autonomy for the people of the West Bank and Gaza, to resolve the Palestinian issue in all its aspects, and to preserve the peace and security of Israel. Let no one doubt our commitment to the security of Israel. In a few days we will observe an historic event when Israel makes another major withdrawal from the Sinai and when Ambassadors will be exchanged between Israel and Egypt. . . .

We've increased and strengthened our naval presence in the Indian Ocean, and we are now making arrangements for key naval and air facilities to be used by our forces in the region of northeast Africa and the Persian Gulf. . . .

In the weeks ahead, we will further strengthen political and military ties with other nations in the region. We believe that there are no irreconcilable differences between us and any Islamic nation. We respect the faith of Islam, and we are ready to cooperate with all Moslem countries. . . .

The crises in Iran and Afghanistan have dramatized a very important lesson: Our excessive dependence on foreign oil is a clear and present danger to our Nation's security. The need has never been more urgent. At long last, we must have a clear, comprehensive energy policy for the United States. . . .

The single biggest factor in the inflation rate last year, the increase in the inflation rate last year, was from one cause: the skyrocketing prices of OPEC [Organization of Petroleum Exporting Countries] oil. We must take whatever actions are necessary to reduce our dependence on foreign oil.

✪ E S S A Y S

This chapter's three essays explore different aspects of U.S. relations with the Middle East—cultural, strategic, and economic—during the Cold War era. In the first essay Michelle Mart of Pennsylvania State University, Berks Campus, examines how popular culture and gender ideology helped shape U.S.-Israeli relations. From Israel's founding in the late 1940s through 1960, she posits, Americans encountered a highly favorable view of the new state and its citizens in the press, best-selling fiction, and Hollywood films. The media portrayed Israel as a vital, masculine society, made in America's own image as a hardened, freedom-loving, frontier nation. Mart contrasts Israel's positive image with the unflattering characterizations made of Arabs, a nonwestern people of color, typically portrayed as cowardly yet dangerous predators. Mart concludes that the gendering of Israel helped promote the belief that the new nation could qualify as a tough-minded Cold War ally and a bulwark against Communism in a highly volatile region of the world.

In the second essay, Douglas Little of Clark University studies the pivotal 1960s when U.S. activity in the Middle East deepened. Washington joined in strategic partnerships with Israel, Iran, and Saudi Arabia, the "three pillars" of U.S. policy in the region. According to Little, President John F. Kennedy hoped to modify traditional Cold War policy by reaching out to the nonaligned regime of Egypt's Nasser and pursuing an Arab-Israeli accord. Nasser's continued support for radical nationalists, however, alienated both Israel and conservative Arabs and undermined Kennedy's initiatives. Little maintains that Kennedy's successor, Lyndon Johnson, guided by both Cold War and domestic politics, changed course and adopted a pro-Israeli posture that featured the sale of advanced weapons to Tel Aviv and U.S. support for Israel in the June 1967 War. The U.S. embrace of Israel, however, was not open-ended. Professor Little notes that the administration pressed the Jewish state to curb its nuclear-weapons program and accept U.N. Resolution 242. Johnson also cemented alliances with Iran and Saudi Arabia, two of the region's most conservative oil-producing Islamic states. While Johnson's approach advanced U.S. interests in the short run, Little observes that festering tensions continued to plague the region and threatened a superpower showdown.

The last selection is drawn from Daniel Yergin's Pulitzer Prize winning history of the oil industry, *The Prize* (1992). An independent historian and an expert on energy issues, Yergin examines President Carter's response to Iran's Islamic revolution of 1979 and the revolution's impact on the U.S. and world economies. Yergin explains how massive oil profits in the 1970s strained Iranian society and generated political upheaval. He faults the Carter administration for standing by Shah Reza Pahlavi in spite of accumulating evidence that the autocratic ruler lacked popular support. Nor did the Carter White House anticipate the tumult's destabilizing effect on international oil markets. According to Yergin, Carter's decision to grant the ailing Shah refuge in the United States underestimated anti-American sentiment in revolutionary Iran, led to the take-over of the U.S. embassy in Tehran in November 1979, and destroyed Carter's presidency. Yergin concludes that the oil shocks of the 1970s, and the accompanying hostage crisis, demonstrated America's relative decline in world power.

Popular Culture, Gender, and America's Special Relationship with Israel

MICHELLE MART

Ever since the formation of Israel in 1948, the United States has had a unique relationship with the Jewish state based on a mix of American foreign policy goals, domestic politics, political idealism, and religious and cultural affiliation. Yet, close ties between the United States and Israel were far from inevitable and, indeed, have been construed by some observers as politically, economically, or strategically questionable. It therefore makes sense to seek further illumination of this relationship outside the realm of traditional explanations. In the looser but pervasive cultural realm, we may find clues as to why John F. Kennedy and subsequent presidents referred to the American-Israeli relationship as "special." This essay examines the dramatic discursive transformation of Jews and Israel in American popular culture and politics in the 1940s and 1950s from curious minorities to kindred spirits and reliable allies in the Cold War.

The following examination of cultural images—as found in Hollywood films, best-selling fiction, the mainstream press, and the speeches and memos of U.S. policymakers—is not offered as a substitute for treatments of American-Israeli relations that focus on economic pressures or military dangers. Rather, a discursive analysis aims to uncover the framework of cultural ideology whose naturalized myths, goals, and languages are embedded in the political assumptions of foreign policies. As [the historian] Richard Slotkin argues in his discussion of Hollywood Westerns and Cold War foreign policy, there is a "reciprocal" relationship between culture and foreign policy: "Film and event 'speak' to each other —event lending political resonance to the fiction, the fiction providing mythological justification for the particular scenarios of real-world action." Furthermore, these fictional expressions are part of the essential ideological glue of every society. "Without the common frame of discourse a public myth (ideology) provides," Slotkin concludes, "a society can neither generate authoritative analysis of a crisis nor muster a consensus on behalf of future policy." . . .

This essay will focus on one aspect of American cultural ideology; gender. As the contributors to a recent symposium in *Diplomatic History* indicate, an analysis of "gender discourse" is a particularly fruitful and hitherto ignored approach to foreign relations. Gender discourse is not merely words or language; it is a system of meaning in which behavior is polarized into two opposite categories according to which we view the actions of individuals and national states. Gender, as a analytical category, can illustrate symbolic links between the understanding of international relations and cultural structures; such links indicate the mutually reinforcing relationship between the supposedly separate worlds of "objective" politics and "subjective" cultural values. This linkage does not obviate the importance of individual policymakers or political groups in the making of policy. But the individuals or

From Michelle Mart, "Tough Guys and American Cold War Policy," *Diplomatic History* 20 (Summer 1996), pp. 357–380. Reprinted by permission of the publisher.

corporate interests that shape policy work within the parameters of dominant cultural discourses and reflect the values and ideologies of their society. Although it is important to recognize the variations of cultural values and individual rhetoric, it is a mistake to ignore the broader implications of that rhetoric.

A study of gendered images of Israel in the early Cold War is useful in understanding American policy toward the Jewish state for four reasons. First, in the 1950s, widely accepted cultural discourses naturalized "traditional" gender roles in which men were dominant, "masculine," and took responsibility for women. In popular fiction, media, and American foreign policy, the discursive forms simultaneously represented social ideals and political goals. At the same time, traditional gender roles were applied to individuals as well as nations; in these representations, the United States was a masculine country that took responsibility for other, "weaker" nations. Thus, Cold War policies were, in part, phrased in and shaped by a particular gendered discourse and set of sexual politics.

Inevitably, the norm in political discourse and the protagonist in cultural discourse represented traditional masculinity. That which was seen as unmasculine was, therefore, alien or outside the accepted parameters of action and behavior. . . .

The second reason that an examination of gendered discourse is useful for understanding American policy toward Israel is that a gendered understanding of national identity became particularly relevant in the early years of the Cold War, because social values and ideology were treated as legitimate concerns in the success or failure of American diplomacy. Foreign policies, such as the Truman Doctrine and NSC-68, continually defined the Cold War as a contest between "two ways of life" in which the United States would demonstrate its moral and social superiority. In the 1940s and 1950s, the American "way of life" included clearly defined gender roles. At the same time, within the framework of Cold War ideology, political alliances often implied a certain degree of cultural similarity and kinship; therefore, understanding the cultural components of nation identity is highly relevant to the study of international relations.

Third, Israel and Jews came to be included in the image of a masculine America ready to fight the Cold War. This equation was surprising. In the popular culture and political speech of the mid-to-late 1940s, Jews and Israelis were treated—relative to their later depiction—as "outsiders." Yet, within a decade, Jews and Israelis had become "insiders" and, thus, subject to a different set of political assumptions. This transition from outsider to insider status was reflected in the Jewish/Israeli role in cultural discourse. In the mid-1940s, for example, traditional American stereotypes of Jews and Israelis questioned the masculinity of Jewish men. As Jews became insiders, these stereotypes were replaced by another set of images emphasizing Jewish masculinity and similarity to other American men. There is an inherent connection between the construction of Jewish/Israeli masculinity and the perception of Jews as insiders, as similar to Americans, to be judged by similar political and social ideals: Israelis would not have been seen as insiders if they had not measured up to an image of traditional masculinity. Moreover, the emergence of Israelis as "insiders" had a powerful effect on the political assumptions of U.S. policymakers.

Finally, while Jews were increasingly depicted as masculine insiders in American popular and political culture, Arabs were increasingly depicted as unmasculine outsiders. An examination of gendered images of Jews and Israelis in the 1940s and 1950s thus reveals a symbiotic stigmatization of Arabs as the adversaries of Israelis. To a certain extent, the view that Israelis were like Americans was predicated on the image of a non-Western, undemocratic, racially darker, and unmasculine—in other words, alien—enemy. Beginning with the founding of the Jewish state, the sympathies of many Americans in the Arab-Israeli dispute lay with the Israelis, whose leaders were considered fellow Westerners. Nevertheless, in the late 1940s and early 1950s, American policy as well as media coverage of the Middle East reflected a good deal of ambivalence about the merits on both sides of the dispute. This ambivalence seemed to disappear from public discourse by the late 1950s as Arabs came to serve as the symbolic inverse of Israeli insider status. The measurement of masculinity was the most vivid expression of the differing status of Israelis and Arabs in public culture.

The images of Jewish masculinity—the depiction of Jews as fighters, as masculine sex symbols, as underdogs who triumph over their enemies, and as protective father figures—were applied to the State of Israel as a whole and contrasted sharply with the image of Israel's enemies; thus, they had broad implications for the way Americans viewed Israelis and the American-Israeli relationship.

In the first half of the twentieth century, Jews were described in American culture by a whole set of stereotypes that set them apart as different and made them "outsiders" in American culture. Many Americans used the outsider images to scapegoat Jews for imagined or real ills in their lives. Anti-Semitism in the United States peaked soon after World War II and the popular postwar images of Jews, therefore, were informed by these stereotypes. One set of stereotypes depicted Jewish men as unmasculine because they were seen as physically awkward, presumably weak, and lacking standard white American male sexual appeal and as unable or unwilling to fight. The stereotypes of Jews as unmasculine were well known in the public culture at midcentury and could be referred to in shorthand. For example, in two popular works of fiction, Edward Dmytryk's 1947 film *Crossfire* and Irwin Shaw's 1948 novel *The Young Lions,* references to grown men (indeed, soldiers) as "Jew-boy" are instantly understood as common expressions and inflammatory insults; they signal that the speakers are bigoted individuals using outdated language. Similarly, in Shaw's novel, when soldiers are telling jokes about Jews, it is clear that all of the characters are familiar with the insults.

Following the postwar trend of assimilation and a celebration of universalism, many writers and filmmakers sought to break down the idea that Jews were outsiders. One principal way in which they tried to make Jews more accepted was to demolish common stereotypes that challenged Jewish masculinity. The familiar challenges to Jewish masculinity had rested on presumptions of physical or "racial" as well as behavioral differences between Jews and Americans. In the late nineteenth and early twentieth centuries, those who believed in eugenics and the popular scientific "proofs" of Anglo-Saxon superiority deemed Jews—along with many other minorities— genetically inferior to the majority of Americans. The most concrete political expression of these beliefs was seen in the 1924 immigration laws restricting immigrants of the "Hebrew race" and in the restrictive quotas and exclusions that operated throughout American society as late as the 1950s. Not surprisingly, as anti-Semitism decreased from the 1940s to the 1960s, the definition of Jews as a race declined dramatically.

The stereotypes of Jews as racial aliens included physical characteristics, such as a frail physique, distinctive facial features (including a large, unattractive nose), and offensive body odors as well as a foreign accent. These characteristics were common in the stock Jewish villain characters of popular fiction. Yet many postwar writers denied the validity of these physical images. Norman Mailer's Joey Goldstein of *The Naked and the Dead,* in contrast to the stereotypical Jew, is physically strong and has a good mechanical sense. Moreover, it is no accident that Roth, the other Jew in Mailer's platoon, who wears his physical weakness as a badge of Jewish identity, falls to his death when he comes to believe the stereotypes about him; meanwhile, Goldstein, the "new" Jew, survives. Another Jewish survivor, Irwin Shaw's Noah, knows the importance of overcoming the physical image of popular stereotypes. He says, "I want every Jew to be treated as if he weighed two hundred pounds."

In addition to these physical stereotypes, many Americans viewed Jews as different from the American masculine norm because they supposedly behaved differently. Incorporating the centuries of Jewish exclusion from landowning, farming, and army service, modern American images of Jews failed to include physical prowess or courageous action. For example, respondents to surveys in the late 1930s and 1940s who reported negative views of Jews cited justifications for their opinions such as the Jewish "refusal to do manual labor" and a tendency of Jews to avoid army service or to get "soft jobs in the army." In popular fiction, Jews had often been stereotyped as cowards. The blockade-running Jewish captain from Leon Uris's *Exodus* explains why he has to prove his masculinity through his daring actions: "I'm supposed to be a coward because I'm a Jew. . . . These guys over here are fighting my battle for respect." In the postwar period, many author's—eager to challenge the image of lambs who had gone placidly to their Holocaust slaughter—were especially strident in their denouncement of the stereotype of the unmasculine Jew who refused to fight. For example, in his 1947 novel *My Glorious Brothers,* Howard Fast writes, "[the Greeks] . . . no longer regarded the Jew as a meek and gentle scholar who would sooner die on the Sabbath day than lift a hand in his defense."

Two of the most popular postwar fictional efforts to counter ideas that Jews were racially or behaviorally different were Laura Hobson's 1947 best-selling novel and award-winning film *Gentleman's Agreement* and the film *Crossfire.* In particular, the stories challenged the stereotype that Jewish men did not make good fighters. The villain of *Crossfire,* a soldier named Monty, murders a Jew named Samuels in an anti-Semitic rage, later asserting that Samuels and others like him "played it safe during the war." Yet, the audience learns that the Jewish victim was discharged from the army after being wounded. The Jewish character in *Gentlemen's Agreement* is also a soldier who did his part in the war.

The characters in Mailer's and Shaw's popular World War II novels were also patriotic contributors to their country's war effort. Shaw's hero, Noah, enlists when war breaks out and becomes an exemplary soldier. Nevertheless, he suffers brutal beatings when he confronts his fellow soldiers about their anti-Semitic taunts. Despite his small size, Noah has proved his masculinity; he is a fully American hero and calls to the reader to identify with him more than with any other character.

Similarly, the blond, blue-eyed, and thoroughly un-Semitic Goldstein of *The Naked and the Dead* has "overcome" his weakness and Jewishness by demonstrating his success as an American soldier.

Jewish characters use their fighting ability to overcome anti-Semitism as well as to recast the history of the Holocaust. The images of wartime destruction were still vivid in American culture in the late 1940s. The Holocaust appeared not only as a tragic episode of World War II, but it came to embody lessons about how to treat dictators and the nature of good and evil. Jews were at the center of this event, both as the ultimate victims and as heroic survivors. Ironically, Jews in the postwar period first symbolized a complete lack of masculinity for their role as victims and then masculine resurgence in their survival and construction of a new state.

During the late 1940s and early 1950s, the "tough Jew" was introduced to fiction as a character and role model. The term belongs to Paul Breines, who uses it to describe a type of Israeli/Jew who became prominent in American popular fiction after the 1967 victory enhanced the Israeli military reputation to legendary proportions. The ideal of a "tough Jew" was built on a set of traits long prized in American culture. Thus, tough Jews are "insiders" in American culture because they are seen to exemplify characteristics of ideal masculinity. This tough ideal of masculinity changed at different times in American history. For example, sociologist Rupert Wilkinson argues that, in its twentieth-century incarnation, the American tough guy is "masterful, dynamic, can take it, a stand up guy, a realist." According to Breines and other critics, Jewish characters with these traits appear in American fiction after Leon Uris created a Jewish superman in his 1958 novel *Exodus*; they argue that the tough Jew is the direct heir of Leon Uris.

Although *Exodus* is a major cultural landmark in the images of Israel and Jews, images of tough Israelis and Jews are found throughout the decade before Uris wrote the novel; their prevalence and acceptability paved the way for Uris and made *Exodus* a cultural touchstone. In 1947 and 1948, Irwin Shaw, Norman Mailer, and Laura Hobson created tough, honorable Jewish soldiers who were similar to other Americans. The characters in the novels *My Glorious Brothers, The Wall,* and *The Last Temptation* and in the films *The Sword in the Desert* and *The Juggler* display even greater physical prowess and machismo.

By the mid-1950s, the toughness of Jewish men was no longer a defensive response to Jewish victimhood and weakness, as it was in such novels as *The Young Lions* (1948). Physical prowess and battle skills now filled the iconographic contours of non-Jewish, American male heroes. The much-maligned, popular genre of biblical fiction in the late 1940s and 1950s illustrates the emphasis placed on the physical attributes of Jewish men. The heroes of biblical fiction have powerful necks, broad shoulders, and muscular physiques; they are the opposite of the stereotypical weak Jewish man. The physically powerful, masculine Jews are drawn in sharp contract to their enemies. In an early example of the biblical genre, Howard Fast writes that Greece's representative in Judea wears "a dainty little skirt and a dainty little tunic, and plead[s] with the world to examine the little he had under the skirt."

While emphasizing the fighting ability of the ancient Jews, most of these biblical narratives situate the audience in a position of the Jewish male protagonist who is threatened by the sexual wiles of a non-Jewish woman. The Jewish man as a sex symbol and pursuer of female attention further proved that Jews were similar to the ideal American man. This hyper-heterosexuality was an essential part of normality during the Cold War, when any sign of homosexuality was seen as a denial of masculine responsibility and an invitation to Communist subversion. Moreover, Hollywood has long used heterosexual temptation and resistance as a metaphorical test for strength of character and morality. The coded filmic language was therefore easily interpreted in the biblical films. This was especially true in the 1940s and 1950s when the film noir genre with this sexual subplot was at its most explicit. In biblical films and novels, the audience identifies with the Jewish man and, by extension, Jewish ethics; the pagan woman or religion is viewed as a threat to the moral order. In contrast, the Jewish women are mothers or symbolic mother figures; the inviolable maternal icon is the corallary to the iconographically masculine hero and the sexual temptress.

In addition to their physical attributes and ability to withstand the temptations of the flesh, the Jews of biblical films demonstrate their masculinity through their spiritual strength, a strength that many Americans felt as their own. That the Jews shared a religious heritage with most Americans was not insignificant in 1950s America. Dwight Eisenhower, who slept with a Bible by his bedside during his eight years in the White House, argued that "Our government makes no sense unless it is founded in a deeply religious faith—I don't care what it is." Eisenhower and many of his contemporaries felt that there was an inherent bond between Christians and Jews. Years later, Thomas Friedman termed the familiarity between Americans and Israelis "intuitive," because "we hear about [the Jews and Israel] every weekend in churches and synagogues across the Western world." Importantly, the Judeo-Christian heritage was for many a sign of strength in the face of "godless" communism and the emptiness of Soviet materialism. Agreeing with the sentiments of his boss, John Foster Dulles, once described by Samuel Flagg Bemis as "the only religious leader, lay or clerical, ever to become Secretary of State," argued that Jews and Americans both had gained strength from their spiritual identity: "Our Amerian history, like Hebrew history, is also rich in the story of men who through faith, wrought mightily." Finally, the identification between modern Americans and ancient Hebrews carries over to modern Jews and Israelis, because of the underlying message that modern Jews are the inheritors of and, indeed, the unique embodiment of ancient values and culture.

Also in the fiction of the mid- and late 1950s, the heroism of individual Jews and Israelis came to stand for the character of the State of Israel as a whole. The Jewish state was usually described in masculine terms. For example, the name "sabra" (a native-born Jewish Palestinian or Israeli) captured the popular imagination and became ubiquitous in Amerian fiction and journalism as a description of Israelis who were simultaneously tough and tender; the term refers to a desert cactus that is tough and prickly on the outside, sweet and tender on the inside. Moreover, the dual image was the ideal response to the helpless victims of the Holocaust. Israelis would defend themselves when threatened, but they still embodied the traditional characteristics of Jewish tenderness, sentimentality, and moral righteousness. *The Sword in the Desert,* *The Juggler,* and *The Last Temptation* all have their share of sabras. By the end of the decade, Ari, in Uris's *Exodus,* and his fellow hypermasculine Israelis summarize the virtues of the prototypical sabras. . . .

In an apparent challenge to traditional gender roles in postwar fiction, not all sabras are men. Many women in these novels and films also prove themselves to be tough Jews. One Kibbutz member in *The Juggler* easily carries a rifle, protecting her European male companion on a hike through the surrounding hills. The main character in *The Last Temptation,* Deborah, survives her husband's wrongful execution and becomes a pioneer fighting for the State of Israel; she is exhilarated by her own strength: "She was a gladiator now. She had slain dragons." Despite the impression that "sabra" may be a unisex category, it does not break down traditional gender roles but reinforces them. These women characters are judged to be tough to the extent that they are masculinized. The tough women have to sacrifice some of their own femininity in order to fight for their country. Deborah, conscious of her new role as defender of the state, turns down a proposal of marriage from her American lover after she unsuccessfully tries to picture herself as an American housewife. In *Exodus,* Kitty—a "real" American woman, so the narrator continually reminds us—compares herself with the coarse, unfeminine sabras such as Ari's sister. It is no accident that Ari's hypermasculinity is not satisfied by the tough Israeli women, and he finds himself drawn to the American.

Importantly, the fictional counterparts to these tough Israelis were their cowardly, unmasculine Arab adversaries. In contrast to the brave, controlled, and heroic Jews, the Arabs "swarm[ed]," "shriek[ed]," had "unnatural fear[s]," and were driven into "frenz[ies]." The Arabs were almost always caricatures rather than characters. A corollary stereotype in American fiction to the unmasculine Arab is the licentious Arab male. The prevalent image of sex-crazed Arabs not only reflects the gendered construction of a sexual threat but also the racist fears of sexuality of the darker Other. This type of character was unmanly because he was out of control—a wild monster as opposed to a mature adult.

Language signifying a link between sexual values and international politics was common in nonfiction discourse as well. One 1948 magazine article made the following distinction between Israelis and Arabs: "the Jews were too tough, too smart, and too vigorous for the divided and debilitated Arab world to conquer." Seven years later, an article in *Time* about Israel linked masculinity with Western political orientation: "Both Israel and Turkey were virile, modern and westward-looking inhabitants of an old, static and inward-looking region. . . . Turkey admires Israel's tough little army as the region's second best force . . . while Israelis see Turkey as the only other Middle East power of military significance." The article repeats what were, by 1955, increasingly familiar political and cultural descriptions of Israel's tough army and the country as an island in a hostile sea. Similarly, press accounts that celebrated Israel's new "realism" and "sobriety" attested to the state's masculine, unsentimental character. In addition to realism, another sign of masculinity was "maturity." As Barbara Ehrenreich argues, in 1950s parlance, "maturity" was a measure of masculinity: "Maturity was not dull," she concludes, "but 'heroic.' " Conforming to the stereotype of unmasculine Arabs, Egyptian leader Gamal Abdel Nasser, in contrast, uniformly labeled a "dictator," was deemed "immature" by journalists.

A corollary to this image of Israeli realism and toughness was the idea of a pioneering people achieving miraculous development in the desert. The image of Israel as a nation of pioneers was widespread in American culture. Israel's president, Chaim Weizmann, articulated a typical version of this image to Harry Truman in 1948: "Our pioneers have done yeoman work in opening up the semi-arid country."

Moreover, the idea that Israel was a nation of tough pioneers paralleled American cultural mythology and, therefore, reinforced an identification between the two countries. For example, in a 1957 letter to the president defending Israel's policy in the Suez war, Leonard Finder, a friend of Dwight Eisenhower, revealed the implications of this identification: "Israel's predicament is reminiscent of that of American pioneers a century ago when confronted with hostile Indians." Similar language was found in journalistic accounts; for example, in a 1948 article introducing Americans to the value of collectivized farms in Israel, *Time* magazine noted that "many are stockaded forts, built to protect pioneer settlers from Arab attacks."

The image of Israeli pioneers resonated with the mythic heritage of the Western frontier. Because it reminded Americans of their own rugged past, it allowed many to salve the anxiety that, with affluence, postwar American society was becoming "soft." . . . In the years of debate leading up to the formation of Israel in 1948, the helplessness of the Jewish refugees was emphasized in press and political accounts. This image of helplessness continued after the state was founded and is illustrated by what came to be one of the most potent images of Israel: the country as a newborn baby.

The metaphor implied a special relationship between Israel and the United States in which the latter was a parent to the baby state. This metaphor established Israel's insider status in two important ways. First, Israel is seen as an offspring or creation of the Untied States; there is no more fundamental expression of insider status. Similarly, Israel's status as a modern, Western power was affirmed when it was also dubbed a "child of the United Nations." Second, the metaphor made Israel integral to an assertion of American masculinity through the idea of symbolic immortality. Nancy Hartsock has pointed out that the search for immortality as a component of masculine ideology is often reflected in images of male birth. She writes that such images have been important in the history of war, such as in the creation of the atom bomb, or "Oppenheimer's baby." Interestingly, she notes, when Henry Stimson telegrammed Winston Churchill about successful detonation, he wrote "Babies satisfactorily born"; furthermore, the code for successful atom and hydrogen bomb tests was "It's a boy."

In the typology of Israel as a newborn baby, President Harry Truman played an essential role. Three days after the formation of Israel, Assistant Secretary of State Robert Lovett wrote that, while "the President's political advisors, having failed to . . . make the President a father of the new state, have determined at least to make him the midwife." That same day, Rabbi Samuel Thurman, of St. Louis, who had met Truman years before, wrote to the president: "America is now at Israel's cradle—virtually, as its mother. As such, it has a high responsibility—I trust, of no little maternal affection and concern. There is much nursing and nurturing to be done to make the new nation live and grow." The chief rabbi of Israel concurred with Thurman, telling the American president that "God put you in your mother's womb so that you could be the *instrument* to bring the rebirth of Israel." . . .

The metaphor of a baby Israel is not wholly inconsistent with the emphasis on Israel as a tough fighter. Both metaphors implied Israel's acceptance as an insider according to American masculine ideology. At the same time, the image of Israel as an infant was a flexible metaphor that signaled the nation's moral innocence and its presumed growth to maturity. The bridge between a new baby and a tough fighter was a third, equally prevalent, metaphor: Israel as an adolescent David facing a powerful Goliath. Not surprisingly, one common image of masculinity in American culture is of the gutsy underdog (as long as he is successful in his struggle). In fiction and nonfiction, the remarkable aspect of Israel's independence struggle was that the Jews banded together against heavy odds to fight for their land. During the war of independence, the myth quickly grew in the American media and among the partisans of Israel that the Jews faced overwhelming odds. The fictional descriptions of Israeli military abilities paralleled those found in the press; journalists frequently used phrases such as Israel's "tough little army." To be sure, Israel was not in fact a kid with slingshot facing a sword-wielding giant. CIA figures from 1948 showed that the Arab forces from Transjordan, Iraq, Egypt, Syria, Lebanon, Saudi Arabia, and Palestine totaled less than half the number of the Israeli forces. Ironically, the image of Israel as a youthful David coexisted with the idea that the Jewish state and Turkey were the only viable military allies in the region.

In the years after 1948, journalists and fiction writers continued to emphasize that the "young" Israel was continually threatened by its more numerous and brutal neighbors. Just weeks before the 1955 Czech-Egyptian arms deal was announced, a story on the Gaza raids began with a biblical quotation about retaliation for "transgressions" from Gaza and was told from the perspective of "young Israeli farmers who labor, gun in hand, in nearby desert settlements." After the arms deliveries, the press frequently mentioned how Israelis were "ringed by" Arabs and their "shiploads of arms from the communists." Similarly, stories explaining Israeli retaliation for border raids noted that "Every Israeli sleeps within 20 miles of an Arab knife." Another account of Israel's relationship with its neighbors argued that, "like the new kid in the rough neighborhood, Israel had to fight from the start." Many of the thousands of pro-Zionist letters to the White House drew a picture of a self-reliant state fighting against unfair circumstances and uneven odds. A typical letter came from American Federation of Labor president William Green, who wrote of tough, battle-tested, and deserving Israelis: "[Jerusalem] had been sanctified by the heroic defense which was made against the Arab attacks." Finally, popular fictional works that told the story of Israel's founding and early years *all* reiterated this David and Goliath story; these works included *The Last Temptation, The Sword in the Desert, The Juggler,* and *Exodus*. The idea that Israel was an innocent nation beset by hostile neighbors reflected Americans' perceptions of their own country's situation in the Cold War: threatened by expansionist communism. . . .

From sex symbols to tough fighters to youthful underdogs, Israelis filled the contours of stereotypical American masculinity. The Jews of popular discourse also proved themselves to be insiders in American culture through their image as sage fathers. Conforming to a gendered understanding of family roles and affirming their role as progenitors, Jews were depicted as strong fathers in their own right and inheritors of a patrilinial bond that they shared with the next generation. In Sholem Asch's *A Passage in the Night* and Myron Kaufmann's *Remember Me to God,* two rabbis fill the role of wise counselors to their youthful, rebellious charges. These rabbis make it clear that the young men's identity is based on the heritage that they received from their own fathers. The ideal father is not only wise, but he wants to protect his family. He demonstrates what were deemed the essential qualities of masculinity: maturity and responsibility. In *Gentleman's Agreement,* Phil, a reporter who pretends to be Jewish in order to investigate anti-Semitism, is most deeply wounded when his son is insulted for being Jewish. The character's Jewish friend, who has also had his masculinity and ability to protect his family challenged, says, "Now you know it all. Well you can quit being Jewish now. That's all there is to it." Given the centrality of the traditional family as a symbol of all that is good in Cold War America, it is not surprising that the moral struggle in many of these novels is over the sanctity and the future of the family. . . .

The Jews in popular discourse are also fathers to the "infant" State of Israel. In *Exodus*, Ari fiercely watches over the new nation. Twice Uris describes him with the biblical passage "Behold he that keepeth Israel shall neither slumber nor sleep." The same passage was used in a *Time* magazine article to describe Prime Minister David Ben Gurion. Israel's military strength in the face of Arab threats was personified in the frequent press profiles of Ben Gurion, who became a larger than life father figure. For example, one 1956 article in *Time* said that he "looks like an Old Testament patriarch" and was "a prophet who packs a pistol." Ben Gurion was described as a "watchman" over Israel and often pictured in a majestic profile. At the same time, most accounts include descriptions of his plain clothes, frugal habits, and long work days; clearly, Ben Gurion did not lead a "soft" life. One article describing him in May 1948 read, "The roughened hands of a laborer will hold the reins of government." As a symbol for all Jews, Ben Gurion's "tough past" was emphasized, and he was quoted saying, "Suffering makes a people greater." . . .

As Jews and Israelis proved their ability as fighters—both in the biblical tales as well as in the war of independence and the Suez war—they became more valuable as members of the Western, anti-Communist camp. U.S. policy in the Middle East (especially after 1955) became increasingly concerned with Cold War rivalries. Zionist supporters and Israelis saw the direction of U.S. policy and argued that Israel, unlike the Arab states, was a fellow democracy and would soon end its attempts to remain neutral in the Cold War. Prominent New York Democrat and former cabinet secretary Henry Morgenthau, for example, had assured Secretary of State Dean Acheson that Israel was "definitely on our side in the present East-West conflict." Many congressmen viewed Israel as Cold War ally long before the White House did. A typical view was expressed by Democratic Congressman William Barrett of Pennsylvania, who wired Eisenhower regarding arms for Israel in early 1956; he referred to the state as "our democratic *bulwark* in the Middle East." For years, congressmen had referred to Israel as a "bastion" for "freedom and peace." Media descriptions of Israel had consistently highlighted the similarity of political interests between Israel and America and the military value of the former to the latter; after Egypt accepted Soviet arms, positive descriptions of Israel's fighting ability became even more frequent.

Yet, long before the 1955 Czech arms sale, the suitability of Egypt as a Cold War ally was compromised by a whole set of images that set off Arabs as outsiders and challenged their masculinity. The references to Arab cowardice in *The Sword in the Desert* and, later, in *The Last Temptation* and *Exodus* reinforced the construction of an image of Jewish masculinity. Israelis became more valuable as democratic allies in the Middle East as they proved their mettle as fighters in opposition—both militarily and rhetorically—to the cowardly Arabs. One contemporary critic, agreeing with [the scholar] Walter Laqueur's warning about the vulnerability of the Arab states to

Communist subversion, concluded that communism might come to power because there was "nothing *virile* enough to resist it." A group of congressmen argued that the United States could not count on the Arabs, who "had proved themselves thoroughly unreliable during the last war." Moreover, Arabs were considered by some to be unprincipled fighters, described as "marauder," "irregulars," "devious," and willing to engage in "ambush[es]." During the Suez crisis, many news stories labeled the fighting ability of Egypt's army poor. And, one article reported that the army was "ill trained" and fought "mostly with windy communiques." . . .

In postwar America, the most vivid and widely understood designation of insider status in cultural and political discourse was the fulfillment of the masculine ideal. A gendered analysis of images of Israel in this period illustrates how ideas about the state were powerfully transformed along with changing ideas of Jewish masculinity. From the late 1940s to the late 1950s, Jews and Israelis were increasingly depicted as tough, pragmatic, masculine fighters similar to Americans. Within gendered Cold War discourse they, therefore, came to be perceived as valuable allies for the United States—not merely as a weak minority or a new nation to be protected. Popular fiction, media, and Washington foreign policies show evidence of this discursive transformation of Jews and Israelis. Fiction and nonfiction alike used familiar rhetorical codes to signal with whom the audience should identify and to evoke commonalities between Israelis and Americans. Ultimately, the foundation of the close political and military relationship between the two countries was reinforced by the emergence of masculine Israelis and their status as insiders in American political culture.

Cold War, Domestic Politics, and America's Strategic Ties with Israel, Iran, and Saudi Arabia

DOUGLAS LITTLE

The Sixties were a pivotal period in America's emerging relationship with the Middle East. The preceding decade and a half had been marked by unprecedented regional turmoil that defied the best efforts of the Truman and Eisenhower administrations to restore order. The discovery of rich new oil fields in Saudi Arabia and neighboring states had highlighted the growing economic importance of the Persian gulf as early as 1945. The creation of Israel, the gradual erosion of British and French influence, and the rising tide of Arab nationalism soon generated chronic political instability that flared into military crisis at Suez in November 1956. And America's deepening commitment to containing Russia along the "northern tier" that stretched from Turkey through Iran to Pakistan helped make the Middle East a central arena of the Cold War by the late 1950s.

John F. Kennedy hoped to reshape U.S. policy in the Middle East by downplaying global considerations and focusing instead on such regional obstacles to peace

From Douglas Little, "A Fool's Errand: America and the Middle East, 1961–1969," in *The Diplomacy of the Crucial Decade: American Foreign Relations in the 1960s* by Diane Kunz. Copyright © 1994 by Columbia University Press. Reprinted with permission of the publisher.

as the smoldering Arab-Israeli conflict and the chronic economic underdevelopment that plagued much of the Muslim world. To nudge Egyptian President Gamal Abdel Nasser and Israeli Prime Minister David Ben Gurion toward peace, Kennedy would provide Egypt with shiploads of surplus wheat and would sell Israel surface-to-air missiles. To inoculate the region's oil-rich sheikdoms and monarchies against revolutionary change, the Kennedy administration would promote social reform and political modernization from Tripoli to Teheran. And to avoid driving the Muslim radicals into the Kremlin's orbit, Kennedy would resort to personal diplomacy predicated on even-handed treatment of both the Arab states and Israel. By late 1963, however, this bold plan for the Middle East had been derailed by bitter disputes between Arab radicals and conservatives and by a deepening conviction among the Israelis and their friends on Capitol Hill that Kennedy's rapprochement with Nasser was foolish in the extreme.

Lyndon Johnson shared these grave doubts about Kennedy's recent initiatives and took steps as early as the spring of 1964 to distance himself from Middle East policies he regarded as increasingly foolhardy. Troubled by Nasser's flirtation with the Kremlin and by his vocal support for anti-Western liberation movements from the banks of the River Jordan to the shores of the Red Sea, Johnson suspended U.S. wheat shipments to Egypt in 1965 and moved to isolate the Arab radicals. By the spring of 1967, America had clearly chosen sides in the Middle East, quietly aligning itself with both Israel and Nasser's conservative Muslim rivals. . . .

Kennedy . . . was no neophyte when it came to the Middle East. Two visits to Israel had left Congressman Kennedy with an abiding respect for Zionist pioneers like Ben Gurion, who were carving a Jewish state out of an extremely hostile political and geographic environment. Four years on the Foreign Relations Committee had left Senator Kennedy with grave doubts about the Eisenhower administration's tendency to write Nasser and other Arab nationalists off as mere Soviet stooges. And the overwhelming support candidate Kennedy received from American Jews during the extraordinarily tight 1960 election left him with renewed appreciation for the potential importance of Middle Eastern diplomacy in domestic political affairs. "Kennedy was the most knowledgeable man on the Middle East in the top echelon of his administration," [NSC staffer] Robert Komer recalled shortly after the tragedy in Dallas. "The President was his own Secretary of State in dealing with what we might loosely call Middle East affairs."

Soviet gains elsewhere in the Third World had convinced the new president that there was little time to waste in the Middle East. Fidel Castro, Patrice Lumumba, and other left-wing nationalists had recently come to power in Latin America and Africa with the Kremlin's blessing, and just days before Kennedy entered the Oval Office Khrushchev had trumpeted Soviet support for wars of national liberation around the globe. Well aware that the UAR [United Arab Republic, formed by Egypt and Syria in 1958] had been buying Russian arms for five years, Kennedy used personal diplomacy to signal Nasser early on that the New Frontier would embrace a "fair-minded and even-handed" approach to the Middle East. Convinced that the road to regional stability ran through Cairo, Kennedy initiated a cordial correspondence with Nasser in which American economic aid for the UAR was implicitly linked to the Egyptian leader's willingness to tone down his anti-Israeli rhetoric. By mid-summer, Ambassador [John] Badeau reported that Nasser was eager to place the Arab-Israeli confrontation "in the icebox" so that he might focus on more pressing matters closer to home like economic development and social reform. Syria's unexpected secession from the UAR in September 1961 constituted a serious blow to Nasser's prestige and prompted speculation in Cairo and other Arab capitals that the CIA had orchestrated events in Damascus. By delaying U.S. recognition of the new Syrian government and by continuing to hint that large amounts of American economic aid might soon be on the way to Egypt, however, the Kennedy administration managed to keep its rapprochement with Nasser on track during the autumn of 1961.

Early in the New Year, JFK sent two high-ranking emissaries to Cairo to put the finishing touches on a three-year agreement to provide Egypt with half a billion dollars in surplus American wheat under the auspices of Public Law 480 (PL-480), the Food for Peace Program. Chester Bowles, Kennedy's ambassador-at-large to the Third World, arrived in Cairo in mid-February 1962. Finding the Egyptians far more pragmatic and far less ideological than he had imagined, Bowles saw little danger that the UAR would gravitate into the Kremlin's orbit. Indeed, the real danger was that the United States might miss a unique opportunity to employ economic leverage to accelerate Egypt's tilt toward the West. "If Nasser can gradually be led to forsake the microphone for the bulldozer," Bowles cabled the White House at the end of his visit, "he may assume a key role in bringing the Middle East peacefully into our modern world." Edward S. Mason, a Harvard specialist in international development who paid a visit to Cairo at Kennedy's request a month later, drew much the same conclusion. By fostering "effective economic cooperation with the UAR," Mason believed that the United States could prevent the spread of "political and social unrest" in the Arab world and avoid "increasing dependence on the Soviet Union which Nasser is currently loathe to see happen." Kennedy accepted Bowles and Mason's recommendations and initialed the three-year PL-480 wheat deal on June 30, 1962.

Closer relations between Washington and Cairo produced little joy in Israel. Unpersuaded that Nasser was seriously committed to an accommodation between Arab and Jew, Prime Minister Ben Gurion suspected that the Egyptians had placed their crusade against Israel on the back burner, not in the refrigerator. Ben Gurion shared his suspicions with Kennedy in May 1961 when the two men met at New York City's Waldorf Astoria. Kennedy replied that Israel must be more flexible in handling the plight of the 500,000 Palestinian refugees who huddled in squalid camps that dotted Jordan's strategically important West Bank.

After reluctantly agreeing to cooperate with the United Nations in resolving the refugee question, Ben Gurion pressed for a quid pro quo. Claiming that the recent arrival of Soviet tanks and bombers in Cairo had created a dangerous military imbalance in the Middle East, Ben Gurion asked Kennedy to sell Israel several batteries of HAWK anti-aircraft missiles. The president listened carefully, not least because he feared that in the absence of a conventional deterrent against Arab aggression, Israel might soon develop nuclear weapons. Six months earlier, during the waning days of the Eisenhower administration, the CIA had confirmed that Israel was building a large nuclear reactor at Dimona in the Negev desert capable of producing enough weapons-grade plutonium to build a small atomic bomb. . . . Although the minutes of his meeting with Ben Gurion at the Waldorf in May remain classified, Kennedy apparently insisted that the prime minister reaffirm his earlier pledge that the Dimona facility would be used only for peaceful purposes before the Pentagon began to review Israel's request for HAWK missiles.

Convinced that an equitable solution to the Palestinian question would do more to ensure Israel's security than would U.S. arms, Kennedy quietly arranged for U.N. Secretary General Dag Hammarskjold to ask Joseph Johnson, head of the Carnegie Endowment for Peace, to develop a refugee resettlement plan. After shuttling among Middle Eastern nations for nearly a year, in July 1962 Johnson unveiled a scheme calling for the resettlement of up to 100,000 Palestinians inside Israel in exchange for Arab pledges to settle their differences with the Israelis peacefully. To win Israel's approval, the United States was prepared secretly to "provide financial help (plus a security guarantee)." The reaction in Israel was predictable. Unwilling to accept what would amount to a "fifth column" inside the Jewish state, Ben Gurion and Foreign Minister Golda Meir insisted that bilateral U.S. military aid for Israel, not multilateral U.N. diplomatic initiatives with the Arabs, was the key to regional peace and stability.

The Johnson Plan would almost certainly have been dead on arrival had not the Kennedy administration linked it to something the Israelis wanted badly— HAWK missiles. Kennedy sent Myer Feldman [the president's deputy special counsel and liaison to Jewish leaders and pro-Israeli members of Congress] to Israel to inform Ben Gurion and Meir that the United States was prepared to sell them an antiaircraft system on favorable credit terms provided that the Israelis agreed to consider the refugee scheme and renewed their earlier pledge not to go nuclear. Once Israel agreed to review the Johnson Plan and to permit outside inspection of the Dimona reactor, Washington approved the HAWK sale in mid-September, just six weeks before the off-year Congressional elections. Because Kennedy had taken pains to inform Nasser about the arms deal in advance, there was little anti-American invective in the Egyptian press. By the autumn of 1962, Kennedy had every reason to be pleased with the results of his Middle East initiative. Wheat for Egypt, weapons for Israel, and a liberal dose of his own legendary personal magic for both Nasser and Ben Gurion raised hopes in Washington for a comprehensive regional settlement before the end of Kennedy's first term.

Before the year was out, however, Washington's even-handed policies were drawing heavy fire from Muslim conservatives who regarded the rapprochement with Cairo as shockingly naive. American relations with Iran, Saudi Arabia, and other traditional regimes in the Middle East had soured considerably after Kennedy signalled his support for political and social change. The Shah of Iran, for example, bitterly resented American calls for political liberalization after riots rocked Teheran in May 1961. Although he grudgingly agreed to trim his military spending in order to concentrate on "the task of building a strong anti-Communist society through social reform and economic development," the Shah reminded Kennedy and Rusk during an April 1962 visit to Washington that "we are not your stooges." Saudi Arabia's King Saud and Libya's King Idris likewise bridled at U.S. pressure to liberalize their regimes. . . .

Not surprisingly, rumors that Britain might scale back its presence East of Suez prompted the Shah and other Middle East autocrats to question whether America would be prepared to fill the ensuing vacuum. To be sure, Kennedy had stood firm in the face of Iraqi efforts to topple the Emir of Kuwait in July 1961 and supported a

British show of force designed to signal continued Western support for the oil-rich regimes that rimmed the Persian Gulf. But by mid-1962, many Muslim conservatives feared that America's rapprochement with Egypt and Kennedy's calls for change might spark revolutions of rising expectations from Tripoli to Teheran. Ominous events in Yemen, an archaic land at the southwest tip of the Arabian Peninsula, soon confirmed that such fears were not far-fetched. On September 26, Colonel Abdallah al-Sallal and other pro-Nasser Yemeni officers overthrew Imam Mohammad al-Badr, proclaimed a republic, and laid claim to disputed territory next door in Saudi Arabia and Britain's Aden protectorate. Bankrolled by the House of Saud and the British, al-Badr mounted a guerrilla war against the new republic regime. After Sallal requested Nasser's support in combating al-Badr's insurgents, the first contingent of what would become a 70,000-man Egyptian expeditionary force armed with tanks and planes left for Yemen in early October. . . .

Like the Saudis, the Israelis had always believed that Kennedy's trust in Nasser was misplaced. Egyptian intervention in Yemen deepened Ben Gurion and Meir's doubts about the Johnson Plan to resettle thousands of Arab refugees in Israel, as did Palestinian efforts to overthrow Jordan's King Hussein in January 1963. After military coups spearheaded by the Ba'ath, a pan-Arab socialist party with links to Nasser, brought radical anti-Israel regimes to power in Syria and Iraq later that winter, Israel scuttled the Johnson Plan and focused instead on building up its arsenal to combat Arab encirclement. By mid-March the CIA worried that the wave of radicalism sweeping the Arab world might accelerate Israel's plans to develop a nuclear deterrent, with disastrous implications for American interests in the Middle East.

Kennedy moved to prevent such an eventuality by distancing himself from Egypt, by reassuring Israel, and by seeking a regional arms limitation agreement. When pro-Nasser demonstrators nearly toppled King Hussein in April, Kennedy moved the Sixth Fleet into the Eastern Mediterranean and warned Egypt to stop meddling in Jordan. A few weeks later he reiterated America's longstanding commitment to the territorial integrity and independence of all states in the Middle East, including Israel. And in June, Kennedy sent John J. McCloy, his special coordinator for disarmament, to Cairo to urge that Nasser begin disengaging from Yemen and that he curb Egypt's arms purchases from the Soviet Union.

When McCloy returned empty-handed, Kennedy began to reconsider his entire even-handed approach to the Middle East. By early October, Kennedy was willing to give informal but explicit assurances to both Levi Eshkol, Ben Gurion's more moderate successor, and Crown Prince Faisal that the United States would provide military assistance in the event of an Egyptian attack on Israel or Saudi Arabia. He also warned Nasser that unless UAR troops pulled out of Yemen and unless Arab radicals ceased their anti-Israel diatribes, irresistible pressure would mount on Capitol Hill to reverse Washington's rapprochement with Cairo. Kennedy's prophecy was fulfilled two weeks later when the Senate adopted Ernest Gruening's amendment to the 1963 foreign aid bill, banning Food for Peace shipments to any nation engaged in aggressive action against any country receiving U.S. economic or military assistance. Oil company lobbyists fearful that Nasser would use Yemen as a springboard for an all-out assault on Saudi Arabia had worked closely with friends of Israel to round up the votes necessary to cut off American aid for Egypt. By the time Kennedy left for

Dallas in November 1963, then, mounting inter-Arab friction in Yemen, growing concerns about Israel's nuclear capability, and congressional second-guessing about foreign aid had led him to shift away from his earlier even-handed Middle East policies and toward an approach based on closer relations with Israel and the muslim conservatives. Lyndon B. Johnson would accelerate that shift.

Like most vice presidents, Lyndon Johnson had been overshadowed by the man in the White House. Although his role in shaping foreign policy during the Kennedy years was relatively limited, when he entered the Oval Office in late 1963 Johnson brought with him strong views and considerable knowledge about the Middle East. One of the most outspoken congressional supporters of the Jewish state from its inception in 1948 through 1960, Senator Johnson had been more sympathetic than his colleague from Massachusetts toward Israel in the aftermath of the 1956 Suez crisis. Less tolerant of Third World nationalism than Kennedy, Vice President Johnson returned from an August 1962 visit to Iran, Lebanon, and Turkey convinced that America must do more to prevent "communist expansion to the oil of the Middle East" by reversing Soviet inroads in Egypt and elsewhere in the "chaotic Arab world."

President Johnson surrounded himself with friends and advisers who shared his own more pro-Israel and anti-Soviet attitudes toward the Middle East. He selected Minnesota Senator Hubert H. Humphrey, a vocal supporter of Israel, as his running mate in 1964, named Arthur Goldberg, an ardent Zionist, as U.S. ambassador to the United Nations in 1965, and appointed the avowedly pro-Israel Rostow brothers to key posts in 1966—Walt as [McGeorge] Bundy's successor as national security adviser and Eugene as Under Secretary of State. Johnson's "kitchen cabinet" included Supreme Court Justice Abe Fortas, a staunch friend of Israel, and other prominent members of the American Jewish community, including Democratic party fundraisers Abe Feinberg and Arthur Krim. AIPAC's [American-Israeli Political Action Committee] Isaiah "Si" Kenen was a frequent visitor to the White House, as was Ephraim "Eppie" Evron, Israel's deputy chief of mission in Washington. . . .

Nasser's encouragement for the anti-Israel crusade waged by West Bank Palestinians, his calls for revolutionary change among the sheikdoms and monarchies of the Arab East, and his support for a variety of pro-Soviet liberation movements helped bring Egypt's relations with America to the breaking point during 1964. Just two months after Kennedy's death, Nasser unveiled plans to create a Palestine Liberation Organization (PLO), whose chief objective was to be the destruction of Israel. Worse still, during the spring of 1964, Egypt secretly began to funnel aid to Marxist rebels who sought to sabotage Britain's plans to convert its Aden protectorate into an independent pro-Western South Arabian Federation. The Kremlin's hand in all this loomed larger in May, when Soviet premier Nikita Khrushchev echoed Nasser's support for the PLO and called for the "liquidation of foreign military bases in Libya, Oman, Cyprus, [and] Aden." . . .

Pressure had been building among Israel's friends on Capitol Hill for months for Johnson to invoke the Gruening amendment and cut off all PL-480 wheat shipments to Egypt. As late as September 1964 the White House remained reluctant to cancel the UAR's Food for Peace allotment because in the past the Egyptians had responded to American economic pressure by moving closer to the Soviets. But Nasser's unwillingness to halt plans to buy guided missiles from the Kremlin and his vitriolic attacks on U.S. intervention in the Congolese civil war later that fall tested the limits of Johnson's patience. After pro-Nasser students burned the United States Information Agency offices in Cairo to the ground on November 26, Johnson summoned the Egyptian ambassador to the White House and exploded: "How can I ask Congress for wheat for you when you burn down our library?" When Egyptian MIGs downed an unarmed American cargo plane that had strayed into UAR airspace three weeks later, killing its two-man crew, Washington hinted that there would be no further U.S. aid until Cairo made amends. Outraged by what he regarded as a crude attempt at diplomatic blackmail, Nasser told a huge crowd gathered on the banks of the Suez Canal on December 23 that "those who do not accept our behavior can go and drink from the sea." Lest Johnson miss the point, Nasser added: "And if the Mediterranean is not enough to slake their thirsts, . . . they can carry on with the Red Sea." . . .

Inspired by Nasser's strident rhetoric, Yasser Arafat and other PLO radicals formed Fatah, a paramilitary group that by mid-1965 was staging hit-and-run raids inside Israel from bases on the West Bank. Eight months later a "radical military clique" including Colonel Hafez al-Assad staged a bloody coup in Syria, embraced the Palestinian cause, and established "close ties with the Communist bloc." . . .

The rising tide of Arab radicalism merely confirmed Israel's judgment that Kennedy's earlier rapprochement with Nasser had been misguided and highlighted the necessity of consummating the special relationship between Israel and America that Lyndon Johnson was rumored to favor. "You have lost a very great friend," the new president told an Israeli diplomat shortly after Kennedy's death. "But you have found a better one." The Israelis wasted little time ascertaining whether Johnson meant what he said. Pointing out that Kennedy had promised that the United States would preserve the military balance in the Middle East, Israeli Prime Minister Levi Eshkol requested American M-48 battle tanks and A-4 Skyhawk jet fighters in early 1964 to offset recent Soviet arms deliveries to Nasser.

Nevertheless, many in Washington questioned whether Israel really needed such sophisticated weaponry. The Pentagon, for example, saw no numerical imbalance between the Arab and Israeli arsenals and suspected that Eshkol sought to drive a wedge between Egypt and America in order to upgrade Israel's "tactical offensive capabilities." The State Department agreed and urged Johnson not to sell Israel tanks or planes but rather to launch a new round of regional arms limitations talks instead. . . .

The White House worked for eight months to arrange a three-cornered arms deal calling for the United States to ship 250 new M-48s to West Germany, which in turn would transfer 250 older tanks from its own arsenal to Israel. Once news of the arrangement leaked to the press, however, West German Chancellor Ludwig Erhard backed out in early 1965, prompting Israel to renew its request to purchase tanks directly from the United States. U.S. officials balked, and tensions mounted in February after Eshkol learned that America was considering arms sales to Jordan,whose military policies were influenced increasingly by King Hussein's half-million Palestinian subjects bent on the destruction of Israel. Eager to resolve the problem, Johnson sent diplomatic troubleshooter Averell Harriman and NSC Middle East expert Robert Komer to Israel in late February. Eshkol and his cabinet refused to acquiesce in U.S. arms sales to Jordan unless the Johnson administration provided comparable weapons to Israel. Worse still, the Israelis evidently hinted that they were prepared to develop a nuclear deterrent against Arab aggression. . . .

Determined to "keep up pressure on Israel not to go nuclear," Secretary of State Dean Rusk recommended that Johnson approve the sale of M-48 tanks to Israel in April 1965. Lest the Israelis forget the major reason for this relatively more accommodating American policy on arms sales, however, Rusk reminded them on April 21 that "we continue unalterably opposed to [the] proliferation [of] nuclear weapons." No sooner was the tank deal completed than Israel moved to upgrade its air force by requesting supersonic F-4 Phantom jets capable of carrying atomic bombs. Once again Washington urged the Israelis to seek aircraft in Bonn and Paris, and once again they came up empty-handed. To avoid another lengthy round of haggling during an election year, Johnson approved the sale of 48 slower A-4 Skyhawks on March 23, 1966. . . .

While some American policymakers struggled to prevent events in Jordan from transforming an Arab-Israeli cold peace into a hot war, others pondered how best to shore up the sagging Western position in the Persian Gulf. Britain's deepening financial woes forced Whitehall reluctantly to announce the abandonment of its huge naval base at Aden in February 1966 and the liquidation of the rest of its military installations east of Suez a year later. Having tried unsuccessfully to persuade the British to reconsider, the Johnson administration scrambled to prevent a vacuum in a region whose strategic and economic importance was growing rapidly. By the mid-1960s, Saudi Arabia, Iran, and their smaller neighbors were exporting 3.5 billion barrels of petroleum annually, one-third of the Free World's output. Although the United States still received less than 10 percent of its oil from the Middle East, skyrocketing domestic consumption meant that American imports were bound to increase. Moreover, nearly three-quarters of Western Europe's petroleum imports continued to originate in the Persian Gulf, while Japan relied on Saudi and Iranian crude to meet almost all its energy needs. . . .

Among those most eager to replace Britain as guardian of the gulf was the Shah of Iran, who hoped to use his burgeoning oil revenues to purchase American arms and recapture the glory of the ancient Persian empire. Iranian-American relations had begun to improve in the months following Kennedy's death. Gambling that Johnson would be less interested in social reform than in the security of the Persian Gulf and its oil, as early as 1964 the Shah moved to position himself as America's most likely Muslim partner. In short order, he signed an accord with the United States that granted American extraterritorial privileges in Iran in exchange for a $200 million military aid package. After the agreement prompted fiery protests by Islamic fundamentalists like the Ayatollah Ruhallah Khomeini and left-wing nationalists like the Mujahadeen i-Khalq, the Shah unleashed his secret police, the dreaded SAVAK, to restore order with Washington's blessing.

By early 1966, the Iranian monarch made no secret that he was willing to assume Britain's mantle in the Persian Gulf and to supply Israel with all the oil it needed, provided the United States permitted Iran to purchase jet aircraft and other sophisticated weaponry. Pleased by Iran's emergence as a regional power, top U.S officials nevertheless worried that the Shah's proposed military spending spree would divert resources away from economic development and destabilize his regime. As a result, the Johnson administration adopted what U.S. Ambassador Armin Meyer termed a "papa knows best attitude" and insisted that the Shah scale back his arms request. The Shah refused, holding out instead for another $200 million arms package including supersonic F-4 Phantoms and hinting darkly that should he come up empty-handed in Washington, he might be forced to turn to Moscow. Unwilling to risk opening the door to fresh Kremlin inroads in the region, the White House changed course in August 1966 and adopted policies aimed, in the words of national security adviser Walt Rostow, at "keeping the Shah from going overboard." Before the year was out, Lyndon Johnson had approved a multi-million dollar arms deal and opened wide America's arsenal for its new found Iranian proxy.

The Shah's Iran was by no means the only conservative Muslim regime eager to cooperate with the United States in stabilizing the situation in the Persian Gulf. Since the early 1960s, Saudi Arabia, the largest and most thinly populated of the Arab oil states, had been seeking sophisticated weapons and other concrete signs of American support for its territorial integrity. The Johnson administration was quick to oblige newly crowned King Faisal, who had finally wrested the Saudi throne from his ailing brother Saud in a March 1964 palace coup. Nine months later, for example, a contingent from the U.S. Army Corps of Engineers arrived in Saudi Arabia to supervise the construction of a network of roads and military installations essential for the desert kingdom's internal security. When Faisal sought to upgrade his air force in April 1965, White House advisers thought it wise to "help him buy US planes" in order to "protect our billion dollar oil investment." And after Egyptian jets based in Yemen strafed targets inside Saudi Arabia later that year, Washington agreed to sell Riyadh ten batteries of HAWK surface-to-air missiles.

A tacit Saudi-American alliance blossomed during 1966. Early in the new year U.S. officials encouraged King Faisal to pursue plans for an "Islamic Pact" among traditional Middle Eastern regimes determined to combat Nasser's brand of revolutionary nationalism. When Faisal visited the White House in June 1966, LBJ personally reaffirmed earlier American pledges to protect the territorial integrity of Saudi Arabia. Johnson also promised to work with Faisal "to fill the gap the British will leave in South Arabia and the Persian Gulf." . . . Like Israel's Levi Eshkol and the Shah of Iran, King Faisal was emerging as one of America's staunchest allies in a very troubled part of the world.

By the autumn of 1966, top U.S. officials had begun to worry that growing ideological polarization in the Middle East might easily ignite the smoldering Arab-Israeli conflict into full-blown military conflagration. In September, Johnson himself commissioned a special report that "revealed a pattern of serious Soviet advances" in the Arab world, particularly in Egypt, Iraq, and Syria, where pressure for a showdown with Israel was mounting rapidly. As the year drew to a close, Radio Cairo was beaming fiery calls for the liberation of Palestine onto the West Bank, Iraqi pilots were learning to fly Soviet MIGs, and Syrian leaders were encouraging Yasser Arafat's Fatah to step up its raids on Israeli villages. . . .

The diplomatic witch's brew simmering in the Middle East that spring finally boiled over in early May. Claiming that Israel had mobilized twelve divisions for an assault on the [Syrian] Golan Heights, the Kremlin advised Nasser on May 13 that he might soon have to come to the aid of Syria. The Israelis denied that they had moved troops to the Syrian frontier and dismissed Moscow's allegations as a blend of misinformation and disinformation, a verdict borne out by recent scholarship.

Nasser, however, accepted the Soviet warning at face value and ordered Egyptian troops to prepare for a showdown with Israel. . . .

. . . Responding to fresh reports from Moscow and Damascus that Israel was about to strike Syria, Nasser sent troops across the Sinai on May 17 to replace the U.N. Emergency Force that had patrolled the no-man's-land between Egypt and Israel for a decade. "Some pretty militant public threats from Israel by Eshkol and others" had persuaded top U.S. officials that "the Soviet advice to the Syrians that the Israelis were planning to attack was not far off." As a result, Johnson warned Eshkol on May 18 that Israel must "not put a match to this fuse." Relieved by Israeli assurances that they did "not intend any military action," during the next forty-eight hours the White House pressed the Kremlin to use its influence among the Arabs "in the cause of moderation" and urged U.N. Secretary General U Thant to renew his efforts to secure a peaceful resolution of the Middle East crisis. As late as May 21, Johnson believed that if Israel continued "to display steady nerves," hostilities could be averted. The next day, however, Nasser escalated the crisis by prohibiting Israeli vessels from using the Straits of Tiran that connected the Gulf of Aqaba with the Red Sea. Reminding Johnson that President Eisenhower had pledged a decade earlier to keep the straits open to Israeli shipping, Eshkol let it be known that his government would regard Nasser's closure of the international waterway as an act of war.

While the Johnson administration scrambled to prevent Eshkol from taking pre-emptive action on May 23, an avalanche of letters and telegrams urging that Washington unleash Israel swamped the White House mailroom. Abe Feinberg, Arthur Krim, and other influential friends of Israel privately pressed their case inside the Oval Office. Johnson went on national television to denounce Nasser's action as "illegal and potentially disastrous to the cause of peace." He signalled America's continued support for Israel by releasing the long-awaited M-113 armored personnel carriers. And he urged the Israelis to be patient while he organized a multinational flotilla to challenge the Egyptian blockade.

The mood at the NSC meeting that Johnson convened the next day to review America's options, however, was very grim. "The issue in the Middle East today," the State Department explained in a background paper, "is whether Nasser, the radical states and their Soviet backers are going to dominate the area." . . . With Britain scaling back its presence east of Suez and with Egypt and Russia sponsoring the PLO, FLOSY [Front for the Liberation of South Yemen], and other Arab liberation movements, some expected America to "back down as a major power" in the Middle East. To prevent the erosion of U.S. credibility in the region, the State Department recommended quiet encouragement for Israel, Iran, and Saudi Arabia. . . .

According to General Earle Wheeler, Chairman of the Joint Chiefs of Staff, the presence of Egyptian submarines and attack planes in the Red Sea made it "harder to open the Gulf of Aqaba than we first thought." Although key portions of the NSC minutes have been "sanitized," some U.S. officials evidently feared that Israel was prepared to use "unconventional weapons" against Nasser's forces. Even without going nuclear, however, Wheeler was certain that "the Israelis can hold their own." CIA director Richard Helms agreed and warned that the biggest danger America faced was being "fully blackballed in the Arab world as Israel's supporter." . . .

For the next week, the White House worked nonstop to preserve peace. Johnson cabled Soviet premier Alexei Kosygin to urge the Kremlin to apprise Nasser of just how explosive the situation had become. He exhorted U.N. Secretary General U Thant to redouble his efforts to find a compromise between Arab and Jew. And he asked Robert Anderson, a Texas businessman and diplomatic troubleshooter who had served as Eisenhower's secret Middle East emissary during the mid-1950s, to fly to Cairo to discuss opening a private back-channel between Nasser and the White House. Anderson reported on June 2 that the Egyptian leader had promised not to attack Israel and actually seemed quite eager for a negotiated settlement. Hinting that he might be willing to refer the dispute over the Straits of Tiran to the World Court, Nasser agreed to send Vice President Zakaria Mohieddin to Washington for secret talks before the week was out.

But early on the morning of June 5, Israeli jets streaked across the Nile delta and destroyed Nasser's air force while it was still on the runway. When the guns fell silent six days later, Israel controlled not only Gaza and the Sinai but also the Golan Heights and the West Bank. In retrospect, the rationale behind Israel's surprise attack seems clear. On May 30, King Hussein had flown to Cairo, where he and Nasser announced an alliance between Jordan and Egypt, thus confronting Israeli military planners with the specter of a two-front war. More important, once the Israelis learned that Vice President Mohieddin would visit Washington, they suspected an American diplomatic doublecross that might leave Nasser in control of the Straits of Tiran and Israel bottled up in the Gulf of Aqaba. Israeli ambassador Avraham Harman raised these concerns with State Department officials on June 2, prompting Secretary of State Rusk to recall Johnson's earlier warning that Israel must not act alone. But when Harman discussed the Middle East crisis with Abe Fortas a few hours later, those cautionary words seemed far less categorical. According to Fortas, Johnson believed that "Rusk will fiddle while Israel burns." Lest the Israeli diplomat miss the point, Fortas added: "If you're going to save yourself, do it yourself." Israel did just that three days later.

Although Johnson evidently signalled his acquiescence in an Israeli first strike at the last moment, he soon had good reason to worry that the splendid little war would spiral into a superpower confrontation. Moments after the fighting erupted on June 5, Dean Rusk had flashed word to Soviet Foreign Minister Andrei Gromyko that the United States was working for a ceasefire under U.N. auspices. Once Israeli armor rolled across the Sinai on June 6 and into the West Bank the next day, Washington expected Israel to halt its offensive. . . .

Before the shooting stopped, however, Israel wished to settle one last score with Syria, which had taken Nasser's advice and stayed out of the war. Well aware that the Israelis had long coveted the Golan Heights that towered over the Sea of Galilee, the Pentagon apparently instructed the U.S.S. *Liberty*, a lightly armed intelligence ship stationed off the Sinai coast, to monitor Israeli military activities along the Syrian frontier. Just after noon on June 8, three waves of Israeli planes and torpedo boats attacked the surveillance vessel, ripping huge holes in its hull and leaving 34 sailors dead and another 171 wounded. While the *Liberty* limped back to port, Israel apologized for what it termed a tragic case of mistaken identity, an explanation many in Washington found hard to believe. Dean Rusk, for example, called the attack "literally incomprehensible," while Clark Clifford, a senior member of Bundy's

Special Committee and a longtime friend of Israel, snapped that it was "inconceivable it was [an] accident." In any case, just fifteen hours after the first rockets destroyed the *Liberty's* eavesdropping equipment and just eight hours after the ceasefire was supposed to have gone into effect, Israel launched a lightning assault on Syria which brought Israeli troops within sight of Damascus. The CIA believed that this move was "aimed at overthrowing the left-wing Baathist party which the Israelis blame for starting the entire Middle East crisis."

Few in Washington expected Moscow to stand aside while Israel accomplished its goal. "The Soviets [had] hinted," Dean Rusk recalled in his memoirs, "that if the Israelis attacked Syria, they would intervene with their own forces." Not surprisingly, the White House-to-Kremlin "Hot Line" lit up three times on June 10 with messages indicating that Soviet military action was imminent. Johnson moved swiftly to forestall such an eventuality. First, he sent word to Eshkol that he expected an effective ceasefire "without delay." Then he moved elements of the U.S. Sixth Fleet from Athens to the Eastern Mediterranean, where "Soviet submarines monitoring the Fleet's operations would report immediately to Moscow." In the end, Israel halted its offensive, Russia edged away from intervention, and everyone relaxed a bit as it became clear that the fighting was petering out."

Yet the lessons were clear. First, America's special relationship with Israel and Russia's special relationship with Nasser and the Arab radicals had brought the two superpowers perilously close to the brink of war. To prevent a replay, Lyndon Johnson and Soviet premier Alexei Kosygin would open a dialogue on the Middle East during their mini-summit at Glassboro, New Jersey in late June. Second, America's interests in the region were certain to be targeted by resurgent Arab revolutionary nationalists bent on avenging the recent military debacle. . . .

A more sharply defined American approach to the Middle East based on three pillars—Saudi Arabia, Iran, and Israel—had begun to take shape shortly after the guns fell silent in June 1967. Assuaging Saudi anger over U.S. acquiescence in Israel's preemptive war was absolutely essential if ARAMCO [Arabian-American Oil Company] and other U.S. firms were to retain their petroleum concessions in the Arab world. Led by the House of Saud, the Arabs had imposed an embargo on all oil shipments to America and Britain on June 6. A week later, Persian Gulf petroleum exports had plummeted sixty percent, the American-owned Trans-Arabian Pipeline that carried Saudi crude to the Eastern Mediterranean had been dynamited, and left-wing oil workers had shut down refineries from Baghdad to Beirut. U.S. and U.K. officials managed to lessen the impact of the embargo by convening an "Emergency Oil Supply Committee" to help Standard Oil of New Jersey, British Petroleum, and other multinational giants divert Western Hemisphere crude to Western Europe. What finally killed the embargo, however, was growing friction between the conservative Arabs who controlled oil production and the radical Arabs who brandished the oil weapon. Convinced that "restrictions on oil export are harming the Arab producers more than the boycotted nations," the Saudis permitted ARAMCO to resume operations in late June. . . .

. . . Grateful that the Saudis had lifted their oil boycott, Johnson authorized the Pentagon to provide the House of Saud with a $25 million package of nonlethal military equipment including four C-130 transport aircraft on June 30. Seven weeks later the State Department agreed to expedite the export licenses the Saudis required to purchase another $50 million worth of HAWK missiles from the Raytheon company. Although the Shah of Iran may not have been a good Arab, or even an Arab at all, the Johnson administration certainly regarded his refusal to embargo oil shipments to Israel and the United States during the Six Day War as a Persian sign of good faith that, like Faisal's, was well worth rewarding. During the last half of 1967, Washington stepped up its economic aid for Iran and encouraged the Shah to work closely with Saudi Arabia in planning for regional defense. . . .

Top U.S. officials continued to wrestle with how best to handle Israel throughout the summer of 1967. Acquiescing in Israel's seizure of East Jerusalem, the West Bank, and the Golan Heights, Rusk told the NSC Special Committee on June 14, could "create a revanchism for the rest of the 20th c[entury]." Even worse, many in Washington feared that a lengthy territorial stalemate would "probably increase pressure favoring going nuclear in both Israel and the Arab states." In light of these concerns, President Johnson placed the Middle East at the top of the agenda during his hastily scheduled summit meeting with Soviet Premier Alexei Kosygin at Glassboro, New Jersey, in late June. Unless America could persuade Israel "to withdraw its forces back to the original [prewar] armistice line," Kosygin warned Johnson, "hostilities were certain to break out again." Likening the Arab-Israeli dispute to a family disagreement between younger siblings, Johnson maintained that "it was up to the older brothers to provide proper guidance." This meant, he continued, Soviet-American agreement to work through the United Nations to resolve the territorial question plus fresh efforts by Washington and Moscow to achieve regional arms limitation. Although Kosygin refused to discuss arms limitation until the Kremlin was able to redress the military imbalance created by Israel's destruction of Egypt's arsenal in the Six Day War, he did pledge to cooperate with Johnson in arranging a U.N.-backed territorial settlement.

By early autumn, the elements of a "peace for land" compromise had begun to take shape at U.N. headquarters in New York City. In exchange for Arab acknowledgment of both Israel's right to exist and its right to use the Straits of Tiran, the Israelis would return those areas they had seized from their neighbors in June. Because this fell considerably short of the formal settlement complete with peace treaties and diplomatic recognition that the Israelis desired, however, they balked at restoring the prewar status quo and insisted that some territorial adjustments were necessary to ensure their security. As a result, before the U.N. Security Council adopted Resolution 242 on November 22 calling for "withdrawal of Israeli armed forces from all territories occupied in the recent conflict," the United States arranged to have the word "all" stricken, creating enough ambiguity to permit Israel to stake a claim to parts of the West Bank and the Golan Heights.

Having thus demonstrated America's commitment to Israeli security, Washington was disappointed by Israel's unwillingness to comply speedily with Resolution 242. Nor were American policymakers happy about rumors that Israel was secretly pursuing its nuclear option at Dimona. . . .

. . . Well into the fall, top U.S. officials insisted that Israel must take concrete steps to implement Resolution 242 . . . before the White House would authorize the sale of the F-4 Phantoms Eshkol had requested in January. With the PLO escalating its operations and with the 1968 presidential election looming, however, pro-Israeli pressure groups on Capitol Hill and Main Street lobbied hard for the release of the suspersonic jets on Israel's wish list. Although Johnson had renounced his own plans for a second term in March, Abe Feinberg and other influential friends of Israel insisted that selling the Jewish state Phantoms might provide just enough swing votes to keep California and New York in the Democratic column in what was expected to be an extraordinarily close election in November. In early October, AIPAC persuaded seventy U.S. senators to sign an open letter urging the president to provide Israel with F-4s as soon as possible. After receiving fresh assurances that Israel accepted the peace-for-land principles outlined in U.N. Resolution 242 and that Israel would not be the first nation to introduce nuclear weapons into the Middle East, Johnson informed Eshkol in late November that the Israelis would soon receive the Phantom jets they had long coveted.

By the time Lyndon Johnson handed the Oval Office over to Richard Nixon and returned home to the banks of the Padernales in January 1969, then, he and his advisers regarded Israel—and Iran and Saudi Arabia too—as strategic assets essential to the containment of Soviet influence in the Muslim world. This meant opening wide the door of America's conventional arsenal to the Israelis both to ensure that they outgunned the Arab radicals and to discourage them from going nuclear. It meant placing a higher premium on military security and political stability than on social reform in Iran, Saudi Arabia, and other oil-rich states threatened by revolutionary change. It meant terminating American efforts to woo Nasser with surplus wheat, technical assistance, and personal diplomacy. But despite AIPAC and oil industry support for the new three pillars approach, it did not mean that the Johnson administration had succumbed to interest group politicking. Rather, when it came to the Middle East, strategic concerns like nuclear nonproliferation and secure access to Persian Gulf petroleum were at least as important in shaping Johnson's policies as domestic political considerations.

Not long after Johnson returned to the Lone Star State, however, his quest for regional stability began to unravel. From the Suez Canal to the banks of the River Jordan, Arab and Israeli forces waged an escalating "war of attrition." From Tripoli to Teheran, the Organization of Petroleum Exporting Countries (OPEC) was beginning to challenge western control of Middle East oil. And from Radio Cairo came word that several thousand Soviet military advisers were on their way to Egypt, where they would help Nasser rebuild the war machine Israel had crippled in June 1967. Bedeviled by intractable Arab-Israeli tensions, increasingly polarized by Soviet-American rivalry, soon to be enriched by growing oil revenues, the Middle East was rapidly becoming a battleground where East confronted West and North confronted South. In the long run, then, Johnson's Middle East policies were no more successful than Kennedy's. A quarter century after Big Daddy from the Padernales left office, a nuclear-armed Israel sits atop a Palestinian powderkeg on the West Bank, radical regimes in Baghdad and Teheran threaten western access to Persian Gulf oil, and 50,000 U.S. troops stand guard in Saudi Arabia to prevent the House of Saud from going the way of Iran's Pahlavi dynasty. Will the end of the Cold War, the start of Israeli-Palestinian peace talks, and changing patterns of American petroleum consumption tempt new fools to undertake an old errand on the outside chance the world may call them genius?

Oil, Revolution, and Jimmy Carter's Iran Debacle

DANIEL YERGIN

On the last day of 1977, President Jimmy Carter, en route from Warsaw to New Delhi in the course of a hectic three-continent trip, arrived in Tehran. He said he had asked Mrs. Carter where she wanted to spend New Year's Eve, and she had said with the Shah and his wife, so delightful a time had the Carters had when the royal couple visited Washington six weeks earlier. Yet there were reasons of realpolitik as much as sentiment behind their choice. Carter had been impressed by the Shah. The Shah, for his part, was taking significant steps toward liberalization and was talking about human rights. With a new understanding between the two men, Carter was now in position to better appreciate the strategic roles of Iran and its leader than when he had first come into office. Iran was a fulcrum country, essential to stability in the region. It was a critical element in counterbalancing Soviet power and ambitions in the area, as well as those of radical and anti-Western forces. It was central to the security of the world's oil supplies, both as one of the world's two major exporters and as a regional power.

Carter also wanted to show his gratitude to the Shah for his progress on human rights and his switch of position on oil prices, which was seen as a major concession on the part of the monarch. Moreover, the President was regretful and embarrassed over the rioting and tear gas that had greeted the Shah's arrival on the South Lawn of the White House, and he wanted to clear up any misunderstandings, within Iran and outside the country, and firmly underline American support. So, at a New Year's Eve banquet, he rose to offer a memorable toast. "Iran, because of the great leadership of the Shah, is an island of stability in one of the more troubled areas of the world," he said. "This is a great tribute to you, Your Majesty, and to your leadership, and to the respect and the admiration and the love which your people give you." On that strong and hopeful note, the President and the Shah welcomed the momentous New Year of 1978.

Not everyone saw the same island of stability that the President had described. Shortly after Carter's visit, the president of one of the independent American oil companies active in Iran came back from a trip to Tehran. He had a confidential message he urgently wanted to share with one of his directors. "The Shah," he said, "is in big trouble." . . .

It had become evident in the mid-1970s that Iran simply could not absorb the vast increase in oil revenues that was flooding into the country. The petrodollars, megalomaniacally misspent on extravagant modernization programs or lost to waste and corruption, were generating economic chaos and social and political tension throughout the nation. The rural populace was pouring from the villages into the already-overcrowded towns and cities; agricultural output was declining, while food imports were going up. Inflation had seized control of the country, breeding all the inevitable discontents. A middle manager or a civil servant in Tehran spent up to 70 percent of his salary on rent. Iran's infrastructure could not cope with the pressure suddenly thrust upon it; the backward railway system was overwhelmed; Tehran's streets were jammed with traffic. The national electricity grid could not meet demand, and it broke down. . . .

Iranians from every sector of national life were losing patience with the Shah's regime and the pell-mell rush to modernization. Grasping for some certitude in the melee, they increasingly heeded the call of traditional Islam and of an ever more fervent fundamentalism. The beneficiary was the Ayatollah Khomeini, whose religious rectitude and unyielding resistance made him the embodiment of opposition to the Shah and his regime and indeed to the very character and times of Iran in the mid-1970s. Born around 1900 in a small town 180 miles from Tehran, Khomeini came from a family of religious teachers. His father had died a few months after his birth, killed on the way to a pilgrimage by a government official, it was said by some. His mother died when he was in his teens. Khomeini turned to religious studies and, by the 1930s and 1940s, was a popular lecturer on Islamic philosophy and law, promulgating the concept of an Islamic Republic under the stern control of the clergy.

For many years, Khomeini had regarded the Pahlavi regime as both corrupt and illegitimate. But he did not become politically active until about the age of sixty, when he emerged as a leading figure in the opposition to the "White Revolution," as the Shah's reform program was called. In 1962, Khomeini expressed outrage at the proposal that places in local assemblies no longer be restricted exclusively to male Moslems. When, under the rubric of the White Revolution, the government redistributed large estates, including the vast holdings of the Shiite clergy, Khomeini came forward as one of the most unyielding opponents, landing in jail more than once and eventually ending up in exile in Iraq. His hatred of the Shah was matched only by his detestation of the United States, which he regarded as the main prop of the Pahlavi regime. His denunciations from exile in Iraq were cast in the rhetoric of blood and vengeance; he seemed to be driven by an unadulterated anger of extraordinary intensity, and he himself became the rallying point for the growing discontent. The words of other, more moderate ayatollahs were overwhelmed by the exile's harsh and uncompromising voice.

Another dimension of opposition had emerged. With Jimmy Carter's capture of the Democratic nomination and then the Presidency in 1976, human rights became a major issue in United States foreign policy, and the human rights record of the Shah was not good. It was also typical of much of the Third World, and better than that of some other countries in the region. A member of the International Commission of Jurists, who was a leading critic of the Shah and who investigated human rights conditions in Iran in 1976, concluded that the Shah was "way down the list of tyrants. He would not even make the A-list." Still, Savak, the Iranian secret police, was brutal, quick, and particularly nasty in its torture; it was also callous, stupid, intrusive, pervasive, and arbitrary. None of this fit the image of the Great Civilization, the Iran that was pursing its ambition to be a world power—and whose Shah was lecturing the industrial world on its own character flaws. Thus, Iran's human rights record became more visible and much more reported upon than the abuses in other developing countries, contributing further to the growing hostility, both inside Iran and out, to the Shah and his regime. . . .

Attacks by the police and army on critics of the regime only served to swell and broaden the ranks of those antagonistic to the Shah. The withdrawal of subsidies to the Shia religious establishment alienated and further angered the clergy. Indeed, overt opposition was becoming part of the fabric of national life. Yet all through the first half of 1978, its significance was discounted. Yes, the Shah told the British ambassador, the situation was serious, but he was determined to press ahead with liberalization. His most implacable enemies, and the most powerful, were the mullahs, with their hold on the minds of the masses. "There could be no compromise with them," he said. "It was a straightforward confrontation and one side had to lose." The Shah made it clear that he could not imagine being on the losing side.

In the U.S. government, too, hardly anyone could imagine that the Shah might fail. For Washington, any alternative was virtually unthinkable. After all, Iran's powerful monarch had sat on his throne for thirty-seven years. He was courted throughout the world. He was modernizing his country. Iran was one of the world's two great oil powers, with wealth far beyond anything it had known only a few years earlier. The Shah was a critical ally, a regional policeman in a crucial area, the "Big Pillar." How could he possibly be toppled?

American intelligence on Iran was constrained. As the United States became more dependent on the Shah, there was less willingness to risk his ire by trying to find out what was happening among the opposition that he despised. In Washington, there were surprisingly few people with the requisite analytic skills on Iran. And until late in the day, there did not seem to be great demand among the "consumers" of intelligence, as senior American national security officials are sometimes called, for analyses of the stability of the Shah's regime, either because they thought it unnecessary or because they feared, at some level, that the conclusions might be too unpalatable. "You couldn't *give* away intelligence on Iran," was the comment of one frustrated intelligence analyst. . . .

And yet there were at that very moment various signs, some particularly grisly, of the fury of the forces that were rising against the Shah. Over a period of two weeks in August 1978, half a dozen movie theaters around the country were set afire by fundamentalists opposed to "sinful" movies. In mid-August, in Abadan, the home of the great refinery, about five hundred people were crowded into a theater when some group locked the doors and incinerated the trapped moviegoers. Though uncertainty remained, it was thought that the perpetrators were fundamentalists. In early September, bloody demonstrations took place in Tehran itself. That was the turning point. From then on, the Shah's government began to collapse as an effective ruling force. Still, the Shah pushed on with his liberalization, including talk of free elections in June 1979.

To those with access to the monarch, something seemed to be wrong with the Shah himself. He appeared distant and more isolated. Rumors had circulated for years about his health. Did he have cancer? Or an incurable venereal disease? On September 16, the British ambassador went to see the Shah again. "I was worried by the change in his appearance and manner. He looked shrunken; his face was yellow and he moved slowly. He seemed exhausted and drained of spirit." The fact of the matter was that the Shah did have cancer, specifically a form of leukemia, which French doctors had first diagnosed in 1974. But the seriousness of the illness was kept for several years from both the Shah and his wife. As it was, he insisted upon the greatest secrecy for his treatment. Later, some in Washington suspected that elements in the French government would nonetheless have had to know. The British government and most certainly the American did not know. Had they been informed of the fact and nature of his ailment, the calculations on many accounts might have been different. . . .

As the weeks passed, more and more of the country went on strike, including oil industry technicians. In early October 1978, at Iran's urging, Ayatollah Khomeini was expelled from Iraq; after all, the Ba'thist regime in Baghdad had to worry about its own Shiite population. Denied refuge in Kuwait, Khomeini went to France and established himself and his entourage in a suburb of Paris. The Iranian government may have thought, out of sight, out of mind, but it was mistaken. France provided Khomeini and his followers with access to the direct-dial international phone service that the Shah had installed in Tehran, greatly facilitating communication. The elderly, irate cleric, who knew so little of the Western world and held it in such scorn, nevertheless proved himself a master of propaganda in front of the media that camped at his door. . . .

The Iranian oil industry was in a state of escalating chaos. The main production area was known as "The Fields." . . .

The impact of the strikes was felt immediately. Iran was the second-largest exporter of oil after Saudi Arabia. Of the upwards of 5.5 million barrels produced daily in Iran, about 4.5 million were exported; the rest were consumed internally. By early November, exports had been reduced to less than a million barrels per day, and thirty tankers were waiting in line at the loading facilities at Kharg Island for oil that was not there at a time when, in the international market, the winter demand surge was beginning. Petroleum companies, responding to the general softness in the market, had been letting their inventories fall. Would there be a shortage on the world market? Moreover, the stability of Iran itself depended upon oil revenues; they were the basis of the country's entire economy. The head of the National Iranian Oil Company [Osco] went south to The Fields to seek a dialogue with the striking oil workers—or so the thought. When he got there, he was mobbed by angry strikers. He immediately decided to forgo negotiations and instead fled the country. There seemed to be no way to end the strike.

Trying to contain the growing chaos, the Shah took a critical step that he had always wanted to avoid; he installed a military government. This was his last chance, but he put a weak general in charge. The general immediately suffered a heart attack and never asserted authority. The new government was able, at least temporarily, to restore some order in the oil industry and get production going again. Soldiers now also moved into Osco's headquarters at Ahwaz, where they coexisted uneasily with the striking workers, who continued to camp in the corridors.

As events tumbled toward their conclusion, the policy of the United States, Iran's most important ally, was in confusion, disarray, and shock. During most of 1978 senior officials of the Carter Administration had been distracted and preoccupied by other momentous and demanding developments: the Camp David peace accords with Egypt and Israel, strategic arms negotiations with the Soviets, normalization of relations with China. American policy had been based on the premise that Iran was a reliable ally and would be the Big Pillar in the region. Out of deference to the Shah and because of the desire not to anger him, American officials had kept their distance from the various opponents of his regime, which meant that they lacked channels of communication to the emerging opposition. There was not even any reporting to Washington on what the Ayatollah was actually saying on those by-now-famous tapes. Some in Washington insisted that the unrest in Iran was a secret, Soviet-orchestrated plot. And, as always, there was the same question: What could the United States government do, whatever the case? Only a few American officials thought that the Iranian military could withstand the persistence of nationwide strikes and the defection of religiously minded soldiers. Indeed, the last few months of 1978 saw a fierce bureaucratic battle over policy waged in Washington. How to bolster the Shah or assure continuity to a friendly successor regime? How to support the Shah without being so committed as to assure an antagonistic relationship with his successors, should he fall? How to disengage, if disengagement were required, without undermining the Shah, in case he could survive politically? Indecision and vacillation in Washington resulted in contradictory signals to Iran: The Shah should hang tough, the Shah should abdicate, military force should be used, human rights must be observed, the military should stage a coup, the military should stand aside, a regency should be established. . . .

So great was the lack of coherence that one senior official, who had been involved in every Middle Eastern crisis since the early 1960s, noted the "extraordinary" fact that the "first systematic meeting" at a high level on Iran was not convened until early November—very late in the day. On November 9, William Sullivan, the American ambassador in Tehran, finally confronted the unpleasant realities in a dramatic message to Washington entitled "Thinking the Unthinkable." Perhaps the Shah would not be able to survive after all, he said; the United States should begin to consider contingencies and alternatives. But in Washington, where the bureaucratic battles continued to rage, there was no meaningful reaction, save that President Carter sent hand-written notes to his Secretary of State, National Security Advisor, Secretary of Defense, and Director of Central Intelligence to ask why he had not been previously informed of the situation inside Iran. Ambassador Sullivan, meanwhile, came to the conclusion that the United States faced the situation in Iran "with no policy whatsoever."

December 1978 was a month for mourning, processions, and self-flagellation in the Shiite creed. The high point was the holiday of Ashura, marking the martyrdom of the iman Hussein and symbolizing unremitting resistance to a tyrant without legitimacy. Khomeini promised that it would be a month of vengeance and "torrents of blood." He called for new martyrs. "Let them kill five thousand, ten thousand, twenty thousand," he declared. "We will prove that blood is more powerful than the sword." Huge demonstrations were held across the country, some truly awe-inspiring in size. All of the opposition seemed to have united, and the Army was crumbling away. The Shah was running out of options. . . .

At the end of December, there was reluctant agreement in the ruling circles that a coalition government would be formed, and that the Shah would leave Iran, ostensibly for medical treatment abroad. But there could be little doubt of what was really happening. The Pahlavi dynasty appeared to be finished. So, virtually, at least for the time being, was petroleum production in The Fields. In the week after Christmas, Osco decided to evacuate all its Western employees. Hardly privy to what was going on either in Tehran in the immediate vicinity of the Peacock Throne or in Washington, the expatriates assumed that their exit was only temporary, a matter of weeks or months at the most, until order was restored. Thus, they were strictly limited to only two suitcases. They left their houses intact, with pretty much everything in place, for their return. . . .

At midday on January 16, [1979,] the Shah appeared at Tehran airport. "I am feeling tired and need a rest," he said to a small group that had gathered, maintaining the pathetic fiction that he was only going on a vacation. Then he boarded his plane and left Tehran for the last time, carrying with his luggage a casket of Iranian soil. His first stop would be Egypt.

With the Shah's departure, all of Tehran erupted into the kind of jubilation that had not been seen since the Shah's own return in triumph in 1953. Car horns blared, headlights were flashed, windshield wipers decorated with pictures of Khomeini swished back and forth, crowds shouted and cheered and danced in the streets, and newspapers were handed out rapid-fire with the unforgettable banner headline "The Shah Is Gone." In Tehran and throughout the country, the great equestrian statues of his father, and of himself, were pulled from their pedestals by wild crowds, and the Pahlavi dynasty and its era crumbled into dust.

And who would rule? A coalition government had been left behind in Tehran, headed by a long-time opponent of the Shah. But on February 1, Khomeini arrived back in Tehran in a chartered Air France 747. Seats on the plane had been sold to Western reporters to finance the flight, while Khomeini himself spent the trip resting on a carpet on the floor of the first-class cabin. He brought with him a second government, a revolutionary council headed by Mehdi Bazargan, whose own credentials as an opponent of the Shah were impeccable. Indeed, in 1951, twenty-eight years earlier, Bazargan had been chosen by Mohammed Mossadegh to be head of the nationalized oil industry, and it was he who had then immediately gone to the oil fields in person with the stamps and wooden sign that said "National Iranian Oil Company." Subsequently, he had served his time in jail under the Shah. And now, despite Khomeini's lasting hatred of Mossadegh as a secularist nationalist, Bazargan was, given the conjunction of political forces, the Ayatollah's candidate to lead the new Iran. So, for a brief time, there were two rival governments in Tehran. But, of course, there could only be one government. In the second week of February, fighting broke out at an air force base in the suburbs of Tehran between non-commissioned officers called "homafars," who were sympathetic to the revolution, and troops of the Imperial Guard. The military support for the coalition government collapsed, and Mehdi Bazargan was in. The American defense attaché provided a succinct summary of the situation in a message to Washington: "Army surrenders; Khomeini wins. Destroying all classified." . . .

The old regime was gone in Iran, and the new one was in power, though most uneasily; there were already bitter struggles for control. And from Iran, as if it had been shaken by a violent earthquake, a giant tidal wave surged around the world. All were swept up in it; nothing and no one escaped. When the wave finally spent its fury two years later, the survivors would look around and find themselves beached on a totally new terrain. Everything was different; relations among all of them were altered. The wave would generate the Second Oil Shock, carrying prices from thirteen to thirty-four dollars a barrel, and bringing in massive changes not only in the international petroleum industry but also, for the second time in less than a decade, in the world economy and global politics.

The new oil shock passed through several stages. The first stretched from the end of December 1978, when Iranian oil exports ceased, to the autumn of 1979. The loss of Iranian production was partly offset by increases elsewhere. Saudi Arabia pushed up production from its self-imposed ceiling of 8.5 million barrels per day to 10.5 by the end of 1978. It lowered its output to 10.1 million barrels per day in the first quarter to 1979, but that was still well above its 8.5 million "ceiling." Other OPEC countries also boosted output. When all of that was figured in, free world oil production in the critical first quarter of 1979 was about 2 million barrels per day below the last quarter of 1978.

There was, then, an actual shortage, which was not surprising. After all, Iran was the second-largest exporter in the world. Yet when measured against world demand of 50 million barrels per day, the shortage was no more than 4 to 5 percent. Why should a 4 or 5 percent loss of supplies have resulted in a 150 percent increase in price? The answer was the panic, which was triggered by five circumstances. The first was the apparent growth of oil consumption and the signal that it gave to the market. Demand had risen smartly from 1976 onward; the impact of conservation and non-OPEC oil was not yet clear, and it was assumed by virtually all that demand was going to continue to rise.

The second factor was the disruption of contractual arrangements within the oil industry, resulting from the revolution in Iran. Despite major upheavals, world oil had remained an integrated industry. However, the ties were no longer the formal ones of ownership, but rather the looser ties of long-term contracts. The Iranian interruption hit companies unevenly, depending upon their dependence on Iran, and led to disruptions of the contractual flow of supplies. That rupture sent hosts of new buyers hurtling into the marketplace, scrambling to secure the same number of barrels that they had lost. All would do anything they could to avoid being caught short. Here was the real end of the classic integrated oil industry. The links between upstream and downstream were, at last, severed. What had been the fringe, the spot market, became the center. And what had been a somewhat disreputable activity, trading, would now become a central preoccupation.

A third factor was the contradictory and conflicting policies of consumer governments. The international energy-security system, which had been promoted by [Secretary of State Henry A.] Kissinger at the 1974 Washington Energy Conference, was still in development, with many aspects yet untested. Actions taken by governments for domestic reasons would be read as major international policies, adding to the stress and tension in the marketplace. While governments were pledging to cooperate to dampen prices, companies from those nations would feverishly be bidding up the price.

Fourth, the upheaval presented the oil exporters with the opportunity to capture additional rents, enormously large rents. Once again, they could assert their power and influence on the world stage. Most, though not all of them, kept pushing the price up at every opportunity, and some manipulated supplies to further agitate the market and gain additional revenues.

Finally, there was the sheer power of emotion. Uncertainty, anxiety, confusion, fear, pessimism—those were the sentiments that fueled and governed actions during the panic. After the fact, when all the numbers were sorted out, when the supply and demand balance was retrospectively dissected, such emotions seemed irrational; they didn't make sense. Yet at the time they were indubitably real. The whole international oil system seemed to have broken down; it was not out of control. And what gave the emotions additional force was the conviction that a prophecy had been fulfilled. The oil crisis expected for the mid-1980s had arrived in 1979, the second phase of the turmoil unleashed in 1973–74 [when OPEC placed an embargo on oil exports to the U.S. and other supporters of Israel during the October 1973 war]. This was not a temporary disruption, but the early arrival of a deeper oil crisis, which would mean permanently high prices. And there was the unanswered question of how far the Iranian Revolution would advance. The French Revolution had reached across all of Europe to the very gates of Moscow before it spent its force. Would the Iranian Revolution reach into nearby Kuwait, to Riyadh, and on to Cairo and beyond? Religious fundamentalism wed to feverish nationalism had caught the Western world by surprise. Though it was still incomprehensible and unfathomable, one of its driving forces was obvious: a rejection of the West and of the modern world. That recognition led to an icy, pervasive fear.

It was the buyers, stunned by the unfolding spectacle, fearing a repetition of 1973, gripped by panic, who inadvertently made the shortage worse by building up inventories—as they had done in 1973. . . .

The rush to build inventories by oil companies, reinforced by consumers, resulted in an additional three million barrels per day of "demand" above actual consumption. When added to the two million barrels per day of net lost supplies, the outcome was a total shortfall of five million barrels per day, which was equivalent to about 10 percent of consumption. In sum, the panic buying to build inventories more than doubled the actual shortage and further fueled the panic. That was the mechanism that drove the price from thirteen to thirty-four dollars a barrel. . . .

The efforts of Western governments to mobilize cutbacks in demand, to blunt the upward price spiral, were proving insufficient. Yet they were loath to invoke the newly devised emergency oil sharing system of the International Energy Agency for fear that it would introduce more rigidity into the market. And, in any case, it was unclear whether the official trigger point for the system, a 7 percent shortfall, had actually been reached. Governments were torn between two fundamental objectives: obtaining relatively low-priced oil and guaranteeing secure supplies at any price. Once they had been able to do both. But now they found that these two objective were contradictory. Governments talked the first but, when domestic pressures began to be felt, pursued the second.

The top priority was to keep domestic consumers, who happened to be voters, supplied. Energy questions had become, explained a European energy minister, "short, short, short-run politics." The various Western governments became promoters and champions of aggressive worldwide acquisition hunts, either indirectly through companies or directly through state-to-state deals. The result was suspicion, accusation, finger pointing, and anger among those supposedly allied nations. For the consuming countries as well as for the oil companies, it appeared to be every man for himself. Prices continued to climb.

To the American public the reemergence of gas lines, which snaked for blocks around gasoline stations, became the embodiment of the panic. The nightmare of

1973 had returned. Owing to the disruption of Iranian supplies, there was, in fact, a shortage of gasoline. Refineries that had been geared to Iranian light and similar crudes could not produce as much gasoline and other lighter products from the heavier crude oils to which they were forced to turn as substitutes. Inventories of gasoline were low in California, and after news reports and rumors of spot shortages, all 12 million vehicles in the state seemed to show up at once at gasoline stations to fill up. Emergency regulations around the country made matters worse. Some states, in an effort to avoid running out of supplies, prohibited motorists from buying more than five dollars worth of gasoline at any one time. The results were exactly the opposite of what was intended, for it meant that motorists had to come back to gas stations that much more frequently. Meanwhile, price controls limited the conservation response; and indeed, if gasoline prices had been decontrolled, the gas lines might have disappeared rather quickly. At the same time, the federal government's own allocation system froze distribution patterns on a historical basis and denied the market the flexibility to move supplies around in response to demand. As a result, gasoline was in short supply in major urban areas, but there were more than abundant supplies in rural and vacation areas, where the only shortage was of tourists. In sum, the nation, through its own political immobilism, was rationing gasoline through the mechanism of gas lines. And, to make matters worse, gas lines themselves helped beget gas lines. A typical car used seven-tenths of a gallon an hour idling in a gas line. One estimate suggested that America's motorists in the spring and summer of 1979 may have wasted 150,000 barrels of oil a day waiting in line to fill their tanks! . . .

The gas lines marked the beginning of the end of the Presidency of Jimmy Carter. He was one more victim of the revolution in Iran and the upheaval in the oil market. Carter had come to Washington two years earlier, in 1977, with a paradoxical persona that reflected the two sides of his experience: a naval officer turned peanut farmer, and a born-again Christian. He was the Preacher, seeking a moral rehabilitation of post-Watergate America with his unembroidered, down-to-earth Presidency. He was also the Engineer, trying to micromanage the intricacies of the American political machine and to show his command over both big issues and little details.

Carter would have seemed particularly well-suited to leadership in the midst of the 1979 panic; after all, his agenda and interests as both Preacher and Engineer had converged on energy and oil, making them the number-one domestic focus of his Administration. And now he confronted the crisis he had been warning against. But there would be no reward nor credit given to the prophet, only blame. By mid-March of 1979, two months into the crisis, Eliot Cutler, his chief White House energy adviser, was already warning of the "darts and arrows coming at us from all directions—from people who want to get rid of the regulatory structure, from people concerned about inflation, from people who want a sexy and affirmative program, from people who don't want the oil companies to profiteer, and generally from people who want to make life politically miserable for us." Shortly after, there came the accident at Three Mile Island [nuclear power plant], and the anxious nation saw photographs of the nuclear engineer, Jimmy Carter, wearing little yellow safety booties, tramping through and personally inspecting the control room of the damaged plant.

In April, Carter delivered a major speech on energy policy that merely intensified the barrage. He announced a decontrol of oil prices, which was certain to infuriate liberals, who tended to blame almost everything bad on the oil companies. And he coupled decontrol with a "windfall profits tax" on excess oil company earnings, which was no less sure to anger conservatives, who blamed the panic on government meddling, controls, and overweening regulations.

A special Presidential task force on energy met repeatedly in secrecy to try to figure out some solution to the gasoline shortage. The only quick way to fight the global oil disruption, and end the gas lines before they ended the Carter Presidency, was to get the Saudis to increase their output again. In June the American ambassador to Riyadh delivered an official letter for President Carer as well as a more personal handwritten note. Both implored the Saudis to increase output. The ambassador also met for several hours with Prince Fahd, the head of the Supreme Petroleum Council, seeking a commitment to boost production and try to hold down the price. That same month, Carter went to Vienna to complete negotiation of the SALT II arms control agreement with Soviet President Leonid Brezhnev. The signing of SALT II, in negotiation for seven years through three administrations, might have been celebrated as a landmark achievement. But not then. It simply did not count. The only thing that mattered was the gas lines—and they were Carter's fault. . . .

. . . Carter himself departed for his next foreign trip, to Tokyo to meet the leaders of the other major Western countries for an economic summit. Fearing the impact of the oil shortage on the overall health of the international economy, the seven leaders of the Western world turned Tokyo into an all-energy summit. It was also a very nasty one. Tempers were badly frayed. "This is the first day of the economic summit, and one of the worst days of my diplomatic life," Carter wrote in his diary. The conference discussions were harsh and acrimonious. Even lunch, Carter noted, "was very bitter and unpleasant." German Chancellor Helmut Schmidt "got personally abusive toward me. . . . He alleged that American interference in the Middle East trying to work for a peace treaty was what had caused the problems with oil all over the world." As for Britain's Prime Minister Margaret Thatcher, Carter found her "a tough lady, highly opinionated, strong-willed, cannot admit that she doesn't know something."

Carter's next stop was supposed to be a vacation in Hawaii. But Stuart Eizenstat, the chief White House domestic policy adviser, feared that a holiday now would be a political disaster of the first order. He thought that the Presidential party, which had been traveling abroad for most of a month, did not comprehend the mood of the country. . . .

So, on the last day of the Tokyo Summit, Eizenstat dispatched a grim, depressing memorandum to Carter about the continuing gas shortage: "Nothing else has so frustrated, confused, angered the American people—or so targeted their distress at you personally." He added, "In many respects, this would appear to be the worst of times. But I honestly believe that we can change this to a time of opportunity." The exhausted Carter canceled Hawaii and, returning from Tokyo, found that his approval rating in the polls had plummeted to 25 percent, matched only by Nixon's in the final days before his resignation. He retreated to Camp David, in the Maryland mountains, where, equipped with a 107-page dissection of the national mind by Patrick Caddell, his favorite pollster, he aimed to meditate on the nation's future. He also met with a cross-section of American leaders and embraced a new book that found "narcissism" at the heart of America's problems.

In July, the Saudis pushed up their output from 8.5 to 9.5 million barrels per day. They had heeded the implorings from the Untied States and had responded to their assessment of their own security interests. The Saudi boost would help ease the shortage over the next few months, but it was not a long-term solution, nor, as events had suggested over the previous couple of months, something on which to base America's and the Western world's entire well-being. Nor could the extra supplies do much immediately to cool the hot temper of the American public.

As a result, Carter was compelled to do something, and to be seen doing something—something big, something positive, something that seemed to offer that long-term solution. He embraced the concept of a vast synthetic fuels plan, essentially based on the hundred-billion-dollar program put forward by Nelson Rockefeller in 1975. This would be the "sexy and affirmative program" that was desperately needed, and his staff worked feverishly to turn it into a specific proposal. Some voices were raised in doubt. The *New York Times* reported in a front-page story on July 12 that a new study from a group of researchers at the Harvard Business School argued that the United States could reduce its oil imports much more cheaply and quickly through a program of energy conservation than through synthetic fuels. Others warned that a synthetic fuel program would have enormous adverse environmental consequences. But in the speech he delivered in July to a distraught nation on America's "crisis of confidence," Carter announced his own plan to make 2.5 million barrels per day of synthetic fuels by 1990, primarily out of coal and shale oil. He had originally wanted to propose 5 million barrels per day, but had been talked out of it. Though he did not use the word, his address became known as Carter's "malaise" speech.

Carter also wanted to make changes in his own Cabinet, and in particular, to force the resignations of two of its members, Treasury secretary Michael Blumenthal and Health Secretary Joseph Califano. His political advisers, Hamilton Jordan and Jody Powell, had convinced him that the two Cabinet officers were disloyal. Stuart Eizenstat argued otherwise to the President, saying that he had worked with the two men every day and that they were committed to the Administration. Eizenstat urged the President more strongly than he had ever urged him on any other matter not to fire Califano, who had strong political support, and Blumenthal, who was the Administration's chief inflation fighter. But Carter had already made up his mind. They would have to go. But how? Just before a Cabinet meeting, Carter told a few of his senior staff that he had decided to have all his Cabinet members submit their resignations and then he would keep only those he still wanted. Some of the staff members fervently tried to dissuade him. Such an action could create a panic. No, the President insisted, it would be seen as positive by a crisis-weary nation, the turning over of the welcome new leaf.

Carter immediately went into a tense Cabinet meeting dominated by the grim situation that the Administration found itself in. As worked out beforehand, Secretary of State Cyrus Vance proposed that all cabinet secretaries submit their resignations so that Carter could begin afresh. The President concurred. A few minutes later,

Robert Strauss, the Middle East peace negotiator, walked in and, not knowing what had just transpired and why the room was so somber, jokingly said that everybody ought to resign. His remark was greeted with silence. Finally, one of the other cabinet secretaries leaned over and whispered, "Bob, shut up." They had all just resigned.

Altogether, five people left the cabinet, some fired and some resigning. The aim was to bolster Presidential leadership. It had quite the opposite effect. The sudden news of the departures sent tremors of uncertainty throughout the country and the Western world. Over lunch that day, the national editor of the *Washington Post* muttered darkly that America's central government had just collapsed. . . .

All the while, buyers continued their quest for oil to build up inventories and fill storage tanks to the very brim in the face of uncertainty and fear for the future. The assumption was that demand was continuing to grow. It was a fatal miscalculation. In fact, a decline had already set in, reflecting the first effects of conservation as well as an economic downturn, but the fall was almost imperceptible at first. And buying remained frantic. As Shell's supply coordinator observed, "Every negotiation with a producer government was a finger-biting exercise: there was one dominant thought in the mind of company presidents and negotiators alike—to hold on to term oil and limit the need for spot acquisition. The suppliers of course sensed this, and a cat-and-mouse dialectic began. . . . Both the terms of contracts and the prices that had to be paid became continuously worse." . . .

Thus, in the summer and early fall of 1979, the world oil market was in a state of anarchy whose global effects far exceeded those of the early 1930s. . . . And while the pockets of the producers and traders swelled with money, consumers were forced to dip ever deeper into their own pockets to pay the price of panic. For many of the exultant exporters, it was another great victory for oil power. There was no limit, they thought, to what the market would bear and what they would earn. Some in the Western world gloomily began to fear that what was at stake was not only the price of the world's most important commodity, not only economic growth and the integrity of the world economy, but perhaps even the international order and world society as they knew it.

Shortly after 3:00 A.M. Washington time, on November 4, 1979, Elizabeth Ann Swift, the political officer in the United States embassy in Tehran, got through by phone to the Operations Center, the communications nerve point on the seventh floor of the State Department in Washington, D.C. Her words jolted the officials at the Washington end of the line out of the slumberous quiet. It was already midmorning in Tehran, and Swift reported that a large mob of young Iranians had broken into the embassy compound, surrounded the chancery building, and were forcing their way into other buildings. An hour and a half later, Swift was back on the line to say that the attackers had set fire to part of the embassy. Still another half hour later, she reported that some of the invaders had threatened to kill two unarmed Americans just outside the room, that the table and sofa blocking the door had been pulled aside, and that the Iranians had burst into the office, even as the embassy officials desperately continued to try to make contact by phone with someone of authority in the Iranian government. The hands of the Americans were now being tied, Swift continued in a professional, almost matter-of-fact way to the shocked listeners at the other end. "We're going down" were her last words, before one of the young Iranians, a picture of Khomeini pinned to his shirt, grabbed the phone out of her hand. And then

Swift, along with the other Americans, all now blindfolded, was led into captivity. The line remained open for a long time, though no one was there. Then it went dead.

Some sixty-three Americans—the skeleton staff that had remained at the embassy after the personnel had been scaled down from the fourteen hundred officials of the Shah's time—were taken hostage by a large, rowdy, violent band of zealots who were thereafter known to the world as "students." Some of the Americans were soon released, leaving fifty in captivity. The Iranian Hostage Crisis had begun, and the Second Oil Shock entered a new phase with an even more dire geopolitical cast.

The specific grievance of the hostage takers focused on Mohammed Pahlavi and America's relation to him. His father, Reza Shah, had found a place of exile in South Africa. Not so the son, who, in his own exile, turned into a modern version of the Flying Dutchman. He could find refuge in no port and seemed cursed to wander forever. He went to Egypt, to Morocco, to the Bahamas, to Mexico. But no one wanted him to stay; he was a reject, a pariah, a figure to whom very little world sympathy attached, and virtually no government wanted to risk the ire of the unfathomable new Iran. All the courting of a few years earlier, all the flattery, the ingratiation, the respectful premiers and supplicating cabinet ministers from the industrial nations, the bowing and scraping of the powerful around the world—it was as if none of that had ever happened. To make matters worse, cancer and related illnesses were ravaging the Shah's body. Remarkably, it was only at the end of September 1979, more than eight months *after* he was forced to leave Iran, that senior American officials first learned that the Shah was seriously ill, and only on October 18 did they discover that it was cancer. Carter had adamantly refused to allow the Shah to enter the United States for medical treatment. But, at last, after months of controversy and acrimony at the highest levels of his Administration, compounded by a vigorous campaign by Henry Kissinger, John McCloy, David Rockefeller, and others, the Shah was admitted. He arrived in New York City on October 23. Though he was checked into the New York Hospital, Cornell Medical Center, under a pseudonym, which just happened to be the real name of U.S. Undersecretary of State David Newsom, to the latter's discomfort, his presence was immediately known and widely reported.

A few days later, while the Shah was under treatment in New York, Carter's national security adviser, Zbigniew Brzezinski, was attending the celebration of the twenty-fifth anniversary of the Algerian revolution in Algiers. There he met with the new Iranian Prime Minister, Mehdi Bazargan, and his foreign and defense ministers. The subject of discussion was how the United States might relate to the reborn Iran. The United States, insisted Brzezinski, would not engage in nor support any conspiracies against Iran. Bazargan and his ministers protested the admission of the Shah to the United States. They insisted that Iranian doctors be allowed to examine him, to determine if he was really ill, or if it was only a ruse to disguise a plot.

The news reports of the Algiers meeting, coming on top of the Shah's arrival in the United States, alarmed Bazargan's theocratic and more radical rivals, as well as young militant fundamentalists. The Shah was the enemy and the archvillain. His presence in the United States stoked memories of 1953, of Mossadegh's fall [through a C.I.A. backed coup], of the Shah's flight to Rome and his triumphant return to the throne, and it aroused fear that the United States was about to stage another coup and again restore the Shah. After all, the Great Satan—the United States—was capable of carrying out the worst abominations. And here was Bazargan trucking with Zbigniew Brzezinski, one of the chief agents of the Great Satan, and a mere week and half after the Shah's arrival in New York. For what purpose?

Thus was provided the impetus, and pretext, for the invasion of the embassy. Perhaps it was only intended, originally, as a sit-in, but it soon turned into an occupation and a mass kidnaping, as well as a bizarre circus, complete with vendors in front of the embassy selling revolutionary tape cassettes, shoes, sweatshirts, hats, and boiled sugar beets. The occupiers even took to answering the embassy phone, "Nest of spies." It appeared that the Ayatollah Khomeini and his immediate circle had some idea of the planned assault and encouraged it. That they took advantage of it, seizing on the event for their own purposes, was quite clear. They would use the ensuing crisis to dispose of Bazargan and all others with Western and secular taints, to consolidate their own power, to eliminate their opponents, including what Khomeini called "American-loving rotten brains," and to put in place the elements of the theocratic regime. Until all of that was done, the hostage crisis would grind on for almost fifteen months—444 days, to be precise. Every day, Americans read about "America in Captivity." Each night, Americans were subjected to the televised spectacle of "America Held Hostage," including the repetitive chorus of the zealots chanting "Death to America." Ironically, with its late-night programs on the hostage crisis, ABC finally found a way to compete successfully against Johnny Carson [Jay Leno's predecessor] and the *Tonight Show*.

The hostage crisis transmitted a powerful message: that the shift of power in the world oil market in the 1970s was only part of a larger drama that was taking place in global politics. The Untied States and the West, it seemed to say, were truly in decline, on the defensive, and, it appeared, unable to do anything to protect their interests, whether economic or political. As Carter succinctly summed matters up two days after the hostage seizure, "They have us by the balls." Iran was not the only scene of unrest. The hapless United States was under attack by a variety of opponents in the Middle East who wanted to eject the United States from the area. Later in November 1979, a few weeks after the hostage taking, some seven hundred armed fundamentalists, bitterly opposed to the Saudi government and its links to the West, seized the Great Mosque in Mecca, in what was supposed to be the first stage of an uprising. They were dislodged only with difficulty. The larger Saudi uprising never materialized, but the assault did send shock waves through the Islamic world. In early December, there was a Shia protest in al-Hasa, in the heart of the oil region in the eastern part of Saudi Arabia. Then came another dramatic and much larger shock a few weeks later in December. The Soviet Union invaded Afghanistan, Iran's neighbor to the east, rocking both the Gulf States and the West. Russia, it now seemed to many, was still intent on fulfilling its century-and-a-half-old ambitions to drive toward the Gulf, and was taking advantage of the disarray of the West to position itself to capture as many of the spoils of the Middle East as it could. The bear was also becoming bolder; it was the first large-scale use of Soviet military forces beyond the communist bloc since World War II.

President Carter responded in January 1980 by enunciating what became known as the Carter Doctrine: "Let our position be absolutely clear. An attempt by any outside force to gain control of the Persian Gulf region will be regarded as an assault on the vital interests of the United States of America, and such an assault will be repelled by any means necessary, including military force." The Carter Doctrine made more explicit what American presidents had been saying as far back as Harry Truman's pledge to Ibn Saud in 1950. With even more historical resonance, it also bore striking similarities to the Lansdowne Declaration of 1903, by which the British Foreign Secretary of the day had warned off Russia and Germany from the Persian Gulf.

Carter had earned great respect in the oil world in 1977, his first year in the Presidency, as the man who had forced the Shah to bend, to recant his commitment to higher prices. Carter had been the magician who had tamed the Shah and transformed him from a price hawk into a compliant dove. He had engineered the Camp David accords between Israel and Egypt. Now all those achievements were overwhelmed. The Shah was an outcast, the Iranian Revolution had sparked the oil panic of 1979, and Carter's Presidency continued to be cursed by events in Iran, with Carter himself held hostage, in political terms, by the gang of "student" militants in Tehran. . . .

The hostage crisis had even wider ramifications. It served to demonstrate the apparent weakness, even nakedness, of the consuming countries—in particular, of the United States, whose power was the basis of the postwar political and economic order. And it seemed to establish that world mastery really did lie in the hands of the oil exporters. At least that was the appearance.

🌐 F U R T H E R   R E A D I N G

Isaac Alteras, *Eisenhower and Israel* (1993)
Irvine Anderson, *Aramco, the United States, and Saudi Arabia* (1981)
Geoffrey Aronson, *From Sideshow to Center Stage: U.S. Policy Toward Egypt, 1946–1956* (1986)
George Ball and Douglas Ball, *The Passionate Attachment* (1992) (on U.S.-Israeli relations)
Hashim S. H. Behbehani, *The Soviet Union and Arab Nationalism* (1986)
Abraham Ben-Zvi, *The United States and Israel* (1993)
Ian J. Bickerton and Carla L. Klausner, *A Concise History of the Arab-Israeli Conflict* (1998)
James A. Bill, *The Eagle and the Lion: The Tragedy of American-Iranian Relations* (1988)
H. W. Brands, *Into the Labyrinth* (1994)
———, *The Specter of Neutralism* (1990)
George W. Breslauer et al., *Soviet Strategy in the Middle East* (1990)
Thomas A. Bryson, *Seeds of the Middle East Crisis: The United States Role in the Middle East Crisis During World War II* (1981)
Noam Chomsky, *The Fateful Triangle: The United States, Israel, and the Palestinians* (1983)
Kathleen Christison, *Perceptions of Palestine* (1999)
Michael J. Cohen, *Truman and Israel* (1990)
Chester L. Cooper, *The Lion's Last Roar: Suez, 1956* (1978)
Alexander DeConde, *Ethnicity, Race, and American Foreign Policy* (1992)
John Drambell, *The Carter Presidency* (1993)
"Fifty Years of U.S.-Israeli Relations: A Roundtable," *Diplomatic History*, 22 (1998), 231–283
Glenn Frankel, *Beyond the Promised Land* (1996)
Steven Z. Freiberger, *Dawn over Suez* (1992)
Thomas L. Friedman, *From Beirut to Jerusalem* (1989)
Mark J. Gasiorowski, *U.S. Foreign Policy and the Shah* (1991)
Fawaz A. Gerges, *America and Political Islam* (1999)

James F. Goode, *The United States and Iran, 1946–1951* (1989)

Stephen Green, *Taking Sides: America's Secret Relations with a Militant Israel* (1984)

Peter Grose, *Israel in the Mind of America* (1983)

Peter L. Hahn, *United States, Great Britain, and Egypt, 1945–1956* (1991)

———, "The View from Jerusalem: Revelations about U.S. Diplomacy from the Archives of Israel," *Diplomatic History,* 22 (1998), 509–532

Robert F. Hunter, *The Palestinian Uprising* (1993)

Victor Israelyan, *Inside the Kremlin During the Yom Kippur War* (1995)

Robert Kaplan, *The Arabists* (1993)

Burton I. Kaufman, *The Arab Middle East and the United States* (1995)

Gabriel Kolko, *Confronting the Third World* (1988)

Bruce R. Kuniholm, *The Origins of the Cold War in the Near East* (1980)

Diane B. Kunz, *The Economic Diplomacy of the Suez Crisis* (1991)

George Lenczowski, *American Presidents and the Middle East* (1990)

Douglas Little, "From Even-handed to Empty-handed: Seeking Order in the Middle East," in Thomas G. Paterson, ed., *Kennedy's Quest for Victory* (1989), pp. 156–177

———, "Gideon's Band: America and the Middle East Since 1945," *Diplomatic History,* 18 (1994), 513–540

———, "The Making of a Special Relationship: The United States and Israel, 1957–1968," *International Journal of Middle East Studies,* 25 (1993), 563–585

Wm. Roger Louis, *The British Empire in the Middle East, 1945–1951* (1984)

Yehuda Lukacs and Abdullah M. Battah, eds., *The Arab-Israeli Conflict* (1988)

Mark H. Lytle, *The Origins of the Iranian-American Alliance* (1987)

Robert J. McMahon, "Eisenhower and the Third World," *Political Science Quarterly,* 101 (1986), 453–473

David Makovsky, *Making Peace with the PLO* (1996)

Gail E. Meyer, *Egypt and the United States* (1980)

Aaron David Miller, *Search for Security: Saudi Arabian Oil and American Foreign Policy, 1939–1949* (1980)

Benny Morris, *Israel's Border Wars, 1949–1956* (1993)

Kenneth Morris, *Jimmy Carter: American Moralist* (1996)

Donald Neff, "Nixon's Middle East Policy: From Balance to Bias," *Arab Studies Quarterly,* 12 (1990), 121–152

———, *Warriors for Jerusalem* (1984)

———, *Warriors at Suez* (1981)

A. F. K. Organski, *The $36 Billion Bargain* (1990) (on U.S. aid to Israel)

David Painter, *Oil and the American Century* (1986)

Richard B. Parker, *The Politics of Miscalculation in the Middle East* (1993)

Thomas G. Paterson, "Threat to the Middle East? The Eisenhower Doctrine," in Paterson, *Meeting the Communist Threat* (1988), pp. 159–190

William B. Quandt, *Peace Process* (1993)

Stephen J. Randall, *United States Foreign Oil Policy, 1919–1948* (1985)

Bernard Reich, *Securing the Covenant: United States-Israeli Relations After the Cold War* (1995)

Cheryl A. Rubenberg, *Israel and the American National Interest* (1986)

Barry Rubin, *Cauldron of Turmoil* (1992)

———, ed., *From War to Peace: Arab-Israeli Relations, 1973–1993* (1994)

———, *Paved with Good Intentions: The American Experience and Iran* (1980)

Nadav Safran, *Israel: The Embattled Ally* (1981)

———, *Saudi Arabia* (1988)

Edward W. Said, *Orientalism* (1978)

———, *The Question of Palestine* (1979)

Yezid Sayigh, *Armed Struggle and the Search for State: The Palestinian National Movement, 1949   1993* (1998)

David Schoenbaum, *The United States and the State of Israel* (1993)

Mohammed Shadid, *The United States and the Palestinians* (1981)

Avi Shlaim, *War and Peace in the Middle East* (1994)
Gary Sick, *All Fall Down: America's Tragic Encounter with Iran* (1984)
Charles D. Smith, *Palestine and the Arab-Israeli Conflict* (1996)
John Snetsinger, *Truman, the Jewish Vote, and the Creation of Israel* (1974)
Steven L. Spiegel, *The Other Arab-Israeli Conflict* (1985)
Michael Stoff, *Oil, War, and American Security* (1980)
Robert Stookey, *America and the Arab States* (1975)
Michael W. Suleiman, ed., *U.S. Policy on Palestine: From Wilson to Clinton* (1995)
Mark Tessler, *A History of the Israeli-Palestinian Conflict* (1995)
Seth P. Tillman, *The United States in the Middle East* (1982)
Rod Troester, *Jimmy Carter as Peacemaker* (1996)
Paul J. White and William S. Logan, eds., *Remaking the Middle East* (1997)

CHAPTER
14

The Cold War Ends and the Post–Cold War Era Begins

After the tragedy of Vietnam, the Watergate constitutional crisis, and the waning of détente, President Jimmy Carter pledged to revive U.S. prestige and power. Carter initially attempted to reenergize Soviet-American détente, but at the close of his administration (1977–1981), the Cold War had become as contentious as ever: Strategic Arms Limitation Talks (SALT) had reached an impasse; the Soviet Union's invasion of its neighbor Afghanistan had prompted a new version of containment, the Carter Doctrine; Moscow and Washington had exchanged barbs over human-rights violations; and plans had been set in motion to install American Pershing II and cruise missiles in NATO countries in Western Europe to counter Soviet SS-20 missiles, raising the nuclear arms race to new levels of danger. At the same time, Carter worried that if Americans continued to neglect their mounting domestic prob-lems, including their dependency on foreign energy sources—the "energy crisis"—the United States might lose its preeminent international status.

Contemptuous of the message of decline, Republican candidate Ronald Reagan charged during the 1980 presidential election that Carter had let American power slip. Ultimately triumphing over Carter, Reagan began his presidency with denunci-ations of the Soviet Union in raw anticommunist rhetoric. Blaming most of the world's problems on Moscow, the Reagan administration (1981–1989) discouraged arms-control talks, and, under the Reagan Doctrine, stepped up U.S. aid to anti-communist movements around the world. Reagan sent U.S. troops to Lebanon and Grenada, ordered bombing raids against Libya, financed the contra *war against the government in Nicaragua (partly by illegal, secret arms sales to Iran), armed radical Muslim rebels with Stinger missiles in Afghanistan, tolerated death-squad human-rights abuses in El Salvador, announced the Strategic Defense Initiative (SDI, or "Star Wars"), and introduced the largest peacetime military budget in history.*

All the while, like President Eisenhower three decades earlier, Reagan dispar-aged reliance on nuclear weapons for defense in an overarmed world that seemed unlikely to survive a nuclear holocaust. As Reagan wrestled with this question, his most hawkish advisers left the administration toward the end of the 1980s. In late 1987, Washington and Moscow reached agreement on the Intermediate-Range Nuclear Forces Treaty (INF) to disband all American and Soviet intermediate-range

591

missiles. Although the treaty covered only 4 percent of superpower arsenals, it ranked as the world's first nuclear arms reduction accord.

Pleased with the hardliners' departure and the INF, critics nonetheless argued that the huge budget deficits and soaring federal debt spelled trouble: that the United States's failure to invest on the homefront in education, technology, the urban infrastructure, and the environment condemned the nation to steady economic and social decline. Reagan would hear nothing of it. America, he declared, was "standing tall." His administration's massive and rapid military buildup, Reagan insisted, had forced the Soviets to the bargaining table.

While Reagan turned to military solutions for international questions, and as the debate about decline gained intensity in the United States, momentous changes rocked the international system. A new, younger, reform-minded generation of Soviet officials came to power in 1985 under the bold leadership of General Secretary of the Communist party Mikhail Gorbachev. He launched perestroika ("restructuring") to improve economic performance and glasnost ("openness") to liberalize politics, and he pledged to reduce the military establishment (in 1988 he unilaterally reduced Soviet military forces). Under the "new thinking" in the Kremlin, Gorbachev also vowed to settle regional conflicts (all Soviet troops were gone from Afghanistan by 1989), to stop the nuclear arms race by eliminating all nuclear weapons (announced in early 1986), and to meet the U.S. president to temper the Cold War (the first summit convened in 1985).

Long simmering protest in the communist-ruled countries of Eastern Europe and East Germany exploded in this new atmosphere of Gorbachev reform. Having reduced Soviet forces in Eastern Europe, Gorbachev made it clear to all the world that he would not suppress dissent in the Warsaw Pact nations. Thus, communist regimes collapsed one after another in 1989—in Poland, Hungary, East Germany, Czechoslovakia, and Romania. In November, one of the infamous pillars of the Cold War, the Berlin Wall, came down. Caught in the storm he had unleashed, Gorbachev himself yielded power to more liberal compatriots. The Soviet Communist party disbanded, and the Union of Soviet Socialist Republics dissolved in 1991. Free-market capitalism, it seemed, had defeated statist communism.

In the decade that followed the collapse of the Berlin Wall, no single conflict or international issue provided a label to identify America's role in the world. Whereas containment of the Soviet Union and bipolarity had for almost fifty years defined U.S. global policy, the post–Cold War era became characterized by a proliferation of threats, some new and many that were carried over from the past. When the Iraqi dictator Saddam Hussein sent invading forces to annex his oil-rich neighbor Kuwait in August 1990, President George Bush (1989–1993) assembled an international military coalition that in early 1991 ousted Hussein's troops. In the afterglow of "Operation Desert Storm," Bush boasted that the "gloomsayers" who predicted decline had been proven wrong, and that the United States stood poised to lead a "new world order" based on self-determination and collective security. The world actually descended into vicious local rivalries and wars that powerful nations seemed unable to stop. Competing factions in the famine-plagued African nations of Somalia resisted U.S. military intervention in 1992 and 1993. In Haiti, beginning in 1994, Washington led a United Nations force to reinstall a government deposed by the military, only to witness a rekindling of violence as U.S. troops withdrew. And in Yugoslavia the splintering of the former communist state generated bloodletting among rival ethnic groups, the emergent states of Bosnia and Croatia, and the Serbian-led central government in Yugoslavia. A U.S.-led, NATO peacekeeping force, deployed in 1995, helped contain the fighting, but an enduring political settlement remained elusive. In response to Serbian attacks against ethnic Albanians in the Yugoslav province of Kosovo, the Clinton administration and NATO (expanded to include the former Soviet satellites of the Czech Republic, Hungary, and Poland) condemned Belgrade's brutal policies of "ethnic cleansing" and in March 1999 launched massive airstrikes against Yugoslavia to force a negotiation of Kosovo's political status. The military intervention posed a major test of NATO's role in the post–Cold War era.

In fact, the post–Cold War world confronted a myriad of security threats. Nuclear proliferation ranked among the most ominous as so-called rogue states such as communist North Korea and Iraq (despite Operation Desert Storm) sought nuclear capability, and several regional powers—most notably India, Pakistan, and Israel—either tested nuclear weapons or flexed their nuclear muscle. Acid rain, global warming, and deforestation endangered the world's environment, and international terrorism remained a constant threat. Cross-border drug trafficking also took center stage, especially with the U.S. invasion of Panama in 1989–1990 and the arrest of Panamanian president Manuel Noriega on narcotics charges.

The end of the Cold War and the demise of Soviet communism also sparked a renewed dedication to the expansion of capitalism. President William J. Clinton, who was elected in 1992 promising domestic reform and economic revitalization, placed special emphasis on trade treaties such as the North American Free Trade Agreement or NAFTA (approved by Congress in 1993). Recessions in Japan and East Asia in the late 1990s, Russia's post-communist financial morass, and the persistence of world hunger, poverty, and disease generated fears that the United States might falter in a globalized economy. When critics on the homefront charged that trade liberalization undermined U.S. industries and jobs, and that U.S. nation-building efforts abroad cost a great deal and produced mixed results, the administration denounced the "new isolationism" and drew analogies to the 1930s when high tariffs had spawned depression, dictatorship, and war, and when America's "isolationist" policies failed to halt aggression. As the twenty-first century neared, Washington seemed more committed than ever to a major global and interventionist role for the United States.

The Cold War ended after almost a half century, and its disorderly aftermath has continued to destabilize world politics. Why and how did it end? Who won? And why has the impact of its ending been so catastrophic? Observers vigorously debate the reasons for this startling turnabout in international history. In explaining the stunning changes in Soviet policies that helped end the Cold War, some point to external factors while others identify internal conditions in the U.S.S.R. Some observers claim that Reagan's huge military expansion, including SDI, and his staunch anti-Sovietism compelled Moscow to change—in short, that the United States won the Cold War by forcing the Soviet Union's collapse.

Other analysts, who emphasize external factors, argue instead that what counted most in ending the Cold War was not confrontation but engagement and compromise. Congress placed restraints on Reagan's confrontationism, an international antinuclear peace movement gained momentum, and Western Europe's pursuit of détente, often against U.S. wishes, also helped to end the Cold War. Some interpretations applaud the courageous people of Eastern Europe, not U.S. policies, for rolling back the Soviet empire. Still other writers argue that the Cold War ceased because of the decline of both superpowers, which exhausted themselves waging the long conflict and suffered setbacks in an increasingly interdependent world in which formidable challenges arose from allies and enemies alike. The great-power drive to restore faltering international positions generated the Soviet-American cooperation necessary to end a Cold War that neither side was winning.

Analysts who explain changes in the Soviet Union by emphasizing internal factors spotlight the decay of the Soviet system after years of mismanagement by a corrupt communist bureaucracy. They explore the history of anti-Stalinist reformers who waited their turn to lead and finally got it under Gorbachev. In short, a courageous Gorbachev determined to revive his nation, not a Reagan determined to undermine it, ended the Cold War. Some scholars argue that Reagan's rhetoric and policies actually delayed the end of the Cold War by undercutting the reformers—by emboldening Kremlin hawks who sought to counter U.S. military expansion and to ice arms-control talks.

The transition from the Cold War to the post–Cold War era has been rough, and except for pronouncements that the United States favored democracy and free markets abroad, no new doctrines with the evocative quality of containment have emerged to define a grand strategy for U.S. foreign policy. Domestic turmoil, including a vigorous but failed Republican campaign in 1998–1999 to impeach and convict President Clinton, and continued problems in education and the environment, raised questions about the United States's ability to lead effectively. As the twenty-first century approached, a major debate formed on the classic question of how and to what extent the United States should use its power in world affairs.

 D O C U M E N T S

In Document 1, comprising press conference comments from January 19, 1981, the newly inaugurated president Ronald Reagan denounces the Soviet Union, setting the Cold War confrontational style of his administration. In a March 23, 1983, speech, Reagan explains U.S. military expansion. Portions of his case, including his call for a new defensive system to blunt nuclear weapons (later called the Strategic Defense Initiative, or SDI), are reprinted here as Document 2. Document 3 is a statement by General Secretary Mikhail Gorbachev on November 21, 1985, at a press conference after meeting with Reagan at the Geneva summit conference. In office for only a few months, Gorbachev chides the U.S. president for escalating the arms race, seeking world supremacy, and operating under the mistaken notion that the Soviets would fold.

Reagan and Gorbachev met again at Reykjavík, Iceland, in October 1986. They came close to a major agreement on terminating the nuclear arms race, but Gorbachev would not accept SDI, which he saw as threatening, and Reagan would not abandon the system, which he saw as defensive. Their opposing positions are presented in Documents 4 and 5, both televised addresses—Reagan's on October 13 and Gorbachev's on October 22. Document 6, a concluding part of Yale University historian Paul Kennedy's best-selling book *The Rise and the Fall of the Great Powers* (1987), discusses the relationship between military spending and the relative economic decline of the United States, and concludes that "imperial overstretch" had weakened America's economy and eroded its national security. Document 7, from interviews conducted during 1987–1989 with Georgi Arbatov, one of the reformers who emerged with Gorbachev, provides a glimpse of the "new thinking" in the Soviet Union. A member of the Communist party's Central Committee and his nation's preeminent Americanist scholar, Arbatov headed the USA Institute, a think tank in Moscow.

President George Bush responded with military force to one of the early international crises of the post–Cold War era: Iraq's invasion of Kuwait in August 1990. In Document 8, an address to Congress on September 11, 1990, Bush emphasized both principle and the U.S. interest in Persian Gulf oil to rally the nation to resist Iraq's aggression and build a "new world order" based on the rule of law. The administration of President William J. Clinton proved no less committed to advancing American influence and values abroad. Document 9 consists of remarks given by President Clinton at a breakfast meeting on October 6, 1995, a day after signing a ceasefire agreement for wartorn and ethnically divided Bosnia. In his comments, the president trumpeted America's role as a peacemaker and world leader, and warned against the danger of isolationism.

1. President Ronald Reagan Denounces the Soviet Union, 1981

So far détente's been a one-way street that the Soviet Union has used to pursue its own aims. I don't have to think of an answer as to what I think their intentions are; they have repeated it. I know of no leader of the Soviet Union since the revolution, and including the present leadership, that has not more than once repeated in the various Communist congresses they hold their determination that their goal must be the promotion of world revolution and a one-world Socialist or Communist state, whichever word you want to use.

Now, as long as they do that and as long as they, at the same time, have openly and publicly declared that the only morality they recognize is what will further their cause, meaning they reserve unto themselves the right to commit any crime, to lie, to cheat, in order to attain that, and that is moral, not immoral, and we operate on a different set of standards, I think when you do business with them, even at a détente, you keep that in mind.

2. Reagan Touts U.S. Military Power and Introduces the Strategic Defense Initiative, 1983

Since the dawn of the atomic age, we've sought to reduce the risk of war by maintaining a strong deterrent and by seeking genuine arms control. "Deterrence" means simply this: making sure any adversary who thinks about attacking the United States, or our allies, or our vital interests, concludes that the risks to him outweigh any potential gains. Once he understands that, he won't attack. We maintain the peace through our strength; weakness only invites aggression. . . .

For 20 years the Soviet Union has been accumulating enormous military might. They didn't stop when their forces exceeded all requirements of a legitimate defensive capability. And they haven't stopped now. During the past decade and a half, the Soviets have built up a massive arsenal of new strategic nuclear weapons—weapons that can strike directly at the United States. . . .

Another example of what's happened: In 1978 the Soviets had 600 intermediate-range nuclear missiles based on land and were beginning to add the SS-20—a new, highly accurate, mobile missile with 3 warheads. We had none. Since then the Soviets have strengthened their lead. By the end of 1979, when Soviet leader Brezhnev

---

Document 1 can be found in *Public Papers of the Presidents, Ronald Reagan, 1981* (Washington, D.C.: U.S. Government Printing Office, 1982), p. 57.

Document 2 can be found in *Public Papers of the Presidents, Ronald Reagan, 1983* (Washington, D.C.: U.S. Government Printing Office, 1984), Book I, pp. 437–443.

declared "a balance now exists," the Soviets had over 800 warheads. We still had none. A year ago this month, Mr. Brezhnev pledged a moratorium, or freeze, on SS-20 deployment. But by last August, their 800 warheads had become more than 1,200. We still had none. Some freeze. At this time Soviet Defense Minister [Dmitri] Ustinov announced "approximate parity of forces continues to exist." But the Soviets are still adding an average of 3 new warheads a week, and now have 1,300. These warheads can reach their targets in a matter of a few minutes. We still have none. So far, it seems that the Soviet definition of parity is a box score of 1,300 to nothing, in their favor.

So, together with our NATO allies, we decided in 1979 to deploy new weapons, beginning this year, as a deterrent to their SS-20's and as an incentive to the Soviet Union to meet us in serious arms control negotiations. We will begin that deployment late this year. At the same time, however, we're willing to cancel our program if the Soviets will dismantle theirs. This is what we've called a zero-zero plan. The Soviets are now at the negotiating table—and I think it's fair to say that without our planned deployments, they wouldn't be there. . . .

Some people may still ask: Would the Soviets ever use their formidable military power? Well, again, can we afford to believe they won't? There is Afghanistan. And in Poland, the Soviets denied the will of the people and in so doing demonstrated to the world how their military power could also be used to intimidate.

The final fact is that the Soviet Union is acquiring what can only be considered an offensive military force. They have continued to build far more intercontinental ballistic missiles than they could possibly need simply to deter an attack. Their conventional forces are trained and equipped not so much to defend against an attack as they are to permit sudden, surprise offensives of their own. . . .

I know that all of you want peace, and so do I. I know too that many of you seriously believe that a nuclear freeze would further the cause of peace. But a freeze now would make us less, not more, secure and would raise, not reduce, the risks of war. It would be largely unverifiable and would seriously undercut our negotiations on arms reduction. It would reward the Soviets for their massive military buildup while preventing us from modernizing our aging and increasingly vulnerable forces. With their present margin of superiority, why should they agree to arms reductions knowing that we were prohibited from catching up? . . .

The calls for cutting back the defense budget come in nice, simple arithmetic. They're the same kind of talk that led the democracies to neglect their defenses in the 1930's and invited the tragedy of World War II. We must not let that grim chapter of history repeat itself through apathy or neglect. . . .

This approach to stability [deterrence] through offensive threat [retaliation] has worked. We and our allies have succeeded in preventing nuclear war for more than three decades. In recent months, however, my advisers, including in particular the Joint Chiefs of Staff, have underscored the necessity to break out of a future that relies solely on offensive retaliation for our security. . . .

If the Soviet Union will join with us in our effort to achieve major arms reduction, we will have succeeded in stabilizing the nuclear balance. Nevertheless, it will still be necessary to rely on the specter of retaliation, on mutual threat. And that's a sad commentary on the human condition. Wouldn't it be better to save lives than to avenge them? Are we not capable of demonstrating our peaceful intentions by applying all our abilities and our ingenuity to achieving a truly lasting stability? I think we are. Indeed, we must.

After careful consultation with my advisers, including the Joint Chiefs of Staff, I believe there is a way. Let me share with you a vision of the future which offers hope. It is that we embark on a program to counter the awesome Soviet missile threat with measures that are defensive. Let us turn to the very strengths in technology that spawned our great industrial base and that have given us the quality of life we enjoy today.

What if free people could live secure in the knowledge that their security did not rest upon the threat of instant U.S. retaliation to deter a Soviet attack, that we could intercept and destroy strategic ballistic missiles before they reached our own soil or that of our allies?

I know this is a formidable, technical task, one that may not be accomplished before the end of this century. Yet, current technology has attained a level of sophistication where it's reasonable for us to begin this effort. It will take years, probably decades of effort on many fronts. There will be failures and setbacks, just as there will be successes and breakthroughs. And as we proceed, we must remain constant in preserving the nuclear deterrent and maintaining a solid capability for flexible response. But isn't it worth every investment necessary to free the world from the threat of nuclear war? We know it is. . . .

I clearly recognize that defensive systems have limitations and raise certain problems and ambiguities. If paired with offensive systems, they can be viewed as fostering an aggressive policy, and no one wants that. But with these considerations firmly in mind, I call upon the scientific community in our country, those who gave us nuclear weapons, to turn their great talents now to the cause of mankind and world peace, to give us the means of rendering these nuclear weapons impotent and obsolete.

Tonight, consistent with our obligations of the ABM [Anti-Ballistic Missile] treaty and recognizing the need for closer consultation with our allies, I'm taking an important first step. I am directing a comprehensive and intensive effort to define a long-term research and development program to begin to achieve our ultimate goal of eliminating the threat posed by strategic nuclear missiles. This could pave the way for arms control measures to eliminate the weapons themselves. We seek neither military superiority nor political advantage. Our only purpose—one all people share—is to search for ways to reduce the danger of nuclear war.

3. General Secretary Mikhail Gorbachev Identifies U.S. Delusions, 1985

I attempted to explain to the President [Reagan] in a frank and straightforward discussion that, as it seems to me, much in American policy in relation to the USSR is based on delusions. On the one hand, it is hoped that the arms race and its escalation will exhaust the Soviet Union economically, undermine its influence in the

This document can be found in M. S. Gorbachev, *Speeches and Writings* (Oxford: Pergamon Press, 1986), I, 284–285.

world and thus free the hands of the United States. History has put such prophets to shame—even at a time when our society had a far smaller potential than today's, and smaller possibilities in general. Today, however, they are enormous. So delusions on this score only hamper the conduct of a realistic policy.

On the other hand, there were also delusions in the area of military plans. Attempts were made to outstrip us. Intercontinental ballistic missiles were put into regular service. This was followed by a Soviet response. After a slight delay, it is true, but it did follow. Then multiple nuclear warheads came on the scene. A Soviet response followed. We have always been able to meet any challenge.

Today, it seems to me, the illusions lingering in US military circles have been adopted to a certain extent by the political circles; by the President in particular. It is only a likelihood, of course, so I am not positive about it, but we do have such an impression.

It is evidently believed in the United States that it now has a definite edge on the Soviet Union in certain types of technology, computers and electronics. So again a desire has arisen to seize on this "edge" and achieve military superiority. President [Lyndon] Johnson's well known phrase to the effect that the nations that will rule outer space will rule the earth is again in current usage. Someone is evidently itching for a fight and is being consumed by ambition for world supremacy.

It is the old ambition of days of yore. The world has changed very much since then.

Thus, speaking of the so called technological edge which is to be realized through SDI and thus create a predicament for the Soviet Union, I must give this answer: this is just another delusion. We will meet this challenge.

4. Reagan Defends SDI After the Reykjavík Summit Meeting, 1986

We proposed the most sweeping and generous arms control proposal in history. We offered the complete elimination of all ballistic missiles—Soviet and American—from the face of the Earth by 1996. While we parted company with this American offer still on the table, we are closer than ever before to agreements that could lead to a safer world without nuclear weapons. . . .

Some years ago, the United States and the Soviet Union agreed to limit any defense against nuclear missile attacks to the emplacement in one location in each country of a small number of missiles capable of intercepting and shooting down incoming nuclear missiles, thus leaving our real defense—a policy called mutual assured destruction, meaning if one side launched a nuclear attack, the other side could retaliate. And this mutual threat of destruction was believed to be a deterrent against either side striking first. So here we sit, with thousands of nuclear warheads targeted on each other and capable of wiping out both our countries. The Soviets deployed the few antiballistic missiles around Moscow as the treaty permitted. Our

This document can be found in *Public Papers of the Presidents, Ronald Reagan, 1986* (Washington, D.C.: U.S. Government Printing Office, 1989), Book II, pp. 1367–1370.

country didn't bother deploying because the threat of nationwide annihilation made such a limited defense seem useless.

For some years now we've been aware that the Soviets may be developing a nationwide defense. They have installed a large, modern radar at Krasnoyarsk, which we believe is a critical part of a radar system designed to provide radar guidance for antiballistic missiles protecting the entire nation. Now, this is a violation of the ABM treaty. Believing that a policy of mutual destruction and slaughter of their citizens and ours was uncivilized, I asked our military, a few years ago, to study and see if there was a practical way to destroy nuclear missiles after their launch but before they can reach their targets, rather than just destroy people. Well, this is the goal for what we call SDI, and our scientists researching such a system are convinced it is practical and that several years down the road we can have such a system ready to deploy. Now incidentally, we are not violating the ABM treaty, which permits such research. If and when we deploy, the treaty also allows withdrawal from the treaty upon 6 months' notice. SDI, let me make it clear, is a nonnuclear defense. . . .

I offered a proposal that we continue our present [SDI] research. And if and when we reached the stage of testing, we would sign, now, a treaty that would permit Soviet observation of such tests. And if the program was practical, we would both eliminate our offensive missiles, and then we would share the benefits of advanced defenses. I explained that even though we would have done away with our offensive ballistic missiles, having the defense would protect against cheating or the possibility of a madman, sometime, deciding to create nuclear missiles. After all, the world now knows how to make them. I likened it to our keeping our gas masks, even though the nations of the world had outlawed poison gas after World War I. We seemed to be making progress on reducing weaponry, although the General Secretary [Gorbachev] was registering opposition to SDI and proposing a pledge to observe ABM for a number of years. . . .

The Soviets had asked for a 10-year delay in the deployment of SDI programs. In an effort to see how we could satisfy their concerns—while protecting our principles and security—we proposed a 10-year period in which we began with the reduction of all strategic nuclear arms, bombers, air-launched cruise missiles, intercontinental ballistic missiles, submarine-launched ballistic missiles and the weapons they carry. They would be reduced 50 percent in the first 5 years. During the next 5 years, we would continue by eliminating all remaining offensive ballistic missiles, of all ranges. And during that time, we would proceed with research, development, and testing of SDI—all done in conformity with ABM provisions. At the 10-year point, with all ballistic missiles eliminated, we could proceed to deploy advanced defenses, at the same time permitting the Soviets to do likewise.

And here the debate began. The General Secretary wanted wording that, in effect, would have kept us from developing the SDI for the entire 10 years. In effect, he was killing SDI. And unless I agreed, all that work toward eliminating nuclear weapons would go down the drain—canceled. I told him I had pledged to the American people that I would not trade away SDI, there was no way I could tell our people their government would not protect them against nuclear destruction. . . .

I realize some Americans may be asking tonight: Why not accept Mr. Gorbachev's demand? Why not give up SDI for this agreement? Well, the answer, my friends, is simple. SDI is America's insurance policy that the Soviet Union would keep the commitments made at Reykjavík. SDI is America's security guarantee if the Soviets should—as they have done too often in the past—fail to comply with their solemn commitments. SDI is what brought the Soviets back to arms control talks at Geneva and Iceland. SDI is the key to a world without nuclear weapons. The Soviets understand this. They have devoted far more resources, for a lot longer time than we, to their own SDI. The world's only operational missile defense today surrounds Moscow, the capital of the Soviet Union.

What Mr. Gorbachev was demanding at Reykjavík was that the United States agree to a new version of a 14-year-old ABM treaty that the Soviet Union has already violated. I told him we don't make those kinds of deals in the United States. And the American people should reflect on these critical questions: How does a defense of the United States threaten the Soviet Union or anyone else? Why are the Soviets so adamant that America remain forever vulnerable to Soviet rocket attack? As of today, all free nations are utterly defenseless against Soviet missiles—fired either by accident or design. Why does the Soviet Union insist that we remain so—forever?

5. Gorbachev Criticizes SDI After the Reykjavík Summit Meeting, 1986

Reykjavík generated not hopes alone. Reykjavík also highlighted the hardships on the road to a nuclear-free world. . . .

Quarters linked with militarism and arms race profits are clearly scared. They are doing their utmost to cope with the new situation and, coordinating their actions, are trying in every way to mislead the people, to control the sentiment of broad sections of the world public, to suppress their quest for peace, to hinder governments from taking a clear-cut position at this decisive moment in history. . . .

Far-reaching and interconnected, they [the Soviet proposals presented at the Reykjavík meeting] constitute an integrated package and are based on the program we announced on 15 January for the elimination of nuclear weapons by the year 2000.

The first proposal is to cut by half all strategic arms, without exception.

The second proposal is to fully eliminate Soviet and US medium-range missiles in Europe and immediately set about talks on missiles of this type in Asia, as well as on missiles with a range of less than a thousand kilometres. We suggested freezing the number of such missiles immediately.

The third proposal is to consolidate the ABM Treaty and to start full-scale talks on a total ban on nuclear tests. . . .

The US Administration is now trying in every possible way to convince people that a possible major success with concrete agreements was not achieved owing to Soviet unyieldingness over the program of the so-called Strategic Defence Initiative (SDI).

This document can be found in M. S. Gorbachev, *Speeches and Writings* (Oxford: Pergamon Press, 1986), II, 64–70.

It is even being asserted that we allegedly lured the President into a trap by putting forward "breathtaking" proposals on cutting down strategic offensive arms and medium-range missiles, and that later on we ostensibly demanded in an ultimatum form that SDI be renounced.

But the essence of our stand and of our proposals is as follows: we are for reduction and then complete elimination of nuclear weapons and are firmly against a new stage in the arms race and against its transfer to outer space.

Hence we are against SDI and are for consolidation of the ABM Treaty.

It is clear to every sober-minded person that if we embark upon the road of deep cuts and then complete elimination of nuclear weapons, it is essential to rule out any opportunity for either the Soviet or US side to gain unilateral military superiority.

We perceive the main danger of SDI precisely in a transfer of the arms race to a new sphere, and in endeavours to go out into space with offensive arms and thereby achieve military superiority.

SDI has become an obstacle to ending the arms race, to getting rid of nuclear weapons, and is the main obstacle to a nuclear-free world. . . .

In upholding the position that thwarted the reaching of agreement in Reykjavík, the President asks rhetorical questions: Why do the Russians so stubbornly demand that America forever remain vulnerable to a Soviet missile strike? Why does the Soviet Union insist that we remain defenceless forever?

I am surprised at such questions, I must say. They have the air of indicating that the American President has an opportunity to make his country invulnerable, to give it secure protection against a nuclear strike.

As long as nuclear weapons exist and the arms race continues, he does not have such an opportunity. The same, naturally, applies to ourselves.

If the President counts on SDI in this respect, he does so in vain. The system would be effective only if all missiles were eliminated. But then, one might ask, why the anti-missile defence altogether? Why build it? I need not mention the money wasted, the cost of the system—according to some estimates, it will run into several trillion dollars.

So far, we have been trying to persuade America to give up that dangerous undertaking. We are urging the American Administration to look for invulnerability and for protection in another way—the way of total elimination of nuclear weapons and the establishment of a comprehensive system of international security that would preclude all war—nuclear and conventional. . . .

It is hard to reconcile oneself to the loss of a unique chance—that of saving mankind from the nuclear threat. Bearing precisely this in mind, I told the press conference in Reykjavík that we did not regard the dialogue as closed and hoped that President Reagan, on returning home, would consult Congress and the American people and adopt decisions logically necessitated by what had been achieved in Reykjavík.

Quite a different thing has happened. Besides distorting the entire picture of the Reykjavík negotiations—I will speak about that later—they have in recent days taken actions that look simply wild in the normal human view after such an important meeting between the two countries' top leaders.

I mean the expulsion of another fifty-five Soviet embassy and consular staff from the United States. We will take measures in response, of course—very tough measures on an equal footing. We are not going to put up with such outrageous practices. But for now let me say the following.

What kind of government is this? What can one expect from it in other affairs in the international arena? To what limits does the unpredictability of its actions go?

It turns out that it has no constructive proposals on key disarmament issues and that it does not even have a desire to maintain the atmosphere essential for a normal continuation of the dialogue. It appears that Washington is not prepared for any of these. . . .

An unattractive portrait of the Administration of that great country, of an Administration quick to take disruptive actions, is coming into view. Either the President is unable to cope with an entourage which literally breathes hatred for the Soviet Union and for everything that may lead international affairs into a calm channel or he himself wants that. At all events, there is no keeping the "hawks" in the White House in check. And this is very dangerous. . . .

Let me say once again: when SDI is preferred to nuclear disarmament, only one conclusion is possible: it is that through that military program efforts are being made to disprove the axiom of international relations of our epoch expressed in the simple and clear-cut words under which the US President and I put our signatures last year [at the Geneva summit conference]. Here are those words: nuclear war must not be fought and it cannot be won.

Let me say in conclusion: the Soviet Union has put the maximum of goodwill into its proposals. We are not removing these proposals, they still stand! Everything that has been said by the way of their substantiation and development remains in force.

6. Paul Kennedy on "Imperial Overstretch" and the Relative Decline of the United States, 1987

Although the United States is at present still in a class of its own economically and perhaps even militarily, it cannot avoid confronting the two great tests which challenge the *longevity* of every major power that occupies the "number one" position in world affairs: whether, in the military/strategic realm, it can preserve a reasonable balance between the nation's perceived defense requirements and the means it possesses to maintain those commitments; and whether, as an intimately related point, it can preserve the technological and economic bases of its power from relative erosion in the face of the ever-shifting patterns of global production. This test of American abilities will be the greater because it, like Imperial Spain around 1600 or the British Empire around 1900, is the inheritor of a vast array of strategical commitments which had been made decades earlier, when the nation's political, economic, and military capacity to influence world affairs seemed so much more assured. In consequence, the United States now runs the risk, so familiar to historians of the rise and fall of previous Great Powers, of what might roughly be called "imperial overstretch"; that is to say, decision-makers in Washington must face the awkward and enduring fact that the sum total of the United States' global interests and obligations is nowadays far larger than the country's power to defend them all simultaneously. . . .

This brings us, inevitably, to the delicate relationship between slow economic growth and high defense spending. The debate upon "the economics of defense spending" is a highly controversial one, and—bearing in mind the size and variety of the American economy, the stimulus which can come from large government contracts, and the technical spin-offs from weapons research—the evidence does not point simply in one direction. But what is significant for our purposes is the comparative dimension. Even if (as is often pointed out) defense expenditures formed 10 percent of GNP under Eisenhower and 9 percent under Kennedy, the United States' relative share of global production and wealth was at that time around *twice* what it is today; and, more particularly, the American economy was not then facing the challenges to either its traditional or its high-technology manufactures. Moreover, if the United States at present continues to devote 7 percent or more of its GNP to defense spending while its major economic rivals, especially Japan, allocate a far smaller proportion, then *ipso facto* the latter have potentially more funds "free" for civilian investment; if the United States continues to invest a massive amount of its R&D activities into military-related production while the Japanese and West Germans concentrate upon commercial R&D; and if the Pentagon's spending drains off the majority of the country's scientists and engineers from the design and production of goods for the world market while similar personnel in other countries are primarily engaged in bringing out better products for the civilian consumer, then it seems inevitable that the American share of world manufacturing will steadily decline, and also likely that its economic growth rates will be slower than in those countries dedicated to the marketplace and less eager to channel resources into defense.

It is almost superfluous to say that these tendencies place the United States on the horns of a most acute dilemma over the longer term. Simply because it is *the* global superpower, with far more extensive military commitments than a regional Power like Japan or West Germany, it requires much larger defense forces—in just the same way as imperial Spain felt it needed a far larger army than its contemporaries and Victorian Britain insisted upon a much bigger navy than any other country. Furthermore, since the USSR is seen to be the major military threat to American interests across the globe and is clearly devoting a far greater proportion of *its* GNP to defense, American decision-makers are inevitably worried about "losing" the arms race with Russia. Yet the more sensible among these decision-makers can also perceive that the burden of armaments is debilitating the Soviet economy; and that if the two superpowers continue to allocate ever-larger shares of their national wealth into the unproductive field of armaments, the critical question might soon be: "Whose economy will decline *fastest*, relative to such expanding states as Japan, China, etc.?" A low investment in armaments may, for a globally overstretched Power like the United States, leave it feeling vulnerable everywhere; but a very heavy investment in armament, while bringing greater security in the short term, may so erode the commercial competitiveness of the American economy that the nation will be *less* secure in the long term.

7. Georgi Arbatov Explains the "New Thinking" in the Soviet Union, 1989

Personally I share the radical view that *perestroika* means building a new model of Soviet socialism. We have to go all the way in democratization, *glasnost,* and economic reforms, not halfway. This bothers some people, but the reasons aren't hard to understand. The Soviet Union is a young country—just over seventy years old. During those years we have lived through so many extraordinary circumstances— the Revolution, the Civil War, Stalinism, the world war, the Cold War—that our structures, psychology, and behavior acquired extraordinary characteristics. It was like growing up under martial law. Even Stalinism was shaped by extraordinary circumstances—the threats of German fascism and Japanese militarism in the 1930s, the burden of the Cold War. So it's not surprising that we haven't yet built the socialist model we intended and believe in.

Now we have to rid ourselves of all those things that arose in those extraordinary times—things in which we used to believe, things we thought were intrinsic to socialism. This isn't easy, partly because many people will believe in all those things but also because the old economic model worked rather well in its time and for certain purposes. If the old economic model had completely failed, if the country had not developed from being a very backward country, it would be easier to change today. It would be easier to give up the obsolete thinking and policies that led the country into a dead end and that had such a negative impact on international relations. I can't think of any other country or government that now is so self-critical and demanding in looking at its own past and learning from the sufferings of the past.

That's why I argue against some of our officials who are guarded or worried about *glasnost.* The anti-*glasnost* tradition was imposed on the country during Stalinism, and it has had very negative effects in our domestic policies—but also in foreign policy. In fact, improvements brought by the Twentieth Party Congress back in the 1950s barely touched foreign policy. I don't mean that everything in our foreign policy stagnated in the years that followed. There were achievements— the beginnings of détente, arms control steps, and other things. But the tradition of secrecy, silence, and the absence of *glasnost* fossilized much of our defense and foreign policy thinking and decision making. When I argue for greater openness, some of our people say that exposing our problems will hurt us abroad. I tell them that the world knew about our problems before *glasnost;* we can't hide them. Moreover, *glasnost* has helped us abroad because more people there understand we are serious about our reforms. If there is an attempt to curtail *glasnost*, it will be harmful and counterproductive. . . .

The main priority of our foreign policy is to create the best international circumstances for the reforms going on inside our country. For us, economic and social progress is the most important thing. Of course, there still are some people here

From *Voices of Glasnost: Interviews with Gorbachev's Reformers* by Stephen F. Cohen and Katrina vanden Heuvel. Copyright © 1989 by Stephen F. Cohen and Katrina vanden Heuvel. Reprinted by permission of W. W. Norton & Company, Inc.

who cling to old ideas about the priority of promoting revolutions abroad—people who still think we can work miracles when foreign Marxists ask us for help. But it doesn't work. The best way to influence other countries is by reforming our own system. *Perestroika* involves a new way of thinking about foreign policy which begins with seeing realities as they are, not as we want them to be. We must face the truth, no matter how bitter it is. Our basic conception of the world has changed. We no longer view it in terms of "we" and "they" but as one humanity that has to live or die together. The nuclear world is too fragile for the use of military force, any kind of serious misbehavior, any geopolitical adventures, or an unlimited arms race. That is a basic principle of our new thinking. . . .

I should say first that we do not claim to have invented all the ideas of the new thinking. Some of them originated years ago outside the Soviet Union with people such as [the scientist] Albert Einstein, [the philosopher] Bertrand Russell, and [the Swedish politician] Olof Palme. We are developing them, along with our own ideas, into a full program for international conduct. To mention just a few of these ideas, we now believe that what unites different countries, their common interests, is more important than the conflicts and differences between them. We also realized that we relied too much on military power for security. Both the Soviet Union and the United States have far more military power than they can use for any reasonable purpose. Militarism on the part of all countries is the real danger. We all must rely for security more on political means—on negotiations, for example. Our mutual task is to reverse the militarization of life. We have no need for all these weapons and huge armies. We also now understand that we cannot obtain national security at the expense of the other side—at your [U.S.] expense—and the same is true for you. This is our concept of mutual security. Our security depends on you feeling secure, and yours depends on us feeling secure. Now we also understand better that the lagging economic development of the Third World is a global problem, and despite our limited resources we have to make our contribution to solving this problem.

More generally, the Soviet Union no longer can live in economic autarchy, isolated from the world economy. Interdependence can only increase. All of these new perceptions make us favor more multilateral efforts, particularly through the United Nations. My own view is that the two superpowers have to be more democratic in their thinking about the world. The Soviet Union and the United States represent only about 10 percent of the world population. We can't and shouldn't try to do everything. And the rest of the world should not be held hostage to U.S.-Soviet relations. . . .

We think [military] sufficiency is enough. Of course, we want some kind of equality, but not in numerical terms. We don't have to have as many airplanes as you have. We don't need them. All we need is enough so that you know it would be folly to start a war.

But we have gone beyond this. We want to create a nonnuclear world or a world with very few nuclear weapons. And we understand that we cannot have these major reductions in nuclear weapons without major reductions in conventional weapons. You can see how serious we are about this from Gorbachev's unilateral reductions in our conventional forces. So far as we are concerned, the door is wide open for even larger reductions through negotiations.

Unfortunately, there is a good deal of hypocrisy on your side. Your authorities complain that we have superiority in conventional weapons. Perhaps we do in some categories and we are prepared to build down in these areas. But you've been complaining about this for forty years, despite the fact that the West's GNP is two and a half times bigger than ours. If you really thought we had such superiority, why didn't you catch up? Your automobile and tractor industries are much stronger than ours. Why didn't they build tanks? No, I think you've used this scare about alleged Soviet superiority to hold your NATO alliance together and to justify building an absolutely irrational number of nuclear weapons.

We are arguing that both sides must adopt a new policy to replace the arms race. The side that is ahead in a weapons category should build down rather than the lagging side build up. This is the reasonable way to solve the problem of imbalances. Unfortunately, the human mind has a tendency to lag behind. Politics and diplomacy do especially. Our task is to bring your perceptions into accord with realities, particularly in foreign and military policy. Since 1985 Gorbachev has proposed getting rid of nuclear weapons. We have liberated ourselves from our own old thinking about nuclear and conventional weapons. President Gorbachev and President Reagan made some important progress on nuclear weapons. But our new thinking seems to have put America in an awkward position. Suddenly we start accepting American proposals and you don't know what to do. We're still getting too many negative responses from you. . . .

I know that some Americans dislike them [Soviet domestic reforms] and I understand why. Since 1945 many American institutions have needed a foreign enemy—an evil empire. Indeed, the general framework of American foreign policy has been constructed on the premise of this enemy. The Cold War was built on a kind of black-and-white, religious fundamentalism. There was the American paradise and the Soviet hell. When hell disappears, when the enemy image erodes, the whole structure becomes shaky. Some Americans fear this. But they will just have to find ways to live without the image of the Soviet enemy. America also needs *perestroika* and new thinking of her own. . . .

But, you know, there is so much ideology about us in America. It's a great irony. You've always accused us of being too ideological, but there's no country in the world more ideological than the Untied States, despite your professed pragmatism. Mr. Reagan's presidency brought this ideological impulse to the fore. We too tended to over-ideologize our foreign policy, but our new thinking is based on realism. For example, that all these weapons are dangerous and useless. Your ideology—or illusions—seem to persist, which is one reason why you can't let go of the enemy image so easily. . . .

The Cold War is a living corpse. It died sometime in the 1960s and has been kept alive by political injections of myths and fantasies about the Soviet threat—like a body kept alive on an artificial heart-and-lung machine. It is time to lay it to rest. Neither of us can any longer afford to squander money on fake problems, false stereotypes, and pointless suspicions. Both of us have plenty of real problems at home. . . .

I'm not confident that you will have new thinking in the United States, but I think your economic problems are going to force a change in your foreign policy anyway. Can you imagine the same amount of military spending and indebtedness over the next eight years? Also, to continue the Cold War you will need a partner. We won't be that partner. So while we may lose valuable time, I think things will be better in the United States.

8. President George Bush Declares a New World Order During the Persian Gulf Crisis, 1990

We stand today at a unique and extraordinary moment. The crisis in the Persian Gulf, as grave as it is, also offers a rare opportunity to move toward an historic period of cooperation. Out of these troubled times, . . . a new world order can emerge: a new era—freer from the threat of terror, stronger in the pursuit of justice, and more secure in the quest for peace. An era in which the nations of the world, East and West, North and South, can prosper and live in harmony. A hundred generations have searched for this elusive path to peace, while a thousand wars raged across the span of human endeavor. Today that new world is struggling to be born, a world quite different from the one we've known. A world where the rule of law supplants the rule of the jungle. A world in which nations recognize the shared responsibility for freedom and justice. A world where the strong respect the rights of the weak. This is the vision that I shared with President Gorbachev in Helsinki. He and other leaders from Europe, the Gulf, and around the world understand that how we manage this crisis today could shape the future for generations to come.

The test we face is great, and so are the stakes. This is the first assault on the new world that we seek, the first test of our mettle. Had we not responded to this first provocation with clarity of purpose, if we do not continue to demonstrate our determination, it would be a signal to actual and potential despots around the world. America and the world must defend common vital interests—and we will. America and the world must support the rule of law—and we will. America and the world must stand up to aggression—and we will. And one thing more: In the pursuit of these goals America will not be intimidated.

Vital issues of principle are at stake. Saddam Hussein is literally trying to wipe a country [Kuwait] off the face of the Earth. We do not exaggerate. Nor do we exaggerate when we say Saddam Hussein will fail. Vital economic interests are at risk as well. Iraq itself controls some 10 percent of the world's proven oil reserves. Iraq plus Kuwait controls twice that. An Iraq permitted to swallow Kuwait would have the economic and military power, as well as the arrogance, to intimidate and coerce its neighbors—neighbors who control the lion's share of the world's remaining oil reserves. We cannot permit a resource so vital to be dominated by one so ruthless. And we won't.

Recent events have surely proven that there is no substitute for American leadership. In the face of tyranny, let no one doubt American credibility and reliability.

This document can be found in "Address to Congress on Persian Gulf Crisis," 11 September 1990, *Public Papers of the Presidents of the United States, George Bush, 1990* (Washington, D.C.: U.S. Government Printing Office, 1991), Book II, pp. 1218–1222.

9. President William J. Clinton Applauds America's Globalism and Warns Against a New Isolationism, 1995

You know, in 1991 I sought the presidency because I believed it was essential to restore the American dream for all Americans and to reassert America's leadership in the post-cold-war world. As we move from the industrial to the information age, from the cold war world to the global village, we have an extraordinary opportunity to advance our values at home and around the world. But we face some stiff challenges in doing so as well. . . .

We see the benefits of American leadership in the progress now being made in Bosnia. In recent weeks, our military muscle through NATO, our determined diplomacy throughout the region, have brought the parties closer to a settlement than at any time since this terrible war began 4 years ago. Yesterday, we helped to produce an agreement on a Bosnia-wide cease-fire. Now, the parties will come to the United States to pursue their peace talks mediated by our negotiating team and our European and Russian counterparts.

We have a long way to go, and there's no guarantee of success. But we will use every ounce of our influence to help the parties make a peace that preserves Bosnia as a single democratic state and protects the rights of all citizens, regardless of their ethnic group.

If and when peace comes, the international community's responsibility will not end. After all the bloodshed, the hatred, the loss of the last years, peace will surely be fragile. The international community must help to secure it. The only organization that can meet that responsibility strongly and effectively is NATO. And as NATO's leader, the United States must do its part and send in troops to join those of our allies under NATO command with clear rules of engagement. If we fail, the consequences for Bosnia and for the future of NATO would be severe. We must not fail.

The United States will not be sending our forces into combat in Bosnia. We will not send them into a peace that cannot be maintained, but we must use our power to secure that peace. I have pledged to consult with Congress before authorizing our participation in such an action. These consultations have already begun.

I believe Congress understands the importance of this moment and of American leadership. I'm glad to see [Republican] Chairman [Robert] Livingston here at the head table today. As I have said consistently for 2 years, we want and welcome congressional support. But in Bosnia as elsewhere, if the United States does not lead, the job will not be done.

We also saw the benefits of America's leadership last week at the White House where leaders from all over the Middle East gathered to support the agreement between Israel and the Palestinian Authority. For nearly a half-century now, Democratic and Republican administrations have worked to facilitate the cause of peace in the Middle East. The credit here belongs to the peacemakers. But we should all be proud that at critical moments along the way, our efforts helped to make the difference between failure and success.

This document can be found in "Remarks at Freedom House," 6 October 1995, *Public Papers of the Presidents of the United States, William J. Clinton, 1995* (Washington, D.C.: U.S. Government Printing Office, 1996), Book II, pp. 1544–1551.

It was almost exactly a year ago that the United States led the international effort to remove Haiti's military regime and give the people of Haiti a real chance at democracy. We've succeeded because we've backed diplomacy with sanctions and ultimately with force. We've succeeded because we understood that standing up for democracy in our own hemisphere was right for the Haitian people and right for America.

American efforts in Bosnia, the Middle East, and Haiti and elsewhere have required investments of time and energy and resources. They've required persistent diplomacy and the measured use of the world's strongest military. They have required both determination and flexibility in our efforts to work as leaders and to work with other nations. And sometimes they've called on us to make decisions that were, of necessity, unpopular in the short run, knowing that the payoff would not come in days or weeks but in months or years. Sometimes they have been difficult for many Americans to understand because they have to be made, as many decisions did right after World War II, without the benefit of some overarching framework, the kind of framework the bipolar cold war world provided for so many years.

To use the popular analogy of the present day, there seems to be no mainframe explanation for the PC world in which we're living. We have to drop the abstractions and dogma and pursue, based on trial and error and persistent experimentation, a policy that advances our values of freedom and democracy, peace, and security. . . .

The results of . . . responsible [U.S.] leadership [during the 1940s] were truly stunning: victory in the war and the construction of a post . . . war world. Not with abstract dogma but again, over a 5-year period, basing experience on new realities, through trial and error with a relentless pursuit of our own values, we created NATO, the Marshall Plan, Bretton Woods, the institutions that kept the peace in Europe, avoided nuclear conflict, helped to spread democracy, brought us unparalleled prosperity, and ultimately ensured the triumph of freedom in the cold war. . . .

Throughout what we now call the American century, Republicans and Democrats disagreed on specific policies, often heatedly from time to time, but we have always agreed on the need for American leadership in the cause of democracy, freedom, security, and prosperity. Now that consensus is truly in danger, and interestingly enough, it is in danger in both parties. Voices from the left and the right are calling on us to step back from, instead of stepping up to, the challenges of the present day. They threaten to reverse the bipartisan support for our leadership that has been essential to our strength for 50 years. Some really believe that after the cold war the United States can play a secondary role in the world, just as some thought we could after World War II, and some made sure we did after World War I.

But if you look at the results from Bosnia to Haiti, from the Middle East to Northern Ireland, it proves once again that American leadership is indispensable and that without it our values, our interests, and peace itself would be at risk.

It has now become a truism to blame the current isolationism on the end of the cold war because there is no longer a mainframe threat in this PC world. . . .

Let me say again, the once bright line between domestic and foreign policy is blurring. If I could do anything to change the speech patterns of those of us in public life, I would almost like to stop hearing people talk about foreign policy and domestic policy and instead start discussing economic policy, security policy, environmental policy, you name it.

When you think about the world and the way that you live in it, you readily see that the foreign-domestic distinction begins to evaporate in so many profound ways. And if we could learn to speak differently about it, the very act of speaking and thinking in the way we live, I believe, would make isolationism seem absolutely impossible as an alternative to public policy. . . .

The isolationists are simply wrong. The environment we face may be new and different, but to meet it with the challenges and opportunities it presents and to advance our enduring values, we have to be more engaged in the world, not less engaged in the world. That's why we have done everything we could in our administration to lead the fight to reduce the nuclear threat, to spread democracy in human rights, to support peace, to open markets, to enlarge and defend the community of nations around the world, to share our aspirations and our values. . . .

. . . But this isolationist backlash, which is present in both parties, is very real. And if you look at it from the point of view of people who feel threatened by the changes in the world, it is even completely understandable. So it is important that we not simply condemn it. It is even more important that we explain the way the world is working. And as the world works its way through this period of transition toward a new order of things in which we can garner all of the benefits of change and technology and opportunity and still reinforce the importance of giving everybody a chance, giving all families the chances to be strong, solidifying communities, as we work our way through this period, it is more and more important that we not simply condemn the isolationists but that we seek to explain how the world works and why we must be engaged and lead.

Condemnation is not enough. Characterization is not enough. We must work through these issues. The American people are good people. They have common sense. They care when people are being murdered around the world. They understand that a war somewhere else could one day involve our sons and daughters. They know that we cannot simply pretend that the rest of the world is not there. But many of them have their own difficulties. We must work and work and work on the basic values and interests and arguments until we beat back the forces of isolation, with both intense passion and reason.

 E S S A Y S

In the first essay, Thomas G. Paterson, a historian at the University of Connecticut, probes the external and internal factors that intersected to change both American and Soviet policies, end the Cold War, and usher in the post–Cold War era. He studies the costs of the long conflict for the United States and the Soviet Union, and the changes in the international system that undermined the power of both countries. Moscow and Washington reversed course and ended the Cold War to stem their decline and to recover their sagging international positions. Although the dawning of the post–Cold War era witnessed a renewed U.S. drive for influence, Paterson concludes that given their substantial domestic problems by the early 1990s, it can hardly be said that either the United States or the Soviet Union won the Cold War.

In the second essay, a statement representative of the Reagan victory school, the historian John Lewis Gaddis of Yale University disagrees with Paterson's perspective on the ending of the Cold War. Gaddis trumpets Reagan's restoration of national self-confidence, the U.S. military buildup, the bargaining chip value of SDI, and the United States's negotiation from a position of strength for "spooking" the Soviets. For Gaddis, Reagan stands tall as a skillful visionary whose toughness paid off.

The third essay, by the political scientists Daniel Deudney of the University of Pennsylvania and G. John Ikenberry of Princeton University, disputes Gaddis and the peace-through-strength thesis. These authors note Reagan's distaste for nuclear weapons and argue that ultimately Reagan's "soft" policies became more influential than his "hard" policies. They also credit a large peace movement in the West and improving East-West economic relations for tempering the Cold War. As for the question of victory, Deudney and Ikenberry posit that what triumphed at the end of the Cold War was not Reagan's free market capitalism but rather the welfare-state ideas of Western European social democracy.

The final essay, by Samuel P. Huntington, a professor of international relations and strategic studies at Harvard University, analyzes America's quest for global hegemony in the post–Cold War era. Huntington argues that the contemporary world system is neither unipolar, bipolar, or multipolar, but rather a hybrid "uni-multipolar" system with one superpower and multiple regional powers. He faults the Bush and Clinton administrations for too often acting unilaterally and failing to use U.S. power to elicit multilateral cooperation in settling international disputes. Huntington warns that attempts to impose American values and dominance through economic sanctions and military interventions have generated deep resentment overseas, especially among peoples whose cultural practices differ from those that prevail in the United States.

Superpower Decline and Hegemonic Survival

THOMAS G. PATERSON

Simply put, the Cold War ended because of the relative decline of the United States and the Soviet Union in the international system from the 1950s through the 1980s. The Cold War waned because the contest had undermined the power of its two major protagonists. In acts of hegemonic survival in a world of mounting challenges on several fronts, they gradually moved toward a cautious cooperation whose urgent goals were nothing less than the restoration of their economic well-being and the preservation of their diminishing global positions.

At least three sources or trends explain this gradual decline and the consequent attractions of détente. The first was the burgeoning economic costs of the Cold War. Challenges to the leadership of the two major powers from within their spheres of influence constitute the second source. The third was the emergence of the Third World, which brought new players into the international game, further diffused power, and eroded bipolarism. The three elements combined to weaken the standing of the two adversaries and ultimately to persuade Soviet and American leaders to halt their nations' descent by ending the Cold War. The Soviet Union fell much harder than the United States, but the implications of decline became unmistakable for both: The Cold War they made in the 1940s had to be unmade if the two nations were to remain prominent international superintendents.

From *On Every Front: The Making and Unmaking of the Cold War,* Revised Edition by Thomas G. Paterson. Copyright © 1992, 1979 by W. W. Norton & Company, Inc. Reprinted by permission of W. W. Norton & Company, Inc.

The first source was the economic burden that the long confrontation inflicted on the United States and the Soviet Union. . . . In the postwar years the United States used its abundant economic resources to spur the recovery of its allies and to build an international military network. The costs of maintaining and expanding its global interests climbed dramatically: $12.4 billion for the Marshall Plan, $69.5 billion for the Korean War, $22.3 billion for the Alliance for Progress, $172.2 billion for the Vietnam War. In the years from 1946 through 1987 the United States dispensed more than $382 billion in economic and military foreign aid. International organizations in which the United States was prominent, such as the World Bank, offered another $273 billion in assistance.

The United States also spent billions of dollars for CIA operations. . . . Expenses also mounted for the maintenance of occupying forces in Germany, Japan, and elsewhere. U.S. Information Agency propaganda activities proved expensive, too, as witnessed by the Voice of America's $640 million expenditure in the 1970s.

Security links stretched across the globe. After the Rio Pact (1947) and NATO (1949) came the ANZUS Pact with Australia and New Zealand (1951), the defense treaty with Japan (1952), the South East Asia Treaty Organization (SEATO, 1954), and the Baghdad Pact for the Middle East (1955). . . . In 1959, moreover, one million Americans were stationed overseas; in 1970 the number was nearly nine hundred thousand; and by 1985 the United States still had more than half a million armed forces personnel abroad.

Alliance building, military expansion, clandestine operations, and interventionism spawned galloping defense budgets amounting to trillions of dollars over four decades. U.S. military spending stood at $13.5 billion in 1949, averaged $40 billion a year in the 1950s, rose to $54 billion in 1960 and $90 billion in 1970 (largely because of the Vietnam War), and soared to $155 billion in 1980. By 1988 the military budget alone had reached more than $300 billion. In the mid-1980s the Defense Department was spending an average of $28 million an hour, twenty-four hours a day, seven days a week. Nuclear-arms development and ever more sophisticated technology [also] drove up the cost of waging the Cold War. . . .

America's massive military spending chipped away at the nation's infrastructure, contributing to the relative decline of the United States and stimulating the movement toward Soviet-American détente. Defense spending demanded capital, which the federal government had to borrow, forcing up interest rates, which in turn slowed economic development. Persistent deficit spending by the federal government drove up the federal debt, which stood at $257 billion in 1950, $286 billion in 1960, $371 billion in 1970, and $908 billion in 1980. By 1986 the debt had reached a staggering $2.1 trillion. . . .

Military spending constantly drew funds away from other categories so essential to the overall well-being of the nation—what economists call "opportunity costs." Domestic troubles mounted: lower productivity, falling savings rate, sagging agricultural sector, inadequately skilled labor force with an increasing number of functional illiterates, drug abuse, decaying cities, growing high school dropout rates, a health care system that failed to cover large numbers of people, and weak conservation programs that left the U.S. economy vulnerable to sharp swings in prices of imported raw materials. . . .

The United States also became a debtor nation with a serious balance of payments problem and a widening trade deficit. . . . International economic crises—high oil prices in the 1970s and massive Third World debt in the 1980s—added to America's woes. Debt-ridden nations curbed their purchases of American products and suspended debt payments. By 1985 the U.S. trade deficit had reached a remarkable $148.5 billion. . . . By 1989 the U.S. foreign debt hit $650 billion. . . .

Although the American economy during the Cold War grew in absolute numbers, the U.S. share of the world's material resources declined relative to other nations. . . . Between 1960 and 1973 the U.S. economic growth rate compared with that of all other countries was 4 percent versus 5.6 percent, and from 1973 to 1980 2 percent versus 3.6 percent. In the decade of the 1970s ninety-eight nations had higher rates of economic growth than the United States. In 1979 and 1980 the U.S. growth rate dropped to minus 0.2 percent; by comparison, Japan's stood at 4.2 percent and West Germany's at 1.8, and the world rate was 2 percent. The U.S. share of gross world product also declined: from approximately 40 percent in 1950 to about 22 percent in 1980. Japan doubled its share in the same period to 9 percent. From the 1950s to the 1980s the American share of world exports slumped while West Germany's and Japan's shares jumped. The American rate for productivity growth (output per worker) also descended; for 1950–1970 the rate was 2.68 percent, then for 1970–1980 it dropped to 1.17 percent, and for 1980–1986 it stood at 1.53 percent. For the same periods Japan's and West Germany's rates ranked higher than the U.S. rate. The American share of world industrial production also fell, and the United States lost its lead in televisions, automobiles, semiconductors, and machine tools. . . .

Measurable economic decline compelled American policy makers, however reluctantly at times, to take steps toward ending the Cold War. By relieving domestic troubles, détente seemed to offer continuation of America's world-class status. Détente might make expensive interventions and ever-growing arsenals less necessary. It also promised greater trade with both the Soviet Union and the People's Republic of China. . . .

The Cold War also cost the Soviet Union a great deal—indeed, much more than it cost the United States—and this burden persuaded Moscow to seek détente. . . . The Soviet Union also became a big military spender, in part to catch up in the strategic arms race. . . .

Foreign ventures, too, strained Soviet resources. In the 1950s Moscow began to lend funds to Third World nations—to India for a steel plant, to Egypt for the Aswan Dam. The Warsaw Pact; aid to the People's Republic of China (until halted by Moscow in the early 1960s); support for Egypt (until the Soviets were evicted in 1972), Syria, and other Middle Eastern states; and subsidies to Fidel Castro's Cuba (which averaged close to five billion dollars during the 1980s) also drew heavily on Soviet funds. North Vietnam received more than eight billion dollars in Soviet aid from 1965 to 1975. The Soviet Union subsidized its Eastern European client states, probably spending at least seventeen billion dollars a year by the early 1980s. The invasions of Hungary in 1956 and Czechoslovakia in 1968 and the ten-year war in Afghanistan from 1979 to 1989 cost dearly. . . .

To pay for its large Red Army encamped in Eastern Europe and along the tense border with China, the considerable expansion of its navy, and its interventions, foreign aid, and nuclear weaponry, the Kremlin shortchanged the nation's domestic development. . . . The nation's overall industrial and agricultural rates of growth slackened. In the 1950s the rate of Soviet economic growth stood at 5.9; from 1960 to 1973 the rate declined to 4.9 percent; from 1973 to 1980 the rate dropped even more to 2.6 percent; and for 1981 to 1985 the rate plummeted further to 1.9. . . .

Low productivity and shoddy craftsmanship stemmed from poor labor morale, alcoholism, high absenteeism, and a stultifying Communist party bureaucracy. "They pretend to pay us and we pretend to work" went the joke. Air and water pollution, crumbling plants, inefficient and hence dismal agricultural output, and declining life expectancy rates also plagued the Soviet Union through the Cold War decades. Shabbily manufactured tractors and trucks required inordinate maintenance; factory breakdowns and lack of spare parts slowed production. . . .

"There are real sources of trouble" in the Soviet Union, admitted Georgi Arbatov, director of Moscow's Institute for United States and Canadian Studies. "The Cold War just prevents us from dealing with them," he explained. "Neither of us can any longer afford to squander money on fake problems, false stereotypes, and pointless suspicions. Both of us have plenty of real problems at home." In 1987, for example, the Chernobyl nuclear plant accident spewed radioactive fallout across Europe and raised anew doubts about Soviet workmanship, management skills, and governmental competence. . . .To save the Soviet economy, the expensive arms race had to be stopped, for military spending was eating up at least a quarter of the nation's budget. . . .

In addition to the economic burden of the Cold War, another significant source accounted for the great powers' decline and their movement toward détente: challenges to their hegemony from independent-minded client states and allies. Some allies, such as West Germany and France, advanced détente on their own. Others made so much trouble that the hegemonic powers welcomed détente as a means to discipline them—Moscow's eagerness to build Soviet-American cooperation as a counterweight to China, for example. The two great powers also embraced détente as a means to reassert mastery, as in the 1970s, when Moscow hoped that the United States would accept the Soviet Union's preeminent influence in Eastern Europe and Washington hoped that détente would create a great-power "equilibrium" that would help reduce radical revolution in the American sphere. Sometimes détente afforded a great power an apparent opportunity to exploit division within a sphere in order to contain or weaken its adversary. The USSR, for example, attempted to encourage France to spoil U.S. plans for Western Europe, and the United States played its "China card" against the Soviet Union. . . .

The United States, too, faced challenges from within its far-flung sphere of influence, although with less disarray than that experienced by the Soviets [in dealing with Eastern European nationalism and the Sino-Soviet schism]. Europe became for Americans a source not only of friends but also of rivals, who themselves marched in the direction of ending the Cold War. . . .

Such expressions of independence by allies became common during the Vietnam era, when NATO partners failed to support the long U.S. war in Southeast Asia. The British, complained the always pungent President Lyndon B. Johnson, could at least have sent a platoon of bagpipers. . . . Some jittery Europeans also believed that American policy makers preferred to use European territory as a nuclear battleground. Under the weight of such strains the American sphere of influence in Europe progressively frayed.

The nationalism and independent decision making of West Germany also shook the American sphere and advanced détente. Many West Germans scorned Americans when the United States did not knock down the Berlin Wall after it went up in 1961, and Chancellor Konrad Adenauer became suspicious that Moscow and Washington would cut deals at Germany's expense. Soon France and Germany seemed to be competing to see which could first establish détente with the Soviet Union. When Willy Brandt became chancellor in 1969, the Federal Republic of Germany displayed unusual independence by making overtures to Moscow. Brandt's Eastern policy *(Ostpolitik)* led in 1970 to a Soviet-German nonaggression treaty, which especially reduced friction over Berlin. Two years later, in an early gesture toward reunification, the two Germanys opened diplomatic channels. Kissinger bristled at this "new form of classic German nationalism," but he nonetheless endorsed Brandt's efforts because most allies did. "We could best hold the Alliance together," he recalled, "by accepting the principle of détente. . . ."

Greatly expanded Western European trade with and investment in the Soviet sphere of influence beginning in the late 1940s also drew back the "iron curtain" in a seemingly irreversible process of economic détente. After the divisive Suez crisis, for example, America's European allies sought more energy independence from the Middle East—and from the United States. The Soviet Union, to Washington's dismay, became an alternative oil and natural gas source. . . .

The diminution of America's power could be measured even in the most conspicuous arena of its hegemony—Latin America. . . . Clear signs of hemispheric independence became evident when Venezuela helped found the Organization of Petroleum Exporting Countries (OPEC) [in 1960] and nationalized American-owned oil companies. American-owned multinational corporations faced higher taxes, terrorism, expropriation, and regulations on the hiring of nationals. . . . During the Vietnam War, when the United States appeared "unreliable as a security partner," Brazil began to import weapons from European suppliers; later it developed its own profitable weapons-exporting business. U.S. hegemony in the Western Hemisphere had rested in part on U.S. dominance in arms production and weapons sales. Washington witnessed another setback in the 1970 election of the Marxist President Salvador Allende in Chile and in Peru's defiant 1970s purchases of Soviet MiGs. The 1979 victory of the radical Sandinistas over the longtime U.S. ally Anastasio Somoza in Nicaragua and Argentina's selling of grain to the Soviet Union in 1980 during a U.S.-imposed embargo against the Soviets provided further evidence of diminished U.S. power in the hemisphere. Although the CIA helped depose Allende in 1973, this American success and the U.S. military interventions in the Dominican Republic (1965), Grenada (1983), and Panama (1989) attested not to U.S. strength but to the loosening of its imperial net. Western Hemispheric nations, overall, boldly questioned the "hegemonic presumption" of the United States.

The most serious defiance to the United States came from Cuba's Fidel Castro. . . . Castro survived the [missile] crisis, consolidated his power, and promised revolution all over Latin America. Cuba remained a Soviet ally, although Havana frequently followed an independent foreign policy. Cuban-American hostility persisted despite some steps toward improved relations in the 1970s.

As he cultivated détente in the early 1970s, President Nixon identified five power centers in the world: the United States, the Soviet Union, China, Japan, and the Common Market. Under détente, he declared, each center should maintain order among smaller states in its region of responsibility. Because the "five great economic superpowers will determine the economic future," Nixon explained, "and, because economic power will be the key to other kinds of power, [they will determine] the future of the world. . . ." For the United States, détente seemed to offer opportunities to determine the future—to discipline its Latin American sphere under a global system of great-power management and to deter Soviet inroads or assistance to rebel groups like the insurgent Sandinistas in Nicaragua by threatening to withdraw the economic benefits the Soviets sought from détente. Détente beckoned as a means to reestablish U.S. control of its most traditional sphere. In 1984 the President's Commission on Central America warned that if the United States ever revealed symptoms of decline in its own neighborhood, it would experience the "erosion of our power to influence events worldwide that would flow from the perception that we were unable to influence vital events close to home."

If the erosion of American and Soviet power stemmed from the fracturing of their spheres, so, too, was it due to the rise of the Third World. After the Second World War a cavalcade of colonies broke from their imperial rulers. From 1943 to 1989 no fewer than ninety-six countries gained independence and entered the international system as new states. . . . Undersecretary of State George W. Ball recalled [that diplomats] necessarily had to focus "on problems involving the bits and pieces of disintegrating empires." . . .

When many Third World nations formed a nonaligned movement to challenge the two Cold Warriors and to press for an end to their dangerous competition, the international system fragmented, bipolarism eroded, and the relative power of the United States and the Soviet Union diminished accordingly. After the 1955 Bandung Conference, many Third World nations in Asia, Africa, and the Middle East declared their neutralism in the Cold War. Third World expressions of alienation from the two superpowers came in many other forms, including Pan-Arabism and Muslim fundamentalism, [and] the Group of 77 in the United Nations. . . .

By sheer force of numbers Third World states became a formidable bloc in world forums. The United States gradually became isolated in the United Nations. In the Security Council, for example, the United States, losing the majority vote its sphere members had long provided, had to cast its first veto in 1970, and by the 1980s it was averaging four vetoes a year. The United States became the largest caster of nay votes in the General Assembly, where it frequently had to contend with setbacks like the 108–9 vote to condemn its invasion of Grenada. In the 1950s General Assembly members voted 70 percent of the time with the United States; in the 1970s the coincidence rate fell to 30 percent, and by the early 1980s to 20 percent. . . .

All of this tugging and pulling jolted the international system. . . . International affairs became more fluid, more unpredictable, less secure, and less manageable. . . . Détente was born in part as a response to this disorderly, pluralistic world. With the United States suffering Third World setbacks in Vietnam, Iran, Nicaragua, and elsewhere, and the Soviet Union stumbling in Egypt and Afghanistan, among other places, Washington and Moscow looked less and less like superpowers. The declining powers in this transforming international system sought to hold their positions by moving from confrontation to cooperation. Détente seemed to promise a restoration of great-power control, a reassertion of great-power tutelage. If détente was embraced as a means to reduce the costs of the Cold War and to meet challenges from sphere members, it also became attractive as a means to deal with the volatile Third World. As President Jimmy Carter once said, Americans had to put their "inordinate fear of Communism" behind them in order to address long-term Third World crises. For the United States, détente with the Soviet Union also offered a "fulcrum or base from which to exert American diplomatic leverage" in the Third World. In 1990, during the Gulf War, when Soviet-American cooperation marshaled a worldwide condemnation of Iraq after it had invaded neighboring Kuwait, Secretary of State James Baker expressed what leaders before him had been saying about the virtues of détente: "When the United States and the Soviet Union lead, others are likely to follow.". . .

The United States and the Soviet Union, bedeviled by Cold War–induced economic problems, independent-minded allies, and contentious Third World nations, gradually moved in fits of truculence and accommodation toward détente and the ultimate end of the Cold War. By the late 1960s, remembered Henry Kissinger, America had to operate "in much more complex conditions than we had ever before faced." That time "marked the end of the period of American predominance based on overwhelming nuclear and economic supremacy." Indeed, he continued, "the Soviet nuclear stockpile was inevitably approaching parity. The economic strength of Europe and Japan was bound to lead them to seek larger political influence. The new, developing nations pressed their claims to greater power and participation." If the world further "tilted against us," he feared, America's strong, if no longer preeminent, position in the international balance of power would falter. In this unsettled environment, détente became even more attractive. Détente did not mean that Soviet-American rivalry would cease, but rather that judicious great-power cooperation, located somewhere between hostile obstructionism and friendly coexistence, would reduce world tensions. Moscow and Washington cautiously endorsed détente as a process to stem the erosion of their power. . . .

U.S. entry into the Persian Gulf War of 1990 and 1991, following Iraq's brutal invasion and annexation of oil-rich Kuwait, exposed a core feature of the immediate post–Cold War international order: the U.S. drive to recoup lost influence, to reestablish credibility, to reaffirm a counterrevolutionary posture, to reassert the great-power status that the prolonged Cold War had eroded. . . . President George Bush claimed that the new war in the Middle East was the first post–Cold War "test of our mettle." The president claimed that "recent events have surely proven that there is no substitute for American leadership" in the world. And "let no one doubt our staying power." The *Wall Street Journal* welcomed the outbreak of war because a U.S. victory "lets America, and above all its elite, recover a sense of self-confidence and self-worth." During Operation Desert Storm proud Americans ballyhooed the destructive power of their high-tech air war, the credibility of their military forces, the skill with which an international coalition was created, and the swiftness of victory. "This is the end of the decline," cheered an official of the conservative American Enterprise Institute. . . .

Although it became fashionable to say that America had won "the sucker and won it big," and it became evident that democratization and capitalism were ascending, the Cold War actually had no winners. Both the United States and the Soviet Union had spent themselves into weakened conditions. Both had paid tremendous prices for making and waging the Cold War. That is why President Gorbachev launched his restructuring programs and why President Bush, echoing Carter and Reagan, made the case for American "renewal" and "renewed credibility." Each major power, in groping for an end to the Cold War, was seeking structures of stability at home and abroad to stem the decline—and collapse—that other complex societies had suffered in the past.

Hanging Tough Paid Off

JOHN LEWIS GADDIS

The time has come to acknowledge an astonishing development: during his eight years as president, Ronald Reagan has presided over the most dramatic improvement in U.S.-Soviet relations—and the most solid progress in arms control—since the Cold War began. History has often produced unexpected results, but this one surely sets some kind of record.

Reagan was not an enthusiast for arms control before entering the White House: indeed his 1976 and 1980 campaigns appeared to reject that enterprise altogether in favor of a simpler search for national security through military superiority over the Soviet Union. That arms control has not only survived but prospered under his leadership ought to make us take a fresh look, both at the administration he headed and at the arms control process itself as it has traditionally been understood.

That process had taken on several distinctive characteristics by the end of the 1970s:

Pessimism. It is now almost forgotten (perhaps even by themselves) that Richard Nixon and Henry Kissinger had originally portrayed the SALT I [Strategic Arms Limitation Talks] negotiations as a way to reduce the effects of America's military decline, stemming from a Soviet strategic buildup in the mid-1960s, to which the United States, because of the Vietnam War, had at first been too distracted and then too divided to respond. Arms control carried with it the tacit assumption that, in this situation, SALT was, at best, a way of minimizing the damage. Coincident but unrelated events had reinforced, by the end of the 1970s, the association of arms control with visions of U.S. military inferiority. These developments included the energy crisis and ensuing double-digit inflation; the erosion of presidential authority that began with Watergate and continued under Ford and Carter; the collapse of old allies in Iran and Nicaragua; and, most dramatically, the juxtapostition of American ineffectiveness in the Tehran hostage crisis with apparent Soviet purposefulness in invading Afghanistan.

Complexity. The Partial Test Ban Treaty of 1963 took 10 days to negotiate and fills just over two pages in the Arms Control and Disarmament Agency's published version. SALT I took two-and-a-half years to negotiate; the text is 18 pages. The unratified SALT II Treaty required almost seven years to negotiate; the resulting text and accompanying statements fill 31 pages of text. With arms control agreements becoming so complex that the experts themselves—to say nothing of average citizens—were finding them difficult to understand, it was reasonable to begin to wonder by the end of the 1970s how one would actually know whether they coincided with the national interest, or how to be sure that the Soviets understood them in precisely the same way.

Insularity. As the SALT process became more complex it appeared to take on a life of its own, insulated from outside events. Despite increasingly detailed provisions for verification, arms control still depended to a considerable extent upon trusting the Soviets. But that was becoming harder to do. After 1975 Moscow openly violated the Helsinki Agreement's human rights provisions; indirect military intervention in Angola, Somalia, and Ethiopia suggested at a minimum an unwillingness to cooperate with the West in managing regional conflicts; the Kremlin appeared determined to push the limits of SALT I as far as possible as it continued its buildup of strategic weapons. Yet the SALT II negotiations proceeded, apparently unaffected by these less than reassuring signs.

Illogic. The SALT process seemed to be based on two propositions generally accepted within the arms control community, but that laymen found less and less plausible when tested against the simpler standards of common sense. One was implied in the very term "arms control"; why not "arms reduction"? And why did "strategic arms limitation" agreements seem to do so little actual "limiting"? The other had to do with the assertion that safety could come only through vulnerability, and that defense, therefore, at least in the nuclear realm, was bad. However rational the experts may have found these precepts, they did not appear rational to the average citizen, and as the nuclear standoff showed signs of stretching endlessly into the future, people became uncomfortable with them.

Whether these criticisms of arms control were fair is not the point. What is important is the skill with which Ronald Reagan focused on them during his campaigns for the presidency. And even more important was the way he incorporated them, after January 1981, into a new approach to arms control that would in time, and against conventional wisdom, produce impressive results. The principal means by which he accomplished this were as follows:

Rebuilding self-confidence. There are rare moments in history when public moods reverse themselves almost overnight. One occurred in March 1933, when Franklin Roosevelt replaced Herbert Hoover in the White House; another took place in Great Britain in May 1940, when Winston Churchill became prime minister; still another occurred in Western Europe in June 1947, when Secretary of State George C. Marshall announced the economic recovery plan that came to bear his name. The mood reversal that followed Reagan's January 1981 inauguration was by no means as dramatic as these, but it occurred: long before the new administration had completed its military buildup, before Paul Volcker and the Federal Reserve Board had checked inflation, and before OPEC's disarray had turned the energy crisis into an oil glut, the *perception* had become widespread that events were beginning to break Washington's way. And that made a big difference.

It has since become commonplace to criticize Reagan for having placed greater emphasis on imagery than on substance during his years as president. But leadership begins with the creation of self-confidence, and that—as Roosevelt, Churchill, and Marshall all knew—is a psychological process depending less upon the rational calculation of tangible gains than upon the ability to convince people that however bad things may be at the moment, time is on their side. Reagan managed during his first months in office to project—and therefore to instill—a degree of self-confidence that went well beyond anything his predecessor had achieved. Without that shift from pessimism to optimism, much of what followed could hardly have taken place.

Spooking the Soviets. The second element in the Reagan strategy proceeded logically from the first—to persuade the Kremlin that time was working against it. Nor was it so difficult to do, because events were beginning to demonstrate precisely this: Afghanistan was revealing the costs of what [the historian] Paul Kennedy has called "strategic overstretch"; "Solidarity" had brought Poland to the edge of open rebellion; economic stagnation was becoming a serious problem inside the Soviet Union; and an increasingly sclerotic Kremlin leadership was responding to these difficulties with near catatonic immobility. In one sense, Reagan was lucky to have come into office at a trough in American fortunes and a peak in those of the Soviets. Things could not get much worse, and were likely to get better. But more than luck is involved in the ability to recognize that such trends are under way, and to capitalize upon them. Reagan's leadership proved decidedly superior to Carter's in that respect.

Several subsequent Reagan administration actions sought to reinforce the idea that time no longer favored Moscow. The U.S. military buildup was launched with the intention of so straining an already inefficient economy that the Soviet leadership would have little choice but to make substantial concessions on arms control. Similar intentions lay behind the Strategic Defense Initiative. The vision of a shift from deterrence to a defense based on American technological superiority would, it was thought, shock the Soviets into contemplating for the first time significant reductions in their own long-range strategic forces.

At the same time, the administration was skillfully defusing both the U.S. nuclear freeze movement and opposition to the deployment of Pershing II and cruise missiles in Western Europe by calling for actual *reductions* in nuclear weapons, and by holding out, through SDI, the prospect of ultimately making them obsolete altogether. To the extent that the Soviets had counted on such groups to constrain administration freedom of action—and they almost certainly had—the effect again was to demonstrate that time was no longer on Moscow's side.

Negotiation from strength. A third element in the Reagan strategy was the principle that negotiations should take place only from a position of strength. The idea dates from the Truman administration's military buildup following the outbreak of the Korean War. Over the years it had come to be understood as a way of evading negotiations altogether, since "strength" was so relative a concept that one might never actually attain it and since adversaries would presumably never negotiate from "weakness." There was reason to believe, at the outset of the Reagan years, that this devious approach was alive and well. Presidential subordinates gleefully put forward "killer" proposals for arms control talks, while the Pentagon swallowed huge military appropriations without any indication that "strength" was about to be achieved.

An important characteristic of Reagan's leadership, however, was that he was *not* devious; when he spoke of the possibility that a military buildup might actually lead to reductions in strategic weapons, he appears to have meant precisely what he said. He also understood, perhaps instinctively, a point George Kennan had been arguing: that the arms control process had become too complex while producing too little, and that the only way to rebuild a domestic consensus in support of it was to hold out clear, simple, and sweeping objectives, such as a 50 percent cut in strategic weapons on both sides.

With the 1984 elections coming up and with indications that Congress would resist further defense budget increases, it could be argued that the administration had little choice but to appear to seek negotiations with the Soviets. Certainly some Reagan advisers felt that negotiations so protracted as to produce no results were almost as desirable as having no negotiations at all. But what many of Reagan's subordinates did not understand—and what those who seek to explain what subsequently happened will have to comprehend—is that while the president may have shared their conservatism, he did not share their cynicism. For him the only question was with whom to negotiate.

Responding to Gorbachev. It is difficult to see that much could have been accomplished in this respect until a functional Soviet leadership had been established. That happened in March 1985, and a fourth element in the Reagan strategy soon emerged, which was to acknowledge Mikhail Gorbachev as a new kind of Soviet leader whose chief priority was internal reform, and with whom one could, in the realm of external affairs, find common interests.

The White House was therefore ready to respond when Gorbachev began modifying long-standing Soviet positions on arms control in a way quite consistent with what the Reagan strategy had anticipated. Neither critics on the left, who had favored negotiations for their own sake, nor those on the right, who had sought negotiations from strength, were in any position to object. The long-stalemated arms control process suddenly accelerated, producing by the final year of the Reagan administration not only an Intermediate-range Nuclear Forces (INF) Treaty that contained unprecedented Soviet concessions on asymmetrical reductions and on-site verification, but substantial progress as well toward agreement on deep cuts in long-range strategic systems, and at least the possibility of a grand compromise that would delay if not defer altogether the deployment of SDI.

There were, to be sure, deficiencies in the Reagan strategy. Characteristically, the president found it easier to think of SDI as he had advertised it—as a first step toward abolishing nuclear weapons altogether—than as the successful bargaining chip it turned out to be. This created an opportunity for Gorbachev to endorse nuclear abolition by the year 2000 and thus to align himself with the president against Reagan's own skeptical advisers. There were few signs of progress toward conventional arms limitation, or toward restricting nuclear testing. Little thought had been given to how the United States might respond if the relaxation of controls that perestroika required were to produce actual rebellions among Soviet nationality groups, or within Eastern Europe. And almost no thought appeared to have been given to the relationship between national security and national solvency—an issue to which Gorbachev himself seemed keenly attuned.

Still, the [doomsday] clock on the front cover of the *Bulletin* [*of the Atomic Scientists*] was set back, a year ago, for the first time since 1972. That symbolic act ought to make us think critically—and without preconceptions—about how we got to that point. It was not by means of arms control as traditionally practiced: the old SALT process would never have survived the Reagan administration's insistence on asymmetrical reductions instead of symmetrical limitations, on intrusive rather than remote verification, and on the virtues of strategic defense as opposed to mutual vulnerability. Strength this time did lead to negotiations, bargaining chips did produce bargains, and "hanging tough" did eventually pay off.

The Soviets deserve much of the credit for what happened. They made most of the concessions, a pattern not likely to be repeated often in the future. It was the Reagan administration, however, that assessed correctly the potential for Soviet concessions. And because of the way it came about, this new approach to arms control has won firmer domestic support within the United States than the SALT process ever did; witness the caution both sides showed in not making it an issue during the otherwise hotly contested 1988 presidential election. How valid the approach will be in years to come remains to be seen, but as Reagan leaves office it would be uncharitable—and historically irresponsible—to begrudge the strategic vision of an administration once thought by many of us to have had none at all.

Engagement and Anti-Nuclearism, Not Containment, Brought an End to the Cold War

DANIEL DEUDNEY AND G. JOHN IKENBERRY

In assessing the rest of the world's impact on Soviet change, a remarkably simplistic and self-serving conventional wisdom has emerged in the United States. This new conventional wisdom, the "Reagan victory school," holds that President Ronald Reagan's military and ideological assertiveness during the 1980s played the lead role in the collapse of Soviet communism and the "taming" of its foreign policy. In that view the Reagan administration's ideological counter-offensive and military buildup delivered the knock-out punch to a system that was internally bankrupt and on the ropes. The Reagan Right's perspective is an ideologically pointed version of the more broadly held conventional wisdom on the end of the Cold War that emphasizes the success of the "peace-through-strength" strategy manifest in four decades of Western containment. After decades of waging a costly "twilight struggle," the West now celebrates the triumph of its military and ideological resolve.

From "Who Won the Cold War?" by Daniel Deudney and G. John Ikenberry from *Foreign Policy,* No. 87 (Summer 1992), pp. 123–128, 130–138. Reprinted with permission from *Foreign Policy.* Copyright © 1992 by the Carnegie Endowment for International Peace.

The Reagan victory school and the broader peace-through-strength perspectives are, however, misleading and incomplete—both in their interpretation of events in the 1980s and in their understanding of deeper forces that led to the end of the Cold War. It is important to reconsider the emerging conventional wisdom before it truly becomes an article of faith on Cold War history and comes to distort the thinking of policymakers in America and elsewhere. . . .

The Cold War's end was a baby that arrived unexpectedly, but a long line of those claiming paternity has quickly formed. A parade of former Reagan administration officials and advocates has forthrightly asserted that Reagan's hard-line policies were the decisive trigger for reorienting Soviet foreign policy and for the demise of communism. As former Pentagon officials like Caspar Weinberger and Richard Perle, columnist George Will, neoconservative thinker Irving Kristol, and other proponents of the Reagan victory school have argued, a combination of military and ideological pressures gave the Soviets little choice but to abandon expansionism abroad and repression at home. In that view, the Reagan military buildup foreclosed Soviet military options while pushing the Soviet economy to the breaking point. Reagan partisans stress that his dramatic "Star Wars" initiative put the Soviets on notice that the next phase of the arms race would be waged in areas where the West held the decisive technological edge.

Reagan and his administration's military initiatives, however, played a far different and more complicated role in inducing Soviet change than the Reagan victory school asserts. For every "hardening" there was a "softening": Reagan's rhetoric of the "Evil Empire" was matched by his vigorous anti-nuclearism; the military buildup in the West matched by the resurgence of a large popular peace movement; and the Reagan Doctrine's toughening of containment was matched by major deviations from containment in East-West economic relations. Moreover, over the longer term, the strength marshaled in containment was matched by mutual weakness in the face of nuclear weapons, and efforts to engage the USSR were as important as efforts to contain it.

Perhaps the greatest anomaly of the Reagan victory school is the "Great Communicator" himself. The Reagan Right ignores that his anti-nuclearism was as strong as his anticommunism. Reagan's personal convictions on nuclear weapons were profoundly at odds with the beliefs of most in his administration. Staffed by officials who considered nuclear weapons a useful instrument of statecraft and who were openly disdainful of the moral critique of nuclear weapons articulated by the arms control community and the peace movement, the administration pursued the hardest line on nuclear policy and the Soviet Union in the postwar era. Then vice president George Bush's observation that nuclear weapons would be fired as a warning shot and Deputy Under Secretary of Defense T. K. Jones's widely quoted view that nuclear war was survivable captured the reigning ethos within the Reagan administration.

In contrast, there is abundant evidence that Reagan himself felt a deep antipathy for nuclear weapons and viewed their abolition to be a realistic and desirable goal. Reagan's call in his famous March 1983 "Star Wars" speech for a program to make nuclear weapons impotent and obsolete was viewed as cynical by many, but actually it expressed Reagan's heartfelt views, views that he came to act upon. As *Washington Post* reporter Lou Cannon's 1991 biography points out, Reagan was deeply disturbed by nuclear deterrence and attracted to abolitionist solutions. "I know I speak for people everywhere when I say our dream is to see the day when nuclear weapons will be banished from the face of the earth," Reagan said in November 1983. . . .

Contrary to the conventional wisdom, the defense buildup did not produce Soviet capitulation. The initial Soviet response to the Reagan administration's buildup and belligerent rhetoric was to accelerate production of offensive weapons, both strategic and conventional. That impasse was broken not by Soviet capitulation but by an extraordinary convergence by Reagan and Mikhail Gorbachev on a vision of mutual nuclear vulnerability and disarmament. On the Soviet side, the dominance of the hardline response to the newly assertive America was thrown into question in early 1985 when Gorbachev became general secretary of the Communist party after the death of Konstantin Chernenko. Without a background in foreign affairs, Gorbachev was eager to assess American intentions directly and put his stamp on Soviet security policy. Reagan's strong antinuclear views expressed at the November 1985 Geneva summit were decisive in convincing Gorbachev that it was possible to work with the West in halting the nuclear arms race. The arms control diplomacy of the later Reagan years was successful because, as *Washington Post* journalist Don Oberdorfer has detailed in *The Turn: From the Cold War to a New Era* (1991), Secretary of State George Shultz picked up on Reagan's strong convictions and deftly side-stepped hardline opposition to agreements. In fact, Shultz's success at linking presidential unease about nuclear weapons to Soviet overtures in the face of right-wing opposition provides a sharp contrast with John Foster Dulles's refusal to act on President Dwight Eisenhower's nuclear doubts and the opportunities presented by Nikita Khrushchev's détente overtures.

Reagan's commitment to anti-nuclearism and its potential for transforming the U.S.-Soviet confrontation was more graphically demonstrated at the October 1986 Reykjavík summit when Reagan and Gorbachev came close to agreeing on a comprehensive program of global denuclearization that was far bolder than any seriously entertained by American strategists since the Baruch Plan of 1946. The sharp contrast between Reagan's and Gorbachev's shared skepticism toward nuclear weapons on the one hand, and the Washington security establishment's consensus on the other, was showcased in former secretary of defense James Schlesinger's scathing accusation that Reagan was engaged in "casual utopianism." But Reagan's anomalous anti-nuclearism provided the crucial signal to Gorbachev that bold initiatives would be reciprocated rather than exploited. Reagan's anti-nuclearism was more important than his administration's military buildup in catalyzing the end of the Cold War.

Neither anti-nuclearism nor its embrace by Reagan have received the credit they deserve for producing the Soviet-U.S. reconciliation. Reagan's accomplishment in this regard has been met with silence from all sides. Conservatives, not sharing Reagan's anti-nuclearism, have emphasized the role of traditional military strength. The popular peace movement, while holding deeply antinuclear views, was viscerally suspicious of Reagan. The establishment arms control community also found Reagan and his motives suspect, and his attack on deterrence conflicted with their desire to stabilize deterrence and establish their credentials as sober participants in security policy making. Reagan's radical anti-nuclearism should sustain his reputation as the ultimate Washington outsider.

The central role of Reagan's and Gorbachev's anti-nuclearism throws new light on the 1987 Treaty on Intermediate-range Nuclear Forces, the first genuine disarmament treaty of the nuclear era. The conventional wisdom emphasizes that this agreement was the fruit of a hard-line negotiating posture and the U.S. military buildup. Yet the superpowers' settlement on the "zero option" was not a vindication of the hard-line strategy. The zero option was originally fashioned by hardliners for propaganda purposes, and many backed off as its implementation became likely. The impasse the hard line created was transcended by the surprising Reagan-Gorbachev convergence against nuclear arms.

The Reagan victory school also overstates the overall impact of American and Western policy on the Soviet Union during the 1980s. The Reagan administration's posture was both evolving and inconsistent. Though loudly proclaiming its intentions to go beyond the previous containment policies that were deemed too soft, the reality of Reagan's policies fell short. As Sovietologists Gail Lapidus and Alexander Dallin observed in a 1989 *Bulletin of the Atomic Scientists* article, the policies were "marked to the end by numerous zigzags and reversals, bureaucratic conflicts, and incoherence." Although rollback had long been a cherished goal of the Republican party's right wing, Reagan was unwilling and unable to implement it.

The hard-line tendencies of the Reagan administration were offset in two ways. First, and most important, Reagan's tough talk fueled a large peace movement in the United States and Western Europe in the 1980s, a movement that put significant political pressure upon Western governments to pursue far-reaching arms control proposals. That mobilization of Western opinion created a political climate in which the rhetoric and posture of the early Reagan administration was a significant political liability. By the 1984 U.S. presidential election, the administration had embraced arms control goals that it had previously ridiculed. Reagan's own anti-nuclearism matched that rising public concern, and Reagan emerged as the spokesman for comprehensive denuclearization. Paradoxically, Reagan administration policies substantially triggered the popular revolt against the nuclear hardline, and then Reagan came to pursue the popular agenda more successfully than any other postwar president.

Second, the Reagan administration's hardline policies were also undercut by powerful Western interests that favored East-West economic ties. In the early months of Reagan's administration, the grain embargo imposed by President Jimmy Carter after the 1979 Soviet invasion of Afghanistan was lifted in order to keep the Republican party's promises to Midwestern farmers. Likewise, in 1981 the Reagan administration did little to challenge Soviet control of Eastern Europe after Moscow pressured Warsaw to suppress the independent Polish trade union Solidarity, in part because Poland might have defaulted on multibillion dollar loans made by Western banks. Also, despite strenuous opposition by the Reagan administration, the NATO allies pushed ahead with a natural gas pipeline linking the Soviet Union with Western Europe. That a project creating substantial economic interdependence could proceed during the worst period of Soviet-U.S. relations in the 1980s demonstrates the failure of the Reagan administration to present an unambiguous hard line toward the Soviet Union. More generally, NATO allies and the vocal European peace movement moderated and buffered hard-line American tendencies.

In sum, the views of the Reagan victory school are flawed because they neglect powerful crosscurrents in the West during the 1980s. The conventional wisdom simplifies a complex story and ignores those aspects of Reagan administration policy inconsistent with the hard-line rationale. Moreover, the Western "face" toward the Soviet Union did not consist exclusively of Reagan administration policies, but encompassed countervailing tendencies from the Western public, other governments, and economic interest groups.

Whether Reagan is seen as the consummate hardliner or the prophet of anti-nuclearism, one should not exaggerate the influence of his administration, or of other short-term forces. Within the Washington beltway, debates about postwar military and foreign policy would suggest that Western strategy fluctuated wildly, but in fact the basic thrust of Western policy toward the USSR remained remarkably consistent. Arguments from the New Right notwithstanding, Reagan's containment strategy was not that different from those of his predecessors. Indeed, the broader peace-through-strength perspective sees the Cold War's finale as the product of a long-term policy, applied over the decades.

In any case, although containment certainly played an important role in blocking Soviet expansionism, it cannot explain either the end of the Cold War or the direction of Soviet policy responses. The West's relationship with the Soviet Union was not limited to containment, but included important elements of mutual vulnerability and engagement. The Cold War's end was not simply a result of Western strength but of mutual weakness and intentional engagement as well.

Most dramatically, the mutual vulnerability created by nuclear weapons overshadowed containment. Nuclear weapons forced the United States and the Soviet Union to eschew war and the serious threat of war as tools of diplomacy and created imperatives for the cooperative regulation of nuclear capability. Both countries tried to fashion nuclear explosives into useful instruments of policy, but they came to the realization—as the joint Soviet-American statement issued from the 1985 Geneva summit put it—that "nuclear war cannot be won and must never be fought." Both countries slowly but surely came to view nuclear weapons as a common threat that must be regulated jointly. Not just containment, but also the overwhelming and common nuclear threat brought the Soviets to the negotiating table. In the shadow of nuclear destruction, common purpose defused traditional antagonisms.

A second error of the peace-through-strength perspective is the failure to recognize that the West offered an increasingly benign face to the communist world. Traditionally, the Soviets' Marxist-Leninist doctrine held that the capitalist West was inevitably hostile and aggressive, an expectation reinforced by the aggression of capitalist, fascist Germany. Since World War II, the Soviets' principal adversaries had been democratic capitalist states. Slowly but surely, Soviet doctrine acknowledged that the West's behavior did not follow Leninist expectations, but was instead increasingly pacific and cooperative. The Soviet willingness to abandon the Brezhnev Doctrine in the late 1980s in favor of the "Sinatra Doctrine"—under which any East European country could sing, "I did it my way"—suggests a radical transformation in the prevailing Soviet perception of threat from the West. In 1990, the Soviet acceptance of the de facto absorption of communist East Germany into West Germany involved the same calculation with even higher stakes. In accepting the German reunification, despite that country's past aggression, Gorbachev acted on the assumption that the Western system was fundamentally pacific. As Russian foreign minister Andrei Kozyrev noted subsequently, that Western countries are pluralistic democracies "practically rules out the pursuance of an aggressive foreign policy." Thus the Cold War ended despite the assertiveness of Western hardliners, rather than because of it.

The second front of the Cold War, according to the Reagan victory school, was ideological. Reagan spearheaded a Western ideological offensive that dealt the USSR a death blow. For the Right, driving home the image of the Evil Empire was a decisive stroke rather than a rhetorical flourish. Ideological warfare was such a key front in the Cold War because the Soviet Union was, at its core, an ideological creation. According to the Reagan Right, the supreme vulnerability of the Soviet Union to ideological assault was greatly underappreciated by Western leaders and publics. In that view, the Cold War was won by the West's uncompromising assertion of the superiority of its values and its complete denial of the moral legitimacy of the Soviet system during the 1980s. Western military strength could prevent defeat, but only ideological breakthrough could bring victory.

Underlying that interpretation is a deeply ideological philosophy of politics and history. The Reagan Right tended to view politics as a war of ideas, an orientation that generated a particularly polemical type of politics. As writer Sidney Blumenthal has pointed out, many of the leading figures in the neoconservative movement since the 1960s came to conservatism after having begun their political careers as Marxists or socialists. That perspective sees the Soviet Union as primarily an ideological artifact, and therefore sees struggle with it in particularly ideological terms. The neoconservatives believe, like Lenin, that "ideas are more fatal than guns." . . .

The end of the Cold War indeed marked an ideological triumph for the West, but not of the sort fancied by the Reagan victory school. Ideology played a far different and more complicated role in inducing Soviet change than the Reagan school allows. As with the military sphere, the Reagan school presents an incomplete picture of Western ideological influence, ignoring the emergence of ideological common ground in stimulating Soviet change.

The ideological legitimacy of the Soviet system collapsed in the eyes of its own citizens not because of an assault by Western ex-leftists, but because of the appeal of Western affluence and permissiveness. The puritanical austerity of Bolshevism's "New Soviet Man" held far less appeal than the "bourgeois decadence" of the West. For the peoples of the USSR and Eastern Europe, it was not so much abstract liberal principles but rather the Western way of life—the material and cultural manifestations of the West's freedoms—that subverted the Soviet vision. Western popular culture—exemplified in rock and roll, television, film, and blue jeans—seduced the communist world far more effectively than ideological sermons by anticommunist activists. As journalist William Echikson noted in his 1990 book *Lighting the Night: Revolution in Eastern Europe,* "instead of listening to the liturgy of Marx and Lenin, generations of would-be socialists tuned into the Rolling Stones and the Beatles."

If Western popular culture and permissiveness helped subvert communist legitimacy, it is a development of profound irony. Domestically, the New Right battled precisely those cultural forms that had such global appeal. V. I. Lenin's most potent ideological foils were John Lennon and Paul McCartney, not Adam Smith and Thomas Jefferson. The Right fought a two-front war against communism abroad and hedonism and consumerism at home. Had it not lost the latter struggle, the West may not have won the former. . . .

The Reagan victory school argues that the renewed emphasis on free-market principles championed by Reagan and then British prime minister Margaret Thatcher led to a global move toward market deregulation and privatization that the Soviets desired to follow. By rekindling the beacon of laissez-faire capitalism, Reagan illuminated the path of economic reform, thus vanquishing communism.

That view is misleading in two respects. First, it was West European social democracy rather than America's more free-wheeling capitalism that attracted Soviet reformers. Gorbachev wanted his reforms to emulate the Swedish model. His vision was not of laissez-faire capitalism but of a social democratic welfare state. Second, the Right's triumphalism in the economic sphere is ironic. The West's robust economies owe much of their relative stability and health to two generations of Keynesian intervention and government involvement that the Right opposed at every step. As with Western popular culture, the Right opposed tendencies in the West that proved vital in the West's victory. . . .

Behind the debate over who "won" the Cold War are competing images of the forces shaping recent history. Containment, strength, and confrontation—the trinity enshrined in conventional thinking on Western foreign policy's role in ending the Cold War—obscure the nature of these momentous changes. Engagement and interdependence, rather than containment, are the ruling trends of the age. Mutual vulnerability, not strength, drives security politics. Accommodation and integration, not confrontation, are the motors of change.

That such encouraging trends were established and deepened even as the Cold War raged demonstrates the considerable continuity underlying the West's support today for reform in the post-Soviet transition. Those trends also expose as one-sided and self-serving the New Right's attempt to take credit for the success of forces that, in truth, they opposed. In the end, Reagan partisans have been far more successful in claiming victory in the Cold War than they were in achieving it.

America's Misguided Quest for Unipolar Hegemony in the Post–Cold War World

SAMUEL P. HUNTINGTON

There is now only one superpower. But that does not mean that the world is *unipolar*. A unipolar system would have one superpower, no significant major powers, and many minor powers. As a result, the superpower could effectively resolve important international issues alone, and no combination of other states would have the power to prevent it from doing so. For several centuries the classical world under Rome, and at times East Asia under China, approximated this model. A *bipolar* system like the Cold War has two superpowers, and the relations between them are central to international politics. Each superpower dominates a coalition of allied states and competes with the other superpower for influence among nonaligned countries. A *multipolar* system has several major powers of comparable strength that cooperate and compete with each other in shifting patterns. A coalition of major states is necessary to resolve important international issues. European politics approximated this model for several centuries.

Contemporary international politics does not fit any of these three models. It is instead a strange hybrid, a *uni-multipolar* system with one superpower and several major powers. The settlement of key international issues requires action by the single superpower but always with some combination of other major states; the single superpower can, however, veto action on key issues by combinations of other states. The United States, of course, is the sole state with preeminence in every domain of power—economic, military, diplomatic, ideological, technological, and cultural—with the reach and capabilities to promote its interests in virtually every part of the world. At a second level are major regional powers that are preeminent in areas of the world without being able to extend their interests and capabilities as globally as the United States. They include the German-French condominium in Europe, Russia in Eurasia, China and potentially Japan in East Asia, India in South Asia, Iran in Southwest Asia, Brazil in Latin America, and South Africa and Nigeria in Africa. At a third level are secondary regional powers whose interests often conflict with the more powerful regional states. These include Britain in relation to the German-French combination, Ukraine in relation to Russia, Japan in relation to China, South Korea in relation to Japan, Pakistan in relation to India, Saudi Arabia in relation to Iran, and Argentina in relation to Brazil.

The superpower or hegemon in a unipolar system, lacking any major powers challenging it, is normally able to maintain its dominance over minor states for a long time until it is weakened by internal decay or by forces from outside the system, both of which happened to fifth-century Rome and nineteenth-century China. In a multipolar system, each state might prefer a unipolar system with itself as the single dominant power but the other major states will act to prevent that from happening, as was often the case in European politics. In the Cold War, each superpower quite explicitly preferred a unipolar system under its hegemony. However, the dynamics of the competition and their early awareness that an effort to create a unipolar system by armed force would be disastrous for both enabled bipolarity to endure for four decades until one state no longer could sustain the rivalry.

In each of these systems, the most powerful actors had an interest in maintaining the system. In a uni-multipolar system, this is less true. The United States would clearly prefer a unipolar system in which it would be the hegemon and often acts as if such a system existed. The major powers, on the other hand, would prefer a multipolar system in which they could pursue their interests, unilaterally and collectively, without being subject to constraints, coercion, and pressure by the stronger superpower. They feel threatened by what they see as the American pursuit of global hegemony. American officials feel frustrated by their failure to achieve that hegemony. None of the principal power-wielders in world affairs is happy with the status quo. . . .

American officials quite naturally tend to act as if the world were unipolar. They boast of American power and American virtue, hailing the United States as a benevolent hegemon. They lecture other countries on the universal validity of

American principles, practices, and institutions. At the 1997 G-7 summit in Denver, President Clinton boasted about the success of the American economy as a model for others. Secretary of State Madeleine K. Albright has called the United States "the indispensable nation" and said that "we stand tall and hence see further than other nations." This statement is true in the narrow sense that the United States is an indispensable participant in any effort to tackle major global problems. It is false in also implying that other nations are dispensable—the United States needs the cooperation of some major countries in handling any issue—and that American indispensability is the source of wisdom.

Addressing the problem of foreign perceptions of American "hegemonism," Deputy Secretary of State Strobe Talbott set forth this rational: "In a fashion and to an extent that is unique in the history of Great Powers, the United States defines its strength—indeed, its very greatness—not in terms of its ability to achieve or maintain dominance over others, but in terms of its ability to work *with* others in the interests of the international community as a whole. . . . American foreign policy is consciously intended to advance *universal* values [his italics]." The most concise statement of the "benign hegemon" syndrome was made by Deputy Secretary of the Treasury Lawrence H. Summers when he called the United States the "first nonimperialist superpower"—a claim that manages in three words to exalt American uniqueness, American virtue, and American power.

American foreign policy is in considerable measure driven by such beliefs. In the past few years the United States has, among other things, attempted or been perceived as attempting more or less unilaterally to do the following: pressure other countries to adopt American values and practices regarding human rights and democracy; prevent other countries from acquiring military capabilities that could counter American conventional superiority; enforce American law extraterritorially in other societies; grade countries according to their adherence to American standards on human rights, drugs, terrorism, nuclear proliferation, missile proliferation, and now religious freedom; apply sanctions against countries that do not meet American standards on these issues; promote American corporate interests under the slogans of free trade and open markets; shape World Bank and International Monetary Fund policies to serve those same corporate interests; intervene in local conflicts in which it has relatively little direct interest; bludgeon other countries to adopt economic policies and social policies that will benefit American economic interests; promote American arms sales abroad while attempting to prevent comparable sales by other countries; force out one U.N. secretary-general and dictate the appointment of his successor; expand NATO initially to include Poland, Hungary, and the Czech Republic and no one else; undertake military action against Iraq and later maintain harsh economic sanctions against the regime; and categorize certain countries as "rogue states," excluding them from global institutions because they refuse to kowtow to American wishes.

In the unipolar moment at the end of the Cold War and the collapse of the Soviet Union, the United States was often able to impose its will on other countries. That moment has passed. The two principal tools of coercion that the United States now attempts to use are economic sanctions and military intervention. Sanctions work, however, only when other countries also support them, and that is decreasingly the case. Hence, the United States either applies them unilaterally to the detriment of its economic interests and its relations with its allies, or it does not enforce them, in which case they become symbols of American weakness.

At relatively low cost the United States can launch bombing or cruise missile attacks against its enemies. By themselves, however, such actions achieve little. More serious military interventions have to meet three conditions: They have to be legitimated through some international organization, such as the United Nations where they are subject to Russian, Chinese, or French veto; they also require the participation of allied forces, which may or may not be forthcoming; and they have to involve no American casualties and virtually no "collateral" casualties. Even if the United States meets all three conditions, it risks stirring up not only criticism at home but widespread political and popular backlash abroad.

American officials seem peculiarly blind to the fact that often the more the United States attacks a foreign leader, the more his popularity soars among his countrymen who applaud him for standing tall against the greatest power of earth. The demonizing of leaders has so far failed to shorten their tenure in power, from [Cuba's] Fidel Castro (who has survived eight American presidents) to [Yugoslavia's] Slobodan Milošević and [Iraq's] Saddam Hussein. Indeed, the best way for a dictator of a small country to prolong his tenure in power may be to provoke the United States into denouncing him as the leader of a "rogue regime" and a threat to global peace. . . .

In acting as if this were a unipolar world, the United States is also becoming increasingly alone in the world. American leaders constantly claim to be speaking on behalf of "the international community." But whom do they have in mind? China? Russia? India? Pakistan? Iran? The Arab world? The Association of Southeast Asian Nations? Africa? Latin America? France? Do any of these countries or regions see the United States as the spokesman for a community of which they are a part? The community for which the United States speaks includes, at best, its Anglo-Saxon cousins (Britain, Canada, Australia, New Zealand) on most issues, Germany and some smaller European democracies on many issues, Israel on some Middle Eastern questions, and Japan on the implementation of U.N. resolutions. These are important states, but they fall far short of being the global international community.

On issue after issue, the United States has found itself increasingly alone with one or a few partners, opposing most of the rest of the world's states and peoples. These issues include U.N. dues; sanctions against Cuba, Iran, Iraq, and Libya; the land mines treaty; global warming; an international war crimes tribunal; the Middle East; the use of force against Iraq and Yugoslavia; and the targeting of 35 countries with new economic sanctions between 1993 and 1996. On these and other issues, much of the international community is on one side and the United States is on the other. The circle of governments who see their interests coinciding with American interests is shrinking. This is manifest, among other ways, in the central lineup among the permanent members of the U.N. Security Council. During the first decades of the Cold War, it was 4:1—the United States, the United Kingdom, France, and China against the Soviet Union. After Mao's communist government took China's seat, the lineup became 3:1:1, with China in a shifting middle position. Now it is 2:1:2, with the United States and the United Kingdom opposing China and Russia, and France in the middle spot. . . .

. . . At a 1997 Harvard conference, scholars reported that the elites of countries comprising at least two-thirds of the world's people—Chinese, Russians, Indians, Arabs, Muslims, and Africans—see the United States as the single greatest external threat to their societies. They do not regard America as a military threat but as a menace to their integrity, autonomy, prosperity, and freedom of action. They view the United States as intrusive, interventionist, exploitative, unilateralist, hegemonic, hypocritical, and applying double standards, engaging in what they label "financial imperialism" and "intellectual colonialism," with a foreign policy driven overwhelmingly by domestic politics. For Indian elites, an Indian scholar reported, "the United States represents the major diplomatic and political threat. On virtually every issue of concern to India, the United States has 'veto' or mobilizational power, whether it is on nuclear, technological, economic, environmental, or political matters. That is, the United States can deny India its objectives and can rally others to join it in punishing India." Its sins are "power, hubris, and greed." From the Russian perspective, a Moscow participant said, the United States pursues a policy of "coercive cooperation." All Russians oppose "a world based on a dominant U.S. leadership which would border on hegemony." In similar terms, the Beijing participant said Chinese leaders believe that the principal threats to peace, stability, and China are "hegemonism and power politics," meaning U.S. policies, which they say are designed to undermine and create disunity in the socialist states and developing countries. Arab elites see the United States as an evil force in world affairs, while the Japanese public rated in 1997 the United States as a threat to Japan second only to North Korea.

Such reactions are to be expected. American leaders believe that the world's business is their business. Other countries believe that what happens in their part of the world is their business, not America's, and quite explicitly respond. As [South African president] Nelson Mandela said, his country rejects another state's having "the arrogance to tell us where we should go or which countries should be our friends. . . . We cannot accept that a state assumes the role of the world's policeman" In a bipolar world, many countries welcomed the United States as their protector against the other superpower. In a uni-multipolar world, in contrast, the world's only superpower is automatically a threat to other major powers. . . .

The interplay of power and culture will decisively mold patterns of alliance and antagonism among states in the coming years. In terms of culture, cooperation is more likely between countries with cultural commonalities; antagonism is more likely between countries with widely different cultures. In terms of power, the United States and the secondary regional powers have common interests in limiting the dominance of the major states in their regions. Thus the United States has warned China by strengthening its military alliance with Japan and supporting the modest extension of Japanese military capabilities. The U.S. special relationship with Britain provides leverage against the emerging power of a united Europe. America is working to develop close relations with Ukraine to counter any expansion of Russian power. With the emergence of Brazil as the dominant state in Latin America, U.S relations with Argentina have greatly improved and the United States has designated Argentina a non-NATO military ally. The United States cooperates closely with Saudi Arabia to counter Iran's power in the Gulf and, less successfully, has worked with Pakistan to balance India in South Asia. In all these cases, cooperation serves mutual interest in containing the influence of the major regional power.

This interplay of power and culture suggests that the United States is likely to have difficult relations with the major regional powers, though less so with the European Union and Brazil than with the others. On the other hand, the United States should have reasonably cooperative relations with all the secondary regional powers, but have closer relations with the secondary regional powers that have similar cultures (Britain, Argentina, and possibly Ukraine) than those that have different cultures (Japan, South Korea, Saudi Arabia, Pakistan). Finally, relations between major and secondary regional powers of the same civilization (the EU and Britain, Russia and Ukraine, Brazil and Argentina, Iran and Saudi Arabia) should be less antagonistic than those between countries of different civilizations (China and Japan; Japan and Korea; India and Pakistan; Israel and the Arab states).

What are the implications of a uni-multipolar world for American policy?

First, it would behoove Americans to stop acting and talking as if this were a unipolar world. It is not. To deal with any major global issue, the United States needs the cooperation of at least some major powers. Unilateral sanctions and interventions are recipes for foreign policy disasters. Second, American leaders should abandon the benign-hegemon illusion that natural congruity exists between their interests and values and those of the rest of the world. . . .

Third, while the United States cannot create a unipolar world, it is in U.S. interests to take advantage of its position as the only superpower in the existing international order and to use its resources to elicit cooperation from other countries to deal with global issues in ways that satisfy American interests. . . .

Fourth, the interaction of power and culture has special relevance for European-American relations. The dynamics of power encourage rivalry; cultural commonalities facilitate cooperation. The achievement of almost any major American goal depends on the triumph of the latter over the former. The relation with Europe is central to the success of American foreign policy, and given the pro- and anti-American outlooks of Britain and France, respectively, America's relations with Germany are central to its relations with Europe. Healthy cooperation with Europe is the prime antidote for the loneliness of American superpowerdom.

Richard N. Haass has argued that the United States should act as a global sheriff, rounding up "posses" of other states to handle major international issues as they arise. Haass handled Persian Gulf matters at the White House in the Bush administration, and this proposal reflects the experience and success of that administration in putting together a heterogeneous global posse to force Saddam out of Kuwait. But that was then, in the unipolar moment. What happened then contrasts dramatically with the Iraqi crisis in the winter of 1998, when France, Russia, and China opposed the use of force and America assembled an Anglo-Saxon posse, not a global one. In December 1998 support for U.S. and British air strikes against Saddam was also limited and criticism widespread. Most strikingly, no Arab government, including Kuwait, endorsed the action. Saudi Arabia refused to allow the United States to use its fighter planes based there. Efforts at rallying future posses are far more likely to resemble what happened in 1998 than what happened in 1990–91. Most of the world, as Mandela said, does not want the United States to be its policeman.

As a multipolar system emerges, the appropriate replacement for a global sheriff is community policing, with the major regional powers assuming primary responsibility for order in their own regions. Haass criticizes this suggestion on the grounds that the other states in a region, which I have called the secondary regional powers, will object to being policed by the leading regional powers. As I have indicated, their interests often do conflict. But the same tension is likely to hold in the relationship between the United States and major regional powers. There is no reason why Americans should take responsibility for maintaining order if it can be done locally. While geography does not coincide exactly with culture, there is considerable overlap between regions and civilizations. . . .

In the multipolar world of the 21st century, the major powers will inevitably compete, clash, and coalesce with each other in various permutations and combinations. Such a world however, will lack the tension and conflict between the superpower and the major regional powers that are the defining characteristic of a uni-multipolar world. For that reason, the United States could find life as a major power in a multipolar world less demanding, less contentious, and more rewarding than it was as the world's only superpower.

FURTHER READING

David Armstrong and Erik Goldstein, eds., *The End of the Cold War* (1990)

Anders Åslund, *Gorbachev's Struggle for Economic Reform* (1989)

Richard J. Barnet and John Cavanagh, *Global Dreams: Imperial Corporations and the New World Order* (1994)

Donald C. Baucom, *The Origins of SDI, 1944–1983* (1992)

Coral Bell, *The Reagan Paradox* (1989)

C. Fred Bergsten and William R. Cline, *The United States–Japan Economic Problem* (1987)

Larry Berman, ed., *Looking Back on the Reagan Presidency* (1990)

William C. Berman, *America's Right Turn* (1994)

Michael A. Bernstein et al., eds., *Understanding American Economic Decline* (1994)

Michael R. Beschloss and Strobe Talbott, *At the Highest Levels* (1993)

Seweryn Bialer and Michael Mandelbaum, eds., *Gorbachev's Russia and American Foreign Policy* (1988)

Sidney Blumenthal and Thomas B. Edsall, eds., *The Reagan Legacy* (1988)

Paul Boyer, ed., *Reagan as President* (1990)

Lea Brilmayer, *American Hegemony* (1994)

Roger Buckley, *US-Japan Alliance Diplomacy* (1992)

Dan Caldwell, *The Dynamics of Domestic Politics and Arms Control* (1991)

David Callahan, *Between Two Worlds: Realism, Idealism, and American Foreign Policy After the Cold War* (1994)

David P. Calleo, *Beyond American Hegemony* (1987)

Colin Campbell and Bert A. Rockman, *The Bush Presidency* (1991)

Lou Cannon, *President Reagan* (1991)

James Chace, *The Consequences of the Peace* (1992)

Stephen F. Cohen, "Gorbachev and the Soviet Reformation," in Stephen F. Cohen and Katrina Vanden Heuvel, eds., *Voices of Glasnost* (1989), pp. 13–32

Michael Cox, *U.S. Foreign Policy after the Cold War* (1999)

Bruce Cumings, "'Revising Post-Revisionism,'" *Diplomatic History*, 17 (1993), 539–569

Robert Dallek, *Ronald Reagan* (1984)

Dusko Doder and Louise Branson, *Gorbachev* (1990)

Theodore Draper, *A Very Thin Line* (1991) (Iran-Contra)

Michael Duffy and Dan Goodgame, *Marching in Place* (1992)

Matthew Evangelista, "Sources of Moderation in Soviet Security Policy," in Philip E.
      Tetlock et al., eds., *Behavior, Society, and Nuclear War* (1991), pp. 254–354

——, *Unarmed Forces: The Transnational Movement to End the Cold War* (1999)

Lawrence Freedman and Efraim Karsh, *The Gulf Conflict, 1990–1991* (1992)

Michael A. Freney and Rebecca S. Hartley, *United Germany and the United States* (1991)

Robert Gates, *From the Shadows* (1996)

John Lewis Gaddis, *The Long Peace* (1987)

——, "The Tragedy of Cold War History," *Diplomatic History,* 17 (1993), 1–16

——, *The United States and the End of the Cold War* (1992)

——, *We Now Know* (1997)

Jeffrey E. Garten, *A Cold Peace* (1992)

Raymond L. Garthoff, *The Great Transition* (1994)

——, *Détente and Confrontation* (1985)

Charles Gati, *The Bloc That Failed* (1990)

Alexander George et al., eds., *U.S.-Soviet Security Cooperation* (1988)

Misha Glenny, *The Fall of Yugoslavia* (1992)

Fred I. Greenstein, ed., *The Reagan Presidency* (1983)

Fred Halliday, *From Kabul to Managua* (1989)

Jim Hanson, *The Decline of the American Empire* (1993)

Erwin C. Hargrove, *Jimmy Carter as President* (1988)

Jonathan Haslam, *The Soviet Union and the Politics of Nuclear Weapons in Europe,
      1969–87* (1990)

Stanley Hoffman, *World Disorders* (1999)

Michael J. Hogan, ed., *The End of the Cold War* (1992)

Samuel P. Huntington, *The Clash of Civilizations and the Remaking of the World Order*
      (1996)

William G. Hyland, *Clinton's World* (1999)

Michael Ignatieff, "Fault Lines," *New York Times Book Review*, December 1, 1996, 13.

John G. Ikenberry, "The Myth of Post Cold War Chaos," *Foreign Affairs*, 75 (1996), 79–91

Harold James and Marla Stone, eds., *When the Wall Came Down: Reactions to German
      Unification* (1992)

Bruce Jentleson, *With Friends Like These: Reagan, Bush, and Saddam* (1994)

Robert Jervis and Seweryn Bialer, eds., *Soviet-American Relations After the Cold War*
      (1991)

Haynes Johnson, *Sleepwalking Through History* (1991)

Robert H. Johnson, *Improbable Dangers* (1995)

Sheila K. Johnson, *The Japanese Through American Eyes* (1990)

Charles O. Jones, *The Trusteeship Presidency* (1988) (Carter)

Robert G. Kaiser, *How Gorbachev Happened* (1991)

William W. Kaufmann, *Glasnost, Perestroika, and U.S. Defense Spending* (1990)

Charles W. Kegley, ed., *The Long Postwar Peace* (1991)

George F. Kennan, "On American Principles," *Foreign Affairs,* 74 (1995), 116–126

Paul Kennedy, *Preparing for the Next Century* (1993)

Michael T. Klare and Peter Kornbluh, eds., *Low-Intensity Warfare* (1988)

William Kristol and Robert Kagan, "Toward a Neo-Reaganite Foreign Policy," *Foreign
      Affairs,* 75 (1996), 18–32

David E. Kyvig, *Reagan and the World* (1990)

Richard Ned Lebow and Janice Gross Stein, "Reagan and the Russians," *Atlantic Monthly,*
      273 (February 1994), 35–37

——, *We All Lost the Cold War* (1994)

Robert J. Lieber, ed., *Eagle Adrift* (1997)

Edward T. Linenthal, *Symbolic Defense* (1989) (SDI)

Allen Lynch, *The Cold War Is Over—Again* (1992)

Sean M. Lynn-Jones, ed., *The Cold War and After* (1991)

Michael Mandlebaum, "Foreign Policy as Social Work," *Foreign Affairs,* 75 (1996), 16–32

Thomas E. Mann, *A Question of Balance* (1990) (Congress)

Michael MccGwire, *Perestroika and Soviet National Security* (1991)

Thomas J. McCormick, *America's Half-Century* (1989)

Jeff McMahan, *Reagan and the World* (1986)

Robert J. McMahon, "Making Sense of American Foreign Policy during the Reagan Years," *Diplomatic History,* 19 (1995) 367–384

Walter Mead, *Mortal Splendor* (1987)

Richard A. Melanson, *Reconstructing Consensus* (1991)

Morris Morley, *Crisis and Confrontation* (1988)

Henry R. Nau, *The Myth of America's Decline* (1990)

John Newhouse, *War and Peace in the Nuclear Age* (1989)

Janne E. Nolan, *Guardians of the Arsenal* (1989)

Joseph S. Nye, Jr., *Bound to Lead* (1990)

Kenneth A. Oye et al., eds., *Eagle Defiant* (1983)

———, *Eagle in a New World* (1992)

———, *Eagle Resurgent?* (1987)

Herbert S. Parmet, *George Bush* (1998)

Joseph E. Persico, *Casey* (1990)

Eric F. Petersen, "The End of the Cold War: A Review of Recent Literature," *History Teacher,* 26 (1993), 471–485

John Prados, *Presidents' Secret Wars* (1986)

Thomas Risse-Kappen, "Did 'Peace Through Strength' End the Cold War? Lessons from INF," *International Security,* 16 (1991), 162–188

Nicholas X. Rizopolous, ed., *Sea-Changes* (1990)

Michael Rogin, *Ronald Reagan* (1987)

Richard Rosecrance, *America's Economic Resurgence* (1990)

Michael Schaller, *Reckoning with Reagan* (1992)

Arthur M. Schlesinger, Jr., "Back to the Womb?: Isolationsim's Renewed Threat," *Foreign Affairs,* 74 (1995) 2–8

Gaddis Smith, *Morality, Reason, and Power* (1986) (Carter)

Steven K. Smith and Douglas A. Wertman, *US–Western European Relations During the Reagan Years* (1992)

Leonard S. Spector, *Nuclear Ambitions* (1990)

Ronald Steel, *Temptations of a Superpower* (1995)

"The Strange Death of Soviet Communism," *National Interest,* no. 31 (1993), special issue

Ralph Summy and Michael E. Salla, *Why the Cold War Ended* (1995)

Strobe Talbott, *The Russians and Reagan* (1984)

Gregory F. Treverton, *America, Germany, and the Future of Europe* (1992)

Robert W. Tucker and David C. Hendrickson, *The Imperial Temptation* (1992)

Garry Wills, "Habits of Hegemony," *Foreign Affairs,* 78 (1999), 50–59

Daniel Wirls, *Buildup* (1992)

Philip Zelikow and Condoleeza Rice, *Germany Unified and Europe Transformed* (1995)